of radios worldwide. Meanwhile, our products have garnered industry and international acclaim and our company a reputation for quality and customer service.

Today, our Shortwave products can be found at more than 1,000 of your favorite department stores, specialty retailers, and electronics chains in North America. Recently, we've taken our success and experience a step further – by expanding our product offering to include "design-driven" consumer electronics under the Etón brand.

Even though our Etón Corporation name may be new to you, our products aren't. We're still the same company that makes the Grundig Shortwave radios that you've trusted and enjoyed for years. The next time you see a Grundig radio, remember the Etón story behind it.

"Tune-in" below to see our current product line

www.etoncorp.com

Brookstone

G2000A, G1000A
Page 48

M100, M300
Page 54

FR200
Page 60

The Future of Etón
Page 66

TABLE OF CONTENTS

World Band Radio

How PASSPORT Began

The concept for what was to become PASSPORT TO WORLD BAND RADIO was simple enough. In our established role with frequency management, IBS had accumulated a wealth of data on shortwave spectrum occupancy, but there was a hitch: It was scribbled onto charts by hand and was barely legible.

Something similar had been photocopied for limited government use by the late Roger Legge of the Voice of America. Alas, it, too, was a "pencil special." However, both were invaluable tools not available to the general public, or even most frequency managers. This needed to change.

New Technology Creates Opportunity

By 1981 it was becoming apparent that we should be able to produce printed spectrum charts on a mini- or micro-computer, as they were known. DEC was working on its desktop Rainbo computer line to be equipped with hard drives in lieu of huge floppies, so we placed an order. Alas, the Rainbo ran into intractable development woes.

By now desperate, we looked into getting an IBM PC-XT, just emerging from development. But we needed something right away, so one of us drove out to sweet talk a young IBM sales lady in the next state. Bending rules, she sold us the lone preview unit they had just received. It was possibly the first XT ever sold, and it saved the day.

Fortunately, one team member had prior mainframe database experience and drew up software specs for a recently hired programmer. By January 1984 the first modest result appeared: a 64-page graphics display of the tropical bands from 2.3-5.1 MHz, along with propagation charts from SUNY astronomy professor David Meisel. It was called Radio Database International, and sold perhaps 300 copies.

But not everybody was enamored with our exercise, and we found ourselves on the receiving end of a lawsuit from a firm associated with an established publication. The buzz from industry cognoscenti was that we could not survive against the might of such an organization, and they were nearly right. But thanks mainly to such invaluable friends-in-need as Don Jensen and Noel Green—along with indignation and stubbornness bordering on insanity—we emerged intact, even if legal expenses left us buried in debt.

How Passport Began

"Hail Mary" Software

Our initial database programs were Hail Mary specials that gave a grim new dimension to the concept of software bugs. Still, with enough patience and tricks we muddled through. One year, though, that was almost not enough.

In the earliest editions, the Blue Pages' masters were generated on a noisy professional dot-matrix printer that was tractor-fed with preprinted forms. These had to be perfectly aligned at all times, with the print head's path being kept to within a gnat's fraction of a millimeter.

A complete printout took over 20 hours. It couldn't be stopped or it would completely abort, and keeping the forms lined up on the fly required the fingers of a safecracker. This meant that somebody had to eyeball and guide the output for hours on end—all while the printer was screeching away like bees on a dentist's drill. Whoever monitored the printer came away looking like Charles Manson.

Time and again, the printout for the book aborted, but the key person to keep this functioning had to catch an urgent flight for overseas. With the final possible printout about one-third completed, he turned the rest over to a hapless colleague and hopped onto the plane. If this printout failed, the deadline for the printers' last courier would pass, our "print slot" would be missed and the book delayed by weeks.

Fortunately, Murphy took a holiday. The printout worked and the book got out on time. We had survived another near-death experience, and that night corks were enthusiastically popped on both sides of the Atlantic.

English Cavalry to the Rescue

We obviously couldn't go like this forever, so it was with great relief that our longtime colleague John Campbell tore into the issue. Then head of the computer science department at Exeter University in England, he collared a couple of eager students to design and implement a new system. One, Richard Mayell, would become our resident IT maven, and continues in that capacity to this day.

World Band Grows, Defying Predictions

Since then PASSPORT has expanded to cover the breadth of topics and formats you see today. Yet, none of this would have been possible without the expansion in shortwave listening that has taken place over the past two decades. Armchair prognosticators have declared the death of shortwave since Harry Truman's day, but in full disrespect of their wisdom the field continues to enlarge.

Who knows? With technological advances and a growing thirst for global knowledge, the best may be yet to come.

— *Lawrence Magne*

International Broadcasting Services, Ltd.

ISSN 0897-0157

OUR READER IS THE MOST IMPORTANT PERSON IN THE WORLD!

Editorial

Editor in Chief	Lawrence Magne
Editor	Tony Jones
Assistant Editor	Craig Tyson
Consulting Editor	John Campbell
Founder Emeritus	Don Jensen
PASSPORT REPORTS	George Heidelman, Lawrence Magne, Chuck Rippel, Danny Wu, Dave Zantow, George Zeller
WorldScan® Contributors	Gabriel Iván Barrera (Argentina), James Conrad (U.S.), David Crystal (Israel), Alok Dasgupta (India), Graeme Dixon (New Zealand), Nicolás Eramo (Argentina), Paulo Roberto e Souza (Brazil), Alokesh Gupta (India), Jose Jacob (India), *Jembatan DX*/Juichi Yamada (Japan), Anatoly Klepov (Russia), Marie Lamb (U.S.), *Radio Nuevo Mundo* (Japan), Célio Romais (Brazil), Nikolai Rudnev (Russia), David Walcutt (U.S.)
WorldScan® Software	Richard Mayell
Laboratory	Robert Sherwood
Artwork	Gahan Wilson, cover
Graphic Arts	Bad Cat Design; Paul Wright, layout
Printing	D.B. Hess

Administration

Publisher	Lawrence Magne
Associate Publisher	Jane Brinker
Offices	IBS North America, Box 300, Penn's Park PA 18943, USA; www.passband.com; Phone +1 (215) 598-9018; Fax +1 (215) 598 3794; mktg@passband.com
Advertising & Media Contact	Jock Elliott, IBS Ltd., Box 300, Penn's Park PA 18943, USA; Phone +1 (215) 598-9018; Fax +1 (215) 598 3794; media@passband.com

Bureaus

IBS Latin America	Tony Jones, Casilla 1844, Asunción, Paraguay; schedules@passband.com; Fax +1 (215) 598 3794
IBS Australia	Craig Tyson, Box 2145, Malaga WA 6062; Fax +61 (8) 9342 9158; addresses@passband.com
IBS Japan	Toshimichi Ohtake, 5-31-6 Tamanawa, Kamakura 247-0071; Fax +81 (467) 43 2167; ibsjapan@passband.com

Library of Congress Cataloging-in-Publication Data

Passport to World Band Radio.
1. Radio Stations, Shortwave—Directories. I. Magne, Lawrence
TK9956.P27   2003   384.54'5   03-22739
ISBN 0-914941-84-4

Tune in the world with Icom!

computer not included

New IC-R5

Compact, filled with features! Winning performance!

150 kHz – 1.3 GHz* • AM, FM, WFM • 1250 Alphanumeric Memories • CTCSS/DTCS Decode • Weather Alert • Dynamic Memory Scan (DMS) • Preprogrammed TV & Shortwave • Weather Resistant • 2 AA Ni-Cds • PC Programmable

IC-R3

See & Hear all the action!

• 500 kHz – 2.45 GHz* • AM, FM, WFM, AM-TV, FM-TV • 450 Alphanumeric Memories • CTCSS with Tone Scan • 4 Level Attenuator • Telescoping Antenna with BNC Connector • 2" Color TFT Display with Video/Audio Output • Lithium Ion Power • PC Programmable

IC-R10

Advanced performance!

500 kHz – 1.3 GHz* • AM, FM, WFM, USB, LSB, CW • 1000 Alphanumeric Memories • Attenuator • Backlit Display & Key Pad • VSC (Voice Scan Control) • 7 Different Scan Modes • Beginner Mode • Band Scope • Includes AA Ni-Cds & Charger • PC Programmable

New Software
IC-PCR1000 BON

Turn your PC into a wide band receiver!

• 100 kHz – 1.3 GHz* • AM, FM, WFM, USB, LSB, CW • Unlimited Memory Channels • Real Time Band Scope • IF Shift • Noise Blanker • Digital AFC • Voice Scan Control • Attenuator • Tunable Bandpass Filters • AGC Function • S Meter Squelch • CTCSS Tone Squelch • Computer Controlled DSP w/optional UT-106

download frequencies
www.icomreceivers.com
right from the web

IC-R75

Pull out the weak signals

• 30 kHz - 60.0 MHz* • AM, FM, S-AM, USB, LSB, CW, RTTY • 101 Alphanumeric Memory Channels • Twin Passband Tuning (PBT) • Commercial Grade • Synchronous AM Detection (S-AM) • Optional DSP with Noise Reduction Auto Notch Filter • Triple Conversion • Up to Two Optional Filters • Front Mounted Speaker • Large Display • Well Spaced Keys and Dials • PC Remote Control with ICOM Software for Windows® (RSR75)

IC-R8500

The expert's choice

• 100 kHz - 2.0 GHz* • AM, FM, WFM, USB, LSB, CW • 1000 Alphanumeric Memories • Commercial Grade • IF Shift • Noise Blanker • Audio Peak Filter (APF) • Selectable AGC Time Constant • Digital Direct Synthesis (DDS) • RS-232C Port for PC Remote Control with ICOM Software for Windows® (RSR8500)

Don't miss anything!

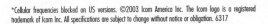
www.icomamerica.com

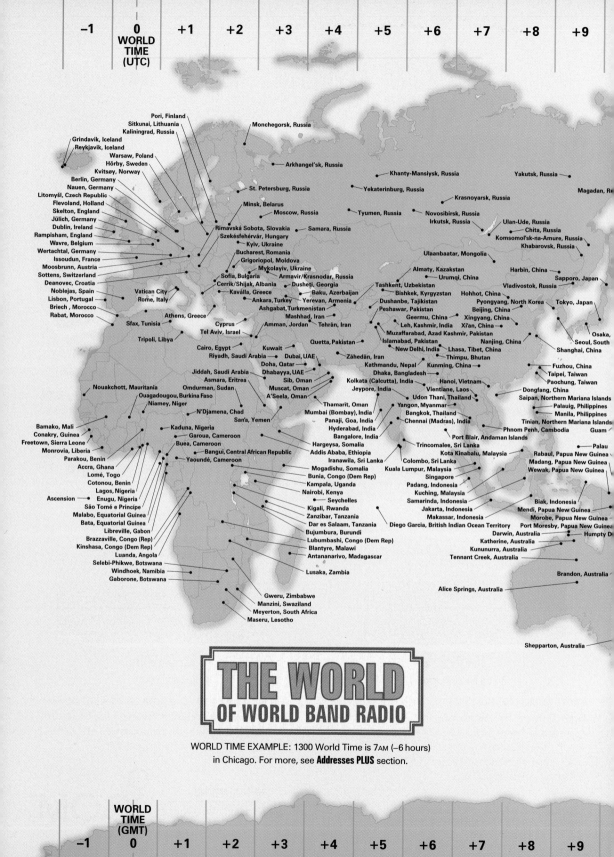

THE WORLD
OF WORLD BAND RADIO

WORLD TIME EXAMPLE: 1300 World Time is 7AM (–6 hours) in Chicago. For more, see **Addresses PLUS** section.

Top time zone scale: –1 | 0 WORLD TIME (UTC) | +1 | +2 | +3 | +4 | +5 | +6 | +7 | +8 | +9

Bottom time zone scale: –1 | 0 WORLD TIME (GMT) | +1 | +2 | +3 | +4 | +5 | +6 | +7 | +8 | +9

City labels:

Pori, Finland
Sitkunai, Lithuania
Kaliningrad, Russia
Grindavik, Iceland
Reykjavik, Iceland
Warsaw, Poland
Hörby, Sweden
Kvitsøy, Norway
Berlin, Germany
Nauen, Germany
Litomyšl, Czech Republic
Flevoland, Holland
Skelton, England
Jülich, Germany
Dublin, Ireland
Rampisham, England
Wavre, Belgium
Wertachtal, Germany
Issoudun, France
Moosbrunn, Austria
Sottens, Switzerland
Deanovec, Croatia
Noblejas, Spain
Lisbon, Portugal
Briech, Morocco
Rabat, Morocco
Vatican City
Rome, Italy
Athens, Greece
Sfax, Tunisia
Tripoli, Libya

Monchegorsk, Russia
Arkhangel'sk, Russia
St. Petersburg, Russia
Minsk, Belarus
Moscow, Russia
Rimavská Sobota, Slovakia
Szekésfehérvár, Hungary
Kyiv, Ukraine
Bucharest, Romania
Grigoriopol, Moldova
Mykolayiv, Ukraine
Sofia, Bulgaria
Cerrik/Shijak, Albania
Kaválla, Greece
Ankara, Turkey
Cyprus
Tel Aviv, Israel
Cairo, Egypt
Riyadh, Saudi Arabia
Kuwait
Doha, Qatar
Jiddah, Saudi Arabia
Dubai, UAE
Dhabayya, UAE
Sib, Oman
Muscat, Oman
A'Seela, Oman

Samara, Russia
Dusheti, Georgia
Armavir/Krasnodar, Russia
Baku, Azerbaijan
Yerevan, Armenia
Ashgabat, Turkmenistan
Mashhad, Iran
Amman, Jordan
Tehrän, Iran
Zähedän, Iran
Quetta, Pakistan

Khanty-Mansiysk, Russia
Yekaterinburg, Russia
Tyumen, Russia
Almaty, Kazakstan
Tashkent, Uzbekistan
Bishkek, Kyrgyzstan
Dushanbe, Tajikistan
Peshawar, Pakistan
Leh, Kashmir, India
Muzaffarabad, Azad Kashmir, Pakistan
Islamabad, Pakistan
New Delhi, India
Kathmandu, Nepal
Dhaka, Bangladesh
Kolkata (Calcutta), India
Jeypore, India
Thamarit, Oman
Mumbai (Bombay), India
Panaji, Goa, India
Hyderabad, India
Bangalore, India
Hargeysa, Somalia
Addis Ababa, Ethiopia
Iranawila, Sri Lanka
Mogadishu, Somalia
Colombo, Sri Lanka
Trincomalee, Sri Lanka
Kota Kinabalu, Malaysia
Kuala Lumpur, Malaysia
Singapore
Padang, Indonesia
Kuching, Malaysia
Samarinda, Indonesia
Jakarta, Indonesia
Makassar, Indonesia
Diego Garcia, British Indian Ocean Territory

Krasnoyarsk, Russia
Novosibirsk, Russia
Irkutsk, Russia
Ulaanbaatar, Mongolia
Urumqi, China
Hohhot, China
Geermu, China
Xingyang, China
Lhasa, Tibet, China
Thimpu, Bhutan
Kunming, China
Hanoi, Vietnam
Vientiane, Laos
Udon Thani, Thailand
Yangon, Myanmar
Bangkok, Thailand
Chennai (Madras), India
Port Blair, Andaman Islands

Yakutsk, Russia
Magadan, Re
Ulan-Ude, Russia
Chita, Russia
Komsomol'sk-na-Amure, Russia
Khabarovsk, Russia
Harbin, China
Vladivostok, Russia
Sapporo, Japan
Pyongyang, North Korea
Beijing, China
Xi'an, China
Tokyo, Japan
Nanjing, China
Osaka,
Seoul, South
Shanghai, China
Fuzhou, China
Taipei, Taiwan
Paochung, Taiwan
Dongfang, China
Saipan, Northern Mariana Islands
Palauig, Philippines
Manila, Philippines
Tinian, Northern Mariana Islands
Guam
Phnom Penh, Cambodia
Palau
Rabaul, Papua New Guinea
Madang, Papua New Guinea
Wewak, Papua New Guinea
Biak, Indonesia
Mendi, Papua New Guinea
Morobe, Papua New Guinea
Port Moresby, Papua New Guinea
Darwin, Australia
Humpty D
Katherine, Australia
Kununurra, Australia
Tennant Creek, Australia
Brandon, Australia
Alice Springs, Australia
Shepparton, Australia

Bamako, Mali
Conakry, Guinea
Freetown, Sierra Leone
Monrovia, Liberia
Parakou, Benin
Accra, Ghana
Lomé, Togo
Cotonou, Benin
Lagos, Nigeria
Ascension
Enugu, Nigeria
São Tomé e Prínçipe
Malabo, Equatorial Guinea
Bata, Equatorial Guinea
Libreville, Gabon
Brazzaville, Congo (Rep)
Kinshasa, Congo (Dem Rep)
Luanda, Angola
Selebi-Phikwe, Botswana
Windhoek, Namibia
Gaborone, Botswana

Nouakchott, Mauritania
Ouagadougou, Burkina Faso
Niamey, Niger
N'Djamena, Chad
Kaduna, Nigeria
Garoua, Cameroon
Buea, Cameroon
Bangui, Central African Republic
Yaoundé, Cameroon
San'a, Yemen
Asmara, Eritrea
Omdurman, Sudan

Bunia, Congo (Dem Rep)
Kampala, Uganda
Nairobi, Kenya
Seychelles
Kigali, Rwanda
Zanzibar, Tanzania
Dar es Salaam, Tanzania
Bujumbura, Burundi
Lubumbashi, Congo (Dem Rep)
Blantyre, Malawi
Antananarivo, Madagascar
Lusaka, Zambia

Gweru, Zimbabwe
Manzini, Swaziland
Meyerton, South Africa
Maseru, Lesotho

Port Blair, Andaman Islands

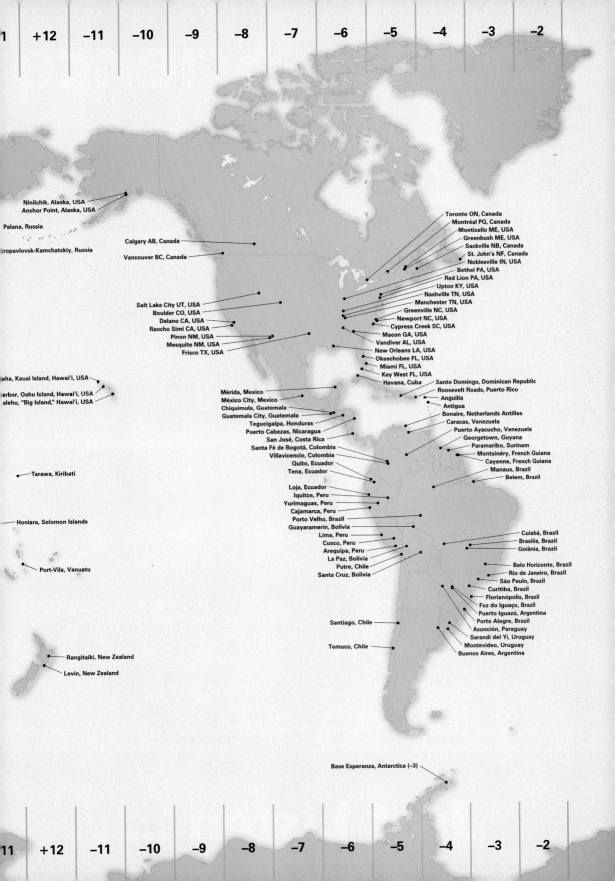

+12 −11 −10 −9 −8 −7 −6 −5 −4 −3 −2

Ninilchik, Alaska, USA
Anchor Point, Alaska, USA

Palana, Russia

ropavlovsk-Kamchatskiy, Russia

Calgary AB, Canada

Vancouver BC, Canada

Toronto ON, Canada
Montréal PQ, Canada
Monticello ME, USA
Greenbush ME, USA
Sackville NB, Canada
St. John's NF, Canada
Noblesville IN, USA
Bethel PA, USA
Red Lion PA, USA
Upton KY, USA
Nashville TN, USA
Manchester TN, USA
Greenville NC, USA
Newport NC, USA
Cypress Creek SC, USA
Macon GA, USA
Vandiver AL, USA
New Orleans LA, USA
Okeechobee FL, USA
Miami FL, USA
Key West FL, USA
Havana, Cuba

Salt Lake City UT, USA
Boulder CO, USA
Delano CA, USA
Rancho Simi CA, USA
Pinon NM, USA
Mesquite NM, USA
Frisco TX, USA

aha, Kauai Island, Hawai'i, USA
arbor, Oahu Island, Hawai'i, USA
alehu, "Big Island," Hawai'i, USA

Santo Domingo, Dominican Republic
Roosevelt Roads, Puerto Rico
Anguilla
Antigua
Bonaire, Netherlands Antilles
Caracas, Venezuela
Puerto Ayacucho, Venezuela
Georgetown, Guyana
Paramaribo, Surinam
Montsinéry, French Guiana
Cayenne, French Guiana
Manaus, Brazil
Belem, Brazil

Mérida, Mexico
México City, Mexico
Chiquimula, Guatemala
Guatemala City, Guatemala
Tegucigalpa, Honduras
Puerto Cabezas, Nicaragua
San José, Costa Rica
Santa Fé de Bogotá, Colombia
Villavicencio, Colombia
Quito, Ecuador
Tena, Ecuador

Tarawa, Kiribati

Loja, Ecuador
Iquitos, Peru
Yurimaguas, Peru
Cajamarca, Peru
Porto Velho, Brazil
Guayaramerín, Bolivia
Lima, Peru
Cusco, Peru
Arequipa, Peru
La Paz, Bolivia
Putre, Chile
Santa Cruz, Bolivia

Honiara, Solomon Islands

Cuiabá, Brazil
Brasília, Brazil
Goiânia, Brazil

Port-Vila, Vanuatu

Belo Horizonte, Brazil
Rio de Janeiro, Brazil
São Paulo, Brazil
Curitiba, Brazil
Florianópolis, Brazil
Foz do Iguaçu, Brazil
Puerto Iguazú, Argentina
Porto Alegre, Brazil
Asunción, Paraguay
Sarandí del Yí, Uruguay
Montevideo, Uruguay
Buenos Aires, Argentina

Santiago, Chile

Temuco, Chile

Rangitaiki, New Zealand

Levin, New Zealand

Base Esperanza, Antarctica (−3)

11 +12 −11 −10 −9 −8 −7 −6 −5 −4 −3 −2

Radio ... Science

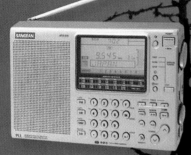

Sangean ATS909

**The Ultimate Features &
Performance In A
Portable SW Receiver!**

306 Memory Presets
• AM/FM/SW/True Upper &
Lower SSB • AM/FM Stereo
Through Headphones
• Dual Time Clock With Alarm

Sangean ATS818ACS

**High Performance SW
With Built-In
Cassette Recorder/Player**

54 Memory Presets
• AM/FM/SW/SSB •
Programmable Cassette
Recorder • AM/FM Stereo
Through Headphones

Sangean ATS505P

**Most Features &
Best Performance
For The Price!**

Superb Audio Quality
• AM/FM/SW/SSB • 45 Memory
Presets • Auto Memory Search &
Store • Dual Time Clock With Alarm
• AC Adapter & SW Antenna Incl.

Just Listen ...™

For The Mind

Myanmar I: Freedom Takes A Holiday

by Manosij Guha

Burma shines as an unspoiled land of teak forests and fertile river plains. The size of Texas, it is also home to hard working and hospitable natives eager to show off their country. Little wonder that Kipling, Orwell and Conrad all wrote longingly of their visits to this ruby of the Orient.

But times have changed, and Burma—now called Myanmar—is cursed with an oppressive military dictatorship. Corrupt, incompetent and repressive, the government has kept everyday Burmese living in fear and impoverishment while the ruling elite lives in opulence.

Foreign Rule Shaken Off

Burma's present condition echoes its past, when incumbent kings massacred rivals to hasten and secure their ascendance to the throne. After numerous wars, mainly between Mons and Thais, Burma was annexed in stages up to 1885 and ultimately became a province of British India. In 1937 the British allowed Burma to separate from India and practice a degree of self-government.

Still not satisfied, early in the Second World War the Burma Independence Army joined forces with Japan against the British. But in 1945, as the fortunes of war were running against Japan, the renamed Burma National Army flip-flopped and helped the British drive out the Japanese. Burma was then rewarded with full independence. A parliamentary democracy was established in 1948, with U Nu as prime minister.

Military Government Installed

In 1962 the army overthrew the U Nu government and installed a military regime led by the eccentric General Ne Win, who established the xenophobic "Burmese Way to Socialism." After a brief dalliance with democracy, Ne Win's Myanmar turned its back on the outside world.

Ne Win's administration became unpopular because of his idiosyncratic rule, including economic policies based on his belief in numerology. Deepening poverty drove the population to sporadic protests, culminating in mass demonstrations in September 1988. After six months of pro-democracy unrest in which thousands of protesters were killed, the armed forces regained direct control of the country by establishing the State Law and Order Restoration Council (SLORC), the much-feared Tatmadaw government.

At this war memorial, built in 1962 to honor fallen soldiers, former foes lie side by side. M.Guha

Daw Aung San Suu Kyi leads the struggle for Burmese democracy.

DVB

A state of emergency was proclaimed, the constitution and civil rights were suspended, and the country was branded with a new name—The Union of Myanmar. This was to be a transitional government, so promises were made to hold free and fair elections to keep the pro-democracy forces at bay.

These promises were not kept. As a result, the opposition united as the National League for Democracy headed by the charismatic leadership of Daw Aung San Suu Kyi, daughter of a national hero. Despite the machinations of the military rulers, the opposition won a landslide victory in the ensuing election in May 1990.

Taken aback by this outcome, the SLORC refused to relinquish power. Instead, it imprisoned the elected leaders, placed Aung San Suu Kyi under house arrest and threw dissidents into jail. According to Amnesty International as many as 1,200 political prisoners languish in Burmese prisons, sometimes in cells formerly used to house dogs.

Ms. Kyi's ancestral house on University Avenue in Yangon has been cordoned off, and is kept under constant surveillance. Efforts have also been made under the guise of the Election Law to disqualify her as an elected leader because of her marriage to a non-citizen. Yet, she has continued to resist detention and to bring the world's attention to the plight of the Burmese people. For her peaceful perseverance she was honored with the Nobel Peace Prize in 1991.

The prestigious award had a positive effect. She was released in 2002 after one-and-a-half years of house arrest and traveled around the country to rejuvenate her political party. However, on May 30, 2003 she was arrested yet again on dubious charges, ostensibly for her own protection. This time she was held in a two-room hut on the grounds of the infamous Insein prison in the outskirts of Yangon, where *poun san*, an Orwellian behavior modification regimen, is practiced to break prisoners' will. International pressure in the form of arms and travel embargos by the western world would seem to have little effect on the junta's stance.

Curbside gambling helps Yangon's unemployed pass away the time.

M. Guha

Repression Continues

The minority Muslim population lives in even greater fear. To avoid persecution Muslims often use Buddhist names, even though the capital city has mosques where the faithful can pray. "I can't even use my own given name," laments a Muslim taxi driver.

After over 40 years of rule and still lacking popular support, Burma's xenophobic authorities live in a growing state of paranoia. Myanmar has mounted an intelligence offensive against foreigners, including local diplomatic missions and their staffs. Diplomatic personnel posted to Yangon complain of being watched and assume that their phones are being tapped. They must also obtain permission to travel more than 25 kilometers from the General Post Office in Yangon. Government functionaries, however well-meaning they may be, face restrictions on their contacts with foreigners and are subject to interrogation about their activities.

Foreign residents and visitors are also watched. As larger numbers of tourists come to Myanmar, intelligence gathering has had to become more selective. Official attention is now focused on those foreigners

This village woman has carried her marigolds for miles to arrive before her competition.   M. Guha

known to be critical of the regime—or who are in positions of influence, such as journalists and academics.

Universities have traditionally been hotbeds of dissent, so the government has moved them to the boondocks so students are removed from the political mainstream and cannot partake in anti-junta activities. One troublesome university has even been relocated to an island, where it can be accessed only by one bridge. When political unrest is expected, the authorities simply close the bridge.

Crickets and other insects make popular Burmese delicacies, like french fries. The crunchy critters are deep fried in oil seasoned with garlic and ginger.   M. Guha

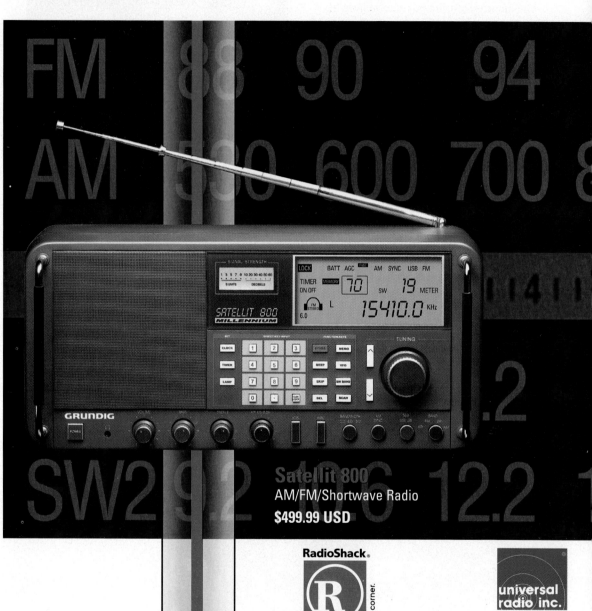

Satellit 800
AM/FM/Shortwave Radio
$499.99 USD

Satellit 800

The Satellit 800 continues Grundig's legendary tradition of high-performance, top-of-the-line portable radios. An advanced digital tuner, with its extensive frequency range (100-30,000 KHz, 87-108 MHz, and 118-136 MHz), covers Longwave, Medium Wave (AM), FM-Stereo, and VHF aircraft band. SSB circuitry enables listening to two-way amateur radio communications. The large, 6" x 3.5" backlit LCD display shows all information with excellent clarity and contrast.

Key features include:
- Multiple tuning choices with direct frequency entry, up/down buttons, and traditional weighted tuning knob
- 70 programmable memory presets with memory scan feature for your favorite stations
- Three built-in bandwidths (6.0, 4.0, 2.3 KHz), using electronically switched IF filters, help to minimize interference
- Synchronous detector (usable from 100-30,000 kHz) improves quality of amplitude modulated signals in the AM and Shortwave bands, minimizing the effects of fading distortion, adjacent frequency interference, and noise
- Dual clocks with timers for waking up in the morning, or sending timed outputs to your favorite recording device

www.etoncorp.com

West Marine
We make boating more fun!™

HAM RADIO OUTLET

GROVE

G2000A, G1000A
Page 48

M100, M300
Page 54

FR200
Page 60

etón
GRUNDIG North America

The Future of Etón
Page 66

Power lines skip by rural residents in Burma, so they don't benefit the very villages over whose land they pass. M. Guha

The ruling junta doesn't make it any easier to leave the country, either. Passports cost a princely sum, and at least one family member is held back to force the emigrant to conform to the law of the land. Overseas workers are also taxed ten percent of their income before remittances even reach their families. Myanmar and the United States are among the few countries, along with the wannabe Basque nation of Euzkadi, with an overseas "citizenship income tax."

"People leaving the country have to pay hefty back taxes," says Maung, my friendly guide who like many of his countrymen uses only one name for fear of reprisals. Paranoia overwhelms him, and he is forever looking at his rearview mirror to check if his shiny Nissan is being followed. Like perhaps half of the Burmese population, he listens regularly to world band stations from the United States and Europe, and knows their times and frequencies by heart. Although, strictly speaking, it is not illegal to tune to world band programs, it is an invitation to trouble should the authorities get wind of it.

Domestic Media Tightly Controlled

Fax machines require an official license, so they are relatively scarce. Telephone conversations and telex messages are recorded, and connections are sometimes cut when uncomfortable subjects are being touched upon. This was dramatically exemplified in May 1996 when a BBC World Service broadcast to Burma carrying a live telephone interview with Aung San Suu Kyi went dead about halfway through the scheduled program.

Telephones and the Internet are so over-priced that they are beyond the reach of most people, limiting communication with the outside world. Both are the provinces of state-run companies, where corrupt officials demand fees which drive the rates up even higher.

Wallowing in wealth, the state-run Internet company is located in swank offices opposite the university in Yangon, which ironically was once the crucible of the pro-democracy movement. However, most of the operation is not devoted to technical matters, but to control. Almost every website with an iota of news, current affairs or dissent is blocked and replaced with an official warning. Even foreign email is usually verboten, although some slips through. While I was in Yangon on assignment for this story, I was able to communicate undetected with the editorial office for several days via an Internet kiosk.

Could Myanmar be among the next dictatorships to be overthrown by outside military force? Probably not, as there appears to be no evidence that Myanmar has undertaken any activity towards acquiring weapons of mass destruction or supporting Muslim terrorists. Britain's Tony Blair explicitly ruled out overthrowing the "Burmese lot" several months ago, and Washington has demonstrated zero interest in such a venture.

Outsiders Provide Hard Currency

Unable to correct the democratic imbalance, the ruling junta has decided to court foreign investors in a bid to replenish its coffers with hard currency. A major effort is being made to attract tourists, and visas are now valid for two months. Temporary residence permits for businessmen are easier to obtain, as well.

An icon of the colonial era is St. Mary's Cathedral, now in derelict condition. Given state coolness toward minority religions, the small Christian community finds it difficult to hold its flock together. M. Guha

Individual travelers are also being allowed instead of chaperoned groups. Yet, anything remotely smacking of news gathering or journalism is prohibited, and violators have their material confiscated and are summarily deported.

A system of dual currency ensures that most of the tourist dollars end up in the coffers of the government. This has resulted in a roaring black market in foreign exchange, which has become an industry in itself thanks to the yawning disparity between official and black market rates.

Inside the sanctum sanctorum of Buddhism's holiest shrines, the Shwedagon Paya. Here, worshipers throng the central courtyard day and night. M. Guha

Tanakha—young boys and girls apply white paste to their faces during an auspicious occasion. It not only brings good luck, it's good for the skin.

M. Guha

Crime and Corruption, but Urban Streets Safe

Yangon—known over the centuries as Dagon, Yangon and Rangoon—is the nation's capital on the bank of the wide river of the same name. Myanmar's largest city, it is home to six million people.

Yangon's attractive center is dominated by wide, tree-lined boulevards with minimal traffic. These thoroughfares bisect lovely green parks alongside buildings with European facades reminiscent of the colonial era. Prime attractions are the shimmering gold-plated domes of a myriad pagodas, with the majestic Shwedagon Paya ruling the roost from its hilltop vantage. One of the cavernous pagodas, Chaukhtatgyi Paya, houses a 20-story reclining Buddha that took five years to build. This elephantine statue is adorned with diamonds and jewels to the tune of 18 million dollars.

Trishaw—*saika*—a contraption made from a modified bicycle to take a third wheel and passenger seat.

M. Guha

Selling vegetables is not a route to prosperity, but it helps families steer clear of Myanmar's worst poverty. M. Guha

There is more traffic and bustle in the suburbs, especially in markets with trishaws, or *saika*, and dangerously over-loaded jitneys. These are the prime means of public transportation.

Violent crime is almost nonexistent, thanks to tough law enforcement and harsh penalties. Walking around the streets is thus a safe learning experience in itself. On one hand, visitors are greeted with wide smiles and it is not difficult to launch into animated conversations despite the language barrier. On the other hand, citizens are randomly accosted by corrupt policemen who have no qualms about extorting a few hundred kyats from, say, a cab driver for an "imaginary" traffic infraction.

Even though gasoline is rationed to two gallons a day, Yangon's roads are filled with shiny Japanese cars. This is aided by Japan's Suzuki, which operates a factory here in concert with a state-run holding company. Still, prices are steep. A typical car is priced around $20,000, with an additional $10,000 tacked on as import duty. This encourages a

roaring black market in stolen cars and car parts. Thanks to the sticky fingers of border guards, cars spirited away from affluent parts of Southeast Asia make their way via Chiang Mai, Thailand to the streets of Yangon, where they fetch astronomical prices.

Opium Traffic and Sexual Enslavement

As Myanmar roosts near the back door of China, it is also the Middle Kingdom's dumping ground. Drug lords and under-world elements find safe haven until their money runs out and they can't buy sanctu-ary any more. Opium is cultivated en masse by poor farmers in border areas to feed the frenzied drug markets in China and the western world, with Thailand serving as the conduit. About half the heroin in the streets of America is believed to emanate from the Golden Triangle, with Myanmar being the largest producer of opium after Laos.

Another form of illicit trafficking tied into Thailand is the ensnaring each year of thousands of young Burmese women and children into prostitution. Representatives of organized crime go from village to village within poor rural areas of Myanmar, spinning tales of well-paid jobs in agriculture, construction, factories and household service for young women willing to emigrate to Thailand.

Once these trusting girls or their parents take the bait, they are forced into a brutal life of sex slavery until they die, escape or acquire AIDS. Somehow, the law-and-order mindset of Burma's police has failed to make a dent in this flourishing traffic in human flesh. Indeed, girls who escape captivity and return to Myanmar are reportedly charged with "unlawfully leaving Myanmar" and are routinely repatriated to their pimps in Thailand.

Sexual abuse of attractive young women doesn't end there. Burmese soldiers are notorious for raping women in the countryside, usually after arresting them following a setup where illegal items have been planted on them or their bicycles. Because raped women are considered unfit for marriage by Burmese society, the victims sometimes wind up marrying their attackers.

Burmese youngsters also suffer in other ways. According to a report by the Belgium-based International Confederation of Free Trade Unions, "The worst forms of child labor—whether in the army, the construction industry, domestic work, or elsewhere—are present throughout Burma." Almost 35 percent of primary school teachers are unqualified, and schools often use textbooks dating back forty years or more. Even though the law states that education is free, most students have to pay schools and teachers for additional night "tuition" to keep up.

"Burmah teak" has long been valued for its fine grain, which puts it at a premium in the world timber market. M. Guha

Cracks in The Bamboo Curtain

Although world band radio is the primary way the Burmese get wind of forbidden news and culture, other media are increasingly chipping away at Myanmar's information curtain. For the wealthy elite and the growing numbers of tourists, upmarket hotel rooms in Yangon provide satellite television carrying CNN and BBC World. Paradoxically, the state-run television now even collaborates with CNN.

Even while the culture police maintain their established stranglehold in many arenas, movies are now treated more gently. Vintage Hollywood imports such as "Cliffhanger" loom from cinema billboards, with images of Sylvester Stallone peering down. Equally popular are Bombay's Bollywood hits, which like their Hollywood counterparts convey a message splendidly contrary to the geriatric junta's tired propaganda.

The world has taken notice of Myanmar's plight, but thus far to little effect. Diplomatic relations have been curtailed and trade sanctions imposed, yet the junta has scarcely budged.

Bogyoke Aung San Road and its surrounding market harken back to the colonial era. M. Guha

There is another path: news and ideas from beyond Myanmar's borders. These, rather than organizational pressure, may yet turn the tide. This subject is covered in Part II of our exclusive report from Myanmar.

Next: *World band radio in Burma.*

www.passband.com

Yangon's finest historic lodging is at the Strand Hotel, built by the British and still resplendent in Burmah teak and polished brass. M. Guha

GRUNDIG North America

GRUNDIG   YB 400PE

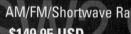
40 STATION MEMORIES   SSB

LW/MW/SW/FM STEREO PLL SYNTHESIZED·DUAL CONVERSION

YB 400PE
AM/FM/Shortwave Radio
$149.95 USD

GRUNDIG North America

YB 400PE

This high-performance PLL synthesized, dual-conversion receiver pulls in AM, FM-Stereo, Shortwave, and Longwave, including continuous coverage from 520-30,000 KHz. Even Ham radio two-way communications can be heard using the SSB circuitry. Its highly sensitive auto-tuning system stops even on weak stations within the international Shortwave broadcast bands. Its 40 programmable memory presets allow quick, easy access to your favorite stations.

Key features include:
- Easy tuning with direct frequency entry, up/down buttons, and auto-scan
- Multifunction LCD displays time, frequency, band, alarm wake time, and sleep timer
- Sleep timer, dual clocks, and dual alarm modes wake you with beeper or radio play
- Built-in antennas for complete portability and socket for supplementary Shortwave antennas • Includes AC adaptor, earphones, carrying pouch, supplementary Shortwave wire antenna, and batteries

www.etoncorp.com

universal radio inc.

West Marine
We make boating more fun!™

G2000A, G1000A
Page 48

M100, M300
Page 54

FR200
Page 60

etón
GRUNDIG North America

The Future of Etón
Page 66

Myanmar II: Battle of The Earwaves

by Manosij Guha

Like the genesis of broadcasting elsewhere in the British Indian empire, the first station in Burma, as Myanmar was then called, was privately owned.

It was fired up in 1926 by Radio Club of Burma experimenters in the capital, Rangoon. A feeble 40 Watts was pumped into the mediumwave AM band on 667 kHz, but a viable audience never developed. Swimming in red ink, it shut down in 1930.

Burmese world band radio surfaced a few years later when the British colonial government approved the use of two transmitters of 1.5 kW and 1.0 kW. These had been originally used for telephone and telegraph communication between India and Burma, but were modified for this pioneering world band foray.

This unit of clandestine Kachin fighters for the OSS was dubbed "Knothead," a name inspired by Archie comic books. The OSS was the precursor of the CIA.

Allen Richter,
Wellington Radio Club

War Introduces Propaganda Efforts

The advent of World War II gave rise to an urgent new mission: broadcasting Allied propaganda. A 10 kW Marconi transmitter was installed at a new facility in the Rangoon suburb of Mingaladon, where the Allied perspective was belted out in English, Burmese and Hindustani—the majority language on the Indian subcontinent.

When Burma was overrun by the Japanese in 1942, the station was equipped with a 10 kW mediumwave AM transmitter and another of 5 kW for world band to support the expanding Japanese Empire. Programming was in Burmese, Japanese, English, Hindustani and Chinese, reflecting the diverse diaspora involved in the War effort.

When war heated up in the Southeast Asian theater in 1945, the Burmese anti-Japanese resistance set up a mobile radio broadcast station on the front lines. This "Burmese Revolutionary Army Broadcasting Station" aired a menu of news and music for resistance troops. Much of the station's expertise came from members of Detachment 101 of "Wild Bill" Donovan's legendary Office of Strategic Services (precursor to the CIA), which trained Kachin volunteers in communication operations.

News of the capture of Sandoway is posted on OSS Detachment 101's blackboard.

Allen Richter,
Wellington Radio Club

About this time, Japan's own occupation broadcast facilities were periodically being used by the Free India (Azad Hind) provisional government in Rangoon. Messages were aired from its leader, Subhas Chandra Bose, to Indian listeners across the Bay of Bengal.

This 1942 transceiver did the trick for the OSS in Burmese jungles—around 200 were cobbled together during World War II. Small, light and reliable, the electronics were from an Allied Radio store stripped bare, then sent over by OSS staff in Washington. The chassis and cabinet were made from aluminum skins of crashed C-47 transport planes.

Allen Richter, Wellington Radio Club

Later the same year, after the Japanese fled Burma, the Psychological Warfare Team of the British Civil Administration for Burma reestablished broadcasting operations. Transmitters, all Marconi, included two of 7.5 kW for world band and one of 5 kW for mediumwave AM, which reactivated daily programs in English, Burmese and Hindustani. These were also used for a few months by the Allied forces' Radio SEAC (South East Asia Command), which was later relocated to Ceylon—today's Sri Lanka.

Using this framework, the Burma Broadcasting Service was established on February 15, 1946, operating in English and Burmese daily on 6035 and Tuesday-Sunday on 9540 kHz. It aired the same identification of "Voice of Burma," or "Myanma Athan," used when the facilities were turned over to the pre-independence Burmese civil government. "Burma Broadcasting Service, Rangoon" was also used often as an on-air ID.

Radio Mandalay Appears

Around 1950, for a brief period there was a regional world band station, Radio Mandalay, operating in the northern city of the same name. It used a 1 kW shortwave transmitter on 7370 kHz, probably the old unit BBS relocated from Rangoon. It operated for three-and-a-half hours (five hours Saturday) with programs in English and Burmese, but had vanished for good by late 1951.

Burma Broadcasting Service Monopoly

Given the secretive nature of the BBS and the lack of access to it, much information about the workings of the station remains unconfirmed. Nonetheless, some credible research has been undertaken by Paul Blackburn for *Broadcasting in Asia and the Pacific* (Temple University).

Unlike other stations in the region which have grown by leaps and bounds, the BBS has scarcely expanded except to enhance transmitter power. Blackburn writes, "Although Burmese broadcasting in the late 1940s was not unlike that of other countries of the region, most others greatly expanded their radio facilities and programming efforts and started television stations during the 1950s and 1960s. Meanwhile, Burma remained content with its single Rangoon radio station, its modest level of programming... This relative non-development has been due not so much to a lack of technical resources or trained personnel, as to a conscious policy by the Burmese government... to apply the bulk of its resources for information activities to other forms of programming, especially the print media... Security considerations, as well as cost, appear to be major reasons for reluctance to open regional stations."

The government claims that much of the population owns radios, but regular listeners to the BBS, now called Radio Myanmar (Myanma Radio & Television),

A broadcast of the "Democratic Voice of Burma" gets underway at modern studios in Oslo, Norway. DVB

total only four million—around ten percent of adults and adolescents. This speaks volumes about the lack of popularity of the state media.

Radio Myanmar got a boost in signal strength when a new 50 kW world band transmitter was first tested in 1957. In 1958 two more such transmitters were added, along with a new 50 kW mediumwave AM sender. An FM transmission link now feeds the world band and mediumwave AM transmitters at Yaegu, while simultaneously serving listeners in Yangon.

Studios Hidden in Secrecy

Radio Myanmar's well-guarded studios and administrative offices are secreted within a tree-lined enclave on Pyay Road which is barely visible on the way to the airport. A staff of 300 prepares all programming, including for the Defence Forces Station in Taunggyi that's currently off the air, but they are prevented by junta rules from speaking publicly with foreigners. "We have to take permission from the minister for every-thing," laments an exasperated U Ko Ko Htay, the station's genial director-general.

We circumvented the restrictions by a series of "gate meetings," where a surprising amount of information was exchanged amid profuse apologies. Almost as bad as the official hassles, though, were swarms of thirsty mosquitoes. Even pungent fumes from a Burmese cigar failed to drive off the persistent bloodsuckers.

World Band's Times, Channels

The flagship National Service of Radio Myanmar is heard mornings at 0030-0245 (0300 weekends) World Time on 7185 kHz. Even on a cheap portable, this puts in a sizeable signal, signing on at daybreak with marching music or vocals eulogizing the ruling junta. This lively fare normally blares out from corner smoke shops throughout Yangon, all but acting as a neighborhood wake-up call. The service resumes after a short break, moving to 9731 kHz at 0330 (earlier on weekends) until 0830.

Programs are usually in the national language, today called Myanma but tradi-tionally known as Burmese or Bamar. Rounding out the roster are also three daily English segments squeezed in at 0200-0245

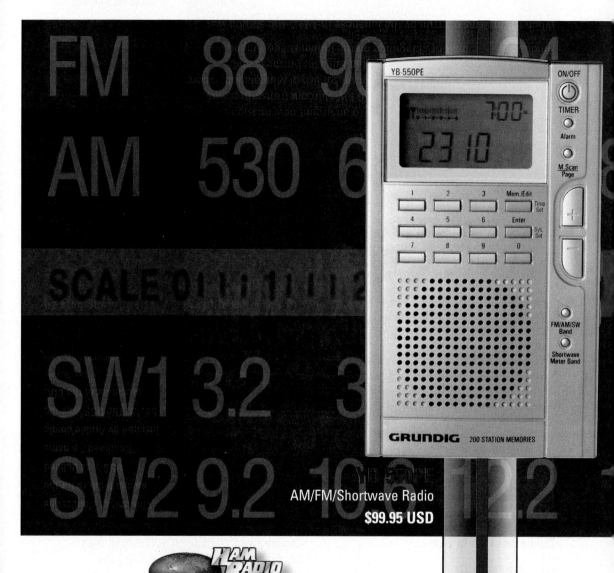

YB-550PE

ON/OFF

TIMER

Alarm

M.Scan Page

Time Set

Sys. Set

Enter

FM/AM/SW Band

Shortwave Meter Band

GRUNDIG   200 STATION MEMORIES

AM/FM/Shortwave Radio
$99.95 USD

YB 550PE

Unique features define the model YB 550PE, such as 200 randomly programmable memory presets with user-defined memory page customizing, digital fine-tuning control, and favorite station wake-up memory. Through its PLL synthesized digital tuner, receive AM, FM-Stereo, and Shortwave with excellent sensitivity and selectivity. Enjoy the entire Shortwave spectrum that includes all 14 international broadcast bands and continuous Shortwave coverage of 520-29,999 KHz. Its auto-tuning system stops even on weak stations within the international Shortwave spectrum, or with the direct frequency entry system, go instantly to any frequency in its tuning range.

Key features include:
- Signal strength and battery power level indicators
- Digital clock with selectable 12/24 hour clock display format
- LCD with display light that shows simultaneous display of frequency and clock
- Alarm with snooze feature and 10-90 minute sleep timer
- Includes built-in antennas, sockets for supplementary Shortwave and FM antennas, earphones, and optional AC adaptor

www.etoncorp.com

G2000A, G1000A
Page 48

M100, M300
Page 54

FR200
Page 60

The Future of Etón
Page 66

Webmaster Thida keeps the "Democratic Voice of Burma" alive and kicking online at www.dvb.no.

DVB

(weekends 0300), 0700-0830 and 1430-1600 World Time. The National Service is aired on 5985 kHz evenings at 0930-1600.

Broadcasts for minorities contain educational material, and are aired late afternoons and evenings at 0930-1330 World Time on 5040 kHz. This appears to use an older transmitter with lower power and frequency instability of plus or minus 0.6 kHz. Here, too, most programs are in Myanma, sometimes with additional programming until as late as 1530, when English-language lessons are offered.

Antennas Beyond View

The government's shortwave transmitting station is located in the secluded hamlet of Yaegu, about an hour's drive from the capital of Yangon. This appears to be a shared military-civilian area, and is off

---

JAM SESSIONS, SOUR NOTES

Early communist and Karen clandestine broadcasts prompted the Burmese government to acquire jamming capability. Although these rebel operations ceased many years ago, the Defense Forces Broadcasting Unit at Taunggyi in Shan State, where the jamming facilities are located, continues to target foreign stations. In recent years it has unleashed its noisome hardware to disturb the Burmese-language services of the BBC World Service, the Voice of America, and the "Democratic Voice of Burma" which from 1995 has been transmitted via leased-time facilities in Europe, East Africa and Central Asia.

As the government continues to maintain strict control over domestic radio, people have turned to the Burmese-language broadcasts of the BBC, VOA, and more recently Radio Free Asia, as well as religious stations such as FEBC. This gives millions of Burmese their daily fix on news, current affairs and happenings in the "real" world beyond their borders, as well as hope and inspiration.

Jamming's Limited Impact

To cope with these beefy signals from abroad, in 1995 the Myanmar army upgraded to more sophisticated jamming equipment, presumably from China. Yet, the military's efforts to control the airwaves have not been particularly effective. In part this reflect's world band radio's unsurpassed ability to overcome deliberate interference. But part of the blame lies with the Burmese jamming effort, which has tended to be ineffectively operated.

Prof. Andrew Selth of the Strategic and Defence Studies Centre at the Australian National University in Canberra has pored over this subject. His 1997 report, "Burma's Intelligence Apparatus," states, "Despite several attempts over the past 50 years, the Burmese government does not appear to have been able to develop a capability regularly or effectively to jam offending radio broadcasts. For example, there have been several clandestine broadcasting ventures since 1948, including the Karen insurgent's Radio Kawthulay, the Parliamentary Democracy Party's Patriotic Youth Front Radio, and the Communist Party of Burma's clandestine 'Voice of the People of Burma.' Yet few of these stations appear to have been subject to consistent or successful jamming operations.

"In late 1995, however, the SLORC attempted to jam Burmese-language programs produced by the BBC and the Voice of America, probably using the one-kilowatt transmitter at Taunggyi operated by the Defense Forces Broadcasting Unit . It is also possible that at the same time jamming was directed against the opposition 'Democratic Voice of Burma.' These attempts were only partly successful, however, and did not last very long, possibly because of the negative publicity these actions generated. It is possible that the Tatmadaw has only recently acquired the technical capability to jam multiple radio broadcasts and has not yet mastered it, or been able to generate sufficient power to implement it effectively."

With the proper mix of transmitter location, power and frequency management, for half a century world band stations have been able to wriggle past even the most intense and sophisticated attempts at jamming. This is one of world band's great strengths, and the Taunggyi operation is simply not up to its mission except, to a degree, within the range of its groundwave. Given Myanmar's size and the number of signals beamed to it, even a greatly expanded jamming effort would produce only limited results.

Jamming Enhances Station's Credibility

Still, any attempt at jamming does manage to achieve one thing, even if it is hardly what was intended. Like forbidden fruit, it enhances the credibility of the very broadcasters the authorities are trying to squash. For example, when the Voice of America's Russian broadcasts were jammed during the Cold War, they were held in high esteem by listeners within the USSR. However, after the United States and the Soviet Union reached agreement to end the jamming, Russian listeners' regard for VOA programs took a dive, as they were no longer worthy of censorship by the ruling authorities.

Inside the majestic
Shwedagon Paya lies the
crown jewel of all
Buddhist pagodas.

M. Guha

**Disguised, I was
able to slip past
the armed
checkpoint.**

limits to foreigners. To slip through as far as the facility's armed checkpoint, I disguised myself to blend in with locals.

The approach to the complex is cut off from the arterial roads miles ahead—access is closely watched, so even the hardiest of guides and drivers keeps a healthy distance.

Photography is forbidden. Simply carrying a camera can incur the wrath of gun-toting militiamen, sometimes followed by imprisonment and deportation.

At the army checkpoint, all that was visible were expansive green rice fields with farmers toiling away and the occasional water buffalo. However, it is an open secret in the area as to what is actually going on. Discreet inquires in a roadside café with an obliging "citizen" and in a lobby with a Chinese businessman revealed that there are six active shortwave transmitters, each rated at 50 kW. While the three older units are manufactured by RCA and were installed between 1957 and 1960, the others date from a Chinese grant in the early 1990s. These are standard Chinese government-issue communications units made by the Beijing BBEF Electronics Group Co. Ltd. at its plant in the Chaoyang District outside Beijing. They are likely of the type TBH-452 with pulse-step modulation, automatic tuning and a wideband transistorized RF driver stage, operable from 3.9 to 22 MHz.

Given Myanmar's existing broadcasting requirements, a complement of six transmitters means that about half are available for other purposes—military, intelligence or civilian telecommunications, or the jamming of hostile military communications. Perhaps this explains why the site is treated with secrecy worthy of Los Alamos.

Burmese Army Station

For over 40 years until spring of 2003, the Burmese army broadcast from Taunggyi, the same site where the government jams foreign and clandestine world band stations. Although Myanmar's jamming is cloaked in secrecy and closed to outsiders, nearly 20 years ago the distinguished AWR broadcaster and expert Dr. Adrian Peterson managed to visit the facility. Given the stagnation of Myanmar's transmitting infrastructure, his observations continue to have relevance even now.

I met with Dr. Peterson at a radio convention at Kulpsville, Pennsylvania in 2003. He explains, "Back in the early part of 1985 I visited this station, which is located in a small army camp on the eastern edge of the regional city, Taunggyi. A Burmese doctor who was fluent in English drove me into the station and also acted as translator.

"This station was established in 1962 and I would suggest that the original transmitter was a 1 kW unit operating at 500 Watts on 5060 kHz. In 1987, a 10 kW NEC transmitter from Japan was installed and the frequency was moved to 6570 kHz. Programming was locally produced in regional languages in half-hour time blocks, though some programming was also prepared by BBS (now Radio Myanmar, MRTV) in Rangoon (now Yangon)."

Peterson goes on, "The station is run by a comparatively small detachment of communication personnel in the army, and they are operating the station on behalf of the Burmese (Myanmar) government. I would suggest that it is not really a propaganda station, but a legitimate news and information station with programming for minority peoples, particularly those in strategic border areas. I imagine that it was off the air for a few years, not by design, but simply because they did not have funding to procure spare parts."

Given the secrecy surrounding the army station, it's impossible to ascertain why it went "dark" in the spring of 2003. Those closest to the operation speculate that it may result from a malfunction, or perhaps equipment is being overhauled, modified or replaced. Whatever, until then the Defense Forces station operated at 0130-0430, 0630-0930 and 1330-1630 World Time on 6570 kHz, with 10 kW of power. Informed sources tell PASSPORT that all programming was prepared at Radio Myanmar in Yangon at the MRTV studios by a separate department dedicated to this purpose. Most programs were pre-recorded, with tapes being sent to Taunggyi on a weekly basis. This explains why the bulk of programming was non-topical, consisting of talks, eulogies, official government statements, soulful songs and local music.

Waves from the Wild Side

Given the turbulent political history of Burma, it comes as little surprise that clandestine radio operations became a prime activity among dissident groups. The first recorded attempts appear to have been made around 1949 by the Karen Nation Defence Foundation, which sought to establish an independent Karen republic and secede from the Burmese union.

Over the years clandestine separatist stations have provided Burmese radio listeners with a rich variety of alternatives to bland state media. The most strident offerings came from the "Voice of the People of Burma," run by the China-backed Burma Communist Party. It started in April 1972, putting out a powerful signal from facilities in Yunnan, southern China. It operated at 0030-0130 and 1200-1300 World Time on approximately 5110 kHz, going off at times that varied from one day to the next. Underscoring its Chinese affiliation, it sometimes signed off with the exact version of the "Internationale" aired by Radio Peking.

In this traditional religious procession, bearers carry alms and gifts for monks at the local Buddhist monastery. M. Guha

This station was the chief means for the communists to reach people in government-held areas. Its daily broadcasts featured revolutionary music, news from the civil war and party propaganda in Burmese, Chinese, Shan, Kachin, Karen, Wa and, occasionally, other tribal languages. In 1978, following policy changes in China after the death of Mao Zedong and the rise to power of Deng Xiaoping, the Chinese welcome mat was withdrawn. The station was forced to move its transmitters to party headquarters at Panghsang in the Wa Hills of northeastern Burma, where it later withered away from lack of support.

A more palatable station was affiliated with the anti-communist, anti-socialist People's Patriotic Party (PPP), founded in 1966. It was led by U Nu, the country's first Prime Minister, who had escaped to neighboring Thailand after a military coup in 1962. This organization broadcast from Bima, a small border village then claimed by both Burma and Thailand. At the time, PASSPORT's predecessor team was unable to confirm rumors that the PPP was covertly supported by funds channeled through the CIA station in Bangkok.

The broadcasts identified as the "National United Liberation Front Radio" from startup in February 1971 until October 1973. Afterwards, until early December of 1974, it identified as "Patriotic Youth Front Radio," representing a loose coalition that included minority groups. After mid-December it became known as "Patriotic Voice Radio," operating at roughly 0030-0115 and 1230-1315 World Time on 7195-7240v kHz, with a second announced frequency on 49 meters that could not be traced by monitors.

Quite different was the Karen National Liberation Army, based along the Thai border in the Kawthulay region; thus, the station's name, "Voice of Kawthulay." The Karens, a Christian minority opposed to the communists in the north, set up their own broadcasting station at the rebel base of Maw Po Kay in the Karen state in early 1983. It was closed down in January 1984 when government forces destroyed their transmitters.

Several attempts to air clandestine broadcasts were also made between 1988 and 1995 by various ethnic and other opposition forces. All emanated from within Myanmar, notably along the borders with China, India and Thailand. Yet, most failed because of poor reception and limited coverage, or they were simply overrun by the government army.

Myanmar government authorities also tried their hand at "black" clandestine propaganda by airing broadcasts falsely claiming

THE OSLO CONNECTION

Foreign and religious broadcasts have long been directed towards Myanmar, where they find appreciative audiences. Yet, there has also been a need for a surrogate station—one the Burmese could call their own.

The opportunity for this finally came about in 1991, when Daw Aung Sang Suu Kyi was awarded the Nobel Peace Prize. Being in captivity, she was unable to attend the ceremony in Oslo. Instead, a delegation of pro-democracy Burmese leaders, including journalism students, met with the Norwegian government.

Station a Consequence of Prize

A proposal was put forward for an independent radio station directed towards Burma under the aegis of the Norwegian Burma Council and the Worldview organization. From that came "Democratic Myanmar a-Than," or the Democratic Voice of Burma (DVB). It was inaugurated on July 19, 1992 from studios and offices at Radio Norway International, using Norwegian Telecom transmitters at Kvitsøy. Reception was good and listener response encouraging.

Turntable antenna, Kvitsøy.
Norkring

Added financial support allowed the station to recruit more staff, expand programming and hire transmitting facilities in Germany, Madagascar, New Zealand, Taiwan, Tajikistan and Uzbekistan—even, briefly, the Pacific islands of Palau. The combined effect of this judiciously placed horsepower allowed the DVB to be easily heard throughout Myanmar.

250 kW transmitter at Jülich, Germany
DT

to be from the separatist Karen National Union. Going by the pseudonym "Thabye (Victory) Radio," this Maymo-language station was heard around 1995 with signals emanating from Yangon.

According to ClandestineRadio.com, a watchdog body of unofficial radio, the most recent bout of Myanmar-based clandestine radio operations was in December 1998 when a station appeared that was allegedly run by one "Kallar-Hpyu Liberation Front," a student-run insurgent group reportedly based in Hsipaw.

World Band Pitches the Ball

World band broadcasts to Myanmar now play an even greater role in guiding public opinion. Such credible outlets as the BBC World Service and the "Democratic Voice of Burma" can be discreetly heard in taxis in Yangon, as well as in isolated villages where they blare from cheap radios tied to the horns of water buffalo.

Over time the people of Myanmar, with the help of international opinion, will almost certainly dismantle their dictatorship. World

FM 88 90 94

AM 530 600

SCALE 0 1 2

SW1 3.2 3.

SW2 9.2 10.6

S350
AM/FM/Shortwave Radio
$99.95 USD

RadioShack®
just around the corner.

THE SHARPER IMAGE®

Incorporating a sensitive, high-performance analog tuner with digital frequency readout, the S350 receives AM, FM-Stereo, and continuous Shortwave coverage of 3,000 to 28,000 KHz, including all 14 international broadcast bands. Its classic analog tuning knob with superimposed fine-tuning control makes it a pleasure to operate, and the variable RF gain control, wide/narrow bandwidth selector and low pass filter give you complete control over incoming signals. Operates on 4 'D' batteries for long battery life.

Key features include:
- Multifunction LCD shows digital frequency, clock, and more
- Alarm and 1-90 minute sleep timer
- Variable, independent bass and treble controls
- Left/right line-level outputs (stereo in FM)
- Includes built-in antennas, sockets for supplementary Shortwave and FM antennas, convertible nylon handle/carrying strap, earphones, and optional AC adaptor

www.etoncorp.com

Brookstone®

G2000A, G1000A
Page 48

M100, M300
Page 54

FR200
Page 60

The Future of Etón
Page 66

Nelson Ku, studio manager for the "Democratic Voice of Burma," oversees the recording of the day's broadcast.

DVB

band radio is working to bring this about, just as it succeeded in doing during the Cold War.

Reporters, Agents and Listeners Unearth News

"We don't call ourselves a clandestine broadcaster because there is no secret that DVB is based in Norway and run by exile activists who have interest in journalism," asserts Aye Chan Naing, chief editor at the DVB. "Nowadays, we are taking both opposition and government officials on the air. We also have weekly program contributors within Burma, and they are doing it openly."

The DVB's main office has a staff of ten who gather news, create programs and maintain a website (www.dvb.no). There are also five reporters in Thailand and two in India, where there are many Burmese in exile, plus stringers in northern Burma. In New Delhi there is another small studio and news bureau where a staff of five prepares news, features and ethnic programs.

Unlike foreign international broadcasters, the DVB's role is to provide local news about Burma with the aim of strengthening the nascent democracy movement. "The BBC and VOA have a more neutral line in

broadcasting than us," acknowledges Aye Chan Naing. "We try to avoid propaganda and not give false information; we try to stick to the facts and be objective, but still our aim is to achieve democracy in Burma.

"We mostly use telephones to call in and ask for information," he continues. "We ask for news from local people, diplomats in Rangoon, NGOs and opposition forces. We also call government offices, police stations to check information. Officially, we don't have anyone in Burma, but our correspondents do have their own secret contacts inside the country."

Publicity Squashes Human Rights Abuse

The DVB has already succeeded in reducing human rights abuses by the ruling junta. "We have inside information from the military that they have instructed their front-line officers not to commit human rights violations—beatings and shootings and things like that—in front of the public in villages and so on," he reveals. "The reason they gave for that is that some of the foreign broadcasters are describing them in very much detail, with the name and registration number of the officer."

Audience Now in the Millions

"We get all our news from DVB," affirms Maung, my friendly taxi driver and self-styled guide in Yangon. "They are our people and they get all news from here." He is so religious about listening to the nightly broadcast that he insists on making a whistlestop at his modest home to tune in, and he's not alone. In addition to reaching thousands of Burmese expats, the DVB musters an estimated audience of nearly four million within Myanmar. It is a mighty force to be reckoned with.

RADIO ...
Anywhere, Anytime

FREEPLAY SUMMIT
**True Alternative Power
In A Digital Travel Radio**

**AM/FM/SW 5.95-15.6 MHz
• Wind-Up Dynamo And Solar
Panel • Built-In Battery Pack
• 30 Station Presets
• Snooze/Alarm**

FREEPLAY PLUS
**Best Alternative Power Radio
— With LED Flashlight!**

**AM/FM/SW 3.0-18.1 MHz
• Wind-Up Baylis Clockwork
Generator And Solar Panel
• Built-In Battery Pack
• Magnetic LED Flashlight**

1-800-522-8863
ccrane.com

C. CRANE COMPANY INC.

FREE CATALOG

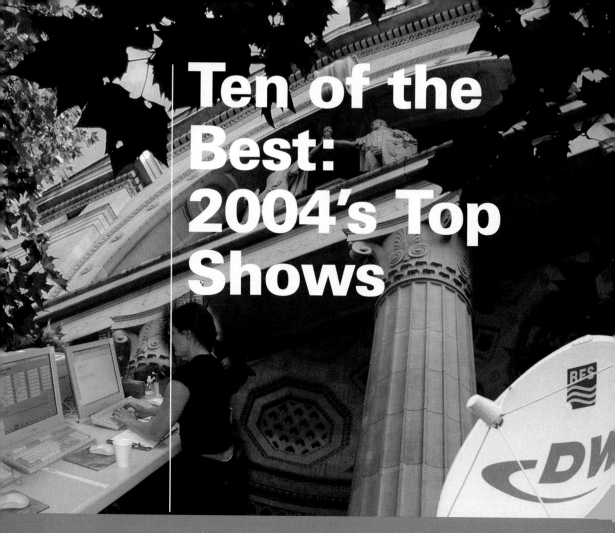

Ten of the Best: 2004's Top Shows

The unhomogenized airwaves of world band radio offer all kinds of good stuff. Yet, some programs really stand out. So, here are ten of the very best shows as selected by PASSPORT's listening panel for your enjoyment.

All times and days are in World Time. "Winter" and "summer" refer to seasons in the Northern Hemisphere, where summer takes place in the middle of the year.

"World Music Live"
Deutsche Welle

Nearly all world music shows have a downside, no matter how good they are. Whether it's a program of CDs or an extravaganza like the Canadian Broadcasting

Corporation's "Global Village," the abrupt switch from one musical style to another can be like going from chili to sushi.

No so with Deutsche Welle's "World Music Live," which features the same performers throughout. Whether it's African dance music from Mozambique or a sedate Chinese folk ensemble, it's a half hour of uninterrupted pleasure. Performances are top rate and the audio is excellent, hardly a surprise given DW's technical capabilities. As the title suggests, all music is recorded live, so it's the real McCoy.

Deutsche Welle doesn't specifically target *North America*, but listeners in the eastern and southern United States often have good reception of the 2100-2200 broadcast to West Africa. Luckily, "World Music Live" is aired then, so try 2130 Monday. The best winter frequency is 15410 kHz; summer, choose between 11865 and 15205 kHz.

Rick Fulker produces "World Music Live" and "Focus on Folk" for Deutsche Welle. DW

Listeners in *Europe* have six opportunities: 1730 Monday and 0730, 0930, 1030, 1230 and 1430 Tuesday, all on 6140 kHz.

There's no official slot for the *Middle East*, but the 1930 Monday broadcast on 11865 kHz winter, and 13590 kHz summer, should do the trick. This broadcast is targeted at East Africa, but is also well heard in parts of the Middle East.

Southern Africa: 0530 Tuesday, winter on 11805 and 12045 kHz, and summer on 12045 and 13755 kHz.

There's no airing for *East Asia*, but *Southeast Asia* gets its chance at 2330 Monday (Tuesday morning local date in the target area). Winter frequencies are 7250, 9815 and 12035 kHz; replaced summer by 9890 and 17860 kHz.

Listeners in *Australasia* should try the Southeast Asia broadcast.

"People in the Know"
China Radio International

China Radio International is coming of age. The quality of its programs is rapidly catching up with its already high technical standards, and "People in the Know" is an excellent example of how far the station has come.

"People in the Know" is an offshoot of an earlier show called "Talk to the Minister," and takes a look at controversial topics concerning China. The format is simple: interviews with experts, government ministers, leaders of national and international organizations, or anyone else "in the know." Whether it's Sino-Japanese relations or floating the Chinese currency on world markets, there's plenty of knowledgeable comment, as well as the occasional hard truth.

The first opportunity for *eastern North America* is at 2331 Sunday on 5990 (nominally to the Caribbean) and 13680 kHz. The next airing is

Guan Juanjuan produces and hosts the informative "People in the Know," aired weekly over China Radio International. CRI

four hours later at 0331 on 9690 kHz, with further repeats at 0431 on 9730 or 9755 kHz, and 1331 on 9570 kHz (all Monday, World Time).

First slot for *western North America* is 0331 Monday (Sunday evening local American date) on 9690 and 9790 kHz; with repeats the same day at 0431 on 9560 (summer) and 9730 or 9755 kHz; 0531 (winter) on 9560 kHz; 1331 (summer) on 7405 kHz; 1431 on 7405 and 17720 kHz; and 1531 on 7405 (winter) and 17720 kHz.

All broadcasts for other areas are aired Monday.

Europe has three choices: 2031 and 2131 winter on 5965 and 9840 kHz, and summer on 11790 and 15110 kHz; plus 2231 winter on 7170 kHz, replaced summer by 9880 kHz and autumn by 7175 kHz.

In the *Middle East*, tune in at 1931 winter on 9585 kHz, and summer on 13790 kHz. For *southern Africa* there's 1431 and 1531 on 13685 and 15125 kHz; 1631 winter on 13650 kHz, and midyear on 9570 kHz; 1731

on 9570, 9695 and 11910 kHz; and 2131 on 11640 and 13630 kHz.

There's nothing for *East Asia*, but *Southeast Asia* has two slots: 1231 on 9730 and 11980 kHz, and 1331 on 11980 and 15180 kHz.

In *Australasia* it's 0931 and 1031 on 11730 (or 17690) and 15210 kHz; 1231 on 9760, 11760 and 15415 kHz; and 1331 on 11760 and 11900 kHz.

"Documentary"
Radio Netherlands

A good radio documentary is like a good movie—it leaves a lasting impression. And so it is with Radio Netherlands' award-winning "Documentary." Solid research and editing combined with first-class production techniques make for a good show.

Offbeat or mainstream, historical or contemporary, each production bears the unmistakable hallmark of Radio Nether-

UPDATE YOUR LISTENING SCHEDULES MONTHLY WITH MONITORING TIMES, *the leading shortwave magazine.*

If it's on the radio, it's in *Monitoring Times*!

Do you own a radio, a shortwave receiver, a scanning receiver, or a ham radio? Then *Monitoring Times*® is your magazine! Open a copy of *MT*, and you will find 92 pages packed with news, information, and tips on getting more out of your radio listening. In fact, it's the most comprehensive radio hobby magazine in the U.S., and you can have it all for only $26.95 per year!

But that's not all... if you have a computer, then you need...

... MT EXPRESS!

Now you can receive the world's favorite monitoring magazine over the Internet! No postal delays and no lost or torn issues. And you can get every issue faster – anywhere in the world – than U.S. postal subscribers!

For a mere $19.95 (U.S. funds), or only $11 if you have a print subscription, MT Express delivers to your computer – in brilliant color – the entire Monitoring Times magazine in PDF format.

Free software lets you navigate through the magazine or click from the index, even search by keywords! Print it out on your computer printer, or use compatible text readers for the visually impaired.

MT EXPRESS on-line subscription: US $19.95 (or US $11 for current print subscribers)

Receive your free sample now by visiting http://www.monitoringtimes.com

Annual Subscription Rates to Print Version
U.S. Second Class Mail, US $26.95
U.S. First Class Mail, US $57.95
Canadian Surface Mail, US $39.50
Canadian Air Mail, US $51.50
Foreign International, US $58.50
Foreign Air Mail, US $88.95

6 month, 2 year, and 3 year subscriptions available.

Sample copy available in Europe for US$4.75 (allow six weeks for delivery).

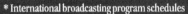

* International broadcasting program schedules
* World hotbed frequencies
* Shortwave and Longwave DXing
* Satellite broadcasting
* Pirate and clandestine stations
* Two-way communications
* Listening tips from the experts
* Frequency lists and loggings
* News-breaking articles
* Exclusive interviews
* New product reviews
* Feature articles
...and much, much more!

Published by Grove Enterprises, Inc.

800-438-8155
www.grove-ent.com
828-837-9200 fax: 828-837-2216
7540 Highway 64 West
Brasstown, NC 28902

Or you can order by emailing
order@grove-ent.com with a
Visa, Mastercard or Discover

Radio Netherlands producer Eric Beauchemin has won numerous international awards for his compelling documentaries focusing on the plight of children in the Third World. RNW

lands' small documentary team. What often distinguishes their documentaries from other productions is the human element. Tragedy, poignancy and joy enrich many of these programs.

The first airing for *eastern North America* is at 1230 Wednesday (one hour earlier in summer) on 5965 and 9890 kHz, with repeats later the same day at 0030 on 9845 kHz and 0130 on 6165 kHz. *Western North America* gets just one shot, 0430 Thursday (Wednesday evening local date) on 6165 and 9590 kHz.

These days there's nothing for *Europe* or the *Middle East*, but there are three Wednesday slots for *southern Africa*: 1830 on 6020 kHz, and 1930 and 2030 on 7120 kHz.

In *East* and *Southeast Asia* it's 1030 Wednesday on 7260 (winter), 12065 and (summer) 13710 kHz. *Australasia* has the same slot, but on 9785 kHz. The channels for Asia also provide good reception in parts of Australasia.

"Folk Box"
Voice of Russia

Some shows seem eternal, yet never lose their appeal. One of the oldest—still as fresh as a spring flower—is the venerable "Folk Box," dating from when the Voice of Russia was still known as Radio Moscow.

From Karelia to Kamchatka, Russia is a treasure trove of folk music that's a joy to the ears. Wedding songs, balalaikas, Cossack choirs...even throat singing. So it's no surprise that "Folk Box" continues to be a favorite with world band listeners.

Winter in *North America*, try 0231 Tuesday (Monday evening local American date) on 6155, 7180, 9765, 13665 and 15445 kHz; and 0531 Thursday on 7125, 7180, 12010, 12020, 13665, 15445 and 15595 kHz. In summer, one hour earlier, it's 0131 Tuesday on 9665, 9725, 11825, 17660 and 17690 kHz; and 0431 Thursday on 9665, 11750, 17565, 17650, 17660 and 17690 kHz.

Deutsche Welle's "Inside Europe" provides the best news about Europe. Its team includes producer Barbara Gruber (bracelet) and studio manager Lukas Alpert, along with presenter Helen Seeney, originally from Australia.   DW

Europe also has two winter slots: 2131 Thursday on 5950, 6175, 7300, 7340 and 7390 kHz; and 1831 Friday on 7290 and 7340 kHz. Summer, it's 2030 Thursday on 9480, 9775, 12030, 12070 and 15455 kHz; and 1731 Friday on 9775 and 9890 kHz.

Winter in the *Middle East* there's 1631 Thursday on 6005 and 9830 kHz, and 1831Friday on 9830 kHz. For summer, try 1531 Thursday on 7325 kHz, and 1731 Friday on 11985 kHz.

In *Southeast Asia* winter, tune in at 1531 Monday on 6205 and 11500 kHz; 0831 Tuesday on 17495, 17525, 17655 and 17665 kHz; or 0931 Thursday on 17495, 17525 and 17665 kHz. Summer options are 1431 Monday on 7390, 12055, 15560 and 17645 kHz; and 0731 Tuesday and 0831 Thursday on 17495, 17525 and 17635 kHz.

Australasia has two opportunities: winter at 0831 Tuesday and 0931 Thursday on 15275, 17495, 17525 and 17665 kHz; and midyear one hour earlier on 17495, 17525, 17635 and 21790 kHz.

"Inside Europe"
Deutsche Welle

There are several worthwhile programs about Europe, but the best is Deutsche Welle's 55-minute weekly roundup, "Inside Europe." Topics are as wide-ranging as they are interesting: historical preservation, controversial treatment for drug addicts, women's rights in the corporate world, profiles of European rock bands, French canal beaches—there's something fresh every week.

G2000A

Designed by the legendary F.A. Porsche, the G2000A's sleek sculpted lines and soft leather ca reminiscent of its automotive design heritage. With its digitally synthesized PLL tuner, capture FM-Stereo, and all 14 international broadcast bands, including Shortwave coverage of 2.3-7.4 and 9.4-26.1 MHz. Use the convenient auto-tuning system or with the direct frequency entry system, go instantly to any frequency in its tuning range.

Key features include:
- Easy tuning with direct frequency entry, up/down buttons, and auto-scan
- Sleep timer and dual alarm with beeper or radio play
- 20 programmable memory presets with memory scan feature for your favorite stations
- Protective leather snap-on cover and stand
- Powered by 3 AA batteries or optional AC adaptor

G2000A
AM/FM/Shortwave Radio
$79.95 USD

 RadioShack.
You've got questions. We've got answers.®

Herrington

NormThon

The Etón Story
Inside Front Cover

Satellit 800
Page 16

YB 400PE
Page 24

YB 550PE
Page 30

S350
Page 3

G1000A

Small enough to fit a coat pocket, this perfect travel radio keeps you informed via local and international stations when you're on the go, helps you fall asleep with its sleep-timer, and then wakes you to your favorite station in the morning.

Its analog tuner with digital frequency readout pulls in AM, FM-stereo, and 8 Shortwave bands (49, 41, 31, 25, 22, 19, 16 and 13 meters). The digital display shows frequency, time, sleep time, and activation of the alarm and sleep timer.

Key features include:
- Alarm and 1-60 minute sleep timer
- Built-in antennas including telescopic antenna FM and Shortwave reception and internal ferrite bar antenna for AM (MW)
- Protective snap-on cover and stand
- Earphone and DC sockets
- Operates on 2 AA batteries or optional AC adaptor

G1000A
AM/FM/Shortwave Radio
$49.95 USD

www.etoncorp.com

Magellan's
AMERICA'S LEADING SOURCE OF TRAVEL SUPPLIES℠

good guys

G2000A, G1000A
Page 48

M100, M300
Page 54

FR200
Page 60

The Future of Etón
Page 66

As the station no longer beams to *North America*, try 0605 Sunday when the show gets its airing to West Africa. Best bet is 15410 kHz in winter, and 17860 kHz in summer, both via the Deutsche Welle relay station in Rwanda. Reception is best in the southern United States and Caribbean.

Unlike North America, *Europe* has an abundance of opportunities: 0705, 0905, 1105, 1405, 1705 and 1805 Saturday, repeated 0605 Sunday, all on 6140 kHz.

The *Middle East* gets an early slot: 0405 Sunday, winter on 9545 kHz and summer on 11945 kHz. For *southern Africa* it's 2005 Saturday, winter on 13780 and 15205 kHz, and midyear on 9780 and 17810 kHz.

Listeners in *East Asia* get their chance at 2205 Saturday (Sunday local date in the target area), winter on 5955 and 6165 kHz, and summer on 9720 and 15605 kHz. *Southeast Asia* gets an earlier time, 1105 Saturday, winter on 17670 and 21650 kHz, and summer on 15110 and 17820 kHz. In *Australasia*, try the broadcast for Southeast Asia.

"Voices from Other Lands"
China Radio International

In "Voices from Other Lands," foreigners who work in or visit China take part in a chatty 25 minutes that's part interview, part discussion. It may be a media consultant in post-war Iraq, a lone skier who has crossed the Antarctic, or an Englishman helping to restore the Great Wall.

Originally just ten minutes long, the show's mix of informality and good subject matter have earned it the extended slot it now occupies.

In *North America*, easterners can tune in at 2331 Wednesday on 5990 (nominally to the Caribbean) and 13680 kHz. All other airings are Thursday, World Time: 0331 (Wednesday evening local American date) on 9690 kHz; 0431 on 9730 or 9755 kHz; and 1331 on 9570 kHz.

For *western North America*, same date, there's 0331 on 9690 and 9790 kHz; 0431 on 9560 (summer) and 9730 or 9755 kHz; 0531 (winter) on 9560 kHz; 1331 (summer) on 7405 kHz; 1431 on 7405 and 17720 kHz; and 1531 on 7405 (winter) and 17720 kHz.

All broadcasts to other areas are aired Thursday.

Europe has two direct broadcasts: 2031 and 2131 winter on 5965 and 9840 kHz, and summer on 11790 and 15110 kHz. A relay via Moscow can be heard one hour later at 2231 winter on 7170 kHz, summer on 9880 kHz and autumn on 7175 kHz.

For the *Middle East* it's 1931 winter on 9585 kHz, and summer on 13790 kHz. In *southern Africa*, choose from 1431 and 1531 on 13685 and 15125 kHz; 1631 winter on 13650 kHz, and midyear on 9570 kHz; 1731 on 9570, 9695 and 11910 kHz; and 2031 on 11640 and 13630 kHz.

There's nothing for *East Asia*, but listeners in *Southeast Asia* have two slots: 1231 on 9730 and 11980 kHz, and 1331 on 11980 and 15180 kHz.

In *Australasia*, take your pick from 0931 and 1031 on 11730 (or 17690) and 15210 kHz; 1231 on 9760, 11760 and 15415 kHz; and 1331 on 11760 and 11900 kHz.

"Newsline"
Radio Netherlands

Few stations can match the news-gathering resources of the BBC World Service or Voice of America, and Radio Netherlands is no exception. Yet, its half-hour "Newsline" is as interesting and newsworthy as anything produced by its Anglo-American colleagues.

Rather than try and compete with the likes of the BBC, Radio Netherlands has wisely chosen another route—fewer reports, but more in-depth coverage.

"Newsline" is prepared at Radio Netherlands' modern newsroom.
RNW

All editions are heard Monday through Friday, local date in the target areas.

In *North America*, easterners can tune in at 1200 (one hour earlier in summer) on 5965 and 9890 kHz; and 0000 on 9845 kHz. A repeat broadcast at 0100 on 6165 kHz usually gives reasonable reception, although it is beamed farther west. The airing for *western North America* is three hours later at 0400 on 6165 and 9590 kHz.

There's nothing for *Europe* or the *Middle East*, but *southern Africa* gets three slots: 1800 on 6020 kHz, and 1900 and 2000 on 7120 kHz.

For *East* and *Southeast Asia* it's 1000 on 7260 (winter), 12065 and (summer) 13710 kHz. *Australasia* has the same slot, but on 9785 kHz. Asian channels also provide good reception in parts of Australasia.

"The World This Weekend"
CBC/Radio Canada International

In-depth news coverage tends to slacken on weekends, but events roll on and often get missed. Many folks would like to be kept informed, but without having to sacrifice weekend entertainment.

Radio Canada International comes to the rescue with the Canadian Broadcasting Corporation's "The World This Weekend." Part news, part background reports and part documentary, it offers a week's worth of newsworthy events packed into 30 must-hear minutes.

Unfortunately for the rest of the world, "The World This Weekend" is broadcast only to the *Americas*: Saturday and Sunday winter at 2300-2330 on 5960, 9590, 11865 and 13730 kHz; and summer one hour earlier on 6140, 9590, 11920, 15170, 15455 and 17880 kHz.

"Audio Book Club"
Voice of Russia

The Voice of Russia's "Audio Book Club" is a hybrid, somewhere between storytelling and theater. It is also a simple and friendly introduction to Russian literature, both classical and modern.

It opens with a summary of a book and its author, with the remaining time given over to reading an extract. Partial dramatization gives the story an extra dimension, while Russian music is used to create an authentic background. Occasionally, the regular format is replaced by a serialized radio adaptation of a short story.

"Audio Book Club" is not edge-of-your-seat theater, but it's good armchair listening.

Winter in *North America*, dial in at 0331 Saturday (Friday evening local American date) on 6155, 7180, 13665 and 15445 kHz; and 0431 Monday and 0531 Friday on 7125, 7180, 12010, 12020, 13665, 15445 and 15595 kHz. In summer, one hour earlier, it's 0231 Saturday on 9665, 9725, 17660 and 17690 kHz; and 0331 Monday and 0431 Friday on 9665, 11750, 17565, 17650, 17660 and 17690 kHz.

Europe has just one airing: 2031 Thursday winter on 5950, 6175, 7290, 7340 and 7390 kHz; and summer, one hour earlier, on 9480, 9775, 11675, 12030 and 12070 kHz.

Winter in the *Middle East*, go for 1631 Wednesday on 6005 and 9830 kHz; and summer one hour earlier on 7325 kHz.

Voice of Russia's editorial staff (front, from left): Tatyana Shvetsova ("Moscow Yesterday and Today," "Audio Book Club," "Christian Message from Moscow"), Lyubov Tsarevskaya ("This Is Russia"), Olga Troshina (Letters Dept.), Larisa Avrutina and Elena Biryukova (Music Dept.); back: Olga Shapovalova (Music), Branislav Siljkovic (announcer), Elena Osipova (Letters), Anatoly Morozov (assistant director) and Elena Frolovskaya (Letters). VoR

In *Southeast Asia* winter, tune in at 0631 Sunday and 0731 Thursday on 17655 and 17665 kHz, and 0831 Wednesday on 17495, 17525, 17655 and 17665 kHz. Summer choices are 0631 Thursday on 17525 and 17635 kHz, and 0731 Wednesday on 17495, 17525 and 17635 kHz.

Australasia has three winter slots: 0631 Sunday and 0731 Thursday on 15275, 17665 and 21790 kHz; and 0831 Wednesday on 15275, 17495, 17525 and 17665 kHz. Midyear, there's 0531 Sunday and 0631 Thursday on 17635 and 21790 kHz; and 0731 Wednesday on 17495, 17525, 17635 and 21790 kHz.

"Focus on Folk"
Deutsche Welle

When a radio show's content is entertaining, it can take off by itself without fancy production tricks. And so it is with "Focus on Folk," the tongue-tricking title of this window on German folk music.

"Focus on Folk" and the Voice of Russia's "Folk Box" both feature national grass roots music, but that's where the similarity ends. "Folk Box" covers a huge range of styles, from the sublime to the curious, and is unique on the world bands. "Focus on Folk," on the other hand, is a hum-along, foot-tapping, stein-clinking 30 minutes of relaxing entertainment. Old and new songs, a yodeling trumpet, the traditional accordion or a band playing a Souza march— it's fun music.

There's no broadcast for *North America*, but listeners in the eastern United States and Caribbean can eavesdrop on Friday's 2130 broadcast to West Africa. Best winter frequency is 15410 kHz; summer, choose between 11865 and 15205 kHz.

Europe: 1730 Friday, and 0830, 1030, 1230 and 1430 the following Monday, all on 6140 kHz.

"Focus on Folk" presenter Angelika Ditscheid in the studio with Irene Quaile, Deutsche Welle's features editor. DW

Nothing's officially scheduled for the *Middle East*, but try 1930 Friday on 11865 kHz winter and 13590 kHz summer. This is targeted at East Africa, but is also well heard in parts of the Middle East.

Southern Africa: 0530 Saturday, winter on 11805 and 12045 kHz, and summer on 12045 and 13755 kHz.

There's *nichts* for *East Asia*, but *Southeast Asia* gets its chance at 2330 Friday (Saturday morning local date in the target area). Winter frequencies are 7250, 9815 and 12035 kHz; replaced summer by 9890 and 17860 kHz. Listeners in *Australasia* should try this, too.

———————————

Prepared by the staff of PASSPORT TO WORLD BAND RADIO.

M100 PE

Travel with the world in your hand. Small enough to fit in your palm, yet powerful enough to receive AM, FM-Stereo and 6 Shortwave bands (49, 41, 31, 25, 19 and 16 meters). Enjoy the classic analog tuner with tuning dial and needle display.

Key features include:
- Palm-sized and weighing less than 5 ounces
- Built-in antennas including telescopic antenna FM and Shortwave reception and internal ferrite bar antenna for AM (MW)
- Operates on 2 AA batteries
- Includes earphones, belt clip, and pouch

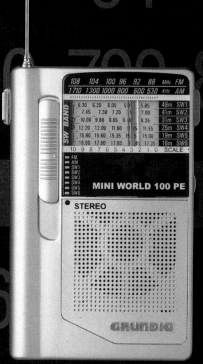

M100 PE
AM/FM/Shortwave Radio
$29.95 USD

AM/FM/SW ANTENNA

M300 BAND RECEIVER

etón

M300
AM/FM/Shortwave Radio
$39.95 USD

With its convenient digital frequency readout, this 4 ounce, shirt-pocket sized analog tuner pulls in AM, FM-stereo and 7 Shortwave bands (49, 41, 31, 25, 22, 19 and 16 meters). The digital display shows frequency, time, and activation of the alarm and sleep timer.

Key features include:
- Push button on/off control
- Built-in antennas including telescopic antenna FM and Shortwave reception and internal ferrite bar antenna for AM (MW)
- Operates on 2 AA batteries or optional AC adaptor
- Includes earphones, carrying strap, and pouch

www.etoncorp.com

Brookstone®

EDWARDS LUGGAGE
ADVENTURES IN TRAVEL

G2000A, G1000A
Page 48

M100, M300
Page 54

FR200
Page 60

etón
GRUNDIG North America

The Future of Etón
Page 66

Compleat Idiot's Guide to Getting Started

Ramping Up: Three World Band "Musts"

World band radio isn't conventional radio, so it calls for some new approaches. Here are the three key "musts" to hear the world successfully.

"Must" #1: **World Time and Day**

World band schedules use a single time, *World Time*. World band radio is global, with stations broadcasting around-the-clock from virtually every time zone. Imagine the chaos if each station used its local time to indicate when you should tune in. Ergo, World Time.

World Time, or Coordinated Universal Time (UTC), is also known as Greenwich Mean Time (GMT) or, in the military, "Zulu." It is announced in 24-hour format, so 2 PM is 1400 ("fourteen hundred") hours. Most major international broadcasters announce World Time at the hour. On the Internet World Time is given at various sites, including http://time5.nrc.ca/webclock_e.shtml.

Around North America, you can also hear World Time over standard time stations WWV in Colorado, WWVH in Hawaii and CHU in Ottawa. WWV and WWVH are on 5000, 10000 and 15000 kHz, with WWV also on 2500 and 20000 kHz. CHU is on 3330, 7335 and 14670 kHz.

See PASSPORT'S sidebar to set your 24-hour clock. For example, if you live on the East Coast of the United States, *add* five hours winter (four hours summer) to your local time to get World Time. So, if it is 8 PM EST (the 20th hour of the day) in New York, it is 0100 hours World Time.

> **Most radios work well simply with their built-in antennas.**

Adjust your radio's 24-hour clock. No clock? Get one now unless you enjoy doing weird computations in your head (it's 6:00 PM here, so add five hours to make it 11:00 PM, which on a 24-hour clock converts

to 23:00 World Time—but, whoops, it's summer so I should have added four hours instead of five...). The best money you'll ever spent.

Don't forget to "wind your calendar," because at midnight a new *World Day* arrives. This can trip up even experienced listeners—sometimes radio stations, too. So if it is 9 PM EST Wednesday in New York, it is 0200 hours World Time *Thursday*.

"Must" #2: Finding Stations

PASSPORT shows station schedules three ways: by country, time of day and frequency. By-country is best to tune to a given station. "What's On Tonight," the time-of-day section, is like *TV Guide* and has program descriptions. The by-frequency Blue Pages help tell you what you're hearing when you're dialing around the bands.

PASSPORT'S THREE-MINUTE START

Too swamped to read the manual? Try this:

1. Night is the right time, so wait until evening when signals are strongest. In a concrete-and-steel building put your radio by a window or balcony.

2. Make sure your radio is plugged in or has fresh batteries. Extend the telescopic antenna fully and vertically. Set the DX/local switch (if there is one) to "DX," but otherwise leave the controls the way they came from the factory.

3. Turn on your radio. Set it to 5900 kHz and begin tuning slowly toward 6200 kHz; you can also try 9400-9990 kHz. You should hear stations from around the world.

Other times? Read "Best Times and Frequencies for 2004."

SETTING YOUR WORLD TIME CLOCK

PASSPORT's "Addresses PLUS" lets you arrive at the local time in another country by adding or subtracting from World Time. Use that section to determine the time within a country you are listening to.

This box, however, gives it from the other direction—what to add or subtract from your local time so you can determine World Time. Use this to set your World Time clock.

Wherever in the world you live, you can also use Addresses PLUS, instead of this sidebar, to determine World Time simply by reversing the time difference. For example, Addresses PLUS states that Burundi's local time is "World Time +2." So if you're in Burundi, to set your World Time clock you would take Burundi time *minus* two hours.

WHERE YOU ARE	TO DETERMINE WORLD TIME
North America	
Newfoundland St. John's NF, St. Anthony NF	Add 3½ hours, 2½ summer
Atlantic St. John NB, Battle Harbour NF	Add 4 hours, 3 summer
Eastern New York, Atlanta, Toronto	Add 5 hours, 4 summer
Central Chicago, Mexico City, Nashville, Winnipeg	Add 6 hours, 5 summer
Mountain Denver, Salt Lake City, Calgary	Add 7 hours, 6 summer
Pacific San Francisco, Vancouver	Add 8 hours, 7 summer
Alaska	Add 9 hours, 8 summer
Hawaii	Add 10 hours
Central America & Caribbean	
Bermuda	Add 4 hours, 3 summer
Barbados, Puerto Rico, Virgin Islands	Add 4 hours
Bahamas, Cuba	Add 5 hours, 4 summer
Jamaica	Add 5 hours
Costa Rica	Add 6 hours
Europe	
United Kingdom, Ireland, Portugal	Same time as World Time winter, subtract 1 hour summer

Continental Western Europe; parts of Central and Eastern Continental Europe	Subtract 1 hour, 2 hours summer
Elsewhere in Continental Europe: Belarus, Bulgaria, Cyprus, Estonia, Finland, Greece, Latvia, Lithuania, Moldova, Romania, Russia (Kaliningradskaya Oblast), Turkey, Ukraine	Subtract 2 hours, 3 summer
Moscow	Subtract 3 hours, 4 summer

Mideast & Africa

Côte d'Ivoire, Ghana, Guinea, Liberia, Mali, Morocco, Senegal, Sierra Leone	World Time exactly
Angola, Benin, Chad, Congo, Nigeria, Tunisia	Subtract 1 hour
Egypt, Israel, Jordan, Lebanon, Syria	Subtract 2 hours, 3 summer
South Africa, Zambia, Zimbabwe	Subtract 2 hours
Ethiopia, Kenya, Kuwait, Saudi Arabia, Tanzania, Uganda	Subtract 3 hours
Iran	Subtract 3½ hours, 4½ summer

Asia & Australasia

Pakistan	Subtract 5 hours
India	Subtract 5½ hours
Bangladesh, Sri Lanka	Subtract 6 hours
Laos, Thailand, Vietnam	Subtract 7 hours
China (including Taiwan), Malaysia, Philippines, Singapore	Subtract 8 hours
Japan, Korea	Subtract 9 hours
Australia: *Victoria, New South Wales, Tasmania*	Subtract 11 hours local summer, 10 local winter (midyear)
Australia: *South Australia*	Subtract 10½ hours local summer, 9½ hours local winter (midyear)
Australia: *Queensland*	Subtract 10 hours
Australia: *Northern Territory*	Subtract 9½ hours
Australia: *Western Australia*	Subtract 8 hours
New Zealand	Subtract 13 hours local summer, 12 hours local winter (midyear)

FR200

Requiring no external power source, the FR200 is a versatile multi-purpose tool for keeping informed, entertained, and safe. Combining AM/FM/Shortwave radio and flashlight in one, the FR200 operates without batteries – powered by its built-in hand-crank generator – allowing you to listen to news, music, and international programming from anywhere, including places where power is a problem.

Key features include:

- AM/FM/Shortwave Tuning (SW1, 3.2-7.6MHz; SW2, 9.2-22MHz)
- Hand-crank power generator recharges internal Ni-MH battery
- Built-in flashlight perfect for emergencies or camping
- Splash-proof ABS cabinet withstands your adventures and abuse
- Can also operate on 3 AA batteries or optional AC adaptor

RadioShack®
just around the corner.

Herrington

Magellan's
AMERICA'S LEADING SOURCE OF TRAVEL SUPPLIES™

FR200
AM/FM/Shortwave Radio
$39.95 USD

www.etoncorp.com

RESTORATION
H A R D W A R E

BED BATH &
BEYOND

G2000A, G1000A
Page 48

M100, M300
Page 54

FR200
Page 60

etón
GRUNDIG North America

The Future of Etón
Page 66

BEST TIMES AND FREQUENCIES FOR 2004

With world band, if you dial randomly you're just as likely to get dead air as a program. That's because some world band segments are alive and kicking only by day, while others spring to life at night. Others fare better at certain times of the year.

This guide is most accurate if you're listening from north of Africa or South America. Even then, what you'll actually hear will vary—depending upon your location, where the station transmits from, the time of year and your radio (*see* Propagation in PASSPORT'S Glossary). Although world band is active around the clock, signals are usually best from an hour or two before sunset until sometime after midnight. Too, try a couple of hours on either side of dawn. **Nighttime** refers to your local hours of darkness, plus dawn and dusk.

A number of official frequency segments are allocated for broadcasting. Broadcasters may also operate "out-of-band" as secondary users, provided they do not cause harmful interference to primary users—typically fixed-service utility stations.

Very Limited Reception Nighttime

2 MHz (120 meters) **2300-2495 kHz**—overwhelmingly domestic stations, plus 2496-2504 kHz for time stations only.

Limited Reception Nighttime

3 MHz (90 meters) **3200-3400 kHz**—overwhelmingly domestic stations.

Good-to-Fair in Europe and Asia except Summer Nights; Elsewhere, Limited Reception Nighttime

4 MHz (75 meters) **3900-4050 kHz**—international and domestic stations, primarily not in or beamed to the Americas; 3900-3950 kHz mainly Asian and Pacific transmitters; 3950-4000 kHz also includes European and African transmitters; 4001-4050 kHz currently out-of-band.

Distant Reception Nighttime; Regional Reception Daytime

5 MHz (60 meters) **4750-4995 kHz** and **5005-5100 kHz**—mostly domestic stations, plus 4996-5004 kHz for time stations only; 5061-5100 kHz currently out-of-band.

Excellent Nighttime; Regional Reception Daytime

6 MHz (49 meters) **5730-6300 kHz**—5730-5899 kHz and 6201-6300 kHz currently out-of-band.

Good Nighttime; Regional Reception Daytime

7 MHz (41 meters) **6890-6990 kHz** and **7100-7600 kHz**—6890-6990 kHz and 7351-7600 kHz currently out-of-band; 7100-7300 kHz no American-based transmitters and few transmissions targeted to the Americas. Some years hence, the 7100 kHz lower parameter may shift to 7200 kHz, with 7200-7300 kHz rather than 7100-7300 kHz being for outside the Americas.

9 MHz (31 meters) **9250-9995 kHz**—9250-9399 kHz and 9901-9995 kHz currently out-of-band, plus 9996-10004 kHz for time stations only.

Feodor Brazhnikov tunes in the world from Siberia, where he is active in the Irkutsk DX Circle (irkutsk.com/radio).

IDXC

World band frequencies are usually given in kilohertz (kHz), but some stations use Megahertz (MHz). The only difference is three decimal places, so 6170 kHz is the same as 6.17 MHz, 6175 kHz identical to 6.175 MHz, and so on.

You're used to hearing FM and other stations at the same spot on the dial, day and night, or Webcasts at the same URLs.

But things are a lot different when you roam the international airwaves.

World band radio is like a global bazaar where a variety of merchants come and go at different times of the day and night. Where you once tuned in, say, a French station, hours later you might find a Russian or Chinese broadcaster roosting on that same spot.

Good Almost Anytime

11 MHz (25 meters) **11500-12200 kHz**—11500-11599 kHz and 12101-12200 kHz currently out-of-band.

Good Daytime; Variable Summer Nighttime

13 MHz (22 meters) **13570-13870 kHz**

15 MHz (19 meters) **15005-15825 kHz**—15005-15099 kHz and 15801-15825 kHz currently out-of-band, plus 14996-15004 kHz for time stations only.

Good Daytime; Variable, Limited Reception Summer Nighttime

17 MHz (16 meters) **17480-17900 kHz**

19 MHz (15 meters) **18900-19020 kHz**

21 MHz (13 meters) **21450-21850 kHz**

Rare, if Any, Reception Daytime

25 MHz (11 meters) **25670-26100 kHz**

RTC, the Training Centre for radio professionals from developing countries and Eastern Europe G. Poppin

Or on a nearby perch. If you suddenly hear interference from a station on an adjacent channel, it doesn't mean something is wrong with your radio; it probably means another station has begun broadcasting on a nearby frequency. There are more stations on the air than there is space for them, so sometimes they try to outshout each other.

To cope with this, purchase a radio with superior adjacent-channel rejection—selectivity—and lean towards radios with synchronous selectable sideband. PASSPORT REPORTS, a major section of this book, tells you which stand out.

Because world band is full of surprises from one listening session to the next, experienced listeners do a lot of surfing of the airwaves. Daytime, you'll find most stations above 11500 kHz; at night, below 12200 kHz.

If a station can't be found or fades out, there is probably nothing wrong with your radio. The atmosphere's sky-high ionosphere deflects world band signals down to earth, where they bounce off water or land back up to the ionosphere, then back up and back down again like a dribbled basketball until they get to your radio. This is why world band radio is so unencumbered—its signals don't rely on cables or satellites or the Internet, just layers of ionized gases which have enveloped our planet for millions of years. World band is free from regulation,

WORLD TIME CLOCKS

Some radios include a World Time clock displayed fulltime—this is best. Other radios may have World Time clocks, but to see the time you have to press a button when the radio is in use. Because World Time uses the 24-hour format, digital clocks are easier to read than hands.

MFJ Enterprises manufactures several 24-hour clocks—conventional or atomic-synchronized, some with seconds displayed numerically—from $9.95 to $79.95 at MFJ or radio dealers. Sharper Image also offers three clocks in the $39.95-49.95 range.

Other 24-hour clocks run up to $2,000, including models designed primarily for professional applications. Nearly all the pricier models display seconds and even split-seconds numerically, while many synchronize with an official atomic clock standard.

Sharper Image's World Time "Woody Clock" shows date, day and temperature. Hourly chime and announcement, too.

Ontario DX Association (odxa.on.ca) members team up to unearth rarely heard stations. Foreground is John Fisher, while from the left are Mark Coady, Bernie Rataj and Brian Smith.

Harold Sellers

free from taxes, free from fees—and largely free from ads, as well.

But nature's ionosphere, like the weather, changes constantly, so world band stations have to adjust accordingly. The result is that broadcasters operate within different frequency ranges, depending upon the time of day and season of the year.

That same changeability can work in your favor, especially if you like to eavesdrop on signals not intended for your part of the world. Sometimes stations from exotic locales—places you would not ordinarily hear—become surprise arrivals at your radio, thanks to the shifting characteristics of nature's ionosphere.

"Must" #3: The Right Radio

Choose carefully, but you shouldn't need a costly set. Avoid cheap radios, as they suffer from one or more major defects. With one of the better-rated portables you'll be able to hear much more of what world band has to offer.

Look for a radio with digital frequency display, which is far and away the easiest to tune—all radios tested for PASSPORT REPORTS have digital displays, but analog (slide-rule-tuning) models are still sold. Also, get a radio that tunes at least 4750-21850 kHz with no significant gaps or "holes." Otherwise, you may not be able to tune in some stations.

You won't need an exotic outside antenna unless you're using a tabletop model. All portables, and to some extent portatops, are designed to work well off their built-in telescopic antennas. If you want to enhance weak-signal sensitivity, clip several yards or meters of insulated wire onto that antenna.

If you just want to hear the major stations, you'll do fine with a moderately priced portable. Beyond that, portatop models have a better chance of bringing in faint and difficult signals—and usually sound better, too. Tabletop receivers are aimed at experienced DX enthusiasts, so they tend to be unnecessarily costly and complex for most program listeners to operate.

Prepared by Jock Elliott, Tony Jones and Lawrence Magne.

the Future of Etón

Since Etón's founding in 1984, the world had changed by leaps and bounds.

Political, economical, social, and technological changes have made information one of the most sought after commodities in the world. As the lives of people around the world become more intertwined, information is the key to keeping informed about the events around you.

At Etón, our goal for the future is to continue to be the gateway for information for people around the world. Radio is a medium that is more relevant today than ever. By serving as a instrument for people around the globe to broadcast to each other, sharing news and culture, radio's future is even brighter than its past.

As we continue to innovate into the future, we promise to provide our customers the products they need to access the information

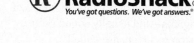

hey want. We pledge to explore leading-edge applications that deliver information better, faster, and more comprehensively than ever before.

With the information age upon us moving forward at the speed of technology, Etón Corporation will continue to be there, bringing you products that fulfill your needs and our mission — linking you to the world.

Etón bringing you:
- Innovative Design and Performance
- Quality Products at an Exceptional Value
- Outstanding Customer Service
- Industry's Only Dedicated Toll-Free Helpline
- Widely Available at Fine Retailers in North America

www.etoncorp.com

G2000A, G1000A
Page 48

M100, M300
Page 54

FR200
Page 60

The Future of Etón
Page 66

First Tries: Ten Easy Catches

Surveys show that most listeners tune to only a handful of easily heard stations. In that spirit, here are ten powerhouses that can be enjoyed nearly anywhere. Several have first-rate programs, and each is in English.

To minimize confusion, all times and days are in World Time. "Winter" and "summer" refer to seasons in the Northern Hemisphere, where summer takes place in the middle of the year.

Remember, easy catches aren't always the best bets. A confidential audience survey performed awhile back with our assistance showed Radio Australia and the U.S. Armed Forces Radio and TV Service to be strong favorites among North American listeners. These weren't the easiest of catches then or now.

In addition to coverage of hot-and-bothered political topics, Radio France Internationale keeps in touch with France's vast cultural heritage.
Toshi Ohtake

EUROPE

France

Radio France Internationale zeros in on audiences in Africa, the Middle East and southern Asia. Yet, thanks to the scattering properties of shortwave its English broadcasts are heard far and wide. Since the summer of 2003, RFI has been aired over three new relays—Ascension Island, United Arab Emirates and South Africa—further extending the reach of its signals.

RECOMMENDED PROGRAM: All are first-rate.

North America: Nothing aimed this way, but shoot for 0600-0630 winter weekdays on 11710 kHz; 0700-0800 year-round on 15605 kHz; and 1600-1700 winter on 17815 kHz, replaced summer by 15160 kHz. These emanate from RFI relays in Gabon and South Africa, and are intended for West Africa. Still, they are widely heard in parts of North America—especially along the East Coast.

Middle East: 1400-1500 on 17620 kHz winter, and 17515 kHz summer; also 1600-1730 winter on 11615 kHz and summer on 15605 kHz.

South Asia: 1400-1500 on 7175 or 9580 kHz in winter, and 11610 kHz in summer. This channel can also be heard in western parts of *Southeast Asia* and *Australia*.

Africa: RFI's popular broadcasts to Africa are audible at 0400-0430 weekdays on two or more frequencies from 9550, 9805, 11700, 11910, 11995 and 13610 kHz; 0500-0530 weekdays on any two channels from 11685, 11850, 13610, 15155 and 17800 kHz; 0600-0630 weekdays on two or more frequencies from 11665, 11725, 15155,

> **Radio France Internationale beams mostly to Africa but is heard far and wide.**

17800 and 21620 kHz; 0700-0800 on 15605 kHz; 1200-1230 on 17815 and 21620 or 25820 kHz; 1600-1700 on any four frequencies from 9730, 11615, 15160, 15605, 17605, 17815 and 17850 kHz; and 1700-1730 on any two channels from 11615, 15605 and 17605 kHz.

Germany

In 2003 **Deutsche Welle,** the Voice of Germany, unceremoniously dumped its North American and Australasian listeners in a move mimicking that of the BBC World Service two years earlier. Facing tough budget decisions, the station decided that direct English broadcasts to these regions were dispensable. Although this move had been in the works for some time, it wound up being implemented just as U.S.-German relations began falling to a post-WW II low.

From this dubious decision came two positive developments: The former 45-minute broadcasts were increased to a full hour, and German and world music were added to balance the news-oriented content of the shorter broadcasts. The station still specializes in German and European news, as well as spotlighting German life and culture, but its flagship "NewsLink" program now airs regional editions for Africa and Asia.

RECOMMENDED PROGRAMS: "Inside Europe" and "World Music Live."

North and Central America: The best opportunity for listeners in the eastern and southern United States and the Caribbean is the broadcast for West Africa at 2100-2200. Try 15410 kHz in winter, and 11865 and 15205 kHz in summer. For night owls, the 0600-0700 broadcast to the same region should also provide reasonable reception, especially to the south. Best winter frequency is 15410 kHz, and 17860 kHz in summer.

Europe: 0600-1900 year-round on 6140 kHz.

Middle East: 0400-0500 winter on 9545 kHz and summer on 11945 kHz. The 1900-2000 broadcast to East Africa can also be heard well in some parts of the region. Try 11865 kHz in winter and 13590 kHz in summer.

Southern Africa: 0500-0600 winter—summer in the Southern Hemisphere—on 11805 and 12045 kHz; and midyear on 12045 and 13755 kHz. The evening transmission airs at 2000-2100 winter on 13780 and 15205 kHz, and midyear on 9780 and 17810 kHz.

East Asia: A 30-minute Asian edition of "NewsLink" can be heard at 1000-1030 winter on 6205 kHz, and summer on 17615 and 17715 kHz. A full one-hour broadcast airs at 2200-2300, winter on 5955 and 6165 kHz and summer on 9720 and 15605 kHz.

Southeast Asia: 1100-1200 winter on 17670 and 21650 kHz, and summer on 15110 and 17820 kHz; and 2300-2400 winter on 7250, 9815 and 12035 kHz; replaced summer by 9890 and 17860 kHz.

Australasia: There's nothing specifically for Australasia, but transmissions to Southeast Asia provide adequate reception when there's no interference from other stations.

Netherlands

Radio Nederland—often called **Radio Netherlands**—is another station which was "restructured" in 2003. English broadcasts were retimed, and there was a shakeup in the program department that resulted in the loss of some key staff. Nevertheless, most shows have been retained, albeit with fewer airings, while the station continues with the same high standards as before.

RECOMMENDED PROGRAMS: "Newsline" and "Documentary."

Eastern North America: 1200-1255 (one hour earlier in summer) on 5965 and 9890 kHz, 1900-2055 (weekends only) on 15315 and 17725 kHz, 0000-0055 on 9845 kHz, and 0100-0155 on 6165 kHz.

THE VERY BEST IN SHORTWAVE RADIOS

YB 400PE AM/FM/ Shortwave Radio

…s high-performance PLL synthesized, dual-conversion YB 400PE receiver pulls in AM, FM-Stereo, …ortwave, and Longwave, including continuous coverage from 520-30,000 KHz. Even Ham radio two-way …mmunications can be heard using the SSB circuitry. Its highly sensitive auto-tuning system stops even on …ak stations within the international Shortwave broadcast bands. Its 40 programmable memory presets …w quick, easy access to your favorite stations. **Key features include:**

…asy tuning with direct frequency entry, up/down buttons, and auto-scan
…ultifunction LCD displays time, frequency, band, alarm wake time, and sleep timer
…leep timer, dual clocks, and dual alarm modes wake you with beeper or radio play
…uilt-in antennas for complete portability and socket for supplementary Shortwave antennas
…ncludes AC adaptor, earphones, carrying pouch, supplementary Shortwave wire antenna, and batteries

$149.95

Satellit 800 AM/FM/ Shortwave Emergency Radio

The Satellit 800 continues Grundig's legendary tradition of high-performance, top-of-the-line portable radios. An advanced digital tuner, with its extensive frequency range (100-30,000 KHz, 87-108 MHz, and 118-136 MHz), covers Longwave, Medium Wave (AM), FM-Stereo, and VHF aircraft band. SSB circuitry enables listening to two-way amateur radio communications. The large, 6" x 3.5" backlit LCD display shows all information with excellent clarity and contrast. **Key features include:**

• Multiple tuning choices with direct frequency entry, up/down buttons, and traditional weighted tuning knob
• 70 programmable memory presets with memory scan feature for your favorite stations
• Three built-in bandwidths (6.0, 4.0, 2.3 KHz), using electronically switched IF filters, help to minimize interference
• Synchronous detector (usable from 100-30,000 kHz) improves quality of amplitude modulated signals in the AM and Shortwave bands, minimizing the effects of fading distortion, adjacent frequency interference, and noise
• Dual clocks with timers for waking up in the morning, or sending timed outputs to your favorite recording device

$499.95

S350 AM/FM/ Shortwave Radio

…corporating a sensitive, high-performance analog tuner with digital frequency readout, the S350 receives …M, FM-Stereo, and continuous Shortwave coverage of 3,000 to 28,000 KHz, including all 14 international …oadcast bands. Its classic analog tuning knob with superimposed fine-tuning control makes it a pleasure to …erate, and the variable RF gain control, wide/narrow bandwidth selector and low pass filter give you …mplete control over incoming signals. Operates on 4 'D' batteries for long battery life.

…ey features include:
…Multifunction LCD shows digital frequency, clock, and more
…Alarm and 1-90 minute sleep timer
…Variable, independent bass and treble controls
…Left/right line-level outputs (stereo in FM)
…Includes built-in antennas, sockets for supplementary Shortwave and FM antennas, convertible nylon …handle/carrying strap, earphones, and optional AC adaptor

$99.95

FR200 AM/FM/ Shortwave Emergency Radio

Requiring no external power source, the FR200 is a versatile multi-purpose tool for keeping informed, entertained, and safe. Combining AM/FM/Shortwave radio and flashlight in one, the FR200 operates without batteries – powered by its built-in hand-crank generator – allowing you to listen to news, music, and international programming from anywhere, including places where power is a problem.

Key features include:
• AM/FM/Shortwave Tuning (SW1, 3.2-7.6MHz; SW2, 9.2-22MHz)
• Hand-crank power generator recharges internal Ni-MH battery
• Built-in flashlight perfect for emergencies or camping
• Splash-proof ABS cabinet withstands your adventures and abuse
• Can also operate on 3 AA batteries or optional AC adaptor

$39.95

Western North America: 1900-2055 (weekends only) on 15315 and 17875 kHz, and 0400-0455 daily on 6165 and 9590 kHz.

Southern Africa: 1800-1855 on 6020 kHz, and 1900-2055 on 7120 kHz.

East and Southeast Asia: 1000-1055 winter on 7260 and 12065 kHz, and summer on 12065 and 13710 kHz.

Australia and the Pacific: 1000-1055 on 9785 kHz. Frequencies for East and Southeast Asia are also widely heard within the region.

Russia

More culturally oriented than most world band stations, the **Voice of Russia** is also one of the friendliest. Despite operating on a razor-thin budget, many of its programs are listener favorites.

RECOMMENDED PROGRAMS: "Folk Box" and "Audio Book Club."

Eastern North America: 0200-0600 winter on 6155 (0200-0400), 7125 (0400-0600), 7180 and (0200-0300) 9765 kHz; summer, one hour earlier, it's 9665 kHz at 0100-0500, 9725 kHz at 0100-0300, 11750 kHz at 0300-0500, and 11825 at 0100-0200. During winter afternoons, try frequencies beamed to Europe—some make it to eastern North America.

Until he died last September, Boris Belitsky was the Voice of Russia's science correspondent.   VoR

Western North America: Best bets for winter are: 0200-0400 on 12020, 13665 and 15445 kHz; and 0400-0600 on 12010, 12020, 13665, 15445, 15595 and (till 0500) 17595 kHz. For summer reception, one hour earlier, use 17660 and 17690 kHz at 0100-0300; and 17565, 17650, 17660 and 17690 kHz at 0300-0500.

Europe: Winter airings are 1800-1900 on 7290 and 7340 kHz; 1900-2000 on 5950, 6175, 6235, 7290, 7340 and 7360 kHz; and 2000-2200 on 5950, 6175, 6235, 7290 (till 2100), 7300 (from 2100), 7340 and 7390 kHz. Summer options are 1700-1800 on 9775 and 9890 kHz; 1800-1900 on 9480, 9775, 9890, 11630, and 11675 kHz; and 1900-2100 on 9480, 9775, 9890, 11675 (till 2000), 12030, 12070 and (from 2000) 15455 kHz [5950 and 6175 kHz (winter) and 9480 and 11675 kHz (summer) are also available weekends during the first hour].

Middle East: 1600-1900 (1500-1800 in summer). Winter, there's 6005 kHz (1600-1700), 9470 kHz (1700-1800), and 9830 kHz (1600-1900). In summer, use 7325 kHz at 1500-1600, 15540 kHz at 1600-1700, and 11985 kHz at 1600-1800.

Southern Africa: Officially, there's virtually nothing beamed this way, but winter try 9875 kHz at 1500-1600, and 9875 and 11510 kHz at 1900-2000. Midyear, go for 11510 kHz at 1700-1900. These channels are for East Africa, but often make it farther south.

Southeast Asia: 0600-1000 winter on 17495 (from 0800), 17525 (from 0800), 17655 (till 0900) and 17665 kHz; and 0600-0900 summer on 17495 (from 0700), 17525 and 17635 kHz; 1500-1600 winter on 6205 and 11500 kHz; 1400-1500 summer on 7390, 12055, 15560 and 17645 kHz; and 1500-1600 summer on 11500 kHz.

Australasia: 0600-0800 winter on 15275, 17665 and 21790 kHz; and 0800-1000 on 15275, 17495, 17525, 17655 (till 0900) and

17665 kHz. Midyear, 0500-0900 on 17495 (from 0700), 17525 (from 0700), 17635 and 21790 kHz.

United Kingdom

The **BBC World Service** is the station that was. Since the masterful John Tusa was edged out as managing director in 1992, there has been a steady decline in the quality of its programs. Falling credibility and rising incompetence flourish at the highest levels, and there is little evidence of a turnaround. Although a number of good programs persist, they are mostly remnants of when Britannia ruled the airwaves through professionalism and earned trust.

Not satisfied with eroded standards of content, World Service management has also shifted delivery to North America and Australasia from hours-long blocks of news and entertainment, primarily via world band, to segments of news inserted within local stations' programs. Nevertheless, the BBC can still be widely heard on world band in most parts of the world, and the breadth and depth of its news reporting in times of international crisis can still be difficult to match. It also offers a wider range of entertainment than any other world band station.

RECOMMENDED PROGRAM: "Charlie Gillett."

North America: There are no longer any broadcasts officially targeted at the United States and Canada; these were dropped in July 2001. Nevertheless, the BBC continues to be well-heard throughout much of the region.

Best for eastern North America is the powerful service for the Caribbean: 1000-1100 on 6195 kHz, 1100-1400 on 6195 and 15190 kHz, 1400-1700 on 15190 kHz, and 2100-0500 on 5975 kHz. The transmission for South America at 2100-0300

England comes to you daily over the BBC.   Mike Wright

on 12095 kHz is also heard in parts of North America, but tends to suffer from teletype interference unless your radio has synchronous selectable sideband (*see* PASSPORT REPORTS). Too, some daytime frequencies for Europe, Africa and the Mideast can be heard— particularly during summer—but times vary, depending on your location and the time of year.

For nighttime and early morning reception in western North America, tune to the BBC's East Asia stream on 9740 kHz (1000-1600); reception is especially good on the West Coast. Winter evenings, try 9525 kHz (0100-0400) and 6135 kHz (0400-0600), replaced summer by 11835 kHz at 0100-0500—these are targeted at nearby Mexico.

Europe: A powerhouse 0300-2300 on 6195, 9410, 12095, 15485, 15565 and 17640 kHz, with times varying for each channel. Three frequencies—12095 (part of the time), 15565 and 17640 kHz— carry a separate program stream intended for the Mideast.

Middle East: 0200-2000. Key frequencies— times for each vary seasonally—are 9410, 11760, 12095, 15310, 15565, 15575 and 17640 kHz. 12095, 15565 and 17640 kHz are mainly intended for Eastern Europe, but provide acceptable reception in northern parts of the Mideast.

Southern Africa: 0300-2200 on, among others, 3255, 6005, 6190, 11940, 12095, 21470 and 21660 kHz—times vary for each channel.

East and Southeast Asia: 0000-0300 on 6195 (till 0200), 15280 and 15360 kHz; 0300-0500 on 15280, 15360, 17760 and 21660 kHz; 0500-0900 on 11955, 15280 (till 0530), 15360, 17760 and 21660; 0900-1030 on 6195, 9605, 9740, 15360, 17760 and 21660 kHz; 1030-1400 on 6195, 9740 and 17760 kHz; 1400-1600 on 6195, 7160 and 9740 kHz; 1600-1700 on 3915, 6195 and 7160 kHz; and 1700-1800 (to Southeast Asia) on 3915 and 7160 kHz. Local mornings, it's 2100-2200 on 3915, 5965, 6110 and 6195 kHz; 2200-2300 on 5965, 6195, 7105, and 11955 kHz; and 2300-2400 on 3915, 5965, 6035 (from 2330), 6195, 7105, 11685 11945, 11955 and 15280 kHz.

Australasia: Like North America, Australasia is no longer an official target for BBC broadcasts. Fortunately, some transmissions for Southeast Asia are easily heard in Australia and New Zealand. Best bets: 0500-0900 on 11955 and 15360 kHz and 0900-1600 on 9740 kHz. At 2200-2300, 12080 kHz is also available for the southwestern Pacific.

ASIA

China

China Radio International is among the few stations to offer genuine worldwide reception. It continues to install new transmitters on home soil, while at the same time increasing its relays overseas. Technically one of the best, CRI now focuses on getting its programs up to a similar level. Since August 2003, English broadcasts for some regions have been progressively extended from one to two hours.

RECOMMENDED PROGRAMS: "Voices from Other Lands" and "People in the Know."

Eastern North America: 0100-0200 on 9580 and 9790 kHz, 0300-0400 on 9690 kHz, 0400-0500 on 9730 or 9755 kHz, 1300-1400 on 9570 kHz, and 2300-2400 on 5990 (better to the south) and 13680 kHz.

Western North America: 0300-0400 on 9690 and 9790 kHz, 0400-0500 on 9730 or 9755 kHz, 0500-0600 (0400-0500 in summer) on 9560 kHz, 1400-1600 on 7405 (1300-1500 in summer) and 17720 kHz, and 2300-2400 on 13680 kHz.

Europe: 2000-2200 winter on 5965 and 9840 kHz, and summer on 11790 and 15110 kHz. A relay via Moscow can be heard winter at 2200-2300 on 7170 kHz, and summer on 9880 kHz (replaced by 7175 kHz in autumn).

Middle East: 1900-2000 winter on 9585 kHz, and summer on 13790 kHz.

Southern Africa: 1400-1600 on 13685 and 15125 kHz; 1600-1700 winter on 13650 kHz, and midyear on 9570 kHz; 1700-1800 on 9570, 9695 and 11910 kHz; and 2000-2130 on 11640 and 13630 kHz.

Asia: (Southeast) 1200-1300 on 9730 and 11980 kHz; and 1300-1400 on 11980 and 15180 kHz; (South) 1400-1500 on 9700, 11675 and 11765 kHz; and 1500-1600 on 7160 and 9785 kHz.

Australasia: 0900-1100 on 11730 (or 17690) and 15210 (or 15250) kHz; 1200-1300 on 9760, 11760 and 15415 kHz; and 1300-1400 on 11760 and 11900 kHz.

China (Taiwan)

Radio Taiwan International (formerly Radio Taipei International) is in a period of flux. Not only did the station assume a new name in 2003, but also it is considering major changes to its broadcasts. Depending on listener feedback, the station may consolidate its two hours of daily programming into just half that amount. Popular features would be retained and the amount

JRC **NRD-545**

Legendary Quality. Digital Signal Processing. Awesome Performance.

With the introduction of the NRD-545, Japan Radio raises the standard by which high performance receivers are judged.

Starting with JRC's legendary quality of construction, the NRD-545 offers superb ergonomics, virtually infinite filter bandwidth selection, steep filter shape factors, a large color liquid crystal display, 1,000 memory channels, scan and sweep functions, and both double sideband and sideband selectable synchronous detection. With high sensitivity, wide dynamic range, computer control capability, a built-in RTTY demodulator, tracking notch filter, and sophisticated DSP noise control circuitry, the NRD-545 redefines what a high-performance receiver should be.

JRC *Japan Radio Co., Ltd.*

Japan Radio Company, Ltd., New York Office —
2125 Center Ave., Suite 208, Fort Lee, NJ 07024
Voice: 201 242 1882   Fax: 201 242 1885

Japan Radio Company, Ltd. — Nittochi Nishi-Shinjuku Bldg.
10-1 Nishi-Shinjuku 6 chome, Shinjuku-ku, Tokyo 160-0023, Japan
Voice: 81 3 3348 3858   Fax: 81 3 3348 3935

- LSB, USB, CW, RTTY, FM, AM, AMS, and ECSS (Exalted Carrier Selectable Sideband) modes.

- Continuously adjustable bandwidth from 10 Hz to 9.99 kHz in 10 Hz steps.

- Pass-band shift adjustable in 50 Hz steps up or down within a ±2.3 kHz range.

- Noise reduction signal processing adjustable in 256 steps.

- Tracking notch filter, adjustable within ±2.5 kHz in 10 Hz steps, follows in a ±10 kHz range even when the tuning dial is rotated.

- Continuously adjustable AGC between 0.04 sec and 5.1 sec in LSB, USB, CW, RTTY, and ECSS modes.

- 1,000 memory channels that store frequency, mode, bandwidth, AGC, ATT, and (for channels 0–19) timer on/off.

- Built-in RTTY demodulator reads ITU-T No. 2 codes for 170, 425, and 850 Hz shifts at 37 to 75 baud rates. Demodulated output can be displayed on a PC monitor through the built-in RS-232C interface.

- High sensitivity and wide dynamic range achieved through four junction-type FETs with low noise and superior cross modulation characteristics.

- Computer control capability.

- Optional wideband converter unit enables reception of 30 MHz to 2,000 MHz frequencies (less cellular) in all modes.

Radio Taiwan International studios. The station changed its name in 2003 from Radio Taipei International.

CBS/RTI

of time given to Chinese language lessons would be reduced. If this comes about, it would be in marked contrast to the expansion of rival China Radio International.

RECOMMENDED PROGRAM: "Jade Bells and Bamboo Pipes."

North America: 0200-0400 on 5950 and 9680 kHz; and, for western North America, 0700-0800 on 5950 kHz.

Europe: 1800-1900 on 3955 kHz; and 2200-2300 winter on 9355 kHz, replaced summer by 15600 kHz.

Middle East: There is nothing specifically targeted at the Mideast, but try the 2200-2300 broadcast to Europe via RTI's North American relay.

Southern Africa: Another area which is not officially targeted. Best options are 0300-0400 on 15320 kHz and 1400-1500 on 15265 kHz (for Southeast Asia), plus the 1600-1800 broadcast for South Asia on 11550 (or 11560) kHz.

Asia: (East) 0200-0300 on 15465 kHz, and 1200-1300 on 7130 kHz; *(Southeast)* 0200-0400 on 11875 and 15320 kHz; 1100-1200 on 7445 kHz; and 1400-1500 on 15265 kHz; *(South)* 1600-1800 on 11550 or 11560 kHz.

Australasia: 0800-0900 on 9610 kHz.

Japan

With relays on five continents, **Radio Japan**—like China Radio International—can be heard just about anywhere. However, unlike CRI's predominantly talk programming, Radio Japan offers a balanced menu of news and entertainment.

RECOMMENDED PROGRAM: "Japan Musical Treasure Box."

Eastern North America: Best bets are 0000-0100 on 6145 kHz, 1100-1200 on 6120 kHz, and 1500-1600 summer on 11705 kHz. All are via the Canadian relay at Sackville, New Brunswick.

Western North America: 0500-0600 on 6110 kHz; 0600-0700 winter on 11690 kHz, and summer on 13630 kHz; 1700-1800 summer on 9505 kHz; and 2100-2200 on 17825 kHz. Listeners in Hawaii can tune in at 0600-0700 on 17870 kHz, and 2100-2200 on 21670 kHz. For Central America there's 0300-0400 on 17825 kHz.

Europe: 0500-0600 on 5975 kHz; 0500-0700 on 7230 kHz; 1000-1100 on 17585; 1700-1800 on 11970 kHz; 2100-2200 on 6055 (summer), 6180 (winter) and 11830 kHz.

Middle East: 0100-0200 on 11880 and 17560 kHz; and 1400-1500 on 17755 kHz.

Southern Africa: 1700-1800 on 15355 kHz.

Asia: 0000-0015 on 13650 and 17810 kHz; 0100-0200 on 11860, 15325, 17810 and 17845 kHz; 0500-0600 on 11715, 11760, 15195 and 17810 kHz; 0600-0700 on 11740 and 15195 kHz; 1000-1200 on 9695 and 15590 kHz; 1400-1500 on 7200 and 9845 (or 11730) kHz; and 1500-1600 on 7200, 9750 and 9845 (or 11730) kHz. Transmissions to Asia are often heard in other parts of the world, as well.

Australasia: 0100-0200 on 17685 kHz; 0300-0400 on 21610 kHz; 0500-0700 and 1000-1100 on 21755 kHz; and 2100-2200 winter on 11920 kHz, replaced midyear by 6035 kHz.

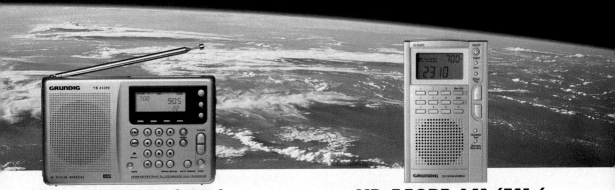

NORTH AMERICA

Canada

After years of tempestuous existence and near-extinction, **Radio Canada International** now sails through calmer waters. Though still heavily reliant on domestic programs from its parent CBC organization, over the last year there has been a boost in RCI's in-house output.

RECOMMENDED PROGRAMS: "Global Village" and "The World This Weekend."

North America: Morning reception is much better in eastern North America than farther west, but evening broadcasts propagate more widely. Winter, morning broadcasts air at 1300-1400 weekdays, 1400-1600 (daily) and 1600-1700 Saturday and Sunday, all on 9515, 9640 and 17710 kHz. In summer these transmissions are one hour earlier, on 9515, 13655 and 17800 kHz. During winter, evening broadcasts air at 2300-0100 on 5960 and 9590 kHz; and 0200-0300 on 6040 and 9755 kHz. The summer schedule is 2200-2400 on 6140, 9590 and 15455 kHz; and 0100-0200 on 9755, 15170 and 15305 kHz.

Europe: 2100-2230 winter on 5850, 6045 (from 2200) and 9770 kHz; and 2000-2130 summer on 5850, 5995 (till 2100), 11690 (till 2100), 15325 and 17870 kHz.

Middle East: 2100-2200 winter on 7425 kHz; and summer, 2000-2100 on 12035 kHz, and 2100-2130 on 7235 kHz.

Asia: To East Asia at 1200-1300 winter on 9795 and 11730 kHz, and summer on 9660 (or 9795) and 15190 kHz; to Southeast Asia at 0000-0100 winter on 9755 and 11895 kHz, summer on 9640 and 15205 kHz; and 1200-1300 winter on 11730 kHz, summer on 15190 kHz; to South Asia at 0200-0300 on 15150 (winter), 15510 (summer) and 17860 kHz; and 1500-1600 winter on 9635 and 11935 kHz, replaced summer by 15455 and 17720 kHz.

United States

In some respects, the **Voice of America** is not unlike the BBC World Service. Both are state funded, both were once highly respected broadcasters, and both are now being widely criticized.

That's where the similarities end. The BBC enjoys a high level of independence—its problems are of its own making. However, the VOA is the target of pressure from politicians with inconsistent and sometimes naive ideas on how it should be run. Those political currents have been made even trickier by non-VOA radio and TV operations recently established by Washington officialdom.

RECOMMENDED PROGRAM: "Music Time in Africa," one of the oldest and finest programs to grace the world band airwaves.

North America: There is a widespread misconception that because the VOA isn't beamed to an American audience, it can't be heard within the United States. In reality, it booms in on world band, allowing American taxpayers to hear firsthand what their government is telling the world in their name and on their dime. The two best times to listen are when the VOA broadcasts to South America and the Caribbean. The morning schedule is 1000-1100 daily on 5745, 7370 and 9590 kHz; while the evening broadcasts airs at 0000-0200 Tuesday through Saturday—local weekday evenings in the Americas—on 5995, 6130, 7405, 9455, 9775, 11695 (till 0100), 13740 (0130-0200), and (0000-0130) 13790 kHz. The African Service can also be heard in parts of North America; try 0300-0500 on 9575 kHz, 0500-0630 (till 0700 weekends) on 6035 kHz, 1800-2200 winter on 15580 kHz, 1900-2200 summer on 15445 kHz, and 2000-2200 winter on 17895 kHz.

There's not much for *Europe*, but try 0400-0700 winter on 7170 kHz, and summer on

9530 kHz; 0500-0700 winter on 11825 kHz; 1500-1700 winter on 15205 kHz; and 1700-2100 summer on 9760 kHz.

Middle East: 0400-0700 winter on 11825 (from 0500) and 15205 kHz; 0400-0700 summer on 11965 and 15205 kHz; 1400-1500 (winter) on 15205 kHz; 1500-1700 on 9575 (winter), 9700 (summer) and 15205 kHz; 1700-1800 winter on 6040, 9760 and 15205 kHz; summer on 9700 and 9760 kHz; 1800-2100 winter on 6040 (till 1900), 9690 (from 1900) and 9760 kHz; summer on 6095 (from 2000), 6160 (1900-2000), 9760, and (till 1900) 9770; and 2100-2200 on 6040, 6095 (summer), 9595 (winter) and 9760 kHz.

Southern Africa: 0300-0500 on 6080, 7105 (till 0400), 7340 (to 0330), 7415 (winter), 9575, 9885 (till 0430), and (midyear) 17895 kHz; 0500-0630 (till 0700 weekends) on 11835 and 12080 (or 13710) kHz; 1600-1700 on 13710 (winter), 15225 (or 15485), 15240 (or 15410) and 17895 kHz; 1700-1800 on 15240 (or 15410) and 17895 kHz; and 1800-2200 on 7415 (from 1900, winter only), 15240 (or 15410), 15445 (midyear, from 1900), 15580 and 17895 kHz.

East and Southeast Asia: 0800-1000 winter on 11995, 13605 and 15150 kHz; summer on 11930, 13620, 13760 and 15150 kHz; 1000-1100 winter on 15250 and 15425 kHz; summer on 13620, 15240 and 15425 kHz; 1100-1300 winter on 6110, 9760, 11705, 15250 and 15425 kHz; summer on 6160, 9760, 13610, 15160, 15240 and 15425 kHz; 1300-1500 winter on 6110, 9760, 11705 and 15425 kHz; summer on 5955, 6160, 15160 and 15425 kHz; 1700-1800 weekdays, winter on 6045, 9525, 9795 and 11955 kHz; summer on 6045, 7215, 9770 and 9785 kHz; 1900-2000 on 15180 kHz; 2100-2200 on 15185 and 17820 kHz; 2200-2400 on 7215, 9770 (summer), 9890 (winter), 15185, 15290, 15305 and 17820 kHz; and 0000-0100 on

Passport's Toshimichi Ohtake visits with Kim Elliott at the Voice of America. K.A. Elliott

7215, 9770 (summer), 9890 (winter), 15185, 15290 and 17820 kHz.

Australasia: 1000-1200 on 5985 (winter), 9645 (from 1100), 9770 (midyear), 11720 (winter) and 15425 kHz; 1200-1500 on 9645 (till 1400), 11715 (till 1300, winter only) and 15425 kHz; 1700-1800 weekdays on 5990 and (midyear) 7170 or (winter) 15255 kHz; 1900-2000 on 9525 and 11770 (or 11870) kHz; 2100-2200 on 9670 (winter), 9705 (midyear), 11870 and 17735 (or 17740) kHz; 2200-2400 on 9705 (midyear), 9770 (winter), 11760 and 17735 (or 17740) kHz; and 0000-0100 on 11760 and 17740 kHz.

Prepared by Tony Jones and the staff of PASSPORT TO WORLD BAND RADIO.

www.passband.com

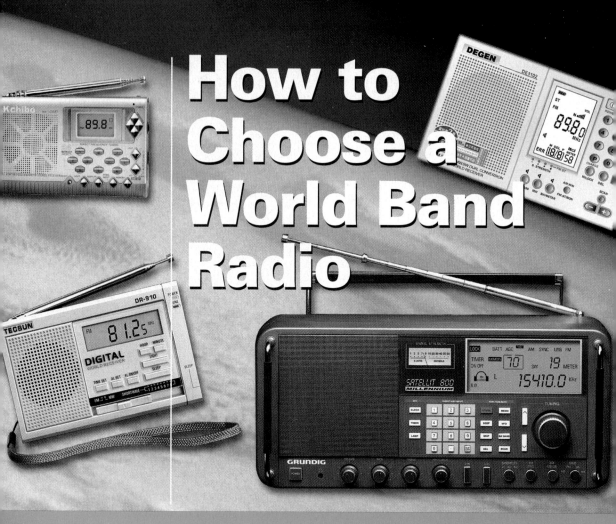

How to Choose a World Band Radio

Some electronic products are almost commodities. Use a little horse sense and you can find something suitable without fuss or bother.

Not so world band receivers, which often vary greatly from model to model. As usual, money talks, but even that's a fickle barometer. Fortunately, many perform well and we rate them accordingly. Yet, even among models with comparable star ratings it helps to choose a radio that satisfies your individual requirements.

No Elbow Room

World band radio is a jungle: 1,100 channels, with stations scrunched cheek-by-jowl. It's much more crowded than FM or mediumwave AM, and to make matters worse a global voyage can wear down signals, making them weak and quavery. To cope, a radio has to perform exceptional electronic gymnastics. Some succeed, others don't.

This is why PASSPORT REPORTS was created. At International Broadcasting Services we've tested hundreds of world band radios and accessories since 1977. These evaluations include rigorous hands-on use by listeners, plus specialized lab tests we've developed over the years. These form the basis of PASSPORT REPORTS, and for some popular premium receivers and antennas there are also the soup-to-nuts Radio Database International White Papers®.

Four-Point Checklist

✔ **Price.** Do you want to hear big stations, or flush out soft voices from exotic lands? Powerful evening signals, or weaker signals by day? Decide, then choose a radio that surpasses your needs by a good notch or so—this helps ensure against disappointment without wasting money.

Once the novelty wears thin, most people give up on cheap radios— they're clumsy to tune, often receive poorly and can sound terrible. That's why we don't cover analog-tuned models. Yet, even some digitally tuned models can disappoint.

Most find satisfaction with portables selling for $80-200 in the United States or £70-130 in the United Kingdom with a rating of ⚫⚫¾ or more. If you're looking for elite performance, shoot for a portable or

The Etón Mini 300, also sold as the Grundig Mini 300 and Tecsun R-919, is one of a growing number of low-cost pocket portables geared to the air traveler.

FEATURES FOR SOLID PERFORMANCE

A signal should not just be audible, but actually sound pleasant. Radios can incorporate features to help bring this about—most are to keep out unwanted sounds, while others enhance audio quality. Of course, just because a feature exists doesn't mean it functions properly, but we check for this in PASSPORT REPORTS.

"Must" Features for Quality Reception

Full world band coverage from 2300-26100 kHz is best, although 3200-21850 kHz or even 4750-21850 kHz is usually adequate. If coverage is less, look at "Best Times and Frequencies for 2004" elsewhere in this book to ensure that important world band segments are fully covered.

Synchronous selectable sideband greatly enhances rejection of adjacent-channel interference while reducing fading distortion. This advanced feature is found on some models selling for $150 or £110 and up.

Especially if a receiver doesn't have synchronous selectable sideband, it helps to have two or more *bandwidths* for superior adjacent-channel rejection. Some premium models incorporate this *and* synchronous selectable sideband—a killer combo. Multiple bandwidths are found on a number of models over $80 or £70.

Multiple conversion or *double conversion* helps reject spurious "image" signals—unwanted growls, whistles, dih-dah sounds and the like. Few models under $100 or £70 have it; nearly all over $150 or £100 do.

Other Helpful Attributes

High-quality speakers are an aural plus, as are *tone controls*—preferably continuously tunable with separate bass and treble adjustments. For world band reception, *single-sideband* (SSB) reception capability is only marginally relevant, but it is essential for utility or "ham" signals, as well as reception of low-powered signals from the popular U.S. Armed Forces Radio & Television Network. On costlier models you'll get it whether you want it or not.

Not satisfied with the available speaker quality? Try feeding your receiver's audio line output, if it has one, through a high-quality computer or other outboard amplified speaker.

Heavy-hitting tabletop models are designed to flush out all but the most stubborn signal, but they usually require experience to operate and are overkill for casual listening. Among these look for a tunable *notch filter* to zap howls; *passband offset* (a/k/a *passband tuning* and *IF shift*) for superior adjacent-channel rejection and audio contouring, especially in conjunction with synchronous selectable sideband; and multiple *AGC* decay rates. At electrically noisy locations a *noise blanker* is essential; some work much better than others.

Digital signal processing (DSP) is the latest attempt to enhance mediocre signal quality. Until recently it has been much smoke, little fire, but the technology has improved considerably. Watch for more DSP receivers to appear, but don't worship at their altar.

With portables and portatops an *AC adaptor* reduces operating costs and may improve weak-signal performance—usually the best performers and values are those that come with a radio. Some of these are poorly made and cause hum, but most are quite good. With tabletop models an *inboard AC power supply* is preferable but not essential.

Looking ahead, *digital shortwave transmission* from Digital Radio Mondiale (www.drm.org) is being actively implemented, although ready-to-use receivers are not yet available. Early adopters with a technical bent should consider the WiNRADiO G303i or Ten-Tec RX-320 reviewed in this PASSPORT REPORTS. However the DRM tests fare, it will be years, if then, before existing analog transmissions are phased out in favor of digital.

AC adaptors save batteries. Some work worldwide.

portatop rated ✪✪✪¾ or better—at least $350 or £300—or consider a five-star tabletop model.

✔ **Location.** Signals tend to be strongest in and around Europe, next-strongest in eastern North America. Elsewhere in the Americas, or in Hawaii or Australasia, you'll need a receiver that's unusually sensitive to weak signals—some sort of accessory antenna helps, too.

✔ **Which features?** Divide features between those which affect performance and those that impact operation (see sidebars), but be wary of judging a radio mainly by its features. Indeed, among lower-cost models, radios with relatively few features often significantly outperform those laden with goodies.

✔ **Where to buy?** Whether you buy in a store, by phone or on the Web makes little difference. That's because world band receivers don't test well in stores except in the handful of world band showrooms with proper outdoor antennas and little electrical noise. Even then, long-term satisfaction is

hard to gauge from a spot test, so visits at different times are advisable.

One thing a store lets you get a feel for is ergonomics—how intuitive a radio is to operate. You can also get a thumbnail idea of world band fidelity by listening to mediumwave AM stations or a superpower world band station.

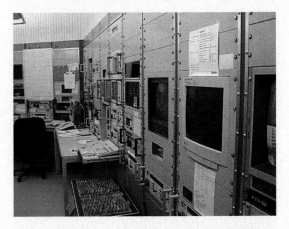

Deutsche Welle's Bockhacken monitoring station uses professional-grade receivers.

T. Ohtake

USEFUL OPERATING FEATURES

A "must" to find stations quickly is *digital frequency readout*, found on virtually all models tested by PASSPORT. A *24-hour clock* for World Time simplifies knowing when to tune in; many receivers have them built in. Best is if it can be read while the frequency is being displayed, but if your favorite radio doesn't include a World Time clock then spring for a standalone 24-hour clock or watch. Seconds displayed digitally are a nice touch to help be alert for station IDs.

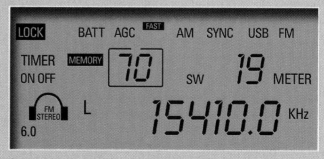

Other important features: direct-access tuning via *keypad* and *station presets* ("memories"); and any

Sophisticated receiver displays show several operating parameters, including tuned frequency.

combination of a *tuning knob*, up/down *slewing controls* or *"signal-seek" scanning* to search for stations. A few models have handy *one-touch presets* buttons, like a car radio. Quick access to *world band segments* is another ergonomic bonus.

Presets are important because world band stations, unlike locals, don't stay on the same frequency throughout the day. Being able to store the multiple frequencies of a broadcaster makes it easy to hear it at various hours. With sophisticated receivers, presets should be able to store not only frequency, but also such other parameters as bandwidth, mode and AGC settings.

Useful but less important is an *on/off timer*—a couple of timer-controlled models even come with built-in cassette recorders. Also, look for an *illuminated display* and a good *signal-strength indicator*, either as an analog meter or digital display, as you prefer. Travelers prefer portables with power-lock switches or recessed power buttons that keep the radio from going on accidentally, although the lock on some Chinese portables doesn't prevent display illumination from coming on accidentally.

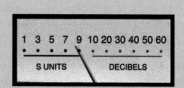

For signal strength readings, world band monitors tend to prefer an analog meter to a digital display.

When ergonomics stand out, bad or good, this is mentioned in the individual receiver's evaluation in PASSPORT REPORTS. In general, receivers with comparable levels of performance that have many controls are easier to operate than like comparable receivers with few controls, especially if the latter's operation involves complex tree-type software menus.

Portables for 2004

Portables are what most of us purchase, even if we also own something fancier. They are handy, affordable and usually do the trick.

In Europe and along the east coast of North America, evening signals come in so well that virtually any well-rated portable should be all you'll need. Even if you live elsewhere or listen during the day, when signals are weaker, a top-ranked portable can be boosted by a simple outdoor wire antenna.

When You're Away

World band makes for unbeatable outdoor entertainment, as well as a global link when you're traveling. For these and emergency situations (see separate article), only a portable will do.

They come in various sizes. Compact and pocket portables are the radio equivalents of Palm-type handhelds, while some larger portables are more like smaller laptop computers. There are compact models with three or more stars that sell for around the equivalent of $150 to $200—you can't go wrong with these workhorses. Aim your sights at models rated only slightly under three stars, and you can cut that price in half.

Off to the friendly skies? Pocket models are ideal for red-eye warriors, and their limited speaker audio can be overcome with earbuds. Yet, some "compact-compacts" sell for peanuts and are good enough for many.

To reflect advances in technology and quality, this year we've trimmed the overall rating of a number of mid-level and lesser models. Although we've raised the ratings bar a notch, the radios themselves haven't changed and sometimes are available at better prices than before.

Find major updates to the 2004 PASSPORT REPORTS at Passband.com.

New for 2004

What's new this year isn't a radio, but a country. In the mid-1970s the center of gravity for world band radios shifted to Japan, which ruled for two decades. Now, in 2004, China has assumed this role, turning out new models faster than the market has seen in years.

Grundig's spectacular sales success in North America now rests with radios made not in Europe, but in China by Tecsun Electronics. Also, most of Sangean's production has been moved from Taiwan to China, helping keep the firm's prices competitive.

For 2004 a new Chinese firm, Degen, has entered the market by significantly reducing the price for quality portables. Thanks to these new models, the era of the serious under-$100 portable is finally here.

When Longwave Is Useful

The longwave band is still used for domestic broadcasts in Europe, North Africa and Russia. If you live or travel in rural areas there, longwave coverage may be a plus. Otherwise, forget it.

Fix or Toss?

Portables aren't meant to be friends for life, and are priced accordingly. The most robust models are usually not ready for the landfill until a decade or more of use, whereas pedestrian portables may give only a few years of regular service. Rarely are they worth fixing unless they are fairly new.

If you purchase a new portable that is defective, insist upon an immediate exchange without a restocking fee—manufacturers' repair facilities tend to have a disappointing record, and a defective sample shouldn't be restocked. That having been said, Etón/Grundig and Sangean America in the United States and Canada provide better in-warranty service than most, and Etón/Grundig also has a useful toll-free help line. Yet, even their post-warranty service can disappoint. If quality of service is important to you, consider a tabletop model, instead.

Shelling Out

Street prices are given, including European and Australian VAT/GST where applicable. These vary plus or minus, so take them as the general guide they are meant to be. Shortwave specialty outlets and a growing number of other retailers have attractive prices, whereas duty-free shopping is not always the bargain you might expect.

David Heim, electronics deputy editor at *Consumer Reports* and quoted in *Reader's Digest*, suggests bluntly, "Look for stuff that's been factory refurbished." In North America refurbished Grundig portables are occasionally available from world band specialty vendors—these are cited in PASSPORT REPORTS' reviews—and try your pot luck if you are near a Sony outlet store.

We try to stick to plain English, but specialized terms can be useful. If you come across something that's not clear, check with PASSPORT's glossary.

Findings Apply Worldwide

PASSPORT REPORTS evaluates nearly every digitally tuned portable available in the world that meets reasonable minimum standards. We go wherever is necessary to obtain radios, so our findings are applicable globally with geographical provisos given as appropriate. Here, then, are the results of our hands-on and laboratory tests of current models.

What PASSPORT's Ratings Mean

Star ratings: ✪✪✪✪✪ is best. Stars reflect overall performance and meaningful features, plus to some extent ergonomics and perceived build quality. Price, appearance, country of manufacture and the like

---

TIPS FOR GLOBETROTTING

Post-9/11 air travel with a world band radio is unlikely to pose unusual difficulty if you take some common-sense steps. To minimize hassles with airport security personnel:

- Bring a portable, not a portatop or tabletop model—terrorists like big radios. Best is a pocket or compact model.
- Stow your radio in a carry-on bag, not in checked luggage or on your person.
- Take along fresh batteries so you can demonstrate that the radio actually works.
- If asked what the radio is for, say for personal use.
- If traveling in zones of war or civil unrest, or off the beaten path in much of Africa or parts of South America, take along a radio you can afford to lose and which fits inconspicuously in a pocket.
- If traveling to Bahrain, avoid taking a radio which has the word "receiver" on its cabinet. Security personnel may think you're a spy.
- If traveling to Malaysia, Bahrain or Saudi Arabia, don't take a model with single-sideband capability—or at the very least take steps to disguise this capability so it is not visually apparent.

Theft? Radios, cameras, binoculars, laptop computers and the like are almost always stolen to be resold. The more worn the item looks—affixing scuffed stickers helps—the less likely it is to be confiscated by corrupt inspectors or stolen by thieves.

are not taken into account. To facilitate comparison, portable rating standards are quite similar to those used for the portatop, tabletop and professional models reviewed elsewhere in this PASSPORT.

A rating of at least OO½ should please most who listen to major stations regularly during the evening. However, for casual use on trips virtually any small portable may suffice.

Passport's Choice. La crème de la crème. Our test team's personal picks of the litter—digitally tuned portables we would buy or have bought for our personal use. Unlike star ratings, these choices are unapologetically subjective.

●: A relative bargain, with decidedly more performance than the price would suggest.

Tips for Using This Section

Models are listed by size; and, within size, in order of world band listening suitability. Street selling prices are cited, including VAT/GST where applicable. Versions designed for certain few countries might not receive single-sideband signals and/or may have reduced tuning ranges. Refer to PASSPORT's glossary to understand specialized terms.

Unless otherwise indicated, each digital model has:

- Tuning by keypad, up/down slewing keys, station presets and signal-seek tuning/scanning.
- Digital frequency readout to the nearest kilohertz or five kilohertz.
- Coverage of the world band shortwave spectrum from at least 3200-26100 kHz.
- Coverage of the usual 87.5-108 MHz FM band. No coverage of the Japanese and other FM bands below 87 MHz.
- Coverage of the AM (mediumwave) band in selectable 9 and 10 kHz channel increments from about 530-1705 kHz. No coverage of the 153-279 kHz longwave band.

- Adequate image rejection, almost invariably resulting from double-conversion circuitry.
- No synchronous selectable sideband or single-sideband demodulation. However, when there is synchronous selectable sideband, the unwanted sideband is rejected approximately 25 dB via phase cancellation, not IF filtering.

POCKET PORTABLES
Perfect for Travel, Marginal for Home

Pocket portables weigh under a pound, or half-kilogram, and are between the size of an audio cassette jewel box and a handheld calculator. They operate off two to four ordinary small "AA" (UM-3 penlite) batteries. These diminutive models are ideal to carry on your person, but listening to tiny speakers can be tiring. If you plan on listening for long periods or to music, opt for using headphones or earpieces, or look into one of the better compact models.

OOO *Passport's Choice*
(see ☞)
Sony ICF-SW100S

Price: $359.95 in the United States. €329.00 in Germany.

Pro: Tiny, easily the smallest tested, but with larger-radio performance and features. High-tech synchronous selectable sideband generally performs well, reducing adjacent-channel interference and selective-fading distortion on world band, longwave and mediumwave AM signals, while adding slightly to weak-signal sensitivity and audio crispness (*see* Con). Single bandwidth, especially when synchronous selectable sideband is used, exceptionally effective at adjacent-channel rejection. Relatively good audio, provided supplied earbuds or outboard audio are used (*see* Con). FM stereo through earbuds. Numerous helpful tuning features, including keypad, two-speed slewing, signal-seek-then-resume

• **AC adaptor.** An outboard AC adaptor is virtually a necessity except on trips. Those provided by the manufacturer are usually best and should be free from hum and noise. Some are multivoltage and operate almost anywhere in the world. ☞ Beware of "switching" type power supplies, as these disrupt radio signals. In principle no radio manufacturer should be offering switching power supplies for use with radios, but in recent months we have seen some examples of this. PASSPORT REPORTS mentions when an AC adaptor causes problems.

• **Adjacent-channel rejection—I:** *selectivity, bandwidth.* World band stations are packed together about twice as tightly as ordinary mediumwave AM stations, so they tend to slop over and interfere with each other—experimental digital broadcasts, now being tested, are even worse at causing interference to neighboring channels. Radios with superior selectivity are better at rejecting this, but at a price: better selectivity also means less high-end ("treble") audio response and muddier sound. So, having more than one bandwidth allows you to choose between tighter selectivity (narrow bandwidth) when it is warranted, and more realistic audio (wide bandwidth) when it is not.

• **Adjacent-channel rejection—II:** *synchronous selectable sideband.* This is the first major advance in world band listening quality in decades, but few world band engineers have figured it out properly. With powerful stations "out in the clear," sync has little audible impact. However, for tougher signals it improves audio quality by minimizing selective-fading distortion, while reducing adjacent-channel interference by selecting the better half (the better sideband) of a signal. *Bonus:* this feature also helps considerably in reducing distortion with fringe mediumwave AM stations at twilight and even at night.

• **Ergonomics.** Some radios are easy to use because they don't have complicated features. Yet, even sophisticated models can be designed to operate intuitively. Choose accordingly—there's no reason to take the square root and cube it just to hear a radio station.

• **Single-sideband demodulation.** If you are interested in hearing non-broadcast shortwave signals—"hams" and utility stations—single-sideband circuitry is *de rigueur.* Too, the popular low-powered U.S. Armed Forces Radio-Television Service (AFRTS/AFN) can be heard only on receivers with single-sideband capability. No portable excels, but those which stand out are cited in PASSPORT REPORTS .

• **Speaker audio quality.** Unlike many portatop and tabletop models, few portables have rich, full audio through their speakers. However, some are much better than others, and with many models you can connect a good set of amplified PC speakers for home listening.

• **Tuning features.** Digitally tuned models are so superior to analog that these are now the only radios normally tested by PASSPORT . Look for such handy tuning aids as direct-frequency access via keypad, station presets (programmable channel memories), up-down tuning via tuning knob and/or slewing keys, band/segment selection, and signal-seek or other (e.g., presets) scanning. These make the radio easier to tune—no small point, given that a hundred or more channels may be audible at a time.

• **Weak-signal sensitivity.** Sensitivity is important if you live in a weak-signal location or tune to DX or daytime stations. Because of cutbacks in recent years, this also has become relevant for hearing some stations, such as the BBC and Deutsche Welle, within North America and Australasia. On the other hand, most portables have enough sensitivity to pull in major stations evenings if you're in such places as Europe or North Africa—even the east coast of North America.

☞ A simple outboard antenna (sidebar) enhances sensitivity, as well as the signal-to-noise ratio, on nearly any good portable.

• **World Time clock.** A World Time clock—24-hour format—is a "must." You can obtain these separately, but many radios have them built in; the best display time whether the radio is on or off.

scanning (*see* Con), five handy "pages" with ten station presets each. Station presets can display station name. Tunes in relatively precise 0.1 kHz increments. Good single-sideband performance (*see* Con). Good dynamic range. Worthy ergonomics for size and features. Illuminated display. Clock for many world cities, which can be made to work as a *de facto* World Time 24-hour clock (*see* Con). Timer and sleep delay. Travel power lock. Japanese FM (most versions) and longwave bands. Amplified outboard antenna, included, in addition to usual built-in antenna, enhances weak-signal reception (*see* Con). Weak-battery indicator; about 16 hours from a set of batteries (*see* Con). High-quality travel case for radio. *Except for North America:* AC adaptor comes with American and European plugs and adjusts automatically to local voltages worldwide.

Con: Tiny speaker, although innovative, has mediocre sound, limited loudness and little tone shaping. Closing clamshell reduces speaker loudness and high-frequency response. Weak-signal sensitivity could be better, although included outboard active antenna helps. Expensive. No tuning knob. Clock not readable when station frequency displayed. As "London Time" is used by the clock for World Time, the summertime clock adjustment cannot be used if World Time is to be displayed accurately. Rejection of images, and 10 kHz "repeats" when synchronous selectable sideband off, could be better. In some urban locations, FM signals from 87.5 to 108 MHz can break through into world band segments with distorted sound, e.g. between 3200 and 3300 kHz. Synchronous selectable sideband tends to lose lock if batteries weak, or if NiCd cells are used. Synchronous selectable sideband

alignment can vary with temperature, factory alignment and battery voltage, causing synchronous selectable sideband reception to be slightly more muffled in one sideband than the other. Some readers report BFO pulling causes audio quavering, not found in our test units. Batteries run down faster than usual when radio off. Tuning in 0.1 kHz increments means that non-synchronous single-sideband reception can be mis-tuned by up to 50 Hz, so audio quality varies. Signal-seek scanner sometimes stops 5 kHz before a strong "real" signal. No meaningful signal-strength indicator. Included accessory antenna performs less well than another Sony accessory antenna, the AN-LP1. Mediumwave AM reception only fair. Mediumwave AM channel spacing adjusts peculiarly. Flimsy battery cover. No batter-

Sony's stealthy ICF-SW100S/E is awash in advanced technology. When closed, it's as discreet as a travel clock.

ies (two "AA" required). *North America:* AC adaptor only 120 Volts.

☞ The above star rating reflects mediocre speaker audio quality. Through earpieces, the rating rises to ✪✪✪¹⁄₈.

☞ In early production samples, the cable connecting the two halves of the "clamshell" case tended to lose continuity with extended use because of a very tight radius and an unfinished edge; this was successfully resolved with a design change in 1997. eBay buyers and owners of early units who encounter this problem should go to www.tesp.com/sw100faq.htm for repair tips.

Verdict: This jewel among world band radios is a shoehorning *tour de force*—don't leave Langley without it. Its synchronous selectable sideband and effective bandwidth filter provide superior adjacent-channel rejection. Speaker and, to a lesser extent, weak-signal sensitivity keep it from being all it could have been, and the accessory

The new Mini 300/R-919 is pocket-sized, with high sensitivity but low image rejection.

antenna isn't Sony's latest or best. Yet, this Japanese-made gem rules the pocket category, and even outperforms most compact models.

✪✪✪ *Passport's Choice*
Sony ICF-SW100E

Price: *ICF-SW100E:* £179.95 in the United Kingdom. €269.00 in Germany. *ACE-30 220V AC adaptor:* £24.95 in the United Kingdom. €25.50 in Germany. *AC adaptor:* £24.95 in the United Kingdom.

Verdict: This version, not available in North America, includes only a case, tape-reel-type passive antenna and earbuds. Otherwise, it is identical to the Sony ICF-SW100S, above.

New for 2004

✪⅝ ☾
Grundig Mini 300, Etón Mini 300, Tecsun R-919

Price: *Mini 300:* $39.95 in the United States. $49.95CAD in Canada. Price not yet established in the United Kingdom.

Pro: Weak-signal sensitivity quite reasonable. Pleasant room-filling audio for such a small package (*see* Con). Clock/alarm-timer with one-hour sleep delay (*see* Con). FM in stereo with earbuds, included. Low battery consumption. Soft carry case affixes to belt or purse strap. Two "AA" batteries included.

Con: Analog tuned with a digital frequency counter, so lacks tuning except by thumbwheel, which is somewhat touchy. Does not tune 120, 75, 90, 60, 15, 13 and 11 meter segments; misses small bits of tuned world band segments. Poor image rejection. Audio lacks bass response. Telescopic antenna does not rotate or swivel. Antenna's plastic base protrudes even when antenna collapsed. Displays in nonstandard XX.XX MHz/XX.XX₅ MHz format. Display not illuminated. Minor drift when hand grasps back of cabinet. Frequency counter noise slightly audible when finger placed over LCD during mediumwave AM reception. Some FM overloading in strong-signal environments. Clock in 12-hour format, displays only when radio off. No port for AC adaptor. *North America:* Toll-free tech support.

Verdict: Best of the really inexpensive portables, even though it comes up short on daytime frequency coverage, lacks display illumination and its clock isn't in World Time format. But thanks to true pocket size, nice weak-signal sensitivity and decent audio quality it is hard to resist for casual use on trips.

❂½
Kaiwa KA-818, Tecsun R-818

Price: $34.95 or less in the United States. $46.95CAD in Canada.

Pro: Reasonable weak-signal sensitivity for low-cost pocket model. Clock with timer/alarm (*see* Con).

Con: Analog tuned with a digital frequency counter, so lacks tuning except by thumbwheel, which is somewhat touchy. Does not tune 120, 75, 90, 60, 22, 15, 13 or 11 meter segments; misses some expanded coverage of other world band segments. Poor image rejection. Frequency counter completely omits last digit so, say, 9575 kHz appears as either 9.57 or 9.58 MHz. Clock in 12-hour format only, displays only when radio off. Display not illuminated. Mediocre speaker audio quality. Telescopic antenna does not rotate or swivel. Mediumwave AM lacks weak-signal sensitivity. Pedestrian FM, with spurious signals. On one of our new units the telescopic antenna immediately fell apart. Two "AA" batteries not included. Few vendors in America and Europe. Warranty only 90 days in United States and various other countries.

Verdict: Performance brings up the rear, but price, size and alarm make this Chinese-made model worth consideration for casual use on trips.

The Tecsun R-818 is also sold as the Kaiwa KA-818. Cheap, tiny, tinny.

New for 2004

❂¼
Kaide KK-989

Price: $24.95 in the United States.

Pro: Very small, ideally sized for air travel and has handy built-in belt clip. Clock with timer/alarm (*see* Con).

Con: Mediocre weak-signal sensitivity; helps considerably to clip a few yards of wire to the built-in antenna. Tinny audio. Analog tuned with a digital frequency counter, so lacks tuning except by thumbwheel, which is very touchy. Does not tune 120, 75, 90, 60, 15, 13 or 11 meter segments; omits coverage of nearly all the 1605-1705 kHz mediumwave AM X-band; which frequencies are missed varies with battery voltage and from sample to sample. Poor image rejection. Frequency counter completely omits last digit so, say, 9575 kHz appears as either 9.57 or 9.58 MHz. Clock in 12-hour format only, displays only when radio off. Display not illuminated. Telescopic antenna does not rotate or swivel. If hand is placed on rear of cabinet, world band drifts considerably; mediumwave AM drifts, too, but less badly. Frequency counter buzzes faintly on mediumwave AM; if finger placed over LCD

This Kaide needs aid. Rock-bottom price, rock-bottom performance.

display, buzz becomes strong and is also audible on lower world band frequencies. FM overloads in presence of strong signals, remediable by shorting antenna (which also reduces weak-signal sensitivity). Mediocre FM weak-signal sensitivity. Poor mediumwave AM weak-signal sensitivity. When first turned on, radio always reverts to FM band. FM in mono only. Three "AAA" batteries not included; "AAA" cells require more frequent replacement than standard "AA" cells, raising the cost of operation. No port for AC adaptor. In the United States, no warranty information comes with radio; best purchased from dealer who will swap if DOA. Although radio purchased from U.S. dealer, operating instructions only in Chinese. Country of manufacture not indicated on radio or box, but almost certainly is China.

Verdict: Nicely sized, and priced for every budget. Yet, with a long roster of significant drawbacks the Kaide KK-989 is a disappointment. Worst of the cheaps.

COMPACT PORTABLES

Nice for Travel, Okay for Home

Compact portables are the most popular because of their intersection of price, performance, size and speaker audio. They tip in at one to two pounds, under a kilogram, and are typically sized less than 8 x 5 x 1.5 inches, or 20 x 13 x 4 cm. Like pocket models, they feed off "AA" (UM-3 penlite) batteries—but, usually, more of them. They travel almost as well as pocket models, but sound better through their larger speakers. They can also suffice as basic home sets.

✪✪✪¼ *Passport's Choice*
Sony ICF-SW07

Price: $399.95 in the United States. £229.95 in the United Kingdom.

Pro: Best non-audio performance among travel-worthy compact portables. Eye popper. High-tech synchronous selectable sideband generally performs very well; reduces adjacent-channel interference and selective-fading distortion on world band, longwave and mediumwave AM signals while adding slightly to weak-signal sensitivity. Unusually small and light for a compact model. Numerous tuning aids, including pushbutton access of frequencies for four stations stored on a replaceable ROM, keypad, two-speed up/down slewing, 20 station presets (ten for world band) and "signal-seek, then resume" tuning. Clamshell design aids in handiness of operation, and is further helped by illuminated LCD readable from a wide variety of angles. Hump on the rear panel places the keypad at a convenient operating angle. Comes with AN-LP2 outboard "tennis racquet" antenna, effective in enhancing weak-signal sensitivity on world band; this antenna, unlike the AN-LP1, has automatic preselector tuning. Good single sideband performance (*see* Con). Clock covers most international time zones, as well as World Time. Outstanding reception of weak and crowded FM stations, with limited urban FM overloading resolved by variable-level attenuator. FM stereo through earpieces, included. Japanese FM (most versions) and longwave bands. Above-average reception of mediumwave AM band. Travel power lock. Closing clamshell does not interfere with speaker. Low-battery indicator. Presets information is non-volatile, can't be erased when batteries changed. Two turn-on times for alarm/clock radio. Sixty-minute sleep delay. Hinged battery cover can't be misplaced. AC adaptor.

Con: Pedestrian speaker audio quality, made worse by the lack of a second, wider, bandwidth and meaningful tone control. Lacks tuning knob. Display shows time and tuned frequency, but not both at the same time. Tuning resolution of 0.1 kHz above 1620 kHz means that non-synchronous single-sideband reception can be mis-tuned by up to 50 Hz, so audio quality varies. Synchronous selectable sideband tends to lose lock if batteries weak, or if NiCd cells are used. Synchronous selectable sideband alignment can vary with temperature, factory alignment and battery voltage, causing synchronous selectable sideband reception to be slightly more muffled in one sideband than the other. No meaningful signal-strength indicator. LCD frequency/time numbers relatively small for size of display, with only average contrast. AN-LP2 accessory antenna has to be physically disconnected for proper mediumwave AM reception. 1621-1705 kHz portion of American AM band and 1705-1735 kHz potential public service segment are erroneously treated as shortwave, although this does not harm reception quality. Low battery indicator misreads immediately after batteries installed; clears up when radio is turned on. No batteries (two "AA" required). UTC, or World Time, displays as "London" time even during the summer, when London is an hour off from World Time. DST key can change UTC in error.

☞ The ICF-SW07 is no longer listed on Sony of America's Website, nor that of Sony Canada or Sony Deutschland. However, U.S. radio dealers report that they continue to obtain stock on a regular basis. This model

The flip-open Sony ICF-SW07 bests all other travel portables. You'll flip at the price, too.

is listed as Sony's "Flagship World Band Receiver" on the Website of Sony United Kingdom.

Verdict: Speaker audio aside, this Japanese-made model is the best compact model for travel—and a killer eyeful.

✪✪✪⅛ ℂ *Passport's Choice*
Sony ICF-SW7600GR

Price: *ICF-SW7600GR:* $169.95 in the United States. $299.00CAD in Canada. £129.95 in the United Kingdom. €169.00 in Germany. $509.00AUD in Australia. *MW 41-680 120V regulated AC adaptor (aftermarket, see below):* $19.95 in the United States.

Pro: One of the great values in world band radio. Far and away the least-costly model available with high-tech synchronous selectable sideband; this generally performs well, reducing adjacent-channel interference and selective-fading distortion on world band, longwave and mediumwave AM signals (*see* Con). Single bandwidth, especially when synchronous selectable sideband is used, exceptionally effective at adjacent-channel rejection. Seemingly robust—similar predecessor had superior quality of components and assembly for price class, and held up unusually well.

Numerous helpful tuning features, including keypad, two-speed up/down slewing, 100 station presets and "signal-seek, then resume" tuning. For those with limited hearing of high-frequency sounds, such as some men over the half-century mark, speaker audio quality may be preferable to that of Grundig Yacht Boy 400PE (*see* Con). Single-sideband performance arguably the best of any portable; analog clarifier, combined with LSB/USB switch, allow single-sideband signals (e.g., AFRTS, utility, amateur) to be tuned with uncommon precision, and thus with superior carrier phasing and the resulting natural-sounding audio. Dual-zone 24-hour clock with single-zone readout, easy to set. Slightly smaller and lighter than most other compact models. Reel-in outboard passive antenna accessory aids slightly with weak-signal reception. Simple timer with

COMING UP

There are a number of Chinese portables in the works. Arguably the most interesting are the Degen DE1106, a planned model that's still many months away, and the flagship lap model DE1108 that is scheduled to go into production in late 2004. Kchibo also has a flagship portable, the KK-S500, due out soon. The 'S500 appears to be long on operating features, but be on your toes as nothing is being indicated about performance.

The Grundig Satellit 900 should be on the market in North America by early 2004, but is not scheduled to replace the existing and quite different Satellit 800. Factual information has been virtually impossible to come by, but it would appear to be a sophisticated lap portable priced slightly higher than the Sony ICF-SW77. In addition to world band, it may also receive certain commercial satellite broadcasters.

Best guess is that the S-900 is being engineered by the R.L. Drake Company in Ohio in cooperation with China's Tecsun. If so, it should have such important performance features as synchronous selectable sideband. Given the early QA track record of the Satellit 800, it would probably be sensible to wait several months until the "shakedown cruise" is over.

In 2005, after much delay, Sangean may yet introduce its ATS 636, which would be similar to the ATS 909, but pocket-sized.

DRM: Success or Failure?

Digital Radio Mondiale (DRM) world band broadcasts are being tested, but are unintelligible on conventional world band radios—special receivers are needed. DRM-capable portables are already in the works, and should start to appear at fairly steep prices.

Experiments have proven to our ears that DRM's digital broadcasts succeed in producing improved fidelity, which of course is their *raison d'être*. Indeed, they can sound quite impressive even by FM standards. However, to date they appear to be audible only with very powerful signals fed into unusually sensitive receivers, preferably with long outdoor antennas. DRM signals also have been spectrum-wasteful, disrupting any number of nearby channels to the point where they are no longer usable. DRM broadcasts are also relatively easily jammed. Too, as the brainchild of mainly European technocrats, DRM has been abysmally marketed.

These are not encouraging signs, but DRM is still experimental and continues to hold much promise. The next couple of years should sort out whether it will soar as a major advance or flop like AM stereo.

sleep delay. Illuminated LCD has high contrast when read head-on or from below. Travel power lock. Superior reception of difficult mediumwave AM stations. Superior FM capture ratio aids reception when band congested, including helping separate co-channel stations. FM stereo through ear-pieces or headphones. Japanese FM (most versions) and longwave bands. Superior battery life. Weak-battery indicator. Stereo line output for recording, FM home transmitters and outboard audio systems. Hinged battery cover can't be mislaid.

Con: Audio lacks tonal quality for pleasant world band or mediumwave AM music reproduction, and speaker audio tiring for any type of FM program. Weak-signal sensitivity, although respectable, not equal to that of the top handful of top-rated portables; helped considerably by extra-cost Sony AN-LP1 active antenna reviewed elsewhere in this edition. Image rejection adequate, but not excellent. Three switches, including those for synchronous selectable sideband, located unhandily at the side of the cabinet. No tuning knob. When using up/down slewing buttons, muting slows down manual bandscanning. No meaningful signal-strength indicator. Synchronous selectable sideband holds lock decently, but less well on weak signals than in Sony's larger models; too, it tends to lose lock even more if batteries weak or if NiCd cells used. Synchronous selectable sideband alignment can vary with temperature, factory alignment and battery voltage, causing synchronous selectable sideband reception to be slightly more muffled in one sideband than the other. No AC adaptor included, while in North America the new optional Sony AC-E60A "switching" adaptor causes serious interference to radio signals and, incredibly, is labeled "Not for use with radios"; Universal Radio offers its own MW 41-680 to remedy this, and presumably other firms will be offering something similar in due course. Radio's adaptor socket is of an unusual size, making it difficult to find a

Sony's ICF-SW7600GR is the most affordable portable with synchronous selectable sideband. ¡Muy robusto!

suitable third-party AC adaptor. 1621-1705 kHz portion of American AM band and 1705-1735 kHz potential public-service segment are erroneously treated as short-wave, although this does not harm reception quality. Even though it has a relatively large LCD, same portion of display is used for clock and frequency digits; thus, clock doesn't display when frequency is shown, although pressing the EXE key allows time to replace frequency for nine seconds. No earphones or earpieces. No batteries (four "AA" needed).

Verdict: The robust Sony ICF-SW7600GR provides surprising bang for the buck, even though it is manufactured in high-cost Japan. Its advanced-tech synchronous selectable sideband is a valuable feature that other portable manufacturers have yet to engineer properly—even some professional models costing thousands of dollars still haven't got it right. To find this operating feature at this price is without parallel.

Top drawer single-sideband reception for a portable, too, along with superior tough-signal FM and mediumwave AM reception. But it has warts: Musical audio quality through the speaker is only *ordinaire* and the factory's new optional AC adaptor should be avoided.

New for 2004

✪✪✪ ✪ *Passport's Choice*
Degen DE1102, Kaito KA1102

Price: *KA1102:* TBA, but presumably under $90 in the United States.

Pro: Unusually small and light for a sophisticated compact model; only a skosh larger and one ounce (28 grams) heavier than its simpler sibling '1101. Two bandwidths, both well chosen. A number of helpful tuning features, including keypad, up/down slewing (1 or 5 kHz steps for world band, 1 or 9/10 kHz for mediumwave AM), carousel selector for 49-16 meter segments, and "signal seek" frequency scanning (*see* Con) and memory scanning; also, ten 19-preset "pages" provide 190 station presets, of which 133 can be used for shortwave (*see* Con). Auto-store function automatically stores presets; works on all bands. Tunable BFO allows for precise signal phasing during single-sideband reception (*see* Con). No muting during manual shortwave bandscanning in 1 or 5 kHz steps, or mediumwave AM bandscanning in 1 kHz steps. PLL and BFO relatively free from drift during single-sideband operation (*see* Con). Above-average weak-signal sensitivity and image rejection. Little circuit "hiss." Superior speaker audio quality, intelligibility and loudness for size. Four-LED signal-strength indicator for mediumwave AM and shortwave (*see* Con); three-level signal-strength indicator for FM (fourth LED becomes stereo indicator). World Time 24-hour clock displays seconds numerically when radio is off; when on, time (sans seconds) flashes on briefly when key is held down; user may choose 12-hour format, instead. Unusually appropriate for use in the dark, as display and keypad illuminated by pleasant blue light which works only in dark (*see* Con). Clicky keys have superior tactile feel. LCD has excellent contrast when viewed from sides or below. Alarm with keypad-selectable 1-99 minute sleep delay (*see* Con). AC adaptor (120V Kaito, 220V

Degen). Travel power lock. Rechargeable NiMH batteries (3 x "AA"), included, can be charged within the radio; station presets and time not erased during charging. Switchable bass boost supplements high-low tone switch, significantly improves FM audio (*see* Con). Low battery consumption except with FM bass boost. Battery-level indicator. Battery cover hinged to avoid being misplaced. Superior FM weak-signal sensitivity. Excellent FM capture ratio aids reception when band congested, including helping separate co-channel stations. FM in stereo through earbuds, included (*see* Con). FM 70-108 MHz coverage includes 76-90 MHz Japanese FM band and 70-74 MHz portion of 66-74 MHz low band still used within some former Warsaw Pact countries. Includes short external wire antenna accessory, which in many locations is about the most that can be used without generating overloading.

Con: Speaker audio, except FM, quality lacks low-frequency ("bass") response as compared to larger models. Bass-boost circuit, which could relieve this on world band, works only on FM. Dynamic range, although at least average for a compact portable, not anywhere equal to that of the sibling '1101; overloads easily with a significant outdoor antenna, although not with the built-in antenna or a short outboard antenna. Not so straightforward to operate as some other portables; for example, single-sideband mode works only when presets "page 9" is selected (or SSB button is held in manually), even if no presets are to be chosen (in any event, presets don't store mode); otherwise, "ERR" is displayed; manufacturer says this is to prevent its Chinese consumers, who are unfamiliar with single sideband, from turning on the BFO accidentally and thus becoming confused. Slight warble in audio with ECSS reception, varies with how many signal-strength LEDs are being illuminated; LEDs can't be turned off. Volume at earphone jack sometimes inadequate with weak or undermodulated signals; variable-level earphone jack misleadingly described as "line out." Power button activates a 99-minute sleep delay; to turn the radio on fulltime, a second key must be pressed immediately afterwards. No tuning knob. No LSB/USB switch. Displays in nonstandard XX.XX MHz/XX.XXx MHz format. Signal-strength indicator overreads. Little-used 2 MHz (120 meter) world band segment not covered. Clock doesn't display when frequency is shown, although pushbutton allows time to replace frequency briefly. Always-on LCD/keypad illumination with AC adaptor, as described in owner's manual, did not function on test sample. LCD/keypad illumination dim and uneven. Rear panel on our sample reads only 522-1620 kHz as mediumwave AM coverage when 520-1710 kHz is also user-selectable. *Kaito:* Warranty only 90 days.

☞ The sole sample tested was from a small pre-production run; these not infrequently have issues that may evolve by the time of actual production. This sample was provided by the manufacturer because the book's press deadline prevented our usual acquisition procedure.

Degen has expressed interest in possibly making changes to the '1102 before starting production, so our findings should emphatically be regarded as tentative. We will evaluate the production version when it becomes available and post any new findings at www.passband.com.

Verdict: Although we have yet to test an off-the-shelf production unit, this appears to be another price and performance winner from Degen.

Evaluation of New Model: The '1102 is Degen's second serious world band offering planned for sale outside China (the simpler DE101 is available only in China), and like the original '1101 it sets a new standard for what is available at lip-smacking low cost. Nothing else under $100 with single-sideband capability even comes close. And like the '1101, the '1102 is diminutive and

Degen offers Audi performance at Beetle prices. Its DE1102 demodulates single sideband signals.

light enough for travel while sounding decent enough for home use.

Helpful Features Include Single Sideband

This latest model comes with an AC adaptor and includes three NiMH "AA" batteries that recharge inside the radio, as well as an accurate battery-level indicator. Like the '1101, it is a power miser, and this is aided by LCD and keypad illumination that works only in the dark. For tuning in the dark, the illumination of keys as well as the usual LCD makes the '1102 unusually appropriate for tuning in the dark. However, although the illumination is a pleasant blue, it is uneven and dim. The battery cover is sensibly hinged so it can't be misplaced.

The '1102 is not as straightforward to use as its '1101 sibling, nor does it have the '1101's standout dynamic range or separate earphone and line-out sockets. However, it demodulates single-sideband signals and offers a four-level signal-strength indicator, although synchronous selectable sideband is absent. There's no LSB/USB switch, yet single-sideband reception is quite good, in part because the variable BFO control is analog, allowing for precise phasing with a station's frequency.

However, there is a small catch. Portables rarely do well with ECSS tuning, and the '1102 is no exception. Performance is limited by minor warbling in concert with the signal-strength indicator as various of the four LEDs go on and off during signal fading. The resulting incremental rises and falls in current drain are just enough to pull the BFO very slightly out of phase with the tuned frequency. This also impacts regular single-sideband reception, but it's virtually impossible to hear.

Convoluted Switch-On Procedures

Overall, ergonomics are pretty reasonable, but there's one exception: single-sideband reception. It can be switched on only when presets "page 9" is selected, even if you have no interest in choosing a preset. This is particularly odd, as none of the presets store mode. The SSB button can be held in manually to avoid bringing up "page 9," but the user has to keep pushing the button until patience wears thin.

Why such a roundabout procedure? The radio's engineer tells PASSPORT that its Chinese customers are not familiar with single sideband, and might be confused were the SSB circuitry to be activated. They also feel that nobody but professionals is interested in receiving SSB. So, they have added steps to constrain its use.

The '1102 also continues the recent and peculiar Chinese concept that when the power button is pressed, the radio doesn't stay on indefinitely; instead, a sleep-delay timer turns off power after 99 minutes. The radio can run fulltime, but only if two buttons are pressed in quick sequence.

Granted, some world band programs are excruciatingly dull, but it's hard to see how the primary purpose of any world band radio should be to help lull people to sleep.

Various Tuning Choices

The illuminated keypad is laid out in customary telephone format, and its clicky keys, although small, have excellent tactile response. Other tuning features include up/down slewing (1 or 5 kHz steps for world band, 1 or 9/10 kHz for mediumwave AM), carousel selector for 49-16 meter segments, and "signal seek" frequency scanning and memory scanning. In addition, there are ten 19-preset "pages" that offer 190 station presets, of which 133 can be used for shortwave. There is an auto-store function which automatically loads presets, but no tuning knob.

Worthy Performance, Signal Indicator

The '1102 has adequate dynamic range—typical or better for a compact portable—but it is not in the same exceptional league as the '1101. However, image rejection is excellent and there are two well-chosen bandwidths. Sensitivity is above average, and there is a four-LED signal-strength indicator; with FM this becomes a three-level indicator, as the fourth becomes a stereo light.

The '1102, although small, comes with a decent-sized speaker having room-filling sound. It lacks bass response, but the radio still has better audio quality through its speaker than most models of its size, and there's little circuit hiss. There is bass boost for FM and it helps bring aural life to this small radio, but it can't be switched in for use on world band.

The nominal line output socket is also supposed to double as an earphone socket, but winds up doing neither properly. It is tied into the volume control, so it isn't really a line output, and for earphones has inadequate level with weak or undermodulated signals. The '1101's separate sockets are the only way to go for these two very different functions.

Superior FM and Mediumwave AM

The '1102 performs nicely on FM in rural fringe areas, as well as in suburban locations where the band is congested. There is also slightly less than the usual level of overloading when there are one or more nearby FM transmitters. It tunes not only the usual 87-108 MHz FM band, but also the Japanese 76-90 MHz band and the 70-74 MHz portion of the 66-74 MHz FM band found within some former Warsaw Pact countries.

Mediumwave AM performance is quite good overall, with long-distance reception being aided by dual bandwidths. Both the Degen and Kaito versions tune mediumwave AM in user-selectable 9/10 kHz increments, with the latter setting allowing coverage up to 1710 kHz.

Degen radios are too new to have a frequency-of-repair record, but visual inspection suggests that build quality is probably at least average. This isn't academic, as the Kaito warranty is for only 90 days, and post-warranty repair outside China could be problematic.

As Degen's products are already being sold by Kaito under that name, the '1102 could eventually materialize under even more brand names.

●●● ⊘ _Passport's Choice_
Grundig Yacht Boy 400PE

Price: _YB-400PE:_ $149.95 in the United States. $199.95CAD in Canada. £99.95 in the United Kingdom. $279.00AUD in Australia. _YB-400PE refurbished units, as available:_ $99.95 in the United States. $169.00CAD in Canada.

Pro: Speaker audio quality tops in size category for those with sharp hearing. Two bandwidths, both well-chosen. Ergonomically superior, a pleasure to operate. A number of helpful tuning features, including keypad, up/down slewing, 40 station presets, "signal seek" frequency scanning and scanning of station presets. Signal-strength indicator. Dual-zone 24-hour clock, with one zone shown at all times; however, clock displays seconds only when

radio is off. Illuminated display. Alarm with simple sleep delay. Tunable BFO allows for superior signal phasing during single-sideband reception (_see_ Con). Reel-in outboard wire antenna supplements telescopic antenna. Generally superior FM performance, especially in weak-signal locations. FM in stereo through head-phones. Longwave. AC adaptor. _North America:_ Toll-free tech support.

Con: Circuit noise ("hiss") can be slightly intrusive with weak signals. No tuning knob. At many locations there can be break-through of powerful AM or FM stations into the world band spectrum. Keypad not in telephone format. No LSB/USB switch, and single-sideband reception is below par. No batteries (six "AA" needed).

☞ Refurbished units reportedly include gift and similar returns from department stores and other outlets where customers tend to be unfamiliar with world band radio. Everything but the radio itself is supposed to be replaced. Limited availability.

☞ At present there are no plans to sell the Yacht Boy 400 under the Etón name.

Verdict: This popular receiver is one of the better values for hearing world band programs and tough FM catches, even if

The best-selling Grundig Yacht Boy 400PE has superior audio and is a pleasure to operate.

single-sideband isn't all it could be. Superior speaker audio quality and simplicity of operation set this Chinese-made compact receiver apart—even though circuit noise with weak signals could be lower.

✪✪⅞
Sangean ATS 909, Sangean ATS 909 "Deluxe", Roberts R861

Price: *ATS 909:* $259.95 in the United States. $369.00CAD in Canada. £139.95 in the United Kingdom. €169.00 in Germany. *ATS 909 "Deluxe":* $289.90 in the United States. *Multivoltage AC adaptor:* £16.95 in the United Kingdom. *R861:* £199.95 in United Kingdom.

Pro: Exceptionally wide range of tuning facilities, including hundreds of world band station presets (one works with a single touch) and tuning knob. Tuning system uses 29 "pages" and alphanumeric station descriptors for world band. Two voice bandwidths. Tunes single-sideband signals in unusually precise 0.04 kHz increments without having to use a fine-tuning control, making this one of the handiest and most effective portables for listening to these signals (*see* Con). Shortwave dynamic range slightly above average for portable, allowing it to perform unusually well with an outboard antenna (*see* Con). Travel power lock.

Sangean's ATS 909 is a favorite for snaring "utility" and amateur stations. It thrives on an outboard antenna.

24-hour clock shows at all times, and can display local time in various cities of the world (*see* Con). Excellent 1-10 digital signal-strength indicator. Low-battery indicator. Clock radio feature offers three "on" times for three discrete frequencies. Sleep delay. FM sensitive to weak signals (see Con) and performs well overall, has RDS feature, and is in stereo through earpieces, included. Illuminated display. Superior ergonomics, including tuning knob with tactile detents. Longwave. *ATS 909 (North American units), ATS 909 "Deluxe" and Roberts:* Superb, but relatively heavy, multivoltage AC adaptor with North American and European plugs. ANT-60 reel-in outboard wire antenna. Sangean service provided by Sangean America on models sold under its name. *ATS 909 "Deluxe," available only from C. Crane Company):* Enhanced tuning knob operation and elimination of muting between stations.

Con: Weak-signal sensitivity with built-in telescopic antenna not equal to that of comparable models; usually remediable with ANT-60 accessory antenna (provided) or other suitable external antenna. Tuning knob tends to mute stations during bandscanning; C. Crane Company offers a "Deluxe" modification to remedy this. Larger and heavier than most compact models. Signal-seek tuning, although flexible and relatively sophisticated, tends to stop on few active shortwave signals. Although scanner can operate out-of-band, reverts to default (in-band) parameters after one pass. When entering a new page, there is an initial two-second wait between when preset is keyed and station becomes audible. Although synthesizer tunes in 0.04 kHz increments, frequency readout only in 1 kHz increments. Software oddities; e.g., under certain conditions, alphanumeric station descriptor may stay on full time. Page tuning system enjoyed by some users, but cumbersome for others. Speaker audio quality only so-so, not aided by three-level treble-cut tone control. No carrying handle or strap. The 24-hour clock set up to display home time, not World Time, although this is easily overcome by not using world-cities-time feature or by creative setup of World/Home display to London/Home. Clock does not compensate for daylight (summer) time in each displayed city. FM can overload in high-signal-strength environments, causing false "repeat" signals to appear; capture ratio average. Heterodyne interference, possibly related to the digital display, sometimes interferes with reception of strong mediumwave AM signals. Battery consumption well above average; would profit from lower current draw or larger (e.g., "C") cell size. No batteries (four "AA" required). Tilt panel flimsy. *Sangean:* AC adaptor lacks UL approval.

☞ Frequencies pre-programmed into "pages" vary by country of sale. It is useful to keep a couple of empty pages to aid in editing, deleting or changing pre-programmed page information.

Verdict: Like the tabletop Icom IC-R75, this feature-laden portable is a favorite among radio enthusiasts who regularly tune utility and ham signals. It includes a wide range of handy operating features and superior single-sideband performance, and is the only Sangean model still made exclusively in Taiwan. Although high battery consumption and insufficient weak-signal sensitivity lower its rating as a portable, when used as at home as a *de facto* tabletop connected to household current and an external antenna it becomes a more tempting choice.

New for 2004

❶❷⅛ ⓒ *Passport's Choice*
Degen DE1101, Kaito KA1101

Price: *KA1101:* $69.99 in the United States.

Pro: Exceptional dynamic range for a compact portable. Unusually small and light for a compact model. Two bandwidths, both well chosen. A number of helpful tuning features, including keypad, up/down slewing and "signal seek" frequency scanning (*see* Con); also, 50 station presets of which ten are for 3,000-10,000 kHz and ten for 10,000-26,100 kHz; others are for FM, FML and mediumwave AM. Above-average weak-signal sensitivity and image rejection. Little circuit "hiss." Superior intelligibility and loudness for size. World Time 24-hour clock displays seconds numerically when radio is off; when on, time (sans seconds) flashes on briefly when key is held down. Illuminated display, works only in dark. Clicky keys have superior tactile feel. LCD has excellent contrast when viewed from sides or below. Alarm with keypad-selectable 1-99 minute sleep delay (*see* Con). AC adaptor (120V Kaito, 220V Degen). Rechargeable NiMH batteries (3 x "AA"), included, can be charged within the radio; station presets and time not erased during charging. Low battery consumption. Battery-level indicator. Battery cover hinged to avoid being misplaced. Travel power lock. Superior FM weak-signal sensitivity. Excellent FM capture ratio aids reception when band congested, including helping separate co-channel stations. aids reception when band congested. FM in stereo through earbuds, included. "FML" covers 76-90 MHz Japanese FM band and 70-74 MHz portion of 66-74 MHz low band still used within some former Warsaw Pact countries. Line output socket (separate from earphone socket) for recording, FM home transmitters and outboard audio systems. *Kaito:* Mediumwave AM 9/10 channel steps user-selectable, tunes up to 1710 kHz.

Con: Speaker audio quality lacks low-frequency ("bass") response as compared to larger models. Power button activates a 99-minute sleep delay; to turn the radio on fulltime, a second key must be pressed immediately afterwards. Station presets, slewing and scanning require pressing bandswitch carousel button up to four times when tuning from below 10 MHz to

Degen's price-busting DE1101 debuted in America in late 2003 as the Kaito KA1101.

knockout bargain. Engineered and manufactured in China, it is one of the smallest compact models tested, and has exceptional dynamic range. It comes with an enviable grab-bag of features and accessories, right down to inboard rechargeable batteries.

Evaluation of New Model: Degen is new to world band, and it's off to a rip-roaring start. At under $70, its initial model available outside China, the '1101, is among the best small-portable bargains to be found. Nothing else other than its sibling '1102 equals its intersection of price, performance, features and included accessories.

Superior Power Traits

For starters, this is not your usual radio with an empty battery cavity. Not only does it come with an AC adaptor, it also includes NiMH "AA" batteries that recharge inside the radio, as well as a battery-level indicator. It underreads when the radio is on, but is accurate when off.

The '1101 is a power miser, too, with low battery drain aided by a tiny sensor that prevents LCD illumination except in the dark. Even the battery cover is hinged so it can't be misplaced.

Ergonomics A Mixed Bag

Still, not everything about the DE1101's concern with power warrants kudos. When you press the power button, the radio doesn't stay on indefinitely. Instead, a sleep-delay timer turns off power after 99 minutes. Fortunately, the radio can run fulltime, but only if two buttons are pressed. There is a pushbutton travel power lock

The keypad is laid out in familiar telephone format, and its clicky keys, although small, have excellent tactile response. Other helpful tuning features include 50 station presets (20 for shortwave), up/down slewing and "signal-seek" frequency scanning. World band tuning is in handy 5 kHz steps, al-

above 10 MHz and *vice versa*. No tuning knob. Tunes world band only in 5 kHz steps and displays in nonstandard XX.XX MHz/XX.XX5 MHz format. Digital buzz under some circumstances, such as when antenna is touched. Spurious signals can appear when user's hand is pressed over back cover. With our unit, microprocessor locked up when batteries removed for over a day; resolved by pressing tiny reset button. No signal-strength indicator (what appears to be an LED tuning indicator is actually an ambient-light sensor to disable LCD illumination except when it's dark). Clock doesn't display when frequency is shown, although pushbutton allows time to replace frequency briefly. Little-used 2 MHz (120 meter) world band segment not covered. On Degen unit tested, FM sounded best when tuned 50 kHz above nominal frequency on LCD; this would appear to be a sample-to-sample issue. *Kaito:* Warranty only 90 days. *Degen:* Upper limit of mediumwave AM tuning is 1620 kHz, rather than the 1705 kHz band upper limit in the Americas, Australia and certain other areas. Mediumwave AM tunes only in 9 kHz steps, making it ill-suited for use in the Americas.

Verdict: The new gray-painted Degen DE1101, sold in North America as the aluminum-colored Kaito KA1101, is a

though there is no finer resolution or clarifier control for optimum reception of off-channel stations. No tuning knob or single-sideband demodulation, either.

The '1101 has an "SW1" band for 3,000-10,000 kHz and "SW2" for 10,000-26,100 kHz—an archaic concept dropped long ago on most better world band portables. Station presets, slewing and scanning are tied into this arrangement, so you have to push the bandswitch button four times when you need to choose from presets (or "hop the divider" with slew/scan controls) within SW1 if the radio is currently tuned to SW2; for going from SW1 to SW2, only one button push is needed. Thankfully, SW1/SW2 bandswitching is automatic when the keypad is used.

On our unit, when batteries were removed for a day or more the radio refused to operate until the microprocessor reset mini-button was depressed.

Solid Performance for Money, Size

The '1101 has surprising dynamic range for a compact portable, thanks in part to a double-balanced mixer. As a result overloading rarely occurs in North America, even when the radio is connected to a serious external antenna. Even in high-signal regions, such as Europe, the '1101's resistance to overloading stands out. Oddly, this exceptional dynamic range performance is not found on the costlier and newer Degen DE1102.

Double conversion circuitry, heretofore unheard of anywhere near this price, virtually banishes images; other types of spurious signals are rarely encountered unless the operator's hand is pressed firmly over the back cover. Two well-chosen bandwidths—radios around this price usually have only one—allow the user to choose between enhanced adjacent-channel rejection and broadband audio response. Sensitivity is above average, although

intelligibility of weaker signals suffering from fast fading is not up to that of the best larger models. There is no signal-strength indicator.

The '1101, although small, comes with a decent-sized speaker with room-filling sound. It lacks bass response, but the radio still has better audio through its speaker than most models of its size, and there's little circuit hiss. If you want better audio quality, you'll have to spring for a Yacht Boy 400 or a larger model.

A line output socket allows for recording or feeding an amplified speaker or home FM transmitter, although its fixed level is too low to be of much practical use. There is also a stereo headphone jack, and earbuds are included.

Superior FM Performance, Coverage

The '1101 performs nicely on FM in rural fringe areas, as well as in suburban locations where the band is congested, although our sample's frequency readout was mildly out of alignment. There is also slightly less than the usual level of overloading when there are one or more nearby FM transmitters. It tunes not only the usual 87-108 MHz FM band, but also a separate "low FM" band from 70-95.5 MHz that includes the Japanese 76-90 MHz band and the 70-74 MHz portion of the 66-74 MHz FM band still used within some former Warsaw Pact countries.

Mediumwave AM performance is quite good overall, with long-distance reception being aided by dual bandwidths. The Kaito version tunes mediumwave AM to 1710 kHz in user-selectable 9/10 kHz increments. However, the Degen tunes no higher than 1620 kHz and only in the 9 kHz increments appropriate outside the Western Hemisphere.

Degen is new to world band radio, so it has no track record for reliability—mean time between failures (MTBF), observed, if you will. Yet, visual inspection suggests that build quality is probably at least average. This is no small point, considering that the Kaito warranty is for only for 90 days, and that obtaining post-warranty repair would seem to be a wishful proposition outside China.

Degen, unlike Grundig and Sony, has chosen to follow the same path as Sangean by manufacturing for other firms under their brand names. Accordingly, in principle the '1101 and other Degen models could eventually appear under even more brand names.

New Version for 2004

★★¾ ✪
Sangean ATS 606AP, Panasonic RF-B55, Roberts R876, Sanyo MB-60A

Price: *ATS 606AP:* $139.95 in the United States. $199.00CAD in Canada. £109.95 in the United Kingdom. €95.00 in Germany. *RF-B55:* £109.95 in the United Kingdom. €149.00 in Germany. *R876:* £129.95 in the United Kingdom. *MB-60A:* R1,000.00 in South Africa.

Pro: Relatively diminutive for a compact model. Single bandwidth reasonably effective at adjacent-channel rejection, while providing reasonable audio bandwidth. Speaker audio quality better than most for size (*see* Con). Weak-signal

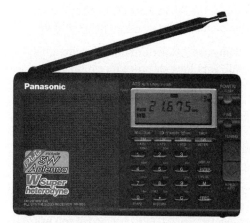

The Sangean ATS 606AP is also available under Panasonic, Roberts and Sanyo brand names.

sensitivity at least average. Various helpful tuning features, including keypad, 54 station presets, slewing, signal-seek tuning and meter band selection. Keypad has superior feel and tactile response. Easy to operate. Longwave. Dual-zone 24-hour clock. Illuminated LCD. Alarm. 15/30/45/60-minute sleep delay. Travel power lock (*see* Con). Multi-level battery strength indicator; also, weak-battery warning. Stereo FM through earphones or earbuds. Above-average FM weak-signal sensitivity and selectivity. Above-average capture ratio aids reception when band congested, including helping separate co-channel stations. Memory scan (*see* Con). Rubber feet reduce sliding while tilt panel in use. *R876 and ATS 606AP:* UL-approved 120/230V AC adaptor, with American and European plugs, adjusts to proper AC voltage automatically; also ANT-60 reel-in outboard wire antenna. *ATS 606AP:* In North America, service provided by Sangean America to models sold under its name. *RF-B55:* Cabinet and controls not painted, so should maintain their appearance unusually well. Country of manufacture (Taiwan) specified on radio and box.

Con: No tuning knob. Speaker audio quality lacks low-frequency ("bass") response as compared to larger models. Clock not readable while frequency displayed. No meaningful signal-strength indicator. Keypad not in telephone format. Power lock doesn't disable LCD illumination button. No carrying strap or handle. No batteries (three "AA" needed). *ATS 606AP:* Country of manufacture (China) not specified on radio or box. *RF-B55:* No AC adaptor or reel-in antenna included, although the owner's manual says that the radio is supposed to come with an "external antenna." Not available within the Americas.

Verdict: This classic continues to hold its own among travel-friendly models. Now, it is available in separate Chinese-made and Taiwanese-made versions.

Observation on Latest (Panasonic) Version: Until now, Panasonic receivers were invariably designed and manufactured by Panasonic, but no longer—the RF-B55, available in parts of Europe and the former Soviet Union, is merely a re-badged Sangean. It is relatively pricey, too, as it lacks the AC adaptor and reel-in antenna found in the Sangean incarnation.

One other difference helps explain the higher price: While the Sangean version is made in China, the Panasonic RF-B55 is labeled under the tilt panel, as well as on the cardboard box, as being made in Taiwan. An official Sangean spokesman confirms that all Sangean products made for Panasonic are manufactured at Sangean's Taiwan facilities.

Otherwise, there have been no significant changes since our last test.

✪✪⅝
Sangean ATS 505P, Roberts R9914

Price: *ATS 505P:* $129.95 in the United States. $179.00CAD in Canada. £79.95 in the United Kingdom. €95.00 in Germany. $199.00AUD in Australia. *R9914:* £99.95 in the United Kingdom. IAC adaptor: £16.95 in the United Kingdom.

Pro: Numerous helpful tuning features, including two-speed tuning knob, keypad, station presets (*see* Con), up/down slewing, meter-band carousel selection, signal-seek tuning and scanning of presets (*see* Con). Automatic-sorting feature arranges station presets in frequency order. Analog clarifier with center detent and stable circuitry allows single-sideband signals to be tuned with uncommon precision and to stay properly tuned, thus allowing for superior audio phasing for a portable (*see* Con). Illuminated LCD. Dual-zone 24/12-hour clock. Alarm with sleep delay. Modest battery consumption. Nine-level battery-reserve indicator. Travel power lock (*see* Con). FM stereo through earbuds, included.

Longwave. AC adaptor. Tape measure antenna.

Con: Bandwidth slightly wider than appropriate for a single-bandwidth receiver. Large for a compact. Only 18 world band station presets, divided up between two "pages" with nine presets apiece. Tuning knob tends to mute stations during bandscanning by knob, especially when tuning rate is set to fine (1 kHz); muting with coarse (5 kHz) tuning is much less objectionable. Keys respond slowly, needing to be held down momentarily rather than simply tapped. Stop-listen-resume scanning of station presets wastes time. Pedestrian overall single-sideband reception because of excessively wide bandwidth and occasional distortion caused by AGC timing. Clock does not display independent of frequency. No meaningful signal-strength indicator. No carrying handle or strap. Country of manufacture (China) not specified on radio or box. Travel power lock does not deactivate LCD illumination key. No batteries (four "AA" needed).

Verdict: An okay portable that demodulates single-sideband signals.

✪✪⅝   ✐
Sony ICF-SW35

Price: $89.95 in the United States. $149.99CAD in Canada. £79.95 in the United Kingdom. €105.00 in Germany. $269.00AUD in Australia. *AC-E45HG 120V AC adaptor:* $19.95 in the United States.

Pro: Superior reception quality, with excellent adjacent-channel rejection (selectivity) and image rejection. Fifty world band station presets, which can be scanned within five "pages." Signal-seek-then-resume scanning works unusually well. Two-speed slewing. Illuminated display. Dual-zone 24-hour clock. Dual-time alarm. Sleep delay (60/45/30/15 minutes). Travel power lock. FM stereo through headphones, not included. Weak-battery indicator.

The ATS 505P is the least costly Sangean receiver that demodulates single-sideband signals.

Japanese FM (most versions) and longwave bands.

Con: No keypad or tuning knob. Synthesizer muting and poky slewing degrade bandscanning. Speaker audio quality clear, but lacks low-frequency response ("bass"). Clock not displayed independent of frequency. LCD lacks contrast when viewed from above. No jacks for recording or outboard antenna. AC adaptor is extra and pricey. No batteries (three "AA" required).

Verdict: The Sony ICF-SW35 has superior rejection of images, which are the bane of most other under-$100 models. This Chinese-made compact lacks a keypad, which is partially overcome by a large

Sony's ICF-SW35, tuning for tortoises.

number of station presets and effective scanning. Overall, a decent choice only if you listen to a predictable roster of stations.

New for 2004

✪✪⅜

Grundig YB-550PE, Etón YB-550PE, Tecsun PL-230, Tecsun PL-200 (see ☞)

Price: *Grundig:* $99.95 in the United States. $129.95CAD in Canada. *Etón:* Price not yet established in the United Kingdom.

Pro: Very good selectivity. Above-average dynamic range. Several handy tuning aids, including 200 station presets with eight pages where user selects how many presets per page; also, meter band selector. For world band, slew buttons tune in 5 kHz increments, while a fine-tuning (encoder) thumbwheel—the PL-200 uses a tuning knob, instead—tunes shortwave and mediumwave AM in 1 kHz increments. Illuminated LCD. World Time clock (*see* Con) with alarm, clock radio and 1-90 minute sleep delay; may also be set to 12-hour format. Clock readout separate from frequency display, shows whether radio on or off. Signal-seek scanner searches world band segments or preset channels (*see* Con). Five-level signal-strength indicator. Battery-strength indicator. FM stereo with earbuds, provided. Japanese FM. Travel power lock. Setting to allow for optimum performance from either regular or rechargeable batteries. *YB-550PE and PL-230:* Generally pleasant audio (*see* Con). Stylish. Removable tilt panel (*see* Con). LCD easy to read. *PL-200:* Handy size for travel—almost a pocket model. Tilt panel on back of case. Choice among three colors (red, gray, silver). *PL-230 and PL-200:* AC adaptor/battery charger and rechargeable "AA" batteries included. *YB-550PE:* Three "AA" alkaline batteries included. *North America (Grundig YB-550PE):* Toll-free tech support.

Con: Weak-signal sensitivity only fair. Mediocre image rejection. Signal-seek scanner stops only on very strong signals.

Power button activates 90-minute sleep delay; works as full-time "on" control only if held down for two seconds, a minor inconvenience. Takes an additional five seconds to fully turn on (or boot up). Keypad has small, cramped keys with little travel. *YB-550PE:* No AC adaptor included. *YB-550PE and PL-230:* Audio crispness on FM through headphones not fully up to Grundig standard. Keypad has oddly placed zero key. Telescopic antenna placement on right side disallows tilting to left. Snap-on tilt panel must be removed to replace batteries. Battery cover comes loose easily if tilt panel not attached. One of our two units displayed FM 50 Hz high, whereas world band frequencies on both samples were 1 kHz high. *PL-200:* Relatively small speaker lacks bass response. Currently not available outside China.

☞ PASSPORT's Tecsun PL-200 was received just as we were going to press, so was tested only briefly and at just one location. It gave out disruptive fixed-pitch howls on numerous frequencies within the shortwave spectrum, and to a lesser degree within the mediumwave AM band. Although the problem sounded like birdies and was not images, unlike true birdies it appeared not as an internally generated open carrier but apparently as modulation superimposed on transmitted carriers; e.g., as found on world band signals. It could not be resolved by changing any of the various system set codes.

This is almost certainly a sample, shipping or early-production problem—or even transitory—and there was no time to obtain a second unit from China or do a thorough investigative analysis in the lab or at other locations. So, the PL-200 cannot yet be given a verifiable rating. However, this issue aside, it earns the same overall star rating as its fraternal twins.

To check for this, simply bandscan within one or more world band segments with a number of audible stations. If it's there, you'll hear it loud and often—it's nothing subtle. If, as is likely, it's not there, you've got a good one.

The new Grundig YB550PE, also available through Etón.

☞ The Tecsun PL-230 is essentially identical to the YB-550PE except for color and the inclusion of rechargeable batteries and an AC adaptor/charger.

Verdict: Although they look quite different, the two YB-550PE models, along with their Tecsun PL-230 lookalike, share the same circuit design with the much smaller Tecsun PL-200.

Under-$100 radios used to look blah and often sound that way, but no more. The stylish YB-550PE/PL-230 is an agreeable set that's straightforward to use and full of software conveniences. However, images and

The travel-sized Tecsun PL-200 appears to have the same circuitry as the Etón/Grundig YB-550PE, but layout and features differ.

weak-signal sensitivity keep it from being all that it could have been.

Evaluation of New Models: For years radio manufacturers turned out the equivalent of the PC "beige box"—undistinguished and indistinguishable except on the inside. But just as this is changing with PCs, so it is with Etón/Grundig's line of world band radios.

The new YB-550PE/PL-230 is a pleasant performer, to be sure, but then so, too, are a number of other models. What sets it apart is an element of visual pizzazz—you don't feel like you have to hide it in a drawer when company stops by. It's also why this radio is likely to be on Father's Day and holiday gift lists.

The '550PE/'230 and '200 also have a degree of software pizzaz. Among software-driven convenience features are page presets which allow the user to define the number of presets per page, which is especially useful when scanning a page to find the strongest frequency. Too, while most radios simply limp along off rechargeable batteries, which produce about a third of a Volt less per cell, these receivers have a software adjustment for when rechargeables are being used. Tecsun even provides the necessary rechargeable batteries and AC adaptor/charger with the PL-230 and PL-200.

The '200's landscape format and keypad layout are handier than what's on the '550PE/'230, although the '200's relatively small speaker lacks the low-end audio

The Sony ICF-SW40's slide-rule "dial" is actually digital.

reproduction of the others. Alas, our PL-200 gave off loud howls on various frequencies throughout the shortwave spectrum and to some degree within the mediumwave AM band. Something this obvious is almost certainly a sample, shipping or early-production problem, but until this is verified we can't give the radio an unqualified rating. However, this issue aside, the '200 merits the same overall star ranking as the '550PE/'230.

The PL-200's small size—within a skosh of a pocket model and even smaller than Degen's offerings—makes it tempting for use on trips. After all, the current crop of pocket models consists of an excellent but pricey Sony, on one hand, and a number of modest offerings, on the other. Tecsun's PL-200, although slightly larger and heavier, potentially fills this gap.

✪✪⅜
Sony ICF-SW40

Price: $119.95 in the United States. £89.95 in the United Kingdom. *AC-E45HG 120V AC adaptor:* $19.95.

Pro: Technologically unintimidating for analog traditionalists, as its advanced digital tuning circuitry is disguised to look like slide-rule, or analog, tuning. World Time 24-hour clock. Two "on" timers and sleep delay. Travel power lock. Illuminated LCD. Japanese FM band (most versions).

Con: Single bandwidth is relatively wide, reducing adjacent-channel rejection. No keypad. Lacks coverage of 1625-1705 kHz portion of North American and Australian mediumwave AM band and 1705-1735 kHz potential public service segment. AC adaptor, much-needed, is extra and overpriced. No batteries (three "AA" required).

Verdict: If you're turned off by things digital and complex, Sony's Japanese-made ICF-SW40 will feel like an old friend. Otherwise, forget it.

✪✪⅜
Sangean ATS 404, Roberts R881

Price: *Sangean:* $99.95 in the United States. $129.00CAD in Canada. £64.95 in the United Kingdom. €69.00 in Germany. *ADP-808 120V AC adaptor:* $10.95 in the United States. *Roberts:* £79.95 in the United Kingdom.

Pro: Superior weak-signal sensitivity. Several handy tuning features. Stereo FM through earpieces, included. Dual-zone 24/12-hour clock displays seconds numerically. Alarm with sleep delay. Travel power lock. Illuminated LCD. Battery indicator.

Con: Poor image rejection. No tuning knob. Overloading, controllable by shortening telescopic antenna on world band and collapsing it on mediumwave AM band. Picks up some internal digital hash. Tunes only in 5 kHz increments. No signal-strength indicator. Frequency and time cannot be displayed simultaneously. Power lock does not disable LCD illumination. No handle or carrying strap. AC adaptor extra. Country of manufacture (China) not specified on radio or box. No batteries (four "AA" needed).

Verdict: Look elsewhere.

The Sangean ATS 404's sensitivity and dynamic range make it best suited to western North America.

FM through earbuds, included. *North America:* Toll-free tech support.

Con: Mediocre image rejection. No tuning knob. Few station presets; e.g., only six for 2300-7800 kHz range. Tunes world band only in 5 kHz steps and displays in non-standard XX.XX MHz/XX.XX₅ MHz format. Keypad entry of even channels with all digits (e.g., 6 - 1 - 9 - 0, Enter) tunes radio 5 kHz higher (e.g., 6195); remedied by not entering trailing zero (e.g., 6 - 1 - 9, Enter). Unhandy carouseling "MW/SW1/SW2/FM" control required for tuning within 2300-7800 kHz *vs.* 9100-26100 kHz range or *vice versa.* Clock not displayed independent of frequency; button alters which one is visible. Nigh-useless signal-strength

✪✪⅜
Etón Yacht Boy 300PE, Grundig Yacht Boy 300PE, Tecsun PL757A

Price: *YB-300PE:* $79.95 in the United States. $99.95CAD in Canada. Price not yet established in the United Kingdom. *YB-300PE refurbished units, as available:* $59.95 in the United States.

Pro: Sensitive to weak world band and FM signals. Various helpful tuning features. World Time 24-hour clock with alarm, clock radio and 10-90 minute sleep delay (*see* Con). Illuminated LCD (*see* Con). 120V AC adaptor (North America) and supplementary antenna. Travel power lock (*see* Con). Stereo

From 2004 some Grundigs will be sold outside North America under the "Etón" name, among them the Yacht Boy 300.

indicator. LCD illumination not disabled by travel power lock.

Verdict: Except for LCD illumination being permanently enabled, this Chinese-made model is priced and sized for air travel, especially where signals are weak.

✪⅛ ✇
Kchibo KK-E200

Price: $64.95 in the United States. $89.95CAD in Canada.

Pro: Pleasant audio for size and price. Various helpful tuning features, including keypad (*see* Con), 12 world band station presets (*see* Con), up/down slewing, meter-band carousel selection and signal-seek tuning. High-contrast illuminated LCD (*see* Con) indicates which preset is in use. Agreeable selectivity and weak-signal sensitivity for price class. Sleep delay, shutoff selectable from 10-90 minutes. World Time 24-hour clock. Travel power lock (*see* Con). AC adaptor (*see* Con). FM stereo through earbuds, included. Pleasant FM performance for price and size class. Control to reset scrambled microprocessor. Hinged battery cover to prevent misplacing (*see* Con).

Con: Image rejection only fair. Dynamic range mediocre, sometimes overloads even with built-in antenna. Does not receive important 7305-9495 kHz chunk of world band spectrum. Does not receive 1621-1705 kHz portion of expanded AM band in the Americas and Australia and the 1705-1735 kHz potential public service segment. No tuning knob. Tunes world band only in 5 kHz steps and displays in nonstandard XX.XX MHz/XX.XX5 MHz format. Unhandy carouseling "MW/SW1/SW2/FM" control required when shifting from tuning within 2300-7300 kHz *vs.* 9500-26100 kHz range or *vice versa*. No signal-strength indicator. Annoying one-second pause when tuning from one channel to the next. Only six station presets for each of the four "bands" (FM/MW-AM/SW1/SW2). Dreadful mediumwave AM performance, with circuit noise drowning out weak stations and degrading stronger ones. AC adaptor sometimes produces slight hum. Tilt panel flimsy; also, hard to open with short finger-nails. Clock doesn't display when frequency is shown, although pushbutton allows time to replace frequency. No alarm or other awakening function. Keypad not in telephone format. Fragile battery-cover hinge pins snap off easily. LCD illumination only fair. Power lock doesn't disable LCD light button. Using 9/10 kHz mediumwave AM channel switch erases station presets and clock setting. No weak-battery indicator; radio goes abruptly silent when batteries weaken. No batteries (three "AA" needed). Box claims "fancy leather cover," but it is ordinary vinyl. No indication of county of manufacture (China) on product, box or manual. "Chinglish" owner's manual occasionally puzzles. Warranty only 90 days in North America.

Verdict: The stylish Kchibo KK-E200 comes with useful accessories omitted on models costing much more. Its speaker audio quality is pleasant for its size and price, too. Although it lacks full frequency coverage, has no alarm and is overly muted for bandscanning, the 'E200 is cheap and an eyeful.

The Kchibo KK-E200 is an inexpensive eyeful with satisfactory performance.

✪⅞
Grundig G2000A "Porsche Design," Grundig Porsche P2000, Grundig Yacht Boy P2000

Price: *G2000A:* $79.95 in the United States. $99.95CAD in Canada. £84.95 in the United Kingdom. *P2000:* £84.95 in the United Kingdom. $199.00AUD in Australia. *G2ACA 120V AC adaptor:* $12.95 in the United States.

Pro: One of the most functionally attractive world band radios on the market, with generally superior ergonomics that include an effective and handy lambskin protective case. Superior adjacent-channel rejection—selectivity—for price and size class. Keypad (in proper telephone format), handy meter-band carousel control, signal-seek and up/down slew tuning. Twenty station presets, of which ten are for world band and the rest for FM and mediumwave AM stations. FM stereo through earpieces, included. World Time 24-hour clock. Timer/alarm with sleep delay. Illuminated display. Travel power lock. Microprocessor reset control. *North America:* Toll-free tech support.

Con: Pedestrian audio. Weak-signal sensitivity mediocre between 9400-26100 kHz, improving slightly between 2300-7400 kHz. Poor image rejection. Does not tune such important world band ranges as 7405-7550 and 9350-9395 kHz. Tunes world band only in 5 kHz steps and displays in nonstandard XX.XX MHz/XX.XX₅ MHz format. No tuning knob. Annoying one-second pause when tuning from one channel to the next. Old-technology SW1/SW2 switch complicates tuning. Protruding power button can get in the way of nearby slew-tuning and meter-carousel keys. Using 9/10 kHz mediumwave AM channel switch erases station presets and clock setting. Leather case makes it difficult to retrieve folded telescopic antenna. Magnetic catches weak on leather case. No carrying strap. Signal-strength indicator nigh useless. Clock not displayed separately from frequency. No batteries (three "AA" required).

The stylish Grundig G2000A "Porsche Design" includes a lambskin wraparound.

☞ At present there are no plans to sell this model under the Etón name.

Verdict: This German-styled, Chinese-manufactured portable is the ultimate in tasteful design, but performance is another story.

New for 2004

✪¾   🅒
Grundig G1000A, Etón G1000A, Tecsun DR-910

Price: $49.95 in the United States. $69.95CAD in Canada. Price not yet established in the United Kingdom.

Pro: Clock/timer with one-hour sleep delay (*see* Con). Illuminated LCD has bigger digits than most models of this size. Tilt panel. FM

The new Grundig/Etón G1000A is inexpensive.

in stereo with earbuds, included. Two "AA" batteries included. Superior carrying case.

Con: Analog tuned with a digital frequency counter, so lacks tuning except by thumbwheel, which is slightly touchy. Does not tune 120, 75, 90, 60, 15 and 11 meter segments; misses a small amount of expanded coverage of 41 and 31 meter segments. Poor image rejection. Audio lacks bass response. Clock in 12-hour format, displays only when radio off. Displays in nonstandard XX.XX MHz/XX.XX5 MHz format. "Play" in bandswitch allows wiggling to slightly alter frequency readout. FM overloads in presence of strong signals, remediable by shorting antenna (which also reduces weak-signal sensitivity). On our units, FM frequency misread by 100 kHz (half a channel). If finger placed over LCD display, buzzing audible on mediumwave AM and lower world band frequencies. *North America:* Toll-free tech support.

Verdict: More spit and polish, and better daytime frequency coverage, than truly cheaper alternatives. It's also backed up by a solid warranty from a reputable company. The G1000A occupies a spot between "throwaway" models that are passable performers, and more highly rated models that cost more.

The jWIN JX-M14 is so cheap that it's hard to resist when traveling where things "disappear." Bring along a length of antenna wire, though, as it struggles with weaker signals.

New for 2004

✪½
jWIN JX-M14

Price: $29.95 or less in the United States.

Pro: Clock with timer/alarm (*see* Con). Tilt panel. Earbuds included (in separate bubble pack).

Con: Mediocre weak-signal sensitivity; helps considerably to clip a few yards of wire to the built-in antenna. Mediocre selectivity. Analog tuned with a digital frequency counter, so lacks tuning except by thumbwheel, which is stiff. Does not tune 120, 75, 90, 60, 15, 13 or 11 meter segments; misses a small amount of expanded coverage of 49 and 41 meter segments. Poor image rejection. Audio lacks bass response. Frequency counter completely omits last digit so, say, 9575 kHz appears as either 9.57 or 9.58 MHz. Clock in 12-hour format only, displays only when radio off. Display not illuminated. If hand is placed on rear of cabinet, world band drifts up to 10 kHz. LCD buzzes on mediumwave AM; if finger placed over LCD, buzz also audible on lower world band frequencies. Mediumwave weak-signal sensitivity uninspiring. FM overloads in strong-signal environments, remediable by shorting antenna (which also reduces weak-signal sensitivity). When first turned on, radio always reverts to FM band. FM in mono only. Two "AA" batteries not included. Warranty in the United States only 90 days and requires $12 advance payment for "return shipping"; add to that the owner's cost to ship, and warranty is of dubious value; best purchased from dealer who will swap if DOA.

Verdict: At almost a throwaway price, the Chinese-made jWIN JX-M14 is a passable portable for casual use on trips or as a stocking stuffer, provided a hank of wire is clipped on to give world band signals a boost.

✪½
Kchibo KK-S320

Price: $ 54.99 plus shipping in the United States.

Pro: Even more compact than its costlier KK-E200 cousin, with better mediumwave AM performance and greater audio crispness. Agreeable weak-signal sensitivity. Sleep delay, shutoff selectable up to 90 minutes (*see* Con) and single-event on/off timer. High contrast LCD indicates which preset is in use. AC adaptor. FM stereo via earbuds, included.

Con: No coverage of 120, 90, 75, 60, 16, 15, 13 and 11 meter (2, 3, 4, 5, 17, 19, 21 and 25 MHz) segments, with only partial coverage of 49 and 19 meters (6 and 15 MHz). No keypad or tuning knob; other tuning alternatives cumbersome, especially with "out-of-band" frequencies. Only five station presets for each of the three "bands" (FM/MW-AM/SW). "Signal seek" scanning works only within limited frequency

The Kchibo KK-S320 is cheapo, but not enough. Similar performers sell for less.

NUMBERS: SONY ICF-SW77	
Max. Sensitivity/Noise Floor	0.16 μV, **S**/–133 dBm, **E** (2)
Blocking	121 dB, **G**
Bandwidths *(Shape Factors)*	6.0 *(1:1.9,* **E***)*, 3.3 *(1:2.0,* **G***)* kHz
Ultimate Rejection	70 dB, **G**
Front-End Selectivity	— (3)
Image Rejection	80 dB, **E**
First IF Rejection	80 dB, **E**
Dynamic Range/IP3 (5 kHz)	64 dB, **F**/–37 dBm, **F**
Dynamic Range/IP3 (20 kHz)	82 dB, **F**/–10 dBm, **G**
Phase Noise	122 dBc, **E**
AGC Threshold	2.0 μV, **G**
Overall Distortion, sync	2.3%, **E**/3.3%, **G** (4)

IBS Lab Ratings: **S** Superb **E** Excellent **G** Good **F** Fair **P** Poor

(1) Measurements flat from 5-29 MHz, but drop to 0.75 μV, **F**/-118 dBm, **F** at 2 MHz.

(2) Sensitivity varies considerably by frequency at 2 MHz and between 10-29.9 MHz; *viz.*, from 0.16 μV to 1.40 μV, **S** - **G**. Noise floor varies by frequency from –133 dBm to –117 dBm, **E** - **G**. Neither measurement could be made at 5 MHz because of spurious responses, noise and leakage.

(3) Cannot be determined.

(4) Wide/narrow bandwidths.

segments. Radio cannot be turned on permanently; rather, the power button activates the 90-minute-or-less sleep-delay timer, forcing the radio to turn itself off after no more than an hour and a half. After radio powers up, slewing buttons cannot be used nor the frequency displayed, until the user presses a preset or band key once, or presses the display key three times. Poor dynamic range, with overloading a major problem at night. Poor adjacent-channel selectivity. "Floating birdie" sometimes appears in various world band segments. Mediocre image rejection. Poor dynamic range for nighttime listening in many parts of the world. Does not receive 1621-1710 kHz portion of expanded mediumwave AM band in the Americas. Tunes world band only in 5 kHz steps. Displays only in nonstandard XX.XX/XX.XX5 MHz format. Display not illuminated. Clock uses 12-hour format, not suitable for World Time. Tilt panel hard to open. Clock doesn't display when frequency is shown, although pushbutton allows time to replace frequency. No travel power lock. No signal-strength indicator. No weak-battery indicator; radio goes abruptly silent when batteries start to flag. No batteries included (three "AA" needed). Microprocessor sometimes freezes up, requiring activation of reset button; this also erases the station presets and clock setting stored in memory. No indication of county of manufacture

(China) on product, box or manual. "Chinglish" owner's manual occasionally puzzles. FM performance pedestrian. Not easily purchased in the Americas or most other parts of the world. Warranty period not yet apparent.

Verdict: Conveniently smaller than its KK-E200 cousin, and priced to move. Yet, the KK-S320's cumbersome tuning, inadequate shortwave coverage and rudimentary world band performance make it a dubious choice.

✪⅜
Bolong HS-490

Price: RMB360 (about $45) in China.

Pro: World Time 24-hour clock (*see* Con). Reel-type outboard passive antenna accessory. AC adaptor. Illuminated display. Alarm with sleep-delay timer. FM stereo (*see* Con) via earbuds, included.

Con: Seemingly impossible to find outside China. Requires patience to get a station, as it tunes world band only via 10 station presets and multi-speed up/down slewing/scanning. Tunes world band only in 5 kHz steps and displays in nonstandard XX.XX MHz/XX.XX5 MHz format. Poor image rejection. So-so adjacent-channel rejection (selectivity). World Time 24-hour clock not displayed independent of frequency. Does not receive relatively unimportant 6200-7100 kHz portion of world band spectrum. Does not receive 1615-1705 kHz portion of expanded AM band in the Americas and Australia or the 1705-1735 kHz potential public service segment. No signal-strength indicator. No travel power lock. Mediumwave AM 9/10 kHz tuning increments not selectable, which may make for inexact tuning in some parts of the world other than where the radio was purchased. FM selectivity and capture ratio mediocre. FM stereo did not trigger on our unit.

The Bolong HS-490 is a classic in China.

Verdict: Made by a joint venture between Xin Hui Electronics and Shanghai Huaxin Electronic Instruments. No prize, but at one time this was the #1 selling digital world band radio in China.

LAP PORTABLES

Pleasant for Home, Acceptable for Travel

A lap portable is probably your best bet for use primarily around the home and yard, plus on occasional trips. They are large enough to perform well, usually sound better than compact models, yet are not too big to fit into a carry-on or briefcase. Most take 3-4 "D" (UM-1) or "C" (UM-2) cells, plus sometimes a couple of "AA" (UM-3) cells for memory backup.

These are typically just under a foot wide— that's 30 cm—and weigh in around 3-5 pounds, or 1.4-2.3 kg. For air travel, that's okay if you are a dedicated listener, but a bit much otherwise.

Look for Grundig to be entering the high end of this market in 2004 (*see* sidebar).

✪✪✪¾
Sony ICF-SW77, Sony ICF-SW77E

Price: $469.95 in the United States. €489.00 in Germany. *Padded carrying case #0395:* $29.95 from Universal Radio in the United States.

The best portable since the Sony ICF-2010 was dropped is another Sony, the ICF-SW77.

Pro: A rich variety of tuning and other features, including sophisticated "page" tuning that some enjoy but others dislike; includes 162 station presets, two-speed tuning knob, signal-seek tuning (*see* Con), keypad tuning and meter-band access. Synchronous selectable sideband is exceptionally handy to operate; it significantly reduces selective-fading distortion and adjacent-channel interference on world band, longwave and mediumwave AM signals; although the sync chip part number was changed not long back, its performance is virtually unchanged (*see* Con). Two well-chosen bandwidths (6.0 kHz and 3.3 kHz) provide superior adjacent-channel rejection. Excellent image rejection and first-IF rejection, both 80 dB. Excellent-to-superb weak-signal sensitivity (noise floor -133 dBm, sensitivity 0.16 microvolts) in and around lower-middle portion of shortwave spectrum where most listening is done (*see*

WHAT ABOUT SONY ICF-2010 PARTS?

The last of the Sony ICF-2010 models was manufactured in late 2002. Not only is this legendary model sorely missed, but Sony no longer appears to stock parts for it.

Thankfully, there is an alternative—Part Solver at www.partsolver.com or 1-877-627-2787, which apparently has purchased Sony's inventory of '2010 parts. Included in its roster of 155 thingies for the '2010 are the 2SK152 front-end FET ($6.89) that is prone to blow from static charges entering via the antenna. Too, they carry replacement telescopic antennas ($19.15). Both are worth keeping on hand should your '2010 act up in the years to come, when parts may not be so readily available.

MAKE YOUR PORTABLE "HEAR" BETTER

Regardless of which portable you own, you can boost weak-signal sensitivity on the cheap. How cheap? Nothing, for starters.

Look for "sweet spots" to place your radio: near windows, appliances, telephones, building I-beams and the like. If your portable has an AC adaptor, try that, then batteries; sometimes the adaptor works better, sometimes batteries. Places to avoid are near computers and other appliances with microprocessors; also, light dimmers, non-incandescent lighting and cable TV or telephone lines. Sometimes power lines and cords can be noisy, too.

Outdoor Antenna Optional

An outdoor antenna isn't necessary, but it can help. With compact and smaller portable receivers, simplest is often best, as sophisticated wire antennas can cause "overloading." Run several meters or yards of ordinary insulated wire to a tree, then clip one end to your set's telescopic antenna with an alligator or claw clip available from RadioShack and such. It's fast and cheap, yet effective.

If you are in a weak-signal location, such as central or western North America or Australia, and want stronger signals, even better is to erect an inverted-L (so-called "longwire") antenna. These are available in the United States at RadioShack (278-758, $9.99) and worldwide at radio specialty outlets. Powerful versions can be constructed from detailed instructions found in the RDI White Paper, *PASSPORT Evaluation of Popular Outdoor Antennas*. Antenna length is not critical, but keep the lead-in wire reasonably short.

Use an outdoor antenna only when needed—disconnect during thunder, snow or sand storms and when the radio is off. And don't touch any antenna during dry weather, as you might discharge static electricity into vulnerable electronic circuitry.

Creative Indoor Solutions

All antennas work best outdoors, away from electrical noises inside your home. If your supplementary antenna has to be indoors, run it along the middle of a window with Velcro, tape or suction cups. In a reinforced-concrete building which absorbs radio signals, you can affix a long whip or telescopic car antenna sticking outdoors, like a flag wall mast, onto a windowsill or balcony rail. Antennas like these are all but invisible, but work well because they reach away from the building.

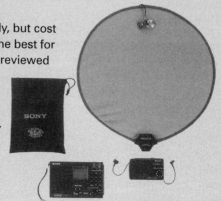

Amplified ("active") antennas are small and handy, but cost more. Many are made for tabletop models, but the best for portables is the Sony AN-LP1 portable loop. It is reviewed in PASSPORT REPORTS' article on active antennas, and despite what Sony's literature says it works nicely with the Sony ICF-SW77. A pricier alternative is AOR's portable WL500 loop, new for 2004.

If you want your portable to snare more weak stations, look into the Sony AN-LP1 portable active antenna.

Con). Superb overall distortion, almost always under one percent. Dynamic range (82 dB) and third-order intercept point (-10 dBm) fairly good at 20 kHz separation (see Con). Tunes in very precise 0.05 kHz increments; displays in 0.1 kHz increments; these and other factors make this model superior to any other portable for single-sideband reception, although portatop and tabletop models usually fare better yet. Continuous bass and treble tone controls, a rarity. Two illuminated multi-function liquid crystal displays. Dual-zone clock, displays separately from frequency. Station name appears on LCD when station presets used. 10-level signal-strength indicator (see Con). Excellent stability, less than 20 Hz drift after ten-second warmup. Excellent weak-signal sensitivity (noise floor -130 dBm, sensitivity 0.21 microvolts) within little-used 120 meter segment (see Con). Flip-up chart for calculating time differences. VCR-type five-event timer controls radio and optional outboard recorder alike. Superior FM audio quality. Stereo FM through earpieces, included. Japanese FM (most versions) and longwave bands. AC adaptor, hum-free, and reel-in outboard antenna. Rubber strip helps prevent sliding.

Con: Large and heavy, very nearly a field portable. "Page" tuning system relatively complex to operate; many find that station presets can't be accessed simply. World band and mediumwave AM audio slightly muffled even when wide bandwidth in use. Synthesizer chuffing degrades reception quality during bandscanning by knob. Dynamic range (64 dB) and third-order intercept point (-37 dBm) only fair at 5 kHz separation. Weak-signal sensitivity varies from fair to superb, depending on where between 2 and 30 MHz receiver is being tuned. Synchronous selectable sideband holds lock reasonably. Synchronous selectable sideband tends to lose lock if batteries weak, or if NiCd cells are used. Synchronous selectable sideband alignment can vary with temperature, factory alignment and battery voltage,

causing synchronous selectable sideband reception to be slightly more muffled in one sideband than the other. Signal-seek tuning skips over weaker signals. Flimsy 11-element telescopic antenna (the older version of the 'SW77 had nine elements). LCD characters small for size of receiver. Display illumination does not stay on with AC power. Unusual tuning knob design disliked by some. On mediumwave AM band, relatively insensitive, sometimes with spurious sounds during single-sideband reception; this doesn't apply to world band reception, however. Mundane reception of difficult FM signals. Signal-strength indicator grossly overreads, covering only a 20 dB range with maximum reading at only 3 microvolts. AGC threshold, 2 microvolts (good). Painted surfaces can wear off with heavy use. Getting harder to find outside the United States. No batteries (four "C" required).

☞ For those seeking to have their ICF-SW77 repaired, a helpful source at Sony of America suggests: Sony Service Center, 1504 Grundy's Lane, MD #12, Bristol PA 19007 USA.

Verdict: The Japanese-made '77 has been a strong contender among portables since it was improved some time back, and for single-sideband reception it is the best portable by a skosh. It's also one of the very few models with continuously tuned bass and treble controls. Ergonomics, however, are a mixed bag, so if you're interested consider trying it out first.

✪✪
Roberts R827

Price: *Roberts:* £159.95 in the United Kingdom.

Pro: Superior overall world band performance. Numerous tuning features, including 18 world band station presets. Two bandwidths for good fidelity/interference tradeoff. Analog clarifier with center detent and stable circuitry allows single-sideband

The Roberts R827 is available in and around the United Kingdom. It is pleasant, with no dazzle or fuss.

signals to be tuned with uncommon precision, thus allowing for superior audio phasing for a portable (*see* Con). Illuminated display. Signal-strength indicator. Dual-zone 24-hour clock, with one zone displayed separately from frequency. Alarm/timer with sleep delay. Travel power lock. FM stereo through headphones. AC adaptor. Longwave.

Con: Tends to mute when tuning knob turned quickly, making bandscanning difficult. Keypad not in telephone format. Touchy variable control for single-sideband fine tuning. Does not come with tape-recorder jack. No batteries (four "D" and three "AA" needed). Country of manufacture (now China) not specified on radio or box.

Verdict: This is a decent, predictable radio—performance and features, alike—and reasonably priced. Sangean no longer makes this model under its own name, and we were unable to find out whether they will continue to manufacture it for Roberts once the existing inventory is exhausted.

New for 2004

✪✪¼ ✪ *Passport's Choice*
Etón S350, Grundig S350, Tecsun BCL-2000

Price: *S350:* $99.95 in the United States. $149.95CAD in Canada. Price not yet established in the United Kingdom. *S350*

refurbished units, as available: $129.00CAD in Canada. *Franzus FR-22 120>220V AC transformer for BCL-2000:* $15-18 in the United States.

Pro: Speaker audio quality substantially above the norm for world band portables, regardless of price. Separate bass and treble tone controls, a rarity at any price, help shape audio frequency response. Unusually powerful audio, suitable for relatively noisy ambient listening environments. Two bandwidths, well-chosen, are a real and pleasant surprise at this price; they provide effective and flexible adjacent-channel rejection *vis-à-vis* fidelity. Sensitive to weak signals, and exceptionally free from circuit noise ("hiss"). No chuffing while tuning. Relatively intuitive to operate, even for newcomers. World Time clock (*see* Con) with alarm, clock radio and 1-90 minute sleep delay; may also be set to 12-hour format. Four-level (eight bar) signal-strength indicator. Battery-level indicator. Low battery consumption, combined with four "D" cells, reduces need for battery replacement. Most comfortable carrying handle of any world band radio tested; also seconds as a shoulder strap. Brightly illuminated LCD has high contrast, is visible from a variety of angles. LCD illumination may be left on fulltime or timed to turn off. Attractive. FM reception quality above average. FM in stereo through headphones. RCA phono sockets provide stereo line output for recording, FM home transmitters and outboard audio systems. Mediumwave AM reception better than most. *North America:* Toll-free tech support. *BCL-2000:* Built-in 220V AC power supply eliminates need for outboard AC adaptor. *S350:* Outboard 120V AC adaptor, included, can be left behind on trips, making the S350 lighter than the BCL-2000.

Con: Analog tuned with a digital frequency counter, so lacks tuning except by pair of concentric (fast/slow) tuning knobs. This results in an unusually high degree of frequency drift, typically 1-4 kHz in the first half-hour, but greater with some samples in certain frequency ranges. Poor image rejection. Power button activates 90-minute sleep-delay timer; works as full-time "on" control only if held down for three seconds, a minor inconvenience. Lacks such helpful tuning aids as station presets, keypad and scanning. Unhandy "MW/SW1/SW2/SW3" switch must often be used to tune mediumwave AM and shortwave spectra. Some user-correctable nighttime overloading in high-signal-strength parts of the world. Does not tune relatively unused 2 MHz (120 meter) tropical world band segment. Mediumwave AM frequency readout can be off by up to 2 kHz. Clock not displayed independent of frequency; button allows time to replace frequency for three seconds. Nominal 30 MHz low-pass filter has such high apparent insertion loss as to be useless except as a de facto attenuator. Poor visual indication of adjustment position of volume, tone and RF gain controls (user-remediable with paint or Wite-Out). Batteries (4 x "D") not included. *S350:* AC adaptor less handy than built-in power supply. *BCL-2000:* Mediumwave AM misses the 1650-1705 kHz portion of the X-band and 1705-1735 kHz potential public-service segment.

☞ Beware of a quasi-counterfeit clone labeled "ECB 2000," also produced in China.

Verdict: Tecsun's BCL-2000—sold in North America as the Grundig S350 and in Europe as the Etón S350—is full of welcome surprises, as well as the other variety. Its flaws are obvious and real: drift, images and a paucity of tuning aids, so it receives a modest star rating.

Why, then, is something like this cited as a "Passport's Choice"? Because for pleasant listening to news, music and entertainment over the world band airwaves, it is hard to beat—its audio quality just isn't equaled by

The Grundig S350, a/k/a Etón S350 and Tecsun BCL-2000, is drifty but has the best audio of any portable. Superior FM and mediumwave AM performance, too.

any other portable. If you want something that sounds as good but performs better, dig deep and spring for a Grundig Satellit 800 portatop.

Evaluation of New Model (current version): This new offering from Tecsun's factory uses four beefy "D" cells, which along with low current drain helps reduce the need for battery changes. There is also a clever carrying strap that doubles as a comfortable padded handle—it's the best we've come across. Additionally for travelers, there's an easy-to-use 24/12-hour clock-radio timer. It is not displayed independent of frequency, but a button

Tecsun's BCL-2000 comes in three colors, including eye-popping metallic red with black trim.

allows time to replace frequency for three seconds on the LCD.

Many modern world band radios use synthesized tuning, but not this model, which uses analog tuning coupled to a digital frequency counter. As a result, operation is fairly simple or frustratingly inadequate, depending on your perspective. Tuning is only by two-speed knob and a pair of switches having three "bands" for shortwave: approximately 2925-8150 ("SW1"), 7840-17325 ("SW2") and 16835-28495 ("SW3") kHz—no station presets, no slew or scan controls, no keypad, no RS232 port. There are two continuous tone controls, bass and treble, along with RF gain and volume controls. Add to that seven buttons for power, clock/timer and LCD illumination, along with an IC-reset detent, and that's the full roster except for low-pass-filter and mono-stereo switches on the cabinet's right side.

The LCD's backlight can stay on for eight or fewer seconds, or be kept on continuously. If you've bandscanned in the dark with timed LCD illumination, you'll appreciate being able to leave it lit.

Ergonomics are reasonable, including a high-contrast LCD with battery-level display and four-level signal-strength indicator (eight bars, but they operate in pairs); that battery level tends to underread when the radio is on, but otherwise is accurate. Nevertheless, ergonomics would have fared even better had the volume and RF gain locations been swapped. Too, the black-on-black knob indicator detents are nigh invisible; Wite-Out or paint resolves this.

The power switch turns out to be a sleep-delay control that shuts the radio off up to 90 minutes later. Fortunately, units produced from May, 2003 onward allow the radio to stay on fulltime, provided the power button is held down for three seconds or more.

"Getting from here to there" with the concentric two-speed (4:1) tuning knob and short-wave bandswitch is fast and easy, although even the "slow" (inner) knob requires a steady hand. As the radio doesn't demodulate single-sideband signals, this arrangement works reasonably well. Also, the analog tuning circuitry precludes rhythmic chuffing during tuning—a plus for bandscanning.

However, this tuning scheme utilizes a maze of string, gears and pulleys connected to potentially drifty variable capacitors. The typical result, even on the latest version: shortwave frequency drift of 1-4 kHz within the initial 30 minutes, occasionally more depending on the sample and the tuned frequency. Compounding this, the chip used for the frequency counter's reading drifts with changes in temperature. Finally, center-tuning by ear on mediumwave AM can result in an additional +1-2 kHz frequency error on top of all the rest.

We had heard from China that drift would be reduced in units produced by the summer of 2003. Yet, by well into the last half of the year new units continued to be driftmasters. It's been decades since we've come across a radio that wanders like this. Thankfully, this is user-correctable through periodic tweaking of the tuning knob, and after the first half hour drift is considerably reduced.

Poor image rejection results in "ghost" signals appearing 910 kHz below fundamental signals. Better-performing radios just don't do this, but at this price few models have worthy image rejection. A high-"Q" tunable active preselector, such as the MFJ-1020C (*see* PASSPORT REPORTS' reviews of active antennas), should help by peaking reception within a narrow band of frequencies, although we haven't specifically tested this combination.

Exceptional Audio Quality

Even though the speaker is unbaffled and only three-inches (75 mm), audio quality is markedly superior to that found on the vast majority of world band portables. This is aided by continuous bass and treble controls—a rarity, even among costly world band tabletop models—and there's plenty of power for room-filling sound.

Sensitivity to weak world band signals with the built-in telescopic antenna is very good. This is a major plus for reception in much of the world and, thanks in part to analog tuning, circuit noise is virtually nil.

Because dynamic range is not great, there can be overloading in and around bands that are awash in powerful signals. In the Americas, Asia, Australasia and much of Africa this is a limited issue. However, in Europe, North Africa and the Near East there are times when signal input needs to be reduced to cope with overloading. The "SW LPF" switch, nominally a 30 MHz low-pass filter, appears to act, instead, as an attenuator, perhaps as a result of insertion loss. It or the RF gain control can be used to reduce overloading—and sensitivity—as can shortening the telescopic antenna.

Selectivity, or adjacent-channel rejection, is much better than is customarily found on low-cost portables. Two well-chosen bandwidths provide flexibility in balancing interference rejection against audio fidelity.

This combination of high sensitivity, flexible selectivity and superior audio makes for unusually pleasant listening to world band programs. It's like a good baseball pitcher—he may not be able to hit as well as his teammates, but all is forgiven when he blows away hitters.

Mediumwave AM Improved

This radio's mediumwave AM performance now has much going for it, including worthy sensitivity with low circuit noise, directionality from the built-in ferrite rod antenna, flexible and appropriate selectivity, and superior audio quality. However, early-production units suffered from horrendous images and other spurious signals, especially at night. The "May 2003 version" was just as flawed, but by late summer the samples we tested were performing pretty much as they should, with only a weakened smattering of spurious signals appearing mainly as varying-pitch whistles.

The BCL-2000's coverage is approximately 520-1640 kHz, which misses the 1650-1705 kHz portion of the X-band found in the Americas and Australia, as well as the 1705-1735 kHz potential public service segment. The S350, on the other hand, tunes the entire band and then some—about 520-1745 kHz.

FM Reception Generally Superior

FM acquits itself very well. Sensitivity is quite good, while selectivity and capture ratio are at least average. There is only slight overloading in the presence of powerful nearby transmitters.

Audio quality isn't in the same league as something from Bose, but is unusually pleasant for a world band portable, and this makes all the difference on FM. Early versions had only mono FM from the earphone socket, but since last May it has been stereo, as has been the line output for recording, FM home transmitters and outboard audio systems.

Visual inspection suggests that the quality of construction is typical, but only time will tell.

Bottom Line

The Grundig S350/Tecsun BCL-2000 is not for world band DXers, nor for those chasing utility or ham signals. But for the silent majority of several million in North America and half a billion beyond who listen to news and entertainment over the world band airwaves, it is a bargain, with superior FM and mediumwave AM thrown in. It is straightforward to operate, has excellent sound and is priced to move.

World Band Cassette Recorders

What happens if your favorite show comes on at an inconvenient time? Why, tape it, of course, with a world band cassette recorder—just like on your VCR.

Two models are offered, and there's no question which is better: the Sony. Smaller, too, so it is less likely to raise eyebrows among airport security personnel. But there's a whopping price difference over the Sangean.

✪✪✪⅛ *Passport's Choice*
Sony ICF-SW1000T

Price: *ICF-SW1000T:* $449.95 in the United States. £359.95 as available in the United Kingdom. €439.00 in Germany. *AC-E30HG 120V AC adaptor:* $19.95.

Pro: Built-in recorder in rear of cabinet, with two events of up to 90 minutes each, selectable in ten-minute increments. Relatively compact for travel, also helpful to avoid airport security hassles. High-tech synchronous selectable sideband; this generally performs well, reducing adjacent-channel interference and selective-fading distortion on world band, longwave and mediumwave AM signals while adding slightly to weak-signal sensitivity (*see* Con). Single bandwidth, especially when

The only world band cassette recorder with timed events is Sony's ICF-SW1000T.

synchronous selectable sideband is used, exceptionally effective at adjacent-channel rejection. Numerous helpful tuning features, including keypad, two-speed up/down slewing, 32 station presets and signal-seek scanning. Thirty of the 32 station presets are within three easy-to-use "pages" so stations can be clustered. Weak-signal sensitivity above average up to about 16 MHz. Demodulates single-sideband signals (*see* Con). World Time 24-hour clock, easy to set (*see* Con). Sleep delay, 10-90 minutes. Illuminated LCD readable from a wide variety of angles. Travel power lock, also useful to keep recorder from being inadvertently switched on while cabinet being grasped (*see* Con). Easy on batteries. Records on both sides of tape without having to flip cassette (provided FWD is selected along with the "turning-around arrow"). Auto record level (*see* Con). "ISS" switch helps radio avoid interference from recorder's bias circuitry. FM stereo through earphones; earbuds included. Japanese FM (most versions) and longwave bands. Tape-reel-type outboard passive antenna accessory. Dead-battery indicator. Lapel mic (*see* Con).

Con: Pedestrian speaker audio quality. Synchronous selectable sideband tends to lose lock if batteries not fresh, or if NiCd cells are used. Synchronous selectable sideband alignment can vary with temperature, factory alignment and battery voltage, causing synchronous selectable sideband reception to be slightly more muffled in one sideband than the other. No tuning knob. Clock not readable when radio switched on except for ten seconds when key is pushed. No meaningful signal-strength indicator, which negates its otherwise obvious role for traveling technical monitors. No recording-level indicator or tape counter. Slow rewind. Fast forward and reverse use buttons that have to be held down. No built-in mic; outboard (lapel) mic is mono. Reception is interrupted for a good two seconds when recording first commences. No pause control. Single lock deactivates controls for radio and recorder alike; separate locks would have been preferable. Tuning resolution of 0.1 kHz allows single-sideband signals to be mis-tuned by up to 50 Hz. Frequency readout to 1 kHz, rather than 0.1 kHz tuning increment. Lacks flip-out tilt panel; instead, uses less handy plug-in tab. FM sometimes overloads. Telescopic antenna exits from the side, which limits tilting choices for FM. Misleading location of battery springs makes it easy to insert one of the two "AA" radio batteries in the wrong direction, albeit to no ill effect. No batteries (three "AA" required, two for radio and one for recorder). AC adaptor costs extra. Increasingly hard to find outside United States.

Verdict: Strictly speaking, Sony's pricey ICF-SW1000T is the world's only true world band cassette recorder. Made in Japan, it is an innovative little package with surprisingly good battery life and build quality.

✪✪ ✐
Sangean ATS-818ACS, Roberts RC828

Price: *Sangean:* $224.95 in the United States. $289.00CAD in Canada. £199.95 in the United Kingdom. €189.00 in Germany. *AC adaptor:* £16.95 in the United Kingdom. *Roberts:* £219.95 in the United Kingdom.

Pro: Built-in cassette recorder. Price low relative to competition. Superior overall world band performance. Numerous tuning features, including 18 world band station presets. Two bandwidths for good fidelity/interference tradeoff. Analog clarifier with center detent and stable circuitry allows single-sideband signals to be tuned with uncommon precision, thus allowing for superior audio phasing for a portable (*see* Con). Illuminated display. Signal-strength indicator. Dual-zone 24-hour clock, with one zone displayed separately from frequency. Alarm/timer with sleep delay.

Cheaper than Sony's 'SW1000T is the Sangean ATS-818ACS, which Roberts markets in the U.K. as the RC828.

Travel power lock. Stereo through headphones. Longwave. Built-in condenser mic. *Most versions:* AC adaptor.

Con: Recorder has no multiple recording events, just one "on" time (quits when tape runs out). Tends to mute when tuning knob turned quickly, making bandscanning difficult (the C. Crane Company offers a $20.00/$29.95 modification to remedy this). Wide bandwidth a bit broad for world band reception without synchronous selectable sideband. Keypad not in telephone format. Touchy single-sideband clarifier. Recorder has no level indicator and no counter. Fast-forward and rewind controls installed facing backwards. No batteries (four "D" and three "AA" needed). Country of manufacture (now China) not specified on radio or box.

Verdict: A great buy, although recording is only single-event with no timed "off."

The PASSPORT *portable-radio review team: Lawrence Magne and David Zantow; also, Tony Jones and Danny Wu, with laboratory measurements performed independently by Rob Sherwood. Additional feedback from Hanno Olinger, Lars Rydén, Craig Tyson, Chewei Wang and George Zeller.*

Light's Out: Radios for Emergencies

It's all but certain: There will be times when the world around you will be disrupted. Whether it be plague or terrorism, darkness or the ravages of nature, you'll need immediate access to trusted information.

When all else fails, world band radio is there—it's the one medium that gets through freely, no matter what. Like an emergency room, the worse things get the more important it becomes.

World band soars through the air direct from stations to your ears without gatekeepers or censorship. That's because its far-reaching signals don't rely on satellites, cables or other man-controlled intermediaries. Instead, they bounce off invisible layers in the earth's atmosphere that are no more subject to humancontrol than the wind.

Even if evildoers, pranksters or agencies try to disrupt a world band station, you stand a good chance of hearing what is being said. That's why world band radios are outlawed in gulags like North Korea.

Which to Choose, Avoid

If you already have a world band portable or portatop, perhaps you don't need to look any further. After all, if you keep extra batteries on hand your existing radio should serve nicely in a crisis.

If you don't already own a world band radio, purchase a portable that works for both routine listening and emergency use. Favor models that can process single-sideband signals. These allow for eavesdropping on aeronautical and other "utility" communications, as well as the U. S. Armed Forces Radio and Television Service. Also, look for illuminated LCDs, *de rigeur* for tuning around in the dark.

What to avoid? Cheap radios lacking digital frequency readout—their imprecise dials make stations hard to find, and most are marginal performers. Also think twice about wind-up radios. They seem promising on paper, but provide substandard reception.

The world continues to wait for a wind-up model that's more than a novelty. Yet, there is cause for hope, as the track record has been one of improvement. The first Baygen and Freeplay crank radios, for example, were analog-tuned with limited frequency coverage. Today's Summit fares much better.

Grundig has also trudged down this path. They once offered a flashlight that incorporated virtually the worst radio we have ever come across. It bombed, but they stuck with the concept and now have a sales blockbuster with their FR-200 radio/flashlight.

Make Sure It Works

You need to ensure that your radio actually works in your basement or other safe nook. Head outdoors and tune to several foreign stations that are weak but intelligible. Jot down their frequencies, then go to your shelter and see how well they come in. If reception is comparable, you're all set. If not, put up a simple outdoor wire antenna. Cut it to a convenient length, then run its feedline into your hideaway. Of course, keep PASSPORT handy so you'll know what's on—a flashlight, too, so you can read it.

> **Sometimes extra batteries are all you need.**

MILLIONS SOLD?

Grundig FR-200, Grundig FR200G, Etón FR-200, Etón FR200G, Tecsun Green-88

Wind-up radios with world band coverage have become major post-9/11 sellers. Indeed, the Etón Corporation claims to sell over a million of their Grundig FR-200 wind-up multiband radios each year in North America alone, and they are ramping up to release it in Europe as the Etón FR-200. Tecsun, which manufactures this analog-readout radio for Etón, already offers it in China. There, it's known as the Green-88, and includes a testosterone-tingling camouflage carrying case.

This cranky radio has surfaced in a palette of colors, including yellow, gray, brown and green. But it doesn't take much green to own. In the United States it sells for under $40, while in Canada figure $10 more. Its replaceable NiMH battery pack is charged not only by crank-driven dynamo, but in the slightly costlier "G" version there's also an AC adaptor. Even better, should the battery pack go dead the dynamo is designed to power the radio by itself.

Have Crank, Will Travel

During the North American blackout of 2003 RadioShack was the most popular store in town, with legions of customers grasping for radio batteries. The analog-readout Grundig FR-200/Etón FR-200/Tecsun Green-88 eliminates this concern, as it requires no consumer batteries. However, it does allow you to install these as backup, even if the battery cover opens too easily, allowing these cells and the rechargeable battery pack to flop out.

That rechargeable pack is juiced by turning a hand crank, like on Ford's earliest cars. But after weeks of playing Mr. Crankit with this radio, your wrists may start to look like Sammy Sosa's. There's a reason cars come with electric starters.

The FR-200 tunes mediumwave AM well beyond the upper band limit of 1705 kHz, as well as FM (including NTSC channel 6 audio) and two shortwave "bands": 3.2-7.6 MHz and 9.2-22 MHz. The front panel also has a bright flashlight to keep the boogie man at bay, but world band reception is, well, elemental.

The good news is that although FM overloads in strong-signal environments, both it and mediumwave AM perform reasonably well. Problem is, the FR-200/Green-88's analog frequency readout crams hundreds of world band stations into a couple of inches or five centimeters of dial space. Global signals thus can be hunted down only by blind man's bluff, and even then you don't know whether you're hearing the station's signal or its less-dependable image "repeat" 900 kHz or so down. As to being able to hear single-sideband signals, forget it.

Sensitivity to weak world band signals is marginal. Adjacent-channel rejection (selectivity) is equally dismal—image rejection, too. Yet, audio quality is pleasant on all bands and the price can't be beat.

For emergencies the FR-200/Green-88 suffices and is eminently affordable. It provides bare-bones performance and operation, and comes with a travel-grade carrying case, earbuds and a one-year warranty.

Retested for 2004
✪¼
Freeplay Summit

Price: $99.95 in the United States. £59.00 in the United Kingdom. €119.95 in Germany.

Pro: Relatively technologically advanced for an emergency radio. Powered by a rechargeable battery pack which, in turn, is juiced by a cranked alternator, solar energy (*see* Con) and an AC adaptor that adjusts to line voltage anywhere in the world (*see* Con). NiMH battery pack replaceable, although manufacturer claims radio will run even if battery no longer takes a charge. Reasonably pleasant audio quality. Timed LCD illumination. Low-battery and crank-charge indicators. World Time clock with alarm and sleep functions can also display in 12-hour format. Includes carrying pouch, worldwide AC adapter with three types of power plugs, and reel-in antenna. Travel power lock. Mediumwave AM includes 9/10 kHz tuning steps. FM includes NTSC channel 6 audio. Longwave. More stylish than most. Two-year warranty.

Con: Poor sensitivity on world band using built-in but undersized telescopic antenna; reel-in accessory antenna, included, helps to a degree. Poor selectivity. Poor image rejection. Shortwave coverage of 5.95-15.6 MHz omits 120, 75, 90, 60, 16, 15, 13 and 11 meter world band segments, along with lower end of 49 meters and upper end of 19 meters. Inconvenient to tune, what with no keypad, no tuning knob and "signal-seek" scanning that stops only at very powerful world band signals; this essentially leaves only single-speed (slow) up/down slewing and five world band presets to navigate the ether. Mutes for a second whenever slew button pressed, an annoyance when bandscanning. Does not continuously display frequency, reverts back to clock after ten seconds. Diminutive AC adaptor disturbs reception with vigorous noise and hum; best is to limit its use to charging the radio's battery, then disconnect it from the wall. Tunes world band only in 5 kHz steps and displays in nonstandard XX.XX MHz/XX.XX5 MHz format.

Freeplay Summit

David Zantow

LCD hard to read in low light without turning on illumination, which fades away after four seconds. Solar charger has relatively limited output. FM overloads in strong-signal environments. No handle or carrying strap.

☞ For the alternator to fully charge the battery for 15-20 hours' use takes over half an hour of nonstop cranking—a Schwarzeneggerian feat. Fortunately, the radio operates properly, for less time, with the battery only partially charged.

☞ The first unit we purchased was almost deaf to world band and FM signals. A second sample did better and forms the basis of our findings.

Verdict: Yes, its world band performance is mediocre and it is bereft of most tuning aids. Nevertheless, the Chinese-made Freeplay Summit is the most acceptable emergency radio we have come across. Performs quite reasonably on FM and mediumwave AM, too.

Evaluation of Retested Unit: The Freeplay Summit, like today's other emergency radios, is not powered directly from a spring-wound dynamo as was its Baygen ancestor. Instead, it uses a hand-cranked alternator to recharge a battery pack that, in turn, powers the radio.

The Summit is tiresome to tune and performs only passably. Yet, were the facade of civilization to be stripped away for weeks on end, this self-powered receiver would be extremely valuable to have on hand.

The PASSPORT *emergency-radio review team: Lawrence Magne and David Zantow.*

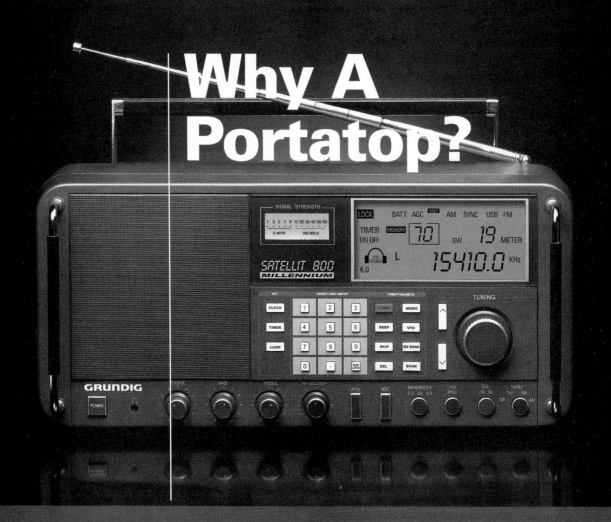

Why A Portatop?

Most of us buy a world band radio not for just a room, but for our entire home property. Yet, portables rarely sound as pleasant as tabletop models, nor do most cut the mustard with really tough signals. Solution: Combine various characteristics of portables and tabletops into one high-performance package—a portatop—which can be serviced, like tabletops, for years to come.

Drawbacks? A portatop is larger and costlier than a portable, and goes through batteries with abandon. If you're comfortable with that, you'll find performance and fidelity approaching that of a good tabletop receiver.

Pay Less

Consumer Reports' David Heim, deputy editor for electronics, suggests in *Reader's Digest*, "Look for stuff that's been factory refurbished." That's sound advice, but the Grundig Satellit 800 portatop takes this one step further. In the United States, it is often available refurbished not at the factory in China, but by the venerable R.L. Drake Company in Ohio. Drake engineered the '800, and normally manufactures only high-grade electronics products. When it says something is right, odds are pretty good that it's right.

S-800 vs. S-900

The forthcoming Grundig Satellit 900 will be a shortwave-and-satellite lap portable having limited kinship with the Satellit 800 portatop, which Grundig plans to keep in its lineup for years to come. Similar names, different radios.

What PASSPORT's Rating Symbols Mean

Star ratings: ✪✪✪✪✪ is best. Stars reflect overall performance and meaningful features, plus to some extent ergonomics and build quality. Price, appearance, country of manufacture and the like are not taken into account. With portatop models there is a balanced emphasis on listening quality, on one hand, and the ability to flush out tough, hard-to-hear signals on the other. Nevertheless, to facilitate comparison the portatop rating standards are very similar to those used for the professional, tabletop and portable models reviewed elsewhere in this PASSPORT.

Passport's Choice. La crème de la crème. Our test team's personal picks of the litter—models we would buy or have bought for our personal use.

✪: A relative bargain, with decidedly more performance than the price would suggest.

> A portatop provides near-tabletop performance in emergencies.

✪✪✪✪⅜ ✪ 📄 *Passport's Choice*
Grundig Satellit 800, Grundig Satellit 800 EU, Tecsun HAM-2000

Price: *S-800:* $499.95 including 120V AC adaptor and headphones in the United States. CAN$599.99 including 120V AC adaptor and headphones in Canada. *S-800 refurbished units, as available:* $399.95 in the United States. *S-800 EU:* £549.00 including 240V AC adaptor and headphones in the United Kingdom. €849.00 including 240V AC adaptor and headphones in Germany.

Pro: Outstanding price, especially in North America and China, for level of performance. Superior, room-filling tonal quality by world band, even if not audiophile, standards—whether with the internal speaker, outboard speakers or headphones; only receiver tested that comes with full-size audiophile-style padded headphones. Tonal shaping aided by continuous separate bass and treble tone controls, a rarity among world band receivers at any price. Excellent-performing synchronous selectable sideband, with 27 dB of unwanted-sideband rejection; this reduces adjacent-channel interference and selective-fading distortion with world band, longwave and mediumwave AM signals. Synchronous selectable sideband also boosts recoverable audio from some of the weakest of signals, and halves overall distortion from 5.3% in the ordinary AM mode to 2.4% on audio frequencies from 100-3,000 Hz. Three voice/music bandwidths; wide measures around 7 kHz, while medium and narrow measure in the vicinity of 5.8 kHz and 2.6 kHz (*see* Con). Bandwidths generally have excellent shape factors (*see* Con) and excellent ultimate rejection; all bandwidths are selectable independent of mode (or dependent, if the user prefers), and work in concert with the synchronous selectable sideband feature to provide superior adjacent-channel rejection. Slow/fast AGC decay (*see* Con). Numerous helpful tuning aids, including 70 tunable station presets that store many variables (*see* Con); also, presets may be scanned (*see* Con). Excellent ergonomics, including many dedicated, widely spaced controls; exceptionally smooth knob tuning aided by ball bearings (*see* Con); and foolproof frequency entry. Superb LCD with huge, bold characters has high contrast and can be viewed clearly from virtually any angle; it is even readable by many with faltering eyesight (*see* Con). Analog signal-strength indicator, a rarity at this price, has gradations in useful S1-9/+60 dB standard (*see* Con). Single-sideband reception above the portable norm (*see* Con), with rock-solid frequency stability and 50 Hz tuning increments. High- and low-impedance inputs for 0.1-30 MHz external antennas. Weak-signal shortwave sensitivity with

NUMBERS: GRUNDIG SATELLIT 800/TECSUN HAM-2000

Max. Sensitivity/Noise Floor	0.43 μV, **G**/-124 dBm, **G** [1]
Blocking	132 dB, **E**
Bandwidths *(Shape Factors)*	7.1 *(1:1.6,* **E***)*, 5.8 *(1:1.6,* **E***)*, 2.6 *(1:2.2,* **G***)* kHz
Ultimate Rejection	75 dB, **E**
Front-End Selectivity	**F**
Image Rejection	65 dB, **G**
First IF Rejection	83 dB, **E**
Dynamic Range/IP3 (5 kHz)	67 dB, **F**/-26 dBm, **G** [2]
Dynamic Range/IP3 (20 kHz)	92 dB, **E**/+11 dBm, **S** [2]
Phase Noise	111 dBc, **G**
AGC Threshold	0.8 μV, **S**
Overall Distortion, sync	2.4%, **E**

IBS Lab Ratings: **S** Superb   **E** Excellent   **G** Good   **F** Fair   **P** Poor

(1) Sample-to-sample variation from 0.23 to 0.43 μV, -129 to -124 dBm.

(2) Estimated, as ability to measure limited by birdies, phase noise and other mixing products.

Grundig's Satellit 800 portable is a refined version of the discontinued Drake SW8A (shown), which in turn was inspired by the Philips D2999.

built-in telescopic antenna equal to or better than that of top-rated portables. Weak-signal shortwave sensitivity with an external antenna can be boosted by setting antenna switch to "whip," thus adding preamplification (and, in such locations as Europe evenings, sometimes generating overloading as well). Superior blocking performance aids consistency of weak-signal sensitivity. Generally superior dynamic range and third-order intercept point to the extent they can be measured amidst receiver phase noise and such. Two-event on/off timer and two 24-hour clocks (*see* Con). Large, tough telescopic antenna includes spring-loaded detents for vertical, 45-degree and 90-degree swiveling; also rotates freely 360 degrees (*see* Con). Clever display and signal strength meter illumination—with batteries in use, light automatically comes on for 15 seconds either at the touch of any button or when receiver is knob or slew tuned; 15-second illumination cycle can be aborted by pushing the light button a second time. FM—mono through built-in speaker, stereo through outboard speakers, headphones and line output—performs well, although capture ratio only average and nearby FM transmitters may cause some overloading. Covers longwave down to 100 kHz. Built-in ferrite rod antenna may be used for 0.1-1.8 MHz. Covers the 118-137 MHz aeronautical band, but only in the AM mode without synchronous selectable sideband; performs about as well as a simple handheld scanner. Excellent, long carrying handle. Comes with AC adaptor—120V AC or 220V AC, depending upon where radio is sold; otherwise, alkaline batteries need changing every 35 hours or so, about 25 cents per hour. Battery-strength indicator (*see* Con). Rack-type handles protect front panel should radio fall over. *North America:* Repairs in and out of one-year warranty are performed by the R.L. Drake Company, long known for superior service (*see* Con). Excellent toll-free tech support.

Con: Huge (20 3/8 inches—517 mm—wide) and weighty (15 pounds or 6.8 kg with batteries). Plastic cabinet and other components are of portable-radio quality, not in the same radiophile-hardware league as found on tabletop models. Synthesizer phase noise, only fair, slightly impacts reception of weak-signals adjacent to powerful signals and in other circumstances; also, limits ability to make certain laboratory measurements accurately. Lacks notch filter, noise blanker, passband

tuning and digital signal processing (DSP)
found on some tabletop models. When
ungrounded (e.g., AC adaptor is not connected to a grounded AC socket) and powered
by batteries, there is vigorous "hash" while
the tuning knob is being handled within some
portions of the mediumwave AM band; this
ceases when the tuning knob is released, and
reception quality of the received station is not
affected. Each key push must each be done
within three seconds, lest receiver wind up
being mis-tuned or placed into an unwanted
operating mode. No signal-seek frequency
scanning. Signal-strength indicator greatly
underreads, although arguably this is
preferable to the overreading often found with
other models. Outboard AC adaptor in lieu of
inboard power supply. Single sideband's 50
Hz synthesizer increments allow tuning to be
out of phase by up to 25 Hz, diminishing
audio fidelity. Fast AGC decay setting is handy
for bandscanning, but sometimes causes
distortion with powerful signals; remedied by
going to slow AGC when no longer actively
bandscanning. Numerous modest birdies on
longwave, mediumwave AM, shortwave and
FM bands; these rarely cause heterodyne
interference to world band signals, approximately one time in 250 they might heterodyne

utility, ham and Eastern Hemisphere
mediumwave signals. Spurious signal on
20,000 kHz obscures WWV reception.
Ergonomics, although excellent, are not ideal;
e.g., no rows and columns of dedicated
buttons for station presets, as was found on
the Sony ICF-2010. Sharp bevel on tuning
knob. Neither clock displays when frequency
is shown; however, pushbutton allows time to
replace frequency on the display for three
seconds. Both clocks in 24-hour format and
neither displays seconds numerically; 12-hour
format not selectable for local time. For faint-
signal DXing, recoverable audio with an
outboard antenna, although good, not fully
equal to that of most tabletop and professional models. Using the built-in antenna,
sensitivity to weak signals is not of DX caliber
in the mediumwave AM band; remedied by
using Terk AM Advantage or similar accessory
antenna. Some frontal (only) radiation of
digital noise from LCD, rarely causes problem
in actual use. No adjustable feet or elevation
rod to angle receiver upwards for handy
operation. When receiver leaned backward,
the telescopic antenna, if angled, spins to the
rear. Battery-strength indicator doesn't come
on until immediately before radio mutes from
low battery voltage. Misleading location of

battery spring clips makes it easy to insert half the batteries in the wrong direction, albeit to no permanent ill effect. Battery cover may come loose if receiver bumped in a specific and unusual manner. Antenna switches located unhandily on rear panel. "USB" on LCD displays as "LISB." No schematic or repair manual available, making service difficult except at authorized repair facilities. No batteries (6 "D" needed). *Tecsun:* "HAM" a confusing name, as world band radio has nothing to do with hams, who are licensed to transmit to each other.

☞ Of the several batches manufactured in 2002, field reports suggest that around three appear to have had a higher than usual defect rate. Production batches in 2003 appear to have been consistently manufactured to proper standards, and in mid-2003 an Etón spokesperson stated that the Satellit 800 is not having QC problems.

☞ Refurbished Grundig units reportedly include gift and similar types of returns from department stores and other outlets where customers tend to be unfamiliar with world band radio. Refurbishing is done at Drake's facility in Ohio (see introduction to article).

☞ At present there are no plans to sell the Satellit 800 under the Etón name.

Verdict: The Grundig Satellit 800/Tecsun HAM-2000 is a benchmark receiver, being the first ever to offer such a level of near-tabletop performance at a near-portable price. Its audio quality and ergonomics are also commendable, but for proper mediumwave AM performance the radio should be grounded.

📄 An *RDI WHITE PAPER* is available for this model.

The PASSPORT *portatop review team includes Lawrence Magne, Tony Jones, Craig Tyson and George Zeller, with Avery Comarow, George Heidelman, John Wagner. Laboratory measurements by Robert Sherwood.*

Tabletop Receivers for 2004

Tabletop receivers flush out tough game—faint stations swamped by competing signals. That's why they are prized by radio aficionados known as "DXers," an old telegraph term meaning long distance. But tabletop models aren't for everybody, and it shows. Even in palmy North America and Europe, tabletop unit sales are minimal even while the roster of choices is as great as ever.

Virtually all models are pricier than portables or portatops, yet less expensive than professional sets reviewed in PASSPORT REPORTS. For that money you tend to get not only excellent performance, but also ruggedness. Tabletop models are not only manufactured to a higher standard than portables and portatops, but also are relatively easy to service and are backed up by knowledgeable repair facilities.

What you rarely find in a tabletop is reception of the everyday 87.5-108 MHz FM band—for this coverage in a premium receiver, look to a portatop.

Tabletop sets, like portatop and professional models, are heavy artillery for where signals are routinely weak—places like the North American Midwest and West, or Australia and New Zealand. Even elsewhere there can be a problem when signals pass over or near the geomagnetic North Pole. To check, place a string on a globe—a conventional map won't do—between you and the station's transmitter, as given in the Blue Pages. If the string passes near or above latitude 60° north, beware.

Weak Signals More Commonplace

Some programs formerly heard during your local prime time are now audible only during the day. These signals tend to be weaker, especially when not beamed to your part of the world. However, thanks to the scattering properties of shortwave, you can still eavesdrop on many of these "off-beam" signals. But it's harder, and that's where a superior receiver's longer reach comes in.

However, if you are already using a portable with an outdoor antenna and it is being disrupted by electrical noise from nearby motors, dimmers and such, you may not benefit from a tabletop model. Its superior circuitry boosts local noise as much as signals. However, an active loop antenna may reduce this noise; these are evaluated elsewhere in PASSPORT REPORTS.

Give Your Signals A Boost

In high-rise buildings, portables can disappoint. Reinforced buildings soak up signals, while local broadcast and cellular transmitters can interfere.

Here, a good bet for tough stations is a well-rated tabletop or portatop model fed by a homebrew insulated-wire antenna along, or just outside, a window or balcony. Also, try an ordinary telescopic car antenna that juts out, like a wall flag mast, out a window or balcony ledge.

Another alternative is to amplify these homebrew antennas with an active preselector. You can also try amplified ("active") antennas that have reception elements and amplifiers in separate modules. These devices are also reviewed in PASSPORT REPORTS.

If you don't live in an apartment, consider a first-rate passive (unamplified) outdoor wire antenna, usually under $100. Performance findings and installation tips are in the Radio Database International White Paper, *Popular Outdoor Antennas*, and are summarized in this PASSPORT REPORTS.

Find major updates to the 2004 PASSPORT REPORTS at www.passband.com.

Complete Findings Now Available

Our unabridged laboratory and hands-on test results for each receiver are too exhaustive to reproduce here. However, they are available for selected current and classic models as PASSPORT'S Radio Database International White Papers—details on availability are elsewhere in this book.

Tips for Using this Section

Receivers are listed in order of suitability for listening to difficult-to-hear world band stations; important secondary consideration is given to audio fidelity, ergonomics and perceived build quality. Street selling prices are cited, including British and Australian VAT/GST where applicable. Prices vary, so take them as the general guide they are meant to be.

Unless otherwise stated, all tabletop models have the following characteristics. See PASSPORT'S glossary to understand terms used.

- Digital frequency synthesis and display.
- Full coverage of at least the 155-29999 kHz longwave, mediumwave AM and shortwave spectra—including all world band frequencies—but no coverage of the FM broadcast band (87.5-108 MHz). Models designed for sale in certain countries have reduced shortwave tuning ranges.
- A wide variety of helpful tuning features.
- Synchronous selectable sideband via high-rejection IF filtering (not lower-rejection phase cancellation), which greatly reduces adjacent-channel interference and selective-fading distortion.

☞ ECSS: Many tabletop models can tune to the nearest 10 Hz or even 1 Hz, allowing the user to use the receiver's single-sideband circuitry to manually phase its BFO (internally generated carrier) with the station's transmitted carrier. Called "ECSS" (exalted-carrier, selectable-sideband) tuning, this can be used in lieu of synchronous selectable sideband. However, in addition to the relative inconvenience of this technique, unlike synchronous selectable sideband, which re-phases continually and perfectly, ECSS is always slightly out of phase. This causes at least some degree of harmonic distortion to music and speech, while tuning to the nearest Hertz can generate slow-sweep fading (for this reason, mis-phasing by two or three Hertz may provide better results).

- Proper demodulation of modes used by non-world-band shortwave signals, except for models designed to be sold in certain countries. These modes include single sideband (LSB/USB) and CW ("Morse code"); also, with suitable ancillary devices, radioteletype (RTTY), frequency shift key (FSK) and radiofax (FAX).
- Meaningful signal-strength indication.
- Illuminated display.

What PASSPORT'S Rating Symbols Mean

Star ratings: ✪✪✪✪✪ is best. Stars reflect overall performance and meaningful features, plus to some extent ergonomics and perceived build quality. Price, appearance, country of manufacture and the like are not taken into account. With tabletop models there is a slightly greater emphasis on the ability to flush out tough, hard-to-hear signals, as this is one of the main reasons these sets are chosen. Nevertheless, to facilitate comparison the tabletop rating standards are very similar to those used for the professional, portatop and portable models reviewed elsewhere in this PASSPORT.

Passport's Choice La crème de la crème. Our test team's personal picks of the litter—models we would buy or have bought for our personal use. Unlike star ratings, these choices are unapologetically subjective.

✪: A relative bargain, with decidedly more performance than the price would suggest. However, none of these receivers is cheap.

✪✪✪✪✪ 📃 *Passport's Choice*
Drake R8B

Drake's R8B has outstanding performance and worthy ergonomics, with superior factory service.

Price: R8B: $1,499.00 in the United States. $2,299.00CAD in Canada. *MS8 Speaker:* US$59.00 in the United States. $75.00CAD in Canada. *VHF Converter:* US$269.00 plus $20 installation in the United States. $399.00CAD plus installation in Canada. *R8B Technical Manual:* $39.95 in the United States. *Aftermarket metal tuning knob (see ☞):* $9.50 shipped within the United States, $14.50 elsewhere.

Pro: Superior all-round performance for listening to world band programs and hunting DX catches, as well as utility,

amateur and mediumwave AM signals. Mellow, above-average audio quality, especially with suitable outboard speaker or headphones (*see* Con). Synchronous selectable sideband excels at reducing distortion caused by selective fading, as well as at diminishing or eliminating adjacent-channel interference; also has synchronous double sideband. Five well-

NUMBERS: TOP TABLETOPS

	Drake R8B	AOR AR7030
Max. Sensitivity/Noise Floor	0.21 μV, **Ｅ**[1]/–130 dBm, **Ｅ**[1]	0.2 μV, **Ｅ**/–128 dBm, **Ｇ**
Blocking	136 dB, **Ｓ**	>130 dB, **Ｅ**
Shape Factors, voice BWs	1:1.96–1:2.70, **Ｇ**	1:1.52–1:1.96, **Ｅ**
Ultimate Rejection	75 dB, **Ｅ**	90 dB, **Ｓ**
Front-End Selectivity	Half octave, **Ｅ**	High/low pass, **Ｆ**
Image Rejection	>90 dB, **Ｓ**	>100 dB, **Ｓ**
First IF Rejection	>90 dB, **Ｓ**	95 dB, **Ｓ**
Dynamic Range/IP3 (5 kHz)	77 dB, **Ｅ**/–17 dBm, **Ｅ**	82 dB, **Ｅ**/+1 dBm, **Ｓ**
Dynamic Range/IP3 (20 kHz)	93 dB, **Ｅ**/+8 dBm, **Ｅ**	100 dB, **Ｓ**/+28 dBm, **Ｓ**
Phase Noise	113 dBc, **Ｇ**	130 dBc, **Ｓ**
AGC Threshold	0.55 μV, **Ｅ**	2.25 μV, **Ｇ**
Overall Distortion, sync	0.6%, **Ｓ**	2.0%, **Ｅ**
Stability	25 Hz, **Ｅ**	30 Hz, **Ｅ**
Notch filter depth	55 dB, **Ｓ**	55 dB, **Ｓ**

IBS Lab Ratings: **Ｓ**Superb **Ｅ**Excellent **Ｇ**Good **Ｆ**Fair **Ｐ**Poor

(1) Preamp on; 0.45 μV **Ｇ**/–124 dBm **Ｇ** with preamp off.

chosen bandwidths, four suitable for world band. Highly flexible operating controls, including a powerful tunable AF notch filter (tunes to 5,300 Hz AF, but *see* Con) and an excellent passband offset control. Best ergonomics of any five-star model (*see* Con). Tunes and displays in precise 10 Hz increments. Slow/fast/off AGC with superior performance characteristics. Exceptionally effective noise blanker. Helpful tuning features include 1,000 station presets and sophisticated scanning functions; presets can be quickly accessed via the tuning knob and slew buttons. Built-in switchable preamplifier. Accepts two antennas, selectable via front panel. Two 24-hour clocks, with seconds displayed numerically and two-event timer (*see* Con). Helpful operating manual. Power cord detaches handily from receiver, making it easy to replace. Fifteen-day money-back trial period if ordered from factory. Superior factory service.

Con: Virtually requires a good outboard speaker for non-headphone listening, although the optional Drake MS8 outboard speaker not equal to the receiver's audio potential; try a good amplified computer speaker or high-efficiency passive speaker instead. Slight bassiness in audio, remediable through careful choice of the right outboard speaker. Neither clock shows when frequency displayed. Lightweight tuning knob lacks any trace of flywheel effect (see ☞, below); this, along with thin cabinet metal and mechanical frequency encoder in lieu of optical encoder used in original R8, exude an aura of cheesiness; nevertheless, years-long track record indicates that reliability is at least average. No IF output. Otherwise-excellent tilt bail difficult to open. Notch filter does not tune below 500 Hz (AF). Not available from dealers outside North America. When changing from 90-132V to 180-264V AC, a resistor must be removed from receiver, which for some users will require a technician. Optional VHF converter difficult to

install; best is to have this done when receiver is purchased.

☞ A limited supply of aftermarket metal tuning knobs for the R8B is available from http://home.att.net/~maghakian/wsb/html/view.cgi-home.html-.html or mikemaghakian@yahoo.com. However, it provides little improvement, and the finger dimple is small. Better for additional tuning feel is simply to glue BBs into the back of the factory plastic knob.

Verdict: There are other models that are superior to the American-made Drake R8B in some respects. Yet, this is the only non-professional receiver tested that gets everything right, where something important isn't missing or sputtering and ergonomics are worthy. This means there's little point spending money on such performance-enhancing accessories as the Sherwood SE-3 Mk III D, although a better—outboard—speaker can allow the receiver to live up to its fidelity potential.

While a number of other manufacturers have been lowering their prices, Drake has been raising theirs. Still, the R8B remains priced at the low end of the five-star category of tabletop and professional models.

📃 An *RDI WHITE PAPER* is available for this model.

✪✪✪✪✪   *Passport's Choice*
AOR AR7030, AOR AR7030+3

Price: *AR7030:* £799.00 in the United Kingdom. €1,148.00 in Germany. *AR7030+3:* $1,469.95 in the United States. £949.00 in the United Kingdom. €1,298.00 in Germany. *UPNB7030 Noise Blanker & Notch Upgrade:* $329.95 in the United States. €280.70 in Germany.

Pro: In terms of sheer performance for program listening, as good a radio as we've ever tested. Except for sensitivity to weak signals (*see* Con), easily overcome, the same comment applies to DX reception. Exceptionally quiet circuitry. Superior audio quality when used with a first-rate outboard speaker or audio system. Synchronous selectable sideband performs exceptionally well at reducing distortion caused by selective fading, as well as at diminishing or eliminating adjacent-channel interference; also has synchronous double sideband. Best dynamic range of any consumer-grade radio tested. Nearly all other lab measurements are top-drawer. Four voice bandwidths (2.3, 7.0, 8.2 and 10.3 kHz), with cascaded ceramic filters, come standard; up to six, either ceramic or mechanical, upon request (*see* Con). Advanced tuning and operating features aplenty, including passband tuning. Tunable audio (AF) notch and noise blanker now available, albeit as an option; notch filter extremely effective, with little loss of audio fidelity. Built-in preamplifier (*see* Con). Automatically self-aligns and centers all bandwidth filters for optimum performance, then displays the actual measured bandwidth of each. Remote keypad (*see* Con). Accepts two antennas. IF output. Optional improved processor unit now has 400 memories, including 14-character alphanumeric readout for station names. World Time 24-hour clock, which displays seconds, calendar and timer/sleep-delay features. Superior mediumwave AM performance. Variety of bandwidth, on-site diagnostic and field (battery) operation options. Superior service at the factory in England.

Con: Unusually convoluted ergonomics, including tree-logic operating scheme, especially in +3 version; once the initial glow of ownership has passed, this may become tiresome. Remote control unit, which has to be aimed carefully at either the front or the back of the receiver, is required to use certain features, such as direct frequency entry; not all panelists were enthusiastic about this arrangement, wishing that a mouse-type umbilical cable

The AOR AR7030+3 offers top-flight performance, with ergonomics that you'll either love or hate.

had been used instead. Although the remote keypad can operate from across a room, the LCD characters are too small to be seen from such a distance. LCD omits certain important information, such as signal strength, when radio in various status modes. Sensitivity to weak signals good, as are related noise-floor measurements, but could be a bit better; a first-rate antenna, as indicated elsewhere in this PASSPORT, overcomes this. Because of peculiar built-in preamplifier/attenuator design in which the two are linked, receiver noise rises slightly when preamplifier used in +10 dB position, or attenuator used in -10 dB setting; however, +3 version remedies this. When six bandwidths used (four standard ceramics, two optional mechanicals), ultimate rejection, although superb with widest three bandwidths, cannot be measured beyond -80/-85 dB on narrowest three bandwidths because of phase noise; still, ultimate rejection is excellent or better with these narrow bandwidths. Lacks, and would profit from, a bandwidth of around 4 or 5 kHz; a Collins mechanical bandwidth filter of 3.5 kHz (nominal at -3 dB, measures 4.17 kHz at -6 dB) is an option worth considering. Such Collins filters, in the two optional bandwidth slots, measure as having poorer shape factors (1:1.8 to 1:2) than the standard-slot ceramic filters (1:1.5 to 1:1.6). LCD emits some digital electrical noise, potentially a problem only if an amplified (active) antenna is used with its pickup element (e.g. telescopic rod) placed near the receiver. Minor microphonics (audio feedback), typically when internal speaker is used, noted in laboratory; in actual listening, however, this is not noticeable; in any event, this is moot when an outboard speaker is used. Uses outboard AC adaptor instead of built-in power supply.

☞ Mechanical encoders on the '7030 used to have an above-average failure rate, seemingly because of corrosion on contacts. Starting from serial number 102050, with production as of late July, 1999, AOR has replaced the original Bourns mechanical encoder with a metal-encased version from Alps—the AR7030 now uses only Alps mechanical encoders, whereas the AR7030+3 uses Alps mechanical and Bourns optical encoders. A conversion kit for earlier units is available for £20 plus shipping, although it requires skill to install. Similarly, features of the +3 version can be incorporated into existing regular models by skilled technicians.

Verdict: If you enjoy the BMW 745i, you'll be right at home with the AOR AR7030. Like the 745i, it not only has Star Trek ergonomics, but also performs right up there with the very best. It is said that the 745i makes you a better driver than you really are, so it just may be that the AR7030 will make you a better DXer than you really are.

Designed by John Thorpe and manufactured in England, the '7030 is an even better performer, and more robust, in its +3 incarnation. But those Bimmer iDrive-type ergonomics, already peculiar and cumbersome in the "barefoot" version, are even more challenging in the +3. For some, this is not a problem—indeed, it can provide a certain satisfaction. But for a number of others it's just not worth the bother, and that includes our panelists. As a result the '7030 is reportedly a slow seller, but among its community of owners it is usually praised as the *ne plus ultra*.

Ergonomics and slightly limited sensitivity to weak signals aside, the '7030 is arguably the best choice—certainly among the best of choices—for serious DXing available on the scotch side of a professional-grade model. This is a receiver you'll really need to lay your hands on before you'll know whether it's love or hate—or something between.

✪✪✪✪½
Japan Radio NRD-545

Price: $1,799.95 in the United States. $3,699.00CAD in Canada. £1,395.00 in the United Kingdom. €1,995.00 in Germany. $3,799.00AUD in Australia. *NVA-319 external speaker:* $199.95 in the United States. £189 in the United Kingdom. €295.00 in Germany. *CHE-199 VHF-UHF converter:* $369.95 in the United States. £269 in the United Kingdom. €449.00 in Germany. *CGD-197 frequency stabilizer:* $99.95 in the United States. €149.00 in Germany.

Pro: Superior build quality, right down to the steel cabinet with machined screws. Easily upgraded by changing software ROMs. Fully 998 bandwidths provide unprecedented flexibility. Razor-sharp skirt selectivity, especially with voice bandwidths. Outstanding array of tuning aids, including 1,000 station presets (*see* Con). Wide array of reception aids, including passband offset, excellent manual/automatic tunable notch, and synchronous selectable sideband having good lock. Superb reception of single-sideband and other "utility" signals. Demodulates C-Quam AM stereo signals, which then need to be fed through an external audio amplifier, not provided (the headphone jack can't be used for this, as it is monaural). Highly adjustable AGC in all modes requiring BFO (*see* Con). Tunes in ultra-precise 1 Hz increments, although displays only in 10 Hz increments. Ergonomics, including the physical quality of tuning knob and other controls, among the very best. Some useful audio shaping.

Computer interface with NRD Win software (*see* Con); among other things, is effective at processing RTTY signals. Virtually no spurious radiation of digital "hash." Hiss-free audio-out port for recording or feeding low-power FM transmitter to hear world band around the house. Internal AC power supply is quiet and generates little heat. Power cord detaches handily from receiver, like on a PC, making it easy to replace. Includes a "CARE package" of all needed metric plugs and connectors, along with a 12V DC power cord.

Con: Ultimate rejection only fair, although average ultimate rejection equivalent is 10-15 dB better; this unusual gap comes about from intermodulation (IMD) inside the digital signal processor, and results in audible "monkey chatter" under certain reception conditions. Audio quality sometimes tough sledding in the unvarnished AM mode—using synchronous selectable sideband helps greatly. No AGC adjustment in AM mode or with synchronous selectable sideband, and lone AGC decay rate too fast. Dynamic range only fair. Synchronous selectable sideband sometimes slow to kick in. Notch filter won't attenuate heterodynes (whistles) any higher in pitch than 2,500 Hz AF. Noise reduction circuit only marginally useful. Signal-strength indicator overreads at higher levels. Frequency display misreads by up to 30 Hz, especially at higher tuned frequencies, and gets worse as the months pass by. Station presets don't store synchronous-AM settings. Audio amplifier lacks oomph with some poorly modulated signals. No IF output, nor can one be retrofitted. NRD Win software, at least the current v1.00, handles only uploads, not downloads, and works only on com port 1 that is usually already in use. World Time 24-hour clock doesn't show when frequency displayed. No tilt bail or feet. Anti-reflective paint on buttons and knobs becomes shiny with wear.

The best tabletop DSP receiver is the NRD-545, manufactured alongside Japan Radio's professional-grade communications gear.

Verdict: In many ways Japan Radio's NRD-545 is a remarkable performer, especially for utility and tropical-bands DXing. With its first-class ergonomics and the fine feel of superior construction quality, it is always a pleasure to operate. Yet, more is needed to make this the ultimate receiver it could be. By now Japan Radio should have issued a ROM upgrade to remedy at least some of these long-standing issues, but *nada* as yet.

Whether "monkey chatter" and other manifestations of DSP overload are an issue varies markedly from one listening situation to another—some hear it, others don't. It depends on the type of signals being received, what part of the world you are in and your own aural perceptions. Among our panelists, all noticed it eventually, but reaction varied from "no big deal" to howls of derision.

✪✪✪✪⅜
Japan Radio "NRD-545SE"

Price: *NRD-545SE:* $1,899.00 in the United States. *Retrofit to change an existing receiver to "SE":* $104.00 plus receiver shipping both ways.

Pro: Dynamic range, 5 kHz, improves from 66 dB to 73 dB.

Con: Not available outside North America. *With 8 kHz replacement filter:* Audio bandwidth reduced by 20 percent at the high end. *With 6 kHz replacement filter (not tested):* Audio bandwidth reduced by about 40 percent at the high end.

☞ For all except those who confine their listening to tough DX or utility catches, the 8 kHz filter is a preferable choice over the 6 kHz option.

Verdict: Sherwood Engineering, an American firm, replaces the stock DSP protection filter with one of two narrower filters of comparable quality. In principle, this should provide beaucoup decibels of audible improvement in the "monkey chatter" encountered on the '545 from adjacent-channel signals. Alas, we couldn't hear the difference, but did notice an unwelcome reduction in audio crispness with world band signals—as well as, of course, with mediumwave AM reception.

Not everyone agrees. Some readers have tried this modification and take exception to our comments. They are pleased with the result.

The "SE" modification yields a slight improvement in close-in dynamic range, but bottom line to our ears is nice try, no cigar. Adventurous DXers may wish to consider the 6 kHz filter-replacement option in lieu of the 8 kHz option tested.

For utility DXing, as well as intense world band DXing, the reduction in high-end audio response is not a real issue. For these applications, the "SE" may represent a marginal improvement over the stock '545.

New for 2004

★★★★ Ⓒ

Icom IC-R75/Icom IC-R75E (Kiwa version)

Price (Kiwa modifications): *Synchronous detector upgrade:* $45.00 in the United States. *Audio upgrade:* $35.00 in the United States.

Pro: Synchronous detection performance improved slightly, with synchronous selectable sideband actually being somewhat functional with a narrow-bandwidth

setting. Added crispness marginally improves audio quality with wide IF bandwidth settings. Generally high-quality parts and installation. Exceptionally fast turnaround from Kiwa.

Con: When sync loses lock during deep fades, there is a heterodyne squeal or warble not evident before modification; slow AGC setting occasionally helps ameliorate this. Audio muffled when selectable synchronous sideband in upper-sideband setting, although lower sideband sounds appropriate. Slight increase in audible hiss with narrow bandwidth settings. Modifications may invalidate Icom's warranty, and they are not readily undone.

Verdict: The two tested Kiwa modifications, particular that for the synchronous detector, provide a slight improvement in the popular Icom IC-R75's performance. They are reasonably priced, but are best deferred until the factory warranty has expired.

Observations with Modified Receiver: Over the years Icom's IC-R75 has come down in price to the point where it has become one of the best-selling tabletops on the market. Its performance with utility and ham signals is top-notch, making it a true bargain for monitoring non-broadcast transmissions. Alas, its synchronous selectable sideband performance is as bad as we've ever encountered, and this limits the 'R75's attractiveness for listening to world band broadcasters.

Enter the small American firm of Kiwa Electronics, which offers two modifications to help overcome the 'R75's world band performance deficiencies. The synchronous detector upgrade is achieved via the installation of a small "potted" cube affixed to the back microprocessor shield (photo). As two pins of the sync chip are lifted and wired to the module, undoing the modification is no simple task.

The audio upgrade is achieved by changing a few capacitors. This is less difficult to undo than the sync mod, but requires yeoman soldering skills. Consequently, either modification is best put off until after the manufacturer's warranty expires. Unless the tech at Icom is in a magnanimous mood, either Kiwa modification may invalidate the receiver's warranty.

Just as the 'R75 has become popular because of its price, so, too, have the Kiwa modifications. The Sherwood SE-3 Mk III D device works wonders, but costs nearly as much as the receiver, making it a non-starter. Viewed in that context, the modest improvements provided by the upgrades become relatively interesting.

The stock 'R75's synchronous selectable sideband performance is pitiful. While the Kiwa upgrade doesn't turn this sow's ear into a silk purse or even a cotton tote bag, there is a degree of audible improvement and the price is right.

We ordered the modifications to our 'R75 "blind" so, we hoped, results wouldn't be tainted by our status as reviewers. Kiwa's workmanship and turnaround were both excellent.

Icom's IC-R75 is eminently affordable and a favorite for eavesdropping on utility communications. Modifications available, too.

✪✪✪✪⅜ *Ⓒ*
Icom IC-R75/Icom IC-R75E

Price: *Receiver only:* $599.95 in the United States, sometimes lower depending on factory rebates and twofer offers. $1,199.00CAD in Canada. £649.00 in the United Kingdom. €749.00 in Germany. $1,649.00AUD in Australia. *UT-106 DSP unit:* $139.95 in the United States, although on past special occasions it has been bundled for free with the R75. $250.00CAD in Canada. £79.95 in the United Kingdom. €99.00 in Germany. $179.00AUD in Australia. *Icom Replacement Bandwidth Filters (e.g., FL-257 3.3 kHz):* $159.95 in the United States. €165.00 in Germany. *SP-20 amplified audio-shaping speaker:* $219.95 in the United States. £164.95 (€264) in the United Kingdom.

Pro: Dual passband offset acts as variable bandwidth and a form of IF shift (*see* Con). Reception of faint signals alongside powerful competing ones aided by excellent ultimate selectivity and good blocking. Excellent front-end selectivity, with seven filters for the shortwave range and more for elsewhere. Two levels of preamplification, 10 dB and 20 dB, can be switched off. Excellent weak-signal sensitivity and good AGC threshold with +20 dB preamplification. Superior rejection of spurious signals, including images. Excellent stability, essential for unattended reception of RTTY and certain other types of utility transmissions. Excels in reception of utility and ham signals, as well as world band signals tuned via "ECSS" technique. Ten tuning steps. Can tune and display in exacting 1 Hz increments (*see* Con). Adjustable UT-106 DSP audio accessory with automatic variable notch filter, normally an extra-cost option, helps to a degree in improving intelligibility, but not pleasantness, of some tough signals; also, it reduces heterodyne ("whistle") interference. Fairly good ergonomics, including smooth-turning weighted tuning knob; nice touch is spinning finger dimple, even if it doesn't spin very well. "Control Central" LCD easy to read and evenly illuminated by 24 LEDs with dimmer. Adjustable AGC—fast, slow, off. Tuning knob uses reliable optical encoder normally found only on professional receivers, rather than everyday mechanical variety. Low overall distortion. Pleasant and hiss-free audio with suitable outboard speaker; audio-shaping amplified Icom SP-20, although pricey, works well for a number of applications. 101 station presets. Two antenna inputs, switchable. Digital bar graph signal-strength indicator, although not as desirable as an analog meter, is unusually linear above S-9 and can be set to hold a peak reading briefly. Audio-out port for recording or feeding low-power FM transmitter to hear world band around the house (*see* Con). World Time 24-hour clock, timer and sleep delay (*see* Con). Tunes to 60 MHz, including 6 meter VHF ham band. Tilt bail (*see* Con).

Con: Synchronous detector virtually non-functional; operates only with modification by user or specialty firm, or by addition of a specialized auxiliary device. Dual passband offset usually has little impact on received world band signals and is inoperative when synchronous detection is in use. DSP's automatic variable notch tends not to work with AM-mode signals not received via "ECSS" technique (tuning AM-mode signals as though they were single sideband). Mediocre audio through internal speaker, and no tone control to offset slightly bassy reproduction that originates prior to the audio stage; audio improves to pleasant with an appropriate external speaker, especially one that offsets the receiver's slight bassiness. Suboptimal audio recovery with weak AM-mode signals having heavy fading; largely remediable by "ECSS" tuning and switching off AGC. Display misreads up to 20 Hz, somewhat negating the precise 1 Hz tuning. Keypad requires frequencies to be entered in MHz format with decimal or trailing zeroes, a pointless inconvenience. Some knobs small. Uses outboard "floor brick" AC adaptor in lieu of internal power supply; adaptor's emission field may be picked up by nearby indoor antennas or unshielded antenna lead-in wiring, which can cause minor hum on received signals (remediable by moving antenna or using

shielded lead-in cable). Can read clock or presets IDs or frequency, but no more than one at the same time. RF/AGC control operates peculiarly. Tilt bail lacks rubber protection for furniture surface. Keyboard beep appears at audio line output. No schematic provided.

Verdict: The Japanese-made Icom IC-R75, formerly $800 in the United States, is now an excellent value. It is a first-rate receiver for unearthing tough utility and ham signals, as well as world band signals received via manual "ECSS" tuning. Nothing else equals it on the sunny side of a kilobuck.

Its hopeless synchronous detector performance is very slightly improved by modifications from such specialty firms as Kiwa (see preceding review). Alternatively, the Sherwood SE-3 Mk III D device can entirely replace the 'R75's synchronous and audio circuits. Problem is, the accessory costs as much as the receiver. Thankfully, the 'R75's exacting frequency steps allow for easy "ECSS" tuning of world band signals as though they were single sideband.

✪✪✪✪⅛
Ten-Tec RX-350

Price: *RX-350:* $1,199.00 in the United States. £1,099.00 (€1725) in the United Kingdom. *302R external keypad/tuning knob:* $139.00 in the United States. £129.00 (€203) in the United Kingdom. *307B external speaker:* $98.00 in the United States. £89.00 (€140) in the United Kingdom.

Pro: Receiver is unlikely to become dated for some time, as many aspects of performance and operation can be readily updated, thus far and presumably always for free, by downloading revised firmware from the manufacturer's website (*see* Con); except for clock, all memory, including for firmware, is non-volatile and thus not dependent on battery backup. Lowest-cost tabletop model available with genuine DSP bandwidth filtering. A superb choice of no less than 34 bandwidths, including at least a dozen suitable for world band reception. Numerous helpful tuning features—front-panel tuning knob; up/down frequency and band slewing; 1024 station presets divided into eight banks with alphanumeric station indicators; sophisticated scanning; optional keypad/tuning knob; and two VFOs. Optional external keypad/tuning knob is handy, comfortable and works well (*see* Con); it allows for frequency entry not only in Megahertz, but also in kilohertz via the enter key if the leading zero is entered first for frequencies under 10000 kHz. Tuning knobs on receiver and outboard keypad both use a reliable optical encoder normally found only on professional receivers, rather than the everyday mechanical variety. Tunes and displays in ultra-precise 1 Hz increments (*see* Con). Superior close-in (5 kHz separation) dynamic range/IP3. Excellent passband offset works in all non-FM modes, providing (in addition to the handy AML/AMU settings) selectable sideband for the synchronous detector (*see* Con). Generally worthy ergonomics with large display and seven useful tuning steps; also, bandwidths and station presets conveniently selectable by knob (*see* Con), and controls have good tactile feel—especially the large, weighted metal tuning knob with rubber edging (*see* Con). Punchy, above-average audio with low overall distortion adds to enjoyment of music and enhances intelligibility, especially with suitable external speaker (*see* Con). Audio-out port for recording or feeding low-power FM transmitter to hear world band around the house. Unlike a number of other DSP receivers, does not make static crashes sound harsh; additionally, DSP noise reduction feature can moderate static noise a bit more. DSP noise reduction also of some use in improving aural quality of certain received signals (*see* Con). Receiver emits very little radiated digital "hash," so inverted-L antennas with single-wire feedlines and proximate loop antennas don't suffer from noise pickup. Rock stable,

Promised fixes to the Ten-Tec RX-350 have not materialized, as the firm is involved with other projects.

essential for unattended reception of RTTY and certain other types of utility transmissions. Notch filter automatic, effective over a wide range (0.1 to over 8.0 kHz AF), and can attenuate more than one heterodyne at a time (*see* Con). AGC threshold, originally poor, improved to excellent in latest version. Signal-strength indicator unusually accurate (*see* Con). More likely than most other models to be adaptable to possible future digital world band transmissions. Soft and hard microprocessor resets provide useful flexibility in case receiver's "computer" gets its knickers in a twist. AC power supply is inboard, where it belongs, and does not run hot. Tilt bail places receiver at handy angle for operation (*see* Con). Timer. Manufacturer has an exemplary record for

Some report problems with the Ten-Tec RX-350's display board, made in China. Fortunately, it is easily accessed.

customer support and factory repair.

Con: Poor front-end selectivity; so, for example, local mediumwave AM stations can cross-modulate with other local stations and even world band stations 4 MHz and below. RF preamplifier cannot be switched off to help prevent overloading. Our receiver froze up periodically; also, when going from memory channels back to a VFO, display showed invalid frequencies in the 45 to 94 MHz range (*see* ☞). Significant phase noise kept us from meaningfully measuring dynamic range/IP3 at 20 kHz separation; it also precluded plausible skirt-selectivity and ultimate rejection measurements. Synchronous selectable sideband loses lock easily during fades, albeit without causing whistling. Circuit hiss with widest bandwidths, a common syndrome with DSP receivers, although the noise reduction feature helps. Spectrum display of marginal utility—limited visual indication, poor contrast, significant time lag and it mutes the receiver during sweep; potentially the most useful range shown in the owner's manual is 120 kHz, but this does not appear in the receiver's menu. Keypad costs extra, even though it is virtually a necessity; it also comes with a remote tuning knob that some may find redundant and which adds to size and cost. Optional outboard keypad has intermittent frequency-entry hesitation. On one unit the display misread up to 30 Hz, somewhat negating the precise 1 Hz tuning; other samples did better. Ineffective noise blanker—DSP, not IF—unnecessarily complicated to turn on as instructed via menu (not indicated in the owner's manual, but the key combination of Alt NR can turn it on more simply), and its 1-7 adjustment needs to be at 5 or above to really work. AM-mode signals, whether received in the conventional AM mode or synchronous, sound harsh with fast AGC. No AGC off. Friction when turning knobs, at least with samples tested; remediable by easing knobs slightly away from front panel (with tuning knob, remove rubber edging to access hex screw). Passband offset requires many turns of the knob to shift the setting significantly with AM-mode or synchronous (SAM) reception, although not in other modes. Automatic notch filter can't be tuned manually in CW and RTTY reception modes, so the notch automatically impacts the desired signal along with any heterodyne(s). Signal-strength indicator's format, using numeric decibels and a short displayed scale, generally disliked by panelists. Noise reduction not adjustable, and solitary setting sometimes reduces intelligibility. Audio control in original version required more than three turns from soft to loud, although revised version uses the traditional single turn; however, as a result the audio scale display now shows 25 percent when the control is set to 100 percent. Unusual 9-pin-to-9-pin serial cable needed to download software not included with receiver. A number of commonly used controls are on the left, inconvenient for northpaws. No IF output. User reports in 2003 tell of display illumination flickering, then failing, necessitating factory a $55 repair; display board (photo) is made in China. Tilt bail lacks protective rubber sheathing. Neither speaker wire can connect to ground, so an external speaker should not have a grounded cabinet (the 307B is appropriate in this regard).

☞ Two of our three units tested suffered from periodic freezing, or lockup, and occasional peculiar display readings. All were resolved by turning the receiver off, then back on again after no more than ten minutes, but re-downloading the firmware made no difference. The manufacturer insists these are sample defects, although to us it appears to have the earmarks of an inherent, but remediable, firmware cause.

Verdict: Ten-Tec indicated a year back that it would shortly resolve the RX-350's poor front-end with a hardware fix, and last year even retrofitted our original receiver with an advance version of a front-end selectivity enhancement. Software fixes for various other problems were expected before long, as well.

Alas, none of this appears to have come to pass, nor is there any credible way of knowing when or if improvements will be made so this interesting model can reach its potential. Given that Ten-Tec is reportedly occupied with tasks for military and intelligence clients, fixes to this consumer-grade product appear to be *tempus incognitum*.

✪✪✪✪
Icom IC-R8500A

Price: *IC-R8500A-02 (no cellular reception):* $1,499.95 in the United States, the exact price depending on factory rebates, if any, available at the time. *IC-R8500A:* $1,749.95 for government use or export in the United States. $2,599.00CAD in Canada. £1,349.00 in the United Kingdom. €1,398.00 in Germany. $3,480.00AUD in Australia. *CR-293 frequency stabilizer:* $269.95 in the United States. €119.00 in Germany. *External speakers:* Up to three Icom speakers available worldwide, with prices ranging from under $65 to $220 or equivalent. *Sherwood SE-3 Mk III D:* $549.00 in the United States.

Pro: Wide-spectrum multimode coverage from 0.1-2000 MHz includes longwave, mediumwave AM, shortwave and scanner frequencies. Physically very rugged, with professional-grade cast-aluminum chassis and impressive computer-type innards. Generally superior ergonomics, with generous-sized front panel having large and well-spaced controls, plus outstanding tuning knob with numerous tuning steps. 1,000 station presets and 100 auto-write presets have handy naming function. Superb weak-signal sensitivity. Pleasant, low-distortion audio aided by audio peak filter. Passband tuning ("IF shift"). Unusually

readable LCD. Tunes and displays in precise 10 Hz increments. Three antenna connections. Clock-timer, combined with record output and recorder-activation jack, make for superior hands-off recording of favorite programs, as well as for feeding a low-power FM transmitter to hear world band around the house.

Con: No synchronous selectable sideband. Bandwidth choices for world band and other AM-mode signals leap from a very narrow 2.7 kHz to a broad 7.1 kHz with nothing between, where something is most needed; third bandwidth is 13.7 kHz, too wide for world band, and no provision is made for a fourth bandwidth filter. Only one single-sideband bandwidth. Unhandy carousel-style bandwidth selection with no permanent indication of which bandwidth is in use. Poor dynamic range, surprising at this price point. Passband tuning ("IF shift") does not work in the AM mode, used by world band and mediumwave AM-band stations. No tunable notch filter. Built-in speaker mediocre. Uses outboard AC adaptor instead of inboard power supply.

☞ The Icom IC-R8500 is available in two similarly priced versions. That sold to the public in the United States is blocked so it cannot receive the 824-849 and 869-894 MHz cellular bands. In the U.S., the un-blocked version is sold only to government-approved organizations, although Canadian mail-order firms will ship this version to customers in the United States

Good broadband performance costs, and the Icom IC-R8500 is no exception. Performance improves with modifications.

☞ Also tested with Sherwood SE-3 Mk III D aftermarket accessory, which proved to be outstanding at adding selectable synchronous sideband. It also provides passband tuning in the AM mode used by nearly all world band stations. Adding the SE-3 and replacing the widest bandwidth with a 4 to 5 kHz bandwidth filter dramatically improve performance on shortwave, mediumwave AM and longwave.

Verdict: The large Icom IC-R8500 is a scanner that happens to cover world band, rather than *vice versa*.

As a standalone world band radio, this Japanese-made wideband receiver makes little sense. Yet, it is well worth considering if you want an all-in-one scanner that also serves as a shortwave receiver.

New for 2004
✪✪✪✪
AOR AR5000A+3

Price: *AR5000A+3 (cellular-blocked version) receiver:* about $2,100.00 in the United States. *AR5000A+3 (full-coverage version) receiver:* $2,469.95 in the United States. $3,799.00CAD in Canada. £1,799.00 in the United Kingdom. €2,298.00 in Germany. $4,600.00AUD in Australia. *Collins 6 kHz mechanical filter (recommended):* $99.95 in the United States. £76.00 in the United Kingdom. *SDU-5500 spectrum display unit:*

New for 2004 is AOR's AR5000A+3. This broadband model features synchronous detection and a steep price tag.

$1,099.95 in the United States. $2,099CAD in Canada. €1,198.00 in Germany.

Pro: Ultra-wide-spectrum multimode coverage from 0.01-3,000 MHz includes longwave, mediumwave AM, shortwave and scanner frequencies. Helpful tuning features include 2,000 station presets in 20 banks of 100 presets each. Narrow bandwidth filter and optional Collins wide filter both have superb skirt selectivity (standard wide filter's skirt selectivity unmeasurable because of limited ultimate rejection). Synchronous selectable and double sideband (*see* Con). Front-end selectivity, image rejection, IF rejection, weak-signal sensitivity, AGC threshold and frequency stability all superior. Exceptionally precise frequency readout to nearest Hertz. Most accurate displayed frequency measurement of any receiver tested to date. Superb circuit shielding results in virtually zero radiated digital "hash." IF output (*see* Con). Automatic Frequency Control (AFC) works on AM-mode, as well as FM, signals. Owner's manual, important because of operating system, unusually helpful.

Con: Synchronous detector loses lock easily, especially if selectable sideband feature in use, greatly detracting from the utility of this high-tech feature. Substandard rejection of unwanted sideband with selectable synchronous sideband. Overall distortion rises when synchronous detector used. Ultimate rejection of "narrow" 2.7 kHz bandwidth filter only 60 dB. Ultimate rejection mediocre (50 dB) with standard 7.6 kHz "wide" bandwidth filter, improves to an uninspiring 60 dB when replaced by optional 6 kHz "wide" Collins mechanical filter. Installation of optional Collins filter requires expertise, patience and special equipment. Poor dynamic range. Cumbersome ergonomics. No passband offset. No tunable notch filter. Needs good external speaker for good audio quality. World Time 24-hour clock does not show when frequency displayed. IF output frequency 10.7 MHz instead of standard 455 kHz.

Verdict: Unbeatable in some respects, inferior in others—it comes down to what use you will be putting the radio. The optional 6 kHz Collins filter is strongly recommended, but it should be installed by your dealer at the time of purchase. Although some AOR receivers are engineered and made in the United Kingdom, this model is designed and manufactured in Japan.

Changes for 2004: The "A" model, new for 2004, has tuning extended to 3.0 GHz (formerly 2.6 GHz). Also, the audio output is squelch controlled. All else remains as before.

New for 2004

✪✪✪✪

Palstar R30 Series/Sherwood

Price: *Sherwood SE-3 Mk III D:* $549.00 in the United States. *Palstar R30x:* See below.

Pro: SE-3 provides nearly flawless synchronous selectable sideband, reducing adjacent-channel interference while enhancing audio fidelity. Foolproof installation; plugs right into the Palstar's existing IF output.

Con: Buzz occasionally heard during weak-signal reception. SE-3 costs roughly as much as a regular Palstar receiver.

Verdict: If you're going to spend $550 to upgrade a $500-650 receiver, you may as well spring for a Drake R8B.

Premium Version Tested for 2004

✪✪✪✪ ✐

Palstar R30, Palstar R30C, Palstar R30CC

Price: *R30:* $495.00 in the United States. £449.00 in the United Kingdom. €663.70 in Germany. *R30C (not tested):* $575.00 in the United States. *R30CC:* $650.00 in the United States.

The Palstar R30 series is offered with ceramic and/or mechanical bandwidth filters. Battery backup is useful for emergencies.

☞ The R30 uses ceramic bandwidth filters, whereas the R30C, not tested, uses a Collins mechanical filter for the narrow bandwidth. The R30CC goes one step further and uses Collins mechanical filters for both bandwidths.

☞ As we have not actually tested the "C" version, this report not specifically refer to that version. However, the "C" narrow filter is identical to that in the "CC" version, whereas the wide filter is the same as that in the basic R30.

☞ The Lowe HF-350, which we can no longer find for sale new, was a variation of the Palstar R30. It also used ceramic filters, but the wide bandwidth was narrower— nominally 4 kHz, although in practice it was probably closer to 5 kHz. If you find a unit for sale, it should go for about the same price as the basic Palstar R30.

Pro: Generally good dynamic range. Overall distortion averages 0.5 percent, superb, in single-sideband mode (in AM mode, averages 2.9 percent, good, at 60% modulation and 4.4 percent, fair, at 95% modulation) (*see* Con, *R30CC*). Every other performance variable measures either good or excellent in PASSPORT's lab; four variables measure slightly better, two slightly worse than in our tests for PASSPORT 2001; also, former "birdies" now nearly all gone. Excellent AGC performance with AM-mode and single-sideband signals. Robust physical construction of cabinet and related hardware. Microprocessor section well shielded to minimize radiation of digital "hash." Features include selectable slow/fast AGC decay (*see* Con), 20-100 Hz/100-500 Hz VRIT (slow/fast variable-rate incremental tuning) knob, 0.5 MHz slewing and 455 kHz IF output. One hundred non-volatile station presets, using a generally well-thought-out scheme (*see* Con); they store frequency, bandwidth, mode, AGC setting and attenuator setting; also, presets displayed by channel number or frequency. Excellent illuminated analog signal-strength meter reads in useful S1-9/+60 dB standard and is reasonably accurate (*see* Con). LCD and signal-strength indicator illumination can be switched off. Also operates from ten firmly secured "AA" internal batteries (*see* Con). Lightweight and small (*see* Con). Good AM-mode sensitivity within longwave and mediumwave AM bands. Audio line output has suitable level and is properly located on back panel. Self-resetting circuit breaker for outboard power (e.g., AC adaptor); fuse used with internal batteries and comes with spare fuses. Tilt bail quite useful (*see* Con). Optional AA30A and AM-30 active anten-nas, evaluated elsewhere in this PASSPORT REPORTS. *R30:* Superb skirt selectivity (1:1.4) and ultimate rejection (90 dB); bandwidths measure 7.7 kHz and 2.7 kHz, using ceramic filters. *R30:* Pleasant audio quality with wide (7.7 kHz) bandwidth (*see* Con). *R30CC:* Virtually superb skirt selectivity (1:1.4 wide and 1:1.5 narrow) and ultimate rejection (90 dB); bandwidths measure 6.3 kHz and 2.6 kHz, using Collins mechanical filters. Adjacent-channel 5 kHz heterodyne whistles largely absent with wide bandwidth (*see* Con, *R30CC*).

Con: No keypad for direct frequency entry, not even as an outboard mouse-type option; only some of the very cheapest of portables now don't come with or offer a keypad. No 5 kHz tuning step choice to aid in bandscanning. Lacks control to hop from one world band segment to another; instead, uses 0.5 MHz fast-slew increments.

No synchronous selectable sideband without pricey Sherwood SE-3 Mk III D aftermarket accessory (see preceding review). ECSS tuning can be up to 10 Hz out of phase because of 20 Hz minimum tuning increment. Mechanical tuning encoder play gives tuning knob sloppy feel, making precise ECSS tuning difficult; an optical encoder could have helped avoided this while adding to reliability. Lacks features found in top-gun receivers, such as tunable notch filter, noise blanker, passband tuning and adjustable RF gain. Recovered audio fine with most signals, but with truly weak signals is not of the DX caliber found with top-gun receivers. No visual indication of which bandwidth is being used. No tone controls. Small identical front-panel buttons, including the MEM button which if accidentally pressed can erase a preset. Station presets not as intuitive or easy to select as with various other models; lacks frequency information on existing presets during memory storage. Lightweight plastic tuning knob lacks mass to provide good tuning feel. No AGC off. No RF gain control. Uses AC adaptor instead of built-in power supply. High battery consumption. Batteries frustratingly difficult to install, requiring partial disassembly of the receiver and care not to damage speaker connections or confuse polarities. Receiver's lightness and tilt bail's lack of rubber sheathing allow it to slide around, especially when tuning knob pushed to change VRIT increments; the added weight of batteries helps slightly. Unsheathed tilt bail digs into some surfaces. Mono headphone jack produces output in only one ear of stereo 'phones (remedied by user-purchased mono-to-stereo adaptor). Signal-strength meter illumination dims when volume turned high with AM-mode signals; LCD illumination unaffected. Three bulbs used for illumination are soldered into place, making replacement difficult, although they should last a very long time. *R30:* Wide bandwidth slightly broad for a model lacking synchronous selectable sideband, often allowing adjacent-channel (5 kHz) heterodyne whistles to be heard; largely remedied by detuning 1-2 kHz, which unlike with some receivers doesn't significantly increase distortion. *R30CC:* Intermittent microphonics in AM mode when using narrow bandwidth and internal speaker. Audio frequency response with wide filter makes for slightly muffled audio as compared with R30; largely remedied by detuning 1-2 kHz, which unlike with some receivers doesn't significantly increase distortion. Factory Website doesn't give "C" or "CC" prices until order form/basket is brought up.

☞ Works best when grounded.

Verdict: Although the Ohio-made Palstar R30 family of receivers is woefully lacking in tuning and performance features, what it sets out to do, it tends to do to a high standard. If you can abide the convoluted battery installation procedure and don't mind having to add an outboard antenna, it can also be used as a field portable.

Nevertheless, this receiver lacks a distinct identity. Although the audio is fairly pleasant, especially in the basic version, it doesn't have the synchronous selectable sideband needed to make it a premium listener's radio.

Its lack of operating features is especially disappointing; it even omits a keypad, something routinely found on portables costing a fraction as much. And its lack of signal-tweaking features, along with pedestrian weak-signal recovered audio, preclude it from use with serious DX.

But not everybody fits neatly into routine categories. One size doesn't fit all, and to that end the R30's straightforward concept and physical robustness adds diversity and choice to the roster of available models.

Evaluation of Changes for 2004—All Versions: The entire Palstar R30 series has undergone a number of small spit-and-polish improvements over the three years that have passed since our last test. The result is not enough to change the overall standing of the receiver, but there is 7 dB better blocking, 6 dB improvement in image rejection and an almost complete banishment of "birdies"; other measurement differences, both better and worse, were close enough to be considered sample-to-sample variations. There's also a 455 kHz IF output and other nice touches lacking in the earliest production samples.

Most companies leave a model alone except for urgent changes, but Palstar goes further and also attends to the small points. This is a good sign.

Evaluation of "CC" Version for 2004: The version we had tested in the past was the basic R30, which uses ceramic filters for the two bandwidths. For 2004 we tested the "CC" incarnation, which uses Collins mechanical filters for both bandwidths. The versions are otherwise identical, and insertion loss is the same whether Collins or ceramic filters are installed—ultimate rejection is also a superb 90 dB in both instances.

Say "Lotus" or "Ferrari" to a sports car buff, and you'll hear how they were *la crème de la crème*. Say "Collins mechanical filter" to a radio buff, and you can also expect high fives.

Does the Collins option live up to its billing?

The -6 dB bandwidths and -6/-60 dB shape factors of the narrow ceramic filter (2.7 kHz, 1:1.4) and mechanical filter (2.6 kHz/1:1.5) are similar enough that it's hard to see the point in the costlier mechanical option. Too, with the mechanical filter we encountered intermittent audio microphonics in the AM mode with the built-in speaker; none was noted in our earlier tests of the ceramic version. Current samples of the basic and "C" versions would have to be tested to ascertain the degree that microphonics may result from Collins filters, and if so whether the "C" and "C" versions are both affected.

The wide ceramic and mechanical filters both have the same shape factors (1:1.4), but the -6 dB bandwidth measurements are another story. The ceramic filter has a bandwidth of 7.7 kHz, whereas the mechanical is 6.3—1.4 kHz narrower. This allows the "CC" version to keep 5 kHz adjacent-channel heterodynes at bay in nearly all situations. It also muffles the audio somewhat, but this is largely overcome by detuning by one or two kilohertz; with some receivers this causes an exponential rise in distortion, but not here.

There is a compromise model offered, the R30C, with one ceramic and one mechanical bandwidth filter. Alas, it's the narrow bandwidth with the mechanical, the reverse of what would do the most good. However, Palstar is a family operation that might respond positively to a customer request to have a "C" unit equipped with the mechanical filter in the wide, rather than the usual narrow, position.

✪✪✪¾ ✐
Yaesu FRG-100

Price: *FRG-100:* $599.95 in the United States. $999.00CAD in Canada. £449.00 in the United Kingdom. *TCXO-4 frequency stabilizer:* $99.00 in the United States. €49.00 in Germany.

Pro: Excellent performance in many respects. Includes three bandwidths, a noise blanker, selectable AGC, two attenuators, the ability to select 16 pre-programmed

The Yaesu FRG-100 is affordable and proven, but lacks a keypad for direct tuning.

world band segments, two clocks, on-off timers, 52 tunable station presets that store frequency and mode data, a variety of scanning schemes and an all-mode squelch.

Con: No keypad for direct frequency entry, and no aftermarket keypad appears to be available any longer. No synchronous selectable sideband. Lacks features found in "top-gun" receivers: passband tuning, notch filter, adjustable RF gain. Simple controls and display, combined with complex functions, can make certain operations confusing. Dynamic range only fair. Uses AC adaptor instead of built-in power supply.

Verdict: While sparse on features, the Yaesu FRG-100 succeeds in delivering worthy performance within an attractive price class.

▤ An *RDI WHITE PAPER* is available for this model.

Retested for 2004
✪✪✪ ✐
Yaesu VR-5000

Price: *VR-5000 Receiver, including single-voltage AC adaptor:* Currently $619.95 in the United States, but price varies markedly over time. $1,099.00CAD in Canada. £599.00 in the United Kingdom. €749.00 in Germany. *DSP-1 digital notch, bandpass and noise reduction unit:* $119.95 in the United States. $199.00CAD in Canada. £79.00 in the United Kingdom. €98.00 in Germany. *DVS-4 16-second digital audio recorder:* $47.00 in the United States. $80.00CAD in Canada. £29.00 in the United Kingdom. €39.00 in Germany. *FVS-1A voice synthesizer:* $43.00 in the United States. $75.00CAD in Canada. £38.00 in the United Kingdom. €55.00 in Germany. *RadioShack 22-504 aftermarket 120V AC>13.8V DC power supply:* $39.99 in the United States.

Pro: Unusually wide frequency coverage, 100 kHz through 2.6 GHz (U.S. version omits cellular frequencies 869-894 MHz). Two thousand alphanumeric-displayed station presets, which can be linked to any of up to 100 groupings of presets. Up to 50 programmable start/stop search ranges. Large and potentially useful "band scope" spectrum display (see Con). Bandwidths have superb skirt selectivity, with shape factors between 1:1.3 and 1:1.4. Wide AM bandwidth (17.2 kHz) allows local mediumwave AM stations to be received with superior fidelity (see Con). Flexible software settings provide a high degree of control over selected parameters. Sophisticated scanning choices, although they are of limited use because of false signals generated by receiver's inadequate dynamic range (see Con). Dual-receive function, with sub-receiver circuitry feeding "band scope" spectrum display; when display not in use, two signals may be monitored simultaneously, provided they are within 20 MHz of each other. Sensitivity to weak signals excellent-to-superb within shortwave spectrum, although combined with receiver's inadequate dynamic range this tends to cause overloading when a worthy antenna is used (see Con). Appears to be robustly constructed. External spectrum display, fed by receiver's 10.7 MHz IF output, can perform very well for narrow-parameter scans (see Con). Two 24-hour clocks, both of which are shown except when spectrum display mode not in use; one clock tied into an elementary map display and database of time in a wide choice of world cities. On-off timer allows for up to 48 automatic events. Sleep-delay/alarm timers. Lightweight and compact. Multi-level display dimmer. Optional DSP unit includes adjustable notch filtering, a bandpass feature and noise reduction (see Con). Tone control. Built-in "CAT" computer control interface (see Con).

Con: Exceptionally poor dynamic range (49 dB at 5 kHz separation, 64 dB at 20 kHz) and IF/image rejection (as low as 30 dB) for a tabletop model; for listeners in such high-signal parts of the world as Europe, North Africa and eastern North America, this shortcoming all but cripples reception of shortwave signals unless a very modest

Yaesu's VR-5000 brings affordability to broadband receivers.

antenna is used; the degree to which VHF-UHF is degraded depends *inter alia* upon the extent of powerful transmissions in the vicinity of the receiver. No synchronous selectable sideband, a major drawback for world band and mediumwave AM listening, but not for shortwave utility/ham, VHF or UHF reception. Has only one single-sideband bandwidth, a relatively broad 4.0 kHz. Wide AM bandwidth (17.2 kHz) of no use for shortwave reception. For world band listening, the middle (8.7 kHz) AM bandwidth lets through adjacent-channel 5 kHz heterodyne, while narrow bandwidth (consistently 3.9 kHz, not the 4.0 kHz of the SSB bandwidth) produces muffled audio. Line output level low. Audio distorts at higher volume settings. Limited bass response. Audio hissy, especially noticeable with a good outboard speaker. DSP-1 option a mediocre overall performer and adds distortion. Phase noise measures 94 dBc, poor. AGC threshold measures 11 microvolts, poor. No adjustment of AGC decay. Single-sideband AGC decay too slow. Most recent sample's (firmware v1u.17) tuning encoder sometimes has rotational delay that requires three clicks instead of one to commence down-frequency tuning when reversing direction from clockwise to counterclockwise. Mediocre tuning-knob feel. Signal-strength indicator has only five levels and overreads; an alternative software-selectable signal-strength indicator—not easy to get in and out of—has no markings other than a single reference level. Built-in spectrum display's dynamic range only 20 dB (-80 to -100 dBm), with a very slow scan rate. Single-sideband frequency readout of latest sample more accurate, but after warmup LSB is still 70 Hz and USB 100 Hz off. Long learning curve: Thirty buttons (often densely spaced, lilliputian and multi-function)—along with carouseling mode/tune-step selection and a menu-driven command scheme—combine to produce ergonomics that are not intuitive. Only one low-impedance antenna connector, inadequate for a wideband device that calls for multiple antennas. Longwave sensitivity mediocre. Clocks don't display seconds numerically. Marginal display contrast. Although four LEDs used for backlighting, the result is unevenly distributed. Uses AC adaptor instead of built-in power supply; adaptor and receiver both tend to run warm. Repeated microprocessor lockups, sometimes displayed as "*ERROR* LOW VOLTAGE," even though the receiver now comes with a 7.2V NiCd battery pack to help prevent this; unplugging set for ten minutes resolves problem until it occurs again, but the only permanent solution appears to be replacing the receiver's AC adaptor with a properly bypassed and regulated non-switching AC adaptor/DC power supply of at least one ampere that produces no less than 13.5V DC—certainly no less than 13.2V DC—and no more than 13.8V DC (we use a lab power supply, but in North America the RadioShack 22-504 appears promising). Even with aforementioned battery, clock has to be reset if power fails. Squelch doesn't function through audio line output (for recording, etc.). Line output gain is somewhat low. Sub-receiver doesn't feed line output. Computer interface lacks viable command structure, limiting usefulness. Tilt feet have inadequate rise. Owner's manual (0104q-DY) doesn't cover all receiver functions, so user has to learn much by trial and error. *United States:* Based on our recent experiences, customer support appears to be indifferent.

Verdict: With existing technology, DC-to-daylight receivers which provide excellent shortwave performance are costly to produce, and thus expensive.

The relatively affordable wideband Yaesu VR-5000 tries to overcome this. This Japanese-made model acts as a VHF/UHF scanner as well as a shortwave receiver, but falls woefully shy for world band reception in strong-signal parts of the world. Elsewhere, it fares better on shortwave, especially if a modest antenna is used. VHF/UHF performance depends on the number and strength of local transmitters.

Observations with Latest Sample: Some minor changes have been made to the firmware, operating manual and even hardware. By and large, these have been marginally for the better, and they underscore Yaesu's commitment to improving existing models. Yet, the main difference is for the worse, at least on our sample: rotational delay with the tuning encoder.

Yaesu has made a good faith effort to combine a scanner and shortwave receiver into one affordable box. On a business level this concept may seem to make good sense, but most world band listeners and DXers should look elsewhere. By shopping carefully, for less money you can purchase a conventional world band radio and separate scanner that cover the same frequencies, yet perform much better.

✪✪✪   ⓔ
AKD Target HF-3M, NASA HF-4/HF-4E/S, SI-TEX NAV-FAX 200

Price: *HF-3M/HF-4/HF-4E:* £149.95 in the United Kingdom. €199.00 in Germany. *HF-4E/S:* £159.95 in the United Kingdom. €299.00 in Germany. *PA30 antenna:* €35.30 in Germany. *NAV-FAX 200 (www.si-tex.com):* $399.00 in the United States. *SI-TEX ACNF 120V AC adaptor:* $19.95 in the United States.

Pro: Superior rejection of images. Third-order intercept point for superior strong-signal handling capability. Bandwidths have superb ultimate rejection. *HF-4/HF-4E/HF-4E/S:* Two AM-mode bandwidths. Illuminated LCD. *Except*

NAV-FAX 200: Comes with DOS software for weatherfax ("WEFAX") reception using a PC; software upgrade may be in the offing. *NAV-FAX 200:* Comes with Mscan Meteo Pro Lite software (www.mscan.com) for WEFAX, RTTY and NAVTEX reception using a PC with Windows XP or earlier. Comes with wire antenna and audio patch cable. Two-year warranty, with repair facility in Florida.

Con: No keypad, and variable-rate tuning knob is difficult to control. Broad skirt selectivity. Single-sideband bandwidth relatively wide. Volume control fussy to adjust. Synthesizer tunes in relatively coarse 1 kHz increments, supplemented by an analog fine-tuning "clarifier" control. Only ten station presets. Single sideband requires both tuning controls to be adjusted. No synchronous selectable sideband, notch filter or passband tuning. Frequency readout off by 2 kHz in single-sideband mode. Uses AC adaptor instead of built-in power supply. No clock, timer or sleep-delay feature. *HF3M:* Band-widths not selectable independent of mode. Only AM-mode bandwidth functions for world band reception. LCD not illuminated. *Except*

Simple and robust, the SI-TEX NAV-FAX 200 is geared to maritime needs.

NAV-FAX 200: Apparently not available outside United Kingdom.

Verdict: Pleasant world band performance at an affordable price, although numerous features are absent and operation is more frustrating than on many other models. Logical for yachting.

The PASSPORT *tabletop-model review team consists of Lawrence Magne, David Zantow and George Zeller; also, George Heidelman, Tony Jones, Chuck Rippel and David Walcutt, with Craig Tyson. Laboratory measurements by J. Robert Sherwood.*

ROLL YOUR OWN

Most shortwave kits are novelties, but there is one exception: Ten-Tec's small 1254 world band radio, $195. Parts quality appears to be excellent, and assembly runs at least 24 hours. It has 15 station presets, but lacks keypad, signal-strength indicator, synchronous selectable sideband, tilt bail, LSB/USB settings and adjustable AGC. Tuning increments are 500 Hz for single sideband and 5 kHz for AM-mode, and an analog clarifier for tweaking between these increments.

Phase noise, front-end selectivity and longwave/mediumwave AM sensitivity are poor. Bandwidth is 5.6 kHz, and there is worthy ultimate rejection, image rejection, world band sensitivity, blocking, AGC threshold and frequency stability. Dynamic range and first IF rejection are fair, while overall distortion is good—with an external speaker, audio is pleasant.

The Ten-Tec 1254 is a fun weekend project, and the manufacturer's track record for hand-holding means that when you're through the radio should really work.

Heathkit may be gone, but kits aren't. Ten-Tec's 1254 is a fun weekend project.

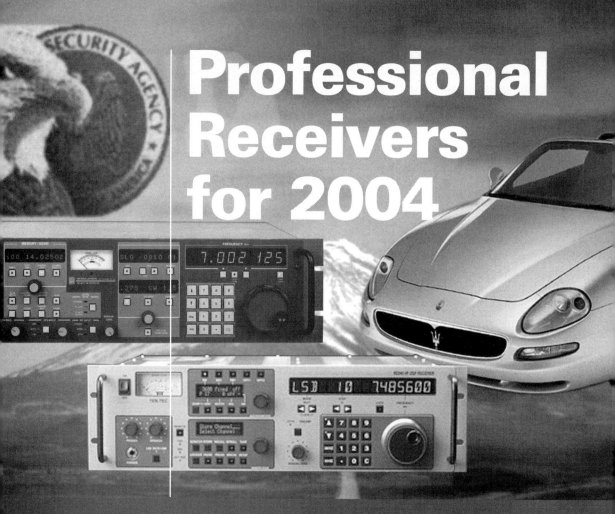

Professional Receivers for 2004

Maseratis of World Radio

Professional-grade receivers are designed for commercial, maritime, surveillance and military organizations. Their requirements have much in common with the needs of world band listening. Yet, there are enough differences that these specialized models are not always as suitable for world band use as consumer-grade offerings.

Some variants make for better results, others worse. But when it all comes together, as it does with the models tested for this PASS-PORT, professional hardware has the greatest potential to excel in snaring DX rarities.

Three Categories

There are three basic categories of professional receivers: easy for human operation, complex for human operation and no human operation.

The first are designed so personnel can tune "utility" signals with minimal training. After all, if an AWACS plane takes shrapnel and the radioman is unable to function, the more straightforward a radio is to operate, the more likely it is that other crew members will be able to carry on. Trouble is, simplicity of operation can also result in performance compromises, making these potentially inferior choices for world band cognoscenti.

The second category goes to the other extreme, with features and performance that are "no holds barred." These assume a high degree of operator skill, and are the type of professional receiver we analyze in PASSPORT REPORTS. If only the very best will do, they are worth considering if you aren't put off by their complexity of operation and sticker shock.

Simplest are "black box" professional receivers, which have virtually no controls. These are operated remotely or by computers, often at hush-hush surveillance facilities. We don't cover this category, as some of the best models are available only to U.S. Federal agencies or NATO organizations. However, consumer-grade versions are evaluated elsewhere within PASSPORT REPORTS.

The Icom IC-R9000L and Japan Radio NRD-301A, reviewed in past editions, have been discontinued. However, the RDI White Paper for the '9000 will continue to be made available.

Find major updates to the 2004 PASSPORT REPORTS at www. passband.com.

Shared Characteristics

All professional receivers should be physically and electrically robust, with resistance to hostile environments and rough handling, as well as having a superior mean time between failures (MTBF). Additionally, their components need to be consistent enough that board swapping and other field repairs can be accomplished easily and without disturbing performance.

The two professional models reviewed in this PASSPORT REPORTS were developed to replace the erstwhile consumer-grade Icom IC-R71A reviewed in a Radio Database International White Paper that's still available. Years ago, the tabletop 'R71A was used by the U.S. National Security Agency for offshore surveillance, but it was not made to NATO spec and had certain other limitations. Thankfully, the two models designed to replace it are as good as it gets for shortwave DXing.

Good Antenna and Low Noise Essential

Top-rated, properly erected antennas are an absolute "must" for professional receivers to reach their potential. For test results and installation information, peruse the Radio Database International White Paper, *Evaluation of Popular Outdoor Antennas*, as well as reviews of antennas found elsewhere in this PASSPORT REPORTS.

If reception at your location is already disrupted by electrical noise even when a suitable antenna is in use, a better receiver would be a waste of money. Before buying, try eliminating the source of noise, or reorienting or replacing your antenna.

Volts with Jolts

Professional receivers tend to be unusually rugged, and often include MOV surge protection before the AC power supply. Nevertheless, it helps to plug your pricey receiver into a non-MOV surge arrestor, such as those manufactured by Zero-Surge (www.zerosurge.com) and Brick Wall (www.brickwall.com).

Any receiver's outdoor antenna always should be fed through a top-caliber static protection device, but this is especially important with the Watkins-Johnson WJ-8711A if it isn't equipped with the 8711/PRE option. Prudent operators also disconnect outdoor antennas from the receiver when thunderstorms threaten.

DSP Audio Qualities

In principle, there is no reason DSP (digital signal processing) receivers can't produce audio quality equal to, and in some respects better than, conventional models. Witness the audio quality of digital CDs, for example.

But a multi-stage receiver is much more complex than a CD, so it requires a great deal of processing horsepower. Today's DSP receivers still fall short in this regard, one result being that audio quality is not all it could be. In particular, static crashes tend to sound harsher.

Helping offset this is that hard-core DXers often find recoverable audio to be slightly greater with DSP receivers. Of course, this same benefit should continue to accrue should overall audio quality be improved through greater microprocessor power.

For tuning world band the Sherwood SE-3 accessory is nearly a "must" for most current and recently discontinued professional receivers. While the Sherwood device doesn't fundamentally resolve the DSP audio issue, it tames it considerably while also providing high-quality synchronous selectable sideband. These are enormous pluses, but there are downsides, too: extra cost, added operating complexity and a BFO that is not fully as stable as those on professional receivers.

Tips for Using this Section

Professional receivers are listed in order of suitability for listening to difficult-to-hear world band stations. Important secondary consideration is given to audio fidelity, ergonomics and reception of utility signals. We cite actual selling prices as of when we go to press, including European VAT and Australian GST where applicable.

Unless otherwise stated, all professional models have the following characteristics. Refer to PASSPORT's glossary to understand specialized terms.

- Digital signal processing, including digital frequency synthesis and display.
- Full coverage of at least the 5-29999 kHz VLF/LF/MF/HF portions of the radio spectrum, encompassing all the longwave, mediumwave AM and shortwave portions—including all world band frequencies—but no coverage of the standard FM broadcast band (87.5-108 MHz).
- A wide variety of helpful tuning features, including tuning and frequency display in 1 Hz increments.

- Synchronous selectable sideband via high-rejection IF filtering (not lower-rejection phasing), which greatly reduces adjacent-channel interference and fading distortion. On some models this is referred to as "SAM" (synchronous AM).

☞ ECSS: Professional models tune to the nearest 1 Hz, allowing the user to use the receiver's single-sideband circuitry to manually phase its BFO (internally generated carrier) with the station's transmitted carrier. Called "ECSS" (exalted-carrier, selectable-sideband) tuning, this can be used with AM-mode signals in lieu of synchronous selectable sideband. However, in addition to the relative inconvenience of this technique, unlike synchronous detection, which re-phases continually and essentially perfectly, ECSS is always slightly out of phase. This causes at least some degree of harmonic distortion to music and speech, while tuning to the nearest Hertz can generate slow-sweep fading (for this reason, high-pass audio filtering or mis-phasing by two or three Hertz may provide better results).

- Proper demodulation of modes used by non-world-band—utility and amateur—shortwave signals. These modes include single sideband (LSB/USB and sometimes ISB) and CW ("Morse code"); also, with suitable ancillary devices, radioteletype (RTTY), frequency shift key (FSK) and radiofax (FAX). Digital world band broadcasts (DRM) are not yet appropriately demodulated.

- Meaningful signal-strength indication.
- Illuminated display.
- Superior build quality, robustness and sample-to-sample consistency as compared to consumer-grade tabletop receivers.
- Audio output for recording or low-power FM retransmission to hear world band around your domicile.

What PASSPORT's Rating Symbols Mean

Star ratings: ✪✪✪✪✪ is best. Stars reflect overall performance and meaningful features, plus to some extent ergonomics and build quality. Price, appearance, country of manufacture and the like are not taken into account. With professional models there is a strong emphasis on the ability to flush out tough, hard-to-hear signals, as this is usually the main reason these sets are chosen by world band enthusiasts. Nevertheless, to facilitate comparison professional receiver rating standards are very similar to those used for the table-top, portatop and portable models reviewed elsewhere in this PASSPORT.

Passport's Choice. La crème de la crème. Our test team's personal picks of the litter—models we would buy or have bought for our personal use.

Retested for 2004

✪✪✪✪✪ *Passport's Choice*
Watkins-Johnson WJ-8711A

Price (receiver, factory options; prices change often): *WJ-8711A: $5,500.00 plus shipping worldwide. 871Y/SEU DSP Speech Enhancement Unit: $1,200.00. 8711/PRE Sub-Octave Preselector: $1,100.00. 871Y/DSO1 Digital Signal Output Unit: $1,150.00.*

Price (aftermarket options): *Hammond RCBS1900517BK1 steel cabinet and 1421A mounting screws and cup washers: $120-140 in the United States from manufacturer (www.hammondmfg.com/rackrcbs.htm) or Newark Electronics (www.newark.com). Sherwood SE-3 MK III accessory: $549.00 plus shipping worldwide.*

Pro: Proven robust. BITE diagnostics and physical layout allows technically qualified

users to make most repairs on-site. Users can upgrade receiver performance over time by EPROM replacement. Exceptional overall performance. Unsurpassed reception of feeble world band DX signals, especially when mated to the Sherwood SE-3 synchronous selectable sideband device and the WJ-871Y/SEU noise-reduction unit (*see* Con). Unusually effective "ECSS" reception, tuning AM-mode signals as though they were single sideband. Superb reception of non-AM mode "utility" stations. Generally superior audio quality when coupled to the Sherwood SE-3 fidelity-enhancing accessory, the W-J speech enhancement unit and a worthy external speaker (*see* Con). Unparalleled bandwidth flexibility, with no less than 66 outstandingly high-quality bandwidths. Trimmer on back panel allows frequency readout to be user-aligned against a known frequency standard, such as WWV/WWVH or a laboratory device. Extraordinary operational flexibility—virtually every receiver parameter is adjustable. One hundred station presets. Synchronous detection, called "SAM" (synchronous AM), reduces selective-fading distortion with world band, mediumwave AM and longwave signals, and works even on very narrow voice bandwidths (*see* Con). Rock stable. Built-in preamplifier. Tunable notch filter. Effective noise blanking. Highly adjustable scanning of both frequency ranges and channel presets. Easy-to-read displays. Large tuning knob. Can be fully and effectively computer and remotely controlled. Passband shift (*see* Con).

Numerous outputs for data collection and ancillary hardware, including 455 kHz IF output which makes for instant installation of Sherwood SE-3 accessory and balanced line outputs (connect to balanced hookup to minimize "hash" radiation). Remote control and dial-up data collection; Windows control software available from manufacturer. Among the most likely of all world band receivers tested to be able to be retrofitted for eventual reception of digital world band broadcasts. Inboard AC power supply, which runs unusually cool, senses incoming current and automatically adjusts to anything from 90-264 VAC, 47-440 Hz—a plus during brownouts or with line voltage or frequency swings. Superior-quality factory service (*see* Con). Comprehensive and well-written operating manual, packed with technical information and schematic diagrams. Hammond aftermarket cabinet is exceptionally robust.

Con: Static crashes and modulation-splash interference sound noticeably harsher than on analog receivers, although this has been improved in latest operating software. Synchronous detection not sideband-selectable, so it can't reduce adjacent-channel interference (remediable by Sherwood SE-3). Basic receiver has mediocre audio in AM mode; "ECSS" tuning or synchronous detection, along with the speech enhancement unit (W1 noise-reduction setting), required to alleviate this. Some clipping distortion in the single-sideband mode. Complex to operate to full advantage. Circuitry puts out a high degree of digital noise ("hash"), relying for the most part on the panels for electrical shielding; one consequence is that various versions emanate hash through the nonstandard rear-panel audio terminals, as well as through the signal-strength meter and front-panel headphone jack—this problem is lessened when the Sherwood SE-3 is used. Antennas with shielded (e.g., coaxial) feedlines are less likely to pick up receiver-generated hash. Passband shift operates only in CW mode. Jekyll-and-Hyde ergonomics: sometimes wonderful, sometimes awful. Front-panel rack "ears" protrude, with the right "ear" getting in the way of the tuning knob; fortunately, these are easily removed. Mediocre front-end selectivity, remediable by 8711/PRE option (with minor 2.5 dB insertion loss); e.g. for those living near mediumwave AM transmitters. 871Y/SEU option reduces audio gain and is extremely difficult to install; best to have all options factory-installed. Signal-strength indicator's gradations in dBm only. No DC power input. Each receiver is built on order (david.feinstein@signia-idt.com), so it can take up to four months for delivery. Factory service can take as much as two months. Cabinet extra, available from Hammond and Premiere. Plastic feet have no front elevation and allow receiver to slide around. Available only through U.S. manufacturer (+1-301/948-7550); receiver and factory options have been subjected to a number of price increases since 2000.

☞ In 1999 Watkins-Johnson in Gaithersburg, Maryland was taken over by Marconi, the British electronics giant. Months later, this entity was swallowed up by British Aerospace; as a result, Watkins-Johnson became "BAE Systems," but that wasn't the end of it: On November 1, 2002, BAE Systems Gaithersburg was incorporated into goliath Integrated Defense Technologies. Thus, what was originally and for decades known as Watkins-Johnson is now "Signia-IDT." Receivers designed before July, 2000 continue to carry the legacy "WJ" prefix, but later models are preceded by "SI," so even the venerable Watkins-Johnson name appears to be headed for the historical dust heap.

Verdict: The American-made WJ-8711A is, by a skosh, the ultimate machine for down-and-dirty world band DXing when money is no object; after all, fully tricked out this receiver costs as much as a used car. Had there not been digital hash, inexcusable at this price—and had there been better audio quality, a tone control, passband shift and synchronous selectable sideband—the '8711A would have been even better, especially for program listening. Fortunately, the Sherwood SE-3 accessory remedies virtually all these problems and improves DX reception, to boot; W-J's optional 871Y/SEU complements, rather than competes with, the SE-3 for improving recovered audio.

Overall, the WJ-8711A DSP receiver, properly configured, is as good as it gets. It is exceptionally well-suited to demanding connoisseurs with the appropriate financial wherewithal—provided they seek an exceptional degree of manual receiver control.

Observations on Latest Unit: Various small improvements have emerged in the most recent production. The trimmer to adjust the frequency readout has been moved from within the receiver to the rear panel, where it can be handily accessed. Too, in PASSPORT's prior test cycle our unit's tuning knob had rotational play that caused a slight pause when reversing direction; there is no trace of this annoyance in this year's sample. Also, the owner's manual now comes in handy CD-ROM format, as well as the traditional printed tome.

Not all changes have been for the better. The main microprocessor IC is no longer installed in a socket, making it impractical to upgrade or replace in the field. And there was one sample defect: A front-panel key occasionally stuck.

In past tests, we have housed the receiver in a Ten-Tec cabinet that no longer appears to be available. So, this time we sprung for the Hammond offering, and found it to be even better—thick, heavy and tough enough for the next world war.

✪✪✪✪✪ *Passport's Choice*
Ten-Tec RX-340

Price: $3,950.00 in the United States. £3,799.00 (€5,450) in the United Kingdom. *Hammond RCBS1900513GY2 or RCBS1900513BK1 13" deep cabinet (www.hammondmfg.com/rackrcbs.htm):* $99.95 in the United States. *Ten-Tec #307G external speaker:* $98.95 in the United States. *Sherwood SE-3 MK III accessory:* $549.00 plus shipping worldwide.

Pro: Appears to be robust (*see* Con). BITE diagnostics and physical layout allows technically qualified users to make most repairs on-site. Users can upgrade receiver performance over time by replacing one or another of three socketed EPROM chips (currently v1.10A). Superb overall performance, including for reception of feeble world band DX signals, especially when mated to the Sherwood SE-3 device; in particular, superlative image and IF rejection, both >100 dB. Few birdies.

Audio quality usually worthy when receiver coupled to the Sherwood SE-3 accessory and a good external speaker. Average overall distortion in single-sideband mode a breathtakingly low 0.2 percent; in other modes, under 2.7 percent. Exceptional bandwidth flexibility, with no less than 57 outstandingly high-quality bandwidths having shape factors of 1:1.33 or better; bandwidth distribution exceptionally good for world band listening and DXing, along with other activities (*see* Con). Tunes and displays accurately in ultra-precise 1 Hz increments. Extraordinary operational flexibility—virtually every receiver parameter is adjustable; for example, the AGC's various time constants have 118 million possible combinations, plus pushbutton AGC "DUMP" to temporarily deactivate AGC (*see* Con). Worthy front-panel ergonomics, valuable given the exceptional degree of manual operation; includes easy-to-read displays (*see* Con). Also, large, properly weighted rubber-track tuning knob with fixed dimple and Oak Grigsby optical encoder provide superior tuning "feel" and reliability. Attractive front panel. Two hundred station presets, 201 including the scratchpad. Synchronous selectable sideband, called "SAM" (synchronous AM), reduces selective-fading distortion, as well as at diminishing or eliminating adjacent-channel interference, with world band, mediumwave AM and longwave signals; with earlier software lock was easily lost, but from v1.10A it now holds lock acceptably (*see* Con). Built-in half-octave

Ten-Tec's RX-340 competes toe-to-toe with the Watkins-Johnson WJ-8711A, but costs less and has superior customer support.

preselector comes standard. Built-in preamplifier (*see* Con). Adjustable noise blanker, works well in most situations (*see* Con). Stable as Gibraltar, as good as it gets. Tunable DSP notch filter with exceptional depth of 58 dB (*see* Con). Passband shift (passband tuning) works unusually well (*see* Con). Unusually effective "ECSS" reception by tuning AM-mode signals as though they were single sideband. Superb reception of "utility" (non-AM mode) stations using a wide variety of modes and including fast filters for delay-critical digital modes. Highly adjustable scanning of both frequency ranges and channel presets. Can be fully and effectively computer and remotely controlled. Numerous outputs for data collection and ancillary hardware, including 455 kHz IF-out for instant hookup of

NUMBERS: PROFESSIONAL RECEIVERS

	Watkins-Johnson WJ-8711A	Ten-Tec RX-340
Max. Sensitivity/Noise Floor	0.13 µV, **S**/–136 dBm, **E**	0.17 µV, **S**/–132 dBm, **E**[1]
Blocking	123 dB, **G**	109 dB, **F**
Shape Factors, voice BWs	1:1.21-1:1.26, **S**	1:1.15-1:1.33, **S**
Ultimate Rejection	>80 dB, **E**	70 dB, **G**
Front-End Selectivity	Wideband, **F**/Half octave, **E**[2]	Half octave, **E**
Image Rejection	80 dB, **E**	>100 dB, **S**
First IF Rejection	— [3]	>100 dB, **S**
Dynamic Range/IP3 (5 kHz)	74 dB, **G**/–18 dBm, **E**	46 dB, **F**/–53 dBm, **P**
Dynamic Range/IP3 (20 kHz)	99 dB, **S**/+20 dBm, **S**	84 dB, **G**/+4 dBm, **E**
Phase Noise	115 dBc, **G**	113 dBc, **G**
AGC Threshold	0.1 µV, **P**	0.3 µV, **G**[4]
Overall Distortion, sync	8.2%, **P**	2.6%, **G**
Notch filter depth	58 dB, **S**	58 dB, **S**

IBS Lab Ratings: **S** Superb   **E** Excellent   **G** Good   **F** Fair   **P** Poor

(1) Preamp on. With preamp off, 0.55 µV, **G**/–122 dBm, **G**.
(2) **F** standard/**E** with optional preselector.
(3) Adequate, but could not measure precisely.
(4) Preamp on. With preamp off, 1.3 µV, **G**.

Sherwood SE-3 accessory. Remote control and dial-up data collection. Superb analog signal-strength indicator (*see* Con). Among the most likely of all world band receivers tested to be able to be retrofitted for eventual reception of digital world band broadcasts. Inboard AC power supply senses incoming current and automatically adjusts to anything from 90-264 VAC, 48-440 Hz—a plus during brownouts or with line voltage or frequency swings. Superior control of fluorescent display dimming (*see* Con). Superior factory service, reasonably priced by professional standards, with prompt turnaround and helpful online/phone tech support. Comprehensive and well-written operating manual, packed with technical information and schematic diagrams.

Con: Synchronous selectable sideband loses lock relatively easily; e.g., if listening to one sideband and there is a strong signal impacting the other sideband, lock can be momentarily lost; resolved by Sherwood SE-3 fidelity device. DSP microprocessor limitations result in poor dynamic range/IP3 at 5 kHz signal spacing. Blocking, phase noise and ultimate rejection all pretty good, but not of professional caliber. Complex to operate to full advantage. Static crashes sound harsher than on analog receivers. Not all bandwidths available in all modes. Spurious signals noted around 6 MHz segment (49 meters) at night at one test location having superb antennas. Synchronous selectable sideband, although recently improved, doesn't hold lock quite as well as some other models. When 9-10 dB preamplifier turned on, AGC acts on noise unless IF gain reduced by 10 dB. Notch filter does not work in AM, synchronous selectable sideband or ISB modes. Passband shift tunes only plus or minus 2 kHz and does not work in the ISB or synchronous selectable sideband modes; remediable with Sherwood SE-3. Audio

quality and synchronous selectable sideband's lock both profit from Sherwood SE-3 accessory and good outboard speaker. Occasional "popping" sound, notably when synchronous selectable sideband or ISB in use—DSP overload? No AGC off except by holding down DUMP button. Noise blanker not effective at some test locations; for example, other receivers work better in reducing noise from electric fences. Audio power, especially through headphones, could be greater. On our unit, right-channel headphone audio cuts out at full volume. On our unit, occasional minor buzz from internal speaker. Keypad not in telephone format. Some ergonomic clumsiness when going back and forth between the presets and VFO tuning; too, "Aux Parameter" and "Memory Scan" knobs touchy to adjust. Signal-strength indicator illuminated less than display. Digital hash from fluorescent display emits from front of receiver, although not elsewhere. On our latest unit, stick-on decal with front-panel markings has peeled loose above the main display, and pushing it back into place hasn't helped; this has not been a problem on other units. No DC power input. Cabinet extra.

Verdict: With an exceptional degree of manual control, the Ten-Tec RX-340, when coupled to fidelity-enhancing hardware, is a superb DSP receiver for those who want no-compromise performance for years to come. It's a sensible value, too—with bells and whistles, it costs considerably less than a fully equipped WJ-8711A. Great factory service, too.

_____

The PASSPORT *professional-model review team consists of Tony Jones, Lawrence Magne, Chuck Rippel, David Walcutt, David Zantow and George Zeller. Laboratory measurements by J. Robert Sherwood.*

Receivers for PCs and Digital Broadcasts

Much of the enjoyment of world band comes from using a variety of knobs and buttons to unearth stations and enhance their reception quality. But one size doesn't fit all. A small but visible group prefers to have their receivers controlled by a PC.

These receivers have no physical controls, so only computers can operate them. Marrying short-wave receivers to PCs allows the performance of each to enhance the capabilities of the other. Yet, benefits are offset by drawbacks, such as convoluted hardware configurations and radio interference from PC hardware—monitors and cables are prime culprits. Professional receiving facilities are set up to avoid these issues, but for a person at home it's a lot tougher.

Sales reflect this. Although proponents of PC-controlled receivers are enthusiastic and voluble, especially on the Internet, there appears to be far more smoke than fire. Reliable industry sources report that actual sales levels have been consistently modest following the initial months after product introduction.

Capable of DRM Reception

For the moment, however, some PC receivers offer a special advantage over conventional models: reception of Digital Radio Mondiale (DRM) world band broadcasts, which will be increasingly offered over the coming months. These receivers need add-ons for DRM, but if you want a pioneering taste of advanced technology they can put you at the leading edge before DRM-ready portables appear. DRM may or may not succeed, but even if it ultimately joins quadrophonic sound and AM stereo in the historical junk heap, your receiver will still give top-drawer reception of traditional world band signals.

PASSPORT's tests have unearthed two offerings that excel with world band and can adapted to receive DRM: the surprising new WiNRADiO G303i and the bargain-priced Ten-Tec RX-320D. The three-star Icom IC-PCR1000 also works as a VHF+ scanner, making it an attractive value for broad-spectrum monitors. The WiNRADiO 1500e, once around the equivalent of $600 world-wide, has been replaced by the similar but reportedly slightly improved 1550e. The 1500e performed better as a scanner than as a world band receiver, and thus was given only a two-star rating in prior editions of PASSPORT REPORTS.

Remember, though, that no matter how carefully a PC receiver is tested its performance depends to some degree upon the individual PC. This increases the odds that you'll encounter an unwelcome surprise, so it's always best to purchase on a fully returnable basis.

Accurate time? PC receiver clocks derive their data from PC clocks, which are notoriously inaccurate. A good remedy is About Time, free from www.arachnoid.com/abouttime/index.html. Over the years we have found it to be stable with Windows NT, 2000 and XP.

Our tests take place in a Windows environment, as that's where PC receivers are oriented. If you're using Mac or Linux, check manufacturers' websites for the latest on non-Windows operating software.

New for 2004

✪✪✪✪ ❷ *Passport's Choice*
WiNRADiO G303i
WiNRADiO G303i-PD/P

Price: *G303:* $499.95 in the United States. $789.00CAD in Canada. £440.00 (€508) in the United Kingdom. €645.00 in Germany. $995.00AUD in Australia. *G303i-PD/P:* $599.95 in the United States. $929.00CAD in Canada. £439.95 (€638) in the United Kingdom. €745 in Germany. $1,195.00AUD in Australia.

Pro: Plug and play aids installation. Once receiver is installed, the included software loads without problem; easily installed software updates available for free from manufacturer's Website, and third-party

Until now, WiNRADiO's PC receivers were disappointing world band performers. That's all changed with the G303i, new for 2004.

Here, the WiNRADiO G303i looks like a "real" receiver, but it is actually a PC screen image.

software can be developed. Optional plug-in being developed to allow for reception of digital (DRM) world band broadcasts. Superb stability, almost unexcelled. Tunes and displays in ultra-precise 1 Hz increments. A thousand station presets which can be clustered into any of 16 groups (see Con—Other). Excellent shape factors (1:1.6, 1:1.8) for 5.0 kHz and 3.2 kHz bandwidths aid selectivity/adjacent-channel rejection; 1.8 kHz bandwidth measures with good shape factor (1:2.3); additional bandwidths available in the PD/P version perform similarly. Excellent shortwave sensitivity (0.21 µV)/noise floor (-130 dBm), good mediumwave AM and longwave sensitivity (0.4 µV)/noise floor (-125 dBm). Potentially excellent audio quality (see below). Excellent dynamic range (90 dB) and third-order intercept point (+5 dBm) at 20 kHz signal separation points (see Con—Other). Phase noise excellent (see Con—Other). Image rejection excellent. Spurious signals essentially absent. Screen, and operation in general, unusually pleasant and intuitive. Single-sideband performance generally excellent (see Con—AGC/AVC). AGC fast, medium, slow and off. Spectrum display shows real-time signal activity, performs commendably and in particular provides signal strength readings to within plus or minus 3 dB. Spectrum scope sweeps between two user-chosen frequencies, displays the output while receiver mutes, then a mouse click can select a desired "peak"; it works quickly and well, and when the step size is set to small (e.g., 1 kHz),

resolution is excellent and quite useful. Large signal-strength indicator highly accurate, as good as we've ever tested; display is both numeric and a digitized "analog meter"; reads out as "S" meter, in dBm or in microvolts. Two easy-to-read on-screen clocks for World Time and local time, display seconds numerically, as well as date (see Con—Other). Superior and timely free factory assistance via email, seemingly seven days a week. *G303i-PD/P:* Continuously adjustable bandwidths from 1Hz to 15 kHz (single sideband/ECSS 1 Hz to 7.5 kHz), with bandwidth presets, aid greatly in providing optimum tradeoff between audio fidelity and adjacent-channel interference rejection. AVC settings, limited to "on-off" in standard version, allow for control over decay and attack times. Improved audio quality in some test configurations. Demodulates ISB signals used by a small proportion of utility stations. SINAD and THD indicators. AF squelch for FM mode.

Pro/Con—Sound: Outstanding freedom from distortion aids in providing good audio quality with appropriate sound cards/chips and speakers; sound quality and level can run the gamut from excellent to awful, depending on the PC's sound card or chipset, which needs to be full duplex. Sound Blaster 16 cards are recommended by manufacturer, but not all models work. During our tests the $130 Sound Blaster Audigy 2 performed with considerable distortion—it doesn't offer full duplex operation for the line input—whereas the $43 Sound Blaster PCI 512 worked splendidly. (ISA sound cards perform terribly; quite sensibly, these are not recommended by the manufacturer.) All input settings for the audio card need to be carefully set to match the settings within the receiver's software. If wrong, there may be no audio or it may be grossly distorted. Indeed, a sound card isn't always necessary, as some sound chipsets commonly found within PCs produce excellent audio with the G303i. Another reason the chipset may be preferable is that Sound Blaster manuals recommend that if there is an audio chipset on the motherboard, it first be disabled in the BIOS and all related software uninstalled—potentially a Maalox Moment. However, even with a suitable board or chipset installed, the user must carefully set the AGC and AVC (automatic volume control, termed "Audio AGC" on the G303i) for distortion-free audio. Powerful amplified speakers provide room-filling sound and allow the AVC to be kept off, thus reducing band noise that can be intrusive when it is on.

Con—AGC/AVC: Weak-signal reception can be compromised by the AGC, which "sees" 10-15 kHz of spectrum within the IF upon which to act. So, if an adjacent world band channel signal is 20 dB or more stronger than a desired weak signal, the AGC's action tends to cause the adjacent signal to mask the desired signal. Inadequate gain with the AVC ("Audio AGC") off, but the aggressive AVC adds listening strain with single-sideband signals, as it tends to increase band noise between words or other modulation peaks. Powerful outboard amplified speakers help reduce the need for the additional audio gain brought about by the AVC and thus are desirable, but be prepared for jumps in volume when you tune to strong stations. Reception sometimes further improves if the AGC is switched off and IF gain is manually decreased, but the operator then has to "ride" the volume control to smooth out major fluctuations. Manual ECSS tuning frequently helps, too. During moments of transient overload, the AVC can contribute to the creation of leading-edge "pops" with powerful signals (slightly more noticeable in the PD/P version). Single-sideband performance, particularly within crowded amateur bands, can be even more audibly compromised by the aforementioned out-of-passband AGC action. Dynamic range/IP3 at 5 kHz signal separation points couldn't be measured with AGC on, as test signals trigger the AGC and keep the receiver from going into

overload; measurement with the AGC off resulted in exceptionally poor numbers (45 db/-62 dBm). Phase noise poor when measured close-in for the same reason.

Con—Other: No outboard version available; requires installation within a vacant PCI card slot inside computer. No synchronous selectable sideband, and double-sideband "AMS" mode loses lock easily. First IF rejection only fair. Front-end selectivity, although adequate for most uses, could be better. Station presets ("memory channels") store only frequency and mode, not bandwidth, AGC or attenuation settings. No passband offset or tunable notch filter. Emits a pop-screech sound when first brought up or when switching from standard to professional demodulator. Uses only SMA antenna connection, typically found on handheld devices rather than tabletop receivers; an SMA-to-BNC adapter is included, but for the many shortwave antennas with neither type of plug a second adaptor or changed plug is needed. World Time clock tied into computer's clock, which may not be accurate without periodic adjustment. On our sample, country of manufacture not found on receiver, box or enclosed printed matter. Erratum sheet suggests that a discone antenna be used; this is fine for reception above roughly 25 MHz; however, in our tests we confirmed that conventional shortwave antennas provide much broader frequency coverage with the G303i, just as they do with other shortwave receivers.

☞ Minimum of 1 GHz Pentium recommended by manufacturer, although in the process of checking this out we obtained acceptable results using 400 MHz and 500 MHz Pentium II with Windows 2000—provided your PC is not multitasking, in which case 2 GHz or more helps keep the PC from bogging down. Primary testing was done using various desktop Pentium IV PCs at 1.5-2.4 GHz, 256-512 MHz RAM and Windows 2000, XP-Home and XP-Pro operating systems. WiNRADiO operating software used during tests were v1.07, v1.14, v1.25 and v1.26.

Verdict: The G303i is a vast improvement in shortwave performance over WiNRADiO wide-spectrum models we have tested to date. Overall, it is the best among PC receivers tested, especially in the highly desirable Professional Demodulator version. It can also be configured for reception of DRM digital broadcast signals, and is a pleasure to operate.

The G303i provides laboratory-quality spectrum displays and signal-strength indication. These spectrum-data functions are top drawer, regardless of price or type of receiver, and that's just the beginning of things done well. The few significant warts: AGC/AVC behavior, possible audio hassles during installation, and the absence of synchronous selectable sideband.

Nevertheless, WiNRADiO's G303i is currently the *ne plus ultra* in PC receivers for world band reception. For serious spectrum monitoring, it may be as good as it gets.

Evaluation of New Model: WiNRADiO models we have tested in the past have showed marked deficiencies, even allowing for their broadband design. So it was a pleasant surprise to find that their new

NUMBERS: TOP PC RECEIVERS

	WiNRADiO G303i	Ten-Tec RX-320D
Max. WB Sensitivity	0.21 μV	0.31 to 0.7 μV **E**-**F**[1]
Noise Floor, WB	-130 dBm **E**	-126 to -119 dBm **G**-**F**[2]
Blocking	120 dB **G**	>146 dB **S**
Shape Factors, voice BWs	1:1.6 **E**-1:2.4 **G**	n/a[3]
Ultimate Rejection	70 dB **G**	60 dB **G**
Front-End Selectivity	**G**	**F**
Image Rejection	85 dB **E**	60 dB **G**
First IF Rejection	52 dB **F**	60 dB **G**
Dynamic Range/IP3 (5 kHz)	45 dB **P**/-62 dBm **P**	n/a[3]
Dynamic Range/IP3 (20 kHz)	90 dB **E**/+5 dBm **E**	n/a[3]
Phase Noise	124 dBc **E**[4]	106 dBc **F**
AGC Threshold	2.7 to 8.0 μV **G**-**P**	4.0 μV **G**
Overall Distortion, voice	<1.0% **S**	<1% **S**
Stability	5 Hz, **S**	80 Hz, **G**
Notch filter depth	n/a	n/a

(1) Excellent 60 meters and up.
(2) Good 60 meters and up.
(3) Could not be measured accurately because of synthesizer noise and spurious signals, but appears to be very good.
(4) Worse at close-in measurement.

IBS Lab Ratings: Superb   Excellent   Good Fair   Poor

G303i wasn't an also-ran. Instead, it has turned out to be the class valedictorian.

For starters, WiNRADiO engineered the G303i to function only below 30 MHz. This opened the way to a high-performance design at an affordable price, even if the VHF-and-above scanner market had to be foregone. Next, they attended to the many points large and small that, when pulled together, can make or break a receiver. The end result is a clear winner, the best of the PC receiver offerings.

The G303i comes only as a plug-in internal card, thus the "I" designation; no outboard variation is offered. Plug-and-play installation is straightforward, and software updates are easily downloaded from the manufacturer's Website. The only potential pitfall during installation is with audio (see Pro/Con—Sound).

Sensible Operation, Great Scope

Once the receiver is successfully installed, it is a honey to operate. The operating screen is agreeably ergonomic, and includes one of the best signal-strength indicators we've come across. There's also an excellent real-time spectrum display, which also includes a "spectrum scope" function to sweep between two chosen frequencies. So many receivers have spectrum displays with serious compromises, but not here. For example, the G303i's spectrum scope signal-strength readings have gnat's-hair accuracy, within 3 dB from -30 dBm to -100 dBm. It actually displays an 80 dB range, which is state of the art. The large signal-strength indicator is similarly spot-on—and when is the last time you have come across one that reads out both numerically and as a (digitized) meter...and displays in "S" units, dBm or microvolts? It just doesn't get any better than this.

Among other goodies are two clocks with dates and numeric seconds, and a thousand station presets. In the regular version there are four voice bandwidths, but the Professional Demodulator incarnation offers a continuous range of bandwidths anywhere between 1 Hz and 15 kHz (7.5 kHz for single-sideband signals). That PD version, sometimes labeled simply as "P," has other virtues (see Pro), including sophisticated control over AGC action—important, given the nature of this receiver's AGC. The PD/P version is around twenty percent more, but it makes for such an improvement that none of our test panel could imagine opting for the bareback offering.

Yet, even the PD/P version doesn't have synchronous selectable sideband, and the receiver's synchronous double sideband (AMS) loses lock with disconcerting ease. Manual ECSS works well as a fallback, even if it is less handy and inherently has a degree of phase mismatch.

Weak-signal sensitivity, ultimate selectivity, wide dynamic range, phase noise, blocking, stability and overall distortion all measure good or better in our lab, and are confirmed by thankful ears.

Unusual AGC/AVC Combination

However, front-end selectivity is only fair, and some aspects of receiver design result in odd AGC threshold measurements and poor close-in dynamic range and phase noise readings (otherwise, phase noise is excellent).

Why? The wide up-conversion filter allows the AGC to act not only on the desired signal, but also on nearby signals. Depending on reception circumstances and the PC's audio configuration, as well as how judiciously the receiver is operated, this can result in low audio, excessive hiss, distortion, or reduced intelligibility of weak signals. Fortunately, this is primarily an issue with single-sideband signals within crowded amateur bands. With world band the impact is more subtle, especially if powerful amplified outboard PC speakers are used; for example:

WiNRADiO also makes outboard models with broadband coverage.

Presumably to make up for the suboptimal AGC, the G303i comes with what it calls "Audio AGC," but which old timers will recall as AVC, or automatic volume control. AVC faded from use decades ago because it acts too late in a radio's circuitry to provide best results, and the WiNRADiO's AVC is no exception. With the AVC off, the G303i's's audio is weak, but this can be somewhat circumvented by feeding the PC's audio to genuinely powerful outboard amplified speakers—not those dinky things you got for free with your last PC. This allows the AVC to be kept off most of the time, and/or for the AGC to be turned off and the manual IF gain throttled back to maximize reception quality.

Still, for weak signals it can become a Hobson's choice. Leave off the AVC, and you may not hear useful audio from a given weak signal. Turn on the AVC, and band noise rises between words on single-sideband signals; in the AM mode, used for world band, the problem is similar but much less pronounced. Either way, the AVC exaggerates background band noise, especially static, during pauses in modulation. As the G303i is so lacking in gain with signals weaker than S7, there is often little choice but to turn on the AVC and live with its aggressive effects. Fortunately, in the PD/P version the slow AVC can be increased from a nominal default value of four seconds to nine seconds, which to our ears

is an improvement. (For the record, however WiNRADiO measures these seconds, the actual time constants appear to be much shorter than nominal.)

Thus, operator patience, skill and experience can reduce this problem. But for world band DXing and the reception of hams, the AGC/AVC configuration is the G303i's Achilles' heel.

A possible solution put forth to us by Sherwood Engineering is the installation of an internal DSP chip within the G303i. The final filtering and detection of the 12 kHz final IF would be internal to the radio card. This would free the receiver from having to rely on the PC's sound card or chip for anything other than audio amplification.

Thus, the receiver's one major flaw—the AGC's not operating on the DSP-filtered final IF—would be ended. The messy AVC circuit would be eliminated altogether, and the radio would be simpler to operate. If this were the case and worthy synchronous selectable sideband were incorporated, the G303i could be one of the best available receivers of any type, not just the best PC radio.

DRM to Use Plug-in

With the receiver installed, and after you've become familiar with its one notable shortcoming, you're ready to rock 'n' roll—and not just with traditional world band signals. World band broadcasts using the Digital Radio Mondiale system are now beginning to appear and will soon be audible worldwide. No consumer radios yet exist that can receive these, but a plug-in is being engineered by WiNRADiO that is to allow the G303i to receive DRM transmissions.

DRM may or may not succeed. Yet, even if it doesn't you will have been able to partake of a piece of radio history. And your receiver will still be able to do yeoman's duty with conventional analog signals.

Enhanced for 2004

✪✪✪ ☺ *Passport's Choice*
Ten-Tec RX-320D

Price: *RX-320D:* $320.00 plus shipping worldwide. *DRM software:* €60.00 worldwide from www.drmrx.org/purchase.php. *Third-party control software:* Free-$99 worldwide.

Pro: The "D" version's 12 kHz IF output allows the receiver to receive digital (DRM) world band broadcasts by using DRM software purchased separately from Germany. Superior dynamic range. Apparently superb bandwidth shape factors (*see* Con). In addition to the supplied factory control software, third-party software is available, often for free, and may improve operation. Up to 34 bandwidths with third-party software. Tunes in extremely precise 1 Hz increments (10 Hz with tested factory software); displays to the nearest Hertz, and frequency readout is easily user-aligned. Large, easy-to-read digital frequency display and faux-analog frequency bar. For PCs with sound cards, outstanding freedom from distortion aids in providing good audio quality with most but not all cards and speakers. Fairly good audio, but with limited treble, also available through radio for PCs without sound cards. Superb blocking performance helps maintain consistently good world band sensitivity. Passband offset (*see* Con). Spectrum display with wide variety of useful sweep widths (*see* Con). World Time on-screen clock (*see* Con). Adjustable AGC decay. Thousands of station presets, with first-rate memory configuration, access and sorting—including by station name and frequency. Only PC-controlled model tested which returns to last tuned frequency when PC turned off. Superior owner's manual. Outstanding factory help and repair support.

Con: No synchronous selectable sideband, although George Privalov's Control Panel Program now automates retuning of drifty

Ten-Tec's RX320D is DRM ready, with the necessary extra-cost software available from Germany.

AM-mode signals received as "ECSS." Some characteristic "DSP roughness" in the audio under certain reception conditions. Synthesizer phase noise measures only fair; among the consequences are that bandwidth shape factors cannot be measured exactly. Some tuning ergonomics only fair as compared with certain standalone receivers. No tunable notch filter. Passband offset doesn't function in AM mode. Signal-strength indicator, calibrated 0-80, too sensitive, reading 20 with no antenna connected and 30 with only band noise being received. Mediocre front-end selectivity can allow powerful mediumwave AM stations to "ghost" into the shortwave spectrum, thus degrading reception of world band stations. Uses AC adaptor instead of built-in power supply. Spectrum display does not function with some third-party software and is only a so-so performer. Mediumwave AM reception below 1 MHz suffers from reduced sensitivity, and longwave sensitivity is atrocious. No internal speaker on outboard receiver module. World Time clock tied into computer's clock, which may not be accurate without periodic adjustment. Almost no retail sources outside the United States.

☞ PASSPORT's four-star rating is for the RX-320D with third-party control software. With factory software the rating is slightly lower.

Verdict: The American-made Ten-Tec RX-320D is one of the best non-professional PC receivers, yet even with DRM software it not much more costly than some portables. It is also less chancy to install to full operating advantage than is the top-rated WiNRADiO G303i.

✪✪✪
Icom IC-PCR1000

Price: *IC-PCR1000:* $399.95 in the United States. $799.00CAD in Canada. £319.95 in the United Kingdom. $977.00AUD in Australia. €449.00 in Germany. *UT-106 DSP Unit:* $139.95 in the United States. £82.00 in the United Kingdom. US$175 in Australia.

Pro: Wideband frequency coverage. Spectrum display with many useful sweep widths for shortwave, as well as good real-time performance. Tunes and displays in extremely precise 1 Hz increments. Comes with reasonably performing control software (*see* Con). Excellent sensitivity to weak signals. AGC, adjustable, performs well in AM and single-sideband modes. Nineteen banks of 50 memories each, with potential for virtually unlimited number of memories. Passband offset (*see* Con). Powerful audio with good weak-signal readability and little distortion (*see* Con).

Con: Poor dynamic range. Audio quality, not pleasant, made worse by presence of circuit hiss. No line output to feed PC sound card and speakers, so no alternative to using receiver's audio. No synchronous selectable sideband. Only two AM-mode bandwidths—8.7 kHz (nominal 6 kHz) and 2.4 kHz (nominal 3 kHz)—both with uninspiring shape factors. Synthesizer phase noise, although not measurable, appears to be only fair; among the effects of this are that bandwidth shape factors cannot be exactly measured. Mediocre blocking slightly limits weak-signal sensitivity when frequency segment contains powerful signals. Tuning ergonomics only fair as compared with some standalone receivers. Automatic tunable notch filter with DSP audio processing (UT-106, not tested) an extra-cost option. Lacks passband offset in AM mode. Uses AC adaptor instead of built-in power supply. Spectrum display mutes audio when single-sideband or CW signal being received. No clock. Mediocre inboard speaker, remediable by using outboard speaker. Sparse owner's manual.

☞ Icom has been known to include Bonito RadioCom software with "select packages" of the 'PCR1000. This nominally provides more flexible audio shaping and the ability to record programs onto hard drive.

Verdict: Among tested PC-controlled receivers, the Japanese-made Icom IC-PCR1000 is the most appropriate for wideband frequency coverage. Its spectrum display is worthy, as well.

Icom's IC-PCR1000 is the least costly way to obtain worthwhile broadband reception.

Robert Sherwood and David Zantow, with Lawrence Magne and Chuck Rippel; also, Craig Tyson.

WHERE TO FIND THE INDEX TO TESTED RADIOS

PASSPORT REPORTS evaluates nearly every digitally tuned receiver on the market. Here's where they are found, with those that are new, forthcoming, revised, rebranded or retested in **bold**.

Comprehensive PASSPORT® Radio Database International White Papers® are available for the many popular premium receivers. Each RDI White Paper®—$6.95 in North America, $9.95 airmail elsewhere, including shipping—contains virtually all our panel's findings and comments during hands-on testing, as well as laboratory measurements and what these mean to you. These unabridged reports are available from key world band dealers, or you can contact our 24-hour VISA/MC order channels (www.passband.com, autovoice +1 215/598-9018, fax +1 215/598 3794), or write us at PASSPORT RDI White Papers, Box 300, Penn's Park, PA 18943 USA.

▤ *Radio Database International White Paper® available.*

Passive Antennas: Overhead Champs

World band radio's appeal includes unfettered reception without wires. War or peace, censorship or freedom—it's always there. Yet, for the best in world band performance an outdoor antenna helps, and most are made from . . . wires.

Not just any old wires. If you spring for a serious outdoor antenna:

- Match it to the type of receiver—simple antennas for simple por-

tables, sophisticated antennas for sophisticated tabletops.

- Purchase the best of the type you want—price differences among similar antennas are small.

- Erect it—preferably outdoors—safely and for best performance.

Goal: To Improve Signal-to-Noise

A properly erected outdoor antenna almost always helps with

weaker signals by providing more signal and overcoming local electrical noises and receiver circuit noise. The result—more signal, less noise—is an improvement in the signal-to-noise ratio.

This is essential, as more signal strength means little if background noise also goes up. Noise can be from local sources—appliances, fluorescent lights, computers, dimmers and the like—as well as from "hiss" and other noise generated within your receiver.

Antennas Don't Always Help

It's no surprise that stations already booming in aren't going to do much better with an improved antenna. Your receiver's signal-strength indicator may read higher, but its automatic-gain control (AGC) ensures that what you hear isn't going to sound much different than it does with your existing antenna.

If you are using an everyday portable, forget sophisticated antennas—outdoor or indoor, passive or active. Make do with the radio's built-in telescopic antenna, or for more oomph use a simple inverted-L wire outdoor antenna (see below) or the Sony AN-LP1 active loop reviewed in PASSPORT REPORTS' coverage of active antennas.

At the other extreme, tabletop receivers usually don't even come with built-in antennas, as proximate antennas—those on or near the receiver—can't cut the mustard. A first-rate remote outboard antenna is as essential to elite receivers as high-octane fuel is to a Maserati.

Inverted-L Alternatives

What about inverted-L antennas, sometimes referred to as "longwires"? They are simple and inexpensive, and for most radios they provide excellent results, even doing reasonably well on mediumwave AM.

Simple inverted-L antennas of moderate length are available at radio stores—these usually rate three stars, sometimes four, but they're much too short to qualify as genuine longwires. Among the available inverted-L antennas in the United States is Radio Shack's ten-buck Outdoor Antenna Kit (278-758) with wire, insulators and other goodies, plus loose change for a claw/alligator clip or other connector.

That's if you want basic. World band specialty stores in North America, the European Union, Australasia and beyond stock inverted-L antennas and components made from higher-quality materials. They are priced accordingly; for example, £25.95 (€38) in the United Kingdom for the Watson SWL Long Wire Antenna Kit.

At full length, an inverted-L antenna can be too long for some portables, causing overloading from hefty incoming signals. Experiment, but as a rough rule of thumb the less costly the portable, the shorter an inverted-L antenna should be. However, unlike other antenna types the inverted-L may be readily shortened to avoid overloading, or just to shoehorn it into a yard.

Homemade versions, detailed in the RDI White Paper on outdoor antennas, can run over 200 feet, or 60 meters—world band and amateur radio vendors usually sell the necessary specialized parts. These long inverted-L antennas can perform as well with tabletop receivers as the Alpha Delta DX-Ultra, sometimes better because their enormous capture wavelength tends to improve the signal-to-noise ratio. But they are a nightmare to keep erect during ice storms and other extremes of weather, and heavy ice can also stretch the wire and cause it to sag like Mother Sill's chest.

Unamplified vs. Amplified

Outboard antennas come in two flavors: unamplified or "passive" (typically outdoor), and amplified or "active" (indoor, outdoor or both).

An unamplified antenna consists of wire or another metal receiving element to provide a radio signal directly to the receiver. It has no electrical amplification.

An amplified or active antenna, on the other hand, typically uses a much shorter rod or wire receiving element, plus one or more stages of electrical amplification to make up for the relatively modest signal coming from the diminutive receiving element.

Amplified antennas are popular because they are compact—for apartments, ideal. Even some homeowners prefer them because they can be easy to erect and are relatively inconspicuous. A couple even outperform passive antennas with staticky tropical world band signals.

But amplified antennas, reviewed in this PASSPORT REPORTS, have four potential drawbacks. First, their short receiving elements usually don't provide the signal-to-noise enhancement that comes when longer elements are used. Second, the antenna's amplifier can generate noise of its own. Third, the antenna's amplifier can itself overload, with results comparable to those found when a receiver overloads . . . a mishmash of jumbled-sounding stations up and down the dial. Indeed, if the antenna amplifier's gain is excessive it can overload the receiver, making stations as incoherent as overloaded tipplers at Tillie's Tavern.

Finally, many amplified antennas have mediocre front-end selectivity, and thus are prone to commingling signals from local mediumwave AM broadcasters with those from world band radio stations. This makes them potentially bad news for the very urban areas in which apartment dwellers and powerful radio/TV signals coexist in close proximity.

Of course, if you're an apartment dweller with high-quality receiving gear, there is little choice—your antenna options are dictated by where you live. Unless you have access to a long roof or parcel of ground and the blessing of your landlord or tenants' association, you'll usually have to make do with an amplified antenna simply because there's no legitimate alternative.

Still, determined apartment dwellers have put their creative juices to full use with a wide variety of hidden or camouflaged outdoor wire antennas, such as "clotheslines." Or they have simply capitalized on urban apathy by erecting a thin-wire outdoor antenna, then seeing what happens. If one of these creative short-wire antennas is feeding a tabletop receiver, results are enhanced if it is mated to the $79.95 MFJ-1020C reviewed in the next chapter.

If you want something similarly James Bondish but ready-to-go, the SGC Stealth Antenna Kit (not tested) can be had for a mere £349.95 (€510 or $555) in the United Kingdom when on special sale, £489.00 (€715 or $780) when it's not. Aston-Martin and blonde are extra.

Protection During Storms

An effective static protector is essential during nearby thunderstorms, windy snowfalls and sandstorms. These generate static charges, sparks that can be strong enough to send your radio to the repair shop. Among the best static protectors, or lightning arrestors, are those made by Alpha Delta Communications.

Of course, it's a good idea to have a surge arrestor on your receiver's power line, too, just as with a PC.

Installation Basics

As an incidental effect of the lobbying of the American Radio Relay League and other radio organizations, Americans are unlikely to encounter legal prohibitions on erecting world band antennas. However, covenants or deed restrictions, increasingly common in gated communities, may limit what you can do. In general, though, the rule of reason applies: Outdoor wire antennas should be neither unsightly nor particularly visible. If you want to annoy neighbors, put out pink flamingos.

Most antennas are robustly constructed to withstand ice buildup during storms. However, those which require guying need hardware comparable in strength to that of the antenna. Also consider using a pair of bungee straps at the antenna's ends to provide elasticity in the event of heavy ice buildup.

Performance Freebie

Antenna location is one of the quiet little secrets of world band radio. An antenna erected out in the fresh air—high up, away from electrical lines, communications cables and other sources of noise—improves the "noise" portion of the signal-to-noise ratio, and it doesn't cost a dime extra. Emerging digital technologies are creating so much RF pollution that antenna location should become even more important in coming years.

You wouldn't bathe in dirty water, so don't place your antenna where it is electrically "dirty."

Fry Chickens, Not Yourself

Safety is paramount during installation, especially to avoid falls or making contact with potentially lethal electrical utility and other lines. The job should be well-done, not you.

There's much more to this than we can cover here, but it's detailed in the RADIO DATABASE INTERNATIONAL report, *Evaluation of Popular Outdoor Antennas*. Also, check out www.universal-radio.com/catalog/sw_ant/safeswl.html.

Which Are Best?

For that RDI White Paper, we tested a number of popular outdoor wire antennas for shortwave listening, and three are summarized here. All are dipoles, most of which rely on traps for frequency resonance. Three mounting layouts are used:

- End-fed sloper, with the antenna pitched about 30 degrees from horizontal.
- Center-fed tapered wing, with a tall (about 20 feet or 6 meters) mounting amidships and two end mountings which are lower.
- Center-fed horizontal, hung between two points of comparable height.

Passive antennas are among the most difficult devices to evaluate properly. For starters, quality of reception is frequency-dependent, so any overall rating is only a generalization. Also, performance depends on how well an antenna is erected, and even the type of soil, moisture and bedrock immediately underneath.

So, don't be afraid to experiment by "rolling your own" or buying something that, tests be damned, you feel might do unusually well at your location. After all, there are numerous designs on the market, and what's offered varies markedly by country. Thankfully, most are affordable enough to experiment with.

Indeed, in the real world of tradeoffs and compromises the determining factor may simply be yard space. Consider, too, that some antennas are almost kits, while others come ready to erect. Do you have the time or patience for the former?

Star Ratings

PASSPORT'S star ratings mean the same thing regardless of whether an antenna is active or passive. This is to help you compare a passive antenna with an active antenna, or *vice versa*.

✪✪✪✪¾ *Passport's Choice*
Alpha Delta DX-Ultra

Price: $119.95 in the United States. $200.00CAD in Canada. Coaxial cable extra.

Pro: Best overall performer of any antenna tested, passive or active. Little variation in performance from one world band segment to another. Rugged construction. Comes with built-in static protection. Wing design appropriate for certain yard layouts. Covers mediumwave AM band.

Con: Assembly a major undertaking, with stiff wire having to be bent and fed through spacer holes, then affixed. Unusually lengthy,

The Alpha Delta DX-Ultra antenna is a chore to assemble and erect. Yet, once it's installed it holds up like the Pyramids.

80 feet or 25 meters. Coaxial cable lead-in not included. Relatively heavy, adding to erection effort. Warranty only six months.

Verdict: The Alpha Delta DX-Ultra rewards sweat equity—it is really more of a kit than a finished product. First, you have to purchase the needed lead-in cable and other hardware bits, then assemble, bend and stretch the many stiff wires, section-by-section.

Because the wire used should outlast the Pyramids, assembly is a trying and unforgiving exercise. Each wire needs to be rigorously and properly affixed, lest it slip loose and the erected antenna comes tumbling down, as it did at one of our test sites.

While all outdoor antennas require yard space, the Ultra is the longest manufactured antenna tested. It is also relatively heavy, making installation an even more tiresome chore than it already is. In ice-prone climates, be sure any trees or poles attached to the antenna are sturdy.

But if you have the yard space and don't object to leaping assembly and erection hurdles, you are rewarded with a robust antenna that is outperformed only by hugely long inverted-L antennas and professional-grade antennas beyond the financial reach of even the most enthusiastic listener.

✪✪✪✪½ *Passport's Choice*
Alpha Delta DX-SWL Sloper

Price: $79.95 in the United States. $135.00CAD in Canada. Coaxial cable and static protector extra.

Pro: Rugged construction. Sloper design uses traps to keep the length down to 60 feet (18 meters), make it suitable for certain yard layouts. Covers mediumwave AM band.

Con: Requires assembly, a significant exercise. Does not include static protection. Coaxial cable lead-in not included. Warranty only six months.

☞ A greatly shortened version, the 40-foot (12 meter) DX-SWL-S (not tested), is available for $69.95, with coaxial cable and static protector extra. Its nominal coverage is 3.2-22 MHz, omitting the little-used 2 MHz (120 meter) world band segment. Although both Sloper versions nominally don't cover the 25 MHz (11 meter) world band segment, our measurements of the full-length Sloper show excellent results there (25650-26100 kHz).

Verdict: An excellent choice where space is limited, but a chore to assemble.

Alpha Delta's DX-SWL Sloper requires only one high spot.

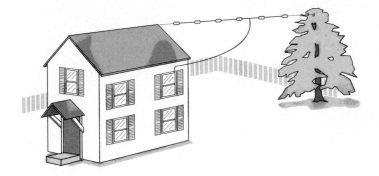

The Eavesdropper Model T comes fully assembled, with everything needed for erection and lightning protection.

✪✪✪✪⅛ *Passport's Choice*
Eavesdropper Model T, Eavesdropper Model C

Price: *Model T:* $89.95, complete, in the United States. *Model C:* $89.95 in the United States. Coaxial cable extra.

Pro: Unusually compact at 43 feet or 13 meters, it fits into many yards. Comes with built-in static protection. One-year warranty, after which repairs made "at nominal cost." *Model T:* Easiest to install of any Passport's Choice antenna—unpack, and it's ready to hang. Comes with ribbon lead-in wire, which tends to have less signal loss than coaxial cable. *Model C:* Easier than most to install, with virtually everything included and assembled but the coaxial cable lead-in.

Con: Some performance drop within the 2 MHz (120 meter) and 3 MHz (90 meter) tropical world band segments. *Model C:* Coaxial cable lead-in not included.

☞ Eavesdropper also makes the $89.95 sloper antenna, not tested by us, similar to the Alpha Delta DX-SWL Sloper. It comes with a static arrestor, but no coaxial cable lead-in.

Verdict: If your teeth gnash when you see packages saying, "Some Assembly Required," take heart. The Eavesdropper T, unlike the Alpha Delta alternatives, comes "ready to go" and is straightforward to erect. At most, you might want to get a pair of bungee straps to provide storm flexibility at the ends.

The size is user-friendly, too. There's no getting around the rule that the longer the antenna, the more likely it is to do well at low frequencies. However, the Eavesdropper's original designer, the late Jim Meadow, told PASSPORT some years back that their research showed little tuning taking place below 4.7 MHz, while on the other hand many folks had problems with yard space, or just wanted a shorter antenna less likely to come down in an ice storm. So, he designed the Eavesdropper to be relatively compact, yet perform optimally above 4.7 MHz while still doing decent service lower down.

Our tests confirm this. The Eavesdropper horizontal trap dipoles perform quite nicely above 4.7 MHz, with a notch less gain than Alpha-Delta models in the 2 MHz and 3 MHz tropical world band segments.

In practice the ribbon lead-in wire used by the T version works very well, using phasing to cancel out much electrical noise. Too, it stands up to the weather and usually has less signal loss than the coaxial cable used by its C sibling, which is preferable only when significant electrical noise is near the feedline.

Otherwise, the T version should get the nod.

Prepared by Stephen Bohac, Jock Elliott, Tony Jones, Lawrence Magne and David Walcutt.

Active Antennas: Where Space Is Limited

Whether you listen by day, when signals are weaker, or just enjoy flushing out tough catches, a good outboard antenna can make all the difference. Trouble is, the most effective world band antennas are passive—unamplified—and require yard space. If you have little or no room outdoors, or are in an apartment or hotel, something else is needed.

That "something" is an active antenna. These include a small "whip" or loop, or a short wire—the receiving element—to snare signals from the airwaves. But because these elements are not lengthy, signals they feed to the receiver tend to be weak. If something weren't done to overcome this, it would be like powering an F-150 with a golf cart engine.

Active antennas resolve this by electrically amplifying signals before they get to the receiver. Although a lengthy passive wire antenna has inherent advantages, compact active antennas can do a surprisingly good job. The challenge is to sort out winners from losers.

Improved Performance

Active antennas used to be considered strictly as also-rans. Pioneering models were noisy, overloaded easily, generated harmonic "false" signals and suffered from the ravages of outdoor use. They quickly earned a reputation for failing to deliver what serious listeners demanded.

In recent years, and again for 2004, this has been changing for the better—the introduction of robust, well-engineered models has altered the game considerably. While none yet equals a proper outdoor wire antenna, the gap has closed considerably. Indeed, one manufacturer's offerings can outperform passive wire antennas in lower frequencies during high-static months.

Testing has been limited to antennas likely to perform satisfactorily under a wide range of circumstances. In addition to these tested models, there are elementary amplified antennas for portables available at low cost from various vendors. In general, the weaker the overall signal strengths at your location, the greater the chances these rudimentary offerings may meet your needs.

> **Active antennas used to be also-rans, but no more.**

Proximate vs. Remote

Active antennas are either proximate or remote. A proximate model requires that the receiving element be located very near the receiver, as it is mounted on a control box close to the radio. Remote models allow the receiving element to be placed some distance away—either indoors or, with some models, outdoors where reception is superior.

Remote units are almost always the better bet, as they allow a receiving element to be placed where electrical noise is low and incoming

For the ultimate in mediumwave AM DX, mount a Wellbrook ALA 1530 antenna atop a rotor. This Yaesu G-5550 is best, as it tilts and rotates to optimize the desired station while rejecting others.

Photos: pp. 189–191 Chuck Rippel; pp. 193, 195–204 Robert Sherwood.

signals are strong. Proximate models give you no choice unless you are willing to move the entire receiver to where reception happens to be optimum, which may not be a satisfactory place to listen.

If you choose a proximate model, remember that many radios put out some degree of electrical "hash," or noise. Typically, this racket radiates forward from the receiver's digital display, so it is best to locate a proximate antenna behind or to either side of the radio. These antennas are also more prone than remote varieties to pick up electrical noise from indoor devices that electronically pollute.

Loops Can Improve Signal-to-Noise Ratio

Proximate loop antennas, such as the AOR LA-350, and indoor-remote loops, such as the AOR WL500 and Sony AN-LP1, are less prone to pick up local electrical noise. For one thing, to varying degrees they can be aimed away from the source of any disruptive noise. Too, they are less likely to pick up atmospheric static from thunderstorms near and far. This can be a real plus, improving the signal-to-noise ratio considerably under the right circumstances, notably within lower frequency segments during the warmer months.

Wellbrook models, especially when placed outdoors, are particularly effective in this regard. In part that's because, unlike the unbalanced LA-350, they are balanced. During high-static summer months, their superior signal-to-noise ratios can make the difference between hearing a pileup of static crashes and copying readable DX.

Preselection vs. Broadband

Broadband electronic amplifiers have the potential for all sorts of mischief. Some add noise and spurious signals, especially from the mediumwave AM band; others may overload a receiver with too much gain.

Either way, this tends to be less of a problem at night because of reduced local transmitting powers.

A partial solution is to have effective tunable or switchable preselection. Preselection limits the band of frequencies which get full amplification, and in so doing reduces the odds of spurious signals being created by the antenna or the receiver. Preselectors with high "Q" also improve image rejection in some receivers.

Problem is, preselection adds to manufacturing cost. And because it usually requires manual tuning, it can increase operating complexity—although it doesn't have to. As indicated in our review of the Sony ICF-SW07 elsewhere in PASSPORT REPORTS, preselection can be automated if the antenna and receiver are designed to work together. So far only the 'SW07 can do this.

A simplified variant of preselection is to substantially reduce gain at frequencies below around two Megahertz with a high-pass filter, or within a given (mediumwave AM) frequency range with a band rejection filter. This is a great help in keeping powerful local mediumwave AM stations from disrupting world band reception.

How Much Is Too Much?

A natural tendency is to judge an active antenna by how much gain it provides, as shown on a receiver's signal-strength indicator. This can be misleading.

For one thing, with a first-rate receiver and passive outdoor wire antenna there is rarely any need for electrical gain between the antenna and receiver. In principle, a good active antenna should replicate that "natural" level of gain—or, better, the signal-to-noise ratio. Too little gain, then overall circuit noise appears, if only from the receiver. Too much gain and the receiver's dynamic range, and/or possibly that of the antenna's amplifier, is strained unnecessarily.

AC Can Cause Hum, Buzz

Active antennas work best when powered by battery. This eliminates all possibility of hum and buzzing caused, directly or indirectly, by an AC-to-DC power supply or adaptor. Problem is, using batteries is impractical with most models.

In some cases it helps, instead, to keep AC adaptors and cords as far as possible from an antenna's receiving element and feedline. However, to the extent hum results from power supply diodes not being properly bypassed, changing the location of the adaptor or its cords may not make any difference.

Steps You Can Take

Antenna performance is one part technology, one part geography-geology, and one part installation. This report covers the first, with tips on the third, but in the end all we can do is boost your odds of success. After all, much of the outcome depends on where you live and what you do once the antenna arrives.

WHERE TO INSTALL A REMOTE ANTENNA

The good news is that if a top-rated active antenna is installed properly, it can perform very well. The bad news is that if you have room outdoors to mount it optimally, you may also have room for a passive wire antenna that will perform better, yet. Probably cheaper, too.

Here are a few practical tips on placement of weather-resistant remote models. As always with antennas, creativity rules—don't be afraid to experiment.

- If you can mount your antenna's receiving element outdoors, try to do it in the clear, especially away from anything metal. Use a nonconductive mast or capped PVC pipe, as metal masts or pipes are likely to degrade performance. Optimum height from ground is usually around 10-25 feet or 3-8 meters, but keep in mind that "ground" refers to electrical ground, which includes non-wooden roofs and the like.

  If this is not feasible, try a nearby tree. This works less well because tree sap is electrically conductive, but is a reasonable fallback, especially with hardwood deciduous varieties. Ensure that leaves and branches can't brush against the antenna's receiving element under most weather conditions.

- If outdoor mounting is impractical, then have the receiving element protrude out into the fresh air as much as possible. Even if you are in a high-rise building, this can work so long as a window opens or there is a balcony. For example, if your antenna's receiving element is a whip, you can stick it away from the building 45 degrees or so, like a flag mast. If that is too visible, try using a string or rope to pull it up, out of view, by day.

  If you are in a house with an attic, especially if it has no foil-lined insulation along the pitched roof and assuming the roof is not metal, this can often work in lieu of an outdoor placement. Indeed, with the large Wellbrook models this is a tempting alternative to placement within a room, especially if a rotor is used.

- If all these choices are impractical, then at least place the receiving element up against a large window. Glass blocks signals much less than masonry or metal, or even insulation foil and aluminum siding.

Antenna location and installation details can make all the difference. Consider experimenting with different locations before doing a permanent setup, and if your receiver has multiple antenna inputs don't be afraid to see which work best.

Best for Portables: Travel Loops

Most active antennas are designed for use with tabletop models, but not all. The Sony AN-LP1, great for use at home and on trips, continues to be an exceptional value for use with nearly any portable, and is even more convenient in its 'LP2 incarnation mated to the 'SW-07 receiver. From late 2001 through mid-2003 the popular 'LP1 was in very short supply, but later in 2003 production apparently was increased substantially. The future is anybody's guess.

For 2004 there is a second choice, the AOR WL500. It's pricier and slightly less handy for trips than Sony's offering, but it performs slightly better.

Small Outdoor Area?

If you own a tabletop or portatop and don't have space outdoors for a full-fledged passive wire antenna—but have enough room for a short outdoor wire—consider the MFJ-1020C. It succeeds only modestly with its proximate built-in antenna. However, it does well as an active preselector when used with a short wire antenna, especially if the wire is placed outdoors. If this makes sense at your location, this combo can provide superior performance at an affordable price.

Best for Tabletops: Wellbrook Loops

The two tested Wellbrook models are among the least compact and are inconvenient to order, but they run away with PASSPORT's honors for use with tabletop

and portatop models. They outperform other active antennas under typical reception conditions, and they are in a league unto themselves during high-static reception.

What PASSPORT's Ratings Mean

Star ratings: ✪✪✪✪✪ is best for any type of antenna, but in reality even the best of active antennas don't yet merit more than four stars when compared against passive antennas. To help with in making a purchase decision, star ratings for active antennas may now be compared directly against those for passive antennas found elsewhere in this PASSPORT REPORTS. Stars reflect overall performance on shortwave and meaningful features, plus to some extent ergonomics and build quality. Price, appearance, country of manufacture and the like are not taken into account.

Passport's Choice. La crème de la crème. Our test team's personal picks of the litter—models we would buy or have bought for our personal use.

✿: A relative bargain, with decidedly more performance than the price would suggest.

Active antennas are listed in descending order of merit. Unless otherwise indicated each has a one-year warranty.

New for 2004
✪✪✪✪ *Passport's Choice*
Wellbrook ALA 330S

Remote, broadband, outdoor-indoor, 2.3-30 MHz

Price: *ALA 330S:* £189.95 plus £10.00 shipping in the United Kingdom and Eire. £189.95 plus £25.00 shipping elsewhere. *'330 to '330S Upgrade Kit:* £80.00 plus £5.00 shipping in the United Kingdom and Eire. £80.00 plus £15.00 shipping elsewhere.

Pro: Best signal-to-noise ratio, including at times reduced pickup of thunderstorm static, on all shortwave frequencies, of any active model tested; low-noise/low-static pickup characteristics most noticeable below 7.5 MHz, especially during local summer, when it sometimes outperforms sophisticated outdoor wire antennas. Balanced loop design inherently helps reduce pickup of local electrical noise; additionally, aluminum loop receiving element can be affixed to a low-cost TV rotor to improve reception by directionally nulling local electrical noise and, to a lesser degree, static. Sometimes, rotatability also can slightly reduce co-channel shortwave interference below about 5 MHz. Superior build quality, including rigorous weather-proofing (*see* Con). Supplied AC adaptor, properly bypassed and regulated, is among the best tested for not causing hum or buzzing. Although any large loop is inherently susceptible to inductive pickup of local thunderstorm static, during our tests the antenna's amplifier never suffered static damage during storms; indeed, even nearby one kilowatt shortwave transmissions have not damaged the antenna amplifier. Protected circuitry, using an easily replaced 315 mA slow-blow fuse. Threaded flange on "S" version improves mounting of loop receiving element (*see* Con).

Con: Only moderate gain for reception within such modest-signal areas as Western Hemisphere, Asia and Australasia—a drawback only with receivers having relatively noisy circuitry. Slightly less gain than ALA 1530 within little-used 2.3-2.5 MHz (120 meter) tropical world band segment, a drawback only with receivers having relatively noisy circuitry. Mediumwave AM coverage is possible, even though the antenna is designed only for shortwave; as expected, reception suffers from mediocre sensitivity, while longwave sensitivity is poor, being down around 25 dB compared to the '1530. Flange for loop receiving element has metric pipe thread-

The Wellbrook ALA 330S is an improvement over earlier versions. It's the best active antenna for world band, but is larger than most.

ing; most U.S. users will need to re-thread. Loop receiving element, about one meter across, is large and cumbersome to ship, although loop is slightly smaller than in the prior version. Mounting mast and optional rotor add to cost and complexity. BNC connector at the receiving element's base is open to the weather and thus needs to be user-sealed with Coax Seal, electrical putty or similar. Encapsulated amplifier makes repair impossible. Manufacturer cautions against allowing high winds to stress mounting flange, or sunlight to damage head amplifier; however, our penultimate unit survived 90+ mph Rocky Mountain winds until the pipe coupling to which we had attached the antenna snapped. Adaptor supplied for 117V AC runs hot after being plugged in for a few hours, while amplifier tends to run slightly warm. No coaxial cable supplied. Available for purchase or export only two cumbersome ways: via Sterling cheque or International Money Order through the English manufacturer (www.wellbrook.uk.com), or with credit card via an English dealer's unsecured email address (sales@shortwave.co.uk); however, as we go to press the "Shortwave Shop" Website (www.shortwave.co.uk) is under construction, so things may yet improve.

☞ A kit is available from the manufacturer in Wales to convert the earlier ALA 330 to the "S" version.

Verdict: The more we use this antenna, the more we like it, especially for its ability to reduce the impact of static and noise on weak signals below 7.5 MHz. For 2004 it is even slightly more effective at recovering audio from faint signals. If its dimensions and purchase hurdles don't deter you, you will not find a better active model than the Welsh-made Wellbrook ALA 330S.

For limited-space situations, and even to complement passive wire antennas on large properties, the '330S is hard to equal. However, if your receiver tends to sound "hissy" with weak signals, then it probably needs an antenna which provides even more gain than does the '330S so it can help overcome the receiver's inherent hissiness. Of course, with top-rated tabletop models this is not an issue.

Ideally, mounting should be outdoors with a rotor, although this is more important with the ALA 1530 model (*see* below) when used for longwave and mediumwave AM reception. In the real world of limited options, worthy results on shortwave can be expected indoors sans rotor or with manual rotation, provided the usual caveats are followed for placement of the reception element.

What's not to like? An ordering procedure that's inconvenient and démodé. There are no dealers outside the United Kingdom, and as we go to press there is as yet no secure way for those beyond U.K. borders to order by credit card on the Web.

Evaluation of Improved Version: Over the past few years Wellbrook's ALA 330 has been an exceptional performer—the more we've used it, the more we have come to appreciate how it helps squeeze readable copy out of emaciated signals. This is the pleasant consequence of quiet circuitry and, occasionally, significantly reduced pickup of static relative to the received signal. This has always been especially noticeable within the lower world band segments below 7.5 MHz.

The Wellbrook ALA 330S, new for 2004, goes a step further—as well it should, considering that the price has been boosted by fully 46 percent. This new version comes with a damping resistor on the loop's output transformer, a modestly quieter head amplifier and additional gain in the interface box alongside the receiver. Taken together, these audibly improve AGC operation on weak signals, with the greater overall gain being especially noticeable above 13 MHz.

The '330S is not intended for use with mediumwave AM signals; that's the job of the Wellbrook ALA 1530. Nevertheless, on mediumwave AM the '330S has a few decibels more gain than the '330. That's because even though the loop is slightly smaller, reducing pickup, the greater amplification more than makes up the difference.

That added gain over the '330—up to 9 dB between 2 and 30 MHz—also benefits world band, especially above about 14 MHz. It also allows a receiver's AGC to work better with weak signals between 2 and 30 MHz, so the operator doesn't have to fiddle as often with the volume/AF gain control.

For small lots and garden apartments, and to a lesser extent other apartments, the Wellbrook ALA 330S is tough to beat. Yet, even if you reside on an acre or more of land with multiple wire antennas, as we do at one test site, the '330S makes sense. As a second antenna, it can specialize in extracting audio out of static, particularly with weak signals in the tropical band segments and 49 meters.

✪✪✪⅛ *Passport's Choice*
Wellbrook ALA 1530, Wellbrook ALA 1530P

Remote, broadband, outdoor-indoor, 0.15-30 MHz

Price: *ALA 1530:* £129.95 plus £10.00 shipping in the United Kingdom. £129.95 plus £25.00 shipping elsewhere. *ALA 1530P (not tested):* £129.95 plus £10.00 shipping in the United Kingdom. £129.95 plus £25.00 shipping elsewhere. *Yaesu G-5550/G-5550B twin-axis rotor:* $619.95 in the United States. $1,060.00CAD in Canada. £559.00 in the United Kingdom. €659.00 in Germany.

Wellbrook antennas can be used indoors, but reach their full potential when mounted outside up and away from sources of electrical noise.

Pro: Unlike Wellbrook's former ALA 330, the established ALA 1530 covers not only shortwave, but also mediumwave AM and longwave nominally down to 150 kHz—even to 30 kHz with reduced sensitivity (*see* Con). Mediumwave AM and longwave performance superb when '1530 coupled to a Yaesu G-5500/G-5550B rotor, which has twin-axis directionality; rotor can also slightly reduce co-channel shortwave interference below about 5 MHz. Very nearly the best signal-to-noise ratio among active models tested, including reduced pickup of thunderstorm static. Balanced loop design inherently helps reduce pickup of local electrical noise. Low-noise/low-static pickup characteristic most noticeable below 7.5 MHz during summer, when it sometimes outperforms sophisticated outdoor wire antennas. Slightly more gain than ALA 1530 within little-used 2.3-2.5 MHz (120 meter) tropical world band segment, a plus only with receivers having relatively noisy circuitry. Superior build quality, including rigorous weatherproofing (*see* Con). Supplied AC adaptor, properly bypassed and regulated, is among the best tested for not causing hum or buzzing. Although any large loop's amplifier is inherently susceptible to inductive pickup of local thunderstorm static, during our tests the antenna's amp never suffered static damage during storms; indeed, even nearby one kilowatt shortwave transmissions did no damage to the antenna amplifier. Protected circuitry, using an easily replaced 315 mA slow-blow fuse.

Con: Extended frequency range can result in mediumwave AM signals surfacing within the shortwave spectrum, degrading reception—usually a more significant issue in urban and suburban North America than elsewhere (even an unsophisticated rotor can help by turning the antenna perpendicular to an offending mediumwave AM signal's axis); this tends to be less of a problem at night because of reduced local transmitting powers. Prone to overloading some receivers in locations rich with strong mediumwave AM signals; this also tends to be less of a problem at night because of reduced local transmitting powers. Only moderate gain for reception within such modest-signal areas as Western Hemisphere, Asia and Australasia—a drawback only with receivers having relatively noisy circuitry. Balanced loop receiving element, about one meter across, not easy to mount and is large and cumbersome to ship.

Mounting mast and optional rotor add to cost and complexity of erection. BNC connector at the receiving element's base is open to the weather and thus needs to be user-sealed with Coax Seal, electrical putty or similar. Encapsulated amplifier makes repair impossible. Manufacturer cautions against allowing high winds to stress mounting flange or sunlight to damage head amplifier; however, after a summer of wind and sun at one outdoor test location, nothing untoward has materialized. Adaptor supplied for 117V AC runs hot after being plugged in for a few hours, while amplifier tends to run slightly warm. No coaxial cable supplied. Available for purchase or export only two cumbersome ways: via Sterling cheque or International Money Order through the English manufacturer (www.wellbrook.uk.com), or with credit card via an English dealer's unsecured email address (sales@shortwave.co.uk); however, as we go to press the "Shortwave Shop" Website (www.shortwave.co.uk) is under construction, so things may yet improve.

☞ If your receiver has antenna inputs with varying impedances, experiment to see which provides the greatest signal strength. Also, at times an antenna tuner can improve signal level as much as 6 dB.

☞ Mediumwave AM and longwave performance directionality may suffer if the '1530 is not mounted well away from other antennas.

☞ The "P" version, not tested by us, uses a semi-rigid plastic loop rather than aluminum. It is intended for indoor use only.

Verdict: Interested in distant broadcast goodies below the shortwave spectrum, as well as world band? The Wellbrook ALA 1530 is hard to beat, so long as you don't live near local mediumwave AM transmission facilities. A rotor is *de rigeur* for nulling co-channel interference below 1.7

MHz, and also can help with tropical world band stations. As with all Wellbrook loop antennas, the '1530 excels in rejecting noise and static, particularly below 7.5 MHz.

Keep in mind that the '1530 is the sibling of the former ALA 330, not the newer—and costlier—ALA 330S.

❂❂❂½ *Passport's Choice*
RF Systems DX-One Professional Mark II

Remote, broadband, outdoor-indoor, 0.02-60 MHz

Price: *DX-One antenna:* $669.95 in the United States. £295.00 in the United Kingdom. €498.00 in Germany. $1,170.00AUD in Australia. *AK-1 pole mounting bracket:* $22.95 in the United States; similar brackets widely available.

Pro: Outstanding dynamic range. Very low noise. Outputs for two receivers. Comes standard with switchable band rejection filter to reduce the chances of mediumwave AM signals ghosting into the shortwave spectrum. Receiving element has outstanding build quality. Coaxial connector at head amplifier is completely shielded from the weather by a clever mechanical design. Superior low noise, high gain performance on mediumwave AM.

Con: Unbalanced design makes antenna susceptible to importing buzz at some locations; this is especially noticeable because of otherwise-excellent performance. AC power supply not bypassed as well as it could be, causing slight hum on some signals. More likely than most antennas to exacerbate fading, even though design nominally reduces fading effects. No coaxial cable supplied. Mounting bracket extra. Output position for 10 dB gain measures +6 dB. Warranty only six months.

Verdict: Substantially improved over the discontinued original version, the pricey new RF Systems DX-One Professional Mark

II is now a superior performer. As with any antenna with a small capture area that has an unbalanced design, at some locations it will be prone to pick up local electrical noise. Made in the Netherlands.

New for 2004

✪✪✪¼ *Passport's Choice*
AOR WL500

Remote, manual preselection, indoor/ portable, 0.155-1.71 MHz + 3.1-30 MHz

Price: *WL500, 3.1-30 MHz:* $198.95 in the United States. *Optional 500LM, 0.155-1.71 MHz:* $74.95 in the United States.

Pro: Very good for use with portable receivers; also works well with portatop and tabletop models. Can be easily assembled and disassembled during airline and other travel, although its transportability is not so clever as that of the Sony AN-LP1 (the '500 uses zip cord held in place by a two-piece wooden rod with wing nuts on the ends); except for the two rod parts, which could be sharpened and used as weapons, it is handy for hospital, prison or other institutional use where an antenna must be stashed away periodically. Excellent gain. As compared to proximate antennas and most other indoor-remote antennas, somewhat lower pickup of local electrical noise. Modest battery consumption (16 mA) allows for use without an AC adaptor; this prevents added hum and noise (*see* Con). Screw configuration to access battery cavity unlikely to be stripped with use (*see* Con).

Con: One of only two remote models tested which can't be mounted outdoors during inclement weather. Possible sensitivity to static charges (*see* , below). Some birdies and tweets, possibly from incipient spurious oscillation. Two rod parts could be thought of by airport security as potential weapons, so should be stowed as checked luggage. Performs only marginally within little-used 2 MHz (120 meter) tropical world band

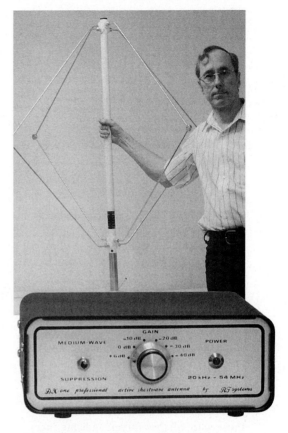

The Mark II RF Systems DX-One Professional is improved over the original.

segment. Requires manual peaking when significantly changing received frequency, although not as often as some other models thanks to fairly low circuit "Q." Changing 9V battery calls for unscrewing six annoyingly tiny screws to remove protective plate. AC adaptor not available from AOR for continuous-use applications, although manufacturer states that one eventually will be offered in certain as-yet-unspecified markets (alternatively, an outboard rechargeable battery can be used). Comes with only a BNC connector for the receiver; user has to modify the antenna-to-receiver cable or obtain adaptors for other types of receiver inputs. Comes with two wing nuts that are easily lost on trips; frequent travelers should obtain spares in advance. Optional longwave/mediumwave receiving

The collapsible AOR WL500 is one of the few active antennas that is truly portable.

element performs poorly, not recommended.

☞ Our first sample ceased functioning in a low-humidity environment when the operator's hand apparently discharged static electricity onto the connector to the antenna range switch. This happened as he reached to adjust it from high to low range, damaging circuitry within the control box at the opposite end of the cable. However, those who sell the antenna indicate that there have been no other known failures of this sort, but this is a new model so it's not yet certain whether the '500's interface unit is genuinely sensitive to static charges.

☞ Although the lower tuning parameter of the WL500 is nominally 3.5 MHz, tests show that performance remains equally good down to just below 3.1 MHz.

Verdict: For the traveling listener or DXer focused on reception quality, the new AOR WL500 is a welcome but pricey alternative to the Sony AN-LP1. Overall, it slightly outperforms the Sony, but it lacks the Sony's spit and polish for mounting and packing on trips. Both are made in Japan.

As of when we go to press, we could not find the '500 for sale outside the United States. This should change over the coming months.

Evaluation of New Model: Loops have a real advantage as active antennas, as they tend to pick up less of the electrical noise that is increasingly present within buildings. The new AOR WL500 is no exception. With its receiving element mounted on a building's window, it rejects local electrical noise better than nearly any other model of proximate or indoor-remote active antenna.

The '500's gain is commendable, too, and its low current consumption makes battery power reasonably convenient, thus preventing AC hum and buzzing that can degrade reception. So although the '500 introduces some spurious signals, by and large it is a superior performer.

Compared to other high-performance active antennas, it's handy for travel, too. You shove together two sticks to create one rod, push two eyelets onto studs at the ends of the rod, tighten a pair of wing nuts, mount the assembled receiving element, hook it to the control box, then connect the control box to the radio. Nevertheless, it doesn't have the Sony AN-LP1's clever folding design and comes with only a BNC connector, so it doesn't equal the Sony as the *ne plus ultra* in user convenience.

For the road warrior who flits from one hotel to the other, the AN-LP1's convenience is hard to beat. But AOR's new WL500 is the obvious choice for the traveling DXer or fastidious listener toting a serious portable, portatop or small tabletop receiver.

✪✪✪
Dressler ARA 100 HDX

Remote, broadband, outdoor-indoor, 0.04-40 MHz

Price: $529.95 in the United States. £325.00 on special order in the United Kingdom.

Pro: Superior build quality, with fiberglass whip and foam-encapsulated head amplifier to resist the weather (*see* Con). Very good gain below 20 MHz (*see* Con). Superior signal-to-noise ratio. Handy detachable "N" connector on bottom. AC adaptor with properly bypassed and regulated DC output is better than most.

Con: Even though it has an amplifier with superior dynamic range, tends to overload in urban/suburban environments awash in powerful mediumwave AM signals unless antenna element mounted close to the ground; this tends to be less of a problem at night because of reduced local transmitting powers. Encapsulated design makes most repairs impossible. Above 20 MHz gain begins to fall off slightly. Body of antenna runs slightly warm. "N" connector at the head amplifier/receiving element exposed to weather, needs to be sealed with Coax Seal, electrical putty or similar by user. Gain control cumbersome to adjust; fortunately, in practice it is rarely needed. Reader reports suggest that ordering direct from the factory can be a frustrating experience.

☞ Star rating applies only when used where there is not significant ambient mediumwave RF, as the Dressler ARA 100 HDX, unless mounted close to the ground, is prone to overloading at locations rich with strong mediumwave AM signals or low-band VHF-TV stations. At some locations, even mounting the antenna on the ground does not eliminate overloading.

Verdict: The robust Dressler ARA 100 HDX, made in Germany, is an excellent but costly low-noise antenna so long as you are not located near one or more powerful mediumwave AM or low-band VHF-TV transmitters.

New for 2004
✪✪✪❷ *Passport's Choice*
MFJ-1020C (with short wire element)

Remote, manual preselection, outdoor-indoor, 0.3-40 MHz

Dressler antennas perform nicely when not close to mediumwave AM or low-band VHF-TV transmitters.

Price: *MFJ-1020C (without antenna wire or insulators):* $79.95 in the United States. $125.00CAD in Canada. £89.95 in the United Kingdom. $229.00AUD in Australia.

The new MFJ-1020C can be used "as is" or as an active preselector.

MFJ-1312D 120 VAC adaptor: $14.95 in the United States. *Radio Shack 278-758 "Outdoor Antenna Kit":* $9.99 in the United States.

Pro: Superior dynamic range, so functions effectively with an outboard wire receiving element, preferably mounted outdoors, in lieu of built-in telescopic antenna element. Sharp preselector peak unusually effective in preventing overloading. Works best off battery (*see* Con). Choice of PL-259 or RCA connections. 30-day money-back guarantee if purchased from manufacturer.

Con: Preselector complicates operation; tune control needs adjustment even with modest frequency changes, especially within the mediumwave AM band. Knobs small and touchy to adjust. High current draw (measures 30 mA), so battery runs down quickly. Removing sheet-metal screws often to change battery should eventually result in stripping unless great care is taken. AC adaptor, optional, causes significant hum on many received signals.

☞ The '1020C serves little or no useful purpose as a tunable preselector for *long* inverted-L or other normally passive wire antennas. It cannot be used as an unamplified preselector; e.g., to improve front-end selectivity with significant wire antennas. Trying to do something similar by using the amplified unit at reduced gain does not improve the signal-to-noise ratio, nor does it improve dynamic range (reduce potential to overload), as the gain potentiometer is only an output pad (with a measured 40 dB range).

☞ Two manufacturing flaws found on one of our "B" version units tested in the past, but this year's "C" unit had no defects. The owner's manual warns of possible "taking off" if the gain is set too high, but during our tests using a variety of receivers we encountered oscillation with only one model.

Verdict: The '1020C has a little secret: It's only okay the way the manufacturer sells it as a proximate active antenna, but as a preselector with an outdoor random-length wire antenna it is a worthy low-cost performer. Simply collapse (or, better, remove) the built-in telescopic antenna, then connect the outboard wire antenna to the '1020C's external antenna input. For this, Radio Shack's "Outdoor Antenna Kit" or equivalent works fine, with the receiving element cut down to a convenient length.

Alas, the optional AC adaptor introduces hum much of the time, battery drain is considerable, and changing the built-in battery is inconvenient and relies on wear-prone sheet-metal screws. Best bet, unless you're into experimenting with power supplies: Skip the adaptor and use a large outboard rechargeable battery.

Peso for peso, the MFJ-1020C fed by a remote wire receiving element is the best buy among active antennas. The rub is the use of several yards or meters of wire, preferably outdoors, makes it something of a hybrid requiring more space than usual. But for many row houses, townhouses, ground-floor and rooftop apartments with a patch of space outdoors it can be a godsend. If visibility is an issue, use ultra-thin wire for the receiving element, or consider it as an environmentally friendly alternative to power lines as a resting spot for birds.

Evaluation of New Version: Thanks to the use of a JFET in place of a dual-gate MOSFET and a changed value of a coupling capacitor from 2 to 12 pF, the "C" version of the MFJ-1020 performs slightly better than the "B" predecessor as a proximate antenna (see review below) and as a remote antenna using a short wire element. It also adds 10 MHz of coverage within the low end of the VHF spectrum, but the AC adaptor degrades reception.

✪✪✪
Dressler ARA 60 S (conditional, see ☞)

Remote, broadband, outdoor-indoor, 0.04-60/100 MHz

Price: $289.95 in the United States. £169.00 in the United Kingdom. €184.00 in Germany.

Pro: Superior build quality, with fiberglass whip and foam-encapsulated head amplifier to resist weather (*see* Con). Very good and consistent gain, even above 20 MHz. AC adaptor with properly bypassed and regulated DC output is better than most.

Con: Encapsulated design makes most repairs impossible. RG-58 coaxial cable permanently attached on antenna end, making user replacement impossible. Gain control cumbersome to adjust; fortunately, in practice it is rarely needed. Reader reports suggest that ordering direct from the factory can be a frustrating experience.

☞ Comments about overloading in the above review of the ARA 100 HDX likely apply to the '60 S, as well.

Verdict: Very similar to the ARA 100 HDX—even its dynamic range and overloading performance are virtually identical. This makes the German-made ARA 60 S an excellent lower-cost alternative to the ARA 100 HDX.

✪✪¾ ✪ *Passport's Choice*
Sony AN-LP1

Remote, manual preselection, indoor/portable, 3.9-4.3 + 4.7-25 MHz

Price: $89.95 in the United States. £69.95 in the United Kingdom. €99.95 in Germany.

Pro: Excellent for use with portable receivers. Very good overall performance, including generally superior gain (*see* Con), especially within world band segments—yet surprisingly free from side effects. Battery operation, so no internally caused hum or noise (*see* Con). Clever compact folding

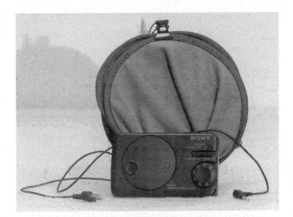

For portables, the Sony AN-LP1 is a solid performer and stows neatly. Reasonably priced, but sometimes hard to find.

design for airline and other travel; also handy for hospital, prison or other institutional use where an antenna must be stashed away periodically. Can be used even with portables that have no antenna input jack (*see* Con). Plug-in filter to reduce local electrical noise (*see* Con). Low battery consumption (*see* Con). Powered by the radio when used with Sony ICF-SW7600G or ICF-SW1000T portables.

Con: One of only two remote models tested which can't be mounted outdoors during inclement weather. Functions acceptably on shortwave only between 3.9-4.3 MHz and 4.7-25 MHz, with no mediumwave AM coverage. Gain varies markedly throughout the shortwave spectrum, in large part because the preselector's step-tuned resonances lack variable peaking. Preselector bandswitching complicates operation slightly. Battery operation only—no AC power supply, not even a socket for an AC adaptor—although battery drain is minimal. Consumer-grade plastic construction with no shielding. When clipped onto a telescopic antenna instead of fed through an antenna jack, the lack of a ground connection reduces performance. Plug-in noise filter unit reduces signal strength by several decibels.

☞ Sony recommends that the AN-LP1 not be used with the Sony ICF-SW77 receiver. However, our tests indicate that so long as the control box and loop receiving element are kept reasonably away from the radio, the antenna performs well.

☞ The Sony ICF-SW07 compact portable comes with an AN-LP2 antenna. This is virtually identical in concept and performance to the AN-LP1, except that because it is designed solely for use with the 'SW07 it has automatic preselection to simplify operation. At present the AN-LP2 cannot be used with other radios, even those from Sony.

Verdict: A real winner if the shoe fits. This is the handiest model for travelers wanting superior world band reception on portables—and it is truly portable. It is often a worthy choice for portatop and tabletop models, as well, provided you don't mind battery-only operation. This Japanese-made device has generally excellent gain, low noise and few side effects. Priced right, too.

There is limited frequency coverage—90/120 meter DXers should look elsewhere—and the loop receiving element cannot be mounted permanently outdoors. Too, the

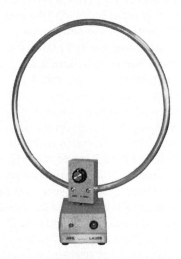

AOR's LA-350 helps reduce electrical noise.

lack of variable preselector peaking causes gain to vary greatly by frequency; this especially limits utility DX performance. Otherwise, the Sony AN-LP1 is nothing short of a bargain.

✪✪¾
AOR LA-350

Proximate, manual preselection, indoor, 0.2-1.6 MHz and 2.5-33 MHz

Price: *LA-350 antenna, with two shortwave elements:* $299.95 in the United States. £199.00 in the United Kingdom. €349.00 in Germany. *350L longwave element, 350M mediumwave AM element:* $72.95 each in the United States. £49.00 in the United Kingdom. €79.95 in Germany.

Pro: Above-average gain. Some directivity below 10 MHz, directionally nulling local electrical noise and static. Sometimes, rotatability can also slightly reduce co-channel shortwave interference; as is the norm with loop antennas, this modest nulling of co-channel skywave interference is best at frequencies below 5 MHz. Rotatability can also improve reception by directionally nulling local electrical noise. Small, easy to rotate. Antenna elements easy to swap (*see* Con). Relatively easy to peak by ear or signal-strength indicator (*see* Con).

Con: Proximate model, so receiving element has to be placed near receiver. Unbalanced design results in local electrical noise being passed into receiver at some locations; owner's manual says a better AC adaptor can reduce this, but a $300 product should come equipped with the proper adaptor. Requires change of antenna elements when going from 3-9 MHz range to 9-33 MHz range or *vice versa*; separate (optional) elements for mediumwave AM and longwave also require shuffling. Reduced performance within 2 MHz (120 meter) world band segment. Requires manual peaking when significantly changing received frequency. Phone plug, which connects antenna elements to the head amplifier, lacks lock washer and thus may loosen; easily remedied with Loctite. User has to supply BNC female-to-PL239 male adaptor, needed to connect antenna to many models of tabletop receivers. Owner's manual says BNC-to-BNC cable comes with antenna, but was not packed with our unit.

Verdict: The '350's unbalanced design makes it more susceptible to local electrical noise pickup than either Wellbrook model, and the supplied AC adaptor doesn't help. It also requires manual swapping of loop heads and circuit peaking. This having been said, where local electrical noise doesn't intrude the '350's superior gain, handy size and ease of rotation make it an effective choice for indoor use.

The Ameco TPA is one of the best proximate antennas tested.

✪✪½ ℄
Ameco TPA

Proximate, manual preselection, indoor, 0.22-30 MHz

Price: $69.95 in the United States.

Pro: Highest recovered signal with the longest supplied whip of the four proximate models tested. Most pleasant unit to tune to proper frequency. Superior ergonomics, including easy-to-read front panel with good-sized metal knobs (*see* Con). Superior gain below 10 MHz.

Con: Proximate model, so receiving element has to be placed near receiver. Above 15 MHz gain slips to slightly below average. Overloads with external antenna; because gain potentiometer is in the first stage, decreasing gain may increase overloading as current drops through the FET. Preselector complicates operation, compromising otherwise-superior ergonom-

ics. No rubber feet, slides around in use; user-remediable. No AC adaptor. Consumer-grade plastic construction with no shielding. Comes with no printed information on warranty; however, manufacturer states by telephone that it is the customary one year.

Verdict: The Ameco TPA, made in the United States, is one of the best proximate models tested for bringing in usable signals with the factory-supplied whip—signal recovery was excellent. However, when connected to an external antenna it overloads badly, and reducing gain doesn't help.

✪✪½
McKay Dymek DA100E, McKay Dymek DA100EM, Stoner Dymek DA100E, Stoner Dymek DA100EM

Remote, broadband, indoor-outdoor-marine, 0.05-30 MHz

Price: *DA100E:* $179.95 in the United States. *DA100EM (marine version, not tested):* $199.95 in the United States.

Pro: Respectable gain and noise. Generally good build quality, with worthy coaxial cable and an effectively sealed receiving element; marine version (not tested) appears to be even better yet for resisting weather. Jack for second antenna when turned off. Minor gain rolloff at higher shortwave frequencies. *DA100EM (not tested):* Weather-resistant fiberglass whip and brass fittings help ensure continued optimum performance.

Con: Slightly higher noise floor compared to other models. Some controls may confuse initially. Dynamic range among the lowest of any model tested; for many applications in the Americas this is adequate, but for use near local transmitters, or in Europe and other strong-signal parts of the world, the antenna is best purchased on a returnable basis. *DA100E:* Telescopic antenna allows moisture and avian waste penetration between segments, and thus potential resistance and/or spurious signals; user should seal these gaps with Coax Seal, electrical

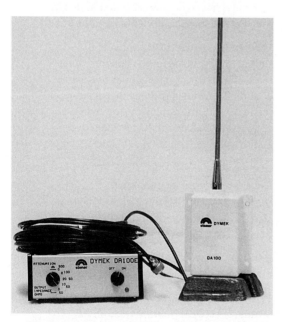

The Dymek DA100 "E" series is the latest in a design which has evolved over two decades. One version is especially for marine use.

putty or similar. Telescopic antenna could, in principle, be de-telescoped by birds, ice and the like, although we did not actually encounter this. Warranty only 30 days.

Verdict: The DA100E is a proven "out of the box" choice, with generally excellent weatherproofing and coaxial cable. Because its dynamic range is relatively modest, it is more prone than some other models to overload, especially in an urban environment or other high-signal-strength location. In principle the extra twenty bucks for the marine version should be a good investment, provided its fiberglass whip is not too visible for your location.

✪✪ ¼
MFJ 1024

Remote, broadband, indoor-outdoor, 0.05-30 MHz

Price: $139.95 in the United States. $220.00CAD in Canada. £149.95 in the United Kingdom. $349.00AUD in Australia.

Pro: Overall good gain and low noise. A/B selector for quick connection to another receiver. "Aux" input for passive antenna. 30-day money-back guarantee if purchased from manufacturer.

Con: Significant hum with supplied AC adaptor; remedied when we substituted a suitable aftermarket adaptor. Non-standard power socket complicates substitution of AC adaptor; also, adaptor's sub-mini plug can spark when inserted while the adaptor is plugged in; adaptor should be unplugged beforehand. Dynamic range among the lowest of any model tested; for many applications in the Americas it is adequate, but for use near local transmitters, or in Europe and other strong-signal parts of the world, antenna is best purchased on a returnable basis. Slightly increased noise floor compared to other models. Telescopic antenna allows moisture and avian waste penetration between segments, and thus potential resistance and/or spurious signals; user should seal these gaps with Coax Seal, electrical putty or similar. Telescopic antenna could, in principle, be de-telescoped by birds, ice and the like after installation, although we did not actually encounter this. Control box/ amplifier has no external weather sealing to protect from moisture, although the printed circuit board nominally comes with a water-resistant coating. Coaxial cable to receiver not provided. Mediocre coaxial cable provided between control box and receiving element. On our unit, a coaxial connector came poorly soldered from the factory.

Verdict: The MFJ 1024, made in America, performs almost identically to the Stoner Dymek DA100E, but sells for $40 less. However, that gap lessens if you factor in the cost of a worthy AC adaptor—assuming you can find or alter one to fit the unusual power jack—and the quality of the 1024's coaxial cable is not in the same league.

New for 2004

✪✪¼
MFJ-1020C

Proximate, manual preselection, indoor, 0.3-40 MHz

Price: *MFJ-1020C:* $79.95 in the United States. $125.00CAD in Canada. £89.95 in the United Kingdom. $229.00AUD in Australia. *MFJ-1312D 120 VAC adaptor:* $14.95 in the United States.

Pro: Rating rises to three stars if converted from a proximate to a remote model by connecting a wire to the external antenna input; see separate review, above. Superior dynamic range, and sharp preselector peak unusually effective in preventing overloading.

MFJ's remote active antenna, the 1024, suffers from hum with the supplied AC adaptor. Some aftermarket adaptors work better.

Works best off battery (*see* Con). Choice of PL-259 or RCA connections. 30-day money-back guarantee if purchased from manufacturer.

Con: Proximate model, so receiving element has to be placed near receiver (can be converted, *see* Pro). Preselector complicates operation; tune control needs adjustment even with modest frequency changes, especially within the mediumwave AM band. Knobs small and touchy to adjust. High current draw (measures 30 mA), so battery runs down quickly. Removing sheet-metal screws often to change battery should eventually result in stripping unless great care is taken. AC adaptor, optional, causes significant hum on many received signals.

☞ Two manufacturing flaws found on one of our "B" version units tested in the past, but this year's "C" unit had no defects. The owner's manual warns of possible "taking off" if the gain is set too high, but during our tests using a variety of receivers we encountered oscillation with only one model.

Verdict: The MFJ-1020C, made in the United States, is okay as a proximate antenna with its own telescopic antenna. However, it works very well when coupled to a random-length wire in lieu of the built-in telescopic antenna; see the separate review earlier in this article.

Alas, the optional AC adaptor introduces hum much of the time, battery drain is considerable, and changing the built-in battery is inconvenient and relies on wear-prone sheet-metal screws. Best bet, unless you're into experimenting with power supplies: Skip the adaptor and use a large outboard rechargeable battery.

Evaluation of New Version: Thanks to the use of a JFET in place of a dual-gate MOSFET and a changed value for a coupling capacitor, the "C" version of the MFJ-1020 performs slightly better than the "B" predecessor, with significantly better gain and less noise. It also adds 10 MHz of coverage within the low end of the VHF spectrum. Too bad that it doesn't come with an AC adaptor of comparable caliber.

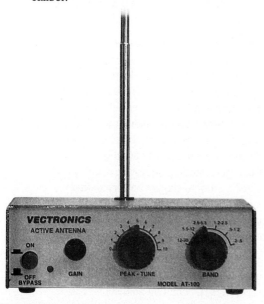

The Vectronics AT-100 works nicely on some receivers, poorly on others.

✪✪
Vectronics AT-100

Proximate, manual preselection, indoor, 0.3-30 MHz

Price: $79.95 in the United States. $109.00CAD in Canada. £79.95 in the United Kingdom.

Pro: Good—sometimes excellent—gain (*see* Con), especially in the mediumwave AM band. Good dynamic range. Most knobs are commendably large.

Con: Proximate model, so receiving element has to be placed near receiver. No AC power; although it accepts an AC adaptor, the lack of polarity markings complicates adaptor choice (it is center-pin positive). Preselector complicates operation, especially as it is stiff to tune and thus awkward to peak. Our unit oscillated badly with some receivers, limiting usable gain—although it was more stable with other receivers, and thus appears to be a function of the load presented by a given receiver.

Verdict: If ever there were a product that needs to be purchased on a returnable basis, this is it. With one receiver, this American-made model gives welcome gain and worthy performance; with another, it goes into oscillation nearly at the drop of a hat.

✪¾
Sony AN-1

Remote, broadband, indoor-outdoor, 0.15-30 MHz

Price: $99.95 in the United States. £69.95 in the United Kingdom. €119.00 in Germany.

Pro: Connects easily to any portable or other receiver, using supplied cables and inductive coupler. Unusually appropriate for low-cost portables lacking an outboard antenna input. Only portable-oriented model tested with weather resistant remote receiving element. Unlike Sony AN-LP1, it covers entire shortwave spectrum, plus mediumwave AM and longwave. AC adaptor jack, although antenna designed to run on six "AA" batteries. Good quality coaxial cable. Coaxial cable user-replaceable once head unit is disassembled. Switchable high-pass filter helps reduce intrusion of mediumwave AM signals into shortwave spectrum; rolloff begins at 3 MHz. Receiving element's bracket allows for nearly any mounting configuration (*see* Con).

Con: Poor gain, with pronounced reduction as frequency increases. Mediocre mediumwave AM performance. Clumsy but versatile mounting bracket makes installation tedious. No AC adaptor.

☞ The AN-1 reportedly has been discontinued, but is still available at some dealers.

☞ Sony offers a number of active antennas in various world markets. All appear to be similar to the AN-1, except for the very different AN-LP1.

Verdict: The Japanese-made Sony AN-1 has feeble gain, rendering it practically useless on higher frequencies and little better below. However, for outdoor mounting and use on lower frequencies it provides passable performance.

⭐ ¾
Palstar AA30/AA30A/AA30P/AM-30

Proximate, manual preselection, indoor, 0.3-30 MHz

Price: *AA30/AA30A:* $99.95 from Ohio factory, $69.95 elsewhere in the United States. £69.95 in the United Kingdom. *AA30P (not tested):* €96.50 in Germany. *AM-30 (not tested):* £69.95 in the United Kingdom.

Pro: Moderate-to-good gain. Tuning control easily peaked. Can be powered directly by the Palstar R30/R30C and Lowe HF-350 tabletop receivers, an internal battery or an AC adaptor.

The Sony AN-1 lacks gain. It reportedly is no longer being manufactured.

Con: Spurious oscillation throughout 14-30 MHz range. Overloads with external antenna. Proximate model, so receiving element has to be placed near receiver. Preselector complicates operation. No AC adaptor.

☞ At present, the AA30A's cabinets are silk screened simply as "AA30," although the accompanying owner's manual refers to the "AA30A."

☞ The Palstar AM-30, not tested, is sometimes sold in Europe. It appears to be comparable to the AA30A.

Verdict: Oscillation makes this a dubious choice except for reception below 14 MHz. Manufactured in the United States.

Palstar's active antenna disappoints at higher frequencies, but has good gain.

New for 2004

★¾ ◯
MFJ-1022

Proximate, broadband, indoor, 0.3-200 MHz

Price: *MFJ-1022:* $49.95 in the United States. £55.95 in the United Kingdom. $119.00AUD in Australia. *MFJ-1312D 120 VAC adaptor:* $14.95 in the United States.

Pro: Unusually broadband coverage reaches well into VHF spectrum. Considerable gain, peaking at 22.5 MHz, audibly helps signals that do not suffer from intermodulation. Idiot-proof to operate. Works best off battery (*see* Con). 30-day money-back guarantee if purchased from manufacturer.

The new MFJ-1022 is inexpensive and easy to operate.

Con: Proximate model, so receiving element has to be placed near receiver. Broadband design results in local mediumwave AM stations ghosting up to 2.7 MHz, and to a lesser degree up through the 3 MHz (90 meter) tropical world band segment at many locations; this often drops at night because of reduced local transmitting powers. Broadband design and high gain not infrequently results in intermodulation products/spurious signals and hiss between reasonable-level signals, and sometimes mixing with weaker signals. Within tropical world band segments, modest-level static from nearby thunderstorms, when coupled with overloading from local mediumwave AM signals, sometimes cause odd background sounds that are not heard with other antennas. High current draw (measures 35 mA), so battery runs down quickly. Removing sheet-metal screws often to change battery should eventually result in stripping unless great care is taken. AC adaptor, optional, causes significant hum on many received signals.

Verdict: Priced to move and offering broadband coverage, this compact antenna from MFJ couldn't be simpler to operate—one button, that's it. For helping to improve the listening quality of modest-strength international broadcasting signals, it works quite nicely. But don't expect to do much DXing, especially of the tropical world band segments unless you live well away from any mediumwave AM stations, and maybe not even then. Forget the AC adaptor and stick to batteries.

Prepared by Robert Sherwood, with George Heidelman, Chuck Rippel and David Zantow; also, Lawrence Magne, with Carl Silberman.

WHERE TO FIND THE INDEX TO TESTED ANTENNAS

PASSPORT REPORTS evaluates many antennas on the market. Here's where they are found, with those that are new, revised or retested in **bold**.

A comprehensive PASSPORT® Radio Database International White Paper®, *PASSPORT Evaluation of Popular Outdoor Antennas*, is available for $6.95 in North America, $9.95 airmail elsewhere, including shipping. It contains virtually all our panel's findings and comments during testing, along with details for proper installation and instructions for inverted-L construction. This unabridged report is available from key world band dealers, or you can contact our 24-hour VISA/MC order channels (www.passband.com, autovoice +1 215/598-9018, fax +1 215/598 3794), or write us at PASSPORT RDI White Papers, Box 300, Penn's Park, PA 18943 USA.

What's On Tonight?

PASSPORT's Hour-by-Hour Guide to World Band Shows

With world band radio, an avalanche of news and entertainment comes tumbling at you day and night. To sort out what's on and when, here is PASSPORT'S hour-by-hour guide to English-language programs, with symbols to highlight the best:

■ Station superior, most shows excellent

● Show worth hearing

Some stations provide schedules, others don't. Yet, even among those that do, their information isn't always credible or complete. To resolve this, PASSPORT monitors stations around the world, firsthand, to detail schedule activity throughout the year. Additionally, to be as useful as possible, PASSPORT'S schedules consist not just of observed activity, but also that which we have creatively opined will appear well into the year ahead. This predictive material is based on decades of experience, and is original from us. Although this is inherently less exact than real-time data, it has proven to be a real help over the years.

Primary frequencies are given for North America, Western Europe, East Asia and Australasia, plus the Middle East, Southern Africa and Southeast Asia. If you want secondary and seasonal channels, or frequencies for other parts of the world, check out "Worldwide Broadcasts in English" and the Blue Pages.

To eliminate confusion, World Time and World Day are used—both explained in "Compleat Idiot's Guide to Getting Started" and the glossary. Seasons are those in the Northern Hemisphere ("summer" July, etc.; "winter" January, etc.).

Tivoli's waterside restaurant is frequented by senior members of the genial Danish Shortwave Clubs International.   T. Ohtake

0000-0559
North America—Evening Prime Time
Europe & Mideast—Early Morning
Australasia & East Asia—Midday and Afternoon

00:00

■**BBC World Service for the Americas.** Tuesday through Saturday winter (weekday evenings in the Americas), opens with five minutes of *news*. This is followed by the long-running *Outlook* and the 15-minute ●*Off the Shelf* (readings from world literature). Best of the weekend shows is ●*One Planet* (the environment) at 2306 Monday. Summer programming starts with *News*, then it's a mixed bag of features. Recommended are ●*Everywoman* (0006 Monday), ●*Charlie Gillett* (world music, 0032 Thursday) and the eclectic ●*John Peel* (0006 Saturday). Continuous programming to North America and the Caribbean on 5975 kHz. Listeners in eastern North America can also try 12095 kHz, targeted at South America; a radio with synchronous selectable sideband helps reduce teletype interference. Farther west, try 11835 kHz in summer.

■**BBC World Service for East and Southeast Asia.** Starts with 20 minutes of *World Briefing*, followed by ●*Sports Roundup*. Except for Sunday, ●*World Business Report/Review* can then be heard on the half-hour. The final 15-minute slot is taken by ●*Analysis* (Tuesday, Wednesday, Friday and Saturday), ●*From Our Own Correspondent* (Thursday) and ●*Letter from America* on Monday. The only 30-minute show is *Agenda* at 0030 Sunday. Audible in East Asia on 15280, 15360 and (till 0030) 17615 kHz; and in Southeast Asia on 3915 (to 0030), 6195, 7105 (to 0030) and 15360 kHz.

■**Radio Netherlands.** Tuesday through Saturday (weekday evenings in North America) there's ●*Newsline* (current events) followed by a feature on the half-hour: ●*Research File* (Tuesday), ●*EuroQuest* (Wednesday), ●*Documentary* (Thursday), *Dutch Horizons* (Friday), and *A Good Life* (Saturday). On the remaining days, a six-minute *news*

00:00–00:00

bulletin is followed Sunday by *Europe Un-zipped*, *Insight* and *Amsterdam Forum*; and Monday by *Wide Angle*, *The Week Ahead* and *Vox Humana*. Fifty-five minutes to eastern North America on 9845 kHz.

Radio Bulgaria. Winter only at this time. *News*, music and features. Tuesday through Saturday (weekday evenings in North America), the news is followed by *Events and Developments*, replaced Sunday by *Views Behind the News* and Monday by the delightfully exotic ●*Folk Studio*. The next slot consists of weekly features. Take your pick from *Plaza/Walks and Talks* (Monday), *Magazine Economy* (Tuesday), *Arts and Artists* (Wednesday), *History Club* (Thursday), *The Way We Live* (Friday), *DX Programme* (Saturday) and *Answering Your Letters*, a listener-response show, on Sunday. Tuesday through Sunday, the broadcast ends with *Keyword Bulgaria*. Sixty minutes to eastern North America and Central America on 7400 and 9400 kHz. One hour earlier in summer.

Radio Canada International. Winter only at this time. Tuesday through Saturday (weekday evenings in North America), it's the final hour of the CBC domestic service news program ●*As It Happens*, which features international stories, Canadian news and general human interest features. Weekends, you can hear two of Canada's best radio shows—Sunday's ●*Quirks and Quarks* (science) and Monday's ●*Global Village* (world music), both from the CBC's domestic output. To North America on 5960 and 9590 kHz, and one hour earlier in summer. For a separate year-round broadcast to Asia, see the next item.

Radio Canada International. Tuesday through Saturday, it's ●*The World At Six*; and a shortened version of ●*As It Happens*, both news-oriented programs. These are replaced Sunday by ●*Quirks and Quarks* (a science show) and Monday by *Tapestry*. One hour to Southeast Asia winter on 9755 and 11895 kHz, and summer on 9640 and 15205 kHz. Also heard in parts of East Asia, especially during summer.

Radio Japan. *News*, then Tuesday through Saturday (weekday evenings local American date) it's *Songs for Everyone* followed by *Japan*

and the *World 44 Minutes* (an in-depth look at current trends and events in Japan and elsewhere). This is replaced Sunday by *Hello from Tokyo*, and Monday by *Weekend Japanology* and *Sight and Sounds of Japan*. One hour to eastern North America on 6145 kHz via the powerful relay facilities of Radio Canada International in Sackville, New Brunswick. A separate 15-minute news bulletin for Southeast Asia is aired on 13650 and 17810 kHz.

Radio Exterior de España ("Spanish National Radio"). Tuesday through Saturday (local weekday evenings in the Americas), there's Spanish and international *news*, commentary, Spanish pop music, a review of the Spanish press, and a general interest feature. Weekends, it's all features, including rebroadcasts of some of the weekday programs. Sixty minutes to eastern North America winter on 6055 kHz, and summer on 6055 or 15385 kHz. Popular with many listeners.

Radio for Peace International, Costa Rica. Continues with a six-hour cyclical block of social conscience and counterculture programming audible in Europe and the Americas on 7445 kHz.

Radio Ukraine International. Summer only at this time. Ample coverage of local issues, including news, sports, politics and culture. Worth hearing is ●*Music from Ukraine*, which fills most of the Monday (Sunday evening in the Americas) broadcast. Sixty minutes to western Europe and eastern North America on 9810 or 12040 kHz. One hour later in winter. Budget and technical limitations have reduced audibility of this station to only a fraction of what it used to be.

Radio Australia. *World News*, then a feature. Monday's offering—unusual, to say the least—is *Awaye*, a program dealing with indigenous affairs. This is replaced Tuesday by *Science Show* and Wednesday by *The National Interest* (topical events). Thursday's *Background Briefing* (investigative journalism) and Friday's historical *Hindsight* complete the weekday lineup. *Feedback* (a listener-response show) and *Country Breakfast* fill the Saturday slots, and Sunday's feature is *The Europeans*. Targeted at Asia and the Pacific on 9660,

12080, 15240, 15415, 17580, 17750 (from 0030), 17775, 17795 and 21740 kHz. In North America (best during summer) try 17580, 17795 and 21740 kHz; and in East Asia go for 15240 kHz. For Southeast Asia there's 15415, 17750 and 17775 kHz.

Radio Prague, Czech Republic. Summer only at this time. *News,* then Tuesday through Saturday (weekday evenings in the Americas), there's *Current Affairs* and one or more features: *Talking Point* (Tuesday); *Witness* and *One on One* (Wednesday); *ABC of Czech* and either *Czechs in History* or *Spotlight* (Thursday); *Economics Report* (Friday); and *Stepping Out* and *The Arts* on Saturday. Weekends there's Sunday's *Insight Central Europe,* and Monday's *Mailbox* and *ABC of Czech* followed by *Encore* (classical music), *Magic Carpet* (Czech world music) or *Czech Books.* Thirty minutes to eastern North America and the Caribbean on 7345 and 9440 kHz. One hour later in winter.

Voice of America. The first 60 minutes of a two-hour broadcast to the Caribbean and Latin America which is aired Tuesday through Saturday (weekday evenings in the Americas). *News Now,* a rolling news format covering political, business and other developments. On 5995, 6130, 7405, 9455, 9775, 11695 and 13790 kHz. The final hour of a separate service to East and Southeast Asia and Australasia (see 2200) can be heard in Asia on 7215, 9770 (or 9890), 11760, 15185, 15290 and 17820 kHz; and in Australasia on 11760 and 17740 kHz.

Radio Thailand. *Newshour.* Thirty minutes to eastern and southern Africa, winter on 9680 kHz and summer on 9570 kHz.

All India Radio. The final 45 minutes of a much larger block of programming targeted at East and Southeast Asia, and heard well beyond. To East Asia on 9950, 11620 and 13605 kHz; and to Southeast Asia on 9705, 11620 and 13605 kHz.

■**Deutsche Welle,** Germany. *News,* then Tuesday through Saturday it's the comprehensive ●*NewsLink for Asia*—commentary, interviews, background reports and analysis. This is followed by *Insight* and *Business German* (Tuesday), *World in Progress* (Wednes-

day), *Money Talks* (Thursday), *Environment* (Friday), and *Spectrum* (Saturday). Sunday fare is *Religion and Society, German by Radio,* and *Asia This Week;* replaced Monday by *Mailbag.* Sixty minutes to South Asia winter on 7290 and 9880 kHz; and summer on 7130, 9505 and 9825 kHz. Also audible in parts of North America.

Radio Cairo, Egypt. The final half hour of a 90-minute broadcast to eastern North America. *Arabic by Radio* can be heard on the hour, and there's a daily *news* bulletin at 0015. See 2300 for more specifics. Easy reception on 9900 or 11725 kHz.

XERMX—Radio México Internacional. Tuesday through Saturday winter (weekday evenings in North America) there's an English summary of the Spanish-language *Antena Radio,* replaced on the remaining days by *Talking Mexico* (interviews). Thirty minutes to southwestern parts of the United States on 9705 and 11770 kHz.

Radio New Zealand International. A friendly package of *news* and features sometimes replaced by live sports commentary. Part of a much longer broadcast for the South Pacific, but also heard in parts of North America (especially during summer) on 17675 kHz.

AFRTS Shortwave, USA. Network news, live sports, music and features in the upper-sideband mode from the Armed Forces Radio & Television Service. Transmitted from modestly powered U.S. Navy stations around the globe. Try 4319, 5765, 6350, 6458.5, 10320, 12579, 12689.5 and 13362 kHz.

00:30

Radio Vilnius, Lithuania. A half hour that's heavily geared to news and background reports about events in Lithuania. Of broader appeal is *Mailbag,* aired every other Sunday (Saturday evenings local American date). For some Lithuanian music, try the next evening, towards the end of the broadcast. To eastern North America winter on 7325 kHz and summer on 11690 kHz.

Voice of the Islamic Republic of Iran. A one-hour package of news, commentary and features, with the accent heavily on Islam and Islamic culture. Lighter than what it used to be, but probably not to the taste of the average listener. One hour to North and Central America winter on 6120 and 9580 kHz, and summer on 9590 and 11920 kHz.

Radio Thailand. *Newshour.* Thirty minutes to central and eastern North America winter on 13695 kHz, and summer on 15395 kHz.

01:00

■**BBC World Service for the Americas.** Winter, starts with *News*, then it's a mixed bag of features. Top choices are ●*Everywoman* (0006 Monday), ●*Charlie Gillett* (world music, 0032 Thursday) and the eclectic ●*John Peel* (0006 Saturday). Pick of the summer shows is Sunday's ●*Play of the Week* (world theater at its best). Other interesting programs include ●*Health Matters* (0106 Tuesday) and ●*One Planet* (same time Friday). Continuous programming to North America and the Caribbean on 5975 kHz, and to western North America and Central America winter on 9525 kHz, and summer on 11835 kHz. In parts of eastern North America, 12095 kHz (nominally to South America) is also audible; a radio with synchronous selectable sideband helps reduce teletype interference.

■**BBC World Service for East and Southeast Asia.** Monday through Saturday, there's five minutes of *World News*, replaced Sunday by a half hour of *The World Today*. Tuesday through Saturday at 0105, look for *Outlook*, one of the BBC's longest running shows (though not as good as it used to be). Monday, this gives way to *Talking Point* (a call-in show). On weekdays, the final 15 minutes carry ●*Off the Shelf*, serialized readings from the best of world literature. At the same time Saturday you can hear *Write On* (a listener-response program), and the religious *In Praise of God* can be heard at 0130 Sunday. Continuous to East Asia on 15280 and 15360 kHz, and to Southeast Asia on 6195 and 15360 kHz.

Radio Canada International. Summer only at this time. *News*, followed Tuesday through Saturday (weekday evenings local American date) by *Canada Today*. The Sunday opener is *Business Sense*, replaced Monday by a listener-response show, *The Mailbag*. On the half-hour there's *Spotlight* (Monday and Thursday), *Media Zone* (Tuesday), *The Mailbag* (Wednesday), *Business Sense* (Friday) and *Sci-Tech File* on Saturday and Sunday. Sixty minutes to North, Central and South America on 9755, 15170 and 15305 kHz. One hour later in winter.

■**Radio Netherlands.** Repeat of the 0000 broadcast; see there for specifics. Fifty-five minutes to North America on 6165 kHz.

Radio Slovakia International. Wednesday through Saturday (Tuesday through Friday evenings in the Americas), starts with *News* and *Topical Issue*. These are followed by features. Regulars include *Tourist News* (Wednesday), *Business News* and *Currency Update* (Thursday), *Culture News* (Friday) and *Regional News* (Saturday). Tuesday's news is followed by *Insight Central Europe*. Sunday's lineup includes *Front Page* and *Sports News*; and Monday there's *Sunday Newsreel* and *Listeners' Tribune*. A friendly half hour to eastern North America and the Caribbean on 5930 and 6190 (or 7230) kHz, and to South America on 9440 kHz.

Radio Austria International. Tuesday through Saturday (weekday evenings in the Americas), the 15-minute ●*Report from Austria* is aired at 0115, and then repeated at 0145. Sunday and Monday, it's a similar arrangement, with *Insight Central Europe* airing at 0105 and 0135. The remainder of the one-hour broadcast is in German. To eastern North America winter on 7325 kHz, and summer on 9870 kHz. Also to Central America winter on 9870 kHz (two hours earlier in summer).

Radio Budapest, Hungary. Summer only at this time. *News* and features, most of which are broadcast on a non-regular basis. Thirty minutes to North America on 9590 kHz. One hour later in winter.

Radio Prague, Czech Republic. *News*, then Tuesday through Saturday (weekday evenings in the Americas), there's the in-depth *Current Affairs* and a feature or two: *Talking Point* (Tuesday), *Witness* and *One on One* (Wednesday), *ABC of Czech* and either *Czechs in History* or *Spotlight* (Thursday), *Economics Report*

01:00–01:00

(Friday) and *Stepping Out* and *The Arts* on Saturday. Winter, the Sunday news is followed by *Insight Central Europe*, which is replaced summer by *Magazine, Letter from Prague* and a repeat of Wednesday's *One on One*. Monday's lineup is *Mailbox* and *ABC of Czech* followed by *Encore* (classical music), *Magic Carpet* (Czech world music) or *Czech Books*. Thirty minutes to eastern and central North America and the Caribbean on 6200 and 7345 kHz.

RAI International—Radio Roma, Italy. Actually starts at 0055. *News* and Italian music make up this 20-minute broadcast to North America on 9675 and 11800 kHz.

Radio Japan. *News*, then Tuesday through Saturday it's *Songs for Everyone* and *Japan and the World 44 Minutes* (an in-depth look at trends and events in Japan and beyond). This is replaced Sunday by *Pop Joins the World*, and Monday by *Hello from Tokyo*. One hour to East Asia on 17845 kHz; to South Asia on 15325 kHz; to Southeast Asia on 11860 and 17810 kHz; to Australasia on 17685 kHz; to South America on 17835 kHz; and to the Mideast on 11880 and 17560 kHz. The broadcast on 17685 kHz has different features after 0115.

Radio for Peace International, Costa Rica. Continues with a six-hour cyclical block of social-conscience and counterculture programming audible in Europe and the Americas on 7445 kHz.

China Radio International. Starts with *News,* followed Monday through Friday (Sunday through Thursday evenings in the Americas) by special reports—current events, sports, business, culture, science and technology and press clippings. The rest of the broadcast is devoted to features. Regulars include ●*People in the Know* (Monday), *Biz China* (Tuesday), *China Horizons* (Wednesday), ●*Voices from Other Lands* (Thursday), and *Life in China* on Friday. Weekends, the news is followed by a shorter series of reports (current events and sport) and two features. Saturday there's *Cutting Edge*, and *Listeners' Garden* (listener mail, Chinese folk music, a preview of the next week's programs, and a Chinese language lesson); replaced Sunday by *Reports on Developing Countries* and *In the Spotlight*, a series of mini-features: *Cultural*

Carousel, In Vogue, Writings from China, China Melody and *Talking Point*. One hour to North America on 9580 and 9790 kHz, via CRI's Cuban and Canadian relays.

Voice of Vietnam. A relay via the facilities of Radio Canada International. Begins with *news*, then there's *Commentary* or *Weekly Review*, followed by short features and some pleasant Vietnamese music (especially at weekends). Thirty minutes to eastern North America, with reception better to the south. On 6175 kHz. Repeated at 0230 on the same channel.

Voice of Russia World Service. Summer only at this hour, and the start of a four-hour block of programming for North America. *News*, then Tuesday through Saturday (weekday evenings in North America), there's *Commonwealth Update*. This is replaced Sunday and Monday by *Moscow Mailbag*. The second half-hour contains some interesting fare, with just about everyone's favorite being Tuesday's ●*Folk Box*. Other shows include Friday's ●*Music at Your Request* (or ●*Music Around Us*), ●*Moscow Yesterday and Today* (Sunday), Wednesday's ●*Jazz Show*, and Saturday's evocative ●*Christian Message from Moscow*. Best for eastern North America are 9665, 9725 and 11825 kHz; farther west, use 17660 and 17690 kHz.

Radio Habana Cuba. The start of a two-hour cyclical broadcast to North America. Tuesday through Sunday (Monday through Saturday evenings in North America), the first half hour consists of international and Cuban *news* followed by *RHC's Viewpoint*. The next 30 minutes consist of a *news* bulletin and the sports-oriented *Time Out* (five minutes each) plus a feature: *Caribbean Outlook* (Tuesday and Friday), *DXers Unlimited* (Wednesday and Sunday), the *Mailbag Show* (Thursday) and *Weekly Review* (Saturday). Monday, the hour is split between *Weekly Review* and *Mailbag Show*. To eastern and central North America on 6000 and 9820 kHz. May also be available on 6195 or 9505 kHz.

Voice of Korea, North Korea. It's no longer the ranting Radio Pyongyang of old, and the announcers are softer-spoken, but the Voice of Korea has still a long way to go before being accepted as a serious broadcaster. For now, it's of curiosity value only, but with North Korea rattling its nuclear sabers, this broadcasting dinosaur could yet provide some surprises. One hour to East Asia on 3560, 4405, 6195, 7140 and 9345 kHz; and to Central and South America on any three channels from 6520, 7580, 11735, 13760 and 15180 kHz.

Radio Australia. Part of a 24-hour service to Asia and the Pacific, but which can also be heard at this time in parts of North America (better to the west). Begins with world *news*, then Tuesday through Saturday there's *Asia Pacific* (regional current events), replaced Sunday by *Correspondents' Report*. Weekdays on the half-hour, there's yet more reporting: *Health Report* (Monday), *Law Report* (Tuesday), *Religion Report* (Wednesday) and *Media Report* (Thursday). Friday brings some relief, with *Sports Factor*. Weekend fare consists of Saturday's *Arts Talk* and Sunday's musical *Oz Sounds*. Targeted at Asia and the Pacific on 9660, 12080, 15240, 15415, 17580, 17750, 17775 (till 0130), 17795 and 21725 kHz. In North America (best during summer) try 17580 and 17795 kHz; in East Asia go for 15240 and 21725 kHz; and best for Southeast Asia are 15415, 17750 and 17775 kHz. Some channels may carry a separate sports service on winter Saturdays.

Voice of America. The second and final hour of a two-hour broadcast to the Caribbean and Latin America which is aired Tuesday through Saturday (weekday evenings in the Americas). *News Now*, a rolling news format covering political, business and other developments. On the half-hour, a program in "Special" (slow-speed) English is carried on 7405, 9775 and 13740 kHz; with mainstream programming continuing on 5995, 6130 and 9455 kHz.

Radio Ukraine International. Winter only at this time; see 0000 for specifics. Sixty minutes of informative programming targeted at Europe, eastern North America and West Asia. Poor reception in most areas due to limited transmitter availability. Try 5905 kHz for eastern North America, 7420 kHz for West Asia, and 9610 kHz in eastern Europe. One hour earlier in summer.

Radio France Internationale covers the old and the new within l'Hexagone.   M. Guha

Radio New Zealand International. Continues with *news* and features sometimes replaced by live sports commentary. Part of a much longer broadcast for the South Pacific, but also heard in parts of North America (especially during summer) on 17675 kHz.

Radio Tashkent, Uzbekistan. Monday through Saturday, opens with *News*, replaced Sunday by *Significant Events of the Week*. The remaining fare consists mainly of features, with Monday's broadcast largely devoted to exotic Uzbek music. On the remaining days there's *Economic Commentary* (Tuesday), a program for women (Wednesday and Sunday), *Echo of History* (Wednesday), *Uzbekistan and the World* and *Man and Society* (Thursday) and a program for shortwave listeners on Friday. The week ends with a Saturday sports program followed by *In the World of Literature*. A half hour to West and South Asia, and occasionally heard in North America. Aired winter on two or more frequencies from 5975, 6165, 7135 and 7160 kHz; and summer on 7190 and 9715 kHz.

AFRTS Shortwave, USA. Network news, live sports, music and features in the upper-sideband mode from the Armed Forces Radio & Television Service. Transmitted from modestly powered U.S. Navy stations around the globe. Try 4319, 5446.5, 5765, 6350, 6458.5, 7507, 10320, 12133.5, 12579, 13362 and 13855 kHz.

01:30–02:00

Deutsche Welle also uses television. Arabic service editors Samir Matar (glasses) and Dr. Ibrahim Mohamed prepare the day's videocast. DW

01:30

Radio Sweden. Tuesday through Saturday, it's *news* and features in *Sixty Degrees North*, concentrating heavily on Scandinavian topics. Several of the features rotate from week to week, but a few are fixtures. Tuesday's *SportScan* is replaced Wednesday by *Close Up* or an alternative feature, and Thursday by special features. Friday's carousel is *Nordic Lights*, *GreenScan* (the environment), *Heart Beat* (health), and *S-Files*, with *Weekly Review* filling the Saturday slot. The Sunday rotation is *Network Europe*, *Spectrum*, *Sweden Today* and *Studio 49*; while Monday's offering is *In Touch with Stockholm* (a listener-response program) or the musical *Sounds Nordic*. Thirty minutes to South Asia and beyond on 9435 kHz. May also use 12060 kHz in winter. Also to North America, summer only, on 9495 kHz.

Voice of the Islamic Republic of Iran. Repeat of the 0030 broadcast. One hour to North and Central America winter on 6120 and 9580 kHz, and summer on 9590 and 11920 kHz.

RTE Overseas, Ireland. A half-hour information bulletin from Radio Telefís Éireann's domestic Radio 1. To Central America (and well heard in parts of North America) on 6155 kHz.

01:45

Radio Tirana, Albania. Tuesday through Sunday (Monday through Saturday evenings in North America) and summer only at this time. Approximately 15 minutes of *news* and

commentary from this small Balkan country. To North America on 6115 and 7160 kHz. One hour later in winter.

02:00

■BBC World Service for the Americas. Starts with *News*, then it's a mixed bag of features. Pick of the winter shows is Sunday's ●*Play of the Week* (world theater at its best). Other interesting programs include ●*Health Matters* (0106 Tuesday) and ●*One Planet* (same time Friday). Summer, opens with 30 minutes of *The World Today*, then Monday through Saturday (Sunday through Friday evenings in the Americas) there's 13 minutes of ●*World Business Report* followed most days by ●*Analysis* (current events). The exceptions are Thursday's ●*From Our Own Correspondent* and Monday's *Instant Guide*. Sunday programming consists of either an extra 30 minutes of ●*Play of the Week* or news coverage in *The World Today*. Continues to North America and the Caribbean on 5975 kHz. Also to western North America and Central America winter on 9525 kHz, and summer on 11835 kHz. In parts of eastern North America, 12095 kHz (nominally to South America) is also audible; a radio with synchronous selectable sideband helps reduce teletype interference.

■BBC World Service for East Asia. Weekdays, the first half hour consists of *News* and an arts show, *Meridian*. In a brutal switch from highbrow to lowbrow, the next 30 minutes are a mixed bag of popular music and *Westway*, a soap. Weekends there's 30 minutes of *The World Today*, with Saturday's *Global Business* or Sunday's ●*From Our Own Correspondent* completing the hour. Continuous to East Asia on 15280 and 15360 kHz, and to Southeast Asia on 15360 kHz.

Radio Cairo, Egypt. Repeat of the 2300 broadcast, and the first hour of a 90-minute potpourri of *news* and features about Egypt and the Arab world. To North America on 11780 kHz.

Radio Argentina al Exterior—RAE Tuesday through Saturday only (local weekday evenings in the Americas). A freewheeling presentation of news, press review, short features and local Argentinian music. Not the easiest station to tune, but popular with many of those who can hear it. Fifty-five minutes nominally to North America on 11710 kHz, but tends to be best heard in the southern U.S. and the Caribbean. Sometimes pre-empted by live soccer commentary in Spanish.

Radio Budapest, Hungary. Winter only at this time. *News* and features, most of which are broadcast on a non-regular basis. Thirty minutes to North America on 9835 kHz. One hour earlier in summer.

Wales Radio International. This time summer Saturdays only (Friday evenings American date). News, reports and music from the Welsh principality. Thirty minutes to North America on 9795 kHz, and one hour later in winter.

Radio Canada International. *News*, followed Tuesday through Saturday (weekday evenings local American date) by *Canada Today*. This is replaced Sunday by *Business Sense*, and Monday by *The Mailbag* (a listener-response show). On the half-hour there's *Spotlight* (Monday and Thursday), *Media Zone* (Tuesday), *The Mailbag* (Wednesday), *Business Sense* (Friday) and *Sci-Tech File* on Saturday and Sunday. One hour winter to North, Central and South America on 6040, 9755 and 11725 kHz; and year round to South Asia on 15150 (winter), 15510 (summer) and 17860 kHz.

Radio Bulgaria. Summer only at this time. Starts with *news*, then Tuesday through Saturday (weekday evenings in North America) there's *Events and Developments*, replaced Sunday by *Views Behind the News* and Monday by 15 minutes of Bulgarian exotica in ●*Folk Studio*. Additional features include *Answering Your Letters* (a listener-response show, Monday), *Plaza/Walks and Talks* (Tuesday), *Magazine Economy* (Wednesday). *Arts and Artists* (Thursday), *History Club* (Friday), *The Way We Live* (Saturday) and *DX Programme*, a Sunday show for radio enthusiasts. Wednesday through Monday, the broadcast ends with *Keyword Bulgaria*. Sixty minutes to eastern North America and Central America on 9400 and 11900 kHz. One hour later in winter.

Radio Prague, Czech Republic. Winter only at this time. *News*, then Tuesday through

Saturday (weekday evenings in the Americas), it's a combination of *Current Affairs* and one or more features: *Talking Point* (Tuesday), *Witness* and *One on One* (Wednesday), *ABC of Czech* and either *Czechs in History* or *Spotlight* (Thursday), *Economics Report* (Friday), and *Stepping Out* and *The Arts* on Saturday. Weekends, Sunday's news is followed by *Magazine*, *Letter from Prague* and a repeat of Wednesday's *One on One*. The Monday lineup consists of *Mailbox* and *ABC of Czech* followed by *Encore* (classical music), *Magic Carpet* (Czech world music) or *Czech Books*. A half hour to North America on 6200 and 7345 kHz. One hour earlier in summer.

Voice of Croatia. Summer only at this time. "Croatia Today," nominally 20 minutes of news, reports and interviews. Actual length varies. To eastern North America and South America on 9925 kHz. One hour later in winter.

Radio Taiwan International. Opens with 15 minutes of *News*, and weekdays closes with *Let's Learn Chinese*, which has a series of segments for beginning, intermediate and advanced learners. In between, there are either one or two features, depending on which day it is. Monday (Sunday evening in North America) it's the pleasurable and exotic ●*Jade Bells and Bamboo Pipes* (Taiwanese music); Tuesday's slots are *Culture Express* and *Trends*; Wednesday brings *Taiwan Today* and *Instant Noodles*; Thursday, there's *Discover Taiwan* and *New Music Lounge*; and Friday's presentations are *Taipei Magazine* and *People*. These are replaced Saturday by *Groove Zone* and *Kaleidoscope*, and Sunday by *Hakka World* and *Mailbag Time*. One hour to North America on 5950 and 9680 kHz; and to Southeast Asia on 11875 and 15320 kHz. For a separate service to East Asia, see the next item.

Radio Taiwan International. Like the broadcast for Southeast Asia and the Americas, opens with 15 minutes of *News*, and weekdays closes with *Let's Learn Chinese*. However, the features are different: *Taiwan Economic Journal* and *Stage, Screen and Studio* (Monday), ●*Jade Bells and Bamboo Pipes* (Tuesday), *New Music Lounge* and the esoterically titled *Confucius and Inspiration Beyond* (Wednesday), *News Talk* and *Life Unusual* (Thursday), and Friday's *Formosa*

02:00–02:00

Outlook and *Taiwan Gourmet.* Saturday's pairing of *Kaleidoscope* and *Mailbag Time* is replaced Sunday by *Hakka World* and *Asia Pacific.* Sixty minutes to East Asia on 15465 kHz.

Voice of Russia World Service. Winter, the start of a four-hour block of programming to North America; summer, it's the beginning of the second hour. *News,* features and music to suit all tastes. Winter fare includes *Commonwealth Update* (0211 Tuesday through Saturday), replaced Sunday and Monday by *Moscow Mailbag.* The second half-hour includes ●*Folk Box* (Tuesday), ●*Jazz Show* (Wednesday),●*Music at Your Request* or ●*Music Around Us* (Friday), ●*Christian Message from Moscow* (Saturday), ●*Moscow Yesterday and Today* (Sunday) and *Timelines* (Monday). In summer, *News and Views* replaces *Commonwealth Update* and Sunday's *Moscow Mailbag,* with *Sunday Panorama* and *Russia: People and Events* filling the Monday spots. There's a news summary on the half-hour, then ●*Audio Book Club* (Saturday), *Songs from Russia* (Sunday), *This is Russia* (Monday), *Kaleidoscope* (Tuesday), *Musical Tales of St. Petersburg* and *Russia: People and Events* (Wednesday), ●*Moscow Yesterday and Today* (Thursday) or Friday's *Russian by Radio.* Note that these days are World Time; locally in North America it will be the previous evening. For eastern North America winter, tune to 6155, 7180 and 9765 kHz; summer, it's 9665 and 9725 kHz. Listeners in western states should go for 12020, 13665 and 15455 kHz in winter; and 17660 and 17690 kHz in summer.

Radio Habana Cuba. The second half of a two-hour broadcast to eastern and central North America. Tuesday through Sunday (Monday through Saturday evenings in North America), opens with 10 minutes of international *news.* Next comes *Spotlight on the Americas* (Tuesday through Saturday) or Sunday's *The World of Stamps.* The final 30 minutes consists of news-oriented programming. The Monday slots are *From Havana* and ●*The Jazz Place* or *Breakthrough* (science). On 6000 and 9820 kHz. May also be available on 6195 or 9505 kHz.

Radio Station Belarus/Radio Minsk. Monday, Wednesday and Friday through

Sunday, summer only at this time. See 0300 for details. Thirty minutes to Europe on 5970 and 7210kHz. One hour later in winter. Sometimes audible in eastern North America.

Radio Australia. Continuous programming to Asia and the Pacific, but well heard in parts of North America (especially to the west). Begins with *World News,* then Monday through Friday it's *The World Today* (comprehensive coverage of world events). Weekends, there's Saturday's *Background Briefing* and *Earthbeat,* replaced Sunday by *Margaret Throsby* (interviews and music). Targeted at Asia and the Pacific on 9660, 12080, 15240, 15415, 15515, 17580, 17750 and 21725 kHz. Best heard in North America (especially during summer) on 15515 and 17580 kHz; in East Asia on 15240 and 21725 kHz; and in Southeast Asia on 15415 and 17750 kHz. Some of these channels carry a separate sports service on summer (midyear) weekends and winter Saturdays.

Radio for Peace International, Costa Rica. Continues with a six hour cyclical block of social-conscience and counterculture programming audible in Europe and the Americas on 7445 kHz.

Radio Korea International, South Korea. Opens with 10 minutes of *news,* then Tuesday through Saturday (weekday evenings in the Americas), a commentary. This is followed by 30 minutes (45 on Saturday) of *Seoul Calling.* Tuesday through Friday, the broadcast closes with a 15-minute feature: *Korea, Today and Tomorrow, Korean Kaleidoscope, Wonderful Korea* and *Seoul Report,* respectively. Sunday, the news is followed by *Worldwide Friendship* (a listener-response program), and Monday by *Korean Pop Interactive.* Sixty minutes to North America on 9560 and 15575 kHz, and to East Asia on 11810 kHz.

Voice of Korea, North Korea. Repeat of the 0100 broadcast. One hour to South East Asia on 9325 (or 11845) and 11335 (or 15230) kHz. Also audible in parts of East Asia on 3560 kHz.

Radio Romania International. *News,* commentary, press review and features on Romania. Regular spots include Wednesday's *Youth Club* (Tuesday evening, local American

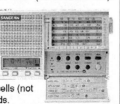

02:00–03:00

date), Thursday's *Romanian Musicians*, and Friday's *Listeners Letterbox* and ●*Skylark* (Romanian folk music). Fifty-five minutes to North America winter on 9550 and 11830 kHz, and summer on 9510 and 11940 kHz; to East Asia winter on 11740 and 15290 kHz, and summer on 11810 and 15105 kHz; and to Australasia winter on 11940 and 15370 kHz, and midyear on 15180 and 17815 kHz.

AFRTS Shortwave, USA. Network news, live sports, music and features in the upper-sideband mode from the Armed Forces Radio & Television Service. Transmitted from modestly powered U.S. Navy stations around the globe. Try 4319, 5446.5, 5765, 6350, 6458.5, 7507, 10320, 12133.5, 12579, 13362 and 13855 kHz.

02:30

Radio Sweden. Tuesday through Saturday (weekday evenings in North America), it's *news* and features in *Sixty Degrees North*, with the accent heavily on Scandinavian topics. See 0330 for full program details. Sunday there's *Network Europe*, *Spectrum* (the arts), *Sweden Today* or *Studio 49*. A listener-response program, *In Touch with Stockholm*, is aired on the first Monday of each month, and replaced by *Sounds Nordic* on the remaining weeks. Thirty minutes to North America on 9495 kHz.

Radio Tirana, Albania. Tuesday through Sunday (Monday through Saturday evenings in North America) and summer only at this time. Thirty minutes of Balkan news and music to

Part of the old radio house still stands on Gonsiori Street in Tallinn, Estonia.   A. Mujunen

North America on 6115 and 7160 kHz. One hour later during winter.

Radio Budapest, Hungary. Summer only at this time. *News* and features, not many of which are broadcast on a regular basis. Thirty minutes to North America on 9570 kHz. One hour later in winter.

Voice of Vietnam. Repeat of the 0100 broadcast; see there for specifics. A relay to eastern North America via the facilities of Radio Canada International on 6175 kHz. Reception is better to the south.

02:45

Radio Tirana, Albania. Tuesday through Sunday (Monday through Saturday local American date) and winter only at this time. Approximately 15 minutes of *news* and commentary from one of Europe's least known countries. To North America on 6115 and 7160 kHz. One hour earlier in summer.

Vatican Radio. Actually starts at 0250. Concentrates heavily, but not exclusively, on issues affecting Catholics around the world. Twenty minutes to eastern North America on 7305 and 9605 kHz.

03:00

■**BBC World Service for the Americas.** Winter, opens with 30 minutes of *The World Today*, then Monday through Saturday (Sunday through Friday evenings in the Americas) there's 13 minutes of ●*World Business Report* followed most days by ●*Analysis* (current events). The exceptions are Thursday's ●*From Our Own Correspondent* and Monday's *Instant Guide*. Sunday programming consists of either an extra 30 minutes of ●*Play of the Week* or news coverage in *The World Today*. Summer programming starts with *News*, then Tuesday through Friday (Monday through Thursday evenings in the Americas) is followed by *Outlook* and the 15-minute ●*Off the Shelf* (also aired Monday). Best of the weekend programs is ●*From Our Own Correspondent* at 0306 Sunday. Continues to North America and the

Caribbean on 5975 kHz; also to western North America and Central America winter on 9525 kHz, and summer on 11835 kHz.

■BBC World Service for Southern Africa. Same as the service for the Mideast until 0330, then Monday through Friday it's *Network Africa*, a fast-moving breakfast show. This is replaced Saturday by *African Quiz* or *This Week and Africa*, and Sunday by *Postmark Africa*. The first 60 minutes of a 19-hour block of programming. On 3255, 6005, 6190 and 7125 kHz.

■BBC World Service for East and Southeast Asia. Monday through Saturday, starts with five minutes of *news*. Best of the weekday features which follow are ●*One Planet* and *People and Places* (Monday), *Discovery* and *Essential Guide* (Tuesday), Wednesday's excellent combo of ●*Health Matters* and ●*Everywoman*, Thursday's ●*Focus on Faith* (0330) and Friday's *Sports International* and *Pick of the World*. On Saturday, the news is followed by 55 minutes of *Wright Round the World*. The Sunday lineup consists of *World Briefing*, ●*Sports Roundup* and *Science in Action*. Audible in East Asia on 15280, 15360 (to 0330), 17760 and 21660 kHz. For Southeast Asia there's only 15360 kHz until 0330.

Voice of Croatia. Winter only at this time. Approximately 20 minutes (sometimes less) of news and reports in "Croatia Today." To eastern North America on 7280 or 9925 kHz; and to South America on 9925 kHz. One hour earlier in summer.

Wales Radio International. This time winter Saturdays only (Friday evenings American date). News, interviews and music from the land of the bards. Thirty minutes to North America on 9735 kHz, and one hour earlier in summer.

Radio Taiwan International. Opens with 15 minutes of *News*, and closes weekdays with *Let's Learn Chinese*. The remaining airtime is taken up by features. Monday (Sunday evening in North America) there's *Taiwan Economic Journal* followed by *Stage, Screen and Studio*; Tuesday's slot goes to ●*Jade Bells and Bamboo Pipes* (Taiwanese music); Wednesday's combo

is *New Music Lounge* and *Confucius and Inspiration Beyond*; Thursday brings *News Talk* and *Life Unusual*; and Friday's menu is *Formosa Outlook* and *Taiwan Gourmet*. Weekends, there's Saturday's *Kaleidoscope* and *Mailbag Time*, and Sunday's *Hakka World* and *Asia Pacific*. One hour to North America on 5950 and 9680 kHz, and to Southeast Asia on 11875 and 15320 kHz. A separate transmission to South America (a repeat of the 0200 broadcast to North America) is aired on 15215 kHz.

China Radio International. Starts with *News*, followed Monday through Friday (Sunday through Thursday evenings in the Americas) by special reports—current events, sports, business, culture, science and technology and press clippings. The rest of the broadcast is devoted to features. Regulars include ●*People in the Know* (Monday), *Biz China* (Tuesday), *China Horizons* (Wednesday), ●*Voices from Other Lands* (Thursday), and *Life in China* on Friday. Weekends, the news is followed by a shorter series of reports (current events and sport) and two features. Saturday there's *Cutting Edge*, and *Listeners' Garden* (listener mail, Chinese folk music, a preview of the next week's programs, and a Chinese language lesson); replaced Sunday by *Reports on Developing Countries* and *In the Spotlight*, a series of mini-features: *Cultural Carousel*, *In Vogue*, *Writings from China*, *China Melody* and *Talking Point*. One hour to North America on 9690 and 9790 kHz.

Radio Ukraine International. Summer only at this time, and a repeat of the 0000 broadcast; see there for specifics. Sixty minutes to western Europe and eastern North America on 9810 or 12040 kHz. One hour later in winter. Often poor reception due to budget and technical limitations.

Voice of America. Three and a half hours (four at weekends) of continuous programming aimed at an African audience. Monday through Friday, there's the informative and entertaining ●*Daybreak Africa*, with the second half-hour taken up by *News Now*—a mixed bag of sports, science, business and other news and features. Weekends, it's a full hour of *News Now*. Although beamed to Africa,

03:00–03:00

this service is widely heard elsewhere, including parts of the United States. Best for southern Africa are 6080, 7105, 7415 (or 17895), 9575 and 9885 kHz. In the United States, try 9575 kHz.

Voice of Russia World Service. Continuous programming to North America at this hour. *News*, then winter it's *News and Views*—except Monday (Sunday evening in North America) when *Sunday Panorama* and *Russia: People and Events* are aired instead. At 0331, there's ●*Audio Book Club* (Saturday), *Songs from Russia* and *You Write to Moscow* (Sunday), *This is Russia* (Monday), *Kaleidoscope* (Tuesday), *Musical Tales of St. Petersburg* and *Russia: People and Events* (Wednesday), ●*Moscow Yesterday and Today* (Thursday) and *Russian by Radio* on Friday. In summer, the news is followed by a feature: *Science and Engineering* (Monday and Thursday), *Musical Tales of St. Petersburg* (Tuesday), *Moscow Mailbag* (Wednesday and Saturday) and *Newmarket* (business) on Friday. More features follow a brief news summary on the half-hour: ●*Audio Book Club* (Monday), *XX Century: Footprints in History* (Tuesday, Thursday and Saturday), and unscheduled features on Wednesday and Friday. Pride of place at this hour goes to Sunday's 45-minute ●*Music and Musicians*. In eastern North America, choose between 6155 and 7180 kHz in winter, and 9665 and 11750 kHz in summer. In western North America, the situation is a little better— for winter, try 12020, 13665 and 15445 kHz; in summer, pick from 17565, 17650, 17660 and 17690 kHz.

Radio Station Belarus/Radio Minsk. Monday, Wednesday and Friday through Sunday, winter only at this time. Thirty minutes of local *news* and interviews, plus a little Belarusian music. All transmissions at this hour are repeats of broadcasts originally aired Tuesday or Thursday evenings. To Europe on 5970 and 7210 kHz, and one hour earlier in summer. Sometimes heard in eastern North America.

Radio Australia. *World News*, then Monday through Friday there's *Regional Sports*, *Pacific Focus* and a 20-minute music feature—*Oz Music Show* (Monday), *Music Deli* (music from different cultures, Tuesday), *Blacktracker* (indigenous music and stories, Wednesday), *Australian*

Country Style (Thursday), and *Jazz Notes* (Friday). Saturday, the out-of-town *Rural Reporter* is paired with *In the Pipeline*, and Sunday's *Feedback* (a listener-response show) is followed by some cutting scientific commentary in ●*Ockham's Razor*. Continuous to Asia and the Pacific on 9660, 12080, 15240, 15415, 15515, 17580, 17750 and 21725 kHz. Also heard in North America (best in summer) on 15515 and 17580 kHz. In East Asia, tune to 15240 or 21725 kHz; for Southeast Asia, there's 15415 and 17750 kHz. Some of these channels carry a separate sports service at weekends.

Radio Habana Cuba. Repeat of the 0100 broadcast. To eastern and central North America on 6000 and 9820 kHz. May also be available on 6195 or 9505 kHz.

Radio Thailand. *News Magazine*. Thirty minutes to western North America winter on 15460 kHz, and summer on 15395 kHz.

Radio Prague, Czech Republic. Summer only at this hour; see 0400 for program specifics. A half hour to North America on 7345 and 9870 kHz. This is by far the best opportunity for listeners in western states. One hour later in winter.

Radio Cairo, Egypt. The final half-hour of a 90-minute broadcast to North America on 11780 kHz.

Radio Bulgaria. Winter only at this time; see 0200 for specifics. A distinctly Bulgarian potpourri of news, commentary, interviews and features, plus a fair amount of music. Not to be missed is the musical ●*Folk Studio* at 0310 Monday (Sunday evening local American date). Sixty minutes to eastern North America and Central America on 7400 and 9400 kHz. One hour earlier in summer.

Radio Japan. *News*, then weekdays it's *Songs for Everyone* and *Asian Top News*. These are followed by a 35-minute feature: *Japan Music Treasure Box* (Monday), Japanese language lessons (Tuesday and Thursday), *Japan Musicscape* (Wednesday), and *Music Beat* (Japanese popular music) on Friday. *Weekend Japanology* and *Sight and Sounds of Japan* fill the Saturday slot, and *Hello from Tokyo* is aired Sunday. Sixty minutes to Australasia on 21610 kHz, and to Central America on 17825 kHz.

Radio New Zealand International. Continues with *news* and features targeted at a regional audience. Part of a much longer transmission for the South Pacific, but also heard in parts of North America (especially during summer) on 17675 kHz. Often carries commentaries of local sporting events. Popular with many listeners.

Voice of Korea, North Korea. Not quite the old-time communist station it was, but the "Great Leader" and "Unrivaled Great Man" continue to be revered. Worth the occasional listen to see if there's any improvement. One hour to East Asia on 4405, 6195, 7140 and 9345 kHz.

Voice of Turkey. Summer only at this time. *News*, followed by *Review of the Turkish Press* and features (some of them unusual) with a strong local flavor. Selections of Turkish popular and classical music complete the program. Fifty minutes to Europe and North America on 9650 or 11655 kHz, and to the Mideast on 7270 kHz. One hour later during winter.

Radio for Peace International, Costa Rica. Continues with a variety of counterculture and social-conscience features. Audible in Europe and the Americas on 7445 kHz.

AFRTS Shortwave, USA. Network news, live sports, music and features in the upper-sideband mode from the Armed Forces Radio & Television Service. Transmitted from modestly powered U.S. Navy stations around the globe. Try 4319, 5446.5, 5765, 6350, 6458.5, 7507, 10320, 12133.5, 12579, 13362 and 13855 kHz.

03:30

Emirates Radio, Dubai. *News*, then a feature devoted to Arab and Islamic history or culture. Twenty minutes to North America on 12005, 13675 and 15400 kHz; heard best during the warm-weather months.

Radio Sweden. Winter only at this time. Tuesday through Saturday (weekday evenings local American date), it's *news* and features in *Sixty Degrees North*, concentrating heavily on Scandinavian topics. Several of the features

rotate from week to week, but a few are fixtures. Tuesday's *SportScan* is replaced Wednesday by *Close Up* or an alternative feature, and Thursday by a special feature. Friday's rotating lineup is *Nordic Lights*, *GreenScan* (the environment), *Heart Beat* (health), and *S-Files*, and *Weekly Review* fills the Saturday slot. The Sunday rotation is *Network Europe*, *Spectrum*, *Sweden Today* and *Studio 49*; while Monday's offering is *In Touch with Stockholm* (a listener-response program) or the musical *Sounds Nordic*. Thirty minutes to western North America on 9495 kHz, and one hour earlier in summer.

Radio Prague, Czech Republic. Summer only at this time. See the 0400 winter broadcast for North America for program specifics. Thirty minutes to the Mideast and South Asia on 11600 and 15620 kHz. One hour later in winter.

Radio Budapest, Hungary. This time winter only. *News* and features, most of which are broadcast on a non-regular basis. Thirty minutes to North America on 9835 kHz. One hour earlier in summer.

Voice of Vietnam. A relay via the facilities of Radio Canada International. Begins with *news*, then there's *Commentary* or *Weekly Review*, followed by short features and some pleasant Vietnamese music (particularly at weekends). A half hour to western North America on 6175 kHz.

Radio Tirana, Albania. Tuesday through Monday (Monday through Saturday evenings local American date) and winter only at this time. *News*, features and lively Albanian music. Thirty minutes to North America on 6115 and 7160 kHz. One hour earlier in summer.

04:00

■**BBC World Service for the Americas.** Winter, starts with *News*, then Tuesday through Friday (Monday through Thursday evenings in the Americas) is followed by *Outlook* and the 15-minute ●*Off the Shelf* (also aired Monday). Best of the weekend programs is ●*From Our Own Correspondent* at 0306 Sunday. The summer opener is *World Briefing*, with *The World Today* completing the hour

04:00–04:00

Monday through Friday (Sunday through Thursday evenings in North America). This is replaced Saturday by ●*Reporting Religion*, and Sunday by *Letter from America* and *The Instant Guide*. Continuous programming to western North America and Central America on 5975, (winter) 6135 and (summer) 11835 kHz.

■BBC World Service for Europe. Identical to the service for the Americas, except for 0430 summer Saturdays, when ●*Weekend* replaces ●*Assignment*. Continuous to Europe and North Africa on 6195, 9410 and (summer) 12035 kHz.

■BBC World Service for Southern Africa. Thirty minutes of ●*The World Today*, followed Monday through Friday by *Network Africa*. Weekends at 0430, look for Saturday's *Talkabout Africa* or Sunday's *African Perspective*. Continues on 3255, 6190, 7125 and (winter) 11765 kHz.

■BBC World Service for East Asia. Monday through Friday, it's 50 minutes of news and current events in *The World Today*, then ●*Sports Roundup* closes the hour. On the remaining days, *The World Today* is cut to 30 minutes, and is followed by Saturday's ●*Assignment* (or another documentary), and Sunday's ●*Omnibus* or light entertainment (including the unique ●*Brain of Britain* for part of the year). Continuous to East Asia on 15280, 17760 and 21660 kHz.

Erik Bettermann, Director-General of Deutsche Welle, in front of the new DW headquarters in Bonn.   DW

■Radio Netherlands. Tuesday through Saturday (weekday evenings in North America), opens with ●*Newsline* (current events). A feature follows on the half-hour: ●*Research File* (Tuesday), ●*EuroQuest* (Wednesday), ●*Documentary* (Thursday), *Dutch Horizons* (Friday), and *A Good Life* (Saturday). On the remaining days, a six-minute *news* bulletin is followed Sunday by *Europe Unzipped*, *Insight* and *Amsterdam Forum*; and Monday by *Wide Angle*, *The Week Ahead* and *Vox Humana*. Fifty-five minutes to western North America on 6165 and 9590 kHz.

Radio Habana Cuba. Repeat of the 0200 broadcast. To east and central North America on 6000 and 9820 kHz. May also be available on 6195 or 9505 kHz.

Flanders Radio International, Belgium. Summer only at this time. See 0500 for program specifics. Thirty minutes to western North America on 15565 kHz. One hour later in winter.

Radio Prague, Czech Republic. Winter only at this time. *News*, then Tuesday through Saturday (weekday evenings in the Americas) there's *Current Affairs* and one or more features: *Talking Point* (Tuesday), *Witness* and *One on One* (Wednesday), *ABC of Czech* and either *Czechs in History* or *Spotlight* (Thursday), *Economics Report* (Friday), and *Stepping Out* and *The Arts* on Saturday. The Sunday lineup is *Magazine*, *Letter from Prague* and a repeat of Wednesday's *One on One*; and Monday there's *Mailbox* and *ABC of Czech* followed by *Encore* (classical music), *Magic Carpet* (Czech world music) or *Czech Books*. Thirty minutes to North America on 5915 and 7345 kHz. By far the best opportunity for western states. One hour earlier in summer.

■Radio France Internationale. Weekdays only at this time. Starts with a bulletin of African *news* and an international newsflash. Next, there's a review of the French dailies, an in-depth look at events in Africa, the main news event of the day in France, and sports. Thirty information-packed minutes to East Africa on any two channels from 9550, 9805, 11700, 11910, 11995 and 13610 kHz. Heard well beyond the intended target area.

Radio Ukraine International. Winter only at this time, and a repeat of the 0100 broadcast. Ample coverage of local issues, including news, sports, politics and culture. Well worth a listen is ●*Music from Ukraine*, which fills most of the Monday (Sunday evening in the Americas) broadcast. Sixty minutes to Europe on 7285 and 9610 kHz; to eastern North America on 5905 kHz, and to West Asia on 7420 kHz. One hour earlier in summer. Budget and technical limitations have greatly reduced the audibility of this station.

Radio Australia. *World News*, then Monday through Friday it's music and interviews with *Margaret Throsby*. Weekend fare consists of *Pacific Focus* followed by Saturday's *The Buzz* or Sunday's *Arts Talk*. Continuous to Asia and the Pacific on 9660, 12080, 15240, 15415, 15515, 17580, 17750 (from 0530) and 21725 kHz. Should also be audible in parts of North America (best during summer) on 15515 and 17580 kHz. In East Asia, choose between 15240 and 21725 kHz; for Southeast Asia, there's 15415 and 17750 kHz. Some channels carry separate sports programming at weekends.

■**Deutsche Welle,** Germany. *News*, followed Tuesday through Saturday by the comprehensive and well produced ●*NewsLink for Africa*— commentary, interviews, background reports and analysis. On the half-hour there's *Insight* and *Business German* (Tuesday), *World in Progress* (Wednesday), *Money Talks* (Thursday), *Environment* (Friday) and *Spectrum* (Saturday). Sunday brings ●*Inside Europe*, replaced Monday by *Mailbag*. Sixty minutes to East and Central Africa winter on 6180, 9545 and 9710 kHz; and summer on 7225, 11945 and 15410 kHz. Good winter reception in the Mideast on 9545 kHz, and summer on 11945 kHz.

Voice of America. Directed to Africa and the Mideast, but widely heard elsewhere. *News Now*—a mixed bag of sports, science, business and other news and features. Weekdays on the half-hour, the African service leaves the mainstream programming and carries its own ●*Daybreak Africa*. To North Africa winter on 7170 kHz, and summer on 9530 kHz (also heard in southern Europe); and to the Mideast on 11965 (summer) and 15205 kHz. For

southern Africa there's 6080, 7415 (or 17895), 9575 and (till 0430) 9885 kHz. In the United States, try 9575 kHz.

Radio Romania International. Similar to the 0200 transmission (see there for specifics). Fifty-five minutes to North America winter on 9550 and 11830 kHz, and summer on 9510 and 11940; and to South Asia winter on 15335 and 17735 kHz, and summer on 17735 and 21480kHz.

Voice of Turkey. Winter only at this time. See 0300 for specifics. Fifty minutes to Europe and North America on 6020 kHz, and to the Mideast on 7240 kHz. One hour earlier in summer.

Kol Israel. Summer only at this time. *News* for 15 minutes from Israel Radio's domestic network. To Europe and eastern North America on 9435 and 15640 kHz, and to Australasia on 17600 kHz. One hour later in winter.

China Radio International. Repeat of the 0300 broadcast (see there for specifics); one hour to North America winter on 9730 kHz, and summer on 9560 and 9755 kHz.

Radio New Zealand International. Continues with regional programming for the South Pacific. Part of a much longer broadcast, which is also heard in parts of North America (especially during summer) on 15340 or 17675 kHz. Sometimes carries commentaries of local sports events.

Radio for Peace International, Costa Rica. Part of a six-hour cyclical block of predominantly social-conscience and counterculture programming. Audible in Europe and the Americas on 7445.

Voice of Russia World Service. Continues to North America at this hour. *News*, then a feature. Winter, there's *Science and Engineering* (Monday and Thursday), *Musical Tales of St. Petersburg* (Tuesday), *Moscow Mailbag* (Wednesday and Saturday) and *Newmarket* (business) on Friday. More features follow a brief news summary on the half-hour: ●*Audio Book Club* (Monday), *XX Century: Footprints in History* (Tuesday, Thursday and Saturday), and unscheduled features on Wednesday and

04:00–05:00

Friday. Not to be missed at this hour is Sunday's 45-minute ●*Music and Musicians*. The summer schedule has plenty of variety, and includes ●*Jazz Show* (0431 Monday), ●*Music at Your Request* and ●*Music Around Us* (same time Tuesday), the business-oriented *Newmarket* (0411 Thursday), *Science and Engineering* (same time Wednesday and Saturday), ●*Folk Box* (0431 Thursday), ●*Audio Book Club* (0431 Friday), *Moscow Mailbag* (0411 Tuesday and Friday), the retrospective ●*Moscow Yesterday and Today* (0431 Wednesday) and *Kaleidoscope* (0431 Sunday). Note that these days are World Time; locally in North America it will be the previous evening. In eastern North America, tune to 7125 and 7180 kHz in winter, and 9665 and 11750 kHz in summer. Best winter bets for the West Coast are 12010, 12020, 13665, 15445, 15595 and 17595 kHz; in summer, choose from 17565, 17650, 17660 and 17690 kHz.

AFRTS Shortwave, USA. Network news, live sports, music and features in the upper-sideband mode from the Armed Forces Radio & Television Service. Transmitted from modestly powered U.S. Navy stations around the globe. Try 4319, 5446.5, 5765, 6350, 6458.5, 7507, 10320, 12133.5, 12579, 13362 and 13855 kHz.

04:30

Radio Prague, Czech Republic. Winter only at this time. See the 0400 broadcast to North America for program specifics. Thirty minutes to the Mideast and South Asia on 9865 and 11600 kHz. One hour earlier in summer.

05:00

■BBC World Service for the Americas. Winter only at this time. Starts with the daily *World Briefing*, then Monday through Friday (Sunday through Thursday evenings in North America), *The World Today* completes the hour. This is replaced Saturday by ●*Reporting Religion*, and Sunday by *Letter from America* and *The Instant Guide*. The final hour to western North America and Central America on 6135 kHz.

■BBC World Service for Europe. Monday through Friday, a full hour of news in ●*The World Today*. Weekends, the second half hour is replaced Saturday by ●*Weekend* (winter) or *Arts in Action* (summer), and Sunday by ●*Reporting Religion* and ●*Letter from America*. Continuous to Europe and North Africa on 6195, 9410 and (summer) 12095 kHz.

■BBC World Service for Africa. ●*The World Today*, then weekdays on the half-hour there's a continuation of *Network Africa*. Weekends, the final 30 minutes are filled by Saturday's *African Quiz* or *This Week and Africa*, and Sunday's *Artbeat*. Continuous programming on 3255 (midyear), 6190, 11765 and (winter) 11940 kHz.

■BBC World Service for East and Southeast Asia and the Pacific. Starts with 30 minutes of ●*The World Today*. Thereafter, it's a mixed bag of features. Favorites are ●*Off the Shelf* (serialized readings from world literature, 0545 weekdays) and ●*Reporting Religion* and ●*Letter from America* (0130 and 0145 Sunday). Continuous to East Asia on 15280 (till 0530), 15360, 17760 and 21660 kHz; and to Southeast Asia on 9740 and 15360 kHz. Heard in Australasia on 15360 kHz.

Flanders Radio International, Belgium. Winter only at this time. Tuesday through Saturday (weekday evenings in North America), starts with *News*. The rest of the broadcast is a mix of current events, reports and Belgian music. Sunday, these are replaced by the entertaining ●*Music from Flanders*, and Monday by *Radio World*, *Tourism* and *Brussels 1043* (a listener-response program). A half hour to western North America on 9590 kHz. One hour earlier in summer.

■Deutsche Welle, Germany. *News*, then Tuesday through Saturday it's ●*NewsLink for Africa*—commentary, interviews, background reports and analysis. The second half-hour features ●*World Music Live* (Tuesday), *Arts on the Air* (Wednesday), *Living in Germany* and *Europe on Stage* (Thursday), *Cool* (a well produced youth show, Friday) and ●*Focus on Folk* (Saturday). On Sunday there's *Religion and Society*, *German by Radio* and *Africa This Week*; and Monday's fare is *Hard to Beat* (sport), *Inspired Minds* and either *Hits in*

Germany or *Melody Time*. Sixty minutes to East, Central and southern Africa, winter on 9565, 11805, 12045 and 15410 kHz; and summer on 9700, 11925, 12045, 13755 and 15410 kHz. Best winter channels for southern Africa are 11805 and 12045 kHz; in summer (winter in the Southern Hemisphere) choose from 12045 and 13755 kHz.

■**Radio France Internationale.** Monday through Friday only at this time. Similar to the 0400 broadcast, but without the international newsflash. A half hour to East Africa (and heard well beyond) on any two channels from 11685, 11850, 13610, 15155 and 17800 kHz.

Vatican Radio. Summer only at this time. Twenty minutes of programming oriented to Catholics. To Europe on 4005, 5890 and 7250 kHz. One hour later in winter.

Radio Japan. *News*, then Monday through Friday there's *Japan and the World 44 Minutes* (an in-depth look at current trends and events). This is replaced Saturday by *Hello from Tokyo* and Sunday by *Pop Joins the World*. One hour to Europe on 5975 and 7230 kHz; to East Asia on 11715, 11760 and 15195 kHz; to Southeast Asia on 17810 kHz; to Australasia on 21755 kHz; and to western North America on 6110 kHz.

China Radio International. This time winter only. Repeat of the 0300 broadcast (see there for specifics); one hour to North America on 9560 kHz via a Canadian relay.

Voice of America. Continues with the morning broadcast to Africa and the Mideast. *News Now*—a mixed bag of sports, science, business and other news and features. To North Africa (and audible in southern Europe) on 7170 kHz in winter, and 9530 kHz in summer; to the Mideast on 11825 (winter), 11965 (summer) and 15205 kHz; and to the rest of Africa on 5970, 6035, 6080, 7195 (summer), 7295 (winter), 9630 (summer) and 12080 kHz. In the United States, try 6035 kHz.

Radio Habana Cuba. The start of a two-hour broadcast for the East Coast and western North America. Tuesday through Sunday (Monday through Saturday evenings in North America), the first half hour consists of

Simo Soininen inside the control room of I Foni tis Helladas, the Voice of Greece. S. Soininen.

international and Cuban news followed by *RHC's Viewpoint*. The next 30 minutes consist of a news bulletin and the sports-oriented *Time Out* (five minutes each) plus a feature: *Caribbean Outlook* (Tuesday and Friday), *DXers Unlimited* (Wednesday and Sunday), the *Mailbag Show* (Thursday) and *Weekly Review* (Saturday). Monday, the hour is split between *Weekly Review* and *Mailbag Show*. In the east, use 9550 kHz; in the west, 9820 kHz (also audible in parts of Australasia). May also be available on 11760 kHz.

Radio Austria International. Summer Sundays only, and actually starts at 0505. See 0600 for more details. To the Mideast on 17870 kHz, and one hour later in winter.

Voice of Nigeria. Monday through Friday, opens with *VON Scope*, a half hour of *news* and press comment. Weekends, a five-minute news summary is followed by Saturday's *VON Link-up* or Sunday's *This Week on VON*. On the half-hour, there's the daily *Moving On*. The first 60 minutes of a longer broadcast to West Africa (and heard in parts of North America, especially in winter) on 7255 kHz, and to North Africa and Europe on 15120 or 17800 kHz.

Radio New Zealand International. Continues with regional programming for the South Pacific. Part of a much longer broadcast, which is also heard in parts of North America (especially during summer) on 11820 or 15340 kHz.

05:00–05:30

Radio Australia. *World News*, then Monday through Friday there's *Pacific Beat* (background reporting on events in the Pacific)— look for a sports bulletin at 0530. Weekends, the news is followed by *Pacific Focus* and Saturday's *Lingua Franca* and *Business Weekend* or Sunday's *Fine Music Australia*. Continuous to Asia and the Pacific on 9660, 12080, 15240, 15415, 15515, 17580, 17750 (from 0530) and 21725 kHz. In North America (best during summer) try 15515 and 17580 kHz. Best for East Asia are 15240 and 21725 kHz; in Southeast Asia use 15415 or 17750 kHz. Some channels carry alternative sports programming at weekends.

Voice of Russia World Service. Winter, the final 60 minutes of a four-hour block of programming to North America; summer, the first of four hours to Australasia. Opens with *News*, followed winter by features. These includes ●*Jazz Show* (0431 Monday), ●*Music at Your Request* and ●*Music Around Us* (same time Tuesday), the business-oriented *Newmarket* (0411 Thursday), *Science and Engineering* (same time Wednesday and Saturday), ●*Folk Box* (0431 Thursday), ●*Audio Book Club* (0431 Friday), *Moscow Mailbag* (0411 Tuesday and Friday), the retrospective ●*Moscow Yesterday and Today* (0431 Wednesday) and *Kaleidoscope* (0431 Sunday). Note that these days are World Time; locally in

Sylvia Acksteiner anchors "Journal" for Deutsche Welle. DW

North America it will be the previous evening. Tuesday through Saturday summer, there's *Focus on Asia and the Pacific*, replaced Sunday by *Science and Engineering* and Monday by *Moscow Mailbag*. On the half-hour, look for *This is Russia* (Friday), ●*Audio Book Club* (Sunday), ●*Moscow Yesterday and Today* (Thursday), ●*Christian Message from Moscow* (Saturday), *Russian by Radio* (Monday and Wednesday) and *Kaleidoscope* on Tuesday. Winter only to eastern North America on 7125 and 7180 kHz, and to western parts on 12010, 12020, 13665, 15445 and 15595 kHz. Available summer to Australasia on 15275, 17635, 17685, 17795 (also heard in Southeast Asia) and 21790 kHz.

Radio for Peace International, Costa Rica. Continues with a six-hour cyclical block of social-conscience and counterculture programming. Audible in Europe and the Americas on 7445 kHz.

Kol Israel. Winter only at this time. *News* for 15 minutes from Israel Radio's domestic network. To Europe and eastern North America on any two channels from 6280, 7475, 9435 and 11605 kHz, and to Australasia on 15640 or 17600 kHz. One hour earlier in summer.

AFRTS Shortwave, USA. Network news, live sports, music and features in the upper-sideband mode from the Armed Forces Radio & Television Service. Transmitted from modestly powered U.S. Navy stations around the globe. Try 4319, 5446.5, 5765, 6350, 6458.5, 7507, 10320, 12133.5, 12579, 13362 and 13855 kHz.

05:30

Emirates Radio, Dubai. See 0330 for program details. Twenty minutes to East Asia and Australasia on 15435, 17830 and 21700 kHz. Frequencies may vary a little.

Radio Thailand. Thirty minutes of *news* and short features relayed from one of the station's domestic services. To Europe winter on 13780 kHz, and summer on 21795 kHz.

0600-1159
Australasia & East Asia—Evening Prime Time
Western North America—Late Evening
Europe & Mideast—Morning and Midday

06:00

■**BBC World Service for Europe.** Monday through Friday winter, a full hour of *The World Today* (news and current events). Weekends, it's reduced to 30 minutes and followed by Saturday's ●*People and Politics* or Sunday's ●*Agenda*. Summer weekdays, you can hear 20 minutes of *World Briefing* followed by ●*Sports Roundup*, ●*World Business Report* and ●*Analysis* (replaced Monday by ●*Letter from America* and Thursday by ●*From Our Own Correspondent*). Saturday and Sunday, the first half hour is the same as during the week, with the final 30 minutes being filled with the same features as winter. Continuous to Europe and North Africa on 6195, 9410, 12095 and (summer) 15485 kHz.

■**BBC World Service for Southern Africa.** Identical to the service for the Mideast at this hour. Continuous programming on 6190, 11765 and 11940 kHz.

■**BBC World Service for East and Southeast Asia and the Pacific.** Five minutes of *news*, then Monday through Friday there's an arts show, *Meridian*. The next half hour consists mostly of a mixed bag of music and light entertainment. Exceptions are winter Thursdays (●*Omnibus*) and summer Mondays (●*Omnibus* and *Composer of the Month*). Weekends, starts with *World Briefing* and ●*Sports Roundup*, then it's either Saturday's ●*People and Politics* or Sunday's *Westway* (a soap). Continuous to East Asia on 15360, 17760 and 21660 kHz; to Southeast Asia on 9740 and 15360 kHz; and to Australasia on 15360 kHz.

■**Deutsche Welle, Germany.** *News*, then Tuesday through Saturday it's ●*NewsLink for Africa*—commentary, interviews, background reports and analysis. This is followed by *Insight* and *Business German* (Tuesday), *World in Progress* (Wednesday), *Money Talks* (Thursday), *Environment* (Friday), and

Spectrum (Saturday). Sunday fare is ●*Inside Europe*, replaced Monday by *Mailbag*. Sixty minutes to West Africa winter on 7225, 11785 and 15410 kHz; and summer on 9780, 15275 and 17860 kHz. Also year round to Europe on 6140 kHz.

Radio Habana Cuba. The second half of a two-hour broadcast for the East Coast and western North America. Tuesday through Sunday (Monday through Saturday evenings in North America), opens with 10 minutes of international news. Next comes *Spotlight on the Americas* (Tuesday through Saturday) or Sunday's *The World of Stamps*. The final 30 minutes consists of news-oriented programming. The Monday slots are *From Havana* and ●*The Jazz Place* or *Breakthrough* (science). Tune to 9550 kHz in the east, and 9820 kHz out west. May also be available on 11760 kHz. Listeners in Australasia can try 9820 kHz, as it's also beamed their way.

Radio Japan. *News*, then weekdays it's *Songs for Everyone* and *Asian Top News*. This is followed by a 35-minute feature: *Japan Music Treasure Box* (Monday), Japanese language lessons (Tuesday and Thursday), *Japan Musicscape* (Wednesday), and *Music Beat* (Japanese popular music) on Friday. On the remaining days, *Pop Joins the World* fills the Saturday slot and *Weekend Japanology* and *Sight and Sounds of Japan* are aired on Sunday. One hour to Europe on 7230 kHz; to East Asia on 15195 kHz; to Southeast Asia on 11740 kHz; to Australasia on 21755 kHz; and to Hawaii on 17870 kHz (this channel has different programming after 0615). Also to western North America winter on 11690 kHz, and summer on 13630 kHz.

Radio Austria International. Winter Sundays only. The 25-minute *Insight Central Europe* is aired at 0605, and then repeated at 0635. The remainder of the one-hour broadcast is in German. To the Mideast on 17870 kHz, and one hour earlier in summer.

06:00–06:00

■**Radio France Internationale.** Weekdays only at this time. Similar to the 0400 broadcast (see there for specifics), but includes a report on the day's main international story. A half hour to East Africa on any two channels from 11665, 11725, 15155, 17800 and 21620 kHz.

Voice of America. Final segment of the transmission to Africa and the Mideast. Monday through Friday, the mainstream African service carries just 30 minutes of ●*Daybreak Africa*, with other channels carrying a full hour of *News Now*—a mixed bag of sports, science, business and other news and features. Weekend programming is the same to all areas—60 minutes of *News Now*. To North Africa (and easily heard in southern Europe) on 5995 and 7170 kHz in winter, and 9530 and 9760 kHz in summer; to the Mideast on 11825 (winter), 11965 (summer) and 15205 kHz; and to mainstream Africa on, among others, 6035, 6080, 7290 (summer), 7295 (winter), 11995 and 12080 kHz. In the United States, try 6035 kHz.

Radio Australia. Opens with *News*, then the weekday lineup is *Regional Sports*, *Pacific Focus* and a 20-minute feature—*Oz Music Show* (Monday), *Music Deli* (music from different cultures, Tuesday), *Blacktracker* (indigenous music and stories, Wednesday), *Australian Country Style* (Thursday), and *Jazz Notes* (Friday). Saturday's pairing is *Feedback* (a listener-response program) and *Oz Sounds*, replaced Sunday by *The Europeans*. Continuous to Asia and the Pacific on 9660, 12080, 15240, 15415, 15515, 17580, 17750 and 21725 kHz. Listeners in western North America should try 15515 and 17580 kHz. In East Asia, tune to 15240 or 21725 kHz; for Southeast Asia, use 15415 or 17750 kHz. Some channels carry an alternative sports program until 0700 on weekends (0800 midyear).

Radio New Zealand International. Continues with regional programming for the South Pacific. Part of a much longer broadcast, which is also heard in parts of North America (especially during summer) on 11820 or 15340 kHz.

Voice of Russia World Service. *News*, then winter it's *Focus on Asia and the Pacific* (Tuesday through Saturday), *Science and Engineering* (Sunday), and *Moscow Mailbag* (Monday). On the half-hour, look for *This is Russia* (Friday), ●*Audio Book Club* (Sunday), ●*Moscow Yesterday and Today* (Thursday), ●*Christian Message from Moscow* (Saturday) and *Russian by Radio* on Monday and Wednesday. In summer, the news is followed by *Science and Engineering* (Monday and Friday), the business-oriented *Newmarket* (Wednesday and Saturday), and a listener-response program, *Moscow Mailbag*, on the remaining days. The second half hour is mostly a combination of *Russia: People and Events*, ●*Russian Treasures* (a gem of a classical music program) and the religious *Daily Reflections*. Continuous programming to Australasia and Southeast Asia. Winter in Australasia (local summer in the Southern Hemisphere), tune to 15275, 15470, 17655, 17665 and 21790 kHz; midyear, go for 15490, 17635, 17685, 17795 and 21790 kHz. For Southeast Asia, there's 11770, 17655 and 21485 kHz in winter, and 15490 and 17795 kHz in summer.

Radio for Peace International, Costa Rica. Continues with counterculture and social-conscience programs. Audible in Europe and the Americas on 7445 kHz.

Vatican Radio. Winter only at this time. Twenty minutes with a heavy Catholic slant. To Europe on 4005, 5890 and 7250 kHz. One hour earlier in summer.

Voice of Croatia. Summer only at this time. A short bulletin of news from and about Croatia. To western North America on 9925 kHz; and to Australasia on 9470 and 13820 kHz. One hour later in winter.

Voice of Malaysia. *News*, followed Monday, Wednesday, Friday and Sunday by a two-minute Malayan language lesson (replaced by a local pop hit on Tuesday). The next 33 minutes are given over to *Hits All the Way*. Saturday, it's the 35-minute *Mailbag*. The hour is rounded off with a feature: *New Horizon* (Monday), *ASEAN Focus* (Tuesday), *Malaysia in Perspective* (Wednesday), *Personality* (Thursday), *News and Views* (Friday), and *Weekly Roundup* and *Current Affairs* on the weekend. The first hour of a 150-minute broadcast to Southeast Asia and Australasia on 6175, 9750 and 15295 kHz.

AFRTS Shortwave, USA. Network news, live sports, music and features in the upper-sideband mode from the Armed Forces Radio & Television Service. Transmitted from modestly powered U.S. Navy stations around the globe. Try 4319, 5446.5, 5765, 6350, 6458.5, 7507, 10320, 12133.5, 12579, 13362 and 13855 kHz.

06:30

Radio Bulgaria. Summer only at this time. Thirty minutes of *news*, commentary, short features and enjoyable Bulgarian music. To Europe on 11600 and 13600 kHz. One hour later during winter.

06:40

Radio Romania International. Actually starts at 0636. A 17-minute broadcast to western Europe winter on 7145, 9510, 9570, 11790 and 11940 kHz; and summer on 7105, 9625, 9550 and 11775 kHz.

07:00

■**BBC World Service for Europe.** Winter, you can hear 20 minutes of *World Briefing* followed by ●*Sports Roundup*, then weekdays there's ●*World Business Report* and ●*Analysis* (replaced Monday by ●*Letter from America* and Thursday by ●*From Our Own Correspondent*). Weekends, these give way to Saturday's *Arts in Action* and Sunday's ●*Assignment* (or substitute documentary). Monday through Saturday summer, starts with *News*, then the long-running *Outlook* (except Monday, when there's *Talking Point*, a call-in show). Weekdays, the final 15 minutes go to ●*Off the Shelf* (readings from the best of world literature); Saturday, the slot is filled by *Write On*. Sunday's lineup is *World Briefing*, ●*Sports Roundup* and ●*Assignment* (or an alternative documentary). Continuous to Europe and North Africa on 6195, 9410, 12095, 15485 and 15565 kHz.

■**BBC World Service for East and Southeast Asia and the Pacific.** Monday through Saturday, starts with five minutes of *news*, then it's all features. Best of the bunch are *Discovery* (science, 0705 Monday), Tuesday's pairing of ●*Health Matters* and ●*Everywoman*, Wednesday's ●*Focus on Faith* (0730) and Friday's ●*One Planet* (0705). The Sunday

Adventist World Radio is headquartered at "White Gate" in suburban London. AWR

lineup consists of *World Briefing*, ●*Sports Roundup* and ●*Assignment* (or its temporary replacement). Continuous to East Asia on 15360, 17760 and 21660 kHz; to Southeast Asia on 9740 and 15360 kHz; and to Australasia on 15360 kHz.

■**Deutsche Welle, Germany.** *News*, followed weekdays by the excellent ●*NewsLink* — commentary, interviews, background reports and analysis. The second half-hour features *Spectrum* (Monday), ●*World Music Live* (Tuesday), *Arts on the Air* (Wednesday), *Living in Germany* and *Europe on Stage* (Thursday) and *Cool* (a youth show, Friday). Weekend fare consists of Saturday's ●*Inside Europe* and Sunday's *Hard to Beat* (sport), *Inspired Minds* and either *Hits in Germany* or *Melody Time*. Sixty minutes to Europe on 6140 kHz.

■**Radio France Internationale.** Starts with a bulletin of African *news*. Next, there's a review of the French dailies, an in-depth look at events in Africa, the main news event of the day in France, and sports. The broadcast ends with a 25-minute feature— *French Lesson, Crossroads, Voices, Rendez-Vous, World Tracks, Weekend* or *Club 9516* (a listener-response program). One hour to West Africa on 15605 kHz, via RFI's Gabon relay. Also audible in parts of North America.

Flanders Radio International, Belgium. Summer only at this time; see 0800 for specifics. Thirty minutes to western Europe on 5985 kHz, and one hour later in winter.

07:30–07:00

Radio Prague, Czech Republic. Summer only at this time. See 0800 for specifics. Thirty minutes to Europe on 9880 and 11600 kHz. One hour later in winter.

Voice of Croatia. Winter only at this time. A short bulletin of news from and about Croatia. To western North America on 7285 or 9925 kHz; and to Australasia on 9470 and 13820 kHz. One hour earlier in summer.

Radio Slovakia International. Tuesday through Friday, starts with *News* and *Topical Issue*, then features. Regulars include *Tourist News* (Tuesday), *Business News* and *Currency Update* (Wednesday), *Culture News* (Thursday) and *Regional News* (Friday). Monday's news is followed by *Insight Central Europe*. The Saturday lineup includes *Front Page* and *Sports News*; and Sunday's features are *Sunday Newsreel* and *Listeners' Tribune*. Thirty minutes to Australasia on 9440 (midyear), 13715 (winter), 15460 and 17550 kHz.

Radio Australia. *World News*, then Monday through Friday it's *Pacific Beat* (background reporting on events in the Pacific)—look for the latest sports news at 0730. *Asia Pacific* and *Business Report* are aired Saturday, with *Correspondents' Report* and *In Conversation* filling the Sunday slots. Continuous to Asia and the Pacific on 9660, 12080, 15240, 15415, 17580, 17750 and 21725 kHz. Listeners in western North America can try 15240 and 17580 kHz (best during summer), while East Asia is served by 15240 and 21725 kHz. For Southeast Asia, take your pick from 15415 and 17750 kHz.

Voice of Malaysia. Starts weekdays with 45 minutes of *Fascinating Malaysia*, replaced Saturday by *Malaysia Rama* and *Malaysia in Perspective*, and Sunday by *ASEAN Melody* and *Destination Malaysia*. Not much doubt about where the broadcast originates! The hour ends with a 15-minute feature. Continuous to Southeast Asia and Australasia on 6175, 9750 and 15295 kHz.

Radio for Peace International, Costa Rica. Continues with a six-hour cyclical block of social-conscience and counterculture programming. Audible in Europe and the Americas on 7445 kHz.

Voice of Russia World Service. Continuous programming to Southeast Asia and Australasia. *News*, then a variety of features. The winter lineup includes *Science and Engineering* (Monday and Friday), the business-oriented *Newmarket* (Wednesday and Saturday), and a listener-response program, *Moscow Mailbag*, on the remaining days. The second half hour is mostly a combination of *Russia: People and Events*, ●*Russian Treasures* and the religious *Daily Reflections*. Summer, the news is followed by the informative ●*Update* on Tuesday, Thursday and Saturday. Other offerings include *Science and Engineering* (Wednesday), *Moscow Mailbag* (Friday) and Monday's masterpiece, ●*Music and Musicians*. On the half-hour, there's some of the Voice of Russia's best—●*Audio Book Club* (Wednesday), ●*Moscow Yesterday and Today* (Friday), *Songs from Russia* (Sunday), ●*Folk Box* (Tuesday) and *This is Russia* on Thursday. Mondays, it's a continuation of ●*Music and Musicians*. Well heard in Australasia winter (local summer) on 15275, 15470, 17655, 17665 and 21790 kHz; and midyear on 17495, 17525, 17635, 17675, 17685 and 17795 kHz. For Southeast Asia, there's 11770, 17655 and 21485 kHz in winter, and 15490, 17685 and 17795 kHz in summer.

Radio New Zealand International. Continues with regional programming for the South Pacific. Part of a much longer broadcast, which is also heard in parts of North America (especially during summer) on 9885 or 11675 kHz.

Radio Taiwan International. Opens with 15 minutes of *News*, and Monday through Friday closes with *Let's Learn Chinese*, which has a series of segments for beginning, intermediate and advanced learners. The remaining airtime is devoted to features. Monday (Sunday evening in North America) there's the exotic ●*Jade Bells and Bamboo Pipes* (Taiwanese music); Tuesday's slots are *Culture Express* and *Trends*; Wednesday's features are *Taiwan Today* and *Instant Noodles*; Thursday's combo is *Discover Taiwan* and *New Music Lounge*; and Friday brings *Taipei Magazine* and *People*. These are replaced Saturday by *Groove Zone* and *Kaleidoscope*, and Sunday by *Hakka World* and *Mailbag Time*. One hour to western North America on 5950 kHz.

AFRTS Shortwave, USA. Network news, live sports, music and features in the upper-sideband mode from the Armed Forces Radio & Television Service. Transmitted from modestly powered U.S. Navy stations around the globe. Try 4319, 5446.5, 5765, 6350, 6458.5, 7507, 10320, 12133.5, 12579, 13362 and 13855 kHz.

07:30

Swiss Radio International. *Swissinfo*—news, reports, and a short feature at weekends (replaced weekdays by music). A half hour to North and West Africa winter on 9885 and 13790 kHz, and summer on 13650 and 15545 kHz; also to southern Africa winter on 17665 kHz, and 21750 kHz midyear.

Radio Bulgaria. This time winter only. See 0630 for specifics. Often includes exotic Bulgarian folk music. Thirty minutes to Europe on 12000 and 13600 kHz. One hour earlier during summer.

08:00

■BBC World Service for Europe. Monday through Saturday winter, starts with *News*, then the long-running *Outlook* (except Monday, when there's *Talking Point*, a call-in show). Weekdays, the final 15 minutes are given to ●*Off the Shelf* (readings from the best of world literature), replaced Saturday by *Write On*. Sunday's lineup is ●*From Our Own Correspondent* and *The Greenfield Collection* (classical music). Summer weekdays, opens with five minutes of *News*, then *Meridian* (an arts program). The second half hour is a mixed bag of popular music or *Westway* (a soap). Saturday has youth-oriented programming, and Sunday's lineup is the same as winter. Continuous to Europe and North Africa on 9410 (winter), 12095, 15485 and 15565 kHz. kHz.

■BBC World Service for East and Southeast Asia and the Pacific. Starts with *news*, then weekdays, a feature: ●*Omnibus* (winter Mondays), alternative pop (Tuesday), *The Greenfield Collection* (classical music, Wednesday), jazz (Thursday), *Composer of the Month* (summer Fridays) and light entertainment on winter Fridays and summer Mondays. *World*

Learning (an educational program) follows on the half-hour. The Saturday lineup is variable, but tends to have youth-oriented programming most of the year. Sunday spots are ●*From Our Own Correspondent* and *Arts in Action*. Continuous to East Asia on 15360, 17760 and 21660 kHz; to Southeast Asia on 9740 and 15360 kHz; and to Australasia on 15360 kHz.

■Deutsche Welle, Germany. *News*, then Monday through Friday there's commentary, interviews, background reports and analysis in ●*NewsLink*. On the half-hour, look for *Focus on Folk* (Monday), *Insight* followed by *Business German* (Tuesday), *World in Progress* (Wednesday), *Money Talks* (Thursday) and *Environment* (Friday). Saturday's lineup is *Religion and Society*, *German by Radio* and ●*Network Europe*, replaced Sunday by *Mailbag*. Sixty minutes to Europe on 6140 kHz.

Flanders Radio International, Belgium. Winter only at this time. Monday through Friday, starts with *News*. The rest of the broadcast is a mix of current events, reports and Belgian music. Saturday, these are replaced by *Network Europe*, and Sunday by *Radio World*, *Tourism* and *Brussels 1043* (a listener-response program). Thirty minutes to Europe on 5985 kHz. One hour earlier in summer.

Voice of Malaysia. *News* and commentary, then *Golden Oldies*. The final half hour of a much longer transmission targeted at Southeast Asia and Australasia on 6175, 9750 and 15295 kHz.

Radio Prague, Czech Republic. Winter only at this time. *News*, then Monday through Friday it's the in-depth *Current Affairs* and one or more features: *Talking Point* (Monday), *Witness* and *One on One* (Tuesday), *ABC of Czech* and either *Czechs in History* or *Spotlight* (Wednesday), *Economics Report* (Thursday), and *Stepping Out* and *The Arts* (Friday). Weekends, the news is followed by Saturday's *Insight Central Europe* or Sunday's *Mailbox* and *ABC of Czech* followed by *Encore* (classical music), *Magic Carpet* (Czech world music) or *Czech Books*. Thirty minutes to Europe on 7315 (or 11600) and 9880 kHz. One hour earlier in summer.

Voice of the Mediterranean, Malta. Summer Sundays only at this time. Sixty minutes of mostly cultural features: *A Thinker's Thoughtful Think*, *The Sovereign Palaces*, *Malta Today*, and *Short Stories with a Maltese Background*. The broadcast ends with *Weekly News Update*. To Europe on 9605 kHz, and one hour later in winter.

Radio Australia. Part of a 24-hour service to Asia and the Pacific, but which can also be heard at this time throughout much of North America. Begins with a bulletin of *World News*, then Monday through Friday there's an in-depth look at current events in *PM*. Weekends, the news is followed by *Grandstand Wrap*, a roundup of the latest Australian sports action, with Saturday's *Earthbeat* or Sunday's *Innovations* filling the second half hour. On 5995, 9580, 9710, 12080, 13605, 15240, 15415, 17750 (from 0830) and 21725 kHz. Audible in parts of North America on 9580 and 15240 kHz. Best for East Asia is 21725 kHz, with 15415 and 17750 kHz the channels for Southeast Asia.

Voice of Russia World Service. Continuous programming to Southeast Asia and Australasia. Winter, *News* is followed by ●*Update* on Tuesday, Thursday and Saturday. Other features include *Science and Engineering* (Wednesday), *Moscow Mailbag* (Friday) and Monday's outstanding ●*Music and Musicians* (classical music). On the half-hour, there's some of the Voice of Russia's best—●*Audio Book Club* (Wednesday), ●*Moscow Yesterday and Today* (Friday), ●*Folk Box* (Tuesday), *Songs from Russia* (Sunday), *Kaleidoscope* (Saturday), and Thursday's *This is Russia*. In summer, ●*Update* is only available on Wednesday and Friday. It is replaced Monday by *Science and Engineering*, Tuesday by *Focus on Asia*, Thursday by *Newmarket* and Saturday by *Moscow Mailbag*. Sunday's offering is the 45-minute ●*Music and Musicians*—a jewel among classical music shows. Choice pickings from the second half hour include ●*Moscow Yesterday and Today* (Monday), ●*Folk Box* (Thursday), ●*Jazz Show* (Friday) and Saturday's ●*Christian Message from Moscow*. For Australasia winter (local Oz summer), use 15275, 15470, 17495, 17525, 17655 and 17665 kHz; midyear, take your pick from 17495, 17525, 17635, 17675, 17685 and 17795 kHz. In Southeast Asia, there's 11770, 17655 and 21485 (or 21810) kHz in winter, and 15490, 17495, 17675, 17685 and 17795 kHz in summer.

Radio Taiwan International. Opens with 15 minutes of *News*, and weekdays closes with *Let's Learn Chinese*, which has a series of segments for beginning, intermediate and advanced learners. The remaining airtime is taken up by features. Monday's offering is the exotic ●*Jade Bells and Bamboo Pipes* (Taiwanese music); Tuesday, there's *Culture Express* and *Trends*; Wednesday's features are *Taiwan Today* and *Instant Noodles*; the Thursday combo is *Discover Taiwan* and *New Music Lounge*; and Friday brings *Taipei Magazine* and *People*. These are replaced Saturday by *Groove Zone* and *Kaleidoscope*, and Sunday by *Hakka*

France

Guha

World and *Mailbag Time*. One hour to Australasia on 9610 kHz.

Radio New Zealand International. Continues with regional programming for the South Pacific. Part of a much longer broadcast, which is also heard in parts of North America (especially during summer) on 9885 or 11675 kHz.

Radio Korea International, South Korea. Opens with 10 minutes of *news*, then Monday through Friday, a commentary. This is followed by 30 minutes (45 on Friday) of *Seoul Calling*. Monday through Thursday, the broadcast closes with a 15-minute feature: *Korea, Today and Tomorrow*, *Korean Kaleidoscope*, *Wonderful Korea* and *Seoul Report*, respectively. Saturday's news is followed by *Worldwide Friendship* (a listener-response show), and Sunday by *Korean Pop Interactive*. Sixty minutes to Europe on 13670 kHz, and to Southeast Asia on 9570 kHz.

Voice of America. The first of several hours of programming to East Asia. *News Now*—a mixed bag of sports, science, business and other news and features. Winter on 11995, 13605 and 15150 kHz; and summer on 11930, 13620, 13760 and 15150 kHz.

AFRTS Shortwave, USA. Network news, live sports, music and features in the upper-sideband mode from the Armed Forces Radio & Television Service. Transmitted from modestly powered U.S. Navy stations around the globe. Try 4319, 5446.5, 5765, 6350, 6458.5, 7507, 10320, 12133.5, 12579, 13362 and 13855 kHz.

08:10

Voice of Armenia. Summer Sundays only. Twenty minutes of Armenian *news* and culture. To Europe on 15270 kHz, and to the Mideast on 4810 kHz. One hour later in winter.

08:30

Swiss Radio International. *Swissinfo*—news, reports, and a short feature at weekends (replaced weekdays by music). Thirty minutes to southern Africa on 21770 kHz.

09:00

■**BBC World Service for Europe.** Monday through Saturday winter, opens with five minutes of *News*, then weekdays it's *Meridian* (an arts show). The second half hour is a mixed bag of popular music or *Westway* (a soap). Saturday has youth-oriented programming, replaced Sunday by *World Briefing*, ●*Reporting Religion* and *In Praise of God*. Summer (except Sunday), starts with *News*, then weekdays there's an interesting collection of features: ●*One Planet* and *People and Places* (Monday), *Discovery* and *Essential Guide* (Tuesday), ●*Health Matters* and ●*Everywoman* (Wednesday),●*Focus on Faith* (0930 Thursday) and *Sports International* and *Pick of the World* on Friday. Saturday brings *World Briefing*, ●*Letter from America* and *Global Business*, and Sunday's programming is the same as winter. Continuous to Europe and North Africa on 12095, 15485 and 15565 kHz.

■**BBC World Service for East and Southeast Asia and the Pacific.** Winter, starts with *World Briefing*, then weekdays it's ●*Sports Roundup*. The lineup for the 0945 feature is ●*Analysis* (Tuesday, Wednesday and Friday), ●*From Our Own Correspondent* (Thursday) and *Write On* (a listener-response program, Monday). Saturday features are ●*Analysis* and *Global Business*, and Sunday there's ●*Reporting Religion* and *In Praise of God*. Monday through Friday summer, there's one hour of *World Update*; Saturday, it's *World Briefing* followed by ●*Letter from America* and *Global Business*; and Sunday's programs are the same as winter. To East Asia on 9740, 11945, 15360, 17760 and 21660 kHz; to Southeast Asia on 6195, 9740 and 15360 kHz; and to Australasia on 15360 kHz.

■**Deutsche Welle,** Germany. *News*, then Monday through Friday it's the excellent ●*NewsLink* —commentary, interviews, background reports and analysis. The second half-hour features *Spectrum* (Monday), ●*World Music Live* (Tuesday), *Arts on the Air* (Wednesday), *Living in Germany* and *Europe on Stage* (Thursday) and *Cool* (a well produced youth show, Friday). Weekend features are

09:00–09:30

Saturday's ●*Inside Europe* and Sunday's *Hard to Beat* (sport), *Inspired Minds* and either *Hits in Germany* or *Melody Time*. Sixty minutes to Europe on 6140 kHz.

China Radio International. Starts with *News*, followed Monday through Friday by special reports—current events, sports, business, culture, science and technology and press clippings. The rest of the broadcast is devoted to features. Regulars include ●*People in the Know* (Monday), *Biz China* (Tuesday), *China Horizons* (Wednesday), ●*Voices from Other Lands* (Thursday), and *Life in China* on Friday. Weekends, the news is followed by a shorter series of reports (current events and sport) and two features. Saturday there's *Cutting Edge*, and *Listeners' Garden* (listener mail, Chinese folk music, a preview of the next week's programs, and a Chinese language lesson); replaced Sunday by *Reports on Developing Countries* and *In the Spotlight*, a series of mini-features: *Cultural Carousel*, *In Vogue*, *Writings from China*, *China Melody* and *Talking Point*. One hour to Australasia on 11730 (or 17690) and 15210 kHz.

Radio New Zealand International. Continuous programming for the islands of the South Pacific, where the broadcasts are targeted. On 9885 or 11675 kHz. Audible in much of North America, especially in summer.

Voice of Russia World Service. Winter only at this time. *News*, followed by ●*Update* on Wednesday and Friday. This is replaced Monday by *Science and Engineering*, Tuesday by *Focus on Asia*, Thursday by *Newmarket* and Saturday by *Moscow Mailbag*. Sunday's offering is the 45-minute ●*Music and Musicians*—not to be missed if you are an aficionado of classical music. Choice pickings from the second half hour include ●*Moscow Yesterday and Today* (Monday), ●*Folk Box* (Thursday) ●*Jazz Show* (Friday) and Saturday's ●*Christian Message from Moscow*. The Tuesday and Wednesday slots are also worth a listen. To Australasia on 15275, 15470, 17495, 17525 and 17665 kHz; and to Southeast Asia on 11770, 17495 and 21485 (or 21810) kHz.

Voice of the Mediterranean, Malta. Winter Sundays only at this time; see 0800 for specifics. Sixty minutes to Europe on 9630 kHz. One hour earlier in summer.

Radio Prague, Czech Republic. Summer only at this time. See 1000 for specifics. Thirty minutes to South Asia and West Africa on 21745 kHz, and heard well beyond. One hour later in winter.

Radio Australia. *World News*, then weekdays it's a call-in show, *Australia Talks Back*. This is replaced Saturday by *Science Show* and *Business Weekend*, and Sunday by *The National Interest* (topical events). Continuous to Asia and the Pacific on 9580, 11880 or 17750 (from 0930) and 21820 kHz; and heard in North America on 9580 kHz. Best for East and Southeast Asia is 11880 (or 17750) kHz, and listeners in Europe should try 21820 kHz.

Voice of America. Opens with *news*, then it's music: *American Gold* (Monday), *Roots and Branches* (Tuesday), *Classic Rock* (Wednesday), *Top Twenty* (Thursday), *Country Hits* (Friday) and jazz at the weekend. Continuous programming to East Asia winter on 11995, 13605 and 15150 kHz; and summer on 11930, 13620, 13760 and 15150 kHz.

AFRTS Shortwave, USA. Network news, live sports, music and features in the upper-sideband mode from the Armed Forces Radio & Television Service. Transmitted from modestly powered U.S. Navy stations around the globe. Try 4319, 5446.5, 5765, 6350, 6458.5, 7507, 10320, 12133.5, 12579, 13362 and 13855 kHz.

09:10

Voice of Armenia. Winter Sundays only. Twenty minutes of Armenian *news* and culture. To Europe on 15270 kHz, and to the Mideast on 4910 kHz. One hour earlier in summer.

09:30

Radio Vilnius, Lithuania. A half hour that's mostly *news* and background reports about events in Lithuania. Of broader appeal is *Mailbag*, aired every other Sunday. For a little Lithuanian music, try the second half of Monday's broadcast. To western Europe on 9710 kHz.

Voice of the Straits, China. Thursday and Friday only. The 30-minute *Focus on China* covers cultural, economic and social developments in the country. Priority is given to business news, but there are often interesting items on environmental and other legislation—from broadcasting to family planning. Formerly on Friday and Sunday, the program moved to a new schedule in summer 2002. To East and Southeast Asia on 6115 and 11590 kHz, and well heard in much of Australasia and beyond.

10:00

■**BBC World Service for the Americas.** Monday through Friday winter, opens with a half hour of *World Update* (news and current events) and closes with 15 minutes of ●*Sports Roundup*. In between, you can hear ●*Letter from America* (Monday), ●*Analysis* (Tuesday, Wednesday and Friday) and ●*From Our Own Correspondent* on Thursday. Weekends, the first 30 minutes are divided between *World Briefing* and ●*Sports Roundup*, with the second half hour consisting of Saturday's *Science in Action* or Sunday's ●*Agenda*. In summer, the weekday lineup is *World Briefing*, ●*World Business Report* and ●*Sports Roundup*, with weekend programs the same as in winter. To the Caribbean on 6195 kHz, and audible in much of the southern and eastern United States. Listeners farther west can tune to the Asian stream on 9740 kHz.

■**BBC World Service for Europe.** Winter weekdays, opens with *News*, then there's an interesting collection of features: ●*One Planet* and *People and Places* (Monday), *Discovery* and *Essential Guide* (Tuesday), ●*Health Matters* and ●*Everywoman* (Wednesday),●*Focus on Faith* (0930 Thursday) and *Sports International* and *Pick of the World* on Friday. Saturday brings *World Briefing*, ●*Letter from America* and *Global Business*; and Sunday there's *World Briefing*, ●*Sports Roundup* and ●*Agenda*. In summer, starts with *World Briefing*, then Monday through Friday there's ●*World Business Report* and ●*Sports Roundup*. Weekends, ●*Sports Roundup* moves to 1020 and is followed by Saturday's ●*Science in*

Action or Sunday's ●*Weekend*. Continuous to Europe and North Africa on 12095, 15485 and 15565 kHz.

■**BBC World Service for East and Southeast Asia and the Pacific.** Monday through Friday, the format is *World Update* (*World Briefing* in summer), ●*World Business Report* and ●*Sports Roundup*. Saturday's *news* bulletin is followed by *Jazzmatazz* and *The Greenfield Collection* (a classical music request show), and Sunday's feature is a first-rate concert of classical music—not to be missed if you appreciate top-notch performances. Continuous to East Asia on 9740 and (till 1030) 15360, 17760 and 21660 kHz; to Southeast Asia on 6195, 9740 and (till 1030) 15360 kHz. For Australasia there's 15360 kHz. Well heard in western North America on 9740 kHz.

■**Deutsche Welle,** Germany. *News*, then Monday through Friday, ●*NewsLink for Asia*. The lineup for the second half-hour is ●*Focus on Folk* (Monday), ●*World Music Live* (Tuesday), *Arts on the Air* (Wednesday), *Living in Germany* and *Europe on Stage* (Thursday) and *Cool* (a youth show) on Friday. Saturday fare consists of *Religion and Society*, *German by Radio* and *Asia This Week*; and Sunday there's *Hard to Beat* (sport), *Inspired Minds* and either *Hits in Germany* or *Melody Time*. Sixty minutes to Europe on 6140 kHz, with the first 30 minutes also available for East Asia on 6205 and 17820 kHz in winter, and 17615 and 17715 kHz in summer.

■**Radio Netherlands.** Monday through Friday it's ●*Newsline*, then a feature: ●*Research File* (Monday), ●*EuroQuest* (Tuesday), ●*Documentary* (Wednesday), *Dutch Horizons* (Thursday) and *A Good Life* (Friday). Weekend fare consists of a six-minute *news* bulletin followed by Saturday's *Europe Unzipped*, *Insight* and *Amsterdam Forum*; or Sunday's *Wide Angle*, *The Week Ahead* and *Vox Humana*. Fifty-five minutes to East and Southeast Asia and Australasia on 7260 (winter), 9785, 12065 and (summer) 13710 kHz. Recommended listening.

Radio Australia. *World News*, then weekdays there's *Asia Pacific* and a feature on the half-hour. Monday, it's health; Tuesday, law; Wednesday, religion; Thursday, media; and Friday, sport. Saturday's lineup consists of *Pacific Review* and *In Conversation*, replaced Sunday by *The Buzz* and *Rural Reporter*. Continuous to Asia and the Pacific on 9580, 11880 (or 17750) and 21820 kHz; and heard in North America on 9580 kHz. Listeners in East and Southeast Asia should tune to 11880 (or 17750) kHz, and 21820 kHz is often heard in Europe.

Radio Prague, Czech Republic. Winter only at this time. *News*, then Monday through Friday there's *Current Affairs* and a feature or two: *Talking Point* (Monday), *Witness* and *One on One* (Tuesday), *ABC of Czech* and either *Czechs in History* or *Spotlight* (Wednesday), *Economics Report* (Thursday) and *Stepping Out* and *The Arts* (Friday). On Saturday the news is followed by *Magazine*, *Letter from Prague* and a repeat of Tuesday's *One on One*. Sunday's lineup is *Mailbox* and *ABC of Czech* followed by *Encore* (classical music), *Magic Carpet* (Czech world music) or *Czech Books*. Thirty minutes to South Asia and West Africa on 21745 kHz, but audible well beyond. One hour earlier in summer.

Radio Japan. *News*, then Monday through Friday it's *Songs for Everyone* and *Japan and the World 44 Minutes* (an in-depth look at current trends and events). This is replaced Saturday by *Hello from Tokyo*, and Sunday by *Weekend Japanology* and *Sight and Sounds of Japan*. One hour to Asia on 15590 kHz, to Southeast Asia on 9695 kHz, to Eastern Europe on 17585 kHz, and to Australasia on 21755 kHz.

RTE Overseas, Ireland. A half-hour information bulletin from Radio Telefís Éireann's domestic Radio 1. To Australasia on 15280 kHz.

Voice of Mongolia. Most days, it's *news*, reports and short features, all with a local flavor. The entire Sunday broadcast is devoted to exotic Mongolian music. Thirty minutes to Southeast Asia and Australasia on 12085 (or 9615) kHz. Often well heard in parts of the United States during March and September.

Voice of Vietnam. Begins with *news*, then there's *Commentary* or *Weekly Review* followed by short features and pleasant Vietnamese music (especially at weekends). Thirty minutes to Southeast Asia on 9840 and 12020 kHz.

Voice of America. The first of the VOA's daily broadcasts to the Caribbean. *News Now*—a mixed bag of sports, science, business and other news and features. On 5745, 7370 and 9590 kHz. For a separate service to Asia and Australasia, see the next item.

Voice of America. The ubiquitous *News Now*, but unlike the service to the Caribbean, this is part of a much longer broadcast. To East and Southeast Asia winter on 15250 and 15425 kHz, and summer on 13620, 15240 and 15245 kHz. In Australasia, tune to 5985 (or 9770), 11720 (midyear) and 15425 kHz.

China Radio International. Repeat of the 0900 broadcast, but with news updates. One hour to Australasia on 11730 (or 17690) and 15210 kHz.

All India Radio. *News*, then a composite program of commentary, press review and features, interspersed with exotic Indian music. One hour to East Asia on 13710, 15235 (or 15020) and 17800 kHz, and to Australasia on 13710, 17510 and 17895 kHz. Also beamed to Sri Lanka on 15260 kHz.

Voice of Korea, North Korea. Not the Radio Pyongyang of old, but the Voice of Korea has a long way to go before being accepted as a serious broadcaster. Still, there are small signs of change. Worth the occasional listen to see if there are any surprises. One hour to Central America on 9335 and 11710 kHz; and to Southeast Asia on 9850 (or 13650) and 11735 kHz. Also audible in parts of East Asia on 3560 kHz.

AFRTS Shortwave, USA. Network news, live sports, music and features in the upper-sideband mode from the Armed Forces Radio & Television Service. Transmitted from modestly powered U.S. Navy stations around the globe. Try 4319, 5446.5, 5765, 6350, 6458.5, 7507, 10320, 12133.5, 12579, 13362 and 13855 kHz.

10:30

Radio Prague, Czech Republic. This time summer only. Repeat of the 0700 broadcast but with different programming on Saturday;

10:30–11:00

see 1130 for program specifics. A half hour to northwestern Europe on 9880 and 11615 kHz. One hour later during winter.

Emirates Radio, Dubai. *News*, then a feature dealing with one or more aspects of Arab life and culture. To Europe and North Africa on 13675, 15370, 15395 and 21605 kHz. Some frequencies tend to be a little variable

11:00

■**BBC World Service for the Americas.** Starts weekends with *World Briefing* and *British News* (replaced weekdays by special programming for the Caribbean) and most days ends with ●*Sports Roundup*. The remaining programs change according to season. Continuous programming to eastern North America and the Caribbean on 6195 and 15190 kHz. Listeners farther west should tune to the Asian stream on 9740 kHz.

■**BBC World Service for Europe.** Winter, identical to the service for the Americas, except that *Arts in Action* replaces ●*Agenda* at 1130 Sunday. Monday through Saturday summer, there's *World Briefing, British News,* ●*Analysis* (replaced Monday be ●*Letter from America* and Thursday by ●*From Our Own Correspondent*) and ●*Sports Roundup* (preempted Friday by *Football Extra*). Sunday, there's more of the same during the first 30 minutes, with *Arts in Action* completing the hour. Continuous to Europe and North Africa on 12095, 15485 and 15565 kHz.

Belgium

Guha

■**BBC World Service for East and Southeast Asia and the Pacific.** Weekdays there's five minutes of *news*, then a pair of features: ●*Health Matters* and ●*Everywoman* (Monday), *Science View* and ●*Focus on Faith* (Tuesday), *Sports International* and *Pick of the World* (Wednesday), ●*One Planet* and *People and Places* (Thursday), and *Discovery* and *Essential Guide* on Friday. Some of the BBC's better offerings. Weekends, opens with *World Briefing* and *British News*, then it's Saturday's ●*Science in Action* or Sunday's first half hour of ●*Play of the Week* (the best in world theater). Continuous to East Asia on 9740, 9815 and 15280 kHz; to Southeast Asia on 6195 and 9740 kHz; and to Australasia on 9740 kHz (also heard in western North America).

■**Radio Netherlands.** Summer only at this time. Monday through Friday, opens with ●*Newsline* (current events) which is replaced weekends by a *news* bulletin. The final 25 minutes (more at weekends) is devoted to features. The lineup includes ●*Research File* (science, Monday), ●*EuroQuest* (Tuesday), the award winning ●*Documentary* (Wednesday), *Dutch Horizons* (Thursday) and *A Good Life* on Friday. Weekends, there's Saturday's *Europe Unzipped, Insight* and *Amsterdam Forum*; replaced Sunday by *Wide Angle, The Week Ahead* and *Vox Humana*. Fifty-five minutes to eastern North America on 5965 and 9890 kHz. One hour later in winter.

■**Deutsche Welle,** Germany. *News*, then weekdays there's the comprehensive ●*NewsLink for Asia*—commentary, interviews, background reports and analysis. This is followed by *Spectrum* (Monday), *Insight* and *Business German* (Tuesday), *World in Progress* (Wednesday), *Money Talks* (Thursday) and *Environment* (Friday). Saturday's feature is the 55-minute ●*Inside Europe*, replaced Sunday by *Mailbag*. Sixty minutes year round to Europe on 6140 kHz. Also to Southeast Asia winter on 17670 and 21650 kHz, and summer on 15110 and 17820 kHz.

Radio Taiwan International. Opens with 15 minutes of *News*, and closes weekdays with *Let's Learn Chinese*. The remaining airtime is taken up by features. Monday, there's *Taiwan Economic Journal* followed by *Stage, Screen and*

Studio; Tuesday, ●*Jade Bells and Bamboo Pipes*; Wednesday, *New Music Lounge* and *Confucius and Inspiration Beyond*; Thursday, *News Talk* and *Life Unusual*; and Friday, *Formosa Outlook* and *Taiwan Gourmet*. The Saturday slots go to *Kaleidoscope* and *Mailbag Time*, replaced Sunday by *Hakka World* and *Asia Pacific*. Sixty minutes to Southeast Asia on 7445 kHz.

Radio Australia. *World News*, with the remainder of the first half hour going to *Asia Pacific* (replaced Sunday by *Correspondents' Report*). Monday through Friday, the next 30 minutes consist of a sports bulletin and *Life Matters* (personal and social issues). Weekends, there's *Fine Music Australia* (classical music) at 1130 Saturday, and *Business Report* at the same time Sunday. Continuous to East Asia and the Pacific on 5995, 6020, 9580, 11880, 12080 and 21820 kHz; and heard in much of North America on 6020 and 9580 kHz. Listeners in Europe should try 21820 kHz.

Radio Ukraine International. Summer only at this time. An hour's ample coverage of just about all things Ukrainian, including news, sports, politics and culture. A popular feature is ●*Music from Ukraine*, which fills most of the Sunday broadcast. Sixty minutes to western Europe on 15415 kHz. One hour later in winter.

HCJB—Voice of the Andes, Ecuador. The first hour of a religious broadcast to North and South America on 15115 kHz.

Voice of America. A mixed bag of sports, science, business and other news and features. Continuous to East and Southeast Asia winter on 6110, 9760, 11705, 15250 and 15425 kHz; and summer on 6160, 9760, 13610, 15160, 15240 and 15425 kHz. For Australasia there's 5985 (or 9770), 9645, 11720 (winter) and 15425 kHz.

Radio Japan. *News*, then weekdays it's *Songs for Everyone* and *Asian Top News*. These are followed by a 35-minute feature: *Japan Music Treasure Box* (Monday), Japanese language lessons (Tuesday and Thursday), *Japan Musicscape* (Wednesday), and *Music Beat* (Japanese popular music) on Friday. *Pop Joins the World* fills the Saturday slot, and is replaced Sunday by *Hello from Tokyo*. One hour to eastern North America on 6120 kHz;

to Asia on 15590 kHz; and to Southeast Asia on 9695 kHz.

Xizang [Tibet] People's Broadcasting Station, China. Monday through Saturday only. *Holy Tibet* describes itself as "a window to life in Tibet," and is a 20-minute package of information and local popular music. Sometimes acknowledges listeners' reception reports at the end of the program. Original editions are aired on Monday, Wednesday and Friday, and repeated at the same time the next day. Well heard in East and Southeast Asia and parts of Australasia (South America, too). On 4905, 4920, 5240, 6110, 6130, 6200, 7385 and 9490 kHz.

Radio Singapore International. A three-hour package for Southeast Asia, and widely heard beyond. Starts with ten minutes of *news* (five at weekends), then Monday through Friday there's *Business and Market Report*, replaced Saturday by *Insight*, and Sunday by *Business World*. These are followed on the quarter-hour by several mini-features, including a daily news and weather bulletin on the half-hour. Monday's lineup is *Young Expressions*, *The Write Stuff*, *Youth Beat* and *E-Z Beat*; Tuesday brings *A World of Our Own*, *On the Line from Silicone Valley*, *Hong Kong: Dragon City*, and *E-Z Beat*; Wednesday offers *Perspective*, *Eco Watch*, *On Second Thought* and *Classic Gold*; Thursday has *Frontiers*, *Eco-Watch*, *Potluck*, *Singapore Scene* and *Love Songs*; and Friday's list includes *Asian Journal*, *Indonesian Media Watch*, *Arts Arena*, *Science and Technology Watch* and *Classic Gold*. Saturday, expect *Insight*, *Regional Press Review*, *Frontiers*, *A Current Affair*, *Family Ties* and *Straight Talk*; replaced Sunday by *Comment*, *Youth Beat*, *Snapshots*, *A Current Affair* and *Instrumentals*. On 6150 and 9600 kHz.

CBC North-Québec, Canada. Summer only at this time; see 1200 for specifics. Intended for a domestic audience, but also heard in the northeastern United States on 9625 kHz.

Voice of Vietnam. Repeat of the 1000 transmission. A half hour to Southeast Asia on 7285 kHz.

Voice of the Islamic Republic of Iran. News, commentary and features, and a little

11:00–11:30

Radio Netherlands presents news from Europe and beyond. M. Guha

Iranian music. Strongly reflects an Islamic point of view. One hour to West, South and Southeast Asia, and widely heard elsewhere. Winter on 15385, 15460 15480, 21470 and 21730 kHz; and summer on 15450, 15550, 15600, 21470 and 21730 kHz.

AFRTS Shortwave, USA. Network news, live sports, music and features in the upper-sideband mode from the Armed Forces Radio & Television Service. Transmitted from modestly powered U.S. Navy stations around the globe. Try 4319, 5446.5, 5765, 6350, 6458.5, 7507, 10320, 12133.5, 12579, 13362 and 13855 kHz.

11:30

Radio Korea International, South Korea. Opens with 10 minutes of *news*, then Monday through Friday, a commentary. This is followed by 30 minutes (45 on Friday) of *Seoul Calling*. Monday through Thursday, the broadcast closes with a 15-minute feature: *Korea, Today and Tomorrow*, *Korean Kaleidoscope*, *Wonderful Korea* and *Seoul Report*, respectively. On Saturday, the news is followed by *Worldwide Friendship* (a listener-response program), and Sunday by *Korean Pop Interactive*. Sixty minutes to eastern North America on 9650 kHz via their Canadian relay.

Radio Bulgaria. Summer only at this time. Thirty minutes of *news*, commentary, short features and enjoyable Bulgarian music. To Europe on 11700 and 15700 kHz. One hour later during winter.

Flanders Radio International, Belgium. Monday through Friday, starts with *News*. The rest of the broadcast is a mix of current events, reports and Belgian music. Saturday, these are replaced by the entertaining ●*Music from Flanders*, and Sunday by *Radio World*, *Tourism* and *Brussels 1043* (a listener-response program). Thirty minutes to East Asia and Australasia winter on 7390 kHz, and summer on 9865 kHz.

Radio Prague, Czech Republic. Winter only at this time. *News*, then Monday through Friday it's *Current Affairs* plus a feature or two. Monday's *Talking Point* is replaced Tuesday by *Witness* and *One on One* (interviews), and Wednesday by *ABC of Czech* and either *Czechs in History* or *Spotlight*. The business-oriented *Economic Report* fills the Thursday slot, with *Stepping Out* and *The Arts* sharing the Friday bill. On Saturday there's *Magazine*, *Letter from Prague* and a repeat of Tuesday's *One on One*. The Sunday lineup is *Mailbox* (a listener-response show), *ABC of Czech* and *Encore* (classical music), *Magic Carpet* (Czech world music) or *Czech Books*. Thirty minutes to northwestern Europe on 11640 kHz, and to East Africa on 21745 kHz. The latter channel is also audible in parts of the Mideast. The European broadcast is one hour earlier in summer, but there is no corresponding transmission for East Africa.

Wales Radio International. Winter Saturdays only at this time. Thirty minutes of news, interviews and music for Australasia on 17625 kHz. One hour later in summer (Oz winter).

Radio Sweden. Summer only at this time; see 1230 for program details. Thirty minutes to eastern North America (one hour later in winter) on 17840 kHz, and to East Asia and Australasia (two hours later in winter) on 17505 kHz.

1200-1759
Western Australia & East Asia—Evening Prime Time
North America—Morning and Lunchtime
Europe & Mideast—Afternoon and Early Evening

12:00

■**BBC World Service for the Americas.** A full hour of news and current events in ●*Newshour*, except for the first 20 minutes Monday through Friday, when there's alternative programming for the Caribbean. Continuous to North America and the Caribbean on 6195 and 15190 kHz. Listeners in western states may get a better signal from the Asian stream on 9740 kHz.

■**BBC World Service for Europe.** Winter, you can hear the daily ●*Newshour*—60 minutes of news and current events. Monday through Friday summer, starts with a *news* bulletin and is followed by *Outlook* and a 15-minute feature. Weekends, the news is followed by Saturday's *Wright Round the World* or Sunday's *The Alternative* (popular music) and *Global Business*. Continuous to Europe and North Africa on 12095, 15485 and 15565 kHz.

■**BBC World Service for East and Southeast Asia and the Pacific.** Monday through Friday, five minutes of *news* are followed by *Outlook* (news and human interest stories). The hour ends with a 15-minute feature. Saturday fare consists of a *news* bulletin, some light entertainment (●*Brain of Britain* part of the year) and the excellent ●*Assignment* (or alternative documentary). Sunday, it's the final part of ●*Play of the Week*, which runs till 1230 or 1300. If the former, ●*Agenda* takes over the second half hour. Continuous to East Asia on 6195, 9740, 9815 (summer) and 15280 kHz; to Southeast Asia on 6195 and 9740 kHz; and to Australasia on 9740 kHz. Also audible in western North America on 9740 kHz.

Radio Canada International. Summer weekdays only at this time. The Canadian Broadcasting Corporation's *The Current*. To eastern North America and the Caribbean on 9515, 13655 and 17800 kHz. For a separate year-round service to Asia, see the next item.

Radio Canada International. *News*, then Tuesday through Friday, *Sounds Like Canada*. Saturday's slot goes to *Richter on Radio*, replaced Sunday by ●*Global Village* (an extravaganza of world music), and Monday by ●*Quirks and Quarks* (an irreverent look at science). One hour to East and Southeast Asia winter on 9795 and 11730 kHz, and summer on 9660 (or 9795) and 15190 kHz.

■**Radio Netherlands.** Winter only at this time; see 1100 for specifics. Fifty-five minutes to eastern North America on 5965 and 9890 kHz. One hour earlier in summer.

■**Deutsche Welle,** Germany. *News*, then Monday through Friday it's ●*NewsLink for Asia*. The next 30 minutes consist of ●*Focus on Folk* (Monday), ●*World Music Live* (Tuesday), *Arts on the Air* (Wednesday), *Living in Germany* and *Europe on Stage* (Thursday) and the youth-oriented *Cool* (Friday). Weekends, the Saturday news is followed by *Religion and Society*, *German by Radio* and *Asia This Week*; and Sunday by *Hard to Beat* (sport), *Inspired Minds* and either *Hits in Germany* or *Melody Time*. Sixty minutes to Europe on 6140 kHz.

Radio Tashkent, Uzbekistan. Monday through Saturday, opens with *News*, replaced Sunday by *Significant Events of the Week*. Other programs include *Uzbekistan and the World* (Monday), *Life in the Village* and *Political Commentary* (Thursday), a listener-response show (Saturday) and *Traditions and Values* on Sunday. Programs of Uzbek music are aired on Tuesday, Wednesday and Friday. To South and Southeast Asia, and also heard in parts of Europe and Australasia. Thirty minutes winter on 5060, 5975, 6025 and 9715 kHz; and summer on 7285, 9715, 15295 and 17775 kHz. Best for Southeast Asia is 9715 kHz in winter, and 17775 kHz in summer.

■**Radio France Internationale.** Opens with a *news* bulletin, then there's a 25-minute

12:00–12:00

feature— *French Lesson, Crossroads, Voices, Rendez-Vous, World Tracks, Weekend* or *Club 9516* (a listener-response program). A half hour to West Africa on 17815 kHz, and to East Africa on 21620 or 25820 kHz.

Radio Polonia, Poland. This time summer only. Sixty minutes of news, commentary, features and music—all with a Polish accent. Weekdays, starts with *News from Poland*—a potpourri of news, reports, interviews and press review. This is followed Monday by *Focus* (an arts program) and *Chart Show* (a look at Polish pop music); Tuesday by *A Day in the Life* (interviews) and *Request Show*; Wednesday by *Around Poland* and *The Best of Polish Radio* (or *Bookworm*); Thursday by *Letter from Poland* and *Multimedia Show*; and Friday by *Business Week* and *High Note* (or an alternative classical music feature). The Saturday broadcast begins with *From the Weeklies*, and is followed by *Insight Central Europe* (a joint-production with other stations of the region) and *Soundcheck* (new Polish music releases). The Sunday lineup includes *Europe East* (correspondents' reports) and *In Touch*, a listener-response program. To western Europe on 9525 and 11820 kHz. One hour later in winter.

Radio Austria International. Summer only at this time. Weekdays, the 15-minute ●*Report from Austria* is aired at 1215, and then repeated at 1245. Saturday and Sunday, it's a similar arrangement, with *Insight Central Europe* airing at 1205 and 1235. The remainder of the one-hour broadcast is in German. To Asia and

Australasia on 21780 kHz, and one hour later in winter. For a separate broadcast to Europe, see the next item.

Radio Austria International. Summer only at this time. Similar to the broadcast for Asia and Australasia, but with no ●*Report from Austria* at 1215 (only at 1245). To Europe on 6155 and 13730 kHz, and one hour later in winter.

Radio Australia. *World News*, then Monday through Thursday it's *Late Night Live* (round-table discussion). On the remaining days, there's Friday's *Sound Quality* (music), Saturday's *The Spirit of Things*, and Sunday's *Country Club* (not all country music comes from Nashville!). Continuous to Asia and the Pacific on 5995, 6020, 9580, 11650, 11880 and 21820 kHz; and well heard in much of North America on 6020 and 9580 kHz. Listeners in Europe should try 21820 kHz.

Radio Ukraine International. Winter only at this time. See 1100 for specifics. Sixty minutes to Europe on any two channels from 11720, 11840, 15520 and 17760 kHz, and to Central Asia on 11825 kHz. One hour earlier in summer. Tends to be irregular due to financial limitations.

CBC North-Québec, Canada. Part of an 18-hour multilingual broadcast for a domestic audience, but which is also heard in the northeastern United States. Weekend programming at this hour is in English, and features *news* followed by the enjoyably eclectic ●*Good Morning Québec* (Saturday) or *Fresh Air*

"Made in Germany" is Deutsche Welle's business magazine, anchored by Andrea Sanke. DW

(Sunday). Starts at this time winter, but summer it is already into the second hour. On 9625 kHz.

HCJB—Voice of the Andes, Ecuador. The second hour of a religious broadcast to North and South America on 15115 kHz.

Radio Singapore International. Continuous programming to Southeast Asia and beyond. Starts with five minutes of *news*, then it's mostly the same programs as the previous hour (see 1100) but on different days of the week. On 6150 and 9600 kHz.

Radio Taiwan International. Opens with 15 minutes of *News*, and weekdays closes with *Let's Learn Chinese*, which has a series of segments for beginning, intermediate and advanced learners. The remaining airtime is devoted to features. Monday's offering is the exotic ●*Jade Bells and Bamboo Pipes* (Taiwanese music); Tuesday's slots are *Culture Express* and *Trends*; Wednesday's features are *Taiwan Today* and *Instant Noodles*; Thursday, there's *Discover Taiwan* and *New Music Lounge*; and Friday brings *Taipei Magazine* and *People*. These are replaced Saturday by *Groove Zone* and *Kaleidoscope*, and Sunday by *Hakka World* and *Mailbag Time*. One hour to East Asia on 7130 kHz.

Voice of America. A mixed bag of current events, sports, science, business and other news and features. Continuous to East and Southeast Asia winter on 6110, 9760, 11705, 15250 and 15425 kHz; and summer on 6160, 9760, 13610, 15160, 15240 and 15425 kHz. For Australasia there's 9645, 11715 (winter) and 15425 kHz.

China Radio International. Starts with *News*, followed Monday through Friday by special reports—current events, sports, business, culture, science and technology and press clippings. The rest of the broadcast is devoted to features. Regulars include ●*People in the Know* (Monday), *Biz China* (Tuesday), *China Horizons* (Wednesday), ●*Voices from Other Lands* (Thursday), and *Life in China* on Friday. Weekends, the news is followed by a shorter series of reports (current events and sport) and two features. Saturday there's *Cutting Edge*, and *Listeners' Garden* (listener mail, Chinese

folk music, a preview of the next week's programs, and a Chinese language lesson); replaced Sunday by *Reports on Developing Countries* and *In the Spotlight*, a series of mini-features: *Cultural Carousel, In Vogue, Writings from China, China Melody* and *Talking Point*. One hour to Southeast Asia on 9730 and 11980 kHz, and to Australasia on 9760, 11760 and 15415 kHz.

AFRTS Shortwave, USA. Network news, live sports, music and features in the upper-sideband mode from the Armed Forces Radio & Television Service. Transmitted from modestly powered U.S. Navy stations around the globe. Try 4319, 5446.5, 5765, 6350, 6458.5, 7507, 10320, 12133.5, 12579, 13362 and 13855 kHz.

12:15

Radio Cairo, Egypt. The start of a 75-minute package of news, religion, culture and entertainment, much of it devoted to Arab and Islamic themes. The initial quarter hour consists of virtually anything, from quizzes to Islamic religious talks, then there's *news* and commentary, followed by political and cultural items. To South and Southeast Asia on 17775 kHz.

12:30

Radio Bulgaria. This time winter only; see 1130 for specifics. Thirty minutes to Europe on 12000 and 15700 kHz. One hour earlier in summer.

Radio Bangladesh. *News*, followed by Islamic and general interest features and pleasant Bengali music. Thirty minutes to Southeast Asia, also heard in Europe, on 7185 and 9550 kHz. Frequencies may vary slightly, and one transmitter is often off the air.

Voice of Vietnam. Repeat of the 1000 transmission. A half hour to Southeast Asia on 9840 and 12020 kHz. Frequencies may vary slightly.

Radio Thailand. Thirty minutes of *news* and short features to Southeast Asia and Australasia, winter on 9810 kHz and summer on 9860 kHz.

13:00–13:00

Voice of Turkey. This time summer only. Fifty-five minutes of *news*, features and Turkish music. To Europe on 17830 kHz, and to Southeast Asia and Australasia on 17595 kHz. One hour later in winter.

Radio Sweden. Monday through Friday, it's *news* and features in *Sixty Degrees North*, concentrating heavily on Scandinavian topics. The Monday slot goes to *SportScan*, replaced Tuesday by *Close Up* or an alternative feature, and Wednesday by special features. Thursday's shows rotate from week to week— *Nordic Lights*, *GreenScan*, *Heart Beat* or *S-Files*, while Friday offers a review of the week's news. Saturday's slot is filled by *Network Europe*, *Spectrum* (the arts), *Sweden Today* or *Studio 49;* and Sunday there's *In Touch with Stockholm* (a listener-response program) or the musical *Sounds Nordic*. Thirty minutes to North America winter on 18960 kHz, and summer on 17840 kHz. Also summer only to Asia and the Pacific on 13580 and 17505 kHz.

Wales Radio International. Summer Saturdays only at this time. News, interviews and local music from Britain's westernmost region. Thirty minutes to Australasia on 17845 kHz, and one hour earlier in winter.

13:00

■BBC World Service for the Americas. Weekdays, a five-minute *news* bulletin is followed by the long-running *Outlook* and the enjoyable ●*Off the Shelf* (readings from world literature). Saturday fare consists of *World Football* (soccer) and a music feature, replaced Sunday by jazz or other music and the religious *In Praise of God*. Continuous programming to North America and the Caribbean on 6195 and 15190 kHz. The Asian stream on 9740 kHz is likely to provide better reception in western North America.

■BBC World Service for Europe. Monday through Friday winter, starts with a *news* bulletin, then it's *Outlook* (news and human interest stories) and a 15-minute feature. Weekends, the news is followed by Saturday's *Wright Round the World* or Sunday's *The Alternative* (popular music) and *Global Business*. Summer weekdays, five minutes of

news are followed by an arts show, *Meridian* (except Monday, when ●*Omnibus* is aired in its place). The next half hour consists of a mixed bag of music and light entertainment. Saturday, there's 60 minutes of news and current events in ●*Newshour*, reduced Sunday to a half hour, and complemented by *Sportsworld*. Continuous to Europe and North Africa on 12095, 15485 and 15565 kHz.

■BBC World Service for East and Southeast Asia and the Pacific. Fifty minutes of ●*Newshour* (a full hour on weekends), with ●*World Business Report* occupying the remaining 10-minute weekday slot. To East and Southeast Asia on 6195 and 9740 kHz, and to Australasia on 9740 kHz (also audible in western North America).

Radio Canada International. Monday through Friday winter, and daily in summer. Winter, it's the Canadian Broadcasting Corporation's *The Current.* Summer weekdays there's *Sounds Like Canada*, replaced Saturday by *The House* (a look at Canadian politics) and Sunday by the first 60 minutes of *The Sunday Edition*. To eastern North America and the Caribbean winter weekdays on 9515, 13655 and 17710 kHz; and summer on 9515, 13655 and 17800 kHz.

China Radio International. Repeat of the 1200 broadcast; see there for specifics. One hour to Southeast Asia on 11980 and 15180 kHz; and to Australasia on 11760 and 11900 kHz. Also available to eastern North America on 9570 kHz; and summer only to western North America on 7405 kHz.

■Deutsche Welle, Germany. *News*, then weekdays it's ●*NewsLink* —commentary, interviews, background reports and analysis. Next, on the half-hour, there's *Spectrum* (Monday), *Insight* and *Business German* (Tuesday), *World in Progress* (Wednesday), *Money Talks* (Thursday) and *Environment* (Friday). Saturday's feature is the 55-minute ●*Concert Hour*, replaced Sunday by *Mailbag*. Sixty minutes to Europe on 6140 kHz.

Radio Polonia, Poland. This time winter only. *News*, commentary, music and a variety of features. See 1200 for specifics. Sixty minutes to Europe on 6095 and 9525 kHz. One hour earlier in summer.

The Ultimate in Technology

GRUNDIG

Satellit 800 AM/FM/Shortwave Radio
"The Best Radio on the Planet"

55 years of outstanding performance and service establishes Grundig as a leader in consumer audio. Decades of making the Satellit series radio defines them as the benchmark in shortwave technology. The Satellit's extensive frequency coverage includes Long wave, AM-broadcast and Shortwave, covered continuously from 100-30,000 KHz.; FM-stereo broadcast, 87-108 MHz.; VHF aircraft band, 118-137 MHz.

ENGINEERED FOR THE BEST POSSIBLE RECEPTION
- Single sideband (SSB) circuitry for listening to two-way communications, such as ham radio.
- Three built-in bandwidths, using electronically switched IF filters: 6.0, 4.0, 2.3 KHz.
- Synchronous detector for improved quality of AM and shortwave broadcast signals. Minimizes fading distortion and adjacent frequency interference.
- Selectable fast and slow AGC mode.
- High dynamic range, allowing for detection of weak signals in the presence of nearby strong signals.
- Excellent sensitivity and selectivity.
- Digital frequency display to 100 Hertz accuracy on AM, SW and VHF aircraft bands. 50 Hz when SSB used.
- A real tuning knob, like on traditional radios, but with ultra-precise digital tuning and with absolutely no audio muting when used.

- A modern, direct-frequency-entry keypad for instant frequency access and push buttons for fixed-step tuning.
- 70 programmable memories, completely immune to loss due to power interruptions. Memory scan feature.

LEGENDARY GRUNDIG AUDIO
- Outstanding audio with separate bass and treble tone control.
- FM stereo with headphones or external amplified stereo speakers.
- Includes high quality stereo headphones.
- Multiple audio outputs: line level output for recording, stereo headphone output.

FULL ANTENNA CAPABILITIES
- Built in telescopic antenna for SW, FM and VHF aircraft band.
- External antenna connections for the addition of auxiliary antennas, e.g. professionally engineered shortwave antennas; long-wire shortwave antennas; specialized AM broadcast band antennas for enthusiasts of AM DX'ing; FM broadcast band antennas; VHF air band antennas.

MORE HIGHLY DESIRABLE FEATURES
- Large, informational LCD display of operational parameters, measuring a massive 6 1/2" x 3 1/2". Easy to read and illuminated.
- Dual, 24 hour format clocks and dual programmable timers.
- An elegant, calibrated, analog signal strength meter.
- Auto backlight shutoff to conserve battery life.
- Low battery indicator.
- Operates on six internal "D" cell batteries or the included 110V AC adapter (220V AC adapter is available).
Dimensions: 21" L x 8 1/2" H x 9 1/2" W
Weight: 14.5 lb.

Yacht Boy 400PE

Yacht Boy 400PE
AM/FM/SW Radio

- Digital Dual-Superhet tuner • 1.711-30 MHz SW range • SSB with fine tuning control • 40 random presets • Direct frequency entry • Manual and auto tuning • Built-in antennas • Supplementary SW antenna • SW antenna jack • FM stereo with headphones • LCD shows frequency, time and more • Dual 24 hour clocks • Alarm • Sleep timer • Battery operated or included AC adapter.

Dimensions: 7 3/4"W x 4 5/8"H x 1 3/8"D.

S350

Grundig's ALL NEW
AM/FM/SW Field Radio

- Sensitive analog tuner with digital frequency readout • 2.3-27.41 MHz SW range • Fine tuning control • RF gain control • Low-pass filter • Built-in antennas • External antenna jacks • Stereo line level out • Separate bass, treble control • Digital clock with alarm • Sleep timer • Headphone jack • Uses 4 D cell batteries or included AC adapter.

Dimensions: 10 1/2"W x 6 1/2"H x 3 1/2"D.

Yacht Boy 300PE

Yacht Boy 300PE
AM/FM/SW Radio

- LCD displays time, frequency and memory station • Display light for momentary illumination • Digital PLL synthesized receiver • Direct frequency entry system for instant access to station • 24 station memory presets • Sleep timer and alarm • FM/SW 360 degree rotary telescopic antenna / MW ferrite bar antenna • External antenna jack for improved shortwave reception • Includes: AC adapter, carrying strap, case, earphones and three AA batteries.

Dimensions: 5 3/4"W x 3 1/2"H x 1 1/8"D

FR200 Emergency Radio

FR200
AM/FM/SW Radio

- Four Band Tuning – AM/FM/SW1/SW2 • Built in power generator • 90 seconds of cranking generates over an hour of power • 2 1/2" diameter speaker • Emergency light • Fine tuning knob • DC jack, earphone jack

Dimensions: 6 3/4"W x 5 3/4"H x 2 1/8"D

13:00–13:00

Radio Prague, Czech Republic. Summer only at this hour. *News,* then Monday through Friday there's *Current Affairs* and one or more features: *Talking Point* (Monday), *Witness* and *One on One* (Tuesday), *ABC of Czech* and either *Czechs in History* or *Spotlight* (Wednesday), *Economics Report* (Thursday) and *Stepping Out* and *The Arts* (Friday). On Saturday the news is followed by *Insight Central Europe,* and Sunday by *Mailbox* and *ABC of Czech* followed by *Encore* (classical music), *Magic Carpet* (Czech world music) or *Czech Books.* Thirty minutes to northern Europe on 13580 kHz, and to South Asia (audible in parts of the Mideast) on 21745 kHz. There is no corresponding broadcast in winter.

Radio Jordan. Summer only at this time. The first hour of a partial relay of the station's domestic broadcasts, beamed to Europe on 11690 kHz. Continuous till 1630 (1730 in winter).

Radio Korea International, South Korea. Opens with 10 minutes of *news,* then Monday through Friday, a commentary. This is followed by 30 minutes (45 on Friday) of *Seoul Calling.* Monday through Thursday, the broadcast closes with a 15-minute feature: *Korea, Today and Tomorrow, Korean Kaleidoscope, Wonderful Korea* and *Seoul Report,* respectively. On Saturday, the news is followed by *Worldwide Friendship* (a listener-response program), and Sunday by *Korean Pop Interactive.* Sixty minutes to Southeast Asia on 9570 and 13670 kHz.

Radio Austria International. Winter only at this time. Starts weekdays at 1315, and weekends at 1305. See 1200 for more details. To Asia and Australasia on 17855 kHz, and one hour earlier in summer. For a separate broadcast to Europe, see the next item.

Radio Austria International. Winter only at this time. Similar to the broadcast for Asia and Australasia, but the weekday start is 1345. See 1200 for more details. To Europe on 6155 and 13730 kHz, and one hour earlier in summer.

Radio Cairo, Egypt. The final half-hour of the 1215 broadcast, consisting of listener participation programs, Arabic language lessons and a summary of the latest news. To South and Southeast Asia on 17775 kHz.

CBC North-Québec, Canada. Continues with multilingual programming for a domestic audience. *News,* then winter Saturdays it's the second hour of ●*Good Morning Québec,* replaced Sunday by *Fresh Air.* In summer, the news is followed by *The House* (Canadian politics, Saturday) or *The Sunday Edition.* Weekday programs are mainly in languages other than English. Audible in the northeastern United States on 9625 kHz.

Radio Australia. Monday through Friday, there's a quarter-hour of *news* followed by 45 minutes of World Music in ●*The Planet.* Weekends, after five minutes of *news,* it's either Saturday's *Science Show* or the second part of Sunday's *Country Club.* Continuous programming to Asia and the Pacific on 5995, 6020, 9580, 11650, 11660 (from 1330), 11880 (till 1330) and 21820 kHz; and easily audible in much of North America on 6020 and 9580 kHz. In Europe, try 21820 kHz.

Radio Singapore International. The third and final hour of a daily broadcasting package to Southeast Asia and beyond. Starts with a five-minute bulletin of the latest *news,* then most days it's music: *Singapop* (local talent, Monday and Thursday); *Rhythm in the Sun* (Tuesday and Sunday); *Spin the Globe* (world music, Wednesday and Saturday); and *Hot Trax* (new releases, Friday). There's more news on the half-hour, then a short feature. Monday's offering is *Family Ties,* replaced Tuesday by *The Write Stuff.* Wednesday's feature is *Potluck;* Thursday has *Call from America;* and Friday it's *Snapshot.* These are followed by the 15-minute *Newsline.* Weekend fare is made up of Saturday's *On the Line from Silicone Valley, On Second Thought* and *Arts Arena;* and Sunday's *A World of Our Own* and *Limelight.* The broadcast ends with yet another five-minute news update. On 6150 and 9600 kHz.

Voice of Korea, North Korea. Uninspiring programs from the last of the old-time communist stations. But with North Korea rattling its nuclear sabers, this broadcasting fossil could yet provide some surprises. One hour to Europe on 7505 (or 13760) and 11335 (or 15245) kHz; and to North America on 9335 and 11710 kHz.

Voice of America. Opens with *news*, then it's music: *American Gold* (Monday), *Roots and Branches* (Tuesday), *Classic Rock* (Wednesday), *Top Twenty* (Thursday), *Country Hits* (Friday) and jazz at the weekend. Continuous programming to East and Southeast Asia winter on 6110, 9760, 11705 and 15425 kHz; and summer on 5955, 6160, 15160 and 15425 kHz. For Australasia there's 9645 and 15425 kHz.

AFRTS Shortwave, USA. Network news, live sports, music and features in the upper-sideband mode from the Armed Forces Radio & Television Service. Transmitted from modestly powered U.S. Navy stations around the globe. Try 4319, 5446.5, 5765, 6350, 6458.5, 7507, 10320, 12133.5, 12579, 13362 and 13855 kHz.

13:30

Emirates Radio, Dubai. *News,* then a feature on an Arab or Islamic theme. Twenty minutes to Europe and North Africa (also audible in eastern North America) on 13630, 13675, 15395 and 21605 kHz. The higher frequencies tend to vary slightly.

Voice of Turkey. This time winter only. *News,* then *Review of the Turkish Press* and features (some of them unusual) with a strong local flavor. Selections of Turkish popular and classical music complete the program. Fifty-five minutes to Europe on 15145 kHz, and to Southeast Asia and Australasia on 15195 kHz. One hour earlier in summer.

Radio Sweden. See 1230 for program details. Thirty minutes to North America summer on 17840 kHz. Also to Asia and Australasia winter on 9430 kHz, and year round on 17505 kHz.

Voice of Vietnam. Begins with *news,* then there's *Commentary* or *Weekly Review,* followed by short features and pleasant Vietnamese music (particularly at weekends). A half hour to Europe winter on 7145 (or 7185) and 9730 kHz, and summer on 11630 and 13740 kHz.

All India Radio. The first half hour of a 90-minute block of regional and international *news,* commentary, exotic Indian music, and a variety of talks and features of general interest. To Southeast Asia and beyond on 9690, 11620 and 13710 kHz.

Radio Tashkent, Uzbekistan. Monday through Saturday, opens with *News,* replaced Sunday by *Significant Events of the Week.* Other programs include *Nature and Us* and *Cooperation* (Monday), *Political Commentary* and *Youth Program* (Wednesday), a feature for women (Thursday), *Parliamentary Herald* (Friday) a show for shortwave listeners (Saturday) and *Interesting Meetings* on Sunday. Programs of Uzbek music are aired on Tuesday, Friday and Saturday, and a competition with prizes on Thursday and Saturday. To South and Southeast Asia, and also heard in parts of Europe and Australasia. Thirty minutes winter on 5060, 5975, 6025 and 9715 kHz; and summer on 7285, 9715, 15295 and 17775 kHz. Best for Southeast Asia is 9715 kHz in winter, and 17775 kHz in summer.

14:00

■**BBC World Service for the Americas.** *News,* then weekdays it's a series of 25-minute arts programs. The second half hour is much more lowbrow—popular music. By far the best are Monday's ●*Charlie Gillett* (world music) and Thursday's ●*John Peel* (eclectic and raw). Weekend programming consists of a five-minute *news* bulletin followed by Saturday's live *Sportsworld* or a Sunday call-in show, *Talking Point.* Continuous to North America and the Caribbean on 15190 kHz. Listeners in the western United States may get better reception from the Asian stream on 9740 kHz.

■**BBC World Service for Europe.** Winter weekdays, five minutes of *news* are followed by an arts show, *Meridian.* The next half hour consists of a mixed bag of music and light entertainment. Same time summer, the *news* is followed by two features, including some of the BBC's better offerings—*Discovery* and *Essential Guide* (Monday), ●*Health Matters* and ●*Everywoman* (Tuesday), ●*Focus on Faith* (1430 Wednesday), *Sports International* and *Pick of the World* (Thursday) and Friday's ●*One Planet* and *People and Places.* Weekend programs are the same all year: five minutes of *news* followed by Saturday's *Sportsworld* or

Sunday's *Talking Point*, a call-in show. Continuous to Europe and North Africa on 12095, 15485 and 15565 kHz.

■**BBC World Service for East and Southeast Asia and the Pacific.** The weekday lineup is *East Asia Today*, *British News* and ●*Sports Roundup*. Weekends, starts with *news*, then it's either Saturday's live *Sportsworld* or Sunday's call-in show, *Talking Point*. Continuous to East and Southeast Asia on 6195 and 9740 kHz, and to Australasia on 9740 kHz (also audible in western North America).

Radio Japan. *News*, then Monday through Friday it's *Japan and the World 44 Minutes* (an in-depth look at current trends and events). Weekends, there's Saturday's *Weekend Japanology* and *Sight and Sounds of Japan*, and Sunday's *Pop Joins the World*. One hour to the Mideast on 17755 kHz; to Southeast Asia on 7200 kHz; to Australasia on 11840 kHz; to western North America summer on 9505 kHz; and to South Asia winter on 9845 kHz, and summer on 11730 kHz.

■**Radio France Internationale.** Weekdays, opens with international and Asian *news*, then in-depth reports, a look at the main news event of the day in France, and sports. *Asia-Pacific*, replaces the international report on Saturday, and Sunday fare includes a weekly report on cultural events in France and a phone-in feature. These are followed on the half-hour by a 25-minute feature— *French Lesson*, *Crossroads*, *Voices*, *Rendez-Vous*, *World Tracks*, *Weekend* or *Club 9516* (a listener-response program). An hour of interesting and well-produced programming to the Mideast and beyond, winter on 17620 kHz, and summer on 17515 kHz. Also to South Asia winter on 7175 or 9580 kHz, and summer on 11610 kHz.

■**Deutsche Welle, Germany.** *News*, then Monday through Friday there's ●*NewsLink*. This is followed on the half-hour by ●*Focus on Folk* (Monday), ●*World Music Live* (Tuesday), *Arts on the Air* (Wednesday), *Living in Germany* and *Europe on Stage* (Thursday) and the youth-oriented *Cool* (Friday). Weekends, the Saturday news is followed by ●*Inside Europe*; and Sunday by *Hard to Beat* (sport), *Inspired Minds* and either *Hits in Germany* or *Melody Time*. Sixty minutes to Europe on 6140 kHz.

Radio Romania International. First afternoon broadcast for European listeners. *News*, commentary, press review, and features about Romanian life and culture, interspersed with lively Romanian folk music. Fifty-five minutes winter on 11940, 15365 and 17790 kHz; and summer on 15250 and 17735 kHz.

Voice of Russia World Service. Summer only at this time. Eleven minutes of *News*, followed Monday through Saturday by much of the same in *News and Views*. Completing the lineup is *Sunday Panorama* and *Russia: People and Events*. On the half-hour, the lineup includes some of the station's better entertainment features. Try ●*Folk Box* (Monday), ●*Music at Your Request* or an alternative (Tuesday and Thursday), ●*Jazz Show* (Wednesday) and Friday's retrospective ●*Moscow Yesterday and Today*, all of which should please. Making up the roster are Saturday's *Timelines* and Sunday's *Kaleidoscope*. Targeted at South and Southeast Asia at this hour. In the Southeast, choose from 7390, 12055, 15560 and 17645 kHz.

■**Radio Netherlands.** The first 60 minutes of an approximately two-hour block of programming. Monday through Friday there's ●*Newsline* (current events) and a feature on the half-hour: ●*Research File* (Monday), ●*EuroQuest* (Tuesday), ●*Documentary* (Wednesday), *Dutch Horizons* (Thursday) and *A Good Life* (Friday). Weekend programming opens with a *news* bulletin, then it's either Saturday's *Europe Unzipped*, *Insight* and *Amsterdam Forum*; or Sunday's *Wide Angle*, *The Week Ahead* and *Vox Humana*. To South Asia winter on 12070, 12080 and 15595 kHz; and summer on 9890, 11835 and 12075 kHz.

Radio Australia. *World News* is followed Monday through Friday by a continuation of ●*The Planet* (world music), Saturday's *New Dimensions* or Sunday's *Books and Writing*. Continuous to Asia and the Pacific on 5995, 6080, 9580, 11650 and 11660 kHz (5995 and 9580 kHz are audible in North America, especially to the west). In Southeast Asia, use 6080 or 11660 kHz.

Radio Prague, Czech Republic. Winter only at this time. *News*, then weekdays it's *Current Affairs* and one or more features: *Talking Point* (Monday), *Witness* and *One on One* (Tuesday),

ABC of Czech and either Czechs in History or Spotlight (Wednesday), Economics Report (Thursday), and Stepping Out and The Arts (Friday). Weekends, the news is followed by Saturday's Insight Central Europe or Sunday's Mailbox and ABC of Czech followed by Encore (classical music), Magic Carpet (Czech world music) or Czech Books. A friendly half hour to eastern North America and East Africa on 21745 kHz. There is no corresponding summer broadcast.

XERMX—Radio México Internacional. Monday through Friday, summer only at this time. An English summary of the Spanish-language Antena Radio. Thirty minutes to the southwestern United States on 9705 and 11770 kHz. One hour later in winter.

Radio Taiwan International. Opens with 15 minutes of News, and weekdays closes with Let's Learn Chinese. The remaining airtime is devoted to features. Monday's offering is the pleasurable and exotic ●Jade Bells and Bamboo Pipes (Taiwanese music); Tuesday, there's Culture Express and Trends; Wednesday's combo is Taiwan Today and Instant Noodles; Thursday's pairing is Discover Taiwan and New Music Lounge; and Friday brings Taipei Magazine and People. These are replaced Saturday by Groove Zone and Kaleidoscope, and Sunday by Hakka World and Mailbag Time. One hour to Southeast Asia on 15265 kHz.

China Radio International. Starts with News, followed Monday through Friday by special reports—current events, sports, business, culture, science and technology and press clippings. The rest of the broadcast is devoted to features. Regulars include ●People in the Know (Monday), Biz China (Tuesday), China Horizons (Wednesday), ●Voices from Other Lands (Thursday), and Life in China on Friday. Weekends, the news is followed by a shorter series of reports (current events and sport) and two features. Saturday there's Cutting Edge, and Listeners' Garden (listener mail, Chinese folk music, a preview of the next week's programs, and a Chinese language lesson); replaced Sunday by Reports on Developing Countries and In the Spotlight, a series of mini-features: Cultural Carousel, In

Vogue, Writings from China, China Melody and Talking Point. One hour to western North America on 7405 and 17720 kHz; to South Asia on 9700, 11675 and 11765 kHz; and to East Africa on 13685 and 15125 kHz.

All India Radio. The final hour of a 90-minute composite program of commentary, press review, features and exotic Indian music. To Southeast Asia and beyond on 9690, 11620 and 13710 kHz.

Radio Canada International. Winter weekdays it's Sounds Like Canada, replaced summer by Outfront (except for Friday's C'est la Vie). Winter Saturdays, there's a look at Canadian politics in The House; and summer it's the entertaining ●Vinyl Café. On Sunday there's 60 minutes of the three-hour show, The Sunday Edition. To eastern North America and the Caribbean winter on 9515, 13655 and 17710 kHz; and summer on 9515, 13655 and 17800 kHz.

CBC North-Québec, Canada. Continues with multilingual programming for a domestic audience. News, followed winter Saturdays by The House (Canadian politics). In summer, it's The Great Eastern, a magazine for Newfoundlanders. Sundays, there's 60 minutes of the three-hour Sunday Edition. Weekday programs are in languages other than English. Audible in the northeastern United States on 9625 kHz.

Radio Jordan. Winter, starts at this time; summer, it's the second hour of a partial relay of the station's domestic broadcasts, and continuous till 1630 (1730 in winter). Aimed at European listeners but also audible in parts of eastern North America, especially during winter. On 11690 kHz.

Voice of America. The first of several hours of continuous programming to the Mideast. News, current events and short features covering sports, science, business, enter-tainment and other topics. Winter on 15205 kHz, and summer on 15255 kHz. Also the final hour to East and Southeast Asia winter on 6110, 9760, 11705 and 15425 kHz; and summer on 5955, 6160, 15160 and 15425 kHz. The 15425 kHz channel is also available to Australasia.

14:00–15:00

Radio Thailand. Thirty minutes of tourist features for Southeast Asia and Australasia. Winter on 9560 kHz, and summer on 9830 kHz.

AFRTS Shortwave, USA. Network news, live sports, music and features in the upper-sideband mode from the Armed Forces Radio & Television Service. Transmitted from modestly powered U.S. Navy stations around the globe. Try 4319, 5446.5, 5765, 6350, 6458.5, 7507, 10320, 12133.5, 12579, 13362 and 13855 kHz.

14:30

Radio Sweden. Winter only at this time. Monday through Friday, it's *news* and features in *Sixty Degrees North*, concentrating heavily on Scandinavian topics. Several of the features rotate from week to week, but a few are fixtures. Monday's *SportScan* is replaced Tuesday by *Close Up* or an alternative feature, and Wednesday by special features. Thursday's carousel is *Nordic Lights*, *GreenScan* (the environment), *Heart Beat* (health), and *S-Files*; with *Weekly Review* filling the Saturday slot. The Sunday rotation is *Network Europe*, *Spectrum*, *Sweden Today* and *Studio 49*; while Monday's offering is *In Touch with Stockholm* (a listener-response program) or the musical *Sounds Nordic*. Thirty minutes to North America on 18960 kHz, and to Asia and Australasia on 17505 kHz.

15:00

■**BBC World Service for the Americas.** Starts with five minutes of *news*, then features, including some of the BBC's better offerings—●*One Planet* (1505 Monday), *Science in Action* (same time Tuesday), ●*Health Matters* and ●*Everywoman* (Wednesday), ●*Omnibus* (1530 Thursday), *Discovery* (science) and *Sports International* (Friday). Saturday has live action in *Sportsworld*, and Sunday programming is either more sport or the finest in classical music. Continuous programming to the Caribbean and North America on 15190 kHz. In western states, try the Asian stream on 9740 kHz—you may well get better reception.

■**BBC World Service for Europe.** Winter, identical to the service for the Americas. In summer, the format is *World Briefing*, *British News* and ●*Analysis* (except Wednesday, when you can hear ●*From Our Own Correspondent*). Saturday, it's a continuation of *Sportsworld*, and Sunday there's some fine classical music (features vary). Continuous to Europe and North Africa on 9410 (winter), 12095, 15485 and 15565 kHz.

■**BBC World Service for East and Southeast Asia and the Pacific.** *News*, then Monday through Friday, *Meridian* (the arts). The second half hour is totally different—either a soap or popular music. These are replaced Saturday by the live *Sportsworld*, and Sunday by *The Alternative* (popular music) and ●*Omnibus* (winter) or *Composer of the Month* (summer). Continuous to East and Southeast Asia on 6195 and 9740 kHz, and to Australasia on 9740 kHz (also heard in western North America).

China Radio International. See 1400 for program details. Sixty minutes to western North America on 7405 (winter) and 17720 kHz. Also available year round to South Asia on 7160 and 9785 kHz; and to East Africa on 13685 and 15125 kHz.

Radio Austria International. Summer only at this time. Weekdays, starts at 1510; Saturday and Sunday at 1505. See 1600 for more details. To western North America on 15515 or 17865 kHz, and one hour later in winter.

■**Radio Netherlands.** The final 55 minutes of an approximately two-hour broadcast targeted at South Asia. Monday through Friday, starts with a feature and ends with ●*Newsline* (current events). The features are repeats of programs aired during the previous six days, and are all worthy of a second hearing: ●*EuroQuest* (Monday), *A Good Life* (Tuesday), *Dutch Horizons* (Wednesday) ●*Research File* (science, Thursday) and ●*Documentary* (winner of several prestigious awards) on Friday. The weekend format is feature-news-feature, with *Vox Humana* and *Europe Unzipped* on Saturday, and ●*Documentary* and *Wide Angle* on Sunday. To South Asia winter on 12070, 12080 and 15595 kHz; and summer on 9890, 11835 and 12075 kHz.

Radio Australia. *World News*, then weekdays there's *Asia Pacific* and a feature on the half-hour. Monday, it's health; Tuesday, law; Wednesday, religion; Thursday, media; and Friday, sport. These are replaced Saturday by *Melisma* (classical music), and Sunday by *Encounter* and *Business Weekend*. Continuous programming to the Pacific (also well heard in western North America) on 5995, 9580 and 11650 kHz. Additionally available to Southeast Asia on 6080 and 11660 kHz.

■**Deutsche Welle,** Germany. *News*, then weekdays it's ●*NewsLink* —commentary, interviews, background reports and analysis. Next, on the half-hour, there's *Spectrum* (Monday), *Insight* and *Business German* (Tuesday), *World in Progress* (Wednesday), *Money Talks* (Thursday) and *Environment* (Friday). Saturday's features are *Religion and Society*, *German by Radio* and ●*Network Europe*; and the 55-minute ●*Concert Hour* fills the Sunday slot. Sixty minutes to Europe on 6140 kHz.

Voice of America. Continues with programming to the Mideast. A mixed bag of current events, sports, science, business and other news and features. Winter on 9575 and 15205 kHz, and summer on 9700 and 15205 kHz. Also heard in much of Europe.

Radio Canada International. Daily in winter, but weekends only in summer. Winter weekdays there's *Outfront* (except for Friday's *C'est la Vie*), replaced Saturday by the unique ●*Vinyl Café* (readings and music). Summer, the Saturday slot goes to ●*Quirks and Quarks* (a science show with a difference). On the remaining day it's *The Sunday Edition* both winter and summer. To North America and the Caribbean, winter on 9515, 13655 and 17710 kHz; and summer on 9515, 13655 and 17800 kHz. For a separate broadcast to South Asia, see the next item.

Radio Canada International. *News*, then Tuesday through Friday it's *Sounds Like Canada*. On the remaining days there's Saturday's *Richter on Radio*, Sunday's ●*Global Village* (world music) and Monday's ●*Quirks and Quarks*, a science show. Sixty minutes to South Asia winter on 9635 and 11935 kHz, and summer on 15455 and 17720

kHz. Heard well beyond the intended target area, especially to the west.

XERMX—Radio México Internacional. Monday through Friday, winter only at this time. An English summary of the Spanish-language *Antena Radio*. Thirty minutes to the southwestern United States on 9705 and 11770 kHz. One hour earlier in summer.

Radio Japan. *News*, then weekdays it's *Songs for Everyone* and *Asian Top News*. A 35-minute feature completes the broadcast: *Japan Music Treasure Box* (Monday), Japanese language lessons (Tuesday and Thursday), *Japan Musicscape* (Wednesday), and *Music Beat* (Japanese popular music) on Friday. *Pop Joins the World* is aired Saturday, and *Hello from Tokyo* fills the Sunday slot. One hour to East Asia on 9750 kHz; to South Asia winter on 9845 kHz, and summer on 11730 kHz; to Southeast Asia on 7200 kHz; and to eastern North America, summer only, on 11705 kHz.

Voice of Russia World Service. Predominantly news-related fare for the first half-hour, then a mixed bag, depending on the day and season. At 1531 winter, look for ●*Folk Box* (Monday), ●*Jazz Show* (Wednesday), ●*Music at Your Request* or an alternative (Tuesday and Thursday), *Kaleidoscope* (Sunday) and Friday's retrospective ●*Moscow Yesterday and Today*. Summer at this time, look for some listener favorites. The lineup includes *This is Russia* (Monday), ●*Moscow Yesterday and Today* (Tuesday), ●*Audio Book Club* (dramatized reading, Wednesday), the incomparable ●*Folk Box* (Thursday), and *Songs from Russia* on Friday. Weekend fare is split between Saturday's *Kaleidoscope* and Sunday's *Russian by Radio*. To the Mideast summer on 7325 and 11985 kHz; and to Southeast Asia winter on 6205 an 11500 kHz, and summer on 7390 and 11500 kHz.

Voice of Mongolia. *News*, reports and short features dealing with local issues, with Sunday featuring lots of exotic Mongolian music. Thirty minutes to West and Central Asia on 9720 or 12015 kHz, and sometimes heard beyond.

15:00–16:00

Radio Jordan. A partial relay of the station's domestic broadcasts, beamed to Europe on 11690 kHz. Continuous till 1630 (1730 in winter). Audible in parts of eastern North America, especially during winter.

Voice of Korea, North Korea. Repeat of the 1300 broadcast. One hour to Europe on 7505 (or 13760) and 11335 (or 15245) kHz; and to North America on 9335 and 11710 kHz.

AFRTS Shortwave, USA. Network news, live sports, music and features in the upper-sideband mode from the Armed Forces Radio & Television Service. Transmitted from modestly powered U.S. Navy stations around the globe. Try 4319, 5446.5, 5765, 6350, 6458.5, 7507, 10320, 12133.5, 12579, 13362 and 13855 kHz.

15:30

Voice of the Islamic Republic of Iran. A one-hour broadcast of news, commentary and features, strongly reflecting an Islamic point of view. To South and Southeast Asia and Australasia winter on 7190, 9610 and 11835 kHz; and summer on 7245, 9635 and 11775 kHz. Frequency usage tends to be a little erratic, though not as much as in the past.

16:00

■BBC World Service for the Americas. Monday through Friday winter, it's *World Briefing, British News,* ●*Analysis* (except Wednesday's ●*From Our Own Correspondent*) and ●*Sports Roundup;* summer, there's ●*Europe Today,* ●*World Business Report* and ●*Sports Roundup.* Weekends, year round, there's a short *news* bulletin followed by live sports. The final hour to the Caribbean and North America on 15190 kHz.

■BBC World Service for Europe. Monday through Saturday, is identical to the service for East and Southeast Asia. Sunday, the winter offering is a concert of classical music (well worth hearing); summer, there's live sports. Continuous to Europe and North Africa on 9410, 12095 and 15565 kHz.

■BBC World Service for East and Southeast Asia. Winter weekdays, there's *World Briefing, British News,* ●*Analysis* (except for Thursday's ●*From Our Own Correspondent*), and ●*Sports Roundup.* These are replaced in summer by ●*Europe Today,* ●*World Business Report* and ●*Sports Roundup.* Saturdays and summer Sundays, a five-minute *news* bulletin is followed by live sports. In winter, the Sunday lineup is *World Briefing, British News,* ●*Reporting Religion* and ●*Sports Roundup.* The final hour to East Asia on 6195 kHz; and continuous to Southeast Asia on 3915 and 7160 kHz.

■Radio France Internationale. The first half hour includes *news* and reports from across Africa, international newsflashes and news about France. Next is a 25-minute feature—*French Lesson, Crossroads, Voices, Rendez-Vous, World Tracks, Weekend* or *Club 9516* (a listener-response program). A fast-moving hour to Africa and the Mideast on any four frequencies from 9730, 11615, 11995, 15160, 15605, 17605, 17815 and 17850 kHz. Best for the Mideast is 11615 kHz in winter, and 15605 kHz in summer.

Radio Austria International. Winter only at this time. Weekdays, the 15-minute ●*Report from Austria* is aired at 1610, and then repeated at 1640. Saturday and Sunday, it's a similar arrangement, with *Insight Central Europe* airing at 1605 and 1635. The remainder of the one-hour broadcast is in German. To western North America on 17865 kHz, and one hour earlier in summer.

Emirates Radio, Dubai. A 15-minute feature on Arab history or culture, and preceded and followed by programming in Arabic. A little later, around 1630, there's a short summary of *news.* To Europe and North Africa (also heard in eastern North America) on 13630, 13675, 15395 and 21605 kHz (the last two frequencies tend to vary a little).

■Deutsche Welle, Germany. *News,* then Monday through Friday it's ●*NewsLink for Asia.* The next 30 minutes consist of *Insight* and *Business German* (Monday), *World in Progress*

GRUNDIG TUNES IN THE WORLD

SATELLIT 800

The World's Most Powerful Radio for the Serious Listener...

The Grundig Satellit legend continues. The pinnacle of over three decades of continu-
ly evolving Satellit series radios, it embodies the dreams and wishes of serious
ortwave listeners the world over. Its continuous frequency coverage of 100-30,000
z means that broadcasts from every corner of the globe are at your finger tips.
ndon, Tokyo, Moscow and many, many more. Listen to ham radio operators com-
inicating across the continent and around the world. Outstanding AM performance.
autiful FM-stereo with the included high quality headphones. And, just for fun, hear
ose planes as they take off and land at your local airport on the VHF 118-136 MHz
craft band. Even if you're new to shortwave, you'll find it a breeze to operate. The

experienced hobbyist will appreciate its host of advanced high-tech features. Use its
built-in antennas, or connect to your favorite external ones. From its massive, easy-
to-read, fully illuminated 6″ x 3.5″ Liquid Crystal Display, elegant traditional analog
signal strength meter, modern PLL circuit designs, to the silky smooth tuning knob
which creates absolutely no audio muting during use, this radio defines the Grundig
tradition. This is the advanced radio for you. Includes a 110V AC adapter (a 220V AC
adapter is available upon request) and high quality headphones. Operates on 6 D cells
(not included). 20.5″ L x 9.4″ H x 8″ W.

YB 400PE: COMPACT POWER

dvance Hi-Tech features, easy to use, exceptional performance in Shortwave,
M and FM. Hear broadcasts from around the world. Catch those hard to
ceive AM and FM stations at home. Turn on the SSB and listen to ham
perators. Digital PLL and Display. Direct Frequency Entry. Auto Tuning.
anual Step Tuning. FM-stereo. 40 memories. 2 Clocks. Alarms. Sleep Timer.
mensions: 7.75″ L x 4.5″ H x 1.5″ W   Weight: 1 lb. 5 oz.

S350: RUGGED FIELD RADIO

Incorporating a sensitive, high-performance analog tuner with digital
frequency readout, the S350 receives AM, FM-Stereo, and continuous
Shortwave coverage of 3,000 to 28,000 KHz, including all 14 international
broadcast bands. Its classic analog tuning knob with superimposed
fine-tuning control makes it a pleasure to operate, and the variable RF
gain control, wide/narrow bandwidth selector and low pass filter give you
complete control over incoming signals. Operates on 4 'D' batteries for
long battery life. Dimensions: 10.5″ L x 6.5″ H x 3.5″ W   Weight: 3 lbs 9 oz.

YB 550PE: THE LATEST INNOVATION

Unique features define the model YB 550PE, such as 200 randomly programmable memory presets with user-defined
memory page customizing, digital fine-tuning control, and favorite station wake-up memory. Through its PLL
synthesized digital tuner, receive AM, FM-Stereo, and Shortwave with excellent sensitivity and selectivity. Enjoy the
entire Shortwave spectrum that includes all 14 international broadcast bands and continuous Shortwave coverage of
520-29.999 KHz. Its auto-tuning system stops even on weak stations within the international Shortwave spectrum,
or with the direct frequency entry system, go instantly to any frequency in its tuning range.
Dimensions: 4.5″ L x 6.5″ H x 1.5″ W   Weight: 14 oz.

LCM

24 Foxwarren Dr., Willowdale
Ontario, Canada M2K 1L3
Tel. (416) 225-8961 / Fax (416) 730-1977

**FOR THE NEWEST
GRUNDIG SHORTWAVE
RADIOS SHOP LCM**

(Tuesday), *Money Talks* (Wednesday), *Environment* (Thursday) and the youth-oriented *Cool* (Friday). Weekends, the Saturday news is followed by *Religion and Society*, *German by Radio* and *Asia This Week*; and Sunday, by *Mailbag*. Sixty minutes to Europe on 6140 kHz. Also to South Asia on 6170, 7225 and (winter) 11695 or (summer) 17595 kHz.

Radio Korea International, South Korea. Opens with 10 minutes of *news*, then Monday through Friday, a commentary. This is followed by 30 minutes (45 on Friday) of *Seoul Calling*. Monday through Thursday, the broadcast closes with a 15-minute feature: *Korea, Today and Tomorrow*, *Korean Kaleidoscope*, *Wonderful Korea* and *Seoul Report*, respectively. On Saturday, the news is followed by *Worldwide Friendship* (a listener-response program), and Sunday by *Korean Pop Interactive*. One hour to East Asia on 5975 kHz, and to the Mideast and much of Africa on 9515 and 9870 kHz.

Radio Taiwan International. Opens with 15 minutes of *News*, and weekdays closes with *Let's Learn Chinese*. In between, there are either one or two features, depending on the day of the week. Monday's exotic and entertaining ●*Jade Bells and Bamboo Pipes* (Taiwanese music) is replaced Tuesday by *Culture Express* and *Trends;* Wednesday by *Taiwan Today* and *Instant Noodles;* Thursday by *Discover Taiwan* and *New Music Lounge;* and Friday by *Taipei Magazine* and *People*. Weekend fare consists of Saturday's *Groove Zone* and *Kaleidoscope*, and Sunday's *Hakka World* and *Mailbag Time*. The first of two hours to South Asia on 11550 kHz, and heard well beyond.

Voice of Korea, North Korea. Uninspiring programs from the last of the old-time communist stations. One hour to the Mideast and Africa on 9975 and 11735 kHz. Also audible in parts of East Asia on 3560 kHz.

Radio Prague, Czech Republic. Summer only at this time. *News*, then Monday through Friday there's *Current Affairs* and a feature or two: *Talking Point* (Monday), *Witness* and *One on One* (Tuesday), *ABC of Czech* and either *Czechs in History* or *Spotlight* (Wednesday), *Economics Report* (Thursday) and *Stepping Out* and *The Arts* (Friday). On Saturday the news is

followed by *Magazine*, *Letter from Prague* and a repeat of Tuesday's *One on One*. Sunday's lineup is *Mailbox* and *ABC of Czech* followed by *Encore* (classical music), *Magic Carpet* (Czech world music) or *Czech Books*. A half hour to Europe on 5930 kHz, and to East Africa on 21745 kHz. The transmission for Europe is one hour later in winter, but there is no corresponding broadcast for East Africa.

Radio Australia. Continuous programming to Asia and the Pacific. At this hour *World News* is followed by *Margaret Throsby* (interviews and music, Monday), *The Comfort Zone* (Tuesday), *Verbatim* (personal experiences) and *Earshot* (Wednesday), *Hindsight* (a look back into history, Thursday), and Friday's show of Australian indigenous music and stories, *Awaye* Saturday brings a continuation of *Melisma*, replaced Sunday by *The National Interest* (topical events). Beamed to the Pacific on 5995, 9580 and 11650 kHz (and well heard in western North America). Additionally available to East and Southeast Asia on 6080, 9475 and 11660 kHz.

Radio Ethiopia. An hour-long broadcast divided into two parts by the 1630 *news* bulletin. Regular weekday features include *Kaleidoscope* and *Women's Forum* (Monday), *Press Review* and *Africa in Focus* (Tuesday), *Guest of the Week* and *Ethiopia Today* (Wednesday), *Ethiopian Music* and *Spotlight* (Thursday) and *Press Review* and *Introducing Ethiopia* on Friday. For weekend listening, there's *Contact* and *Ethiopia This Week* (Saturday), or Sunday's *Listeners' Choice* and *Commentary*. Best heard in parts of Africa and the Mideast, but sometimes audible in Europe. On 7165, 9560 and 11800 kHz.

Radio Jordan. A partial relay of the station's domestic broadcasts, beamed to Europe on 11690 kHz. The final half hour in summer, but a full 60 minutes in winter. Sometimes audible in parts of eastern North America, especially during winter.

Voice of Russia World Service. Continuous programming to the Mideast and West Asia at this hour. *News*, then very much a mixed bag, depending on the day and season. Winter weekdays, there's *Focus on Asia and the Pacific*, with Saturday's *Newmarket* and Sunday's *Moscow Mailbag* making up the week. On the half-hour, choose from *This is*

Russia (Monday), ●*Moscow Yesterday and Today* (Tuesday), ●*Audio Book Club* (dramatized reading, Wednesday), the exotic and eclectic ●*Folk Box* (Thursday), and Friday's *Songs from Russia*. Weekend fare is split between Saturday's *Kaleidoscope* and Sunday's *Russian by Radio*. Summer, the news is followed by the business-oriented *Newmarket* (Monday and Thursday), *Science and Engineering* (Tuesday and Sunday), *Moscow Mailbag* (Wednesday and Friday), and Saturday's showpiece, ●*Music and Musicians*. The features after the half-hour tend to be variable. Audible in the Mideast winter on 6005 and 9830 kHz, and summer on 11985 and 15540 kHz.

Radio Canada International. Winter weekends only at this hour. Saturday there's ●*Quirks and Quarks* (science), and Sunday it's the final hour of *The Sunday Edition*. To North America and the Caribbean on 9515, 13655 and 17710 kHz.

China Radio International. Starts with *News,* followed Monday through Friday by special reports—current events, sports, business, culture, science and technology and press clippings. The rest of the broadcast is devoted to features. Regulars include ●*People in the Know* (Monday), *Biz China* (Tuesday), *China Horizons* (Wednesday), ●*Voices from Other Lands* (Thursday), and *Life in China* (Friday). Weekends, the news is followed by a shorter series of reports (current events and sport) and two features. Saturday there's *Cutting Edge*, and *Listeners' Garden* (listener mail, Chinese folk music, a preview of the next week's programs, and a Chinese language lesson); replaced Sunday by *Reports on Developing Countries* and *In the Spotlight*, a series of mini-features: *Cultural Carousel, In Vogue, Writings from China, China Melody* and *Talking Point*. One hour to eastern and southern Africa winter on 7190 and 13650 kHz, and midyear on 9570 and 11900 kHz.

Voice of America. *News Now*—a mixed bag of news and reports on current events, sports, science, business and more. To the Mideast on 9575 (winter), 9700 (summer) and 15205 kHz summer on 9700 and 15205 kHz.

AFRTS Shortwave, USA. Network news, live sports, music and features in the upper-sideband mode from the Armed Forces Radio & Television Service. Transmitted from modestly powered U.S. Navy stations around the globe. Try 4319, 5446.5, 5765, 6350, 6458.5, 7507, 10320, 12133.5, 12579, 13362 and 13855 kHz.

16:30

Radio Slovakia International. Summer only at this time; see 1730 for specifics. Thirty minutes of friendly programming to western Europe on 5920, 6055 and 7345 kHz. One hour later in winter.

Voice of Vietnam. *News*, then *Commentary* or *Weekly Review* followed by short features and pleasant Vietnamese music (especially at weekends). A half hour to Europe winter on 7145 (or 7185) and 9730 kHz, and summer on 11630 and 13740 kHz.

Xizang [Tibet] People's Broadcasting Station, China. Monday through Saturday only. *Holy Tibet*, which describes itself as "a window to life in Tibet," is a 20-minute package of information and local music—mountains, monasteries, local customs, and (mostly) Tibetan popular music. Sometimes acknowledges listeners' reception reports at the end of the program. Original editions are aired on Monday, Wednesday and Friday, and repeated at the same time the next day. Well heard in East Asia, and sometimes provides fair reception in Europe. On 4905, 4920, 5240, 6110, 6130, 6200, 7385 and 9490 kHz.

Radio Cairo, Egypt. The first 30 minutes of a two-hour mix of Arab music and features on Egyptian and Islamic themes, with *news*, commentary, quizzes, mailbag shows, and answers to listeners' questions. To southern Africa on 9755 kHz.

17:00

■**BBC World Service for Europe.** Identical to the service for Southeast Asia. Continuous to

Europe and North Africa on 6195 and 9410 kHz

■**BBC World Service for Southern Africa.** *News, Focus on Africa,* and ●*Sports Roundup.* Part of a 19-hour daily service on a variety of channels. At this hour, on 3255, 6190 and 15400 kHz.

■**BBC World Service for Southeast Asia.** Monday through Friday winter, there's ●*Europe Today,* ●*World Business Report* and ●*Sports Roundup.* Summer replacements are a five-minute *news* bulletin, *Outlook* (news and human interest stories) and a 15-minute feature (very much a mixed bag). Winter Saturdays, it's *World Briefing, British News* and ●*Sportsworld,* replaced summer by ●*From Our Own Correspondent* and ●*Agenda.* Sunday's winter offerings are *Global Business* and ●*Agenda,* with ●*Play of the Week* filling the summer slot. The final hour to Southeast Asia, on 3915 and 7160 kHz.

Radio Prague, Czech Republic. See 1700 for program specifics. A half hour winter to West Africa on 17485 kHz, and summer to Central Africa on 21745 kHz. Also year round to Europe on 5930 kHz.

■**Deutsche Welle,** Germany. *News,* then Monday through Friday, ●*NewsLink for Asia.* The lineup for the second half-hour is ●*World Music Live* (Monday), *Arts on the Air* (Tuesday), *Living in Germany* and *Europe on Stage* (Wednesday), *Cool* (a youth show, Thursday) and ●*Focus on Folk* (Friday). Saturday's feature is the 55-minute ●*Inside Europe,* replaced Sunday by *Hard to Beat* (sport), *Inspired Minds* and either *Hits in Germany* or *Melody Time.* One hour to Europe on 6140 kHz.

Radio Romania International. *News,* commentary, a press review, and several short features. Music, too. Thirty minutes to Europe winter on 9625 11830, 11940 and 15245 kHz; and summer on 11740, 15365, 15380, 17735 and 17805 kHz.

Radio Australia. Continuous programming to Asia and the Pacific. Starts with *World News,* then Monday through Friday there's *Bush Telegraph,* a light-hearted look at rural and regional issues in Australia. Replaced Satur-

day by *The Spirit of Things,* and Sunday by *New Dimensions.* Beamed to the Pacific on 5995, 9580, 9815 and 11880 kHz; and to East and Southeast Asia on 6080 and 9475 kHz. Listeners in Japan should tune to 9815 kHz. Also audible in parts of western North America on 5995, 9580 and 11880 kHz.

Radio Polonia, Poland. This time summer only. Monday through Friday, opens with *News from Poland*—a compendium of news, reports and interviews. A couple of features complete the broadcast. Monday's combo is *Around Poland* and *The Best of Polish Radio* (or *Bookworm*); Tuesday, it's *Letter from Poland* and *Multimedia Show*; Wednesday, *A Day in the Life* (interviews) and *High Note* (or an alternative classical music program); Thursday, *Focus* (the arts in Poland) and *Soundcheck* (new Polish music releases); and Friday, *Business Week* and *In Touch,* a listener-response show. The Saturday broadcast begins with *Europe East* (correspondents' reports), and is followed by *From The Weeklies* and *Chart Show.* Sundays, it's five minutes of *news* followed by *Insight Central Europe* (a joint-production with other stations of the region) and *Request Show.* Sixty minutes to western Europe on 5995 and 7285 kHz. One hour later during winter.

Radio Jordan. Winter only at this time. The final 30 minutes of a partial relay of the station's domestic broadcasts. To Europe on 11690 kHz.

Voice of Russia World Service. *News,* then it's a mixed bag, depending on the day and season. Winter, the news is followed by the business-oriented *Newmarket* (Monday and Thursday), *Science and Engineering* (Tuesday and Sunday), and *Moscow Mailbag* (Wednesday and Friday). The choice of features for the second half hour is somewhat variable. In summer, the news is followed by a series of features: *Moscow Mailbag* (Monday, Thursday and Saturday), *Newmarket* (Tuesday and Friday), *Science and Engineering* (Wednesday) and Sunday's jewel, *Music and Musicians* On the half-hour, the lineup includes *Kaleidoscope* (Monday), ●*Music at Your Request* or an alternative (Tuesday), ●*Moscow Yesterday and Today* (Wednesday), Friday's ●*Folk Box* and Saturday's *Songs from Russia.* Summer only to

Europe on 9775 and 9890 kHz, plus weekends on 9480 and 11675 kHz. For the Mideast, tune to 9470 and 9830 kHz in winter, and 11985 kHz in summer. In Southern Africa, try 11510 kHz midyear.

Radio Japan. *News*, then weekdays it's *Songs for Everyone* and *Japan and the World 44 Minutes* (in-depth reporting). Saturday's feature is *Hello From Tokyo*, replaced Sunday by *Pop Joins the World*. One hour to Europe on 11970 kHz; to southern Africa on 15355 kHz; and to western North America summer on 9505 kHz.

Radio Taiwan International. The final 60 minutes of a two-hour block of programs to South Asia. Opens with 15 minutes of *News*, and closes weekdays with *Let's Learn Chinese*. The remaining airtime is taken up be features. Monday, there's *Taiwan Economic Journal* followed by *Stage, Screen and Studio*; Tuesday, ●*Jade Bells and Bamboo Pipes*; Wednesday, *New Music Lounge* and *Confucius and Inspiration Beyond*; Thursday, *News Talk* and *Life*

Unusual; and Friday, *Formosa Outlook* and *Taiwan Gourmet*. The Saturday slots go to *Kaleidoscope* and *Mailbag Time*, replaced Sunday by *Hakka World* and *Asia Pacific*. On 11550 kHz.

China Radio International. Repeat of the 1600 transmission; see there for specifics. One hour to eastern and southern Africa on 7150 (winter), 9570, 9695, 11910 and (midyear) 11920 kHz.

Voice of Vietnam. Summer only at this time. Thirty minutes to western Europe via an Austrian relay on 9725 kHz. See 1800 for specifics. One hour later in winter.

Voice of America. Continuous programming to the Mideast and North Africa. *News*, then Monday through Friday it's the interactive *Talk to America*. Weekends, there's the ubiquitous *News Now*. Winter on 6040, 9760 and 15205 kHz; and summer on 9700 and 9760 kHz. For a separate service to Africa, see the next item.

17:00–17:45

Voice of America. Programs for Africa. Monday through Saturday, identical to the service for Europe and the Mideast (see previous item). Sunday, there's *Reporters Roundtable* and the entertaining ●*Music Time in Africa*. Audible well beyond where it is targeted. Winter on 13710, 15240, 15445 and 17895 kHz; and summer on 9850, 15410 and 15580 kHz. For yet another service (to East Asia and the Pacific), see the next item.

Voice of America. Monday through Friday only. *News*, followed by the interactive *Talk to America*. Sixty minutes to Asia on 5990, 6045, 6110, 6160, 7170, 7215, 9525, 9645, 9670, 9770, 9785, 9795, 11955, 12005 and 15255 kHz, some of which are seasonal. For Australasia, try 9525 and 15255 kHz in winter, and 7170 and 11770 kHz midyear.

■**Radio France Internationale.** An additional half-hour (see 1600) of predominantly African fare. Monday through Friday, focuses on *news* from the eastern part of Africa. Weekends, there's *Spotlight on Africa*, health issues, features on French culture, sports, media in Africa, and a phone-in feature, *On-Line*. To East Africa (and heard well in parts of the Mideast) on any two channels from 11615, 15605 and 17605 kHz.

Radio Cairo, Egypt. See 1630 for specifics. Continues with a broadcast to southern Africa on 9755 kHz.

AFRTS Shortwave, USA. Network news, live sports, music and features in the upper-sideband mode from the Armed Forces Radio & Television Service. Transmitted from modestly powered U.S. Navy stations around the globe. Try 4319, 5446.5, 5765, 6350, 6458.5, 7507, 10320, 12133.5, 12579, 13362 and 13855 kHz.

17:30

Radio Slovakia International. Tuesday through Friday, starts with *News* and *Topical Issue*, then features. Regulars include *Tourist News* (Tuesday), *Business News* and *Currency Update* (Wednesday), *Culture News* (Thursday) and *Regional News* (Friday). Monday's news is followed by *Insight Central Europe*. The Saturday lineup includes *Front Page* and *Sports*

News; and Sunday's features are *Sunday Newsreel* and *Listeners' Tribune*. A friendly half hour to western Europe on 5915, 6055 and 7345 kHz. One hour earlier in summer.

Radio Bulgaria. Summer only at this time. See 1830 for specifics. Thirty minutes to Europe on 9400 and 11900 kHz. One hour later in winter.

Radio Sweden. Summer only at this hour; see 1830 for program details. Thirty minutes of Scandinavian fare for Europe, Monday through Saturday, on 6065 kHz, and for western Europe and West Africa Sunday on 13580 kHz. One hour later in winter.

Swiss Radio International. *Swissinfo*—news, reports, and a short feature at weekends (replaced weekdays by music). Thirty minutes to the Mideast and East Africa winter on 9755, 13790 and 15555 kHz; and summer on 13750, 15515 and 17870 kHz.

Flanders Radio International, Belgium. Summer only at this time. See 1830 for program specifics. Thirty minutes to Europe on 9925, 13690 and 13710 kHz; and to the Mideast on 13710 kHz. One hour later in winter.

Voice of the Mediterranean, Malta. Monday through Saturday only at this hour. Starts with a cultural feature and ends with *Bits and Pieces* and *Today in History*. Monday's feature is *Cultural Café*, replaced on other days by *Human Dimension* (Tuesday), *Insight* (Wednesday), *Contemporary Mediterranean Writers* (Thursday), *The Wonderful World of Opera* (Friday) and *Cultural Notebook* on Saturday. Thirty minutes to Europe winter on 9850 kHz, and summer on 6185 or 9605 kHz.

17:45

All India Radio. The first 15 minutes of a two-hour broadcast to Europe, Africa and the Mideast, consisting of regional and international *news*, commentary, a variety of talks and features, press review and exotic Indian music. Continuous till 1945. To Europe on 7410, 9950 and 11620 kHz; to West Africa on 9445, 13605 and 15155 kHz; and to East Africa on 11935, 15075 and 17670 kHz.

1800-2359
Europe & Mideast—Evening Prime Time
East Asia—Early Morning
Australasia—Morning
Eastern North America—Afternoon and Suppertime
Western North America—Midday

18:00

BBC World Service for Europe. Monday through Friday winter, *News* is followed by *Outlook* (news and human interest stories) and a mixed bag of 15-minute features. Weekend fare is *World Briefing*, *British News* and either Saturday's ●*Agenda* or Sunday's ●*Assignment*. Summer weekdays, there's *news*, *Meridian* (the arts) and a soap or popular music. These are replaced Saturday by *World Briefing*, *British News*, *World Business Review* and *Letter from America*. Sunday, it's the final part of ●*Play of the Week*. If it ends at 1820, you also get *British News* and *Assignment* (or an alternative documentary); if it makes it to 1830, you get just the documentary; and if it goes the full hour, just sit back and enjoy it! Continuous to Europe and North Africa on 6195 and 9410 kHz.

■BBC World Service for Southern Africa. Starts weekdays with five minutes of *News*, then it's a couple of features: ●*Health Matters* and ●*Everywoman* (Monday), *Science View* and ●*Focus on Faith* (Tuesday), *Sports International* and *Pick of the World* (Wednesday), ●*One Planet* and *People and Places* (Thursday), and *Discovery* and *Essential Guide* on Friday. Not a bad one among them. Weekends, the first 30 minutes are taken by *World Briefing* and *British News*. After the half-hour, it's Saturday's ●*World Business Review* and ●*Letter from America* or Sunday's ●*Assignment* (sometimes replaced by an alternative documentary). Continuous programming on 3255, 6190 and 15400 kHz.

■Deutsche Welle, Germany. *News*, followed weekdays by commentary, interviews, background reports and analysis in ●*NewsLink for Asia*. The second half-hour consists of features: *Insight* and *Business German* (Monday), *World in Progress* (Tuesday), *Money Talks* (Wednesday), *Environment* (Thursday) and *Spectrum* (Friday). Weekends, there's

Saturday's ●*Inside Europe* and Sunday's *Mailbag*. Sixty minutes to Europe on 6140 kHz.

■Radio Netherlands. The first 60 minutes of an approximately three-hour broadcast targeted at Africa, and heard well beyond. Monday through Friday, the initial 30 minutes are taken up by ●*Newsline* (current events), with a feature occupying the second half-hour: ●*Research File* (Monday), ●*EuroQuest* (Tuesday), ●*Documentary* (Wednesday), *Dutch Horizons* (Thursday) and *A Good Life* on Friday. Weekend fare consists of *news* followed by Saturday's *Europe Unzipped*, *Insight* and *Amsterdam Forum*; or Sunday's *Wide Angle*, *The Week Ahead* and *Vox Humana*. To East Africa on 9895 and (winter) 11655 kHz; and to southern Africa on 6020 kHz.

Radio Kuwait. The start of a three-hour package of *news*, Islamic-oriented features and western popular music. Some interesting features, even if you don't particularly like the music. There is a full program summary at the beginning of each transmission, to enable you to pick and choose. To Europe and eastern North America on 11990 kHz.

Voice of Vietnam. Begins with *news*, which is followed by *Commentary* or *Weekly Review*, short features and some pleasant Vietnamese music (especially at weekends). A half hour to Europe winter on 5955, 7145 (or 7185) and 9730 kHz; and summer on 11630 and 13740 kHz. The 5955 kHz channel is via an Austrian relay, and should provide good reception.

All India Radio. Continuation of the transmission to Europe, Africa and the Mideast (see 1745). *News* and commentary, followed by programming of a more general nature. To Europe on 7410, 9950 and 11620 kHz; to West Africa on 9445, 13605 and 15155 kHz; and to East Africa on 11935, 15075 and 17670 kHz.

Radio Prague, Czech Republic. Winter only at

18:00–18:00

this time. *News*, then Monday through Friday there's *Current Affairs* and one or more features: *Talking Point* (Monday), *Witness* and *One on One* (Tuesday), *ABC of Czech* and either *Czechs in History* or *Spotlight* (Wednesday), *Economics Report* (Thursday) and *Stepping Out* and *The Arts* (Friday). On Saturday the news is followed by *Insight Central Europe*, and Sunday by *Mailbox* and *ABC of Czech* followed by *Encore* (classical music), *Magic Carpet* (Czech world music) or *Czech Books*. A half hour to Europe on 5930 kHz, and to Australasia on 9495 kHz. Europe's broadcast is one hour earlier in summer, but for Australasia it's two hours later.

RTE Overseas, Ireland. A half-hour information bulletin from Radio Telefís Éireann's domestic Radio 1. To the Mideast winter on 9850 kHz and summer on 15585 kHz.

Radio Australia. Sunday through Friday, *World News* is followed by *Pacific Beat* (a news magazine), replaced Saturday by *Lifelong Learning*. As we went to press, the future content of the second half hour was yet to be decided. Part of a continuous 24-hour service, and at this hour beamed to the Pacific on 6080, 7240, 9580, 9815 and 11880 kHz. Additionally available to East Asia on 9475 and 9815 kHz. In western North America, try 9580 and 11880 kHz.

Radio Polonia, Poland. This time winter only. See 1700 for program specifics. *News*, features and music reflecting Polish life and culture. Sixty minutes to Europe on 5995 and 7285 kHz. One hour earlier in summer.

Voice of Russia World Service. Continuous programming to Europe and beyond. Predominantly news-related fare during the initial half hour in summer, but the winter schedule offers a more varied diet. Winter, the *news* is followed by a series of features: *Moscow Mailbag* (Monday, Thursday and Saturday), *Newmarket* (Tuesday and Friday), *Science and Engineering* (Wednesday) and the outstanding ●*Music and Musicians* on Sunday. On the half-hour, the lineup includes *Kaleidoscope* (Monday), ●*Music at Your Request* or an alternative (Tuesday), ●*Moscow Yesterday and Today* (Wednesday), *Folk Box* (Friday) and Saturday's *Songs from Russia*. Summer weekdays, the first half hour consists of news followed by *Commonwealth*

Update, while the features that follow tend to be somewhat variable. The Saturday slots are filled by *Science and Engineering* and *This is Russia*, replaced Sunday by *Musical Portraits of the Twentieth Century* and ●*Christian Message from Moscow* (an insight into Russian Orthodoxy). Best winter bets are 5940 and 6175 (weekends), 7335, 7340 and 9775 kHz; likely summer channels include 7300, 9480, 9775, 9890, 11630 11675 and 11870 kHz. Also available winter only to the Mideast on 9830 kHz. In Southern Africa, try 11510 kHz.

Radio Argentina al Exterior—R.A.E. Monday through Friday only. *News* and short features on Argentina and its people. One of only a handful of stations which still give prominence to folk music. Tangos, too, if you're nostalgic. Fifty-five minutes to Europe on 9690 and 15345 kHz.

Voice of America. Continuous programming to the Mideast and North Africa. *News Now—*reports and features on a variety of topics. On 6040 (winter) and 9760 kHz. For a separate service to Africa, see the next item.

Voice of America. Monday through Friday, it's *News Now* and *Africa World Tonight*. Weekends, there's a full hour of the former. To Africa—but heard well beyond—on 7275, 11920, 11975, 12040, 13710, 15410, 15580 and 17895 kHz, some of which are seasonal.

Radio Cairo, Egypt. See 1630 for specifics. The final 30 minutes of a two-hour broadcast to southern Africa on 9755 kHz.

Radio Taiwan International. Opens with 15 minutes of *News*, and closes weekdays with *Let's Learn Chinese*. The remaining airtime is taken up be features. Monday, there's *Taiwan Economic Journal* followed by *Stage, Screen and Studio*; Tuesday, ●*Jade Bells and Bamboo Pipes*; Wednesday, *New Music Lounge* and *Confucius and Inspiration Beyond*; Thursday, *News Talk* and *Life Unusual*; and Friday, *Formosa Outlook* and *Taiwan Gourmet*. The Saturday slots go to *Kaleidoscope* and *Mailbag Time*, replaced Sunday by *Hakka World* and *Asia Pacific*. One hour to western Europe on 3955 kHz.

AFRTS Shortwave, USA. Network news, live sports, music and features in the upper-sideband mode from the Armed Forces Radio &

18:00–19:00

Television Service. Transmitted from modestly powered U.S. Navy stations around the globe. Try 4319, 5446.5, 5765, 6350, 6458.5, 7507, 10320, 12133.5, 12579, 13362 and 13855 kHz.

18:15

Radio Bangladesh. *News,* followed by Islamic and general interest features; some nice Bengali music, too. Thirty minutes to Europe on 7190 and 9550 kHz, and irregularly on 15520 kHz. Frequencies may be slightly variable.

18:30

Radio Bulgaria. This time winter only. Thirty minutes of *news,* commentary, short features and enjoyable Bulgarian music. Thirty minutes to Europe on 5800 and 7500 kHz. One hour earlier in summer.

Radio Slovakia International. Summer only at this time; see 1930 for program specifics. Thirty minutes of *news* and features with a strong Slovak flavor. To western Europe on 5920, 6055 and 7345 kHz. One hour later in winter.

RTE Overseas, Ireland. A half-hour information bulletin from Radio Telefís Éireann's domestic Radio 1. To North America on 13640 kHz, and to Central and Southern Africa on 21630 kHz.

Flanders Radio International, Belgium. Winter only at this time. Monday through Friday, starts with *News.* The rest of the broadcast is a mix of current events, reports and Belgian music. Saturday, these are replaced by the highly enjoyable ●*Music from Flanders,* and Sunday by *Radio World, Tourism* and *Brussels 1043* (a listener-response program). Thirty minutes to Europe on 7465, 13650 and 13685 kHz; and to the Mideast on 13650 kHz. One hour earlier in summer.

Voice of Turkey. This time summer only. *News,* followed by *Review of the Turkish Press,* then features on Turkish history, culture and international relations, interspersed with enjoyable selections of the country's popular and classical music. Fifty minutes to Western Europe on 9785 kHz. One hour later in winter.

Radio Sweden. Winter only at this time. Monday through Friday, it's *news* and features in *Sixty Degrees North,* concentrating heavily on Scandinavian topics. The Monday slot goes to *SportScan,* replaced Tuesday by *Close Up* or an alternative feature, and Wednesday by special features. Thursday's shows rotate from week to week—*Nordic Lights, GreenScan, Heart Beat* or *S-Files,* while Friday offers a review of the week's news. Saturday's slot is filled by *Network Europe, Spectrum* (the arts), *Sweden Today* or *Studio 49;* and Sunday fare consists of *In Touch with Stockholm* (a listener-response program) or the musical *Sounds Nordic.* Thirty minutes to Europe, Monday through Saturday on 6065 kHz, and Sunday on 5840 kHz. One hour earlier in summer.

19:00

■**BBC World Service for Europe.** Monday through Friday winter, there's *news, Meridian* (the arts) and a soap or popular music. Weekends, the first half hour consists of *World Briefing* and ●*Sports Roundup,* with the final 30 minutes going to Saturday's ●*World Business Review* and ●*Letter from America* or Sunday's *Science in Action.* Summer weekdays, opens with five minutes of *news,* and then it's features: ●*Health Matters* and ●*Everywoman* (Monday), ●*Focus on Faith* (1930 Tuesday), *Sports International* and *Pick of the World* (Wednesday), ●*One Planet* and *People and Places* (Thursday), and *Discovery* and *Essential Guide* on Friday. Some of the BBC's better offerings. Weekend fare is similar to that in winter, except for 1930 Saturday, when there's a 30-minute soap. Continuous to Europe and North Africa on 6195 and 9410 kHz.

■**BBC World Service for Southern Africa.** Monday through Friday, *News* is followed by 25 minutes of *Focus on Africa.* The second half hour consists of popular music or *Westway,* a soap. Weekend programming opens with *World Briefing,* Saturday's ●*Sports Roundup* ●*Science in Action* or Sunday's news bulletin followed by *Wright Round the World.* Continuous on 3255, 6190 and 15400 kHz. The last frequency can often be heard in eastern North America during summer.

■**Radio Netherlands.** The second hour of an approximately three-hour block of programming for Africa. Monday through Friday, starts with a feature and ends with ●*Newsline* (current events). The features are repeats of programs aired during the previous six days, and are worth a second hearing: ●*EuroQuest* (Monday), *A Good Life* (Tuesday), *Dutch Horizons* (Wednesday) ●*Research File* (science, Thursday) and the award-winning ●*Documentary* on Friday. The weekend format is feature-news-features, with *Vox Humana*, *Europe Unzipped* and *Insight* on Saturday, and ●*Documentary*, *Wide Angle* and a program preview on Sunday. Continuous programming on 7120, 9895, 11655 and 17810 kHz. In southern Africa, tune to 7120 kHz. The weekend broadcasts are also available to North America on 15315, 17725 and 17875 kHz. On other days, listeners in the United States should try 17810 kHz, which is via a relay in the Netherlands Antilles.

Radio Australia. Begins with *World News*, then Sunday through Thursday it's *Pacific Beat* (in-depth reporting on the region). Friday's slots go to *Pacific Focus* and *In Conversation*, replaced Saturday by *Earthbeat* (the environment) and *Lingua Franca*. Continuous to Asia and the Pacific on 6080, 7240, 9500, 9580, 9815 and 11880 kHz. Listeners in western North America should try 9580 and 11880 kHz, and best for East Asia are 6080 and 9500 kHz.

Radio Kuwait. See 1800; continuous to Europe and eastern North America on 11990 kHz.

Kol Israel. Summer only at this time. Twenty-five minutes of even-handed and comprehensive news reporting from and about Israel. To Europe and North America on 11605, 15615 and 17545 kHz; and to Africa and South America on 15640 kHz. One hour later in winter.

All India Radio. The final 45 minutes of a two-hour broadcast to Europe, Africa and the Mideast (see 1745). Starts off with *news*, then continues with a mixed bag of features and Indian music. To Europe on 7410, 9950 and 11620 kHz; to West Africa on 9445, 13605 and 15155 kHz; and to East Africa on 11935, 15075 and 17670 kHz.

Radio Budapest, Hungary. Summer only at this time. *News* and features, few of which are broadcast on a regular basis. Thirty minutes to Europe on 3975, 6025 and 11720 kHz. One hour later in winter.

Voice of the Mediterranean, Malta. Saturday through Thursday, summer only, at this time (Friday programs are in Arabic). See 2000 for program specifics. Sixty minutes to Europe on 12060 kHz, and one hour later in winter.

■**Deutsche Welle,** Germany. *News*, then Monday through Friday there's ●*NewsLink for Africa*. The second half-hour consists of ●*World Music Live* (Monday), *Arts on the Air* (Tuesday), *Living in Germany* and *Europe on Stage* (Wednesday), the youth-oriented *Cool* (Thursday) and ●*Focus on Folk* (Friday). Weekends, the Saturday news is followed by *Religion and Society*, *German by Radio* and *Asia This Week*; and Sunday by *Hard to Beat* (sport), *Inspired Minds* and either *Hits in Germany* or *Melody Time*. One hour to Central and East Africa winter on 6180, 11865, 13590 and 13780 kHz; and summer on 6180, 7225, 11965 and 13590 kHz. Heard well in parts of the Mideast on 11865 kHz in winter, and 13590 kHz in summer.

Voice of Russia World Service. Continuous programming to Europe at this hour. *News*, then winter weekdays there's *Commonwealth Update* (news and reports from and about the CIS), replaced Saturday by *Science and Engineering*, and Sunday by *Musical Portraits of the Twentieth Century*. Monday through Saturday summer, it's *News and Views*, with *Sunday Panorama* and *Russia: People and Events* filling the Sunday slots. Winter weekends at 1931, there's Saturday's *This is Russia*, and Sunday's emotive ●*Christian Message from Moscow*. During the week, the feature lineup is somewhat variable. Summer offerings at this time are mostly a combination of *Russia: People and Events*, the aptly-titled ●*Russian Treasures* and the religious *Daily Reflections*. Winter choices are 5940, 5950, 6175, 7340, 7360, 7440 and 9775 kHz; in summer, try 7440, 9480, 9685, 9775, 9890, 11675, 12030 and 12070 kHz.

China Radio International. Repeat of the 1600 transmission. One hour to the Mideast winter on 9585 kHz, and summer on 13790

19:00–19:30

kHz. Also year round to North Africa on 9440 kHz.

Radio Thailand. A 60-minute package of *news*, features and (if you're lucky) enjoyable Thai music. To Northern Europe winter on 9535 kHz, and summer on 7155 kHz.

Voice of Korea, North Korea. For now, of curiosity value only. An hour of old-style communist programming to Europe on 7505 (or 13760) and 11335 (or 15245) kHz; and to North America on 11710 kHz. Also heard in parts of East Asia on 4405 kHz.

Voice of Vietnam. Repeat of the 1800 transmission (see there for specifics). A half hour to Europe winter on 7145 (or 7185) and 9730 kHz, and summer on 11630 and 13740 kHz.

Voice of America. Continuous programming to the Mideast and North Africa. *News Now*—news and reports on a wide variety of topics. On 9760 and (summer) 9770 kHz. Also heard in Europe. For a separate service to Africa, see the next item.

Voice of America. *News Now*, then Monday through Friday it's *World of Music*. Best of the weekend programs is ●*Music Time in Africa* at 1930 Sunday. Continuous to most of Africa on 6035, 7375, 7415, 11920, 11975, 12040, 15410, 15445 and 15580 kHz, some of which are seasonal. For yet another service, to Australasia, see the following item.

Voice of America. Sixty minutes of news and reports covering a variety of topics. One hour to Australasia on 9525, 11870 and 15180 kHz.

Radio Korea International, South Korea. Opens with 10 minutes of *news*, then Monday through Friday, a commentary. This is followed by 30 minutes (45 on Friday) of *Seoul Calling*. Monday through Thursday, the broadcast closes with a 15-minute feature: *Korea, Today and Tomorrow, Korean Kaleidoscope, Wonderful Korea* and *Seoul Report*, respectively. On Saturday, the news is followed by *Worldwide Friendship* (a listener-response program), and Sunday by *Korean Pop Interactive*. Sixty minutes to East Asia on 5975 kHz, and to Europe on 7275 kHz.

AFRTS Shortwave, USA. Network news, live sports, music and features in the upper-sideband mode from the Armed Forces Radio & Television Service. Transmitted from modestly powered U.S. Navy stations around the globe. Try 4319, 5446.5, 5765, 6350, 6458.5, 7507, 10320, 12133.5, 12579, 13362 and 13855 kHz.

19:30

Radio Slovakia International. Tuesday through Friday, starts with *News* and *Topical Issue*, then features. Regulars include *Tourist News* (Tuesday), *Business News* and *Currency Update* (Wednesday), *Culture News* (Thursday) and *Regional News* (Friday). Monday's news is followed by *Insight Central Europe*. The Saturday lineup includes *Front Page* and *Sports News*; and Sunday's features are *Sunday Newsreel* and *Listeners' Tribune*. Thirty minutes to western Europe on 5915, 6055 and 7345 kHz. One hour earlier in summer.

Swiss Radio International. *Swissinfo*—news, reports, and a short feature at weekends (replaced weekdays by music). Thirty minutes to Africa winter on 9755, 13660, 15485 and 17660 kHz; and summer on 11815, 13645, 13795 and 15220 kHz. In southern Africa, choose between 13660 and 17660 kHz in winter, and 11815 and 15220 kHz midyear.

Voice of Turkey. Winter only at this time. See 1830 for program details. Some unusual programs and friendly presentation make for worthy listening. Fifty minutes to Europe on 5980 kHz. One hour earlier in summer.

Voice of the Islamic Republic of Iran. A one-hour broadcast of news, commentary and features with a strong Islamic influence. To Europe winter on 6110 and 7320 kHz; and summer on 11670 and 11860 kHz. Also to southern Africa winter on 11695 and 15140 kHz, and midyear on 9800 and 11750 kHz.

Flanders Radio International, Belgium. Summer only at this time; see 2030 for program specifics. Thirty minutes to Europe on 9925 and 13690 kHz, and one hour later in winter.

Radio Sweden. Summer only at this time, and a repeat of the 1730 broadcast. See 1830 for program details. Thirty minutes to Europe on 6065 kHz, and one hour later in winter.

RAI International—Radio Roma, Italy. Actually starts at 1935. Approximately 12 minutes of *news*, then some Italian music. Twenty minutes to western Europe winter on 5965 and 9845 kHz, and summer on 5970 and 9745 kHz.

Radio Station Belarus/Radio Minsk. Tuesday and Thursday, summer only at this time. See 2030 for specifics. Thirty minutes to Europe on 7105 and 7210 kHz. One hour later in winter.

19:40

Voice of Armenia. Monday through Saturday, summer only at this time. Twenty minutes of Armenian *news* and culture. To Europe on 9960 kHz, and to the Mideast on 4810 kHz. One hour later in winter.

19:50

Vatican Radio. Summer only at this time. Twenty minutes of programming oriented to Catholics. To Europe on 4005, 5890 and 7250 kHz. One hour later in winter.

20:00

■**BBC World Service for Europe.** Monday through Friday winter, the format is *News* and two features. These include ●*Health Matters* and ●*Everywoman* (Monday), ●*Focus on Faith* (1930 Tuesday), *Sports International* and *Pick of the World* (Wednesday), ●*One Planet* and *People and Places* (Thursday), and *Discovery* and *Essential Guide* on Friday. Weekends, there's Saturday's ●*From Our Own Correspondent* and *Westway* (a soap), replaced Sunday by popular music and light entertainment. In summer, it's ●*Newshour*, the standard for all in-depth news shows from international broadcasters. One hour to Europe and North Africa on 6195 and 9410 kHz.

■**BBC World Service for Southern Africa.** Fifty minutes of ●*Newshour*, with ●*Sports Roundup* closing the hour. Continuous programming on 3255, 6190 and 15400 kHz. The last frequency is often audible in eastern North America during summer.

■**Deutsche Welle,** Germany. *News*, then Monday through Friday there's the in-depth ●*NewsLink for Africa*. The second half-hour consists of features: *Insight* and *Business German* (Monday), *World in Progress* (Tuesday), *Money Talks* (Wednesday), *Environment* (Thursday) and *Spectrum* (Friday). Weekends, there's Saturday's ●*Inside Europe* and Sunday's *Mailbag*. One hour to East, Central and southern Africa, winter on 13590, 13780, 15205 and 15410 kHz; and summer on 9780, 15205 and 17810 kHz. Best winter bet for southern Africa is 13780 kHz, with 9780 kHz the summer choice.

Voice of the Mediterranean, Malta. Saturday through Thursday, winter only, at this hour. Sixty minutes of mostly cultural features: *This Week in History*, *Art Focus* and *Travelogue* (Monday); *Cultural Café*, *Insight* and *Malta and Beyond* (Tuesday); *Showcase of Malta*, *Cultural Notebook* and *Malta, Remains of Atlantis* (Wednesday); *VOM Bookshelf* and *Malta's Ways and Music* (Thursday); *The World of Operetta*, *More Malta Memories* and *Random Reflections* (Saturday); and *A Thinker's Thoughtful Think*, *The Sovereign Palaces*, *Malta Today*, *Short Stories with a Maltese Background* and *Weekly News Update* on Sunday. To Europe on 7440 kHz, and one hour earlier in summer.

Radio Canada International. Summer only at this time. *News*, then Monday through Friday it's *Canada Today*. Saturday's *Business Sense* and Sunday's *Mailbag* (a listener-response show) complete the week. On the half-hour there's *Spotlight* (Wednesday and Sunday), *Media Zone* (Monday), *The Mailbag* (Tuesday), *Business Sense* (Thursday) and *Sci-Tech File* on Saturday and Sunday. Sixty minutes to Europe, Africa and the Mideast on 5850, 5995, 11690, 11965, 12015, 12035, 15325 and 17870 kHz. One hour later during winter.

■**Radio Netherlands.** The final 55 minutes of an approximately three-hour broadcast targeted at Africa. Monday through Friday, opens with a feature: ●*Research File* (Monday), ●*EuroQuest* (Tuesday), ●*Documentary* (Wednesday), *Dutch Horizons* (Thursday) and *A Good Life* (Friday). ●*Newsline* (current events) and *Press Review* complete the broadcast. On weekends there's a six-minute *news* bulletin and either Saturday's *Europe Unzipped* and *Insight* or Sunday's *Wide Angle* and a program preview. To southern Africa on 7120 kHz; and to West Africa on 9895, 11655 (summer) and 17810 kHz. Weekend programming is also available for North America on 15315, 17725 and 17875 kHz. On other days, listeners in the United States can try 17810 kHz, which is via a relay in the Netherlands Antilles.

Radio Damascus, Syria. Actually starts at 2005. *News*, a daily press review, and different features for each day of the week. These can be heard at approximately 2030 and 2045, and include *Arab Profile* and *Palestine Talk* (Monday), *Syria and the World* and *Listeners Overseas* (Tuesday), *Around the World* and *Selected Readings* (Wednesday), *From the World Press* and *Reflections* (Thursday), *Arab Newsweek* and *Cultural Magazine* (Friday), *Welcome to Syria* and *Arab Civilization* (Saturday), and *From Our Literature* and *Music from the Orient* (Sunday). Most of the transmission, however, is given over to Syrian and some western popular music. One hour to Europe, sometimes audible in eastern North America, on 12085 and 13610 kHz. Low audio level is often a problem.

Swiss Radio International. Repeat of the 1930 broadcast. Thirty minutes to Africa winter on 9755, 13660, 15485 and 17660 kHz; and summer on 11815, 13645, 13795 and 15220 kHz. In southern Africa, choose between 13660 and 17660 kHz in winter, and 11815 and 15220 kHz midyear.

Radio Australia. Starts with *World News*, then Sunday through Thursday there's a continuation of *Pacific Beat* (in-depth reporting). Friday fare consists of *Pacific Review* and *Country Breakfast*, and Saturday, *Australia All Over* (a popular show from the Radio National domestic service). Continuous programming to the Pacific on 9580, 9815 and 11880 kHz; and to East and Southeast Asia on 9500 kHz. In western North America, try 9580 and 11880 kHz.

Voice of Russia World Service. Continuous programming to Europe at this hour. *News*, then Monday through Saturday winter it's *News and Views*, with *Sunday Panorama* and *Russia: People and Events* completing the

lineup. In summer, these are replaced by a variety of features. Pick from *Science and Engineering* (Monday and Thursday), *Newmarket* (Wednesday and Saturday), *Moscow Mailbag* (Tuesday and Friday), and the 47-minute ●*Music and Musicians* on Sunday. Winter on the half-hour, it's mostly a combination of *Russia: People and Events*, ●*Russian Treasures* (gems of classical music) and the religious *Daily Reflections*. Best of the summer offerings at this time are Thursday's ●*Folk Box*, Friday's ●*Jazz Show* and Tuesday's ●*Music at Your Request* or its alternative. Other features include *Songs from Russia* (Monday), *Musical Portraits of the Twentieth Century* (Wednesday) and Saturday's *Russian by Radio*. Winter on 5940, 5950, 6175, 7335, 7340, 7390 and 9775 kHz; and summer on 9480, 9775, 9890, 11675, 12030, 12070 and 15455 kHz. Some channels are audible in eastern North America.

Radio Kuwait. The final sixty minutes of a three-hour broadcast to Europe and eastern North America (see 1800). Regular features at this time include *Theater in Kuwait* (2000), *Saheeh Muslim* (2030) and *News in Brief* at 2057. On 11990 kHz.

Radio Exterior de España ("Spanish National Radio"). Weekdays only at this time. Spanish and international *news*, commentary, Spanish pop music, a review of the Spanish press, and a general interest feature. Sixty minutes to Europe winter on 9690 kHz, and summer on 15290 kHz; and to North and West Africa winter on 9595 kHz, and summer on 9570 kHz.

Radio Budapest, Hungary. Winter only at this time. *News* and features, most of which are broadcast on a non-regular basis. Thirty minutes to Europe on 3975 and 6025 kHz. One hour earlier in summer.

China Radio International. Starts with *News*, followed Monday through Friday by special reports—current events, sports, business, culture, science and technology and press clippings. The rest of the broadcast is devoted to features. Regulars include ●*People in the Know* (Monday), *Biz China* (Tuesday), *China Horizons* (Wednesday), ●*Voices from Other Lands* (Thursday), and *Life in China* (Friday).

Weekends, the news is followed by a shorter series of reports (current events and sport) and two features. Saturday there's *Cutting Edge*, and *Listeners' Garden* (listener mail, Chinese folk music, a preview of the next week's programs, and a Chinese language lesson); replaced Sunday by *Reports on Developing Countries* and *In the Spotlight*, a series of mini-features: *Cultural Carousel*, *In Vogue*, *Writings from China*, *China Melody* and *Talking Point*. One hour to Europe winter on 5965 and 9840 kHz, and summer on 11790 and 15110 kHz. Also available to eastern and southern Africa on 11640 and 13630 kHz; and to North and West Africa on 9440 kHz.

Kol Israel. Winter only at this time. Twenty-five minutes of *news* and in-depth reporting from and about Israel. To Europe and North America on any three channels from 6280, 7520, 9435 and 11605 kHz; and to Southern Africa and South America on 15640 kHz. One hour earlier in summer.

Radio Prague, Czech Republic. Summer only at this time. *News*, then Monday through Friday there's *Current Affairs* and one or two features: *Talking Point* (Monday), *Witness* and *One on One* (Tuesday), *ABC of Czech* and either *Czechs in History* or *Spotlight* (Wednesday), *Economics Report* (Thursday) and *Stepping Out* and *The Arts* (Friday). On Saturday the news is followed by *Magazine*, *Letter from Prague* and a repeat of Tuesday's *One on One*. Sunday's lineup is *Mailbox* and *ABC of Czech* followed by *Encore* (classical music), *Magic Carpet* (Czech world music) or *Czech Books*. Thirty minutes to western Europe on 5930 kHz, and to Southeast Asia and Australasia on 11600 kHz. One hour later in winter.

Voice of America. Continuous programming to the Mideast and North Africa. *News*, reports and capsulated features covering everything from politics to entertainment. On 6095 (winter), 9760, and (summer) 9770 kHz. For African listeners there's the weekday *Africa World Tonight*, replaced weekends by *Nightline Africa*, on 6035, 7275, 7375, 7415, 11715, 11855, 15410, 15445, 15580, 17725 and 17755 kHz, some of which are seasonal. Both transmissions are heard well beyond their target areas, including parts of North America.

AFRTS Shortwave, USA. Network news, live sports, music and features in the upper-sideband mode from the Armed Forces Radio & Television Service. Transmitted from modestly powered U.S. Navy stations around the globe. Try 4319, 5446.5, 5765, 6350, 6458.5, 7507, 10320, 12133.5, 12579, 13362 and 13855 kHz.

20:30

Radio Sweden. Winter only at this time. Monday through Friday, it's *news* and features in *Sixty Degrees North*, concentrating heavily on Scandinavian topics. Monday there's *SportScan*, replaced Tuesday by *Close Up* or an alternative feature, and Wednesday by special features. Thursday's shows rotate from week to week—*Nordic Lights*, *GreenScan*, *Heart Beat* or *S-Files*, while Friday offers a review of the week's news. Saturday's slot is filled by *Network Europe*, *Spectrum* (the arts), *Sweden Today* or *Studio 49*; and the Sunday lineup is *In Touch with Stockholm* (a listener-response program) or the musical *Sounds Nordic*. Thirty minutes to Europe (one hour earlier in summer) on 6065 kHz, and to Asia and Australasia (one hour later in summer) on 9400 kHz.

Voice of Vietnam. *News*, then it's either *Commentary* or *Weekly Review*, which in turn is followed by short features. Look for some pleasant Vietnamese music towards the end of the broadcast (more at weekends). A half hour to Europe winter on 7145 (or 7185) and 9730 kHz, and summer on 11630 and 13740 kHz.

Radio Thailand. Fifteen minutes of *news* targeted at Europe. Winter on 9535 kHz, and summer on 9680 kHz.

Flanders Radio International, Belgium. Winter only at this time. Monday through Friday, starts with *News*. The rest of the broadcast is a mix of current events, reports and Belgian music. Saturday, these are replaced by the entertaining ●*Music from Flanders*, and Sunday by *Radio World*, *Tourism* and *Brussels 1043* (a listener-response program). Thirty minutes to Europe on 7465 kHz. One hour earlier in summer.

20:30–21:00

Voice of Turkey. This time summer only. *News*, followed by *Review of the Turkish Press* and features (some of them unusual) with a strong local flavor. Selections of Turkish popular and classical music complete the program. Fifty minutes to Southeast Asia and Australasia on 9525 kHz. One hour later during winter.

Radio Station Belarus/Radio Minsk. Tuesday and Thursday only at this time. Thirty minutes of local *news* and interviews, plus a little Belarusian music. To Europe on 7105 and 7210 kHz. Occasionally heard in eastern North America during winter.

Wales Radio International. Summer Fridays only at this time. News, interviews and music from the Welsh hills and valleys. Thirty minutes to Europe on 7325 kHz, and one hour later in winter.

Radio Habana Cuba. The first half of a 60-minute broadcast. Monday through Saturday, there's international and Cuban news followed by *RHC's Viewpoint*. This is replaced Sunday by *Weekly Review*. To Europe on 11670 or 11760 kHz, and to the Caribbean on 6195 or 9550 kHz..

Radio Tashkent, Uzbekistan. Monday through Saturday, opens with *News*, replaced Sunday by *Significant Events of the Week*. Other programs include *Uzbekistan and the World* (Monday), *Life in the Village* and *Political Commentary* (Thursday), a listener-response show (Saturday) and *Traditions and Values* on Sunday. Programs of Uzbek music are aired on Tuesday, Wednesday and Friday. To Europe winter on two or more frequencies from 5025, 7105, 7185 and 11905 kHz; and summer on 5025 and 11905 kHz.

RAI International—Radio Roma, Italy. Actually starts at 2025. Twenty minutes of *news* and Italian music to the Mideast. Winter on 5985, 9710 and 11880 kHz; and summer on 6185, 9670 and 11880 kHz.

20:45

Voice of Armenia. Monday through Saturday, winter only at this time. Actually starts at 2040. Twenty minutes of Armenian *news* and culture. To Europe on 9960 kHz, and to the Mideast on 4910 kHz. The channel for Europe sometimes produces fair reception in parts of eastern North America. One hour earlier in summer.

All India Radio. The first 15 minutes of a much longer broadcast, consisting of a press review, Indian music, regional and international *news*, commentary, and a variety of talks and features of general interest. Continuous till 2230. To Western Europe on 7410, 9445, 9950 and 11620 kHz; and to Australasia on 9575, 9910, 11620 and 11715 kHz. Early risers in Southeast Asia can try the channels for Australasia.

Vatican Radio. Winter only at this time, and actually starts at 2050. Twenty minutes of predominantly Catholic fare. To Europe on 4005, 5890 and 7250 kHz. One hour earlier in summer.

21:00

■**BBC World Service for the Americas.** Winter weekdays, opens with five minutes of *news*, then a features double-bill (except on 5975 kHz, which has *Caribbean Report* until 2130). Pick of the features are *Science in Action* (2005 Monday), ●*Health Matters* and ●*Everywoman* (Tuesday), ●*Omnibus* (2030 Wednesday), *Discovery* (science) and *Sports International* (Thursday) and ●*One Planet* (Friday). Summer at the same time the lineup is *News*, ●*World Business Report*, *British News*, ●*Sports Roundup* and ●*Analysis* (replaced Wednesday by ●*From Our Own Correspondent*). Winter weekends, look for 60 minutes of ●*Newshour*, which is replaced summer by a bulletin of *news* and several short features. The Saturday slots are ●*World Business Review*, *British News*, ●*Sports Roundup* and *Patterns of Faith*; and the Sunday lineup is *Global Business*, ●*Sports Roundup* and *Write On*. To the Caribbean and eastern and southern parts of the United States on 5975 kHz. 12095 kHz, targeted at South America, is also audible in some areas; a radio with synchronous selectable sideband helps reduce teletype interference.

BBC World Service for Europe. Winter programming consists of ●*Newshour*, the BBC's flagship in-depth news show. In summer, weekday format is *News*, ●*World Business Report*, *British News*, ●*Sports Roundup* and ●*Off the Shelf* (readings from world literature). Saturday, the news is followed by *Jazzmatazz* and *Composer of the Month*; Sunday, by popular music and light entertainment. Continuous to Europe and North Africa on 6195 and 9410 kHz.

BBC World Service for Southern Africa. Winter, there's a full 60 minutes of ●*Newshour*. In summer, the weekday lineup is *News*, ●*World Business Report*, *British News*, ●*Sports Roundup* and ●*Analysis* (replaced Wednesday by ●*From Our Own Correspondent*). Weekends, opens with five minutes of *News*, then Saturday it's ●*World Business Review*, *British News*, ●*Sports Roundup* and ●*Letter from America*. These are replaced Sunday by *Global Business*, ●*Sports Roundup* and ●*Reporting Religion*. The final 60 minutes of a 19-hour block of programming. On 3255, 6005 and 6190 kHz.

■**BBC World Service for East and Southeast Asia.** Identical to the service for Southern Africa. To East Asia on 5965, 6195 and (summer) 11945 kHz; and to Southeast Asia on 3915 and 6195 kHz.

Radio Exterior de España ("Spanish National Radio"). Summer weekends only at this time. Features, including rebroadcasts of programs aired earlier in the week. One hour to Europe on 9840 kHz, and to North and West Africa on 9570 kHz. One hour later in winter.

Radio Ukraine International. Summer only at this time. *News*, commentary, reports and interviews, covering multiple aspects of Ukrainian life. Saturdays feature a listener-response program, and most of Sunday's broadcast is a showpiece for Ukrainian music. Sixty minutes to western Europe on 5905 kHz. One hour later in winter. Should be easily heard despite the station's technical limitations.

Radio Canada International. A full hour winter, but only 30 minutes in summer. Winter weekdays there's *Canada Today*, with

Saturday's *Business Sense* and Sunday's *Mailbag* (a listener-response show) the weekend replacements. A feature completes the hour: *Spotlight* (Wednesday and Sunday), *Media Zone* (Monday), *The Mailbag* (Tuesday), *Business Sense* (Thursday) and *Sci-Tech File* on Saturday and Sunday. Sixty minutes to Europe, Africa and the Mideast on 5850, 7235, 7425, 9770, 9805 and 13650 kHz; and one hour earlier during summer. In summer, the weekday ●*World at Six* is replaced Saturday by *Media Zone* and Sunday by *Sci-Tech File*. Choose from 5850, 7235, 13690, 15325 and 17870 kHz. One hour later in winter.

Radio Prague, Czech Republic. Winter only at this time. See 2000 for program details. *News* and features on Czech life and culture. A half hour to western Europe (and easily audible in parts of eastern North America) on 5930 kHz, and to Southeast Asia and Australasia on 9430 kHz. One hour earlier in summer.

Radio Bulgaria. This time summer only. Starts with *news*, then Monday through Friday there's *Events and Developments*, replaced Saturday by *Views Behind the News* and Sunday by 15 minutes of Bulgarian exotica in ●*Folk Studio*. Additional features include *Walks and Talks* (Monday), *Magazine Economy* (Tuesday), *Arts and Artists* (Wednesday), *History Club* (Thursday), *The Way We Live* (Friday) and *DX Programme*, a Saturday slot for radio enthusiasts. Sunday, look for *Answering Your Letters*, a listener-response show. Tuesday through Saturday, the broadcast ends with *Keyword Bulgaria*. Sixty minutes to Europe on 5800 and 7500 kHz. One hour later during winter.

China Radio International. Repeat of the 2000 transmission; see there for specifics. One hour to Europe winter on 5965 and 9840 kHz, and summer on 11790 and 15110 kHz. A 30-minute shortened version is also available for eastern and southern Africa on 11640 and 13630 kHz.

Voice of Russia World Service. Winter only at this time. *News*, then *Science and Engineering* (Monday and Thursday), the business-oriented *Newmarket* (Wednesday and Saturday), *Moscow*

Mailbag (Tuesday and Friday) or Sunday's excellent ●*Music and Musicians*. Best of the second half hour are Thursday's ●*Folk Box*, Friday's ●*Jazz Show* and Tuesday's ●*Music at Your Request* or its alternative. Other features include *Songs from Russia* (Monday) and Saturday's *Russian by Radio*. The final 60 minutes for Europe on 5940, 5950, 6175, 7300, 7335, 7340 and 7390 kHz, and one hour earlier in summer. Some channels are audible in eastern North America.

Radio Budapest, Hungary. Summer only at this time. *News* and features, few of which are broadcast on a regular basis. Thirty minutes to Europe on 6025 kHz, and to southern Africa on 11890 kHz. One hour later in winter.

Radio Japan. *News*, then Monday through Friday (Tuesday through Saturday local date in Australasia) it's *Songs for Everyone* and *Asian Top News*. A 35-minute feature completes the hour: *Japan Music Treasure Box* (Monday), Japanese language lessons (Tuesday and Thursday), *Japan Musicscape* (Wednesday), and *Music Beat* (Japanese popular music) on Friday. *Weekend Japanology* and *Sight and Sounds of Japan* fill the Saturday slots, and *Hello from Tokyo* is aired Sunday. Sixty minutes to Europe on 6055 (summer), 6090 (winter), 6180 and 11830 kHz; to Australasia winter on 11920 kHz, and midyear on 6035 kHz; to western North America on 17825 kHz; to Hawaii on 21670 kHz; and to Central Africa on 11855 kHz. The broadcast on 17825 kHz has different programming after 2115.

Radio Australia. *World News*, then Sunday through Thursday there's a look at current events in *AM* (replaced Friday by a listener-response program, *Feedback*). Next, on the half-hour, there's a daily feature—*In the Pipeline* (Sunday), *Health Report* (Monday), *Innovations* (Tuesday), *Religion Report* (Wednesday), and the musical *Oz Sounds* on Thursday. Saturday, it's the final part of *Australia All Over* plus the 15-minute *Asia Sunday*. Continuous to the Pacific on 7240, 9580 (till 2130), 9660, 11880, 12080, 17715 and 21740 kHz; and to East and Southeast Asia (till 2130) on 9500 kHz. Listeners in North America should try 11880, 17715 and 21740 kHz.

■**Deutsche Welle,** Germany. *News*, then weekdays there's ●*NewsLink for Africa*. On the half-hour you can listen to ●*World Music Live* (Monday), *Arts on the Air* (Tuesday), *Living in Germany* and *Europe on Stage* (Wednesday), the youth-oriented *Cool* (Thursday) and ●*Focus on Folk* (Friday). Weekends, the Saturday news is followed by *Religion and Society*, *German by Radio* and *Asia This Week*; and Sunday by *Hard to Beat* (sport), *Inspired Minds* and either *Hits in Germany* or *Melody Time*. One hour to West Africa, and audible in much of eastern and southern North America. Winter on 9615, 13780 and 15410 kHz; and summer on 9440, 11865 and 15205 kHz. In North America, try 15410 kHz in winter, and 11865 and 15205 kHz in summer.

Radio Romania International. *News*, commentary, press review and features. Regular spots include *Youth Club* (Tuesday), *Romanian Musicians* (Wednesday), and Thursday's *Listeners' Letterbox* and ●*Skylark* (Romanian folk music). Fifty-five minutes to Europe winter on 5955, 7105, 7215 and 9690 kHz; and summer on 9510, 9725, 11740 and 11940 kHz.

Radio México Internacional. Summer only at this time, when there's a daily 30-minute feature. The lineup consists of *Mosaic of Mexico* (Monday and Friday), *DXperience* (for radio enthusiasts, Tuesday and Sunday), *Regional Roots and Rhythms* (Wednesday), *Mirror of Mexico* (Thursday) and Saturday's *Magical Trip*. Best heard in western and southern parts of the United States on 9705 and 11770 kHz.

Radio Korea International, South Korea. Summer only at this time. Opens with 10 minutes of *news*, then Monday through Friday, a commentary and 15-minute feature: *Korea, Today and Tomorrow* (Monday), *Korean Kaleidoscope* (Tuesday), *Wonderful Korea* (Wednesday), *Seoul Report* (Thursday) and *Seoul Calling* (Friday). On Saturday, the news is followed by *Worldwide Friendship* (a listener-response program), and Sunday by *Korean Pop Interactive*. Thirty minutes to Europe on 3955 kHz, and one hour later in winter.

Voice of Korea, North Korea. Not quite the old-time communist station it was, but the

"Beloved Leader" and "Unrivaled Great Man" continue to feature prominently. Despite a few changes for the better, the Voice of Korea still has a long way to go before being accepted as a serious broadcaster. In the meantime, the uninspiring programs continue. One hour to Europe on 7505 (or 13760) and 11335 (or 15245) kHz.

Radio Habana Cuba. The final 30 minutes of a one-hour broadcast. Monday through Saturday, there's a news bulletin and the sports-oriented *Time Out* (five minutes each), then a feature: *Caribbean Outlook* (Monday and Thursday), *DXers Unlimited* (Tuesday and Saturday), the *Mailbag Show* (Wednesday) and *Weekly Review* (Friday). These are replaced Sunday by a longer edition of *Mailbag Show*. To Europe on 11670 or 11760 kHz, and to the Caribbean on 6195 or 9550 kHz.

XERMX—Radio México Internacional. Monday, Wednesday and Friday, summer only at this time. Fifteen minutes of *Regional Roots and Rhythms*. Programs on the remaining days are in Spanish. To the southwestern United States on 9705 and 11770 kHz. One hour later in winter.

Voice of America. Opens with *news*, then it's music: *American Gold* (Monday), *Roots and Branches* (Tuesday), *Classic Rock* (Wednesday), *Top Twenty* (Thursday), *Country Hits* (Friday) and jazz at the weekend. To the Mideast on 6040, 6095 (summer), 9595 (winter) and 9760 kHz; to Africa on (among others) 6035, 7375, 7415, 11715, 11975, 13670, 13710, 15410, 15445, 15580, 17725 and 17895 kHz (some of which are seasonal); to East and Southeast Asia on 15185 and 17820 kHz; and to Australasia on 9670 (or 9705), 11870 and 17735 (or 17740) kHz. In the United States, try 15580 and 17895 kHz in winter, and 15445 kHz in summer.

All India Radio. Continues to Western Europe on 7410, 9445, 9950 and 11620 kHz; and to Australasia on 9575, 9910, 11620 and 11715 kHz. Look for some authentic Indian music from 2115 onwards. The European frequencies are audible in parts of eastern North America, while those for Australasia are also heard in Southeast Asia.

21:15

Radio Damascus, Syria. Actually starts at 2110. *News*, a daily press review, and a variety of features (depending on the day of the week) at approximately 2130 and 2145. These include *Arab Profile* and *Economic Affairs* (Sunday), *Camera and Masks* and *Selected Readings* (Monday), *Reflections* and *Back on the Stage* (Tuesday), *Listeners Overseas* and *Palestine Talking* (Wednesday), *From the World Press* and *Arab Women in Focus* (Thursday), *Arab Newsweek* and *From Our Literature* (Friday), and *Human Rights* and *Syria and the World* (Saturday). The transmission also contains Syrian and some western popular music. Sixty minutes to North America and Australasia on 12085 and 13610 kHz. Audio level is often very low.

BBC World Service for the Caribbean. *Caribbean Report*, although intended for listeners in the area, can also be clearly heard throughout much of eastern North America. This brief, 15-minute program provides comprehensive coverage of Caribbean economic and political affairs, both within and outside the region. Monday through Friday only, on 11675 and 15390 kHz.

Radio Cairo, Egypt. The start of a 90-minute broadcast highlighting Arab and Egyptian themes. The initial quarter-hour of general programming is followed by *news*, commentary and political items. This in turn is followed by a cultural program until 2215, when the station again reverts to more general fare. A big signal to Europe on 9990 kHz.

AFRTS Shortwave, USA. Network news, live sports, music and features in the upper-sideband mode from the Armed Forces Radio & Television Service. Transmitted from modestly powered U.S. Navy stations around the globe. Try 4319, 5446.5, 5765, 6350, 6458.5, 7507, 10320, 12133.5, 12579, 13362 and 13855 kHz.

21:30

BBC World Service for the Falkland Islands. *Calling the Falklands* has been running for such a long time, it's a little surprising it's still on the air. This twice-

21:30–22:00

weekly transmission for a small community in the South Atlantic consists of news and short features, and is one of the curiosities of world band radio. Audible for 15 minutes Tuesday and Friday on 11680 kHz, and easily heard in parts of eastern North America.

Radio Station Belarus/Radio Minsk. Tuesday and Thursday, winter only, at this time. See 2030 for specifics. Thirty minutes to Europe on 7105 and 7210 kHz. One hour earlier in summer.

Wales Radio International. Winter Fridays only at this time. News, interviews and music from westernmost Britain. Thirty minutes to Europe on 7325 kHz, and one hour earlier in summer.

Radio Tashkent, Uzbekistan. Monday through Saturday, opens with *News*, replaced Sunday by *Significant Events of the Week*. Other programs include *Nature and Us* and *Cooperation* (Monday), *Political Commentary* and *Youth Program* (Wednesday), a feature for women (Thursday), *Parliamentary Herald* (Friday) a show for shortwave listeners (Saturday) and *Interesting Meetings* on Sunday. Programs of Uzbek music are aired on Tuesday, Friday and Saturday, and a competition with prizes on Thursday and Saturday. To Europe winter on two or more frequencies from 5025, 7105, 7185 and 11905 kHz; and summer on 5025 and 11905 kHz.

Radio Tirana, Albania. Monday through Saturday, summer only at this time. *News*, short features and some lively Albanian music. Thirty minutes to Europe on 7130 and 9540 kHz. One hour later in winter.

Voice of Turkey. This time winter only. *News*, followed by *Review of the Turkish Press* and features (some of them unusual) with a strong local flavor. Selections of Turkish popular and classical music complete the program. Fifty minutes to Southeast Asia and Australasia on 9525 kHz. One hour earlier in summer.

Radio Sweden. Summer only at this time. Thirty minutes of predominantly Scandinavian fare (see 2230 for specifics). To Europe on 6065 kHz, and to Southeast Asia and Australasia on 11650 kHz.

Voice of the Islamic Republic of Iran. A one-hour package of news, commentary and features with a distinctly Islamic slant. A little Iranian music, too. Not the lightest of programming, but an interesting alternative to what is heard from Western media. To Australasia winter on 9780 and 11740 kHz, and summer on 9870 and 13665 kHz.

22:00

■BBC World Service for the Americas. Monday through Friday winter, five minutes of *news* are followed by ●*World Business Report*, *British News*, ●*Sports Roundup* and ●*Analysis* (replaced Wednesday by ●*From Our Own Correspondent*). Summer, it's a full hour of *The World Today*, with the exception of Friday, when the final 30 minutes are taken up by ●*People and Politics*. Weekend programs are year round, with *The World Today* filling the first half hour, followed by Saturday's ●*From Our Own Correspondent* or Sunday's ●*Agenda*. Continuous programming to the Caribbean and eastern North America on 5975 kHz. Also audible in some areas on 12095 kHz, beamed to South America; a radio with synchronous selectable sideband helps reduce teletype interference.

BBC World Service for Europe. Winter weekdays, there's *News*, ●*World Business Report*, *British News*, ●*Sports Roundup* and ●*Off the Shelf* (readings from world literature). Weekends, *News* is followed by *Jazzmatazz* and ●*Omnibus* (Saturday), and *Meridian* (the arts) and ●*Weekend* on Sunday. Summer, it's news and current events in *The World Today*, reduced to 30 minutes Friday and Saturday, when it is followed by ●*People and Politics* and ●*From Our Own Correspondent*, respectively. The final 60 minutes of a 19-hour block of programming to Europe and North Africa. On 6195 kHz.

■BBC World Service for East and Southeast Asia and the Pacific. Sunday through Thursday (local Asian weekdays), it's a full hour of news and current events in ●*The World Today*. Friday and Saturday, there's 30 minutes of the same, followed by ●*People and Politics* and ●*From Our Own Correspondent*, respectively. Continuous to East Asia on 5965 and 6195 kHz; to Southeast Asia on 6195, 7110, 9660 and 11955 kHz; and to Australasia on 9660, 11955 and 12080 kHz.

■**Deutsche Welle,** Germany. *News,* then Monday through Friday (Tuesday through Saturday local date in the target area) it's ●*NewsLink for Asia*—commentary, interviews, background reports and analysis. The second half-hour consists of features: *Insight* and *Business German* (Monday), *World in Progress* (Tuesday), *Money Talks* (Wednesday), *Environment* (Thursday) and *Spectrum* (Friday). Weekends, there's Saturday's ●*Inside Europe* and Sunday's *Mailbag.* One hour to East Asia winter on 5955 and 6165 kHz, and summer on 9720 and 15605 kHz.

Radio Bulgaria. This time winter only. See 2100 for specifics. News and culture from the Balkans—don't miss ●*Folk Studio* (Bulgarian music) at 2210 Sunday. Sixty minutes to Europe, also heard in parts of eastern North America, on 5800 and 7500 kHz. One hour earlier in summer.

Radio Cairo, Egypt. The second half of a 90-minute broadcast to Europe on 9990 kHz; see 2115 for program details.

Radio Exterior de España ("Spanish National Radio"). Winter weekends only at this time. Features, including repeats of programs aired earlier in the week. One hour to Europe on 9680 kHz, and to North and West Africa on 9595 kHz. One hour earlier in summer.

Flanders Radio International, Belgium. Monday through Friday, starts with *News.* The rest of the broadcast is a mix of current events, reports and Belgian music. Saturday, these are replaced by the entertaining ●*Music from Flanders,* and Sunday by *Radio World, Tourism* and *Brussels 1043* (a listener-response program). Thirty minutes to North America winter on 11730 (or 13685) kHz, and summer on 15565 kHz.

China Radio International. Repeat of the 2000 transmission (see there for specifics), but with news updates. One hour to Europe winter on 7170 kHz, summer on 9880 kHz, and autumn on 7175 kHz.

Voice of America. The beginning of a three-hour block of programs to East and Southeast Asia and the Pacific. The ubiquitous *News Now*—news and reports on current events, sports, science, business, entertainment and more. To East and Southeast Asia on 7215, 9705, 9770, 11760, 15185, 15290, 15305, 17735 (or 17740) and 17820 kHz; and to Australasia on 15185, 15305 and 17735 kHz. The first half hour is also available weekday evenings to Africa on 7340, 7375 and 7415 kHz.

RAI International—Radio Roma, Italy. Actually starts at 2205. Twenty-five minutes of *news* and Italian music to East Asia on 11895 kHz.

Radio Australia. *News,* followed Sunday through Thursday by *AM* (current events) and, on the half-hour, a feature. The lineup starts with Sunday's *Australian Music Show* (contemporary music) and ends with Thursday's *Jazz Notes.* In between, there's *Music Deli* (samplings from different cultures, Monday); *Blacktracker* (contemporary aboriginal music, Tuesday); and *Australian Country Style* (Oz's response to Nashville, Wednesday). Friday's features are *Asia Pacific* and a later-than-usual edition of *AM;* and Saturday's pairing is *Correspondents' Report* and *Business Report.* Continuous programming to the Pacific on 17715, 17795 and 21740 kHz (audible in parts of North America, especially during summer), and to Southeast Asia on 13620, 15230 and 15240 kHz.

Radio Taiwan International. Opens with 15 minutes of *News,* and weekdays closes with *Let's Learn Chinese,* which has a series of segments for beginning, intermediate and advanced learners. The remainder of the broadcast is devoted to features. Monday, you can listen to the pleasurable and exotic ●*Jade Bells and Bamboo Pipes* (Taiwanese music); and Tuesday to *Culture Express* and *Trends.* Wednesday's slots are *Taiwan Today* and *Instant Noodles;* Thursday's pairing is *Discover Taiwan* and *New Music Lounge;* and Friday brings *Taipei Magazine* and *People.* These are replaced Saturday by *Groove Zone* and *Kaleidoscope,* and Sunday by *Hakka World* and *Mailbag Time.* Sixty minutes to western Europe,

22:00–22:30

winter on 9355 kHz, and summer on 15600 kHz.

Radio Tirana, Albania. Monday through Saturday, winter only at this time. Thirty minutes of news, short features and Albanian music. To Europe on 7130 and 9540 kHz. One hour earlier in summer.

Radio Budapest, Hungary. Winter only at this time. *News* and features, most of which are broadcast on a non-regular basis. Thirty minutes to Europe on 6025 kHz, and to southern Africa on 11965 kHz. One hour earlier in summer.

Voice of Turkey. Summer only at this time. *News,* followed by *Review of the Turkish Press* and features with a strong local flavor. Selections of Turkish popular and classical music complete the program. Fifty minutes to Europe and eastern North America on 9830 and 12000 kHz. One hour later during winter.

Radio Canada International. Summer only at this hour, and a relay of CBC domestic programming. Monday through Friday, opens with ●*The World at Six;* Saturday and Sunday, ●*The World This Weekend.* On the half-hour there's the weekday ●*As It Happens,* Saturday's *Madly Off in All Directions* (sometimes replaced by another comedy show), and Sunday's *The Inside Track.* Sixty minutes to North America on 6140, 9590 and 15455 kHz. The first half hour is also available to the Caribbean and South America on 11920, 15170 and 17880 kHz. One hour later in winter. For a separate winter service to Europe, see the next item.

Radio Canada International. Winter only at this time. Weekdays, it's ●*The World at Six;* Saturday, *Media Zone;* and Sunday, *Sci-Tech File.* Thirty minutes to Europe and North and West Africa on 5850, 6045, 9770, 9805 and 12005 kHz. One hour earlier in summer.

Radio Korea International, South Korea. Winter only at this hour. See 2100 for specifics Thirty minutes to Europe on 3955 kHz, and one hour earlier in summer.

Radio Ukraine International. Winter only at this time. A potpourri of things Ukrainian, with the Sunday broadcast often featuring some excellent music. Sixty minutes to Europe and

beyond on two or more channels from 5905, 6020, 7240 and 9560 kHz. Often mediocre reception due to financial and technical limitations. One hour earlier in summer.

Radio for Peace International, Costa Rica. Counterculture and social-conscience programs. to Europe and North America on 7445 kHz.

XERMX—Radio México Internacional. Monday, Wednesday and Friday, winter only at this time. Fifteen minutes of *Regional Roots and Rhythms.* Programs on the remaining days are in Spanish. To the southwestern United States on 9705 and 11770 kHz. One hour earlier in summer.

All India Radio. The final half-hour of a transmission to Western Europe and Australasia, consisting mainly of news-related fare. To Western Europe on 7410, 9445, 9950 and 11620 kHz; and to Australasia on 9575, 9910, 11620 and 11715 kHz. Frequencies for Europe are audible in parts of eastern North America, while those for Australasia are also heard in Southeast Asia.

AFRTS Shortwave, USA. Network news, live sports, music and features in the upper-sideband mode from the Armed Forces Radio & Television Service. Transmitted from modestly powered U.S. Navy stations around the globe. Try 4319, 5446.5, 5765, 6350, 6458.5, 7507, 10320, 12133.5, 12579, 13362 and 13855 kHz.

22:30

Radio Sweden. Monday through Friday, it's *news* and features in *Sixty Degrees North,* concentrating heavily on Scandinavian topics. The Monday slot goes to *SportScan,* replaced Tuesday by *Close Up* or an alternative feature, and Wednesday by special features. Thursday's shows rotate from week to week—*Nordic Report, GreenScan, Heart Beat* or *S-Files,* while Friday offers a review of the week's news. Saturday's carousel is *Network Europe, Spectrum* (the arts), *Sweden Today* or *Studio 49;* and Sunday fare consists of *In Touch with Stockholm* (a listener-response program) or the musical *Sounds Nordic.* Thirty minutes to Europe on 6065 kHz. One hour earlier in summer.

Radio Prague, Czech Republic. *News*, then Monday through Friday there's *Current Affairs* followed by one or two features. Monday's *Talking Point* is replaced Tuesday by *Witness* and *One on One* (interviews); Wednesday's lineup is *ABC of Czech* followed by *Spotlight* or *Czechs in History*; Thursday brings *Economic Report*; and Friday's features are *Stepping Out* (nightlife in Prague) and *The Arts*. Saturday fare is either the summer *Insight Central Europe* or the winter combo of *Magazine, Letter from Prague* and a repeat of Tuesday's *One on One*. Sunday's features are *Mailbox* and *ABC of Czech* followed by *Encore* (classical music), *Magic Carpet* (Czech world music) or *Czech Books*. A half hour to eastern North America winter on 7345 kHz, and summer on 11600 and 13580 kHz; also to West Africa winter on 9435 kHz.

22:45

All India Radio. The first 15 minutes of a much longer broadcast, consisting of Indian music, regional and international *news*, commentary, and a variety of talks and features of general interest. Continuous till 0045. To East Asia on 9950, 11620 and 13605 kHz; and to Southeast Asia on 9705, 11620 and 13605 kHz.

23:00

■BBC World Service for the Americas. Monday through Thursday winter, a full hour of *The World Today*. On the remaining days, it's reduced to 30 minutes and followed by *Global Business* (Friday), *Arts in Action* (Saturday) or Sunday's *Pick of the Week*. Summer weekdays, opens with five minutes of *news*. Next comes the long-running *Outlook*, and the hour is rounded off with a 15-minute feature (very much a mixed bag). Saturday brings ●*Play of the Week* (world theater at its best), replaced Sunday by the same programs as in winter. Continuous to the Caribbean and eastern North America on 5975 kHz. Also audible in some areas on 12095 kHz, targeted at South America; a radio with synchronous selectable sideband helps reduce teletype interference.

■BBC World Service for East and Southeast Asia and the Pacific. Sunday through Thursday (weekday mornings in Asia), it's the second hour of *The World Today*, a breakfast news show for the region. On the remaining days there's 30 minutes of the same, followed by Friday's *Global Business* or Saturday's *Arts in Action*. Continuous to East Asia on 5965, 6035, 6195, 11945, 11955 and 15280 kHz; to Southeast Asia on 3915, 6195, 7105 and 11955 kHz; and to Australasia on 11955 kHz.

Voice of Turkey. Winter only at this hour. See 2200 for program details. Fifty minutes to Europe on 6020 kHz, and to eastern North America on 9655 kHz. One hour earlier in summer.

■Deutsche Welle, Germany. *News*, then Monday through Friday (Tuesday through Saturday local date in the target area), it's ●*NewsLink for Asia*. The lineup for the second half-hour is ●*World Music Live* (Monday), *Arts on the Air* (Tuesday), *Living in Germany* and *Europe on Stage* (Wednesday), *Cool* (a youth show, Thursday) and ●*Focus on Folk* (Friday). Weekends, Saturday's news is followed by *Religion and Society, German by Radio* and *Asia This Week*; and Sunday there's *Hard to Beat* (sport), *Inspired Minds* and either *Hits in Germany* or *Melody Time*. Sixty minutes to Southeast Asia winter on 7250, 9815 and 12035 kHz; and summer on 9890 and 17860 kHz.

Radio Australia. *World News*, followed Sunday through Thursday by *Asia Pacific* (replaced Friday by *Lingua Franca*, and Saturday by some sharp scientific commentary in ●*Ockham's Razor*). On the half-hour, look for a feature. *Earthbeat* (the environment) occupies the Sunday slot, and is replaced Monday by *The Buzz*. Then come Tuesday's *Arts Talk*, Wednesday's *Rural Reporter*, Thursday's *Media Report*, Friday's *Sports Factor*, and Saturday's *Innovations*. Continuous to the Pacific on 9660, 12080, 17715, 17795 and 21740 kHz; and to Southeast Asia on 13620, 15230 and 15240 kHz. Listeners in North America should try 17715, 17795 and 21740 kHz, especially during summer.

Radio Canada International. Summer weekdays, the final hour of ●*As It Happens*. Winter, it's the first 30 minutes of the same, preceded by the up-to-the-minute news

23:00–23:30

program ●*World at Six.* Summer weekends, look for ●*Quirks and Quarks* (science, Saturday) and ●*Global Village* (world music, Sunday). Winter, there's ●*The World This Weekend* followed by Saturday's *Madly Off in All Directions* (comedy) or Sunday's *The Inside Track.* To North America and the Caribbean winter on 5960 and 9590 kHz, and summer on 6140, 9590 and 15455 kHz.

China Radio International. Starts with *News,* followed Sunday through Thursday by special reports—current events, sports, business, culture, science and technology and press clippings. The rest of the broadcast is devoted to features. Regulars include ●*People in the Know* (Sunday), *Biz China* (Monday), *China Horizons* (Tuesday), ●*Voices from Other Lands* (Wednesday), and *Life in China* on Thursday. On Friday and Saturday the news is followed by a shorter series of reports (current events and sport) and two features. Friday brings *Cutting Edge*, and *Listeners' Garden* (listener mail, Chinese folk music, a preview of the next week's programs, and a Chinese language lesson); replaced Saturday by *Reports on Developing Countries* and *In the Spotlight*, a series of mini-features: *Cultural Carousel, In Vogue, Writings from China, China Melody* and *Talking Point.* One hour to the United States and Caribbean on 5990 and 13680 kHz via CRI's Cuban and Canadian relays.

Radio for Peace International, Costa Rica. Continues with a six-hour cyclical block of social-conscience and counterculture programming audible in Europe and the Americas on 7445 kHz.

Radio Cairo, Egypt. The first hour of a 90-minute broadcast to eastern North America. A ten-minute *news* bulletin is aired at 2315, with the remaining time taken up by short features on Egypt, the Middle East and Islam. For the intellectual listener there's *Literary Readings* at 2345 Monday, and *Modern Arabic Poetry* at the same time Friday. More general fare is available in *Listener's Mail* at 2325 Thursday and Saturday. Easy reception on 9900 (or 11725) kHz.

Radio Austria International. Summer only at this time. Monday through Friday, the 15-minute ●*Report from Austria* is aired at 2315, and then repeated at 2345. Weekends, it's a similar arrangement, with *Insight Central Europe* airing at 2305 and 2335. The remainder of the one-hour broadcast is in German. To Central America on 9870 kHz (two hours later in winter), and to South America on 13730 kHz (one hour later in winter).

Radio Romania International. *News,* commentary and features, plus some enjoyable Romanian music. Fifty-five minutes to Europe on 7195 (winter), 9570 and (summer) 11775 kHz; also to eastern North America winter on 9510 and 11940 kHz, and summer on 11740 and 15105 kHz.

Radio Bulgaria. Summer only at this time. *News,* music and features. Monday through Friday (weekday evenings in North America), the news is followed by *Events and Developments,* replaced Saturday by *Views Behind the News* and Sunday by the enjoyable and exotic ●*Folk Studio.* The next slot consists of weekly features. Take your pick from *Plaza/Walks and Talks* (Sunday), *Magazine Economy* (Monday), *Arts and Artists* (Tuesday), *History Club* (Wednesday), *The Way We Live* (Thursday), *DX Programme* (Friday) and *Answering Your Letters,* a listener- response show, on Saturday. Monday through Saturday, the broadcast ends with *Keyword Bulgaria.* Sixty minutes to eastern North America on 9400 and 11900 kHz. One hour later during winter.

Voice of America. Continues with programs aimed at East Asia and the Pacific on the same frequencies as at 2200.

AFRTS Shortwave, USA. Network news, live sports, music and features in the upper-sideband mode from the Armed Forces Radio & Television Service. Transmitted from modestly powered U.S. Navy stations around the globe. Try 4319, 5446.5, 5765, 6350, 6458.5, 7507, 10320, 12133.5, 12579, 13362 and 13855 kHz.

23:30

Radio Prague, Czech Republic. Winter only at this time. See 2230 for specifics. Saturday programming at this hour is *Insight Central*

Europe. A half hour to eastern North America on 5915 and 7345 kHz, and one hour earlier in summer.

Radio Vilnius, Lithuania. A half hour that's mostly *news* and background reports about events in Lithuania. Of broader appeal is *Mailbag,* aired every other Saturday. For some Lithuanian music, try the second half of Sunday's broadcast. To eastern North America on 9875 kHz.

Swiss Radio International. *Swissinfo*—news, reports, and a short feature at weekends (replaced weekdays by music). Thirty minutes to South America on 9885, (winter) 11660 and (summer) 11905 kHz. This slot is far and away the best opportunity for listeners in North America, which is not targeted directly.

XERMX—Radio México Internacional. Summer only at this time. Monday through Friday there's an English summary of the Spanish-language *Antena Radio,* replaced weekends by *Talking Mexico* (interviews).Thirty minutes to the southwestern United States on 9705 and 11770 kHz. One hour later in winter.

All India Radio. Continuous programming to East and Southeast Asia. A potpourri of *news,* commentary, features and exotic Indian music. To East Asia on 9950, 11620 and 13605 kHz; and to Southeast Asia on 9705, 11620 and 13605 kHz.

Voice of Vietnam. *News,* then *Commentary* or *Weekly Review.* These are followed by short features and some pleasant Vietnamese music. A half hour to Southeast Asia on 9840 and 12020 kHz. Frequencies may vary slightly.

Prepared by Tony Jones and the staff of PASSPORT TO WORLD BAND RADIO.

Addresses PLUS—2004

Station Postal and Email Addresses . . . PLUS Webcasts, Websites, Who's Who, Phones, Faxes, Bureaus, Future Plans, Items for Sale, Giveaways . . . PLUS Summer and Winter Times in Each Country!

Much of PASSPORT shows how stations reach out to you, but Addresses PLUS explains how you can reach out to stations. It also details, country by country, how broadcasters go beyond world band radio to inform and entertain.

Verifications and Souvenirs

When radio broadcasting was in its infancy, listeners sent in "applause" cards to let stations how well they were being received. To say "thanks," stations would reply with a letter or illustrated card verifying ("QSLing" in Morse code) that the station the listener heard was, in fact, theirs. While they were at it, some would throw in a free souvenir—station calendar, pennant or sticker.

This still goes on today, although obtaining QSLs is tougher than it used to be; you can learn how to provide feedback to stations by looking under "Verification" in PASSPORT's glossary. Some stations also sell goods—radios, CDs, publications, clothing, tote bags, caps, watches, clocks, pens, knives, letter openers, lighters, refrigerator magnets and keyrings.

Return Postage Varies

Most broadcasters reply to listener correspondence—even email—through the postal system. That way, they can send out printed schedules, verification cards and other "hands-on" souvenirs. Major stations usually do this for free, but smaller ones often seek reimbursement for postage.

Most effective, especially for Latin American and Indonesian stations, is to enclose some unused (mint) stamps from the station's country. These are available from Plum's Airmail Postage, 12 Glenn Road, Flemington NJ 08822 USA, plumdx@msn.com, phone +1 (908) 788-1020, fax +1 (908) 782 2612. One way to help ensure your return-postage stamps will be put to the intended use is to affix them onto a pre-addressed return airmail envelope. The result is a self-addressed stamped envelope, or SASE.

You can also prompt reluctant stations by donating one U.S. dollar, preferably hidden from prying eyes by a piece of foil-covered carbon paper or the like. As cash tends to get stolen, registration can help—but not always. In some countries registered mail is a prime target for would-be thieves, especially in parts of Latin America.

International Reply Coupons (IRCs), which recipients may exchange locally for air or surface stamps, are available at a number of post offices worldwide, particularly in large cities. Alas, they're increasingly hard to find, relatively costly, not fully effective, and aren't accepted by postal authorities in some countries.

Stamp Out Crime

Yes, even nowadays mail theft is a problem in several countries. We identify these, and for each one offer proven ways to help avoid theft. Remember that a few postal employees are stamp collectors, and in

Some stations give free souvenirs to corresponding listeners.

Boats docked near the Central Station, Malmö. Radio Sweden has a long record of helpful interaction with listeners.
T. Ohtake

certain countries they freely steal mail with unusual stamps. When in doubt, use everyday stamps or, even better, a postal meter or PC-generated postage. Another option is to use an aerogram.

¿Que Hora Es?

World Time, explained elsewhere in this book, is essential if you want to find out when your favorite station is on. But if you want to know what time it is in any given country, World Time and Addresses PLUS work together to give you local times within each country.

So that you don't have to wrestle with seasonal changes in your own time, we give local times for each country in terms of hours' difference from World Time, which stays the same year- round. For example, if you look below under "Albania," you'll see that country is World Time +1; that is, one hour ahead of World Time. So, if World Time is 1200, the local time in Albania is 1300 (1:00 PM). On the other hand, México City is World Time -6; that is, six hours behind World Time. If World Time is 1200, in México City it's 6:00 AM.

Times shown in parentheses are for the middle of the year—roughly April-October; specific dates of seasonal-time changeovers for individual countries can be obtained at www.timeanddate.com/worldclock.

Spotted Something New?

Has something changed since we went to press? A missing detail? Please let us know! Your update information, especially photocopies of material received from stations, is highly valued. Contact the IBS Editorial Office, Box 300, Penn's Park, PA 18943 USA, fax +1 (215) 598 3794, email addresses@passband.com.

Muchas gracias to the kindly folks and helpful organizations mentioned at the end of this chapter for their tireless cooperation in the preparation of this section. Without them, none of this would have been possible.

Using PASSPORT'S Addresses PLUS Section

Stations included: All stations are listed if known to reply, however erratically. Also, new stations which possibly may reply to correspondence from listeners.

Leased-time programs: Private organizations/NGOs that lease program time, but which possess no world band transmitters of their own, are usually not listed. However, they may be reached by contacting the stations over which they are heard.

Postal addresses. Communications addresses are given. These sometimes differ from the physical transmitter locations given in the Blue Pages.

Email addresses and Websites. Given in Internet format. Periods, commas and semicolons at the end of an address listing are normal sentence punctuation, not part of the address, and "http://" is used only when there is no "www."

Phone and fax numbers. To help avoid confusion, telephone numbers are given with hyphens, fax numbers without. All are configured for international dialing once you add your country's International access code (011 in the United States and Canada, 010 in the United Kingdom, and so on). For domestic dialing within countries outside the United States, Canada and the Caribbean, replace the country code (1-3 digits preceded by a "+") by a zero.

Giveaways. If you want freebies, say so politely in your correspondence. These are usually available only until supplies run out.

Webcasting. World band stations which simulcast and/or provide archived programming over the Internet are indicated by 🖥.

Unless otherwise indicated, stations:

- Reply regularly within six months to most listeners' correspondence in English.
- Provide, upon request, free station schedules and verification ("QSL")

postcards or letters (see "Verification" in the glossary). We specify when other items are available for free or for purchase.

• Do not require compensation for postage costs incurred in replying to you. Where compensation is required, details are provided.

Local times. These are given in difference from World Time. For example, "World Time -5" means that if you subtract five hours from World Time, you'll get the local time in that country. Thus, if it were 1100 World Time, it would be 0600 local time in that country. Times in (parentheses) are for the middle of the year—roughly April-October. For exact changeover dates, see the above explanatory paragraph.

ALBANIA   World Time +1 (+2 midyear)

▣ **Radio Tirana,** External Service, Rruga Ismail Qemali Nr. 11, Tirana, Albania. Phone: (general) +355 (42) 23-239; (Phone/fax, Technical Directorate) +355 (42) 26203. Fax: (External Service) +355 (42) 23650; (Technical Directorate) +355 (42) 27 745. Email: (general) radiotirana@ radiotirana.net; radiotirana@interalb.net; (Technical Directorate) 113566.3011@compuserve.com; (Mandija) imandija@icc-al.org; or dcico@artv.tirana.al. Web: (general) www.radiotirana.net; http://rtsh.sil.at; (RealAudio from Radio Tirana 1, domestic service) http://rtsh.sil.at/online.htm. Contact: Astrit Ibro, Director of External Services; Adriana Bislea, English Department; Clara Ceska; Marjeta Thoma; Pandi Skaka, Producer; or Diana Koci; (Technical Directorate) Irfan Mandija, Technical Director ARTV; (Frequency Management) Mrs. Drita Cico, Head of RTV Monitoring Center. May send free stickers and postcards. Replies from the station are again forthcoming, but it is advisable to include return postage ($1 should be enough).
Trans World Radio—see Monaco.

ANGOLA   World Time +1

Rádio Ecclésia, Rua Comandante Bula 118, São Paulo, Luanda, Angola; or Caixa Postal 3579, Luanda, Angola. Phone: (general) +244 (2) 443-041; (studios) +244 (2) 445-484. Fax: +244 (2) 443 093. Email: ecclesia@snet.co.ao. Web: http://recclesia.org. Contact: Fr. Antônio Jaca, General Manager. A Catholic station founded in 1954 and which broadcast continuously from March 1955 until closed by presidential decree in 1978. Reestablished in March 1997, when it was granted a permit to operate on FM. Experimented with shortwave transmissions via Radio Nederland facilities during July 2000, but these were terminated for technical reasons. Restarted transmissions in April 2001 via facilities of Germany's Deutsche Telekom (see) and switched to a South African relay in May 2002. Eventually hopes to resume shortwave broadcasts via its own transmitter, if and when the current tight regulations in Angola are relaxed. According to press reports, the shortwave equipment has already been purchased by the Episcopal Conference of Portugal.

▣ **Rádio Nacional de Angola,** Caixa Postal 1329, Luanda, Angola. Fax: +244 (2) 391 234. Email: (general, including reception reports) diop@rna.ao; (Magalhães) josela30@ hotmail.com; (technical) rochapinto@rna.ao Web: (includes RealAudio) www.rna.ao; if the audio link doesn't work, try www.netangola.com/p/default.htm. Contact: Júlio Mendonça, Diretor dos Serviços de Programas; [Ms.] Josefa Canzuela Magalhães, Departamento de Intercâmbio e Opinião Pública; or Manuel Rabelais, Diretor Geral; (technical) Cândido Rocha Pinto, Diretor dos Serviços Técnicos. Replies irregularly. Best is to correspond in Portuguese and include $1, return postage or 2 IRCs.

ANTARCTICA   World Time -3 Base Antárctica Esperanza

Radio Nacional Arcángel San Gabriel—LRA36, Base Esperanza, V9411XAD Antártida Argentina, Argentina. Phone/fax: +54 (2964) 421 519. Email: lra36@infovia. com.ar. Return postage required. Replies to correspondence in Spanish, and sometimes to correspondence in English and French, depending on who is at the station (the staff changes each year, usually around February). If no reply, try sending your correspondence (but don't write the station's name on the envelope) and 2 IRCs via the helpful Gabriel Iván Barrera, Casilla 2868, C1000WBC Buenos Aires, Argentina.

ANGUILLA   World Time -4

Caribbean Beacon, Box 690, Anguilla, British West Indies. Phone: +1 (264) 497- 4340. Fax: +1 (264) 497 4311. Contact: Monsell Hazell, Chief Engineer. $2 or return postage helpful. Relays Dr. Gene Scott's University Network—see USA.

ANTIGUA   World Time -4

BBC World Service—Caribbean Relay Station, P.O. Box 1203, St. John's, Antigua. Phone: +1 (268) 462-0994. Fax: +1 (268) 462 0436. Contact: (technical) David George. Nontechnical correspondence should be sent to the BBC World Service in London (see).
Deutsche Welle—Relay Station Antigua—same address and contact as BBC World Service, above. Nontechnical correspondence should be sent to Deutsche Welle in Germany (see).

ARGENTINA   World Time -3

Radio Baluarte, Casilla de Correo 45, 3370 Puerto Iguazú, Provincia de Misiones, Argentina. Phone: +54 (3737) 422-557. Email: icnfuturo@hotmail.com. Contact: Hugo Eidinger, Director. Free tourist literature. Return postage helpful. The same programs are aired on 1610 kHz (Radio Maranatha) and 101.7 MHz (Radio Futuro), and all three outlets are believed to be unlicensed. However, given the current radio licensing situation in the country, this is not unusual.

Radiodifusión Argentina al Exterior—RAE, Casilla de Correos 555, C1000WAF Buenos Aires, Argentina. Phone/fax: +54 (11) 4325-6368; (technical) +54 (11) 4325-5270. Email: (general) rae@radionacional.gov.ar; (technical) operativa@radionacional. gov.ar; (Marcela Campos) camposrae@fibertel.com.ar (this address is to be phased out). Web: www.radionacional.gov.ar/rae.asp. Contact: (general) John Anthony Middleton, Head of English Team; María Dolores López, Spanish Team; (administration) Marcela G. R. Campos, Directora; (technical) Gabriel Iván Barrera, DX Editor. Return postage (2 IRCs) appreciated. The station asks listeners not to send currency notes, as it's a breach of local postal regulations. Reports covering at least 20-30 minutes of reception are appreciated.

Radio Nacional Buenos Aires, Maipú 555, C1006ACE Buenos Aires, Argentina. Phone: +54 (11) 4325-9100. Fax: (management—Gerencia General) +54 (11) 4325 9433; (Director) +54 (11) 4325-4590, +54 (11) 4322-4313; (technical—Gerencia Operativa) +54 (11) 4325-5270. Email: (general) info@ radionacional.gov.ar; (Director) direccion@radionacional.gov.ar, or mariogiorgi@uol.com.ar; (technical) operativa@radionacional.gov.ar. Web: www.radionacional.gov.ar. Contact: (general) Lic.Adelina O. Moncalvillo, Directora Ejecutiva; (technical) Alberto Enríquez. Return postage (2 IRCs) helpful. Prefers correspondence in Spanish, and usually replies via RAE (see above). If no reply, try sending your correspondence (but don't write the station's name on your envelope) and 2 IRCs via the helpful Gabriel Iván Barrera, Casilla 2868, C1000WBC Buenos Aires, Argentina.

ARMENIA   World Time +4 (+5 midyear)

🔊**Public Radio of Armenia/Voice of Armenia,** Radio Agency, Alek Manoukyan Street 5, 375025 Yerevan, Armenia. Phone: +374 (1) 551-143. Fax: +374 (1) 554 600. Email: (General Director) president@mediaconcern.am; (Foreign Broadcasts Department, reception reports and comments on programs) pr@armradio.am. Web: (includes Windows Media) www.armradio.am. Contact: V. Voskanian, Deputy Editor-in-Chief; R. Abalian, Editor-in-Chief; Armenag Sansaryan, International Relations Bureau; Laura Baghdassarian, Deputy Manager, Radioagency; or Armen Amiryan, Director. Free postcards and stamps. Requests 2 IRCs for postal reply. Replies slowly.

ASCENSION   World Time exactly

BBC World Service—Atlantic Relay Station, English Bay, Ascension (South Atlantic Ocean). Fax: +247 6117. Contact: (technical) Jeff Cant, Staff Manager; M.R. Watkins, A/Assistant Resident Engineer; or Mrs. Nicola Nicholls, Transmitter Engineer. Nontechnical correspondence should be sent to the BBC World Service in London (see).

AUSTRALIA   World Time +11 (+10 midyear) Victoria (VIC), New South Wales (NSW), Australian Capital Territory (ACT) and Tasmania (TAS); +10:30 (+9:30 midyear) South Australia (SA); +10 Queensland (QLD); +9:30 Northern Territory (NT); +8 Western Australia (WA)

Australian Broadcasting Corporation Northern Territory HF Service—ABC Radio 8DDD Darwin, Administrative Center for the Northern Territory Shortwave Service, ABC Box 9994, GPO Darwin NT 0820, Australia. Phone: +61 (8) 8943-3222; (engineering) +61 (8) 8943-3209. Fax: +61 (8) 8943 3235 or +61 (8) 8943 3208. Contact: (general) Tony Bowden, Branch Manager; (administration) Carole Askham, Administrative Of-

ficer; (technical) Peter Camilleri or Yvonne Corby. Free stickers and postcards. "Traveller's Guide to ABC Radio" for $1. T-shirts US$20. Three IRCs or return postage helpful.

BBC World Service via Radio Australia—For verification direct from the Australian transmitters, contact John Westland, Director of English Programs at Radio Australia (see). Nontechnical correspondence should be sent to the BBC World Service in London (see).

CDRS—Community Development Radio Service, ARDS, Box 1671, Nhulunbuy NT 0881, Australia; or (street address) 19 Pera Circuit, Nhulunbuy NT 0880, Australia. Phone: +61 (8) 8987-3910. Fax: +61 (8) 8987 3912. Email: (general) nhulun@ards.com.au; (technical) dale@ards.com.au. Web: www.ards.com.au/cdrsframe.htm. Contact: Dale Chesson, Radio Service Manager.

EDXP News Report, 404 Mont Albert Road, Mont Albert, Victoria 3127, Australia. Phone/fax: +61 (3) 9898-2906. Email: info@edxp.org. Web: http://edxp.org. Contact: Bob Padula. "EDXP News Report" is compiled by the "Electronic DX Press" and aired over a number of world band stations. Focuses on shortwave broadcasters beaming to, or located in Asia and the Pacific. Currently broadcast by Adventist World Radio, HCJB-Australia, HCJB-Ecuador, WINB, WWCR, WHRA, KWHR, WHRI, Radio Vlaanderen International and Radio Korea International. Verifies postal reports with full-detail "EDXP" QSL cards showing Australian fauna, flora, and scenery. Return postage required: four 50c stamps within Australia, and one IRC or US dollar elsewhere. Email reports are confirmed with animated Web-delivered QSLs.

HCJB Australia, P.O. Box 291, Kilsyth VIC 3137, Australia. Phone: +61 (3) 9761-4844. Fax: +61 (3) 9761 4061. Email: wilcom@netcon.net or office@hcjb.org.au. Contact: Dennis Adams; or Ian Williams, Technical Director.

VERIFICATION OF RECEPTION REPORTS: Voice of the Great Southland, GPO Box 691, Melbourne VIC 3001, Australia. Email: english@hcjb.org.au. One IRC required for postal reply. *NEW DELHI ADDRESS:* Voice of the Great Southland, P.O. Box 9149, Patparganj, New Delhi- 110 091, India.

🔊**Radio Australia**

STUDIOS AND MAIN OFFICES: GPO Box 428G, Melbourne VIC 3001, Australia. Phone: ("Openline" voice mail for listeners' messages and requests) +61 (3) 9626-1825; (switchboard) +61 (3) 9626-1800; (English programs) +61 (3) 9626-1922; (marketing manager) +61 (3) 9626 1723; (engineering) +61 (3) 9626-1914. Fax and Faxpoll: (general) +61 (3) 9626 1899; (engineering) +61 (3) 9626 1917. Email: (general) english@ra.abc.net.au; (marketing manager) hutchins.andria@abc.net.au; (engineering) holmes.nigel@a2.abc.net.au; (Radio Australia transmissions and programs) raelp@radioaus.abc.net.au; (Pacific Services) rapac@radioaus.abc.net.au; (Internet and Web Coordinator) naughton.russell@a2.abc.net.au. Web: (includes RealAudio) www.abc.net.au/ra. Contact: (general) John Westland, Head, English Language Programming; Roger Broadbent, Producer "Feedback"; Tony Hastings, Director of Programs; Caroline Bilney, Information Officer; Kirsty Boyle, Transmission Performance Officer; Andria Hutchins, Marketing Manager; or Jean-Gabriel Manguy, General Manager; (technical) Nigel Holmes, Transmission Manager, Transmission Management Unit. Free stickers and sometimes pennants and souvenirs available. On-air language courses available in Chinese, Indonesian, Khmer and Vietnamese. Course notes available at cost price. Radio Australia will attempt to answer listener's letters even though this will largely depend on the availability of resources and a reply may no longer be possible in all cases. All reception reports received by Radio Australia will now be forwarded to the Australian Radio DX Club for assessment and checking. ARDXC will forward completed QSLs to Radio Australia for mailing. For further information, contact John Westland, Director of English Programs at Radio Australia (Email: westland.john@a2.abc.net.au); or John Wright, Secretary/Editor, ARDXC (Email: dxer@fl.net.au). Plans to add new aerials and re-locate 250 kW transmitters.

NEW YORK BUREAU, NONTECHNICAL: Room 2260, 630 Fifth Avenue, New York NY 10020 USA. Phone: (representative) +1 (212) 332-2540; or (correspondent) +1 (212) 332-2545. Fax: +1 (212) 332 2546. Contact: Maggie Jones, North American Representative.

LONDON BUREAU, NONTECHNICAL: 54 Portland Place, London WIN 4DY, United Kingdom. Phone: +44 (20) 7631-4456. Fax: (administration) +44 (20) 7323 0059, (news) +44 (20) 7323 1125. Contact: Robert Bolton, Manager.

BANGKOK BUREAU, NONTECHNICAL: 209 Soi Hutayana off Soi Suanplu, South Sathorn Road, Bangkok 10120, Thailand. Fax: +66 (2) 287 2040. Contact: Nicholas Stuart.

SAN FRANCISCO OFFICE, SCHEDULES: 2654 17th Avenue, San Francisco CA 94116 USA. Phone: +1 (415) 564-9968. Email: GPoppin@aol.com. Contact: George Poppin. This address, a volunteer office, only provides Radio Australia schedules to listeners. All other correspondence should be sent directly to the main office in Melbourne.

◙**Voice International Limited** (formerly Christian Voice International Australia)
MAIN OFFICE: Voice International TM, P.O. Box 1104, Buderim, QLD 4556, Australia; or (street address) Killick Street, Kunda Park, QLD 4556, Australia. Phone: +61 (7) 5477-1555. Fax: +61 (7) 5477 1727. Email: (general) voice@voice.com.au; (DXer contact) dxer@voice.com.au; (Hindi Service) mail@thevoiceasia.com. (Edmiston) mike.edmiston@voice.com.au; (Moti) raymoti@voice.com.au. Web: www.voice.com.au; (Hindi Service, includes MP3) www.the voiceasia. com. Contact: (general) Mike Edmiston, Director; Raymond Moti, Station Manager; or Richard Daniel, Corporate Relations Manager.

ADDRESSES IN INDIA: The Voice, P.O. Box 1, Kangra, Pin Code 176001, Himachal, India; or The Voice, P.O. Box 2, Ludhiana, Pin Code 141008, Punjab, India.

TRANSMITTER SITE: Voice International, PMB 5777, Darwin NT 0801, Australia. Phone: (general) +61 (8) 8981-6591 or (operations manager) +61 (8) 8981-8822. Fax: +61 (8) 8981 2846. Contact: Mrs. Lorna Manning, Site Administrator; or Robert Egoroff, Operations Manager.

AUSTRIA   World Time +1 (+2 midyear)

◙**Radio Afrika International** (if reactivated), Radio Afrika Center, Heigerleinstrasse 7, A-1160 Vienna, Austria. Phone/fax: +43 (1) 4944-033. Email: radio.afrikas@sil.at. Web: (includes RealAudio) www.radioafrika.net. Contact: Mathurin Butusolua; Alexis Neuberg. Suspended transmissions on shortwave in June 2003, but remains on mediumwave AM and the Internet. Is looking for new partners and donors to resume on shortwave.

◙**Radio Austria International,** Listener Service, Argentinierstrasse 30a, A-1040 Vienna, Austria. Phone: +43 (1) 50101-16060; (frequency management) +43 (1) 87878-12629. Fax: +43 (1) 50101 16066; (frequency management) +43 (1) 87878 12773. Email: (frequency schedules, comments, reception reports) roi.service@orf.at; (frequency management) hfbc@orf.at. Web: (includes RealAudio) http://roi.orf.at. Contact: (general) Vera Bock, Listener Service; (English Department) David Ward; (technical) Ing. Ernst Vranka, Frequency Manager; Ing. Klaus Hollndonner, Chief Engineer; Martin

Cargnelli, Monitoring Department.
WASHINGTON NEWS BUREAU: 1206 Eaton Ct. NW, Washington DC 20007 USA. Phone: +1 (202) 822-9570. Contact: Eugen Freund.

AZERBAIJAN   World Time +4 (+5 midyear)

Radio Dada Gorgud/Voice of Azerbaijan, Medhi Hüseyin küçäsi 1, 370011 Baku, Azerbaijan. Phone: +994 (12) 398-585. Fax: +994 (12) 395 452. Email: root@aztv.baku.az. Web: (State TV and Radio Broadcasting Company parent organization) www.aztv.az. Contact: Mrs. Tamam Bayatli-Öner, Director; Kamil Mamedov, Director of Division of International Relations; or Arzu Abdullayev. May run station contests at various times during the year. Free postcards, and occasionally, books. $1 or return postage helpful. Replies irregularly to correspondence in English.

BANGLADESH   World Time +6

Bangladesh Betar
NONTECHNICAL CORRESPONDENCE: External Services, Bangladesh Betar, Shahbagh Post Box No. 2204, Dhaka 1000, Bangladesh; (physical address) Betar Bhaban Sher-e-Bangla Nagar, Agargaon Road, Dhaka 1207, Bangladesh. Phone: (director general) +880 (2) 8615-294; (Rahman Khan) +880 (2) 8613-949; (external services) +880 (2) 8618-119. Fax:(director general) +880 (2) 8612 021. Email: (Office of Director General) dgbetar@bd.drik.net; (external services) ts-betar@ bdonline.com. Contact: Mrs. Dilruba Begum, Director, External Services; Ashfaque-ur Rahman Khan, Director - Programmes; or (technical) Muhammed Nazrul Islam, Station Engineer. $1 helpful. For further technical contacts, *see* below.

RESEARCH AND RECEIVING CENTRE: Bangladesh Betar, 121 Kazi Nazrul Islam Avenue, Dhaka-1000, Bangladesh. Phone: +880 (2) 8625-538 or +880 (2) 8626-175. Fax: +880 (2) 8612 021. Email: rrc@aitlbd.net or dgbetar@bd.drik.net. Contact: Md. Kamal Uddin.

TECHNICAL CORRESPONDENCE: National Broadcasting Authority, NBA Bhaban, 121 Kazi Nazrul Islam Avenue, Shahabagh, Dhaka 1000, Bangladesh. Phone: +880 (2) 500-143/7, +880 (2) 500-490, +880 (2) 500-810, +880 (2) 505-113 or +880 (2) 507-269; (Shakir) +880 (2) 818- 734; (Das) +880 (2) 500-810. Fax: +880 (2) 817 850; (Shakir) +880 (2) 817 850. Email: dgradio@drik.bgd.toolnet.org, or rrc@aitlbd.net. Contact: Syed Abdus Shakir, Chief Engineer; (reception reports) Manoranjan Das, Station Engineer, Dhaka; or Muhammed Romizuddin Bhuiya, Senior Engineer (Research Wing). Verifications not common from this office.

BELARUS   World Time +2 (+3 midyear)

Belarusian Radio—*see* Radio Station Belarus, below, for details.
Radio Grodno (Hrodna)—contact via Radio Station Belarus, below.
Radio Mogilev (Mahiliou)—contact via Radio Station Belarus, below.
◙**Radio Station Belarus/Radio Minsk,** 4, Krasnaya St., Minsk 220807, Republic of Belarus. Phone: (domestic Belarusian Radio) +375 (17) 239-5810; (external services, general) +375 (17) 239-5830; (English Service) +375 (17) 239-5831; (German Service) +375 (17) 239-5875. Fax: (all services) +375 (17) 284 8574. Email: (domestic Belarusian Radio) tvr@tvr.by; (external services) radio-minsk@tvr.by. Web: (includes Windows

Media) www.tvr.by. Contact: Natalia Khlebus, Director; Grigori Mityushnikov, Editor, English Service; Ilia Dohel, English Program Director; Elena Khoroshevich, German Program Editor; or Jürgen Eberhardt, German Program Editor. Free Belarus stamps.

BELGIUM   World Time +1 (+2 midyear)

▣RTBF-International, B-1044 Brussels, Belgium. Phone: +32 (2) 737-4024. Fax: +32 (2) 737 3032. Email: relint.r@rtbf.be, or rtbfi@rtbf.be. Web: (RTBF-International) www.rtbf.be/ri; ("La Première") www.rtbf.be/premiere; (RealAudio) www.rtbf.be/jp. Contact: Jean-Pol Hecq, Directeur des Relations Internationales (or "Head, International Service" if writing in English). Broadcasts are essentially a relay of news and information programs from the domestic channel "La Première" of RTBF (Radio-Télévision Belge de la Communauté Française). Return postage not required. Accepts email reports.

▣Radio Vlaanderen Internationaal (RVI)

NONTECHNICAL AND GENERAL TECHNICAL: B-1043 Brussels, Belgium; (English Section) RVI, Brussels Calling, B-1043 Brussels, Belgium. Phone: +32 (2) 741-5611, +32 (2) 741-3806/7 or +32 (2) 741-3802. Fax: +32 (2) 741-4689. Email: info@rvi.be. Web: (includes RealAudio, Windows Media and online reception report form) www.rvi.be. Contact (general) Deanne Lehman, Producer, "Brussels 1043" letterbox program; Ximena

Prieto, Head, Foreign Languages Desk; Maryse Jacob, Head, French Service; Martina Luxen, Head, German Service; or Wim Jansen, Station Manager; (general technical) Frans Vossen, Producer, "Radio World." Sells RVI T-shirts (large/extra large) for 400 Belgian francs. May send free music CD.

FREQUENCY MANAGEMENT OFFICE: BRTN, August Reyerslaan 52, B-1043 Brussels, Belgium. Phone: +32 (2) 741-5020. Fax: +32 (2) 741 5567. Email: (De Cuyper) hector.decuyper@vrt.be. Contact: Hector De Cuyper, Frequency Manager.

TRANSMITTER DOCUMENTATION PROJECT (TDP), P.O. Box 1, B-2310 Rijkevorsel, Belgium. Phone: +32 (3) 314-7800. Fax: +32 (3) 314 1212. Email: info@transmitter.org. Web: www.broadcast.be. Contact: Ludo Maes. A free online publication by Belgian Dxer Ludo Maes. TDP lists all current and past shortwave transmitters used worldwide in country order with station name, transmitter site & geographical coordinates, transmitter type, power and year of installation etc. Also brokers leased airtime over world band transmitters, and verifies reception reports for client stations.

BENIN   World Time +1

Office de Radiodiffusion et Télévision du Benin, Boite Postale 366, Cotonou, Benin. Phone: +229 301-096, +229 301-347. Fax: +229 302 184, +229 300 448. Email: info@ortb.org.

TIPS FOR EFFECTIVE CORRESPONDENCE

Write to be read. Be interesting and helpful from the recipient's point of view, yet friendly without being chummy. Comments on specific programs are almost always appreciated, even if you are sending in what is basically a technical report.

Incorporate language courtesies. Using the broadcaster's tongue is always a plus—Addresses PLUS indicates when it is a requirement—but English is usually the next-best bet. When writing in any language to Spanish-speaking countries, remember that what gringos think of as the "last name" is actually written as the penultimate name. Thus, Juan Antonio Vargas García, which can also be written as Juan Antonio Vargas G., refers to Sr. Vargas; so your salutation should read, *Estimado Sr. Vargas*.

What's that "García" doing there, then? That's *mamita's* father's family name. Latinos more or less solved the problem of gender fairness in names long before Anglos.

But, wait—what about Portuguese, used by all those stations in Brazil? Same concept, but in reverse. *Mamá's* father's family name is penultimate, and the "real" last name is where English-speakers are used to it, at the end.

In Chinese, the "last" name comes first. However, when writing in English, Chinese names are sometimes reversed for the benefit of *weiguoren*—foreigners. Use your judgement. For example, "Li" is a common Chinese last name, so if you see "Li Dan," it's "Mr. Li." But if it's "Dan Li"—and certainly if it's been Westernized into "Dan Lee"—he's already one step ahead of you, and it's still "Mr. Li" (or Lee). Less widely known is that the same can also occur in Hungarian. For example, "Bartók Béla" for Béla Bartók.

If in doubt, fall back on the ever-safe "Dear Sir" or "Dear Madam," or use email, where salutations are not expected. And be patient—replies by post usually take weeks, sometimes months. Slow responders, those that tend to take many months to reply, are cited in Addresses PLUS, as are erratic repliers.

Web: www.ortb.org. Contact: (Cotonou) Damien Zinsou Ala Hassa; Emile Desire Ologoudou, Directeur Generale; or Leonce Goohouede; (technical) Anastase Adjoko, Chef de Service Technique. Return postage, $1 or IRC required. Replies irregularly and slowly to correspondence in French.

PARAKOU REGIONAL STATION: ORTB-Parakou, Boite Postale 128, Parakou, Benin. Phone: +229 610-773, +229 611-096, +229 611080. Fax: +229 610 881. Contact: (general) J. de Matha, Le Chef de la Station; (technical) Léon Donou, Chef des Services Techniques. Return postage required. Replies tend to be extremely irregular, and a safer option is to send correspondence to the Cotonou address.

BHUTAN   World Time +6

Bhutan Broadcasting Service

STATION: Department of Information and Broadcasting, Ministry of Communications, P.O. Box 101, Thimphu, Bhutan. Phone: +975 (2) 323-071/72. Fax: +975 (2) 323 073. Email: (News and Current Affairs) news@bbs.com.bt; (Kinga Singye) ks@bbs.com.bt; (Thinley Tobgay Dorji) thinley@bbs.com.bt; (Sonam Tobgay) toby@bbs.com.bt. Web: (includes news and songs in MP3) www.bbs.com.bt. Contact: (general) Thinley Tobgay Dorji, News Coordinator; or Kinga Singye, Executive Director; (technical) Dorji Wangchuk, Station Engineer. Two IRCs, return postage or $1 required. Replies irregularly; correspondence to the U.N. Mission (*see* following) may be more fruitful.

UNITED NATIONS MISSION: Permanent Mission of the Kingdom of Bhutan to the United Nations, Two United Nations Plaza, 27th Floor, New York NY 10017 USA. Fax: +1 (212) 826 2998. Contact: Mrs. Kunzang C. Namgyel, Third Secretary; Mrs. Sonam Yangchen, Attaché; Ms. Leki Wangmo, Second Secretary; or Hari K. Chhetri, Second Secretary. Free newspapers and booklet on the history of Bhutan.

BOLIVIA   World Time -4

NOTE ON STATION IDENTIFICATIONS: Many Bolivian stations listed as "Radio..." may also announce as "Radio Emisora..." or "Radiodifusora..."

Paitití Radiodifusión—*see* Radio Paitití, below.

Radio Abaroa (if reactivated), Calle Nicanor Gonzalo Salvatierra 249, Riberalta, Beni, Bolivia. Contact: René Arias Pacheco, Director. Return postage or $1 required. Replies occasionally to correspondence in Spanish.

Radio Animas (if reactivated), Chocaya, Animas, Potosí, Bolivia. Contact: Julio Acosta Campos, Director. Return postage or $1 required. Replies irregularly to correspondence in Spanish.

Radio Camargo—*see* Radio Emisoras Camargo, below.

Radio Centenario "La Nueva"

MAIN OFFICE: Casilla 818, Santa Cruz de la Sierra, Bolivia. Phone: +591 (33) 529-265. Fax: +591 (3) 524 747. Email: mision.eplabol@scbbs-bo.com. Contact: Napoleón Ardaya B., Director. May send a calendar. Free stickers. Return postage or $1 required. Audio cassettes of contemporary Christian music and Bolivian folk music $10, including postage; CDs of Christian folk music $15, including postage. Replies to correspondence in English and Spanish.

U.S. BRANCH OFFICE: LATCOM, 1218 Croton Avenue, New Castle PA 16101 USA. Phone: +1 (412) 652-0101. Fax: +1 (412) 652 4654. Contact: Hope Cummins.

Radio Eco (when operating)

MAIN ADDRESS: Correo Central, Reyes, Ballivián, Beni, Bo-

livia. Contact: Gonzalo Espinoza Cortés, Director. Free station literature. $1 or return postage required. Replies to correspondence in Spanish.

ALTERNATIVE ADDRESS: Rolmán Medina Méndez, Correo Central, Reyes, Ballivián, Bolivia.

Radio Eco San Borja (if reactivated), Correo Central, San Borja, Ballivián, Beni, Bolivia. Email: gonzaloeco@hotmail.com. Contact: Gonzalo Espinoza Cortés, Director. Free station poster promised to correspondents. Return postage appreciated. Replies slowly to correspondence in Spanish.

Radio Emisoras Ballivián (when operating), Correo Central, San Borja, Beni, Bolivia. Replies to correspondence in Spanish, and sometimes sends pennant.

Radio Emisora Padilla—*see* Radio Padilla, below.

Radio Emisoras Camargo, Casilla Postal 9, Camargo, Provincia Nor-Cinti, Chuquisaca, Bolivia. Email: jlgarpas@hotmail.com. Web: www.radiocamargo.cjb.net. Contact: Pablo García B., Gerente Propietario. Return postage or $1 required. Replies slowly to correspondence in Spanish.

Radio Emisoras Minería—*see* Radiodifusoras Minería.

🔊**Radio Fides,** Casilla 9143, La Paz, Bolivia. Fax: +591 (2) 237 9030. Email: rafides@fidesbolivia.com (rafides@caoba.entelnet.bo may also work). Web: (includes RealAudio) http://fidesbolivia.com. Contact: R.P. Eduardo Pérez Iribarne, S.J., Director. Replies occasionally to correspondence in Spanish.

Radio Guanay (when operating), Calle Boston de Guanay 123, Guanay, La Paz, Bolivia.

Radio Illimani (when operating), Casilla 1042, La Paz, Bolivia. Phone: +591 (2) 237-6364. Fax: +591 (2) 235 9275. Email: illimani@communica.gov.bo. Contact: Gabriel Astorga Guachala. $1 required, and your letter should be registered and include a tourist brochure or postcard from where you live. Replies irregularly to friendly correspondence in Spanish.

Radio Juan XXIII [Veintitrés], Avenida Santa Cruz al frente de la plaza principal, San Ignacio de Velasco, Santa Cruz, Bolivia. Phone: +591 (3962) 2087. Phone/fax: +591 (3962) 2188. Contact: Pbro. Elías Cortezón, Director; or María Elffy Gutiérrez Méndez, Encargada de la Discoteca. Return postage or $1 required. Replies occasionally to correspondence in Spanish.

🔊**Radio La Cruz del Sur,** Casilla 1408, La Paz, Bolivia. Phone: +591 (2) 222-0541. Fax: +591 (2) 224 3337. Email: cruzdelsur@zuper.net. Web: (includes Real Audio) www.geocities.com/cruzdelsur2000. Contact: Carlos Montesinos, Director. Pennant $1 or return postage. Replies slowly to correspondence in Spanish.

Radio La Palabra (when operating), Parroquia de Santa Ana de Yacuma, Beni, Bolivia. Phone: +591 (3848) 2117. Contact: Padre Yosu Arketa, Director. Return postage required. Replies to correspondence in Spanish.

Radio Mallku (formerly Radio A.N.D.E.S.), Casilla No. 16, Uyuni, Provincia Antonio Quijarro, Departamento de Potosí, Bolivia. Phone: +591 (2693) 2145. Email: (FRUTCAS parent organization) frutcas@hotmail.es. Contact: Freddy Juárez Huarachi, Director; Erwin Freddy Mamani Machaca, Jefe de Prensa y Programación. Spanish preferred. Return postage in the form of two U.S. dollars appreciated, as the station depends on donations for its existence. Station owned by La Federación Unica de Trabajadores Campesinos del Altiplano Sud (FRUTCAS).

Radio Minería—*see* Radiodifusoras Minería.

Radio Mosoj Chaski, Casilla 4493, Cochabamba, Bolivia. Phone: +591 (442) 220-641 or +591 (442) 220-644. Fax: +591 (442) 251 041. Email: chaski@bo.net. Contact: Paul G. Pittman, Administrator. Replies to correspondence in Spanish and English.

NORTH AMERICAN OFFICE: Quechuan Radio, c/o SIM USA, P.O. Box 7900, Charlotte NC 28241 USA.

Radio Movima (if reactivated), Calle Baptista No. 24, Santa Ana de Yacuma, Beni, Bolivia. Contact: Rubén Serrano López, Director; Javier Roca Díaz, Director Gerente; or Mavis Serrano, Directora. Return postage or $1 required. Replies irregularly to correspondence in Spanish.

Radio Nacional de Huanuni, Casilla 681, Oruro, Bolivia. Contact: Rafael Linneo Morales, Director General; or Alfredo Murillo, Director. Return postage or $1 required. Replies irregularly to correspondence in Spanish.

Radio Norte (if reactivated), Calle Warnes 195, 2ᵈᵒ piso del Cine Escorpio, Montero, Santa Cruz, Bolivia. Phone: +591 (3922) 20-970. Fax: +591 (3922) 21 062. Contact: Leonardo Arteaga Ríos, Director.

Radio Padilla (if reactivated), Padilla, Chuquisaca, Bolivia. Contact: Moisés Palma Salazar, Director. Return postage or $1 required. Replies to correspondence in Spanish.

Radio Paitití, Casilla 172, Guayaramerín, Beni, Bolivia. Contact: Armando Mollinedo Bacarreza, Director; Luis Carlos Santa Cruz Cuéllar, Director Gerente; or Ancir Vaca Cuéllar, Gerente-Propietario. Free pennants. Return postage or $3 required. Replies irregularly to correspondence in Spanish.

☞**Radio Panamericana,** Casilla 5263, La Paz, Bolivia; (physical address) Av. 16 de Julio, Edif. 16 de Julio, Of. 902, El Prado, La Paz, Bolivia. Phone: +591 (2) 231-2644, +591 (2) 231-1383 or +591 (2) 231-3980. Fax: +591 (2) 233-4271. Email: pana@panamericanabolivia.com. Web: (includes RealAudio) www.panamericanabolivia.com. Contact: Daniel Sánchez Rocha, Director. Replies irregularly, with correspondence in Spanish preferred. $1 or 2 IRCs helpful.

Radio Perla del Acre (when operating), Casilla 7, Cobija, Departamento de Pando, Bolivia. Return postage or $1 required. Replies irregularly to correspondence in Spanish.

Radio Pío XII [Doce], Siglo Veinte, Potosí, Bolivia. Phone: +591 (258) 20-250. Fax: +591 (258) 20 544. Email: radiopio@nogal.oru.entelnet.bo. Contact: Pbro. Roberto Durette, OMI, Director General; or José Blanco. Return postage necessary. As mail delivery to Siglo Veinte is erratic, latters may be sent instead to: Casilla 434, Oruro, Bolivia; to the attention of Abenor Alfaro Castillo, periodista de Radio Pío XX [Phone: +591 (252) 76-1630].

Radio San Gabriel, Casilla 4792, La Paz, Bolivia. Phone: +591 (22) 414-371. Phone/fax: +591 (22) 411 174. Email: rsg@fundayni.rds.org.bo; (technical) remoc@entelnet.bo. Contact: (general) Hno. [Brother] José Canut Saurat, Director General; or Sra. Martha Portugal, Dpto. de Publicidad; (technical) Rómulo Copaja Alcón, Director Técnico. $1 or return postage helpful. Free book on station, Aymara calendars and *La Voz del Pueblo Aymara* magazine. Replies fairly regularly to correspondence in Spanish. Station of the Hermanos de la Salle Catholic religious order.

Radio San Miguel, Casilla 102, Riberalta, Beni, Bolivia. Phone: +591 (385) 8268 or +591 (385) 8363. Fax: +591 (385) 8268. Contact: Félix Alberto Rada Q., Director; or Gerin Pardo Molina, Director. Free stickers and pennants; has a different pennant each year. Return postage or $1 required. Replies irregularly to correspondence in Spanish. Feedback on program "Bolivia al Mundo" (aired 0200-0300 World Time) especially appreciated.

Radio Santa Ana, Calle Sucre No. 250, Santa Ana de Yacuma, Beni, Bolivia. Contact: Mario Roberto Suárez, Director; or Mariano Verdugo. Return postage or $1 required. Replies irregularly to correspondence in Spanish.

Radio Santa Cruz, Emisora del Instituto Radiofónico Fé y Alegría (IRFA), Casilla 672 (or 3213), Santa Cruz, Bolivia. Phone: +591 (33) 521-814. Fax: +591 (33) 532 257. Email: irfacruz@roble.scz.entelnet.bo. Contact: Padre Francisco Flores, S.J., Director General; Srta. María Yolanda Marcó Escobar, Secretaria de Dirección; Señora Mirian Suárez, Productor, "Protagonista Ud."; or Lic. Silvia Nava S. Free pamphlets, stickers and pennants. Welcomes correspondence in English, French and Spanish, but return postage required for a reply.

Radio Tacana, Tumupasa, Provincia Inturralde, Departamento de La Paz, Bolivia. Station of the Consejo Indígena del Pueblo Tacana (CIPTA).

Radio Yura (La Voz de los Ayllus), Casilla 326, Yura, Provincia Quijarro, Departamento de Potosí, Bolivia. Phone: +591 (281) 36-216. Email: canal18@cedro.pts.entelnet.bo. Contact: Rolando Cueto F., Director.

Radiodifusoras Minería, Casilla de Correo 247, Oruro, Bolivia. Phone: +591 (252) 77-736. Contact: Dr. José Carlos Gómez Espinoza, Gerente Propietario; or Srta. Costa Colque Flores, Responsable del programa "Minería Cultural." Free pennants. Replies to correspondence in Spanish.

Radiodifusoras Trópico, Casilla 60, Trinidad, Beni, Bolivia. Contact: Eduardo Avila Alberdi, Director. Replies slowly to correspondence in Spanish. Return postage required for reply.

BOTSWANA   World Time +2

Radio Botswana, Private Bag 0060, Gaborone, Botswana. Phone: +267 352-541 or +267 352- 861. Fax: +267 357 138. Contact: (general) Ted Makgekgenene, Director; or Monica Mphusu, Producer, "Maokaneng/Pleasure Mix"; (technical) Kingsley Reetsang, Principal Broadcasting Engineer. Free stickers, pennants and pins. Return postage, $1 or 2 IRCs required. Replies slowly and irregularly.

Voice of America/IBB—Botswana Relay Station
TRANSMITTER SITE: Voice of America, Botswana Relay Station, Moepeng Hill, Selebi- Phikwe, Botswana; or VOA-Botswana Transmitting Station, Private Bag 38, Selebi-Phikwe, Botswana. Phone: +267 810-932. Contact: Station Manager. This address for specialized technical correspondence only, although some reception reports may be verified, depending on who is at the site. During 2001, a number of verifications were received from Gabriel Tjitjo, Supervisor, Transmission Plant. All other correspondence should be directed to the regular VOA or IBB addresses (*see* USA).

BRAZIL   World Time -1 (-2 midyear) Atlantic Islands; -2 (-3 midyear) Eastern, including Brasília and Rio de Janeiro; -3 (-4 midyear) Western; -4 Northwestern; -5 Acre. There are often slight variations from one year to the next. Information regarding Daylight Saving Time can be found at http://pcdsh01.on.br.

NOTE: Postal authorities recommend that, because of the level of theft in the Brazilian postal system, correspondence to Brazil be sent only via registered mail.

Emissora Rural A Voz do São Francisco, Caixa Postal 8, 56300-000 Petrolina PE, Brazil. Email: emissorarural@silcons.com.br. Contact: Maria Letecia de Andrade Nunes. Return postage necessary. Replies to correspondence in Portuguese.

Rádio Alvorada, Rua Dom Bosco 145, 86060-340 Londrina PR, Brazil. Phone: +55 (43) 3347- 0606. Fax: +55 (43) 3347

0303. Email: pascom@arquidiocesedelondrina.com.br. Web: www.dialogocomdeus.com.br/radio.html. Contact: Padre Silvio Andrei, Diretor; or Sonia López. $1 or return postage. Replies to correspondence in Portuguese.

Rádio Alvorada, Rua Governador Leopoldo Neves 516, 69151-460 Parintins AM, Brazil. Phone: +55 (92) 533-2002, +55 (92) 533-3097. Fax: +55 (92) 533 2004. Email: alvorada@jurupari.com.br. Contact: Raimunda Ribeira da Motta, Diretora; or M. Braga. Return postage required. Replies occasionally to correspondence in Portuguese.

Rádio Alvorada, Avenida Ceará 2150, Jardim Nazle, 69900-460 Rio Branco AC, Brazil. Phone: +55 (68) 226-2301. Email: severian_jose@brturbo.com. Contact: José Severiano, Diretor. Occasionally replies to correspondence in Portuguese.

◪Rádio Araguaia—FM sister-station to Rádio Anhanguera (*see* next entry) and sometimes relayed via the latter's shortwave outlet. Web: (general) www.opopular.com.br/araguaia; (RealAudio) www2.opopular.com.br/radio.htm. Usually identifies as "Araguaia FM."

Rádio Anhanguera, BR-157 Km. 1103, Zona Rural, 77804-970 Araguaína TO, Brazil. Return postage required. Occasionally replies to correspondence in Portuguese. Sometimes airs programming from sister-station Rádio Araguaia, 97.1 FM (*see* previous item) or from the Rede Somzoomsat satellite network.

◪Rádio Anhanguera, Caixa Postal 13, 74823-000 Goiânia GO, Brazil. Web: (RealAudio only) www2.opopular.com.br/radio.htm. Contact: Rossana F. da Silva; or Eng. Domingo Vicente Tinoco. Return postage required. Replies to correspondence in Portuguese. Although—like its namesake in Araguaína (*see*, above)—a member of the Sistema de Rádio da Organização Jaime Câmara, this station is also an affiliate of the CBN network and often identifies as "CBN Anhanguera," especially when airing news programming.

Rádio Aparecida, Avenida Getulio Vargas 185, 12570-000 Aparecida SP, Brazil; or Caixa Postal 2, 12570-970 Aparecida SP, Brazil. Phone/fax: +55 (12) 564-4400. Email: (nontechnical) radioaparecida@redemptor.com.br; (Macedo) cassianomac@yahoo.com. Web: www.radioaparecida.com.br. Contact: Padre C. Cabral; Savio Trevisan, Departamento Técnico; Cassiano Alves Macedo, Producer, "Encontro DX" (aired 2200 Saturday; one hour earlier when Brazil on DST); Ana Cristina Carvalho, Secretária da Direção; Padre César Moreira; or João Climaco, Diretor Geral. Return postage or $1 required. Replies occasionally to correspondence in Portuguese.

◪Rádio Bandeirantes, Rua Radiantes 13, Bairro Morumbi, 01059-970 São Paulo SP, Brazil. Phone: +55 (11) 3745 7552. Fax: +55 (11) 3743 5391. Email: (general) rbnoar@band.com.br; (Huertas) ahuertas@band.com.br; (Dorin) ldorin@band.com.br. Web: (includes Windows Media) www.radiobandeirantes.com.br. Contact: Augusto Huertas, Coordenador Técnico; or Luciano Dorin, Apresentador. Free stickers, pennants and canceled Brazilian stamps. $1 or return postage required.

Rádio Baré Ondas Tropicais, Av. Carvalho Leal 250, Cachoeirinha, 69065-000 Manaus AM, Brazil; or Avenida Humaitá 336, Cachoeirinha, 69065-000 Manaus AM, Brazil. Phone: +55 (92) 231-1299; +55 (92) 231-1379. Fax: +55 (92) 234 0161. Email: proclip@argo.com.br. Contact: Rosivaldo Ferreira, Diretor da agência PROCLIP. A service for listeners in the interior of the state of Amazonas, produced and managed by PROCLIP, a local advertising agency. Replies to correspondence in Portuguese.

Rádio Brasil, Caixa Postal 625, 13000-000 Campinas, São Paulo SP, Brazil. Contact: Wilson Roberto Correa Viana, Gerente. Return postage required. Replies to correspondence in Portuguese.

Rádio Brasil Central, Caixa Postal 330, 74001-970 Goiânia GO, Brazil. Contact: Ney Raymundo Fernández, Diretor Administrativo; Sergio Rubens da Silva; or Arizio Pedro Soárez, Diretor Gerente. Free stickers. $1 or return postage required. Replies to correspondence in Portuguese.

Rádio Brasil Tropical, Caixa Postal 405, 78005-970 Cuiabá MT, Brazil (street address: Rua Joaquim Murtinho 1456, 78020-830 Cuiabá MT, Brazil). Phone: +55 (65) 321-6882 or +55 (65) 321-6226. Fax: +55 (65) 624 3455. Email: rcultura@terra.com.br. Contact: Klécius Antonio dos Santos, Diretor Comercial; or Roberto Ferreira, Gerente Comercial. Free stickers. $1 required. Replies to correspondence in Portuguese. Shortwave sister-station to Rádio Cultura de Cuiabá (*see*).

Rádio Caiari, Rua das Crianças, Bairro Areal da Floresta, 78912-210 Porto Velho RO, Brazil. Phone: +55 (69) 227-8849. Fax: +55 (69) 210 2321. Email: caiari@enter-net.com.br. Contact: Carlos Alberto Diniz Martins, Diretor Geral; or Ronaldo Rocha, Diretor Executivo. Free stickers. Return postage helpful. Replies irregularly to correspondence in Portuguese.

◪Rádio Canção Nova, Caixa Postal 57, 12630-000 Cachoeira Paulista SP, Brazil; (physical address) Rua João Paulo II s/n, Alto da Bela Vista, 12630-000 Cachoeira Paulista SP, Brazil. Phone: +55 (12) 560-2022. Fax: +55 (12) 561 2074. Email: (nontechnical) radio@cancaonova.org.br; (Director) adriana@cancaonova.org.br; (reception reports) alemfronteiras@cancaonova.com. Web: (includes RealAudio) www.cancaonova.org.br/cnova/radio. Contact: (general) Benedita Luiza Rodrigues; Ana Claudia de Santana; or Valera Guimarães Massafera, Secretária; (administration) Adriana Pereira, Diretora da Rádio; (reception reports) Eduardo Moura, Apresentador do programa "Além Fronteiras," aired 2200 UTC Saturday (one hour earlier when Brazil is on DST). Free stickers, pennants and station brochure sometimes given upon request. May send magazines. $1 helpful.

Rádio Capixaba, Caixa Postal 509, 29000-000 Vitória ES, Brazil; or (street address) Av. Santo Antônio 366, 29025-000 Vitória ES, Brazil. Email: radiocap@terra.com.br. Contact: Jairo Gouvea Maia, Diretor; or Sr. Sardinha, Técnico. Replies occasionally to correspondence in Portuguese.

◪Rádio Clube de Dourados, Rua Ciro Mello 2045, Dourados MS, Brazil. Web: (Windows Media only) www.douranet.com.br/netshow/clube.asx. Replies irregularly to correspondence in Portuguese.

Rádio Clube de Rondonópolis (when operating), Caixa Postal 190, 78700-000 Rondonópolis MT, Brazil. Contact: Canário Silva, Departamento Comercial; or Saúl Feliz, Gerente-Geral. Return postage helpful. Replies to correspondence in Portuguese.

Rádio Clube de Varginha, Caixa Postal 102, 37000-000 Varginha MG, Brazil. Email: sistemaclube@varginha.com.br. Contact: Mariela Silva Gómez. Return postage necessary. Replies to correspondence in Spanish and Portuguese.

◪Rádio Clube do Pará, Av. Almirante Barroso 2190 - 3º andar, 66093-020 Belém PA, Brazil. Phone: +55 (91) 3084-0138. Fax: +55 (91) 276 2848. Email: timaocampeao@expert.com.br. Web: (includes Windows Media) www.radioclubedopara.com.br. Contact: Edyr Paiva Proença, Diretor Geral; or José Almeida Lima de Sousa. Return postage required. Replies irregularly to correspondence in Portuguese.

Radio Clube Paranaense, Rua Rockefeller 1311, Prado Velho, 80230-130 Curitiba PR, Brazil. Phone: +55 (41) 332-2772.

Email: clubeb2@onda.com.br. Web: www.clubeb2.com.br. Contact: Vicente Mickosz, Superintendente.

Rádio Copacabana (when operating), Rua Visconde Inhauma 37 - 12° andar, Rio de Janeiro. Phone: +55 (21) 233-9269 or +55 (21) 263-8567. Replies slowly to correspondence in Portuguese.

Rádio Congonhas, Praça Basílica 130, 36404-000 Congonhas MG, Brazil. Replies to correspondence in Portuguese.

Rádio Cultura Araraquara, Avenida Feijó 583 (Centro), 14801-140 Araraquara SP, Brazil. Phone: +55 (16) 232-3790. Fax: +55 (16) 232 3475. Email: ouvintes@culturafmam.com.br (cultura@techs.com.br may also work). Web: (includes Windows Media) www.culturafmam.com.br. Contact: Antonio Carlos Rodrigues dos Santos, Diretor Artistico e Comercial. Return postage required. Replies slowly to correspondence in Portuguese.

Rádio Cultura de Campos (when operating), Caixa Postal 79, 28100-970 Campos RJ, Brazil. $1 or return postage necessary. Replies to correspondence in Portuguese.

Rádio Cultura de Cuiabá—AM sister-station of Rádio Brasil Tropical (*see*) and whose programming is partly relayed by RBT. Email: rcultura@terra.com.br. Web: www.grupocultura.com.br.

Rádio Cultura Filadelfia, Rua Antonio Barbosa 1353, Caixa Postal 89, 85851-090 Foz do Iguaçu PR, Brazil. Phone: +55 (45) 523-2930. A Finnish listener reported receiving a reply from Andre Antero (andreantero@hotmail.com); however, this person's connection with the station is unknown.

Rádio Cultura Ondas Tropicais, Rua Barcelos s/n - Praça 14, 69020-200 Manaus AM, Brazil. Phone: +55 (92) 621-0015. Fax: +55 (92) 633 3332, +55 (92) 633 2829. Web: (FUNTEC parent organization) www.tvculturaamazonas.br. Contact: Luíz Fernando de Souza Ferreira; or Maria Jerusalem dos Santos, Chefe da Divisão de Rádio. Replies to correspondence in Portuguese. Return postage appreciated. Station is part of the FUNTEC (Fundação Televisão e Rádio Cultura do Amazonas) network.

Rádio Cultura São Paulo, Rua Cenno Sbrighi 378, Agua Branca, 05036-900 São Paulo, Brazil; or Caixa Postal 11544, 05049-970 São Paulo, Brazil. Phone: (general) +55 (11) 3874-3122; (Cultura AM) +55 (11) 3874-3081; (Cultura FM) +55 (11) 3874-3082. Fax: +55 (11) 3611 2014. Email: (Cultura AM, relayed on 9615 and 17815 kHz) falecom@radiocultura.am.br; (Cultura FM, relayed on 6170 kHz) falecom@radioculturasp.fm.br. Web: (includes Windows Media) www.tvcultura.com.br. Contact: Thais de Almeida Dias, Chefe de Produção e Programação; Eduardo Weber; Sra. Maria Luíza Amaral Kfouri, Chefe de Produção; or Valvenio Martins de Almeida, Coordenador de Produção. $1 or return postage required. Replies slowly to postal correspondence in Portuguese.

Rádio Difusora Acreana, Rua Benjamin Constant 1232, 69900-161 Rio Branco AC, Brazil. Phone: +55 (68) 223-9696. Fax: +55 (68) 223 8610. Email: rda@osite.com.br. Contact: Washington Aquino, Diretor Geral. Replies irregularly to correspondence in Portuguese.

Rádio Difusora Cáceres, Caixa Postal 297, 78200-000 Cáceres MT, Brazil. Contact: Sra. Maridalva Amaral Vignardi. $1 or return postage required. Replies occasionally to correspondence in Portuguese.

Rádio Difusora de Aquidauana, Caixa Postal 18, 79200-000 Aquidauana MS, Brazil. Phone: +55 (67) 241-3956 or +55 (67) 241-3957. Contact: Joel Severino da Silva, Diretor Geral. Free tourist literature and used Brazilian stamps. $1 or return postage required. This station sometimes identifies during the program day as "Nova Difusora," but its sign-off announcement gives the official name as "Rádio Difusora, Aquidauana."

Rádio Difusora de Londrina, Caixa Postal 1870, 86000-000 Londrina PR, Brazil. Contact: Oscar Simões Costa, Gerente Administrativo. Free tourist brochure, which sometimes seconds as a verification. $1 or return postage helpful. Replies irregularly to correspondence in Portuguese.

Rádio Difusora de Macapá, Rua Cândido Mendes 525 - Centro, 68900-100 Macapá AP, Brazil. Phone: +55 (96) 212-1120 or +55 (96) 212-1118. Fax: +55 (96) 212 1116. Email: radio630@hotmail.com. Web: http://macapa-ap.com.br/empresas/rdm.htm. Contact: Paulo Roberto Rodrigues, Gerente. $1 or return postage required. Replies irregularly to correspondence in Portuguese. Sometimes provides stickers, key rings and—on rare occasions—T-shirts.

Rádio Difusora de Poços de Caldas, Rua Rio Grande do Sul 631- 1° andar, Centro, 37701-001 Poços de Caldas MG, Brazil. Phone/fax: +55 (35) 3722-1530. Email: difusora@difusorapocos.com.br. Web: www.difusorapocos.com.br. Contact: (general) Orlando Cioffi, Diretor Geral; (technical) Ronaldo Cioffi, Diretor Técnico. $1 or return postage required. Replies to correspondence in Portuguese.

Rádio Difusora do Amazonas, Av. Eduardo Ribeiro 639 - 20° andar, Centro, 69010-001 Manaus AM, Brazil. Phone: +55 (92) 633-1001. Fax: +55 (92) 234 3750. Email: difusora@internext.com.br. Web: (includes Windows Media) www.difusoramanaus.com.br. Contact: J. Joaquim Marinho, Diretor. Joaquim Marinho is a keen collector and especially interested in Duck Hunting Permit Stamps, stamp booklets and stamp sheets. Will reply to correspondence in Portuguese or English. $1 or return postage helpful.

Rádio Difusora Roraima, Avenida Capitão Ene Garcez 830, São Francisco, 69301-160 Boa Vista RR, Brazil. Phone/fax: +55 (95) 623-2259. Email: radiorr@technet.com.br. Web: www.radiororaima.com.br. Contact: Galvão Soares, Diretor Geral. Return postage required. Replies occasionally to correspondence in Portuguese.

Rádio Difusora Taubaté (when operating), Rua Dr. Sousa Alves 960, 12020-030 Taubaté SP, Brazil. Contact: Emilio Amadei Beringhs Neto, Diretor Superintendente. May send free stickers, pens, keychains and T-shirts. Return postage or $1 helpful.

Rádio Educação Rural, Avenida Mato Grosso 530, Centro, 79002-230 Campo Grande MS, Brazil. Phone: +55 (67) 384-3164, +55 (67) 382-2238 or +55 (67) 384-3345. Contact: Ailton Guerra, Gerente-Geral; Angelo Venturelli, Diretor. $1 or return postage required. Replies to correspondence in Portuguese.

Rádio Educação Rural, Praça São Sebastião 228, 69460-000 Coari AM, Brazil. Phone: +55 (97) 561-2474. Fax: +55 (97) 561 263. Email: radiocoari@portalcoari.com.br. Contact: Lino Rodrigues Pessoa, Diretor Comercial; or Elijane Martins Correa. $1 or return postage helpful. Replies irregularly to correspondence in Portuguese.

Rádio Educação Rural de Tefé, Caixa Postal 21, 69470-000 Tefé AM, Brazil; or (street address) 21Praça Santa Tereza 283, Centro, 69470-000 Tefé AM, Brazil. Phone: +55 (97) 343- 3017. Fax: +55 (97) 343 2663. Email: rert@osite.com.br; fjoaquim@mandic.com.br. Contact: Thomas Schwamborn, Diretor Administrativo.

Rádio Educadora 6 de Agosto, Rua Pio Nazário 31, 69930-000 Xapuri AC, Brazil. Phone: +55 (68) 542-3063. Contact: Francisco Evangelista de Abreu. Replies to correspondence in Portuguese.

Rádio Educadora de Bragança, Praça das Bandeiras s/n, 68600-000 Bragança PA, Brazil. Phone: +55 (91) 425-1295.

Fax: +55 (91) 425 1702. Email: educadora@eletronet.com.br. Contact: José Rosendo de S. Neto; Zelina Cardoso Gonçalves; or Adelino Borges, Aux. Escritório. $1 or return postage required. Replies to correspondence in Portuguese.

Rádio Educadora de Guajará Mirim, Praça Mário Corrêa No.90, 78957-000 Guajará Mirim RO, Brazil. Phone: +55 (69) 541-2274. Fax: +55 (69) 541 6333. Email: educadora@osite.com.br; comercial@radio-educadora.ht.st. Contact: Wilson Charles. Return postage helpful. Replies to correspondence in Portuguese.

Rádio Educadora de Limeira, Caixa Postal 105, 13480-970 Limeira SP, Brazil. Email: (Bortolan) bab@zaz.com.br. Contact: Bruno Arcaro Bortolan, Gerente.

📻**Rádio Gaúcha**, Avenida Ipiranga 1075 - 2º andar, Bairro Azenha, 90160-093 Porto Alegre RS, Brazil. Phone: +55 (51) 3218-6600. Fax: +55 (51) 3218 6680. Email: (general) gaucha@rdgaucha.com.br; (comments on program content) reportagem@rdgaucha.com.br; (technical) gilberto.kussler@rdgaucha.com.br. Web: (includes RealAudio) http://radiogaucha.clicrbs.com.br. Contact: Gilberto Kussler, Gerente Técnico. Replies to correspondence, preferably in Portuguese.

Rádio Gazeta, Avenida Paulista 900, 01310-940 São Paulo SP, Brazil. Phone: +55 (11) 3170- 5757. Fax: +55 (11) 3170 5630. Email: (Fundação Cásper Líbero parent organization) fcl@fcl.com.br. Web: (Fundação Cásper Líbero parent organization) www.fcl.com.br. Contact: Shakespeare Ettinger, Supervisor Geral de Operação; Bernardo Leite da Costa; José Roberto Mignone Cheibub, Gerente Geral; or Ing. Aníbal Horta Figueiredo. Free stickers. $1 or return postage necessary. Replies to correspondence in Portuguese. Currently relays programming from the station's Mediumwave AM station (Gazeta AM) after several years of leasing airtime to the "Deus é Amor" Pentecostal church.

📻**Rádio Globo**, Rua do Russel 434-Glória, 22210-210 Rio de Janeiro RJ, Brazil. Phone: +55 (21) 555-8375. Fax: +55 (21) 558 6385. Email: (administration) gerenciaamrio@radioglobo.com.br. Web: (includes RealAudio) www.radioglobo.com.br/globorio. Contact: Marcos Libretti, Diretor Geral. Replies irregularly to correspondence in Portuguese. Return postage helpful.

📻**Rádio Globo**, Rua das Palmeiras 315, Santa Cecilia, 01226-901 São Paulo SP, Brazil. Phone: +55 (11) 3824-3217. Fax: +55 (11) 3824 3210. Email: (Rapussi) margarete@radioglobo.com.br. Web: (includes RealAudio) www.radioglobo.com.br. Contact: Ademir Dutra, Locutor, "Programa Ademar Dutra"; Margarete Rapussi; Guilherme Viterbo; or José Marques. Replies to correspondence, preferably in Portuguese.

📻**Rádio Guaíba**, Rua Caldas Júnior 219, 90019-900 Porto Alegre RS, Brazil. Phone: +55 (51) 3215-6222. Email: (administration) diretor@radioguaiba.com.br; (technical) centraltecnica@radioguaiba.com.br. Web: (includes RealAudio) www.radioguaiba.com.br. Return postage helpful.

📻**Rádio Guarani** (if reactivated), Avenida Assis Chateaubriand 499, Floresta, 30150-101 Belo Horizonte MG, Brazil. Phone: +55 (31) 3237-6000. Fax: +55 (31) 3237 6656. Email: guarani@guarani.com.br. Web: (includes RealAudio) www.guarani.com.br. Contact: Junara Belo, Setor de Comunicações. Replies slowly to correspondence in Portuguese. Return postage helpful.

Rádio Guarujá, Caixa Postal 45, 88000-000 Florianópolis SC, Brazil. Email: guaruja@radioguaruja.com.br. Web: www.radioguaruja.com.br. Contact: Mario Silva, Diretor; or Rosa Michels de Souza; (technical) Carlos Alberto Silva. Return postage required. Replies irregularly to correspondence in Portuguese. Reception reports should be directed to Carlos

Alberto Silva.

NEW YORK OFFICE: 45 West 46 Street, 5th Floor, Manhattan, NY 10036 USA.

Rádio Guarujá Paulista, Rua José Vaz Porto 175, Vila Santa Rosa, 11431-190 Guarujá SP, Brazil; or (technical, including reception reports) A/C Orivaldo Rampazzo, Rua Montenegro 196, 11410-040 Guarujá SP, Brazil. Phone: +55 (13) 3386-6092. Email: guarujaam@miranet.com.br. Contact: Orivaldo Rampazzo, Diretor. Replies to correspondence in Portuguese. Transmits via facilities of former world band stations in the state of São Paulo, which are fed via the Internet.

Rádio Iguatemi (when operating), Caixa Postal 66, 06001-970 Osasco SP, Brazil. Web: http://radioiguatemi. cidadeinternet.com.br. Sometimes replaces Rádio Mundial (*see*) on 4975 kHz. Both stations belong to the same network, Rede CBS.

REDE CBS PARENT ORGANIZATION: Rede CBS, Av. Paulista, 2200 - 14º andar - Cerqueira César, 01310-300 São Paulo SP, Brazil. Phone: +55 (11) 3016 5999. Fax: +55 (11) 3016 5980. Web: www.redecbs.com.br.

Rádio Inconfidência, Avenida Raja Gabáglia 1666, Luxemburgo, 30350-540 Belo Horizonte MG, Brazil. Phone: +55 (31) 3297-7344. Fax: +55 (31) 3297 7348. Email: inconfidencia@inconfidencia.com.br. Web: www.inconfidencia. com.br. Contact: Isaias Lansky, Diretor; Manuel Emilio de Lima Torres, Diretor Superintendente; Jairo Antolio Lima, Diretor Artístico; or Eugenio Silva. Free stickers and postcards. May send CD of Brazilian music. $1 or return postage helpful.

Rádio Integração (when active), Rua Alagoas 270, Bairro Escola Técnica, 69980-000 Cruzeiro do Sul AC, Brazil. Phone: +55 (68) 322-4637. Fax: +55 (68) 322 6511. Email: rtvi@omegasul.com.br. Contact: Oscar Alves Bandeira, Gerente. Return postage helpful.

Rádio IPB AM, Rua Itajaí 473, Bairro Antonio Vendas, 79041-270 Campo Grande MS, Brazil. Contact: Iván Páez Barboza, Diretor Geral (hence, the station's name, "IPB"); Pastor Laercio Paula das Neves, Dirigente Estadual; Agenor Patrocinio S., Locutor; Pastor José Adão Hames; or Kelly Cristina Rodrigues da Silva, Secretária. Return postage required. Replies to correspondence in Portuguese. Most of the airtime is leased to the "Deus é Amor" Pentecostal church.

Rádio Itatiaia, Rua Itatiaia 117, 31210-170 Belo Horizonte MG, Brazil. Fax: +55 (31) 446 2900. Email: itatiaia@itatiaia.com.br. Web: (includes RealAudio) www.itatiaia.com.br/am/index.html. Contact: Lúcia Araújo Bessa, Assistente da Diretória; or Claudio Carneiro.

Rádio Jornal "A Crítica" (when operating), Av. André Araujo 1024A, Aleixo, 69060-001 Manaus AM, Brazil. Phone: +55 (92) 642-4545. Fax: +55 (92) 642 2484. Contact: Rui Souto de Alencar, Diretor Executivo.

Rádio Liberal (when operating), C.P 498, 66017-970 Belém PA, Brazil; or (street address) Av. Nazaré 350, 66035-170 Belém PA, Brazil. Phone: +55 (91) 213-1500. Fax: +55 (91) 224 5240. Email: radio@radioliberal.com.br. Web: (includes RealAudio) www.radioliberal.com.br. Contact: Flavia Vasconcellos; Advaldo Castro, Diretor de Programação AM; João Carlos Silva Ribeiro, Coordenador de Programação AM. Currently off the air because of difficulty in obtaining parts for the transmitter.

Rádio Marumby, Caixa Postal 296, 88010-970 Florianópolis SC, Brazil; Rua Angelo Laporta 841, C. P. 62, 88020-600 Florianópolis SC, Brazil; or (missionary parent organization) Gideões Missionários da Última Hora—GMUH, Ministério Evangélico Mundial, Rua Joaquim Nunes 244, Caixa Postal 2004, 88340-000 Camboriú SC, Brazil. Email: (GMUH parent organization) gmuh@gmuh.com.br. Web: www.gmuh.com.br/aradio.htm; www.gmuh.com.br/marumby.htm. Contact: Davi Campos, Diretor Artístico; Dr. Cesario Bernardino, Presidente, GMUH; or Jair Albano, Diretor. $1 or return postage required. Free diploma and stickers. Replies to correspondence in Portuguese.

Rádio Marumby, Curitiba—see Rádio Novas de Paz, Curitiba, below.

Rádio Meteorologia Paulista, Rua Capitão João Marques 89, Jardim Centenário, 14940-000 Ibitinga, São Paulo SP, Brazil. Phone: +55 (16) 242-3388. Fax: +55 (16) 242 5056. Email: radio.ibitinga@ibinet.com.br. Web: (includes RealAudio from Ternura FM, relayed several hours each day by Rádio Meteorologia Paulista) www.ibinet.com.br/radioibitinga. Contact: Roque de Rosa, Diretora. Replies to correspondence in Portuguese. $1 or return postage required.

Rádio Missões da Amazônia, Travessa Dr. Lauro Sodré 299, 68250-000 Óbidos PA, Brazil. Phone: +55 (93) 547-1698. Fax: +55 (93) 547-1699. Email: radiomissoes@eunet.com.br. Contact: Max Hamoy; Edérgio de Moras Pinto; or Maristela Hamoy. Return postage required. Replies occasionally to correspondence in Portuguese.

Rádio Mundial, Av. Paulista 2198-Térreo, Cerqueira César, 01310-300 São Paulo, Brazil. Phone: +55 (11) 3016 5999. Email: radiomundial@radiomundial.com. Web: www.radiomundial.com.br. Contact: (nontechnical) Luci Rothschild de Abreu, Diretora Presidente.

REDE CBS PARENT ORGANIZATION: Rede CBS, Av. Paulista, 2200 - 14° andar - Cerqueira César, 01310-300 São Paulo SP,

Brazil. Phone: +55 (11) 3016 5999. Fax: +55 (11) 3016 5980. Web: www.redecbs.com.br.

Rádio Municipal, Avenida Alvaro Maia s/n, 69750-000 São Gabriel da Cachoeira AM, Brazil. Phone/fax: +55 (97) 471-1768. Contact: Luíz dos Santos França, Gerente; or Valdir de Souza Marques. Return postage necessary. Replies to correspondence in Portuguese. Formerly Rádio Nacional de São Gabriel da Cachoeira, prior to the station's transfer from Radiobrás to the local municipality.

Rádio Nacional da Amazônia, SCRN 702/3 Bloco-B, Ed. Radiobrás, 70710-750 Brasília DF, Brazil; or (postal address) Caixa Postal 258, 70359-970 Brasília-DF, Brazil. Phone: +55 (61) 327-1981. Fax: +55 (61) 321 7602. Email: nacionaloc@radiobras.gov.br. Web: (includes Windows Media) www.radiobras.gov.br/nacional. Contact: (general) Luíz Otavio de Castro Souza, Diretor; Fernando Gómez da Câmara, Gerente de Escritório; or Januario Procopio Toledo, Diretor; (technical) Valmira Almeida, Chefe da Divisão de Ondas Curtas da Radiobrás. Free stickers, but no verifications.

Rádio Nacional do Brasil, Caixa Postal 259, 70359-715 Brasília-DF, Brazil. Email: radionacionaldobrasil@radiobras.gov.br. Returned to the air in August 2003 after several years off the air.

Rádio Nacional São Gabriel da Cachoeira—see Rádio Municipal.

Rádio Novas de Paz, Avenida Paraná 1896, 82510-000 Curitiba PR, Brazil; or Caixa Postal 22, 80000-000 Curitiba PR, Brazil. Phone: +55 (41) 257-4109. Contact: João Falavinha Ienzen, Gerente. $1 or return postage required. Replies irregularly to correspondence in Portuguese.

Rádio Nova Visão

STUDIOS: Rua do Manifesto 1373, 04209-001 São Paulo SP, Brazil. Contact: José Eduardo Dias, Diretor Executivo. Return postage required. Replies to correspondence in Portuguese. Free stickers. Relays Rádio Trans Mundial fulltime.

TRANSMITTER: Caixa Postal 551, 97000-000 Santa Maria RS, Brazil; or Caixa Postal 6084, 90000-000 Porto Alegre RS, Brazil. Reportedly issues full-data verifications for reports in Portuguese or German, upon request, from this location. If no luck, try contacting, in English or Dutch, Tom van Ewijck, via email at egiaroll@mail.iss.lcca.usp.br. For further information, see the entry for Rádio Trans Mundial.

Rádio Oito de Setembro (when operating), Caixa Postal 8, 13690-000 Descalvado SP, Brazil. Contact: Adonias Gomes. Replies to corrrespondence in Portuguese.

Rádio Pioneira de Teresina, Rua 24 de Janeiro 150 sul, 64001-230 Teresina PI, Brazil. Phone: +55 (86) 222-8121. Fax: +55 (86) 222 8122. Email: pioneira@webone.com.br. Web: www.radiopioneira.am.br. Contact: Luíz Eduardo Bastos; Padre Tony Batista, Diretor; or Joel Silva. $1 or return postage required. Replies slowly to correspondence in Portuguese.

Rádio Progresso (if reactivated), Estrada do Belmont s/n, B% Nacional, 78903-400 Porto Velho RO, Brazil. Return postage required. Replies occasionally to correspondence in Portuguese.

Rádio Record

STATION: Caixa Postal 7920, 04084-002 São Paulo SP, Brazil. Email: radiorecord@rederecord.com.br. Contact: Mário Luíz Catto, Diretor Geral. Free stickers. Return postage or $1 required. Replies occasionally to correspondence in Portuguese. NEW YORK OFFICE: 630 Fifth Avenue, Room 2607, New York NY 10111 USA.

Rádio Relógio, Rua Paramopama 131, Ribeira, Ilha do Governador, 21930-110 Rio de Janeiro RJ, Brazil. Phone: +55

(21) 467-0201. Fax: +55 (21) 467 4656. Email: radiorelogio@ig.com.br. Web: www.radiorelogio.com.br. Contact: Olindo Coutinho, Diretor Geral; or Renato Castro. Replies occasionally to correspondence in Portuguese.

Rádio RGS—see Rádio Rio Grande do Sul, below.

Rádio Ribeirão Preto, Caixa Postal 1252, 14025-000 Ribeirão Preto SP, Brazil (physical address: Av. 9 de Julho 600, 14025-000 Ribeirão Preto SP, Brazil). Phone/fax: +55 (16) 610- 3511. Contact: Lucinda de Oliveira, Secretária; Luis Schiavone Junior; or Paulo Henríque Rocha da Silva. Replies to correspondence in Portuguese.

Rádio Rio Grande do Sul, Rede Pampa de Comunicação, Rua Orfanatrófio 711, 90840-440 Porto Alegre RS, Brazil. Phone: +55 (51) 233-8311. Fax: +55 (51) 233 4500. Email: pampa@pampa.com.br. All the station's shortwave outlets carry programming from Sistema LBV Mundial (see), to where all program and reception related correspondence should be sent.

🖀**Rádio Rio Mar**, Rua José Clemente 500, Centro, 69010-070 Manaus AM, Brazil. Phone: +55 (92) 633-2295; +55 (92) 633-5005. Fax: +55 (92) 232 7763. Email: riomar@bol.com.br; decom@auxiliadora.g12.br. Web: (includes Windows Media) www.geocities.com/radioriomar. Contact: Jairo de Sousa Coelho, Diretor de Programação e Jornalismo. Replies to correspondence in Portuguese. $1 or return postage helpful.

Rádio Rural Santarém, Rua São Sebastião 622 - Bloco A, 68005-090 Santarém PA, Brazil. Phone: +55 (93) 523-1006. Fax: +55 (93) 523 2685. Email: ruralsonia@hotmail.com. Contact: Edilberto Moura Sena, Diretor Executivo; João Elias B. Bentes, Gerente Geral; or Edsergio de Moraes Pinto. Replies slowly to correspondence in Portuguese. Free stickers. Return postage or $1 required.

🖀**Rádio Trans Mundial**, Caixa Postal 18300, 04626-970 São Paulo SP, Brazil. Phone: +55 (11) 5031-3533. Fax: +55 (11) 5031 5271. Email: (general) rtm@transmundial.com.br; (technical) tecnica@transmundial.com.br; ("Amigos do Rádio" DX-program) amigosdoradio@transmundial.com.br. Web: (includes RealAudio) www.transmundial.com.br. Contact: José Eduardo Dias, Diretor; or Rudolf Grimm, programa "Amigos do Rádio." Sells religious books and casettes and CDs of religious music (from choral to bossa nova). Prices, in local currency, can be found at the Website (click on "catálogo"). Program provider for Rádio Nova Visão—see, above.

Rádio Cacique (when operating), Caixa Postal 486, 18090-970 Sorocaba SP, Brazil. Phone: +55 (15) 231-3712 or (15) 232-2922. Email: Online email form. Web: www.radiocacique.com.br.

🖀**Rádio Senado**, Caixa Postal 070-747, 70359-970 Brasília DF, Brazil; or (physical address) Praça dos Três Poderes, Anexo II, Bloco B, Térreo, 70165-900 Brasília DF, Brazil. Email: radio@senado.gov.br; (Maintenance Engineer) arenato@senado.gov.br. Web: (includes RealAudio) www.senado.gov.br/radio. Contact: Aldo Renato B. de Assis, Engenheiro de Manutenção.

Rádio Universo/Rádio Tupi, Rua Basilio Itiberê 1001, Rebouças, 80215-140 Curitiba PR, Brazil. Email: (Santana) billsantana2000@hotmail.com. Contact: Luíz Andreu Rúbio, Diretor; or Douglas Santana. Replies occasionally to correspondence in Portuguese. Rádio Universo's air time is leased to the "Deus é Amor" Pentecostal church, and programs originate from the Rádio Tupi network. Identifies on the air as "Rádio Tupi, Sistema Universo de Comunicação" or, more often, just as "Rádio Tupi."

Rádio Vale do Rio Madeira (if activated), Rua Júlio de Oliveira 1323, São Pedro, 69800-000 Humaitá AM, Brazil. Phone/fax: +55 (97) 373-2073. Email: radiovrm@dknet.com.br. Although

assigned a shortwave frequency years ago, the station never used it. Now, the station is again proposing to operate on shortwave, but only if it is granted a new frequency, for which it has already applied. In the meantime, broadcasts continue on 670 kHz AM.

Rádio Verdes Florestas, Rua Mário Lobão 81, 69980-000 Cruzeiro do Sul AC, Brazil; or Caixa Postal 53, 69981-970 Cruzeiro do Sul AC, Brazil. Phone: +55 (68) 322-3309, +55 (68) 322- 2634. Email: florestas@nauanet.com.br. Contact: Marlene Valente de Andrade. Return postage required. Replies occasionally to correspondence in Portuguese.

Rádio Voz do Coração Imaculado (if reactivated), Caixa Postal 354, 75001-970 Anápolis GO, Brazil. Contact: P. Domingos M. Esposito A religious station which started shortwave operation in 1999 with the transmitter formerly used by Rádio Carajá. Operation tends to be irregular, as the station is funded entirely from donations.

🖀**Rede SomZoom Sat**—a satellite network based in Fortaleza, Ceará, whose programming is sometimes carried by Brazilian world band stations (usually during night hours). Email: somzoomsat@somzoom.com.br. Web: (includes Windows Media) www.somzoom.com.br/Radio/radio.htm.

🖀**Sistema LBV Mundial**, Legião da Boa Vontade, Av. Sérgio Tomás 740, Bom Retiro, 01131- 010 São Paulo SP, Brazil; or Rua Doraci 90, Bom Retiro, 01134-020 São Paulo SP, Brazil. Phone: 3225-4500. Fax: +55 (11) 3225 4639. Web: (general) http://sistema.lbv.org; (LBV parent organization, includes RealAudio) www.lbv.org. Contact: André Tiago, Diretor; Sandra Albuquerque, Secretária; or Gizelle Almeida, Gerente do Dept. de Rádio. Replies slowly to correspondence in all main languages. Program provider for Radio Rio Grande do Sul (see). NEW YORK OFFICE: 383 5th Avenue, 2nd Floor, New York NY 10016 USA. Phone: +1 (212) 481-1004. Fax: +1 (212) 481 1005. Email: lgw2000@aol.com.

🖀**Voz de Libertação**. Ubiquitous programming originating from the "Deus é Amor" Pentecostal church's Rádio Universo (1300 kHz) in São Bernardo do Campo, São Paulo, and heard over several shortwave stations, especially Rádio Universo, Curitiba (see). A RealAudio feed is available at the "Deus é Amor" Website, www.ipda.org.br.

Voz do Coração Imaculado—see Rádio Voz do Coração Imaculado.

BULGARIA   World Time +2 (+3 midyear)

🖀**Radio Bulgaria**
NONTECHNICAL AND TECHNICAL: P.O. Box 900, BG-1000, Sofia, Bulgaria; or (street address) 4 Dragan Tsankov Blvd., 1040 Sofia, Bulgaria. Phone: (general) +359 (2) 985-241; (Managing Director) +359 (2) 854-604. Fax: (general, usually weekdays only) +359 (2) 871 060, +359 (2) 871 061 or +359 (2) 650 560; (Managing Director) +359 (2) 946 1576; +359 (2) 988 5103; (Frequency Manager) +359 (2) 963 4464. Email: rcorresp1@fon15.bnr.acad.bg; (Nedyalkov) nedyalkov@nationalradio.bg; or rbul1@nationalradio.bg; (English program and schedule information) english@nationalradio.bg (same format for other languages, e.g. french@...; spanish@...). Web: (includes RealAudio) www.nationalradio.bg. Contact: (general) Mrs. Iva Delcheva, English Section; Svilen Stoicheff, Head of English Section; (administration and technical) Anguel H. Nedyalkov, Managing Director; (technical) Atanas Tzenov, Director. Replies regularly, but sometimes slowly. Return postage helpful. Verifies email reports with QSL cards. For concerns about frequency usage, contact BTC, below, with copies to Messrs. Nedyalkov

and Tzenov of Radio Bulgaria.
FREQUENCY MANAGEMENT AND TRANSMISSION OPERATIONS:
Bulgarian Telecommunications Company (BTC), Ltd., 8 Totleben
Blvd., 1606 Sofia, Bulgaria. Phone: +359 (2) 88-00-75. Fax:
+359 (2) 87 58 85 or +359 (2) 80 25 80. Contact: Roumen
Petkov, Frequency Manager; or Mrs. Margarita Krasteva, Ra-
dio Regulatory Department.
Radio Varna, 22 blv. Primorski, 9000 Varna, Bulgaria. Replies
irregularly. Return postage required. If no reply is forthcom-
ing, try sending an email to rcorresp1@bnr.acad.bg.

BURKINA FASO   World Time exactly

Radiodiffusion-Télévision Burkina, B.P. 7029,
Ouagadougou, Burkina Faso. Phone: +226 310- 441. Contact:
(general) Raphael L. Onadia; Tahere Ouedraogo, Le Chef des
Programs; or M. Pierre Tassembedo; (technical) Marcel Teho,
Head of Transmitting Centre. Replies irregularly to correspon-
dence in French. IRC or return postage helpful.

BURMA   —*see* MYANMAR.

BURUNDI   World Time +2

La Voix de la Révolution, B.P. 1900, Bujumbura, Burundi.
Phone: +257 22-37-42. Fax: +257 22 65 47 or +257 22 66 13.
Email: rtnb@cbinf.com. Contact: (general) Grégoire
Barampumba, Head of News Section; or Frederic
Havugiyaremye, Journaliste; (administration) Gérard
Mfuranzima, Le Directeur de la Radio; or Didace Baranderetse,
Directeur Général de la Radio; (technical) Abraham Makuza,
Le Directeur Technique. $1 required.

CAMBODIA   World Time +7

National Radio of Cambodia (when operating)
STATION ADDRESS: 106 Preah Kossamak Street, Monivong
Boulevard, Phnom Penh, Cambodia. Phone: +855 (23) 423-
369 or +855 (23) 422-869. Fax: + 855 (23) 427 319. Contact:
(general) Miss Hem Bory, English Announcer; Kem Yan, Chief
of External Relations; or Touch Chhatha, Producer, Art Department; (administration) In Chhay, Chief of Overseas Service; Som Sarun, Chief of Home Service; Van Sunheng, Deputy
Director General, Cambodian National Radio and Television;
or Ieng Muli, Minister of Information; (technical) Oum Phin,
Chief of Technical Department. Free program schedule. Replies irregularly and slowly. Do not include stamps, currency,
IRCs or dutiable items in envelope. Registered letters stand a
much better chance of getting through. Has been increasingly
off the air in recent years.

CAMEROON   World Time +1

NOTE: Any CRTV outlet is likely to be verified by contacting
via registered mail, in English or French with $2 enclosed, James
Achanyi-Fontem, Cameroon Link, Shortwave Monitors, P.O.
Box 1460, Douala, Cameroon.
Cameroon Radio Television Corporation (CRTV)—Buea
(when operating), P.M.B., Buea (Sud-Ouest), Cameroon. Con-
tact: Ononino Oli Isidore, Chef Service Technique. Three IRCs,
$1 or return postage required.
Cameroon Radio Television Corporation (CRTV)—Garoua
(when operating), B.P. 103, Garoua (Nord/Adamawa),
Cameroon. Contact: Kadeche Manguele. Free cloth pennants.

Three IRCs or return postage required. Replies irregularly and
slowly to correspondence in French.
Cameroon Radio Television Corporation (CRTV)—
Yaoundé (when operating), B.P. 1634, Yaoundé (Centre-Sud),
Cameroon. Phone: +237 221-4035, +237 221-4077 or +237
221-4088. Fax: +237 220 4340. Email: crtv@crtv.cm. Web: (includes RealAudio and Windows Media) www.crtv.cm. Contact:
(technical or nontechnical) Prof. Gervais Mendo Ze, Directeur-
Général; (technical) Eyébé Tanga, Directeur Technique. $1 re-
quired. Replies slowly (sometimes extremely slowly) to
correspondence in French.

CANADA   World Time -3:30 (-2:30 midyear)

Newfoundland; -4 (-3 midyear) Atlantic; -5 (-4 midyear) Eastern,
including Quebec and Ontario; -6 (-5 midyear) Central; except
Saskatchewan; -6 Saskatchewan; -7 (-6 midyear) Mountain; -
8 (-7 midyear) Pacific, including Yukon.
Canadian Broadcasting Corporation (CBC)—English Pro-
grams, P.O. Box 500, Station A, Toronto, Ontario, M5W 1E6,
Canada. Phone: (Audience Relations) +1 (416) 205-3700. Email:
cbcinput@toronto.cbc.ca. Web: (includes RealAudio)
www.radio.cbc.ca. CBC prepares some of the programs heard
over Radio Canada International (*see*).
LONDON NEWS BUREAU: CBC, 43-51 Great Titchfield Street,
London W1P 8DD, England. Phone: +44 (20) 7412-9200. Fax:
+44 (20) 7631 3095.
PARIS NEWS BUREAU: CBC, 17 avenue Matignon, F-75008 Paris,
France. Phone: +33 (1) 4421-1515. Fax: +33 (1) 4421 1514.
WASHINGTON NEWS BUREAU: CBC, National Press Building,
Suite 500, 529 14th Street NW, Washington DC 20045 USA.
Phone: +1 (202) 383-2900. Contact: Jean-Louis Arcand, David
Hall or Susan Murray.
Canadian Broadcasting Corporation (CBC)—French Pro-
grams, Société Radio-Canada, C.P. 6000, succ. centre-ville,
Montréal, Québec, H3C 3A8, Canada. Phone: (Audience Rela-
tions) +1 (514) 597-6000. Email (comments on programs):
auditoire@montreal.radio-canada.ca. Welcomes correspon-
dence sent to this address but may not reply due to shortage
of staff. Web: (includes RealAudio) www.radio-canada.ca. CBC
prepares some of the programs heard over Radio Canada International (*see*).
CBC Northern Quebec Shortwave Service—*see* Radio
Canada International, below.
CFRX-CFRB *MAIN ADDRESS:* 2 St. Clair Avenue West,
Toronto, Ontario, M4V 1L6, Canada. Phone:(main switchboard)
+1 (416) 924-5711; (talk shows switchboard) +1 (416) 872-
1010; (news centre) +1 (416) 924-6717; (CFRB information
access line) +1 (416) 872-2372. Fax: (main fax line) +1 (416)
323 6830; (CFRB news fax line) +1 (416) 323 6816. Email:
(comments on programs) cfrbcomments@cfrb.com; (News Director) news@cfrb.com; (general, nontechnical) info@cfrb.com;
or opsmngr@cfrb.com; (technical) ian.sharp@cfrb.com. Web:
(includes MP3) www.cfrb.com. Contact: (nontechnical) Carlo
Massaro, Information Officer; or Steve Kowch, Operations
Manager; (technical) Ian Sharp, Technical Supervisor. Reception reports should be sent to the verification address, below.
VERIFICATION ADDRESS: Ontario DX Association, P.O. Box 161,
Station 'A', Willowdale, Ontario, M2N 5S8, Canada, or by email:
odxa@compuserve.com. General information about CFRB/
CFRX can be seen at the ODXA Website: www.odxa.on.ca.
General information about CFRB/CFRX reception may be di-
rected to the QSL Manager, Steve Canney, VA3SC (email:
scanney@cogeco.ca). A free CFRB/CFRX information sheet and
an ODXA brochure is enclosed with your verification card.

Christmas Eve in Frankfurt, one of the many events covered by Deutsche Welle. The station offers German language courses to corresponding listeners.

Milan Prezelj

Reports are processed quickly if sent to this address.

CFVP-CKMX, AM 1060, Standard Broadcasting, P.O. Box 2750, Station 'M', Calgary, Alberta, T2P 4P8, Canada. Phone: (general) +1 (403) 240-5800; (news) +1 (403) 240-5844; (technical) +1 (403) 240-5867. Fax: (general and technical) +1 (403) 240 5801; (news) +1 (403) 246 7099. Contact: (general) Gary Russell, General Manager; or Beverley Van Tighem, Executive Assistant; (technical) Ken Pasolli, Technical Director.

CHU. Radio Station CHU, National Research Council of Canada, 1200 Montreal Road, Bldg M-36, Ottawa, Ontario, K1A 0R6, Canada. Phone: +1 (613) 993-5186. Fax: +1 (613) 952 1394. Email: radio.chu@nrc.ca. Web: http://inms-ienm.nrc-cnrc.gc.ca/time_services/shortwave_broadcasts_e.html. Contact: Dr. Rob Douglas; Dr. Jean-Simon Boulanger, Group Leader; or Ray Pelletier, Technical Officer. Official standard frequency and World Time station for Canada on 3330, 7335 and 14670 kHz. Brochure available upon request. Those with a personal computer, Bell 103 compatible modem and appropriate software can get the exact time, from CHU's cesium clock, via the telephone; details available upon request, or direct from the Website. Verifies reception reports with a QSL card.

CKZN, CBC Newfoundland and Labrador, P.O. Box 12010, Station 'A', St. John's, Newfoundland, A1B 3T8, Canada. Phone: +1 (709) 576-5155. Fax: +1 (709) 576 5099. Email: (administration) radiomgt@stjohns.cbc.ca; (engineer) keith_durnford@cbc.ca. Web: (includes RealAudio) www.stjohns.cbc.ca. Contact: (general) Heather Elliott, Communications Officer; (technical) Shawn R. Williams, Manager, Transmission and Distribution; Keith Durnford, Transmission Supervisor; Jerry Brett, Transmitter Department; or Janet Ferweda. Free CBC sticker and verification card with the history of Newfoundland included. Don't enclose money, stamps or IRCs with correspondence, as they will only have to be returned. Relays CBN (St. John's, 640 kHz) except at 1000-1330 World Time (one hour earlier in summer) when programming comes from CFGB Goose Bay.

CFGB ADDRESS: CBC Radio, Box 1029 Station 'C', Happy Valley, Goose Bay, Labrador, Newfoundland A0P 1C0, Canada.

CKZU-CBU, CBC, P.O. Box 4600, Vancouver, British Columbia, V6B 4A2, Canada—for verification of reception reports, mark the envelope, "Attention: Engineering." Phone: (general) +1 (604) 662-6000; (toll-free, U.S. and Canada only) 1-800-961-6161; (engineering) +1 (604) 662-6060. Fax: +1 (604) 662 6350. Email: (general) webmaster@vancouver.cbc.ca; (Newbury) newburyd@vancouver.cbc.ca. Web: (includes RealAudio) www.vancouver.cbc.ca. Contact: (general) Public Relations; (technical) Dave Newbury, Transmission Engineer.

High Adventure Gospel Communication Ministries—*see* Bible Voice Broadcasting, United Kingdom.

Radio Canada International

NOTE: (CBC Northern Quebec Service) The following RCI address, fax and email information for the Main Office and Transmission Office is also valid for the CBC Northern Quebec Shortwave Service, provided you make your communication to the attention of the particular service you seek to contact.

MAIN OFFICE: P.O. Box 6000, Montréal, Quebec, H3C 3A8, Canada; or (street address) 1400 boulevard René Lévesque East, Level B Montréal, Québec, H2L 2M2, Canada. Phone: (general) +1 (514) 597-7500; (Audience Relations, Ms. Maggy Akerblom) +1 (514) 597-7555; (Communications) +1 (514) 597-7551. Fax: (general) +1 (514) 597 7076; (Audience Relations) +1 (514) 597 7760. Email: rci@montreal.radio-canada.ca. Web: (includes Window Media & MP3) www.rcinet.ca. Contact: (general) Maggy Akerblom, Audience Relations; Stéphane Parent, Producer/Host "Le courrier mondial"; Mark Montgomery; or Ian Jones, Producer/Host "The Maple Leaf Mailbag"; (administration) Jean Larin, Director; (technical—verifications) Bill Westenhaver. Free stickers, pennants and lapel pins, when available.

TRANSMISSION OFFICE, INTERNATIONAL SERVICES, CBC TRANSMISSION: Room: B52- 70, 1400 boulevard René Lévesque East, Montréal, Québec, H2L 2M2, Canada. Phone: +1 (514) 597-7618/19. Fax: +1 (514) 284 2052. Email: (Théorêt) gerald_theoret@radio-canada.ca; (Bouliane) jacques_bouliane@radio-canada.ca. Contact: (general) Gérald Théorêt, Frequency Manager, CBC Transmission Management; or Ms. Nicole Vincent, Frequency Management; (administration) Jacques Bouliane, Senior Manager, International Services. This office only for informing about transmitter-related problems (interference, modulation quality, etc.), especially by fax. Verifications not given out at this office; requests for verification should be sent to the main office, above.

TRANSMITTER SITE: CBC, P.O. Box 6131, Sackville New Brunswick, E4L 1G6, Canada. Phone: +1 (506) 536-2690/1.

Fax: +1 (506) 536 2342. Email: ray_bristol@cbc.ca. Contact: Raymond Bristol, Sackville Plant Manager, CBC Transmission. All correspondence not concerned with transmitting equipment should be directed to the appropriate address in Montréal, above. Free tours given during normal working hours.

MONITORING STATION: P.O. Box 460, Station Main Stittsville, Ontario, K2S 1A6, Canada. Phone: +1 (613) 831-4802. Fax: +1 (613) 831 0343. Email: derek.williams@cbc.ca. Contact: Derek Williams, Manager of Monitoring.

Radio Monte-Carlo Middle East (via Radio Canada International)—*see* France.

Shortwave Classroom, R. Tait McKenzie Public School, 175 Paterson Street, Almonte, Ontario, K0A 1A0, Canada. Phone: +1 (613) 256-8248. Fax: +1 (613) 256 4791. Email: carletonn@ucdsb.on.ca. Contact: Neil Carleton, VE3NCE, Editor & Publisher. *The Shortwave Classroom* newsletter was published three times per year as a nonprofit volunteer project for teachers around the world that use shortwave listening in the classroom, or as a club activity, to teach about global perspectives, media studies, world geography, languages, social studies and other subjects. Although no longer published, a set of back issues with articles and classroom tips from teachers around the globe is available for $10.

CENTRAL AFRICAN REPUBLIC   World Time +1

Radio Centrafrique, Radiodiffusion-Télévision Centrafricaine, B.P. 940, Bangui, Central African Republic. Contact: (technical) Jacques Mbilo, Directeur des Services Techniques; or Michèl Bata, Services Techniques. Replies on rare occasions to correspondence in French. Return postage required.

CHAD   World Time +1

Radiodiffusion Nationale Tchadienne—N'djamena, B.P. 892, N'Djamena, Chad. Contact: Djimadoum Ngoka Kilamian; or Ousmane Mahamat. Two IRCs or return postage required. Replies slowly to correspondence in French.

CHILE   World Time -3 (-4 midyear)

Radio Esperanza
OFFICE: Casilla 830, Temuco, Chile. Phone: +56 (45) 213-790. Phone/fax: +56 (45) 367-070. Email: esperanza@telsur.cl. Website: www.acym.cl/radio.htm. Contact: (general) Juanita Cárcamo, Departamento de Programación; Eleazar Jara, Dpto. de Programación; Ramón P. Woerner K., Publicidad; or Alberto Higueras Martínez, Locutor; (verifications) Rodolfo Campos, Director; Juanita Carmaco M., Dpto. de Programación; (technical) Juan Luis Puentes, Dpto. Técnico. Free pennants, stickers, bookmarks and tourist information. Two IRCs, $1 or 2 U.S. stamps appreciated. Replies, often slowly, to correspondence in Spanish or English.
STUDIO: Calle Luis Durand 03057, Temuco, Chile. Phone/fax: +56 (45) 240-161.

Radio Santa María (if reactivated), Apartado 1, Coyhaique, Chile. Phone: +56 (67) 232-398, +56 (67) 232-025 or +56 (67) 231-817. Fax: +56 (67) 231 306. Email: santamaria@ entelchile.net. Contact: Pedro Andrade Vera, Coordinador; Víctor Soto Guzmán, Director. $1 or return postage required. May send free tourist cards. Replies to correspondence in Spanish and Italian.

Radio Parinacota, Casilla 82, Arica, Chile. Phone: +56 (58) 245-889. Phone/Fax: +56 (58) 245 986. Email: rparinacota@

latinmail.com. Contact: Tomislav Simunovich Gran, Director.
Radio Triunfal Evangélica (if reactivated), Calle Las Araucarias 2757, Villa Monseñor Larrain, Talagante, Chile. Phone: +56 (1) 815-4765. Contact: Fernando González Segura, Obispo de la Misión Pentecostal Fundamentalista. Two IRCs required. Replies to correspondence in Spanish.

▣**Radio Voz Cristiana**
ENGINEERING DEPARTMENT: Ryder Street, West Bromwich, West Midlands B70 0EJ, United Kingdom. Phone: +44 (121) 522-6087. Fax: +44 (121) 522 6083. Email: andrewflynn@christianvision.com. Contact: Andrew Flynn, Head of Engineering.
TRANSMISSION FACILITIES: Casilla 395, Talagante, Santiago, Chile. Phone: (Engineering) +56 (2) 855-7046. Fax: +56 (2) 855 7053. Email: (Operations Manager) gisela@vozcristiana.cl; (Engineering) vozing@interaccess.cl; (Frequency Manager) andrewflynn@christianvision.com; (Administration) vozcrist@ interaccess.cl. Contact: Ms. Gisela Vergara, Operations Manager; or Antonio Reyes, Project Engineer. Free program and frequency schedules. Sometimes sends small souvenirs. All QSL requests should be sent to the Miami address, below.
PROGRAM PRODUCTION: P.O. Box 2889, Miami FL 33144 USA; or (street address) 15485 Eagle Nest Lane, Suite 220, Miami Lakes FL 33014 USA. Phone: +1 (305) 231-7704; (Portuguese Service) +1 (305) 231-7742. Fax: +1 (305) 231 7447. Email: (listener feedback) comentarios@vozcristiana.com; (González) david@vozcristiana.com; (Portuguese Service, including reception reports) altasondas@vozcrista.com. Web: (includes RealAudio) www.vozcristiana.com; (Portuguese, includes RealAudio) www.vozcrista.com. Contact: (administration) Juan Mark Gallardo, Director Regional; (technical and nontechnical) David González, Gerente de Programación. Verifies reception reports.

CHINA   World Time +8; still nominally +6 ("Urümqi Time") in the Xinjiang Uighur Autonomous Region, but in practice +8 is observed there, as well.

NOTE: China Radio International, the Central People's Broadcasting Station and certain regional outlets reply regularly to listeners' letters in a variety of languages. If a Chinese regional station does not respond to your correspondence within four months—and many will not, unless your letter is in Chinese or the regional dialect—try writing them c/o China Radio International.

▣**Central People's Broadcasting Station (CPBS)—China National Radio** (Zhongyang Renmin Guangbo Diantai), P.O. Box 4501, Beijing 100866, China. Phone: +86 (10) 6851-2435 or +86 (10) 6851-5522. Fax: +86 (10) 6851 6630. Email: zhangzr@mail.cnradio.com.cn. Web: (includes RealAudio) www.cnr.com.cn. Contact: Wang Changquan, Audience Department, China National Radio. Tape recordings of music and news $5 plus postage. CPBS T-shirts $10 plus postage; also sells ties and other items with CPBS logo. No credit cards. Free stickers, pennants and other small souvenirs. Return postage helpful. Responds regularly to correspondence in English and Standard Chinese (Mandarin). Although in recent years this station has officially been called "China National Radio" in English-language documents, all on- air identifications in Standard Chinese continue to be "Zhongyang Renmin Guangbo Dientai" (Central People's Broadcasting Station). To quote from the Website of China's State Administration of Radio, Film and TV: "The station moved to Beijing on March 25, 1949. It was renamed the Central People's Broadcasting Station (it [sic] English name was changed to China National Radio later on)..."

🖃**China Huayi Broadcasting Corporation**, P.O. Box 251, Fuzhou, Fujian 350001, China. Email: (station) fm1071@chbcnews.com; (Yuan Jia) chrisyuanjia@sohu.com; (Qiao Xiaoli, reception reports) 2883752@163.com, dxswl@21cn.com. Web: (includes Windows Media) www.chbcnews.com (or www.chbc.cn). Contact: Lin Hai Chun, Announcer; Qiao Xiaoli QSL Manager; Yuan Jia, Program Manager; or Wu Gehong. Replies to correspondence in English and Chinese. Reception reports can be sent to Qiao Xiaoli, Feng Jing Xin Cun 3-4-304, Changshu, Jiangsu 215500, China (although verifications are sometimes received direct from the station). Return postage necessary and recordings accepted.

China National Radio—*see* Central People's Broadcasting Station (CPBS), above.

🖃**China Radio International**
MAIN OFFICE, NON-CHINESE LANGUAGES SERVICE: 16A Shijingshan Street, Beijing 100040, China; or P.O. Box 4216, CRI-2 Beijing 100040 China. Phone: (Director's office) +86 (10) 6889-1625; (Audience Relations.) +86 (10) 6889-1617 or +86 (10) 6889-1652; (English newsroom/current affairs) +86 (10) 6889-1619; (Technical Director) +86 (10) 6609-2577. Fax: (Director's office) +86 (10) 6889 1582; (English Service) +86 (10) 6889 1378 or +86 (10) 6889 1379; (Audience Relations) +86 (10) 6889 3175; (administration) +86 (10) 6851 3174; (German Service) +86 (10) 6889 1941; (Spanish Service) +86 (10) 6889 1909. Email: (English) crieng@cri.com.cn; or msg@cri.com.cn; (Chinese) chn@cri.com.cn; (German) ger@box.cri.com.cn (*see* also the entry for the Berlin Bureau, below); (Japanese) jap@cri.com.cn; (Spanish) spa@cri.com.cn; ("Voices from Other Lands" program) voices@box.cri.com.cn. Web: (official, includes RealAudio) www.cri.com.cn; (unofficial, but regularly updated) http://pw2.netcom.com/~jleq/cri1.htm. Contact: Ms. Wang Anjing, Director of Audience Relations, English Service; Ying Lian, English Service; Shang Chunyan, "Listener's Garden"; Yu Meng, Editor; or Li Ping, Director of English Service; (administration) Li Dan, President, China Radio International; Xia Jixuan, Chen Minyi, Chao Tieqi and Wang Dongmei, Deputy Directors, China Radio International; Xin Liancai, Director International Relations, China Radio International. Free bi-monthly *Messenger* newsletter for loyal listeners, pennants, stickers, desk calendars, pins and handmade papercuts. Every year, China Radio International holds contests and quizzes, with the overall winner getting a free trip to China. T-shirts for $8. Two-volume, 820-page set of *Day-to-Day Chinese* language-lesson books $15, including postage worldwide; a 155-page book, *Learn to Speak Chinese: Sentence by Sentence*, plus two cassettes for $15. Two Chinese music tapes for $15. Various other books (on arts, medicine, Chinese idioms etc.) in English available from Audience Relations Department, English Service, China Radio International, 100040 Beijing, China. Payment by postal money order to Mr. Li Yi. Every year, the Audience Relations Department will renew the mailing list of the *Messenger* newsletter. CRI is also relayed via shortwave transmitters in Canada, Cuba, France, French Guiana, Mali, Russia and Spain.
FREQUENCY PLANNING DIVISION: Radio and Television of People's Republic of China, 2 Fuxingmenwai Street, Beijing 100866, China; or P.O. Box 2144, Beijing 100866, China. Phone: (Yang Minmin) +86 (10) 8609-2064; or (Zheng Shuguang & Pang Junhua) +86 (10) 8069-2120. Fax: +86 (10) 6609 2176. Email: (Yang Minmin) pdc@abrs.chinasartft. Contact: Ms. Yang Minmin, Manager, Frequency Coordination; Mr. Zheng Shuguang, Frequency Manager; or Ms. Pang Junhua, Frequency Manager.
MAIN OFFICE, CHINESE LANGUAGES SERVICE: China Radio International, Beijing 100040, China. Prefers correspondence in

Chinese (Mandarin).
MONITORING CENTER: 2 Fuxingmenwai Street, Beijing 100866, China or P.O Box 4502 Beijing 100866, China. Phone: +86 (10) 8609-1745/6. Fax: +86 (10) 8609 2176 or +86 (10) 8609 3269. Email: mc@chinasarft.gov.cn or jczhxjch@public.fhnet.cn.net. Contact: Ms. Zhang Wei, Chief Engineer, Monitoring Department; Zhao Chengping, Monitoring Manager; or Ms. Xu Tao, Deputy Director of Monitoring Department.
ARLINGTON NEWS BUREAU: 2000 South Eads Street APT#712, Arlington VA 22202 USA. Phone: +1 (703) 521-8689. Contact: Mr. Yongjing Li.
BERLIN BUREAU: Berliner Büro, Gürtelstr. 32 B, D-10247 Berlin, Germany. Phone: +49 (30) 2966-8998. Fax: +49 (30) 2966 8997. Email: deyubu@hotmail.com. Correspondence to CRI's German Service can be sent to this office.
CHINA (HONG KONG) NEWS BUREAU: 387 Queen's Road East, Room 1503, Hong Kong, China. Phone: +852 2834-0384. Contact: Ms. He Jincao.
JERUSALEM NEWS BUREAU: Flat 16, Hagdud Ha'ivri 12, Jerusalem 92345, Israel. Phone: +972 (2) 566-6084. Contact: Ms. Liu Suyun.
LONDON NEWS BUREAU: 13B Clifton Gardens, Golders Green, London NW11 7ER, United Kingdom. Phone: +44 (20) 8458-6943. Contact: Ms. Wu Manling.
NEW YORK NEWS BUREAU: 630 First Avenue #35K, New York NY 10016 USA. Fax: +1 (212) 889 2076. Contact: Mr Qian Jun.
SYDNEY NEWS BUREAU: Unit 53, Block A15 Herbert Street, St. Leonards NSW 2065, Australia. Phone: +61 (2) 9436-1493. Contact: Mr. Yang Binyuan.
SAN FRANCISCO OFFICE, SCHEDULES: 2654 17th Avenue, San Francisco CA 94116 USA. Phone: +1 (415) 564-9968. Email: GPoppin@aol.com. Contact: George Poppin. This address, a volunteer office, only provides CRI schedules to listeners. All other correspondence should be sent directly to the main office in Beijing.

Fujian People's Broadcasting Station, 2 Gutian Lu, Fuzhou, Fujian 350001, China. $1 or IRC helpful. Contact: Audience Relations. Replies occasionally and usually slowly. Prefers correspondence in Chinese.

Gannan People's Broadcasting Station, 49 Renmin Xije, Hezuo Zhen, Xiahe, Gian Su 747000, China. Verifies reception reports written in English. Return postage not required.

Gansu People's Broadcasting Station, 226 Donggang Xilu, Lanzhou 730000, China. Phone: +86 (931) 841-1054. Fax: +86 (931) 882 5834. Contact: Li Mei. IRC helpful.

Guangxi Foreign Broadcasting Station, 12 Min Zu Avenue, Nanning, Guangxi 530022, China. Phone: +86 (771) 585-4191, +86 (771) 585-4256 or +86 (771) 585-4403. Email: 101@gxfbs.com or 103@gxfbs.com; (Thanh Mai) thanhmai@gxfbs.com. Web: www.gxfbs.com. Contact: Thanh Mai, Vietnamese Section. Free stickers and handmade papercuts. IRC helpful. Replies irregularly. Broadcasts in Vietnamese and Cantonese to listeners in Vietnam.

Guangxi People's Broadcasting Station (if reactivated), 75 Min Zu Avenue, Nanning, Guangxi 530022, China. Email: gxbs@public.nn.gx.cn. Web: www.gxpbs.com. IRC helpful. Replies irregularly.

Guizhou People's Broadcasting Station (when operating), 259 Qingyun Lu, Guiyang, Guizhou 550002, China. Phone: +86 (851) 582-2495. Fax: +86 (851) 586 9983.

Heilongjiang People's Broadcasting Station, 181 Zhongshan Lu, Harbin, Heilongjiang 150001, China. Phone: +86 (451) 262-7454. Fax: +86 (451) 289 3539. Email: am621@sina.com. Web: www.am621.com.cn. $1 or return postage helpful.

Hubei People's Broadcasting Station, 563 Jiefang Dadao,

Wuhan, Hubei 430022, China.

Hunan People's Broadcasting Station, 27 Yuhua Lu, Changsha, Hunan 410007, China. Phone: +86 (731) 554-7202. Fax: +86 (731) 554 7220.

Jiangxi People's Broadcasting Station, 111 Hongdu Zhong Dadao, Nanchang, Jiangxi 330046, China. Email: gfzq@public.nc.jx.cn. Contact: Tang Ji Sheng, Editor, Chief Editor's Office. Free gold/red pins. Replies irregularly. Mr. Tang enjoys music, literature and stamps, so enclosing a small memento along these lines should help assure a speedy reply.

Nei Menggu (Inner Mongolia) People's Broadcasting Station, 19 Xinhua Darjie, Hohhot, Nei Menggu 010058, China. Web: www.nmrb.com.ch. Contact: Zhang Xiang-Quen, Secretary; or Liang Yan. Replies irregularly.

Qinghai People's Broadcasting Station, 96 Kunlun Lu, Xining, Qinghai 810001, China. Contact: Liqing Fangfang; or Ghou Guo Liang, Director, Technical Department. $1 helpful. Radio Television Hong Kong (when operating), C.P.O Box 70200, Kowloon, Hong Kong, China. Broadcasts weather reports for the South China Sea Yacht Race on even-numbered years, usually around late March, on 3940 kHz. Website for the race is: www.rhkyc.org.hk/chinasearace/home.htm. CAPE D'AGUILAR HF STATION: P.O. Box 9896, GPO Hong Kong, China. Phone: +825 2809- 2434. Fax: +825 2809 2434. Contact: Lam Chi Keung, Assistant Engineer. This station provides the transmission facilities for the weather reports on the South China Sea Yacht Race. See previous entry.

Sichuan People's Broadcasting Station, 119-1 Hongxing Zhonglu, Chengdu, Sichuan 610017, China. Web: www.swww.com.cn/scsb. Replies occasionally.

Voice of Jinling (Jinling zhi Sheng), P.O. Box 268, Nanjing, Jiangsu 210002, China. Fax: +86 (25) 413 235. Contact: Strong Lee, Producer/Host, "Window of Taiwan." Free stickers and calendars, plus Chinese-language color station brochure and information on the Nanjing Technology Import and Export Corporation. Replies to correspondence in Chinese and to simple correspondence in English. $1, IRC or 1 yuan Chinese stamp required for return postage.

Voice of Pujiang (Pujiang zhi Sheng), P.O. Box 3064, Shanghai 200002, China. Phone: +86 (21) 6208-2797. Fax: +86 (21) 6208 2850. Contact: Jiang Bimiao, Editor and Reporter.

Voice of the Strait (Haixia zhi Sheng), P.O. Box 187, Fuzhou, Fujian 350012, China. Email: vos@am666.net. Web: (includes RealAudio) www.vos.com.cn. Replies irregularly to correspondence in English.

Wenzhou People's Broadcasting Station, 19 Xianxue Qianlu, Wenzhou, Zhejiang 325000, China.

Xilingol People's Broadcasting Station, Xilin Dajie, Xilinhot, Nei Menggu 026000, China.

Xinjiang People's Broadcasting Station, 84 Tuanjie Lu, Urümqi, Xinjiang 830044, China. Email: mw738@21cn.com. Web: www.xjbs.com.cn. Contact: Zhao Ji-shu or Ms. Zhao Donglan, Editorial Office. Free tourist booklet, postcards and used Chinese stamps. Replies to correspondence in Chinese and to simple correspondence in English.

Xizang People's Broadcasting Station, 180 Beijing Zhonglu, Lhasa, Xizang 850000, China. Web: http://tibet.goldinfo. com.cn/diantai/diantai.htm. Contact: Lobsang Chonphel, Announcer; Tse Ring Yuzen, President; Tse Ring DeKy; or Miss Wenxin, host of "Tonight's Appointment" program. Free stickers and brochures. Enclosing an English-language magazine may help with a reply. Sometimes announces itself in English as "China Tibet Broadcasting Station" or "Tibet China Broadcasting Station."

Yunnan People's Broadcasting Station, 73 Renmin Xilu, Central Building of Broadcasting and TV, Kunming, 650031 Yunnan,

China. Phone: +86 (871) 531-0270. Fax: +86 (871) 531 0360. Contact: Sheng Hongpeng or F.K. Fan. Free Chinese-language brochure on Yunnan Province, but no QSL cards. $1 or return postage helpful. Replies occasionally.

Zhejiang People's Broadcasting Station, 111 Moganshan Lu, Hangzhou, Zhejiang 310005, China. Phone: +86 (571) 807-7050. Email: radiozjy@163.com. Contact: Yin Weiling, Editor.

CHINA (TAIWAN)   World Time +8

Central Broadcasting System (CBS), 55 Pei'an Road, Tachih, Taipei 104, Taiwan, Republic of China. Phone: +886 (2) 2591-8161 or +886 (2) 2885-6168. Email: cbs@cbs.org.tw. Web (includes RealAudio): www.cbs.org.tw. Contact: Lee Ming, Deputy Director. Free stickers.

China Radio, 53 Min Chuan West Road 9th Floor, Taipei 10418, Taiwan. Phone: +886 (2) 2598-1009. Fax: +886 (2) 2598 8348. Email: (Adams) readams@usa.net. Contact: Richard E. Adams, Station Director. Verifies reception reports. A religious broadcaster, sometimes referred to as "True Light Station," transmitting via leased facilities in Petropavlovsk-Kamchatskiy, Russia.

Radio Taiwan International (RTI), 55 Pei-an Road, Taipei 104, Taiwan, Republic of China. Phone: +886 (2) 2885-6168. Fax: +886 (2) 2886 2294. Email: cbs@cbs.org.tw. Web: (includes RealAudio and online reception report form) www.cbs.org.tw; (under construction) www.rti.org.tw. Contact: (general) Mei-yee Chao, Chief of Listeners' Service Section; (administration) Tenray Chou, Chairman; (technical) Peter Lee, Manager, Engineering Department. May send an annual diary, other publications or an occasional surprise gift. Broadcasts to the Americas are relayed via WYFR's Okeechobee site in the USA. Also uses relay facilities in France and the United Kingdom. Formerly known as Radio Taipei International.
BERLIN OFFICE: Postfach 30 92 43, D-10760 Berlin, Germany.
DAKAR OFFICE: B.P. 687, Dakar, Senegal.
HANOI OFFICE: G.P.O Box 104 Hanoi, Vietnam.
NEW DELHI OFFICE: P. O. Box 4914, Safdarjung Enclave, New Delhi, 110 029 India.
SURABAYA OFFICE: P.O. Box 1024, Surabaya, 60008 Indonesia.

Voice of Asia, P.O. Box 24-777, Taipei, Taiwan, Republic of China. Phone: +886 (2) 2771- 0151, X-2431. Fax: +886 (2) 2751 9277. Web: same as for Radio Taiwan International, above. As of June 2001, broadcasts only in Thai, although previous languages included English.

CLANDESTINE

Clandestine broadcasts are often subject to abrupt change or termination. Being operated by anti- establishment political and/or military organizations, these groups tend to be suspicious of outsiders' motives. Thus, they are more likely to reply to contacts from those who communicate in the station's native tongue, and who are perceived to be at least somewhat favorably disposed to their cause. Most will provide, upon request, printed matter on their cause, though not necessarily in English.

For more detailed information on clandestine stations, refer to the annual publication, *Clandestine Stations List*, about $10 or 10 IRCs postpaid by air, published by the Danish Shortwave Clubs International, Tavleager 31, DK-2670 Greve, Denmark; phone (Denmark) +45 4290-2900; fax (via Germany) +49 6371 71790; email 100413.2375@compuserve.com. For CIA media contact information, *see* USA. Available on the Internet, *The*

Clandestine Radio Intel Webpage specializes in background information on these stations and is organized by region and target country. The page can be accessed at: www.ClandestineRadio.com. Another informative Web page specializing in clandestine radio information and containing a twice monthly report on the latest news and developments affecting the study of clandestine radio is *Clandestine Radio Watch*, found at www.listen.to/qip.

"Al Asr Radio." Email: info@alasr-radio.com. Web: www.alasr-radio.com. Reception reports are best sent to: TDP, P.O. Box 1, 2310 Rijkevorsel, Belgium (*see*).

📻**"Arab Radio."** Web: (includes RealAudio and Windows Media) www.arabicsyradio.org. Successor to the former "Voice of the Homeland" and opposes the Syrian government.

"Ashur Radio" (also known as "Qala D Ashur" and "Voice of Zowaa"). Email: info@zowaa.com; or ashur@zowaa.com. Web: (Zowaa parent organization) www.zowaa.com. Supports the Assyrian Democratic Movement (Zowaa), and is believed to broadcast via facilities in Azerbaijan.

📻**"Ava-ye Ashena"** (if reactivated), Postfach 120228, D-10592 Berlin, Germany. Email: redaction@avayeashena.com; or webmaster@avayeashena.com. Web: (RealAudio) www.avayeashena.com.

📻**"Dat Radio."** Email: info@datradio.com. Web: (includes MP3) www.datradio.com. Opposed to Kazakstan president Nazarbayev.

📻**"Dejen Radio."** Email: (Ethiopian Commentator parent organization) articles@ethiopiancommentator.com. Web: (RealAudio) www.ethiopiancommentator.com/dejenradio/index2.html.

📻**"Democratic Voice of Burma"** ("Democratic Myanmar a-Than") *STATION:* DVB Radio, P.O. Box 6720, St. Olavs Plass, N-0130 Oslo, Norway. Phone: (Director/Chief Editor) +47 (22) 868-486; (Aministration) +47 (22) 868-472. Email: dvbburma@online.no. Web: (includes RealAudio) http://www.dvb.no. Contact: (general) Dr. Anng Kin, Listener Liaison; Aye Chan Naing, Daily Editor; or Thida, host for "Songs Request Program"; (administration) Harn Yawnghwe, Director; or Daw Khin Pyone, Manager; (technical) Saw Neslon Ku, Studio Technician; Petter Bernsten; or Technical Dept. Norwegian kroner requested for a reply, but presumably Norwegian mint stamps would also suffice. Programs produced by Burmese democratic movements, as well as professional and independent radio journalists, to provide informational and educational services for the democracy movement inside and outside Burma. Opposes the current Myanmar government. Transmitted originally via facilities in Norway, but more recently has broadcast from sites in Germany, Madagascar and Central Asia.

AFFINITY GROUPS:

BurmaNet. Email: (BurmaNet News editor, Free Burma Coalition, USA) strider@igc.apc.org; (Web coordinator, Free Burma Coalition, USA) freeburma@pobox.com. Web: (BurmaNet News, USA) http://sunsite.unc.edu/freeburma/listservers.html.

Free Burma Coalition, 1101 Pennsylvania Avenue SE #204, Washington DC 20003 USA Phone: +1 (202) 547-5985. Fax: +1 (202) 544 6118. Email: info@freeburmacoalition.org. Web: www.freeburmacoalition.org.

📻**"Fang Guang Ming Radio"**—successor to "World Falun Dafa Radio" and radio outlet of the Falun Gong movement. Email: editor@falundafaradio.org. Web: (parent organization) www.fgmtv.org; (RealAudio/MP3) www.falundafaradio.org. Reception reports are best sent to: TDP, P.O. Box 1, 2310 Rijkevorsel, Belgium (*see*).

📻**"Hmong Lao Radio,"** P.O. Box 6426, St. Paul MN 55106 USA. Phone: +1 (651) 292-0774. Email: webmaster@laohmongradio.org. Web: (includes Windows Media) www.laohmongradio.org.

"New Horizon" ("Chân Trói Mòi"). Email: ctm@radioctm.com. Nominally a Vietnamese Christian broadcast, and aired via the Jülich facilities of Germany's Deutsche Telekom (*see*). *JAPAN ADDRESS:* P.O. Box 48, Nishi Yodogawa, Osaka 555-8691, Japan. This office forwards reception reports and other correspondence to station personnel in the United States. $1 helpful.

"Information Radio" (when operating), 193rd Special Operations Wing, 81 Constellation Court, Middletown PA 17057 USA. Email: (Shank) edward.shank@paharr.ang.af.mil. Web: (193rd Special Operation Wing parent organization) www.paharr.ang.af.mil. Contact: Lt. Edward Shank, Public Affairs Officer. Psy-ops station operated by the 193rd Special Operations Wing of the Pennsylvania Air National Guard.

"Jakada Radio International" (when operating). Web: www.geocities.com/nac6015/webs/jakada. Headed by Yaro Yusufu Mamman, former Nigerian ambassador to Spain and the Vatican, and now chairman of Nigeria's Alliance for Democracy political party. Reception reports can be verified via TDP, P.O. Box 1, 2310 Rijkevorsel, Belgium (*see*).

"National Radio of the Democratic Saharan Arab Republic"—*see* Radio Nacional de la República Arabe Saharaui Democrática, Western Sahara.

"Qala D Ashur"—*see* "Ashur Radio"

📻**"Radio Anternacional,"** BM Box 1499, London WC1N 3XX, United Kingdom. Phone: +44 (20) 8962-2707. Fax: +44 (20) 8346 2203. Email: radio7520@yahoo.com; (Majedi) azarmajedi@yahoo.com. Web: (includes Windows Media) www.anternacional.org. Contact: Ms. Azar Majedi. A broadcast in Persian sponsored by the Committee for Humanitarian Assistance to Iranian Refugees (CHAIR) and aired via facilities in Moldova. Has ties to the Worker- Communist Party of Iran.

📻**"Radio Barabari"** (if reactived). Web: (includes RealAudio) www.radiobarabari.net.

"Radio Dat"—*see* "Dat Radio"

"Radio Free Afghanistan"—*see* USA.

"Radio Free Bougainville" (when operating), 2 Griffith Avenue, Roseville NSW 2069, Australia. Phone/fax: +61 (2) 9417-1066. Email: svoron@hotmail.com. Contact: Sam Voron, Australian Director. $5, AUS$5 or 5 IRCs required. Station is operated from Panguna, Central Bougainville by members of the Mekamui Defence Force led by Francis Ona. Opposed to the Papua New Guinea government.

"Radio Free Iraq"—*see* USA.

"Radio Free Lebanon"—*see* "Voice of Free Lebanon"

"Radio Freedom, Voice of the Ogadeni People"—*see* "Radio Xoriyo"

"Radio Independent Makumi" (when operating)—*see* "Radio Free Bougainville" (which is sometimes operated under this name) for contact details.

"Radio Insurgente" (when operating). Web: (under construction) www.radioinsurgente.org; (MP3 audio) http://chiapas.mediosindependientes.org; (EZLN parent organization) www.ezln.org. Station of the Ejército Zapatista de Liberación Nacional (Zapatista Army of National Liberation). *ZAPATISTA NATIONAL LIBERATION FRONT:* Frente Zapatista de Liberación Nacional, Zapotecos 7, Col. Obrera, 06800-México, D.F., Mexico. Phone/Fax: +52 (55) 5761-4236. Email: fzln@fzln.org.mx. Web: www.fzln.org.mx.

"Radio International"—*see* "Radio Anternacional"

📻**"Radio Justice,"** P.O. Box 60040, Washington DC 20039 USA.

Email: ethiopians@tisjd.net or tisforjd@aol.com. Web: (includes RealAudio) www.tisjd.net. Successor to the former "Radio Solidarity" and funded by the Tigrean International Solidarity for Justice and Democracy organization.

"Radio Komala," c/o Representation of Komala Abroad, Postfach 800272, D-51002 Köln, Germany. Email: komala_radio@hotmail.com; radiokomala@komala.org. Web: www.komala.org. Replies to correspondence in English. Komala, one of the founder members of the Communist Party of Iran in 1982, left that organization in 2000. It now refers to itself in English as the "Revolutionary Organization of the People of Kurdistan."

"Radio Kurdistan"—see Iraq

"Radio Nacional de la República Arabe Saharaui Democrática"—see Western Sahara.

"Radio New Sudan," SNA/SAF, Culture and Information Office, Neguse Street Nr. 6/8 (or P.O. Box 9257), Asmara, Eritrea. Email: infosaf@eol.com.er. Web: (Sudan Alliance Forces) www.safsudan.com. Contact: Amir Babkir, Sudan Alliance Forces Secretary for Culture and Information. The Sudan Alliance Forces are an opposition guerrilla army of ex-government northern soldiers, affiliated to the Asmara, Eritrea-based National Democratic Alliance (NDA). Opposes the current Sudan government. Claims to operate in liberated areas on the Sudanese side of the Sudan-Eritrea border, but actual site seems to be in Asmara, Eritrea. Formerly known as "Voice of Freedom and Renewal."

"Radio Payam-e Dost" (Bahá'í Radio International), P.O. Box 765, Great Falls VA 22066 USA. Phone: +1 (703) 671-8888. Fax: +1 (301) 292 6947. Email: payam@bahairadio.org. Web: www.bahairadio.org.

"Radio Rainbow" ("Kestedamena rediyo ye selamena yewendimamach dimtse"), c/o RAPEHGA, P.O. Box 140104, D-53056 Bonn, Germany. Contact: T. Assefa. Supposedly operated by an Ethiopian opposition group called Research and Action Group for Peace in Ethiopia and the Horn of Africa. Broadcasts via hired shortwave transmitters in Germany.

"Radio Rhino International-Africa," Voice of the Voiceless International-Uganda, c/o Allerweltshaus, Koernerstr. 77-79, D-50823 Koeln, Germany. Phone: +49 (162) 885-4486. Fax: +49 (221) 991 2907. Email: mail@radiorhino.org. Web: (includes MP3) www.radiorhino.org. Contact: Godfrey Elum Ayoo, Manager. Opposes Ugandan president Yoweri Museveni.

"Radio Sedaye Iran"—see KRSI, USA.

"Radio Station Freedom, Voice of the Communist Party of Iraqi Kurdistan" ("Era ezgay azadiya, dengi hizbi shuyu'i kurdistani iraqa").

KURDISTAN COMMUNIST PARTY-IRAQ (KCPI) PARENT ORGANIZATION: Web: http://user.tninet.se/~lto357q/framse4.

"Radio Voice of Hope"—see Netherlands.

"Radio Voice of the Mojahed"—see "Voice of the Mojahed," later in this section.

"Radio Voice of the People." Email: voxpop@zol.co.zw (if this fails, try the online email form). Web: www.voxpop.co.zw. Airs via Radio Nederland facilities in Madagascar and is opposed to Zimbabwean president Mugabe.

MOVEMENT FOR DEMOCRATIC CHANGE PARENT ORGANIZATION: Harvest House, 6th Floor, N.Mandela Ave/Angwa St, Harare, Zimbabwe. Phone: +263 (91) 367-151/2/3 or +263 (4) 781-138/9. Email: support@mdc.co.zw. Web: www.mdczimbabwe.com.

"Radio VOP"—see "Radio Voice of the People," above.

"Radio Xoriyo," ("Halkani wa Radio Xoriyo, Codkii Ummadda Odageniya"). Email: radioxoriyo@ogaden.com; or ogaden@yahoo.com (some verifications received from these addresses). Web: (includes RealAudio) www.ogaden.com/

Radio_Freedom.htm. Broadcasts are supportive of the Ogadenia National Liberation Front, and hostile to the Ethiopian government. Transmits via facilities of Germany's Deutsche Telekom (see).

"Republic of Iraq Radio, Voice of the Iraqi People" ("Idha'at al-Jamahiriya al-Iraqiya, Saut al-Sha'b al-Iraqi"). Anti-Saddam Hussein "black" clandestine supported by CIA, British Intelligence, the Gulf Cooperation Council and Saudi Arabia. The name of this station has changed periodically since its inception during the Gulf crisis. Via transmitters in Saudi Arabia.

SPONSORING ORGANIZATION: Iraqi National Congress, 17 Cavendish Square, London W1M 9AA, United Kingdom. Phone: +44 (20) 7665-1812; (office in Arbil, Iraq) +873 (682) 346-239. Fax: +44 (20) 7665 1201; (office in Arbil, Iraq) +873 (682) 346 240. Email: pressoffice@inc.org.uk. Web: www.inc.org.uk.

"SW Radio Africa"

UNITED KINGDOM OFFICE: Phone: +44 (20) 8387-1441. Email: (general) views@swradioafrica.com; (technical) tech@swradioafrica.com. Web: (includes Windows Media) www.swradioafrica.com. Zimbabwe's only independent voice. Programs are produced in London and aired 3 hours daily (1600-1900 UTC) into Zimbabwe via a shortwave transmitter and streamed via the website. Programme archives held for 2 weeks. Run by exiled Zimbabweans and opposes the Mugabe government.

"Voice of Biafra International," 733 15th Street NW, Suite 700, Washington DC 20005 USA. Phone: +1 (202) 347-2983. Email: biafrafoundation@yahoo.com; (Nkwocha) oguchi@pacbell.net; oguchi@mbay.net. Web (includes Windows Media): www.biafraland.com/vobi.htm. Contact: Oguchi Nkwocha, M.D.; or Chima Osondu. A project of the Biafra Foundation, Ekwe Nche and the Biafra Actualization Forum.

"Voice of China" ("Zhongguo zhi Yin"), P.O. Box 273538, Concord CA 94527 USA; or (sponsoring organization) Foundation for China in the 21st Century, P.O. Box 11696, Berkeley CA 94701 USA. Web: www.china21century.org/default. asp?menu=xu (click on "VOC"). Contact: Lily Hu, Executive Director. Financial support from the Foundation for China in the 21st Century. Has "picked up the mission" of the earlier Voice of June 4th, but has no organizational relationship with it. Transmits via facilities of the Central Broadcasting System, Taiwan (see).

"Voice of Democratic Eritrea" ("Sawt Eritrea al-Dimuqratiya-Sawtu Jabhat al-Tahrir al- Eritrea"), ELF-RC, Postfach 200434, D-53134 Bonn, Germany. Alternative address: Postfach 1946, D-65409 Ruesselheim, Germany. Phone: +49 (228) 356-181. Email: (Eritrean political opposition) meskerem@erols.com. Web: (includes RealAudio) www.meskerem.net. Contact: Seyoum O. Michael, Member of Executive Committee, ELF-RC; or Neguse Tseggon. Station of the Eritrean Liberation Front-Revolutionary Council, hostile to the government of Eritrea. Transmits via facilities of Deutsche Telekom (see), in Germany.

"Voice of Ethiopia." Email: info@democracyfrontiers.org. Web: www.democracyfrontiers.org. Opposes the Ethiopian government. Reception reports can be sent to: TDP, P.O. Box 1, 2310 Rijkevorsel, Belgium (see).

"Voice of Ethiopian Medhin," P.O. Box 7968, Washington, DC 20044 USA Phone: +1 (301) 565-4011. Fax: +1 (301) 565 4031. Web: (includes RealAudio) www.medhin.com. Broadcast produced by overseas members of the Ethiopian Medhin Democratic Party based in the USA, a broad-based coalition of Ethiopians aiming to democratize their country.

MEDHIN GERMAN BRANCH: Postfach 111423, D-60049 Frankfurt/Main, Germany.

"Voice of Ethiopian Unity"—*see* "Voice of the Democratic Path of Ethiopian Unity."

"Voice of Free Lebanon" ("Sawt lubnan al-hurriyah"), Rassemblement Pour Le Liban, 63 Rue Sainte Anne, F-75002 Paris, France. Phone: +33 (1) 4015-0652. Fax: +33 (1) 4015 0552. Email: radio@tayyar.org. Web: www.tayyar.org. Radio outlet of former Army Commander Michel Awn's Free Patriotic Movement.

"Voice of Iranian Kurdistan" ("Seda-ye Kordestan-e Iran")— Contact one of the PDKI (Democratic Party of Iranian Kurdistan parent organization) offices, below.

PDKI INTERNATIONAL BUREAU: AFK, Boite Postale 102, F-75623 Paris Cedex 13, France. Phone: +33 (1) 4585-6431. Fax: +33 (1) 4585 2093. Email: pdkiran@club-internet.fr; Web: www.pdk-iran.org.

PDKI AUSTRALIAN BUREAU: Web: www.pdkiran.org.

PDKI CANADA BUREAU: P.O. Box 29010, London, Ontario N6K 4L9, Canada. Phone/fax: +1 (519) 680-7784. Email: pdkiontario@pdki.org. Web: www.pdki.org.

PDKI REPRESENTATIVE IN USA: Email: pdkiusa@pdki.org.

"Voice of Iraqi Kurdistan"—*see* Iraq.

"Voice of Jammu Kashmir Freedom" ("Sada-i Hurriyat-i Jammu Kashmir"), P.O. Box 102, Muzaffarabad, Azad Kashmir, via Pakistan. Contact: Islam-ud Din Butt. Pro-Moslem and favors Azad Kashmiri independence from India. Believed to transmit via facilities in Pakistan. Return postage not required. *HARKAT-UL-MUJAHIDEEN SPONSORING ORGANIZATION:* Email: info@harkatulmujahideen.org. Web: www.ummah.net.pk/harkat.

"Voice of Khmer Krom," P.O. Box 121, Pensauken NJ 08110 USA. Email: vokk@khmerkrom.org. Web: (includes RealAudio) http://radio.khmerkrom.org. Targeted at the inhabitants of what used to be South Vietnam, and aired via facilities in Central Asia. Reception reports can be verified from: TDP, P.O. Box 1, 2310 Rijkevorsel, Belgium (*see*).

"Voice of Komalah" ("Seda-ye Komalah"). Email: radiokom@radiokomaleh.com. Web: (includes RealAudio) www.radiokomaleh.com. Station of the Kurdish branch of the Communist Party of Iran.

KOMALAH PARENT ORGANIZATION (KURDISTAN): Email: komalah@hotmail.com.

SWEDISH OFFICE: P.O. Box 750 26, Uppsala, Sweden. Phone/fax: +46 (18) 468-493. Email: komala@cpiran.org.

"Voice of Kurdistan Toilers" ("Aira dengi zahmatkishan-e kurdistana")

KURDISTAN TOILERS PARTY PARENT ORGANIZATION: Email: info@ktp.nu. Web: www.ktp.nu.

"Voice of Mesopotamia" ("Dengê Mezopotamya"), Phone: +32 (53) 648-827/29. Fax: +32 (53) 641 215. Email: info@denge-mezopotamya.com. Web: www.denge-mezopotamya.com. Contact: Ahmed Dicle, Director.

KURDISTAN WORKERS PARTY (PKK, also known as Kadek) SPONSORING ORGANIZATION: Email: serxwebun@serxwebun.com. Web: www.pkk.org.

ADDRESS FOR RECEPTION REPORTS: TDP, P.O. Box 1, 2310 Rijkevorsel, Belgium (*see*).

"Voice of National Salvation" ("Gugugui Sori Pangsong") (if reactivated), Grenier Osawa 107, 40 Nando-cho, Shinjuku-ku, Tokyo, Japan. Phone: + 81 (3) 5261-0331. Fax: +81 (3) 5261 0332. Email: (National Democratic Front of South Korea parent organization) kuguk@alles.or.jp. Web: (National Democratic Front of South Korea parent organization) www.alles.or.jp/~kuguk. Pro- North Korea, pro-Korean unification, and supported by the North Korean government. Via transmitters located in Pyongyang, Haeju and Wongsan. On the air since 1967,

but not always under the same name, the station suspended transmissions on July 31, 2003, expecting a *quid pro quo* from South Korea. When this didn't appear, transmissions were resumed on August 15, consisting of relays from Pyongyang's Korean Central Broadcasting Station, and announcing as "Pyongyang branch of Korean National Democratic Front."

TOKYO OFFICE: NDFSK, Greneir Osawa 107, 40 Nando-cho, Shinjuku-ku, Tokyo, Japan. Phone: +81 (3) 5261-0331. Fax: +81 (3) 5261 0332. Email: ndfsk@campus.ne.jp. Web: www.ndfsk.dyn.to.

PYONGYANG OFFICE: NDFSK Mission in Pyongyang, Munsudong, Taedonggang District, Pyongyang, Democratic People's Republic of Korea. Phone: +850 (2) 381-4292. Fax: +850 (2) 381 4505 (valid only in those countries with direct telephone service to North Korea). Email: ndfskpy@campus.ne.jp.

"Voice of Oromiyaa" ("Sagalee Oromiyaa"). Email: sagaloromo@aol.com. Web: (includes RealAudio) www.voiceoforomiyaa.com.

"Voice of Oromo Liberation" ("Sagalee Bilisummaa Oromoo"), Postfach 510610, D-13366 Berlin, Germany; or SBO, Prinzenallee 81, D-13357 Berlin, Germany. Phone: +49 (30) 494- 1036. Fax: +49 (30) 494 3372. Email: sbo13366@aol.com. Web: (includes RealAudio) www.oromoliberationfront.org/sbo.html. Contact: Taye Teferah, European Coordinator. Occasionally replies to correspondence in English or German. Return postage required. Station of the Oromo Liberation Front of Ethiopia, an Oromo nationalist organization. Via Deutsche Telekom facilities in Germany.

OROMO LIBERATION FRONT USA OFFICE: P.O. Box 73247, Washington DC 20056 USA. Phone: +1 (202) 462-5477. Fax: +1 (202) 332 7011.

"Voice of Palestine, Voice of the Palestinian Islamic Revolution" ("Saut al-Filistin, Saut al- Thowrah al-Islamiyah al-Filistiniyah")—for many years considered a clandestine station, but is now officially listed as part of the Arabic schedule of the Voice of the Islamic Republic of Iran, over whose transmitters the broadcasts are aired. *See* "Iran" for potential contact information. Supports the Islamic Resistance Movement, Hamas, which is anti-Arafat and anti-Israel.

"Voice of Reform" ("Sawt al-Islah"), BM Box: MIRA, London WC1N 3XX, United Kingdom. Phone: +44 (208) 452-0303. Fax: +44 (208) 452 0808. Email: info@islah.org. Web: (RealAudio only) www.myislah.org/radio/newradio.htm. Opposes the government of Saudi Arabia.

"Voice of Southern Azerbaijan" ("Güney Azerbaycan Sesi Radiosu") (when operating). Email: info@cehreganli.com. Web: (includes MP3) www.cehreganli.com/media/radio.html. Supports autonomy for Iran's Southern Azerbaijan province, and broadcasts from within Azerbaijan.

"Voice of the Communist Party of Iraqi Kurdistan"—*see* "Radio Station Freedom"

"Voice of the Communist Party of Iran" ("Seda-ye Hezb-e Komunist-e Iran")

COMMUNIST PARTY OF IRAN SPONSORING ORGANIZATION: C.D.C.R.I., Box 704 45, S- 107 25 Stockholm, Sweden. Phone/fax: +46 (8) 786-8054. Email: cpi@cpiran.org. Web: www.cpiran.org.

"Voice of the Democratic Path of Ethiopian Unity," Finote Democracy, P.O. Box 88675, Los Angeles CA 90009 USA. Email: efdpu@finote.org. Web: (includes RealAudio) www.finote.org. Transmits via German facilities of Deutsche Telekom (*see*).

EUROPEAN ADDRESS: Finote Democracy, Postbus 10573, 1001 EN, Amsterdam, Netherlands.

"Voice of the Iraqi People" (when operating), BM Al-Tariq, London WC1N 3XX, United Kingdom. Web: www.iraqcp.org/

radicp; (RealAudio) http://icp42.tripod.com/icpradio; (Iraqi Communist Party sponsoring organization) www.iraqcp.org. Not to be confused with "Republic of Iraq Radio, Voice of the Iraqi People" (see).

"Voice of the Islamic Revolution in Iraq," P.O. Box 11365/738, Tehran, Iran; P.O. Box 37155/146, Qom, Iran; or P.O. Box 36802, Damascus, Syria. Anti-Saddam Hussain, and supported by the Shi'ite-oriented Supreme Assembly of the Islamic Revolution of Iraq, led by Mohammed Baqir al-Hakim. Supported by the Iranian government and transmitted via facilities of Islamic Republic of Iran Broadcasting.
SPONSORING ORGANIZATION: Supreme Council for Islamic Revolution in Iraq (SCIRI), 27a Old Gloucester St, London WC1N 3XX, United Kingdom. Phone: +44 (20) 7371-6815. Fax: +44 (20) 7371 2886. Email: info@nidaa-arrafidain.com Web: www.nidaa-arrafidain.com.

"Voice of the Kurdistan People"—*see* Iraq.

☞**"Voice of the Mojahed"** (Seda-ye Mojahed)
Email: (People's Mojahedin Organization of Iran parent organization) mojahed@mojahedin.org. Web: (includes Windows Media) www.mojahedin.org/Pages/seda1/f_seda1.html; (RealAudio only) www.mojahedin.org/Pages/seda; (People's Mojahedin Organization of Iran parent organization) www.mojahedin.org. The main European office of the People's Mojahedin Organization of Iran was raided and closed by the French authorities in 2003, after the organization was classified as "terrorist." However, the PMOI Website was not closed down and continued to operate, albeit with limited functionality.
COLOGNE BUREAU: (if still functioning) Voice of the Mojahed, c/o Heibatollahi, Postfach 502107, 50981 Köln, Germany.

☞**"Voice of the Worker"** ("Seda-ye Kargar"). Web: (includes historical archives in TrueSpeech) www.kvwpiran.org.
WORKER-COMMUNIST PARTY OF IRAN (WPI) PARENT ORGANIZATION: Email: wpi@wpiran.org. Web: www.wpiran.org.
WPI INTERNATIONAL OFFICE: WPI, Office of International Relations, Suite 730, 28 Old Brompton Road, South Kensington, London SW7 3SS, United Kingdom. Phone: +44 (77) 7989- 8968. Fax: +44 (87) 0136 2182. Email: wpi.international.office@ukonline.co.uk.

"Voice of the Worker-Communist Party of Iraq" (Aira dangi kizb-e communist-e kargar-e iraqa") (when operating), WCPI Radio, Zargata, Sulaimania, Iraq. Email: radio@wpiraq.org; (WPCI parent organization) jamal@wpiraq.org. Web: (WCPI parent organization) www.wpiraq.org. Station of the Worker-Communist Party of Iraq.
WCPI CANADIAN OFFICE: P.O. Box 491, Don Mills Postal Station, North York, Ontario M3C 2T4, Canada.
WCPI GERMAN OFFICE: A.K.P.I., Postfach 160244, D-10336 Berlin, Germany.
WCPI SWEDISH OFFICE: W.P.C.I., Box 1211, SE-17224, Sundbyberg, Sweden.

☞**"Voice of Tibet"**
ADMINISTRATIVE OFFICE: Welhavensgate 1, N-0166 Oslo, Norway. Phone: (administration) +47 2211-2700; (studio) +47 2211-1209. Fax: +47 2211 5474. Email: voti@online.no; (Norbu) votibet@online.no. Web: (includes RealAudio) www.vot.org. Contact: Øystein Alme, Project Manager [sometimes referred to as "Director"]; or Chophel Norbu, Project Coordinator.
MAIN EDITORIAL OFFICE: Voice of Tibet, Editor-in-Chief, Narthang Building, Gangchen, Kyishong, Dharamsala-176 215 H.P., India. Phone: +91 (1892) 228-179 or +91 (1892) 222 384. Fax: +91 (1892) 24913. Email: vot@nde.vsnl.net.in. Contact: Sonam Dargyay. A joint venture of the Norwegian Human Rights House, Norwegian Tibet Committee and World-View International. Programs focus on Tibetan culture, education, human rights and news from Tibet. Opposed to Chinese control of Tibet. Those seeking a verification for this program should enclose a prepared card or letter. Return postage helpful. Verifications have been received from both addresses. Broadcasts via transmitters in the former Soviet Union.

"Voice of Zowaa"—*see* "Ashur Radio"

"Voz de la Resistencia" Email: (FARC-EP parent organization) farc-ep@ comision.internal.org; or elbarcino@laneta.apc.org (updated transmission schedules and QSLs available from this address, but correspond in Spanish). Web: www.resistencianacional.org/radio.htm; www.radioresistencia.com; (FARC-EP parent organization) http://burn.ucsd.edu/~farc-ep. Contact: Olga Lucía Marín, Comisión Internacional de las FARC-EP. Station of the Fuerzas Armadas Revolucionarias de Colombia - Ejercito del Pueblo.

COLOMBIA   World Time -5

NOTE: Colombia, the country, is always spelled with two o's. It should never be written as "Columbia."

Alcaravan Radio—*see* La Voz de Tu Conciencia.

☞**Caracol Colombia** (if reactivated)
MAIN OFFICE: Apartado Aéreo 9291, Santafé de Bogotá, D.C., Colombia. Phone: +57 (1) 337- 8866. Fax: +57 (1) 337 7126. Web: (includes RealAudio) www.caracol.com.co/webasp2/homeneo.asp. Contact: Hernán Peláez Restrepo, Jefe Cadena Básica; Efraín Jiménez, Director de Operaciones; or Oscar López M., Director Musical. Free stickers. Replies to correspondence in Spanish and English.
MIAMI OFFICE: 2100 Coral Way, Miami FL 33145 USA. Phone: +1 (305) 285-2477 or +1 (305) 285-1260. Fax: +1 (305) 858 5907.

Caracol Florencia (if reactivated), Apartado Aéreo 465, Florencia, Caquetá, Colombia. Phone: +57 (88) 352-199. Contact: Guillermo Rodríguez Herrera, Gerente; or Vicente Delgado, Operador. Replies occasionally to correspondence in Spanish.

Caracol Villavicencio—*see* La Voz de los Centauros.

Ecos del Atrato (when operating), Apartado Aéreo 196, Quibdó, Chocó, Colombia. Phone: +57 (49) 711-450. Contact: Absalón Palacios Agualimpia, Administrador. Free pennants. Replies to correspondence in Spanish.

La Voz de la Selva—*see* Caracol Florencia.

La Voz de Tu Conciencia, Colombia para Cristo, Apartado Aéreo 95300, Santafé de Bogotá, D.C., Colombia. Phone: +57 (1) 338-4716. Email: info@fuerzadepaz.com. Web: www.fuerza de paz.com/emisoras.asp. Contact: Martin Stendal, Administrador. Station is actually located in Puerto Lleras, in the guerrilla "combat zone." Sometimes carries programming from sister station Alcaravan Radio (1530 kHz).

La Voz de los Centauros (Caracol Villavicencio), Cra. 31 No. 37-71 Of. 1001, Villavicencio, Meta, Colombia. Phone: +57 (986) 214-995; (technical) +57 (986) 662-3666. Fax: +57 (986) 623 954. Contact: Carlos Torres Leyva, Gerencia; or Olga Arenas, Administradora. Replies to correspondence in Spanish.

La Voz del Guaviare, Carrera 22 con Calle 9, San José del Guaviare, Colombia. Phone: +57 (986) 840-153/4. Fax: +57 (986) 840 102. Contact: Luis Fernando Román Robayo, Director General. Replies slowly to correspondence in Spanish.

La Voz del Llano (if reactivated), Calle 41B No. 30-11, Barrio La Grama, Villavicencio, Meta, Colombia; or (postal address in Bogotá) Apartado Aéreo 67751, Santafé de Bogotá, Colombia. Phone: +57 (986) 624-102. Fax: +57 (986) 625 045. Contact: Manuel Buenaventura, Director; Rafael Rodríguez R., or Edgar Valenzuela Romero. Replies occasionally to correspondence in Spanish. $1 or return postage necessary.

Ondas del Orteguaza, Calle 16, No. 12-48, piso 2, Florencia, Caquetá, Colombia. Phone: +57 (88) 352-558. Contact: Sandra Liliana Vásquez, Secretaria; Señora Elisa Viuda de Santos; or Henry Valencia Vásquez. Free stickers. IRC, return postage or $1 required. Replies occasionally to correspondence in Spanish.

Radio Auténtica, Calle 38 No. 32-41, piso 7, Edif. Santander, Villavicencio, Meta, Colombia. Phone: +57 (986) 626-780. Phone/fax: +57 (986) 624-507. Web: (Cadena Radial Auténtica de Colombia parent organization) www.cmb.org.co/cra. Contact: (general) Pedro Rojas Velásquez; or Carlos Alberto Pimienta, Gerente; (technical) Sra. Alba Nelly González de Rojas, Administradora. Sells religious audio cassettes for 3,000 pesos. Return postage required. Replies slowly to correspondence in Spanish.

Radiodifusora Nacional de Colombia (when active)
MAIN ADDRESS: Edificio Inravisión, CAN, Av. Eldorado, Santafé de Bogotá, D.C., Colombia. Phone: +57 (1) 222-0415. Fax: +57 (1) 222 0409 or +57 (1) 222 8000. Email: radio_oc@inravision.com.gov; radiodifusora@hotmail.com. Web: (includes online reception report form) www.inravision.gov.co/seccionradiodifusora/onda1.htm. Contact: Janeth Jiménez M., Coordinadora de Onda Corta; or Dra. Athala Morris, Directora. Free lapel badges, membership in Listeners' Club and monthly program booklet.

CONGO (DEMOCRATIC REPUBLIC)
(formerly Zaïre)

World Time +1 Western, including Kinshasa; +2 Eastern

Radio Bukavu (when active), B.P. 475, Bukavu, Democratic Republic of the Congo. $1 or return postage required. Replies slowly. Correspondence in French preferred.

Radio CANDIP, B.P. 373, Bunia, Democratic Republic of Congo. Letters should preferably be sent via registered mail. $1 or return postage required. Correspondence in French preferred.

Radio Kahuzi, c/o AIMServe, Box 63435 (BUKAVU), Nairobi, Kenya. Email: besi@alltell.net. Contact: Richard & Kathy McDonald.

Radio Lubumbashi, B.P. 7296, Lubumbashi, Democratic Republic of the Congo. Letters should be sent via registered mail. $1 or 3 IRCs helpful. Correspondence in French preferred.

Radio Okapi
Email: info@monuc.org. Web: (includes Windows Media) www.monuc.org/radio. A joint project involving the United Nations Mission in the Democratic Republic of the Congo (MONUC) and the Swiss-based Fondation Hirondelle.
MONUC PUBLIC INFORMATION OFFICES:
(USA) P.O. Box 4653, Grand Central Station, New York NY 10163-4653 USA. Phone: +1 (212) 963-0103. Fax: +1 (212) 963 0205.
(Congo) 12 Av. des Aviateurs, Kinshasa, Gombe, Democratic Republic of the Congo; or B.P. 8811, Kinshasa 1, Democratic Republic of the Congo. Phone: +39 0831 24 5000, X-56372 or X- 56374. Contact: Georges Schleger, VE2EK, Communications Officer & Head of Technical Services.
FONDATION HIRONDELLE: 3, Rue Traversière, CH 1018-Lausanne, Switzerland. Phone: +41 (21) 647- 2805. Fax: +41 (21) 647 4469. Email: info@hirondelle.org.

Radio-Télévision Nationale Congolaise, B.P. 3171, Kinshasa-Gombe, Democratic Republic of the Congo. Letters should be sent via registered mail. $1 or 3 IRCs helpful. Correspondence in French preferred.

CONGO (REPUBLIC)   World Time +1

Radiodiffusion Nationale Congolaise (also announces as "Radio Nationale" or "Radio Congo"), Radiodiffusion-Télévision Congolaise, B.P. 2241, Brazzaville, Congo. Email: (technical) actu_rtnc@hotmail.com. Contact: Roger Olingou. Return postage required, but smallest denomination currency notes (e.g. $1US or 1 euro) reportedly cannot be changed into local currency. Replies irregularly to letters in French (and sometimes English) sent via registered mail.
ALTERNATIVE ADDRESS FOR RECEPTION REPORTS: Direction Générale de Télédiffusion du Congo, B.P. 2912, Brazzaville, Congo. Phone: +242 810-608. Contact: Jean Medard Bokatola.

COSTA RICA   World Time -6

Faro del Caribe—TIFC, Apartado 2710, 1000 San José, Costa Rica. Phone: +506 226-4358, +506 227-5048, +506 286-1755. Fax: +506 227-1725. Email: tifc@farodelcaribe.org, tifccr@racsa.co.cr, radio@farodelcaribe.org; (technical) tecnico@farodelcaribe.org. Web: (includes Real Audio) www.farodelcaribe.org. Contact: Carlos A. Rozotto Piedrasanta, Director Administrativo; or Mauricio Ramires; (technical) Minor Enrique, Station Engineer. Free stickers, pennants, books and bibles. $1 or IRCs helpful.
U.S. OFFICE, NONTECHNICAL: Misión Latinoamericana, P.O. Box 620485, Orlando FL 32862 USA.

Radio Casino, Apartado 287, 7301 Puerto Limón, Costa Rica. Phone: +506 758-0029. Fax: +506 758 3029. Contact: Edwin Zamora, Departamento de Notícias; or Luis Grau Villalobos, Gerente; (technical) Ing. Jorge Pardo, Director Técnico; or Geraldo Moya, Técnico.

Radio Exterior de España—Cariari Relay Station, Cariari de Pococí, Costa Rica. Phone: +506 767-7308 or +506 767-7311. Fax: +506 225 2938.

Radio For Peace International (RFPI), P.O. Box 75, Cuidad Colón, Costa Rica. Phone: +506 249-1821. Fax: +506 249 1095. Email: info@rfpi.org; rfpiradio@yahoo.com. Web: (includes RealAudio and MP3) www.rfpi.org. Contact: James Latham, CEO; Naomi Fowler, Program Director or Emily Morales, Operations Manager. Broadcasts independently produced programming 24 hours a day on issues of social justice and human rights. Replies sometimes slow in coming because of the mail. Monthly RFPI newsletter online, which includes schedules and program information, $40 annual membership ($50 family/organization) in "Friends of Radio for Peace International," station commemorative T-shirts and rain forest T-shirts $20; (VISA/MC). As a totally independent radio station, RFPI actively solicits listener contributions. Free online verification of email reports, but $1 or 3 IRCs required for verification by QSL card. Runs a unique 4 week intensive Peace Journalism course with an option to remain longer and volunteer (information on the www.rfpi.org).
U.S. OFFICE: P.O. Box 3165, Newberg OR 97132-3165 USA. Email: radioforpeace@yahoo.com. T-shirts and other merchandise can be purchased from this address.

Radio Reloj (if reactivated), Sistema Radiofónico H.B., Apartado Postal 341-1000, San José, Costa Rica. Phone: +506 286-2636. Fax: +506 226 5579. Email: info@radioreloj.co.cr. Web: (includes live audio, but registration required) www.radioreloj.co.cr. Contact: Roger Barahona, Gerente; or Francisco Barahona Gómez. Can be very slow in replying. $1 required.

Radio Universidad de Costa Rica, Apartado 1-06, 2060 Universidad de Costa Rica, San Pedro de Montes de Oca, San José, Costa Rica. Phone: (general) +506 207-4727; (studio) +506 225- 3936. Fax: +506 207 5459. Email: radioucr@cariari.ucr.ac.cr. Web: http://cariari.ucr.ac.cr/~radioucr/radioucr. Contact: Marco González Muñoz; Henry Jones, Locutor de Planta; or Nora Garita B., Directora. Marco González is a radio amateur, call-sign TI3AGM. Free postcards, station brochure and stickers. Replies slowly to correspondence in Spanish or English. $1 or return postage required.
University Network—*see* USA.

CROATIA   World Time +1 (+2 midyear)

Croatian Radio-Television (Hrvatska Radio-Televizija, HRT)
MAIN OFFICE: Hrvatska Radio-Televizija (HRT), Prisavlje 3, HR-10000 Zagreb, Croatia. Phone: (operator) +385 (1) 634-3366; (Managing Director) +385 (1) 634-3308; (Technical Director) +385 (1) 634-3663. Fax: (Technical Director) +385 (1) 634 3636. Email: (Managing Director) i.lucev@hrt.hr; (Technical Director) nikola.percin@hrt.hr; (technical, including reception reports) z.klasan@hrt.hr. Web: (includes RealAudio) www.hrt.hr. Contact: (general) Ivanka Lucev, Managing Director; (Technical Director) Nikola Percin.
TRANSMITTING STATION DEANOVEC: P.O Box 3, 10313 Graberje Ivaanicko, Croatia. Phone: +385 (1) 283-0533. Fax: +385 (1) 283 0534. Email: dane.pavlic@oiv.hr. Contact: Dane Pavlic, Head of Station.
TRANSMISSION AUTHORITY: Odasiljaci i Veze D.O.O., Vlaska 106, HR-10000 Zagreb, Croatia. Phone: +385 (1) 464-6160. Fax: +385 (1) 464 6161. Email: Zelimir.Klasan@hrt.hr. Contact: Zelimir Klasan. This independent state-owned company replaces the former Transmitters and Communications Department of HRT.
Voice of Croatia (Glas Hrvatske)—same address as "Hrvatska Radio," above. Phone: (Editor- in-Chief) +385 (1) 634-2602; (Shortwave Technical Coordinator) +385 (1) 634-3428; (Shortwave Technical Coordinator, mobile) +385 9857-7565. Fax: (Editor-in-Chief) +385 (1) 634 3305; (Shortwave Technical Coordinator) +385 (1) 634 3347. Email: (Editor-in-Chief) ivana.jadresic@hrt.hr; (staff) kratki.val@hrt.hr; (Shortwave Technical Coordinator) z.klasan@hrt.hr. Contact: (Editor-in-Chief) Ivana Jadresic; (Shortwave Technical Coordinator, domestic & external) Zelimir Klasan.
Croatian Radio operates two services on world band: the domestic (first) national radio program, transmitted via HRT's Deanovec shortwave station for listeners in Europe and the Mediterranean; and a special service in Croatian, with news segments in English and Spanish for Croatian expatriates, which airs via facilities of Deutsche Telekom (*see*) in Jülich, Germany and is sponsored by the Croatian Heritage Organization. The previous Croatian external broadcasting service known as "Radio Hrvatska" and produced by the Croatian Information Center (Hrvatski Informativni Centar, HIC) was discontinued on October 1st 2000. The external service resumed its transmissions on April 18th 2001 as Glas Hrvatske (Voice of Croatia) under the authority of HRT.
WASHINGTON NEWS BUREAU: Croatian-American Association, 2020 Pennsylvania Avenue NW, Suite 287, Washington DC 20006 USA. Phone: +1 (202) 429-5543. Fax: +1 (202) 429 5545. Email: 73150.3552@compuserve.com. Web: www.hrnet.org/CAA. Contact: Frank Brozovich, President.

CUBA   World Time -5 (-4 midyear)

Radio Habana Cuba, P.O. Box 6240, Habana, Cuba 10600. Phone: (general) +53 (7) 784-954 or +53 (7) 334-272; (English Department) +53 (7) 877-6628; (Coro) +53 (7) 814-243 or (home) +53 (7) 301-794. Fax: (general) +53 (7) 783 518; (English Department) +53 (7) 705 810. Email: (general) radiohc@ip.etecsa.cu; (English Service) radiohc@enet.cu; (Arnie Coro) arnie@radiohc.org. Web: (includes Windows Media and online reception report form) www.radiohc.cu; (includes archived scripts of "DXers Unlimited") www.radiohc.org. Contact: (general) Lourdes López, Head of Correspondence Department; Juan Jacomino, Head of English Service; or Mike La Guardia, Senior Editor; (administration) Ms. Milagro Hernández Cuba, General Director; (technical) Arnaldo Coro Antich, ("Arnie Coro"), Producer, "DXers Unlimited"; or Arturo González, Head of Technical Department. Free wallet and wall calendars, pennants, stickers, keychains and pins. DX Listeners' Club. Free sample *Granma International* newspaper. Contests with various prizes, including trips to Cuba.
Radio Rebelde, Departamento de Relaciones Públicas, Apartado Postal 6277, 10600 Habana 6, Cuba; or (street address) Calle 23 No. 258 entre L y M, El Vedado, Habana, Cuba 10600. For technical correspondence (including reception reports), substitute "Servicio de Onda Corta" in place of "Departamento de Relaciones Públicas." Reception reports can also be emailed to Radio Habana Cuba's Arnie Coro (arnie@radiohc.org) for forwarding to Radio Rebelde. Phone: +53 (7) 831-3514. Fax: +53 (7) 334 270. Email: (nontechnical) webrebelde@rrebelde.icrt.cu. Web (includes RealAudio): www.radiorebelde.com.cu. Contact: Daimelis Monzón; Noemí Cairo Marín; Iberlise González Padua; or Marisel Ramos Soca (all from "Relaciones Públicas"); or Jorge Luis Más Zabala, Director, Relaciones Públicas. Replies slowly, with correspondence in Spanish preferred.

CYPRUS   World Time +2 (+3 midyear)

Bayrak Radio International, BRTK Campus, Dr. Fazil Küçük Boulevard, P.O. Box 417, Lefkosa - T.R.N.C., via Mersin 10, Turkey. Phone: +90 (392) 225-5555. Fax: (general) +90 (392) 225 4581. Email: (general) brt@cc.emu.edu.tr; (technical, including reception reports) tosun@cc.emu.edu.tr. Web: (includes RealAudio) www.brt.gov.nc.tr. Contact: Mustafa Tosun, Head of Transmission Department; Halil Balbaz, Transmitter Manager; Ülfet Kortmaz, Head of Bayrak International.
BBC World Service—East Mediterranean Relay Station, P.O. Box 209, Limassol, Cyprus. Contact: Steve Welch. This address for technical matters only. Other correspondence should be sent to the BBC World Service in London (*see*).
Cyprus Broadcasting Corporation, Broadcasting House, P.O. Box 4824, Nicosia 1397, Cyprus; or (physical address) RIK Street, Athalassa, Nicosia 2120, Cyprus. Phone: +357 (2) 862- 000. Fax: +357 (2) 314 050. Email: rik@cybc.com.cy. Web: (includes RealAudio) www.cybc.com.cy. Contact: (general) Pavlos Soteriades, Director General; or Evangella Gregoriou, Head of Public and International Relations; (technical) Andreas Michaelides, Director of Technical Services. Free stickers. Replies occasionally, sometimes slowly. IRC or $1 helpful.

CZECH REPUBLIC   World Time +1 (+2 midyear)

Radio Prague, Czech Radio, Vinohradská 12, 12099 Prague 2, Czech Republic. Phone: (Czech Department) +420 (2) 2155-2921; (English Department) +420 (2) 2155-2930; (German

Department) +420 (2) 2155-2941; (French Department) +420 (2) 2155-2910; (Spanish Department) +420 (2) 2155-2950. Phone/fax: (Oldrich Cip, technical) +420 (2) 2271-5005. Fax: (all languages) +420 (2) 2155 2903. Email: (general) cr@radio.cz; (Director) Miroslav.Krupicka@radio.cz; (English Department) english@radio.cz; (Program Director) David.Vaughan@radio.cz; (free news texts) robot@radio.cz, writing "Subscribe English" (or other desired language) within the subject line; (technical, chief engineer) cip@radio.cz. Web: (includes RealAudio and MP3) www.radio.cz; (text) ftp://ftp.radio.cz; gopher:// gopher.radio.cz. Contact: (general) Markéta Atanasová; David Vaughan, Editor-in-Chief; (administration) Miroslav Krupička, Director; (technical, all programs) Oldrich Čip, Chief Engineer. Free stickers; also key chains, pens, bookmarks and other souvenirs when available. Samples of *Welcome to the Czech Republic* and *Czech Life* available upon request from Orbis, Vinohradská 46, 120 41 Prague, Czech Republic.

RFE-RL—*see* USA.

DENMARK World Time +1 (+2 midyear)

📻Radio Danmark

MAIN OFFICE: Radioavisen, Rosenørns Allé 22, DK-1999 Frederiksberg C, Denmark. Phone: (office, including voice mail, voice schedules in Danish) +45 3520-5784. Fax: + 45 3520 5781. Email: (schedule and program matters) rdk@dr.dk; (technical matters and reception reports) rdktek@dr.dk. Web: (includes RealAudio) www.dr.dk/rdk. Contact: (general) Jette Hapiach, Audience Communications; (technical) Erik Køie, Technical Adviser. Replies to correspondence in English, German, French, Norwegian, Swedish or Danish. Cassette tapes, CD and MD (not returned), short RealAudio or MP3 or similar email files accepted. Will verify all correct reception reports; although not necessary, return postage ($1, EUR1 or one IRC) appreciated. Uses transmitting facilities of Radio Norway International. All broadcasts are in Danish, and are aired at xx.30-xx.55 24 hours a day. "Tune In" letterbox program aired every second Saturday, hourly 6 times from 11.48 UTC (summer; winter 12.48 UTC).

TRANSMISSION MANAGEMENT AUTHORITY: Broadcast Service Danmark A/S, Banestroget 21, DK-2630 Taastrup, Denmark. Phone: +45 4332-2408. Email: ihl@bsd.dk. Contact: Ib H. Lavrsen, Senior Engineer.

NORWEGIAN OFFICE, TECHNICAL: Details of reception quality may also be sent to the Engineering Department of Radio Norway International (*see*), which operates the transmitters currently used by Radio Danmark.

World Music Radio (when operating), P. O. Box 112, DK-8900 Randers, Denmark. Phone: (Monday through Friday, 0800-1400 World Time) +45 70 222 222. Fax: +45 70 222 888. E-mail: wmr@wmr.dk. URL: www.wmr.dk. Contact: Stig Hartvig Nielsen. Return postage required. An independent station, WMR first went on the air in 1967 from the Netherlands, from where broadcasting continued until August 1973. Later programs were aired via the facilities of Radio Andorra (in 1976 and 1980), Radio Milano International (1982-1983) and Radio Dublin (1983-1989). In 1997, WMR returned to the air between May 31 and August 24 from a new HQ in Denmark, leasing airtime over powerful transmitters in South Africa. These broadcasts ceased due to lack of commercial advertising. The station again tested briefly during 2003 from its own transmitter. Plans to commence regular transmissions possibly in late November 2003 from transmitters of 10 kW located near Karup in Central Jutland, Denmark.

DOMINICAN REPUBLIC World Time -4

Emisora Onda Musical (when active), Pablo Hincado 204 Altos, Apartado Postal 860, Santo Domingo, Dominican Republic. Contact: Mario Báez Asunción, Director. Replies occasionally to correspondence in Spanish. $1 helpful.

Radio Amanecer Internacional, Apartado Postal 4680, Santo Domingo, Dominican Republic. Phone: +1 (809) 688-5600, +1 (809) 688-5609, +1 (809) 688-8067. Fax: +1 (809) 227 1869. Web: www.tricom.net/amanecer. Contact: (general) Señora Ramona C. de Subervi, Directora; (technical) Ing. Sócrates Domínguez. $1 or return postage required. Replies slowly to correspondence in Spanish.

Radio Barahona (when operating), Apartado 201, Barahona, Dominican Republic; or Gustavo Mejía Ricart No. 293, Apto. 2-B, Ensanche Quisqueya, Santo Domingo, Dominican Republic. Phone: +1 (809) 524-4040. Fax: +1 (809) 524 5461. Contact: (general) Rodolfo Z. Lama Jaar, Administrador; (technical) Ing. Roberto Lama Sajour, Administrador General. Free stickers. Letters should be sent via registered mail. $1 or return postage helpful. Replies to correspondence in Spanish.

EMPRESAS RADIOFÓNICAS PARENT ORGANIZATION: Empresas Radiofónicas S.A., Apartado Postal 20339, Santo Domingo, Dominican Republic. Phone: +1 (809) 567-9698. Fax: +1 (809) 472-3313. Web: www.suprafm.com.

Radio Cima Cien (when operating), Apartado 804, Santo Domingo, Dominican Republic. Fax: +1 (809) 541 1088. Contact: Roberto Vargas, Director. Free pennants, postcards, coins and taped music. Roberto likes collecting stamps and coins.

Radio Cristal Internacional, Apartado Postal 894, Santo Domingo, Dominican Republic; or (street address) Calle Pepillo Salcedo No. 18, Altos, Santo Domingo, Dominican Republic. Phone: +1 (809) 565-1460 or +1 (809) 566-5411. Fax: +1 (809) 567 9107. Contact: (general) Fernando Hermón Gross, Director de Programas; or Margarita Reyes, Secretaria; (administration) Darío Badía, Director General; or Héctor Badía, Director de Administración. Seeks reception reports. Return postage of $2 appreciated.

ECUADOR World Time -5 (-4 sometimes, in times of drought); -6 Galapagos

NOTE: According to HCJB's "DX Party Line," during periods of drought, such as caused by "El Niño," electricity rationing

Visitors to Radio Danmark invariably wind up at Copenhagen's Tivoli Park. T. Ohtake

causes periods in which transmitters cannot operate because of inadequate hydroelectric power, as well as spikes which occasionally damage transmitters. Accordingly, many Ecuadorian stations tend to be irregular, or even entirely off the air, during drought conditions.

NOTE: According to veteran Dxer Harald Kuhl in Hard-Core-DX of Kotanet Communications Ltd., IRCs are exchangeable only in the cities of Quito and Guayaquil. Too, overseas air-mail postage is very expensive now in Ecuador; so when in doubt, enclosing $2 for return postage is appropriate.

Emisoras Jesús del Gran Poder (if reactivated), Casilla 17-01-183, Quito, Ecuador. Phone: +593 (2) 251-3077. Contact: Mariela Villarreal; Padre Angel Falconí, Gerente; or Hno. Segundo Cuenca OFM.

Emisoras Luz y Vida, Casilla 11-01-222, Loja, Ecuador. Phone: +593 (7) 570-426. Contact: Hermana [Sister] Ana Maza Reyes, Directora; or Lic. Guida Carrión H., Directora de Programas. Return postage required. Replies irregularly to correspondence in Spanish.

Escuelas Radiofónicas Populares del Ecuador, Juan de Velasco 4755 y Guayaquil, Casilla Postal 06-01-341, Riobamba, Ecuador. Phone: +593 (3) 961-608 or +593 (3) 960-247. Fax: +593 (3) 961 625. Email: admin@esrapoec.ecuanex.net.ec. Web: www.ded.org.ec/essapa01.htm. Contact: Juan Pérez Sarmiento, Director Ejecutivo; or María Ercilia López, Secretaria. Free pennants and key rings. "Chimborazo" cassette of Ecuadorian music for 10,000 sucres plus postage; T-shirts for 12,000 sucres plus postage; and caps with station logo for 8,000 sucres plus postage. Return postage helpful. Replies to correspondence in Spanish.

HCJB World Radio, The Voice of the Andes

STATION: Casilla 17-17-691, Quito, Ecuador. Phone: (general) +593 (2) 226-6808 (X-4441, 1300-2200

World Time Monday through Friday, for the English Dept.); (Frequency Management) +593 (2) 226-6808 (X-4627); (DX Partyline English program, toll-free, U.S. only, for reception reports, loggings and other correspondence) +1 866 343-0791. Fax: (general) +593 (2) 226 7263; (Frequency Manager) +593 (2) 226 3267. Email: (Graham) agraham@hcjb.org.ec; (Frequency Management) irops@hcjb.org.ec or dweber@hcjb.org.ec; (language sections) format is language@hcjb.org.ec; so to reach, say, the Spanish Department, it would be spanish@hcjb.org.ec. Web: (English, includes RealAudio and online reception report form) www.hcjb.org; (Spanish) www.hcjb.org.ec. Contact: (general) English [or other language] Department; (administration) Jim Estes, Director of Broadcasting; Alex Saks, Station Manager; Curt Cole, Programme Director, or Allen Graham, Ecuador National Director; (technical) Douglas Weber, Frequency Manager. Free religious brochures, calendars, stickers and pennants; free email The Andean Herald newsletter. Catch the Vision book $8, postpaid. IRC or unused U.S. or Canadian stamps appreciated for airmail reply.

INTERNATIONAL HEADQUARTERS: HCJB World Radio, Inc., P.O. Box 39800, Colorado Springs CO 80949-9800 USA. Phone: +1 (719) 590-9800. Fax: +1 (719) 590 9801. Email: info@hcjb.org. Contact: Andrew Braio, Public Information; (administration) Richard D. Jacquin, Director, International Operations. Various items sold via U.S. address—catalog available. This address is not a mail drop, so listeners' correspondence, except those concerned with purchasing HCJB items, should be directed to the usual Quito address.

ENGINEERING CENTER: 2830 South 17th Street, Elkhart IN 46517 USA. Phone: +1 (219) 294-8201. Fax: +1 (219) 294 8391.

Email: info@hcjbeng.org. Web: www.hcjbeng.org. Contact: Dave Pasechnik, Project Manager; or Bob Moore, Engineering. This address only for those professionally concerned with the design and manufacture of transmitter and antenna equipment. Listeners' correspondence should be directed to the usual Quito address.

REGIONAL OFFICES: Although HCJB has over 20 regional offices throughout the world, the station wishes that all listener correspondence be directed to the station in Quito, as the regional offices do not serve as mail drops for the station.

La Voz de Saquisilí—Radio Libertador, Calle 24 de Mayo, Saquisilí, Cotopaxi, Ecuador. Phone: +593 (3) 721-035. Contact: Arturo Mena Herrera, Gerente-Propietario, who may also be contacted via his son-in-law, Eddy Roger Velástegui Mena, who is studying in Quito (Email: eddyv@uio.uio.satnet.net). Reception reports actively solicited, and will be confirmed with a special commemorative QSL card. Return postage, in the form of $2 or mint Ecuadorian stamps, appreciated; IRCs difficult to exchange. Spanish strongly preferred.

La Voz del Napo, Misión Josefina, Tena, Napo, Ecuador. Phone: +593 (6) 886-356. Email: coljav20@yahoo.es. Contact: Padre Humberto Dorigatti, Director. Free pennants and stickers. $2 or return postage required. Replies occasionally to correspondence in Spanish.

La Voz del Río Tarqui (when operating), Manuel Vega 653 y Presidente Córdova, Cuenca, Ecuador. Phone: +593 (7) 822-132. Contact: Sra. Alicia Pulla Célleri, Gerente. Replies irregularly to correspondence in Spanish. Has ties with station WKDM in New York.

La Voz del Upano

STATION: Vicariato Apostólico de Méndez, Misión Salesiana, 10 de Agosto s/n, Macas, Provincia de Morona Santiago, Ecuador. Phone: +593 (7) 505-247. Email: radioupano@easynet.net.ec. Contact: Sra. Leonor Guzmán, Directora. Free pennants and calendars. On one occasion, not necessarily to be repeated, sent tape of Ecuadorian folk music for $2. Otherwise, $2 required. Replies to correspondence in Spanish.

QUITO OFFICE: Procura Salesiana, Equinoccio 623 y Queseras del Medio, Quito, Ecuador. Phone: +593 (2) 551-012.

Radio Bahá'í (if reactivated), Casilla 10-02-1464, Otavalo, Imbabura, Ecuador. Phone: +593 (6) 920-245. Fax: +593 (6) 922 504. Contact: (general) William Rodríguez Barreiro, Coordinador; or Juan Antonio Reascos, Locutor; (technical) Ing. Tom Dopps. Free information about the Bahá'í faith, which teaches the unity of all the races, nations and religions, and that the Earth is one country and mankind its citizens. Free pennants. Return postage appreciated. Replies regularly to correspondence in English or Spanish. Enclosing a family photo may help getting a reply. Station is property of the Instituto Nacional de Enseñanza de la Fe Bahá'í (National Spiritual Assembly of the Bahá'ís of Ecuador). Although there are many Bahá'í radio stations around the world, Radio Bahá'í in Ecuador is the only one on shortwave.

Radio Buen Pastor—see Radio El Buen Pastor.

Radio Centinela del Sur (C.D.S. Internacional), Casilla 11-01-106, Loja, Ecuador; or (studios) Olmedo 11-56 y Mercadillo, Loja, Ecuador. Phone: +593 (7) 561-166 or +593 (7) 570-211. Fax: +593 (7) 562 270. Contact: (general) Marcos G. Coronel V., Director de Programas; or José A. Coronel V., Director del programa "Ovación"; (technical) José A. Coronel Illescas, Gerente General. Return postage required. Replies occasionally to correspondence in Spanish.

Radio Centro, Casilla 18-01-574, Ambato, Ecuador. Phone: +593 (3) 822-240 or +593 (3) 841- 126. Fax: +593 (3) 829 824.

Contact: Luis Alberto Gamboa Tello, Director Gerente; or Lic. María Elena de López. Free stickers. Return postage appreciated. Replies to correspondence in Spanish.

Radiodifusora Cultural Católica La Voz del Upano—*see* La Voz del Upano, above.

Radiodifusora Cultural, La Voz del Napo—*see* La Voz del Napo, above.

Radio El Buen Pastor, Asociación Cristiana de Indígenas Saraguros (ACIS), Reino de Quito y Azuay, Correo Central, Saraguro, Loja, Ecuador. Phone: +593 (2) 00-146. Contact: (general) Dean Pablo Davis, Sub-director; Segundo Poma, Director; Mark Vogan, OMS Missionary; Mike Schrode, OMS Ecuador Field Director; Juana Guamán, Secretaria; or Zoila Vacacela, Secretaria; (technical) Miguel Kelly. $2 or return postage in the form of mint Ecuadorian stamps required, as IRCs are difficult to exchange in Ecuador. Station is keen to receive reception reports; may respond to English, but correspondence in Spanish preferred. $10 required for QSL card and pennant.

Radio Federación Shuar (Shuara Tuntuiri), Casilla 17-01-1422, Quito, Ecuador. Phone/fax: +593 (2) 504-264. Contact: Manuel Jesús Vinza Chacucuy, Director; Yurank Tsapak Rubén Gerardo, Director; or Prof. Albino M. Utitiaj P., Director de Medios. Return postage or $2 required. Replies irregularly to correspondence in Spanish.

Radio Interoceánica, Santa Rosa de Quijos, Cantón El Chaco, Provincia de Napo, Ecuador. Email: interoceanic@hotmail.com; (Riera) edwinriera@hotmail.com. Contact: Edwin Riera, Director; Byron Medina, Gerente; or Ing. Olaf Hegmuir. $2 or return postage required, and donations appreciated (station owned by Swedish Covenant Church). Replies slowly to correspondence in Spanish, English or Swedish.

Radio Jesús del Gran Poder—*see* Emisoras Jesús del Gran Poder, above.

Radio La Voz del Río Tarqui—*see* La Voz del Rio Tarqui.

Radio Luz y Vida—*see* Emisoras Luz y Vida, above.

📻**Radio María**
GUAYAQUIL OFFICE: P. Icaza 437 y G. Córdova, Guayaquil, Ecuador. Phone: +593 (4) 568- 172. Fax: +593 (4) 568 176. Email: radiomaria@radiomariaecuador.org. Web: (includes RealAudio) www.radiomariaecuador.org; (Windows Media and MP3 audio) www.radiomaria.org/media/index.asp?LNG=SPA.
QUITO OFFICE: Baquerizo Moreno 281 y Leonidas Plaza, Quito, Ecuador. Phone: +593 (2) 564-714, +593 (2) 564-719 or +593 (2) 558-702. Fax: +593 (2) 237 630. Email: radmaria@andinanet.net
A Catholic radio network currently leasing airtime over La Voz del Napo (*see*), but which is looking into the possiblity of setting up its own shortwave station.

Radio Nacional Espejo (if reactivated), Casilla 17-01-352, Quito, Ecuador. Phone: +593 (2) 21- 366. Email: (Marco Caicedo) mcaicedo@hoy.net. Contact: Marco Caicedo, Gerente; Steve Caicedo; or Mercedes B. de Caicedo, Secretaria. Replies irregularly to correspondence in English and Spanish.

Radio Nacional Progreso (when operating), Casilla V, Loja, Ecuador. Contact: José A. Guamán Guajala, Director del programa "Círculo Dominical." Replies irregularly to correspondence in Spanish, particularly for feedback on "Circulo Dominical" program aired Sundays from 1100 to 1300. Return postage required.

Radio Oriental, Casilla 260, Tena, Napo, Ecuador. Phone: +593 (6) 886-033 or +593 (6) 886- 388. Contact: Luis Enrique Espín Espinosa, Gerente General. $2 or return postage helpful. Reception reports welcome.

Radio Quito, Casilla 17-21-1971, Quito, Ecuador. Phone/fax: +593 (2) 508-301. Email: radioquito@elcomercio.com. Contact: Xavier Almeida, Gerente General; or José Almeida, Subgerente. Free stickers. Return postage normally required, but occasionally verifies email reports. Replies slowly, but regularly.

Sistema de Emisoras Progreso—*see* Radio Nacional Progreso, above.

EGYPT   World Time +2 (+3 midyear)

WARNING: MAIL THEFT. Feedback from PASSPORT readership indicates that money is sometimes stolen from envelopes sent to Radio Cairo.

Egyptian Radio, P.O. Box 1186, 11511 Cairo, Egypt. Email: ertu@ertu.gov.eg. Web: www.ertu.gov.eg. For additional details, *see* Radio Cairo, below.

Radio Cairo
NONTECHNICAL: P.O. Box 566, Cairo 11511, Egypt. Phone: +20 (2) 677-8945. Fax: +20 (2) 575 9553. Email: (Spanish Service) radioelcairoespa@yahoo.com; (French Service) frenchprog@ erti.org; (African services) radiocairo@hotmail.com. Contact: Mrs. Amal Badr, Head of English Programme; Mrs. Sahar Kalil, Director of English Service to North America and Producer, "Questions and Answers"; or Mrs. Magda Hamman, Secretary. Free stickers, postcards, stamps, maps, papyrus souvenirs, calendars and *External Services of Radio Cairo* book. Free booklet and individually tutored Arabic-language lessons with loaned textbooks from Kamila Abdullah, Director General, Arabic by Radio, Radio Cairo, P.O. Box 325, Cairo, Egypt. Arabic-language religious, cultural and language-learning audio and video tapes from the Egyptian Radio and Television Union sold via Sono Cairo Audio-Video, P.O. Box 2017, Cairo, Egypt; when ordering video tapes, inquire to ensure they function on the television standard (NTSC, PAL or SECAM) in your country. Once replied regularly, if slowly, but recently replies have been increasingly scarce. Comments welcomed about audio quality—*see* TECHNICAL, below. Avoid enclosing money (*see* WARNING, above).

TECHNICAL: Broadcast Engineering Department, 24th Floor—TV Building (Maspiro), Egyptian Radio and Television Union, P.O. Box 1186, 11511 Cairo, Egypt. Phone/fax: +20 (2) 574-6840. Email: (general) rtu@idsc.gov.eg or freqmeg@yahoo.com; (Lawrence) niveenl@hotmail.com; (Adib) alviraadib@yahoo.com; or (Helmy) gihanessam@hotmail.com. Contact: Hamdy Emara, Chairman of Engineering Sector; Mrs. Rokaya M. Kamel, Head of Engineering & Training; Mrs. Gihan E. Helmy, Frequency Manager; Mrs. Alvira Adib, Frequency Manager; Mr. Mohsen Sayed, Director of Monitoring & Frequency Management; or Ms. Niveen W. Lawrence, Director of Shortwave Department. Comments and suggestions on audio quality and level especially welcomed. One PASSPORT reader reported that his letter to this address was returned by the Egyptian postal authorities, but we have not received any other reports of returned mail.

EL SALVADOR   World Time -6

Radio Imperial (when operating), Apartado 56, Sonsonante, El Salvador. Fax: +503 450-0189. Contact: (general) Nubia Ericka García, Directora; (technical) Moisés B. Cruz G., Ingeniero. Replies to correspondence in English and Spanish, and verifies reception reports by fax, if number provided. $1 helpful.

ENGLAND —see UNITED KINGDOM.

EQUATORIAL GUINEA World Time +1

Radio Africa
TRANSMISSION OFFICE: Apartado 851, Malabo, Isla Bioko, Equatorial Guinea.
U.S. OFFICE FOR CORRESPONDENCE AND VERIFICATIONS: Pan American Broadcasting, 20410 Town Center Lane #200, Cupertino CA 95014 USA. Phone: +1 (408) 996-2033; (toll-free, U.S. only) 1-800-726-2620. Fax: +1 (408) 252 6855. Email: pabcomain@aol.com. Web: www.radiopanam.com. Contact: (listener correspondence) Terry Kraemer; (general) Carmen Jung, Office and Sales Administrator; or James Manero. $1 in cash or unused U.S. stamps, or 2 IRCs, required for reply.
Radio East Africa—same details as "Radio Africa," above.
Radio Nacional de Guinea Ecuatorial—Bata ("Radio Bata"), Apartado 749, Bata, Río Muni, Equatorial Guinea. Phone: +240 (8) 2592. Fax: +240 (8) 2093. Contact: José Mba Obama, Director. If no response try sending your letter c/o Spanish Embassy, Bata, enclosing $1 for return postage. Spanish preferred.
Radio Nacional de Guinea Ecuatorial—Malabo ("Radio Malabo"), Apartado 195, Malabo, Isla Bioko, Equatorial Guinea. Phone: +240 (9) 2260. Fax: (general) +240 (9) 2097; (technical) +240 (9) 3122. Contact: (general) Román Manuel Mané-Abaga, Jefe de Programación; Ciprano Somon Suakin; or Manuel Sobede, Inspector de Servicios de Radio y TV; (technical) Hermenegildo Moliko Chele, Jefe Servicios Técnicos de Radio y Televisión. $1 or return postage required. Replies irregularly to correspondence in Spanish.

ERITREA World Time +3

Radio UNMEE—see United Nations.
☼**Voice of the Broad Masses of Eritrea** (Dimtsi Hafash), Ministry of Information, Radio Division, P.O. Box 872, Asmara, Eritrea; or Ministry of Information, Technical Branch, P.O. Box 243, Asmara, Eritrea. Phone: +291 (1) 116-084 or +291 (1) 120-497. Fax: +291 (1) 126 747. Email: nesredin1@dehai.org. Web: (including RealAudio) www.dehai.org/dhe/dhe.htm. Contact: Ghebreab Ghebremedhin; or Mehreteab Tesfagiorgis, Technical Director, Engineering Division. Return postage or $1 helpful. Free information on history of the station and about Eritrea.

ETHIOPIA World Time +3

Radio Ethiopia: (external service) P.O. Box 654; (domestic service) P.O. Box 1020—both in Addis Ababa, Ethiopia (address your correspondence to "Audience Relations"). Phone: (main office) +251 (1) 116-427 or +251 (1) 551-011; (engineering) +251 (1) 200-948. Fax: +251 (1) 552 263. Web: www.angelfire.com/biz/radioethiopia. Contact: (external service, general) Kahsai Tewoldemedhin, Program Director; Ms. Woinshet Woldeyes, Secretary, Audience Relations; Ms. Ellene Mocria, Head of Audience Relations; or Yohaness Ruphael, Producer, "Contact"; (administration) Kasa Miliko, Head of Station; (technical) Terefe Ghebre Medhin or Zegeye Solomon. Free stickers and tourist brochures. Poor replier.
Radio Fana (Radio Torch), P.O. Box 30702, Addis Ababa, Ethiopia. Phone: +251 (1) 516-777. Email: radio-fana@telecom.net.et. Contact: Woldu Yemessel, General Manager; Mesfin Alemayehu, Head, External Relations; or Girma Lema,

Head, Planning and Research Department. Station is autonomous and receives its income from non-governmental educational sponsorship. Seeks help with obtaining vehicles, recording equipment and training materials.
Voice of the Tigray Revolution, P.O. Box 450, Mek'ele, Tigray, Ethiopia. Contact: Fre Tesfamichael, Director. $1 helpful.

FINLAND World Time +2 (+3 midyear)

☼**YLE Radio Finland**
MAIN OFFICE: Box 78, FIN-00024 Yleisradio, Finland. Phone: (general, 24-hour English speaking switchboard for both Radio Finland and Yleisradio Oy) +358 (9) 14801; (international information) +358 (9) 1480-3729; (administration) +358 (9) 1480-4320 or +358 (9) 1480-4316; (Technical Customer Service) +358 (9) 1480-3213; (comments on programs) +358 (9) 1480- 5490. Fax: (general) +358 (9) 148 1169; (international information) +358 (9) 1480 3391; (Technical Affairs) +358 (9) 1480 3588. Email: (general) rfinland@yle.fi, or rfinland@aol.com; (comments on programs) christina.rockstroh@yle.fi; (Yleisradio Oy parent organization) fbc@yle.fi; (reception reports) raimoe.makela@yle.fi. To contact individuals, the format is firstname.lastname@yle.fi; so to reach, say, Pertti Seppä, it would be pertti.seppa@yle.fi. Web: (includes RealAudio) www.yle.fi/rfinland; (online reception report form) www.yle.fi/sataradio/receptionreport.html. Contact—Radio Finland: (administration) Juhani Niinistö, Head of International Radio; (comments on programs) Mrs. Christina Rockstroh, Managing Editor, foreign language radio. Contact—Yleisradio Oy parent organization: (general) Marja Salusjärvi, Head of International PR; (administration) Arne Wessberg, Managing Director; or Tapio Siikala, Director for Domestic and International Radio. Sometimes provides free stickers and small souvenirs, as well as tourist and other magazines. For a free color catalog of souvenirs, clothes, toys, timepieces, binoculars, CDs, tapes and other merchandise, contact the YLE Shop, Yleisradio, Pl 77, FIN-00003 Helsinki, Finland. Phone: +358 (9) 1480-3555. Fax: +358 (9) 1480 3466 or go to www.yle.fi/yleshop. Replies to correspondence. For verification of reception reports, see Transmission Facility, below. YLE Radio Finland external broadcasting is a part of YLE and not a separate administrative unit. Radio Finland itself is not a legal entity. NUNTII LATINI (Program in Latin): P.O. Box 99, FIN- 00024 Yleisradio, Finland. Fax: +358 (9) 1480 3391. Email: nuntii.latini@yle.fi. Web: www.yle.fi/fbc/nuntii.html. Six years of Nuntii Latini now available in books I to III at US$30 each from: Bookstore Tiedekirja, Kirkkokatu 14, FIN-00170 Helsinki, Finland; fax: +358 (9) 635 017. VISA/MC/EURO.
NETWORK PLANNING: Digita, Wireless Networks, P.O. Box 135, FIN-00521 Helsinki, Finland. Phone: (Huuhka) +358 (20) 411-7287; (Hautala) +358 (20) 411-7282. Fax: +358 (9) 148 5260. Email: esko.huuhka@digita.fi or kari.hautala@digita.fi. Contact: Esko Huuhka, Head of Network Planning; or Kari Hautala, Frequency Manager.
TRANSMISSION FACILITY: Digita Shortwave Centre, Makholmantie 79, FIN-28660 Pori; or (verifications) Pori SW Base, Preiviikki, FIN-28660 Pori, Finland—Attention: Raimo Mäkelä. (Email: raimoe.makela@yle.fi). Web: (Digita Oy) www.digita.fi; www.yle.fi/sataradio/preiviiki.html. Contact: Kalevi Vahtera, Station Manager; or Raimo Mäkelä (QSL-verifications). Issues full-data verification cards for good reception reports, and provides free illustrated booklets about the transmitting station.
NORTH AMERICAN OFFICE—LISTENER and MEDIA LIAISON: P.O. Box 462, Windsor CT 06095 USA. Phone: +1 (860) 688-5540

or +1 (860) 688-5098. Phone/fax: (24-hour toll-free within U.S. and Canada for recorded schedule and voice mail) 1-800-221-9539. Fax: +1 (860) 688 0113. Email: yleus@aol.com. Contact: John Berky, YLE Finland Transcriptions. Free *YLE North America* newsletter. This office does not verify reception reports.

Scandinavian Weekend Radio, P.O. Box 35, FIN-40321, Jyväskylä, Finland. Phone: (when on air) +358 (400) 995-559. Fax: (when on air) +358 (3) 475 5776. Email: (general) info@swradio.net; (technical) esa.saunamaki@swradio.net; (reception reports) online report form at the station's Website. Web: www.swradio.net. Two IRCs, $2 or 2 euros required for verification card.

FRANCE   World Time +1 (+2 midyear)

⚲Radio France Internationale (RFI)
MAIN OFFICE: B.P. 9516, F-75016 Paris Cedex 16, France; (street address) 116, avenue du président Kennedy, F-75016 Paris, France. Phone: (general) +33 (1) 56-40-12-12; (International Affairs and Program Placement) +33 (1) 44-30-89-32 or +33 (1) 44-30-89-49; (Service de la communication) +33 (1) 42-30-29-51; (Audience Relations) +33 (1) 44-30-89-69/70/71; (Media Relations) +33 (1) 42-30-29-85; (Développement et de la communication) +33 (1) 44-30-89-21; *(Fréquence Monde)* +33 (1) 42-30-10-86; (English Service) +33 (1) 56-40-30-62; (Spanish Department) +33 (1) 42-30-30-48. Fax: (general) +33 (1) 56 40 47 59; (International Affairs and Program Placement) +33 (1) 44 30 89 20; (Audience Relations) +33 (1) 44 30 89 99; (other nontechnical) +33 (1) 42 30 44 81; (English Service) +33 (1) 56 40 26 74; (Spanish Department) +33 (1) 42 30 46 69. Email: (Audience Relations) courrier.auditeurs@rfi.fr; (English Service) english.service@rfi.fr, english.features@rfi.fr; (Spanish Service) service.amerique.latine@rfi.fr. Web: (includes RealAudio) www.rfi.fr. Contact: John Maguire, Editor, English Language Service; J.P. Charbonnier, Producer, "Lettres des Auditeurs"; Joël Amar, International Affairs/Program Placement Department; Arnaud Littardi, Directeur du développement et de la communication; Nicolas Levkov, Rédactions en Langues Etrangères; Daniel Franco, Rédaction en français; Mme. Anne Toulouse, Rédacteur en chef du Service Mondiale en français; Christine Berbudeau, Rédacteur en chef, *Fréquence Monde*; or Marc Verney, Attaché de Presse; (administration) Jean-Paul Cluzel, Président-Directeur Général; (technical) M. Raymond Pincon, Producer, "Le Courrier Technique." Free *Fréquence Monde* bi-monthly magazine in French upon request. Free souvenir keychains, pins, lighters, pencils, T-shirts and stickers have been received by some—especially when visiting the headquarters at 116 avenue du Président Kennedy, in the 16th Arrondissement. Can provide supplementary materials for "Dites-moi tout" French-language course; write to the attention of Mme. Chantal de Grandpre, "Dites-moi tout." "Le Club des Auditeurs" French-language listener's club ("Club 9516" for English-language listeners); applicants must provide name, address and two passport-type photos, whereupon they will receive a membership card and the club bulletin. RFI exists primarily to defend and promote Francophone culture, but also provides meaningful information and cultural perspectives in non-French languages.
TRANSMISSION OFFICE, TECHNICAL: TéléDiffusion de France, Direction de la Production et des Méthodes, Shortwave service, 10 rue d'Oradour sur Glane, 75732 Paris Cedex 15, France. Phone: (Bochent) +33 (1) 5595-1369; or (Meunier) +33 (1) 5595-1161. Fax: +33 (1) 5595 2137. Email: (Bochent) danielbochent@compuserve.com; (Meunier) a_meunier@

compuserve.com. Contact: Daniel Bochent, Head of shortwave service; Alain Meunier, Michel Penneroux, Business Development Manager AM-HF; Mme Annick Daronian or Mme Sylvie Greuillet (short wave service). This office is for informing about transmitter-related problems (interference, modulation quality), and also for reception reports and verifications.
UNITED STATES PROMOTIONAL, SCHOOL LIAISON, PROGRAM PLACEMENT AND CULTURAL EXCHANGE OFFICES:
NEW ORLEANS: Services Culturels, Suite 2105, Ambassade de France, 300 Poydras Street, New Orleans LA 70130 USA. Phone: +1 (504) 523-5394. Phone/fax: +1 (504) 529-7502. Contact: Adam-Anthony Steg, Attaché Audiovisuel. This office promotes RFI, especially to language teachers and others in the educational community within the southern United States, and arranges for bi-national cultural exchanges. It also sets up RFI feeds to local radio stations within the southern United States.
NEW YORK: Audiovisual Bureau, Radio France Internationale, 972 Fifth Avenue, New York NY 10021 USA. Phone: +1 (212) 439-1452. Fax: +1 (212) 439 1455. Contact: Gérard Blondel or Julien Vin. This office promotes RFI, especially to language teachers and others within the educational community outside the southern United States, and arranges for bi-national cultural exchanges. It also sets up RFI feeds to local radio stations within much of the United States.
NEW YORK NEWS BUREAU: 1290 Avenue of the Americas, New York NY 10019 USA. Phone: +1 (212) 581-1771. Fax: +1 (212) 541 4309. Contact: Ms. Auberi Edler, Reporter; or Bruno Albin, Reporter.
WASHINGTON NEWS BUREAU: 529 14th Street NW, Suite 1126, Washington DC 20045 USA. Phone: +1 (202) 879-6706. Contact: Pierre J. Cayrol.
SAN FRANCISCO OFFICE, SCHEDULES: 2654 17th Avenue, San Francisco CA 94116 USA. Phone: +1 (415) 564-9968. Email: GPoppin@aol.com. Contact: George Poppin. This address, a volunteer office, only provides RFI schedules to listeners. All other correspondence should be sent directly to the main office in Paris.

⚲Radio Monte Carlo-Middle East
MAIN OFFICE: Radio Monte Carlo-Moyen Orient, 116 avenue du président Kennedy, F-75116 Paris, France; or B.P. 371, Paris 16, France. Email: contact@rmc-mo.com. Web: (includes RealAudio) www.rmc-mo.com. A station of the RFI group whose programs are produced in Paris and aired via a mediumwave AM transmitter in Cyprus; also via FM in France

Radio France Internationale uses multiple media to cover French arts.   T. Ohtake

and parts of the Middle East. Provides programs for RFI's Arabic service. A daily Arabic program is also broadcast on shortwave to North America via Radio Canada International's Sackville facilitities.

CYPRUS ADDRESS: P.O. Box 2026, Nicosia, Cyprus. Contact: M. Pavlides, Chef de Station. Reception reports have sometimes been verified via this address.

Trans World Radio—*see* Monaco.

Voice of Orthodoxy—*see* Voix de l'Orthodoxie, below.

Voix de l'Orthodoxie, B.P. 416-08, F-75366 Paris Cedex 08, France. Email: irinavo@wanadoo.fr. Contact: Michel Solovieff, General Secretary. An organization that has long broadcast religious programming to Russia via shortwave transmitters in various countries, most recently via Deutsche Telekom (Germany) and Kazakstan. Verifies reception reports, including those written in English.

RUSSIAN OFFICE: Nab. Leitenanta Shmidta 39, St. Petersburg 199034, Russia.

FRENCH GUIANA   World Time -3

Radio France Internationale—Guyane Relay Station, TDF Outre-Mer, Boite Postale 7024, 97307 Cayenne Cedex, French Guiana. Email: (Esnay) fabrice.esnay@tdf.fr. Contact: (technical) Fabrice Esnay, Responsable Groupe Maintenance. Replies to correspondence in French, and verifies reception reports. All correspondence concerning non-technical matters should be sent to the main address (*see*) for Radio France Internationale in France.

⊠RFO Guyane, 43 bis, rue du Docteur-Gabriel-Devèze, B.P. 7013, Cayenne Cedex, French Guiana. Phone: +595 299-900 or +594 299-907. Fax: +594 299 958. Web: (text plus news summaries in Quick-Time audio) www.rfo.fr/guyane/guyane.htm; (streaming in RealAudio, Windows Media and Quick-Time) www.rfo.fr/emissions/emis_s_radio.htm. Contact: (administration) George Chow-Toun, Directeur Régional; (editorial) Claude Joly, Rédacteur en Chef; (technical) Charles Diony, Directeur Technique. Free stickers. Replies occasionally and sometimes slowly; correspondence in French preferred, but English often okay.

GABON   World Time +1

Afrique Numéro Un, B.P. 1, Libreville, Gabon. Fax: +241 742 133. Email: africagc@club- internet.fr. Web: www.africa1.com. Contact: (general) Gaston Didace Singangoye; or A. Letamba, Le Directeur des Programmes; (technical) Mme. Marguerite Bayimbi, Le Directeur [sic] Technique. Free calendars and bumper stickers. $1, 2 IRCs or return postage helpful. Replies very slowly.

RTV Gabonaise, B.P. 10150, Libreville, Gabon. Contact: André Ranaud-Renombo, Le Directeur Technique, Adjoint Radio. Free stickers. $1 required. Replies occasionally, but slowly, to correspondence in French.

GEORGIA   World Time +4 (+5 midyear)

⊠Georgian Radio, TV-Radio Tbilisi, ul. M. Kostava 68, Tbilisi 380071, Republic of Georgia. Phone: (domestic service) +995 (32) 368-362; (external service) +995 (32) 360-063. Fax: +995 (32) 955 137. Email: office@geotvr.ge. Web: (includes MP3) www.geotvr.ge. Contact: (external service) Helena Apkhadze, Foreign Editor; Tamar Shengelia; Mrs. Natia Datuaschwili, Secretary; or Maya Chihradze; (domestic service) Lia Uumlaelsa, Manager; or V. Khundadze, Acting Director of Television and

Radio Department. Replies erratically and slowly, in part due to financial restrictions. Return postage or $1 helpful.

Radio Hara, Rustaveli Ave. 52, II Floor, Apt. 211-212, Tbilisi, Georgia. Email: league@geoconst.org.ge. Contact: Nino Berdznishvili, Program Manager; or Zourab Shengelia. Programs are produced by the Georgian-Abkhazian Relations Institute.

Republic of Abkhazia Radio, Abkhaz State Radio and TV Co., Aidgylara Street 34, Sukhum 384900, Republic of Abkhazia; or Zvanba Street 8, Sukhum 384900, Republic of Abkhazia. However, given the problems in getting mail to Abkhazia, the station requests that reception reports be sent to the following address: National Library of Abkhazia, Krasnodar District, P.O. Box 964, 354000 Sochi, Russia. Phone: +995 (881) 24-867 or +995 (881) 25-321. Fax: +995 (881) 21 144. Contact: Zurab Argun, Director. A 1992 uprising in northwestern Georgia drove the majority of ethnic Georgians from the region. This area remains virtually autonomous from Georgia.

GERMANY   World Time +1 (+2 midyear)

⊠Adventist World Radio

AWR GERMAN LANGUAGE OFFICE: Stimme der Hoffnung, Am Elfengrund 66, D-64297 Darmstadt, Germany. (Reception reports should be addressed to the Technischer Hörerservice.) Phone: (listener services) +49 (6151) 9544-0; (technical) +49 (6151) 954-465. Fax: (listener services) +61 (6151) 954 470; (technical) +61 (6151) 539 3365. Email: (listener services) service@stimme-der-hoffnung.de; (technical) dxer@stimme-der-hoffnung.de. Web: (includes RealAudio) www.stimme-der-hoffnung.de/rs. Contact: (technical) Lothar Klepp. Note that only German should be used to contact this office; all listener mail in English should be sent to: Adventist World Radio, 39 Brendon Street, London W1H 5HD, United Kingdom. *See* other AWR listings under Guam, Guatemala, Kenya, Madagascar, United Kingdom and USA.

AWR EUROPE FREQUENCY MANAGEMENT OFFICE: Postfach 100252, D-64202 Darmstadt, Germany. Phone: (Dedio) +49 (6151) 953-151; (Crillo) +49 (6151) 953-153. Fax: +61 (6151) 953 152. Email: (Dedio) 102555.257@compuserve.com; or dedio@awr.org; (Cirillo) pino@awr.org. Contact: Claudius Dedio, Frequency Coordinator; or Giuseppe Cirillo, Monitoring Engineer.

⊠Bayerischer Rundfunk, Rundfunkplatz 1, D-80300 München, Germany. Phone: +49 (89) 5900-01. Fax: +49 (89) 5900 2375. Email: (general) info@br-online.de; (technical) techinfo@br-mail.de; or techinfo@brnet.de. Web: (includes RealAudio) www.br-online.de. Contact: Dr. Gualtiero Guidi; or Jutta Paue, Engineering Adviser. Free stickers and 250-page program schedule book. Replies to correspondence in English and German. Verifies email reports with QSL cards, if requested.

Christliche Wissenschaft (Christian Science), Radiosendungen, E. Bethmann, P.O. Box 7330, D-22832 Norderstedt, Germany; or CS-Radiosendungen, Alexanderplatz 2, D-20099 Hamburg, Germany. Contact: Erich Bethmann. A program aired intermittently via the Jülich facilities of Deutsche Telekom (*see*).

Deutsche Telekom. *See* "Shortwave Radio Station Jülich—Deutsche Telekom AG."

⊠Deutsche Welle

MAIN OFFICE: Kurt-Schumacher-Str. 3, D-53113 Bonn, Germany; or (postal address) DW, D- 53110, Bonn, Germany. Phone: +49 (228) 429-0; (English Service) +49 (228) 429-4144. Fax: +1 (228) 429 3000; (English Service) +49 (228) 429 4155. Email: online@dw-world.de; (English Service) feedback. english@dw-world.de. To reach specific individuals by email

at Deutsche Welle the format is: firstname.lastname@dw-world.de. For language courses: feedback.radio@dw-world.de. Web: www.dw-world.de. Contact: Erik Bettermann, Director General; or Uta Thofern, Head of English Service. Broadcasts via transmitters in Germany, Antigua, Canada, Madagascar, Portugal, Russia, Rwanda, Singapore and Sri Lanka.
TECHNICAL ADVISORY SERVICE: Phone: +49 (228) 429-3208. Fax: +49 (228) 429 3220. Email: tb@dw-world.de. All technical mail and QSL-reports should be sent to the Technical Advisory Service.
U.S./CANADIAN LISTENER CONTACT OFFICE: 2000 M Street, NW, Suite 335, Washington DC 20036 USA. Phone: +1 (202) 785-5730. Fax: +1 (202) 785 5735.
Deutschlandfunk, Raderberggürtel 40, D-50968 Köln, Germany. Phone: +49 (221) 345-0. Fax: +49 (221) 345 4802. Email: (program information) deutschlandfunk@dradio.de. Web: www.dradio.de/dlf/themen.
DeutschlandRadio-Berlin, Hans-Rosenthal-Platz, D-10825 Berlin Schönberg, Germany. Phone: +49 (30) 8503-0. Fax: +49 (30) 8503 6168. Email: dlrb@dlf.de; online@dlf.de; (program information) deutschlandradioberlin@dradio.de. Web: www.dradio.de/dlrb/index.html. Contact: Dr. Karl-Heinz Stamm; or Ulrich Reuter. Correspondence in English accepted. Sometimes sends stickers, pens, magazines and other souvenirs. Verifies email reports with a QSL card.
Evangeliums-Rundfunk—*see* Monaco (Trans World Radio).
Evangeliums-Radio-Hamburg, Postfach 920741, D-21137 Hamburg, Germany. Phone: +49 (40) 702-7025. Fax: +49 (40) 8540 8861. Email: evangeliums-radio-hamburg@t-online.de. Web: www.evr-hamburg.de. Verifies reports in German, and possibly English. Airs via Deutsche Telekom's Jülich facilities, and locally on FM and cable.
📻infoRADIO, Masurenallee 8 bis 14, D-14057 Berlin, Germany. Phone: +49 (30) 3031-1931. Fax: +49 (30) 3031 1939. Email: info@inforadio.de. Web: (includes RealAudio) www.inforadio.de. Replies to correspondence in German and English and verifies reception reports. No return postage. Does not have its own transmitter, but is relayed by Südwestrundfunk (*see*) on 7265 kHz at 2200-0500 World Time (to 0655 on weekends, and one hour earlier in summer). A station of the Rundfunk Berlin-Brandenburg group.
Shortwave Radio Station Jülich—Deutsche Telekom AG
JÜLICH ADDRESS: Rundfunksendestelle Jülich, Merscher Höhe D-52428 Jülich, Germany. Phone: +49 (2461) 697-310; (Technical Engineer) +49 (2461) 697-330; (Technical Advisor and Sales Management) +49 (2461) 697-340. Fax: (all offices) +49 (2461) 697 372. Email: (Hirte) guenter.hirte@t-systems.com; (Goslawski) roman.goslawski@t-systems.com; (Brodowsky) walter.brodowsky@t-systems.com; (Weyl) ralf.weyl@t-systems.com. Contact: Günter Hirte, Head of Shortwave Radio Station Jülich; Roman Goslawski, Deputy Head of Shortwave Radio Station Jülich; Horst Tobias, Frequency Manager; (technical) Walter Brodowsky, Customer Services; or (nontechnical) Ralf Weyl, Customer Services. Reception reports accepted by mail or fax, and should be clearly marked to the attention of Walter Brodowsky.
KÖLN ADDRESS: Niederlassung 2 Köln, Service Centre Rundfunk, D-50482 Köln Germany. Phone: (Kraus) +49 (221) 575-4000; (Hufschlag) +49 (221) 575-4011. Fax: +49 (221) 575 4090. Email: info@dtag.de. Web: www.dtag.de; www.telekom.de. Contact: Egon Kraus, Head of Broadcasting Service Centre; or Josef Hufschlag, Customer Advisor for High Frequency Broadcasting. This organization operates transmitters on German soil used by Deutsche Welle, as well as those leased to various non-German world band stations.

📻Radio Santec, Marienstrasse 1, D-97070 Würzburg, Germany. Phone: (0800-1600 Central European Time, Monday through Friday) +49 (931) 3903-264. Fax: +49 (931) 3903 195. Email: info@radio-santec.com. Web: (includes RealAudio) www.radio-santec.com. Reception reports verified with QSL cards only if requested. Radio Santec, constituted as a separate legal entity in 1999, is the radio branch of Universelles Leben (Universal Life).
Stimme des Evangeliums, Evangelische Missions-Gemeinden, Jahnstrasse 9, D-89182 Bernstadt, Germany. Phone: +49 (7348) 948-026. Fax: +49 (7348) 948 027. Contact: Pastor Albert Giessler. Replies to correspondence in German, and verifies reception reports. A broadcast of the Evangelical Missions Congregations in Germany, and aired via Deutsche Telekom's Jülich facilities.
📻Südwestrundfunk, Neckarstrasse 230, D-70190 Stuttgart, Germany. Phone +49 (711) 929-0. Fax: +49 (711) 929 2600. Email: (general) info@swr.de; (technical) technik@swr.de. Web: (includes RealAudio and Windows Media) www.swr.de/radio. Sometimes sends stickers and postcards. Return postage not required. This station is the result of a merger between the former Süddeutscher Rundfunk and Südwestfunk. Based in Stuttgart, transmissions under the new banner commenced in September 1998.

GHANA   World Time exactly

WARNING—CONFIDENCE ARTISTS: Attempted correspondence with Radio Ghana may result in requests, perhaps resulting from mail theft, from skilled confidence artists for money, free electronic or other products, publications or immigration sponsorship. To help avoid this, correspondence to Radio Ghana should be sent via registered mail.
📻Ghana Broadcasting Corporation, Broadcasting House, P.O. Box 1633, Accra, Ghana. Phone: +233 (21) 221-161. Fax: +233 (21) 221 153 or +233 (21) 773 227. Web: (not updated) www.gbc.com.gh. Contact: (general) Mrs. Maud Blankson-Mills, Director of Corporate Affairs; (administration) Cris Tackie, Acting Director of Radio; (technical) K.D. Frimpong, Director of Engineering; or E. Heneath, Propagation Department. Replies tend to be erratic, and reception reports are best sent to the attention of the Propagation Engineer, GBC Monitoring Station. Enclosing an IRC, return postage or $1 and registering your letter should improve the chances of a reply.

GREECE   World Time +2 (+3 midyear)

📻Foni tis Helladas (Voice of Greece)
NONTECHNICAL: Hellenic Radio-Television, ERA-5, The Voice of Greece, 432 Mesogion Av., 15342 Athens, Greece; or P.O. Box 60019, 15310 Aghia Paraskevi, Athens, Greece. Phone: +30 (210) 606-6298, +30 (210) 606-6308 or +30 (210) 606-6310. Fax: +30 (210) 606 6309. Email: era5@ert.gr; (Foreign Language News Department) interprogram@ert.gr. Web: www.ert.gr/radio/era5. Contact: Angeliki Barka, Head of Programmes. Ioannis Koutzouradis, Managing Director; or Gina Vogiatzoglou, Programme Director. Free tourist literature.
TECHNICAL: Elliniki Radiophonia—ERA-5, General Technical Directorate, ERT/ERA Hellenic Radio Television SA, Mesogion 402, 15342 Athens, Greece. Phone: (Charalambopoulos) +30 (210) 606-6257; (Vorgias) +30 (210) 606-6256 or +30 (210) 606-6263. Fax: +30 (210) 606 6243. Email: (reception reports) era5@ert.gr; (Vorgias) svorgias@ert.gr; (Charalambopoulos) bcharalabopoulos@ert.gr. Contact:

Charalambos Charalambopoulos or Sotiris Vorgias, Planning Engineer; (administration) Th. Kokossis, General Director; or Nicolas Yannakakis, Director. Technical reception reports may be sent via mail, fax or email. Taped reports not accepted.

Radiophonikos Stathmos Makedonias—ERT-3, Angelaki 2, 546 21 Thessaloniki, Greece. Phone: +30 (310) 244-979. Fax: +30 (310) 236 370. Email: charter3@compulink.gr. Contact: (general) Mrs. Tatiana Tsioli, Program Director; or Lefty Kongalides, Head of International Relations; (technical) Dimitrios Keramidas, Engineer. Free booklets, stickers and other small souvenirs.

GREENLAND

Kalaallit Nunaata Radio (Radio Greenland), P.O. Box 1007, DK-3900 Nuuk, Greenland. Phone: +299 325-333. Fax: +299 325 042. Web: www.knr.gl. Although off world band for many years, the station is reported to be considering replacing its mediumwave AM transmitters with a shortwave transmitter. Since all inhabited areas of the country are now covered by FM signals, it is believed that shortwave would be financially more viable than mediumwave AM to broadcast to the country's fishermen.

GUAM   World Time +10

Adventist World Radio—KSDA
AWR-Asia, P.O. Box 8990, Agat, GU 96928 USA. Phone: +1 (671) 565-2000. Fax: +1 (671) 565 2983. Email: english@awr.org. Web: www.awr.org. Contact: Elvin Vence, Chief Engineer. All listener mail should be sent to: Adventist World Radio, 39 Brendon Street, London W1H 5HD, United Kingdom. Also, *see* AWR listings under Germany, Guatemala, Kenya, Madagascar, United Kingdom and USA.

Trans World Radio—KTWR
MAIN OFFICE, ENGINEERING INQUIRIES & FREQUENCY CO-ORDINATION ONLY: P.O. Box 8780, Agana, GU 96928 USA. Phone: +1 (671) 828-8638. Fax: +1 (671) 828 8636. Email: cwhite@guam.twr.org or ktwrfreq@guam.twr.org. Web: (schedule) www.gospelcom.net/twr/broadcasts/guam.htm. Contact: (technical) Chuck White, Chief Engineer/Station Manager; or George Ross, Frequency Coordinator Manager. This office will also verify email reports with a QSL card. Requests reports covering 15-30 minutes of programming. All English listener mail of a nontechnical nature should now be sent to the Australian office (*see* next entry). Addresses for listener mail in other languages will be found in the broadcasts. Also, *see* USA.
ENGLISH LISTENER MAIL, NONTECHNICAL: Trans World Radio ANZ, 2-6 Albert Street, Blackburn, Victoria 3130, Australia; or P.O. Box 390, Box Hill, Victoria 3128, Australia. Phone: +61 (3) 9878-5922. Fax: +61 (3) 9878 5944. Email: info@twradio.org. Web: www.twradio.org. Contact: John Reeder, National Director.
PROGRAMMING INQUIRES & REGIONAL HEADQUARTERS: Trans World Radio, 75 High Street #04-00 Wisma Sugnomal, Singapore 179435, Singapore.
CHINA (HONG KONG) OFFICE: TWR-CMI, P.O. Box 98697, Tsimshatsui Post Office, Kowloon, Hong Kong. Phone: +852 2780-8336. Fax: +852 2385 5045. Email: (general) info@twr.org.hk; (Ko) simon_ko@compuserve.com; (Lok) joycelok@compuserve.com. Web: www.twr.org.hk. Contact: Simon Ko, Acting Area Director; or Joyce Lok, Programming/Follow -up Director.

NEW DELHI OFFICE: P.O. Box 4310, New Delhi-110 019, India. Contact: N. Emil Jebasingh, Vishwa Vani; or S. Stanley.
TOKYO OFFICE: Pacific Broadcasting Association, C.P.O. Box 1000, Tokyo 100-91, Japan. Phone +81 (3) 3295-4921. Fax: +81 (3) 3233 2650. Email: pba@path.ne.jp. Contact: (administration) Nobuyoshi Nakagawa.

GUATEMALA   World Time -6

Adventist World Radio—Unión Radio (when operating), Apartado de Correo 51-C, Guatemala City, Guatemala. Phone: +502 365-2509. Fax:+502 365 9076. Email: uniradio@infovia.com.gt; mundi@guate.net. Free tourist and religious literature and Guatemalan stamps. Return postage (3 IRCs or $1) appreciated. Correspondence in Spanish preferred. Also, *see* AWR listings under Germany, Guam, Kenya, Madagascar, United Kingdom and USA.
La Voz de Nahualá, Nahualá, Sololá, Guatemala. Phone: +502 763-0115 or +502 763-0163. Contact: (technical) Juan Fidel Lepe Juárez, Técnico Auxiliar; or F. Manuel Esquipulas Carrillo Tzep. Return postage required. Correspondence in Spanish preferred.
Radio Amistad
ADDRESS FOR RECEPTION REPORTS: David Daniell, Asesor de Comunicaciones, Apartado Postal 25, Bulevares MX, 53140 Mexico. Phone/fax: +52 (5) 572-9633. Email: dpdaniell@aol.com. Replies to correspondence in English or Spanish.
Radio Buenas Nuevas, 13020 San Sebastián, Huehuetenango, Guatemala. Contact: Israel G. Rodas Mérida, Gerente. $1 or return postage helpful. Free religious and station information in Spanish. Sometimes includes a small pennant. Replies to correspondence in Spanish.
Radio Chortís, Centro Social, 20004 Jocotán, Chiquimula, Guatemala. Contact: Padre Juan María Boxus, Director. $1 or return postage required. Replies irregularly to correspondence in Spanish.
Radio Coatán—*see* Radio Cultural Coatán, below.
Radio Cultural—TGNA, Apartado 601, 01901 Guatemala City, Guatemala. Phone: +502 472- 1745; (English) +502 471-0807. Fax: +502 440-0260. Email: tgn@radiocultural.com; tgna@guate.net. Web: www.radiocultural.com. Contact: Wayne Berger, Chief Engineer. Free religious printed matter. Return postage or $1 appreciated.
Radio Cultural Coatán, San Sebastián Coatán, Huehuetenango, Guatemala. Contact: Domingo Hernández, Director. On-air identification is frequently "Radio Coatán."
Radio K'ekchi—TGVC, 3ra Calle 7-15, Zona 1, 16015 Fray Bartolomé de las Casas, Alta Verapaz, Guatemala; (Media Consultant) David Daniell, Asesor de Comunicaciones, Apartado Postal 25, Bulevares MX, 53140 Mexico. Phone: (station) +502 950-0299; (Daniell, phone/fax) +52 (5) 572-9633. Fax: (station) +502 950 0398. Email: dpdaniell@aol.com. Contact: (general) Gilberto Sun Xicol, Gerente; Ancelmo Cuc Chub, Director; or Mateo Botzoc, Director de Programas; (technical) Larry Baysinger, Ingeniero Jefe. Free paper pennant. $1 or return postage required. Replies to correspondence in Spanish.
Radio Mam, Acu'Mam, Cabricán, Quetzaltenango, Guatemala. Contact: Porfirio Pérez, Director. Free stickers and pennants. $1 or return postage required. Replies irregularly to correspondence in Spanish.
Radio Maya de Barillas—TGBA, 13026 Villa de Barillas, Huehuetenango, Guatemala. Contact: José Castañeda, Pastor Evangélico y Gerente. Free pennants and pins. Station is very interested in receiving reception reports. $1 or return postage required. Replies occasionally to correspondence in Spanish.

Radio Tezulutlán—TGTZ (when operating), Apartado de Correo 19, Cobán, Alta Verapaz 16001, Guatemala. Phone: +502 952-1928 or +502 951-2848. Fax: +502 951 3080. Email: verapaz@intelnet.net.gt. Web: www. verapaz.com/tezulutlan. Contact: Sergio W. Godoy, Director; or Hno. Antonio Jacobs, Director Ejecutivo. Pennant for donation to specific bank account. $1 or return postage required. Replies to correspondence in Spanish.

Radio Verdad, Apartado Postal 5, Chiquimula, Guatemala. Contact: Dr. Édgar Amílcar Madrid Morales, Gerente. May send free pennants & calendars. Replies to correspondence in Spanish and English; return postage appreciated. An evangelical and educational station.

GUINEA   World Time exactly

Radiodiffusion-Télévision Guinéenne, B.P. 391, Conakry, Guinea. If no reply is forthcoming from this address, try sending your letter to: D.G.R./P.T.T., B.P. 3322, Conakry, Guinea. Phone/fax: +224 451-408. Email: (Conde) issaconde@yahoo.fr. Contact: Issa Conde, Directeur de la radiodiffusion nationale. Return postage or $1 required. Replies very irregularly to postal correspondence in French, but email reports to the Director tend to fare better.

GUYANA   World Time -3

Voice of Guyana, Guyana Broadcasting Corporation, Broadcasting House, P.O. Box 10760, Georgetown, Guyana. Phone: +592 (2) 258-734, +592 (2) 258-083 or +592 (2) 262-691. Fax: +592 (2) 258 756, but persist as the fax machine appears to be switched off much of the time. Contact: (general) Indira Anandjit, Personnel Assistant; or M. Phillips; (technical) Roy Marshall, Senior Technician; or Shiroxley Goodman, Chief Engineer. $1 or IRC helpful. Sending a spare sticker from another station helps assure a reply. Note that when the station's mediumwave AM transmitter is down because of a component fault, parts of the shortwave unit are sometimes 'borrowed' until spares become available. As a result, the station is sometimes off shortwave for several weeks at a time.

HOLLAND   —see NETHERLANDS

HONDURAS   World Time -6

La Voz de la Mosquitia (if reactivated)
STATION: Puerto Lempira, Dpto. Gracias a Dios, Honduras. Contact: Sammy Simpson, Director; or Larry Sexton. Free pennants.
U.S. OFFICE: Global Outreach, Box 1, Tupelo MS 38802 USA. Phone: +1 (601) 842-4615. Another U.S. contact is Larry Hooker, who occasionally visits the station, and who can be reached at +1 (334) 694-7976.
La Voz Evangélica—HRVC
MAIN OFFICE: Apartado Postal 3252, Tegucigalpa, M.D.C., Honduras. Phone: +504 234- 3468/69/70. Fax: +504 233 3933. Email: hrvc@infanet.hn. Web (includes RealAudio): www.hrvc.org. Contact: (general) Srta. Orfa Esther Durón Mendoza, Secretaria; Tereso Ramos, Director de Programación; Alan Maradiaga; or Modesto Palma, Jefe, Depto. Tráfico; (technical) Carlos Paguada, Director del Dpto. Técnico; (administration) Venancio Mejía, Gerente; or Nelson Perdomo, Director. Free calendars. Three IRCs or $1 required. Replies to corre-

spondence in English, Spanish, Portuguese and German.
REGIONAL OFFICE, SAN PEDRO SULA: Apartado 2336, San Pedro Sula, Honduras. Phone: +504 557-5030. Contact: Hernán Miranda, Director.
REGIONAL OFFICE, LA CEIBA: Apartado 164, La Ceiba, Honduras. Phone: +504 443-2390. Contact: José Banegas, Director.
Radio Costeña—relays Radio Ebenezer (1220 kHz mediumwave AM), and all correspondence should be sent to the latter's address: Radio Ebenezer 1220 AM, Apartado 3466, San Pedro Sula, Honduras. Email: ebenezer@globalnet.hn; or pastor@ebenezer.hn. Web: www.ebenezer.hn. Contact: Germán Ponce, Gerente. According to a Swedish DXer, a reply was received from Iván Franco at casasps@yahoo.com, but it's not known what relation this person has with the station.
Radio HRMI, Radio Misiones Internacionales
STATION: Apartado Postal 20583, Comayaguela, M.D.C., Honduras. Phone: +504 233-9029. Contact: Wayne Downs, Director. $1 or return postage helpful.
U.S. OFFICE: IMF World Missions, P.O. Box 6321, San Bernardino CA 92412, USA. Phone +1 (909) 370-4515. Fax: +1 (909) 370 4862. Email: jkpimf@msn.com. Contact: Dr. James K. Planck, President; or Gustavo Roa, Coordinator.
Radio Litoral—HRLW, Apartado Postal 888, La Ceiba, Provincia Atlántida, Honduras. Phone: +504 443-0039. Email: radiolitoral@psinet.hn. Contact: José A. Mejía, Gerente-Propietario; or Antonio Jerome. Free postcards. 1$ or return postage required. Replies to correspondence in Spanish.
Radio Luz y Vida—HRPC, Apartado 369, San Pedro Sula, Honduras. Phone: +504 654-1221. Fax: +504 557 0394. Email: efmhonduras@globalnet.hn. Contact: Don Moore, Station Director; Cristóbal "Chris" Fleck; Ubaldo Zaldívar; or, to have your letter read over the air, "English Friendship Program." Return postage or $1 appreciated.

HUNGARY   World Time +1 (+2 midyear)

📻Radio Budapest
STATION OFFICES: Bródy Sándor utca 5-7, H-1800 Budapest, Hungary. Phone: (general) +36 (1) 328-7339, +36 (1) 328-8328, +36 (1) 328-7357 +36 (1) 328-8588, +36 (1) 328-7710 or +36 (1) 328-7723; (voice mail, English) +36 (1) 328-8320; (voice mail, German) +36 (1) 328-7325; (administration) +36 (1) 328-7503 or +36 (1) 328-8415; (technical) +36 (1) 328-7226 or +36 (1) 328-8923. Fax: (general) +36 (1) 328 8517; (administration) +36 (1) 328 8838; (technical) +36 (1) 328 7105. Email: (English) angol1@kaf.radio.hu; (German) nemet1@kaf.radio.hu; (Spanish) espanol@kaf.radio.hu; (Hungarian Information Resources) avadasz@bluemoon.sma.com; (technical) (Füszfás) Fuszfasla@muszak.radio.hu. Web: (general) www.kaf.radio.hu/index.html; (RealAudio in English, German, Hungarian and Russian) www.wrn.org/ondemand/hungary.html. Contact: (English Language Service) Ágnes Kevi, Correspondence; Louis Horváth, DX Editor; or Sándor Laczkó, Editor; (administration) László Krassó, Director, Foreign Broadcasting; Dr. Zsuzsa Mészáros, Vice-Director, Foreign Broadcasting; János Szirányi, President, Magyar Rádió; or János Simkó, Vice President, Magyar Rádió; (technical) László Füszfás, Deputy Technical Director, Magyar Rádió; Külföldi Adások Főszerkesztősége; or Lajos Horváth, Műszaki Igazgatósá; (Hungarian Information Resources) Andrew Vadasz. Replies irregularly to correspondence in English, but mail in other languages (e.g. Spanish) seems to fare better.
COMMUNICATION AUTHORITY: P.O. Box 75, H-1525 Budapest, Hungary. Phone: +36 (1) 457-7178. Fax: +36 (1) 457 7120 or 36 (1) 356 5520. Email: czuprak@hif.hu. Contact: Ernö Czuprák.

TRANSMISSION AUTHORITY: Ministry of Transport, Communications and Water Management, P.O. Box 87, H-1400 Budapest, Hungary. Phone: +36 (1) 461-3390. Fax: +36 (1) 461 3392. Email: horvathf@cms.khvm.hu. Contact: Ferenc Horváth, Frequency Manager, Radio Communications Engineering Services.

ICELAND   World Time exactly

AFRTS-Armed Forces Radio and Television Service (Shortwave), U.S. Naval Base, 235 Keflavikurflugvöllur, Iceland. Email: keflavik@mediacen.navy.mil.

☞**Ríkisútvarpid**, International Relations Department, Efstaleiti 1, IS-150 Reykjavik, Iceland. Phone: +354 515-3000. Fax: +354 515 3010. Email: isradio@ruv.is. Web: (includes RealAudio) www.ruv.is/utvarpid. Contact: Dóra Ingvadóttir, Head of International Relations; or Markús Öern Antonsson, Director.

INDIA   World Time +5:30

WARNING—MAIL THEFT: Several PASSPORT readers report that letters to India containing IRCs and other valuables have disappeared en route when not registered. Best is either to register your letter or to send correspondence in an unsealed envelope, and without enclosures.

VERIFICATION OF REGIONAL STATIONS: All Indian regional stations can be verified via New Delhi (see All India Radio—External Services Division for contact details), but some listeners prefer contacting each station individually, in the hope of receiving a direct QSL. Well- known Indian DXer Jose Jacob makes the following suggestions: address your report to the station engineer of the respective station; specify the time of reception in both World Time (UTC) and Indian Standard Time (IST); instead of using the SINPO code, write a brief summary of reception quality; and if possible, report on local programs rather than relays of national programming from New Delhi. Jose adds that reports should be written in English, and return postage is not required (although an IRC or mint Indian stamps may sometimes help).

☞**Akashvani—All India Radio**

ADMINISTRATION/ENGINEERING: Directorate General of All India Radio, Akashvani Bhawan, 1 Sansad Marg, New Delhi-110 001, India. Phone: +91 (11) 2342-1006 or +91 (11) 2371-5413; (Director General) +91 (11) 2371-0300 Ext. 102; (Engineer-in-Chief) +91 (11) 2342- 1058 or (Phone/fax) +91 (11) 2342-1459; (Director, Spectrum Management) +91 (11) 2342-1062 or +91 (11) 2342-1145. Fax: +91 (11) 2371 11956; (Director General) +91 (11) 2342 1956. Email: airlive@air.org.in; (Director General) dgair@air.org.in; (Engineer-in-Chief) einc@air.org.in; (Director, Spectrum Management) faair@nda.vsnl.net.in. Website: (includes live audio) www.allindiaradio.org. Contact: (technical) K.M. Paul, Engineer-in-Chief; A.K. Bhatnagar, Director, Spectrum Management; or Devendra Singh, Deputy Director, Spectrum Management.

AUDIENCE RESEARCH: Audience Research Unit, All India Radio, Press Trust of India Building, 2nd floor, Sansad Marg, New Delhi-110 001, India. Phone: (general) +91 (11) 2371- 0033 or +91 (11) 2371-9215; (Director) +91 (11) 2338-6506. Contact: Ramesh Chandra, Director.

CENTRAL MONITORING STATION: All India Radio, Ayanagar, New Delhi-110 047, India. Phone: +91 (11) 2650-2955 or +91 (11) 2650 1763. Contact: P.S. Bhatnagar, Director.

COMMERCIAL SERVICE: Vividh Bharati Service, AIR, P.O. Box 11497, 101 M.K. Road, Mumbai-400 020, India. Phone: +91 (22) 2203-7193.

INTERNATIONAL MONITORING STATION—MAIN OFFICE: International Monitoring Station, All India Radio, Dr. K.S. Krishnan Road, Todapur, New Delhi-110 097, India. Phone: +91 (11) 2584-2939. Contact: B.L. Kasturiya, Deputy Director; D.P. Chhabra or R.K. Malviya, Assistant Research Engineers—Frequency Planning.

NATIONAL CHANNEL: AIR, Gate 22, Jawaharlal Nehru Stadium, Lodhi Road, New Delhi-110 003. Phone: +91 (11) 2584-3825; (station engineer) +91 (11) 2584-3207. Contact: J.K. Das, Director; or V.D. Sharma, Station Engineer.

NEWS SERVICES DIVISION: News Services Division, Broadcasting House, 1 Sansad Marg, New Delhi-110 001, India. Phone: (newsroom) +91 (11) 2342-1006 or +91 (11) 2371-5413; (Special Director General—News) +91 (11) 2371-0084 or +91 (11) 2373-1510; (News on phone in English) +91 (11) 2332-4343; (News on phone in Hindi) +91 (11) 2332-4242. Fax: +91 (11) 2371 1196. Email: nsdair@giasdl01.vsnl.net.in. Contact: B.I. Saini, Special Director General—News.

PROGRAMMING: Broadcasting House, 1 Sansad Marg, New Delhi-110 001 India. Phone: (general) +91 (11) 2371-5411.

RESEARCH AND DEVELOPMENT: Office of the Chief Engineer R&D, All India Radio, 14-B Ring Road, Indraprastha Estate, New Delhi-110 002, India. Phone: (general) +91 (11) 2337-8211/12; (Chief Engineer) +91 (11) 2337 9255 or +91 (11) 2337-9329. Fax: +91 (11) 2331 8329 or +91 (11) 2331 6674. Email: rdair@nda.vsnl.net.in. Web: www.air.kode.net. Contact: B.L. Mathur, Chief Engineer.

TRANSCRIPTION AND PROGRAM EXCHANGE SERVICES: Akashvani Bhawan, 1 Sansad Marg, New Delhi-110 001, India. Phone: (Director, Transcription & Program Exchange Services: V.A. Magazine) +91 (11) 2342-1927. Contact: D.P. Jadav, Director.

All India Radio—Aizawl, Radio Tila, Tuikhuahtlang, Aizawl-796 001, Mizoram, India. Phone: +91 (389) 2322-415. Fax: +91 (389) 2322 114. Email: airzawl@sancharnet.in.

All India Radio—Aligarh, Anoopshahar Road, Aligarh-202 001, Uttar Pradesh, India. Phone: +91 (571) 2401-993. Phone/fax: +91 (571) 2400-972. Email: airaligarh@lycos.com.

All India Radio—Bangalore Shortwave Transmitting Centre

HEADQUARTERS: see All India Radio—External Services Division.

AIR OFFICE NEAR TRANSMITTER: P.O. Box 5096, Bangalore-560 001, Karnataka, India. Phone/fax: +91 (80) 2846-0379. Email: spt@bgl.vsnl.net.in.

All India Radio—Bhopal, Akashvani Bhawan, Shamla Hills, Bhopal-462 002, Madhya Pradesh, India. Phone: +91 (755) 2540-041. Email: airbpl@sancharnet.in.

All India Radio—Chennai

EXTERNAL SERVICES: see All India Radio—External Services Division.

DOMESTIC SERVICE: Avadi, Chennai-100 062, Tamil Nadu, India. Phone/fax: +91 (44) 2638- 3204. Email: airavadi@md5.vsnl.net.in.

All India Radio—External Services Division

MAIN ADDRESS: Broadcasting House, 1 Sansad Marg, P.O. Box 500, New Delhi-110 001, India. Phone: (general) +91 (11) 2371-5411; (Director) +91 (11) 2371-0057. Contact: (general) P.P. Setia, Director of External Services; or S.C. Panda, Audience Relations Officer; (technical) Rakesh Tyagi, Assistant Director Engineering (F.A.). Email (Research Dept.): rdair@giasdl01.vsnl.net.in; (comments on programs) air@kode.net. Web: (includes RealAudio in English and other languages) www.allindiaradio.com; http://air.kode.net; (unofficial, but contains updated schedule information) www.angelfire.com/

in/alokdg/air.html. Free monthly *India Calling* magazine and stickers. Replies erratic. Except for stations listed below, correspondence to domestic stations is more likely to be responded to if it is sent via the External Services Division; request that your letter be forwarded to the appropriate domestic station. *VERIFICATION ADDRESS:* Prasar Bharati Corporation of India, Akashvani Bhawan, Room 204, Sansad Marg, New Delhi-110 001, India; or P.O. Box 500, New Delhi-110 001, India. Fax: +91 (11) 2342 1062 or +91 (11) 2342 1145. Email: faair@nda.vsnl.net.in; or faair@giasdl01.vsnl.net.in; (Bhatnagar) akb@ir.org.in. Contact: A. K. Bhatnagar, Director, Spectrum Management.

All India Radio—Gangtok, Old MLA Hostel, Gangtok-737 101, Sikkim, India. Phone: +91 (359) 222-636. Email: airgtk@dte.vsnl.net.in.

All India Radio—Gorakhpur
NEPALESE EXTERNAL SERVICE: see All India Radio—External Services Division.
DOMESTIC SERVICE: Town Hall, Post Bag 26, Gorakhpur-273 001, Uttar Pradesh, India. Phone/fax: +91 (551) 2337-401. Fax: +91 (551) 2333 618. Email: seairgkp@sancharnet.in.

All India Radio—Guwahati, P.O. Box 28, Chandmari, Guwahati-781 003, Assam, India. Phone/fax: +91 (361) 2540-135. Fax: +91 (361) 2540 378 or +91 (361) 2540 426. Email: airgau@sancharnet.in.

All India Radio—Hyderabad, Rocklands, Saifabad, Hyderabad-500 004, Andhra Pradesh, India. Phone: +91 (40) 2323-4904. Fax: +91 (40) 2323 2239 or +91 (40) 2323 4282. Email: airhyd@hd2.vsnl.net.in.

All India Radio—Imphal, Palau Road, Imphal-795 001, Manipur, India. Phone: +91 (385) 220- 534. Email: airimfal@sancharnet.in.

All India Radio—Itanagar, Naharlagun, Itanagar-791 110, Arunachal Pradesh, India. Phone: +91 (360) 2213-007. Fax: +91 (360) 2213 008 or +91 (360) 2212 933. Email: airitan@sancharnet.in. Verifications direct from the station are difficult to obtain, as engineering is done by staff from the Regional Engineering Headquarters at AIR—Guwahati (*see*); that address might be worth contacting if all else fails.

All India Radio—Jaipur, 5 Park House, Mirza Ismail Road, Jaipur-302 001, Rajasthan, India. Phone: +91 (141) 2366-623. Fax: +91 (141) 2363 196. Email: airjpr@datainfosys.net.

All India Radio—Jammu—*see* Radio Kashmir—Jammu.

All India Radio—Jeypore, Jeypore-764 005, Orissa, India. Phone: +91 (685) 2432-524. Fax: +91 (685) 2432 358. Email: airjeyp@sancharnet.in.

All India Radio—Kohima, P.O. Box 42, Kohima-797 001, Nagaland, India. Phone/fax: +91 (370) 222-121. Fax: +91 (370) 222 109. Email: airkohima@rediffmail.com. Return postage, $1 or IRC helpful.

All India Radio—Kolkata, G.P.O. Box 696, Kolkata—700 001, West Bengal, India. Phone: +91 (33) 2248-9131. Email: aircal@cal.vsnl.net.in.

All India Radio—Kurseong, Mehta Club Building, Kurseong-734 203, Darjeeling District, West Bengal, India. Phone: +91 (3554) 24350. Email: airkurseong@justmailz.com

All India Radio—Leh—*see* Radio Kashmir—Leh.

All India Radio—Lucknow, 18 Vidhan Sabha Marg, Lucknow-226 001, Uttar Pradesh, India. Phone: +91 (522) 2244-130 or +91 (522) 2237-476. Fax: +91 (522) 2237 470. Email: airlko@sancharnet.in. This station now appears to be replying via the External Services Division, New Delhi.

All India Radio—Mumbai
EXTERNAL SERVICES: see All India Radio—External Services Division.

DOMESTIC SERVICE: P.O. Box 13034, Mumbai-400 020, Maharashtra, India. Phone: +91 (22) 2202-9853. Email: (general) sdairmumbai@vsnl.net; (Manuswamy) mindiran@yahoo.co.uk. Contact: Indiran Munuswamy, Superintending Engineer; or Lak Bhatnagar, Supervisor, Frequency Assignments.

All India Radio—New Delhi, P.O. Box 70, New Delhi-110 011, India. Phone: (general) +91 (11) 2371-6249. Fax: +91 (11) 2371 0113. Email: (reception reports) faair@nda.vsnl.net.in. Contact: (technical) V. Chaudhry, Superintending Engineer.

All India Radio—Panaji Shortwave Transmitting Centre
HEADQUARTERS: see All India Radio—External Services Division, above.
AIR OFFICE NEAR TRANSMITTER: P.O. Box 220, Altinho, Panaji-403 001, Goa, India. Phone: +91 (832) 2225-623 or +91 (832) 2230-696. Fax: +91 (832) 2225 662 or +91 (832) 2225 351. Email: airtrgoa@goatelecom.com.

All India Radio—Port Blair, Haddo Post, Dilanipur, Port Blair-744 102, South Andaman, Andaman and Nicobar Islands, Union Territory, India. Phone: +91 (3192) 30-682. Fax: +91 (3192) 230 260. Email: airpb@dte.vsnl.net.in. Registering letter appears to be useful.

All India Radio—Ranchi, 6 Ratu Road, Ranchi-834 001, Jharkhand, India. Phone: +91 (651) 2283-310 or +91 (651) 2208-558. Fax: +91 (651) 2301 666 or +91 (651) 2301 957. Email: seairran@yahoo.co.in.

All India Radio—Shillong, P.O. Box 14, Shillong-793 001, Meghalaya, India. Phone: +91 (364) 2224-443 or +91 (364) 2222-781. Fax: +91 (364) 2222 781. Email: airmegh@sancharnet.in; airnews@sancharnet.in. Free booklet on station's history. Replies tend to be rare, due to a shortage of staff.

All India Radio—Shimla, Choura Maidan, Simla-171 004, Himachal Pradesh, India. Phone: +91 (177) 24809 or +91 (177) 2211-355. Fax: +91 (177) 2204 400. Return postage helpful.

All India Radio—Srinagar—*see* Radio Kashmir—Srinagar.

All India Radio—Thiruvananthapuram, P.O. Box 403, Bhakti Vilas, Vazuthacaud, Thiruvananthapuram-695 014, Kerala, India. Phone: +91 (471) 2325-009. Fax: +91 (471) 2324 406 or +91 (471) 2324 982. Email: airtvpm@md4.vsnl.net.in; (Station Engineer) tvm_airtvpm@sancharnet.in. Contact: (general) K. Srinivasa Raghavan, Station Director; (technical) T.S. Sreekumar, Assistant Station Engineer.

Radio Kashmir—Jammu, Jammu-180 001, Jammu and Kashmir, India. Email: airjammu2002@yahoo.co.uk.

Radio Kashmir—Leh, Leh-194 101, Ladakh District, Jammu and Kashmir, India. Phone: +91 (198) 2252-063. Fax: +91 (198) 2252 234. Email: seairladakh2002@yahoo.co.in.

Radio Kashmir—Srinagar, Sherwani Road, Srinagar-190 001, Jammu and Kashmir, India. Phone: +91 (194) 271-460. Phone/fax: +91 (194) 2452-100. Fax: +91 (194) 2452 168. Email: akashvani@nde.com. Contact: L. Rehman, Station Director; or P.M. Bansal, Station Engineer.

INDONESIA World Time +7 Western: Waktu Indonesia Bagian Barat (Jawa, Sumatera); +8 Central: Waktu Indonesia Bagian Tengal (Bali, Kalimantan, Sulawesi, Nusa Tenggara); +9 Eastern: Waktu Indonesia Bagian Timur (Papua, Maluku)

NOTE: Except where otherwise indicated, Indonesian stations, especially those of the Radio Republik Indonesia (RRI) network, will reply to at least some correspondence in English. However, correspondence in Indonesian is more likely to ensure a reply.

Kang Guru II Radio English, KANGURU, JALF, Kotak Pos 3095, Denpasar 80030, Bali, Indonesia. Phone: +62 (361) 225-243. Fax: +62 (361) 263 509. Email: kangguru@ialfbali.co.id. Web:

www.kanguru.org. Contact: Walter Slamer, Kang Guru Project Manager; or Ogi Yutarini, Administration Officer. Free "KANGURU" magazine. This program is aired over various RRI outlets, including Jakarta and Sorong. Continuation of this project, currently sponsored by Australia's AusAID, will depend upon whether adequate supplementary funding can be made available.

Radio Pemerintah Daerah Kabupaten TK II—RPDK Manggarai, Ruteng, Flores, Nusa Tenggara Timur, Indonesia. Contact: Simon Saleh, B.A. Return postage required.

Radio Pemerintah Daerah Kabupaten Daerah TK II—RSPK Ngada, Jalan Soekarno-Hatta, Bjawa, Flores, Nusa Tenggara Tengah, Indonesia. Phone: +62 (384) 21-142. Contact: Drs. Petrus Tena, Kepala Studio.

Radio Republik Indonesia—RRI Ambon (when operating), Jalan Jendral Akhmad Yani 1, Ambon 97124, Maluku, Indonesia. Phone: +62 (911) 52-740, +62 (911) 53-261 or +62 (911) 53- 263. Fax: +62 (911) 53 262. Contact: Drs. H. Ali Amran or Pirla C. Noija, Kepala Seksi Siaran. A very poor replier to correspondence in recent years. Correspondence in Indonesian and return postage essential.

Radio Republik Indonesia—RRI Banda Aceh (when operating), Kotak Pos 112, Banda Aceh 23243, Aceh, Indonesia. Phone: +62 (651) 22-116/156. Contact: Parmono Prawira, Technical Director; or S.H. Rosa Kim. Return postage helpful.

Radio Republik Indonesia—Bandar Lampung, see RRI Tanjung Karang listing below.

Radio Republik Indonesia—RRI Bandung (when operating), Stasiun Regional 1, Kotak Pos 1055, Bandung 40122, Jawa Barat, Indonesia. Email: rribandung@yahoo.com. Web: www.kanguru.org/rristationprofiles.htm. Contact: Drs. Idrus Alkaf, Kepala Stasiun; Mrs. Ati Kusmiati; or Eem Suhaemi, Kepala Seksi Siaran. Return postage or IRC helpful.

Radio Republik Indonesia—RRI Banjarmasin (when operating), Stasiun Nusantara 111, Kotak Pos 117, Banjarmasin 70234, Kalimantan Selatan, Indonesia. Phone: +62 (511) 268-601 or +62 (511) 261-562. Fax: +62 (511) 252 238. Contact: Jul Chaidir, Stasiun Kepala; or Harmyn Husein. Free stickers. Return postage or IRCs helpful.

Radio Republik Indonesia—RRI Bengkulu, Stasiun Regional 1, Kotak Pos 13 Kawat, Kotamadya Bengkulu 38227, Indonesia. Phone: +62 (736) 350-811. Fax: +62 (736) 350 927. Contact: Drs. Drs. Jasran Abubakar, Kepala Stasiun. Free picture postcards, decals and tourist literature. Return postage or 2 IRCs helpful.

Radio Republik Indonesia—RRI Biak (when operating), Kotak Pos 505, Biak 98117, Papua, Indonesia. Phone: +62 (981) 21-211 or +62 (981) 21-197. Fax: +62 (981) 21 905. Contact: Butje Latuperissa, Kepala Seksi Siaran; or Drs. D.A. Siahainenia, Kepala Stasiun. Correspondence in Indonesian preferred.

Radio Republik Indonesia—RRI Bukittinggi (when operating), Stasiun Regional 1 Bukittinggi, Jalan Prof. Muhammad Yamin 199, Aurkuning, Bukittinggi 26131, Propinsi Sumatera Barat, Indonesia. Phone: +62 (752) 21-319 or +62 (752) 21-320. Fax: +62 (752) 367 132. Contact: Mr. Effendi, Sekretaris; Zul Arifin Mukhtar, SH; or Samirwan Sarjana Hukum, Producer, "Phone in Program." Replies to correspondence in Indonesian or English. Return postage helpful.

Radio Republik Indonesia—RRI Denpasar (when operating), Kotak Pos 3031, Denpasar 80233, Bali, Indonesia. Phone: +62 (361) 222-161 or +62 (361) 223-087. Fax: +62 (361) 227 312. Contact: I Gusti Ngurah Oka, Kepala Stasiun. Replies slowly to correspondence in Indonesian. Return postage or IRCs helpful.

Radio Republik Indonesia—RRI Dili (when operating), Stasiun Regional 1 Dili, Jalan Kaikoli, Kotak Pos 103, Dili 88000, Timor-Timur, Indonesia. Contact: Harry A. Silalahi, Kepala Stasiun; Arnoldus Klau; or Paul J. Amalo, BA. Return postage or $1 helpful. Replies occasionally to correspondence in Indonesian.

Radio Republik Indonesia—RRI Fak Fak, Jalan Kapten P. Tendean, Kotak Pos 54, Fak-Fak 98612, Papua, Indonesia. Phone: +62 (956) 22-519 or +62 (956) 22-521. Contact: Bahrun Siregar, Kepala Stasiun; Aloys Ngotra, Kepala Seksi Siaran; Drs. Tukiran Erlantoko; or Richart Tan, Kepala Sub Seksi Siaran Kata. Station plans to upgrade its transmitting facilities with the help of the Japanese government. Return postage required. Replies occasionally.

Radio Republik Indonesia—RRI Gorontalo, Jalan Jendral Sudirman 30, Gorontalo 96115, Sulawesi Utara, Indonesia. Fax: +62 (435) 821 590/91. Contact: Drs. Bagus Edi Asmoro; Drs. Muhammad. Assad, Kepala Stasiun; or Saleh S. Thalib, Technical Manager. Return postage helpful. Replies occasionally, preferably to correspondence in Indonesian.

⏻Radio Republik Indonesia—RRI Jakarta

STATION: Stasiun Nasional Jakarta, Kotak Pos 356, Jakarta 10110, Daerah Khusus Jakarta Raya, Indonesia; or (street address) Jalan Merdeka Barat 4-5, Jakarta 10110, Indonesia. Phone: +62 (21) 384-9091 or +62 (21) 384-6817. Fax: +62 (21) 345 7132 or +62 (21) 345 7134. Email: rri@rrionline.com; rri@rri-online.com. Web: (includes Windows Media) www.rri.online.com; ("official site," with news in MP3) www.rri-online.com (Note: www.rrionline.com and www.rri- online.com are two very different sites). Contact: Drs. Beni Koesbani, Kepala Stasiun; or Drs. Nuryudi, MM. Return postage helpful. Replies irregularly.

"DATELINE" ENGLISH PROGRAM: see Kang Guru II Radio English.

TRANSMITTERS DIVISION: Jalan Merdeka Barat 4-5, Jakarta 10110 Indonesia. Phone/fax: +62 (21) 385-7831. Email: sruslan@yahoo.com or sruslan@msn.com. Contact: Sunarya Ruslan, Head of Transmitters Division.

"U.N. CALLING ASIA" ENGLISH PROGRAM: Program via RRI Jakarta Programa Ibukota Satu, every Sunday. Contact address same as United Nations Radio (see).

Radio Republik Indonesia—RRI Jambi (when operating), Jalan Jendral A. Yani 5, Telanaipura, Jambi 36122, Propinsi Jambi, Indonesia. Contact: M. Yazid, Kepala Siaran; H. Asmuni Lubis, BA; or Byamsuri, Acting Station Manager. Return postage helpful.

Radio Republik Indonesia—RRI Jayapura, Kotak Pos 1077, Jayapura 99200, Papua, Indonesia. Phone: +62 (967) 33-339. Fax: +62 (967) 33 439. Contact: Harry Liborang, Direktorat Radio; Hartono, Bidang Teknik; or Dr. David Alex Siahainenia, Kepala. Return postage of $1 helpful. Replies to correspondence in Indonesian or English.

Radio Republik Indonesia—RRI Kendari, Kotak Pos 7, Kendari 93111, Sulawesi Tenggara, Indonesia. Phone: +62 (401) 21-464. Fax: +62 (401) 21 730. Contact: H. Sjahbuddin, BA; Muniruddin Amin, Programmer; or Drs. Supandi. Return postage required. Replies slowly to correspondence in Indonesian.

Radio Republik Indonesia—RRI Kupang (Regional I) (when operating), Jalan Tompello 8, Kupang 85225, Timor, Indonesia. Phone: +62 (380) 821-437 or +62 (380) 825-444. Fax: +62 (380) 833 149. Contact: Drs. P.M. Tisera, Kepala Stasiun; Qustigap Bagang, Kepala Seksi Siaran; or Said Rasyid, Kepala Studio. Return postage helpful. Correspondence in Indonesian preferred. Replies occasionally.

Radio Republik Indonesia—RRI Madiun (when operating), Jalan Mayjend Panjaitan 10, Madiun 63133, Jawa Timur, Indonesia. Phone: +62 (351) 464-419, +62 (351) 459-198, +62 (351) 462-726 or +62 (351) 459-495. Fax: +62 (351) 464 964. Web: www.kanguru.org/rristationprofiles.htm. Contact: Sri Lestari, SS or Imam Soeprapto, Kepala Seksi Siaran. Replies to correspondence in English or Indonesian. Return postage helpful.

Radio Republik Indonesia—RRI Makassar, Jalan Riburane 3, Makassar, 90111, Sulawesi Selatan, Indonesia. Phone: +62 (411) 321-853. Contact: H. Kamaruddin Alkaf Yasin, Head of Broadcasting Department; L.A. Rachim Ganie; Ashan Muhammad, Kepala Bidang Teknik; Salam Hormat, Head of Station; or Drs. Bambang Pudjono. Return postage, $1 or IRCs helpful. Replies irregularly and sometimes slowly.

Radio Republik Indonesia—RRI Malang (when operating), Kotak Pos 78, Malang 65140, Jawa Timur, Indonesia; or Jalan Candi Panggung No. 58, Mojolangu, Malang 65142, Indonesia. Email: makobu@mlg.globalxtrem.net. Contact: Drs.Tjutju Tjuar Na Adikorya, Kepala Stasiun; Ml. Mawahib, Kepala Seksi Siaran; or Dra Hartati Soekemi, Mengetahui. Return postage required. Free history and other booklets. Replies irregularly to correspondence in Indonesian.

Radio Republik Indonesia—RRI Manado (when operating), Kotak Pos 1110, Manado 95124 Propinsi Sulawesi Utara, Indonesia. Phone: +62 (431) 863-392. Fax: +62 (431) 863 492. Contact: Costher H. Gulton, Kepala Stasiun; or Untung Santoso, Kepala Seksi Teknik. Free stickers and postcards. Return postage or $1 required. Replies occasionally to correspondence in Indonesian.

Radio Republik Indonesia—RRI Manokwari (when operating), Regional II, Jalan Merdeka 68, Manokwari 98311, Papua, Indonesia. Phone: +62 (962) 21-343. Contact: Eddy Kusbandi, Manager; or Nurdin Mokogintu. Return postage helpful.

Radio Republik Indonesia—RRI Mataram (when operating), Stasiun Regional I Mataram, Jalan Langko 83 Ampenan, Mataram 83114, Nusa Tenggara Barat, Indonesia. Phone: +62 (370) 23-713 or +62 (370) 21-355. Contact: Drs. Hamid Djasman, Kepala; or Bochri Rachman, Ketua Dewan Pimpinan Harian. Free stickers. Return postage required. With sufficient return postage or small token gift, sometimes sends tourist information and Batik print. Replies to correspondence in Indonesian.

Radio Republik Indonesia—RRI Medan (when operating), Jalan Letkol Martinus Lubis 5, Medan 20232, Sumatera, Indonesia. Phone: +62 (61) 324-222/441. Fax: +62 (61) 512 161. Contact: Kepala Stasiun, Ujamalul Abidin Ass; Drs. S. Parlin Tobing, SH, Produsennya, "Kontak Pendengar"; Drs. H. Suryanta Saleh; or Suprato. Free stickers. Return postage required. Replies to correspondence in Indonesian.

Radio Republik Indonesia—RRI Merauke, Stasiun Regional 1, Kotak Pos 11, Merauke 99611, Papua, Indonesia. Phone: +62 (971) 21-396 or +62 (971) 21-376. Contact: (general) Drs. Buang Akhir, Direktur; Achmad Ruskaya B.A., Kepala Stasiun, Drs.Tuanakotta Semuel, Kepala Seksi Siaran; or John Manuputty, Kepala Subseksi Pemancar; (technical) Daf'an Kubangun, Kepala Seksi Tehnik. Return postage helpful.

Radio Republik Indonesia—RRI Nabire (when operating), Kotak Pos 110, Jalan Merdeka 74 Nabire 98811, Papua, Indonesia. Phone: +62 (984) 21-013. Contact: Muchtar Yushaputra, Kepala Stasiun. Free stickers and occasional free picture postcards. Return postage or IRCs helpful.

Radio Republik Indonesia—RRI Padang, Kotak Pos 77, Padang 25111, Sumatera Barat, Indonesia. Phone: +61 (751) 28-363, +62 (751) 21-030 or +62 (751) 27-482. Contact: H.

Hutabarat, Kepala Stasiun; or Amir Hasan, Kepala Seksi Siaran. Return postage helpful.

Radio Republik Indonesia—RRI Palangkaraya (when operating), Jalan M. Husni Thamrin 1, Palangkaraya 73111, Kalimantan Tengah, Indonesia. Phone: +62 (536) 21-779. Fax: +62 (536) 21 778. Contact: Andy Sunandar; Drs.Amiruddin; S. Polin; A.F. Herry Purwanto; Meyiwati SH; Supardal Djojosubrojo, Sarjana Hukum; Dr. S. Parlin Tobing, Station Manager; Murniaty Oesin, Transmission Department Engineer; Gumer Kamis; or Ricky D. Wader, Kepala Stasiun. Return postage helpful. Will respond to correspondence in Indonesian or English.

Radio Republik Indonesia—RRI Palembang (when operating), Jalan Radio 2, Km. 4, Palembang 30128, Sumatera Selatan, Indonesia. Phone: +62 (711) 350-811, +62 (711) 309-977 or +62 (711) 350-927. Contact: Drs. H. Mursjid Noor, Kepala Stasiun; H.Ahmad Syukri Ahkab, Kepala Seksi Siaran; or H.Iskandar Suradilaga. Return postage helpful. Replies slowly and occasionally.

Radio Republik Indonesia—RRI Palu, Jalan R.A. Kartini 39, Palu 94112, Sulawesi Tengah, Indonesia. Phone: +62 (451) 21-621 or +62 (451) 94-112. Contact: Akson Boole; Nyonyah Netty Ch. Soriton, Kepala Seksi Siaran; Gugun Santoso; Untung Santoso, Kepala Seksi Teknik; or M. Hasjim, Head of Programming. Return postage required. Replies slowly to correspondence in Indonesian.

Radio Republik Indonesia—RRI Pekanbaru (when operating), Kotak Pos 51, Pekanbaru 28113, Kepulauan Riau, Indonesia. Phone: +62 (761) 22-081, +62 (761) 23-606 or +62 (761) 25- 111. Fax: +62 (761) 23 605. Contact: (general) Hendri Yunis, ST, Kepala Stasiun, Ketua DPH; Arisun Agus, Kepala Seksi Siaran; Drs. H. Syamsidi, Kepala Supag Tata Usaha; or Zainal Abbas. Return postage helpful.

Radio Republik Indonesia—RRI Pontianak, Kotak Pos 1005, Pontianak 78117, Kalimantan Barat, Indonesia. Phone: +62 (561) 734-987. Fax: +62 (561) 734 659. Contact: Ruddy Banding, Kepala Seksi Siaran; Achmad Ruskaya, BA; Drs. Effendi Afati, Producer, "Dalam Acara Kantong Surat"; Subagio, Kepala Sub Bagian Tata Usaha; Augustwus Campek; Rahayu Widati; Suryadharma, Kepala Sub Seksi Programa; or Muchlis Marzuki B.A. Return postage or $1 helpful. Replies some of the time to correspondence in Indonesian (preferred) or English.

Radio Republik Indonesia—RRI Samarinda, Kotak Pos 45, Samarinda, Kalimantan Timur 75110, Indonesia. Phone: +62 (541) 743-495. Fax: +62 (541) 741 693. Contact: Siti Thomah, Kepala Seksi Siaran; Tyranus Lenjau, English Announcer; S. Yati; Marthin Tapparan; or Sunendra, Kepala Stasiun. May send tourist brochures and maps. Return postage helpful. Replies to correspondence in Indonesian.

Radio Republik Indonesia—RRI Semarang (when operating), Kotak Pos 1073, Semarang 50241, Jawa Tengah, Indonesia. Phone: +62 (24) 831-6686, +62 (24) 831-6661 or +62 (24) 831- 6330. (Phone/fax, marketing) +62 (24) 831-6330. Web: www.kanguru.org/rristationprofiles.htm. Contact: Djarwanto, SH; Drs. Sabeni, Doktorandus; Drs. Purwadi, Program Director; Dra. Endang Widiastuti, Kepala Sub Seksi Periklanan Jasa dan Hak Cipta; H. Sutakno, Kepala Stasiun; or Mardanon, Kepala Teknik. Return postage helpful.

Radio Republik Indonesia—RRI Serui, Jalan Pattimura Kotak Pos 19, Serui 98213, Papua, Indonesia. Phone: +62 (983) 31-150 or +62 (983) 31-121. Contact: Agus Raunsai, Kepala Stasiun; J. Lolouan, BA, Kepala Studio; Ketua Tim Pimpinan Harian, Kepala Seksi Siaran; Yance Yebi-Yebi; Natalis Edowai; Albertus Corputty; or Drs. Jasran Abubakar. Replies occasionally to correspondence in Indonesian. IRC or return postage helpful.

Radio Republik Indonesia—RRI Sibolga (when operating), Jalan Ade Irma Suryani, Nasution No. 11, Sibolga 22513, Sumatera Utara, Indonesia. Phone: +61 (631) 21-183, +62 (631) 22-506 or +62 (631) 22-947. Contact: Mrs. Laiya, Mrs. S. Sitoupul or B.A. Tanjung. Return postage required. Replies occasionally to correspondence in Indonesian.

Radio Republik Indonesia—RRI Sorong
STATION: Kotak Pos 146, Sorong 98414, Papua, Indonesia. Phone: +62 (951) 21-003, +62 (951) 22-111, or +62 (951) 22-611. Contact: Drs. Sallomo Hamid; Tetty Rumbay S., Kasubsi Siaran Kata; Mrs. Tien Widarsanto, Resa Kasi Siaran; Ressa Molle; Mughpar Yushaputra, Kepala Stasiun; Umar Solle, Station Manager; or Linda Rumbay. Return postage helpful. Replies to correspondence in English.
"DATELINE" ENGLISH PROGRAM: See Kang Guru II Radio English.

Radio Republik Indonesia—RRI Sumenep (when operating), Jalan Urip Sumoharjo 26, Sumenep 69411, Madura, Jawa Timur, Indonesia. Phone: +62 (328) 62-317, +62 (328) 21-811, +62 (328) 21-317 or +62 (328) 66-768. Contact: Dian Irianto, Kepala Stasiun. Return postage helpful.

Radio Republik Indonesia—RRI Surabaya, (when operating) Stasiun Regional 1, Kotak Pos 239, Surabaya 60271, Jawa Timur, Indonesia. Phone: +62 (31) 534-1327, +62 (31) 534-2327, +62 (31) 534-1327, +62 (31) 534-5474, +62 (31) 534-0478 or +62 (31) 547-3610. Fax: +62 (31) 534 2351. Contact: Zainal Abbas, Kepala Stasiun; Usmany Johozua, Kepala Seksi Siaran; Drs. E. Agus Widjaja, MM, Kasi Siaran; Pardjingat, Kepala Seksi Teknik; or Ny Koen Tarjadi. Return postage or IRCs helpful.

Radio Republik Indonesia—RRI Surakarta (when operating), Kotak Pos 40, Surakarta 57133, Jawa Tengah, Indonesia. Phone: +62 (271) 634-004/05, +62 (271) 638-145, +62 (271) 654-399 or +62 (271) 641-178. Fax: +62 (271) 642 208. Contact: H. Tomo, B.A., Head of Broadcasting; or Titiek Sudartik, S.H., Kepala. Return postage helpful.

Radio Republik Indonesia—RRI Tanjungkarang, Kotak Pos 24, Bandar Lampung 35213, Indonesia. Phone: +62 (721) 555-2280 or +62 (721) 569-720. Fax: +62 (721) 562 767. Contact: M. Nasir Agun, Kepala Stasiun; Hi Hanafie Umar; Djarot Nursinggih, Tech. Transmission; Drs. Doewadji, Kepala Seksi Siaran; Drs. Zulhaqqi Hafiz, Kepala Sub Seksi Periklanan; or Asmara Haidar Manaf. Return postage helpful. Also identifies as RRI Bandar Lampung. Replies in Indonesian to correspondence in English or Indonesian.

Radio Republik Indonesia—RRI Tanjungpinang, Stasiun RRI Regional II Tanjungpinang, Kotak Pos 8, Tanjungpinang 29123, Kepulauan Riau, Indonesia. Phone: +62 (771) 21-278, +62 (771) 21-540, +62 (771) 21-916 or +62 (771) 29-123. Contact: M. Yazid, Kepala Stasiun; Wan Suhardi, Produsennya, "Siaran Bahasa Melayu"; or Rosakim, Sarjana Hukum. Return postage helpful. Replies occasionally to correspondence in Indonesian or English.

Radio Republik Indonesia—RRI Ternate (when operating), Jalan Sultan Khairun, Kedaton, Ternate 97720 (Ternate), Maluku Utara, Indonesia. Phone: +62 (921) 21-582, +62 (921) 21-762 or +62 (921) 25-525. Contact: (general) Abd. Latief Kamarudin, Kepala Stasiun; (technical) Rusdy Bachmid, Head of Engineering; or Abubakar Alhadar. Return postage helpful.

Radio Republik Indonesia Tual (when operating), Watden, Pulau Kai, Tual 97661 Maluku, Indonesia.

Radio Republik Indonesia—RRI Wamena (when operating), RRI Regional II, Kotak Pos 10, Wamena, Papua 99511, Indonesia. Phone: +62 (969) 31-380. Fax: +62 (969) 31 299. Con-

tact: Yoswa Kumurawak, Penjab Subseksi Pemancar. Return postage helpful.

Radio Republik Indonesia—RRI Yogyakarta (when operating), Jalan Amat Jazuli 4, Kotak Pos 18, Yogyakarta 55224, Jawa Tengah, Indonesia. Fax: +62 (274) 2784. Phone: +62 (274) 512-783/85 or +62 (274) 580-333. Email: rri-yk@yogya.wasantara.net.id. Contact: Phoenix Sudomo Sudaryo; Tris Mulyanti, Seksi Programa Siaran; Martono, ub. Kabid Penyelenggaraan Siaran; Mr. Kadis, Technical Department; or Drs. H. Hamdan Sjahbeni, Kepala Stasiun. IRC, return postage or $1 helpful. Replies occasionally to correspondence in Indonesian or English.

Radio Siaran Pemerintah Daerah TK II—RSPD Halmahera Tengah, Soasio, Jalan A. Malawat, Soasio, Maluku Tengah 97812, Indonesia. Contact: Drs. S. Chalid A. Latif, Kepala Badan Pengelola.

◪**Voice of Indonesia**, Kotak Pos 1157, Jakarta 10001, Daerah Khusus Jakarta Raya, Indonesia. Phone: +62 (21) 720-3467, +62 (21) 355-381 or +62 (21) 349-091. Fax: +62 (21) 345 7132. Email: voi@rri-online.com. Web: (Windows Media only) www.rrionline.com (Note: www.rrionline.com and www.rri-online.com are two different sites). Contact: Anastasia Yasmine, Head of Foreign Affairs Section; or Amy Aisha, Presenter, "Listeners Mailbag." Free stickers and calendars. Be careful when addressing your letters to the station as mail sent to the Voice of Indonesia, Japanese Section, has sometimes been incorrectly delivered to NHK's Jakarta Bureau. Very slow in replying but enclosing 4 IRCs may help speed things up.

IRAN   World Time +3:30 (+4:30 midyear)

◪**Voice of the Islamic Republic of Iran**
MAIN OFFICE: IRIB External Services, P.O. Box 19395-6767, Tehran, Iran; or P.O. Box 19395-3333, Tehran, Iran. Phone: (IRIB Public Relations) +98 (21) 204-001/2/3 and +98 (21) 204-6894/5. Fax: (external services) +98 (21) 205 1635, +98 (21) 204 1097 or + 98 (21) 291 095; (IRIB Public Relations) +98 (21) 205 3305/7; (IRIB Central Administration) +98 (21) 204 1051; (technical) +98 (21) 654 841. Email: (general) irib@dci.iran.com; (all technical matters) sw@irib.com; (Research Centre) iribrec@dci.iran.com; (English Service) englishradio@irib.com (same format for German and Spanish, e.g. germanradio@irib.com); (French Service) radio_fr@irib.ir. *NOTE:* All irib.com addresses may eventually be phased out and replaced by irib.ir. Web: (includes RealAudio) www.irib.com/worldservice. Contact: (general) Hamid Yasamin, Public Affairs; Ali Larijani, Head; or Hameed Barimani, Producer, "Listeners Special"; (administration) J. Ghanbari, Director General; or J. Sarafraz, Deputy Managing Director; (technical) M. Ebrahim Vassigh, Frequency Manager. Free seven-volume set of books on Islam, magazines, calendars, book markers, tourist literature and postcards. Verifications require a minimum of two days' reception data on two or more separate broadcasts, plus return postage. Station is currently asking their listeners to send in their telephone numbers so that they can call and talk to them directly. Upon request they will even broadcast your conversation on air. You can send your phone number to the postal address above or you can fax it to: + 98 (21) 205 1635. If English Service doesn't reply, then try writing the French Service in French.
ENGINEERING ACTIVITIES, TEHRAN: IRIB, P.O. Box 15875-4344, Tehran, Iran. Phone: +98 (21) 2196-6127. Fax: +98 (21) 204 1051, +98 (21) 2196 6268 or +98 (21) 172 924. Contact: Mrs. Niloufar Parviz.
ENGINEERING ACTIVITIES, HESSARAK/KARAJ: IRIB, P.O. Box 155, Hessarak/Karaj, Iran. Phone: (Frequency Control & De-

sign Bureau) +98 (21) 216-3762; (Majid Farahmandnia) +98 (21) 216-3772; or (Yousef Ghadaksaz) +98 (21) 216-3742. Fax: (Frequency Design Bureau) +98 (21) 201 3649. Email: rezairib@dci.iran.com; (Ali Akbar Sabouri) sabouri@takta.net; (Yousef Ghadaksaz) ghadaksaz@irib.com; or (Majid Farahmandnia) farahmand@irib.com. Contact: Yousef Ghadaksaz, Manager of Shortwave Radio Department; Saeed Alavivafa, Head of Shortwave Frequency Management; Ali Akbar Sabouri, Head of Karaj Station; Navid Homayouni, Planning Engineer; M. Ebrahim Vasigh; or Majid Farahmandnia, Manager, Frequency Control and Design Bureau.

SIRJAN TRANSMITTING STATION: P.O. Box 369, Sirjan, Iran. Phone: +98 (21) 216-3744. Contact: Ebrahim Safabahar, Head of Sirjan Station; or Saeed Safizadeh, Technical Engineer.

Mashhad Regional Radio, P.O. Box 555, Mashhad Center, Jomhoriye Eslame, Iran. Contact: J. Ghanbari, General Director.

IRAQ   World Time +3 (+4 midyear)

Radio Kurdistan ("Aira dangi kurdistana, dangi hizbi socialisti democrati kurdistan") (when active). Web: (KSDP parent organization) www.ksdp.net. Station is run by the Kurdistan Socialist Democratic Party.

⚲**Voice of Iraqi Kurdistan** ("Aira dangi Kurdestana Iraqiyah") (when active). Sponsored by the Kurdistan Democratic Party-Iraq (KDP), led by Masoud Barzani, and the National Democratic Iraqi Front. Broadcasts from its own transmitting facilities, reportedly located in the Kurdish section of Iraq. To contact the station or to obtain verification of reception reports, try going via one of the following KDP offices (the Swedish office is known to verify email reception reports):

KURDISTAN-SALAHEDDIN CENTRAL MEDIA AND CULTURE OF-FICE: Phone: +873 (761) 610-320. Fax: +873 (761) 610 321. Email: kdppress@aol.com.

KDP LONDON OFFICE: KDP International Relations Committee-London, P.O. Box 7725, London SW1V 3ZD, United Kingdom. Phone: +44 (20) 7498-2664. Fax: +44 (20) 7498 2531. Email: kdpeurope@aol.com.

KDP MADRID OFFICE: PDK Comité de Relaciones Internacionales-España, Avenida Papa Negro, 20-1º-105ª, E-28043 Madrid, Spain. Phone: +34 (91) 759-9475. Fax: +34 (91) 300 1638. Email: pdk@futurnet.es. Web: http://usuarios.futurnet.es/p/pdk.

KDP WASHINGTON OFFICE: KDP International Relations Committee-Washington, 1015 18th Street, NW, Suite 704, Washington DC 20036 USA. Phone: +1 (202) 331-9505. Fax: +1 (202) 331 9506. Email: kdpusa@aol.com. Contact: Namat Sharif, Kurdistan Democratic Party.

KDP-CANADA OFFICE: Phone: +1 (905) 387-3759. Fax: +1 (905) 387 3756. Email: kdpcanada@hotmail.com. Web: www.geocities.com/Paris/Gallery/3209.

KDP-DENMARK OFFICE: Postbox 437, DK-3000 Helsingor, Denmark; or Postbox 551, DK- 2620 Albertslund, Denmark. Phone/fax: +45 5577-9761. Email: kdpdenmark@hotmail.com. Web: http://members.tripod.com/kdpDenmark.

KDP-SWEDEN OFFICE: Box 2017, SE-145 02 Norsborg, Sweden. Phone: +46 (8) 361-446. Fax: +46 (8) 367 844. Email: party@kdp.pp.se; (Atroushi) atrushi@iname.com. Web: (includes Windows Media) www.kdp.pp.se. Contact: Alex Atroushi, who will verify email reports sent to the "party" address.

Voice of the Kurdistan People—see Voice of the People of Kurdistan, below.

Voice of the People of Kurdistan ("Aira dangi gelli kurdistana"). Email: said@aha.ru; or puk@puk.org. Web: www.aha.ru/~said/dang.htm; (PUK parent organization)

www.puk.org. Official radio station of the Patriotic Union of Kurdistan (PUK) led by Jalal Talabani. Originally called "Voice of the Iraqi Revolution."

PUK GERMAN OFFICE: Patriotische Union Kurdistans (PUK), Postfach 21 0231, D-10502 Berlin, Germany. Phone: +49 (30) 3409-7850. Fax: +49 (30) 3409 7849. Email: pukoffice@pukg.de. Contact: Dara Gafori. Replies to correspondence in English and German, and verifies reception reports.

IRELAND   World Time exactly (+1 midyear)

⚲**Radio Telefís Éireann**, Broadcasting Developments, RTÉ, Dublin 4, Ireland. Phone: (general) +353 (1) 208-3111; (Broadcasting Developments) +353 (1) 208-2350. Audio services available by phone include concise news bulletins: (United States, special charges apply) +1 (900) 420- 2411; (United Kingdom) +44 (891) 871-116; (Australia) +61 (3) 9552-1140; and concise sports bulletins: (United States, special charges apply) +1 (900) 420-2412; (United Kingdom) +44 (891) 871-117; (Australia) +61 (3) 9552-1141. Fax: (general) +353 (1) 208 3082; (Broadcasting Developments) +353 (1) 208 3031. Email: (Pope) popeb@rte.ie. Web: (general, includes RealAudio) www.rte.ie/radio; (RealAudio, some programs) www.wrn.org/ondemand/ireland.html. Contact: Bernie Pope, Reception. IRC appreciated. Offers a variety of video tapes (mostly PAL, but a few "American Standard"), CDs and audio casettes for sale from RTÉ Commercial Enterprises Ltd, Box 1947, Donnybrook, Dublin 4, Ireland. (phone) +353 (1) 208-3453; (fax) +353 (1) 208 2620; (email) celmerch@rte.ie. A full list of what's on offer can be viewed at www.rte.ie/lib/store.html#music. Regular transmissions—see next item—via facilities of VT Merlin Communications (see United Kingdom) in Ascension, Singapore and the United Kingdom, plus Radio Canada International's Sackville site; also irregularly via these and other countries for sports or election coverage.

RTÉ Overseas (Shortwave)—a half-hour information bulletin from RTÉ's (see, above) domestic Radio 1, relayed on shortwave. Phone: +353 (1) 208 3064. Email: (information) lennie.kaye@rte.ie; (reception reports) popeb@rte.ie. Web: www.rte.ie/radio/worldwide.html. Contact: Lennie Kaye; Bernie Pope.

ISRAEL   World Time +2 (+3 midyear)

Bezeq—Israel Telecommunication Corp. Ltd., Engineering and Planning Division, Radio and T.V. Broadcasting Section, P.O. Box 62081, Tel-Aviv 61620, Israel. Phone: +972 (3) 626-4562 or +972 (3) 626-4500. Fax: +972 (3) 626 4559. Email: (Oren) mosheor@bezeq.com. Web: www.bezeq.co.il. Contact: Moshe Oren, Frequency Manager. Bezeq is responsible for transmitting the programs of the Israel Broadcasting Authority (IBA), which inter alia parents Kol Israel. This address only for pointing out transmitter-related problems (interference, modulation quality, network mixups, etc.), especially by fax, of transmitters based in Israel. Does not verify reception reports.

⚲**Galei Zahal (Israel Defence Forces Radio)**, Zahal, Military Mail No. 01005, Israel. Phone: +972 (3) 512-6666. Fax: +972 (3) 512 6760. Email: glz@galatz.co.il. Web: (includes Windows Media) www.glz.msn.co.il.

⚲**Kol Israel (Israel Radio International)**

STUDIOS: Kol Israel, P.O. Box 1082, Jerusalem 91010, Israel. Phone: (general) +972 (2) 530- 2222; (Engineering Dept.) +972 (2) 501-3453; (Hebrew voice mail for Reshet Bet program "The Israel Connection") +972 (3) 765-1929. Fax: (English Service) +972

(2) 530 2424. Email: (general) ask@israel-info.gov.il; (English Service) englishradio@iba.org.il; (correspondence relating to reception problems, only) engineering@israelradio.org; (Reshet Bet program for Israelis abroad) kesherisraeli@yahoo.com. Web: (schedule, RealAudio) www.israelradio.org; (IBA parent organization, including RealAudio in Hebrew and Arabic) www.iba.org.il. Contact: Edmond Sehayeq, Head of Programming, Arabic, Persian and Yemenite broadcasts; Yishai Eldar, Reporter, English News Department; Steve Linde, Head of English News Department; or Sara Gabbai, Head of Western Broadcasting Department; (administration) Yonni Ben- Menachem, Director of External Broadcasting; (technical, frequency management) Raphael Kochanowski, Director of Liaison and Coordination, Engineering Dept. No verifications or freebies, due to limited budget.

SAN FRANCISCO OFFICE, SCHEDULES: 2654 17th Avenue, San Francisco CA 94116 USA. Phone: +1 (415) 564-9968. Email: GPoppin@aol.com. Contact: George Poppin. This address, a volunteer office, only provides Kol Israel schedules. All other correspondence should be sent directly to the main office in Jerusalem.

ITALY   World Time +1 (+2 midyear)

🔲**Italian Radio Relay Service**, IRRS-Shortwave, Nexus-IBA, C.P. 10980, I-20110 Milano, Italy. Phone: +39 (02) 266-6971. Fax: +39 (02) 7063 8151. Email: (general) info@nexus.org; (reception reports) reports@nexus.org; (Cotroneo) aec@nexus.org; (Norton) ron@nexus.org. Web:www.nexus.org/radio.htm; (MP3) http://mp3.nexus.org. Contact: (general) Ms. Anna S. Boschetti, Verification Manager; Alfredo E. Cotroneo, President; (technical) Ron Norton. For budget reasons, this station cannot assure a reply to all listeners' mail. Email correspondence and reception reports by email are answered promptly and at no charge. A number of booklets and sometimes stickers and small souvenirs are available for sale, but check their Website for further details. Two IRCs or $1 helpful.

🔲**Radio Europe**, P.O. Box 12, 20090 Limito di Pioltello, Milan, Italy. Phone: +39 (02) 9210- 0246. Fax: +39 (02) 8645 0149. Email: radioeurope@iol.it. Web: (includes RealAudio) www.alpcom.it/hamradio/freewaves/europe.htm. Contact: Dario Monferini, Foreign Relations Director; or Alex Bertini, General Manager. Pennants $5 and T-shirts $25. $30 for a lifetime membership to Radio Europe's Listeners' Club. Membership includes T-shirt, poster, stickers, flags, gadgets, and so forth, with a monthly drawing for prizes. Application forms available from station. Sells airtime for $20 per hour. Two IRCs or $1 return postage appreciated. Unlicensed, but apparently left alone by the authorities.

🔲**Radio Roma-RAI International** (external services)
MAIN OFFICE: External/Foreign Service, Centro RAI, Saxa Rubra, 00188 Rome, Italy; or P.O. Box 320, Correspondence Sector, 00100 Rome, Italy. Phone: +39 (06) 33-17-2360. Fax: +39 (06) 33 17 18 95 or +39 (06) 322 6070. Email: raiinternational@rai.it. Web: (shortwave) www.raiinternational.rai.it/radio/indexoc.htm. Contact: (general) Rosaria Vassallo, Correspondence Sector; or Augusto Milana, Editor-in-Chief, Shortwave Programs in Foreign Languages; Esther Casas, Servicio Español; (administration) Angela Buttiglione, Managing Director; or Gabriella Tambroni, Assistant Director. Free stickers, banners, calendars and *RAI Calling from Rome* magazine. Can provide supplementary materials, including on VHS and CD- ROM, for Italian-language video course, "Viva l' italiano," with an audio equivalent soon to be offered, as well. Is constructing "a new, more powerful and sophisticated shortwave transmitting cen-

ter" in Tuscany; when this is activated, RAI International plans to expand news, cultural items and music in Italian and various other language services—including Spanish & Portuguese, plus new services in Chinese and Japanese. Responses can be very slow. Pictures of RAI's Shortwave Center at Prato Smeraldo can be found at www.mediasuk.org/rai.

SHORTWAVE FREQUENCY MONITORING OFFICE: RaiWay Monitoring Centre, Centro di Controllo, Via Mirabellino 1, 20052 Monza (MI), Italy. Phone: +39 (039) 388-389. Phone/fax (ask for fax): +39 (039) 386-222. Email: raiway.hfmonitoring@rai.it or cqmonza@rai.it. Contact: Mrs. Lucia Luisa La Franceschina; or Mario Ballabio.

ENGINEERING OFFICE, ROME: Via Teulada 66, 00195 Rome, Italy. Phone: +39 (06) 331- 70721. Fax: +39 (06) 331 75142 or +39 (06) 372 3376. Email: isola@rai.it. Contact: Clara Isola.

ENGINEERING OFFICE, TURIN: Via Cernaia 33, 10121 Turin, Italy. Phone: +39 (011) 810- 2293. Fax: +39 (011) 575 9610. Email: allamano@rai.it. Contact: Giuseppe Allamano, HF Frequency Planning.

NEW YORK OFFICE, NONTECHNICAL: 1350 Avenue of the Americas—21st floor, New York NY 10019 USA. Phone: +1 (212) 468-2500. Fax: +1 (212) 765 1956. Contact: Umberto Bonetti, Deputy Director of Radio Division. RAI caps, aprons and tote bags for sale at Boutique RAI, c/o the aforementioned New York address.

SAN FRANCISCO OFFICE, SCHEDULES: 2654 17th Avenue, San Francisco CA 94116 USA. Phone: +1 (415) 564-9968. Email: GPoppin@aol.com. Contact: George Poppin. This address, a volunteer office, only provides RAI schedules to listeners. All other correspondence should be sent directly to the main office in Rome.

Radio Speranza, Modena (if reactivated), Largo San Giorgio 91, 41100 Modena, Italy. Phone/fax: +39 (059) 230-373. Email: radiosperanza@radiosperanza.it. Web: www.radiosperanza.com. Contact: Padre Luigi Cordioli, Missionario Redentorista. Free Italian- language newsletter. Replies enthusiastically to correspondence in Italian. Return postage appreciated.

RTV Italiana-RAI (domestic service)
ROME: Centro RAI, Saxa Rubra, 00188 Rome, Italy. Fax: +39 (06) 322 6070. Email: grr@rai.it. Web: www.rai.it.

JAPAN   World Time +9

NHK Fukuoka, 1-1-10 Ropponmatsu, Chuo-ku, Fukuoka-shi, Fukuoka 810-8577, Japan. Phone: +81 (92) 724-2800. Web: www.nhk.or.jp/fukuoka.

NHK Nagoya, 13-3 Higashisakura 1-chome, Higashi-ku, Nagoya 461-8725, Japan. Phone: +81 (52) 952-7111. Fax: +81 (52) 952 7268. Web: www.nhk.or.jp/nagoya.

NHK Osaka, 3-43 Bamba-cho, Chuo-ku, Osaka 540-8501, Japan. Fax: +81 (6) 6941 0612. Web: www.nhk.or.jp/osaka. Contact: (technical) Technical Bureau. IRC or $1 helpful.

NHK Sapporo, 1-1-1 Ohdori Nishi, Chuo-ku, Sapporo 060-8703, Japan. Fax: +81 (11) 232 5951. Web: www.nhk.or.jp/sapporo. Sometimes sends postcards, stickers or other small souvenirs.

NHK Tokyo/Shobu-Kuki, 3047-1 Oaza-Sanga, Shobu-cho, Minamisaitama-gun, Saitama 346- 0104, Japan. Fax: +81 (3) 3481 4985 or +81 (480) 85 1508. Web: www.nhk.or.jp. IRC or $1 helpful. Replies occasionally. Letters should be sent via registered mail.

🔲**Radio Japan/NHK World** (external service)
MAIN OFFICE: NHK World, Nippon Hoso Kyokai, Tokyo 150-8001, Japan. Phone: +81 (3) 3465-1111. Fax: (general) +81 (3) 3481 1350; ("Hello from Tokyo" and Production Center) +81

(3) 3465 0966. Email: (general) info@intl.nhk.or.jp; ("Hello from Tokyo" program) hello@intl.nhk.or.jp; (Spanish Section) latin@intl.nhk.or.jp. Web: (includes RealAudio and Windows Media) www.nhk.or.jp/nhkworld. Contact: (administration) Isao Kitamoto, Deputy Director General; Hisashi Okawa, Senior Director International Planning; (general) Yoshiki Fushimi; H. Kawamoto, English Service; Ms. Kyoko Hirotani, Programming Division; or K. Terasaka, Programming Division.

ENGINEERING ADMINISTRATION DEPARTMENT: Nippon Hoso Kyokai, Tokyo 150-8001, Japan. Phone: +81 (3) 5455-5395, +81 (3) 5455-5384, +81 (3) 5455-5376 or +81 (3) 5455-2288. Fax: +81 (3) 3485 0952 or + 81 (3) 3481 4985. Email: (general) rj-freq@eng.nhk.or.jp; yoshimi@eng.nhk.or.jp or kurasima@eng.nhk.or.jp. Contact: Fujimoto Hiroki, Frequency Manager; Akira Mizuguchi, Transmissions Manager; Tetsuya Itsuk or Toshiki Kurashima.

MONITORING SECTION: NHK World/Radio Japan. Fax: +81 (3) 3481 1877.

HONG KONG OFFICE: Phone: +852 2577-5999.

LONDON OFFICE: Phone: +44 (20) 7334-0909.

LOS ANGELES OFFICE: Phone: +1 (310) 816-0300.

NEW YORK OFFICE: Phone: +1 (212) 755-3907.

SINGAPORE OFFICE: Phone: + 65 225-0667.

Radio Tampa, Nikkei Radio Broadcasting Company, 9-15 Akasaka 1-chome, Minato-ku, Tokyo 107-8373, Japan. Fax: +81 (3) 3583 9062. Email: web@tampa.co.jp. Web: (includes Windows Media) www.tampa.co.jp. Contact: H. Nagao, Public Relations; M. Teshima; Ms. Terumi Onoda; or H. Ono. Sending a reception report may help with a reply. Free stickers and Japanese stamps. Plans to drop shortwave broadcasts in favor of satellite transmissions sometime in the future. $1 or 2 IRCs helpful. Formerly known officially as the Nihon Shortwave Broadcasting Company, the name was changed to Nikkei Radio Broadcasting Company on October 1, 2003. The on-air name, Radio Tampa, is also to be changed, possibly in April 2004.

NEW YORK NEWS BUREAU: 1325 Avenue of the Americas #2403, New York NY 10019 USA. Fax: +1 (212) 261 6449. Contact: Noboru Fukui, reporter.

JORDAN   World Time +2 (+3 midyear)

Radio Jordan, P.O. Box 909, Amman, Jordan; or P.O. Box 1041, Amman, Jordan. Phone: (general) +962 (6) 477-4111; (International Relations) +962 (6) 477-8578; (English Service) +962 (6) 475-7410 or +962 (6) 477-3111; (Arabic Service) +962 (6) 463-6454; (Saleh) +962 (6) 474-8048; or (Al-Arini) +962 (6) 474-9161. Fax: (general) +962 (6) 478 8115; (English Service) +962 (6) 420 7862; (Al-Arini) +962 (6) 474 9190. Email: (general) general@jrtv.gov.jo; (programs) rj@jrtv.gov.jo; (schedule) feedback@jrtv.gov.jo; (technical) eng@jrtv.gov.jo; (Director of Radio TV Engineering) arini@jrtv.gov.jo. Web: www.jrtv.com/radio.htm. Contact: (general) Jawad Zada, Director of Foreign Service; Mrs. Firyal Zamakhshari, Director of Arabic Programs; or Qasral Mushatta; (administrative) Hashem Khresat, Director of Radio; Mrs. Fatima Massri, Director of International Relations; or Muwaffaq al-Rahayifah, Director of Shortwave Services; (technical) Youssef Al-Arini, Director of Radio TV Engineering. Free stickers. Replies irregularly and slowly. Enclosing $1 helps.

KENYA   World Time +3

Adventist World Radio, AWR Africa, P.O. Box 42276, Nairobi, Kenya. Phone: +254 (2) 573- 277. Fax: +254 (2) 568 433. Web: www.awr.org. Contact: (general) Samuel Misiani, Regional Director. Free home Bible study guides, program schedule and other small items. Return postage (IRCs or 1$) appreciated. This office will sometimes verify reception reports direct, but replies are slow. Also, *see* AWR listings under Germany, Guam, Guatemala, Madagascar, United Kingdom and USA.

☞Kenya Broadcasting Corporation, P.O. Box 30456, Harry Thuku Road, Nairobi, Kenya. Phone: +254 (2) 334-567. Fax: +254 (2) 220 675. Email: (general) kbc@swiftkenya.com; (management) mdkbc@swiftkenya.com; (technical services) kbctechnical@swiftkenya.com. Web: (general) www.kbc.co.ke; (RealAudio) www.africaonline.co.ke/AfricaOnline/netradio.html. Contact: (general) Henry Makokha, Liaison Office; (administration) Joe Matano Khamisi, Managing Director; (technical) Nathan Lamu, Senior Principal Technical Officer; Augustine Kenyanjier Gochui; Lawrence Holnati, Engineering Division; or Daniel Githua, Assistant Manager Technical Services (Radio). IRC required. Replies irregularly. If all you want is verfication of your reception report(s), you may have better luck sending your letter to: Engineer in Charge, Maralal Radio Station, P.O. Box 38, Maralal, Kenya.

KIRIBATI   World Time +12

Radio Kiribati (when operating), Broadcasting & Publications Authority, P.O. Box 78, Bairiki, Tarawa, Republic of Kiribati. Phone: +686 21187. Fax: +686 21096. Email: bpa@tskl.net.ki. Contact: (general) Atiota Bauro, Programme Organiser; Mrs. Otiri Laboia; Batiri Bataua, News Editor; or Moia Tetoa, Radio Manager; (technical) Tooto Kabwebwenibeia, Broadcast Engineer; Martin Ouma Ojwach, Senior Superintendent of Electronics; Kautabuki Rubeiarki, Senior Technician; or T. Fakaofo, Technical Staff. Cassettes of local songs available for purchase. $1 or return postage required for a reply (IRCs not accepted). Currently off the air due to transmitter problems.

KOREA (DPR)   World Time +9

Voice of Korea, External Service, Korean Central Broadcasting Station, Pyongyang, Democratic People's Republic of Korea (*not* "North Korea"). Phone: +850 (2) 381-6035. Fax: +850 (2) 381 4416. Phone and fax numbers valid only in those countries with direct telephone service to North Korea. Web: (unofficial) www.hikoryo.com/ser/vok.htm. Free publications, pennants, calendars, newspapers, artistic prints and pins. Do not include dutiable items in your envelope. Replies are irregular, as mail from countries not having diplomatic relations with North Korea is sent via circuitous routes and apparently does not always arrive. Indeed, some PASSPORT readers continue to report that mail to the sation results in their receiving anti-communist literature from *South* Korea, which indicates that mail interdiction has not ceased. One way around the problem is to add "VIA BEIJING, CHINA" to the address, but replies via this route tend to be slow in coming. Another gambit is to send your correspondence to an associate in a country—such as China, Ukraine or India—having reasonable relations with North Korea, and ask that it be forwarded. If you don't know anyone in these countries, try using the good offices of the following person: Willi Passman, Oberhausener Str. 100, D-45476, Mülheim, Germany. Send correspondence in a sealed envelope without any address on the back. That should be sent inside another envelope. Include 2 IRCs to cover the cost of forwarding.

Regional Korean Central Broadcasting Stations—Not known to reply, but a long-shot possibility is to try corresponding in Korean to: Korean Central Broadcasting Station, Ministry of Posts and Telecommunications, Chongsung-dong, Moranbong District, Pyongyang, Democratic People's Republic of Korea.

KOREA (REPUBLIC) World Time +9

⊞**Korean Broadcasting System (KBS)**, 18 Yoido-dong, Youngdeungpo-ku, Seoul, Republic of Korea 150-790. Phone: +82 (2) 781-1000. Fax: +82 (2) 781 1698 or +82 (2) 781 2399. Email: pr@kbs.co.kr. Web: (includes Windows Media) www.kbs.co.kr.

⊞**Radio Korea International**

MAIN OFFICE: Overseas Service, Korean Broadcasting System, Yoido-dong 18, Youngdeungpo-ku, Seoul, Republic of Korea 150-790. Phone: (general) +82 (2) 781-3650/60/70; (Engineering Department) +82 (2) 781-5141 or +82 (2) 781-5137; (English Service) +82 (2) 781- 3674/5/6; (German Service) +82 (2) 781-3682/3/9; (Japanese Service) +82 (2) 781-3654/5/6 (Spanish Service) +82 (2) 781-3679/81/97. Fax: +82 (2) 781 3694/5/6; (Engineering Department) +82 (2) 781 5159. Email: (general) rki@kbs.co.kr; (English) english@kbs.co.kr; (German) german@kbs.co.kr; (Japanese) rkijp@kbs.co.kr; (Spanish) spanish@kbs.co.kr. Web: (includes Windows Media) www.rki.kbs.co.kr. Contact: Ms. Shin Joo-Ok, Director Division 1; Ms. Han Hee-Joo, Executive Director; Mr. In-whan Park, Frequency Manager, Engineering Department; or Mr. Chunsoo Lee, Planning Engineer, Engineering Department. QSLs, time/frequency schedule, station stickers, calendars, *Let's Learn Korean* book and a wide variety of other small souvenirs. *History of Korea* is available on CD-ROM (upon request) and via the station's Website.

KUWAIT World Time +3

Ministry of Information, P.O. Box 193, 13002 Safat, Kuwait. Phone: +965 241-5301. Fax: +965 243 4511. Web: www.moinfo.gov.kw. Contact: Sheik Nasir Al-Sabah, Minister of Information.

TRANSMISSION AND FREQUENCY MANAGEMENT SECTION: Ministry of Information, P.O. Box 967 13010 Safat, Kuwait. Phone: +965 241-3590 or +965 241-7830. Fax: +965 241 5498. Email: kwtfreq@yahoo.com. Contact: Ahmed J. Alawdhi, Head of Frequency Section; Abdel Amir Mohamed Ali, Head of Frequency Planning; Nasser Al-Saffar, Frequency Manager; or Muhamad Abdullah, Director of Transmitting Stations.

⊞**Radio Kuwait**, P.O. Box 397, 13004 Safat, Kuwait; (technical) Department of Frequency Management, P.O. Box 967, 13010 Safat, Kuwait. Phone: (general) +965 242-3774; (technical) +965 241-0301. Fax: (general) +965 245 6660; (technical) +965 241 5946. Email: (technical, including reception reports) kwtfreq@hotmail.com; (general) radiokuwait@radiokuwait.org or info@moinfo.gov.kw. Web: (technical) www.moinfo.gov.kw/ENG/FREQ; (RealAudio) www.radiokuwait.org. Contact: (general) Manager, External Service; (technical) Wessam Najaf. Sometimes gives away stickers, calendars, pens or key chains.

KYRGYZSTAN World Time +5 (+6 midyear)

Kyrgyz Radio, Kyrgyz TV and Radio Center, 59 Jash Gvardiya Boulevard, 720300 Bishkek, Kyrgyzstan. Phone: (general) +996 (312) 253-404 or +996 (312) 255-741; (Director) +996 (312) 255-700 or +996 (312) 255-709; (Assemov) +996 (312) 650-7341 or +996 (312) 255-703; (Atakanova) +996 (312) 251-927; (technical) +996 (312) 257-771. Fax: +996 (312) 257 952. Note that from a few countries, the dialing code is still the old +7 (3312). Email: trk@kyrnet.kg. Contact: (administration), Moldoseyit Mambetakunov, Vice-Chairman - Kyrgyz Radio; or Eraly Ayilchiyev, Director; (general) Talant Assemov, Editor -

Kyrgyz/Russian/German news; Gulnara Abdulaeva, Announcer - Kyrgyz/Russian/German news; (technical) Mirbek Uursabekov, Technical Director. Kyrgyz and Russian preferred, but correspondence in English and German can also be processed. For quick processing of reception reports, use email in German to Talant Assemov.

TRANSMISSION FACILITIES: Ministry of Transport and Communications, 42 Issanova Street, 720000 Bishkek, Kyrgyzstan. Phone: +996 (312) 216-672. Fax: +996 (312) 213 667. Contact: Jantoro Satybaldiyev, Minister. The shortwave transmitting station is located at Krasny-Retcha (Red River), a military encampment in the Issk-Ata region, about 40 km south of Bishkek.

Radio Extol. Email: am1467@hotmail.com; (technical) timskar@pisem.net. Contact: Timur Karimov, Technical Department.

LAOS World Time +7

Lao National Radio, Luang Prabang (if reactivated), Luang Prabang, Laos; or B.P. 310, Vientiane, Laos. Return postage required (IRCs not accepted). Replies slowly and very rarely. Best bet is to write in Laotian or French directly to Luang Prabang, where the transmitter is located.

Lao National Radio, Vientiane, Laotian National Radio and Television, B.P. 310, Vientiane, Laos. Phone: +856 (21) 212-429. Fax: +856 (21) 212 430. Email: natradio@laonet.net. Contact: Khoun Sounantha, Manager-in-Charge; Bounthan Inthasai, Director General; Mrs. Vinachine, English/French Sections; Ms. Mativarn Simanithone, Deputy Head, English Section; or Miss Chanthery Vichitsavanh, Announcer, English Section who says, "It would be good if you send your letter unregistered, because I find it difficult to get all letters by myself at the post. Please use my name, and 'Lao National Radio, P.O. Box 310, Vientiane, Laos P.D.R.' It will go directly to me." Sometimes includes a program schedule and Laotian stamps when replying. The external service of this station is currently off shortwave.

LEBANON World Time +2 (+3 midyear)

⊞**Voice of Charity**, Rue Fouad Chéhab, B.P. 850, Jounieh, Lebanon. Phone: +961 (9) 914-901 or +961 (9) 918-090. Email: radiocharity@opuslibani.org.lb. Web: (includes RealAudio) www.radiocharity.org.lb. Contact: Frère Elie Nakhoul, Managing Director. Program aired via facilities of Vatican Radio from a station founded by the Order of the Lebanese Missionaries. Basically, a Lebanese Christian educational radio program. Replies to correspondence in English, French and Arabic, and verifies reception reports.

LESOTHO World Time +2

Radio Lesotho, P.O. Box 552, Maseru 100, Lesotho. Phone: +266 323-371 or +266 323-561. Fax: +266 323 003. Web: www.radioles.co.ls. Contact: (general) Mamonyane Matsaba, Acting Programming Director; or Sekhonyana Motlohi, Producer, "What Do Listeners Say?"; (administration) Ms. Mpine Tente, Principal Secretary, Ministry of Information and Broadcasting; (technical) Lebohang Monnapula, Chief Engineer; Emmanuel Rametse, Transmitter Engineer; or Motlatsi Monyane, Studio Engineer. Return postage necessary, but do not include currency notes—local currency exchange laws are very strict.

LIBERIA World Time exactly

NOTE: Mail sent to Liberia may be returned as undeliverable.
Radio ELWA, c/o SIM Liberia, 08 B.P. 886, Abidjan 08, Côte d'Ivoire. Contact: Moses T. Nyantee, Station Manager; or Chief Technician.
Radio Liberia International (when operating), Liberian Communications Network/KISS, P.O. Box 1103, 1000 Monrovia 10, Liberia. Phone: +231 226-963 or +231 227-593. Fax: (during working hours) +231 226 003. Contact: Issac P. Davis, Engineer-in-Charge/QSL Coordinator. $5 required for QSL card.
Radio Veritas, P.O. Box 3569, Monrovia, Liberia. Phone: +231 226-979. Contact: Steve Kenneh, Manager.

LIBYA World Time +2

Libyan Jamahiriyah Broadcasting Corporation, P.O. Box 9333, Soug al Jama, Tripoli, Libya. Email: info@ljbc.net. Web: www.ljbc.net/radio/radio.htm.
Voice of Africa, P.O. Box 4677, Soug al Jama, Tripoli, Libya. Phone: +218 (21) 444-0112, +218 (21) 444-9106 or +218 (21) 444-9872. Fax: +218 (21) 444 9875. Email: africanvoice@hotmail.com. The external service of Libyan Jamahiriyah Broadcasting identifies as "Voice of Africa" in its English and French programs, while in Arabic it may use the same identification as the domestic service or refer to itself as the "Voice of Libya." Replies slowly and irregularly.
MALTA OFFICE: P.O. Box 17, Hamrun, Malta. Replies tend to be more forthcoming from this address than direct from Libya.

LITHUANIA World Time +2 (+3 midyear)

⛶Lithuanian Radio (if reactivated on shortwave), Lietuvos Radijas, S. Konarskio 49, LT-2600 Vilnius MTP, Lithuania. Phone: (Program Director) +370 (5) 236-3002; (Technical Director) +370 (5) 236-3202. Fax: (administration) +370 (5) 213 5333; (Technical Director) +370 (5) 213 2465. Email: (Litvaitiené) litvaitiene@lrt.lt; (reception reports) peles@lrt.lt. Web: (includes RealAudio and Windows Media) www.lrt.lt. Contact: (general) Ms. Guoda Litvaitiené, Program Director; (technical) Vytautas Marozas, Technical Director.
Radio Vilnius, Lietuvos Radijas, Konarskio 49, LT-2600 Vilnius, Lithuania. Phone: +370 (5) 236-3079. Email: ravil@lrt.lt. Contact: Ms. Ilona Rukiene, Head of English Department. Free stickers, pennants, Lithuanian stamps and other souvenirs.

MADAGASCAR World Time +3

Adventist World Radio
ADMINISTRATION: B.P. 700, Antananarivo, Madagascar. Phone: +261 (2022) 404-65.
STUDIO: B.P. 460, Antananarivo, Madagascar.
TECHNICAL AND NON-TECHNICAL (e.g. comments on programs)—see United Kingdom and USA. AWR broadcasts in Malagasy and French on leased airtime from Radio Nederland's Madagascar Relay. Reception reports concerning these broadcasts are best sent to the AWR U.K. office. Also, *see* AWR listings under Germany, Guam, Guatemala, Kenya, United Kingdom and USA.
Radio Madagasikara, B.P. 442 - Anosy, 101 Antananarivo, Madagascar. Phone: +261 2022- 21745. Fax: +261 2022 32715. Email: (Director's Office) mmdir@dts.mg; (Editorial Dept.) mminfo@dts.mg; (Program Dept.) mmprog@dts.mg; (Webmaster) radmad@dts.mg. Web: http://takelaka.dts.mg/radmad. Contact: Mlle. Rakotonirina Soa Herimanitia, Secrétaire de Direction, a young lady who collects stamps;

Mamy Rafenomanantsoa, Directeur; or J.J. Rakotonirina, who has been known to request hi-fi catalogs. $1 required, and enclosing used stamps from various countries may help. Tape recordings accepted. Replies slowly and somewhat irregularly, usually to correspondence in French.
Radio Nederland Wereldomroep—Madagascar Relay, B.P. 404, Antananarivo, Madagascar. Contact: (technical) Rahamefy Eddy, Technische Dienst; or J.A. Ratobimiarana, Chief Engineer. Nontechnical correspondence should be sent to Radio Nederland Wereldomreop in the Netherlands (*see*).

MALAWI World Time +2

Malawi Broadcasting Corporation (when operating), P.O. Box 30133, Chichiri, Blantyre 3, Malawi. Phone: (general) +265 671-222; (transmitting station) +265 694-208. Fax: +265 671 257 or +265 671 353. Email: dgmbc@malawi.net. Web: www.mbcradios.com. Contact: (general) Wilson Bankuku, Director General; J.O. Mndeke; or T.J. Sineta; (technical) Edwin K. Lungu, Controller of Transmitters; Phillip Chinseu, Engineering Consultant; or Joseph Chikagwa, Director of Engineering. Tends to be irregular due to lack of transmitter spares. Return postage or $1 helpful, as the station is underfunded.

MALAYSIA World Time +8

Asia-Pacific Broadcasting Union (ABU), P.O. Box 1164, 59700 Kuala Lumpur, Malaysia; or (street address) 2nd Floor, Bangunan IPTAR, Angkasapuri, 50614 Kuala Lumpur, Malaysia. Phone: (general) +60 (3) 2282-3592; (Programme Department) +60 (3) 2282-2480; (Technical Department) +60 (3) 2282-3108. Fax: +60 (3) 2282 5292. Email: (Office of Secretary-General) sg@abu.org.my; (Programme Department) prog@abu.org.my; (Technical Department) tech@abu.org.my. Web: www.abu.org.my. Contact: (administration) David Astley, Secretary- General; (technical) Sharad Sadhu and Rukmin Wijemanne, Senior Engineers, Technical Department.
Radio Malaysia Kota Kinabalu, RTM Sabah, 2.4 km Jalan Tuaran, 88614 Kota Kinabalu, Sabah, Malaysia. Phone: +60 (88) 213-444. Fax: +60 (88) 223 493. Email: rtmkk@rtm.net.my. Web: www.p.sabah.gov.my/rtm. Contact: Benedict Janil, Director of Broadcasting; Hasbullah Latiff; or Mrs. Angrick Saguman. Registering your letter may help. $1 or return postage required.
⛶Radio Malaysia, Kuala Lumpur
MAIN OFFICE: RTM, Angkasapuri, Bukit Putra, 50614 Kuala Lumpur, Malaysia. Phone: +60 (3) 2282-5333 or +60 (3) 2282-4976. Fax: +60 (3) 2282 4735, +60 (3) 2282 5103 or +60 (3) 2282 5859. Email: sabariah@rtm.net.my or helpdesk@rtm.net.my. Web: www.rtm.net.my. Contact: (general) Madzhi Johari, Director of Radio; (technical) Ms. Aminah Din, Deputy Director Engineering (Radio); Abdullah Bin Shahadan, Engineer, Transmission and Monitoring; or Ong Poh, Chief Engineer. May sell T-shirts and key chains. Return postage required.
ENGINEERING DIVISION: 3rd Floor, Angkasapum, 50616 Kuala Lumpur, Malaysia. Phone: +60 (3) 2285-7544. Fax: +60 (3) 2283 2446. Email: zulrahim@rtm.net.my. Contact: Zulkifli Ab Rahim.
RADIO 1 (MALAY): Wisma Radio Angkasapuri, P.O. Box 11272, 50740 Kuala Lumpur, Malaysia. Phone: +60 (3) 2288-7841 or +60 (3) 2288-7261. Fax: +60 (3) 2284 7593. Email: komit@radio1.com.my. Web: www.rtm.net.my/radio1; (includes Windows Media) www.radio1.com.my.
RADIO 4 (ENGLISH): Same address as Radio 1, above. Phone: +60 (3) 2288-7282/3/4/5 or +60 (3) 2288-7663. Fax: +60 (3)

2284 5750. Email: radio4@rtm.net.my. Web: www.rtm.net.my/radio4.

RADIO 6 (TAMIL): Same address as Radios 1 and 4, above. Phone: +60 (3) 2288-7279. Fax: +60 (3) 2284 9137. Web: www.rtm.net.my/radio6.

TRANSMISSION OFFICE: Controller of Engineering, Department of Broadcasting (RTM), 43000 Kajang, Selangor Darul Ehsan, Malaysia. Phone: +60 (3) 8736-1530 or +60 (3) 8736- 1530/1863. Fax: +60 (3) 8736 1226/7. Email: rtmkjg@rtm.net.my. Contact: Jeffrey Looi; or Ab Wahid Bin Hamid, Supervisor, Transmission Engineering.

Radio Malaysia Sarawak (Kuching), RTM Sarawak, Jalan Satok, 93614 Kuching, Sarawak, Malaysia. Phone: +60 (82) 248-422. Fax: +60 (82) 241 914. Email: rtmkuc@rtm.net.my. Contact: (general) Yusof Ally, Director of Broadcasting; Mohd. Hulman Abdollah; or Human Resources Development; (technical, but also nontechnical) Colin A. Minoi, Technical Correspondence; (technical) Kho Kwang Khoon, Deputy Director of Engineering. Return postage helpful.

Radio Malaysia Sarawak (Miri), RTM Miri, Bangunan Penyiaran, 98000 Miri, Sarawak, Malaysia. Phone: +60 (85) 422-524 or +60 (85) 423-645. Fax: +60 (85) 411 430. Contact: Clement Stia. $1 or return postage helpful.

Radio Malaysia Sarawak (Sibu), RTM Sibu, Bangunan Penyiaran, 96009 Sibu, Sarawak, Malaysia. Phone: +60 (84) 323-566. Fax: +60 (84) 321 717. Contact: Clement Stia, Divisional Controller, Broadcasting Department. $1 or return postage required. Replies irregularly and slowly.

Voice of Islam—Program of the Voice of Malaysia (*see*, below).

Voice of Malaysia, Suara Malaysia, Wisma Radio Angkasapuri, P.O. Box 11272, 50740 Kuala Lumpur, Malaysia. Phone: (general) +60 (3) 2288-7824; (English Service) +60 (3) 2282-7826. Fax: +60 (3) 2284 7594. Email: vom@rtm.net.my; (technical, Kajang transmitter site) rtmkjg@po.jaring.my. Web: www.rtm.net.my/vom/utama.htm. Contact: (general) Mrs. Mahani bte Ujang, Supervisor, English Service; Hajjah Wan Chuk Othman, English Service; (administration) Santokh Singh Gill, Director; or Mrs. Adilan bte Omar, Assistant Director; (technical) Lin Chew, Director of Engineering; (Kajang transmitter site) Kok Yoon Yeen, Technical Assistant. Free calendars and stickers. Two IRCs or return postage helpful. Replies slowly and irregularly.

Studios of Deutsche Welle, Germany.   M. Guha

MALI   World Time exactly

Radiodiffusion Télévision Malienne, B.P. 171, Bamako, Mali. Phone: +223 212-019 or +223 212-474. Fax: +223 214 205. Email: (general) ortm@cafib.com; (Traore) cotraore@sotelma.ml. Contact: Karamoko Issiaka Daman, Directeur des Programmes; (administration) Abdoulaye Sidibe, Directeur General; (Technical) Nouhoum Traore. $1 or IRC helpful. Replies slowly and irregularly to correspondence in French. English also accepted.

MALTA   World Time +1 (+2 midyear)

◪**Voice of the Mediterranean (Radio Melita)**, Chircop Building, Floor 2, Valley Road, Birkirkara BKR 14, Malta; or P.O. Box 143, Valetta CMR 01, Malta. Phone: +356 227-97000. Fax: +356 227 97111. Email: info@vomradio.com. Web: (includes Windows Media) www.vomradio.com. Contact: (management) Richard Muscat, Managing Director; (German Service and listener contact) Ingrid Huettmann; Victoria Farrugia. Letters and reception reports welcomed. May send blank QSL cards, stickers and bookmarks.

MAURITANIA   World Time exactly

Radio Mauritanie, B.P. 200, Nouakchott, Mauritania. Phone: +222 (2) 52287. Fax: +222 (2) 51264. Email: rm@mauritania.mr. Contact: Madame Amir Feu; Lemrabott Boukhary; Madame Fatimetou Fall Dite Ami, Secretaire de Direction; Mr. El Hadj Diagne; or Mr. Hane Abou. Return postage or $1 required. Rarely replies.

MEXICO   World Time -6 (-5 midyear) Central, South and Eastern, including D.F.; -7 (-6 midyear) Mountain; -7 Sonora; -8 (-7 midyear) Pacific

Candela FM—*see* RASA Onda Corta.

La Hora Exacta—XEQK (if reactivated), Real de Mayorazgo 83, Barrio de Xoco, 03330- México D.F., Mexico. Phone: +52 (55) 5628-1731, +52 (55) 5628-1700 Ext. 1648 or 1659. Fax: +52 (55) 5604 8292. Web: www.imer.gob.mx (click on "Radiodifusoras"). Contact: Lic. Santiago Ibarra Ferrer, Gerente.

La Jarocha—XEFT (if reactivated), Apartado Postal 21, 91701- Veracruz, VER, Mexico. Phone: +52 (229) 322-250. Contact: C.P. Miguel Rodríguez Sáez, Sub-Director; or Lic. Juan de Dios Rodríguez Díaz, Director. Free tourist guide to Veracruz. Return postage, IRC or $1 probably helpful. Likely to reply to correspondence in Spanish.

◪**Radio Educación Onda Corta—XEPPM**, Apartado Postal 21-940, 04021-México D.F., Mexico. Phone: (general) +52 (55) 5559-6169. Phone/fax: (Director's Office) +52 (55) 5575- 6566. Email: (general) radioe@conaculta.gob.mx; (Lidia Camacho) lidiac@conaculta.gob.mx. Web: www.cnca.gob.mx/cnca/buena/radio; (includes Windows Media) www.radioeducacion.edu.mx. Contact: (general) Lic. María Del Carmen Limón Celorio, Directora de Producción y Planeación; (administration) Lic. Lidia Camacho Camacho, Directora General; (technical) Ing. Jesús Aguilera Jiménez, Subdirector de Desarrollo Técnico. Free stickers, calendars and station photo. Return postage or $1 required. Replies, sometimes slowly, to correspondence in English, Spanish, Italian or French.

Radio Huayacocotla—XEJN

STATION ADDRESS: "Radio Huaya," Dom. Gutiérrez Najera s/n, Apartado Postal 13, 92600- Huayacocotla, VER, Mexico. Phone: +52 (775) 80067. Fax: +52 (775) 80178. Email:

radiohua@sjsocial.org, or framos@uibero.uia.mx. Web: www.sjsocial.org/Radio/huarad.html. Contact: Pedro Ruperto Albino, Coordinador. Return postage or $1 helpful. Replies irregularly to correspondence in Spanish.

Radio México Internacional—XERMX, Instituto Méxicano de la Radio, Mayorazgo #83, Colonia Xoco, 03330-Mexico D.F., Mexico; or Apartado Postal 21-300, 04021-México, D.F., Mexico. Phone: +52 (55) 5604-7846 or +52 (55) 5628-1720. Fax: +52 (55) 5628 1710. Email: rmi@eudoramail.com. Web: www.imer.gob.mx (click on "Radiodifusoras," then "XERMX"). Contact: Juan Josi Miroz, Host "Mailbag Program." Free stickers, post cards and stamps. Welcomes correspondence, including inquiries about Mexico, in Spanish and English. $1 helpful.

Radio Mil Onda Corta—XEOI, NRM, Avda. Insurgentes Sur 1870, Col. Florida, 01030- México D.F., Mexico; or Apartado Postal 21-1000, 04021-México, D.F., Mexico (this address for reception reports and listeners' correspondence on the station's shortwave broadcasts, and mark the envelope to the attention of Dr. Julián Santiago Díez de Bonilla). Phone: (station) +52 (55) 5662-1000 or +52 (55) 5662-1100; (Núcleo Radio Mil network) +52 (55) 5662-6060, +52 (55) 5663-0739 or +52 (55) 5663 0590. Fax: (station) +52 (55) 5662 0974; (Núcleo Radio Mil network) +52 (55) 5662 0979. Email: info@nrm.com.mx. Web: www.nrm.com.mx/estaciones/radiomil. Contact: (administration) Edilberto Huesca P., Vicepresidente Ejecutivo del Núcleo Radio Mil; or Lic. Gustavo Alvite Martínez, Director; (shortwave service) Dr. Julián Santiago Díez de Bonilla. Free stickers. $1 or return postage required.

Radio Tapachula—XETS (when activated), 7ª Oriente Nº 42, 30700-Tapachula, Chiapas, Mexico. Web: (Radio Núcleo parent organization) www.radionucleo.com.

☒**Radio Transcontinental—XERTA** (when operating), Plaza de San Juan 5, Primer piso, Despacho 2, Esquina con Ayuntamiento, Centro, 06070-México D.F., Mexico. Phone: +52 (55) 5518-4938. Email: xerta@radiodifusion.com. Web: (includes RealAudio) www.misionradio.com. Contact: Verónica Coria Miranda, Representante Ejecutiva.

☒**Radio UNAM [Universidad Autónoma de México]—XEYU** (when operating), Adolfo Prieto 133, Colonia del Valle, 03100-México D.F., Mexico. Phone: +52 (55) 5523-2633. Email: (general) radiounam@www.unam.mx; (Director) fes@servidor.unam.mx. Web: (includes RealAudio and MP3) www.unam.mx/radiounam. Contact: (general) Lic. Fernando Escalante Sobrino, Director General de Radio UNAM; (technical) Ing. Gustavo Carreño, Departamento Técnico. Free tourist literature and stickers. $1 or return postage required. Replies irregularly to correspondence in Spanish.

Radio Universidad—XEXQ, Gral. Mariano Arista 245, Centro Histórico, Apartado Postal 456, 78000-San Luis Potosí, SLP, Mexico. Phone: +52 (444) 826-1345. Fax: +52 (444) 826 1388. Web: www.uaslp.mxmx/rtu. Contact: Lic.María del Pilar Delgadillo Silva; Lic. Leticia Zavala Pérez, Coordinadora; or Lizbeth Deyanira Tapia Hernández, Radio Operadora.

RASA Onda Corta—XEQM (when operating), Apartado Postal 217, 97001-Mérida, YUC, Mexico. Phone: +52 (999) 236-155. Fax: +52 (999) 280 680. Contact: Lic. Bernardo Laris Rodríguez, Director General del Grupo RASA Mérida. Replies irregularly to correspondence in Spanish. Currently relays programs from FM sister station "Candela Tropicaliente," but hopes eventually to produce its own programming based on the best programs of each station in the network.

MOLDOVA   World Time +2 (+3 midyear)

Radio DMR, Rose Luxembourg Street 10, Tiraspol 3300, Republic of Moldova. Web: www.olvia.idknet.com/newweben.htm. Contact: Arkady D Shablienko, Director; Ms.

Antonina N. Voronkova, Editor-in-Chief; Ernest A. Vardanean, Editor and Translator; Vadim A. Rudomiotov, Announcer. Replies to correspondence in English and Russian. Return postage helpful. Broadcasts from the separatist, pro-Russian, "Dniester Moldavian Republic" (also known as "Trans-Dniester Moldavian Republic").

MONACO   World Time +1 (+2 midyear)

Trans World Radio
MAIN OFFICE: B.P. 349, MC-98007 Monte-Carlo, Monaco-Cedex. Phone: +377 (92) 16-56-00. Fax: +377 (92) 16 56 01. Web: (transmission schedule) www.gospelcom.net/twr/broadcasts/europe.htm. Contact: (general) Mrs. Jeanne Olson; (administration) Richard Olson, Station Manager; (Technical) *see* Vienna address, below. Free paper pennant. IRC or $1 helpful. Also, *see* USA. Uses the transmitting facilities of Radio Monte Carlo, across the border in Fontbonne, France.

GERMAN OFFICE: Evangeliums-Rundfunk, Postfach 1444, D-35573 Wetzlar, Germany. Phone: +49 (6441) 957-0. Fax: +49 (6441) 957 120. Email: erf@erf.de; or siemens@arf.de. Web: (includes RealAudio) www.erf.de. Contact: Jürgen Werth, Direktor.

NETHERLANDS OFFICE, NONTECHNICAL: Postbus 176, NL-3780 BD Voorthuizen, Netherlands. Phone: +31 (0) 3429-2727. Fax: +31 (0) 3429 6727. Contact: Beate Kiebel, Manager Broadcast Department; or Felix Widmer.

VIENNA OFFICE, TECHNICAL: Postfach 141, A-1235 Vienna, Austria. Phone: (Schraut) +43 (1) 863-1216: (Dobos) +43 (1) 863-1221; +43 (1) 863-1233; +43 (1) 863-1247 or (Baertschi) +43 (1) 863-1258. Fax: +43 (1) 863 1220. Email: (Menzel) 100615.1511@compuserve.com; (Schraut) twr_euro_bschraut@compuserve.com; bschraut@twr-europe.at; (Baertschi) rbaertsc@twr-europe.net; (Dobos) kdobos@twr-europe.at. Contact: Helmut Menzel, Director of Engineering; Bernhard Schraut, Frequency Manager; Rudolf Baertschi, Technical Director; or Kalman Dobos, Frequency Coordinator.

SWISS OFFICE: Evangelium in Radio und Fernsehen, Witzbergstrasse 23, CH-8330 Pfäffikon ZH, Switzerland. Phone: +41 (951) 0500. Fax: +41 (951) 0540. Email: erf@erf.ch. Web: www.erf.ch.

MONGOLIA   World Time +8 (+9 midyear)

Mongolian Radio (Postal and email addresseses same as Voice of Mongolia, *see* below). Phone: (administration) +976 (11) 323-520 or +976 (11) 328-978; (editorial) +976 (11) 329-766; (MRTV parent organization) +976 (11) 326-663. Fax: +976 (11) 327 234. Email: radiomongolia@magicnet.mn. Contact: A. Buidakhmet, Director.

☒**Voice of Mongolia**, C.P.O. Box 365, Ulaanbaatar 13, Mongolia. Phone: +976 (1) 321-624 or (English Section) +976 (11) 327-900. Fax: +976 (11) 323 096 or (English Section) +976 (11) 327 234. Email: (general) radiomongolia@magicnet.mn, radio-internet@magicnet.mn, or (International Relations Office) mrtv@magicnet.mn. Web: (includes RealAudio) www.mongol.net/vom. Contact: (general) Mrs. Narantuya, Chief of Foreign Service; D. Batbayar, Mail Editor, English Department; N. Tuya, Head of English Department; Dr. Mark Ostrowski, Consultant, MRTV International Relations Department; or Ms. Tsegmid Burmaa, Japanese Department; (administration) Ch. Surenjav, Director; (technical) Ing. Ganhuu, Chief of Technical Department. Correpondence should be directed to the relevant language section and 2 IRCs or 1$ appreciated. Sometimes very slow in replying. Accepts taped reception reports, preferably containing five-minute excerpts of the broadcast(s) reported, but cassettes cannot be returned. Free pennants, postcards, newspapers and Mongolian stamps.

TECHNICAL DEPARTMENT: C.P.O Box 1126, Ulaanbaatar Mongolia. Phone: +976 (11) 363- 584. Fax: +976 (11) 327 900. Email: mrtv@magicnet.mn or aem@mongol.net. Contact: Mr. Tumurbaatar Gantumur, Director of Technical Department; or Ms. Buyanbaatar Unur, Engineer, Technical Center of Transmission System.

MOROCCO   World Time exactly

📻**Radio Medi Un**
MAIN OFFICE: B.P. 2055, Tanger, Morocco (physical location: 3, rue Emsallah, 90000 Tanger, Morocco). Phone/fax: +212 (9) 936-363 or +212 (9) 935-755. Email: (general) medi1@medi1.com; (technical) technique@medi1.com. Web: (includes RealAudio) www.medi1.com; www.medi1.co.ma. Contact: J. Dryk, Responsable Haute Fréquence. Two IRCs helpful. Free stickers. Correspondence in French preferred.
PARIS BUREAU, NONTECHNICAL: 78 Avenue Raymond Poincaré, F-75016 Paris, France. Phone: +33 (1) 45-01-53-30. Correspondence in French preferred.
Radio Mediterranée Internationale—*see* Radio Medi Un.
📻**Radiodiffusion-Télévision Marocaine**, 1 rue El Brihi, Rabat, Morocco. Phone: +212 (7) 766- 881/83/85, +212 (7) 701-740 or +212 (7) 201-404. Fax: +212 (7) 722 047, or +212 (7) 703 208. Email: rtm@rtm.gov.ma; (technical) hammouda@ rtm.gov.ma. Web: (general) www.rtm.gov.ma; (radio) www.rtm.gov.ma/Radiodiffusion/Radiodiffusion.htm; (RealAudio) www.maroc.net/rc/live.htm. Contact: (nontechnical and technical) Ms. Naaman Khadija, Ingénieur d'Etat en Télécommunication; Abed Bendalh; or Rahal Sabir; (technical) Tanone Mohammed Jamaledine, Technical Director; Hammouda Mohammed, Engineer; or N. Read. Correspondence welcomed in English, French, Arabic or Berber.
Voice of America/IBB—Morocco Relay Station, Briech. Phone: (office) +212 (9) 93-24-81. Fax: +212 (9) 93 55 71. Contact: Station Manager. These numbers for urgent technical matters only. Otherwise, does not welcome direct correspondence; *see* USA for acceptable VOA and IBB Washington addresses and related information.

MYANMAR (BURMA)   World Time +6:30

Radio Myanmar
STATION: GPO Box 1432, Yangon-11181, Myanmar; or (street address) 426, Pyay Road, Yangon-11041, Myanmar. Phone: +95 (1) 531-850, +95 (1) 532-814. Fax: +95 (1) 525 428. Web: www.myanmar.com/RADIO_TV.HTM. Contact: Ko Ko Htway, Director.

NAGORNO-KARABAGH   World Time +4 (+5 midyear)

Voice of Justice, Tigranmetz Street 23a, Stepanakert, Nagorno-Karabagh. Contact: Michael Hajiyan, Station Manager. Replies to correspondence in Armenian, Azeri, Russian and German.

NAMIBIA   World Time +2 (+1 midyear)

Radio Namibia/Namibian Broadcasting Corporation, P.O. Box 321, Windhoek 9000, Namibia. Phone: (general) +264 (61) 291-3111; (National Radio—English Service) +264 (61) 291-2440; (German Service) +264 (61) 291-2330; (Schachtschneider)

+264 (61) 291-2188. Fax: (general) +264 (61) 217 760; (German Service) +264 (61) 291 2291; (Duwe, technical) +264 (61) 231 881. Email: (general) webmaster@nbc.com.na. To contact individuals, the format is initiallastname@nbc.com.na; so to reach, say, Peter Schachtschneider, it would be pschachtschneider@nbc.com.na. Web: www.nbc.com.na/index.html. Contact: (technical) Peter Schachtschneider, Manager, Transmitter Maintenance; Joe Duwe, Chief Technician. Free stickers.

NEPAL   World Time +5:45

📻**Radio Nepal**, P.O. Box 634, Singha Durbar, Kathmandu, Nepal. Phone: (general) +977 (1) 223-910, +977 (1) 243-569; (engineering) +977 (1) 225-467. Fax: +977 (1) 221 952. Email: radio@rne.wlink.com.np; (engineering) radio@engg.wlink.com.np. Web: (includes RealAudio in English and Nepali) www.radionepal.org. Contact: (general) S.R. Sharma, Executive Director; M.P. Adhikari, Deputy Executive Director; Jayanti Rajbhandari, Director - Programming; or S.K. Pant, Producer, "Listener's Mail"; (technical) Ram Sharan Kharki, Director - Engineering. 3 IRCs necessary, but station urges that neither mint stamps nor cash be enclosed, as this invites theft by Nepalese postal employees.

NETHERLANDS   World Time +1 (+2 midyear)

📻**Radio Nederland Wereldomroep (Radio Netherlands)**
MAIN OFFICE: P.O. Box 222, 1200 JG Hilversum, The Netherlands. Phone: (general) +31 (35) 672-4211; (English Language Service) +31 (35) 672-4242; (24-hour listener Answerline) +31 (35) 672-4222. Fax: (general) +31 (35) 672 4207, but indicate destination department on fax cover sheet; (English Language Service) +31 (35) 672 4239. Email: (English Service) letters@rnw.nl; ("Media Network") media@rnw.nl. Web: (includes RealAudio, Windows Media and MP3) www.rnw.nl. Contact: (management) Lodewijk Bouwens, Director General; Jan Hoek, Director of Finance and Logistics; Freek Eland, Editor-in-Chief; Mike Shaw, Head of English Language Service; Ginger da Silva, Network Manager English. Full-data verification card for reception reports, following guidelines in the RNW folder, "Writing Useful Reception Reports," available on the Media Network Website. Semi-annual *On Target* newsletter also free upon request, as are stickers and booklets. Other language departments have their own newsletters. Radio Netherlands Music produces concerts heard on many NPR stations in North America, as well as a line of CDs, mainly of classical, jazz, world music and the Euro Hit 40. Most of the productions are only for rebroadcasting on other stations, but recordings on the NM Classics label are for sale. More details are available at www.rnmusic.nl. Visitors welcome, but must call in advance.
PROGRAMME DISTRIBUTION, NETWORK AND FREQUENCY PLANNING: P.O. Box 222, 1200 JG Hilversum, The Netherlands. Phone: +31 (35) 672-4422. Fax: +31 (35) 672 4429. Email: nfp@rnw.nl. Contact: Leo van der Woude, Frequency Manager; or Jan Willem Drexhage, Head of Programme Distribution.
NEW DELHI OFFICE: (local correspondence only) P.O. Box 5257, Chanakya Puri Post Office, New Delhi, 110 021, India. Forwards mail from Indian listeners to the Netherlands every three weeks.
📻**Radio Voice of Hope**, Plot No. 15, Komi Crescent, Lusira, 338829 Kampala, Uganda. Phone: +256 (41) 220-334. Email: webmaster@radiovoiceofhope.net; hope@africaonline.co.ug; or (Namadi) jnamadi@excite.com. Web: (includes RealAudio)

www.radiovoiceofhope.net. Contact: Jane Namadi, Editor. Return postage requested. Programs are produced by the New Sudan Council of Churches (NSCC) at studios in the Netherlands and Uganda. Identifies as "Radio Voice of Hope for the voiceless in southern Sudan." Transmits via the Radio Nederland relay station in Madagascar, and is a project sponsored by the Dutch public broadcaster NCRV and supported by Pax Christi and the Interchurch Organization for Development Corporation.

KENYA ADDRESS: P.O.Box 66168, Nairobi, Kenya. Phone: +254 (2) 446-966 or +254 (2) 448- 141/2. Fax: +254 (2) 447 015. Email: nscc-nbo@maf.org.

NETHERLANDS ANTILLES   World Time -4

Radio Nederland Wereldomroep—Bonaire Relay, P.O. Box 45, Kralendijk, Netherlands Antilles. Contact: Leo Kool, Manager. Nontechnical correspondence should be sent to Radio Nederland Wereldomreop in the Netherlands (*see*).

NEW ZEALAND   World Time +13 (+12 midyear)

☎Radio New Zealand International (Te Reo Irirangi O Aotearoa, O Te Moana-nui-a-kiwa), P.O. Box 123, Wellington, New Zealand. Phone: +64 (4) 474-1437. Fax: +64 (4) 474 1433 or +64 (4) 474 1886. Email: info@rnzi.com. Web: (includes RealAudio and online reception report form) www.rnzi.com. Contact: Florence de Ruiter, Listener Mail; Myra Oh, Producer, "Mailbox"; or Walter Zweifel, News Editor; (administration) Ms. Linden Clark, Manager; (technical) Adrian Sainsbury, Technical Manager. Free stickers, schedule/flyer about station, map of New Zealand and tourist literature available. English/Maori T-shirts for US$20; sweatshirts $40; interesting variety of CDs, as well as music cassettes and spoken programs, in Domestic "Replay Radio" catalog (VISA/MC). Two IRCs or $2 for QSL card, one IRC for schedule/catalog. Email reports verified by email only.

Radio Reading Service—ZLXA, P.O. Box 360, Levin 5500, New Zealand. Phone: (general) +64 (6) 368-2229; (engineering) +64 (25) 985-360. Fax: +64 (6) 368 7290. Email: (general) nzrpd@xtra.co.nz; (Bell) ABell@radioreading.org; (Little) Alittle@radioreading.org; (Stokoe) BStokoe@radioreading.org. Web: www.radioreading.org. Contact: (general) Ash Bell, Manager/Station Director; (administration) Allen J. Little, Executive President; (technical, including reception reports) Brian Stokoe. Operated by volunteers 24 hours a day, seven days a week. Station is owned by the "New Zealand Radio for the Print Disabled Inc." Free brochure, postcards and stickers. $1, return postage or 3 IRCs appreciated.

NICARAGUA   World Time -6

Radio Miskut, Barrio Pancasan, Puerto Cabezas, R.A.A.N., Nicaragua. Phone: +505 (282) 2443. Fax: +505 (267) 3032. Contact: Evaristo Mercado Pérez, Director de Operación y de Programas; or Abigail Zúñiga Fagoth. Replies slowly and irregularly to correspondence in English and Spanish. $2 helpful, as is registering your letter.

NIGER   World Time +1

La Voix du Sahel, O.R.T.N., B.P. 361, Niamey, Niger. Fax: +227 72 35 48. Contact: (general) Adamou Oumarou; Issaka Mamadou; Zakari Saley; Souley Boubacou; or Mounkaïla Inazadan, Producer, "Inter-Jeunes Variétés"; (administration)

Eduardo Moura, who at one time presented "Além Fronteiras" over Rádio Canção Nova, Brazil.

E. Moura

Oumar Tiello, Directeur; (technical) Afo Sourou Victor. $1 helpful. Correspondence in French preferred. Correspondence by males with this station may result in requests for certain unusual types of magazines and photographs.

NIGERIA   World Time +1

WARNING—MAIL THEFT: For the time being, correspondence from abroad to Nigerian addresses has a relatively high probability of being stolen.

WARNING—CONFIDENCE ARTISTS: For years, now, correspondence with Nigerian stations has sometimes resulted in letters from highly skilled "pen pal" confidence artists. These typically offer to send you large sums of money, if you will provide details of your bank account or similar information (after which they clean out your account). Other scams are disguised as tempting business proposals; or requests for money, free electronic or other products, publications or immigration sponsorship. Persons thus approached should contact their country's diplomatic offices. For example, Americans should contact the Diplomatic Security Section of the Department of State [phone +1 (202) 647-4000], or an American embassy or consulate.

Radio Nigeria—Enugu (when operating), P.M.B. 1051, Enugu (Anambra), Phone: +234 (42) 254-137. Fax: +234 (42) 255 354. Nigeria. Contact: Engr. Louis Nnamuchi, Deputy Director Engineering Services. Two IRCs, return postage or $1 required. Replies slowly.

Radio Nigeria—Ibadan, Broadcasting House, P.M.B. 5003, Ibadan, Oyo State, Nigeria. Phone: +234 (22) 241-4093 or +234 (22) 241-4106. Fax: +234 (22) 241 3930. Contact: V.A. Kalejaiye, Technical Services Department; Rev. Olukunle Ajani, Executive Director; Nike Adegoke, Executive Director; or Dare Folarin, Principal Public Affairs Officer. $1 or return postage required. Replies slowly.

Radio Nigeria—Kaduna, P.O. Box 250, Kaduna (Kaduna), Nigeria. Contact: R.B. Jimoh, Assistant Director Technical Service; or Shehu Muhammad, Chief Technical Officer, Studio Link and Outside Broadcasts. May send sticker celebrating 30 years of broadcasting. $1 or return postage required. Replies slowly.

Radio Nigeria—Lagos, P.M.B. 12504, Ikoyi, Lagos, Nigeria. Phone: +234 (1) 269-0301. Fax: +234 (1) 269 0073. Contact: Willie Egbe, Assistant Director for Programmes; Babatunde Olalekan Raji, Monitoring Unit. Two IRCs or return postage helpful. Replies slowly and irregularly.

Voice of Nigeria

ABUJA OFFICE: 6th Floor, Radio House Herbert Macaulay, Garki-Abuja, Nigeria. Phone: +234 (9) 234-6973, +234 (9) 234-4017. Fax: +234 (9) 234 6970. Email: (general) dgovon@nigol.net.ng, vonabuja@rosecom.net; (Idowu) tidowu@yahoo.com. Web: www.voiceofnigeria.org. Contact: Ayodele Suleiman, Director of Programming; Tope Idowu, Editor "Voice Of Nigeria Air-waves" program magazine & Special Assistant to the Director General; Frank Iloye, Station Manager; (technical) Timothy Gyang, Deputy Director, Engineering.

LAGOS OFFICE: P.M.B. 40003, Falomo, Lagos, Nigeria. Phone: +234 (1) 269-3075 or +234 (1) 269-3078. Fax: +234 (1) 269 3078, +234 (9) 269 1944. Email: vonlagos@fiberia.com. Replies from the station tend to be erratic, but continue to generate unsolicited correspondence from supposed "pen pals" (*see WARNING—CONFIDENCE ARTISTS*, above); faxes, which are much less likely to be intercepted, may be more fruitful. Two IRCs or return postage helpful.

NORTHERN MARIANA ISLANDS World Time +10

Far East Broadcasting Company—Radio Station KFBS, P.O. Box 500209, Saipan, Mariana Islands MP 96950 USA. Phone: +1 (670) 322-3841. Fax: +1 (670) 322 3060. Email: saipan@febc.org. Web: www.febc.org. Contact: Robert Springer, Director; or Irene Gabbie, QSL Secretary. Replies sometimes take months. Also, *see* FEBC Radio International, USA.

NORWAY World Time +1 (+2 midyear).

NPT—Norwegian Post and Telecommunications Authority
FREQUENCY MANAGEMENT OFFICE: Statens Teleforvaltning, Dept. TF/OMG, Revierstredet 2, P.O. Box 447 Sentrum, N-0104 Oslo, Norway. Phone: +47 (22) 824-776. Fax: +47 (22) 824 890. Email: (Johnsbråthen) erik.johnsbraten@npt.no; (Ohta) ayumu.ohta@npt.no. Contact: Erik Johnsbråthen, Frequency Manager; or Ayumu Ohta.

Radio Norway, NRK Radio i utlandet, N-0342 Oslo, Norway. Phone: +47 2304-7000. Email: info@nrk.no. Web: (includes RealAudio) www.nrk.no/radionorway.

UKEsenderen, Elgesetergate 1, N-7030 Trondheim, Norway. Email: uka@uka.no. Web: www.uka.ntnu.no. A student station which operates on 7215 kHz for approximately three weeks (mid-October to early November) in odd-numbered years.

OMAN World Time +4

Radio Sultanate of Oman, Ministry of Information, P.O. Box 600, Muscat, Post Code 113, Sultanate of Oman. Phone: +968 602-494 or +968 603-222. Fax: (general) +968 602 055, +968 693 770 or +968 602 831; (technical) +968 604 629 or +968 607 239. Email: (general) tvradio@omantel.net.om; (Frequency Management) sjnomani@omantel.net.om; or abulukman@hotmail.com. Web: (includes RealAudio) www.oman-radio.gov.om. Contact: (Directorate General of Technical Affairs) Abdallah Bin Saif Al-Nabhani, Acting Chief Engineer; Salim Al-Nomani, Director of Frequency Management; or Ahmed Mohamed Al- Balushi, Head of Studio's Engineering. Replies regularly, and responses are from one to two weeks. $1, mint stamps or 3 IRCs helpful.

PAKISTAN World Time +5 (+6 midyear)

Azad Kashmir Radio, Muzaffarabad, Azad Kashmir, Pakistan. Contact: (technical) M. Sajjad Ali Siddiqui, Director of Engineering; or Liaquatullah Khan, Engineering Manager. Regis-tered mail helpful. Rarely replies to correspondence.

Pakistan Broadcasting Corporation—same address, fax and contact details as "Radio Pakistan," below. Web: (includes RealAudio) www.radio.gov.pk.

Radio Pakistan, P.O. Box 1393, Islamabad 44000, Pakistan. Phone: +92 (51) 921-6942 or +92 (51) 921-7321. Fax: +92 (51) 920 1861, +92 (51) 920 1118 or +92 (51) 922 3877. Email: (general) cnoradio@isb.comsats.net.pk; (technical) cfmpbchq@isb.comsats.net.pk (reception reports to this address have been verified with QSL cards). Web: www.radio.gov.pk/exter.html. Contact: (technical) Ahmed Nawaz, Senior Broadcast Engineer, Room No. 324, Frequency Management Cell; Iftikhar Malik, Senior Broadcast Engineer & Frequency Manager, Frequency Management Cell; Ajmal Kokhar, Controller of Frequency Management; Syed Asmat Ali Shah, Senior Broadcasting Engineer; Zulfiqar Ahmad, Director of Engineering; or Nasirahmad Bajwa, Frequency Management. Free stickers, pennants and *Pakistan Calling* magazine. May also send pocket calendar. Replies ir-regularly to postal correspondence; better is to use email if you can. Plans to replace two 50 kW transmitters with 500 kW units if and when funding is forthcoming.

PALAU World Time +9

Radio Station T8BZ (formerly KHBN), P.O. Box 66, Koror, Palau PW 96940. Phone: +680 488-2162. Fax: (main office) +680 488 2163; (engineering) +680 544 1008. Email: (technical) cacciatore@lineone.net. Contact: (technical) Rev. Dr. Bill Burton, Chief Engineer. IRC requested.

PAPUA NEW GUINEA World Time +10

NOTE: Stations are sometimes off the air due to financial or technical problems which can take weeks or months to re-solve.

KBBN ("Krai Bilong Baibel Bradkesting Netwok"), P.O. Box 617, Mt. Hagen W.H.P., Papua New Guinea. Email: bwells@daltron.com.pg. Contact: Brad Wells. A bible radio ministry ini-tially broadcasting on FM, but which eventually hopes to add a shortwave transmitter.

National Broadcasting Corporation of Papua New Guinea, P.O. Box 1359, Boroko 111 NCD, Papua New Guinea. Phone: +675 325-5233, + 675 325-5949 or +675 325-6779. Fax: +675 323 0404, +675 325 0796 or +675 325 6296. Email: pom@nbc.com.pg. Web: www.nbc.com.pg. Contact: (general) Renagi R. Lohia, CBE, Managing Director and C.E.O.; or Ephraim Tammy, Director, Radio Services; (technical) Bob Kabewa, Sr. Technical Officer; or F. Maredey, Chief Engineer. Two IRCs or return postage helpful. Replies irregularly.

Radio Bougainville, P.O. Box 35, Buka, North Solomons Prov-ince (NSP), Papua New Guinea. Contact: Aloysius Rumina, Pro-vincial Programme Manager; Ms. Christine Talei, Assistant Provincial Manager; or Aloysius Laukai, Senior Programme Of-ficer. Replies irregularly.

Radio Central (when operating), P.O. Box 1359, Boroko, NCD, Papua New Guinea. Contact: Steven Gamini, Station Manager; Lahui Lovai, Provincial Programme Manager; or Amos Langit, Technician. $1, 2 IRCs or return postage helpful. Replies ir-regularly.

Radio Eastern Highlands (when operating), P.O. Box 311, Goroka, EHP, Papua New Guinea. Phone: +675 732-1533, +675 732-1733. Contact: Tony Mill, Station Manager; Tonko Nonao, Program Manager; Ignas Yanam, Technical Officer; or Kiri Nige, Engineering Division. $1 or return postage required. Replies irregularly.

Radio East New Britain (when operating), P.O. Box 393, Rabaul, ENBP, Papua New Guinea. Contact: Esekia Mael, Station Manager; or Oemas Kumaina, Provincial Program Manager. Return postage required. Replies slowly.

Radio East Sepik, P.O. Box 65, Wewak, E.S.P., Papua New Guinea. Contact: Elias Albert, Assistant Provincial Program Manager; or Luke Umbo, Station Manager.

Radio Enga, P.O. Box 300, Wabag, Enga Province, Papua New Guinea. Phone: +675 547-1213. Contact: (general) John Lyein Kur, Station Manager; or Robert Papuvo, (technical) Gabriel Paiao, Station Technician.

Radio Gulf (when operating), P.O. Box 36, Kerema, Gulf, Papua New Guinea. Contact: Tmothy Akia, Station Manager; or Timothy Akia, Provincial Program Manager.

Radio Madang, P.O. Box 2138, Madang, Papua New Guinea. Phone: +675 852-2415. Fax: +675 852 2360. Contact: (general) Damien Boaging, Senior Programme Officer; Geo Gedabing, Provincial Programme Manager; Peter Charlie Yannum, Assistant Provincial Programme Manager; or James Steve Valakvi, Senior Programme Officer; (technical) Lloyd Guvil, Technician.

Radio Manus, P.O. Box 505, Lorengau, Manus, Papua New Guinea. Phone: +675 470-9029. Fax: +675 470 9079. Contact: (technical and nontechnical) John P. Mandrakamu, Provincial Program Manager. Station is seeking the help of DXers and broadcasting professionals in obtaining a second hand, but still usable broadcasting quality CD player that could be donated to Radio Manus. Replies regularly. Return postage appreciated.

Radio Milne Bay (when operating), P.O. Box 111, Alotau, Milne Bay, Papua New Guinea. Contact: (general) Trevor Webumo, Assistant Manager; Simon Muraga, Station Manager; or Raka Petuely, Program Officer; (technical) Philip Maik, Technician. Return postage in the form of mint stamps helpful.

Radio Morobe, P.O. Box 1262, Lae, Morobe, Papua New Guinea. Fax: +675 472 6423. Contact: Ken L. Tropu, Assistant Program Manager; Peter W. Manua, Program Manager; Kekalem M. Meruk, Assistant Provincial Program Manager; or Aloysius R. Nase, Station Manager.

Radio New Ireland (when operating), P.O. Box 140, Kavieng, New Ireland, Papua New Guinea. Contact: Otto A. Malatana, Station Manager; or Ruben Bale, Provincial Program Manager. Currently off air due to a shortage of transmitter spares. Return postage or $1 helpful.

Radio Northern (when operating), Voice of Oro, P.O. Box 137, Popondetta, Oro, Papua New Guinea. Contact: Roma Tererembo, Assistant Provincial Programme Manager; or Misael Pendaia, Station Manager. Return postage required.

Radio Sandaun, P.O. Box 37, Vanimo, Sandaun Province, Papua New Guinea. Contact: (nontechnical) Gabriel Deckwalen, Station Manager; Zacharias Nauot, Acting Assistant Manager; Celina Korei, Station Journalist; Elias Rathley, Provincial Programme Manager; Mrs. Maria Nauot, Secretary; (technical) Paia Ottawa, Technician. $1 helpful.

Radio Simbu, P.O. Box 228, Kundiawa, Chimbu, Papua New Guinea. Phone: +675 735-1038 or +675 735-1082. Fax: +675 735 1012. Contact: (general) Jack Wera, Manager; Tony Mill Waine, Provincial Programme Manager; Felix Tsiki; or Thomas Ghiyandiule, Producer, "Pasikam Long ol Pipel." Cassette recordings $5. Free two-Kina banknotes.

Radio Southern Highlands (when operating), P.O. Box 104, Mendi, SHP, Papua New Guinea. Contact: (general) Andrew Meles, Provincial Programme Manager; Miriam Piapo, Programme Officer; Benard Kagaro, Programme Officer; Lucy Aluy, Programme Officer; Jacob Mambi, Shift Officer; or Nicholas Sambu, Producer, "Questions and Answers"; (technical) Ronald Helori, Station Technician. $1 or return postage helpful; or donate a wall poster of a rock band, singer or American landscape.

Radio Western, P.O. Box 23, Daru, Western Province, Papua New Guinea. Contact: Robin Wainetti, Manager; (technical) Samson Tobel, Technician. $1 or return postage required. Replies irregularly.

Radio Western Highlands (when operating), P.O. Box 311, Mount Hagen, WHP, Papua New Guinea. Contact: (general) Anna Pundia, Station Manager; (technical) Esau Okole, Technician. $1 or return postage helpful. Replies occasionally. Often off the air because of theft, armed robbery or inadequate security for the station's staff.

Radio West New Britain, P.O. Box 412, Kimbe, WNBP, Papua New Guinea. Fax: +675 983 5600. Contact: Valuka Lowa, Provincial Station Manager; Darius Gilime, Provincial Program Manager; Lemeck Kuam, Producer, "Questions and Answers"; or Esekial Mael. Return postage required.

Wantok Radio Light—PNG Christian Broadcasting Network *U.S. SPONSORING ORGANIZATION:* Life Radio Ministries, Inc., Joe Emert, P.O. Box 2020, Griffin GA 30223 USA. Phone: +1 (770) 229-9267. Email: jemert@wmvv.com. Web: www.wmvv.com/intmin.htm. Contact: Joe Emert. Currently operates on FM, but has been granted permission to operate a 100 kW shortwave transmitter. A joint project involving Life Radio Ministries, HCJB World Radio and others.

PARAGUAY   World Time -3 (-4 midyear)

Radio América (when operating), Casilla de Correo 2220, Asunción, Paraguay. Fax: +595 (21) 963-149. Email: radioamerica@lycos.com, ramerica@rieder.net.py. Contact: Adán Mur, Asesor Técnico. Replies to correspondence in Spanish and English. Operates on legally assigned 1480 kHz on mediumwave/AM, but is believed to be unlicensed on shortwave.

Radio Nacional del Paraguay (when operating), Blas Garay 241 entre Yegros e Iturbe, Asunción, Paraguay. Phone: +595 (21) 449-213. Fax: +595 (21) 332 750. Free tourist brochure. $1 or return postage required. Replies, sometimes slowly, to correspondence in Spanish.

PERU   World Time -5

NOTE: Obtaining replies from Peruvian stations calls for creativity, tact, patience—and the proper use of Spanish, not form letters and the like.

CPN Radio (if reactivated), Cadena Peruana de Noticias, Gral. Salaverry 156, Miraflores, Lima, Peru. Phone: +51 (1) 446-1554 or +51 (1) 445-7770. Email: webmastercpn@gestion.com.pe. Web: www.cpnradio.com.pe. Contact: Oscar Romero Caro, Gerente General; or Zenaida Solís, Directora de Programas.

Estación C (if reactivated), Casilla de Correo 210, Moyobamba, San Martín, Peru. Contact: Porfirio Centurión, Propietario.

Estación Tarapoto (if reactivated), Jirón Federico Sánchez 720, Tarapoto, Peru. Phone: +51 (94) 522-709. Contact: Luis Humberto Hidalgo Sánchez, Gerente General; or José Luna Paima, Announcer. Replies occasionally to correspondence in Spanish.

Estación Wari (when operating), Calle Nazareno 108, Ayacucho, Peru. Phone: +51 (64) 813- 039. Contact: Walter Muñoz Ynga I., Gerente.

Estación X (Equis) (when operating), Calle Argentina 198, Bagua, Departamento de Amazonas, Peru.

Frecuencia Líder (Radio Bambamarca), Jirón Jorge Chávez 416, Bambamarca, Hualgayoc, Cajamarca, Peru. Phone: (office) +51 (74) 713-260; (studio) +51 (74) 713-249. Contact: (general) Valentín Peralta Díaz, Gerente; Irma Peralta Rojas; or Carlos Antonio Peralta Rojas; (technical) Oscar Lino Peralta Rojas. Free station photos. *La Historia de Bambamarca* book for 5 Soles; cassettes of Peruvian and Latin American folk music for 4 Soles each; T-shirts for 10 Soles each (sending US$1 per Sol should suffice and cover foreign postage costs, as well). Replies occasionally to correspondence in Spanish. Considering replacing their transmitter to improve reception.

Frecuencia San Ignacio (if reactivated), Jirón Villanueva Pinillos 330, San Ignacio, Cajamarca, Peru. Contact: Franklin R. Hoyos Cóndor, Director Gerente; or Ignacio Gómez Torres, Técnico de Sonido. Replies to correspondence in Spanish. $1 or return postage necessary.

Frecuencia VH—*see* Radio Frecuencia VH.

La Super Radio San Ignacio (when operating), Avenida Víctor Larco 104, a un costado del campo deportivo, San Ignacio, Distrito de Sinsicap, Provincia de Otuzco, La Libertad, Peru.

La Voz de Anta, Distrito de Anta, Provincia de Acobamba, Departamento de Huancavelica. Phone: +51 (64) 750-201.

La Voz de la Selva—*see* Radio La Voz de la Selva.

La Voz de San Juan—*see* Radio La Voz de San Juan.

La Voz del Campesino—*see* Radio La Voz del Campesino.

La Voz del Marañón—*see* Radio La Voz del Marañon.

Ondas del Suroriente—*see* Radio Ondas del Suroriente, below.

Radio Adventista Mundial—La Voz de la Esperanza (when operating), Jirón Dos de Mayo No. 218, Celendín, Cajamarca, Peru. Contact: Francisco Goicochea Ortiz, Director; or Lucas Solano Oyarce, Director de Ventas.

Radio Altura (Cerro de Pasco), Casilla de Correo 140, Cerro de Pasco, Pasco, Peru. Phone: +51 (64) 721-875, +51 (64) 722-398. Contact: Oswaldo de la Cruz Vásquez, Gerente General. Replies to correspondence in Spanish.

Radio Altura (Huarmaca), Prolongación San Martín s/n, Huarmaca, Provincia de Huancabamba, Piura, Peru.

Radio Amauta del Perú, (when operating), Jirón Manuel Iglesias s/n, a pocos pasos de la Plazuela San Juan, San Pablo, Cajamarca, Nor Oriental del Marañón, Peru.

Radio Amistad, Manzana I-11, Lote 6, Calle 22, Urbanización Mariscal Cáceres, San Juan de Lurigancho, Lima, Peru. Phone: +51 (1) 392-3640. Email: radioamistad@peru.com. Contact: Manuel Mejía Barboza. Accepts email reception reports.

Radio Ancash, Casilla de Correo 221, Huaraz, Peru. Phone: +51 (44) 721-381,+51 (44) 721- 359, +51 (44) 721-487, +51 (44) 722-512. Fax: +51 (44) 722 992. Contact: Armando Moreno Romero, Gerente General. Replies to correspondence in Spanish.

Radio Andahuaylas, Jr. Ayacucho No. 248, Andahuaylas, Apurímac, Peru. Contact: Sr. Daniel Andréu C., Gerente. $1 required. Replies irregularly to correspondence in Spanish.

Radio Andina, Huáscar 201, Huancabamba, Piura, Peru. According to an on-air announcement, the station is expected to move to Avenida Ramón Castilla 254. Phone: +51 (74) 473-104. Contact: Manuel Campos Ojeda, Director.

Radio Andina, Real 175, Huancayo, Junín, Peru. Phone: +51 (64) 231-123. Replies infrequently to correspondence in Spanish.

Radio Apurímac (when operating), Jirón Cusco 206 (or Ovalo El Olivo No. 23), Abancay, Apurímac, Peru. Contact: Antero Quispe Allca, Director General.

Radio Atlántida

STATION: Jirón Arica 441, Iquitos, Loreto, Peru. Phone: +51 (94) 234-452, +51 (94) 234-962. Contact: Pablo Rojas Bardales.

LISTENER CORRESPONDENCE: Sra. Carmela López Paredes, Directora del prgrama "Trocha Turística," Jirón Arica 1083, Iquitos, Loreto, Peru. Free pennants and tourist information. $1 or return postage required. Replies to most correspondence in Spanish, the preferred language, and some correspondence in English.

Radio Bambamarca—*see* Frecuencia Líder, above.

Radio Bethel—*see* Radio Bethel Arequipa, below.

Radio Bethel Arequipa, Avenida Unión 215, 3er piso, Distrito Miraflores, Arequipa, Peru. Contact: Josué Ascarruz Pacheco. Usually announces as "Radio Bethel" and belongs to the "Movimiento Misionero Mundial" evangelistic organization.

Radio Bolívar, Correo Central, Bolívar, Provincia de Bolívar, Departamento de La Libertad, Peru. Contact: Julio Dávila Echevarría, Gerente. May send free pennant. Return postage helpful.

Radio Cajamarca, Jirón La Mar 675, Cajamarca, Peru. Phone: +51 (44) 921-014. Contact: Porfirio Cruz Potosí.

Radio Chanchamayo (when operating), Jirón Tarma 551, La Merced, Junín, Peru.

Radio Chaski, Baptist Mid-Missions, Apartado Postal 368, Cusco, Peru; or Alameda Pachacútec s/n B-5, Cusco, Peru. Phone: +51 (84) 225-052. Contact: Andrés Tuttle H., Gerente; or Felipe S. Velarde Hinojosa M., Representante Legal.

Radio Chincheros, Jirón Apurímac s/n, Chincheros, Departamento de Apurímac, Peru.

Radio Chota, Jirón Anaximandro Vega 690, Apartado Postal 3, Chota, Cajamarca, Peru. Phone: +51 (44) 771-240. Contact: Aladino Gavidia Huamán, Administrador. $1 or return postage required. Replies slowly to correspondence in Spanish.

Radio Comas, Avenida Estados Unidos 327, Urbanización Huaquillay, km 10 de la Avenida Túpac Amaru, Distrito de Comas, Lima, Peru. Phone: +51 (1) 525-0859; +51 (1) 525-0919. Fax: +51 (1) 525 0094. Email: rtcomas@terra.com.pe. Web: (includes MP3) www.radiocomas.com. Contact: Edgar Saldaña R.; Juan Rafael Saldaña Reátegui (Relaciones Públicas) or Gamaniel Francisco Chahua, Productor-Programador General.

Radio Comercial Naranjos (when operating), Avenida Cajamarca 464, Distrito de Pardo Miguel Naranjos, Provincia de Rioja, San Martín, Peru. Contact: Mario Cusma Vasquez, Propietario; Esperanza Galo Gomez, Gerente Administrativo; or Pepe Vasquez, Jefe de Producciones.

Radio CORA (when operating), Compañía Radiofónica Lima, S.A., Paseo de la República 144, Centro Cívico, Oficina 5, Lima 1, Peru. Phone: +51 (1) 433-5005, +51 (1) 433-1188 or +51 (1) 433-0848. Fax: +51 (1) 433 6134. Email: cora@peru.itete.com; cora@lima.business.com.pe. Contact: (general) Dra. Lylian Ramírez M., Directora de Prensa y Programación; Juan Ramírez Lazo, Director Gerente; or Srta. Angelina María Abie; (technical) Srta. Sylvia Ramírez M., Directora Técnica. Free station sticky-label pads, bumper stickers and may send large certificate suitable for framing. Audio cassettes with extracts from their programs $20 plus $2 postage; women's hair bands $2 plus $1 postage. Two IRCs or $1 required. Replies slowly to correspondence in English, Spanish, French, Italian and Portuguese.

Radio Coremarca (if reactivated), Jirón Jaime de Martínez, Bambamarca, Peru. Contact: Virgilio Carranza Tello, Director. A small educational station, so include return postage with your correspondence.

Radio Cultural Amauta, Jr. Cahuide 278, Apartado Postal 24, Huanta, Ayacucho, Peru. Phone/Fax: +51 (64) 832-153. Email: arca@terra.com.pe or (Montes Sinforoso) montessd@terra.com.pe. Web: (includes RealAudio) www.rca.es.vg. Contact: Demetria Montes Sinforoso (Administradora); Vicente Saico Tinco.

Radio Cusco, Apartado Postal 251, Cusco, Peru. Phone: (general)+51 (84) 225-851; (management) +51 (84) 232-457. Fax: +51 (84) 223 308. Contact: Sra. Juana Huamán Yépez, Administradora; or Raúl Siú Almonte, Gerente General; (technical) Benjamín Yábar Alvarez. Free pennants, postcards and key rings. Audio cassettes of Peruvian music $10 plus postage. $1 or return postage required. Replies irregularly to correspondence in English or Spanish. Station is looking for folk music recordings from around the world to use in their programs.

Radio del Pacífico, Apartado Postal 4236, Lima 1, Peru. Phone: +51 (1) 433-3275. Fax: +51 (1) 433 3276. Contact: J. Petronio Allauca, Secretario, Departamento de Relaciones Públicas; or Julio Villarreal. $1 or return postage required. Replies occasionally to correspondence in Spanish.

Radio El Sol de los Andes, Jirón 2 de Mayo 257, Juliaca, Peru. Phone: +51 (54) 321-115. Fax: +51 (54) 322 981. Contact: Armando Alarcón Velarde.

Radio Estación Uno, Barrio Altos, Distrito de Pucará, Provincia Jaén, Nor Oriental del Marañón, Peru.

Radio Estudio 2000, Distrito Miguel Pardo Naranjos, Provincia de Rioja, Departamento de San Martín, Peru.

Radio Frecuencia VH ("La Voz de Celendín"; "RVC"), Jirón José Gálvez 1030, Celendín, Cajamarca, Peru. Contact: Fernando Vásquez Castro, Propietario.

Radio Frecuencia San Ignacio—*see* Frecuencia San Ignacio.

Radio Horizonte (Chachapoyas), Apartado Postal 69 (or Jirón Amazonas 1177), Chachapoyas, Amazonas, Peru. Phone: +51 (74) 757-793. Fax: +51 (74) 757 004. Contact: Sra. Rocío García Rubio, Ing. Electrónico, Directora; Percy Chuquizuta Alvarado, Locutor; María Montaldo Echaiz, Locutora; Marcelo Mozambite Chavarry, Locutor; Ing. María Dolores Gutiérrez Atienza, Administradora; Juan Nancy Ruíz de Valdez, Secretaria; Yoel Toro Morales, Técnico de Transmisión; or María Soledad Sánchez Castro, Administradora. Replies to correspondence in English, French, German and Spanish. $1 required.

Radio Horizonte (Chiclayo), Jirón Incanato 387 Altos, Distrito José Leonardo Ortiz, Chiclayo, Lambayeque, Peru. Phone: +51 (74) 252-917. Contact: Enrique Becerra Rojas, Owner and General Manager. Return postage required.

Radio Hualgayoc (if reactivated), Jirón San Martín s/n, Hualgayoc, Cajamarca, Peru. Contact: Máximo Zamora Medina, Director Propietario.

Radio Huamachuco (if reactivated), Jirón Bolívar 937, Huamachuco, La Libertad, Peru. Contact: Manuel D. Gil Gil, Director Propietario.

Radio Huanta 2000, Jirón Gervacio Santillana 455, Huanta, Peru. Phone: +51 (64) 932-105. Fax: +51 (64) 832 105. Contact: Ronaldo Sapaico Maravi, Departmento Técnico; or Sra. Lucila Orellana de Paz, Administradora. Free photo of staff. Return postage or $1 appreciated. Replies to correspondence in Spanish.

Radio Huarmaca, Jirón 9 de Octubre 110 frente al Parque Leoncio Prado, Huarmaca, Provincia de Huancabamba, Región Grau, Peru. Contact: Simón Zavaleta Pérez. Return postage helpful.

Radio Ilucán, Jirón Lima 290, Cutervo, Región Nororiental del Marañón, Peru. Phone: +51 (44) 737-010 or +51 (44) 737-231. Email: radioilucan@hotmail.com. Contact: José Gálvez Salazar, Gerente Administrativo. $1 required. Replies occasionally to correspondence in Spanish.

Radio Imagen (when operating), Casilla de Correo 42, Tarapoto, San Martín, Peru; Jirón San Martín 328, Tarapoto, San Martín, Peru; or Apartado Postal 254, Tarapoto, San Martín, Peru. Phone: +51 (94) 522-696. Contact: Adith Chumbe

Vásquez, Secretaria; or Jaime Ríos Tapullima, Gerente General. Replies irregularly to correspondence in Spanish. $1 or return postage helpful.

Radio Integración, Av. Seoane 200, Apartado Postal 57, Abancay, Departamento de Apurímac, Peru. Contact: Zenón Hernán Farfán Cruzado, Propietario.

Radio Internacional (if activated), Apartado Postal 105, Serpost, Cercado, Arequipa, Peru. Email: radiovozdesalvacion@iglesia-dios.org; (Vera) joseveravera@iglesia-dios.org; (Quiroz) pilarquiroz@iglesia-dios.org. Web: www.radiovozdesalvacion.100megas.com/index.html. Contact: José Manuel Vera Vera, Director General; or Hna. [Sister] Pilar Quiroz, Asistente de Programas Internacionales. Plans to operate on 6035 kHz.

Radio Internacional Cristiana—*see* Radio Internacional, above.

Radio Internacional del Perú (if reactivated), Jirón Bolognesi 532, San Pablo, Cajamarca, Peru.

Radio Jaén (La Voz de la Frontera), Calle Mariscal Castilla 439, Jaén, Cajamarca, Peru. Contact: Luis A. Vílchez Ochoa, Administrador.

Radio Juliaca (La Decana), Jirón Ramón Castilla 949, Apartado Postal 67, Juliaca, San Román, Puno, Peru. Phone: +51 (54) 321-372. Fax: +51 (54) 332 386. Contact: Robert Theran Escobedo, Director.

Radio JVL (when operating), Jirón Túpac Amaru 105, Consuelo, Distrito de San Pablo, Provincia de Bellavista, Departamento de San Martín, Peru. Contact: John Wiley Villanueva Lara—a student of electronic engineering—who currently runs the station, and whose initials make up the station name. Replies to correspondence in Spanish. Return Postage required.

Radio La Hora, Av. Garcilaso 180, Cusco, Peru. Phone: +51 (84) 225-615 or +51 (84) 231-371. Contact: (general) Edmundo Montesinos G., Gerente; (reception reports) Carlos Gamarra Moscoso, who is also a DXer. Free stickers, pins, pennants and postcards of Cusco. Return postage required. Replies to correspondence in Spanish. Reception reports are best sent direct to Carlos Gamarra's home address: Av. Garcilaso 411, Wanchaq, Cusco, Peru. The station hopes to increase transmitter power to 2 kw if and when the economic situation improves.

Radio La Inmaculada, Parroquia La Inmaculada Concepción, Frente de la Plaza de Armas, Santa Cruz, Provincia de Santa Cruz, Departamento de Cajamarca, Peru. Phone: +51 (74) 714-051. Contact: Reverendo Padre Angel Jorge Carrasco, Gerente; or Gabino González Vera, Locutor.

Radio Lajas, Jirón Rosendo Mendívil 589, Lajas, Chota, Cajamarca, Nor Oriental del Marañón, Peru. Contact: Alfonso Medina Burga, Gerente Propietario.

Radio La Merced, Junín 163, La Merced, Junín, Peru. Phone: +51 (64) 531-199. Occasionally replies to correspondence in Spanish.

Radio La Oroya, Calle Lima 190, Tercer Piso Of. 3, Apartado Postal 88, La Oroya, Provincia de Yauli, Departamento de Junín, Peru. Phone: +51 (64) 391-401. Fax: +51 (64) 391 440. Email: rlofigu@net.cosapidata.com.pe. Contact: Jacinto Manuel Figueroa Yauri, Gerente-Propietario. Free pennants. $1 or return postage necessary. Replies to correspondence in Spanish.

Radio La Voz, Andahuaylas, Apurímac, Peru. Contact: Lucio Fuentes, Director Gerente.

Radio La Voz de Abancay, Avenida Noviembre Lote 6, Urbanización Micaela Bastidas, Abancay, Departamento de Apurímac, Peru. Contact: Lucio Fuentes, Propietario.

Radio La Voz de Chiriaco (when operating), Jirón Ricardo Palma s/n, Chiriaco, Distrito de Imaza, Provincia de Bagua, Departamento de Amazonas, Peru. Contact: Hildebrando López

Listeners send half a million letters to Deutsche Welle each year. The station makes use of them to evaluate its programs. DW

Pintado, Director; Santos Castañeda Cubas, Director Gerente; or Fidel Huamuro Curinambe, Técnico de Mantenimiento. $1 or return postage helpful.

Radio La Voz de Cutervo (if reactivated), Jirón María Elena Medina 644-650, Cutervo, Cajamarca, Peru.

Radio La Voz de la Selva, Jirón Abtao 255, Casilla de Correo 207, Iquitos, Loreto, Peru. Phone: +51 (94) 265-245. Fax: +51 (94) 264 531. Email: lvsradio@terra.com.pe. Contact: Julia Jáuregui Rengifo, Directora; Marcelino Esteban Benito, Director; Pedro Sandoval Guzmán, Announcer; or Mery Blas Rojas. Replies to correspondence in Spanish.

Radio La Voz de las Huarinjas, Barrio El Altillo s/n, Huancabamba, Piura, Peru. Phone: +51 (74) 473-126 or +51 (74) 473-259. Contact: Alfonso García Silva, Gerente Director (also the owner of the station); or Bill Yeltsin, Administrador. Replies to correspondence in Spanish.

Radio La Voz de Oxapampa (if reactivated), Av. Mullenbruck 469, Oxapampa, Pasco, Peru. Contact: Pascual Villafranca Guzmán, Director Propietario.

Radio La Voz de San Juan (if reactivated), 28 de Julio 420, Lonya Grande, Provincia de Utcubamba, Región Nororiental del Marañón, Peru. Contact: Prof. Víctor Hugo Hidrovo; or Edilberto Ortiz Chávez, Locutor. Formerly known as Radio San Juan.

Radio La Voz de Santa Cruz (if reactivated), Av. Zarumilla 190, Santa Cruz, Cajamarca, Peru.

Radio La Voz del Campesino, Av. San Francisco de Asís s/n, Huarmaca, Provincia de Huancabamba, Piura, Peru. Contact: Hernando Huancas Huancas.

Radio La Voz del Marañón, Jirón Bolognesi 130, Barrio La Alameda, Cajamarca, Nor Oriental del Marañón, Peru. Contact: Eduardo Díaz Coronado.

Radio Libertad de Junín, Cerro de Pasco 528, Apartado Postal 2, Junín, Peru. Phone: +51 (64) 344-026. Contact: Mauro Chaccha G., Director Gerente. Replies slowly to correspondence in Spanish. Return postage necessary.

Radio Líder, Portal Belén 115, 2do piso, Cusco, Peru. Contact: Mauro Calvo Acurio, Propietario.

Radio Lircay (when operating), Barrio Maravillas, Lircay, Provincia de Angaraes, Huancavelica, Peru.

Radio Los Andes (Huamachuco), Pasaje Damián Nicolau 108-110, 2do piso, Huamachuco, La Libertad, Peru. Phone: +51 (44) 441-240 or +51 (44) 441-502. Fax: +51 (44) 441 214. Email: radiolosandes@starmedia.com. Contact: Monseñor Sebastián Ramis Torerns.

Radio Los Andes (Huarmaca), Huarmaca, Provincia de Huancabamba, Región Grau, Peru. Contact: William Cerro Calderón.

Radio Luz y Sonido, Apartado Postal 280, Huánuco, Peru; or (street address) Jirón Dos de Mayo 1286, Oficina 205, Huánuco, Peru. Phone: +51 (64) 512-394 or +51 (64) 518-500. Fax: +51 (64) 511 985. Contact: (technical) Jorge Benavides Moreno; (nontechnical) Pedro Martínez Tineo, Director Ejecutivo; Lic. Orlando Bravo Jesús; or Seydel Saavedra Cabrera, Operador/Locutor. Return postage or $2 required. Replies to correspondence in Spanish, Italian and Portuguese. Sells video cassettes of local folk dances and religious and tourist themes.

Radio Macedonia, Seminario Bautista Macedonia, Casilla 1677, Arequipa, Peru. Phone/Fax: +51 (54) 444-376. Email: (W.A. Gardner) gardner@world-evangelism.com. Contact: W. Austin Gardner; or Chris Gardner. Replies to correspondence in Spanish or English.

U.S. PARENT ORGANIZATION: Macedonia World Baptist Missions Inc., P.O. Box 519, Braselton GA 30517 USA. Phone: +1 (706) 654-2818. Fax: +1 (706) 654 2816. Email: mwbm@mwbm.org. Web: http://mwbm.org.

Radio Madre de Dios, Daniel Alcides Carrión 385, Apartado Postal 37, Puerto Maldonado, Madre de Dios, Peru. Phone: +51 (84) 571-050. Fax: +51 (84) 571 018 or +51 (84) 573 542. Contact: (administration) Padre Rufino Lobo Alonso, Director; (general) Alcides Arguedas Márquez, Director del programa "Un Festival de Música Internacional," heard Mondays 0100 to 0200 World Time. Sr. Arguedas is interested in feedback for this letterbox program. Replies to correspondence in Spanish. $1 or return postage appreciated.

Radio Majestad (if reactivated), Calle Real 1033, Oficina 302, Huancayo, Junín, Peru.

Radio Marañón, Apartado Postal 50, Jaén, Cajamarca, Peru; or (street address) Francisco de Orellana 343, Jaén, Cajamarca, Peru. Phone: +51 (44) 731-147 or +51 (44) 732-168. Fax: +51 (44) 732 580. Email: correo@radiomaranon.org.pe. Web: www.radiomaranon.org.pe. Contact: Francisco Muguiro Ibarra, Director. Return postage necessary. May send free pennant. Replies slowly to correspondence in Spanish and (sometimes) English.

Radio Marginal, San Martín 257, Tocache, San Martín, Peru. Phone: +51 (94) 551-031. Rarely replies.

Radio Máster, Jirón 20 de Abril 308, Moyobamba, Departamento de San Martín, Peru. Contact: Américo Vásquez Hurtado, Director.

Radio Melodía, San Camilo 501, Arequipa, Peru. Phone: +51 (54) 232-071, +51 (54) 232-327 or +51 (54) 285-152. Fax: +51 (54) 237 312. Contact: Hermógenes Delgado Torres, Director; or Señora Elba Alvarez de Delgado. Replies to correspondence in Spanish.

Radio Moderna, Jirón Arequipa 323, 2do piso, Celendín, Cajamarca, Peru.

Radio Mundial Adventista (if activated), Colegio Adventista de Titicaca, Casilla 4, Juliaca, Peru. Currently on mediumwave (AM) only, but hopes to add shortwave sometime in the future.

Radio Naylamp, Avenida Andrés Avelino Cáceres 800, Lambayeque, Peru. Phone: +51 (74) 283-353. Contact: Dr. Juan José Grández Vargas, Director Gerente; or Delicia Coronel Muñoz, who is interested in receiving postcards and the like. Free stickers, pennants and calendars. Return postage necessary.

Radio Nor Andina (when operating), Jirón José Gálvez 602, Celendín, Cajamarca, Peru. Contact: Misael Alcántara Guevara, Gerente; or Víctor B. Vargas C., Departamento de Prensa. Free calendar. $1 required. Donations (registered mail best) sought for the Committee for Good Health for Children, headed by Sr. Alcántara, which is active in saving the lives of hungry youngsters in poverty-stricken Cajamarca Province. Replies irregularly to casual or technical correspondence in Spanish, but regularly to Children's Committee donors and helpful correspondence in Spanish.

Radio Nor Peruana, Emisora Municipal, Jirón Ortiz Arrieta 588, 1er. piso del Concejo Provincial de Chachapoyas, Chachapoyas, Amazonas, Peru. Contact: Carlos Poema, Administrador; or Edgar Villegas, program host for "La Voz de Chachapoyas," (Sundays, 1100- 1300).

Radio Nuevo Horizonte, Consorcio Minero Horizonte, Minera Aurífera Retamas, Distrito de Parcoy, Provincia de Pataz, Departamento de La Libertad, Peru.

Radio Ondas del Huallaga, Jirón Leoncio Prado 723, Apartado Postal 343, Huánuco, Peru. Phone: +51 (64) 511-525 or +51 (64) 512-428. Contact: Flaviano Llanos Malpartida, Representante Legal. $1 or return postage required. Replies to correspondence in Spanish.

Radio Ondas del [Río] Marañón (when operating), Jirón Amazonas 315, Distrito de Aramango, Provincia de Bagua, Departamento de Amazonas, Región Nororiental del Marañón, Peru. Contact: Agustín Tongod, Director Propietario. "Río"—river— is sometimes, but not always, used in on-air identification.

Radio Ondas del Río Mayo, Jirón Huallaga 348, Nueva Cajamarca, San Martín, Peru. Phone: +51 (94) 556-006. Contact: Edilberto Lucío Peralta Lozada, Gerente; or Víctor Huaras Rojas, Locutor. Free pennants. Return postage helpful. Replies slowly to correspondence in Spanish.

Radio Ondas del Suroriente (when operating), Jirón Ricardo Palma 510, Quillabamba, La Convención, Cusco, Peru.

Radio Oriente, Vicariato Apostólico, Avenida Progreso 114, Yurimaguas, Loreto, Peru. Phone: +51 (94) 352-156. Fax: +51 (94) 352 128. Email: rovay@qnet.co.pe. Web: www.dxing.info/radio/oriente. Contact: (general) Sra. Elisa Cancino Hidalgo; or Juan Antonio López-Manzanares M., Director; (technical) Pedro Capo Moragues, Gerente Técnico. $1 or return postage required. Replies occasionally to correspondence in English, French, Spanish and Catalan.

Radio Origen (if reactivated), Acobamba, Departamento de Huancavelica, Peru.

Radio Paccha (if reactivated), Calle Mariscal Castilla 52, Paccha, Provincia de Chota, Departamento de Cajamarca, Peru.

Radio Paucartambo, Emisora Municipal (if reactivated) STATION ADDRESS: Paucartambo, Cusco, Peru. STAFFER ADDRESS: Manuel H. Loaiza Canal, Correo Central, Paucartambo, Cusco, Peru. Return postage or $1 required.

Radio Perú ("Perú, la Radio") STUDIO ADDRESS: Jirón Atahualpa 191, San Ignacio, Región Nororiental del Marañón, Peru. ADMINISTRATION: Avenida San Ignacio 493, San Ignacio, Región Nororiental del Marañón, Peru. Contact: Oscar Vásquez Chacón, Director General; or Idelso Vásquez Chacón, Director Propietario. Sometimes relays the FM outlet, "Estudio 97."

Radio Quillabamba, Jirón Ricardo Palma 432, Apartado Postal 76, Quillabamba, La Convención, Cusco, Peru. Phone: +51 (84) 281-002. Fax: +51 (84) 281 771. Contact: Padre Francisco Javier Panera, Director. Replies very irregularly to correspondence in Spanish.

Radio Reina de la Selva, Jirón Ayacucho 944, Plaza de Armas, Chachapoyas, Región Nor Oriental del Marañón, Peru. Phone: +51 (74) 757-203. Contact: José David Reina Noriega, Gerente General; or Jorge Oscar Reina Noriega, Director General. Re-

plies irregularly to correspondence in Spanish. Return postage necessary.

Radio San Antonio (Callalli), Parroquia San Antonio de Padua, Plaza Principal s/n, Callalli, Departamento de Arequipa, Peru. Contact: Hermano [Brother] Rolando.

Radio San Antonio (Villa Atalaya), Jirón Iquitos s/n, Villa Atalaya, Departamento de Ucayali, Peru. Email: (Zerdin) zerdin@terra.com.pe. Contact: Gerardo Zerdin.

Radio San Francisco Solano (when operating), Parroquia de Sóndor, Calle San Miguel No. 207, Distrito de Sóndor, Huancabamba, Piura, Peru. Contact: Reverendo Padre Manuel José Rosas Castillo, Vicario Parroquial. Station operated by the Franciscan Fathers. Replies to correspondence in Spanish. $1 helpful.

Radio San Ignacio (when operating), Jirón Victoria 277, San Ignacio, Región Nororiental del Marañón, Peru. Contact: César Colunche Bustamante, Director Propietario; or his son, Fredy Colunche, Director de Programación.

Radio San Juan (when operating), Distrito de Aramango, Provincia de Bagua, Departamento de Amazonas, Región Nororiental del Marañón, Peru.

Radio San Juan (when operating), 28 de Julio 420, Lonya Grande, Provincia de Utcubamba, Región Nororiental del Marañón, Peru. Contact: Prof. Víctor Hugo Díaz Hidrovo; or Edilberto Ortiz Chávez, Locutor.

Radio San Miguel, Av. Huayna Cápac 146, Huánchac, Cusco, Peru. Contact: Sra. Catalina Pérez de Alencastre, Gerente General; or Margarita Mercado. Replies to correspondence in Spanish.

Radio San Miguel (when operating), Jirón Alfonso Ugarte 668, San Miguel, Cajamarca, Peru.

Radio San Miguel de El Faique (if reactivated), Distrito de El Faique, Provincia de Huancabamba, Departamento de Piura, Peru.

Radio San Nicolás, Jirón Amazonas 114, Rodríguez de Mendoza, Peru. Contact: Juan José Grández Santillán, Gerente; or Violeta Grández Vargas, Administradora. Return postage necessary.

Radio Santa Mónica, Urbanización Marcavalle P-20, Cusco, Peru. Phone:+ 51 (84) 225-357.

Radio Santa Rosa, Jirón Camaná 170, Casilla 4451, Lima 01, Peru. Phone: +51 (1) 427-7488. Fax: +51 (1) 426 9219. Email: radiosantarosa@terra.com.pe. Web: http://barrioperu.terra.com.pe/radiosantarosa. Contact: Padre Juan Sokolich Alvarado, Director; or Lucy Palma Barreda. Free stickers and pennants. $1 or return postage necessary. 180-page book commemorating station's 35th anniversary $10. Replies to correspondence in Spanish.

Radio Satélite, Jirón Cutervo No. 543, Provincia de Santa Cruz, Cajamarca, Peru. Phone:+51 (74) 714-074, +51 (74) 714-169. Contact: Sabino Llamo Chávez, Gerente. Free tourist brochure. $1 or return postage required. Replies to correspondence in Spanish.

Radio Sicuani, Jirón 2 de Mayo 212, Sicuani, Canchis, Cusco, Peru; or Apartado Postal 45, Sicuani, Peru. Phone: +51 (84) 351-136 or +51 (84) 351-698. Fax: +51 (84) 351 697. Email: cecosda@mail.cosapidata.com.pe. Contact: Mario Ochoa Vargas, Director.

Radio Soledad (if reactivated), Centro Minero de Retama, Distrito de Parcoy, Provincia de Pataz, La Libertad, Peru. Contact: Vicente Valdivieso, Locutor. Return postage necessary.

Radio Sudamérica, Jirón Ramón Castilla 491, tercer nivel, Plaza de Armas, Cutervo, Cajamarca, Peru. Phone: +51 (74) 736-090 or +51 (74) 737-443. Contact: Jorge Luis Paredes Guerra, Administrador; or Amadeo Mario Muñoz Guivar, Propietario.

Radio Superior, Jirón San Martín 229, Provincia de Bolívar, Departamento de La Libertad, Peru.

Radio Tacna, Aniceto Ibarra 436, Casilla de Correo 370, Tacna, Peru. Phone: +51 (54) 714-871. Fax: +51 (54) 723 745. Email: scaceres@viabcp.com. Contact: (nontechnical and technical) Ing. Alfonso Cáceres Contreras, Gerente de Operaciones; (administration) Yolanda Vda. de Cáceres C., Directora Gerente. Free stickers and samples of *Correo* local newspaper. $1 or return postage helpful. Audio cassettes of Peruvian and other music $2 plus postage. Replies irregularly to correspondence in English and Spanish.

Radio Tawantinsuyo, Av. Sol 806, Cusco, Peru. Phone: +51 (84) 226-955 or +51 (84) 228-411. Contact: Iván Montesinos, Gerente. Has a very attractive QSL card, but only replies occasionally to correspondence, which should be in Spanish.

Radio Tarma, Jirón Molino del Amo 167, Apartado Postal 167, Tarma, Peru. Phone/fax: +51 (64) 321-167 or +51 (64) 321-510. Contact: Mario Monteverde Pomareda, Gerente General. Sometimes sends 100 Inti banknote in return when $1 enclosed. Free stickers. $1 or return postage required. Replies irregularly to correspondence in Spanish.

Radio Tayacaja (when operating), Correo Central, Distrito de Pampas, Tayacaja, Huancavelica, Peru. Phone: +51 (64) 220-217, Anexo 238. Contact: (general) J. Jorge Flores Cárdenas; (technical) Ing. Larry Guido Flores Lezama. Free stickers and pennants. Replies to correspondence in Spanish. Hopes to replace transmitter.

Radio Tingo María (when operating), Jirón Callao 115 (or Av. Raimondi No. 592), Casilla de Correo 25, Tingo María, Leoncio Prado, Departamento de Huánuco, Peru. Contact: Gina A. de la Cruz Ricalde, Administradora; or Ricardo Abad Vásquez, Gerente. Free brochures. $1 required. Replies slowly to correspondence in Spanish.

Radio Tropical (if reactivated), Casilla de Correo 31, Tarapoto, Peru. Phone: +51 (94) 522-083 or +51 (94) 524-689. Fax: +51 (94) 522 155. Contact: Mery A. Rengifo Tenazoa, Secretaria; or Luis F. Mori Reátegui, Gerente. Free stickers, occasionally free pennants, and station history booklet. $1 or return postage required. Replies occasionally to correspondence in Spanish.

Radio Unión, Apartado Postal 833, Lima 27, Peru; or (street address) José Pardo 138, Edificio Neptuno - piso 16, Miraflores, Lima, Peru. Contact: Raúl Rubbeck Jiménez, Director Gerente; Juan Zubiaga Santiváñez, Gerente; Natividad Albizuri Salinas, Secretaria; or Juan Carlos Sologuren, Dpto. de Administración, who collects stamps. Free satin pennants and stickers. IRC required, and enclosing used or new stamps from various countries is especially appreciated. Replies irregularly to correspondence and tape recordings, with Spanish preferred.

Radio Uno, Av. Balta 1480, 3er piso, frente al Mercado Modelo, Chiclayo, Peru. Phone: +51 (74) 224-967. Contact: Luz Angela Romero, Directora del noticiero "Encuentros"; Plutarco Chamba Febres, Director Propietario; Juan Vargas, Administrador; or Filomena Saldívar Alarcón, Pauta Comercial. Return postage required.

Radio Uripa, Avenida Túpac Amaru s/n, Uripa, Provincia de Chincheros, Departamento de Apurímac, Peru. Contact: Lorenzo Quispe Nauto, Propietario.

Radio Victoria, Jr.Reynel 320, Mirones Bajo, Lima 1, Peru. Phone: +51 (1) 336-5448. Fax: +51 (1) 427 1195. Email: soermi@mixmail.com. Contact: Marta Flores Ushinahua. This station is owned by the Brazilian-run Pentecostal Church "Dios Es Amor," with local headquarters at Av. Arica 248, Lima; phone: +51 (1) 330-8023. Their program "La Voz de la Liberación" is produced locally and aired over numerous Peruvian shortwave stations.

Radio Virgen del Carmen ("RVC"), Jirón Virrey Toledo 466, Huancavelica, Peru. Phone: +51 (64) 752-740. Contact: Rvdo. Samuel Morán Cárdenas, Gerente.

Radiodifusoras Huancabamba (if reactivated), Calle Unión 409, Huancabamba, Piura, Peru. Phone: +51 (74) 473-233. Contact: Federico Ibáñez Maticorena, Director.

Radiodifusoras Paratón, Jirón Alfonso Ugarte 1090, contiguo al Parque Leoncio Prado, Huarmaca, Provincia de Huancabamba, Piura, Peru. Contact: Prof. Hernando Huancas Huancas, Gerente General; or Prof. Rómulo Chincay Huamán, Gerente Administrativo.

PHILIPPINES   World Time +8

NOTE: Philippine stations sometimes send publications with lists of Philippine young ladies seeking "pen pal" courtships.

DUR2—Philippine Broadcasting Service (when operating), Bureau of Broadcasting Services, Media Center, Bohol Avenue, Quezon City, Philippines. Relays DZRB Radio ng Bayan and DZRM Radio Manila.

☎Far East Broadcasting Company—FEBC Radio International (External Service)
MAIN OFFICE: P.O. Box 1, Valenzuela, Metro Manila, Philippines 0560. Phone: (general) +63 (2) 292-5603, +63 (2) 292-9403 or +63 (2) 292-5790; (International Broadcast Manager) +63 (2) 292-5603 ext. 158. Fax: +63 (2) 292 9430; +63 (2) 291 4982 (International Broadcast Manager) +63 (2) 292 9724, but lacks funds to provide faxed replies. Email: febcomphil@febc.org.ph; (Peter McIntyre) pm@febc.jfm.org.ph; (Larry Podmore) lpodmore@febc.jmf.org.ph; (Chris Cooper) ccooper@febc.org.ph. Web: www.febc.org; www.febi.org. Contact: (general) Peter McIntyre, Manager, International Operations Division; (administration) Carlos Peña, Managing Director; Chris Cooper, International Broadcast Manager; (engineering) Ing. Renato Valentin, Frequency Manager; Larry Podmore, IBG Chief Engineer. Free stickers and calendar cards. Three IRCs appreciated for airmail reply. Plans to add a new 100 kW shortwave transmitter.
INTERNATIONAL SCHEDULLING OFFICE: FEBC, 20 Ayer Rajah Crescent, Technopreneur Center, #09-22, Singapore 139964, Singapore. Phone: +65 6773-9017. Fax: +65 6773 9018. Email: phsu@febi.org. Contact: Peter C. Hsu, International Schedule Manager.
NEW DELHI BUREAU, NONTECHNICAL: c/o FEBC, Box 6, New Delhi-110 001, India.

Radyo Pilipinas, the Voice of Democracy, Philippine Broadcasting Service, 4th Floor, PIA Building, Visayas Avenue, Quezon City 1100, Metro Manila, Philippines. Phone: (general) +63 (2) 924-2620; +63 (2) 920-3963; or +63 (2) 924-2548; (engineering) +63 (2) 924-2268. Fax: +63 (2) 924 2745. Email: pbs.pao@pbs.gov.ph. Contact: (nontechnical) Evelyn Salvador Agato, Officer-in-Charge; Mercy Lumba; Leo Romano, Producer, "Listeners and Friends"; Tanny V. Rodriguez, Station Manager; or Richard G. Lorenzo, Production Coordinator; (technical) Danilo Alberto, Supervisor; or Mike Pangilinan, Engineer. Free postcards and stickers.

Radio Veritas Asia
STUDIOS AND ADMINISTRATIVE HEADQUARTERS: P.O. Box 2642, Quezon City, 1166 Philippines. Phone: +63 (2) 939-0011 to 14, +63 (2) 939-4692. Fax: (general) +63 (2) 938 1940; (Frequency Planning and Monitoring) +63 (2) 939 7556. Email: (Program Dept.) rvaprogram@rveritas-asia.org; (Audience Research) rva-ars@rveritas-asia.org; (technical) technical@rveritas-asia.org. Web: www.rveritas-asia.org. Contact: (administration) Ms. Erlinda G. So, Manager; (general) Ms. Cleofe R.

Labindao, Audience Relations Officer; Mrs. Regie de Juan Galindez; or Msgr. Pietro Nguyen Van Tai, Program Director; (technical) Honorio L. Llavore, Technical Director; Alex M. Movilla, Assistant Technical Director; or Alfonso L. Macaranas, Station Operating Engineer. Free caps, T-shirts, stickers, pennants, rulers, pens, postcards and calendars. Free bi-monthly newsletter *UPLINK*. Return postage appreciated.

TRANSMITTER SITE: Radio Veritas Asia, Palauig, Zambales, Philippines. Contact: Fr. Hugo Delbaere, CICM, Technical Consultant.

BRUSSELS BUREAUS AND MAIL DROPS: Catholic Radio and Television Network, 32-34 Rue de l' Association, B-1000 Brussels, Belgium; or UNDA, 12 Rue de l'Orme, B-1040 Brussels, Belgium.

Voice of Friendship—*see* FEBC Radio International.

PIRATE Pirate radio stations are usually one-person operations airing home-brew entertainment and/or iconoclastic viewpoints. In order to avoid detection by the authorities, they tend to appear irregularly, with little concern for the niceties of conventional program scheduling. Most are found in Europe chiefly on weekends, and mainly during evenings in North America, often just above 6200 kHz, just below 7000 kHz and just above 7375 kHz. These *sub rosa* stations and their addresses are subject to unusually abrupt change or termination, sometimes as a result of forays by radio authorities.

A worthy source of current addresses and other information on American pirate radio activity is: A*C*E, P.O. Box 12112, Norfolk VA 23541 USA (email: pradio@erols.com; Web: www.frn.net/ace/), a club which publishes a periodical ($20/year U.S., US$21 Canada, $27 elsewhere) for serious pirate radio enthusiasts.

For Europirate DX news, try:

SRSNEWS, Swedish Report Service, Ostra Porten 29, SE-442 54 Ytterby, Sweden. Email: srs@ice.warp.slink.se. Web: www-pp.kdt.net/jonny/index.html.

Pirate Connection, P.O. Box 4580, SE-203 20 Malmoe, Sweden; or P.O. Box 7085, Kansas City, Missouri 64113 USA. Phone: (home, Sweden) +46 (40) 611-1775; (mobile, Sweden) +46 (70) 581-5047. Email: etoxspz@eto.ericsson.se, xtdspz@lmd.ericsson.se or spz@exallon.se. Web: www-pp.hogia.net/jonny/pc. Six issues annually for about $23. Related to SRSNEWS, above.

FRS Goes DX, P.O. Box 2727, NL-6049 ZG Herten, Netherlands. Email: FRSH@pi.net; or peter.verbruggen@tip.nl. Web: http://home.pi.net/~freak55/home.htm.

Free-DX, 3 Greenway, Harold Park, Romford, Essex, RM3 OHH, United Kingdom.

FRC-Finland, P.O. Box 82, FIN-40101 Jyvaskyla, Finland.

Pirate Express, Postfach 220342, Wuppertal, Germany.

For up-to-date listener discussions and other pirate-radio information on the Internet, the usenet URLs are: alt.radio.pirate and rec.radio.pirate.

POLAND   World Time +1 (+2 midyear)

Office of Telecommunication Regulation, Rozyckiego 1C, PL-51-608 Wroclaw, Poland. Phone: +48 (71) 348-8866. Fax: +48 (71) 345 9043. Email: w.sega@urt.gov.pl. Web: www.urt.gov.pl. Contact: Wiktor Sega, Deputy Director, Frequency Management Department.

Radio Maryja, ul. _wirki i Wigury 80, PL-87-100 Toru_, Poland. Phone: +48 (56) 655-2361. Fax: +48 (56) 655 2362. Email: radio@radiomaryja.pl; (Kabulska) anna.kabulska@radiomaryja.pl. Web: (includes RealAudio) www.radiomaryja.pl; (Windows Media) http://nyas.radiomaria.org/Poland.asx. Contact: Father Tadeusz Rydzk, Dyrektor; Father Jacek Cydzik; Anna Kabulska,

Secretary; or Malgorzata Zaniewska. Polish preferred, but also replies to correspondence in English. Transmits via facilities in western Russia.

Radio Polonia

STATION: External Service, P.O. Box 46, PL-00-977 Warsaw, Poland. Phone: (general) +48 (22) 645-9305 or +48 (22) 444-123; (English Section) +48 (22) 645-9262; (German Section) +48 (22) 645-9333; (placement liaison) +48 (2) 645-9002. Fax: (general and administration) +48 (22) 645 5917 or +48 (22) 645 5919; (placement liaison) +48 (2) 645 5906. Email: (general): piatka@radio.com.pl; (Polish Section) polonia@radio.com.pl; (English Section) english.section@radio.com.pl; (German Section) deutsche.redaktion@radio.com.pl; (Esperanto Section) esperanto.redakcio@radio.com.pl. Web: (includes RealAudio and Windows Media) www.radio.com.pl/polonia. Contact: (general) Rafał Kiepuszewski, Head, English Section and Producer, "Postbag"; Peter Gentle, Presenter, "Postbag"; or Ann Flapan, Corresponding Secretary; (administration) Jerzy M. Nowakowski, Managing Director; Wanda Samborska, Managing Director; Bogumiła Berdychowska, Deputy Managing Director; or Maciej Lętowski, Executive Manager. On-air Polish language course with free printed material. Free stickers, pens, key rings and possibly T-shirts depending on financial cutbacks. DX Listeners' Club.

TRANSMISSION AUTHORITY: PAR (National Radiocommunication Agency), ul. Kasprzaka 18/20, PL-01-211 Warsaw, Poland. Phone: +48 (22) 608-8139/40, +48 (22) 608-8174 or +48 (22) 608-8191. Fax: +48 (22) 608 8195. Email: the format is initial.last name@par.gov.pl, so to reach, say, Filomena Grodzicka, it would be f.grodzicka@par.gov.pl. Contact: Mrs. Filomena Grodzicka, Head of BC Section; Lukasz Trzos; Mrs. Katalin Jaros; Ms. Urszula Rzepa or Jan Kondej. Responsible for coordinating Radio Polonia's frequencies.

PORTUGAL   World Time exactly (+1 midyear); Azores

World Time -1 (World Time midyear)

RDP Internacional—Rádio Portugal, Apartado 1011, 1001 Lisbon, Portugal; (street address) Av. Eng. Duarte Pacheco 26, 1070-110 Lisbon, Portugal. Phone: (general) +351 (21) 382-0000; (engineering) +351 (21) 382-2000. Fax: (general) +351 (21) 382 0165; (engineering) +351 (21) 387 1381. Email: (general) rdpinternacional@rdp.pt; (reception reports and listener correspondence) isabelsaraiva@rdp.pt, or christianehaupt@rdp.pt; (Frequency Management) teresaabreu@rdp.pt or paulacarvalho@rdp.pt. Web: (includes RealAudio and Windows Media) www.rdp.pt/internacional. Contact: (administration) José Manuel Nunes, Chairman; or Jaime Marques de Almeida, Director; (general) Isabel Saraiva or Christiane Haupt, Listener's Service Department; (technical) Eng. Francisco Mascarenhas, Technical Director; (Frequency Management) Mrs. Teresa Beatriz Abreu, Frequency Manager; or Ms. Paula Carvalho. Free stickers. May also send literature from the Portuguese National Tourist Office.

Radio Trans Europe (transmission facilities), 6° esq., Rua Braamcamp 84, 1200 Lisbon, Portugal. Transmitters located at Sines, and used by RDP Internacional and Germany's Deutsche Welle (*see*).

QATAR   World Time +3

Qatar Radio & Television Corporation (if reactivated), P.O. Box 3939, Doha, Qatar. Phone: (director) +974 86-48-05; (under secretary) +974 864-823; (engineering) +974 864-518;

(main Arabic service audio feed) +974 895-895. Fax: +974 822 888 or +974 831 447. Contact: Jassim Mohamed Al-Qattan, Head of Public Relations. May send booklet on Qatar Broadcasting Service. Occasionally replies, and return postage helpful. *TECHNICAL OFFICE:* Qatar Radio and Television Corporation, P.O. Box 1836, Doha, Qatar. Phone: +974 831-443, +974 864-057 or +974 894-613. Fax: +974 831 447. Contact: Hassan Al-Mass, Abdelwahab Al-Kawary; or Issa Ahmed Al-Hamadi, Head of Frequency Management.

ROMANIA   World Time +2 (+3 midyear)

Radio România Actualitati, Societatea Româna de Radiodifuziune, 60-62 Berthelot St., RO- 70747 Bucharest, Romania. Phone: +40 (21) 615-9350. Fax: +40 (21) 223 2612.
Radio România International
STATION: 60-62 Berthelot St., RO-70747 Bucharest, Romania; P.O. Box 111, RO-70756 Bucharest, Romania; or Romanian embassies worldwide. Phone: (general) +40 (21) 222-2556, +40 (21) 303-1172, +40 (21) 303-1488 or +40 (21) 312-3645; (English Department) +40 (21) 303-1357; (engineering) +40 (21) 303-1193. Fax: (general) +40 (21) 223 2613 [if no connection, try via the office of the Director General of Radio România, but mark fax "Pentru RRI"; that fax is +40 (21) 222 5641]; (Engineering Services) +40 (21) 312 1056/7 or +40 (21) 615 6992. Email: (general) rri@rri.ro; (English Service) engl@rri.ro; (Nisipeanu) mnisipeanu@radio.rornet.ro; (Ianculescu) rianculescu@rri.ro. Web: (includes RealAudio) www.rri.ro. Contact: (communications in English or Romanian) Dan Balamat, "Listeners' Letterbox"; or Ioana Masariu, Head of the English Service; (radio enthusiasts' issues, English only) "DX Mailbox," English Department; (communications in French or Romanian) Doru Vasile Ionescu, Deputy General Director; (listeners' letters) or Dan Dumitrescu; (technical) Sorin Floricu, Head of Broadcasting Department; Radu Ianculescu, HF Planning & Monitoring; or Marius Nisipeanu, Director, Production & Broadcasting. Listeners' Club. Annual contests. Rarely replies. Concerns about frequency management should be directed to the PTT (*see* below), with copies to the Romanian Autonomous Company (*see* farther below) and to a suitable official at RRI.
TRANSMISSION AND FREQUENCY MANAGEMENT, PTT: General Directorate of Regulations, Ministry of Communications, 14a Al. Libertatii, R-70060 Bucharest, Romania. Phone: +40 (21) 400-1312 or +40 (21) 400-177. Fax: +40 (21) 400 1230. Email: marian@snr.ro. Contact: Mrs. Elena Danila, Head of Frequency Management Department.
TRANSMISSION AND FREQUENCY MANAGEMENT, AUTONOMOUS COMPANY: Romanian Autonomous Company for Radio Communications, 14a Al. Libertatii, R-70060 Bucharest, Romania. Phone: +40 (21) 400-1072. Fax: +40 (21) 400 1228 or +40 (1) 335 5965. Email: marian@snr.ro. Contact: Mr. Marian Ionitá, Executive Director of Operations.

RUSSIA   (Times given for republics, oblasts and krays):

- World Time +2 (+3 midyear) Kaliningradskaya;
- World Time +3 (+4 midyear) Adygeya, Arkhangelskaya, Astrakhanskaya, Belgorodskaya, Bryanskaya, Chechnya, Chuvashiya, Dagestan, Ingushetiya, Kabardino-Balkariya, Kalmykiya, Kaluzhskaya, Karachayevo-Cherkesiya, Ivanovskaya, Karelia, Kirovskaya, Komi, Kostromskaya, Krasnodarskiy, Kurskaya, Leningradskaya (including St. Petersburg), Lipetskaya, Mariy-El, Mordoviya, Moskovskaya (including the capital, Moscow), Murmanskaya, Nenetskiy,

Nizhegorodskaya, Novgorodskaya, Severnaya Osetiya, Orlovskaya, Penzenskaya, Pskovskaya, Rostovskaya, Ryazanskaya, Saratovskaya, Smolenskaya, Stavropolskiy, Tambovskaya, Tatarstan, Tulskaya, Tverskaya, Ulyanovskaya, Vladimirskaya, Volgogradskaya, Vologodskaya, Voronezhskaya, Yaroslavskaya;
- World Time +4 (+5 midyear) Samarskaya, Udmurtiya;
- World Time +5 (+6 midyear) Bashkortostan, Chelyabinskaya, Khanty-Mansiyskiy, Komi- Permyatskiy, Kurganskaya, Orenburgskaya, Permskaya, Sverdlovskaya, Tyumenskaya, Yamalo- Nenetskiy;
- World Time +6 (+7 midyear) Altayskiy, Novosibirskaya, Omskaya, Tomskaya;
- World Time +7 (+8 midyear) Evenkiyskiy, Kemerovskaya, Khakasiya, Krasnoyarskiy, Taymyrskiy, Tyva;
- World Time +8 (+9 midyear) Buryatiya, Irkutskaya, Ust-Ordynskiy;
- World Time +9 (+10 midyear) Aginskiy-Buryatskiy, Amurskaya, Chitinskaya, Sakha;
- World Time +10 (+11 midyear) Khabarovskiy, Primorskiy, Yevreyskaya;
- World Time +11 (+12 midyear) Magadanskaya, Sakhalinskaya;
- World Time +12 (+13 midyear) Chukotskiy, Kamchatskaya, Koryakskiy;

VERIFICATION OF STATIONS USING TRANSMITTERS IN ST. PETERSBURG AND KALININGRAD: Transmissions of certain world band stations—such as Radio Rossii and China Radio International—when emanating from transmitters located in St. Petersburg and Kaliningrad, may be verified directly from: World Band Verification QSL Service, Centre for Broadcasting and Radio Communications No. 2 (CRR-2), ul. Akademika Pavlova 13A, 197376 St. Petersburg, Russia. Phone: +7 (812) 234-1002. Fax: +7 (812) 234 2971 during working hours. Contact: Mikhail V. Sergeyev, Chief Engineer; or Mikhail Timofeyev, verifier. Free stickers. Two IRCs required for a reply, which upon request includes a copy of "Broadcast Schedule," which gives transmission details (excluding powers) for all transmissions emanating from three distinct transmitter locations: Kaliningrad-Bolshakovo, St. Petersburg and St. Petersburg-Popovka.

Government Radio Agencies
C.I.S. FREQUENCY MANAGEMENT ENGINEERING OFFICE: General Radio Frequency Center, 25 Pyatnitskaya Str., 113326 Moscow, Russia. Phone: +7 (095) 950-6022; phone/fax: +7 (095) 789-3587. Email: (Titov) titov@vr.ru. Web: (General Radio Frequency Center parent organization) www.grfc.ru. Contact: (general) Mrs. Nina Bykova, Monitoring Coordinator; (administration) Anatoliy T. Titov, Chief of Division for SW and MW Frequency Broadcasting Schedules. This office is responsible for the operation of radio broadcasting in the Russian Federation, as well as for frequency usage of transmitters throughout much of the C.I.S. Correspondence should be concerned only with significant technical observations or engineering suggestions concerning frequency management improvement—not regular requests for verifications. Correspondence in Russian preferred, but English accepted.
CENTRE FOR BROADCASTING AND RADIO COMMUNICATIONS NO. 2 (GPR-2)—see VERIFICATION OF STATIONS USING TRANSMITTERS IN ST. PETERSBURG AND KALININGRAD, above.
STATE RADIO COMPANY: AS Radioagency Co., Pyatnitskaya 25, 115326 Moscow, Russia. Phone: (Staviskaia) +7 (095) 950-6115. Fax: (Staviskaia) +7 (095) 950 6851. Email: (Staviskaia) srm@vr.ru. Contact: Mrs. Rachel Staviskaia, Director of Technical Development.

STATE TRANSMISSION AUTHORITY: Russian Ministry of Tele-communication, ul. Tverskaya 7, 103375 Moscow, Russia. Phone: +7 (095) 201-6568. Fax: +7 (095) 292 7086 or +7 (095) 292 7128. Contact: Anatoly C. Batiouchkine.

STATE TV AND RADIO COMPANY: Russian State TV and Radio Company, Yamskogo polya, 5-ya ul. 19/21, 125124 Moscow, Russia. Phone: +7 (095) 213-1054, +7 (095) 213-1054 or +7 (095) 250-0511. Fax: +7 (095) 250 0105. Contact: Ivan Sitilenlov.

Adgygey Radio—*see* Maykop Radio.

Amur Radio—*see* Blagoveschensk Radio.

Arkhangel'sk Radio, GTRK "Pomorye", ul. Popova 2, 163061 Arkhangel'sk, Arkhangel'skaya Oblast, Russia; or U1PR, Valentin G. Kalasnikov, ul. Suvorov 2, kv. 16, Arkhangel'sk, Arkhangel'skaya Oblast, Russia. Replies irregularly to correspondence in Russian.

Blagoveschensk Radio, GTRK "Amur", per Svyatitelya Innokentiya 15, 675000 Blagoveschensk, Russia. Contact: V.I. Kal'chenko, Chief Engineer.

Buryat Radio—*see* Ulan-Ude Radio.

Kabardino-Balkar Radio—*see* Nalchik Radio.

Kamchatka Rybatskaya—a special service for fishermen off the coasts of China, Japan and western North America; *see* Petropavlovsk-Kamchatskiy Radio for contact details.

Khabarovsk Radio (when operating), GTRK "Dalnevostochnaya", ul. Lenina 4, 682632 Khabarovsk, Khabarovskiy Kray, Russia; or Dom Radio, pl. Slavy, 682632 Khabarovsk, Khabarovskiy Kray, Russia. Web: (program schedule only) www.khb.ru/Afisha/Radio/kabar.htm. Contact: (technical) V.N. Kononov, Glavnyy Inzhener.

Khanty-Mansiysk Radio, GTRK "Yugoriya", ul. Mira 7, 626200 Khanty-Mansiysk, Russia. Contact: (technical) Vladimir Sokolov, Engineer.

Koryak Radio—*see* Palana Radio.

Krasnoyarsk Radio, Krasnoyarskaya GTRK, "Tsentr Rossii", ul. Mechnikova 44A, 666001, Krasnoyarsk 28, Krasnoyarsky Kray, Russia. Email: postmaster@telegid.krasnoyarsk.su. Contact: Valeriy Korotchenko; or Anatoliy A. Potehin, RAØAKE. Free local information booklets in English/Russian. Replies in Russian to correspondence in English or Russian. Return postage helpful.

Kyzyl Radio, GTRK "Tyva", ul. Gornaya 31, 667003 Kyzyl, Respublika Tyva, Russia. Email: tv@tuva.ru. Replies to correspondence in Russian.

Magadan Radio, GTRK "Magadan", ul. Kommuny 8/12, 685024 Magadan, Magadanskaya Oblast, Russia. Contact: Viktor Loktionov or V.G. Kuznetsov. Return postage helpful. Occasionally replies to correspondence in Russian.

Mariy Radio—*see* Yoshkar-Ola Radio.

Mayak—*see* Radiostantsiya Mayak.

Maykop Radio, GTRK "Adygeya", ul. Zhukovskogo 24, 352700 Maykop, Republic of Adygeya, Russia. Contact: A.T. Kerashev, Chairman. English accepted but Russian preferred. Return postage helpful.

Murmansk Radio, GTRK "Murman", per. Rusanova 7, 183032 Murmansk, Murmanskaya Oblast, Russia. Phone: +7 (8152) 561-527. Phone/fax: +7 (8152) 459-770. Fax: +7 (8152) 231 913. Email: tvmurman@sampo.ru; tvmurman@sampo.karelia.ru; murmantv@com.mels.ru. Web: www.sampo.ru/~tvmurman/radio/rmain.html. Contact: D. Perederi (chairman).

Nalchik Radio, GTRK "Kabbalk Teleradio", pr. Lenina 3, 360000 Nalchik, Republic of Kabardino-Balkariya, Russia. Contact: Kamal Makitov, Vice-Chairman. Replies to correspondence in Russian.

Palana Radio, Koryakskaya GTRK "Palana," ul. Obukhova 4, 684620 Palana, Koryakskiy avt. Okrug, Russia.

Perm Radio, Permskaya GTRK "T-7", ul. Tekhnicheskaya 7, 614070 Perm, Permskaya Oblast, Russia. Contact: M. Levin, Senior Editor; or A. Losev, Acting Chief Editor.

Petropavlovsk-Kamchatskiy Radio, GTRK "Kamchatka", ul. Sovetskaya 62, 683000 Petropavlovsk-Kamchatskiy, Kamchatskaya Oblast, Russia. Contact: A.F. Borodin, Head of GTRK "Kamchatka." Email: gtrkbuh@mail.iks.ru. $1 required for postal reply. Replies in Russian to correspondence in Russian or English. Currently inactive on shortwave, apart from a special program for fishermen—*see* Kamchatka Rybatskaya.

Radio Gardarika (when operating), Radio Studio Dom Radio, Ligovsky Prospekt 174, 197002 St. Petersburg, Russia. Email: studiosw@metroclub.ru. Contact: Suvorov Alexey, Shortwave Project Manager. Replies to correspondence in Russian and English. Return postage helpful.

Radio Krishnaloka

STATION: Email: radioveda@mail.ru

MOSCOW CONTACT ADDRESS: ul. Avtozavodskaya, dom 6, kvartira 24 A, Moscow, Russia. Email: schyammohan@ukr.net. Web: www.harekrishna.ru/news/krishnaloka.shtml.

Replies to correspondence in Russian. Station is considering changing its name to

Radio Veda.

⚙**Radio Miks-Master**, ul. Oktyabr'skaya 20/1, 677027 Yakutsk, Respublika Sakha, Russia. Phone: +7 (4112) 420-302. Email: mix_radio@rambler.ru. Web: (includes MP3) http://mixmaster.ykt.ru.

Radio Nalchik—*see* Radio Kabardino-Balkar, above.

⚙**Radio Rossii** (Russia's Radio), GRK "Radio Rossii", Yamskogo Polya 5-YA ul. 19/21, 125124 Moscow, Russia. Phone: +7 (095) 213-1054, +7 (095) 250-0511 or +7 (095) 251-4050. Fax: +7 (095) 250 0105, +7 (095) 233 6449 or +7 (095) 214 4767. Email: mail@radiorus.ru. Web: (includes Windows Media) www.radiorus.ru. Contact: Sergei Yerofeyev, Director of International Operations [sic]; or Sergei Davidov, Director. Free English-language information sheet. For verification of reception from transmitters located in St. Petersburg and Kaliningrad, *see NOTE*, above, shortly after the country heading, "RUSSIA."

Radio Samorodinka (when operating), P.O. Box 898, Center, 101000 Moscow, Russia. Contact: Lev Stepanovich Shishkin, Editor & Director. This station is not licensed, so do not include the station name on the envelope. Mr. Shishkin is fluent in English.

Radio Studio—*see* Radio Gardarika.

Radio Veda—*see* Radio Krishnaloka.

⚙**Radiostantsiya Mayak**, GRK "Mayak", ul. Pyatnitskaya 25, 115326 Moscow, Russia. Phone: +7 (095) 950-6767. Fax: +7 (095) 959 4204. Email: inform@radiomayak.ru. Web: (includes Windows Media) www.radiomayak.ru. Although no longer operating officially on shortwave in Russia, the station is relayed via one or two regional stations in Siberia. Unofficially, Mayak broadcasts are also aired over certain military transmitters in Belarus which operate in the 2, 3 and 5 MHz bands. Correspondence in Russian preferred, but English increasingly accepted.

Radiostantsiya Tikhiy Okean ("Radio Station Pacific Ocean") (when operating), RTV Center, ul. Uborevieha 20A, 690000 Vladivostok, Primorskiy Kray, Russia. Once a regular broadcaster, but now restricted to special transmissions.

Russian Radio International. A joint-project involving the Voice of Russia and Russkoye Radio. Same contact information as for the Voice of Russia.

Sakhalin Radio, GTRK "Sakhalin," ul. Komsomolskaya 209, 693000 Yuzhno-Sakhalinsk, Sakhalinskaya Oblast, Russia. Phone: (Director of Radio) +7 (42422) 729-349. Phone/fax: (GTRK parent company) +7 (42422) 35286. Email: gtrk@sakhalin.ru; (Romanov) romanov@gtrk.sakhalin.su. Web: www.gtrk.ru/RV/radio.htm. Contact: S. Romanov, Director of Radio.

Tatarstan Wave ("Tatarstan Dulkynda"), GTRK "Tatarstan", ul. Gor'kogo 15, 420015 Kazan, Tatarstan, Russia. Phone: (general) +7 (8432) 384-846; (editorial) +7 (8432) 367-493. Fax: +7 (8432) 361 283. Email: root@gtrkrt.kazan.su; postmaster@ stvcrt.kazan.su. Contact: (nontechnical) Hania Hazipovna Galinova. Formerly known as Voice of Tatarstan. *ADDRESS FOR RECEPTION REPORTS:* QSL Manager, P.O. Box 134, 420136 Kazan, Tatarstan, Russia. Contact: Ildus Ibatullin, QSL Manager. Offers an honorary diploma in return for 12 correct reports in a given year. The diploma costs 2 IRCs for Russia and 4 IRCs elsewhere. All reports to the QSL Manager address listed above. Accepts reports in English and Russian. Return postage helpful.

Tura Radio, Evenkiyskaya GTRK "Kheglen", ul. 50 Let Oktyabrya 28, 663370 Tura, Russia.

Tyumen' Radio, GTRK "Region-Tyumen", ul. Permyakova 6, 625013 Tyumen', Tyumenskaya Oblast, Russia. Email: regtumc@sbtx.tmn.ru. Contact: (general) Liliya Vycherova, Advertising Manager; (technical) V.D. Kizerov, Engineer, Technical Center. Sometimes replies to correspondence in Russian. Return postage helpful.

Ufa Radio, GTRK "Bashkortostan", ul. Gafuri 9/1, 450076 Ufa, Respublika Bashkortostan, Russia. Email: gtrk@bashinform.ru. Replies to correspondence in Russian.

Ulan-Ude Radio, Buryatskaya GTRK, ul. Erbanova 7, 670000 Ulan-Ude, Republic of Buryatia, Russia. Contact: Z.A. Telin; Mrs. M.V. Urbaeva, 1st Vice-Chairman; or L.S. Shikhanova.

⬛Voice of Russia, GRK "Golos Rossii", ul. Pyatnitskaya 25, Moscow 115326, Russia. Phone: (Chairman) +7 (095) 950-6331; (International Relations Department) +7 (095) 950-6440; (Technical Department) +7 (095) 950-6115. Fax: (Chairman & World Service in English) +7 (095) 230 2828; Email: letters@vor.ru. Web: (includes RealAudio) www.vor.ru. Contact: (Letters Department, World Service in English) Olga Troshina, Elena Osipova or Elena Frolovskaya; (Chairman) Armen Oganesyan; (International Relations Department) Victor Kopytin, Director; (Technical Department) Ms. Rachel Staviskaya, Director; (World Service in English) Vladimir Zhamkin, Director. For language services other than English contact the International Relations Department. *SAN FRANCISCO OFFICE, SCHEDULES:* 2654 17th Avenue, San Francisco CA 94116 USA. Phone: +1 (415) 564-9968. Email: GPoppin@aol.com. Contact: George Poppin. This address, a volunteer office, only provides Voice of Russia schedules to listeners. All other correspondence should be sent directly to the Voice of Russia in Moscow.

Yakutsk Radio, NVK "Sakha", ul. Ordzhonikidze 48, 677007 Yakutsk, Respublika Sakha, Russia. Contact: (general) Alexandra Borisova; Lia Sharoborina, Advertising Editor; or Albina Danilova, Producer, "Your Letters"; (technical) Sergei Bobnev, Technical Director. Russian books $15; audio cassettes $10. Free station stickers and original Yakutian souvenirs. Replies to correspondence in English.

Yoshkar- Ola Radio, GTRK "Mariy-El", ul. Osipenko 50, 424014 Yoshkar-Ola, Russia. Verifies reports in Russian.

RWANDA   World Time +2

Deutsche Welle—Relay Station Kigali—Correspondence should be directed to the main offices in Germany *(see)*.

⬛Radio Rwanda, B.P. 83, Kigali, Rwanda. Phone: +250 76540. Fax: +250 76185. Email: (Rwandan Information Office) imvaho2002@yahoo.fr. Web: (includes RealAudio) www.orinfor.gov.rw/radiorwanda.htm. Contact: Marcel Singirankabo. $1 required. Rarely replies, with correspondence in French preferred.

SAO TOME E PRINCIPE   World Time exactly

Voice of America/IBB—São Tomé Relay Station, P.O. Box 522, São Tomé, São Tomé e Príncipe. Contact: Manuel Neves, Transmitter Plant Technician. Replies direct if $1 included with correspondence, otherwise all communications should be directed to the usual VOA or IBB addresses in Washington *(see USA)*.

SAUDI ARABIA   World Time +3

⬛Broadcasting Service of the Kingdom of Saudi Arabia, P.O. Box 61718, Riyadh-11575, Saudi Arabia. Phone: (general) +966 (1) 404-2795; (administration) +966 (1) 442-5493. Fax: (general) +966 (1) 402 8177. Web: (MP3 only) www.saudiradio.net. Contact: (general) Mutlaq A. Albegami. Free travel information and book on Saudi history. For technical contacts including Engineering and Frequency Management, see the next entry.

Saudi Arabian Radio & Television, P.O. Box 8525, Riyadh-11492, Saudi Arabia. Phone: (technical & frequency management) +966 (1) 442-5170. Fax: (technical & frequency management) +966 (1) 404 1692. Email: alsamnan@yahoo.com or inform.eng@suhuf.net.sa. Contact: Suleiman Al-Samnan, Director of Engineering and Frequency Management; Suleiman Al-Kalifa, General Manager; Suleiman Al Haidari, Engineer; or Youssef Dhim. This agency is responsible for choosing the frequencies used by the Broadcasting Service of the Kingdom of Saudi Arabia

SERBIA AND MONTENEGRO   World Time +1 (+2 midyear)

⬛ International Radio of Serbia and Montenegro, Hilendarska 2/IV, P.O. Box 200, 11000 Beograd, Serbia and Montenegro. Phone: +381 (11) 324-4455. Fax: +381 (11) 323 2014. Email: radioyu@bitsyu.net. Web: (includes RealAudio) www.radioyu.org. Contact: (general) Milena Jokich, Director & Editor-in-Chief; Aleksandar Georgiev; Aleksandar Popovic, Head of Public Relations; Pance Zafirovski, Head of Programs; (technical) B. Miletic, Operations Department of HF Broadcasting; Technical Department; or Rodoljub Medan, Chief Engineer. Free pennants, stickers, pins and tourist information. $1 helpful. Formerly known as Radio Yugoslavia.

SEYCHELLES   World Time +4

BBC World Service—Indian Ocean Relay Station, P.O. Box 448, Victoria, Mahé, Seychelles; or Grand Anse, Mahé, Seychelles. Phone: +248 78-269. Fax: +248 78 500. Contact: (administration) Peter J. Loveday, Station Manager; (technical) Peter Lee, Resident Engineer; Nigel Bird, Resident Engineer; or Steve Welch, Assistant Resident Engineer. Nontechnical correspondence should be sent to the BBC World Service in London *(see)*.

SIERRA LEONE   World Time exactly

Radio UNAMSIL (when operating), Mammy Yoko Hotel, P.O. Box 5, Freetown, Sierra Leone. Email: info@unamsil.org; or patrickcoker@unamsil.org. Web: (UNAMSIL parent organization) www.unamsil.org. Contact: Patrick Coker or Sheila Dallas, Station Manager & Executive Producer. Station of the United Nations Mission in Sierra Leone.

Sierra Leone Broadcasting Service (when operating), New England, Freetown, Sierra Leone. Phone: +232 (22) 240-123; +232 (22) 240-173; +232 (22) 240-497 or 232 (22) 241-919. Fax: +232 (22) 240 922. Contact: Cyril Juxon-Smith, Officer in Charge; or Henry Goodaig Hjax, Assistant Engineer.

SINGAPORE   World Time +8

BBC World Service—Far Eastern Relay Station, VT Merlin Communications, 51 Turut Track, Singapore 718930, Singapore. Phone: + 65 6793-7511/3. Fax: +65 6793 7834. Email: wuipin@singnet.com.sg. Contact: (technical) Mr. Wui Pin Yong, Operations Manager; or Far East Resident Engineer. Nontechnical correspondence should be sent to the BBC World Service in London (see).

MediaCorp Radio, Farrer Road, P.O. Box 968, Singapore 912899, Singapore; or (street address) Caldecott Broadcast Centre, Caldecott Hill, Andrew Road, Singapore 299939, Singapore. Phone: (general) +65 6251-8622; (Fern) +65 6359-7577; (transmitting station) +65 6793-7651. Fax: +65 6256 9533. Email: (Fern) cherfern@mediacorpradio.com. Web: (includes Windows Media) www.mediacorpradio.com. Contact: (administration) Peh Cher Fern, Corporate Communications Senior Executive. Free regular and Post-It stickers, pens, umbrellas, mugs, towels, wallets and lapel pins. Do not include currency in envelope. Successor to the former Radio Corporation of Singapore.

Radio Singapore International, Farrer Road, P.O. Box 5300, Singapore 912899, Singapore; or (street address) Caldecott Broadcast Centre, Annex Building Level 1, Andrew Road, Singapore 299939, Singapore. Phone: (general) + 65 6359-7662; (English Service) + 65 6359- 7675. Fax: +65 6259 1357 or +65 6259 1380. Email: info@rsi.com.sg; or (English Service) english@rsi.com.sg. Web: (includes Windows Media) www.rsi.com.sg. Contact: (general) Augustine Anthuvan, Assistant Programme Manager, English Service; (technical) Lim Wing Kee, RSI Engineering. Free souvenir T-shirts and key chains to selected listeners. Do not include currency in envelope.

SLOVAKIA   World Time +1 (+2 midyear)

Radio Slovakia International, Mýtna 1, P.O. Box 15, 817 55 Bratislava 15, Slovakia. Phone: (Editor-in-Chief) +421 (2) 5727-3730; (English Service) +421 (2) 5727-3736 or +421 (2) 5727- 2737; (technical) +421 (2) 5727-3251. Fax: +421 (2) 5249 6282 or +421 (2) 5249 8247; (technical) +421 (2) 5249 7659. Email: (English Section) englishsection@slovakradio sk; for other language sections, the format is rsi_language@ slovakradio.sk, where the language is written in English (e.g. rsi_spanish@slovakradio.sk); (Frequency Manager) chocholata@slovakradio.sk. Web: (includes RealAudio and online reception-report form) www.rsi.sk. Contact: Oxana Ferjenčíková, Director of English Broadcasting; (administration) PhDr. Karol Palkovič, Head of External Broadcasting; or Dr. Slavomira Kubickova, Head of International Relations; (technical) Ms. Edita Chocholatá, Frequency Manager. May exchange stamps, recipes and coins.

SOLOMON ISLANDS   World Time +11

Solomon Islands Broadcasting Corporation (Radio Happy Isles), P.O. Box 654, Honiara, Solomon Islands. Phone: +677 20051. Fax: +677 23159 or +677 25652. Email: sibcnews@ solomon.com.sb. Web: (SIBC news in text format) www.sibconline.com.sb. Contact: (general) Julian Maka'a, Producer, "Listeners From Far Away"; Cornelius Teasi; or Silas Hule; (administration) Johnson Honimae, General Manager; (technical) John Babera, Chief Engineer. IRC or $1 helpful. Problems with the domestic mail system may cause delays.

SOMALIA   World Time +3

Radio Baidoa (when operating)
RAHANWEIN RESISTANCE ARMY SPONSORING ORGANIZATION: Email: info@arlaadi.com. Web: www.arlaadi.com; www.arlaadinet.com.
Radio Banaadir—see Radio Banadir, below.
Radio Banadir (when operating), Kaaraan (Beexaani), Mogadishu, Somalia. Phone: +2525 944- 156 or +2525 960-368. Email: radiobanadir@somalinternet.com. Web: (includes RealAudio) www.radiobanadir.com.
Radio Baydhabo—see Radio Baidoa, above.
Radio Galkayo (when operating), 2 Griffith Avenue, Roseville NSW 2069, Australia. Phone/fax: +61 (2) 9417-1066. Email: svoron@hotmail.com. Web: (includes RealAudio and online email form) www. radiogalkayo.com. Contact: Sam Voron, Australian Director. $5, AUS$5 or 5 IRCs required. A community radio station in the Mudug region of northeastern Somalia, and operated by the Somali International Amateur Radio Club. Seeks volunteers and donations of radio equipment and airline tickets.

SOMALILAND   World Time +3

NOTE: "Somaliland," claimed as an independent nation, is diplomatically recognized only as part of Somalia.
Radio Hargeysa, P.O. Box 14, Hargeysa, Somaliland, Somalia. Email: no known direct mail address, but try admin@radiohargeysa.com or radio@somaliland.com. Web: (includes RealAudio) www.radiohargeysa.com; (RealAudio archives only) www.radiosomaliland.com. Contact: Sulayman Abdel-Rahman, announcer. More likely to respond to correspondence in Somali or Arabic.

SOUTH AFRICA   World Time +2

BBC World Service via South Africa—For verification direct from the South African transmitters, contact Sentech (see below). Nontechnical correspondence should be sent to the BBC World Service in London (see).
Channel Africa, P.O. Box 91313, Auckland Park 2006, South Africa. Phone: (executive editor) +27 (11) 714-2255; (technical) +27 (11) 714-2614. Fax: (executive editor) +27 (11) 714 2072. Email: (general) africancan@channelafrica.org; (news desk) news.africa@channelafrica.org; (technical) meyerhelen@channelafrica.org. Web: (includes Windows Media) www.channelafrica.org. Contact: (general) Promise Zamesa, Executive Editor; (technical) Mrs. Helen Meyer, Supervisor Operations. Reception reports are best directed to Sentech (see), which operates the transmission facilities.
Radio Veritas, P.O. Box 53687, Troyeville 2139, South Africa; or (street address) 36 Beelaerts Street, Troyeville 2094, South Africa. Phone: +27 (11) 624-2516; (studio) +27 (11) 614-6225.

Fax: +27 (11) 614 7711. Email: info@radioveritas.co.za; (Fr. Blaser) eblaser@iafrica.com. Web: www.radioveritas.co.za. Contact: Fr. Emil Blaser OP, Director. Return postage helpful. Reception reports can also be directed to Sentech (*see*), which operates the transmission facilities.

🖳**Radiosondergrense (Radio Without Boundaries)**, Posbus 91312, Auckland Park 2006, South Africa. Phone: (general) +27 (89) 110-2525; (live studio on-air line) +27 (89) 110-4553; (station manager) +27 (11) 714-2702. Fax: (general) +27 (11) 714 6445; (station manager) +27 (11) 714 3472. Email: (general) info@rsg.co.za; (Myburgh) sarel@rsg.co.za. Web: (includes Windows Media) www.rsg.co.za. Contact: Sarel Myburgh, Station Manager. Reception reports are best directed to Sentech (*see*, below), which operates the shortwave transmission facilities. A domestic service of the South African Broadcasting Corporation, and formerly known as Afrikaans Stereo. The shortwave operation is scheduled to be eventually replaced by a satellite and FM network.

Sentech (Pty) Ltd, Shortwave Services, Private Bag X06, Honeydew 2040, South Africa. Phone: (general) +27 (11) 475-5600; (shortwave) +27 (11) 475-1596; (Otto) +27 (11) 471-4658 or +27 (11) 471-4537. Fax: (general) +27 (11) 475 5112; (Otto) +27 (11) 471 4758 or +27 (11) 471 4754. Email: (Otto) ottok@sentech.co.za; (Smuts) smutsn@sentech.co.za. Web: (general) www.sentech.co.za; (schedules, unofficial) http://home.mweb.co.za/an/andre46. Contact: Mr. Neël Smuts, Managing Director; Rodgers Gamuti, Client Manager; or Kathy Otto, HF Coverage Planner. Sentech issues its own verification cards, and is the best place to send reception reports for world band stations broadcasting via South African facilities.

South African Radio League—Amateur Radio Mirror International, P.O. Box 90438, Garsfontein 0042, South Africa. Email: armi@intekom.co.za; armi@sarl.org.za. Web: www.sarl.org.za/public/ARMI/ARMI.asp. Amateur Radio Mirror International is a weekly broadcast aired via Sentech's Meyerton facilities.

Trans World Radio Africa
NONTECHNICAL CORRESPONDENCE: Trans World Radio—South Africa, Private Bag 987, Pretoria 0001, South Africa. Phone: +27 (12) 807-0053. Fax: +27 (12) 807 1266. Web: (includes online email form) www.twrafrica.org.
TECHNICAL CORRESPONDENCE: Reception reports and other technical correspondence are best directed to Sentech (*see*, above) or to TWR's Swaziland office (*see*). Also, *see* USA.

SPAIN   World Time +1 (+2 midyear)

🖳**Radio Exterior de España (Spanish National Radio, World Service)**
MAIN OFFICE: Apartado de Correos 156.202, E-28080 Madrid, Spain. Phone: (general) +34 (91) 346-1081/1083; (Audience Relations) +34 (91) 346-1149. Fax: +34 (91) 346 1815. Email: (Director) dir_ree.rne@rtve.es; (Spanish programming, listener feedback) ree.rne@rtve.es. Web: (includes RealAudio, MP3 and Windows Media) www.ree.rne.es. Contact: (Audience Relations) Pilar Salvador M.; (Assistant Director) Pedro Fernández Céspedes; (Director) Francisco Fernández Oria. Free stickers and tourist information. Verification of reception reports is temporarily suspended due to "staffing and budget constraints." Listeners are requested not to send cash or IRCs, since the limited services which still exist are free. An alternative, for those who speak and write Spanish, is to send a reception report on the program "Españoles en la Mar" which is produced in the Canary Islands. Times and frequencies can be found at the REE Website. Reports should be sent to: Programa

"Españoles en la Mar," Apartado Postal 1233, Santa Cruz de Tenerife, Spain. Magazines and small souvenirs are sometimes included with verifications from this address.
TRANSCRIPTION SERVICE: Radio Nacional de España, Servicio de Transcripciones, Apartado 156.200, Casa de la Radio (Prado del Rey), E-28223 Madrid, Spain.
HF FREQUENCY PLANNING OFFICE: Prado del Rey. Pozuelo de Alarcom, E-28223 Madrid, Spain. Phone: (Huerta) +34 (91) 346-1276; (Arlanzón) +34 (91) 346-1639; or (Almarza) +34 (91) 346-1978. Fax: (Huerta & Almarza) +34 (91) 346 1402 or (Alanzón) +34 (91) 346 1275. Email: (Almarza) planif_red2.rne@rtve.es; or (Huerta & Arlanzón) plan_red.rne@rtve.es. Contact: Fernando Almarza, Frequency Planning; Salvador Arlanzón, HF Frequency Manager; or José Maria Huerta, Technical Director.
NOBLEJAS TRANSMITTER SITE: Centro Emisor de RNE en Onda Corta, Ctra. Dos Barrios s/n, E-45350 Noblejas-Toledo, Spain.
COSTA RICA RELAY FACILITY—see Costa Rica.
MOSCOW OFFICE: P.O Box 88, 109044 Moscow, Russia.
WASHINGTON NEWS BUREAU: National Press Building, 529 14th Street NW, Suite 1288, Washington DC 20045 USA. Phone: +1 (202) 783-0768. Contact: Luz Maria Rodríguez.

SRI LANKA   World Time +6:00

Deutsche Welle—Relay Station Sri Lanka, 92/2 D.S. Senanayake Mawatha, Colombo 08, Sri Lanka. Phone: +94 (1) 699-449. Fax: +94 (1) 699 450. Contact: R. Groschkus, Resident Engineer. Nontechnical correspondence should be sent to Deutsche Welle in Germany (*see*).

Radio Japan/NHK, c/o SLBC, P.O. Box 574, Torrington Square, Colombo 7, Sri Lanka. This address for technical correspondence only. General nontechnical listener correspondence should be sent to the usual Radio Japan address in Japan. News-oriented correspondence may also be sent to the NHK Bangkok Bureau (*see* Radio Japan, Japan).

Sri Lanka Broadcasting Corporation (also announces as "Radio Sri Lanka" in the external service), P.O. Box 574, Independence (Torrington) Square, Colombo 7, Sri Lanka. Phone: (general) +94 (1) 697-491 or +94 (1) 697-493; (Director General) +94 (1) 696-140. Fax: (general) +94 (1) 697 150 or +94 (1) 698 576; (Director General) +94 (1) 695 488; (Sooryia, Phone/fax) +94 (1) 696-1311. Email: slbc@sri.lanka.net; slbcweb@sri.lanka.net. Web: www.infolanka.com/people/sisira/slbc.html. Contact: Icumar Ratnayake, Controller, "Mailbag Program"; (SLBC administration) Eric Fernando, Director General; Newton Gunaratne, Deputy Director-General; (technical) H.M.N.R. Jayawardena, Engineer - Training and Frequency Management; Wimala Sooriya, Deputy Director - Engineering; or A.M.W. Gunaratne, Station Engineer, Ekala.

Voice of America/IBB—Iranawila Relay Station.
ADDRESS: Station Manager, IBB Sri Lanka Transmitting Station, c/o U.S. Embassy, 210 Galle Road, Colombo 3, Sri Lanka. Contact: Walter Patterson, Station Manager. Verifies reception reports. Nontechnical correspondence should be sent to the VOA address in Washington.

SUDAN   World Time +3

Sudan National Radio Corporation, P.O. Box 572, Omdurman, Sudan. Phone: (general) +249 (11) 553-151 or +249 (11) 552-100. (Phone/fax, technical) +249 (11) 550- 492. Email: (general) snrc@sudanmail.net; has2000@hotmail.com; (technical) salihb@maktoob.com. Web: www.srtc.info/radio. Contact: (general) Mohammed Elfatih El Sumoal; (technical) Abbas

Sidig, Director General, Engineering and Technical Affairs; Mohammed Elmahdi Khalil, Administrator, Engineering and Technical Affairs; Saleh Al-Hay; Bachir Saleh, Deputy Director of Engineering; or Adil Didahammed, Engineering Department. Replies irregularly. Return postage necessary.

SURINAME   World Time -3

☞**Radio Apintie**, Postbus 595, Paramaribo, Suriname. Phone: +597 400-500, +597 400-450 or +597 401-400. Fax: +597 400 684. Email: apintie@sr.net. Web: (includes Windows Media) www.apintie.sr. Contact: Charles E. Vervuurt, Director. Free pennant. Return postage or $1 required. Email reception reports preferred, since local mail service is unreliable.

SWAZILAND   World Time +2

Trans World Radio—Swaziland
MAIN OFFICE: P.O. Box 64, Manzini, Swaziland. Phone: +268 505-2781/2/3. Fax: +268 505 5333. Email: (Chief Engineer) sstavrop@twr.org; (Mrs. L. Stavropoulos, DX Secretary) lstavrop@twr.org; (Greg Shaw, Follow-up Department) gshaw@twr.org. Web: (transmission schedule) www.gospelcom. net/twr/broadcasts/africa.htm. Contact: (general) Greg Shaw, Follow- up Department; G.J. Alary, Station Director; or Joseph Ndzinisa, Program Manager; (technical) Mrs. L. Stavropoulos, DX Secretary; Chief Engineer. Free stickers, postcards and calendars. A free Bible Study course is available. May swap canceled stamps. $1, return postage or 3 IRCs required. Also, *see* USA.
AFRICA REGIONAL OFFICE: P.O. Box 4232,Kempton Park 1610, South Africa. Phone: +27 (11) 974-2885. Fax: +27 (11) 974 9960. Email: jburnett@twraro.org.za. Contact: James Burnett, Regional Engineer & Frequency Manager; Stephen Boakye-Yiadom, African Regional Director.
CÔTE D'IVOIRE OFFICE: B.P. 2131, Abidjan 06, Côte d'Ivoire.
KENYA OFFICE: P.O. Box 21514 Nairobi, Kenya.
MALAWI OFFICE: P. O. Box 52 Lilongwe, Malawi.
SOUTH AFRICA OFFICE: P.O. Box 36000, Menlo Park 0102, South Africa.
ZIMBABWE OFFICE: P.O. Box H-74, Hatfield, Harare, Zimbabwe.

SWEDEN   World Time +1 (+2 midyear)

IBRA Radio, SE-141 99 Stockholm, Sweden. Phone: +46 (8) 608-9600. Fax: +46 (8) 608 9650. Email: ibra@ibra.se. Web: www.ibra.se; www.ibra.org. Contact: Mikael Stjernberg, Public Relations Manager; or Helene Hasslof. Free pennants and stickers. IBRA Radio's programs are aired over various world band stations, including Trans World Radio and FEBA Radio; and also broadcast independently via transmitters in Germany and Russia. Accepts email reception reports.
☞**Radio Sweden**, SE-105 10 Stockholm, Sweden. Phone: (general) +46 (8) 784-7200, +46 (8) 784-7207, +46 (8) 784-7288 or +46 (8) 784-5000; (listener voice mail) +46 (8) 784-7287; (technical department) +46 (8) 784-7286. Fax: (general) +46 (8) 667 6283; (polling to receive schedule) +46 8 660 2990. Email: (general) radiosweden@sr.se; (In Touch) intouch@p6.sr.se; (schedule on demand) english@rs.sr.se; (Roxström) sarah.roxstrom@rs.sr.se; (Hagström) nidia.hagstrom@rs.sr.se; (Wood) george.wood@p6.sr.se; (Sounds Nordic) sono@p6.sr.se); (Beckman, technical manager) rolf-b@stab.sr.se. Web: (includes RealAudio) www.sr.se/rs.Contact: (general) Nidia Hagström, Host, "In Touch with Stockholm" [include your telephone num-

ber]; Sarah Roxström, Head, English Service; Greta Grandin, Program Assistant, English Service; Gabby Katz, Presenter of Heartbeat; Bill Schiller, Spectrum presenter; George Wood; Olimpia Seldon, Assistant to the Director; or Frida Sjolander, Public Relations and Information; (administration) Finn Norgren, Director General; (technical) Rolf Erik Beckman, Head, Technical Department; or Anders Baecklin, Editor, Technical Administration. T-shirts (three sizes) $10 or £8. Payment for T-shirts may be made by international money order, Swedish postal giro account No. 43 36 56-6 or internationally negotiable bank check.
NEW YORK NEWS BUREAU: Swedish Broadcasting, 747 Third Avenue, 8th floor, New York NY 10022 USA. Phone: +1 (212) 644-1224. Fax: +1 (212) 644 1227. Contact: Elizabeth Johansson.
WASHINGTON NEWS BUREAU: Swedish Broadcasting, 2030 M Street NW, Suite 700, Washington DC 20036 USA. Phone: +1 (202) 785-1727. Contact: Folke Rydén, Lisa Carlsson or Steffan Ekendahl.
TRANSMISSION AUTHORITY: TERACOM, Svensk Rundradio AB, P.O. Box 17666, SE-118 92 Stockholm, Sweden. Phone: (general) +46 (8) 555-420-00; (Wiberg) +46 (8) 555-420-66. Fax: (general) +46 (8) 555 420 01; (Wiberg) +46 (8) 555 20 60. Email: (general) info@teracom.se; (Wiberg) magnus.wiberg@ teracom.se. Web: www.teracom.se. Contact: (Frequency Planning Dept.—Head Office) Magnus Wiberg; (Engineering) Hakan Widenstedt, Chief Engineer. Free stickers; sometimes free T-shirts to those monitoring during special test transmissions. Seeks monitoring feedback for new frequency usages.

SWITZERLAND   World Time +1 (+2 midyear)

European Broadcasting Union, 17A Ancienne Route, CH-1218 Grand-Saconnex, Geneva, Switzerland; or Case Postal 67, CH-1218 Grand-Saconnex, Geneva, Switzerland. Phone: +41 (22) 717-2111. Fax: +41 (22) 747 4000. Email: ebu@ebu.ch. Web: www.ebu.ch. Contact: Mr. Jean Stock, Secretary-General; or Robin Levey, Strategic Information Service Database Manager. Umbrella organization for broadcasters in 49 European and Mediterranean countries.
International Telecommunication Union, Place des Nations, CH-1211 Geneva 20, Switzerland. Phone: (switchboard) +41 (22) 730-5111; (Broadcasting Services Division) +41 (22) 730-5933 or +41 (22) 730-6136; (Terrestrial Services Department) +41 (22) 730-5514. Fax: (general) +41 (22) 733 7256; (Broadcasting Services Division) +41 (22) 730 5785. Email: (schedules and reference tables) brmail@itu.int; (Broadcasting Services Division) jacques.fonteyne@itu.int or pham.hai@itu.int; (Terrestrial Services Department) nedialko.miltchev@itu.int. Web: www.itu.int. Contact: Jacques Fonteyne, Head of Broadcasting Services Division; Hai Pham, Broadcasting Services Division; or Nedialko Miltchev, Engineer, Terrestrial Services Department. The ITU is the world's official regulatory body for all telecommunication activities, including world band radio. Offers a wide range of official multilingual telecommunication publications in print and/or digital formats.
☞**Radio Réveil**, Paroles, Les Chapons 4, CH-2022 Bevaix, Switzerland. Phone: +41 (32) 846- 1655. Fax: +41 (32) 846 2547. Email: contact@paroles.ch. Web (includes RealAudio): www.paroles.ch. An evangelical radio ministry, part of the larger Radio Réveil Paroles de Vie organization, which apart from broadcasting to much of Europe on longwave, mediumwave AM and FM, also targets an African audience via the shortwave facilities of Germany's Deutsche Telekom (*see*).
☞**Swiss Radio International (Swissinfo/SRI)**,

Giacomettistrasse 1, CH-3000 Berne 15, Switzerland. Phone: (general) +41 (31) 350-9222; (English Department) +41 (31) 350-9790; (French Department) +41 (31) 350-9555; (German Department) +41 (31) 350-9535; (Italian Department) +41 (31) 350-9531); (Frequency Management) +41 (31) 350-9734. Fax: (general) +41 (31) 350 9569; (administration) +41 (31) 350 9744 or +41 (31) 350 9581; (Communication and Marketing) +41 (31) 350 9544; (Programme Department) +41 (31) 350 9569; (English Department) +41 (31) 350 9580; (French Department) +41 (31) 350 9664; (German Department) +41 (31) 350 9562; (Italian Department) +41 (31) 350 9678; (Frequency Management) +41 (31) 350 9745. Email: (general) info@swissinfo.ch; (language departments) format is language@swissinfo.ch (e.g. english@swissinfo.ch, german@swissinfo.ch); (marketing) marketing@swissinfo.ch; (technical, including reception reports) technical@swissinfo.ch; (Frequency Management): ulrich.wegmueller@swissinfo.ch. Web: (includes RealAudio and MP3) www.swissinfo.ch. Contact: (general) Nancy Hartmann, English Department; Marlies Schmutz, Listeners' Letters, German Programmes; Thérèse Schafter, Listeners' Letters, French Programmes; Esther Niedhammer, Listeners' Letters, Italian Programmes; Beatrice Lombard, Promotion; Giovanni D'Amico, Audience Officer; (administration) Ulrich Kündig, General Manager; Nicolas Lombard, Director; Walter Fankhauser, Head, Communication and Marketing Services; Rose-Marie Malinverni, Head, Editorial Co-ordination Unit; Ron Grünig, Head, English Programmes; James Jeanneret, Head, German Programmes; Diana Zanotta, German Service; Philippe Zahne, Head, French Programmes; Fabio Mariani, Head, Italian Programmes; (technical) Paul Badertscher, Head, Engineering Services; or Ulrich Wegmüller, Frequency Manager. Free station stickers. Swiss Radio International will gradually phase out its shortwave transmissions by the end of October 2004 in favor of alternative delivery systems such as the internet and to a lesser extent direct satellite broadcasting in English. *WASHINGTON NEWS BUREAU:* 2030 M Street NW, Washington DC 20554 USA. Phone: (general) +1 (202) 775-0894 or +1 (202) 429-9668; (French-language radio) +1 (202) 296-0277; (German-language radio) +1 (202) 7477. Fax: +1 (202) 833 2777. Contact: Christophe Erbeck, reporter.

SYRIA World Time +2 (+3 midyear)

Radio Damascus, Syrian Radio and Television, P.O. Box 4702, Damascus, Syria. Phone: +963 (11) 221-7653. Fax: +963 (11) 222 2692. Email: tv-radio@net.sy; mostafab@scs-net.org. Web: www.rtv.gov.sy. Contact: Mr. Afaf, Director General; Mr. Mazen Al-Achhab, Head of Frequency Department; Adnan Salhab; Mr. Farid Shalash; or Mr. Mohamed Hamida. Free stickers, paper pennants and *The Syria Times* newspaper. Replies can be highly erratic, but as of late have been more regular, if sometimes slow.

TAIWAN —see CHINA (TAIWAN)

TAJIKISTAN World Time +5

Radio Tajikistan, Chapaev Street 31, 734025 Dushanbe, Tajikistan; or English Service, International Service, Radio Tajikistan, P.O. Box 108, 734025 Dushanbe, Tajikistan. Phone: (Director) +992 (372) 210-877 or +992 (372) 277-417; (English Department) +992 (372) 277- 417; (Ramazonov) +992 (372) 277-667 or +992 (372) 277-347. Fax: +992 (372) 211 198. Email: treng@td.silk.org. Web: http://radio.tojikiston.com. Contact: (administration) Mansur Sultanov, Director - Tajik Radio; Nasrullo

Ramazonov, Foreign Relations Department. Correspondence in Russian or Tajik preferred. There is no official policy for verification of listeners' reports, so try sending reception reports and correspondence in English to the attention of Mr. Ramazonov, who is currently the sole English speaker at the station. Caution should be exercised when contacting him via email, as it is his personal account and he is charged for both incoming and outgoing mail. In addition, all email is routinely monitored and censored. Return postage (IRCs) helpful.

Tajik Radio, ul. Chapaeva 31, 734025 Dushanbe, Tajikistan. Contact information as for Radio Tajikistan, above.

TANZANIA World Time +3

Radio Tanzania, Nyerere Road, P.O. Box 9191, Dar es Salaam, Tanzania. Phone: +255 (51) 860-760. Fax: +255 (51) 865 577. Email: radiotanzania@raha.com. Contact: (general) Abdul Ngarawa, Director of Broadcasting; Mrs. Edda Sanga, Controller of Programs; Ms. Penzi Nyamungumi, Head of English Service and International Relations Unit; or Ahmed Jongo, Producer, "Your Answer"; (technical) Taha Usi, Chief Engineer; or Emmanuel Mangula, Deputy Chief Engineer. Replies to correspondence in English.

Voice of Tanzania Zanzibar, Department of Broadcasting, Radio Tanzania Zanzibar, P.O. Box 2503, Zanzibar, Tanzania— if this address brings no reply, try P.O. Box 1178; (Ali Bakari Muombwa, personal address) P.O. Box 2068, Zanzibar, Tanzania. Phone: +255 (54) 231-088. Fax: + 255 (54) 257 207. Contact: (general) Seti Suleiman, Director; Ndaro Nyamwolha; Ali Bakari Muombwa; Abdulrah'man M. Said; or Kassim S. Kassim; (technical) Khalid Hassan Rajab, Shortwave Transmitter Engineer; Nassor M. Suleiman, Maintenance Engineer. $1 return postage helpful.

THAILAND World Time +7

BBC World Service—Asia Relay Station, P.O. Box 20, Muang, Nakhon Sawan 60000, Thailand. Contact: Jaruwan Meesaurtong, Personal Assistant. Verifies reception reports.

Radio Thailand World Service, 236 Vibhavadi Rangsit Road, Din Daeng, Bangkok 10400, Thailand. Phone: +66 (2) 277-7895, +66 (2) 277-4022 X-2223. Phone/fax: +66 (2) 277-6139, +66 (2) 274-9099. Email: (general) radio_thailand@hotmail.com; (Samosorn) amporns@mozart.inet.co.th. Web: www.geocities.com/hsk9th. Contact: Mrs. Amporn Samosorn, Chief of External Services; Mr. Santi Charoenjai, Head of Shortwave Transmitter Station; or Suphachai Chantha.

TUNISIA World Time +1

Arab States Broadcasting Union, 6, rue des Enterpreneurs, Z.I. Ariana Cedex, TN-1080 Tunis, Tunisia. Phone: +216 (71) 703-855. Fax: +216 (71) 704 203. Email: a.suleiman@asbu.intl.tn. Contact: Abdelrahim Suleiman, Director, Technical Department; or Bassil Ahmad Zoubi, Head of Transmission Department.

☐Radiodiffusion Télévision Tunisienne, 71 Avenue de la Liberté, TN-1070 Tunis, Tunisia. Phone: +216 (1) 801-177. Fax: +216 (1) 781 927. Email: info@radiotunis.com. Web: (includes RealAudio) www.radiotunis.com/news.html. Contact: Mongai Caffai, Director General; Mohamed Abdelkafi, Director; Kamel Cherif, Directeur; Masmoudi Mahmoud; Mr. Bechir Betteib, Director of Operations; or Smaoui Sadok, Le Sous-Directeur Technique. Replies irregularly and slowly to correspondence in French or Arabic. $1 helpful. For reception reports try: Le Chef de Service du Controle de la Récepcion de l'Office National de la Télediffusion, O.N.T, Cité Ennassim I, Bourjel, B.P. 399, TN-1080 Tunis, Tunisia. Phone: +216 (1) 801-177. Fax: +216 (1) 781 927. Email: ont.@ati.tn. Contact: Abdesselem Slim.

TURKEY   World Time +2 (+3 midyear)

Meteoroloji Sesi Radyosu (Voice of Meteorology), T.C. Tarim Bakanliği, Devlet Meteoroloji İşleri, Genel Müdürlüğü, P.K. 401, Ankara, Turkey. Phone: +90 (312) 359-7545, X-281. Fax: +90 (312) 314 1196. Email: info@meteor.gov.tr; e-mail@ meteor.gov.tr. Contact: Prof. Atila Dorum. Free tourist literature. Return postage helpful.

Türkiye Polis Radyosu (Turkish Police Radio) (if reactivated), T.C. Içişleri Bakanliği, Emniyet Genel Müdürlüğü, Ankara, Turkey. Tourist literature for return postage. Replies irregularly.

🖷**Voice of Turkey** (Turkish Radio-Television Corporation External Service)

MAIN OFFICE, NONTECHNICAL: TRT External Services Department, TRT Sitesi, Turan Güneş Blv., Or-An Çankaya, 06450 Ankara, Turkey; or P.K. 333, Yenişehir, 06443 Ankara, Turkey. Phone: (general) +90 (312) 490-9800/9801; (English desk) +90 (312) 490-9842. Fax: (English desk) +90 (312) 490 9846. Email: (English desk) englishdesk@trt.net.tr; (Spanish Service) espanol@trt.net.tr. Web: (includes Windows Media) www.trt.net.tr. *WARNING: This site can only be viewed using Microsoft's Internet Explorer, and is not easy to navigate.* Contact: (English and non-technical) Mr. Osman Erkan, Chief, English desk. Technical correspondence, such as on reception quality should be directed to: Ms. Sedef Somaltin *(see next entry below).* On-air language courses offered in Arabic and German, but no printed course material. Free stickers, pennants, and tourist literature.

MAIN OFFICE, TECHNICAL (FOR EMIRLER AND ÇAKIRLAR TRANSMITTER SITES AND FOR FREQUENCY MANAGEMENT): TRT Teknik Yardimcilik, TRT Sitesi, Kat: 5/C, 06109 ORAN, Ankara, Turkey. Phone: +90 (312) 490-1732. Fax: +90 (312) 490 1733. Email: sedef.somaltin@trt.net.tr or kiymet.erdal@ trt.net.tr. Contact: Mr. Haluk Buran, TRT Deputy Director General (Head of Engineering); Ms. Sedef Somaltin, Engineer & Frequency Manager; or Ms. Kiymet Erdal, Engineer & Frequency Manager. The HFBC seasonal schedules can be reached directly from: www.trt.net.tr/duyurufiles/vot.htm.

SAN FRANCISCO OFFICE, SCHEDULES: 2654 17th Avenue, San Francisco CA 94116 USA. Phone: +1 (415) 564-9968. Email: GPoppin@aol.com. Contact: George Poppin. This address, a volunteer office, only provides TRT schedules to listeners. All other correspondence should be sent directly to Ankara.

TURKMENISTAN   World Time +5

Radio Turkmenistan, National TV and Radio Broadcasting Company, Mollanepes St. 3, 744000 Ashgabat, Turkmenistan. Phone: +993 (12) 251-515. Fax: +993 (12) 251 421. Contact: (administration) Yu M. Pashaev, Deputy Chairman of State Television and Radio Company; (technical) G. Khanmamedov; Kakali Karayev, Chief of Technical Department; or A.A Armanklichev, Deputy Chief, Technical Department. This country is currently under strict censorship and media people are closely watched. A lot of foreign mail addressed to a particular person may attract the attention of the security services. Best is not to address your mail to particular individuals but to the station itself.

Mrs. Amporn Samosorn heads the external services of the Radio Thailand World Service.   T. Ohtake

UGANDA   World Time +3

Radio Uganda
GENERAL OFFICE: P.O. Box 7142, Kampala, Uganda. Phone: +256 (41) 257-256. Fax: +256 (41) 256 888. Email: ugabro@infocom.co.ug. Contact: (general) Charles Byekwaso, Controller of Programmes; Machel Rachel Makibuuka; or Mrs. Florence Sewanyana, Head of Public Relations. $1 or return postage required. Replies infrequently and slowly. Correspondence to this address has sometimes been returned with the annotation "storage period overdue"—presumably because the mail is not collected on a regular basis.
ENGINEERING DIVISION: P.O. Box 2038, Kampala, Uganda. Phone: +256 (41) 256-647. Contact: Leopold B. Lubega, Principal Broadcasting Engineer; or Rachel Nakibuuka, Secretary. Four IRCs or $2 required. Enclosing a self addressed envelope may also help to get a reply.

UKRAINE   World Time +2 (+3 midyear)

WARNING-MAIL THEFT: For the time being, letters to Ukrainian stations, especially containing funds or IRCs, are more likely to arrive safely if sent by registered mail.

Government Transmission Authority: RRT/Concern of Broadcasting, Radiocommunication and Television, 10 Dorogajtshaya St., 254112 Kyiv, Ukraine. Phone: +380 (44) 226-2260 or +380 (44) 444-6900. Fax: +380 (44) 440 8722; or +380 (44) 452 6784. Email: (Kurilov) ak@cbrt.freenet.kiev.ua. Contact: Mr. Mykola Kyryliuk, Deputy Director, Technical Operations & Management Centre; Alexej M. Kurilov; Alexey Karpenko; Alexander Serdiuk, Director, Technical Operations & Management Centre; Nikolai P. Kiriliuk, Head of Operative Management Service; or Mrs. Liudmila Deretskaya, Interpreter. This agency is responsible for choosing the frequencies used by Radio Ukraine International.

Radio Ukraine International, Kreshchatik str., 26, 252001 Kyiv, Ukraine. Phone: +380 (44) 228-2534, +380 (44) 229-1757, +380 (44) 229-1883 or (Phone/fax) +380 (44) 228-7356. Fax: +380 (44) 229 4585 or +380 (44) 229 3477. Email: (QSL cards & complete schedules) vsru@nrcu.gov.ua; (reception reports) egorov@nrcu.gov.ua; mo@ukrradio.ru.kiev.ua. Web: www.nrcu.gov.ua/eng/program/vsru/vsru.html. Contact: (administration) Inna Chichinadze, Vice-Director of RUI; or Yulia McGuffie, Deputy Editor-in-Chief. Free stickers, calendars and Ukrainian stamps.

SAN FRANCISCO OFFICE, SCHEDULES: 2654 17th Avenue, San Francisco CA 94116 USA. Phone: +1 (415) 564-9968. Email: GPoppin@aol.com. Contact: George Poppin. This address, a volunteer office, only provides Radio Ukraine International schedules to listeners. All other correspondence should be sent directly to the main office in Kyiv.

UNITED ARAB EMIRATES World Time +4

Emirates Radio, P.O. Box 1695, Dubai, United Arab Emirates. Phone: +971 (4) 370-255. Fax: +971 (4) 374 111, +971 (4) 370 283 or +971 (4) 371 079. Email: radio@dubaitv.gov.ae; radio@dubaidd.org.ae. Web: www.dubaitv.gov.ae. Contact: Ms. Khulud Halaby; or Sameer Aga, Producer, "Cassette Club Cinarabic"; (technical) K.F. Fenner, Chief Engineer—Radio; or Ahmed Al Muhaideb, Assistant Controller, Engineering. Free pennants. Replies irregularly.

UNITED KINGDOM World Time exactly (+1 midyear)

Adventist World Radio, 39 Brendon Street, London W1H 5HD, United Kingdom. Phone: +44 (1344) 401-401. Fax: +44 (1344) 401 419. Email: english@awr.org. Web: www.awr.org. Contact: Bert Smit, European Regional Director; or Victor Hulbert, Director English Listener Mail. All mail addressed to AWR and written in English is processed at this address. Also, see AWR listings under Germany, Guam, Guatemala, Kenya, Madagascar and USA.

BBC Monitoring, Caversham Park, Reading, Berkshire RG4 8TZ, United Kingdom. Phone: (switchboard) +44 (118) 948-6000; (Foreign Media Unit—monitoring) +44 (118) 948-6261; Marketing Department) +44 (118) 948-6289. Fax: (Foreign Media Unit) +44 (118) 946 1993; (Marketing Department) +44 (118) 946 3823. Email: (Marketing Department) marketing@mon.bbc.co.uk; (Foreign Media Unit/World Media) fmu@mon.bbc.co.uk; (Kenny) dave_kenny@mon.bbc.co.uk; (publications and real time services) marketing@mon.bbc.co.uk. Web: www.monitor.bbc.co.uk. Contact: (administration) Andrew Hills, Director of Monitoring; (Foreign Media Unit) Chris McWhinnie, Editor "World Media," Dave Kenny, Chief Sub Editor, "World Media," or Peter Feuilherade; (Publication Sales) Stephen Innes, Marketing. BBC Monitoring produces the weekly publication *World Media* which reports political, economic, legal, organisational, programming and technical developments in the world's electronic media. Its reports are based on material broadcast or published by radio and TV stations, news agencies, Websites and publications; other information issued but not necessarily broadcast by such sources and by other relevant bodies; and information obtained by BBC Monitoring's own observations of foreign media. Available on yearly subscription, costing £410.00. Price excludes postage overseas. *World Media* is also available online through the Internet or via a direct dial-in bulletin board at an annual cost of £425.00. VISA/MC/AX. The Technical Operations Unit provides detailed observations of broadcasts on the long, medium, short wave, satellite bands and Internet. This unit provides tailored channel occupancy observations, reception reports, and updates the *MediaNet* source information database (constantly updated on over 100 countries) and the *Broadcast Research Log* (a record of broadcasting developments compiled daily).

BBC World Service
MAIN OFFICE, NONTECHNICAL: Bush House, Strand, London WC2B 4PH, United Kingdom. Phone: (general) +44 (20) 7240-3456; (Press Office) +44 (20) 7557-2947/1; (International Marketing) +44 (20) 7557-1143. Fax: (Audience Relations) +44 (20) 7557 1258; ("Write On" listeners' letters program) +44 (20) 7436 2800; (Audience and Market Research) +44 (20) 7557 1254; (International Marketing) +44 (20) 7557 1254. Email: (general listener correspondence) worldservice.letters@bbc.co.uk; ("Write

On") writeon@bbc.co.uk. Web: (general, including RealAudio and Windows Media) www.bbc.co.uk/worldservice; (RealAudio) www.broadcast.com/bbc; (entertainment and information) www.beeb.com. Contact: Patrick Condren, Presenter, of "Write On"; Alan Booth, Controller, Marketing & Communications; Miles Palmer, Head of Business Development; or Mark Byford, Chief Executive. Offers *BBC On Air* magazine (*see* below). Also, *see* Antigua, Ascension, Oman, Seychelles, Singapore and Thailand. Does not verify reception reports due to budget limitations.
SAN FRANCISCO OFFICE, SCHEDULES: 2654 17th Avenue, San Francisco CA 94116 USA. Phone: +1 (415) 564-9968. Email: GPoppin@aol.com. Contact: George Poppin. This address, a volunteer office, only provides BBC World Service schedules to listeners. All other correspondence should be sent directly to the main office in London.
TECHNICAL: See VT Merlin Communications.
BBC WORLD SERVICE—PUBLICATION AND PRODUCT SALES
BBC World Service Shop, Bush House Arcade, Strand, London WC2B 4PH, United Kingdom. Phone: +44 (20) 7557-2576. Fax: +44 (20) 7240 4811. Sells numerous audio/video cassettes (video, PAL/VHS only), publications, portable world band radios, T-shirts, sweatshirts and other BBC souvenirs available by mail order to UK addresses only.
"BBC On Air" (monthly program magazine), P.O. Box 76, Bush House, Strand, London WC2B 4PH, United Kingdom. Phone: +44 (20) 7557-2211 or +44 (20) 7557-2803. Fax: +44 (20) 7240 4899. Email: bbconair@bbc.co.uk. Web: www.bbconair.co.uk. Contact: Millie Patrick, Marketing Manager, BBC On Air magazine. Subscription $35 or £22 per year, and can be processed online. VISA/MC/AX/Barclay/EURO/Access, Postal Order, International Money Draft or cheque in pounds sterling or U.S. dollars.
BFBS—British Forces Broadcasting Service (when operating), Services Sound and Vision, Chalfont Grove, Narcot Lane, Chalfont St. Peter, Gerrards Cross, Buckinghamshire SL9 8TN, United Kingdom; or BFBS Worldwide, P.O. Box 903, Gerrards Cross, Buckinghamshire SL9 8TN, United Kingdom. Email: (general) marina.haward@bfbs.com. Web: (includes Windows Media) www.ssvc.com/bfbs. Normally only on satellite and FM, but sometimes hires additional shortwave facilities when British troops are fighting overseas.
Bible Voice Broadcasting
EUROPEAN OFFICE: P. O. Box 2801, Eastbourne BN21 2EQ, United Kingdom. Phone: +44 (1900) 826-522. Email: mail@biblevoice.org.
Web: www.biblevoice.org. Contact: Martin and Liz Thompson.
ALTERNATIVE ADDRESS: Bible Voice Broadcasting Network, P.O. Box 220, Leeds LS26 0WW, United Kingdom.
NORTH AMERICAN OFFICE: High Adventure Gospel Communication Ministries, P.O. Box 425, Station E, Toronto, ON M6H 4E3, Canada.
Phone: +1 (905) 898-5447; (toll-free, U.S. and Canada only) 1-800-550-4670. Email: highadventure@sympatico.ca. Contact: Don and Marty McLaughlin.
Bible Voice Broadcasting is a partnership between Bible Voice (U.K.) and High Adventure Gospel Communication Ministries (Canada).
Commonwealth Broadcasting Association, CBA Secretariat, 17 Fleet Street, London EC4Y 1AA, United Kingdom. Phone: +44 (20) 7583-5550. Fax: +44 (20) 7583 5549. Email: cba@cba.org.uk. Web: www.cba.org.uk. Publishes the annual *Commonwealth Broadcaster Directory* and the quarterly *Commonwealth Broadcaster* (online subscription form available).
Far East Broadcasting Association (FEBA), Ivy Arch Road, Worthing, West Sussex BN14 8BX, United Kingdom. Phone: +44

(1903) 237-281. Fax: +44 (1903) 205 294. Email: reception@feba.org.uk or (Richard Whittington) rwhittington@feba.org.uk. Web: www.feba.org.uk. Contact: Tony Ford, Director of Programming; or Richard Whittington, Schedule Engineer. Normally, does not verify reception reports. Try sending reports to individual program producers (addresses are usually given over the air).

◪IBC-Tamil, 3 College Fields, Prince George's Road, Colliers Wood, London SW19 2PT, United Kingdom. Phone: +44 (20) 8100-0011. Fax: +44 (20) 8100 0003. Email: radio@ibctamil.co.uk. Web: (includes RealAudio) www.ibctamil.co.uk. Contact: A.C. Tarcisius, Managing Director; S. Shivaranjith, Manager; K. Pillai; or Public Relations Officer.

Radio Ezra (when operating). Fax: +44 (1642) 887 546. Email: info@radioezra.com. Web: www.radioezra.com. Contact: John D. Hill. Broadcasts irregularly via transmitters in the former Sovet Union. Welcomes reception reports via fax or email, and verifies with a QSL certificate. Describes itself as a "counter-missionary station." Plans to be back on air late 2003 or early 2004 if sufficient funding is met.

Salama Radio (when operating), The Studio, P.O. Box 126, Chessington, Surrey KT9 2WJ, United Kingdom. Phone/fax: +44 (208) 395-7425. Email: admin@salamaradio.org. Web: www.salamaradio.org. Contact: Dr. Jacob Abdalla, President, Harvestime Ministries; Mrs. Margaret Perera, International Director, Harvestime Ministries. A radio project of Harvestime Ministries.

VT Merlin Communications Limited, 20 Lincoln's Inn Fields, London WC2A 3ED, United Kingdom. Phone: +44 (20) 7969-0000. Fax: +44 (20) 7396 6223. Email: marketing@merlincommunications.com. Web: www.vtplc.com/merlin. Contact: Fiona Lowry, Chief Executive; Rory Maclachlan, Director of International Communications & Digital Services; Ciaran Fitzgerald, Head of Engineering & Operations; Richard Hurd, Head of Transmission Sales; Laura Jelf, Marketing Manager; or Anna Foakes, Marketing Department. VT Merlin Communications (formerly Merlin Communications International) is a provider of communications services to the broadcast, defense and space communications industries worldwide, and delivers over one thousand hours of both short and mediumwave AM broadcasts every day for international and religious broadcasters worldwide. Does not verify reception reports.

◪Wales Radio International, Preseli Radio Productions, Pros Kairon, Crymych, Pembrokeshire, SA41 3QE, Wales, United Kingdom. Phone: +44 (1437) 563-361. Fax: +44 (1239) 831 390. Email: jenny@wri.cymru.net. Web: (includes MP3) http://wri.cymru.net. Contact: Jenny O'Brien. A weekly broadcast via the facilities of VT Merlin Communications (see, above).

◪World Radio Network, P.O. Box 1212, London SW8 2ZF, United Kingdom. Phone: +44 (20) 7896-9000. Fax: + 44 (20) 7896 9007. Email: (general) email@wrn.org; (Ayris) tim.ayris@wrn.org. Web: (includes RealAudio and Windows Media) www.wrn.org. Contact: Tim Ayris, Broadcast Sales Manager for WRN's networks. Provides Webcasts and program placements for international broadcasters.

UNITED NATIONS World Time -5 (-4 midyear)

◪Radio UNMEE
Web: (MP3) www.un.org/Depts/dpko/unmee/radio.htm; (UNMEE general information) www.un.org/Depts/dpko/unmee/unmeeN.htm.
NEW YORK OFFICE: Same contact details as United Nations Radio, below.

ERITREA OFFICE: P.O. Box 5805, Asmara, Eritrea. Phone: +291 (1) 151-908. Email: kellyb@un.org.
ETHIOPIA OFFICE: ECA Building, P.O. Box 3001, Addis Ababa, Ethiopia. Phone: +251 (1) 443-396. Email: gudina@un.org. Contact: Adane Gudina.
Radio service of the United Nations Mission in Eritrea and Ethiopia (UNMEE). Aired via facilities in the United Arab Emirates, and also relayed over Eritrea's national radio, Voice of the Broad Masses of Eritrea.

◪United Nations Radio, Secretariat Building, Room S-850-M, United Nations, New York NY 10017 USA; or write to the station over which UN Radio was heard. Phone: +1 (212) 963-5201. Fax: +1 (212) 963 1307. Email: (general) unradio@un.org; (comments on programs) audio- visual@un.org; (reception reports) smithd@un.org; or (Villanueva) villanueva1@un.org. Web: (general) www.un.org/av/radio; (RealAudio) www.wrn.org/ondemand/unitednations.html; www.internetbroadcast.com/un. Contact: (general) Sylvester E. Rowe, Chief, Radio and Video Service; or Ayman El-Amir, Chief, Radio Section, Department of Public Information; (reception reports) David Smith; or Trixie Villanueva; (technical and nontechnical) Sandra Guy, Secretary. Free stamps and *UN Frequency* publication. Reception reports (including those sent by email) are verified with a QSL card.
GENEVA OFFICE: Room G209, Palais des Nations, CH-1211 Geneva 10, Switzerland. Phone: +41 (22) 917-4222. Fax: +41 (22) 917 0123.
PARIS OFFICE: UNESCO Radio, 7 Place de Fontenoy, F-75007 Paris, France. Fax: +33 (1) 45 67 30 72. Contact: Erin Faherty, Executive Radio Producer.

URUGUAY World Time -3

Banda Oriental—*see* Radio Sarandí del Yi.
◪Emisora Ciudad de Montevideo, Canelones 2061, 11200 Montevideo, Uruguay. Phone: +598 (2) 402-0142 or +598 (2) 402-4242. Fax: +598 (2) 402 0700. Email: online form. Web: (includes MP3) www.emisoraciudaddemontevideo.com.uy. Contact: Aramazd Yizmeyian, Director General. Free stickers. Return postage helpful.
La Voz de Artigas (if reactivated), Av. Lecueder 483, 55000 Artigas, Uruguay. Phone: +598 (772) 2447 or +598 (772) 3445. Fax: +598 (772) 4744. Email: lavozart@adinet.com.uy. Contact: (general) Sra. Solange Murillo Ricciardi, Co-Propietario; or Luis Murillo; (technical) Roberto Murillo Ricciardi, Director. Free stickers and pennants. Replies to correspondence written in English, Spanish, French, Italian and Portuguese.
Radiodifusion Nacional—*see* S.O.D.R.E.
◪Radio Monte Carlo, Av. 18 de Julio 1224 piso 1, 11100 Montevideo, Uruguay. Phone: +598 (2) 901-4433 or +598 (2) 908-3987. Fax: +598 (2) 901 7762. Email: cx20@netgate.com.uy. Contact: Ana Ferreira de Errázquin, Secretaria, Departamento de Prensa de la Cooperativa de Radioemisoras; Gustavo Cirino, Jefe Técnico; Déborah Ibarra, Secretaria; Emilia Sánchez Vega, Secretaria; or Ulises Graceras. Correspondence in Spanish preferred.
◪Radio Oriental—Same mailing address as Radio Monte Carlo, above. Phone: +598 (2) 901- 4433 or +598 (2) 900-5612. Fax: +598 (2) 901 7762. Contact: (technical) José A. Porro, Technician. Correspondence in Spanish preferred. A newspaper report in September 2003 reported that this station had been sold, but no further details were known as we went to press.
◪Radio Sarandí Sport (when operating), Henriqueta Compte y Riqué 1250, 11800 Montevideo, Uruguay. Phone: +598 (2) 208-2612. Email: (general) sport890@sport890.com.uy; (Silva) asilva@claxson.com.uy. Web: (RealAudio only)

www.sport890.com.uy. Contact: (technical) Alejandro Silva, Encargado Técnico.

Radio Sarandí del Yí (when operatin), Sarandí 328, 97100 Sarandí del Yí, Uruguay. Phone/fax: +598 (367) 9155. Email: (owner) norasan@adinet.com.uy. Contact: Nora San Martín de Porro, Propietaria.

Radio Universo, Ferrer 1265, 27000 Castillos, Dpto. de Rocha, Uruguay. Email: am1480@adinet.com.uy. Contact: Juan Héber Brañas, Propietario. Currently only on 1480 kHz mediumwave AM, but has been granted a license to operate on shortwave.

S.O.D.R.E., Radiodifusión Nacional, Casilla 1412, 11000 Montevideo, Uruguay. Phone: +598 (2) 916-1933; (technical) +598 (2) 915-7865. Email: info@sodre.gub.uy. Web: www.sodre.gub.uy. Contact: (management) Julio César Ocampos, Director de Radiodifusión Nacional; (technical) José Cuello, División Técnica Radio. Reception reports may also be sent to the "Radioactividades" program (see, below).

MEDIA PROGRAM: "Radioactividades," Casilla 7011, 11000 Montevideo, Uruguay. Fax: +598 (2) 575 4640. Email: radioact@chasque.apc.org. Web: www.chasque.org/radioact.

USA   World Time -4 Atlantic, including Puerto Rico and Virgin Islands; -5 (-4 midyear) Eastern, excluding Indiana; -5 Indiana, except northwest and southwest portions; -6 (-5 midyear) Central, including northwest and southwest Indiana; -7 (-6 midyear) Mountain, except Arizona; -7 Arizona, -8 (-7 midyear) Pacific; -9 (-8 midyear) Alaska, except Aleutian Islands; -10 (-9 midyear) Aleutian Islands; -10 Hawaii; -11 Samoa

📻Adventist World Radio

HEADQUARTERS: 12501 Old Columbia Pike, Silver Spring MD 20904 USA. Email: english@awr.org. Web: (includes RealAudio and Windows Media) www.awr.org; (Chinese service, English/Chinese text) www.vohc.com—worth a visit just for the graphics. Send all letters and reception reports to: AWR, 39 Brendon Street, London W1H 5HD, United Kingdom.

INTERNATIONAL RELATIONS: Box 29235, Indianapolis IN 46229 USA. Phone/fax: +1 (317) 891-8540. Email: adrian@awr.org. Contact: Dr. Adrian M. Peterson, International Relations Coordinator. Provides publications with regular news releases and technical information. Sometimes issues special verification cards. QSL stamps and certificates also available from this address in return for reception reports.

OPERATIONS AND ENGINEERING: 3060 Noble Court, Boulder CO 80301 USA. Phone: +1 (303) 448-1875. Fax: +1 (303) 998 0259. Email: hodgson@awr.org. Contact: Greg Hodgson

DX PROGRAM: "Wavescan," prepared by Adrian Peterson; aired on all AWR facilities and other stations. Also available in RealAudio at the AWR Website, www.awr.org. Also, see AWR listings under Germany, Guam, Guatemala, Kenya, Madagascar and United Kingdom.

AFNL—American Farsi NetLink (when operating), P.O. Box 1601, Simi Valley CA 93062 USA. Phone: +1 (818) 348-2766, +1 (818) 348-3399. Fax: +1 (818) 348 3627. Email: info@afnl.com; amir@afnl.com. Web: (includes MP3) www.afnl.com. A satellite broadcaster which irregularly hires airtime on shortwave. Has used transmitter facilities in Moldova and Norway.

📻AFRTS-Armed Forces Radio and Television Service (Shortwave), Naval Media Center, NDW Anacostia Annex, 2713 Mitscher Road SW, Washington DC 20373-5819 USA. For verification of reception, be sure to mark the envelope, "Attn: Short Wave Reception Reports." Email: (verifications) qsl@mediacen.navy.mil. Web: www.myafn.net; (AFRTS parent organization) www.afrts.osd.mil; (2-minute news clips in RealAudio): www.defenselink.mil/news/radio; (Naval Media Center) www.mediacen.navy.mil. The Naval Media Center is responsible for all AFRTS broadcasts aired on shortwave.

FLORIDA ADDRESS: NCTS-Jacksonville-Detachment Key West, Building A 1004, Naval Air Station Boca Chica, Key West, FL 33040 USA.

Aurora Communications, Mile 129, Sterling Highway, Ninilchik, Alaska, USA. Plans to commence broadcasts to Russia when circumstances allow.

Broadcasting Board of Governors (BBG), 330 Independence Avenue SW, Room 3360, Washington DC 20237 USA. Phone: +1 (202) 619-2538. Fax: +1 (202) 619 1241. Email: pubaff@ibb.gov. Web: www.ibb.gov/bbg. Contact: Kathleen Harrington, Public Relations. The BBG, created in 1994 and headed by nine members nominated by the President, is the overseeing agency for all official non-military United States international broadcasting operations, including the VOA, RFE-RL, Radio Martí and Radio Free Asia.

📻Christian Science Publishing Society—Shortwave Broadcasts (all locations) Shortwave Broadcasts, P.O. Box 1524, Boston MA 02117-1524 USA. Phone: +1 (617) 450-2929; (toll free, U.S. only) 1-800-288-7090, extension 2929 for Shortwave Helpline to request printed schedules and information. Email: (letters & reception reports) letterbox@csps.com. Web: (includes RealAudio) www.tfccs.com/gv/CSPs/Herald/bdcst/bdcst.jhtml. Contact: Tina Hammers, Frequency & Production Coordinator. Free schedules and information about Christian Science religion. *The Christian Science Monitor* newspaper and a full line of Christian Science books are available from: 1 Norway Street, Boston MA 02115 USA. *Science and Health with Key to the Scriptures* by Mary Baker Eddy is available in English $12.95 paperback; $24-26 in French, German, Portuguese, Russian or Spanish paperback; from Science and Health, P.O. Box 1875, Boston MA 02117 USA.

Christian Science Publishing Society—WSHB Cypress Creek, 1030 Shortwave Lane, Pineland SC 29934 USA. Phone: (general) +1 (803) 625-5551; (station manager) +1 (803) 625-5555; (engineer) +1 (803) 625-5554. Fax: +1 (803) 625 5559. Email: (Station Manager) evansc@wshb.com; (Chief Engineer) centgrafd@wshb.com; (QSL Coordinator) riehmc@wshb.com. Web: www.tfccs.com/GV/shortwave/shortwave_schedule.jhtml. Contact: Catherine Aitken-Smith, Broadcast Director; (technical) C. Ed. Evans, Station Manager; Damian Centgraf, Chief Engineer; Tony Kobatake, Transmission Engineer; or Cindy Riehm, QSL Coordinator. Visitors welcome from 9 to 4 Monday through Friday; for other times, contact transmitter site beforehand to make arrangements. Shortwave Lane address for technical feedback on South Carolina transmissions only; other inquiries should be directed to the Boston address, above.

📻Family Radio Worldwide:

NONTECHNICAL: Family Stations, Inc., 290 Hegenberger Road, Oakland CA 94621-1436 USA; or P.O. Box 2140 Oakland CA 94621-9985 USA. Phone: (general) +1 (510) 568-6200; (toll free, U.S. only) 1-800-543-1495; (engineering) +1 (510) 568-6200 ext. 240. Fax: (main office) +1 (510) 568 6200; (engineering) +1 (510) 562 1023. Email: (general) famradio@familyradio.com; (international department) international@familyradio.com; (shortwave program schedules) shortwave@familyradio.com. Web: (includes RealAudio and MP3) www.familyradio.com. Contact: (general) Harold Camping, General Manager; or David Hoff, Manager of International Department. Free gospel tracts (33 languages), books, booklets, quarterly *Family Radio News* magazine and frequency schedule. 2 IRCs helpful.

TECHNICAL: WYFR—Family Radio, 10400 NW 240th Street, Okeechobee FL 34972 USA. Phone: +1 (863) 763-0281. Fax: +1 (863) 763 8867. Email: (technical) fsiyfr@okeechobee.com; (frequency schedule) wyfr@okeechobee.com. Contact: Dan Elyea, Engineering Manager; or Edward F. Dearborn, Chief Operator; (frequency schedule) Evelyn Marcy.

FEBC Radio International

INTERNATIONAL HEADQUARTERS: Far East Broadcasting Company, Inc., P.O. Box 1, La Mirada CA 90637 USA. Phone: +1 (310) 947-4651. Fax: +1 (310) 943 0160. Email: febc@febc.org. Web: www.febc.org. Operates world band stations in the Northern Mariana Islands, the Philippines and the Seychelles. Does not verify reception reports from this address.

RUSSIAN OFFICE: P.O. Box 2128, Khabarovsk 680020, Russia. Email: khabarovsk@febc.org.

Federal Communications Commission, 445 12th Street SW, Washington DC 20554 USA. Phone: +1 (202) 418-0190; (toll-free, U.S. only) 1-888-225-5322. Fax: +1 (202) 418 0232. Email: (general information and inquiries) fccinfo@fcc.gov; (Freedom of Information Act requests) FOIA@fcc.gov; (Polzin) tpolzin@fcc.gov. Web: (general) www.fcc.gov; (high frequency operating schedules) www.fcc.gov/ib/pnd/neg/hf_web/seasons.html; (FTP) ftp://ftp.fcc.gov/pub. Contact: (International Bureau, technical) Thomas E. Polzin.

Fundamental Broadcasting Network, Grace Missionary Baptist Church, 520 Roberts Road, Newport NC 28570 USA. Phone: +1 (252) 223-6088; (toll-free, U.S. only) 1-800-245-9685; (Robinson) +1 (252) 223-4600. Email: (general) fbn@clis.com; (technical, David Robinson) davidwr@clis.com. Web: (includes MP3) www.fbnradio.com. Contact: Pastor Clyde Eborn; (technical) David Robinson, Chief Engineer. Verifies reception reports if an IRC or (within the USA) an SASE is included. Accepts email reports. A religious and educational non-commercial broadcasting network which operates sister stations WBOH and WTJC.

George Jacobs and Associates, Inc., 8701 Georgia Avenue, Suite 711, Silver Spring MD 20910 USA. Phone: +1 (301) 587-8800. Fax: +1 (301) 587 8801. Email: gja@gjainc.com; or gjainc_20910@yahoo.com. Web: www.gjainc.com. Contact: (technical) Bob German or Mrs. Anne Case; (administration) George Jacobs, P.E. This firm provides frequency management and other engineering services for a variety of private U.S. world band stations.

Gospel for Asia, 1800 Golden Trail Court, Carrollton TX 75010 USA. Phone: +1 (972) 300- 7777; (toll-free, U.S. only) 1-800-946-2742. Email: info@gfa.org. Web: www.gfa.org. Transmits via facilities in Jülich, Germany, and Dhabayya, U.A.E.

CALIFORNIA OFFICE: P.O. Box 1210, Somis, California 93066 USA. Email: gfaradio@mygfa.org. Contact: Rhonda Penland, Coordinator.

CANADIAN OFFICE: 245 King Street E., Stoney Creek, ON L8G 1L9, Canada. Phone: +1 (905) 662-2101. Email: infocanada@gfa.org.

UNITED KINGDOM OFFICE: P.O. Box 166, York YO10 5WA, United Kingdom. Phone: +44 (1904) 643-233. Email: infouk@gfa.org.

Herald Broadcasting—*see* Christian Science Publishing Society.

High Adventure Ministries
MAIN OFFICE: P.O. Box 197569, Louisville KY 40259 USA. Phone: +1 (502) 968-7550; (toll- free, U.S. only) 1-800-517-4673. Fax: +1 (502) 968 7580. Email: mail@highadventure.net. Web: www.highadventure.net. Contact: Jackie Yockey.
CALIFORNIA STUDIO OFFICES: See KVOH.
MIDDLE EAST OFFICE: P.O. Box 53379, Limassol, Cyprus. Phone: +972 (9) 767-0835. Fax: +972 (9) 765 1407. Email: gronberg@zahav.net.il. Contact: Isaac Gronberg.
SINGAPORE OFFICE, NONTECHNICAL: 265B/C South Bridge Road - Eu Yan Sang Annexe, Singapore 058814, Singapore. Phone: + 65 221-2054. Fax: +65 221 2059. Email: csarch@singnet.com.sg. Contact: Cyril Seah.

International Broadcasting Bureau (IBB)—Reports to the Broadcasting Board of Governors (*see*), and includes, among others, the Voice of America, RFE-RL, Radio Martí and Radio Free Asia. IBB Engineering (Office of Engineering and Technical Operations) provides broadcast services for these stations. Contact: (administration) Brian Conniff, Director; or Joseph O'Connell, Director of External Affairs. Web: www.ibb.gov/ibbpage.html.
FREQUENCY AND MONITORING OFFICE, TECHNICAL: IBB/EOF: Spectrum Management Division, International Broadcasting Bureau (IBB), Room 4611 Cohen Bldg., 330 Independence Avenue SW, Washington DC 20237 USA. Phone: +1 (202) 619-1669. Fax: +1 (202) 619 1680. Email: (scheduling) dferguson@ibb.gov; (monitoring) bw@his.com. Web: (general) http://monitor.ibb.gov; (email reception report form) http://monitor.ibb.gov/now_you_try_it.html. Contact: Dan Ferguson (dferguson@ibb.gov); or Bill Whitacre (bw@his.com).

KAIJ
ADMINISTRATION OFFICE: Two-if-by-Sea Broadcasting Co., 22720 SE 410th St., Enumclaw WA 89022 USA. Phone/fax: (Mike Parker, California) +1 (818) 606-1254; (Washington State office, if and when operating) +1 (206) 825 4517. Contact: Mike Parker (mark envelope, "please forward"). Relays programs of Dr. Gene Scott's University Network (*see*). Replies occasionally.
STUDIO: Faith Center, 1615 S. Glendale Avenue, Glendale CA 91025 USA. Phone: +1 (818) 246-8121. Contact: Dr. Gene Scott, President.
TRANSMITTER SITE: RR#3 Box 120, Frisco TX 75034 USA; or Highway 380 West, Prosper TX 75078 USA (physical location: Highway 380, 3.6 miles west of State Rt. 289, near Denton TX; transmitters and antennas located on Belt Line Road along the lake in Coppell TX). Phone: +1 (972) 346-2758. Contact: Walt Green or Fred Bithell. Station encourages mail to be sent to the administration office, which seldom replies, or the studio (*see* above).

KIMF (under construction): International Fellowship of Churches, Radio Station KIMF, 9746 6th Street, Rancho Cucamonga CA 91730 USA.
ALTERNATIVE ADDRESS: IMF World Missions, P.O. Box 6321, San Bernardino CA 92412, USA. Phone +1 (909) 370-4515. Fax: +1 (909) 370 4862. Email: jkpimf@msn.com. Contact: Dr. James K. Planck, President.
TRANSMITTER SITE: Intersection Spring Mesa Road & State Road 506, Pinon NM, USA.

KJES—King Jesus Eternal Savior
STATION: The Lord's Ranch, 230 High Valley Road, Vado NM

88072 USA. Phone: +1 (505) 233-2090. Fax: +1 (505) 233 3019. Email: KJES@aol.com. Contact: Michael Reuter, Manager. $1 or return postage appreciated.
SPONSORING ORGANIZATION: Our Lady's Youth Center, P.O. Box 1422, El Paso TX 79948 USA. Phone: +1 (915) 533-9122.

KNLS—New Life Station
OPERATIONS CENTER: 605 Bradley Ct., Franklin TN 37067 USA (letters sent to the Alaska transmitter site are usually forwarded to Franklin). Phone: +1 (615) 371-8707 ext.140. Fax: +1 (615) 371 8791. Email: knls@aol.com. Web: (includes sample programs in RealAudio) www.knls.org. Contact: (general) Dale Ward, Executive Producer; L. Wesley Jones, Director of Follow-Up Teaching; or Mike Osborne, Senior Producer, English Language Service; (technical) F.M. Perry, Frequency Coordinator. Free *Alaska Calling!* newsletter and station pennants. Free spiritual literature and bibles in Russian, Mandarin and English. Free Alaska books, tapes, postcards and cloth patches. Two free DX books for beginners. Special, individually numbered, limited edition, verification cards issued for each new transmission period to the first 200 listeners providing confirmed reception reports. Stamp and postcard exchange. Return postage appreciated.
TRANSMITTER SITE: P.O. Box 473, Anchor Point AK 99556 USA. Phone: +1 (907) 235-8262. Fax: +1 (907) 235 2326. Contact: (technical) Kevin Chambers, Chief Engineer.

⬛KRSI—Radio Sedaye Iran, Suite 207, 9744 Wilshire Boulevard, Beverly Hills CA 90212- 1812 USA. Phone: +1 (310) 888-2818. Fax: +1 (310) 859 8444. Web: (includes Windows Media and online email form) www.krsi.net. Normally operates via a closed broadcasting system and the Internet, but started shortwave broadcasts during 2000. Broadcasts via facilities in Moldova or France (occasionally both).

⬛KTBN—Trinity Broadcasting Network
GENERAL CORRESPONDENCE: P.O. Box A, Santa Ana CA 92711 USA. Phone: +1 (714) 832-2950. Fax: +1 (714) 730 0661. Email: comments@tbn.org. Web: (Trinity Broadcasting Network, including RealAudio) www.tbn.org; (KTBN) www.tbn.org/watch/how2watch/sw_radio/index.htm. Contact: Dr. Paul F. Crouch, Managing Director. Monthly TBN newsletter. Free booklets, stickers and small souvenirs sometimes available.
TECHNICAL CORRESPONDENCE: Engineering/QSL Department, 2442 Michelle Drive, Tustin CA 92780-7015 USA. Phone: +1 (714) 665-2145. Fax: +1 (714) 730 0661. Email: lreyes@tbn.org. Contact: Laura Reyes, QSL Manager; or Ben Miller, Vice President, Engineering. Responds to reception reports. Write to: Trinity Broadcasting Network, Attention: Superpower KTBN Radio QSL Manager, Laura Reyes, 2442 Michelle Drive, Tustin CA 92780 USA. Return postage (IRC or SASE) helpful. Although a California operation, KTBN's shortwave transmitter is located at Salt Lake City, Utah.

KVOH—Voice of Hope, P.O. Box 100, Simi Valley CA 93062 USA. Phone: +1 (805) 520- 9460; Fax: +1 (805) 520 7823. Email: kvoh@usa.com. Web: www.geocities.com/aleluya01/clock.html. Return postage (IRCs) required. Replies as time permits. Station of High Adventure Ministries (*see*).

⬛KWHR-World Harvest Radio
ADMINISTRATION OFFICE: See WHRI—World Harvest Radio.
TRANSMITTER: Although located 6 1/2 miles southwest of Naalehu, 8 miles north of South Cape, and 2000 feet west of South Point (Ka La) Road (the antennas are easily visible from this road) on Big Island, Hawaii, the operators of this rural transmitter site maintain no post office box in or near Naalehu, and their telephone number is unlisted, Best bet is to contact them via their administration office (*see* WHRI), or to drive in unan-

nounced (it's just off South Point Road) the next time you vacation on Big Island.

Leinwoll (Stanley)—Telecommunication Consultant, 305 E. 86th Street, Suite 21S-W, New York NY 10028 USA. Phone: +1 (212) 987-0456. Fax: +1 (212) 987 3532. Email: stanL00011@aol.com. Contact: Stanley Leinwoll, President. This firm provides frequency management and other engineering services for some private U.S. world band stations, but does not correspond with the general public.

Overcomer Ministry ("Voice of the Last Day Prophet of God"), P.O. Box 691, Walterboro SC 29488 USA. Phone: (0900-1700 local time, Sunday through Friday) +1 (803) 538-3892. Email: (general) brotherstair@overcomerministry.com; (reception reports) overcomer@overcomerministry.com. Web: (includes RealAudio) www.overcomerministry.com. Contact: Brother R.G. Stair. Sample "Overcomer" newsletter and various pamphlets free upon request. Sells a Sangean shortwave radio for $50, plus other items of equipment and various publications at appropriate prices. Via Deutsche Telekom, Germany, and WWCR, USA.

Pan American Broadcasting, 20410 Town Center Lane #200, Cupertino CA 95014 USA. Phone: +1 (408) 996-2033; (toll-free, U.S. only) 1-800-726-2620. Fax: +1 (408) 252 6855. Email: info@panambc.com; pabcomain@aol.com; (Bernald) gbernald@panambc.com. Web: www.panambc.com. Contact: (listener correspondence) Terry Kraemer; (general) Carmen Jung, Office and Sales Administrator; or Gene Bernald. $1 in cash or unused U.S. stamps, or 2 IRCs, required for reply. Operates transmitters in Equatorial Guinea (see) and hires airtime over a number of world band stations, plus Deutsche Telekom facilities in Germany.

Radio Africa International, General Board of Global Ministries, United Methodist Church, 475 Riverside Drive, New York NY 10115 USA. Phone: (toll-free, U.S. only) 1-800-862-4246; (Media Contact) +1 (212) 870 3803. Fax: +1 (212) 870 3748. Email: radio@gbgm-umc.org. Web: (GBGM-UMC parent organization) www.gbgm-umc.org. Contact: Donna Niemann, Executive Producer; Raphael Mbadinga, Senior Producer. Sells calendars, magazines, books, videos and CDs of Christian music. Transmits via Jülich, Germany.

Radio Amani, Afghanistan Peace Association (APA), 41-36 College Point Blvd., Suite #2A, Flushing NY 11355 USA. Phone: +1 (718) 461-6799. Fax: +1 (718) 886 8616. Email: info@afghanistanpeace.com. Web: www.afghanistanpeace.com. Leases airtime over a transmitter in Russia.

Radio Farda—a joint venture between Radio Free Europe-Radio Liberty (see) and the Voice of America (see). Web: (includes RealAudio and Windows Media) www.radiofarda.com. Broadcasts a mix of news, information and popular Iranian and western music to younger audiences in Iran.

Radio Free Afghanistan—a service of Radio Free Europe-Radio Liberty (see). Web: (includes RealAudio) www.azadiradio.org.

Radio Free Asia, Suite 300, 2025 M Street NW, Washington DC 20036 USA. Phone: (general) +1 (202) 530-4999; (vice president of programming) +1 (202) 530-4907; (president) +1 (202) 457-4901; (chief technology officer) +1 (202) 530-4958. Fax: +1 (202) 530 7794 or +1 (202) 721 7468. Email: (individuals) the format is lastnameinitial@rfa.org; so to reach, say the CTO, David Baden, it would be badend@rfa.org; (language sections) the format is language@rfa.org; so to contact, say, the Vietnamese section, address your message to vietnamese@rfa.org; (general) communications@rfa.org. Web: (includes audio in

AudioActive and Real formats) www.rfa.org. Contact: (administration) Richard Richter, President; or Daniel Southerland, Vice President of Editoral; (technical) David M. Baden, Chief Technology Officer; (on-air operations) AJ Janitschek, Manager of Production Support; (reception reports) Ms. Tetiana Iwanciw, Executive Assistant for Technical Operations. RFA, originally created in 1996 as the Asia Pacific Network, is funded as a private nonprofit U.S. corporation by a grant from the Broadcasting Board of Governors (see), a politically bipartisan body appointed by the President of the United States. The purpose of RFA is to deliver accurate and timely news, information, and commentary, and to provide a forum for a variety of opinions and voices from within Asian countries. RFA focuses on events occurring in those countries. RFA seeks to promote the rights of freedom of opinion and expression—including the freedom to seek, receive and impart information and ideas through any medium regardless of frontiers.

HONG KONG OFFICE: Room 904, Massmutal Tower, 38 Gloucester Road, Wanchai, Hong Kong, China.

INDIA OFFICE: Temple Road, PO McLeod Ganj, District Kangra, Dharmsal HP 176 219 India.

KOREA OFFICE: 7F Joongang Ilbo Bldg, 7-Soonwha-dong, Jungku, Seoul Republic of Korea 100-759.

TAIWAN OFFICE: 88 Chunghsiao East Road, Section 2, 10th Floor Suite 1003, Taipei, Taiwan, Republic of China.

THAILAND OFFICE: Maxim House, 112 Witthayu Road, Pathomwan, Bangkok 10330, Thailand.

TURKEY OFFICE: Bayindir Sok 23/2, Kizilay, Ankara, Turkey.

Radio Free Europe-Radio Liberty/RFE-RL

PRAGUE HEADQUARTERS: Vinohradská 1, 110 00 Prague 1, Czech Republic. Phone: +420 (2) 2112-1111; (president) +420 (2) 2112-3000; (news desk) +420 (2) 2112-3629; (public relations) +420 (2) 2112-3012; (technical operations) +420 (2) 2112-3700; (broadcast operations) +420 (2) 2112-3550; (affiliate relations). +420 (2) 2112-2539. Fax: +420 (2) 2112 3013; (president) +420 (2) 2112 3002; (news desk) +420 (2) 2112 3613; (public relations) +420 (2) 2112 2995; (technical operations) +420 (2) 2112 3702; (broadcast operations) +420 (2) 2112 3540; (affiliate operations) +420 (2) 2112 4563. Email: the format is lastnameinitial@rferl.org; so to reach, say, Luke Springer, it would be springerl@rferl.org. Web: (general, including RealAudio) www.rferl.org; (broadcast services) www.rferl.org/bd. Contact: Thomas A. Dine, President; Kestutis Girnius, Managing Editor, News and Current Affairs; Luke Springer, Deputy Director, Technology; Jana Horakova, Public Relations Coordinator; Uldis Grava, Marketing Director; or Christopher Carzoli, Broadcast Operations Director.

WASHINGTON OFFICE: 1201 Connecticut Avenue NW, Washington DC 20036 USA. Phone: +1 (202) 457-6900; (newsdesk) +1 (202) 457-6950; (technical) +1 (202) 457-6963. Fax: +1 (202) 457 6992; (news desk) +1 (202) 457 6997; (technical) +1 (202) 457 6913. Email and Web: see above. Contact: Jane Lester, Secretary of the Corporation; Ken Morehouse, Director of Technology Systems; or Paul Goble, Director of Communications; (news) Oleh Zwadiuk, Washington Bureau Chief. A private nonprofit corporation funded by a grant from the Broadcasting Board of Governors, RFE/RL broadcasts in 21 languages (but not English) from transmission facilities now part of the International Broadcasting Bureau (IBB), see.

Radio Free Iraq—a service of Radio Free Europe-Radio Liberty (see, above). Web: (includes RealAudio) www.rferl.org/bd/iq.

Radio Martí, Office of Cuba Broadcasting, 4201 N.W. 77th

Avenue, Miami FL 33166 USA. Phone: +1 (305) 437-7000; (Director) +1 (305) 437-7117; (Technical Operations) +1 (305) 437-7051. Fax: +1 (305) 437 7016. Email: martinoticias@ocb.ibb.gov. Web: (includes RealAudio and Windows Media) www.martinoticias.com/radio.asp. Contact: (management) Jorge Luis Hernández, Director; (technical) Michael Pallone, Director, Engineering and Technical Operations; or Tom Warden, Chief of Radio Operations.

☎Radio Sawa—the Middle East Radio Network (MERN) of the Voice of America (*see*). Email: comments@radiosawa.com. Web: (includes RealAudio and Windows Media) www.radiosawa.com.

Sudan Radio Service, Education Development Center, 1000 Potomac Street NW, Suite 350, Washington DC 20007 USA. Phone: +1 (202) 572-3700. Fax: +1 (202) 223 4059. Email: srs@edc.org; (Groce) jgroce@edc.org. (Laflin) mlaflin@edc.org. Contact: Jeremy Groce, Radio Programming Advisor, EDC; or Mike Laflin, Director, EDC. Web: (EDC parent organization) www.edc.org.

☎Trans World Radio, International Headquarters, P.O. Box 8700, Cary NC 27512-8700 USA. Phone: +1 (919) 460-3700; (toll-free, U.S. only) 1-800-456-7897. Fax: +1 (919) 460 3702. Email: info2@twr.org. Web: (includes sample programs in RealAudio) www.gospelcom.net/twr. Contact: (general) Jon Vaught, Public Relations; Richard Greene, Director, Public Relations; Joe Fort, Director, Broadcaster Relations; or Bill Danick; (technical) Glenn W. Sink, Assistant Vice President, International Operations. Free "Towers to Eternity" publication for those living in the U.S. Technical correspondence should be sent to the office nearest the country where the transmitter is located—Guam, Monaco or Swaziland. For information on offices in Asia and Australasia, refer to the entry under "Guam." *CANADIAN OFFICE:* P.O. Box 444, Niagara Falls ON, L2E 6T8 Canada. Web: http://twrcan.ca.

☎University Network, P.O. Box 1, Los Angeles CA 90053 USA. Phone: (toll-free, U.S. only) 1- 800-338-3030; (elsewhere, call collect) +1 (818) 240-8151. Web: (includes RealAudio and Windows Media) www.drgenescott.com. Sells audio and video tapes and books relating to Dr. Scott's teaching. Free copies of *The Truth About* and *The University Cathedral Pulpit* publications. Transmits over KAIJ and WWCR (USA); Caribbean Beacon (Anguilla, West Indies); the former AWR facilities in Cahuita, Costa Rica; and a transmitter in Samara, Russia. Does not verify reception reports.

☎USA Radio Network, 2290 Springlake Road, Suite 107, Dallas TX 75234 USA. Toll-free phone (U.S. only) 1-800-829-8111. Email: (complaints/suggestions) tim@usaradio.com; (technical) david@usaradio.com. Web: (includes RealAudio and MP3) www.usaradio.com. Contact: (general) Tim Maddoux. Does not broadcast direct on shortwave, but some of its news and other programs are heard via U.S. stations KWHR, WHRA, WHRI and WWCR.

☎Voice of America—All Transmitter Locations
MAIN OFFICE: 330 Independence Avenue SW, Washington DC 20237 USA. If contacting the VOA directly is impractical, write c/o the American Embassy in your country. Phone: (Office of Public Affairs) +1 (202) 401-7000; (Audience Mail Division) +1 (202) 619-2770; (Africa Division) +1 (202) 619-1666 or +1 (202) 619-2879; (Office of Research) +1 (202) 619-4965; (administration) +1 (202) 619-1088. Fax: (Office of Public Affairs) +1 (202) 619 1241; (Africa Division) +1 (202) 619 1664; (Audience Mail Division and Office of Research) +1 (202) 619 0211. Email: (general business) pubaff@voa.gov; (reception reports and schedule requests) letters@voa.gov; (automatic reply back email

schedules for "VOA News Now") schedule@voanews.com or cwschedule@voa.gov; ("VOA News Now") newsnow@voanews.com; (VOA Special English) special@voa.gov; (VOA English to Africa) africanews@voa.gov. Web: (includes RealAudio) www.voa.gov. Contact: Mrs. Betty Lacy Thompson, Chief, Audience Mail Division, B/K. G759A Cohen; Larry James, Director, English Programs Division; Leo Sarkisian; Rita Rochelle, Africa Division; George Mackenzie, Audience Research Officer; (reception reports) Mrs. Irene Greene, QSL Desk, Audience Mail Division, Room G-759-C. Free stickers and calendars. If you're an American and miffed because you can't receive these goodies from the VOA, don't blame the station—they're only following the law. The VOA occasionally hosts international broadcasting conventions, and as of 1996 has been accepting limited supplemental funding from the U.S. Agency for International Development (AID). Also, *see* Botswana, Greece, Morocco, Philippines, São Tomé e Príncipe, Sri Lanka and Thailand.

Voice of America/IBB—Delano Relay Station, Rt. 1, Box 1350, Delano CA 93215 USA; (physical address) 11015 Melcher Road, Delano CA 93215 USA. Phone: +1 (805) 725-0150. Fax: +1 (805) 725 6511. Email: (Vodenik) jvodenik@del.ibb.gov, k9hsp@juno.com. Contact: (technical) John Vodenik, Engineer. Photos of this facility can be seen at the following Website: www.hawkins.pair.com/voadelano.shtml. Nontechnical correspondence should be sent to the VOA address in Washington.

Voice of America/IBB—Greenville Relay Station, P.O. Box 1826, Greenville NC 27834 USA. Phone: (site A) +1 (252) 752-7115 or (site B) +1 (252) 752-7181. Fax: (site A) +1 (252) 758 8742 or (site B) +1 (252) 752 5959. Contact: (technical) Bruce Hunter, Manager; or Glenn Ruckleson. Nontechnical correspondence should be sent to the VOA address in Washington.

WBCQ—The Planet, 97 High Street, Kennebunk ME 04043 USA. Phone: (Business Office) +1 (207) 985-7547; (studios and transmitters) +1 (207) 538-9180. Email: wbcq@gwi.net. Web: (includes MP3) www.wbcq.com. Contact: Allan H. Weiner, Owner; or Elayne Star, Assistant Manager. Verifies reception reports if 1 IRC or (within USA) an SASE is included.

WBOH—*see* Fundamental Broadcasting Network.

☎WEWN—EWTN Global Catholic Radio
TRANSMISSION FACILITY AND STATION MAILING ADDRESS: 1500 High Road, P.O. Box 176, Vandiver AL 35176 USA.
ENGINEERING AND MARKETING OFFICES: 5817 Old Leeds Rd., Irondale AL 35210 USA.
Phone: (general) +1 (205) 271-2900; (Station Manager) +1 (205) 271-2943; (Chief Engineer) +1 (205) 271-2959; (Marketing Manager) +1 (205) 271-2982; (Program Director, English) +1 (205) 271-2944; (Program Director, Spanish) +1 (205) 271-2900 ext. 2073; (Frequency Manager) +1 (205) 795-5779. Fax: (general) +1 (205) 271 2926; (Marketing) +1 (205) 271 2925; (Engineering and Frequency Management) +1 (205) 271 2953. Email: (general) wewn@ewtn.com; (technical) radio@ewtn.com; (Spanish) rcm@ewtn.com. To contact individuals, the format is initiallastname@ewtn.com; so to reach, say, Thom Price, it would be tprice@ewtn.com. Web: (includes RealAudio and online reception-report form) www.ewtn.com/wewn. Contact: (general) Thom Price, Director of English Programming; or Doug Archer, Director of Spanish Programming; (marketing) Bernard Lockhart, Radio Marketing Manager; (administration) William Steltemeier, President; or Frank Leurck, Station Manager; (technical) Terry Borders, Vice President Engineering; Glen Tapley, Frequency Manager; or Dennis Dempsey, Chief Engineer. Listener correspondence welcomed; responds to correspondence on-air and by mail. Free bumper stickers, program schedules and (some-

times) other booklets or publications. Sells numerous religious books, CDs, audio and video cassettes, T-shirts, sweatshirts and various other religious articles; list available upon request (VISA/MC). IRC or return postage appreciated for correspondence. Although a Catholic entity, WEWN is not an official station of the Vatican, which operates its own Vatican Radio (see). Rather, WEWN reflects the activities of Mother M. Angelica and the Eternal Word Foundation, Inc. Donations and bequests accepted by the Eternal Word Foundation.

◪WHRA-World Harvest Radio
ADMINISTRATION: See WHRI, below.
TRANSMITTER: Located in Greenbush, Maine, but all technical and other correspondence should be sent to WHRI (see next entry).

◪WHRI—World Harvest Radio, LeSEA Broadcasting, 61300 Ironwood Road, South Bend IN 46614 USA. Phone: +1 (219) 291-8200. Fax: (station) +1 (219) 291 9043. Email: whr@lesea.com. Web: (including RealAudio): www.whr.org; (Parent Organization, LeSEA Broadcasting) www.lesea.com. Contact: (listener contact) Joe Brashier; (general manager) Pete Sumrall; (programming or sales) Joe Brashier, Program/Sales coordinator; (technical) Douglas Garlinger, Chief Engineer. World Harvest Radio T-shirts available from 61300 Ironwood Road, South Bend IN 46614 USA. Return postage appreciated.
ENGINEERING DEPARTMENT: P.O. Box 50450, Indianapolis, IN 46250 USA.

WINB—World International Broadcasters, 2900 Windsor Road, P.O. Box 88, Red Lion PA 17356 USA. Phone: (all departments) +1 (717) 244-5360. Fax: +1 (717) 246 0363. Email: info@winb.com. Web: www.winb.com. Contact: (general) Mrs. Sally Spyker, Manager; (sales & Frequency Manager) Hans Johnson; (technical) Fred W. Wise, Technical Director; or John H. Norris, Owner. Return postage helpful outside United States. No giveaways or items for sale.

WJIE Shortwave, P.O. Box 197309, Louisville KY 40259 USA. Phone: +1 (502) 965-1220. Fax: +1 (502) 964 4228. Email: wjiesw@hotmail.com. Web: www.wjiesw.com. Transmitting equipment purchased from former world band station WJCR.

WMLK—Assemblies of Yahweh, 190 Frantz Road, P.O. Box C, Bethel PA 19507 USA. Phone: +1 (717) 933-4518, +1 (717) 933-4880; (toll-free, U.S. only) 1-800-523-3827. Email: (general) aoy@wmlkradio.net; (technical) technician@wmlkradio.net; (Elder Meyer) jacobmeyer@wmlkradio.net; (McAvin) garymcavin@wmlkradio.net. Web: http://wmlkradio.net; (Assemblies of Yahweh parent organization) www.assembliesofyahweh. com. Contact: (general) Elder Jacob O. Meyer, Manager and Producer of "The Open Door to the Living World"; (technical) Gary McAvin, Station Manager. Free The Sacred Name Broadcaster magazine published monthly, stickers and religious material. Bibles, audio and video (VHS) tapes and religious paperback books offered. Enclosing return postage ($1 or IRCs) helps speed things up.

WRMI—Radio Miami International, 175 Fontainebleau Blvd., Suite 1N4, Miami FL 33172 USA; or P.O. Box 526852, Miami FL 33152 USA. Phone: (general) +1 (305) 559-9764; (Engineering) +1 (305) 827-2234. Fax: (general) +1 (305) 559 8186; (Engineering) +1 (305) 819 8756. Email: info@wrmi.net. Web: www.wrmi.net. Contact: (technical and nontechnical) Jeff White, General Manager/Sales Manager; (technical) Indalecio "Kiko" Espinosa, Chief Engineer. Free station stickers and tourist brochures. Sells "public access" airtime to nearly anyone to say virtually anything for $1 per minute.

WRNO WORLDWIDE (when operating)

TRANSMITTER SITE: 4539 I-10 Service Road North, Metairie LA 70006 USA.
GOOD NEWS WORLDWIDE, PARENT ORGANIZATION: P.O. Box 895, Fort Worth TX 76101 USA. Phone: +1 (817) 801-8322. Fax: +1 (817) 492 7015. Email: hope@goodnewsworld.org. Web: www.goodnewsworld.org.

WSHB—see Christian Science Publishing Society.
WTJC—see Fundamental Broadcasting Network.

WWBS, P.O. Box 18174. Macon GA 31209 USA. Phone: +1 (912) 477-3433. Email: (general) wwbsradio@aol.com. Contact: Charles C. Josey; or Joanne Josey. Include return postage if you want your reception reports verified.

WWCR—World Wide Christian Radio, F.W. Robbert Broadcasting Co., 1300 WWCR Avenue, Nashville TN 37218 USA. Phone: (general) +1 (615) 255-1300. Fax: +1 (615) 255 1311. Email: (general) wwcr@wwcr.com; ("Ask WWCR" program) askwwcr@wwcr.com. Web: www.wwcr.com. Contact: (administration) George McClintock, K4BTY, General Manager; Adam W. Lock, Sr., WA2JAL, Head of Operations; or Dawn Keen, Program Director; (technical) William Hair, Chief Engineer. Free program guides, updated monthly. Return postage helpful. For items sold on the air and tapes of programs, contact the producers of the programs, and not WWCR. Replies as time permits. Carries programs from various political organizations, which may be contacted directly.

WWRB—World Wide Religious Broadcasters, c/o Southeast Radio Church, Box 7, Manchester TN 37349-0007 USA. Phone/fax: +1 (931) 841-0492. Email: dfrantz@tennessee.com. Web: www.wwrb.org. Contact: Dave Frantz, Chief Engineer. In its previous incarnation as WWFV, verification policy was that reception reports were to be sent to individual broadcasters (i.e. program producers) with a request to forward the report to the station, which in turn would then verify it.

WWV/WWVB (official time and frequency stations): NIST Radio Station WWV, 2000 East County Road #58, Ft. Collins CO 80524 USA. Phone: +1 (303) 497-3914. Fax: +1 (303) 497 4063. Email: nist.radio@boulder.nist.gov; (Deutch) deutch@ boulder.nist.gov. Web: http://tf.nist.gov/timefreq/stations/wwv.html. Contact: Matt Deutch, Engineer-in-Charge; or John S. Milton. Along with branch sister station WWVH in Hawaii (see below), WWV and WWVB are the official time and frequency stations of the United States, operating over longwave (WWVB) on 60 kHz, and over shortwave (WWV) on 2500, 5000, 10000, 15000 and 20000 kHz.
PARENT ORGANIZATION: National Institute of Standards and Technology, Time and Frequency Division, 325 Broadway, Boulder CO 80305-3328 USA. Phone: +1 (303) 497-5453. Email: (Lowe) lowe@boulder.nist.gov. Contact: John Lowe, Group Leader.

WWVH (official time and frequency station): NIST Radio Station WWVH, P.O. Box 417, Kekaha, Kauai HI 96752 USA. Phone: +1 (808) 335-4361; (live audio) +1 (808) 335-4363. Fax: +1 (808) 335 4747. Email: nistwwvh@gte.net; (Okayama) okayama@boulder.nist.gov. Web: http://tf.nist.gov/stations/wwvh.htm. Contact: (technical) Dean T. Okayama, Engineer-in-Charge. Along with headquarters sister stations WWV and WWVB (see preceding), WWVH is the official time and frequency station of the United States, operating on 2500, 5000, 10000 and 15000 kHz.

WYFR—Family Radio—see Family Radio Worldwide.

UZBEKISTAN   World Time +5

Radio Tashkent, Khorazm Street 49, Tashkent 700047, Uzbekistan. Phone: +998 (71) 139- 9657; (Chief Editor, English Service) +998 (71) 133-9221; (Chief, English Department) +998 (71) 139-9643. Fax: +998 (71) 133 6068. Email: ino@uzpak.uz. Web: http://ino.uzpak.uz. Contact: Sherzat Gulyamov, Director International Service; Mirtuichi Agzamov, Chief of English Department; Ms. Nargiza Kamilova, Chief Editor, English and German Services. Correspondence is welcomed in English, German, Russian, Uzbek and nine other languages broadcast by Radio Tashkent. Reception reports are verified with colorful QSL cards. Free pennants, badges, wallet calendars and postcards. Has quizzes from time to time with prizes and souvenirs. Books in English by Uzbek writers are apparently available for purchase. Station offers free membership to the "Salum Aleikum Listeners' Club" for regular listeners. Now refers to itself as "Radio Tashkent International" in official publications, but still announces as "Radio Tashkent" on the air.

VANUATU   World Time +12 (+11 midyear)

Radio Vanuatu, Information and Public Relations, Private Mail Bag 049, Port Vila, Vanuatu. Phone: +678 22999 or +678 23026. Fax: +678 22026. Contact: Maxwell E. Maltok, General Manager; Ambong Thompson, Head of Programmes; or Allan Kalfabun, Sales and Marketing Consultant, who is interested in exchanging letters and souvenirs from other countries; (technical) K.J. Page, Principal Engineer; Marianne Berukilkilu, Technical Manager; or Willie Daniel, Technician.

VATICAN CITY STATE   World Time +1 (+2 midyear)

⬚Radio Vaticana (Vatican Radio)
MAIN AND PROMOTION OFFICES: 00120 Città del Vaticano, Vatican City State. Phone: (general) +39 (06) 6988-3551; (Director General) +39 (06) 6988-3945; (Programme Director) +39 (06) 6988-3996; (Publicity and Promotion Department) +39 (06) 6988-3045; (technical) +39 (06) 6988-4897; (frequency management) +39 (06) 6988-5258. Fax: (general) +39 (06) 6988 4565; (frequency management) +39 (06) 6988 5062. Email: sedoc@vatiradio.va; sedoc@vaticanradio-us.org; (Director General) dirigen@vatiradio.va; (frequency management) mc6790@mclink.it; or gestfreq@vatiradio.va; (technical direction, general) sectec@vatiradio.va; (Programme Director) dirpro@vatiradio.va; (Publicity and Promotion Department) promo@vatiradio.va; (English Section) englishpr@vatiradio.va; (French Section) magfra@vatiradio.va; (German Section) deutsch@vatiradio.va; (Japanese Section) japan@vatiradio.va. Web: (general, including multilingual news and live broadcasts in RealAudio) www.vatican.va/news_services/radio; www.vaticanradio.org; (RealAudio in English and other European languages, plus text) www.wrn.org/vatican-radio. Contact: (general) Elisabetta Vitalini Sacconi, Promotion Office and schedules; Eileen O'Neill, Head of Program Development, English Service; Fr. Lech Rynkiewicz S.J., Head of Promotion Office; Fr. Federico Lombardi, S.J., Program Director; Solange de Maillardoz, Head of International Relations; Sean Patrick Lovett, Head of English Service; or Veronica Scarisbrick, Producer, "On the Air;" (administration) Fr. Pasquale Borgomeo, S.J., Director General; (technical) Umberto Tolaini, Frequency Manager, Direzione Tecnica; Sergio Salvatori, Assistant Frequency Manager, Direzione Tecnica; Fr. Eugenio Matis S.J., Technical Director; or Giovanni Serra, Frequency Management Department. Correspondence sought on religious and programming matters, rather than the technical minutiae of radio. Free station stickers and paper pennants. Music CDs $13; Pope John Paul II: The Pope of the Rosary double CD/cassette $19.98 plus shipping; "Sixty Years...a Single Day" PAL video on Vatican Radio for

15,000 lire, including postage, from the Promotion Office.
INDIA OFFICE: Loyola College, P.B. No 3301, Chennai-600 03, India. Fax: +91 (44) 2825 7340. Email: (Tamil) tamil@vatiradio.va; (Hindi) hindi@vatiradio.va; (English) india@vatiradio.va.
REGIONAL OFFICE, INDIA: Pastoral Orientation Centre, Box 2251, Palarivattom, Kochi-682 025, Kerala, India. Phone: +91 (484) 280-6227. Email: mediacom@md2.vsnl.net.in; (Malayalam) malayalam@vatiradio.va
JAPAN OFFICE: 2-10-10 Shiomi, Koto-ku, Tokyo 135, Japan. Fax: +81 (3) 5632 4457.
POLAND OFFICE: Warszawskie Biuro Sekcji Polskiej Radia Watykanskiego, ul. Skwer Ks. Kard. S, Warsaw, Poland. Phone: +48 (22) 838-8796.

VENEZUELA   World Time -4

Ecos del Torbes (when operating), Apartado 152, San Cristóbal 5001-A, Táchira, Venezuela. Phone: (general) +58 (276) 438-244; (studio): +58 (276) 421-949. Contact: (general) Licenciada Dinorah González Zerpa, Gerente; Simón Zaidman Krenter; (technical) Ing. Iván Escobar S., Jefe Técnico.
Observatorio Cagigal—YVTO, Apartado 6745, Armada 84-DHN, Caracas 103, Venezuela. Phone: +58 (212) 481-2761. Email: armdhn@ven.net. Contact: Jesús Alberto Escalona, Director Técnico; or Gregorio Pérez Moreno, Director. $1 or return postage helpful.
Radio Amazonas, Av. Simón Bolívar 4, Puerto Ayacucho 7101, Amazonas, Venezuela; or if no reply try Francisco José Ocaña at: Urb. 23 de Enero, Calle Nicolás Briceño, No. 18-266, Barinas 5201-A, Venezuela. Contact: Luis Jairo, Director; or Santiago Sangil Gonzales, Gerente. Francisco José Ocaña is a keen collector of U.S. radio station stickers. Sending a few stickers with your letter as well as enclosing $2 may help.
Radio Nacional de Venezuela (when operating), Final Calle Las Marías, El Pedregal de Chapellín, 1050 Caracas, Venezuela. If this fails, try: Director de la Onda Corta, Apartado Postal 3979, Caracas 1010-A, Venezuela. Phone: +58 (212) 730-6022, +58 (212) 730-6666. Email: ondacortavenezuela@hotmail.com. Contact: Ali Méndez Martínez, Representativo de onda corta. The transmitter site is actually located at Campo Carabobo, near Valencia, some three hours drive from Caracas.
Radio Táchira (when operating), Apartado 152, San Cristóbal 5001-A, Táchira, Venezuela. Phone: +58 (276) 430-009. Contact: Desirée González Zerpa, Directora; Sra. Albertina, Secretaria; or Eleázar Silva Malavé, Gerente.
Radio Valera (when operating), Av. 10 No. 9-31, Valera 3102, Trujillo, Venezuela. Phone: +58 (271) 53-744. Contact: Gladys Barroeta; or Mariela Leal. Replies to correspondence in Spanish. Return postage required. This station has been on the same world band frequency for almost 50 years, which is a record for Latin America.

VIETNAM   World Time +7

Bac Thai Broadcasting Service—contact via Voice of Vietnam—Overseas Service, below.
Lai Chau Broadcasting Service—contact via Voice of Vietnam—Overseas Service, below.
Lam Dong Broadcasting Service, Da Lat, Vietnam. Contact: Hoang Van Trung. Replies slowly to correspondence in Vietnamese. French may also suffice.
Son La Broadcasting Service, Son La, Vietnam. Contact: Nguyen Hang, Director. Replies slowly to correspondence in Vietnamese, but French may also suffice.

Voice of Vietnam—Domestic Service (Dài Tiêng Nói Viêt Nam, TNVN)—Addresses and contact numbers as for all sections of Voice of Vietnam—Overseas Service, below. Contact: Phan Quang, Director General.

Voice of Vietnam—Overseas Service
TRANSMISSION FACILITY (MAIN ADDRESS FOR NONTECHNICAL CORRESPONDENCE AND GENERAL VERIFICATIONS): 58 Quán Sú, Hànôi, Vietnam. Phone: +84 (4) 824-0044. Fax: +84 (4) 826 1122. Email: (including reception reports) btdn.vov@hn.vnn.vn. Web: (English text) www.vov.org.vn/docs1/english; (Vietnamese text and RealAudio in English and Vietnamese) www.vov.org.vn. Contact: Ms. Hoang Minh Nguyet, Director of International Relations.
STUDIOS (NONTECHNICAL CORRESPONDENCE AND GENERAL VERIFICATIONS): 45 Ba Trieu Street, Hànôi, Vietnam. Phone: (director) +84 (4) 825-7870; (English service) +84 (4) 934-2456; (newsroom) +84 (4) 825-5761 or +84 (4) 825-5862. Fax: (English service) +84 (4) 826 6707. Email: btdn.vov@hn.vnn.vn. Contact: Ms. Nguyen Thi Hue, Director, Overseas Service. Voice of Vietnam Overseas Service broadcasts in 11 foreign languages namely English, French, Japanese, Russian, Spanish, Mandarin, Cantonese, Indonesian, Lao, Thai, Khmer and Vietnamese for overseas Vietnamese.
TECHNICAL CORRESPONDENCE: Office of Radio Reception Quality, Central Department of Radio and Television Broadcast Engineering, Vietnam General Corporation of Posts and Telecommunications, Hànôi, Vietnam.
Yen Bai Broadcasting Station—contact via Voice of Vietnam, Overseas Service, above.

WESTERN SAHARA World Time exactly

Radio Nacional de la República Arabe Saharaui Democrática, Directeur d'Information, Frente Polisario, B.P. 10, El-Mouradia, 16000 Algiers, Algeria; or c/o Ambassade de la République Arabe Saharaui Démocratique, 1 Av. Franklin Roosevelt, 16000 Algiers, Algeria. Phone (Algeria): +213 (2) 747-907. Fax, when operating (Algeria): +213 (2) 747 984. Email: rasdradio@yahoo.es. Web: (includes a RealAudio recording made in the station's studios) http://web.jet.es/rasd/amateur4.htm. Contact: Mohammed Baali. Two IRCs helpful. Pro-Polisario Front, and supported by the Algerian government. Operates from Rabuni, near Tindouf, on the Algerian side of the border with Western Sahara.

YEMEN World Time +3

Republic of Yemen Radio, Ministry of Information, P.O. Box 2182 (or P.O. Box 2371), Sana'a-al Hasbah, Yemen. Phone: (general) +967 (1) 230-654, +967 (1) 282-005; (engineering) +967 (1) 230-751. Fax: (general) +967 (1) 230 761; (engineering) +967 (1) 251 628. Email: yradio@y.net.ye or hussein3itu@y.net.ye. Web: (includes RealAudio): www.yradio.gov.ye. Contact: (general) English Service; (administration) Mohammed Dahwan, General Director of Sana'a Radio; Adel Affara; or Abdulrahman Al-Haimi; (technical) Mohammed H. Bather, Engineer; Esmail Hussein Al Nomo, Head of Transmitting Station; Mohamed Al Aryani, Chief Engineer; or Mohamed Al Sammann, Chairman of Engineering Sector.

ZAMBIA World Time +2

The Voice - Africa (formerly Radio Christian Voice)
STATION: Private Bag E606, Lusaka, Zambia. Phone: +260 (1) 274-

251. Fax: +260 (1) 274 526. Email: cvoice@zamnet.zm. Web: (includes MP3) www.voiceglobal.net. Contact: Philip Haggar, Station Manager; Beatrice Phiri; or Lenganji Nanyangwe, Assistant to Station Manager. Free calendars and stickers; pens, as available. Free religious books and items under selected circumstances. Sells T-shirts and sundry other items. $1 or 2 IRCs appreciated for reply. Broadcasts Christian teachings and music, as well as news and programs on farming, sport, education, health, business and children's affairs.
U. K. OFFICE: The Voice, P.O. Box 3040, West Bromwich, West Midlands, B70 0EJ, United Kingdom. Phone:+44 (121) 224-1614. Fax: +44 (121) 224 1613. Email: feedback@voiceafrica.net; (Joynes) sandra@voiceafrica.net. Contact: Sandra Joynes, Office Administrator.

Radio Zambia, Mass Media Complex, Alick Nkhata Road, P.O. Box 50015, Lusaka 10101, Zambia. Phone: (general) +260 (1) 254-989, +260 (1) 253-301 or +260 (1) 252-005; (Public Relations) +260 (1) 254-989, X-216; (engineering) +260 (1) 250-380. Fax: +260 (1) 254 317 or +260 (1) 254 013. Email: (general) znbc@microlink.zm (zambroad@ zamnet.zm may also work); (Nkula, technical) pnkula@yahoo.com. Web: www. znbc.co.zm. Contact: (general) Keith M. Nalumango, Director of Programmes; or Lawson Chishimba, Public Relations Manager; (administration) Duncan H. Mbazima, Director-General; (technical) Patrick Nkula, Director of Engineering; or Malolela Lusambo. Free *Zamwaves* newsletter. Sometimes gives away stickers, postcards and small publications. $1 required, and postal correspondence should be sent via registered mail. Tours given of the station Tuesdays to Fridays between 9:00 AM and noon local time; inquire in advance. Used to reply slowly and irregularly, but seems to be better now.

ZIMBABWE World Time +2

Zimbabwe Broadcasting Corporation, P.O. Box HG444, Highlands, Harare, Zimbabwe; or P.O. Box 2271, Harare, Zimbabwe. Phone: +263 (4) 498-610 or +263 (4) 498-630. Fax: +263 (4) 498 613. Email: zbc@zbc.co.zw; (general enquiries) pr@zbc.co.zw; (news) hnn@zbc.co.zw; (Engineering) hbt@zbc.co.zw. Web: (includes Windows Media) www.zbc.co.zw. Contact: (general) Rugare Sangomoyo; or Lydia Muzenda; (administration) Alum Mpofu, Chief Executive Officer; (news details) Munyaradzi Hwengwere; (Broadcasting Technology, Engineering) Craig Matambo. $1 helpful.

CREDITS: Craig Tyson (Australia), Editor, with Tony Jones (Paraguay). Also, Lawrence Magne (USA), with special thanks to colleagues Gabriel Iván Barrera (Argentina), David Crystal (Israel), Graeme Dixon (New Zealand), Héctor García Bojorge (Mexico), Jose Jacob (India), Marie Lamb (USA), Gary Neal (USA), Fotios Padazopulos (USA), George Poppin (USA), Paulo Roberto e Souza (Brazil) and Célio Romais (Brazil); also the following organizations for their support and cooperation: Jembatan DX/*Juichi Yamada (Japan),* Radio Nuevo Mundo/*Tetsuya Hirahara (Japan) and* RUS-DX/*Anatoly Klepov (Russia).*

Worldwide Broadcasts in English— 2004

Country-by-Country Guide to Best-Heard Stations

Dozens of countries reach out to us in English, and this section gives the times and frequencies where you're likely to hear them. If you want to know which shows are on hour-by-hour, check out "What's On Tonight."

• **When and where:** "Best Times and Frequencies," earlier in this edition, pinpoints where each world band segment is found and gives tuning tips. Best is late afternoon and evening, when most programs are beamed your way. Tune world band segments within the 5730-10000 kHz range in winter, 5730-15800 kHz during summer. Around breakfast, you can also explore segments within the 5730-17900 kHz range for fewer but intriguing catches.

• **Strongest (and weakest) frequencies:** Frequencies shown in italics—say, *5965* kHz—tend to be best, as they are from transmitters that may be located near you. However, other frequencies beamed your way might do almost as well. Some signals not beamed to you can also be heard, especially when they are targeted to nearby parts of the world. Frequencies with no target zones are typically for domestic coverage, so they are unlikely to be heard unless you're in or near that country.

Program Times

Some stations shift broadcast times by one hour midyear, typically April through October. These are indicated by ▭ (one hour earlier) and ▭ (one hour later). Frequencies used seasonally are labeled ▣ for summer (midyear, typically April through October), and ▣ for winter. Stations may also extend their hours of transmission, or air special programs, for national holidays, emergencies or sports events.

Times and days of the week are in World Time, explained in "Setting Your World Time Clock" earlier in this edition, as well as in PASSPORT'S glossary.

> **World band is 24/7, but late afternoon and evening are best.**

Indigenous Music

Broadcasts in other than English? Turn to the next section, "Voices from Home," or the Blue Pages. Keep in mind that stations for kinsfolk abroad sometimes carry delightful chunks of native music. They make for enjoyable listening, regardless of language.

Schedules for Entire Year

To be as useful as possible over the months to come, PASSPORT'S schedules consist not just of observed activity, but also that which we have creatively opined will take place during the forthcoming year. This predictive material is based on decades of experience and is original from us. Although inherently not as exact as real-time data, over the years it's been of tangible value to PASSPORT readers.

M. Wright

ALBANIA

RADIO TIRANA

0245-0300 &	
0330-0400	▣ Tu-Su 6115 & Tu-Su 7160 (E North Am)
1845-1900	▣ M-Sa 9520 (W Europe)
1945-2000	▣ M-Sa 7210 (W Europe)
1945-2000	▣ M-Sa 9510 (W Europe)
2230-2300	▣ M-Sa 7130 & M-Sa 9540 (W Europe)

ARGENTINA

RADIO ARGENTINA AL EXTERIOR-RAE

| 0200-0300 | Tu-Sa 11710 (Americas) |
| 1800-1900 | M-F 9690 (Europe & N Africa), M-F 15345 (Europe) |

ARMENIA

VOICE OF ARMENIA

| 0910-0930 | ▣ Su 4810 (E Europe, Mideast & W Asia), Su 15270 (Europe) |
| 2040-2100 | ▣ M-Sa 4810 (E Europe, Mideast & W Asia), M-Sa 9960 (Europe) |

AUSTRALIA

HCJB AUSTRALIA

0130-0330	15555 (S Asia)
0800-1200	11750 (Australasia)
1230-1700	15390 (S Asia)
1800-2030	11765 (Australasia)

RADIO AUSTRALIA

0000-0130	17775 (SE Asia)
0000-0200	17795 (Pacific & W North Am)
0000-0700	15240 (Pacific & E Asia)
0000-0800	9660 (Pacific), 17580 (Pacific & E Asia)
0000-0900	12080 (S Pacific), 15415 (SE Asia), 21725 (Asia)
0030-0400	17750 (SE Asia)
0200-0700	15515 (Pacific & N America)
0430-0500 &	
0530-0800	17750 (SE Asia)
0700-0800	15240 (Pacific, E Asia & W North Am)
0800-0830	Sa/Su 17750 (SE Asia)
0800-0900	5995 & 9710 (Pacific), 15240 (Pacific & W North Am)
0800-1100	9580 (Pacific & W North Am)
0800-1130	15240 (E Asia)
0830-0900	17750 (SE Asia)
0900-0930	Sa/Su 17750 (SE Asia)
0900-1300	11880 (SE Asia)
0900-1400	21820 (Asia)
0930-1100	17750 (SE Asia)
1100-1200	12080 (S Pacific)
1100-1300	9475 (SE Asia)
1100-1400	5995 (Pacific), 6020 (Pacific & W North Am)
1100-1700	11650 (Pacific)
1100-2130	9580 (Pacific & N America)
1300-1700	11660 (SE Asia)
1400-1800	5995 (Pacific & W North Am), 6080 (SE Asia)
1430-1900	9475 (SE Asia)
1700-2100	9815 (Pacific & E Asia)
1700-2200	11880 (Pacific & W North Am)
1800-2000	6080 (Pacific & E Asia), 7240 (Pacific)
1900-2130	9500 (SE Asia)
2000-2100	F/Sa 6080 & F/Sa 7240 (Pacific)
2000-2200	12080 (S Pacific)
2100-2200	7240 & 9660 (Pacific)
2100-2400	17715 (Pacific & W North Am), 21740 (Pacific & N America)

Radio Australia addresses events in and around Australasia, including the fine arts.   Nova

2200-2330	*15240* (E Asia)
2200-2400	13620 & 15230 (SE Asia), 17795 (Pacific & W North Am)
2300-2400	9660 (Pacific), 12080 (S Pacific)
2330-2400	11695 & 15415 (SE Asia)

VOICE INTERNATIONAL

0800-0900	▥ 13685 (E Asia)
0900-1000	▥ 11955 (SE Asia)
0900-1300	13685 (E Asia)
1300-1500	13685 (S Asia & SE Asia)
1300-1700	▥ 13610 (E Asia)
1500-1700	13665 (S Asia & SE Asia)
1700-2100	▤ 11680 & ▥ 11685 (S Asia & SE Asia)
2100-2300	▥ 9795 (S Asia & SE Asia)

AUSTRIA
RADIO AUSTRIA INTERNATIONAL

0005-0015 ▭	Su/M 13730 (S America)
0015-0030 ▭	13730 (S America)
0035-0045 ▭	Su/M 13730 (S America)
0045-0100 ▭	13730 (S America)
0105-0115	▥ Su/M 7325 & ▤ Su/M 9870 (E North Am), ▥ Su/M 9870 (C America)
0115-0130	▥ 7325 & ▤ 9870 (E North Am), ▥ 9870 (C America)
0135-0145	▥ Su/M 7325 & ▤ Su/M 9870 (E North Am), ▥ Su/M 9870 (C America)
0145-0200	▥ 7325 & ▤ 9870 (E North Am), ▥ 9870 (C America)
0605-0630 &	
0635-0700 ▭	Su 17870 (Mideast)
1205-1215	▤ Sa/Su 21780 (S Asia, SE Asia & Australasia)
1205-1230	▤ Sa/Su 6155 & ▤ Sa/Su 13730 (Europe)
1215-1230	▤ 21780 (S Asia, SE Asia & Australasia)
1235-1245	▤ Sa/Su 21780 (S Asia, SE Asia & Australasia)
1245-1300	▤ M-F 6155 & ▤ M-F 13730 (Europe), ▤ 21780 (S Asia, SE Asia & Australasia)
1305-1315	▥ Sa/Su 17855 (S Asia, SE Asia & Australasia)
1305-1330	▥ Sa/Su 6155 & ▥ Sa/Su 13730 (Europe)
1315-1330	▥ 17855 (S Asia, SE Asia & Australasia)
1335-1345	▥ Sa/Su 17855 (S Asia, SE Asia & Australasia)
1345-1400	▥ M-F 6155 & ▥ M-F 13730 (Europe), ▥ 17855 (S Asia, SE Asia & Australasia)
1605-1630 ▭	Sa/Su *17865/15515* (W North Am)
1610-1625 ▭	M-F *17865/15515* (W North Am)
1635-1700 ▭	Sa/Su *17865/15515* (W North Am)
1640-1655 ▭	M-F *17865/15515* (W North Am)
2305-2315	▤ Su/M 9870 (C America)
2315-2330	▤ 9870 (C America)
2335-2345	▤ Su/M 9870 (C America)
2345-2400	▤ 9870 (C America)

BANGLADESH
BANGLADESH BETAR

1230-1300	7185 & 9550 (SE Asia)
1745-1815 &	
1815-1900	7185 & 9550 (Europe)

BELARUS
RADIO BELARUS/RADIO MINSK

0300-0330 ▭	W/F-M 5970 (W Europe & Atlantic), M/W/F-Su 7210 (N Europe)
2030-2100 &	
2130-2200 ▭	Tu/Th 7105 (Europe), Tu/Th 7210 (N Europe)

BELGIUM
RADIO VLAANDEREN INTERNATIONAAL

0400-0430	▤ *15565* (W North Am)
0500-0530	▥ *9590* (W North Am)
0800-0830 ▭	*5985* (Europe)
1130-1200	▥ *7390* & ▤ *9865* (E Asia)
1730-1800	▤ *9925* (Europe), ▤ *13690* (S Europe & W Africa), ▤ *13710* (S Europe & Mideast)
1830-1900	▥ *7465* (Europe), ▥ *13650* (S Europe & Mideast), ▥ *13685* (S Europe & W Africa)
1930-2000	▤ *9925* (Europe), ▤ *13690* (S Europe & W Africa)
2030-2100	▥ *7465* (Europe)
2200-2230	▥ *11730/13685* & ▤ *15565* (N America)

BULGARIA

RADIO BULGARIA

0000-0100 ◨ 9400 (E North Am)
0000-0100   🆆 7400 (E North Am)
0200-0300   🆂 11900 (E North Am)
0300-0400 ◨ 9400 (E North Am)
0300-0400   🆆 7400 (E North Am)
0630-0700   🆂 11600 (W Europe)
0730-0800 ◨ 13600 (W Europe)
0730-0800   🆆 12000 (W Europe)
1130-1200   🆂 11700 (W Europe)
1230-1300 ◨ 15700 (W Europe)
1230-1300   🆆 12000 (W Europe)
1730-1800   🆂 9400 & 🆂 11900 (W Europe)
1830-1900   🆆 5800 & 🆆 7500 (W Europe)
2200-2300 ◨ 5800 & 7500 (W Europe)
2300-2400   🆂 11900 (E North Am)

CANADA

CANADIAN BROADCASTING CORP—(E North Am)

0000-0300 ◨ Su 9625
0200-0300 ◨ Tu-Sa 9625
0300-0310 &
0330-0609 ◨ M 9625
0400-0609 ◨ Su 9625
0500-0609 ◨ Tu-Sa 9625
1200-1255 ◨ M-F 9625
1200-1505 ◨ Sa 9625
1200-1700 ◨ Su 9625
1600-1615 &
1700-1805 ◨ Sa 9625
1800-2400 ◨ Su 9625
1945-2015,
2200-2225 &
2240-2330 ◨ M-F 9625

CFRX-CFRB—(E North Am)
24 Hr6070
CFVP-CKMX—(W North Am)
0600-0400 ◨ 6030
CKZN—(E North Am)
24 Hr6160
CKZU-CBU—(W North Am)
24 Hr6160

RADIO CANADA INTERNATIONAL

0000-0100 ◨ 9590 (E North Am & C
          America)
0000-0100   🆆 5960 (E North Am & C
          America), 🆂 9640 (E Asia & SE
          Asia), 🆆 9755, 🆆 11895 & 🆂
          15205 (SE Asia)

0100-0200   🆂 9755 (N America & C
          America), 🆂 15170 & 🆂
          15305 (C America & S
          America)
0200-0300   🆆 6040 & 🆆 9755 (E North Am
          & C America), 🆆 11725 (C
          America & S America), 🆆
          15150, 🆂 15510 & 17860 (S
          Asia)
1200-1300   🆂 M-F 9515 (N America & C
          America), 9660/9795 (E Asia),
          🆆 11730 & 🆂 15190 (E Asia &
          SE Asia), 🆂 M-F 17800 (C
          America)
1300-1400 ◨ M-F 13655 (E North Am & C
          America)
1300-1400   🆆 M-F 9515 (E North Am & C
          America), 🆆 M-F 17710 (C
          America)
1300-1500   🆂 9515 (N America & C
          America), 🆂 17800 (C
          America)
1400-1600 ◨ 13655 (E North Am & C
          America)
1400-1600   🆆 9515 (E North Am & C
          America), 🆆 17710 (C
          America)
1500-1600   🆂 Sa/Su 9515 (N America & C
          America), 🆆 9635, 🆆 11935, 🆂
          15455 & 🆂 17720 (S Asia), 🆂
          Sa/Su 17800 (C America)
1600-1700 ◨ Sa/Su 13655 (E North Am & C
          America)
1600-1700   🆆 Sa/Su 9515 (E North Am &
          C America), 🆆 Sa/Su 17710 (C
          America)
2000-2100   🆂 5995 (S Europe & N Africa),
          🆂 11690 (Europe), 🆂 11965 (N
          Africa & W Africa), 🆂 12015 (E
          Africa), 🆂 12035 (Mideast & E
          Africa)
2000-2130   🆂 15325 (W Europe), 🆂 17870
          (W Europe & N Africa)
2100-2130   🆂 7235 (Mideast), 🆆 11725 (N
          Africa), 🆂 13690 (N Africa & W
          Africa)
2100-2200   🆆 7235 (N Africa), 🆆 7425
          (Mideast & E Africa), 🆆 9805
          (C Africa & E Africa), 🆆 13650
          (N Africa)
2100-2230 ◨ 5850 (W Europe)
2100-2230   🆆 9770 (W Europe)

2200-2230 ☑ *6045* (W Europe & N Africa), ☑ *9805* (N Africa & W Africa), ☒ 11920 (C America & S America), ☑ 12005 (W Africa), ☒ 15170 (C America & S America), ☒ 17880 (S America)

2200-2400 ☒ 6140 (E North Am & C America), ☒ 15455 (N America)

2300-2330 ☑ 11865 & ☑ 13730 (C America & S America)

2300-2400 ▱ 9590 (E North Am & C America)

2300-2400 ☑ 5960 (E North Am & C America)

CHINA

CHINA RADIO INTERNATIONAL

0100-0200 *9580* (E North Am), *9790* (W North Am)

0300-0400 *9690* (N America & C America), *9790* (W North Am)

0400-0500 ☑ *9730* & ☒ *9755* (W North Am)

0500-0600 ▱ *9560* (W North Am)

0900-1100 11730/17690 & 15210 (Australasia)

1200-1300 9730 (SE Asia), 9760 & 15415 (Australasia)

1200-1400 11760 (Australasia), 11980 (SE Asia)

1300-1400 *9570* (E North Am), 11900 (Australasia), 15180 (SE Asia)

1400-1500 9700, 11675 & 11765 (South Asia)

1400-1600 ▱ 7405 (W North Am)

1400-1600 *13685* (E Africa & S Africa), *15125* (C Africa & E Africa), *17720* (W North Am)

1500-1600 7160 & 9785 (S Asia)

1600-1700 ☑ 13650 (S Africa)

1600-1800 ☑ 7190 & 9570 (E Africa & S Africa)

1700-1800 9695 (S Africa), ☒ 11920 (E Africa)

1900-2000 ☑ 9585 & ☒ 13790 (Mideast)

1900-2100 9440 (N Africa)

2000-2130 *11640* & *13630* (E Africa & S Africa)

2000-2200 ☑ 5965, ☑ 9840, ☒ 11790 & ☒ 15110 (Europe)

2200-2300 ☑ *7170* & ☒ *9880/7175* (N Europe)

2300-2400 *5990* (C America), *13680* (N America & C America)

CHINA (TAIWAN)

RADIO TAIWAN INTERNATIONAL

0200-0300 *5950* (E North Am), 15465 (E Asia)

0200-0400 *9680* (N America), 11875 & 15320 (SE Asia)

0300-0400 *5950* (W North Am), *15215* (S America)

0700-0800 *5950* (W North Am)

0800-0900 9610 (Australasia)

1100-1200 7445 (SE Asia)

1200-1300 7130 (E Asia)

1400-1500 15265 (SE Asia)

1600-1800 11550/11560 (S Asia)

1800-1900 *3955* (W Europe)

2200-2300 ☑ *9355* & ☒ *15600* (Europe)

COSTA RICA

RADIO FOR PEACE INTERNATIONAL

24 Hr7445 (C America & N America)

CROATIA

VOICE OF CROATIA

0200-0220 ☒ *9925* (E North Am)

0300-0320 ☑ *7285* (N America)

CUBA

RADIO HABANA CUBA

0100-0500 6000 (E North Am), 9820 (N America)

0200-0500 6195/9505 (E North Am)

0500-0700 9550 (E North Am), 9820 & ☒ 11760 (W North Am)

2030-2130 6195/9550 (C America), 11670/11760 (Europe & E North Am)

CZECH REPUBLIC

RADIO PRAGUE

0000-0030 ☒ 7345 (N America & C America), ☒ 9440 (Americas)

0100-0130 6200 (N America & C America), 7345 (N America)

0200-0230 ☑ 6200 (N America & C America), ☑ 7345 (N America)

0300-0330 ☒ 7345 (N America), ☒ 9870 (W North Am & C America)

0330-0400 ☒ 11600 (Mideast), ☒ 15620 (Mideast & S Asia)

0400-0430 ☑ 5915 (W North Am & C America), ☑ 7345 (N America)

Nile polish: Radio Cairo explains ancient Egyptian history. Nova

ECUADOR

HCJB-VOICE OF THE ANDES
1100-1300	15115 (Americas), 21455 USB (Europe & Australasia)

EGYPT

RADIO CAIRO
0000-0030	9900/11725 (E North Am)
0200-0330	11780 (N America)
1215-1330	17775 (S Asia & SE Asia)
1630-1830	9755 (C Africa & S Africa)
2030-2200	15375 (W Africa)
2115-2245	9990 (Europe)
2300-2400	9900/11725 (E North Am)

ETHIOPIA

RADIO ETHIOPIA
1600-1700	7165 & 9560 (E Africa)

FRANCE

RADIO FRANCE INTERNATIONALE
0400-0430	**S** M-F *9550/11910*, **W** M- F *9805*, **S** M-F 11710/13610 & **W** M-F 11995/13610 (E Africa)
0500-0530	**W** M-F *11850* (E Africa & S Africa), **W** M-F 13610/15155 (E Africa), **S** M-F 17800 (E Africa)
0600-0630	**S** M-F *11665*, **W** M-F *11710* & **W** M-F *11725* (W Africa), **W** M-F 15155, M- F 17800 & **S** M-F 21620 (E Africa)
0700-0800	*15605* (W Africa)
1200-1230	*17815* (W Africa), 25820 (E Africa)
1400-1500	**W** *7175/9580* & **S** *11610* (S Asia), **S** 17515 & **W** 17620 (Mideast)
1600-1700	*9730* (S Africa), 11615 (Irr) (N Africa), *11995* (W Africa), *12015* (S Africa), **S** *15160* & **W** *17815* (W Africa), 17850 (C Africa & S Africa)
1600-1730	**W** 11615 & **S** 15605 (Mideast), **W** 15605 & **S** 17605 (E Africa)

GERMANY

DEUTSCHE WELLE
0000-0100	**S** *7130*, **W** *7290*, **S** *9505*, **S** 9825 & **W** 9880 (S Asia)

0430-0500	**W** 9865 (Mideast), **W** 11600 (Mideast & S Asia)
0700-0730	**S** 11600 (W Europe)
0800-0830 ◨	9880 (W Europe)
0800-0830	**W** 11600/7315 (W Europe)
0900-0930	**S** 21745 (S Asia & W Africa)
1000-1030	**W** 21745 (S Asia & W Africa)
1030-1100	**S** 9880 & **S** 11615 (N Europe)
1130-1200	**W** 11640 (N Europe), **W** 21745 (E Africa & Mideast)
1300-1330	**S** 13580 (N Europe), **S** 21745 (S Asia)
1400-1430	**W** 21745 (N America & E Africa)
1600-1630	**S** 21745 (E Africa)
1700-1730 ◨	5930 (W Europe)
1700-1730	**S** 17485 (C Africa), **W** 17485 (W Africa & C Africa)
1800-1830 ◨	5930 (W Europe)
1800-1830	**W** 9495 (E Europe, Asia & Australasia)
2000-2030	**S** 11600 (SE Asia & Australasia)
2100-2130 ◨	5930 (W Europe)
2100-2130	**W** 9430 (SE Asia & Australasia)
2230-2300	**W** 7345 (N America), **W** 9435 (W Africa), **S** 11600 (E North Am), **S** 13580 (N America)
2330-2400	**W** 5915 & **W** 7345 (N America)

0400-0500	[W] *6180* (E Africa & S Africa), [S] 7225 (C Africa & E Africa), [W] *9545* (E Africa & Mideast), [W] 9710 (C Africa & S Africa), [S] *11945* (Mideast & E Africa), [S] 15410 (E Africa)
0500-0600	[W] *9565* & [S] *9700* (C Africa & E Africa), [W] 11805 (S Africa), [S] *11925* (C Africa & S Africa), *12045* & [S] *13755* (S Africa), [S] 15410 & [W] *15410* (C Africa & E Africa)
0600-0700	[W] 7225 & [S] *9780* (W Africa), [W] 11785 (W Africa & C Africa), [S] 15275, [W] *15410* & [S] *17860* (W Africa)
0600-1900	6140 (Europe)
0800-1200	[W] *15440* (Europe)
1000-1030	[W] *6205* (E Asia), [S] *17615* (E Asia & SE Asia), [S] *17715* & [W] *17820* (E Asia)
1100-1200	[S] *15110*, [W] *17670*, [S] *17820* & [W] *21650* (SE Asia)
1600-1700	*6170* & 7225 (S Asia), [W] 11695 (S Asia, SE Asia & Australasia), [S] 17595 (S Asia)
1900-2000	*6180* & [S] *7225* (C Africa & E Africa), [W] 11865 (Mideast & E Africa), [S] *11965* (W Africa, C Africa & E Africa), [S] 13590 (Mideast & E Africa), [W] *13780* (E Africa)
1900-2100	[W] 13590 (E Africa & S Africa)
2000-2100	[S] *9780* & [W] *13780* (S Africa), [S] 15205 (C Africa & E Africa), [W] 15205 (C Africa & S Africa), [W] *15410* (C Africa & E Africa), [S] 17810 (C Africa & S Africa)
2100-2200	[S] 9440, [W] 9615 & [S] *11865* (W Africa), [W] *13780* (W Africa & C Africa), [S] *15205* (W Africa), [W] *15410* (W Africa & C America)
2200-2300	[W] *5955* & [W] *6165* (E Asia), [S] *9720* & [S] *15605* (E Asia & SE Asia)
2300-2400	[W] *7250*, [W] *9815*, [S] *9890*, [W] *12035* & [S] *17860* (SE Asia)

GHANA
GHANA BROADCASTING CORPORATION

0530-0900	4915, 6130/3366
0900-1200	Sa/Su/Holidays 4915
1200-1700	6130
1700-2400	3366, 4915

GREECE
FONI TIS HELLADAS

0830-0900	[S] W-M 15630 & [S] W-M 17900 (W Europe & Atlantic)
0930-1000	[W] W-M 9420 (Europe), [W] W-M 15630 (W Europe & Atlantic)
1600-1700	[S] Sa 9420 (Europe), [S] Sa 15630 (W Europe & Atlantic), [S] Sa *17705* (N America)
1700-1800	[W] Sa 9420 (Europe), [W] Sa 15630 (W Europe & Atlantic), [W] Sa *17705* (N America)
1800-1900	[S] Su 9420 (Europe), [S] Su 15630 (W Europe & Atlantic), [S] Su *17705* (N America)
1830-1900	[S] 12105 (Europe)
1900-2000	[W] Su 5865 (W Europe & Atlantic), [W] Su 9420 (Europe), [W] Su *17705* (N America)
1930-2000	[W] 7475 (Europe)

HUNGARY
RADIO BUDAPEST

0100-0130	[S] 9590 (N America)
0200-0230	[W] 9835 (N America)
0230-0300	[S] 9570 (N America)
0330-0400	[W] 9835 (N America)
1500-1530	[S] Su 9715 (N Europe)
1600-1630	[▭] Su 6025 (Europe)

I Foni tis Helladas reaches Europe and North America, but frequencies are unpredictable. Guha

1600-1630	⊞ Su 9585 (N Europe)
1900-1930	🄢 11720 (W Europe)
2000-2030 ▭	3975 & 6025 (Europe)
2100-2130	🄢 11890 (S Africa)
2200-2230 ▭	6025 (Europe)
2200-2230	⊞ 11965 (S Africa)

INDIA

ALL INDIA RADIO

0000-0045	9705 (SE Asia), 9950 (E Asia), 11620 & 13605 (E Asia & SE Asia)
1000-1100	13710 (E Asia & Australasia), 15235/15020 (E Asia), 15260 (S Asia), 15410 (E Asia), 17510 (Australasia), 17800 (E Asia), 17895 (Australasia)
1330-1500	9690, 11620 & 13710 (SE Asia)
1745-1945	7410 (Europe), 9445 (W Africa), 9950 & 11620 (Europe), 11935 (E Africa), 13605 (W Africa), 15075 (E Africa), 15155 (W Africa), 17670 (E Africa)
2045-2230	7410 & 9445 (Europe), 9575 & 9910 (Australasia), 9950 (Europe), 11620 (Europe & Australasia), 11715 (Australasia)
2245-2400	9705 (SE Asia), 9950 (E Asia), 11620 & 13605 (E Asia & SE Asia)

INDONESIA

VOICE OF INDONESIA

0100-0200	9525 & 11785 (E Asia, SE Asia & Pacific)
0800-0900	11785 (Australasia)
2000-2100	11785 & 15150 (Europe)

IRAN

VOICE OF THE ISLAMIC REPUBLIC

| 0030-0130 | ⊞ 6120, ⊞ 9580, 🄢 9610 & 🄢 9835 (E North Am & C America) |
| 1130-1230 | ⊞ 15385, ⊞ 15460, 🄢 15450 (S Asia), 🄢 15585 & 🄢 15600 (W Asia & S Asia), 21470 & 21730 (S Asia & SE Asia) |

1530-1630	⊞ 7190 (S Asia & SE Asia), 🄢 7240, ⊞ 9610 & 🄢 9635 (S Asia, SE Asia & Australasia), ⊞ 11835 (S Asia & SE Asia)
1930-2030	⊞ 6110 & ⊞ 7320 (Europe), 🄢 9800 (S Africa), 🄢 11670 (Europe), ⊞ 11695 & 🄢 11750 (S Africa), 🄢 11860 (Europe), ⊞ 15140 (S Africa)
2130-2230	⊞ 9780 (Australasia), 🄢 9870 (S Asia, SE Asia & Australasia), ⊞ 11740 (Australasia), 🄢 13665 (SE Asia & Australasia)

IRELAND

RTE OVERSEAS

0130-0200	*6155* (C America)
1000-1030	*15280* (Australasia)
1800-1830	⊞ *9850* & 🄢 *15585* (Mideast)
1830-1900	*13640* (N America), *21630* (C Africa & S Africa)

ISRAEL

KOL ISRAEL

0400-0415	🄢 15640 (W Europe & E North Am)
0500-0515 ▭	9435 (W Europe & E North Am), 17600 (Australasia)
0500-0515	⊞ 6280 & ⊞ 11605/7475 (W Europe & E North Am)
1900-1925	🄢 11605, 🄢 15615 & 🄢 17545 (W Europe & E North Am)
2000-2025 ▭	15640 (S Africa & S America)
2000-2025	⊞ 6280, ⊞ 9435, ⊞ 11605/7520 & ⊞ 13720 (W Europe & E North Am)

ITALY

RAI INTERNATIONAL

0055-0115	9675 & 11800 (N America)
0445-0500	⊞ 5965 (S Europe & N Africa), ⊞ 6100 & 🄢 6110 (N Africa), ⊞ 7230, 🄢 7235 & 🄢 9875 (S Europe & N Africa)
1935-1955	⊞ 5965, 🄢 5970, 🄢 9745 & ⊞ 9845 (W Europe)
2025-2045	⊞ 5985, 🄢 6185, 🄢 9670, ⊞ 9710 & 11880 (Mideast)
2205-2230	11895 (E Asia)

JAPAN
RADIO JAPAN
0000-0015	13650 & 17810 (SE Asia)
0000-0100	*6145* (E North Am)
0100-0200	*11860* (SE Asia), *11880* (Mideast), 15325 (S Asia), 17560 (Mideast), 17685 (Australasia), 17810 (SE Asia), 17835 (S America), 17845 (E Asia)
0300-0400	17825 (C America), 21610 (Australasia)
0500-0600	*5975* (W Europe), *6110* (W North Am), 11715 & 11760 (E Asia), 17810 (SE Asia)
0500-0700	*7230* (Europe), 15195 (E Asia), 21755 (Australasia)
0600-0700	◩ 11690 (W North Am), *11740* (SE Asia), ◪ 13630 (W North Am), 17870 (Pacific)
1000-1100	*17585* (Europe), 21755 (Australasia)
1000-1200	9695 (SE Asia), 15590 (Asia)
1100-1200	*6120* (E North Am)
1400-1500	◪ 9505 (W North Am), *11840* (Australasia), *17755* (Mideast)
1400-1600	7200 (SE Asia), ◩ 9845 & ◪ 11730 (S Asia)
1500-1600	9750 (E Asia), ◪ *11705* (E North Am)
1700-1800	◪ 9505 (W North Am), 11970 (Europe), *15355* (S Africa)
2100-2200	◪ *6035* (Australasia), ◪ *6055* & ◩ *6090* (W Europe), 6180 & ◪ 11830 (Europe), *11855* (C Africa), ◩ *11920* (Australasia), 17825 (W North Am), 21670 (Pacific)

JORDAN
RADIO JORDAN—(W Europe)
1400-1730	▱	11690

KOREA (DPR)
VOICE OF KOREA
0100-0200	3560, 4405 & 6195 (E Asia), 6520/13760 (C America & S America), 7140 (E Asia), 7580/1518 0 (C America & S America), 9345 (E Asia), 11735 (C America & S America)

0200-0300	3560 (E Asia), 9325/11845 & 11335/15230 (SE Asia)
0300-0400	4405, 6195, 7140 & 9345 (E Asia)
1000-1100	3560 (E Asia), 9335 (C America), 9850/13650 (SE Asia), 11710 (C America), 11735 (SE Asia)
1300-1400 &	
1500-1600	7505/13760 (Europe), 9335 (N America), 11335/15245 (Europe), 11710 (N America)
1600-1700	3560 (E Asia), 9975 & 11735 (Mideast & Africa)
1900-2000	7505/13760 & 11335/15245 (Europe), 11710 (N America)
2100-2200	7505/13760 & 11335/15245 (Europe)

KOREA (REPUBLIC)
RADIO KOREA INTERNATIONAL
0200-0300	*9560* (W North Am), 11810 (E Asia), 15575 (N America)
0800-0900	9570 (SE Asia), 13670 (Europe)
1130-1230	*9650* (E North Am)
1300-1400	9570 & 13670 (SE Asia)
1600-1700	5975 (E Asia), 9515 (Mideast & Africa), 9870 (Mideast & E Africa)
1900-2000	5975 (E Asia), 7275 (Europe)
2100-2130	◪ *3955* (W Europe)
2200-2230	◩ *3955* (W Europe)

KUWAIT
RADIO KUWAIT
0500-0800	15110 (S Asia & SE Asia)
1800-2100	11990 (Europe & E North Am)

LITHUANIA
RADIO VILNIUS
0030-0100	◩ 7325 & ◪ 11690 (E North Am)
0930-1000 ▱	9710 (W Europe)
2330-2400	9875 (E North Am)

MALAYSIA
VOICE OF MALAYSIA
0300-0600 &	
0600-0825	6175 & 9750 (SE Asia), 15295 (Australasia)

MALTA

VOICE OF THE MEDITERRANEAN

0800-0900	[S] Su *9605* (Europe)
0900-1000	[W] Su *9630* (Europe)
1730-1800	[S] M-Sa *9605/6185* & [W] M-Sa *9850* (Europe)
1900-2000	[S] Sa-Th *12060* (Europe & N Africa)
2000-2100	[W] Sa-Th *7440* (Europe)

MEXICO

RADIO MEXICO INTERNACIONAL—(W North Am & C America)

0000-0030 ⇦	9705 & 11770
1500-1530 ⇦	M-F 9705 & M-F 11770
2200-2215 ⇦	M/W/F 9705 & M/W/F 11770

MOLDOVA

RADIO DMR—(Europe)

1700-1730 ⇦	W 5960

MONGOLIA

VOICE OF MONGOLIA

1000-1030	9615/12085 (E Asia, SE Asia & Australasia)
1500-1530	9720/12015 (W Asia)

NEPAL

RADIO NEPAL

0215-0225	5005, [S] 6100, 7165/3230
0815-0825	[S] 6100, 7165/3230
1415-1425	5005, [S] 6100, 7165/3230

NETHERLANDS

RADIO NEDERLAND

0000-0055	*9845* (E North Am)
0100-0155	*6165* (N America)
0400-0455	*6165* & *9590* (W North Am)
1000-1055	[W] *7260* (E Asia & Australasia), *9785* (Australasia), [S] *12065* (E Asia & Australasia), [W] *12065* (SE Asia), [S] *13710* (E Asia & Australasia)
1200-1255 ⇦	*5965* & *9890* (E North Am)
1400-1555	[S] *9890*, [S] *11835*, [W] *12070*, [S] *12075*, [W] *12080* & [W] *15595* (S Asia)
1800-1855	*6020* (S Africa)
1800-1955	9895 & [W] *11655* (E Africa)
1900-2055	*7120* (S Africa), [S] 11655 (W Africa), Sa/Su *15315* (N America), Sa/Su *17725* (E North Am), *17810* (W Africa), Sa/Su *17875* (W North Am)
2000-2055	9895 (W Africa)

NEW ZEALAND

RADIO NEW ZEALAND INTERNATIONAL—(Pacific)

0000-0505	17675
0505-0705	[S] 11820 & [W] 15340
0705-1105	[S] 9885 & [W] 11675
1105-1305	[S] 9850 & [W] 15175
1305-1650	6095
1650-1750	[S] M-F 6095 & [W] M-F 11980
1750-1850	[S] M-F 11980 & [W] 15265
1850-2050	[W] 15265
1850-2215	[S] 15160
2050-2215	[W] 17675
2215-2400	17675

NIGERIA

VOICE OF NIGERIA

0500-1000 & 1500-2300	15120/17800 (N Africa & Europe)

OMAN

RADIO SULTANATE OF OMAN

0300-0400	15355 (E Africa)
1400-1500	15140 (Europe & Mideast)

PHILIPPINES

RADYO PILIPINAS—(S Asia & Mideast)

0200-0330	[S] 11885, [W] 12015, 15120 & 15270

POLAND

RADIO POLONIA—(W Europe)

1200-1300	[S] 11820
1300-1400 ⇦	9525
1300-1400	[W] 6095
1800-1900 ⇦	5995 & 7285

ROMANIA

RADIO ROMANIA INTERNATIONAL

0200-0300	**S** 9510 (E North Am), **W** 9550 (N America), **W** 9625, **W** 11740 & **S** 11810 (E Asia), **W** 11830 & **S** 11940 (N America), **W** 11940 (Australasia), **S** 15105 (E Asia), **S** 15180, **W** 15370 & **S** 17815 (Australasia)
0400-0500	**S** 9510 (E North Am), **W** 9550, **W** 11830 & **S** 11940 (N America), **W** 15335, 17735 & **S** 21480 (S Asia)
0600-0700	**W** 9530, **S** 9635, **W** 11830 & **S** 11940 (W North Am)
0637-0656	**W** 9510 (W Europe), **S** 9525 & **S** 9550 (Europe), **W** 9570 (W Europe), **S** 11775, **W** 11790 & **W** 11940 (Europe)
0700-0800	**W** 17720 (N Africa, C Africa & S Africa), **W** 21480 (C Africa & S Africa), **S** 21530 (N Africa, C Africa & S Africa)
1400-1500	**S** 15250, **W** 15365, **S** 17735 & **W** 17790 (W Europe)
1700-1800	**W** 7155 & **W** 9625 (N Europe), **W** 9690 (W Europe), **S** 11740 (N Europe), **W** 11940 (W Europe), **S** 15365 (N Europe), **S** 15380 & **S** 17805 (W Europe)
2100-2200	**W** 5955 (N Europe), **W** 7105 (W Europe), **W** 7215 (N Europe), **S** 9510 & **W** 9690 (W Europe), **S** 9725 & **S** 11740 (N Europe), **S** 11940 (Europe)
2300-2400	**W** 7195 (W Europe), **W** 9510 (E North Am), 9570 (W Europe), **S** 11740 (E North Am), **S** 11775 (N Europe), **W** 11940 & **S** 15105 (E North Am)

RUSSIA

VOICE OF RUSSIA

0100-0200	**S** *11825* (E North Am)
0100-0300	**S** 9725 (E North Am), **S** 17595 (W North Am)
0100-0500	**S** *9665* (E North Am), **S** 12000 (W North Am)
0200-0300	**W** *9765* (E North Am)
0200-0400	**W** 6155 (E North Am)
0200-0500	**W** 13665 & **W** 15445 (W North Am)
0200-0600	**W** *7180* (E North Am), **W** 12020 (W North Am)
0300-0500	**S** 11720 & **S** *11750* (E North Am), **S** 17565, **S** 17650, **S** 17660 & **S** 17690 (W North Am)
0400-0600	**W** *7125* & **W** *7240* (E North Am), **W** 12010, **W** 15595 & **W** 17595 (W North Am)
0500-0900	**S** 17635 (Australasia), **S** 17685 & **S** 17795 (SE Asia & Australasia)
0530-0900	**S** 15490 (SE Asia & Australasia)
0600-0800 ◼	21790 (Australasia)
0600-0800	**S** *17670* (Mideast), **W** 21485 (SE Asia)
0600-0900	**W** 12010 (W Europe), **W** 17655 (SE Asia & Australasia)
0600-1000	**W** 11770 (SE Asia), **W** 15275, **W** 15470 & **W** 17665 (Australasia)
0700-0900	**S** 17675 (SE Asia & Australasia)
0700-1000	**W** 11820 (W Europe)
0800-1000 ◼	*17495* (SE Asia & Australasia), *17525* (Australasia)
0800-1000	**W** 21485/21810 (SE Asia)
1400-1500	**S** 9745 (C Asia & S Asia), **S** 12055 (SE Asia), **S** 15560 & **S** 17645 (S Asia & SE Asia)
1400-1600	**S** 7390 (E Asia & SE Asia)
1500-1600	**W** 6205 (SE Asia), **W** 7315 (W Asia & S Asia), **S** 7325 (Mideast), **W** 7350 (S Asia), *11500* (SE Asia)
1500-1800	**S** 11985 (Mideast)
1500-1900	**W** 7260 (N Pacific & W North Am)
1600-1700 ◼	*4940*, *4965* & *4975* (W Asia & S Asia)
1600-1700	**W** 5890 (S Asia), **W** 6005 (Mideast), **W** 7305, **S** 7350 & **S** 11720 (S Asia), **S** 12055 (W Asia & S Asia), **S** 15540 (Mideast)
1600-1900	**W** 9830 (Mideast)
1700-1800	**W** 9470 (Mideast), **S** Sa/Su 9480 & **S** Sa/Su 11675 (N Europe)
1700-1900	**S** 9745 (E Africa)

1700-2000	◼ 9890 (Europe)
1700-2100	◼ 9775 (Europe)
1800-1900	◻ Sa/Su 5940 (N Europe), ◼ 5950 (Europe), ◻ Sa/Su 6175 (N Europe), ◼ 7300, ◼ 11630 & ◼ 11870 (Europe)
1800-2000 ▭	*11510* (E Africa & S Africa)
1800-2000	◻ 7335 (E Africa), ◻ 9775 (Europe)
1800-2100	◼ 9480 & ◼ 11675 (N Europe)
1800-2200	◻ 6235 (W Europe), ◻ 7335 & ◻ 7340 (Europe)
1900-2000	◻ 7360 (Europe & N Africa), 7440 (Europe), ◻ 9875 (E Africa & S Africa)
1900-2100	◼ 12030 & ◼ 12070 (Europe)
1900-2200	◻ 5940 (N Europe), ◻ 5950 (Europe), ◻ 6175 (N Europe)
2000-2100	◼ 15455 (Europe)
2000-2200	◻ 7390 (Europe), ◻ *15735* (S America)
2030-2100	◻ 9775 (Europe)
2100-2200	◻ 7300 (Europe)

SERBIA AND MONTENEGRO

INTERNATIONAL RADIO OF SERBIA AND MONTENEGRO

0000-0030	◼ M-Sa *9580* (E North Am)
0100-0130	◻ M-Sa *7115* (E North Am)
0200-0230	◻ M-Sa *7130* (W North Am)
0430-0500	◼ *9580* (W North Am)
1330-1400	◻ M-F *11835* (Australasia)
1930-2000 ▭	*6100* (Europe)
2200-2230 ▭	*6100* (W Europe)
2200-2230	◼ Su-F *7230* (Australasia)

SINGAPORE

MEDIACORP RADIO

1400-1600 &	
2300-1100	6150

RADIO SINGAPORE INTERNATIONAL—(SE Asia)

1100-1400	6150 & 9600

SLOVAKIA

RADIO SLOVAKIA INTERNATIONAL

0100-0130	5930, ◼ 6190 & ◻ 7230 (E North Am & C America), 9440 (S America)
0700-0730	◼ 9440, ◻ 13715, 15460 & 17550 (Australasia)
1630-1700	◼ 5920 (W Europe)
1730-1800 ▭	6055 & 7345 (W Europe)
1730-1800	◻ 5915 (W Europe)
1830-1900	◼ 5920 (W Europe)
1930-2000 ▭	6055 & 7345 (W Europe)
1930-2000	◻ 5915 (W Europe)

SOLOMON ISLANDS

SOLOMON ISLANDS BROADCASTING

0000-0030	5020
0030-0038	Sa/Su 5020
0038-0130	5020
0130-0145	Sa/Su 5020
0145-0230	5020
0230-0245	Sa/Su 5020
0240-0330	5020
0330-0338	Sa/Su 5020
0338-0430	5020
0430-0438	Sa/Su 5020
0438-0545	5020
0545-0600	Sa/Su 5020
0600-0648	5020
0648-0700	Sa/Su 5020
0700-0800	5020
0800-0830	Sa/Su 5020
0830-0945	5020
0945-1000	Su-F 5020
1000-1010	5020
1010-1030	Sa/Su 5020
1030-1100,	
1100-1900,	
1900-1930 &	
1945-2030	5020
2030-2045	F/Sa 5020
2045-2130	5020
2130-2138	F/Sa 5020
2138-2230	5020
2230-2238	F/Sa 5020
2238-2330	5020
2330-2345	F/Sa 5020
2345-2400	5020

SOUTH AFRICA

CHANNEL AFRICA

0300-0330	◼ 6035 & ◻ 9525 (E Africa & C Africa)
0400-0430	5955 (S Africa)
0500-0530	11710 (W Africa & C Africa)
0600-0630	15215 (W Africa & C Africa)
1300-1455	◻ Sa/Su 11710 & ◼ Sa/Su 11780 (S Africa), Sa/Su 17725/21620 (C Africa & E Africa), Sa/Su 21760 (W Africa)

1500-1530	17725/17770 (C Africa & E Africa)
1600-1630	9525 (S Africa)
1700-1730 & 1800-1830	[S] 15265 & [W] 17870 (W Africa & C Africa)

SPAIN

RADIO EXTERIOR DE ESPA—A

0000-0100	[W] 6055 & [S] 15385 (N America & C America)
2000-2100	[S] M-F 9570 & [W] M-F 9595 (N Africa & W Africa), [W] M-F 9680/9700 & [S] M-F 15290 (Europe)
2100-2200	[S] Sa/Su 9570 (N Africa & W Africa), [S] Sa/Su 9840 (Europe)
2200-2300	[W] Sa/Su 9595 (N Africa & W Africa), [W] Sa/Su 9680 (Europe)

SRI LANKA

SRI LANKA BROADCASTING CORPORATION

0030-0430	6005, 9770 & 15745 (S Asia)
1230-1530	6005, 9770 & 15745 (S Asia)
1900-2000	Sa *6010* (W Europe)

SWEDEN

RADIO SWEDEN

0130-0200	9435 (S Asia)
0230-0300 & 0330-0400 ⬅	*9490* (N America)
1100-1130	[S] 17505 (E Asia & Australasia)
1230-1300 ⬅	17840/18960 (N America)
1230-1300	[S] 13580 and 17505 (Asia & Australasia)
1330-1400 ⬅	17505 (E Asia & Australasia), 17840/18960 (N America)
1330-1400	[W] 9430 (E Asia & Australasia)
1430-1500 ⬅	17505 (Asia & Australasia), 17840/18960 (N America)
1730-1800	[S] Su 13580 (Europe & Africa)
1830-1900 ⬅	M-Sa 6065 (Europe)
1830-1900	[W] Su 5840 (W Europe & N Africa)
2030-2100 ⬅	6065 (Europe)
2030-2100	[W] 9415 (Australasia)
2130-2200	[S] 11650 (Australasia)
2230-2300 ⬅	6065 (Europe)

Although Swiss Radio International is but a shadow of its former self, it still continues to reach out to traveling countrymen and interested foreigners. Nova

SWITZERLAND

SWISS RADIO INTERNATIONAL

0730-0800	[W] *9885* (N Africa), [S] *13650* (N Africa & W Africa), [W] *13790* (W Africa), [S] *15445* (N Africa), [W] 17665 & [S] 21750 (C Africa & S Africa)
0830-0900	21770 (C Africa & S Africa)
1730-1800	[W] *9755*, [S] *13750*, [W] *13790* & [S] *15515* (Mideast), [W] 15555 & [S] 17870 (Mideast & E Africa)
1930-2030	[W] *9755* (N Africa & W Africa), [S] *11815* (C Africa & S Africa), [S] *13645* (N Africa & W Africa), [W] 13660 (C Africa & S Africa), [S] 13795 (E Africa), [S] *15220* (S Africa), [W] *15485* (E Africa), [W] *17660* (S Africa)
2330-2400	9885, [W] *11660* & [S] *11905* (S America)

SYRIA

RADIO DAMASCUS

2005-2105	12085 & 13610 (Europe)
2110-2210	12085 (N America), 13610 (Australasia)

THAILAND

RADIO THAILAND

0000-0030	🅂 9570 & 🅆 9680 (E Africa & S Africa)
0030-0100	🅆 13695 & 🅂 15395 (E North Am)
0300-0330	🅂 15395 & 🅆 15460 (W North Am)
0530-0600	🅆 13780 & 🅂 21795 (Europe)
1230-1300	🅆 9810 & 🅂 9860 (SE Asia & Australasia)
1400-1430	🅆 9560 & 🅂 9830 (SE Asia & Australasia)
1900-2000	🅂 7155 & 🅆 9535 (N Europe)
2030-2045	🅆 9535 & 🅂 9680 (Europe)

TURKEY

VOICE OF TURKEY

0300-0350	🅂 7270 (Mideast), 🅂 11655/9650 (Europe & N America)
0400-0450	🅆 6020 (Europe & N America), 🅆 7240 (Mideast)
1230-1325	🅂 17595 (S Asia, SE Asia & Australasia), 🅂 17830 (Europe)
1330-1425	🅆 15145 (Europe), 🅆 15195 (S Asia, SE Asia & Australasia)
1830-1920	🅂 9785 (Europe)
1930-2020	🅆 5980 (W Europe)
2130-2220 ▭	9525 (S Asia, SE Asia & Australasia)
2200-2250	🅂 9830 & 🅂 12000 (W Europe & E North Am)
2300-2350	🅆 6020 (W Europe), 🅆 9655 (W Europe & E North Am)

UKRAINE

RADIO UKRAINE

0000-0100	🅂 12040/9810 (E North Am)
0100-0200	🅆 5905/9385 (E North Am), 🅆 9610 (W Asia)
0300-0400	🅂 12040/9810 (E North Am)
0400-0500	🅆 5905/9385 (E North Am), 🅆 6020 (Europe), 🅆 7285 (N Europe)
1100-1200	🅂 15415 (W Europe)
1200-1300	🅆 11825 (C Asia), 🅆 11840, 🅆 13590 & 🅆 17760 (W Europe)
2100-2200	🅂 5905 (W Europe), 🅂 6020 (Europe)
2200-2300	🅆 5905 (W Europe), 🅆 6020 (Europe), 🅆 7240 & 🅆 9560 (W Europe)

UNITED ARAB EMIRATES

EMIRATES RADIO

0330-0350	12005, 13675/13650 & 15400 (E North Am & C America)
0530-0550	15435 (Australasia), 17830 (E Asia), 21700 (Australasia)
1030-1050	13675/13650 (Europe), 15370 (N Africa), 15395 & 21605 (Europe)
1330-1350	13630 (N Africa), 13675/13650, 15395 & 21605 (Europe)
1600-1615	13630 (N Africa) 13675/13650, 15395 & 21605 (Europe)

UNITED KINGDOM

BBC WORLD SERVICE

0000-0030	3915 (SE Asia), 11945 (E Asia)
0000-0100	5970 (S Asia), 9740 (SE Asia), 11955 (S Asia), 17615 (E Asia)
0000-0200	6195 (SE Asia), 9410 (W Asia)
0000-0300	9825 (S America), 🅂 11835 (W North Am & C America), 12095 (S America), 15310 (S Asia), 15360 (SE Asia), 17790 (S Asia)
0000-0400	5975 (C America & N America)
0000-0530	15280 (E Asia)
0100-0300	🅆 11860 (SE Asia), 11955 (S Asia)
0100-0400	🅆 9525 (C America & W North Am)
0200-0300	🅂 6195 (E Europe), 🅆 6195 & 🅂 9410 (Europe), 🅆 9410 (Mideast & W Asia), 9750 (E Africa), 🅂 11760 (Mideast)
0300-0400	6005 (S Africa), 9750, 🅂 12035 & 🅆 12035 (E Africa), 🅂 12095 (E Europe)
0300-0500	3255 (S Africa), 🅂 7120 (W Africa), 🅂 11760 (W Asia), 🅆 11760 (Mideast), 🅆 11765 (W Africa), 🅂 11835 (W North Am & C America), 15360 (SE Asia), 🅂 15575 (Mideast), 17760 & 21660 (E Asia), 21830 (W Asia & S Asia)
0300-0600	6195 (Europe), 15310 (S Asia)
0300-0700	7160 (W Africa & C Africa), 9410 (Europe), 17790 (S Asia)
0300-2200	6190 (S Africa)

Time	Frequency (Region)
0330-0600	*15420* (E Africa)
0400-0500	5975 (W North Am, C America & S America), [W] *12035* & [S] *17640* (E Africa)
0400-0600	[W] *6135* (W North Am & C America), [S] *12095* (Europe)
0400-0720	*6005* (W Africa)
0500-0530	*17885* (E Africa)
0500-0700	*11765* (W Africa), [S] 15565 (E Europe), [W] *15565* (N Europe & E Europe), *17640* (E Africa)
0500-0730	*15575* (W Asia)
0500-0800	*21660* (E Asia)
0500-0900	*11955* (SE Asia), *15360* (E Asia, SE Asia & Australasia)
0500-1000	*17760* (E Asia & SE Asia)
0500-1400	*11760* (Mideast)
0500-1700	*11940* (S Africa)
0530-0600	M-F *17885* (E Africa)
0600-0700	[S] 15485 (W Europe & N Africa)
0600-0800	[W] 6195 (W Europe), Sa/Su *17885* (E Africa)
0600-1700	12095 (Europe)
0600-1800	*15310* (S Asia)
0630-0700	*15400* (W Africa & C Africa)
0700-0800	*11765* & *17830* (W Africa)
0700-0900	[W] 9410 (Europe)
0700-1000	*15400* (W Africa)
0700-1500	17640 (E Europe & W Asia)
0700-1600	*17790* (S Asia)
0700-1700	15485 (W Europe & N Africa)
0700-1800	15565 (E Europe)
0730-0900	Sa/Su *15575* (W Asia)
0800-0900	[S] 21830 (W Asia & S Asia)
0800-1000	*17830* (W Africa & C Africa)
0800-1100	*17885* (E Africa), *21660* (E Asia)
0800-1300	*21470* (S Africa)
0900-1000	*15190* (S America)
0900-1030	*15360* (E Asia)
0900-1100	6195 (SE Asia), *9605* (E Asia)
0900-1200	*15575* (W Asia)
0900-1600	*9740* (SE Asia & Australasia)
1000-1100	Sa/Su *15190* (S America), Sa/Su *15400* (W Africa), Sa/Su *17830* (W Africa & C Africa)
1000-1400	6195 (C America & N America), *17760* (E Asia)
1030-1100	*11945* & *15285* (E Asia)
1100-1130	*15400* (W Africa), *17790* (S America)
1100-1200	17885 (E Africa)
1100-1700	6195 (SE Asia), *15190* (C America & S America)
1100-2100	17830 (W Africa & C Africa)
1200-1400	*17885* (E Africa)
1200-1500	*15575* (Mideast)
1300-1400	*15420* (E Africa)
1300-1900	*21470* (S Africa)
1400-1600	[S] *6135* & [S] *7160* (E Asia), *21660* (E Africa)
1500-1530	*11860, 15420* & *21490* (E Africa)
1500-1600	5975 (S Asia), [W] 9410 (Europe)
1500-2300	*15400* (W Africa)
1600-1700	[S] 9410 (W Europe), 17790 (W Asia & S Asia), [W] *21660* (E Africa)
1600-1800	3915 & 7160 (SE Asia), 9510 (S Asia)
1600-1830	5975 (S Asia)
1615-1700	Sa/Su *11860*, Sa/Su *15420* & Sa/Su *21490* (E Africa)
1700-1745	6005 & 9630 (E Africa)
1700-1800	[S] 15485 (W Europe & N Africa)
1700-1900	12095 (E Europe), *15420* (E Africa)
1700-2200	*3255* (S Africa), 6195 & *9410* (Europe)
1800-2000	*15310* (Mideast)
1830-2100	6005 & 9630 (E Africa)
1900-2100	12095 (S Africa)
2100-2200	3915 (S Asia & SE Asia), 6005 (S Africa), [W] *6110* (E Asia), 6195 (SE Asia), [S] *11945* (E Asia)
2100-2300	[W] *9605* (W Africa)
2100-2400	5965 (E Asia), *5975* (C America & N America), *12095* (S America), [S] *17830* (W Africa)
2115-2130	M-F *11675* & M-F *15390* (C America)
2130-2145	[W] Tu/F 11680 & [S] Tu/F 11720 (Atlantic & S America)
2200-2300	[S] *6195* (W Europe), 7105, 9660 & *11955* (SE Asia), *12080* (S Pacific)
2200-2400	[W] 6195 (N Europe & W Europe), *6195* & *9740* (SE Asia)
2300-2400	*3915* (SE Asia), *11945* (E Asia), *11955* (SE Asia), *15280* (E Asia)

2330-2400   ▣ *6035* & ▣ *9580* (E Asia)

WALES RADIO INTERNATIONAL
0200-0230   ▣ Sa *9795* (N America)
0300-0330   ▣ Sa *9735* (N America)
1130-1200   ▣ Sa *17625* (Australasia)
1230-1300   ▣ Sa *17845* (Australasia)
2030-2100   ▣ F *7325* (Europe)
2130-2200   ▣ F *6010/7325* (Europe)

UNITED NATIONS

UNITED NATIONS RADIO
1730-1745   ▣ M-F *7150* & ▣ M-F *7170* (S
             Africa), M-F *15495* (Mideast),
             M-F *17810* (W Africa & C Africa)

USA

ADVENTIST WORLD RADIO
0030-0100   ▣ *6035*, ▣ *6175*, ▣ *9720* & ▣
             9810 (S Asia)
0200-0230   ▣ *9820* (W Asia & S Asia)
0230-0300   ▣ *7230* (W Asia & S Asia)
0500-0530   ▣ *3215*, ▣ *3345*, ▣ *5960* & ▣
             6015 (S Africa)
0530-0600   ▣ *15105* & ▣ *15345* (W Africa
             & C Africa)
0600-0630   ▣ *15105* & ▣ *15345* (C Africa
             & E Africa)
0630-0700   ▣ M-Th/Sa *15160* (N Africa)
0730-0800   ▣ *9775* (Europe)
0830-0900   ▣ *9660* (Europe), ▣ *17820* (W
             Africa)
0830-0930   ▣ *17780* (W Africa)
0900-0930   ▣ *17670* (W Africa)
1000-1030   ▣ *11705* & ▣ *11930* (SE Asia)
1000-1100   ▣ *11560* & ▣ *11900* (E Asia)
1300-1330   ▣ *9860* & ▣ *17740* (C Asia)
1330-1400   ▣ *11755* & ▣ *11980* (E Asia), ▣
             15275 (S Asia & SE Asia), ▣
             15320 & ▣ *15385* (S Asia), ▣
             M/Tu/Th-Sa *15660* (S Asia &
             SE Asia)
1600-1700   *11560*, ▣ *15215*, ▣ *15235*, ▣
             15480 & ▣ *15495* (S Asia)
1630-1700   ▣ *11975* (S Asia), ▣ *11980* (W
             Asia & S Asia), ▣ *17640* (S Asia)
1730-1800   *9385* & ▣ *12015* (Mideast)
1800-1830   ▣ *3215*, ▣ *3345*, ▣ *5960* & ▣
             7265 (S Africa)
1800-1900   ▣ *9520* & ▣ *11985* (E Africa)
1930-2000   ▣ *7130* (W Europe), ▣ M- Th/
             Sa *11845* (N Africa & W Africa)
2000-2030   ▣ *15295* (C Africa)

2000-2100   ▣ *6060*, ▣ *7105*, ▣ *11750* & ▣
             11980 (E Asia), ▣ *15385* (C
             Africa)
2030-2100   ▣ *5955* (W Europe), ▣ *15295*
             (C Africa & E Africa)
2100-2200   ▣ *9660* & ▣ *15130* (W Africa)
2130-2200   ▣ *11850*, *11980* & ▣ *12010* (E
             Asia)

**AFRTS-ARMED FORCES RADIO & TV
SERVICE**
24 Hr   *4319/12579* USB (S Asia),
             5447 USB (C America), *5765/
             13362* USB & *6350/10320*
             USB (Pacific), *6459/7507* USB
             (C America), *12134* USB
             (Americas), *13855* (Irr) USB
             (Atlantic)

FAMILY RADIO
0000-0100   ▣ 6065 & ▣ 6085 (E North
             Am), ▣ 11720 & ▣ 15130 (S
             America)
0000-0445   9505 (N America)
0100-0200   *15060* (S Asia)
0100-0445   6065 (E North Am)
0200-0300   5985 (C America), ▣ 9985 (S
             America), 11855 (C
             America), ▣ 15255 (S
             America)
0300-0400   11740 (C America)
0400-0500   7355 & ▣ 11580 (Europe)
0400-0600   ▣ 9355 (Europe), 9715 (W
             North Am)
0500-0600   ▣ 6855 (E North Am), ▣ 7520
             (Europe)
0600-0700   ▣ 11530 (C Africa & S Africa),
             ▣ 11530 & ▣ 11580 (Europe),
             ▣ 11580 (C Africa & S Africa)
0600-0745   7355 (Europe)
0700-0745   ▣ 13695 (W Africa)
0700-0900   ▣ 9985 (W Africa)
0800-0900   ▣ 13570 (W Africa)
1000-1245   5950 (E North Am)
1100-1200   ▣ 7355 (C America), ▣ 9555 (S
             America), ▣ 11725 (C
             America), ▣ 11855 (S
             America)
1100-1245   ▣ 5850 (W North Am)
1100-1300   ▣ 11830 (N America)
1200-1300   13695 (E North Am)
1200-1345   ▣ 11970 (W North Am)
1200-1700   ▣ 17750 (W North Am & C
             America)

1300-1500	*11560* (S Asia), W 11740 (E North Am), S 11865 (N America), S 11970 (E North Am)
1300-1700	11830 (N America)
1400-1700	W 17760 (W North Am)
1500-1600	*6280* (S Asia)
1500-1700	*15520* (S Asia)
1600-1645	W 17790 (C Africa)
1600-1700	W 11865 (N America), S 21525 (C Africa & S Africa)
1600-1800	21455 (Europe)
1600-1945	18980 (Europe)
1700-1800	*21680* (C Africa & E Africa)
1900-1945	W 15115 (C Africa), W 15565 (Europe)
1900-2000	S 17750 (Europe)
1900-2100	*3230* (S Africa)
1945-2145	S 18980 (Europe)
2000-2100	*15195* (C Africa)
2000-2200	W 5810 (Europe), W 15565 (W Africa), S 17525 & W 17575 (S America), S 18930 (Europe)
2000-2245	W 7580 (Europe), S 17845 (W Africa)
2200-2245	S 15695 (Europe), S 15770 & W 21525 (C Africa & S Africa)
2200-2345	11740 (N America)
2300-2400	5985 & 11855 (C America), W 15170, S 15255, W 15400 & S 17750 (S America)

HERALD BROADCASTING

0000-0057	W/F-M 9430 (E North Am), M/W/F 15285 (C America & S America)
0100-0157	9430 (N America), M 15285 (C America & S America)
0200-0257	M/Th 7535 (W North Am & C America), Su/M 9430 (N America)
0300-0357	W M 5850, M 7535 & S M 11550 (E Europe)
0400-0457	W M/Tu/Th/Sa 12020 & S M/Tu/Th/Sa 15195 (E Africa & C Africa)
0500-0557	W M 7535 & S M 9450 (E Europe), S 9840 & W 12020 (S Africa)
0600-0657	W M/W/F/Sa 7535 & S M/W/F/Sa 9450 (W Africa & C Africa)
0700-0757	W Tu/Th 7535 & S Tu/Th 9450 (W Africa)
0800-0857	W Sa/Su 7535 (Europe), Sa-Th 9845 (Australasia), S Sa/Su 9860 (Europe)
0900-0957	W Tu/Th 7535 & S Tu/Th 9860 (Europe)
1000-1057	M/W/Th 6095 (E North Am), Su 9455 (S America)
1000-1100	Th-Tu *11780* (E Asia)
1100-1157	Tu/F-Su 6095 (E North Am), M 9455 (C America & S America)
1200-1257	M/W/Th 9430 (E North Am), Sa 9455 (C America & S America)
1200-1300	S *9585* & W *9880* (SE Asia)
1300-1357	Sa-Th 9430 (N America), Tu/F 9455 (W North Am & C America)
1300-1400	W *7340* & S *7460* (S Asia)
1600-1657	Sa 18910 (E Africa)
1700-1800	Tu/Th/Sa 18910 (C Africa)
1800-1857	Su 15665 (E Europe), Su/W 18910 (S Africa)
1900-1957	Su/Tu/Th 15665 (E Europe), 18910 (S Africa)
2000-2057	W Su/M/W/F 15665 & S Su/M/W/F 18910 (Africa)
2100-2157	W W/Sa-M 11650 & S W/Sa-M 15665 (W Europe), W F 15665 & S F 18910 (W Africa & C Africa)
2200-2257	W Su/Th 7510 & S Su/Th 13770 (W Europe), W/Su 15285 (S America)
2300-2357	W Su/W 7510 & S Su/W 13770 (S Europe & W Africa), Su 15285 (S America)

KAIJ—(N America)

0000-0200	5755/13815
0200-1200	5755
1200-1400	5755/13815
1400-2400	13815

KJES

0100-0230	7555 (W North Am)
1300-1400	11715 (N America)
1400-1500	11715 (W North Am)
1800-1900	15385 (Australasia)

KNLS-NEW LIFE STATION—(E Asia)

0800-0900	W 9615/11765 & S 11765
1300-1400	W 9615/11765 & S 11870/11565

KTBN—(E North Am)

0000-0100	W 7505 & S 15590
0100-1500	7505

1500-1600   [W] 7505 & [S] 15590
1600-2400   15590

KWHR-WORLD HARVEST RADIO

0000-0100   Su-F 17510 (E Asia)
0100-0130   17510 (E Asia)
0130-0200   Tu-Sa 17510 (E Asia)
0200-0400   17510 (E Asia)
0400-0530   17780 (E Asia)
0530-0600   Su-F 17780 (E Asia)
0600-0800   17780 (E Asia)
0700-1045   11565 (Australasia)
0800-0900   [W] 9930 & [S] 17780 (E Asia)
0900-1000   [W] Su-F 9930 & [S] Su-F 17780 (E Asia)
1000-1030   Su-F 9930 (E Asia & SE Asia)
1045-1300   Sa/Su 11565 (Australasia)
1130-1230   9930 (E Asia & SE Asia)
1230-1400   Su 9930 (E Asia & SE Asia)
1500-1630   Sa/Su 9930 (E Asia & SE Asia)
2200-2300   17510 (E Asia)
2300-2400   Su-F 17510 (E Asia)

RADIO AFRICA INTERNATIONAL

1700-1900   [W] *11735* (C Africa), *13820* (E Africa), [S] *15715* (C Africa)

UNIVERSITY NETWORK

0000-0200   *13750* (C America)
0000-1200   *5029* (C America), *6150* (C America & S America), *7375* (S America)
24 Hr   *9725* (N America)
0300-1600   [S] *17765* (S Asia)
1200-2400   *11869* (S America)
2000-2400   *13750* (C America)

VOA-VOICE OF AMERICA

0000-0100   *7215*, [S] *9770* & [W] *9890* (SE Asia), Tu-Sa 11695 (C America & S America), *11760* (SE Asia), *15185* (SE Asia & S Pacific), *15290* (E Asia), *17740* (E Asia & S Pacific), *17820* (E Asia)
0000-0130   Tu-Sa 13790 (C America & S America)
0000-0200   Tu-Sa 5995 (C America & S America), Tu-Sa 6130 (C America), Tu-Sa 7405, Tu-Sa 9455 & Tu-Sa 9775 (C America & S America)
0100-0300   [S] *7115*, [W] *7200*, [W] *7255*, [S] *9635*, [W] *9850*, *11705*, [S] *11725*, *11820*, [S] *13650*, [W] *15250*, *17740* & *17820* (S Asia)

0130-0200   Tu-Sa 13740 (C America & S America)
0300-0330   *7340* (C Africa & E Africa)
0300-0400   [W] *4960* (W Africa & C Africa), [W] *6035* (E Africa & S Africa), [S] *7105* & [W] *7265* (C Africa & S Africa)
0300-0430   *9885* (S Africa & C Africa)
0300-0500   *6080* (C Africa & S Africa), [W] *7290* (C Africa & E Africa), [W] *7415* (C Africa & S Africa), *9575* (W Africa & S Africa), [S] *17895* (C Africa & E Africa)
0300-0600   [S] *7290* (C Africa & S Africa)
0400-0500   *4960* (W Africa & C Africa), [W] *9775* (C Africa & E Africa)
0400-0700   [W] *7170* & [S] *9530* (N Africa), [S] *11965* (Mideast), *15205* (Mideast & S Asia)
0500-0600   [W] *9700* (N Africa & W Africa)
0500-0630   *6035* (W Africa & S Africa), [S] *6080* (C Africa & S Africa), [W] *6080* (W Africa), [W] *6105* (W Africa & C Africa), [S] *7195* (N Africa), [W] *7295* (W Africa), [W] *11835* (W Africa & S Africa), [S] *12080* (E Africa & S Africa), [S] *13670* (C Africa & S Africa), [W] *13710* (C Africa & E Africa)
0500-0700   [W] *11825* (Europe & Mideast)
0600-0630   [S] M-F *7290* (W Africa & C Africa), *11995* (C Africa & E Africa)
0600-0700   [W] *5995*, [W] *9760*, [S] *11805* & [W] *11930* (N Africa)
0630-0700   Sa/Su 6035 (W Africa & S Africa), [S] Sa/Su *6080* (C Africa & S Africa), [W] Sa/Su *6080* (W Africa), [W] Sa/Su *6105* (W Africa & C Africa), [S] Sa/Su *7195* (N Africa), [W] Sa/Su *7295* (W Africa), [W] Sa/Su *11835* (W Africa & S Africa), Sa/Su *11995* (C Africa & E Africa), [S] Sa/Su *12080* (E Africa & S Africa), [S] Sa/Su *13670* (C Africa & S Africa), [W] Sa/Su *13710* (C Africa & E Africa)
0700-1000   [S] *13760* (E Asia)

0800-1000 [S] *11930*, [W] *11995*, [W] *13615* & 15150 (E Asia)
0800-1100 [S] *13620* (E Asia)
1000-1100 5745, 7370 & 9590 (C America)
1000-1200 [W] 5985 & [S] 9770 (Pacific & Australasia), [W] *11720* (E Asia & Australasia)
1000-1300 [S] *9830* & [S] *15240* (E Asia), [W] *15240* (E Asia & SE Asia), [W] *15250* (E Asia), [W] *15455* (SE Asia & Pacific)
1000-1500 [S] *15425* (SE Asia & Pacific)
1100-1300 [W] *6110* & [S] *6160* (SE Asia), [S] *13610* (E Asia)
1100-1400 *9645* (SE Asia & Australasia)
1100-1500 *9760* (E Asia, S Asia & SE Asia), [W] *11705* & [S] *15160* (E Asia)
1200-1300 [W] *11715* (E Asia & Australasia)
1300-1500 [W] *15480* (SE Asia & Pacific)
1300-1800 [W] *6110* & [S] *6160* (S Asia & SE Asia)
1400-1800 *7125* (S Asia), [W] *15205* (Mideast & S Asia), [S] *15255* (Mideast), [W] *15395* (S Asia)
1500-1600 [S] *9590* & [S] *9760* (S Asia & SE Asia), [W] *9760* (E Asia, S Asia & SE Asia), [W] *9795*, [S] *9845* & [S] *12040* (E Asia), [W] *15460* (SE Asia), [S] *15550* (SE Asia & Australasia)
1500-1700 [W] *9575* (Mideast & S Asia), [W] *9645* (S Asia), [W] *11995* (E Asia), [S] *15205* (Europe, N Africa & Mideast)
1500-1800 [S] *9700* (Mideast)
1600-1700 [W] *6035* (W Africa), *9760* (S Asia & SE Asia), 13600 (C Africa & E Africa), [S] *13710* (S Africa), [S] *15225*, [S] *15410* & [W] *15485* (C Africa & E Africa), [W] *17640* (E Africa), [W] *17715* (W Africa), [S] *17810* & [W] *17895* (Africa)
1600-1800 [S] *15445* (Africa), [W] *15445* (E Africa)
1600-1900 [S] *17895* (Africa)
1600-2000 [W] *13710* (E Africa & S Africa)
1600-2200 [W] *15240* (Africa)
1700-1800 M-F *5990* (SE Asia & Australasia), [S] M-F *6045* (E Asia), [W] M-F *6045* & [S] M-F *7170* (E Asia & Australasia), [S] M-F *7215* (SE Asia & Pacific), [W] M- F *9525* (E Asia, SE Asia & S Pacific), *9645* (S Asia), [S] M-F *9770* (E Asia), [S] M-F *9785*, [W] M-F *9795* & [W] M-F *11955* (S Asia & SE Asia), [W] M-F *12005* (SE Asia), [W] M-F *15255* (E Asia & S Pacific), [W] *17895* (C Africa & S Africa)
1700-1900 [W] *6040* (N Africa & Mideast)
1700-2100 [S] *9760* (N Africa & Mideast), [W] *9760* (Mideast & S Asia)
1700-2200 [S] *15410* (Africa)
1800-1900 [S] *9770* & [W] *9885* (Mideast)
1800-2000 [W] *17895* (Africa)
1800-2200 [W] *6035* (W Africa), *11975* (C Africa & E Africa), 15580 (W Africa & S Africa)
1900-2000 [W] M-F *5965* & [S] *6160* (Mideast), [S] *7260* (Mideast & W Asia), *9525* (Australasia), [S] M-F *9550*, [S] *9680* & [W] *9785* (Mideast), M-F *9840* & [W] *11720* (Mideast & S Asia), [S] *11770* (Australasia), [S] M-F *11780* (Mideast), [W] *11870* (Australasia), [S] M-F *11970* (E Asia & SE Asia), [W] M-F *11970* (E Asia), [S] M-F *12015* (S Asia & SE Asia), [W] *12015*, [S] *13635* & [W] *13640* (Mideast), *13725* (W Asia & S Asia), *15180* (Pacific), [W] M-F *15205* (Mideast), [S] M-F *15235* & [W] M-F *15410* (E Asia)
1900-2030 *4950* (W Africa & C Africa)
1900-2100 [W] *9690* (Mideast & S Asia), [S] *9770* (N Africa & E Africa)
1900-2200 [W] *7415* (E Africa & S Africa), [S] *15445* (Africa)
2000-2030 *11855* (W Africa)
2000-2100 [S] *17745* & [W] *17885* (W Africa & C Africa)
2000-2200 *6095* (Mideast), [W] *13710* & 17895 (W Africa & C Africa)
2030-2100 Sa/Su *4950* (W Africa & C Africa)
2100-2200 *6040* (Mideast), [S] *9530* (N Africa & E Africa), [W] *9595* (Mideast & S Asia), [W] *9670* (SE Asia & Australasia), *9760* (E Europe & Mideast), *11870* (Australasia)
2100-2400 [S] *9705* (SE Asia), *15185* (SE Asia & S Pacific), [W] *17735* & [S]

	17740 (E Asia & S Pacific), *17820* (E Asia)
2200-2230	▥ M-F *6035* (W Africa), ▥ M-F *7415* (E Africa & S Africa), ▥ M-F *11655* (C Africa & S Africa), M-F *11975* (C Africa & E Africa), ▥ M-F *13710* (W Africa & C Africa)
2200-2300	▥ *6045* (E Asia)
2200-2400	*7215* & ▤ *9770* (SE Asia), ▥ *9770* (SE Asia & Australasia), ▥ *9890* & *11760* (SE Asia), *15290* (E Asia), *15305* (E Asia & SE Asia)
2300-2400	▥ *6180*, ▤ *7190*, ▤ *7200*, ▥ *7205*, ▤ *9545*, *11925*, ▤ *13775* & ▥ *15395* (E Asia)
2330-2400	▥ *7130*, ▤ *7225*, ▤ *7260*, ▥ *9620*, *11805*, ▤ *13735*, ▥ *13745* & *15205* (SE Asia)

WBCQ-"THE PLANET"—(N America)

0000-0500 ▣	5105, 7415 & 9335
0500-0545 ▣	Tu-Su 7415
0545-0700 ▣	F/Su 7415
1300-1400 ▣	Su 17495
1500-2200 ▣	M-F 7415/9335
1800-1900 ▣	M-Sa 17495
1900-2200 ▣	M-F 17495
2200-2400 ▣	M-F 5105, 7415 & M-Sa 9335

WEWN

0000-1000	5825 (N America)
0500-0800	▥ 7570 (Europe)
0600-0900	▤ 9385 (Europe)
1000-1300	▥ 5825 (N America)
1000-1400	▤ 7520 (N America)
1300-1400	▥ 9955 (N America)
1400-1600	9955 (N America)
1600-2000	▥ 17840 (Europe)
1600-2200	13615 (N America)
1700-2000	▤ 17595 (Europe)
2000-2400	17595 (W Africa)
2200-2400	9975 (N America)

WHRA-WORLD HARVEST RADIO

0000-0500	7580 (Europe & Mideast)
0500-1000	▥ 7580 & ▤ 11730 (Africa)
1500-2300 ▣	17650 (Africa)
2300-2400	7580 (Europe & Mideast)

WHRI-WORLD HARVEST RADIO

0000-1000	5745 (E North Am), 7315 (C America)
1000-1045	M-Sa 9495 (N America & C America)

1000-1500	▤ 9850 (E North Am)
1000-1600	▥ 9840 (E North Am)
1045-1300	9495 (N America & C America)
1300-1700	15105 (C America)
1500-1600	▤ 13760 (E North Am & W Europe)
1600-1715	13760 (E North Am & W Europe)
1700-1800	▤ 9495 (N America & C America), ▥ 15105 (C America)
1715-1730	M-Sa 13760 (E North Am & W Europe)
1730-2000	13760 (E North Am & W Europe)
1800-2400	9495 (N America & C America)
2000-2400	5745 (E North Am)

WINB-WORLD INTERNATIONAL BROADCASTERS—(C America & W North Am)

0000-0400	9320/12160
1000-1200	9320
1200-2300	9930/13570
2300-2400	9320/13570

WMLK—(Europe, Mideast & N America)

1600-2100	Su-F 9465

WRMI-RADIO MIAMI INTERNATIONAL

0000-0100 &	
0300-0400 ▣	7385 (N America)
0400-1000 ▣	Tu-Su 7385 (N America)
1000-1045 ▣	Su-F 9955 (C America)
1045-1100 ▣	9955 (C America)
1100-1200 ▣	Su 9955 (C America)
1200-1230 ▣	Sa 9955 (C America)
1230-1300 ▣	Sa/Su 9955 (C America)
1300-2400 ▣	15725 (N America)

WTJC—(N America)

0000-0130 ▣	9370
0130-0145 ▣	Tu-Su 9370
0145-1105 ▣	9370
1105-1120 ▣	M-Sa 9370
1120-2400 ▣	9370

WWBS—(E North Am)

0000-0100	▤ Su/M 11910
0000-0200	▥ Su/M 11900
2300-2400	▤ Sa/Su 11910

WWCR

0000-0100	3210/9475 (E North Am)
0000-0200	5935/13845 (E North Am)
0000-0500	7465 (E North Am)
0000-1200	5070 (E North Am)

0100-0900	3210 (E North Am)
0200-1200	5935 (E North Am)
0500-1400	7465/7560 (E North Am)
0900-1000	▥ 3210/9475 (E North Am)
1000-1100 ▭	Su-F 9475 (E North Am)
1000-1100 ▤	Su-F 15825 (E North Am)
1100-1130 ▤	Sa/Su 15825 (E North Am)
1100-1200 ▥	Su-F 15825 (E North Am)
1130-1200 ▤	15825 (E North Am)
1200-1230 ▤	15825 & ▥ Sa/Su 15825 (E North Am)
1200-1300	5070/12160 (E North Am)
1200-1400	5935/13845 (E North Am)
1230-2100	15825 (E North Am)
1300-1400 ▤	9475 (E North Am)
1300-2200	12160 (E North Am & Europe)
1400-2200	9475 (E North Am)
1400-2400	13845 (E North Am)
2100-2145 ▤	Sa/Su 15825 (E North Am)
2100-2200	▥ 7465 (Irr) & ▥ 15825 (Irr) (E North Am)
2145-2200 ▤	15825 (E North Am)
2200-2245	▤ 9475 & ▥ Sa/Su 9475 (E North Am)
2200-2400	5070/12160 (E North Am & Europe), 7465 (E North Am)
2245-2300	9475 (E North Am)
2300-2400	▥ 3210/9475 (E North Am)

WWRB

0000-0600	5050, 5085 and 6890 (N America & C America)
1600-2300	9320 & 12172 (N America)
2300-2400	5050, 5085 and 6890 (N America & C America)

UZBEKISTAN

RADIO TASHKENT

0100-0130	▥ 5975 (S Asia), ▥ 6165 (W Asia & S Asia), ▥ 7135 & ▥ 7160 (S Asia), ▤ 7190 & ▤ 9715 (W Asia & S Asia)
1200-1230 &	
1330-1400	▥ 5060, ▥ 5975, ▥ 6025, ▤ 7285, 9715 & ▤ 15295 (S Asia), ▤ 17775 (S Asia & SE Asia)
2030-2100	5025, ▥ 7105, ▥ 7185 & 11905 (Europe)
2130-2200	5025, ▥ 7105, ▥ 7185 & ▤ 11905 (Europe)

VATICAN STATE

VATICAN RADIO

0250-0310	7305 (E North Am), 9605 (E North Am & C America)
0600-0620 ▭	4005 (Europe), 5890 (W Europe)
0620-0700 ▭	5890 (W Europe)
0630-0645 ▤	M-Sa 9645 (S Europe & N Africa)
0730-0745 ▭	M-Sa 4005 (Europe), M-Sa 5890 (W Europe), M-Sa 7250 (Europe), M-Sa 11740 (W Europe & N Africa), M-Sa 15595 (Mideast)
0730-0745	▥ M-Sa 9645 (W Europe)
1120-1130 ▭	M-Sa 7250 (Europe), M-Sa 11740 (W Europe)
1615-1630	▤ 7250 (N Europe), ▤ 11810 (Mideast)
1715-1730 ▭	4005 (Europe), 5890 & 9645 (W Europe)
1715-1730	▥ 7250 (Mideast)
2050-2110 ▭	4005 & 5890 (Europe)

VIETNAM

VOICE OF VIETNAM

0100-0130,	
0230-0300 &	
0330-0400	*6175* (E North Am & C America)
1000-1030	9840 & 12020 (SE Asia)
1100-1130	7285 (SE Asia)
1230-1300	9840 & 12020 (SE Asia)
1330-1400 &	
1600-1630	▥ 7145/7185, ▥ 9730, ▤ 11630 & ▤ 13740 (Europe)
1700-1730	▤ *9725* (W Europe)
1800-1830	▥ *5955* (W Europe), ▥ 7145/7185, ▥ 9730, ▤ 11630 & ▤ 13740 (Europe)
1900-1930 &	
2030-2100	▥ 7145/7185, ▥ 9730, ▤ 11630 & ▤ 13740 (Europe)
2330-2400	9840 & 12020 (SE Asia)

YEMEN

REPUBLIC OF YEMEN RADIO—(Mideast & E Africa)

0600-0700 &	
1800-1900	9780

Voices from Home—2004

Country-by-Country Guide to Native Broadcasts

For some listeners, English offerings are merely icing on the cake. Their real interest is in eavesdropping on broadcasts for *nativos*—the home folks. These can be enjoyable regardless of language, especially when they offer traditional music.

Some you'll hear, many you won't, depending on your location and receiving equipment. Keep in mind that native-language broadcasts are sometimes weaker than those in English, so you may need more patience and better hardware. PASSPORT REPORTS shows which radios and antennas work best.

When to Tune

Some broadcasts come in better during the day within world band segments from 9300 to 21850 kHz. However, signals from Latin

America and Africa peak near or during darkness, especially from 4700 to 5100 kHz. See "Best Times and Frequencies" for specifics.

Times and days of the week are in World Time, explained in "Setting Your World Time Clock" and PASSPORT's glossary; for local times in each country, see "Addresses PLUS." Midyear, some stations are an hour earlier (◻) or later (◻) because of daylight saving time, typically April through October. Those used only seasonally are labeled ◼ for summer (midyear) and ◼ for winter (January, etc.). Stations may also extend their hours for holidays, emergencies or sports events.

Frequencies in *italics* may be best, as they come from relay transmitters that might be near you, although other frequencies beamed your way might do almost as well. Some signals not beamed to you can also be heard, especially when they are targeted to nearby parts of the world. Frequencies with no target zones are usually for domestic coverage, so they are the least likely to be heard unless you're in or near that country.

Schedules for Entire Year

To be as useful as possible over the months to come, PASSPORT's schedules consist not just of observed activity, but also that which we have creatively opined will take place during the forthcoming year. This predictive material is based on decades of experience and is original from us. Although inherently not as exact as real-time data, over the years it's been of tangible value to PASSPORT readers.

Great for expats and to revisit favorite places.

Africa's many regional stations make for challenging catches. The toughest are detailed in PASSPORT's Blue Pages.

Nova

ALBANIA—Albanian
RADIO TIRANA
0000-0430	[□]	7270 (E North Am)
0900-1000	[□]	7110 (Europe)
1500-1800	[□]	7270 (Europe)
2130-2300	[□]	7295 (Europe)

ARGENTINA—Spanish
RADIO ARGENTINA AL EXTERIOR-RAE
1200-1400	M-F 15345 (Americas)
2200-2400	M-F 6060 (C America & S America), M-F 11710 & M-F 15345 (Europe)

RADIO NACIONAL
0000-0100	M 11710 (S America)
0000-0230	Su/M 6060 (C America & S America), Su/M 15345 (Americas)
0230-0300	M 6060 (C America & S America), M 15345 (Americas)
0900-1200	6060 (S America), 15345 (Americas)
1800-2000	Su 6060 & Su 11710 (S America), Su 15345 (Europe)
2000-2200	Sa/Su 11710 (Irr) (S America)
2000-2400	Sa/Su 6060 (S America), Sa/Su 15345 (Europe)
2200-2400	Su 11710 (S America)

ARMENIA—Armenian
VOICE OF ARMENIA
0300-0330	[□]	4810 (Irr) (E Europe, Mideast & W Asia), 9965 (S America)
0400-0430	[□]	9965 (Irr) (S America)
0800-0830	[□]	Su 4810 (E Europe, Mideast & W Asia), Su 15270 (Europe)
1930-2000	[□]	M-Sa 4810 (E Europe, Mideast & W Asia), M-Sa 9960 (Europe)

AUSTRIA—German
RADIO AUSTRIA INTERNATIONAL
0000-0015 &		
0030-0045	[□]	Tu-Sa 13730 (S America)
0100-0115 &		
0130-0145		[W] Tu-Sa 7325 & [S] Tu-Sa 9870 (E North Am), [W] Tu-Sa 9870 (C America)
0400-0500		[S] 6155 & [S] 13730 (Europe)
0500-1205		6155 & 13730 (Europe)
0600-0700	[□]	M-Sa 17870 (Mideast)
1200-1215		[S] M-F 21780 (S Asia, SE Asia & Australasia)
1205-1230		[S] M-F 6155, [W] 6155, [S] M-F 13730 & [W] 13730 (Europe)
1230-1245		6155 & 13730 (Europe), [S] M-F 21780 (S Asia, SE Asia & Australasia)
1245-1300		[S] Sa/Su 6155, [W] 6155, [S] Sa/Su 13730 & [W] 13730 (Europe)
1300-1315		[W] M-F 17855 (S Asia, SE Asia & Australasia)
1300-1330		[S] 6155, [W] M-F 6155, [S] 13730 & [W] M-F 13730 (Europe)
1330-1345		6155 & 13730 (Europe), [W] M-F 17855 (S Asia, SE Asia & Australasia)
1345-1400		[S] 6155, [W] Sa/Su 6155, [S] 13730 & [W] Sa/Su 13730 (Europe)
1400-1800		13730 (Europe)
1400-2208		6155 (Europe)
1600-1610 &		
1630-1640	[□]	M-F 17865/15515 (W North Am)
1800-2208		5945 (Europe)
2208-2308		[W] 5945 & [W] 6155 (Europe)
2300-2315 &		
2330-2345		[S] Tu-Sa 9870 (C America)

BANGLADESH—Bangla
BANGLADESH BETAR
1630-1730	7185 & 9550 (Mideast)
1915-2000	7185 & 9550 (Europe)

BELGIUM
RADIO VLAANDEREN INTERNATIONAAL
Dutch
0430-0500		[S] 15565 (W North Am)
0500-0530		[S] 9925 (C Africa)
0530-0600		[W] 9590 (W North Am)
0600-0630		[W] 17730 (C Africa)
0600-0800	[□]	13685 (E Europe & Mideast)
0600-0900	[□]	15195 (Europe)
0800-0900	[□]	13685 (S Europe & W Africa)
1100-1130		[S] 15195 (S Europe & W Africa), [S] 17650 (Europe)
1100-1200	[□]	Su 21630 (C Africa)
1200-1230	[□]	21630 (C Africa)

1200-1230	▣ *7390* & ▣ *9865* (E Asia), ▣ *13685* (S Europe), ▣ *15195* (Europe), ▣ *17690* & ▣ *17695* (SE Asia & Australasia)
1300-1600	▣ Su *15195* (S Europe & W Africa), ▣ Su *17695* (Europe)
1400-1700	▣ Su *13685* (Europe), ▣ Su *15325* (S Europe & W Africa)
1700-1800	▣ *15195* (Europe)
1800-1900	▣ *7195* (S Africa), *9925* (Europe), ▣ *13690* (S Europe & W Africa), ▣ *13710* (S Europe & Mideast)
1900-2000 ▭	*15325* (C Africa)
1900-2000	▣ *7465* (Europe), ▣ *13650* (S Europe & Mideast), ▣ *13685* (S Europe & W Africa), ▣ *13720* (S Africa)
1900-2100 ▭	Sa *5910* (Europe)
2000-2100	▣ *9925* (Europe), ▣ *13690* (S Europe & W Africa)
2100-2200	▣ *5960* (S Europe & W Africa), ▣ *7465* (Europe)
2230-2300	▣ *11730/13685* & ▣ *15565* (N America)

RTBF INTERNATIONAL
French

0400-0530 ▭	M-F *9490* (C Africa)
0530-0600 ▭	*9490* (C Africa), Su 9970 (S Europe)
0600-0700 ▭	Su-F 9970 (S Europe)
0600-0812 ▭	*17580* (C Africa)
0700-1800 ▭	9970 (S Europe)
0812-0906 ▭	Sa/Su *17580* (C Africa)
0906-1100 ▭	Sa *17580* (C Africa)
1100-1200 ▭	M-Sa *21565* (C Africa)
1200-1217 ▭	*21565* (C Africa)
1217-1306 ▭	M-F *21565* (C Africa)
1500-1600	▣ Su-F *17570* (C Africa)
1600-1700	▣ Su-F *15135* (C Africa)
1600-1721	▣ *17570* (C Africa)
1700-1821	▣ *15135* (C Africa)
1800-2100 ▭	M-Sa 9970 (S Europe)
2100-2200 ▭	Sa 9970 (S Europe)

BRAZIL—Portuguese

RADIO BANDEIRANTES

24 Hr	6090, 9645, 11925

RADIO BRASIL CENTRAL

0000-0200 ▭	4985, 11815
0200-0600 ▭	4985 (Irr), 11815 (Irr)
0600-2400 ▭	4985, 11815

RADIO CULTURA

0000-0200 ▭	6170, 9615, 17815
0700-2400 ▭	9615, 17815
0800-2400 ▭	6170

RADIO GUAIBA

0700-0300 ▭	6000, 11785

RADIO NACIONAL DA AMAZONIA

0000-0050	6180
0000-0230 ▭	11780
0230-0700 ▭	Su 11780
0700-0800	▣ 6180
0700-2400 ▭	11780
0800-1950 &	
2110-2400	6180

RADIO NACIONAL DO BRASIL—(Africa)

0500-0700 &	
1900-2100	9665

BULGARIA—Bulgarian

RADIO BULGARIA

0000-0100	▣ 9500 (S America), ▣ 11900 (E North Am)
0100-0200 ▭	9400 (E North Am), 11600 (S America)
0100-0200	▣ 5900 (S America), ▣ 7400 (E North Am)
0400-0430	▣ Sa/Su 7200 (S Europe), ▣ Sa/Su 12000 (W Europe)
0430-0500	▣ 7200 (S Europe), ▣ 12000 (W Europe)
0500-0530 ▭	Sa/Su 7500 (E Europe), Sa/Su 9400 (W Europe), Sa/Su 9500 (E Europe)
0500-0530	▣ Sa/Su 5800 (W Europe), ▣ Sa/Su 5900 (S Europe)
0530-0600 ▭	7500 (E Europe), 9400 (W Europe), 9500 (E Europe)
0530-0600	▣ 5800 (W Europe), ▣ 5900 (S Europe)
1000-1030	▣ 11600 (E Europe), ▣ 11700 (W Europe), ▣ 13600 (E Europe)
1100-1130 ▭	9500 (S Europe), 15700 (W Europe)
1100-1130	▣ 11700 (E Europe), ▣ 12000 (W Europe), ▣ 15200 (E Europe)

1200-1400 [S] 11700 (W Europe)
1300-1500 ⬅ 15700 (W Europe)
1300-1500 [W] 12000 (W Europe)
1500-1600 [S] 7200 (S Europe), [S] 9500 (E Europe), [S] 15700 (Mideast)
1600-1700 ⬅ 7500 (E Europe), 17500 (S Africa)
1600-1700 [W] 9400 (Mideast), [W] 9900 (E Europe)
1800-1900 [S] 6000 (S Europe)
1800-2000 [S] 7200 (W Europe)
1900-2000 [W] 5900 (S Europe)
1900-2100 ⬅ 7400 (Mideast)
1900-2100 [W] 6000 (W Europe)

CANADA—French

CANADIAN BROADCASTING CORP—(E North Am)

0100-0300 ⬅ M 9625
0300-0400 ⬅ Su 9625 & Tu-Sa 9625
1300-1310 &
1500-1555 ⬅ M-F 9625
1700-1715 ⬅ Su 9625
1900-1945 ⬅ M-F 9625
1900-2310 ⬅ Sa 9625

RADIO CANADA INTERNATIONAL

0000-0100 [W] 9755 (E North Am & C America), [W] 11865 (C America & S America), [W] 13640 (E North Am & C America)
1100-1200 [S] 5990 (E North Am), [S] 9515 & [S] 15305 (E North Am & C America)
1200-1300 [S] Sa/Su 5990 (E North Am), [S] Sa/Su 9515, [W] 11805 & [S] Sa/Su 15305 (E North Am & C America)
1300-1400 [W] Sa/Su 11805 & [W] Sa/Su 13655 (E North Am & C America)
1600-1700 [S] 9515, [S] 13650 & [S] 15305 (E North Am & C America)
1900-2000 [S] *5995* (S Europe & N Africa), [S] *15245* (N Africa & W Africa), [S] 15325 (W Europe), [S] 17570 (W Africa), [S] 17870 (W Europe & N Africa)
2000-2100 ⬅ *7235* (N Africa)
2000-2100 [W] 9770 (W Europe), [W] *11725* (W Africa), [W] 13650 (N Africa), [W] 15325 (W Africa)
2130-2200 [S] *7235* (N Africa & W Africa), [S] 9590 & [S] 11920 (E North Am & C America), [S] *13690* (N Africa & W Africa), [S] 15325 (W Europe), [S] 17870 (W Europe & N Africa), [S] 17880 (S America)
2200-2300 [W] *9810* (E Asia & SE Asia), [S] *11755* (W Africa), [S] *11810* (E Asia), [W] *11835* (W Africa), [W] *12045* & [S] *17835* (E Asia & SE Asia)
2230-2300 ⬅ *5850* (W Europe)
2230-2300 [W] *6045* (W Europe & N Africa), [W] 9755 (E North Am & C America), [W] 9770 (W Europe), [W] *9805* (N Africa & W Africa), [W] 11865 (C America & S America), [W] 12005 (W Africa), [W] 13730 (C America & S America)
2300-2400 [S] 5960 (E North Am & C America), [S] 15170 (C America & S America), [S] 17880 (S America)

CHINA RADIO INTERNATIONAL
Chinese

0200-0300 *9580* (E North Am), *9690* (N America & C America), 15435/17680 (S America)
0300-0400 *9720* (W North Am)
0900-1000 9665 (E Asia), 11700 & 11875 (Australasia), [S] 11975 & 15110 (E Asia), 15440 (Australasia)
0900-1100 7360, 15340 & 17785 (SE Asia)
1200-1400 11875 (Australasia), 15340 & 17785 (SE Asia)
1500-1600 [W] 7180, [W] 7265, [S] 11760 & [S] 11825 (S Asia)
1730-1830 [W] 6150 & [W] 7120 (Europe), [W] 7160 (Mideast), [W] 7315 (N Africa), 9645 (W Africa & C Africa), [S] 9685 (Mideast & N Africa), [W] 9745 (Mideast), [S] 11660 (Europe), [S] 11760 (Mideast & N Africa), [S] 11835 (N Africa), [S] 13610 (Europe)

2000-2100	[W] 7220/7660 (E Europe), [W] 7245 (Mideast), [W] 7335 (Europe), 9685 (Mideast), [W] 9720 & [S] 9765 (E Europe), [S] 11610 & [S] 11650 (Mideast & N Africa), [S] 11870 (E Europe), [S] 13775 (Europe), [S] 13790 (Mideast)
2200-2300	[W] 7190 (E Africa & S Africa), [W] 7265 (Mideast & W Asia), 9460 & 9550 (SE Asia), [S] 9585 (Mideast & W Asia), 11945 (SE Asia), [S] 15110 (E Asia), 15260 & 15400 (SE Asia)
2230-2300	*15500* (C Africa & E Africa)
2230-2400	*11975* (N Africa)
2300-2400	*7170* (W Africa)

Cantonese

0400-0500	*9790* (W North Am)
1000-1100	15440 (Australasia), 17755 (SE Asia)
1000-1200	11875 (Australasia)
1100-1200	9590, 15340 & 17785 (SE Asia)
1200-1300	*9570* (E North Am), *11855* (E North Am & C America)
1700-1800	[W] 7220 (E Africa & S Africa), 9770 & [S] 15580 (E Africa)
1900-2000	7255 (Europe), [W] 9720 & [S] 9765 (E Europe), [S] 11895 (Europe)
2300-2400	9460, 9550, 11945, 15100, 15260 & 15400 (SE Asia)

CHINA (TAIWAN)

CENTRAL BROADCASTING SYSTEM- CBS

Amoy

0000-0100	*15440* (W North Am)
0000-0200	11875 (SE Asia)
0600-0700	*9680* (N America)
0600-0800	15580 (SE Asia)
0800-0900	11715 (SE Asia)
1000-1100	11605 (E Asia), 15465 (SE Asia)
1300-1400	11635 & 15465 (SE Asia)
2100-2200	*5950* (E North Am)

Chinese

0100-0200	[W] *11825* & [S] *17845* (S America)

0400-0500	*5950* (W North Am), *9680* (N America), 15270 & 15320 (SE Asia)
0500-0600	*11740* (C America)
0900-1000	11520 (SE Asia), 11605 (E Asia), 11635 (SE Asia), 11715 (Australasia), 15525 (SE Asia)
1100-1200	11715 (Australasia)
1200-1300	11605 (E Asia), 15465 (SE Asia)
1300-1500	7445 (SE Asia)
1500-1700	15265 (SE Asia)
1900-2000	[W] *9355*, 9955 & [S] *15600* (Europe)
2200-2300	*3965* (W Europe)
2200-2400	*5950* (E North Am), 11635 (SE Asia), *15440* (W North Am)

Cantonese

0100-0200	*5950* (E North Am), 15290 (SE Asia), *15440* (W North Am)
0200-0300	15610 (SE Asia)
0500-0600	*5950* (W North Am), *9680* (N America), 15320 & 15580 (SE Asia)
1000-1100	11635 (SE Asia), 11715 (Australasia), 15525 (SE Asia)
1000-1200	15270 (SE Asia)
1200-1400	6105/6060 (E Asia), 11915 (SE Asia)

CROATIA—Croatian

CROATIAN RADIO

0500-1000	[W] 7365 (Europe & Mideast)
0500-1800	[⊡] 9830 (Europe & Mideast)
0500-2400	[⊡] 6165 (Europe)
0900-1000	[S] 13830 (Europe)
1000-2200	13830 (Europe & Mideast)
2200-2300	[S] 13830 (Europe)

VOICE OF CROATIA

0000-0200	[S] *9925* (E North Am & S America)
0000-0300	[W] *7285* (E North Am & S America)
0220-0230 & 0250-0300	[S] *9925* (E North Am & S America)
0300-0400	[S] *9925* (W North Am & S America)

0320-0330 &
0350-0400   ▨ *7285* (N America & S America)
0400-0600   ▨ *7285* (W North Am)
0400-0700   ▧ *9925* (W North Am)
0500-0800   *9470* (Australasia)
0700-1100   ▧ *13820* (Australasia)
0800-1000   ▨ *9470* (Australasia)
2300-2400   ▨ *7285* (S America), ▧ *9925* (E North Am & S America)

CUBA—Spanish

RADIO HABANA CUBA

0000-0100 ▭   Tu-Sa 6000 (E North Am), Tu-Sa 11875 (S America)
0000-0100   6040 (E North Am), 9820 (N America)
0000-0500   5965 (C America & W North Am), 9550 (C America & E North Am), 9600 (S America), 11760 (E North Am), 15230 (S America)
1100-1400   6000 (C America)
1100-1500   11760 (E North Am)
1200-1400   9550 (C America), 15230 (S America)
2100-2300   13750 & 15120 (Europe), 15230 (S America)
2300-2400 ▭   M-F 6000 (E North Am), M-F 11875 (S America)

RADIO REBELDE

24 Hr   5025
0300-0400   6120 (C America)
1000-1300   9600 (C America)
1100-1300   6140/11655 (C America)

CZECH REPUBLIC—Czech

RADIO PRAGUE

0030-0100   ▨ 7345 (N America), ▨ 9440 (S America)
0130-0200   ▧ 6200 (N America & C America), ▧ 7345 (S America)
0230-0300   ▨ 6200 (N America & C America), ▧ 7345 (N America), ▨ 7345 (S America), ▧ 9870 (W North Am & C America)
0330-0400   ▨ 5915 (W North Am & C America), ▨ 7345 (N America)

0830-0900   ▧ 11600 (W Europe), ▧ 21745 (E Africa & Mideast)
0930-1000   ▨ 15255 (W Europe), ▧ 21745 (S Asia & W Africa), ▨ 21745 (E Africa & Mideast)
1030-1100   ▨ 21745 (S Asia & W Africa)
1100-1130   ▧ 11615 (N Europe), ▧ 21745 (S Asia)
1200-1230   ▨ 11640 (N Europe), ▨ 21745 (S Asia, SE Asia & Australasia)
1330-1400 ▭ 6055 (Europe), 7345 (W Europe)
1330-1400   ▧ 13580 (N Europe), ▧ 21745 (S Asia)
1430-1500   ▨ 21745 (N America & E Africa)
1530-1600   ▧ 21745 (E Africa)
1630-1700 ▭ 5930 (W Europe)
1630-1700   ▨ 17485 (W Africa & C Africa)
1730-1800   ▧ 5930 (E Europe, SE Asia & Australasia), ▧ 17485 (C Africa)
1830-1900   ▨ 5930 (W Europe), ▨ 9495 (E Europe, Asia & Australasia)
1930-2000   ▧ 11600 (SE Asia & Australasia)
2030-2100 ▭ 5930 (W Europe)
2030-2100   ▨ 9430 (SE Asia & Australasia)
2100-2130   ▧ 11600 (SE Asia & Australasia), ▧ 13580 (W Africa)
2200-2230   ▨ 5930 (W Europe), ▨ 9435 (W Europe & S America)
2330-2400   ▧ 9440 & ▧ 11615 (S America)

EGYPT—Arabic

EGYPTIAN RADIO

0000-0030 ▭ 11665 (C Africa & E Africa)
0000-0400 ▭ 12050 (Europe & E North Am)
0300-1900 ▭ 15285 (Mideast)
0350-0700 ▭ 9855 (Mideast)
0600-1400 ▭ 11720 (S Europe, N Africa & Mideast)
0700-1100 ▭ 15115 (W Africa)
0700-1200 ▭ 9800 (Mideast)
1100-1600 ▭ 17675 (N Africa)
1100-2400 ▭ 11540 (S Europe, N Africa & Mideast)

1200-2400 ⬛ 12050 (Europe & E North Am)
1900-2400 ⬛ 11665 (C Africa & E Africa)

RADIO CAIRO

0000-0045 11755 & 15590 (S America)
0030-0430 9900/11725 (E North Am)
1015-1215 17775 (Mideast)
1100-1130 17800 (E Africa & S Africa)
1300-1600 15220 (C Africa)
2000-2200 11750 (Australasia)
2330-2400 11755 & 15590 (S America)

FRANCE—French

RADIO FRANCE INTERNATIONALE

0000-0030 🆆 15440 & 🆂 17710 (SE Asia)
0000-0100 🆆 9805 & 🆂 11660 (S Asia & SE Asia), 🆆 12025 (SE Asia), 15200 (S America), 🆂 15535 (SE Asia)
0100-0200 🆆 15440 & 🆂 17710 (S Asia)
0130-0200 🆆 9790 (C America), 🆆 9800 (S America), 9800 & 11665 (C America), 🆂 11995 (S America)
0200-0230 15200 (S America)
0300-0400 🆆 5915 (Mideast & E Africa), 🆆 5945 (E Europe & Mideast), 9550 (Mideast), 🆂 9825, 🆂 11700, 11995 & 🆂 13610 (E Africa)
0300-0500 🆆 7315 (Mideast)
0300-0600 9790 (Africa), 🆆 9845 (E Africa)
0300-0700 7135 (Africa)
0330-0500 🆂 9745 (E Europe)
0400-0430 🆆 Sa/Su 11910, 🆂 11995, 🆆 Sa/Su 11995, Sa/Su 13610 (Irr) & 🆂 Sa/Su 15155 (E Africa)
0400-0445 🆂 7280 (E Europe)
0400-0500 🆆 3965 (N Africa), 4890 (C Africa), 🆂 5925 (N Africa), 🆂 7150 & 🆆 7270 (C Africa & S Africa), 🆆 9805 (C Africa), 11850 (Mideast), 🆂 13780 (Mideast & E Africa)
0400-0600 ⬛ 11685 (Mideast)
0400-0600 🆆 9550 (Mideast), 11700 (C Africa & S Africa), 🆂 15135 (E Africa), 🆆 15210 (Mideast & E Africa), 🆂 15605 (Mideast & W Asia)
0430-0445 🆆 5990 (E Europe)
0430-0500 ⬛ 7280 (E Europe)
0430-0500 🆆 11910, 11995, 13610 (Irr) & 🆂 15155 (E Africa)
0430-0600 ⬛ 6045 (E Europe)
0500-0530 🆆 Sa/Su 13610 (E Africa), 🆆 Sa/Su 15155 (E Africa & S Africa), 🆂 Sa/Su 17800 (E Africa)
0500-0600 6175 (C Africa), 🆆 11995 (E Africa), 🆂 13640 (Mideast & E Africa), 🆂 15300 (C Africa & S Africa), 15605 (N Africa & Mideast)
0500-0700 🆆 11700 (C Africa & S Africa), 🆂 17620 (E Africa)
0530-0600 🆆 13610 (E Africa), 🆆 15155 (E Africa & S Africa), 🆂 17800 (E Africa)
0600-0630 🆂 Sa/Su 11665, 🆆 Sa/Su 11710 & 🆆 Sa/Su 11725 (W Africa), 🆆 Sa/Su 15155, Sa/Su 17800 & 🆂 Sa/Su 21620 (E Africa)
0600-0700 🆆 5925 (N Africa), 🆆 6175 (E Europe), 9790 (N Africa & W Africa), 🆂 9790 (C Africa), 🆆 15135 (Mideast), 15300 (C Africa & S Africa), 15315 (Irr) (W Africa), 🆂 17650 (Mideast), 17770 (C Africa), 🆂 17850 (C Africa & S Africa)
0600-0800 11700 (N Africa & W Africa)
0630-0700 🆂 11665, 🆆 11710 & 🆆 11725 (W Africa), 🆆 15155, 17800 & 🆂 21620 (E Africa)
0700-0800 🆆 7135 (N Africa), 🆆 9790 (N Africa & W Africa), 9790 (C Africa), 9805 (E Europe), 🆆 11975 (N Europe), 15170 (C Africa), 🆂 15300 (N Africa & W Africa), 🆆 15300 (C Africa & S Africa), 15315 & 🆂 17620 (W Africa), 17850 (C Africa & S Africa)
0700-1130 11670 (E Europe)
0800-0900 🆂 15315, 17620 & 🆆 21685 (W Africa)
0800-1000 15300 (N Africa & W Africa), 🆆 21580 (C Africa & S Africa)

0800-1600	11845 (N Africa)
0900-0930	◪ *9715* & ◪ *11670* (S America)
0900-1000	◪ 17620 (W Africa)
0900-1200	21620 & 25820 (E Africa)
0900-1600	*21685* (W Africa)
1000-1100	15155 (E Europe), 15300 (W Africa), 17850 (C Africa & S Africa)
1000-1600	21580 (C Africa & S Africa)
1030-1100	*15435* (S America)
1030-1200	◪ *7140* & ◪ *9830* (E Asia), ◪ *9830*, ◪ *11890* & ◪ *15215* (SE Asia)
1100-1130	◪ 17610 (Irr) (E North Am & C America)
1100-1200	6175 (W Europe & Atlantic), *11600* (SE Asia), ◪ *11670*, *13640* & *15515* (C America), ◪ 17570 (E North Am & C America), *21755* (S Africa)
1100-1300	◪ 17620 (W Africa)
1100-1400	15300 (N Africa & W Africa), *17720* (C Africa)
1130-1200	◪ 17610 (E North Am & C America)
1200-1230	◪ *21760* (W Africa)
1200-1400	*9790* (C Africa)
1230-1300	*15515* (C America), *21760* (W Africa), 25820 (E Africa)
1230-1330	*17860* (C America)
1300-1400	17620 (W Africa), *21645* (C America)
1330-1400	M-Sa *17860* (C America)
1400-1500	17650 (Mideast)
1400-1600	15300 (W Africa)
1500-1600	◪ 15605 (Mideast & W Asia), 17605 & 17620 (E Africa), ◪ 17650 (Mideast), 17850 (C Africa & S Africa), 21620 (E Africa)
1600-1700	*6090* (SE Asia), 11700 (N Africa), ◪ 15300 (W Africa), ◪ 17605 & ◪ 21620 (E Africa)
1600-1800	◪ 15300 (Africa), ◪ 21580 (C Africa & S Africa)
1700-1800	◪ 5960 (N Europe), ◪ 11670 (E Europe), 11700 (Irr) (N Africa), ◪ 15300 (N Africa & W Africa), ◪ 17620 (W Africa & E Africa)
1700-2000	◪ 11965 (W Africa)
1730-1800	◪ 11615 & ◪ 15605 (Mideast), ◪ 15605 & ◪ 17605 (E Africa)
1800-1900	◪ 5900 (E Europe), ◪ 5970 (N Europe), ◪ 11615 (N Africa), ◪ 17620 (E Africa)
1800-2000	◪ 9790 (N Africa & W Africa), ◪ 11615 (W Africa), 11705 (Africa), ◪ 11995 (E Africa), 15300 (Africa), ◪ 15460 (E Africa)
1800-2200	*7160* (C Africa), *11955* (W Africa)
1900-2000	◪ 3965 (Europe), ◪ 6175 (N Europe), ◪ 7315 (N Africa), ◪ 9485 (E Africa), ◪ 17620 (W Africa)
1900-2200	*5925* (C Africa)
2000-2100	◪ 6175 (N Africa), ◪ 15300 (Africa)
2000-2200	◪ 5960 (S Europe), 7315 (N Africa), 9485 (E Africa), 9790 (N Africa & W Africa), ◪ 9790 (C Africa & S Africa), 11995 (E Africa)
2100-2200	◪ 3965 (N Africa), ◪ 5915 (E Europe), 6175 (N Africa), ◪ 9805 (E Europe), ◪ 15300 (C Africa & S Africa)
2200-2300	◪ 9790 (W Africa)
2230-2300	*17620* (S America)
2300-2400	◪ 9805 & ◪ 11660 (S Asia & SE Asia), ◪ *12025* (SE Asia), ◪ *12075* (E Asia), ◪ *15440*, ◪ *15535*, ◪ *15595* & ◪ *17710* (SE Asia)
2330-2400	◪ 9790 (C America), ◪ 9800 (S America), ◪ 11670 (C America), ◪ *11995*, *15200* & *17620* (S America)

GABON—French

AFRIQUE NUMERO UN

0500-2300	9580 (C Africa)
0700-1600	17630 (W Africa)
1600-1900	15475 (W Africa & E North Am)

GERMANY—German

BAYERISCHER RUNDFUNK

0500-2300	◪ 6085

DEUTSCHE WELLE

0000-0200	6075 (Europe), [W] *6075* (N America), [W] *6100* (E North Am), 9545 (S America), [S] 9545 & [S] *9640* (E North Am), [W] *9655* (C America), [S] *11865* (S America), [S] *11960* (W North Am), [W] *13780* (S America), [S] *15275* (C America & S America)
0000-0600	3995 (Europe)
0200-0400	[W] 6075 (Mideast & W Asia), [W] *6100* (N America), [W] 6145 & [S] *9640* (N America & C America), [W] *9870* (C America)
0200-0600	6075 (Europe & N America), [S] 6100 (E North Am), [S] 9735 (N America)
0400-0600	[W] *6100* (W North Am), [W] 6145 (N America), [S] *11970* (W North Am)
0600-0800	[W] 3995 & 6075 (Europe), 9735 & *11985* (Australasia)
0600-1000	9690 & 11795 (Australasia), *21640* & [S] 21840 (SE Asia & Australasia)
0600-1800	13780 (Mideast)
0600-2000	9545 (S Europe & Atlantic)
0800-1000	[W] 9735 (Australasia)
0800-1800	6075 (Europe)
1000-1200	[W] *17650* (E Asia), [W] 21840 (SE Asia & Australasia)
1000-1400	[W] *5910*, [W] *7400* & [S] *7430* (E Asia), [S] *9900* (S Asia & SE Asia), [S] *17485* (SE Asia & Australasia), [W] *17845* & [S] *21640* (E Asia & SE Asia), [S] 21840 (W Asia & C Asia)
1200-1400	[W] 9655 (Europe), [W] *12030* (E Asia), [W] 13780 & [W] 17650 (Asia & Australasia)
1200-1600	[S] *12090/15720* (C Asia)
1400-1600	[W] 6130 & [S] 6180 (Europe), [W] 13780 (S Asia, SE Asia & Australasia), 15275 (S Asia & SE Asia), [W] *17840* (W Asia), [S] 17845 (S Asia & SE Asia)
1400-1800	*9655* (S Asia), [S] 17845 & [S] *21790* (Mideast)
1600-1730	[W] 3995 (Europe)
1600-1800	[W] 11795 & [S] 13780 (S Asia & SE Asia), [W] 13780 (E Africa), [W] *15215* (W Asia), [S] 15275 (S Asia)
1800-2000	[W] 3995 (Europe), 6075 (Europe & E Africa), [W] 9735 (W Africa & E Africa)
1800-2200	[S] *7185* (S Africa), [S] 9735 & [S] 11795 (Africa), [W] 11795 (C Africa & S Africa), [W] *11945* (S Africa), [S] 13780 (Africa), [S] 13810 (W Africa & S America), *17860* (W Africa & C America)
2000-2200	6075 (Europe), 9545 (Atlantic & S America), [W] 9735 (W Africa)
2000-2400	3995 (Europe)
2200-2400	6075 (Europe), [W] *6225* (E Asia), 9545 (S America), *11690* (C America), [S] *11865* (S America), [W] *11955* (N America), [S] 13780 (E North Am), [W] *13780* (S America), [S] *15275* (C America & S America), [S] *15410* (E North Am), [W] *17860* (C America)

German travelers can use world band to keep in touch with home. Nova

DEUTSCHLANDRADIO—(Europe)
24 Hr   6005
SUDWESTRUNDFUNK—(Europe)
24 Hr   7265
0455-2305 ▭ 6030

GREECE—Greek

FONI TIS HELLADAS
0000-0350   7475 (N America)
0000-0400   9420 (W Africa & S America),
              15630 (Mideast, S Asia &
              Australasia)
0000-0550   Ⓦ 5865 (W Europe & Atlantic)
0350-0550   Ⓦ 7475 (N America)
0400-0550   Ⓢ 9420 (Europe)
0400-0600   Ⓢ 15630 (W Europe &
              Atlantic)
0400-0700   17520 (Mideast, S Asia &
              Australasia)
0400-0800   21530 (Mideast, S Asia &
              Australasia)
0550-0650   Ⓢ 9420 (Europe)
0600-0650   15630 (W Europe & Atlantic)

I Foni tis Helladas links Greek expatriates and mariners
to the motherland.   Nova

0600-0800   Ⓦ 9420 (Europe), Ⓦ *11900* & Ⓢ
              15190 (E Asia & Australasia)
0650-0700   Ⓦ 15630 (W Europe &
              Atlantic)
0700-0800   Ⓢ W-M 15630 & Ⓦ 15630 (W
              Europe & Atlantic), Ⓦ 17520
              (Mideast, S Asia &
              Australasia), Ⓢ W-M 17900 (W
              Europe & Atlantic)
0800-0830   W-M 15630 & Ⓢ W-M 17900
              (W Europe & Atlantic)
0800-0930   Ⓦ W-M 9420 (Europe)
0830-0900   Ⓦ W-M 15630 (W Europe &
              Atlantic)
0900-0930   W-M 15630 (W Europe &
              Atlantic)
0930-1000   Ⓢ W-M 15630 (W Europe &
              Atlantic)
1100-1200   Ⓦ W-M 15630 (W Europe &
              Atlantic)
1100-1250   Ⓢ 12105 (Europe), Ⓢ 17900 (W
              Europe & Atlantic)
1100-1300   Ⓦ 9420 (Europe)
1200-1300   Ⓦ 15630 (W Europe &
              Atlantic)
1200-1500   Ⓦ *9825* & Ⓢ *11730* (N America)
1300-1400 ▭ 15650 (Mideast & C Asia)
1300-1600   9420 (Europe), 15630 (W
              Europe & Atlantic)
1600-1700   Ⓢ Su-F 9420 & Ⓦ 9420
              (Europe), Ⓢ Su-F 15630 & Ⓦ
              15630 (W Europe & Atlantic),
              Ⓢ Su-F *17705* & Ⓦ *17705* (N
              America)
1700-1800   Ⓢ 9420 & Ⓦ Su-F 9420
              (Europe), Ⓢ 15630 & Ⓦ Su-F
              15630 (W Europe & Atlantic),
              Ⓢ *17705* & Ⓦ Su-F *17705* (N
              America)
1800-1850   Ⓦ 15630 (W Europe &
              Atlantic)
1800-1900   Ⓢ M-Sa 9420 & Ⓦ 9420
              (Europe), Ⓢ M-Sa 15630 (W
              Europe & Atlantic), Ⓢ M-Sa
              17705 & Ⓦ *17705* (N America)
1900-2000   Ⓦ M-Sa 5865 (W Europe &
              Atlantic), Ⓢ 9420 & Ⓦ M-Sa
              9420 (Europe), Ⓢ *17705* & Ⓦ
              M-Sa *17705* (N America)

1900-2050	**[S]** 12105 (Europe), **[S]** 15630 (W Europe & Atlantic)
2000-2100	**[W]** 7475 & 9420 (Europe)
2000-2200	*17565* (S America), *17705* (N America)
2000-2400	**[W]** 5865 (W Europe & Atlantic)
2100-2300	9420 & **[S]** 12110 (Australasia)
2100-2400	**[S]** 9375 (W Europe & Atlantic), **[W]** 15650 (Australasia)
2300-2400	7475 (W Europe & Atlantic), **[W]** 9420, **[S]** 12105 & **[S]** 12110 (W Africa & S America)

HUNGARY—Hungarian

RADIO BUDAPEST

0000-0100	**[W]** M 9580 (S America), **[S]** 9800 (N America), **[W]** M 12010 (S America)
0100-0200	**[W]** 9835 (N America)
0130-0230	**[S]** 9570 (N America)
0230-0330	**[W]** 9835 (N America)
0500-1300 **[◻]**	6025 (Europe)
1200-1300 **[◻]**	21560 (Australasia)
1300-1400 **[◻]**	M-Sa 6025 (Europe)
1400-1500 **[◻]**	6025 (Europe)
1500-1700 **[◻]**	M-Sa 6025 (Europe)
1700-1800	**[S]** 15275 (S Africa)
1800-1900	**[S]** 7170 (N Europe)
1900-2000 **[◻]**	3975 & 6025 (Europe)
1900-2000	**[W]** 11925 (Australasia)
2000-2100	**[W]** 11785/11895 (S Africa), **[S]** 11890 (N America)
2100-2200	**[S]** 9780 (Australasia)
2200-2300	**[W]** 9825 (N America), **[S]** 9850 & **[S]** 11990 (S America)
2300-2400 **[◻]**	6025 (Europe)
2300-2400	**[W]** 9580, **[S]** Su 9850, **[S]** Su 11990 & **[W]** 12010 (S America)

INDIA—Hindi

ALL INDIA RADIO

0000-0040 &	
0130-0530	9425 & 9470 (S Asia)
0315-0415	11840 (W Asia & Mideast), 13695 (Mideast), 15075 (Mideast & E Africa), 15185 & 17715 (E Africa)
0430-0530	15075, 15185 & 17715 (E Africa)
0930-1200	9425 (S Asia)
1000-1230	9470 (S Asia)
1320-2400	9425 & 9470 (S Asia)
1615-1730	7410 (Mideast & W Asia), 9950 (E Africa), 12025 & 13770 (W Asia & Mideast), 15075 & 17670 (E Africa)
1945-2045	7410, 9950 & 11620 (Europe)
2300-2400	9910, 11740 & 13795 (SE Asia)

ISRAEL

GALEI ZAHAL—(Europe)
Hebrew

24 Hr	6973/15785

KOL ISRAEL
Arabic

0400-2215 **[◻]**	5915 (Mideast & N Africa), 12150 (Mideast & W Asia)

Hebrew

0000-0330	11585 (W Europe & E North Am)
0000-0400	**[S]** 13850 (W Europe & E North Am)
0000-0500	**[W]** 9310 & **[S]** 15760 (W Europe & E North Am)
0000-0600	**[W]** 7545 (W Europe & N America)
0330-0500	**[S]** 11590 (W Europe & E North Am)
0330-0600	**[W]** 11585 (W Europe & E North Am)
0400-0600	**[S]** 17535 (W Europe & E North Am)
0500-1800	15760 (W Europe & E North Am)
0600-1900	17535 (W Europe & E North Am)
1600-1700	**[S]** 11585 (W Europe & E North Am)
1700-2400	11585 (W Europe & E North Am)
1800-2400	**[W]** 9310 & **[S]** 15760 (W Europe & E North Am)
1900-2300	**[W]** 9390 (W Europe & E North Am)
1900-2400	**[S]** 17535 (W Europe & E North Am)
2100-2215 **[◻]**	15640 (S America)
2300-2400	**[W]** 7545 (W Europe & N America)

ITALY—Italian

RAI INTERNATIONAL

0000-0055	9675 (N America), 9840 (S America), 11800 (N America), 12030 (S America)
0130-0230	*6110* (S America), *11765* (C America)
0130-0315	9675 (N America), 9840 (S America), 11800 (N America), 12030 (S America)
0435-0445	◰ 5965 (S Europe & N Africa), ◰ 6100 & ◪ 6110 (N Africa), ◰ 7230, ◪ 7235 & ◪ 9875 (S Europe & N Africa)
0455-0530	◪ 11900 & ◰ 11985 (E Africa)
0630-1300	9670 & 11800 (E Europe)
1000-1100	*11920* (Australasia)
1350-1730	◪ Su 9670 & ◰ Su 9850 (W Europe), Su/Holidays 21520 (N America), Su/Holidays 21535 (S America), Su/Holidays 21710 (C Africa & S Africa)
1400-1425	M-Sa 17780 (N America)
1400-1430	M-Sa 21520 (N America)
1500-1525	M-Sa 9670 (S Europe & N Africa), ◪ M-Sa 11800 (N Africa & Mideast), ◰ M- Sa 11800 (S Europe & N Africa), ◪ M-Sa 11880 (N Africa & Mideast), ◰ M- Sa 11880 (S Europe & N Africa)
1555-1625	M-Sa 9670 & M-Sa 11855 (W Europe)
1700-1800	◰ 6185 (Europe), M-Sa 9670 (S Europe & N Africa), ◪ 9730 (E Africa), 11725 (S Europe & N Africa), ◰ 11875 (E Africa), ◰ 15320, *15320* & ◪ 17880 (C Africa & S Africa)
1820-2020	Sa 11785 (E Africa), ◰ Sa 15250 (N America), ◰ Sa 21550 (S America), ◰ Sa 21710 (C Africa & S Africa)
1830-1905	◰ Su-F 15250, 17780 & ◪ 21520 (N America)
2240-2400	9675 (N America), 9840 (S America), 11800 (N America), 12030 (S America)

RAI-RADIOTELEVISIONE ITALIANA—
(Europe, Mideast & N Africa)

0000-0003,		
0012-0103,		
0112-0203,		
0212-0303,		
0312-0403,		
0412-0500 &		
2300-2400	▭	6060

JAPAN—Japanese

RADIO JAPAN

0200-0300	*11860* (SE Asia), 17825 (C America), 17845 (E Asia), 21610 (Australasia)
0200-0400	*5960* (E North Am), 15325 (S Asia), 17560 (Mideast), 17685 (Australasia), 17835 (S America), ◪ 17875 (W North Am)
0200-0500	15195 (E Asia), 17810 (SE Asia)
0300-0400	*9660* (S America), *11890* (S Asia)
0700-0800	6145, 6165 & 15195 (E Asia), 17870 (Pacific)
0700-0900	17860 (SE Asia)
0700-1000	*11740* (SE Asia), *11920* & 21755 (Australasia)
0800-1000	*9530* (S America), ◰ 9540 (C America), 9825 (Pacific & S America), *11710* (Europe), ◪ 12030 (C America), 15590 (S Asia), *17650* (W Africa), ◪ *21550* (Mideast)
0800-1500	9750 (E Asia)
0900-1500	11815 (SE Asia)
1300-1500	*11705* (E North Am)
1500-1600	9505 (W North Am)
1500-1700	◰ 9535 & ◪ 11895 (C America), *12045* (S Asia), *21630* (C Africa)
1600-1700	◪ 9505 (W North Am), 9750 (E Asia), ◰ 9845 & ◪ 11730 (S Asia)
1600-1800	7140 (Australasia)
1600-1900	6035 (E Asia), 7200 (SE Asia)
1700-1800	*9750* (Europe), *21600* (S America)
1700-1900	*6175* (W Europe), 9835 (Pacific & S America), *11880* (Mideast)
1800-1900	*15355* (S Africa)
1900-2000	◰ 11665 (SE Asia), *11675* (Australasia)

1900-2100	6165 (E Asia)
1900-2400	11910 (E Asia), ☒ 13680 (SE Asia)
2000-2100	☒ 6035 (Australasia), 11830 (Europe), ☒ 11920 (Australasia)
2000-2200	☒ 7225 & 11665 (SE Asia)
2200-2300	6110 (E North Am), 6115 (W Europe), ☒ 11770 (Australasia), 11895 (C America), 15220 (S America), 17825 (W North Am)
2200-2400	☒ 11665 (SE Asia)
2300-2400	17605 (S America)

RADIO TAMPA

0000-0800	3925, Sa/Su 9760
0000-0900	Sa/Su 3945, Sa/Su 6115
0000-1400	6055, 9595
0800-1400 &	
2030-2300	3925
2030-2400	6055, 9595
2300-2400	3925, F/Sa 3945, F/Sa 6115, F/Sa 9760

KOREA (DPR)—Korean

KOREAN CENTRAL BS

0000-0630	6100
0000-0930	9665
0000-1800	2850, 11680
0900-0950	4405, 7140 & 9345 (E Asia)
1200-1250	3560 (E Asia), 9335 (C America), 9850/13650 (SE Asia), 11710 (C America), 11735 (SE Asia)
1400-1450	3560 (E Asia), 9850/13650 & 11735 (SE Asia)
1500-1800	6100
1700-1750	7505/13760 (Europe), 9335 (N America), 11335/15245 (Europe), 11710 (N America)
2000-2050	3560 & 4405 (E Asia), 6520/9640 (C Africa), 6575 & 9325 (E Europe), 9975 & 11735 (Mideast & Africa)
2000-2400	2850, 6100, 9665, 11680
2300-2350	3560 & 7140 (E Asia), 7505/13760 (Europe), 9345 & 9975 (E Asia), 11335/15245 (Europe), 11735 (E Asia)

RADIO PYONGYANG

0000-0050	3560, 4405, 7140 & 9345 (E Asia)
0000-0100	6195 (E Asia)
0000-0925	6250 (E Asia)
0700-0750	4405, 7140 & 9345 (E Asia)
0900-0950	3560 & 6575/11735 (E Asia), 9325 (E Europe & Asia), 9975 (E Asia), 11335/15245 (E Europe)
1000-1050 &	
1200-1250	4405, 7140 & 9345 (E Asia)
1300-1350	4405 (E Asia), 6575 & 9325 (E Europe)
1500-1900 &	
2100-2400	6250 (E Asia)

KOREA (REPUBLIC)—Korean

RADIO KOREA INTERNATIONAL

0100-0200	15575 (N America)
0300-0400	11810 (E Asia)
0700-0800	9535 (Europe)
0900-1000	15210/9640 (Europe)
0900-1100	5975 & 7275 (E Asia), 9570 (SE Asia), 13670 (Europe)
1100-1130	9650 (E North Am)
1200-1300	7275 (E Asia)
1600-1800	7275 (Europe)
1700-1900	5975 (E Asia), 7150 (Mideast)
1800-2000	9870 (Mideast & E Africa), 15575 (Europe)
2100-2300	5975 (E Asia)

KUWAIT—Arabic

RADIO KUWAIT

0000-0530	11675 (W North Am)
0200-1305	6055 (Mideast & W Asia), 15495 (Mideast)
0400-0740	15505 (E Europe & W Asia)
0800-0925	15110 (S Asia & SE Asia)
0930-1605	13620 (Europe & E North Am)
1015-1740	15505 (W Africa & C Africa)
1200-1505	17885 (SE Asia)
1315-1600	15110 (S Asia & SE Asia)
1315-2130	9880 (Mideast)
1615-1800	11990 (Europe & E North Am)
1745-2130	15505 (Europe & E North Am)
1745-2400	15495 (W Africa & C Africa)
1815-2400	9855 (Europe & E North Am)
2145-2400	11675 (W North Am)

LITHUANIA—Lithuanian
RADIO VILNIUS
0000-0030	🔲 7325 & 🔳 11690 (E North Am)
0900-0930 📧	9710 (W Europe)
2300-2330	9875 (E North Am)

MEXICO—Spanish
RADIO EDUCACION
0000-0830 📧	6185
0830-0900 📧	Th-Tu 6185
0900-1200 📧	6185

RADIO MEXICO INTERNACIONAL—(W North Am & C America)
0030-0500 📧	9705 & 11770
0500-0600 📧	Tu-Su 9705 & Tu-Su 11770
1300-1500 📧	9705 & 11770
1500-1530 📧	Sa/Su 9705 & Sa/Su 11770
1530-2200 📧	9705 & 11770
2200-2215 📧	Tu/Th/Sa/Su 9705 & Tu/Th/Sa/Su 11770
2215-2400 📧	9705 & 11770

MOROCCO
RADIO MEDI UN—(Europe & N Africa)
Arabic & French
0500-0400	9575

RTV MAROCAINE
Arabic
0000-0500	🔲 5980 (N Africa), 🔳 11920 (N Africa & Mideast)
0900-2200	15345 (N Africa & Mideast)
1100-1500	15335 (Europe)
2200-2400	7135 (Europe)

Mexico's direct broadcasts supplement Univision for present and former countrymen within the United States. Nova

NETHERLANDS—Dutch
RADIO NEDERLAND
0300-0355	*6165* (N America), *9590* (C America)
0600-0655 📧	7125 (Europe)
0600-0655	*6165* (W North Am)
0600-0855 📧	9895 (S Europe)
0600-0855	🔲 6015 (S Europe)
0600-1755 📧	5955 (W Europe)
0700-0800	🔲 *9625*, 🔳 *9820* & *11655* (Australasia)
0700-0855 📧	11935 (S Europe)
0900-1555 📧	Sa/Su 9895 & Sa/Su 13700 (S Europe)
0930-1015	M-Sa *6020* (C America)
1000-1055	*13820* (E Asia)
1300-1355	🔲 *9865* & 🔳 *9890* (E Asia & SE Asia), 🔲 *12070* (S Asia), *17580* & *17815* (SE Asia), *21480* (S Asia)
1300-1400	🔲 *7375* (E Asia & SE Asia)
1500-1755 📧	13700 (S Europe)
1600-1655	*15335* & *17695* (Mideast)
1600-1755 📧	9895 (S Europe)
1700-1755	*6020* (S Africa), *11655* & 🔳 *15560* (E Africa)
2000-2055	🔲 *11655* (W Africa & C Africa)
2100-2155	*7120* (C Africa), 🔳 *11655* (W Africa), 🔲 *11655* (W Africa & C Africa), *15315* (S America), *17810* (W Africa)
2200-2255	*15315* (S America)
2300-2355	🔲 *6100* (C America & S America), *15315* (S America)

OMAN—Arabic
RADIO SULTANATE OF OMAN
0000-0200	9760 (Europe & Mideast)
0200-0300	🔲 15355 (E Africa)
0200-0400	6085 (Mideast)
0400-0600	9515/9740 (Mideast), 17590 (E Africa)
0600-1000	17630 (Europe & Mideast)
0600-1400	13640 (Mideast)
1400-1800	🔳 13725 & 15375 (E Africa)
1500-1800	15140 (Europe & Mideast)
1800-2000	6190 & 15355 (E Africa)
2000-2200	6085 (E Africa), 13640 (Europe & Mideast)

2200-2400	13755 (Europe & Mideast)
2300-2400	🄂 9760 (Europe & Mideast)

POLAND—Polish

RADIO POLONIA

1130-1200 ▱	7285 (E Europe)
1130-1200	🅆 5965 (N Europe)
1530-1630	🄂 5965 (W Europe)
1630-1730	🅆 6020 (W Europe)
2200-2300 ▱	6050 (E Europe), 7265 (W Europe)

PORTUGAL—Portuguese

RDP INTERNATIONAL

0000-0200	🄂 Tu-Sa 13660 & 🄂 Tu-Sa 15295 (S America)
0000-0300 ▱	Tu-Sa 9715 (E North Am), Tu-Sa 11655 (W North Am), Tu-Sa 13700 (C America)
0000-0300	🅆 Tu-Sa 11980 & 🅆 Tu-Sa 13770 (S America)
0500-0700	🄂 M-F 15585 (W North Am)
0500-0800	🄂 M-F 9840 (Europe)
0500-0900	🄂 M-F 11950 (W Europe)
0500-1200	🄂 M-F 11960 & 🄂 M-F 15555 (W Europe)
0600-0800	🅆 M-F 11675 (W North Am)
0600-0850	🅆 M-F 9755 (Europe)
0600-1300 ▱	M-F 9815 (Europe)
0645-0800	🄂 M-F 11850 (Europe)
0700-0800	🄂 Sa/Su 13640 (Europe)
0700-1300	🄂 Sa/Su 9840 (Europe)
0700-1400	🄂 Sa/Su 13610 (W Europe)
0745-0900	🅆 M-F 11660 (Europe)
0800-0900	🅆 Sa/Su 11875 (Europe)
0800-1100 ▱	Sa/Su 21655 (W Africa & S America), Sa/Su 21830 (E Africa & S Africa)
0800-1200	🄂 13640 (Europe)
0800-1455	🅆 Sa/Su 15575 (W Europe)
0900-1300	🅆 11875 (Europe)
0930-1100 ▱	Sa/Su 11995/9815 (Europe)
1100-1300 ▱	21655 & M-F 21725 (W Africa & S America), 21830 (E Africa & S Africa)
1200-1400	🄂 Sa/Su 13640 (Europe)
1200-2000	🄂 Sa/Su/Holidays 17575 (N America), 🄂 Sa/Su/Holidays 17615/21690 (C America)
1300-1455	🅆 Sa/Su 11875 (Europe)
1300-1500	🄂 M-F 17760 (Mideast & S Asia)
1300-1700 ▱	Sa/Su 21655 & Sa/Su 21800 (W Africa & S America)
1300-1755 ▱	Sa/Su 21830 (E Africa & S Africa)
1300-2100	🅆 Sa/Su/Holidays 15540 (N America), 🅆 Sa/Su/Holidays 17745 (C America)
1400-1600 ▱	M-F 21810 (S Asia)
1400-1600	🄂 Sa/Su 13770 (Europe), 🄂 Sa/Su 15555 (W Europe)
1500-2100	🅆 Sa/Su 13660 (Europe), 🅆 Sa/Su 13790 (W Europe)
1600-1900	🄂 13770, 🄂 15445 & 🄂 M-F 15525 (Europe), 🄂 15555 (W Europe), 🄂 M-F 17650 & 🄂 M-F 17770 (Europe)
1700-1800 ▱	M-F 17680 (E Africa & S Africa)
1700-2000 ▱	21655 & 21800 (W Africa & S America)
1700-2000	🅆 M-F 11800 & 🅆 M-F 13585 (Europe)
1800-1955	🅆 M-F 17745 (Irr) (C America)
1800-2000 ▱	17680 (E Africa & S Africa)
1900-2000	🄂 Sa/Su 13770 (Europe)
1900-2300	🄂 11945 (Irr) (S Africa), 🄂 13720 (Irr) (W Europe), 🄂 15445 (Irr) (Europe), 🄂 15555 (Irr) (W Europe), 🄂 21540 (Irr) (C America)
2000-2100 ▱	Sa/Su 17680 & M-F 17680 (Irr) (E Africa & S Africa), Sa/Su 21800 & M-F 21800 (Irr) (W Africa & S America)
2000-2300	🄂 M-F 15480 (Irr) (N America), 🄂 17575 (Irr) (E North Am), 🄂 Sa/Su 21655 (Irr) (W Africa & S America)
2000-2400	🅆 M-F 11800 (Irr) & 🅆 M-F 11860 (Europe), 🅆 13770 (Irr) (C America)
2100-2400 ▱	17680 (Irr) (E Africa & S Africa), 21800 (Irr) (S America)
2100-2400	🅆 Sa/Su 13660 (Irr) (Europe), 🅆 15540 (Irr) (N America)
2300-2400	🄂 M-F 13660 & 🄂 M-F 15295 (S America)

RUSSIA—Russian

RADIO ROSSII

0000-0700	ⓦ 9700 (E Asia)
0000-1000	ⓢ 15475 (E Asia)
0000-1800 ▱	7220 (N Asia)
0100-0400	ⓢ 11980 (W Africa & S America)
0100-0500	ⓢ 5935 (E Europe), ⓢ 7365 (W Asia & C Asia), ⓢ 12020 (N Europe & E North Am)
0100-0800	ⓢ 12025 (W Asia & C Asia)
0200-0500	ⓦ 6115 (N Europe & E North Am), ⓦ 6125 & ⓦ 7365 (W Asia & C Asia), ⓦ 7380 (W Africa & S America)
0200-0600	ⓦ 5920 (E Europe)
0430-0700	ⓢ 15225 (Europe & W Africa)
0520-0900	ⓦ 12065 (W Asia & C Asia)
0530-0800	ⓦ 9860 (N Europe & E North Am), ⓦ 12075 (Europe & W Africa)
0530-0830	ⓢ 13705 (N Europe & E North Am)
0530-0900	ⓢ 12065 (W Asia & C Asia)
0530-1400	ⓦ 11990 (W Asia & C Asia)
0630-1500 ▱	9720 (Europe)
0730-1200	ⓦ 7440 (E Asia)
0730-1700	ⓢ 17660 (Europe & W Africa)
0820-1500	ⓢ 11655 (W Asia & C Asia)
0830-1500	ⓦ 17600 (Europe & W Africa)
0830-1700	13705 (N Europe & E North Am)
0920-1600	ⓦ 12005 (W Asia & C Asia)
0930-1300	ⓢ 12005 (W Asia)
1030-1500	ⓢ 9655 (E Asia)
1230-1600	ⓦ 7295 (E Asia)
1330-1700	ⓢ 7360 (W Asia & C Asia)
1430-2100	ⓢ 5940 (E Europe)
1430-2200	ⓦ 6125 (W Asia & C Asia)
1520-2100	ⓢ 9490 (N Europe)
1530-1800	ⓦ 11630 (Europe & W Africa)
1530-2200	ⓦ 6060 (Europe)
1620-2200	ⓦ 5895 (N Europe & E Europe)
1700-1800	ⓢ 13705 (N Europe & E North Am)
1730-2100	ⓢ 7355 (W Asia & C Asia), ⓢ 11735 (Europe & W Africa)
1730-2200	ⓦ 7260 (N Europe & E North Am)
1830-2100	ⓢ 9845 (N Europe & E North Am)
1830-2200	ⓦ 7140 (W Europe & Atlantic)
1900-2200	ⓢ 9805 (E Asia)
2000-2300	ⓦ 7295 (E Asia)
2200-2400 ▱	7220 (N Asia)
2230-2400	ⓢ 15475 (E Asia)
2330-2400	ⓦ 9700 (E Asia)

VOICE OF RUSSIA/RUSSIAN RADIO INTERNATIONAL

0100-0300	ⓢ 11720 & ⓢ *11750* (E North Am), ⓢ 12060 & ⓢ 12070 (S America), ⓢ 17565, ⓢ 17620, ⓢ 17660 & ⓢ 17690 (W North Am)
0200-0300	ⓢ 7330 & ⓢ 9480 (S America), ⓢ 17650 (W North Am)
0200-0400	ⓦ *7125* & ⓦ *7240* (E North Am), ⓦ 7260 (Atlantic & C America), ⓦ 7440 (S America), ⓦ 12010, ⓦ 15595, ⓦ 17565 & ⓦ 17595 (W North Am)
0300-0400	ⓦ 7350 (S America)
1200-1300	ⓢ 7390 & ⓢ 11870 (E Asia), ⓢ 13720 (E Asia & SE Asia)
1200-1400	ⓢ 9745 (C Asia & S Asia), ⓢ 11640 (SE Asia), ⓢ 15470 (E Asia), ⓢ 15560 (S Asia & SE Asia)
1200-1500	ⓢ 9470 (E Asia & SE Asia), ⓢ 9920 (C Asia & S Asia)
1300-1400	ⓦ 6145 & ⓢ 7330 (E Asia), ⓢ 17645 (S Asia & SE Asia)
1300-1500	ⓦ 7105 (C Asia), ⓦ 7155 & ⓦ 9450 (E Asia), ⓢ 9490 & ⓦ 9490 (SE Asia), ⓦ 15460 (S Asia & SE Asia)
1300-1900	ⓦ 6185 (C Asia)
1300-2100	ⓢ 7370 (Europe)
1400-1500	ⓦ 6205 (SE Asia), ⓦ 7315 (W Asia & S Asia)
1400-1700	ⓢ 11830 (Mideast)
1400-1800	ⓢ 7315 (W Asia & S Asia)
1400-1900	ⓦ 6045 (W Europe & Atlantic), ⓢ 9820/9450 (Europe)
1500-1600	ⓦ 5890, ⓦ 7350, ⓢ 9745 & ⓢ 12055 (S Asia), ⓢ 15540 (Mideast), ⓢ 15560 (S Asia & SE Asia), ⓢ 17580 (Mideast & E Africa)
1500-1700	ⓦ 7440 (Europe)

1500-1900   ⟦W⟧ 5995 (C Asia)
1500-2100   ⟦W⟧ 7170 (W Europe)
1600-1700   ⟦W⟧ 7315 (W Asia & S Asia), ⟦W⟧ 9470 (Mideast), ⟦W⟧ 12030 (E Europe & Mideast)
1600-1800   ⟦S⟧ 7420 (Europe), ⟦S⟧ 9875 (W Asia)
1700-1800   ⟦S⟧ 5950, ⟦S⟧ 7300 & ⟦S⟧ 11630 (Europe), ⟦S⟧ 15540 (Mideast)
1700-2100   ⟦S⟧ 12055 (Mideast & E Africa)
1800-1900   ⟦W⟧ 5950 & ⟦S⟧ 7360 (Europe), ⟦W⟧ 7360 (Europe & N Africa)
1900-2000   ⟦S⟧ 5950, ⟦S⟧ 11745 & ⟦S⟧ 15350 (Europe), ⟦S⟧ 17685 (S Europe)
1930-2000   ⟦S⟧ 11630 (Europe)
2000-2100   ⟦W⟧ 6145, ⟦W⟧ 7310 & ⟦W⟧ 7380 (Europe), ⟦S⟧ 7390 (Europe & W Africa), ⟦S⟧ 9450 (S Europe), ⟦S⟧ 9890 (Europe), ⟦S⟧ 12000 (Europe & W Africa)
2000-2200   ⟦W⟧ 7355 (E Asia)
2030-2100   ⟦W⟧ 7360 (Europe & N Africa)
2100-2200   ⟦W⟧ 6045 (W Europe & Atlantic), ⟦W⟧ 7370 (S Europe), ⟦W⟧ 9480 (Europe & W Africa)

SAUDI ARABIA—Arabic
BROADCASTING SERVICE OF THE KINGDOM
0300-0600   9580 (Mideast & E Africa), 11820 (N Africa), 15170 (E Europe & W Asia), 15435 (W Asia), 21495 (C Asia & E Asia)
0300-0900   9675 (Mideast)
0600-0800   17895 (C Asia)
0600-0900   15380 (Mideast), 17620/ 17500 (W Asia), 17760 (N Africa)
0600-1500   21505 (N Africa), 21705 (W Europe)
0600-1700   11855 (Mideast & E Africa)
0900-1200   11935 (Mideast), 17615 (SE Asia), 21495 (E Asia & SE Asia)
0900-1600   9675 (Mideast)
1200-1400   15380 (Mideast), 21600 (SE Asia)
1200-1500   17585 (W Asia), 17895 (N Africa)

1200-1600   17760 (N Africa)
1500-1800   11785 (W Asia), 13710 & 15315 (N Africa), 15435 (W Europe)
1600-1800   11710 (N Africa), 15205 (W Europe), 17560 (C Africa & W Africa)
1700-2200   9580 (Mideast & E Africa)
1800-2100   11950 (W Asia)
1800-2300   9555 (N Africa), 9870 & 11820 (W Europe), 11915 (N Africa), 15230 (C Africa & W Africa)

SERBIA AND MONTENEGRO—Serbian
INTERNATIONAL RADIO OF SERBIA & MONTENEGRO
0000-0030   ⟦S⟧ Su *9580* (E North Am)
0030-0100   ⟦W⟧ *7115* & ⟦S⟧ *9580* (E North Am)
0100-0130   ⟦W⟧ Su *7115* (E North Am)
0130-0200   ⟦W⟧ *7115* (E North Am)
1400-1430   ⟦W⟧ *11835* (Australasia)
1500-1530   ⟦W⟧ M-F *11835* (Australasia)
2030-2100   ⟦◻⟧ *6100* (W Europe)
2100-2130   ⟦◻⟧ Sa *6100* (W Europe)
2130-2200   ⟦S⟧ *7230* (Australasia)
2200-2230   ⟦S⟧ Sa *7230* (Australasia)
2330-2400   ⟦S⟧ *9580* (E North Am)

SINGAPORE—Chinese
MEDIACORP RADIO
1400-1600 & 2300-1100   6000
RADIO SINGAPORE INTERNATIONAL—(SE Asia)
1100-1400   6000 & 9560

SLOVAKIA—Slovak
RADIO SLOVAKIA INTERNATIONAL
0130-0200   5930, ⟦S⟧ 6190 & ⟦W⟧ 7230 (E North Am & C America), 9440 (S America)
0730-0800   ⟦S⟧ 9440, ⟦W⟧ 13715, 15460 & 17550 (Australasia)
1530-1600   ⟦S⟧ 5920 (W Europe)
1630-1700   ⟦◻⟧ 6055 & 7345 (W Europe)
1630-1700   ⟦W⟧ 5915 (W Europe)
1900-1930   ⟦S⟧ 5920 (W Europe)
2000-2030   ⟦◻⟧ 6055 & 7345 (W Europe)
2000-2030   ⟦W⟧ 5915 (W Europe)

SPAIN

RADIO EXTERIOR DE ESPAÑA
Galician, Catalan & Basque

1240-1255	[S] M-F *9765* (C America), [S] M-F *15170* (W North Am), [S] M-F 15585 (Europe), [S] M-F 21540 (C Africa & S Africa), [S] M-F 21570 (S America), [S] M-F 21610 (Mideast), [S] M-F 21700 (N America)
1340-1355	[W] M-F *9765* (C America), [W] M-F *15170* (W North Am), [W] M-F 15585 (Europe), [W] M-F 17595 (N America & C America), [W] M-F 21540 (C Africa & S Africa), [W] M-F 21570 (S America), [W] M-F 21610 (Mideast)

Spanish

0000-0200	[S] 11680 & [W] 11945 (S America)
0000-0400	[S] *6020* & [W] *11815* (C America)
0000-0500	9535/9540 (N America & C America), 9620 (S America), [S] 15160 (C America & S America)
0100-0600	6055 (N America & C America)
0200-0600	[S] *3350* (C America), [S] *6125* (W North Am & C America), [W] *11880/3210* (C America & W North Am)
0500-0600	[S] 9710 & [S] 12035 (Europe)
0500-0700	[W] 11890 & [S] 17665 (Mideast)
0600-0700	9710 (Europe)
0600-0800	12035 (Europe)
0600-1300	[W] 13720 (W Europe)
0700-0900	17770 & 21610 (Australasia)
0800-0900	[S] 12035 (Europe)
0800-1000	M-F 21570 (S America)
0900-1240	15585 (Europe), 21540 (C Africa & S Africa), 21610 (Mideast)
1000-1200	*9660* (E Asia)
1000-1240	21570 (S America), [S] M-F 21700 (N America)
1000-1300	M-F *11815* & [W] M-F 17595 (C America)
1100-1240	[S] M-F *9765* (C America), M-F *15170* (W North Am)
1100-1400	[W] M-F *5970* (C America)
1200-1400	*11910* (SE Asia)
1200-1500	Su *15170* (W North Am & C America), Sa/Su 21700 (C America & S America)
1200-1600	[S] Su *9765* & [S] Su *11815* (C America), [W] Su *15125* (C America & S America)
1240-1255	[W] M-F *15170* (W North Am), [S] Sa/Su 15585 & [W] 15585 (Europe), [S] Sa/Su 21540 & [W] 21540 (C Africa & S Africa), [S] Sa/Su 21570 & [W] 21570 (S America), [S] Sa/Su 21610 & [W] 21610 (Mideast)
1255-1340	M-F *15170* (W North Am), 15585 (Europe), 21540 (C Africa & S Africa), 21570 (S America), 21610 (Mideast)
1255-1400	[S] M-F *9765* (C America)
1300-1340	M-F 17595 (N America & C America)
1300-1400	[W] Sa/Su 13720 (W Europe)
1340-1355	[S] M-F *15170* (W North Am), [S] 15585 & [W] Sa/Su 15585 (Europe), [S] M-F 17595 (N America & C America), [S] 21540 & [W] Sa/Su 21540 (C Africa & S Africa), [S] 21570 & [W] Sa/Su 21570 (S America), [S] 21610 & [W] Sa/Su 21610 (Mideast)
1355-1500	M-F 17595 (N America & C America), 21610 (Mideast)
1355-1700	15585 (Europe), 21570 (S America)
1400-1500	[S] M-Sa 17755 & [W] 21540 (C Africa & S Africa)
1500-1600	[W] Su *9765* (C America), Su *17850* (W North Am)
1500-1700	M-Sa 15375/15385 (W Africa & C Africa), 21610 (Mideast)
1500-1800	21700 (C America & S America)
1500-1900	17755 (C Africa & S Africa)
1600-2300	Sa/Su *9765* & [S] Sa/Su *11815* (C America), [W] Sa/Su *15125* (C America & S America), Sa/Su *17850* (W North Am)
1700-1900	17715 (S America)
1700-2000	Sa/Su 9665 (Europe)
1700-2300	7275 (Europe)
1800-2100	Sa/Su 21700 (Irr) (C America & S America)

1900-2100	🗱 Su 17755 & Su 17755 (C Africa & S Africa)
1900-2300	15110 (N America & C America)
2000-2100	🗲 Sa 9665 & 🗱 Sa/Su 9665 (Europe)
2100-2200	🗱 Sa 9665 (Europe), 🗱 M-F 11665 (C Africa)
2200-2300	7270 (N Africa & W Africa), 🗱 Sa 11665 (C Africa)
2300-2400	9535/9540 (N America & C America), 9620, 🗲 11680 & 🗱 11945 (S America), 🗲 15160 (C America & S America

SWITZERLAND

SWISS RADIO INTERNATIONAL
French

0600-0630	🗱 *9885* (N Africa), 🗲 *13650* (N Africa & W Africa), 🗱 *13790* (W Africa), 🗲 *15445* (N Africa), 🗱 17665 & 🗲 21750 (C Africa & S Africa)
1000-1030	21770 (C Africa & S Africa)
1800-1815	🗱 *9755,* 🗱 *11810,* 🗲 à750 & 🗲 *15515* (Mideast), 🗱 15555 & 🗲 17870 (Mideast & E Africa)
2100-2130	🗱 *9820* (N Africa & W Africa), 🗲 *11815* & 🗱 11920 (C Africa & S Africa), 🗲 *13645* (N Africa & W Africa), 🗱 *13660* & 🗲 13795 (E Africa), 🗲 *15220* & 🗱 *17660* (S Africa)
2200-2230	9885, 🗱 *11660* & 🗲 *11905* (S America)

German

0630-0700	🗱 *9885* (N Africa), 🗲 *13650* (N Africa & W Africa), 🗱 *13790* (W Africa), 🗲 *15445* (N Africa), 🗱 17665 & 🗲 21750 (C Africa & S Africa)
0930-1000	21770 (C Africa & S Africa)
2030-2100	🗱 *9820* (N Africa & W Africa), 🗲 *11815* & 🗱 11920 (C Africa & S Africa), 🗲 *13645* (N Africa & W Africa), 🗱 *13660* & 🗲 13795 (E Africa), 🗲 *15220* & 🗱 *17660* (S Africa)
2230-2300	9885, 🗱 *11660* & 🗲 *11905* (S America)

Italian

0700-0730	🗱 *9885* (N Africa), 🗲 *13650* (N Africa & W Africa), 🗱 *13790* (W Africa), 🗲 *15445* (N Africa), 🗱 17665 & 🗲 21750 (C Africa & S Africa)
0900-0930	21770 (C Africa & S Africa)
1630-1700	🗱 *9755,* 🗱 *11810,* 🗲 *13750* & 🗲 *15515* (Mideast), 🗱 15555 & 🗲 17870 (Mideast & E Africa)
1830-1900	🗱 *9820* (N Africa & W Africa), 🗲 *11815* & 🗱 11920 (C Africa & S Africa), 🗲 *13645* (N Africa & W Africa), 🗱 *13660* & 🗲 13795 (E Africa), 🗲 *15220* & 🗱 *17660* (S Africa)
2300-2330	9885, 🗱 *11660* & 🗲 *11905* (S America)

SYRIA—Arabic

RADIO DAMASCUS—(S America)

2215-2315	12085 & 13610

THAILAND—Thai

RADIO THAILAND

0100-0200	🗱 13695 & 🗲 15395 (E North Am)
0330-0430	🗲 15395 & 🗱 15460 (W North Am)
1000-1100	🗱 7285 & 🗲 11805 (SE Asia & Australasia)
1100-1220	4830, 6070 & 7115 (SE Asia)
1330-1400	🗱 7160 & 🗲 11685 (E Asia)
1800-1900	🗲 9695 & 🗱 11855 (Mideast)
2045-2115	🗱 9535 & 🗲 9680 (Europe)

TUNISIA—Arabic

RTV TUNISIENNE

0200-0500	9720 & 12005 (N Africa & Mideast)
0400-0700	7190 (N Africa)
0400-0800	7275 (W Europe)
1200-1600	15450 & 17735 (N Africa & Mideast)
1400-1700	11730 (W Europe)
1400-1900	11950 (N Africa)
1600-2100	9720 & 12005 (N Africa & Mideast)
1700-2300	7225 (W Europe)
1900-2300	7190 (N Africa)

TURKEY—Turkish

VOICE OF TURKEY

0000-0400	🄢 5960 (Mideast), 🄢 11885 (Europe & N America)
0000-0500	🄦 6120 (Mideast), 🄦 7300 (Europe & N America)
0000-0800 ⛶	9460 (Europe, E North Am & C America)
0400-0900	🄢 11750 (Mideast), 🄢 15545 (Mideast & W Asia)
0500-0800 ⛶	17690 (W Asia & C Asia)
0500-1000	🄦 11925 (Mideast), 🄦 15480 (Mideast & W Asia)
0500-1700 ⛶	11955 (Mideast)
0800-1700 ⛶	15350 (Europe)
0800-2200 ⛶	9460 (Europe)
0900-1200	🄢 21715 (W Asia, S Asia & Australasia)
1000-1300	🄦 17720 (W Asia, S Asia & Australasia)
1000-1500	🄢 F 17630 (N Africa)
1100-1600	🄦 F 17860 (N Africa)
1200-1600	🄢 13655 (S Asia, SE Asia & Australasia)
1300-1700	🄦 9500 (SE Asia & Australasia)
1600-2400	🄢 5960 (Mideast)
1700-2200	🄢 7215 (N Africa & W Africa)
1700-2300 ⛶	5980 (Europe), 9560 (S Asia, SE Asia & Australasia)
1700-2400	🄦 6120 (Mideast)
1800-2300	🄦 6185 (N Africa & W Africa)
2200-2400 ⛶	9460 (Europe, E North Am & C America)
2200-2400	🄢 11885 (Europe & N America)
2300-2400	🄦 7300 (Europe & N America)

UKRAINE—Ukrainian

RADIO UKRAINE

0000-0100	🄦 5905/9385 (E North Am), 🄦 9610 (W Asia)
0000-0400	🄢 9620/7420 (W Asia)
0100-0300	🄢 12040/9810 (E North Am)
0200-0400	🄦 5905/9385 (E North Am), 🄦 9610 (W Asia)
0300-0400	🄦 7285 (N Europe)
0400-0700	🄢 7410 (W Europe)
0400-0800	🄦 7420 (Europe)
0500-0700	🄦 7285 (N Europe)
0500-1000	🄦 9600 (S Europe)
0500-1200	🄦 11825 (C Asia)
0500-1600	🄦 6020 (Europe)
0700-1100	🄢 15415 (W Europe)
0700-1200	🄦 13590 & 🄦 17760 (W Europe)
0800-1200	🄦 11840 (W Europe)
1200-1300	🄢 15415 (W Europe)
1300-1400	🄦 11825 (C Asia)
1300-1700	🄢 9620/7420 (W Asia), 🄦 13590 (W Europe)
1400-1800	🄦 7240 (E Europe & W Asia), 🄦 9610 (W Asia)
1600-1700	6020 (Europe)
1700-2200	🄦 7285 (N Europe)
1800-2000	🄢 6020 (Europe), 🄢 11550 (W Europe)
1900-2100	🄦 6020 (Europe), 🄦 7240 (W Europe)
2000-2100	🄦 5905 (S Europe)
2200-2300	🄢 5905 (W Europe), 🄢 6020 (Europe)
2300-2400	🄦 5905, 🄦 7240 & 🄦 9560 (W Europe), 🄢 12040/9810 (E North Am)

Although emigration is not what it once was, overseas Vietnamese have shown a renewed interest in their country of origin. *Nova*

UNITED ARAB EMIRATES—Arabic

EMIRATES RADIO

0000-0200	11950 (Irr), 13675/13650 (Irr) (E North Am & C America)
0200-0330	12005, 13675/13650 & 15400 (E North Am & C America)
0400-0530	15435 (Australasia), 17830 (E Asia), 21700 (Australasia)
0600-1030	13675/13650, 15395 & 21605 (Europe)
1050-1200	15370 (N Africa)
1050-1330	13675/13650, 15395 & 21605 (Europe)
1200-1330	13630 (N Africa)
1350-1600	13630 (N Africa), 13675/ 13650, 15395 & 21605 (Europe)
1615-1630	13630 (N Africa), 21605 (Europe)
1615-2050	13675/13650 & 15395 (Europe)
1630-2050	11950, 13630 (N Africa)
2050-2400	11950 (Irr), 13675/13650 (Irr) (E North Am & C America)

VIETNAM—Vietnamese

VOICE OF VIETNAM

0000-0100	**W** 7145/7185, **W** 9730, **S** 11630 & **S** 13740 (C Africa)
0000-1600	5925, 5975, 7210, 9530
0130-0230	*6175* (E North Am & C America)
0150-1000	9875
0400-0500	*6175* (W North Am)
1600-1700	F 5975, F 9530
1700-1800	**W** 7145/7185, **W** 9730, **S** 11630 & **S** 13740 (Europe)
1730-1830	**S** *9725* (W Europe)
1830-1930	**W** *5955* (W Europe)
1930-2030	**S** *9725* (S Europe)
2030-2130	**W** *5970* (S Europe)
2200-2400	5925, 5975, 7210, 9530

YEMEN—Arabic

REPUBLIC OF YEMEN RADIO

0300-0600	9780 (Mideast & E Africa)
0300-1500	5950 (Mideast)
0700-1800 &	
1900-2208	9780
2208-2308	9780 (Irr)

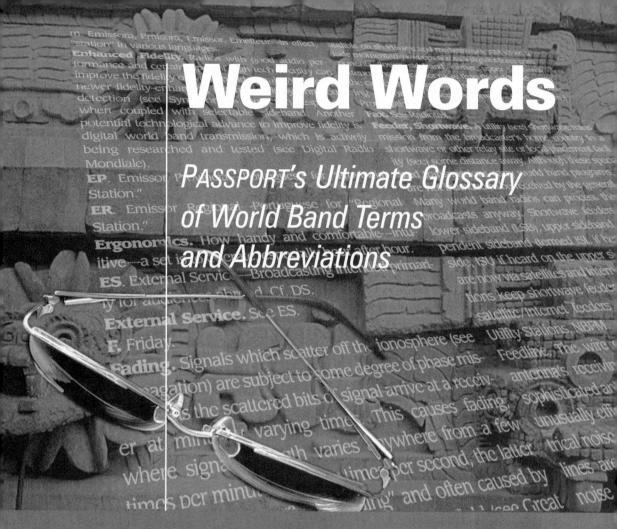

Weird Words

PASSPORT's Ultimate Glossary of World Band Terms and Abbreviations

A rich variety of terms and abbreviations is used in world band radio. Some are specialized and benefit from explanation; several are foreign words that need translation; and yet others are simply adaptations of everyday usage.

Here, then, is PASSPORT's A-Z guide to what's what in world band buzzwords. For a thorough analysis of terms and norms used in evaluating world band radios, see the Radio Database International White Paper, *How to Interpret Receiver Specifications and Lab Tests*.

A. Summer schedule season for world band stations. *See* ◧. *See* HFCC. *Cf.* B.

Active Antenna. An antenna that electronically amplifies signals. Active, or amplified, antennas are typically mounted indoors, but some models can also be mounted outdoors. Active antennas take up relatively little space, but their amplification circuits may introduce certain types of problems that can result in unwanted sounds being heard. *See* Passive Antenna.

Adjacent-Channel Rejection. *See* Selectivity.

AGC. *See* Automatic Gain Control.

AGC Threshold. The threshold at which the automatic gain control (AGC), *see*, chooses to act relates to both listening pleasure and audible sensitivity. If the threshold is too low, the AGC will tend to act on internal receiver noise and minor static, desensitizing the receiver. However, if the threshold is too high, variations in loudness will be uncomfortable to the ear, forcing the listener to manually twiddle with the volume control to do, in effect, what the AGC should be doing automatically. Measured in µV (microvolts).

Alt. Freq. Alternative frequency or channel. Frequency or channel that may be used in place of the regularly scheduled one.

Amateur Radio. *See* Hams.

AM Band. The popular radio band that runs from 520–1705 kHz within the mediumwave spectrum, or Medium Frequency (MF) range of the radio spectrum, from 0.3-3.0 MHz (300-3,000 kHz). Outside North America, it is usually called the mediumwave (MW) band. However, in parts of Latin America it is sometimes called, by the general public and a few stations, *onda larga*—longwave—strictly speaking, a misnomer.

Amplified Antenna. *See* Active Antenna.

Analog Frequency Readout. This type of received-frequency indication is used on radios having needle-and-dial or "slide-rule" tuning. It is much less handy than digital frequency readout. *See* Synthesizer. *Cf.* Digital Frequency Display.

Arrestor. *See* MOV.

Audio Quality. At Passport, audio quality refers to what in computer testing is called "benchmark" quality. This means, primarily, the freedom from distortion of a signal fed through a receiver's entire circuitry—*not* just the audio stage—from the antenna input through to the speaker terminals. A lesser characteristic of audio quality is the audio bandwidth needed for pleasant world band reception of music. Also, *see* Enhanced Fidelity.

Automatic Gain Control (AGC). Smooths out fluctuations in signal strength brought about by fading, a regular occurrence with world band signals. *See* AGC Threshold.

AV. A Voz—Portuguese for "The Voice." In Passport, this term is also used to represent "The Voice of."

B. Winter schedule season for world band stations. *See* ◨. *See* HFCC. *Cf.* A.

Bandwidth. A key variable that determines selectivity (*see*), bandwidth is the amount of radio signal at –6 dB a radio's circuitry will let pass, and thus be heard. With world band channel spacing at 5 kHz, the best single bandwidths are usually in the vicinity of 3 to 6 kHz. Better radios offer two or more selectable bandwidths: at least one of 5 to 9 kHz or so for when a station is in the clear, and one or more others between 2 to 6 kHz for when a station is hemmed in by other signals next to it. Proper selectivity is a key determinant of the aural quality of what you hear, and some newer models of tabletop receivers have dozens of bandwidths. Synchronous selectable sideband (*see*) allows wider bandwidths to be used to provide improved fidelity.

Baud. Measurement of the speed by which radioteletype (*see*), radiofax (*see*) and other digital data are transmitted. Baud is properly written entirely in lower case, and thus is abbreviated as b (baud), kb (kilobaud) or Mb (Megabaud). Baud rate standards are usually set by the international CCITT regulatory body.

BC. Broadcaster, Broadcasters, Broadcasting, Broadcasting Company, Broadcasting Corporation.

Birdie. A silent spurious signal, similar to a station's open carrier, created by circuit interaction within a receiver. The fewer and weaker the birdies within a receiver's tuning range, the better, although in reality birdies rarely degrade reception.

Blocking. The ability of a receiver to avoid being desensitized by powerful adjacent signals or signals from other nearby frequencies. Measured in dB (decibels) at 100 kHz signal spacing.

Boat Anchor. Radio slang for a classic or vintage tube-type communications receiver. These huge, heavy monsters were manufactured mainly from before World War II through the mid-1970s, although a few continued to be available up to a decade later. The definitive reference for collectors of elder receivers is *Shortwave Receivers Past & Present* by Universal Radio.

Broadcast. A radio or television transmission meant for the general public. *Compare* Utility Stations, Hams.

BS. Broadcasting Station, Broadcasting Service.

Cd. Ciudad—Spanish for "City."

Channel. An everyday term to indicate where a station is supposed to be located on the dial. World band channels are spaced exactly 5 kHz apart. Stations operating outside this norm are "off-channel" (for these, Passport provides resolution to better than 1 kHz to aid in station identification).

Chugging, Chuffing. The sound made by some synthesized tuning systems when the tuning knob is turned. Called "chugging" or "chuffing," as it is suggestive of the rhythmic "chuf, chuf" sound of steam locomotives or "chugalug" gulping of beverages.

Cl. Club, Clube.

Coordinated Universal Time. *See* UTC.

Cult. Cultura, Cultural.

Default. The setting at which a control of a digitally operated electronic device, including many world band radios, normally operates, and to which it will eventually return (e.g., when the radio is next switched on).

Digital Frequency Display, Digital Frequency Readout. Indicates that a receiver displays the tuned frequency digitally, usually in kilohertz (*see*). Because this is so much handier than an analog frequency readout, all models included in Passport REPORTS have digital frequency readout. *See* Synthesizer.

Digital Radio Mondiale (DRM). International organization (www.drm.org) heavily involved in the effort to convert world band transmissions from traditional analog mode to digital mode. *See* Mode.

Digital Signal Processing (DSP). Where digital circuitry and software are used to perform radio circuit functions traditionally done using analog circuits. Used on certain world band receivers; also, available as an add-on accessory for audio processing only.

Dipole Antenna. *See* Passive Antenna.

Distortion. *See* Overall Distortion.

Domestic Service. *See* DS.

DS. Domestic Service—Broadcasting intended primarily for audiences in the broadcaster's home country. However, some domestic programs are beamed on world band to expatriates and other kinfolk abroad, as well as interested foreigners. *Compare* ES.

DSP. *See* Digital Signal Processing.

DX, DXers, DXing. From an old telegraph abbreviation for "distance"; thus, to DX is to communicate over a great distance. DXers are those who specialize in finding distant or exotic stations that are considered to be rare catches. Few world band listeners are considered to be regular DXers, but many others seek out DX stations every now and then—usually by bandscanning, which is greatly facilitated by Passport's Blue Pages.

Dynamic Range. The ability of a receiver to handle weak signals in the presence of strong competing signals within or near the same world band segment (*see* World Band Spectrum). Sets with inferior dynamic range sometimes "overload," especially with external antennas, causing a mishmash of false signals up and down—and even beyond—the segment being received. Dynamic range is closely related to the third-order intercept point, or IP3. Where possible, Passport measures dynamic range and IP3 at the traditional 20 kHz and more challenging 5 kHz signal-separation points.

Earliest Heard (or Latest Heard). See key at the bottom of each Blue Page. If the Passport monitoring team cannot establish the definite sign-on (or sign-off) time of a station, the earliest (or latest) time that the station could be traced is indicated by a left-facing or right-facing "arrowhead flag." This means that the station almost certainly operates beyond the time shown by that "flag." It also means that, unless you live relatively close to the station, you're unlikely to be able to hear it beyond that "flagged" time.

EBS. Economic Broadcasting Station, a type of station found in China.

ECSS (Exalted-Carrier Selectable Sideband). Manual tuning of a conventional AM-mode signal, using a receiver's single-sideband circuitry to zero-beat *(see)* the receiver's BFO with the transmitted signal's carrier. The better-sounding of the signal's sidebands is then selected by the listener. *See* Synchronous Detector.

Ed, Educ. Educational, Educação, Educadora.

Electrical Noise. *See* Noise.

Em. Emissora, Emisora, Emissor, Emetteur—in effect, "station" in various languages.

Enhanced Fidelity. Radios with good audio performance and certain types of high-tech circuitry can improve the fidelity of world band signals. Among the newer fidelity-enhancing techniques is synchronous detection *(see* Synchronous Detector*)*, especially when coupled with selectable sideband. Another potential technological advance to improve fidelity is digital world band transmission, which is actively being researched and tested *(see* Digital Radio Mondiale*)*.

EP. Emissor Provincial—Portuguese for "Provincial Station."

ER. Emissor Regional—Portuguese for "Regional Station."

Ergonomics. How handy and comfortable—intuitive—a set is to operate, especially hour after hour.

ES. External Service—Broadcasting intended primarily for audiences abroad. *Compare* DS.

External Service. *See* ES.

F. Friday.

Fax. *See* Radiofax.

Feeder, Shortwave. A utility transmission from the broadcaster's home country to a relay site or placement facility some distance away. Although these specialized transmissions carry world band programming, most are not intended to be received by the general public. Many world band radios can process these quasi-broadcasts anyway. Feeders operate in lower sideband (LSB), upper sideband (USB) or independent sideband (termed ISL if heard on the lower side, ISU if heard on the upper side) modes. Nearly all shortwave feeders have now been replaced by satellite and Internet audio feeders, but an important newcomer—Armed Forces Radio & Television Service—has taken to the air in recent years; the AFRTS is beamed to U.S. Navy ships, where radio operators retransmit the audio shipboard. *See* Single Sideband, Utility Stations, NBFM.

First IF Rejection. A relatively uncommon source of false signals occurs when powerful transmitters operate on the same frequency as a receiver's first intermediate frequency (IF). The ability of receiving circuitry to avoid such transmitters' causing reception problems is called "IF rejection."

FM. *See* NBFM.

Frequency. The standard term to indicate where a station is located within the radio spectrum—regardless of whether it is "on-channel" or "off-channel" *(see* Channel*)*. Below 30 MHz this is customarily expressed in kilohertz (kHz, *see*), but some receivers display in Megahertz (MHz, *see*). These differ only in the placement of a decimal; e.g., 5970 kHz is the same as 5.97 MHz. Either measurement is equally valid, but to minimize confusion PASSPORT and most stations designate frequencies only in kHz.

Frequency Synthesizer. *See* Synthesizer, Frequency.

Front-End Selectivity. The ability of the initial stage of receiving circuitry to admit only limited frequency ranges into succeeding stages of circuitry. Good front-end selectivity keeps signals from other, powerful bands or segments from being superimposed upon the frequency range you're tuning. For example, a receiver with good front-end selectivity will receive only shortwave signals within the range 3200-3400 kHz. However, a receiver with mediocre front-end selectivity might allow powerful local mediumwave AM stations from 520-1700 kHz to be heard "ghosting in" between 3200 and 3400 kHz, along with the desired shortwave signals. Obviously, mediumwave AM signals don't belong on shortwave. Receivers with inadequate front-end selectivity can benefit from the addition of a preselector *(see)* or a high-pass filter.

GMT. Greenwich Mean Time—*See* World Time.

Hams. Government-licensed amateur radio hobbyists who *transmit* to each other by radio, often by single sideband *(see)*, within special amateur bands. Many of these bands are within the shortwave spectrum *(see)*. This spectrum is also used by world band radio, but world band radio and ham radio, which laymen sometimes confuse with each other, are two very separate entities. The easiest way is to think of hams as making something like phone calls, whereas world band stations are like long-distance versions of ordinary mediumwave AM stations.

Harmonic, Harmonic Radiation, Harmonic Signal. Usually, an unwanted weak spurious repeat of a signal in multiple(s) of the fundamental, or "real," frequency. Thus, the third harmonic of a mediumwave AM station on 1120 kHz might be heard faintly on 4480 kHz within the world band spectrum. Stations almost always try to minimize harmonic radiation, as it wastes energy and spectrum space. However, in rare cases stations have been known to amplify a harmonic signal so they can operate inexpensively on a second frequency. Also, *see* Subharmonic.

Hash. Electrical noise. *See* Noise.

High Fidelity. *See* Enhanced Fidelity.

HFCC (High Frequency Co-ordination Conference). Founded in 1990 and headquartered in Prague, the HFCC (www.hfcc.org) helps coordinate frequency usage by some 60 broadcasting organizations from more than 30 countries. These represent about 75 to 80 percent of the global output for international shortwave broadcasting. Coordination meetings take place twice yearly: once each for the "A" (summer) and "B" (winter) schedule seasons.

IBS. International Broadcasting Services, Ltd., publishers of PASSPORT TO WORLD BAND RADIO and other publications.

Image. A common type of spurious signal found on low-cost radios where a strong signal appears at reduced strength, usually on a frequency 900 kHz or 910 kHz lower down. For example, the BBC on 5875 kHz might repeat on 4975 kHz, its "image frequency." *See* Spurious-Signal Rejection.

Independent Sideband. *See* Single Sideband.

Interference. Sounds from other signals, notably on the same ("co-channel") frequency or nearby channels, that are disturbing the one you are trying to hear. Worthy radios reduce interference by having good selectivity *(see)*. Nearby television sets and cable television wiring may also generate a special type of radio interference called TVI, a "growl" heard every 15 kHz or so. Sometimes referred to as QRM, a term based on Morse-code shorthand.

International Reply Coupon (IRC). Sold by selected post offices in most parts of the world, IRCs amount to official international "scrip" that may be exchanged for postage in most countries of the world. Because they amount to an international form of postage repayment, they are handy for listeners trying to encourage foreign stations to write them back. However, IRCs are very costly for the amount in stamps that is provided in return. Too, an increasing number of countries are not forthcoming about "cashing in" IRCs. Specifics on this and related matters are provided in the Addresses PLUS section of this book.

International Telecommunication Union (ITU). The regulatory body, headquartered in Geneva, for all international telecommunications, including world band radio. Sometimes incorrectly referred to as the "International Telecommunications Union." In recent years, the ITU has become increasingly ineffective as a regulatory body for world band radio, with much of its former role having been taken up by the HFCC *(see)*.

Internet Radio. *See* Web radio.

Inverted-L Antenna. *See* Passive Antenna.

Ionosphere. *See* Propagation.

IP3. Third-order intercept point. *See* Dynamic Range.

IRC. *See* International Reply Coupon.

Irr. Irregular operation or hours of operation; i.e., schedule tends to be unpredictable.

ISB. Independent sideband. *See* Single Sideband.

ISL. Independent sideband, lower. *See* Feeder.

ISU. Independent sideband, upper. *See* Feeder.

ITU. *See* International Telecommunication Union.

Jamming. Deliberate interference to a transmission with the intent of discouraging listening. However, shortwave broadcasts are uniquely resistant to jamming. This ability to avoid "gatekeeping" is a major reason why shortwave continues to be the workhorse for international broadcasting. For now, jamming is practiced much less than it was during the Cold War.

Keypad. On a world band radio, like a cell phone, a keypad can be used to control many variables. Radio keypads are used primarily so you can enter a station's frequency for reception, and the best keypads have real keys (not a membrane) in the standard telephone format of 3x4 with "zero" under the "8" key. Many keypads are also used for presets, but this means you have to remember code numbers for stations (e.g., BBC 5975 kHz is "07"); handier radios have separate keys for presets, while some others use LCD-displayed "pages" to access presets.

kHz. Kilohertz, the most common unit for measuring where a station is located on the world band dial if it is below 30,000 kHz. Formerly known as "kilocycles per second," or kc/s. 1,000 kilohertz equals one Megahertz. *See* Frequency. *Cf.* MHz.

Kilohertz. *See* kHz.

kW. Kilowatt(s), the most common unit of measurement for transmitter power (*see*).

LCD. Liquid-crystal display. LCDs, if properly designed, are fairly easily seen in bright light, but require illumination under darker conditions. LCDs—typically monochrome and gray on gray—also tend to have mediocre contrast, and sometimes can be read from only a certain angle or angles, but they consume nearly no battery power.

LED. Light-emitting diode. LEDs have a long life and are very easily read in the dark or in normal room light, but consume more battery power than LCDs and are hard to read in bright ambient light.

Location. The physical location of a station's transmitter, which may be different from the studio location. Transmitter location is useful as a guide to reception quality. For example, if you're in eastern North America and wish to listen to the Voice of Russia, a transmitter located in St. Petersburg will almost certainly provide better reception than, say, one located in Siberia.

Longwave Band. The 148.5–283.5 kHz portion of the low-frequency (LF) radio spectrum used in Europe, the Near East, North Africa, Russia and Mongolia for domestic broadcasting. As a practical matter, these longwave signals, which have nothing to do with world band or other shortwave signals, are not usually audible in other parts of the world.

Longwire Antenna. *See* Passive Antenna.

Loop Antenna. Round (like a hula hoop) or square antenna often used for reception of longwave, mediumwave AM and even shortwave signals. These can be highly directive below around 2 MHz, and even up to roughly 6 MHz. For this reason, most such antennas can be rotated and even tilted manually or with an antenna rotor. Loops tend to have low gain, and thus need electrical amplification in order to reach their potential. When properly designed and mounted, they can produce superior signal-to-noise ratios that help with weak-signal (DX) reception. Strictly speaking, ferrite-rod antennas, found inside nearly every mediumwave AM radio as well as some specialty outboard antennas, are not "loops." However, in everyday parlance these tiny antennas are referred to as "loops" or "loopsticks."

LSB. Lower Sideband. *See* Feeder, Single Sideband.

LV. La Voix, La Voz—French and Spanish for "The Voice." In PASSPORT, this term is also used to represent "The Voice of."

M. Monday.

Mediumwave Band, Mediumwave AM Band, Mediumwave Spectrum. *See* AM Band.

Megahertz. *See* MHz.

Memory, Memories. *See* Preset.

Meters. An outdated unit of measurement used for individual world band segments of the shortwave spectrum. The frequency range covered by a given meters designation—also known as "wavelength"—can be gleaned from the following formula: *frequency (kHz) = 299,792 ÷ meters*. Thus, 49 meters comes out to a frequency of 6118 kHz—well within the range of frequencies included in that segment (*see* World Band Spectrum). Inversely, meters can be derived from the following: *meters = 299,792 ÷ frequency (kHz)*. The figure 299,792 is based on the speed of light as agreed upon internationally in 1983. However, in practice this awkward figure is usually rounded to 300,000 for computational purposes.

MHz. Megahertz, a common unit to measure where a station is located on the dial, especially above 30 MHz, although in the purest sense all measurements above 3 MHz are supposed to be in MHz. Formerly known as "Megacycles per second," or Mc/s. One Megahertz equals 1,000 kilohertz. *See* Frequency. *Cf.* kHz.

Mode. Method of transmission of radio signals. World band radio broadcasts are almost always in the analog AM mode, the same mode used in the mediumwave AM band (*see*). The AM mode consists of three components: two "sidebands," plus one "carrier" that resides between the two sidebands. Each sideband contains the same programming as the other, and the carrier carries no programming, so a few stations have experimented with the single-sideband (SSB) mode. SSB contains only one sideband, either the lower sideband (LSB) or upper sideband (USB), and a reduced carrier. It requires special radio circuitry to be demodulated, or made intelligible, which is the main reason SSB is unlikely to be widely adopted as a world band mode. However, major efforts are currently underway to implement digital-mode world band transmissions (*see* Digital Radio Mondiale). There are yet other modes used on shortwave, but not for world band. These include CW (Morse-type code), radiofax, RTTY (radioteletype) and narrow-band FM used by utility and ham stations. Narrow-band FM is not used for music, and is different from usual FM. *See* Single Sideband, NBFM, ISB, ISL, ISU, LSB and USB.

MOV. Often used in power-line and antenna surge arrestors to shunt static and line-power surges to ground. MOVs perform well and are inexpensive, but tend to lose their effectiveness with use; costlier alternatives are thus sometimes worth considering. On rare occasion they also appear to have been implicated in starting fires, so a UL or other recognized certification is helpful. For both these reasons MOV-based arrestors should be replaced at least once every decade that they are in service.

N. New, Nueva, Nuevo, Nouvelle, Nacional, National, Nationale.

Nac. Nacional. Spanish and Portuguese for "National."

Narrow-band FM. *See* NBFM.

Nat, Natl, Nat'l. National, Nationale.

NBFM. Narrow-band FM, used within the shortwave spectrum by some "utility" stations, including (between 25-30 MHz) point-to-point broadcast station remote links. These links are documented by Guido Schotmans at http://dxing.hypermart.net.

Noise. Static, buzzes, pops and the like caused by the earth's atmosphere (typically lightning), and to a lesser extent by galactic noise. Also, electrical noise emanates from such man-made sources as electric blankets, fish-tank heaters, heating pads, electrical and gasoline motors, light dimmers, flickering light bulbs, non-incandescent lights, computers and computer peripherals, office machines, electric fences, and faulty electric utility wiring and related components. Sometimes referred to as QRN, a term based on Morse-code shorthand.

Noise Floor. *See* Sensitivity.

Notch Filter, Tunable. A useful feature for reducing or rejecting annoying heterodyne interference—the whistles, howls and squeals for which shortwave has traditionally been notorious.

Other. Programs are in a language other than one of the world's primary languages.

Overall Distortion. Nothing makes listening quite so tiring as distortion. PASSPORT has devised techniques to measure overall cumulative distortion from signal input through audio output—not just distortion within the audio stage. This level of distortion is thus equal to what is heard by the ear.

Overloading. *See* Dynamic Range.

Passive Antenna. An antenna that is not electronically amplified. Typically, these are mounted outdoors, although the "tape-measure" type that comes as an accessory with some portables is usually strung indoors. For world band reception, virtually all outboard models for consumers are made from wire, rather than rods or tubular elements. The two most common designs are the inverted-L (so-called "longwire") and trapped dipole (mounted either horizontally or as a "sloper"). These antennas are preferable to active antennas (*see*), and are reviewed in detail in the Radio Database International White Paper, PASSPORT *Evaluation of Popular Outdoor Antennas (Unamplified)*.

PBS. In China, People's Broadcasting Station.

Phase Noise. Synthesizers and other circuits can create a "rushing" noise that is usually noticed only when the receiver is tuned alongside the edge of a powerful broadcast or other carrier. In effect, the signal becomes "modulated" by the noise. Phase noise is a useful measurement if you tune weak signals alongside powerful signals. Measured in dBc (decibels below carrier).

PLL (Phase-Locked Loop). With world band receivers, a PLL circuit means that the radio can be tuned digitally, often using a number of handy tuning techniques, such as a keypad *(see)* and presets *(see)*.

Power. Transmitter power *before* antenna gain, expressed in kilowatts (kW). The present range of world band powers is 0.01 to 1,000 kW.

Power Lock. *See* Travel Power Lock.

PR. People's Republic.

Preselector. A circuit—outboard as an accessory, or inboard as part of the receiver—that effectively limits the range of frequencies which can enter a receiver's circuitry or the circuitry of an active antenna *(see)*; that is, which improves front-end selectivity *(see)*. For example, a preselector may let in the range 15000-16000 kHz, thus helping ensure that your receiver or active antenna will not encounter problems within that range caused by signals from, say, 5730-6250 kHz or local mediumwave AM signals (520-1705 kHz). This range usually can be varied, manually or automatically, according to the frequency to which the receiver is being tuned. A preselector may be passive (unamplified) or active (amplified).

Preset. Allows you to select a station pre-stored in a radio's memory. The handiest presets require only one push of a button, as on a car radio.

Propagation. World band signals travel, like a basketball, up and down from the station to your radio. The "floor" below is the earth's surface, whereas the "player's hand" on high is the *ionosphere*, a gaseous layer that envelops the planet. While the earth's surface remains pretty much the same from day to day, the ionosphere—nature's own passive "satellite"—varies in how it propagates radio signals, depending on how much sunlight hits the "bounce points."

Thus, some world band segments do well mainly by day, whereas others are best by night. During winter there's less sunlight, so the "night bands" become unusually active, whereas the "day bands" become correspondingly less useful *(see* World Band Spectrum). Day-to-day changes in the sun's weather also cause short-term changes in world band radio reception; this explains why some days you can hear rare signals.

Additionally, the 11-year sunspot cycle has a long term effect on propagation, with sunspot maximum greatly enhancing reception on higher world band segments.

PS. Provincial Station, Pangsong.

Pto. Puerto, Porto.

QRM. *See* Interference.

QRN. *See* Noise.

QSL. *See* Verification.

R. Radio, Radiodiffusion, Radiodifusora, Radiodifusão, Radiophonikos, Radiostantsiya, Radyo, Radyosu, and so forth.

Radiofax, Radio Facsimile. Like ordinary telefax (facsimile by telephone lines), but by radio.

Radioteletype (RTTY). Characters, but not illustrations, transmitted by radio. *See* Baud.

RDI. Radio Database International®, a registered trademark of International Broadcasting Services, Ltd.

Receiver. Synonym for a radio, but sometimes—especially when called a "communications receiver"—implying a radio with superior tough-signal or utility-signal performance.

Reduced Carrier. *See* Single Sideband.

Reg. Regional.

Relay. A retransmission facility, often highlighted in "Worldwide Broadcasts in English" and "Voices from Home" in Passport's WorldScan® section. Relay facilities are generally considered to be located outside the broadcaster's country. Being closer to the target audience, they usually provide superior reception. *See* Feeder.

Rep. Republic, République, República.

RN. *See* R and N.

RS. Radio Station, Radiostantsiya, Radiostudiya, Radiophonikos Stathmos.

RT, RTV. Radiodiffusion Télévision, Radio Télévision, and so forth.

RTTY. *See* Radioteletype.

◼ Transmission aired summer (midyear) only; see "HFCC." *Cf.* **◻**

S. San, Santa, Santo, São, Saint, Sainte. Also, South.

Sa. Saturday.

Scan, Scanning. Circuitry within a radio that allows it to bandscan or memory scan automatically.

Season, Schedule Season. *See* HFCC.

Segments. *See* Shortwave Spectrum.

Selectivity. The ability of a radio to reject interference *(see)* from signals on adjacent channels. Thus, also known as adjacent-channel rejection, a key variable in radio quality. *See* Bandwidth. *See* Shape Factor. *See* Ultimate Rejection. *See* Synchronous Detector.

Sensitivity. The ability of a radio to receive weak signals; thus, also known as weak-signal sensitivity. Of special importance if you are listening during the day or tuning domestic tropical band broadcasts—or if you are located in such parts of the world as Western North America, Hawaii or Australasia, where signals tend to be relatively weak. The best measurement of sensitivity is the noise floor.

Shape Factor. Skirt selectivity helps reduce interference and increase audio fidelity. It is important if you will be tuning stations that are weaker than adjacent-channel signals. Skirt selectivity is measured by the shape factor, the ratio between the bandwidth at -6 dB (adjacent signal at about the same strength as the received station) and -60 dB (adjacent signal relatively much stronger). A good shape factor provides the best defense against adjacent powerful signals' muscling their way in to disturb reception of the desired signal.

Shortwave Spectrum. The shortwave spectrum—also known as the High Frequency (HF) spectrum—is that portion of the radio spectrum from 3 MHz through 30 MHz (3,000-30,000 kHz). The shortwave spectrum is occupied not only by world band broadcasts (*see* World Band Segments), but also hams *(see)* and utility stations *(see)*.

Sideband. *See* Mode.

Single Sideband, Independent Sideband. Spectrum- and power-conserving modes of transmission commonly used mainly by utility stations and hams. These transmitted signals consist of one full sideband (lower sideband, LSB; or upper sideband, USB) and a vestigial carrier, but no second sideband. Very few broadcasters use, or are expected ever to use, these modes, although some quasi-broadcasts, such as the American AFRTS, operate in the single-sideband mode. Many world band radios are already capable of demodulating single-sideband transmissions, and some can even process independent-sideband signals. Certain single-sideband transmissions operate with a minimum of carrier reduction, which allows them to be listened to, albeit with some distortion, on ordinary radios not equipped to demodulate single sideband. Properly designed synchronous detectors *(see)* may prevent such distortion. *See* Feeder, Mode.

Site. *See* Location.

Skirt Selectivity. *See* Shape Factor.

Slew Controls. Elevator-button-type up and down controls to tune a radio. On many radios with synthesized tuning, slewing is used in lieu of tuning by knob. Better is when slew controls are complemented by a tuning knob, which is more versatile.

Sloper Antenna. *See* Passive Antenna.

SPR. Spurious (false) extra signal from a transmitter actually operating on another frequency. One such type is harmonic *(see)*.

Spurious-Signal Rejection. The ability of a radio receiver to avoid producing false, or "ghost," signals that might otherwise interfere with the clarity of the station you're trying to hear. *See* Image.

St, Sta, Sto. Abbreviations for words that mean "Saint."

Stability. The ability of a receiver to rest exactly the tuned frequency without drifting.

Static. *See* Noise.

Static Arrestor. *See* MOV.

Su. Sunday.

Subharmonic. A harmonic heard at 1.5 or 0.5 times the operating frequency. This anomaly is caused by the way signals are generated within vintage-model transmitters, and thus cannot take place with modern transmitters. For example, the subharmonic of a station on 3360 kHz might be heard faintly on 5040 or 1680 kHz. Also, *see* Harmonic.

Sunspot Cycle. *See* Propagation.

Surge Arrestor. *See* MOV.

Synchronous Detector. World band radios are increasingly coming equipped with this high-tech circuit that greatly reduces fading distortion. Better synchronous detectors also allow for synchronous selectable sideband; that is, the highly desirable ability to select the less-interfered of the two sidebands of a world band or other AM-mode signal. *See* Mode.

Synchronous Selectable Sideband. *See* Synchronous Detector.

Synthesizer, Frequency. Better world band receivers utilize a digital frequency synthesizer to tune signals. Among other things, such synthesizers allow for pushbutton tuning and presets, and display the exact frequency digitally—pluses that make tuning to the world considerably easier. Virtually a "must" feature. *See* Analog Frequency Readout. *See* Digital Frequency Display.

Target. Where a transmission is beamed, a/k/a target zone.

Th. Thursday.

Third Order Intercept Point. *See* Dynamic Range.

Travel Power Lock. Control which disables the on/off switch to prevent a radio from switching on accidentally.

Transmitter Power. *See* Power.

Trap Dipole Antenna, Trapped Dipole Antenna. *See* Passive Antenna.

Tu. Tuesday.

Ultimate Rejection, Ultimate Selectivity. The point at which a receiver is no longer able to reject adjacent-channel interference. Ultimate rejection is important if you listen to signals that are markedly weaker than are adjacent signals. *See* Selectivity.

Universal Day. *See* World Time.

Universal Time. *See* World Time.

URL. Universal Resource Locator; i.e., the Internet address for a given Webpage.

USB. Upper Sideband. *See* Feeder. *See* Single Sideband.

UTC. Coordinated Universal Time—and, no, it's *never* "Universal Time Coordinated," although for everyday use it's okay to refer simply to "Universal Time." *See* World Time.

Utility Stations. Most signals within the shortwave spectrum are not world band stations. Rather, they are utility stations—radio telephones, ships at sea, aircraft, ionospheric sounders, over-the-horizon radar and the like—that transmit strange sounds (growls, gurgles, dih-dah sounds, etc.). Although these can be picked up on many receivers, they are rarely intended to be utilized by the general public. *Compare* Broadcast, Hams and Feeders.

v. Variable frequency; i.e., one that is unstable or drifting because of a transmitter malfunction or, less often, to avoid jamming or other interference.

Verification. A "QSL" card or letter from a station verifying that a listener indeed heard that particular station. In order to stand a chance of qualifying for a verification card or letter, you should respond shortly after having heard the transmission. You need to provide the station heard with, at a minimum, the following information in a three-number "SIO" code, in which "SIO 555" is best and "SIO 111" is worst:

• **S**ignal strength, with 5 being of excellent quality, comparable to that of a local mediumwave AM station, and 1 being inaudible or at least so weak as to be virtually unintelligible. 2 (faint, but somewhat intelligible), 3 (moderate strength) and 4 (good strength) represent the signal-strength levels usually encountered with world band stations.

• **I**nterference from other stations, with 5 indicating no interference whatsoever, and 1 indicating such extreme interference that the desired signal is virtually drowned out. 2 (heavy interference), 3 (moderate interference) and 4 (slight interference) represent the differing degrees of interference more typically encountered with world band signals. If possible, indicate the names of the interfering station(s) and the channel(s) they are on. Otherwise, at least describe what the interference sounds like.

• **O**verall quality of the signal, with 5 being best, 1 worst.

• In addition to providing SIO findings, you should indicate which programs you've heard, as well as comments on how you liked or disliked those programs. Refer to the Addresses PLUS section of this edition for information on where and to whom your report should be sent, and whether return postage should be included.

• Because of the hassle involved, few stations wish to receive tape recordings of their transmissions.

Vo. Voice of.

🅆 Transmission aired winter only; *see* HFCC. *Cf.* **🅂**

W. Wednesday.

Wavelength. *See* Meters.

Weak-Signal Sensitivity. *See* Sensitivity.

Webcasting. *See* Web Radio.

Web Radio, Webcasts. Broadcasts aired to the public over the Internet's World Wide Web. These thousands of stations worldwide include simulcast FM, mediumwave AM and world band stations, as well as Web-only "stations." Thus far listening to Webcasts for more than brief periods has been limited by phone-line and related costs except within the United States. Although Webcasting was originally completely unfettered, it is increasingly being subject to official gatekeeping, or censorship, as well as copyright and union restrictions. Accordingly, it has been in a state of gradual decline since early 2001. Where Webcasting is headed is anybody's guess, but recent trends suggest that the same entities which are major forces in terrestrial broadcasting will also eventually dominate Webcasting.

World Band Radio. Similar to regular mediumwave AM band and FM band radio, except that world band stations can be heard over enormous distances, and thus often carry news, music and entertainment programs created especially for audiences abroad. World band is also especially difficult to "jam" (*see* Jamming), making it uniquely effective in outflanking official censorship. Some world band stations have regular audiences in the tens of millions, and even over 100 million. Some 600 million people worldwide are believed to listen to world band radio.

World Band Segments. Fourteen slices within the world band spectrum *(see)* and mediumwave spectrum (*see* AM Band) that are used almost exclusively for transmission of world band broadcasts. *See* "Best Times and Frequencies" within this edition.

World Band Spectrum. The portion of the shortwave spectrum *(see)* and mediumwave spectrum between 2.3-26.1 MHz.

World Day. *See* World Time.

World Time. Also known as Coordinated Universal Time (UTC), Greenwich Mean Time (GMT), Zulu time (Z) and "military time." With over 150 countries on world band radio, if each announced its own local time you would need a calculator to figure it all out. To get around this, a single international time—World Time—is used. The differences between World Time and local time are detailed in the Addresses PLUS and Setting Your World Time Clock sections of this edition. World Time can also be determined simply by listening to time announcements on the hour by world band stations—or minute by minute by WWV and WWVH in the United States on such frequencies as 5000, 10000 and 15000 kHz, or CHU in Canada on 3330, 7335 and 14670 kHz. A 24-hour clock format is used, so "1800 World Time" means 6:00 PM World Time. If you're in, say, North America, Eastern Time is five hours behind World Time winters and four hours behind World Time summers, so 1800 World Time would be 1:00 PM EST or 2:00 PM EDT. The easiest solution is to use a 24-hour digital clock set to World Time. Many radios already have these built in, and World Time clocks are also available as accessories. World Time also applies to the days of the week. So if it's 9:00 PM (21:00) Wednesday in New York during the winter, it's 0200 *Thursday* World Time.

WS. World Service.

Zero beat. When tuning a world band or other AM-mode signal in the single-sideband mode, there is a whistle, or "beat," whose pitch is the result of the difference in frequency between the receiver's internally generated carrier (BFO, or beat-frequency oscillator) and the station's transmitted carrier. By tuning carefully, the listener can reduce the difference between these two carriers to the point where the whistle is deeper and deeper, to the point where it no longer audible. This silent sweet spot is known as "zero beat." *See* ECSS.

Printed in USA

PASSPORT's Blue Pages— 2004

Channel Surfer's Guide to World Band Schedules

If you scan the world band airwaves, you'll discover lots more than stations aimed your way. That's because shortwave signals are scattered by the heavens, so you can often hear stations not targeted to your area.

Blue Pages Help Identify Stations

But just dialing around can be frustrating if you don't have a "map"—PASSPORT's Blue Pages. Let's say that you've stumbled across something Asian-sounding on 7410 kHz at 2035 World Time. The Blue Pages show All India Radio beamed to Western Europe, with 250 kW of power from Delhi. These clues suggest this is probably what you're hearing, even if you're not in Europe. You can also see that English from India will begin on that same channel in about ten minutes.

Schedules for Entire Year

Times and days of the week are in World Time; for local times in each country, see "Addresses PLUS." Some stations are shown as one hour earlier (◧) or later (◨) midyear—typically April through October. Stations may also extend their hours for holidays, emergencies or sports events.

To be as useful as possible over the months to come, PASSPORT's schedules consist not just of observed activity, but also that which we have creatively opined will take place during the forthcoming year. This predictive material is based on decades of experience and is original from us. Although inherently not as exact as real-time data, over the years it's been of tangible value to PASSPORT readers.

Guide to Blue Pages Format

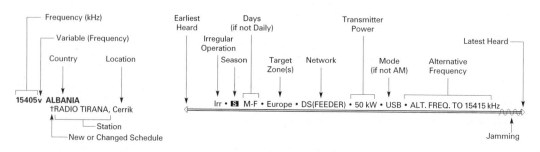

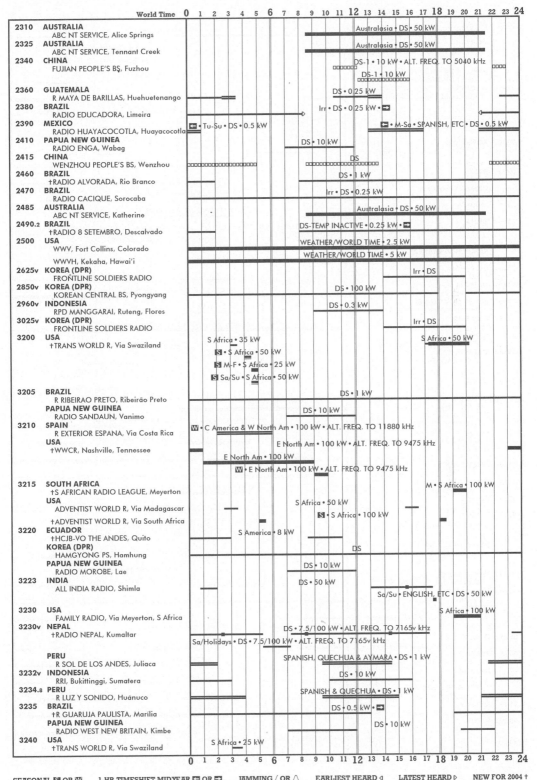

World Time 0 1 2 3 4 5 6 7 8 9 10 11 12 13 14 15 16 17 18 19 20 21 22 23 24

kHz	Country / Station	Schedule
2310	**AUSTRALIA** ABC NT SERVICE, Alice Springs	Australasia • DS • 50 kW
2325	**AUSTRALIA** ABC NT SERVICE, Tennant Creek	Australasia • DS • 50 kW
2340	**CHINA** FUJIAN PEOPLE'S BS, Fuzhou	DS-1 • 10 kW • ALT. FREQ. TO 5040 kHz; DS-1 • 10 kW
2360	**GUATEMALA** R MAYA DE BARILLAS, Huehuetenango	DS • 0.25 kW
2380	**BRAZIL** RADIO EDUCADORA, Limeira	Irr • DS • 0.25 kW • ⇨
2390	**MEXICO** RADIO HUAYACOCOTLA, Huayacocotla	⇦ • Tu-Su • DS • 0.5 kW; ⇦ • M-Sa • SPANISH, ETC • DS • 0.5 kW
2410	**PAPUA NEW GUINEA** RADIO ENGA, Wabag	DS • 10 kW
2415	**CHINA** WENZHOU PEOPLE'S BS, Wenzhou	DS
2460	**BRAZIL** †RADIO ALVORADA, Rio Branco	DS • 1 kW
2470	**BRAZIL** RADIO CACIQUE, Sorocaba	Irr • DS • 0.25 kW
2485	**AUSTRALIA** ABC NT SERVICE, Katherine	Australasia • DS • 50 kW
2490.2	**BRAZIL** †RADIO 8 SETEMBRO, Descalvado	DS-TEMP INACTIVE • 0.25 kW • ⇨
2500	**USA** WWV, Fort Collins, Colorado	WEATHER/WORLD TIME • 2.5 kW
	WWVH, Kekaha, Hawai'i	WEATHER/WORLD TIME • 5 kW
2625v	**KOREA (DPR)** FRONTLINE SOLDIERS RADIO	Irr • DS
2850v	**KOREA (DPR)** KOREAN CENTRAL BS, Pyongyang	DS • 100 kW
2960v	**INDONESIA** RPD MANGGARAI, Ruteng, Flores	DS • 0.3 kW
3025v	**KOREA (DPR)** FRONTLINE SOLDIERS RADIO	Irr • DS
3200	**USA** †TRANS WORLD R, Via Swaziland	S Africa • 35 kW; S Africa • 50 kW; [S] • S Africa • 50 kW; [S] M-F • S Africa • 25 kW; [S] Sa/Su • S Africa • 50 kW
3205	**BRAZIL** R RIBEIRAO PRETO, Ribeirão Preto	DS • 1 kW
	PAPUA NEW GUINEA RADIO SANDAUN, Vanimo	DS • 10 kW
3210	**SPAIN** R EXTERIOR ESPANA, Via Costa Rica	[W] • C America & W North Am • 100 kW • ALT. FREQ. TO 11880 kHz
	USA †WWCR, Nashville, Tennessee	E North Am • 100 kW • ALT. FREQ. TO 9475 kHz; E North Am • 100 kW; [W] • E North Am • 100 kW • ALT. FREQ. TO 9475 kHz
3215	**SOUTH AFRICA** †S AFRICAN RADIO LEAGUE, Meyerton	M • S Africa • 100 kW
	USA ADVENTIST WORLD R, Via Madagascar	S Africa • 50 kW
	†ADVENTIST WORLD R, Via South Africa	[S] • S Africa • 100 kW
3220	**ECUADOR** †HCJB-VO THE ANDES, Quito	S America • 8 kW
	KOREA (DPR) HAMGYONG PS, Hamhung	DS
	PAPUA NEW GUINEA RADIO MOROBE, Lae	DS • 10 kW
3223	**INDIA** ALL INDIA RADIO, Shimla	DS • 50 kW; Sa/Su • ENGLISH, ETC • DS • 50 kW
3230	**USA** FAMILY RADIO, Via Meyerton, S Africa	S Africa • 100 kW
3230v	**NEPAL** †RADIO NEPAL, Kumaltar	DS • 7.5/100 kW • ALT. FREQ. TO 7165v kHz; Sa/Holidays • DS • 7.5/100 kW • ALT. FREQ. TO 7165v kHz
	PERU R SOL DE LOS ANDES, Juliaca	SPANISH, QUECHUA & AYMARA • DS • 1 kW
3232v	**INDONESIA** RRI, Bukittinggi, Sumatera	DS • 10 kW
3234.8	**PERU** R LUZ Y SONIDO, Huánuco	SPANISH & QUECHUA • DS • 1 kW
3235	**BRAZIL** †R GUARUJA PAULISTA, Marília	DS • 0.5 kW • ⇨
	PAPUA NEW GUINEA RADIO WEST NEW BRITAIN, Kimbe	DS • 10 kW
3240	**USA** †TRANS WORLD R, Via Swaziland	S Africa • 25 kW

0 1 2 3 4 5 6 7 8 9 10 11 12 13 14 15 16 17 18 19 20 21 22 23 24

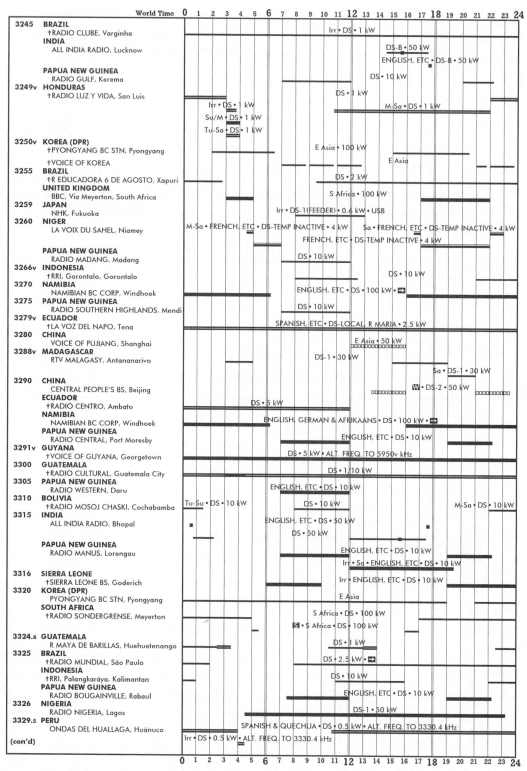

World Time 0 1 2 3 4 5 6 7 8 9 10 11 12 13 14 15 16 17 18 19 20 21 22 23 24

3245 BRAZIL
†RADIO CLUBE, Varginha — Irr • DS • 1 kW

INDIA
ALL INDIA RADIO, Lucknow — DS-B • 50 kW / ENGLISH, ETC • DS-B • 50 kW

PAPUA NEW GUINEA
RADIO GULF, Kerema — DS • 10 kW

3249v HONDURAS
†RADIO LUZ Y VIDA, San Luis — DS • 1 kW / Irr • DS • 1 kW / M-Sa • DS • 1 kW / Su/M • DS • 1 kW / Tu-Sa • DS • 1 kW

3250v KOREA (DPR)
†PYONGYANG BC STN, Pyongyang — E Asia • 100 kW

†VOICE OF KOREA — E Asia

3255 BRAZIL
†R EDUCADORA 6 DE AGOSTO, Xapuri — DS • 2 kW

UNITED KINGDOM
BBC, Via Meyerton, South Africa — S Africa • 100 kW

3259 JAPAN
NHK, Fukuoka — Irr • DS-1(FEEDER) • 0.6 kW • USB

3260 NIGER
LA VOIX DU SAHEL, Niamey — M-Sa • FRENCH, ETC • DS-TEMP INACTIVE • 4 kW / Sa • FRENCH, ETC • DS-TEMP INACTIVE • 4 kW / FRENCH, ETC • DS-TEMP INACTIVE • 4 kW

PAPUA NEW GUINEA
RADIO MADANG, Madang — DS • 10 kW

3266v INDONESIA
†RRI, Gorontalo, Gorontalo — DS • 10 kW

3270 NAMIBIA
NAMIBIAN BC CORP, Windhoek — ENGLISH, ETC • DS • 100 kW • ➡

3275 PAPUA NEW GUINEA
RADIO SOUTHERN HIGHLANDS, Mendi — DS • 10 kW

3279v ECUADOR
†LA VOZ DEL NAPO, Tena — SPANISH, ETC • DS-LOCAL, R MARIA • 2.5 kW

3280 CHINA
VOICE OF PUJIANG, Shanghai — E Asia • 50 kW

3288v MADAGASCAR
RTV MALAGASY, Antananarivo — DS-1 • 30 kW / Sa • DS-1 • 30 kW

3290 CHINA
CENTRAL PEOPLE'S BS, Beijing — W • DS-2 • 50 kW

ECUADOR
†RADIO CENTRO, Ambato — DS • 5 kW

NAMIBIA
NAMIBIAN BC CORP, Windhoek — ENGLISH, GERMAN & AFRIKAANS • DS • 100 kW • ➡

PAPUA NEW GUINEA
RADIO CENTRAL, Port Moresby — ENGLISH, ETC • DS • 10 kW

3291v GUYANA
†VOICE OF GUYANA, Georgetown — DS • 5 kW • ALT. FREQ. TO 5950v kHz

3300 GUATEMALA
†RADIO CULTURAL, Guatemala City — DS • 1/10 kW

3305 PAPUA NEW GUINEA
RADIO WESTERN, Daru — ENGLISH, ETC • DS • 10 kW

3310 BOLIVIA
†RADIO MOSOJ CHASKI, Cochabamba — Tu-Su • DS • 10 kW / DS • 10 kW / M-Sa • DS • 10 kW

3315 INDIA
ALL INDIA RADIO, Bhopal — ENGLISH, ETC • DS • 50 kW / DS • 50 kW

PAPUA NEW GUINEA
RADIO MANUS, Lorengau — ENGLISH, ETC • DS • 10 kW / Irr • Sa • ENGLISH, ETC • DS • 10 kW

3316 SIERRA LEONE
†SIERRA LEONE BS, Goderich — Irr • ENGLISH, ETC • DS • 10 kW

3320 KOREA (DPR)
PYONGYANG BC STN, Pyongyang — E Asia

SOUTH AFRICA
†RADIO SONDERGRENSE, Meyerton — S Africa • DS • 100 kW / S • S Africa • DS • 100 kW

3324.8 GUATEMALA
R MAYA DE BARILLAS, Huehuetenango — DS • 1 kW

3325 BRAZIL
†RADIO MUNDIAL, São Paulo — DS • 2.5 kW • ➡

INDONESIA
†RRI, Palangkaráya, Kalimantan — DS • 10 kW

PAPUA NEW GUINEA
RADIO BOUGAINVILLE, Rabaul — ENGLISH, ETC • DS • 10 kW

3326 NIGERIA
RADIO NIGERIA, Lagos — DS-1 • 50 kW

3329.5 PERU
ONDAS DEL HUALLAGA, Huánuco — SPANISH & QUECHUA • DS • 0.5 kW • ALT. FREQ. TO 3330.4 kHz

(con'd) — Irr • DS • 0.5 kW • ALT. FREQ. TO 3330.4 kHz

0 1 2 3 4 5 6 7 8 9 10 11 12 13 14 15 16 17 18 19 20 21 22 23 24

ENGLISH ▬ ARABIC ▨ CHINESE ▢▢▢ FRENCH ▬ GERMAN ▬ RUSSIAN ═ SPANISH ▬ OTHER ▬

World Time 0 1 2 3 4 5 6 7 8 9 10 11 12 13 14 15 16 17 18 19 20 21 22 23 24

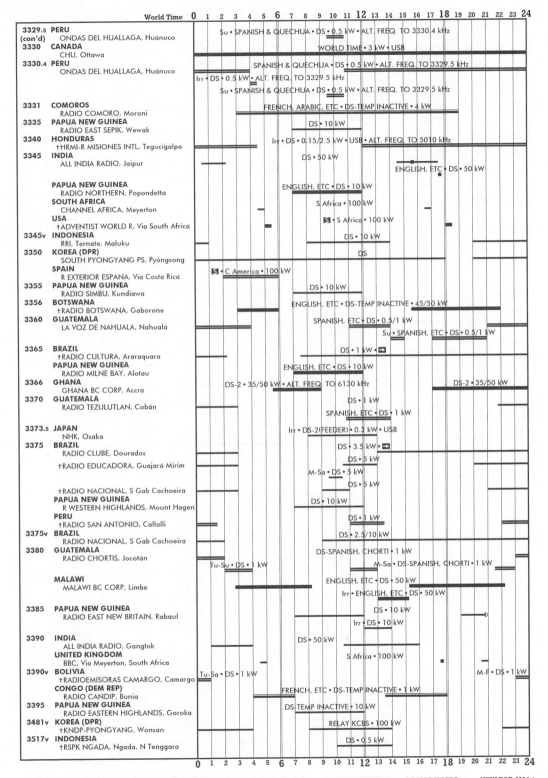

Freq	Country / Station	Schedule
3329.5 (con'd)	PERU — ONDAS DEL HUALLAGA, Huánuco	Su • SPANISH & QUECHUA • DS • 0.5 kW • ALT. FREQ. TO 3330.4 kHz
3330	CANADA — CHU, Ottawa	WORLD TIME • 3 kW • USB
3330.4	PERU — ONDAS DEL HUALLAGA, Huánuco	SPANISH & QUECHUA • DS • 0.5 kW • ALT. FREQ. TO 3329.5 kHz / Irr • DS • 0.5 kW • ALT. FREQ. TO 3329.5 kHz / Su • SPANISH & QUECHUA • DS • 0.5 kW • ALT. FREQ. TO 3329.5 kHz
3331	COMOROS — RADIO COMORO, Moroni	FRENCH, ARABIC, ETC • DS-TEMP INACTIVE • 4 kW
3335	PAPUA NEW GUINEA — RADIO EAST SEPIK, Wewak	DS • 10 kW
3340	HONDURAS — †HRMI-R MISIONES INTL, Tegucigalpa	Irr • DS • 0.15/2.5 kW • USB • ALT. FREQ. TO 5010 kHz
3345	INDIA — ALL INDIA RADIO, Jaipur	DS • 50 kW / ENGLISH, ETC • DS • 50 kW
	PAPUA NEW GUINEA — RADIO NORTHERN, Popondetta	ENGLISH, ETC • DS • 10 kW
	SOUTH AFRICA — CHANNEL AFRICA, Meyerton	S Africa • 100 kW
	USA — †ADVENTIST WORLD R, Via South Africa	S • S Africa • 100 kW
3345v	INDONESIA — RRI, Ternate, Maluku	DS • 10 kW
3350	KOREA (DPR) — SOUTH PYONGYANG PS, Pyŏngsong	DS
	SPAIN — R EXTERIOR ESPANA, Via Costa Rica	S • C America • 100 kW
3355	PAPUA NEW GUINEA — RADIO SIMBU, Kundiawa	DS • 10 kW
3356	BOTSWANA — †RADIO BOTSWANA, Gaborone	ENGLISH, ETC • DS-TEMP INACTIVE • 45/50 kW
3360	GUATEMALA — LA VOZ DE NAHUALA, Nahualá	SPANISH, ETC • DS • 0.5/1 kW / Su • SPANISH, ETC • DS • 0.5/1 kW
3365	BRAZIL — †RADIO CULTURA, Araraquara	DS • 1 kW • ➡
	PAPUA NEW GUINEA — RADIO MILNE BAY, Alotau	ENGLISH, ETC • DS • 10 kW
3366	GHANA — GHANA BC CORP, Accra	DS-2 • 35/50 kW • ALT. FREQ. TO 6130 kHz / DS-2 • 35/50 kW
3370	GUATEMALA — RADIO TEZULUTLAN, Cobán	DS • 1 kW / SPANISH, ETC • DS • 1 kW
3373.5	JAPAN — NHK, Osaka	Irr • DS-2 (FEEDER) • 0.3 kW • USB
3375	BRAZIL — RADIO CLUBE, Dourados	DS • 3.5 kW • ➡
	†RADIO EDUCADORA, Guajará Mirim	DS • 5 kW / M-Sa • DS • 5 kW / DS • 5 kW
	†RADIO NACIONAL, S Gab Cachoeira	
	PAPUA NEW GUINEA — R WESTERN HIGHLANDS, Mount Hagen	DS • 10 kW
	PERU — †RADIO SAN ANTONIO, Callalli	DS • 1 kW
3375v	BRAZIL — RADIO NACIONAL, S Gab Cachoeira	DS • 2.5/10 kW
3380	GUATEMALA — RADIO CHORTIS, Jocotán	DS-SPANISH, CHORTI • 1 kW / Tu-Su • DS • 1 kW / M-Sa • DS-SPANISH, CHORTI • 1 kW
	MALAWI — MALAWI BC CORP, Limbe	ENGLISH, ETC • DS • 50 kW / Irr • ENGLISH, ETC • DS • 50 kW
3385	PAPUA NEW GUINEA — RADIO EAST NEW BRITAIN, Rabaul	DS • 10 kW / Irr • DS • 10 kW
3390	INDIA — ALL INDIA RADIO, Gangtok	DS • 50 kW
	UNITED KINGDOM — BBC, Via Meyerton, South Africa	S Africa • 100 kW
3390v	BOLIVIA — †RADIOEMISORAS CAMARGO, Camargo	Tu-Sa • DS • 1 kW / M-F • DS • 1 kW
	CONGO (DEM REP) — RADIO CANDIP, Bunia	FRENCH, ETC • DS-TEMP INACTIVE • 1 kW
3395	PAPUA NEW GUINEA — RADIO EASTERN HIGHLANDS, Goroka	DS-TEMP INACTIVE • 10 kW
3481v	KOREA (DPR) — †KNDP-PYONGYANG, Wonsan	RELAY KCBS • 100 kW
3517v	INDONESIA — †RSPK NGADA, Ngada, N Tenggara	DS • 0.5 kW

0 1 2 3 4 5 6 7 8 9 10 11 12 13 14 15 16 17 18 19 20 21 22 23 24

SEASONAL S OR W   1-HR TIMESHIFT MIDYEAR ⬅ OR ➡   JAMMING / OR /\   EARLIEST HEARD ◁   LATEST HEARD ▷   NEW FOR 2004 †

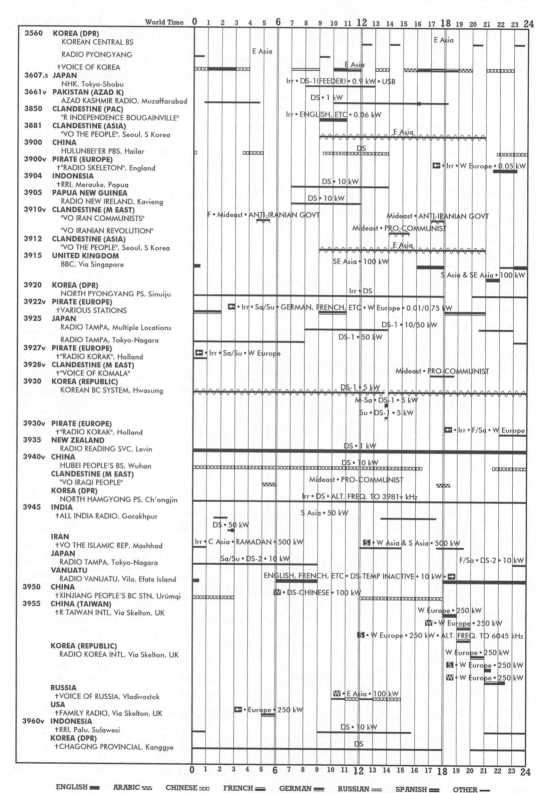

Freq	Country / Station	
3560	**KOREA (DPR)**	
	KOREAN CENTRAL BS	E Asia
	RADIO PYONGYANG	E Asia
	†VOICE OF KOREA	E Asia
3607.5	**JAPAN**	
	NHK, Tokyo-Shobu	Irr • DS-1 (FEEDER) • 0.9 kW • USB
3661v	**PAKISTAN (AZAD K)**	
	AZAD KASHMIR RADIO, Muzaffarabad	DS • 1 kW
3850	**CLANDESTINE (PAC)**	
	"R INDEPENDENCE BOUGAINVILLE"	Irr • ENGLISH, ETC • 0.06 kW
3881	**CLANDESTINE (ASIA)**	
	"VO THE PEOPLE", Seoul, S Korea	E Asia
3900	**CHINA**	
	HULUNBEI'ER PBS, Hailar	DS
3900v	**PIRATE (EUROPE)**	
	†"RADIO SKELETON", England	Irr • W Europe • 0.05 kW
3904	**INDONESIA**	
	†RRI, Merauke, Papua	DS • 10 kW
3905	**PAPUA NEW GUINEA**	
	RADIO NEW IRELAND, Kavieng	DS • 10 kW
3910v	**CLANDESTINE (M EAST)**	
	"VO IRAN COMMUNISTS"	F • Mideast • ANTI-IRANIAN GOVT Mideast • ANTI-IRANIAN GOVT
	"VO IRANIAN REVOLUTION"	Mideast • PRO-COMMUNIST
3912	**CLANDESTINE (ASIA)**	
	"VO THE PEOPLE", Seoul, S Korea	E Asia
3915	**UNITED KINGDOM**	
	BBC, Via Singapore	SE Asia • 100 kW S Asia & SE Asia • 100 kW
3920	**KOREA (DPR)**	
	NORTH PYONGYANG PS, Sinuiju	Irr • DS
3922v	**PIRATE (EUROPE)**	
	†VARIOUS STATIONS	Irr • Sa/Su • GERMAN, FRENCH, ETC • W Europe • 0.01/0.75 kW
3925	**JAPAN**	
	RADIO TAMPA, Multiple Locations	DS-1 • 10/50 kW
	RADIO TAMPA, Tokyo-Nagara	DS-1 • 50 kW
3927v	**PIRATE (EUROPE)**	
	†"RADIO KORAK", Holland	Irr • Sa/Su • W Europe
3928v	**CLANDESTINE (M EAST)**	
	†"VOICE OF KOMALA"	Mideast • PRO-COMMUNIST
3930	**KOREA (REPUBLIC)**	
	KOREAN BC SYSTEM, Hwasung	DS-1 • 5 kW
		M-Sa • DS-1 • 5 kW
		Su • DS-1 • 5 kW
3930v	**PIRATE (EUROPE)**	
	†"RADIO KORAK", Holland	Irr • F/Sa • W Europe
3935	**NEW ZEALAND**	
	RADIO READING SVC, Levin	DS • 1 kW
3940v	**CHINA**	
	HUBEI PEOPLE'S BS, Wuhan	DS • 10 kW
	CLANDESTINE (M EAST)	
	"VO IRAQI PEOPLE"	Mideast • PRO-COMMUNIST
	KOREA (DPR)	
	NORTH HAMGYONG PS, Ch'ongjin	Irr • DS • ALT. FREQ. TO 3981v kHz
3945	**INDIA**	
	†ALL INDIA RADIO, Gorakhpur	S Asia • 50 kW
		DS • 50 kW
	IRAN	
	†VO THE ISLAMIC REP, Mashhad	Irr • C Asia • RAMADAN • 500 kW W Asia & S Asia • 500 kW
	JAPAN	
	RADIO TAMPA, Tokyo-Nagara	Sa/Su • DS-2 • 10 kW F/Sa • DS-2 • 10 kW
	VANUATU	
	RADIO VANUATU, Vila, Efate Island	ENGLISH, FRENCH, ETC • DS-TEMP INACTIVE • 10 kW
3950	**CHINA**	
	†XINJIANG PEOPLE'S BC STN, Urümqi	W • DS-CHINESE • 100 kW
3955	**CHINA (TAIWAN)**	
	†R TAIWAN INTL, Via Skelton, UK	W Europe • 250 kW
		W • W Europe • 250 kW
		S • W Europe • 250 kW • ALT. FREQ. TO 6045 kHz
	KOREA (REPUBLIC)	
	RADIO KOREA INTL, Via Skelton, UK	W Europe • 250 kW
		S • W Europe • 250 kW
		W • W Europe • 250 kW
	RUSSIA	
	†VOICE OF RUSSIA, Vladivostok	W • E Asia • 100 kW
	USA	
	†FAMILY RADIO, Via Skelton, UK	Europe • 250 kW
3960v	**INDONESIA**	
	†RRI, Palu, Sulawesi	DS • 10 kW
	KOREA (DPR)	
	†CHAGONG PROVINCIAL, Kanggye	DS

World Time: 0 1 2 3 4 5 6 7 8 9 10 11 12 13 14 15 16 17 18 19 20 21 22 23 24

ENGLISH ▬ ARABIC ≋ CHINESE □□□ FRENCH ▬ GERMAN ▬ RUSSIAN ═ SPANISH ▬ OTHER ▬

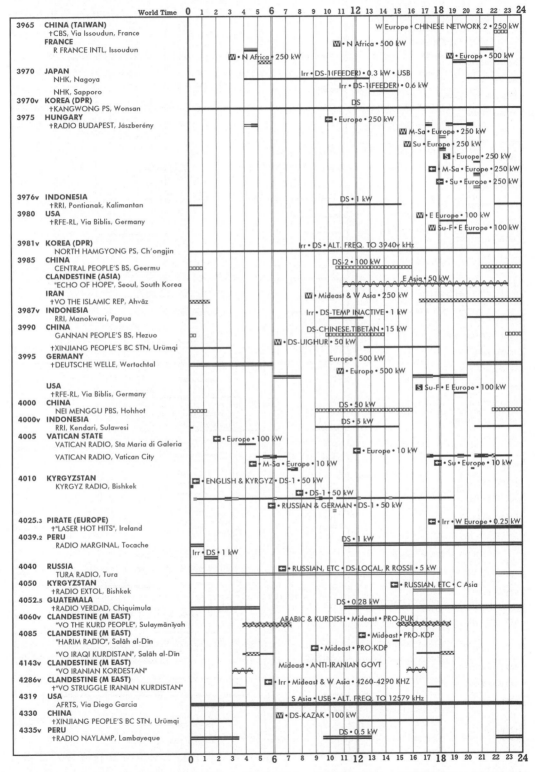

World Time 0 1 2 3 4 5 6 7 8 9 10 11 12 13 14 15 16 17 18 19 20 21 22 23 24

3965 **CHINA (TAIWAN)**
†CBS, Via Issoudun, France　　　W Europe • CHINESE NETWORK 2 • 250 kW
FRANCE
R FRANCE INTL, Issoudun　　　W • N Africa • 500 kW
W • N Africa • 250 kW　　　W • Europe • 500 kW

3970 **JAPAN**
NHK, Nagoya　　　Irr • DS-1 (FEEDER) • 0.3 kW • USB
NHK, Sapporo　　　Irr • DS-1 (FEEDER) • 0.6 kW

3970v **KOREA (DPR)**
†KANGWONG PS, Wonsan　　　DS

3975 **HUNGARY**
†RADIO BUDAPEST, Jászberény　　　⊟ • Europe • 250 kW
W M-Sa • Europe • 250 kW
W Su • Europe • 250 kW
S • Europe • 250 kW
⊟ • M-Sa • Europe • 250 kW
⊟ • Su • Europe • 250 kW

3976v **INDONESIA**
†RRI, Pontianak, Kalimantan　　　DS • 1 kW

3980 **USA**
†RFE-RL, Via Biblis, Germany　　　W • E Europe • 100 kW
W Su-F • E Europe • 100 kW

3981v **KOREA (DPR)**
NORTH HAMGYONG PS, Ch'ongjin　　　Irr • DS • ALT. FREQ. TO 3940v kHz

3985 **CHINA**
CENTRAL PEOPLE'S BS, Geermu　　　DS-2 • 100 kW
CLANDESTINE (ASIA)
"ECHO OF HOPE", Seoul, South Korea　　　E Asia • 50 kW
IRAN
†VO THE ISLAMIC REP, Ahvāz　　　W • Mideast & W Asia • 250 kW

3987v **INDONESIA**
RRI, Manokwari, Papua　　　Irr • DS-TEMP INACTIVE • 1 kW

3990 **CHINA**
GANNAN PEOPLE'S BS, Hezuo　　　DS-CHINESE, TIBETAN • 15 kW
†XINJIANG PEOPLE'S BC STN, Urümqi　　　W • DS-UIGHUR • 50 kW

3995 **GERMANY**
†DEUTSCHE WELLE, Wertachtal　　　Europe • 500 kW
W • Europe • 500 kW

USA
†RFE-RL, Via Biblis, Germany　　　S Su-F • E Europe • 100 kW

4000 **CHINA**
NEI MENGGU PBS, Hohhot　　　DS • 50 kW

4000v **INDONESIA**
RRI, Kendari, Sulawesi　　　DS • 5 kW

4005 **VATICAN STATE**
VATICAN RADIO, Sta Maria di Galeria　　　⊟ • Europe • 100 kW
⊟ • Europe • 10 kW
VATICAN RADIO, Vatican City　　　⊟ • M-Sa • Europe • 10 kW
⊟ • Su • Europe • 10 kW

4010 **KYRGYZSTAN**
KYRGYZ RADIO, Bishkek　　　⊟ • ENGLISH & KYRGYZ • DS-1 • 50 kW
⊟ • DS-1 • 50 kW
⊟ • RUSSIAN & GERMAN • DS-1 • 50 kW

4025.3 **PIRATE (EUROPE)**
†"LASER HOT HITS", Ireland　　　⊟ • Irr • W Europe • 0.25 kW

4039.2 **PERU**
RADIO MARGINAL, Tocache　　　DS • 1 kW
Irr • DS • 1 kW

4040 **RUSSIA**
TURA RADIO, Tura　　　⊟ • RUSSIAN, ETC • DS-LOCAL, R ROSSII • 5 kW

4050 **KYRGYZSTAN**
†RADIO EXTOL, Bishkek　　　⊟ • RUSSIAN, ETC • C Asia

4052.5 **GUATEMALA**
†RADIO VERDAD, Chiquimula　　　DS • 0.28 kW

4060v **CLANDESTINE (M EAST)**
"VO THE KURD PEOPLE", Sulaymānīyah　　　ARABIC & KURDISH • Mideast • PRO-PUK

4085 **CLANDESTINE (M EAST)**
"HARIM RADIO", Salāh al-Dīn　　　⊟ • Mideast • PRO-KDP
"VO IRAQI KURDISTAN", Salāh al-Dīn　　　⊟ • Mideast • PRO-KDP

4143v **CLANDESTINE (M EAST)**
"VO IRANIAN KORDESTAN"　　　Mideast • ANTI-IRANIAN GOVT

4286v **CLANDESTINE (M EAST)**
†"VO STRUGGLE IRANIAN KURDISTAN"　　　⊟ • Irr • Mideast & W Asia • 4260-4290 KHZ

4319 **USA**
AFRTS, Via Diego Garcia　　　S Asia • USB • ALT. FREQ. TO 12579 kHz

4330 **CHINA**
†XINJIANG PEOPLE'S BC STN, Urümqi　　　W • DS-KAZAK • 100 kW

4335v **PERU**
†RADIO NAYLAMP, Lambayeque　　　DS • 0.5 kW

0 1 2 3 4 5 6 7 8 9 10 11 12 13 14 15 16 17 18 19 20 21 22 23 24

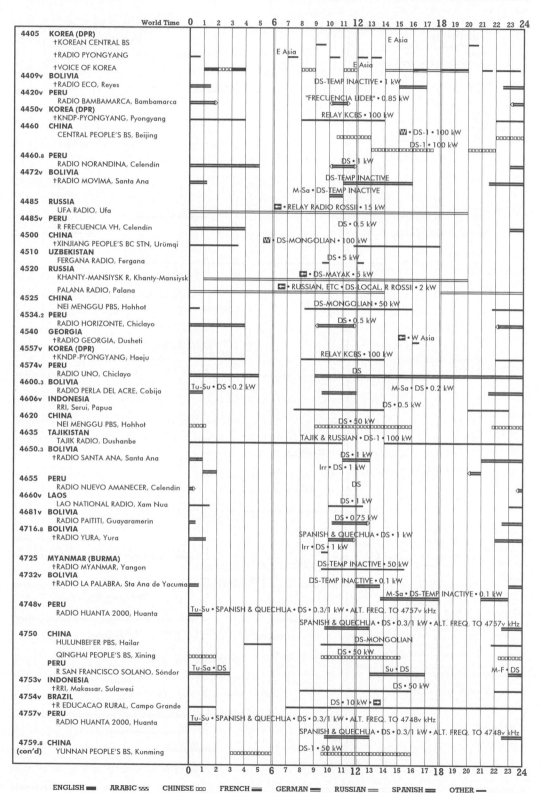

World Time	4405 KOREA (DPR)

4405 **KOREA (DPR)**
  †KOREAN CENTRAL BS — E Asia
  †RADIO PYONGYANG — E Asia
  †VOICE OF KOREA — E Asia
4409v **BOLIVIA**
  †RADIO ECO, Reyes — DS-TEMP INACTIVE • 1 kW
4420v **PERU**
  RADIO BAMBAMARCA, Bambamarca — "FRECUENCIA LIDER" • 0.85 kW
4450v **KOREA (DPR)**
  †KNDP-PYONGYANG, Pyongyang — RELAY KCBS • 100 kW
4460 **CHINA**
  CENTRAL PEOPLE'S BS, Beijing — W • DS-1 • 100 kW — DS-1 • 100 kW
4460.8 **PERU**
  RADIO NORANDINA, Celendin — DS • 1 kW
4472v **BOLIVIA**
  †RADIO MOVIMA, Santa Ana — DS-TEMP INACTIVE — M-Sa • DS-TEMP INACTIVE
4485 **RUSSIA**
  UFA RADIO, Ufa — • RELAY RADIO ROSSII • 15 kW
4485v **PERU**
  R FRECUENCIA VH, Celendin — DS • 0.5 kW
4500 **CHINA**
  †XINJIANG PEOPLE'S BC STN, Urümqi — W • DS-MONGOLIAN • 100 kW
4510 **UZBEKISTAN**
  FERGANA RADIO, Fergana — DS • 5 kW
4520 **RUSSIA**
  KHANTY-MANSIYSK R, Khanty-Mansiysk — • DS-MAYAK • 5 kW
  PALANA RADIO, Palana — • RUSSIAN, ETC • DS-LOCAL, R ROSSII • 2 kW
4525 **CHINA**
  NEI MENGGU PBS, Hohhot — DS-MONGOLIAN • 50 kW
4534.2 **PERU**
  RADIO HORIZONTE, Chiclayo — DS • 0.5 kW
4540 **GEORGIA**
  †RADIO GEORGIA, Dusheti — • W Asia
4557v **KOREA (DPR)**
  †KNDP-PYONGYANG, Haeju — RELAY KCBS • 100 kW
4574v **PERU**
  RADIO UNO, Chiclayo — DS
4600.3 **BOLIVIA**
  RADIO PERLA DEL ACRE, Cobija — Tu-Su • DS • 0.2 kW — M-Sa • DS • 0.2 kW
4606v **INDONESIA**
  RRI, Serui, Papua — DS • 0.5 kW
4620 **CHINA**
  NEI MENGGU PBS, Hohhot — DS • 50 kW
4635 **TAJIKISTAN**
  TAJIK RADIO, Dushanbe — TAJIK & RUSSIAN • DS-1 • 100 kW
4650.3 **BOLIVIA**
  †RADIO SANTA ANA, Santa Ana — DS • 1 kW — Irr • DS • 1 kW
4655 **PERU**
  RADIO NUEVO AMANECER, Celendin — DS
4660v **LAOS**
  LAO NATIONAL RADIO, Xam Nua — DS • 1 kW
4681v **BOLIVIA**
  RADIO PAITITI, Guayaramerin — DS • 0.75 kW
4716.8 **BOLIVIA**
  †RADIO YURA, Yura — SPANISH & QUECHUA • DS • 1 kW — Irr • DS • 1 kW
4725 **MYANMAR (BURMA)**
  †RADIO MYANMAR, Yangon — DS-TEMP INACTIVE • 50 kW
4732v **BOLIVIA**
  †RADIO LA PALABRA, Sta Ana de Yacuma — DS-TEMP INACTIVE • 0.1 kW — M-Sa • DS-TEMP INACTIVE • 0.1 kW
4748v **PERU**
  RADIO HUANTA 2000, Huanta — Tu-Su • SPANISH & QUECHUA • DS • 0.3/1 kW • ALT. FREQ. TO 4757v kHz — SPANISH & QUECHUA • DS • 0.3/1 kW • ALT. FREQ. TO 4757v kHz
4750 **CHINA**
  HULUNBEI'ER PBS, Hailar — DS-MONGOLIAN
  QINGHAI PEOPLE'S BS, Xining — DS • 50 kW
  PERU
  R SAN FRANCISCO SOLANO, Sóndor — Tu-Sa • DS — Su • DS — M-F • DS
4753v **INDONESIA**
  †RRI, Makassar, Sulawesi — DS • 50 kW
4754v **BRAZIL**
  †R EDUCACAO RURAL, Campo Grande — DS • 10 kW •
4757v **PERU**
  RADIO HUANTA 2000, Huanta — Tu-Su • SPANISH & QUECHUA • DS • 0.3/1 kW • ALT. FREQ. TO 4748v kHz — SPANISH & QUECHUA • DS • 0.3/1 kW • ALT. FREQ. TO 4748v kHz
4759.8 **CHINA**
(con'd) YUNNAN PEOPLE'S BS, Kunming — DS-1 • 50 kW

ENGLISH ■■■   ARABIC ⌇⌇⌇   CHINESE ▭▭▭   FRENCH ═══   GERMAN ▬▬▬   RUSSIAN ══   SPANISH ═══   OTHER ▬▬

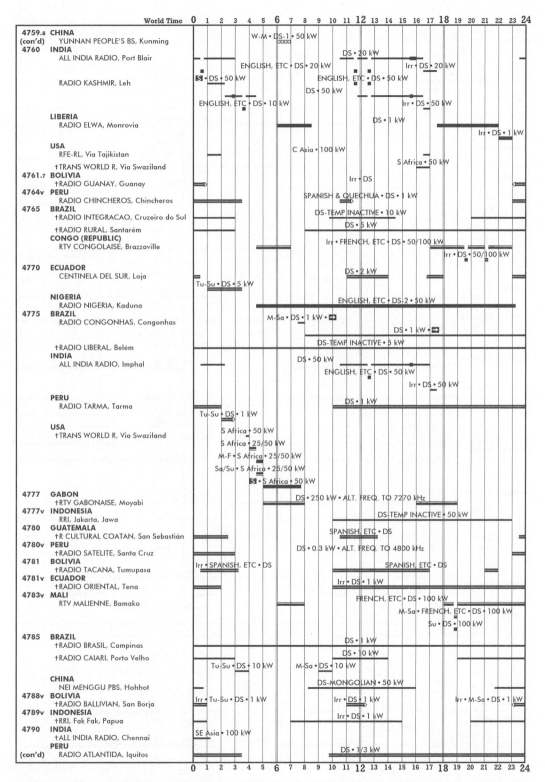

World Time	Station
4759.8 (con'd)	**CHINA** YUNNAN PEOPLE'S BS, Kunming
4760	**INDIA** ALL INDIA RADIO, Port Blair
	RADIO KASHMIR, Leh
	LIBERIA RADIO ELWA, Monrovia
	USA RFE-RL, Via Tajikistan
	†TRANS WORLD R, Via Swaziland
4761.7	**BOLIVIA** †RADIO GUANAY, Guanay
4764v	**PERU** RADIO CHINCHEROS, Chincheros
4765	**BRAZIL** †RADIO INTEGRACAO, Cruzeiro do Sul
	†RADIO RURAL, Santarém
	CONGO (REPUBLIC) RTV CONGOLAISE, Brazzaville
4770	**ECUADOR** CENTINELA DEL SUR, Loja
	NIGERIA RADIO NIGERIA, Kaduna
4775	**BRAZIL** RADIO CONGONHAS, Congonhas
	†RADIO LIBERAL, Belém
	INDIA ALL INDIA RADIO, Imphal
	PERU RADIO TARMA, Tarma
	USA †TRANS WORLD R, Via Swaziland
4777	**GABON** †RTV GABONAISE, Moyabi
4777v	**INDONESIA** RRI, Jakarta, Jawa
4780	**GUATEMALA** †R CULTURAL COATAN, San Sebastián
4780v	**PERU** †RADIO SATELITE, Santa Cruz
4781	**BOLIVIA** †RADIO TACANA, Tumupasa
4781v	**ECUADOR** †RADIO ORIENTAL, Tena
4783v	**MALI** RTV MALIENNE, Bamako
4785	**BRAZIL** †RADIO BRASIL, Campinas
	†RADIO CAIARI, Porto Velho
	CHINA NEI MENGGU PBS, Hohhot
4788v	**BOLIVIA** †RADIO BALLIVIAN, San Borja
4789v	**INDONESIA** †RRI, Fak Fak, Papua
4790	**INDIA** †ALL INDIA RADIO, Chennai
(con'd)	**PERU** RADIO ATLANTIDA, Iquitos

Partial broadcast-schedule annotations (World Time 0–24):

- **CHINA** YUNNAN PEOPLE'S BS, Kunming — W-M • DS-1 • 50 kW
- **INDIA** ALL INDIA RADIO, Port Blair — DS • 20 kW / ENGLISH, ETC • DS • 20 kW / Irr • DS • 20 kW
- RADIO KASHMIR, Leh — S • DS • 50 kW / ENGLISH, ETC • DS • 50 kW / DS • 50 kW / ENGLISH, ETC • DS • 10 kW / Irr • DS • 50 kW
- **LIBERIA** RADIO ELWA, Monrovia — DS • 1 kW / Irr • DS • 1 kW
- **USA** RFE-RL, Via Tajikistan — C Asia • 100 kW
- †TRANS WORLD R, Via Swaziland — S Africa • 50 kW
- **BOLIVIA** †RADIO GUANAY, Guanay — Irr • DS
- **PERU** RADIO CHINCHEROS, Chincheros — SPANISH & QUECHUA • DS • 1 kW
- **BRAZIL** †RADIO INTEGRACAO, Cruzeiro do Sul — DS-TEMP INACTIVE • 10 kW
- †RADIO RURAL, Santarém — DS • 5 kW
- **CONGO (REPUBLIC)** RTV CONGOLAISE, Brazzaville — Irr • FRENCH, ETC • DS • 50/100 kW / Irr • DS • 50/100 kW
- **ECUADOR** CENTINELA DEL SUR, Loja — DS • 2 kW / Tu-Su • DS • 5 kW
- **NIGERIA** RADIO NIGERIA, Kaduna — ENGLISH, ETC • DS-2 • 50 kW
- **BRAZIL** RADIO CONGONHAS, Congonhas — M-Sa • DS • 1 kW • ➡ / DS • 1 kW • ➡
- †RADIO LIBERAL, Belém — DS-TEMP INACTIVE • 5 kW
- **INDIA** ALL INDIA RADIO, Imphal — DS • 50 kW / ENGLISH, ETC • DS • 50 kW / Irr • DS • 50 kW
- **PERU** RADIO TARMA, Tarma — DS • 1 kW / Tu-Su • DS • 1 kW
- **USA** †TRANS WORLD R, Via Swaziland — S Africa • 50 kW / S Africa • 25/50 kW / M-F • S Africa • 25/50 kW / Sa/Su • S Africa • 25/50 kW / S • S Africa • 50 kW
- **GABON** †RTV GABONAISE, Moyabi — DS • 250 kW • ALT. FREQ. TO 7270 kHz
- **INDONESIA** RRI, Jakarta, Jawa — DS-TEMP INACTIVE • 50 kW
- **GUATEMALA** †R CULTURAL COATAN, San Sebastián — SPANISH, ETC • DS
- **PERU** †RADIO SATELITE, Santa Cruz — DS • 0.3 kW • ALT. FREQ. TO 4800 kHz
- **BOLIVIA** †RADIO TACANA, Tumupasa — Irr • SPANISH, ETC • DS / SPANISH, ETC • DS
- **ECUADOR** †RADIO ORIENTAL, Tena — Irr • DS • 1 kW
- **MALI** RTV MALIENNE, Bamako — FRENCH, ETC • DS • 100 kW / M-Sa • FRENCH, ETC • DS • 100 kW / Su • DS • 100 kW
- **BRAZIL** †RADIO BRASIL, Campinas — DS • 1 kW
- †RADIO CAIARI, Porto Velho — DS • 10 kW / Tu-Su • DS • 10 kW / M-Sa • DS • 10 kW
- **CHINA** NEI MENGGU PBS, Hohhot — DS-MONGOLIAN • 50 kW
- **BOLIVIA** †RADIO BALLIVIAN, San Borja — Irr • Tu-Su • DS • 1 kW / Irr • DS • 1 kW / Irr • M-Sa • DS • 1 kW
- **INDONESIA** †RRI, Fak Fak, Papua — Irr • DS • 1 kW
- **INDIA** †ALL INDIA RADIO, Chennai — SE Asia • 100 kW
- **PERU** RADIO ATLANTIDA, Iquitos — DS • 1/3 kW

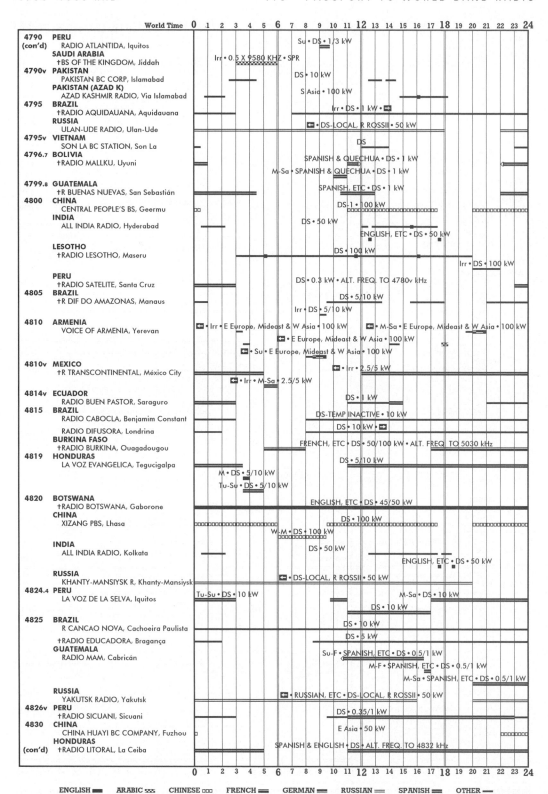

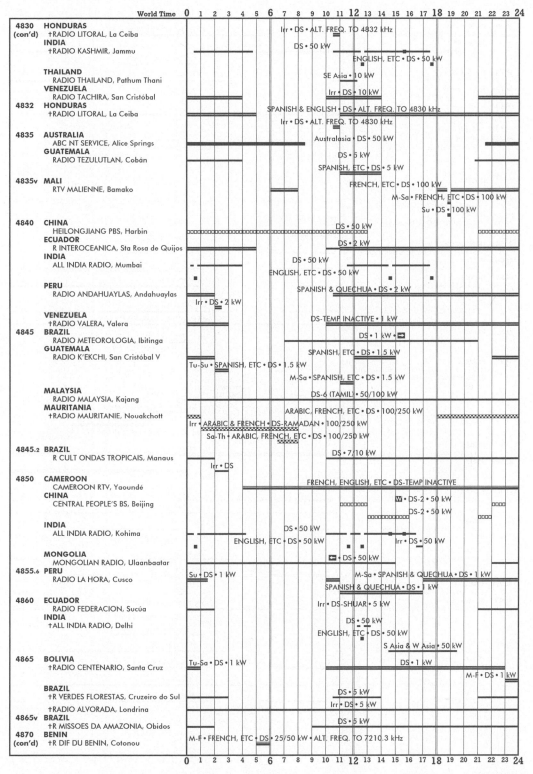

World Time 0 1 2 3 4 5 6 7 8 9 10 11 12 13 14 15 16 17 18 19 20 21 22 23 24

Freq	Country / Station	
4830 (con'd)	HONDURAS †RADIO LITORAL, La Ceiba	Irr • DS • ALT. FREQ. TO 4832 kHz
	INDIA †RADIO KASHMIR, Jammu	DS • 50 kW — ENGLISH, ETC • DS • 50 kW
	THAILAND RADIO THAILAND, Pathum Thani	SE Asia • 10 kW
	VENEZUELA RADIO TACHIRA, San Cristóbal	Irr • DS • 10 kW
4832	HONDURAS †RADIO LITORAL, La Ceiba	SPANISH & ENGLISH • DS • ALT. FREQ. TO 4830 kHz — Irr • DS • ALT. FREQ. TO 4830 kHz
4835	AUSTRALIA ABC NT SERVICE, Alice Springs	Australasia • DS • 50 kW
	GUATEMALA RADIO TEZULUTLAN, Cobán	DS • 5 kW — SPANISH, ETC • DS • 5 kW
4835v	MALI RTV MALIENNE, Bamako	FRENCH, ETC • DS • 100 kW — M-Sa • FRENCH, ETC • DS • 100 kW — Su • DS • 100 kW
4840	CHINA HEILONGJIANG PBS, Harbin	DS • 50 kW
	ECUADOR R INTEROCEANICA, Sta Rosa de Quijos	DS • 2 kW
	INDIA ALL INDIA RADIO, Mumbai	DS • 50 kW — ENGLISH, ETC • DS • 50 kW
	PERU RADIO ANDAHUAYLAS, Andahuaylas	SPANISH & QUECHUA • DS • 2 kW — Irr • DS • 2 kW
	VENEZUELA †RADIO VALERA, Valera	DS-TEMP INACTIVE • 1 kW
4845	BRAZIL RADIO METEOROLOGIA, Ibitinga	DS • 1 kW • →
	GUATEMALA RADIO K'EKCHI, San Cristóbal V	SPANISH, ETC • DS • 1.5 kW — Tu-Su • SPANISH, ETC • DS • 1.5 kW — M-Sa • SPANISH, ETC • DS • 1.5 kW
	MALAYSIA RADIO MALAYSIA, Kajang	DS-6 (TAMIL) • 50/100 kW
	MAURITANIA †RADIO MAURITANIE, Nouakchott	ARABIC, FRENCH, ETC • DS • 100/250 kW — Irr • ARABIC & FRENCH • DS-RAMADAN • 100/250 kW — Sa-Th • ARABIC, FRENCH, ETC • DS • 100/250 kW
4845.2	BRAZIL R CULT ONDAS TROPICAIS, Manaus	DS • 7/10 kW — Irr • DS
4850	CAMEROON CAMEROON RTV, Yaoundé	FRENCH, ENGLISH, ETC • DS-TEMP INACTIVE
	CHINA CENTRAL PEOPLE'S BS, Beijing	W • DS-2 • 50 kW — DS-2 • 50 kW
	INDIA ALL INDIA RADIO, Kohima	DS • 50 kW — ENGLISH, ETC • DS • 50 kW — Irr • DS • 50 kW
	MONGOLIA MONGOLIAN RADIO, Ulaanbaatar	← DS • 50 kW
4855.6	PERU RADIO LA HORA, Cusco	Su • DS • 1 kW — M-Sa • SPANISH & QUECHUA • DS • 1 kW — SPANISH & QUECHUA • DS • 1 kW
4860	ECUADOR RADIO FEDERACION, Sucúa	Irr • DS-SHUAR • 5 kW
	INDIA †ALL INDIA RADIO, Delhi	DS • 50 kW — ENGLISH, ETC • DS • 50 kW — S Asia & W Asia • 50 kW
4865	BOLIVIA †RADIO CENTENARIO, Santa Cruz	Tu-Sa • DS • 1 kW — DS • 1 kW — M-F • DS • 1 kW
	BRAZIL †R VERDES FLORESTAS, Cruzeiro do Sul	DS • 5 kW
	†RADIO ALVORADA, Londrina	Irr • DS • 5 kW
4865v	BRAZIL †R MISSOES DA AMAZONIA, Obidos	DS • 5 kW
4870 (con'd)	BENIN †R DIF DU BENIN, Cotonou	M-F • FRENCH, ETC • DS • 25/50 kW • ALT. FREQ. TO 7210.3 kHz

0 1 2 3 4 5 6 7 8 9 10 11 12 13 14 15 16 17 18 19 20 21 22 23 24

SEASONAL S OR W   1-HR TIMESHIFT MIDYEAR ← OR →   JAMMING / OR ∧   EARLIEST HEARD ◁   LATEST HEARD ▷   NEW FOR 2004 †

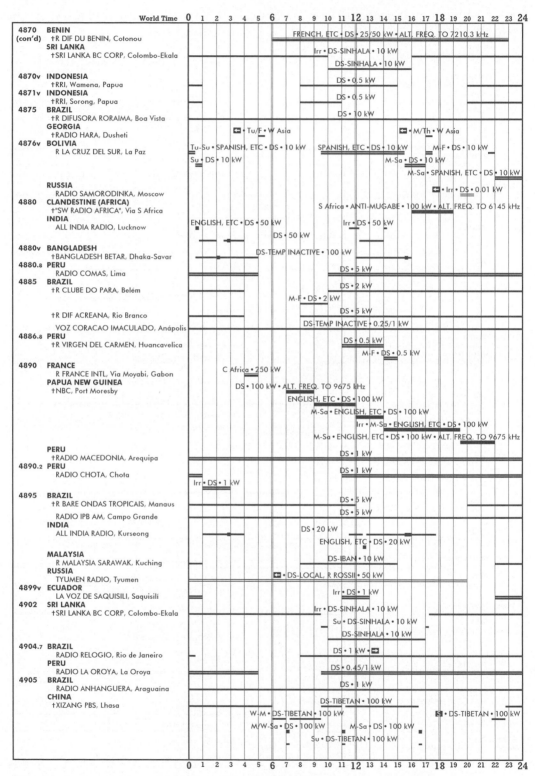

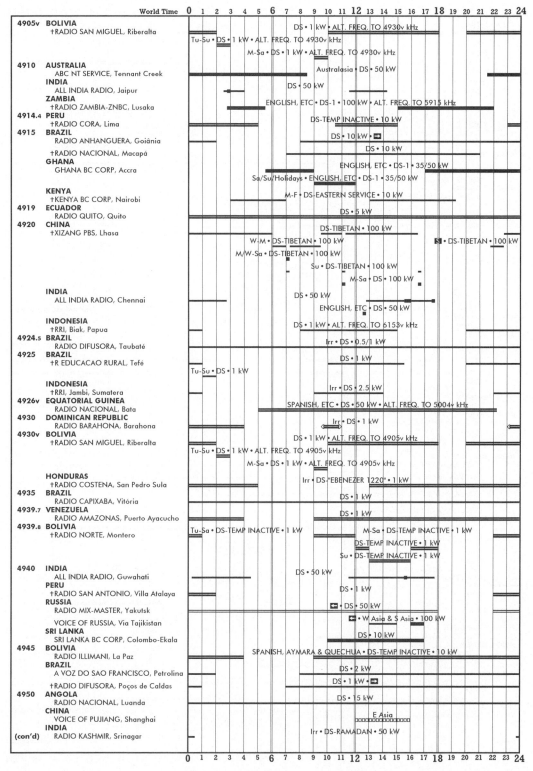

World Time 0 1 2 3 4 5 6 7 8 9 10 11 12 13 14 15 16 17 18 19 20 21 22 23 24

4905v BOLIVIA
†RADIO SAN MIGUEL, Riberalta
DS • 1 kW • ALT. FREQ. TO 4930v kHz
Tu-Su • DS • 1 kW • ALT. FREQ. TO 4930v kHz
M-Sa • DS • 1 kW • ALT. FREQ. TO 4930v kHz

4910 AUSTRALIA
ABC NT SERVICE, Tennant Creek
Australasia • DS • 50 kW
INDIA
ALL INDIA RADIO, Jaipur
DS • 50 kW
ZAMBIA
†RADIO ZAMBIA-ZNBC, Lusaka
ENGLISH, ETC • DS-1 • 100 kW • ALT. FREQ. TO 5915 kHz
4914.4 PERU
†RADIO CORA, Lima
DS-TEMP INACTIVE • 10 kW
4915 BRAZIL
RADIO ANHANGUERA, Goiânia
DS • 10 kW •
†RADIO NACIONAL, Macapá
DS • 10 kW
GHANA
GHANA BC CORP, Accra
ENGLISH, ETC • DS-1 • 35/50 kW
Sa/Su/Holidays • ENGLISH, ETC • DS-1 • 35/50 kW
KENYA
†KENYA BC CORP, Nairobi
M-F • DS-EASTERN SERVICE • 10 kW
4919 ECUADOR
RADIO QUITO, Quito
DS • 5 kW
4920 CHINA
†XIZANG PBS, Lhasa
DS-TIBETAN • 100 kW
W-M • DS-TIBETAN • 100 kW
DS-TIBETAN • 100 kW
M/W-Sa • DS-TIBETAN • 100 kW
Su • DS-TIBETAN • 100 kW
M-Sa • DS • 100 kW
INDIA
ALL INDIA RADIO, Chennai
DS • 50 kW
ENGLISH, ETC • DS • 50 kW
INDONESIA
†RRI, Biak, Papua
DS • 1 kW • ALT. FREQ. TO 6153v kHz
4924.5 BRAZIL
RADIO DIFUSORA, Taubaté
Irr • DS • 0.5/1 kW
4925 BRAZIL
†R EDUCACAO RURAL, Tefé
DS • 1 kW
Tu-Su • DS • 1 kW
INDONESIA
†RRI, Jambi, Sumatera
Irr • DS • 2.5 kW
4926v EQUATORIAL GUINEA
RADIO NACIONAL, Bata
SPANISH, ETC • DS • 50 kW • ALT. FREQ. TO 5004v kHz
4930 DOMINICAN REPUBLIC
RADIO BARAHONA, Barahona
Irr • DS • 1 kW
4930v BOLIVIA
†RADIO SAN MIGUEL, Riberalta
DS • 1 kW • ALT. FREQ. TO 4905v kHz
Tu-Su • DS • 1 kW • ALT. FREQ. TO 4905v kHz
M-Sa • DS • 1 kW • ALT. FREQ. TO 4905v kHz
HONDURAS
†RADIO COSTENA, San Pedro Sula
Irr • DS-"EBENEZER 1220" • 1 kW
4935 BRAZIL
RADIO CAPIXABA, Vitória
DS • 1 kW
4939.7 VENEZUELA
RADIO AMAZONAS, Puerto Ayacucho
DS • 1 kW
4939.8 BOLIVIA
†RADIO NORTE, Montero
Tu-Sa • DS-TEMP INACTIVE • 1 kW
M-Sa • DS-TEMP INACTIVE • 1 kW
DS-TEMP INACTIVE • 1 kW
Su • DS-TEMP INACTIVE • 1 kW
4940 INDIA
ALL INDIA RADIO, Guwahati
DS • 50 kW
PERU
†RADIO SAN ANTONIO, Villa Atalaya
DS • 1 kW
RUSSIA
RADIO MIX-MASTER, Yakutsk
DS • 50 kW
VOICE OF RUSSIA, Via Tajikistan
• W Asia & S Asia • 100 kW
SRI LANKA
SRI LANKA BC CORP, Colombo-Ekala
DS • 10 kW
4945 BOLIVIA
RADIO ILLIMANI, La Paz
SPANISH, AYMARA & QUECHUA • DS-TEMP INACTIVE • 10 kW
BRAZIL
A VOZ DO SAO FRANCISCO, Petrolina
DS • 2 kW
†RADIO DIFUSORA, Poços de Caldas
DS • 1 kW •
4950 ANGOLA
RADIO NACIONAL, Luanda
DS • 15 kW
CHINA
VOICE OF PUJIANG, Shanghai
E Asia
INDIA
(con'd) RADIO KASHMIR, Srinagar
Irr • DS-RAMADAN • 50 kW

0 1 2 3 4 5 6 7 8 9 10 11 12 13 14 15 16 17 18 19 20 21 22 23 24

SEASONAL 🅢 OR 🅦 1-HR TIMESHIFT MIDYEAR ⬅ OR ➡ JAMMING / OR ∧ EARLIEST HEARD ◁ LATEST HEARD ▷ NEW FOR 2004 †

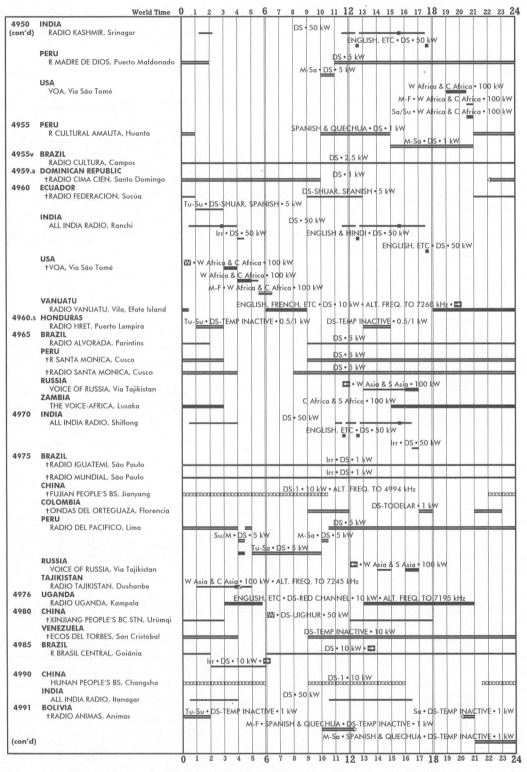

World Time	0 1 2 3 4 5 6 7 8 9 10 11 12 13 14 15 16 17 18 19 20 21 22 23 24

4950 **INDIA**
(con'd) RADIO KASHMIR, Srinagar — DS • 50 kW / ENGLISH, ETC • DS • 50 kW

PERU
R MADRE DE DIOS, Puerto Maldonado — DS • 5 kW / M-Sa • DS • 5 kW

USA
VOA, Via São Tomé — W Africa & C Africa • 100 kW / M-F • W Africa & C Africa • 100 kW / Sa/Su • W Africa & C Africa • 100 kW

4955 **PERU**
R CULTURAL AMAUTA, Huanta — SPANISH & QUECHUA • DS • 1 kW / M-Sa • DS • 1 kW

4955v **BRAZIL**
RADIO CULTURA, Campos — DS • 2.5 kW

4959.8 **DOMINICAN REPUBLIC**
†RADIO CIMA CIEN, Santo Domingo — DS • 1 kW

4960 **ECUADOR**
†RADIO FEDERACION, Sucúa — DS-SHUAR, SPANISH • 5 kW / Tu-Su • DS-SHUAR, SPANISH • 5 kW

INDIA
ALL INDIA RADIO, Ranchi — DS • 50 kW / Irr • DS • 50 kW / ENGLISH & HINDI • DS • 50 kW / ENGLISH, ETC • DS • 50 kW

USA
†VOA, Via São Tomé — W • W Africa & C Africa • 100 kW / W Africa & C Africa • 100 kW / M-F • W Africa & C Africa • 100 kW

VANUATU
RADIO VANUATU, Vila, Efate Island — ENGLISH, FRENCH, ETC • DS • 10 kW • ALT. FREQ. TO 7260 kHz •

4960.5 **HONDURAS**
RADIO HRET, Puerto Lempira — Tu-Su • DS-TEMP INACTIVE • 0.5/1 kW / DS-TEMP INACTIVE • 0.5/1 kW

4965 **BRAZIL**
RADIO ALVORADA, Parintins — DS • 5 kW

PERU
†R SANTA MONICA, Cusco — DS • 5 kW

†RADIO SANTA MONICA, Cusco — DS • 5 kW

RUSSIA
VOICE OF RUSSIA, Via Tajikistan — • W Asia & S Asia • 100 kW

ZAMBIA
THE VOICE-AFRICA, Lusaka — C Africa & S Africa • 100 kW

4970 **INDIA**
ALL INDIA RADIO, Shillong — DS • 50 kW / ENGLISH, ETC • DS • 50 kW / Irr • DS • 50 kW

4975 **BRAZIL**
†RADIO IGUATEMI, São Paulo — Irr • DS • 1 kW

†RADIO MUNDIAL, São Paulo — Irr • DS • 1 kW

CHINA
†FUJIAN PEOPLE'S BS, Jianyang — DS-1 • 10 kW • ALT. FREQ. TO 4994 kHz

COLOMBIA
†ONDAS DEL ORTEGUAZA, Florencia — DS-TODELAR • 1 kW

PERU
RADIO DEL PACIFICO, Lima — DS • 5 kW / Su/M • DS • 5 kW / M-Sa • DS • 5 kW / Tu-Sa • DS • 5 kW

RUSSIA
VOICE OF RUSSIA, Via Tajikistan — • W Asia & S Asia • 100 kW

TAJIKISTAN
RADIO TAJIKISTAN, Dushanbe — W Asia & C Asia • 100 kW • ALT. FREQ. TO 7245 kHz

4976 **UGANDA**
RADIO UGANDA, Kampala — ENGLISH, ETC • DS-RED CHANNEL • 10 kW • ALT. FREQ. TO 7195 kHz

4980 **CHINA**
†XINJIANG PEOPLE'S BC STN, Urümqi — W • DS-UIGHUR • 50 kW

VENEZUELA
†ECOS DEL TORBES, San Cristóbal — DS-TEMP INACTIVE • 10 kW

4985 **BRAZIL**
R BRASIL CENTRAL, Goiânia — DS • 10 kW • / Irr • DS • 10 kW •

4990 **CHINA**
HUNAN PEOPLE'S BS, Changsha — DS-1 • 10 kW

INDIA
ALL INDIA RADIO, Itanagar — DS • 50 kW

4991 **BOLIVIA**
†RADIO ANIMAS, Animas — Tu-Su • DS-TEMP INACTIVE • 1 kW / Sa • DS-TEMP INACTIVE • 1 kW / M-F • SPANISH & QUECHUA • DS-TEMP INACTIVE • 1 kW / M-Sa • SPANISH & QUECHUA • DS-TEMP INACTIVE • 1 kW

(con'd)

0 1 2 3 4 5 6 7 8 9 10 11 12 13 14 15 16 17 18 19 20 21 22 23 24

ENGLISH ▬ ARABIC ⋙ CHINESE ▭▭▭ FRENCH ▬▬ GERMAN ▬▬ RUSSIAN ══ SPANISH ▬▬ OTHER ▬

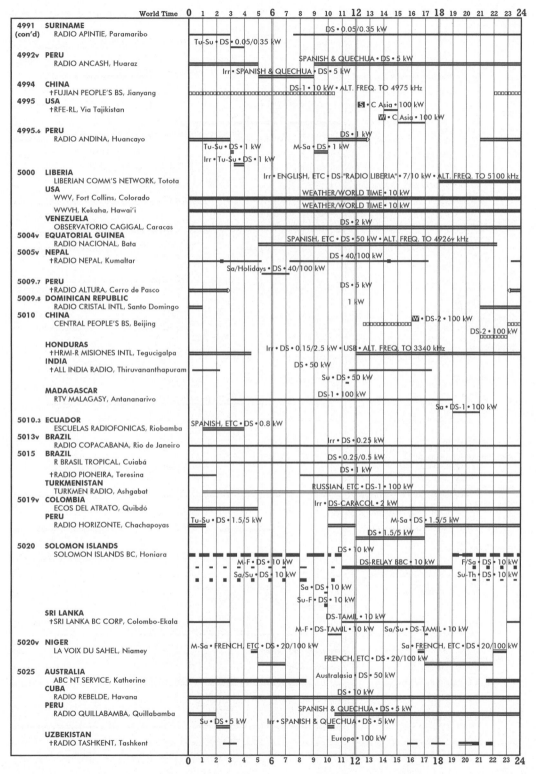

4991	**SURINAME**
(con'd)	RADIO APINTIE, Paramaribo
4992v	**PERU**
	RADIO ANCASH, Huaraz
4994	**CHINA**
	†FUJIAN PEOPLE'S BS, Jianyang
4995	**USA**
	†RFE-RL, Via Tajikistan
4995.6	**PERU**
	RADIO ANDINA, Huancayo
5000	**LIBERIA**
	LIBERIAN COMM'S NETWORK, Totota
	USA
	WWV, Fort Collins, Colorado
	WWVH, Kekaha, Hawai'i
	VENEZUELA
	OBSERVATORIO CAGIGAL, Caracas
5004v	**EQUATORIAL GUINEA**
	RADIO NACIONAL, Bata
5005v	**NEPAL**
	†RADIO NEPAL, Kumaltar
5009.7	**PERU**
	†RADIO ALTURA, Cerro de Pasco
5009.8	**DOMINICAN REPUBLIC**
	RADIO CRISTAL INTL, Santo Domingo
5010	**CHINA**
	CENTRAL PEOPLE'S BS, Beijing
	HONDURAS
	†HRMI-R MISIONES INTL, Tegucigalpa
	INDIA
	†ALL INDIA RADIO, Thiruvananthapuram
	MADAGASCAR
	RTV MALAGASY, Antananarivo
5010.3	**ECUADOR**
	ESCUELAS RADIOFONICAS, Riobamba
5013v	**BRAZIL**
	RADIO COPACABANA, Rio de Janeiro
5015	**BRAZIL**
	R BRASIL TROPICAL, Cuiabá
	†RADIO PIONEIRA, Teresina
	TURKMENISTAN
	TURKMEN RADIO, Ashgabat
5019v	**COLOMBIA**
	ECOS DEL ATRATO, Quibdó
	PERU
	RADIO HORIZONTE, Chachapoyas
5020	**SOLOMON ISLANDS**
	SOLOMON ISLANDS BC, Honiara
	SRI LANKA
	†SRI LANKA BC CORP, Colombo-Ekala
5020v	**NIGER**
	LA VOIX DU SAHEL, Niamey
5025	**AUSTRALIA**
	ABC NT SERVICE, Katherine
	CUBA
	RADIO REBELDE, Havana
	PERU
	RADIO QUILLABAMBA, Quillabamba
	UZBEKISTAN
	†RADIO TASHKENT, Tashkent

Selected programme details:

- DS • 0.05/0.35 kW
- Tu-Su • DS • 0.05/0.35 kW
- SPANISH & QUECHUA • DS • 5 kW
- Irr • SPANISH & QUECHUA • DS • 5 kW
- DS-1 • 10 kW • ALT. FREQ. TO 4975 kHz
- [S] • C Asia • 100 kW
- [W] • C Asia • 100 kW
- DS • 1 kW
- Tu-Su • DS • 1 kW
- M-Sa • DS • 1 kW
- Irr • Tu-Su • DS • 1 kW
- Irr • ENGLISH, ETC • DS "RADIO LIBERIA" • 7/10 kW • ALT. FREQ. TO 5100 kHz
- WEATHER/WORLD TIME • 10 kW
- WEATHER/WORLD TIME • 10 kW
- DS • 2 kW
- SPANISH, ETC • DS • 50 kW • ALT. FREQ. TO 4926v kHz
- DS • 40/100 kW
- Sa/Holidays • DS • 40/100 kW
- DS • 5 kW
- 1 kW
- [W] • DS-2 • 100 kW
- DS-2 • 100 kW
- Irr • DS • 0.15/2.5 kW • USB • ALT. FREQ. TO 3340 kHz
- DS • 50 kW
- Su • DS • 50 kW
- DS-1 • 100 kW
- Sa • DS-1 • 100 kW
- SPANISH, ETC • DS • 0.8 kW
- Irr • DS • 0.25 kW
- DS • 0.25/0.5 kW
- DS • 1 kW
- RUSSIAN, ETC • DS-1 • 100 kW
- Irr • DS-CARACOL • 2 kW
- Tu-Su • DS • 1.5/5 kW
- M-Sa • DS • 1.5/5 kW
- DS • 1.5/5 kW
- DS • 10 kW
- M-F • DS • 10 kW
- DS-RELAY BBC • 10 kW
- F/Sa • DS • 10 kW
- Sa/Su • DS • 10 kW
- Su-Th • DS • 10 kW
- Sa • DS • 10 kW
- Su-F • DS • 10 kW
- DS-TAMIL • 10 kW
- M-F • DS-TAMIL • 10 kW
- Sa/Su • DS-TAMIL • 10 kW
- M-Sa • FRENCH, ETC • DS • 20/100 kW
- Sa • FRENCH, ETC • DS • 20/100 kW
- FRENCH, ETC • DS • 20/100 kW
- Australasia • DS • 50 kW
- DS • 10 kW
- SPANISH & QUECHUA • DS • 5 kW
- Su • DS • 5 kW
- Irr • SPANISH & QUECHUA • DS • 5 kW
- Europe • 100 kW

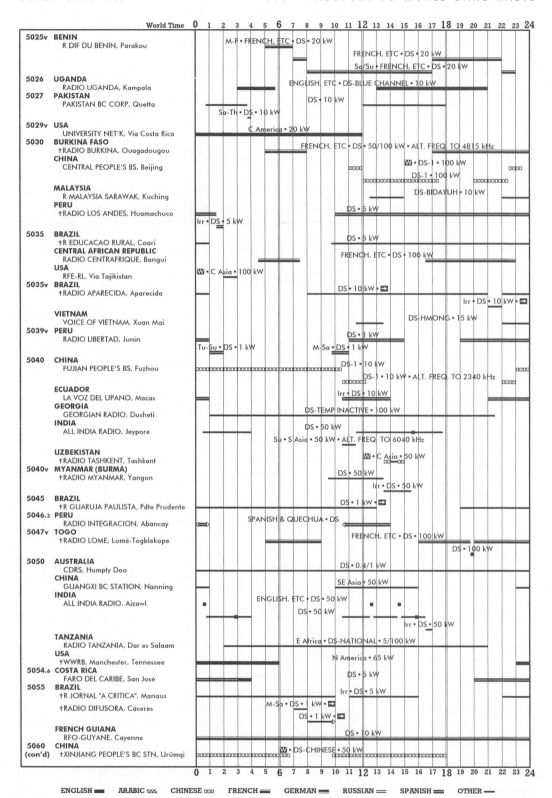

5025v	**BENIN**
	R DIF DU BENIN, Parakou
5026	**UGANDA**
	RADIO UGANDA, Kampala
5027	**PAKISTAN**
	PAKISTAN BC CORP, Quetta
5029v	**USA**
	UNIVERSITY NET'K, Via Costa Rica
5030	**BURKINA FASO**
	†RADIO BURKINA, Ouagadougou
	CHINA
	CENTRAL PEOPLE'S BS, Beijing
	MALAYSIA
	R MALAYSIA SARAWAK, Kuching
	PERU
	†RADIO LOS ANDES, Huamachuco
5035	**BRAZIL**
	†R EDUCACAO RURAL, Coari
	CENTRAL AFRICAN REPUBLIC
	RADIO CENTRAFRIQUE, Bangui
	USA
	RFE-RL, Via Tajikistan
5035v	**BRAZIL**
	†RADIO APARECIDA, Aparecida
	VIETNAM
	VOICE OF VIETNAM, Xuan Mai
5039v	**PERU**
	RADIO LIBERTAD, Junín
5040	**CHINA**
	FUJIAN PEOPLE'S BS, Fuzhou
	ECUADOR
	LA VOZ DEL UPANO, Macas
	GEORGIA
	GEORGIAN RADIO, Dusheti
	INDIA
	ALL INDIA RADIO, Jeypore
	UZBEKISTAN
	†RADIO TASHKENT, Tashkent
5040v	**MYANMAR (BURMA)**
	†RADIO MYANMAR, Yangon
5045	**BRAZIL**
	†R GUARUJA PAULISTA, Pdte Prudente
5046.3	**PERU**
	RADIO INTEGRACION, Abancay
5047v	**TOGO**
	†RADIO LOME, Lomé-Togblekope
5050	**AUSTRALIA**
	CDRS, Humpty Doo
	CHINA
	GUANGXI BC STATION, Nanning
	INDIA
	ALL INDIA RADIO, Aizawl
	TANZANIA
	RADIO TANZANIA, Dar es Salaam
	USA
	†WWRB, Manchester, Tennessee
5054.6	**COSTA RICA**
	FARO DEL CARIBE, San José
5055	**BRAZIL**
	†R JORNAL "A CRITICA", Manaus
	†RADIO DIFUSORA, Cáceres
	FRENCH GUIANA
	RFO-GUYANE, Cayenne
5060	**CHINA**
(con'd)	†XINJIANG PEOPLE'S BC STN, Urümqi

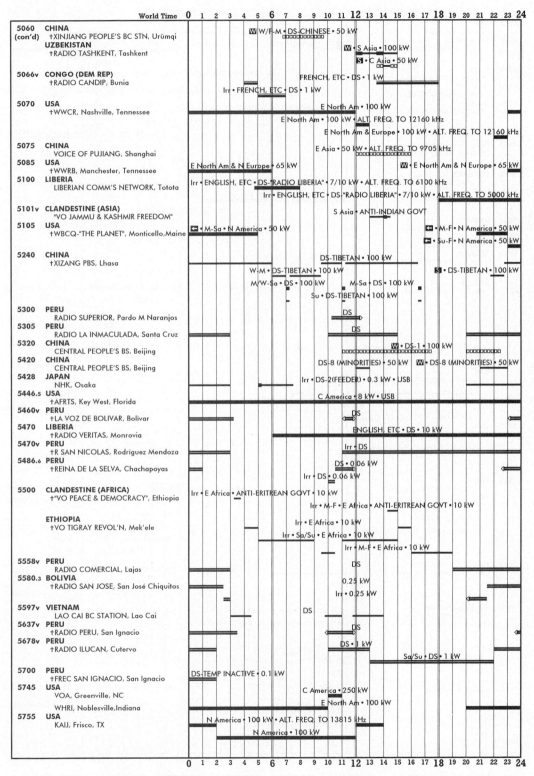

World Time 0 1 2 3 4 5 6 7 8 9 10 11 12 13 14 15 16 17 18 19 20 21 22 23 24

Freq	Country / Station	
5060 (con'd)	CHINA †XINJIANG PEOPLE'S BC STN, Urümqi	W·W/F-M·DS-CHINESE·50 kW
	UZBEKISTAN †RADIO TASHKENT, Tashkent	W·S Asia·100 kW / S·C Asia·50 kW
5066v	CONGO (DEM REP) †RADIO CANDIP, Bunia	FRENCH, ETC·DS·1 kW / Irr·FRENCH, ETC·DS·1 kW
5070	USA †WWCR, Nashville, Tennessee	E North Am·100 kW / E North Am·100 kW·ALT. FREQ. TO 12160 kHz / E North Am & Europe·100 kW·ALT. FREQ. TO 12160 kHz
5075	CHINA VOICE OF PUJIANG, Shanghai	E Asia·50 kW·ALT. FREQ. TO 9705 kHz
5085	USA †WWRB, Manchester, Tennessee	E North Am & N Europe·65 kW / W·E North Am & N Europe·65 kW
5100	LIBERIA LIBERIAN COMM'S NETWORK, Totota	Irr·ENGLISH, ETC·DS·"RADIO LIBERIA"·7/10 kW·ALT. FREQ. TO 6100 kHz / Irr·ENGLISH, ETC·DS·"RADIO LIBERIA"·7/10 kW·ALT. FREQ. TO 5000 kHz
5101v	CLANDESTINE (ASIA) "VO JAMMU & KASHMIR FREEDOM"	S Asia·ANTI-INDIAN GOVT
5105	USA †WBCQ-"THE PLANET", Monticello, Maine	·M-Sa·N America·50 kW / ·M-F·N America·50 kW / ·Su-F·N America·50 kW
5240	CHINA †XIZANG PBS, Lhasa	DS-TIBETAN·100 kW / W-M·DS-TIBETAN·100 kW / S·DS-TIBETAN·100 kW / M/W-Sa·DS·100 kW / M-Sa·DS·100 kW / Su·DS-TIBETAN·100 kW
5300	PERU RADIO SUPERIOR, Pardo M Naranjos	DS
5305	PERU RADIO LA INMACULADA, Santa Cruz	DS
5320	CHINA CENTRAL PEOPLE'S BS, Beijing	W·DS-1·100 kW
5420	CHINA CENTRAL PEOPLE'S BS, Beijing	DS-8 (MINORITIES)·50 kW / W·DS-8 (MINORITIES)·50 kW
5428	JAPAN NHK, Osaka	Irr·DS-2 (FEEDER)·0.3 kW·USB
5446.5	USA †AFRTS, Key West, Florida	C America·8 kW·USB
5460v	PERU †LA VOZ DE BOLIVAR, Bolivar	DS
5470	LIBERIA †RADIO VERITAS, Monrovia	ENGLISH, ETC·DS·10 kW
5470v	PERU †R SAN NICOLAS, Rodriguez Mendoza	Irr·DS
5486.6	PERU †REINA DE LA SELVA, Chachapoyas	DS·0.06 kW / Irr·DS·0.06 kW
5500	CLANDESTINE (AFRICA) †"VO PEACE & DEMOCRACY", Ethiopia	Irr·E Africa·ANTI-ERITREAN GOVT·10 kW / Irr·M-F·E Africa·ANTI-ERITREAN GOVT·10 kW
	ETHIOPIA †VO TIGRAY REVOL'N, Mek'ele	Irr·E Africa·10 kW / Irr·Sa/Su·E Africa·10 kW / Irr·M-F·E Africa·10 kW
5558v	PERU RADIO COMERCIAL, Lajas	DS
5580.3	BOLIVIA †RADIO SAN JOSE, San José Chiquitos	0.25 kW / Irr·0.25 kW
5597v	VIETNAM LAO CAI BC STATION, Lao Cai	DS
5637v	PERU †RADIO PERU, San Ignacio	DS
5678v	PERU †RADIO ILUCAN, Cutervo	DS·1 kW / Sa/Su·DS·1 kW
5700	PERU †FREC SAN IGNACIO, San Ignacio	DS-TEMP INACTIVE·0.1 kW
5745	USA VOA, Greenville, NC	C America·250 kW
	WHRI, Noblesville, Indiana	E North Am·100 kW
5755	USA KAIJ, Frisco, TX	N America·100 kW·ALT. FREQ. TO 13815 kHz / N America·100 kW

0 1 2 3 4 5 6 7 8 9 10 11 12 13 14 15 16 17 18 19 20 21 22 23 24

SEASONAL S OR W   1-HR TIMESHIFT MIDYEAR ⇇ OR ⇉   JAMMING / OR ∧   EARLIEST HEARD ◁   LATEST HEARD ▷   NEW FOR 2004 †

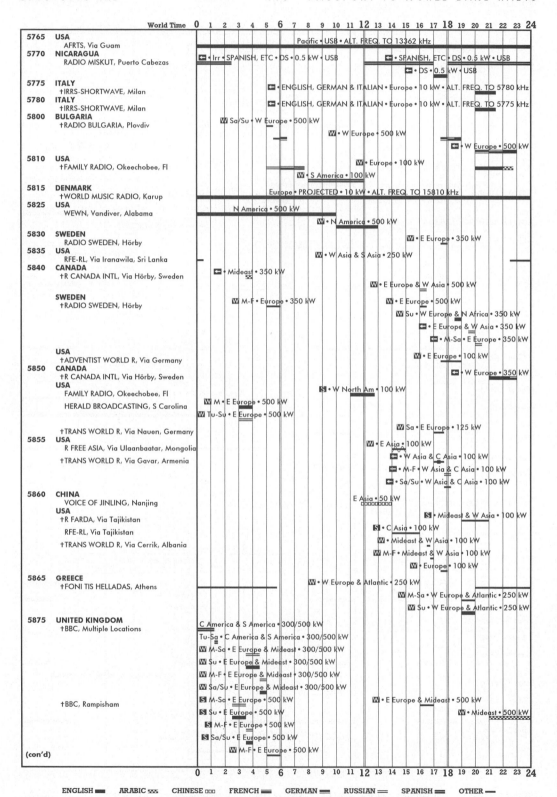

5765 USA	
AFRTS, Via Guam	Pacific • USB • ALT. FREQ. TO 13362 kHz
5770 NICARAGUA	
RADIO MISKUT, Puerto Cabezas	Irr • SPANISH, ETC • DS • 0.5 kW • USB / SPANISH, ETC • DS • 0.5 kW • USB / DS • 0.5 kW • USB
5775 ITALY	
†IRRS-SHORTWAVE, Milan	ENGLISH, GERMAN & ITALIAN • Europe • 10 kW • ALT. FREQ. TO 5780 kHz
5780 ITALY	
†IRRS-SHORTWAVE, Milan	ENGLISH, GERMAN & ITALIAN • Europe • 10 kW • ALT. FREQ. TO 5775 kHz
5800 BULGARIA	
†RADIO BULGARIA, Plovdiv	Sa/Su • W Europe • 500 kW / W • W Europe • 500 kW / W Europe • 500 kW
5810 USA	
†FAMILY RADIO, Okeechobee, Fl	Europe • 100 kW / S America • 100 kW
5815 DENMARK	
†WORLD MUSIC RADIO, Karup	Europe • PROJECTED • 10 kW • ALT. FREQ. TO 15810 kHz
5825 USA	
WEWN, Vandiver, Alabama	N America • 500 kW / W • N America • 500 kW
5830 SWEDEN	
RADIO SWEDEN, Hörby	W • E Europe • 350 kW
5835 USA	
RFE-RL, Via Iranawila, Sri Lanka	W • W Asia & S Asia • 250 kW
5840 CANADA	
†R CANADA INTL, Via Hörby, Sweden	Mideast • 350 kW / W • E Europe & W Asia • 500 kW
SWEDEN	
†RADIO SWEDEN, Hörby	M-F • Europe • 350 kW / W • E Europe • 500 kW / Su • W Europe & N Africa • 350 kW / E Europe & W Asia • 350 kW / M-Sa • E Europe • 350 kW
USA	
†ADVENTIST WORLD R, Via Germany	W • E Europe • 100 kW
5850 CANADA	
†R CANADA INTL, Via Hörby, Sweden	W • E Europe • 350 kW
USA	
FAMILY RADIO, Okeechobee, Fl	S • W North Am • 100 kW
HERALD BROADCASTING, S Carolina	M • E Europe • 500 kW / Tu-Su • E Europe • 500 kW
†TRANS WORLD R, Via Nauen, Germany	Sa • E Europe • 125 kW
5855 USA	
R FREE ASIA, Via Ulaanbaatar, Mongolia	W • E Asia • 100 kW
†TRANS WORLD R, Via Gavar, Armenia	W Asia & C Asia • 100 kW / M-F • W Asia & C Asia • 100 kW / Sa/Su • W Asia & C Asia • 100 kW
5860 CHINA	
VOICE OF JINLING, Nanjing	E Asia • 50 kW
USA	
†R FARDA, Via Tajikistan	S • Mideast & W Asia • 100 kW
RFE-RL, Via Tajikistan	S • C Asia • 100 kW
†TRANS WORLD R, Via Cerrik, Albania	W • Mideast & W Asia • 100 kW / M-F • Mideast & W Asia • 100 kW / W • Europe • 100 kW
5865 GREECE	
†FONI TIS HELLADAS, Athens	W • W Europe & Atlantic • 250 kW / M-Sa • W Europe & Atlantic • 250 kW / Su • W Europe & Atlantic • 250 kW
5875 UNITED KINGDOM	
†BBC, Multiple Locations	C America & S America • 300/500 kW / Tu-Sa • C America & S America • 300/500 kW / M-Sa • E Europe & Mideast • 300/500 kW / Su • E Europe & Mideast • 300/500 kW / M-F • E Europe & Mideast • 300/500 kW / Sa/Su • E Europe & Mideast • 300/500 kW
†BBC, Rampisham	M-Sa • E Europe • 500 kW / E Europe & Mideast • 500 kW / Su • E Europe • 500 kW / Mideast • 500 kW / M-F • E Europe • 500 kW / Sa/Su • E Europe • 500 kW / M-F • E Europe • 500 kW

(con'd)

ENGLISH ▬ ARABIC ▨ CHINESE ▯▯▯ FRENCH ▭ GERMAN ▬ RUSSIAN ═ SPANISH ▬ OTHER ▬

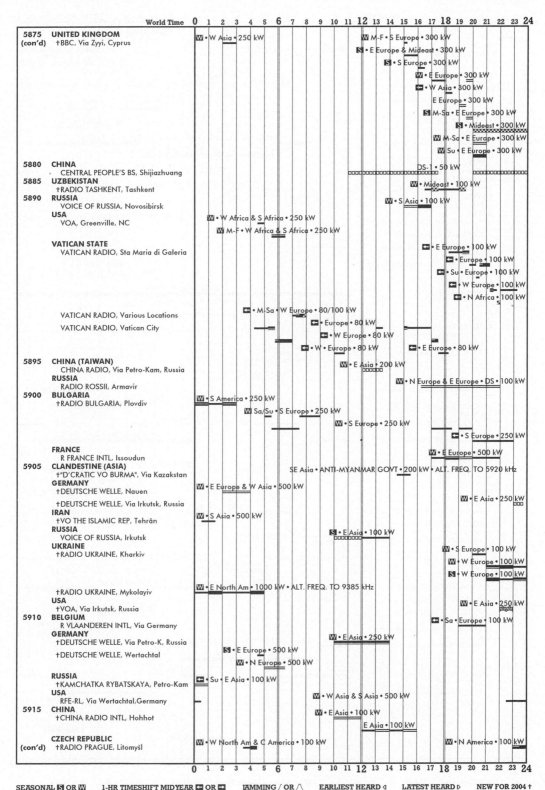

World Time

5875	UNITED KINGDOM
(con'd)	†BBC, Via Zyyi, Cyprus

W • W Asia • 250 kW
W M-F • S Europe • 300 kW
S • E Europe & Mideast • 300 kW
S • S Europe • 300 kW
W • E Europe • 300 kW
• W Asia • 300 kW
E Europe • 300 kW
S M-Sa • E Europe • 300 kW
S • Mideast • 300 kW
W M-Sa • E Europe • 300 kW
W Su • E Europe • 300 kW

5880	CHINA
	CENTRAL PEOPLE'S BS, Shijiazhuang

DS-1 • 50 kW

5885	UZBEKISTAN
	†RADIO TASHKENT, Tashkent

W • Mideast • 100 kW

5890	RUSSIA
	VOICE OF RUSSIA, Novosibirsk
	USA
	VOA, Greenville, NC

W • S Asia • 100 kW
W • W Africa & S Africa • 250 kW
W M-F • W Africa & S Africa • 250 kW

VATICAN STATE
VATICAN RADIO, Sta Maria di Galeria

• E Europe • 100 kW
• Europe • 100 kW
• Su • Europe • 100 kW
• W Europe • 100 kW
• N Africa • 100 kW

VATICAN RADIO, Various Locations

• M-Sa • W Europe • 80/100 kW

VATICAN RADIO, Vatican City

• Europe • 80 kW
• W Europe • 80 kW
• W • Europe • 80 kW
• E Europe • 80 kW

5895	CHINA (TAIWAN)
	CHINA RADIO, Via Petro-Kam, Russia
	RUSSIA
	RADIO ROSSII, Armavir

• E Asia • 200 kW
W • N Europe & E Europe • DS • 100 kW

5900	BULGARIA
	†RADIO BULGARIA, Plovdiv

W • S America • 250 kW
W Sa/Su • S Europe • 250 kW
W • S Europe • 250 kW
• S Europe • 250 kW

FRANCE
R FRANCE INTL, Issoudun

W • E Europe • 500 kW

5905	CLANDESTINE (ASIA)
	†"D'CRATIC VO BURMA", Via Kazakstan
	GERMANY
	†DEUTSCHE WELLE, Nauen
	†DEUTSCHE WELLE, Via Irkutsk, Russia
	IRAN
	†VO THE ISLAMIC REP, Tehrān
	RUSSIA
	VOICE OF RUSSIA, Irkutsk
	UKRAINE
	†RADIO UKRAINE, Kharkiv
	†RADIO UKRAINE, Mykolayiv
	USA
	†VOA, Via Irkutsk, Russia

SE Asia • ANTI-MYANMAR GOVT • 200 kW • ALT. FREQ. TO 5920 kHz
W • E Europe & W Asia • 500 kW
W • E Asia • 250 kW
W • S Asia • 500 kW
S • E Asia • 100 kW
W • S Europe • 100 kW
W • W Europe • 100 kW
S • W Europe • 100 kW
W • E North Am • 1000 kW • ALT. FREQ. TO 9385 kHz
W • E Asia • 250 kW

5910	BELGIUM
	R VLAANDEREN INTL, Via Germany
	GERMANY
	†DEUTSCHE WELLE, Via Petro-K, Russia
	†DEUTSCHE WELLE, Wertachtal
	RUSSIA
	†KAMCHATKA RYBATSKAYA, Petro-Kam
	USA
	RFE-RL, Via Wertachtal, Germany

• Sa • Europe • 100 kW
W • E Asia • 250 kW
S • E Europe • 500 kW
W • N Europe • 500 kW
• Su • E Asia • 100 kW

5915	CHINA
	†CHINA RADIO INTL, Hohhot
	CZECH REPUBLIC
(con'd)	†RADIO PRAGUE, Litomyšl

W • E Asia • 100 kW
E Asia • 100 kW
W • W North Am & C America • 100 kW
W • N America • 100 kW

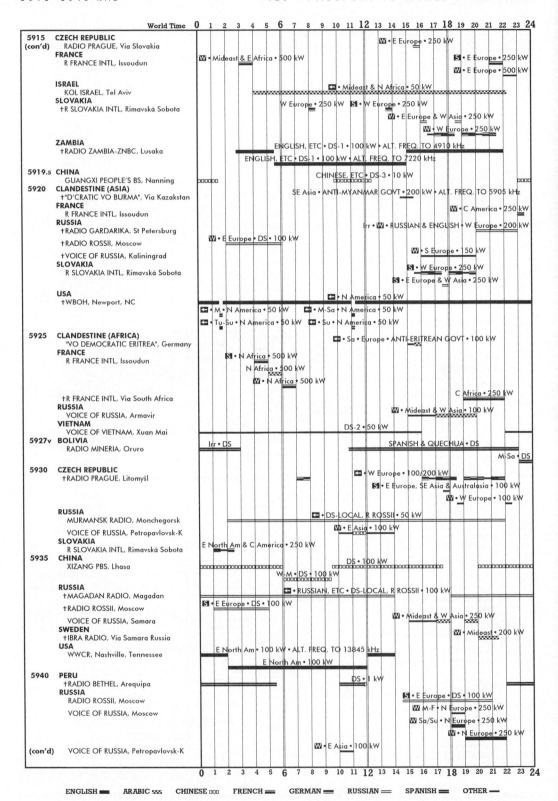

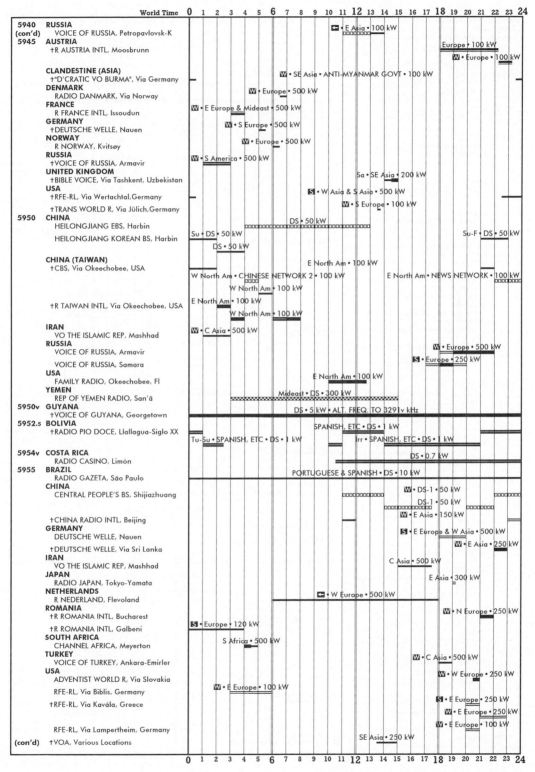

| World Time | 0 1 2 3 4 5 6 7 8 9 10 11 12 13 14 15 16 17 18 19 20 21 22 23 24 |

5940 **RUSSIA**
(con'd) VOICE OF RUSSIA, Petropavlovsk-K — E Asia • 100 kW
5945 **AUSTRIA**
†R AUSTRIA INTL, Moosbrunn — Europe • 100 kW — W • Europe • 100 kW

CLANDESTINE (ASIA)
†"D'CRATIC VO BURMA", Via Germany — W • SE Asia • ANTI-MYANMAR GOVT • 100 kW
DENMARK
RADIO DANMARK, Via Norway — W • Europe • 500 kW
FRANCE
R FRANCE INTL, Issoudun — W • E Europe & Mideast • 500 kW
GERMANY
†DEUTSCHE WELLE, Nauen — W • S Europe • 500 kW
NORWAY
R NORWAY, Kvitsøy — W • Europe • 500 kW
RUSSIA
†VOICE OF RUSSIA, Armavir — W • S America • 500 kW
UNITED KINGDOM
†BIBLE VOICE, Via Tashkent, Uzbekistan — Sa • SE Asia • 200 kW
USA
†RFE-RL, Via Wertachtal, Germany — S • W Asia & S Asia • 500 kW

†TRANS WORLD R, Via Jülich, Germany — W • S Europe • 100 kW
5950 **CHINA**
HEILONGJIANG EBS, Harbin — DS • 50 kW
HEILONGJIANG KOREAN BS, Harbin — Su • DS • 50 kW — Su-F • DS • 50 kW
— DS • 50 kW

CHINA (TAIWAN)
†CBS, Via Okeechobee, USA — E North Am • 100 kW
W North Am • CHINESE NETWORK 2 • 100 kW — E North Am • NEWS NETWORK • 100 kW
W North Am • 100 kW
†R TAIWAN INTL, Via Okeechobee, USA — E North Am • 100 kW
W North Am • 100 kW

IRAN
VO THE ISLAMIC REP, Mashhad — W • C Asia • 500 kW
RUSSIA
VOICE OF RUSSIA, Armavir — W • Europe • 500 kW
VOICE OF RUSSIA, Samara — S • Europe • 250 kW
USA
FAMILY RADIO, Okeechobee, Fl — E North Am • 100 kW
YEMEN
REP OF YEMEN RADIO, San'ā — Mideast • DS • 300 kW
5950v **GUYANA**
†VOICE OF GUYANA, Georgetown — DS • 5 kW • ALT. FREQ. TO 3291v kHz
5952.5 **BOLIVIA**
†RADIO PIO DOCE, Llallagua-Siglo XX — SPANISH, ETC • DS • 1 kW
Tu-Su • SPANISH, ETC • DS • 1 kW — Irr • SPANISH, ETC • DS • 1 kW

5954v **COSTA RICA**
RADIO CASINO, Limón — DS • 0.7 kW
5955 **BRAZIL**
RADIO GAZETA, São Paulo — PORTUGUESE & SPANISH • DS • 10 kW
CHINA
CENTRAL PEOPLE'S BS, Shijiazhuang — W • DS-1 • 50 kW
DS-1 • 50 kW
†CHINA RADIO INTL, Beijing — W • E Asia • 150 kW
GERMANY
DEUTSCHE WELLE, Nauen — S • E Europe & W Asia • 500 kW
†DEUTSCHE WELLE, Via Sri Lanka — W • E Asia • 250 kW
IRAN
VO THE ISLAMIC REP, Mashhad — C Asia • 500 kW
JAPAN
RADIO JAPAN, Tokyo-Yamata — E Asia • 300 kW
NETHERLANDS
R NEDERLAND, Flevoland — W Europe • 500 kW
ROMANIA
†R ROMANIA INTL, Bucharest — W • N Europe • 250 kW
†R ROMANIA INTL, Galbeni — S • Europe • 120 kW
SOUTH AFRICA
CHANNEL AFRICA, Meyerton — S Africa • 500 kW
TURKEY
VOICE OF TURKEY, Ankara-Emirler — W • C Asia • 500 kW
USA
ADVENTIST WORLD R, Via Slovakia — W • W Europe • 250 kW
RFE-RL, Via Biblis, Germany — W • E Europe • 100 kW
†RFE-RL, Via Kavála, Greece — S • E Europe • 250 kW
— W • E Europe • 250 kW

RFE-RL, Via Lampertheim, Germany — W • E Europe • 100 kW
(con'd) †VOA, Various Locations — SE Asia • 250 kW

| | 0 1 2 3 4 5 6 7 8 9 10 11 12 13 14 15 16 17 18 19 20 21 22 23 24 |

SEASONAL 🅂 OR 🅆   1-HR TIMESHIFT MIDYEAR ⇦ OR ⇨   JAMMING / OR /\   EARLIEST HEARD ◁   LATEST HEARD ▷   NEW FOR 2004 †

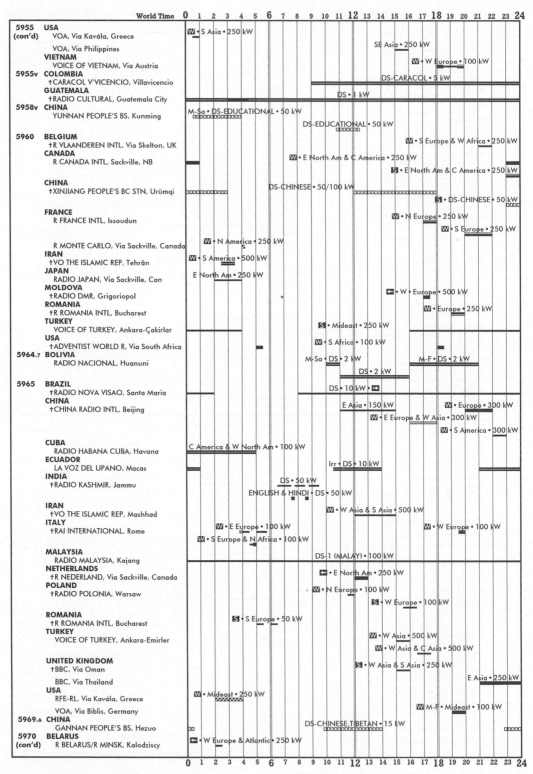

		World Time	0 1 2 3 4 5 6 7 8 9 10 11 12 13 14 15 16 17 18 19 20 21 22 23 24

5955
(con'd)   **USA**
   VOA, Via Kavála, Greece — W • S Asia • 250 kW
   VOA, Via Philippines — SE Asia • 250 kW
VIETNAM
   VOICE OF VIETNAM, Via Austria — W • W Europe • 100 kW
5955v COLOMBIA
   †CARACOL V'VICENCIO, Villavicencio — DS-CARACOL • 5 kW
GUATEMALA
   †RADIO CULTURAL, Guatemala City — DS • 1 kW
5958v CHINA
   YUNNAN PEOPLE'S BS, Kunming — M-Sa • DS-EDUCATIONAL • 50 kW / DS-EDUCATIONAL • 50 kW

5960   **BELGIUM**
   †R VLAANDEREN INTL, Via Skelton, UK — W • S Europe & W Africa • 250 kW
CANADA
   R CANADA INTL, Sackville, NB — W • E North Am & C America • 250 kW / S • E North Am & C America • 250 kW
CHINA
   †XINJIANG PEOPLE'S BC STN, Urümqi — DS-CHINESE • 50/100 kW / S • DS-CHINESE • 50 kW
FRANCE
   R FRANCE INTL, Issoudun — W • N Europe • 250 kW / W • S Europe • 250 kW
   R MONTE CARLO, Via Sackville, Canada — W • N America • 250 kW
IRAN
   †VO THE ISLAMIC REP, Tehrän — W • S America • 500 kW
JAPAN
   RADIO JAPAN, Via Sackville, Can — E North Am • 250 kW
MOLDOVA
   †RADIO DMR, Grigoriopol — W • Europe • 500 kW
ROMANIA
   †R ROMANIA INTL, Bucharest — W • Europe • 250 kW
TURKEY
   VOICE OF TURKEY, Ankara-Çakirlar — S • Mideast • 250 kW
USA
   †ADVENTIST WORLD R, Via South Africa — W • S Africa • 100 kW
5964.7 BOLIVIA
   RADIO NACIONAL, Huanuni — M-Sa • DS • 2 kW / M-F • DS • 2 kW / DS • 2 kW

5965   **BRAZIL**
   †RADIO NOVA VISAO, Santa Maria — DS • 10 kW
CHINA
   †CHINA RADIO INTL, Beijing — E Asia • 150 kW / W • Europe • 300 kW / W • E Europe & W Asia • 300 kW / W • S America • 300 kW
CUBA
   RADIO HABANA CUBA, Havana — C America & W North Am • 100 kW
ECUADOR
   LA VOZ DEL UPANO, Macas — Irr • DS • 10 kW
INDIA
   †RADIO KASHMIR, Jammu — DS • 50 kW / ENGLISH & HINDI • DS • 50 kW
IRAN
   †VO THE ISLAMIC REP, Mashhad — W • W Asia & S Asia • 500 kW
ITALY
   †RAI INTERNATIONAL, Rome — W • E Europe • 100 kW / W • W Europe • 100 kW / W • S Europe & N Africa • 100 kW
MALAYSIA
   RADIO MALAYSIA, Kajang — DS-1 (MALAY) • 100 kW
NETHERLANDS
   †R NEDERLAND, Via Sackville, Canada — E North Am • 250 kW
POLAND
   †RADIO POLONIA, Warsaw — W • N Europe • 100 kW / S • W Europe • 100 kW
ROMANIA
   †R ROMANIA INTL, Bucharest — S • S Europe • 50 kW
TURKEY
   VOICE OF TURKEY, Ankara-Emirler — W • W Asia • 500 kW / W • W Asia & C Asia • 500 kW
UNITED KINGDOM
   †BBC, Via Oman — S • W Asia & S Asia • 250 kW
   BBC, Via Thailand — E Asia • 250 kW
USA
   RFE-RL, Via Kavála, Greece — W • Mideast • 250 kW
   VOA, Via Biblis, Germany — W M-F • Mideast • 100 kW
5969.6 CHINA
   GANNAN PEOPLE'S BS, Hezuo — DS-CHINESE,TIBETAN • 15 kW
5970   **BELARUS**
(con'd)   R BELARUS/R MINSK, Kalodziscy — W • W Europe & Atlantic • 250 kW

	World Time	0 1 2 3 4 5 6 7 8 9 10 11 12 13 14 15 16 17 18 19 20 21 22 23 24

ENGLISH ▬   ARABIC ▨   CHINESE ▭▭▭   FRENCH ▦   GERMAN ▬   RUSSIAN ═   SPANISH ▬   OTHER ▬

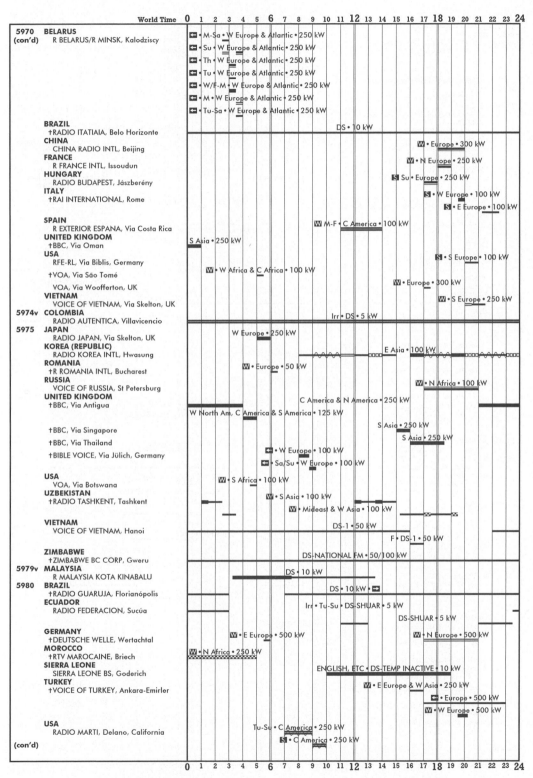

World Time 0 1 2 3 4 5 6 7 8 9 10 11 12 13 14 15 16 17 18 19 20 21 22 23 24

5970
(con'd) BELARUS
R BELARUS/R MINSK, Kalodziscy

- ⇦ M-Sa • W Europe & Atlantic • 250 kW
- ⇦ Su • W Europe & Atlantic • 250 kW
- ⇦ Th • W Europe & Atlantic • 250 kW
- ⇦ Tu • W Europe & Atlantic • 250 kW
- ⇦ W/F-M • W Europe & Atlantic • 250 kW
- ⇦ M • W Europe & Atlantic • 250 kW
- ⇦ Tu-Sa • W Europe & Atlantic • 250 kW

BRAZIL
†RADIO ITATIAIA, Belo Horizonte — DS • 10 kW

CHINA
CHINA RADIO INTL, Beijing — W • Europe • 300 kW

FRANCE
R FRANCE INTL, Issoudun — W • N Europe • 250 kW

HUNGARY
RADIO BUDAPEST, Jászberény — S Su • Europe • 250 kW

ITALY
†RAI INTERNATIONAL, Rome — S • W Europe • 100 kW
— S • E Europe • 100 kW

SPAIN
R EXTERIOR ESPANA, Via Costa Rica — W M-F • C America • 100 kW

UNITED KINGDOM
†BBC, Via Oman — S Asia • 250 kW

USA
RFE-RL, Via Biblis, Germany — S • S Europe • 100 kW

†VOA, Via São Tomé — W • W Africa & C Africa • 100 kW

VOA, Via Woofferton, UK — W • Europe • 300 kW

VIETNAM
VOICE OF VIETNAM, Via Skelton, UK — W • S Europe • 250 kW

5974v COLOMBIA
RADIO AUTENTICA, Villavicencio — Irr • DS • 5 kW

5975 JAPAN
RADIO JAPAN, Via Skelton, UK — W Europe • 250 kW

KOREA (REPUBLIC)
RADIO KOREA INTL, Hwasung — E Asia • 100 kW

ROMANIA
†R ROMANIA INTL, Bucharest — W • Europe • 50 kW

RUSSIA
VOICE OF RUSSIA, St Petersburg — W • N Africa • 100 kW

UNITED KINGDOM
†BBC, Via Antigua — C America & N America • 250 kW
— W North Am, C America & S America • 125 kW

†BBC, Via Singapore — S Asia • 250 kW

†BBC, Via Thailand — S Asia • 250 kW

†BIBLE VOICE, Via Jülich, Germany — ⇦ • W Europe • 100 kW
— ⇦ Sa/Su • W Europe • 100 kW

USA
VOA, Via Botswana — W • S Africa • 100 kW

UZBEKISTAN
†RADIO TASHKENT, Tashkent — W • S Asia • 100 kW
— W • Mideast & W Asia • 100 kW

VIETNAM
VOICE OF VIETNAM, Hanoi — DS-1 • 50 kW
— F • DS-1 • 50 kW

ZIMBABWE
†ZIMBABWE BC CORP, Gweru — DS-NATIONAL FM • 50/100 kW

5979v MALAYSIA
R MALAYSIA KOTA KINABALU — DS • 10 kW

5980 BRAZIL
†RADIO GUARUJA, Florianópolis — DS • 10 kW • ⇨

ECUADOR
RADIO FEDERACION, Sucúa — Irr • Tu-Su • DS-SHUAR • 5 kW
— DS-SHUAR • 5 kW

GERMANY
†DEUTSCHE WELLE, Wertachtal — W • E Europe • 500 kW
— W • N Europe • 500 kW

MOROCCO
†RTV MAROCAINE, Briech — W • N Africa • 250 kW

SIERRA LEONE
SIERRA LEONE BS, Goderich — ENGLISH, ETC • DS-TEMP INACTIVE • 10 kW

TURKEY
†VOICE OF TURKEY, Ankara-Emirler — W • E Europe & W Asia • 250 kW
— ⇦ • Europe • 500 kW
— W • W Europe • 500 kW

USA
RADIO MARTI, Delano, California — Tu-Su • C America • 250 kW
— S • C America • 250 kW

(con'd)

0 1 2 3 4 5 6 7 8 9 10 11 12 13 14 15 16 17 18 19 20 21 22 23 24

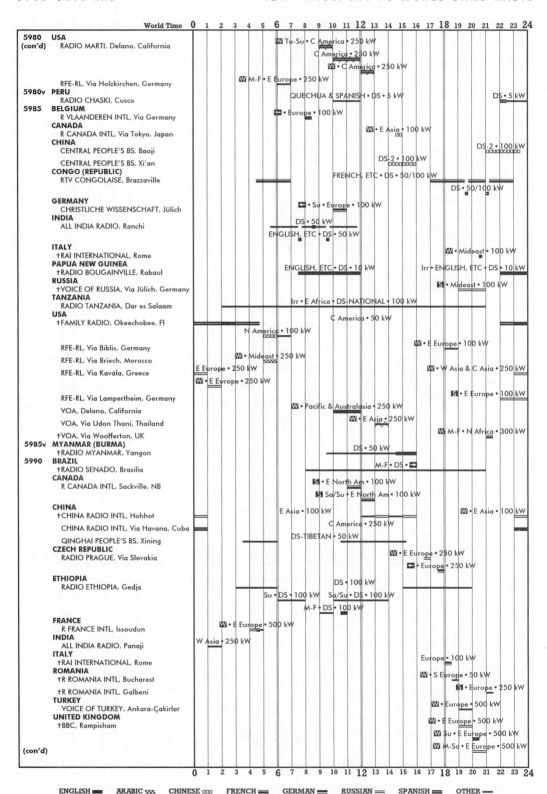

World Time 0 1 2 3 4 5 6 7 8 9 10 11 12 13 14 15 16 17 18 19 20 21 22 23 24

5980 **USA**
(con'd)   RADIO MARTI, Delano, California

          RFE-RL, Via Holzkirchen, Germany
5980v **PERU**
          RADIO CHASKI, Cusco
5985 **BELGIUM**
          R VLAANDEREN INTL, Via Germany
CANADA
          R CANADA INTL, Via Tokyo, Japan
CHINA
          CENTRAL PEOPLE'S BS, Baoji

          CENTRAL PEOPLE'S BS, Xi'an
CONGO (REPUBLIC)
          RTV CONGOLAISE, Brazzaville

GERMANY
          CHRISTLICHE WISSENSCHAFT, Jülich
INDIA
          ALL INDIA RADIO, Ranchi

ITALY
          †RAI INTERNATIONAL, Rome
PAPUA NEW GUINEA
          †RADIO BOUGAINVILLE, Rabaul
RUSSIA
          †VOICE OF RUSSIA, Via Jülich, Germany
TANZANIA
          RADIO TANZANIA, Dar es Salaam
USA
          †FAMILY RADIO, Okeechobee, Fl

          RFE-RL, Via Biblis, Germany

          RFE-RL, Via Briech, Morocco

          RFE-RL, Via Kavála, Greece

          RFE-RL, Via Lampertheim, Germany

          VOA, Delano, California

          VOA, Via Udon Thani, Thailand

          †VOA, Via Woofferton, UK
5985v **MYANMAR (BURMA)**
          †RADIO MYANMAR, Yangon
5990 **BRAZIL**
          †RADIO SENADO, Brasilia
CANADA
          R CANADA INTL, Sackville, NB

CHINA
          †CHINA RADIO INTL, Hohhot

          CHINA RADIO INTL, Via Havana, Cuba

          QINGHAI PEOPLE'S BS, Xining
CZECH REPUBLIC
          RADIO PRAGUE, Via Slovakia

ETHIOPIA
          RADIO ETHIOPIA, Gedja

FRANCE
          R FRANCE INTL, Issoudun
INDIA
          ALL INDIA RADIO, Panaji
ITALY
          †RAI INTERNATIONAL, Rome
ROMANIA
          †R ROMANIA INTL, Bucharest

          †R ROMANIA INTL, Galbeni
TURKEY
          VOICE OF TURKEY, Ankara-Çakirlar
UNITED KINGDOM
          †BBC, Rampisham

(con'd)

0 1 2 3 4 5 6 7 8 9 10 11 12 13 14 15 16 17 18 19 20 21 22 23 24

ENGLISH ▬   ARABIC ░░░   CHINESE □□□   FRENCH ▭   GERMAN ▭   RUSSIAN ═   SPANISH ▬   OTHER ▬

World Time | 0 1 2 3 4 5 6 7 8 9 10 11 12 13 14 15 16 17 18 19 20 21 22 23 24

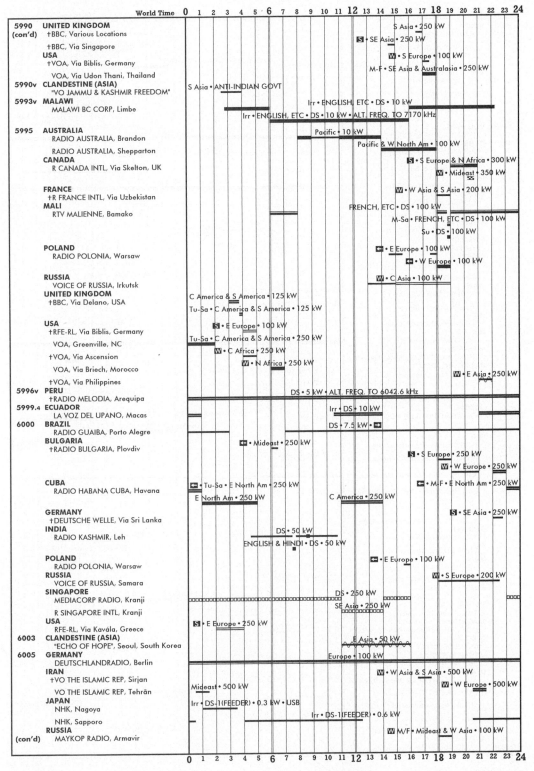

Freq	Station	Schedule
5990 (con'd)	**UNITED KINGDOM** †BBC, Various Locations	S Asia • 250 kW
	†BBC, Via Singapore	🅂 • SE Asia • 250 kW
	USA †VOA, Via Biblis, Germany	🅆 • S Europe • 100 kW
	VOA, Via Udon Thani, Thailand	M-F • SE Asia & Australasia • 250 kW
5990v	**CLANDESTINE (ASIA)** "VO JAMMU & KASHMIR FREEDOM"	S Asia • ANTI-INDIAN GOVT
5993v	**MALAWI** MALAWI BC CORP, Limbe	Irr • ENGLISH, ETC • DS • 10 kW Irr • ENGLISH, ETC • DS • 10 kW • ALT. FREQ. TO 7170 kHz
5995	**AUSTRALIA** RADIO AUSTRALIA, Brandon	Pacific • 10 kW
	RADIO AUSTRALIA, Shepparton	Pacific & W North Am • 100 kW
	CANADA R CANADA INTL, Via Skelton, UK	🅂 • S Europe & N Africa • 300 kW 🅆 • Mideast • 350 kW
	FRANCE †R FRANCE INTL, Via Uzbekistan	🅆 • W Asia & S Asia • 200 kW
	MALI RTV MALIENNE, Bamako	FRENCH, ETC • DS • 100 kW M-Sa • FRENCH, ETC • DS • 100 kW Su • DS • 100 kW
	POLAND RADIO POLONIA, Warsaw	⇦ • E Europe • 100 kW ⇦ • W Europe • 100 kW
	RUSSIA VOICE OF RUSSIA, Irkutsk	🅆 • C Asia • 100 kW
	UNITED KINGDOM †BBC, Via Delano, USA	C America & S America • 125 kW Tu-Sa • C America & S America • 125 kW
	USA †RFE-RL, Via Biblis, Germany	🅂 • E Europe • 100 kW
	VOA, Greenville, NC	Tu-Sa • C America & S America • 250 kW
	†VOA, Via Ascension	🅆 • C Africa • 250 kW
	VOA, Via Briech, Morocco	🅆 • N Africa • 250 kW
	†VOA, Via Philippines	🅆 • E Asia • 250 kW
5996v	**PERU** †RADIO MELODIA, Arequipa	DS • 5 kW • ALT. FREQ. TO 6042.6 kHz
5999.4	**ECUADOR** LA VOZ DEL UPANO, Macas	Irr • DS • 10 kW
6000	**BRAZIL** RADIO GUAIBA, Porto Alegre	DS • 7.5 kW • ⇨
	BULGARIA †RADIO BULGARIA, Plovdiv	⇦ • Mideast • 250 kW 🅂 • S Europe • 250 kW 🅆 • W Europe • 250 kW
	CUBA RADIO HABANA CUBA, Havana	⇦ • Tu-Sa • E North Am • 250 kW E North Am • 250 kW C America • 250 kW ⇦ • M-F • E North Am • 250 kW
	GERMANY †DEUTSCHE WELLE, Via Sri Lanka	🅂 • SE Asia • 250 kW
	INDIA RADIO KASHMIR, Leh	DS • 50 kW ENGLISH & HINDI • DS • 50 kW
	POLAND RADIO POLONIA, Warsaw	⇦ • E Europe • 100 kW
	RUSSIA VOICE OF RUSSIA, Samara	🅆 • S Europe • 200 kW
	SINGAPORE MEDIACORP RADIO, Kranji	DS • 250 kW SE Asia • 250 kW
	R SINGAPORE INTL, Kranji	
	USA RFE-RL, Via Kavála, Greece	🅂 • E Europe • 250 kW
6003	**CLANDESTINE (ASIA)** "ECHO OF HOPE", Seoul, South Korea	E Asia • 50 kW
6005	**GERMANY** DEUTSCHLANDRADIO, Berlin	Europe • 100 kW
	IRAN †VO THE ISLAMIC REP, Sirjan	🅆 • W Asia & S Asia • 500 kW
	VO THE ISLAMIC REP, Tehrān	Mideast • 500 kW 🅆 • W Europe • 500 kW
	JAPAN NHK, Nagoya	Irr • DS-1(FEEDER) • 0.3 kW • USB
	NHK, Sapporo	Irr • DS-1(FEEDER) • 0.6 kW
	RUSSIA (con'd) MAYKOP RADIO, Armavir	🅆 M/F • Mideast & W Asia • 100 kW

0 1 2 3 4 5 6 7 8 9 10 11 12 13 14 15 16 17 18 19 20 21 22 23 24

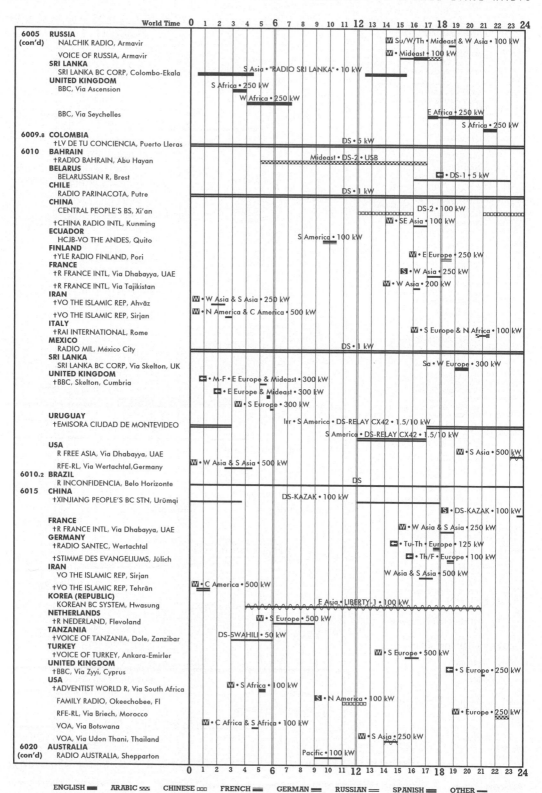

		World Time	0 1 2 3 4 5 6 7 8 9 10 11 12 13 14 15 16 17 18 19 20 21 22 23 24

6005 RUSSIA
(con'd)   NALCHIK RADIO, Armavir — W • Su/W/Th • Mideast & W Asia • 100 kW
     VOICE OF RUSSIA, Armavir — W • Mideast • 100 kW
   SRI LANKA
     SRI LANKA BC CORP, Colombo-Ekala — S Asia • "RADIO SRI LANKA" • 10 kW
   UNITED KINGDOM
     BBC, Via Ascension — S Africa • 250 kW / W Africa • 250 kW
     BBC, Via Seychelles — E Africa • 250 kW / S Africa • 250 kW

6009.8 COLOMBIA
     †LV DE TU CONCIENCIA, Puerto Lleras — DS • 5 kW
6010 BAHRAIN
     †RADIO BAHRAIN, Abu Hayan — Mideast • DS-2 • USB
   BELARUS
     BELARUSSIAN R, Brest — DS-1 • 5 kW
   CHILE
     RADIO PARINACOTA, Putre — DS • 1 kW
   CHINA
     CENTRAL PEOPLE'S BS, Xi'an — DS-2 • 100 kW
     †CHINA RADIO INTL, Kunming — W • SE Asia • 100 kW
   ECUADOR
     HCJB-VO THE ANDES, Quito — S America • 100 kW
   FINLAND
     †YLE RADIO FINLAND, Pori — W • E Europe • 250 kW
   FRANCE
     †R FRANCE INTL, Via Dhabayya, UAE — S • W Asia • 250 kW
     †R FRANCE INTL, Via Tajikistan — W • W Asia • 200 kW
   IRAN
     †VO THE ISLAMIC REP, Ahvāz — W • W Asia & S Asia • 250 kW
     †VO THE ISLAMIC REP, Sirjan — W • N America & C America • 500 kW
   ITALY
     †RAI INTERNATIONAL, Rome — W • S Europe & N Africa • 100 kW
   MEXICO
     RADIO MIL, México City — DS • 1 kW
   SRI LANKA
     SRI LANKA BC CORP, Via Skelton, UK — Sa • W Europe • 300 kW
   UNITED KINGDOM
     †BBC, Skelton, Cumbria — M-F • E Europe & Mideast • 300 kW / E Europe & Mideast • 300 kW / W • S Europe • 300 kW
   URUGUAY
     †EMISORA CIUDAD DE MONTEVIDEO — Irr • S America • DS-RELAY CX42 • 1.5/10 kW / S America • DS-RELAY CX42 • 1.5/10 kW
   USA
     R FREE ASIA, Via Dhabayya, UAE — W • S Asia • 500 kW
     RFE-RL, Via Wertachtal, Germany — W • W Asia & S Asia • 500 kW
6010.2 BRAZIL
     R INCONFIDENCIA, Belo Horizonte — DS
6015 CHINA
     †XINJIANG PEOPLE'S BC STN, Urümqi — DS-KAZAK • 100 kW / S • DS-KAZAK • 100 kW
   FRANCE
     †R FRANCE INTL, Via Dhabayya, UAE — W • W Asia & S Asia • 250 kW
   GERMANY
     †RADIO SANTEC, Wertachtal — Tu-Th • Europe • 125 kW
     †STIMME DES EVANGELIUMS, Jülich — Th/F • Europe • 100 kW
   IRAN
     VO THE ISLAMIC REP, Sirjan — W Asia & S Asia • 500 kW
     †VO THE ISLAMIC REP, Tehrān — W • C America • 500 kW
   KOREA (REPUBLIC)
     KOREAN BC SYSTEM, Hwasung — E Asia • LIBERTY-] • 100 kW
   NETHERLANDS
     †R NEDERLAND, Flevoland — W • S Europe • 500 kW
   TANZANIA
     †VOICE OF TANZANIA, Dole, Zanzibar — DS-SWAHILI • 50 kW
   TURKEY
     †VOICE OF TURKEY, Ankara-Emirler — W • S Europe • 500 kW
   UNITED KINGDOM
     †BBC, Via Zyyi, Cyprus — S Europe • 250 kW
   USA
     †ADVENTIST WORLD R, Via South Africa — W • S Africa • 100 kW
     FAMILY RADIO, Okeechobee, Fl — S • N America • 100 kW
     RFE-RL, Via Briech, Morocco — W • Europe • 250 kW
     VOA, Via Botswana — W • C Africa & S Africa • 100 kW
     VOA, Via Udon Thani, Thailand — W • S Asia • 250 kW
6020 AUSTRALIA
(con'd)   RADIO AUSTRALIA, Shepparton — Pacific • 100 kW

		0 1 2 3 4 5 6 7 8 9 10 11 12 13 14 15 16 17 18 19 20 21 22 23 24

ENGLISH ▬   ARABIC ▨   CHINESE ▫▫▫   FRENCH ═   GERMAN ▬   RUSSIAN ═   SPANISH ▬   OTHER ▬

World Time

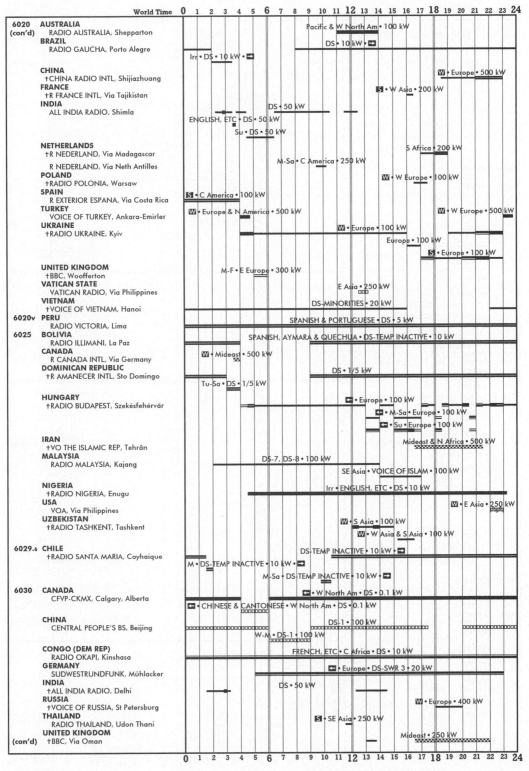

6020 (con'd)	AUSTRALIA
	RADIO AUSTRALIA, Shepparton
	Pacific & W North Am • 100 kW
	BRAZIL
	RADIO GAUCHA, Porto Alegre
	DS • 10 kW • ▣
	Irr • DS • 10 kW • ▣
	CHINA
	†CHINA RADIO INTL, Shijiazhuang
	▣ • Europe • 500 kW
	FRANCE
	†R FRANCE INTL, Via Tajikistan
	▣ • W Asia • 200 kW
	INDIA
	ALL INDIA RADIO, Shimla
	DS • 50 kW
	ENGLISH, ETC • DS • 50 kW
	Su • DS • 50 kW
	NETHERLANDS
	†R NEDERLAND, Via Madagascar
	S Africa • 200 kW
	R NEDERLAND, Via Neth Antilles
	M-Sa • C America • 250 kW
	POLAND
	†RADIO POLONIA, Warsaw
	▣ • W Europe • 100 kW
	SPAIN
	R EXTERIOR ESPANA, Via Costa Rica
	▣ • C America • 100 kW
	TURKEY
	VOICE OF TURKEY, Ankara-Emirler
	▣ • Europe & N America • 500 kW
	▣ • W Europe • 500 kW
	UKRAINE
	†RADIO UKRAINE, Kyiv
	▣ • Europe • 100 kW
	Europe • 100 kW
	▣ • Europe • 100 kW
	UNITED KINGDOM
	†BBC, Woofferton
	M-F • E Europe • 300 kW
	VATICAN STATE
	VATICAN RADIO, Via Philippines
	E Asia • 250 kW
	VIETNAM
	†VOICE OF VIETNAM, Hanoi
	DS-MINORITIES • 20 kW
6020v	PERU
	RADIO VICTORIA, Lima
	SPANISH & PORTUGUESE • DS • 5 kW
6025	BOLIVIA
	RADIO ILLIMANI, La Paz
	SPANISH, AYMARA & QUECHUA • DS-TEMP INACTIVE • 10 kW
	CANADA
	R CANADA INTL, Via Germany
	▣ • Mideast • 500 kW
	DOMINICAN REPUBLIC
	†R AMANECER INTL, Sto Domingo
	DS • 1/5 kW
	Tu-Sa • DS • 1/5 kW
	HUNGARY
	†RADIO BUDAPEST, Szekésfehérvár
	▣ • Europe • 100 kW
	▣ • M-Sa • Europe • 100 kW
	▣ • Su • Europe • 100 kW
	IRAN
	†VO THE ISLAMIC REP, Tehrän
	Mideast & N Africa • 500 kW
	MALAYSIA
	RADIO MALAYSIA, Kajang
	DS-7, DS-8 • 100 kW
	SE Asia • VOICE OF ISLAM • 100 kW
	NIGERIA
	†RADIO NIGERIA, Enugu
	Irr • ENGLISH, ETC • DS • 10 kW
	USA
	VOA, Via Philippines
	▣ • E Asia • 250 kW
	UZBEKISTAN
	†RADIO TASHKENT, Tashkent
	▣ • S Asia • 100 kW
	▣ • W Asia & S Asia • 100 kW
6029.6	CHILE
	†RADIO SANTA MARIA, Coyhaique
	DS-TEMP INACTIVE • 10 kW • ▣
	M • DS-TEMP INACTIVE • 10 kW • ▣
	M-Sa • DS-TEMP INACTIVE • 10 kW • ▣
6030	CANADA
	CFVP-CKMX, Calgary, Alberta
	▣ • W North Am • DS • 0.1 kW
	▣ • CHINESE & CANTONESE • W North Am • DS • 0.1 kW
	CHINA
	CENTRAL PEOPLE'S BS, Beijing
	DS-1 • 100 kW
	W-M • DS-1 • 100 kW
	CONGO (DEM REP)
	RADIO OKAPI, Kinshasa
	FRENCH, ETC • C Africa • DS • 10 kW
	GERMANY
	SUDWESTRUNDFUNK, Mühlacker
	▣ • Europe • DS-SWR 3 • 20 kW
	INDIA
	†ALL INDIA RADIO, Delhi
	DS • 50 kW
	RUSSIA
	†VOICE OF RUSSIA, St Petersburg
	▣ • Europe • 400 kW
	THAILAND
	RADIO THAILAND, Udon Thani
	▣ • SE Asia • 250 kW
	UNITED KINGDOM
	†BBC, Via Oman
	Mideast • 250 kW
(con'd)	

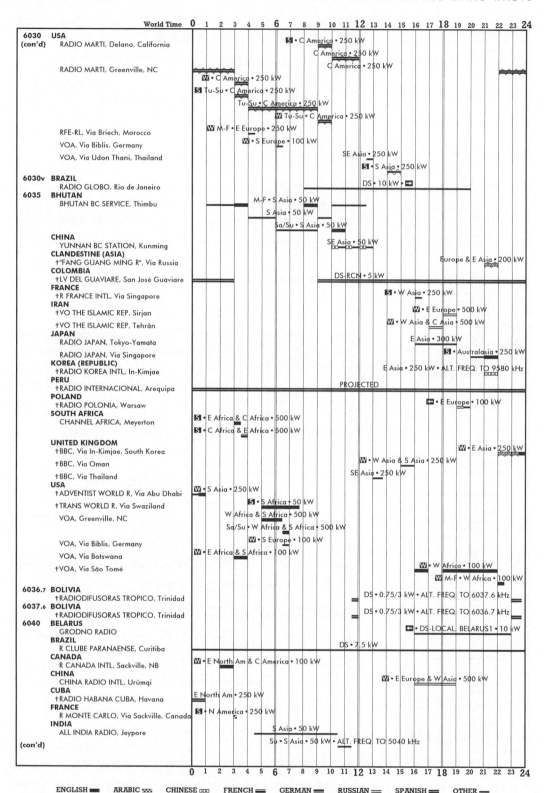

World Time		
6030 USA (con'd)	RADIO MARTI, Delano, California	S • C America • 250 kW / C America • 250 kW / C America • 250 kW
	RADIO MARTI, Greenville, NC	W • C America • 250 kW / S Tu-Su • C America • 250 kW / Tu-Su • C America • 250 kW / W Tu-Su • C America • 250 kW
	RFE-RL, Via Briech, Morocco	W M-F • E Europe • 250 kW
	VOA, Via Biblis, Germany	W • S Europe • 100 kW
	VOA, Via Udon Thani, Thailand	SE Asia • 250 kW / S • S Asia • 250 kW
6030v BRAZIL	RADIO GLOBO, Rio de Janeiro	DS • 10 kW • ➡
6035 BHUTAN	BHUTAN BC SERVICE, Thimbu	M-F • S Asia • 50 kW / S Asia • 50 kW / Sa/Su • S Asia • 50 kW
CHINA	YUNNAN BC STATION, Kunming	SE Asia • 50 kW
CLANDESTINE (ASIA)	†"FANG GUANG MING R", Via Russia	Europe & E Asia • 200 kW
COLOMBIA	†LV DEL GUAVIARE, San José Guaviare	DS-RCN • 5 kW
FRANCE	†R FRANCE INTL, Via Singapore	S • W Asia • 250 kW
IRAN	†VO THE ISLAMIC REP, Sirjan	W • E Europe • 500 kW
	†VO THE ISLAMIC REP, Tehrān	W • W Asia & C Asia • 500 kW
JAPAN	RADIO JAPAN, Tokyo-Yamata	E Asia • 300 kW
	RADIO JAPAN, Via Singapore	S • Australasia • 250 kW
KOREA (REPUBLIC)	†RADIO KOREA INTL, In-Kimjae	E Asia • 250 kW • ALT. FREQ. TO 9580 kHz
PERU	†RADIO INTERNACIONAL, Arequipa	PROJECTED
POLAND	†RADIO POLONIA, Warsaw	⬛ • E Europe • 100 kW
SOUTH AFRICA	CHANNEL AFRICA, Meyerton	S • E Africa & C Africa • 500 kW / S • C Africa & E Africa • 500 kW
UNITED KINGDOM	†BBC, Via In-Kimjae, South Korea	W • E Asia • 250 kW
	†BBC, Via Oman	W • W Asia & S Asia • 250 kW
	†BBC, Via Thailand	SE Asia • 250 kW
USA	†ADVENTIST WORLD R, Via Abu Dhabi	W • S Asia • 250 kW
	†TRANS WORLD R, Via Swaziland	S • S Africa • 50 kW
	VOA, Greenville, NC	W Africa & S Africa • 500 kW / Sa/Su • W Africa & S Africa • 500 kW
	VOA, Via Biblis, Germany	W • S Europe • 100 kW
	VOA, Via Botswana	W • E Africa & S Africa • 100 kW
	†VOA, Via São Tomé	W • W Africa • 100 kW / W M-F • W Africa • 100 kW
6036.7 BOLIVIA	†RADIODIFUSORAS TROPICO, Trinidad	DS • 0.75/3 kW • ALT. FREQ. TO 6037.6 kHz
6037.6 BOLIVIA	†RADIODIFUSORAS TROPICO, Trinidad	DS • 0.75/3 kW • ALT. FREQ. TO 6036.7 kHz
6040 BELARUS	GRODNO RADIO	⬅ • DS-LOCAL BELARUS1 • 10 kW
BRAZIL	R CLUBE PARANAENSE, Curitiba	DS • 7.5 kW
CANADA	R CANADA INTL, Sackville, NB	W • E North Am & C America • 100 kW
CHINA	CHINA RADIO INTL, Urümqi	W • E Europe & W Asia • 500 kW
CUBA	†RADIO HABANA CUBA, Havana	E North Am • 250 kW
FRANCE	R MONTE CARLO, Via Sackville, Canada	S • N America • 250 kW
INDIA	ALL INDIA RADIO, Jeypore	S Asia • 50 kW / Su • S Asia • 50 kW • ALT. FREQ. TO 5040 kHz
(con'd)		

ENGLISH ▬   ARABIC ⁓⁓⁓   CHINESE □□□   FRENCH ═   GERMAN ▬   RUSSIAN ═   SPANISH ═   OTHER ▬

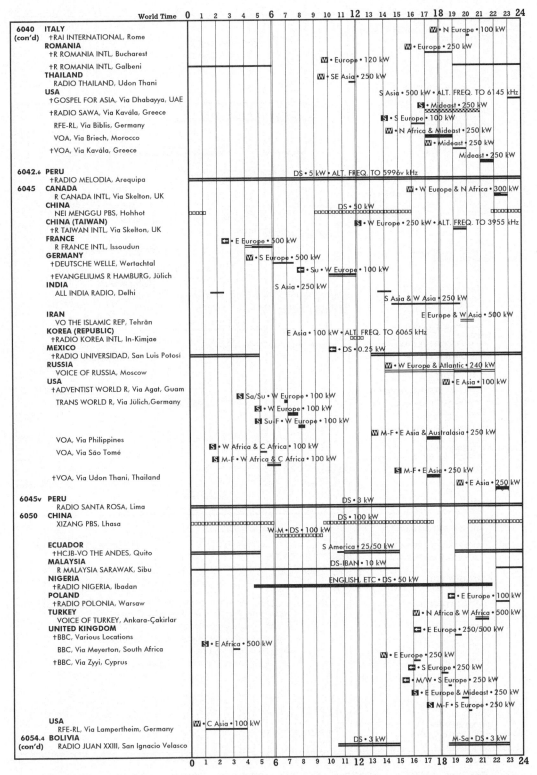

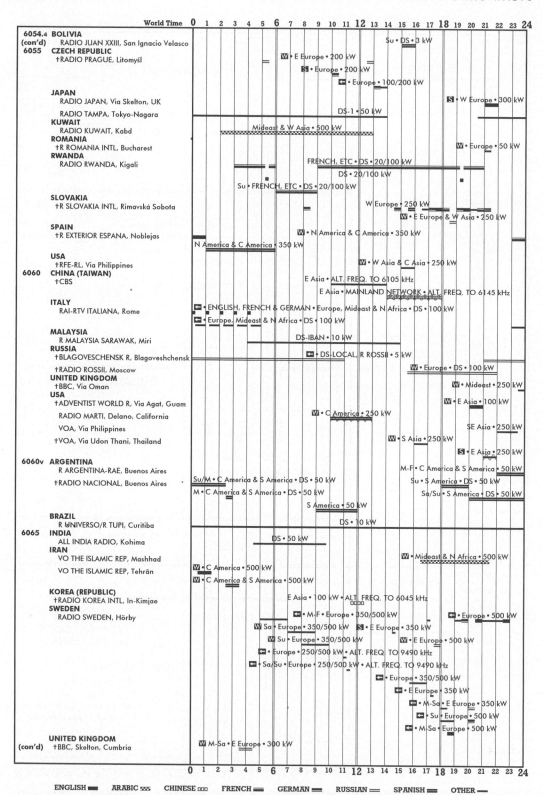

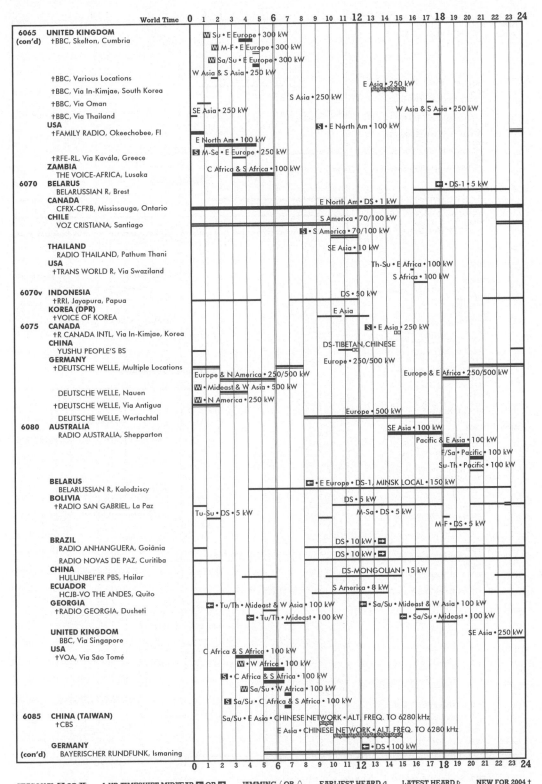

World Time	0 1 2 3 4 5 6 7 8 9 10 11 12 13 14 15 16 17 18 19 20 21 22 23 24
6065 UNITED KINGDOM	
(con'd) †BBC, Skelton, Cumbria	W · Su · E Europe · 300 kW
	W · M-F · E Europe · 300 kW
	W · Sa/Su · E Europe · 300 kW
†BBC, Various Locations	W Asia & S Asia · 250 kW
†BBC, Via In-Kimjae, South Korea	E Asia · 250 kW
†BBC, Via Oman	S Asia · 250 kW
†BBC, Via Thailand	SE Asia · 250 kW W Asia & S Asia · 250 kW
USA	
†FAMILY RADIO, Okeechobee, Fl	S · E North Am · 100 kW
	E North Am · 100 kW
†RFE-RL, Via Kavála, Greece	S M-Sa · E Europe · 250 kW
ZAMBIA	
THE VOICE-AFRICA, Lusaka	C Africa & S Africa · 100 kW
6070 BELARUS	
BELARUSSIAN R, Brest	· DS-1 · 5 kW
CANADA	
CFRX-CFRB, Mississauga, Ontario	E North Am · DS · 1 kW
CHILE	
VOZ CRISTIANA, Santiago	S America · 70/100 kW
	S · S America · 70/100 kW
THAILAND	
RADIO THAILAND, Pathum Thani	SE Asia · 10 kW
USA	
†TRANS WORLD R, Via Swaziland	Th-Su · E Africa · 100 kW
	S Africa · 100 kW
6070v INDONESIA	
†RRI, Jayapura, Papua	DS · 50 kW
KOREA (DPR)	
†VOICE OF KOREA	E Asia
6075 CANADA	
†R CANADA INTL, Via In-Kimjae, Korea	S · E Asia · 250 kW
CHINA	
YUSHU PEOPLE'S BS	DS-TIBETAN,CHINESE
GERMANY	
†DEUTSCHE WELLE, Multiple Locations	Europe · 250/500 kW Europe & E Africa · 250/500 kW
	Europe & N America · 250/500 kW
DEUTSCHE WELLE, Nauen	W · Mideast & W Asia · 500 kW
†DEUTSCHE WELLE, Via Antigua	W · N America · 250 kW
DEUTSCHE WELLE, Wertachtal	Europe · 500 kW
6080 AUSTRALIA	
RADIO AUSTRALIA, Shepparton	SE Asia · 100 kW
	Pacific & E Asia · 100 kW
	F/Sa · Pacific · 100 kW
	Su-Th · Pacific · 100 kW
BELARUS	
BELARUSSIAN R, Kalodziscy	· E Europe · DS-1, MINSK LOCAL · 150 kW
BOLIVIA	
†RADIO SAN GABRIEL, La Paz	DS · 5 kW
	Tu-Su · DS · 5 kW M-Sa · DS · 5 kW
	M-F · DS · 5 kW
BRAZIL	
RADIO ANHANGUERA, Goiânia	DS · 10 kW ·
RADIO NOVAS DE PAZ, Curitiba	DS · 10 kW ·
CHINA	
HULUNBEI'ER PBS, Hailar	DS-MONGOLIAN · 15 kW
ECUADOR	
HCJB-VO THE ANDES, Quito	S America · 8 kW
GEORGIA	
†RADIO GEORGIA, Dusheti	· Tu/Th · Mideast & W Asia · 100 kW · Sa/Su · Mideast & W Asia · 100 kW
	· Tu/Th · Mideast · 100 kW · Sa/Su · Mideast · 100 kW
UNITED KINGDOM	
BBC, Via Singapore	SE Asia · 250 kW
USA	
†VOA, Via São Tomé	C Africa & S Africa · 100 kW
	W · W Africa · 100 kW
	S · C Africa & S Africa · 100 kW
	W · Sa/Su · W Africa · 100 kW
	S · Sa/Su · C Africa & S Africa · 100 kW
6085 CHINA (TAIWAN)	
†CBS	Sa/Su · E Asia · CHINESE NETWORK · ALT FREQ. TO 6280 kHz
	E Asia · CHINESE NETWORK · ALT FREQ. TO 6280 kHz
GERMANY	
(con'd) BAYERISCHER RUNDFUNK, Ismaning	· DS · 100 kW

	0 1 2 3 4 5 6 7 8 9 10 11 12 13 14 15 16 17 18 19 20 21 22 23 24

SEASONAL S OR W 1-HR TIMESHIFT MIDYEAR ⬅ OR ➡ JAMMING / OR ∧ EARLIEST HEARD ◁ LATEST HEARD ▷ NEW FOR 2004 †

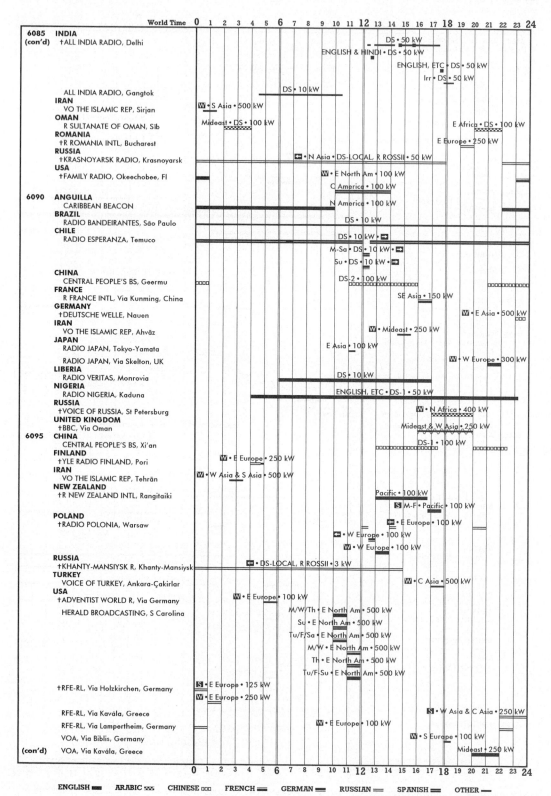

ENGLISH ▬ ARABIC ▨ CHINESE □□□ FRENCH ▬ GERMAN ▬ RUSSIAN ══ SPANISH ▬ OTHER ▬

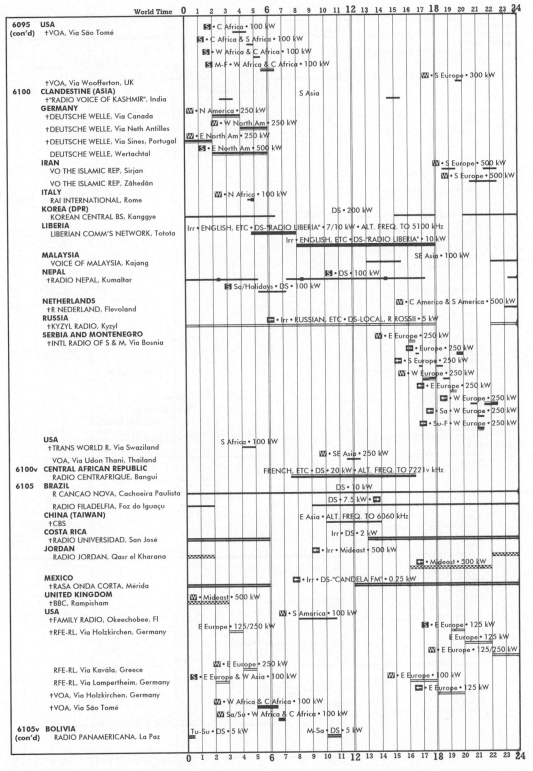

World Time 0 1 2 3 4 5 6 7 8 9 10 11 12 13 14 15 16 17 18 19 20 21 22 23 24

6095 **USA**
(con'd)   †VOA, Via São Tomé
S • C Africa • 100 kW
S • C Africa & S Africa • 100 kW
S • W Africa & C Africa • 100 kW
S • M-F • W Africa & C Africa • 100 kW

†VOA, Via Woofferton, UK   W • S Europe • 300 kW
6100 **CLANDESTINE (ASIA)**
   †"RADIO VOICE OF KASHMIR", India   S Asia
GERMANY
   †DEUTSCHE WELLE, Via Canada   W • N America • 250 kW
   †DEUTSCHE WELLE, Via Neth Antilles   W • W North Am • 250 kW
   †DEUTSCHE WELLE, Via Sines, Portugal   W • E North Am • 250 kW
   DEUTSCHE WELLE, Wertachtal   S • E North Am • 500 kW
IRAN
   VO THE ISLAMIC REP, Sirjan   W • S Europe • 500 kW
   VO THE ISLAMIC REP, Zähedän   W • S Europe • 500 kW
ITALY
   RAI INTERNATIONAL, Rome   W • N Africa • 100 kW
KOREA (DPR)
   KOREAN CENTRAL BS, Kanggye   DS • 200 kW
LIBERIA
   LIBERIAN COMM'S NETWORK, Totota   Irr • ENGLISH, ETC • DS-"RADIO LIBERIA" • 7/10 kW • ALT. FREQ. TO 5100 kHz
   Irr • ENGLISH, ETC • DS-"RADIO LIBERIA" • 10 kW
MALAYSIA
   VOICE OF MALAYSIA, Kajang   SE Asia • 100 kW
NEPAL
   †RADIO NEPAL, Kumaltar   S • DS • 100 kW
   S • Sa/Holidays • DS • 100 kW
NETHERLANDS
   †R NEDERLAND, Flevoland   W • C America & S America • 500 kW
RUSSIA
   †KYZYL RADIO, Kyzyl   ⇦ • Irr • RUSSIAN, ETC • DS-LOCAL, R ROSSII • 5 kW
SERBIA AND MONTENEGRO
   †INTL RADIO OF S & M, Via Bosnia   W • E Europe • 250 kW
   ⇦ • Europe • 250 kW
   ⇦ • S Europe • 250 kW
   W • W Europe • 250 kW
   ⇦ • E Europe • 250 kW
   ⇦ • W Europe • 250 kW
   ⇦ • Sa • W Europe • 250 kW
   ⇦ • Su-F • W Europe • 250 kW

USA
   †TRANS WORLD R, Via Swaziland   S Africa • 100 kW
   VOA, Via Udon Thani, Thailand   W • SE Asia • 250 kW
6100v **CENTRAL AFRICAN REPUBLIC**
   RADIO CENTRAFRIQUE, Bangui   FRENCH, ETC • DS • 20 kW • ALT. FREQ. TO 7221v kHz
6105 **BRAZIL**
   R CANCAO NOVA, Cachoeira Paulista   DS • 10 kW
   RADIO FILADELFIA, Foz do Iguaçu   DS • 7.5 kW • ⇨
CHINA (TAIWAN)
   †CBS   E Asia • ALT. FREQ. TO 6060 kHz
COSTA RICA
   †RADIO UNIVERSIDAD, San José   Irr • DS • 2 kW
JORDAN
   RADIO JORDAN, Qasr el Kharana   ⇦ • Irr • Mideast • 500 kW
   ⇦ • Mideast • 500 kW
MEXICO
   †RASA ONDA CORTA, Mérida   ⇦ • Irr • DS-"CANDELA FM" • 0.25 kW
UNITED KINGDOM
   †BBC, Rampisham   W • Mideast • 500 kW
USA
   †FAMILY RADIO, Okeechobee, Fl   W • S America • 100 kW
   †RFE-RL, Via Holzkirchen, Germany   E Europe • 125/250 kW
   S • E Europe • 125 kW
   E Europe • 125 kW
   W • E Europe • 125/250 kW
   RFE-RL, Via Kavála, Greece   W • E Europe • 250 kW
   RFE-RL, Via Lampertheim, Germany   S • E Europe & W Asia • 100 kW
   W • E Europe • 100 kW
   ⇦ • E Europe • 125 kW
   †VOA, Via Holzkirchen, Germany   W • W Africa & C Africa • 100 kW
   †VOA, Via São Tomé   W • Sa/Su • W Africa & C Africa • 100 kW
6105v **BOLIVIA**
(con'd)   RADIO PANAMERICANA, La Paz   Tu-Su • DS • 5 kW   M-Sa • DS • 5 kW

0 1 2 3 4 5 6 7 8 9 10 11 12 13 14 15 16 17 18 19 20 21 22 23 24

SEASONAL S OR W   1-HR TIMESHIFT MIDYEAR ⇦ OR ⇨   JAMMING / OR ∧   EARLIEST HEARD ◁   LATEST HEARD ▷   NEW FOR 2004 †

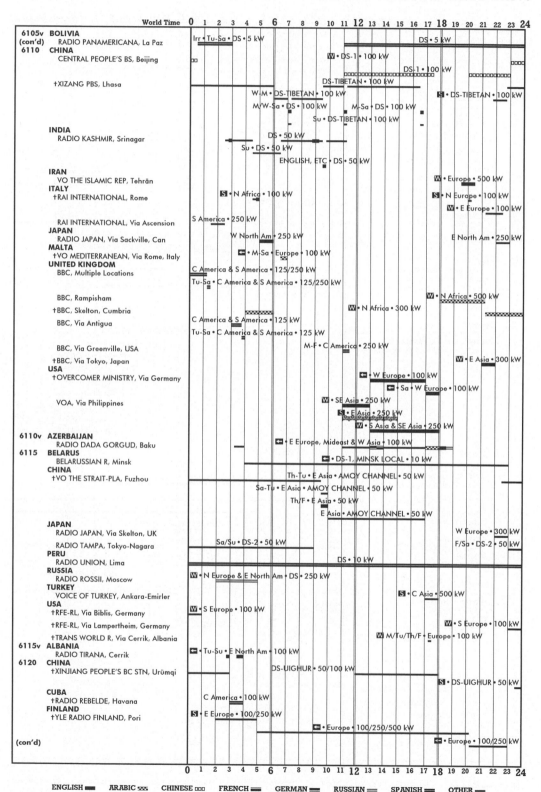

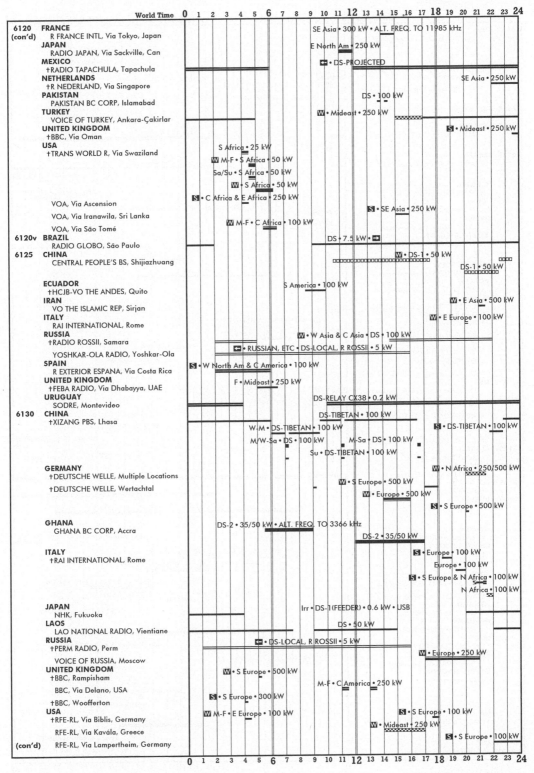

		World Time	0 1 2 3 4 5 6 7 8 9 10 11 12 13 14 15 16 17 18 19 20 21 22 23 24

6120 **FRANCE**
(con'd) R FRANCE INTL, Via Tokyo, Japan — SE Asia • 300 kW • ALT. FREQ. TO 11985 kHz
JAPAN
RADIO JAPAN, Via Sackville, Can — E North Am • 250 kW
MEXICO
†RADIO TAPACHULA, Tapachula — DS-PROJECTED
NETHERLANDS
†R NEDERLAND, Via Singapore — SE Asia • 250 kW
PAKISTAN
PAKISTAN BC CORP, Islamabad — DS • 100 kW
TURKEY
VOICE OF TURKEY, Ankara-Çakirlar — W • Mideast • 250 kW
UNITED KINGDOM
†BBC, Via Oman — S • Mideast • 250 kW
USA
†TRANS WORLD R, Via Swaziland — S Africa • 25 kW
— W M-F • S Africa • 50 kW
— Sa/Su • S Africa • 50 kW
— W • S Africa • 50 kW
VOA, Via Ascension — S • C Africa & E Africa • 250 kW
VOA, Via Iranawila, Sri Lanka — S • SE Asia • 250 kW
VOA, Via São Tomé — W M-F • C Africa • 100 kW

6120v **BRAZIL**
RADIO GLOBO, São Paulo — DS • 7.5 kW •

6125 **CHINA**
CENTRAL PEOPLE'S BS, Shijiazhuang — W • DS-1 • 50 kW
— DS-1 • 50 kW
ECUADOR
†HCJB-VO THE ANDES, Quito — S America • 100 kW
IRAN
VO THE ISLAMIC REP, Sirjan — W • E Asia • 500 kW
ITALY
RAI INTERNATIONAL, Rome — W • E Europe • 100 kW
RUSSIA
†RADIO ROSSII, Samara — W • W Asia & C Asia • DS • 100 kW
YOSHKAR-OLA RADIO, Yoshkar-Ola — • RUSSIAN, ETC • DS-LOCAL, R ROSSII • 5 kW
SPAIN
R EXTERIOR ESPANA, Via Costa Rica — S • W North Am & C America • 100 kW
UNITED KINGDOM
†FEBA RADIO, Via Dhabayya, UAE — F • Mideast • 250 kW
URUGUAY
SODRE, Montevideo — DS-RELAY CX38 • 0.2 kW

6130 **CHINA**
†XIZANG PBS, Lhasa — DS-TIBETAN • 100 kW
— W-M • DS-TIBETAN • 100 kW — S • DS-TIBETAN • 100 kW
— M/W-Sa • DS • 100 kW — M-Sa • DS • 100 kW
— Su • DS-TIBETAN • 100 kW
GERMANY
†DEUTSCHE WELLE, Multiple Locations — W • N Africa • 250/500 kW
†DEUTSCHE WELLE, Wertachtal — W • S Europe • 500 kW
— W • Europe • 500 kW
— S • S Europe • 500 kW
GHANA
GHANA BC CORP, Accra — DS-2 • 35/50 kW • ALT. FREQ. TO 3366 kHz
— DS-2 • 35/50 kW
ITALY
†RAI INTERNATIONAL, Rome — S • Europe • 100 kW
— Europe • 100 kW
— S • S Europe & N Africa • 100 kW
— N Africa • 100 kW
JAPAN
NHK, Fukuoka — Irr • DS-1 (FEEDER) • 0.6 kW • USB
LAOS
LAO NATIONAL RADIO, Vientiane — DS • 50 kW
RUSSIA
†PERM RADIO, Perm — • DS-LOCAL, R ROSSII • 5 kW
VOICE OF RUSSIA, Moscow — W • Europe • 250 kW
UNITED KINGDOM
†BBC, Rampisham — W • S Europe • 500 kW
BBC, Via Delano, USA — M-F • C America • 250 kW
†BBC, Woofferton — S • S Europe • 300 kW
USA
†RFE-RL, Via Biblis, Germany — W M-F • E Europe • 100 kW
— S • S Europe • 100 kW
RFE-RL, Via Kavála, Greece — W • Mideast • 250 kW
(con'd) RFE-RL, Via Lampertheim, Germany — S • S Europe • 100 kW

	0 1 2 3 4 5 6 7 8 9 10 11 12 13 14 15 16 17 18 19 20 21 22 23 24

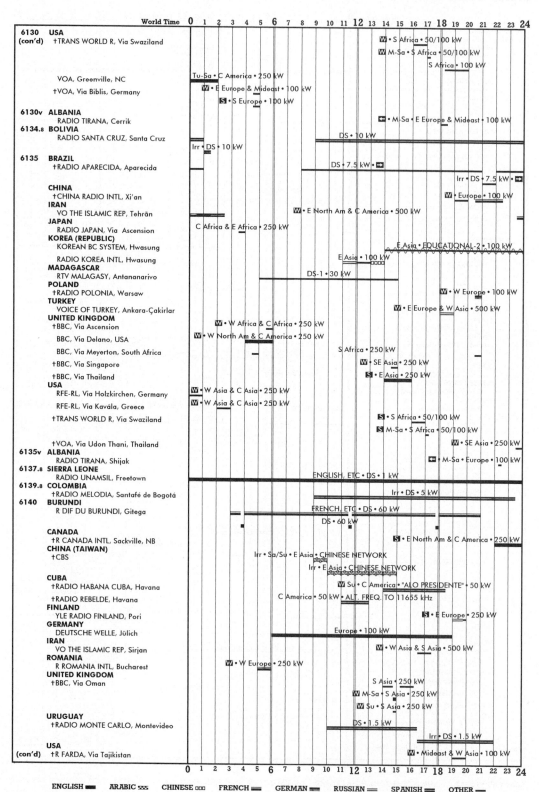

6130 **USA**	
(con'd) †TRANS WORLD R, Via Swaziland	
VOA, Greenville, NC	
†VOA, Via Biblis, Germany	
6130v **ALBANIA**	
RADIO TIRANA, Cerrik	
6134.8 **BOLIVIA**	
RADIO SANTA CRUZ, Santa Cruz	
6135 **BRAZIL**	
†RADIO APARECIDA, Aparecida	
CHINA	
†CHINA RADIO INTL, Xi'an	
IRAN	
VO THE ISLAMIC REP, Tehrān	
JAPAN	
RADIO JAPAN, Via Ascension	
KOREA (REPUBLIC)	
KOREAN BC SYSTEM, Hwasung	
RADIO KOREA INTL, Hwasung	
MADAGASCAR	
RTV MALAGASY, Antananarivo	
POLAND	
†RADIO POLONIA, Warsaw	
TURKEY	
VOICE OF TURKEY, Ankara-Çakirlar	
UNITED KINGDOM	
†BBC, Via Ascension	
BBC, Via Delano, USA	
BBC, Via Meyerton, South Africa	
†BBC, Via Singapore	
†BBC, Via Thailand	
USA	
RFE-RL, Via Holzkirchen, Germany	
RFE-RL, Via Kavála, Greece	
†TRANS WORLD R, Via Swaziland	
†VOA, Via Udon Thani, Thailand	
6135v **ALBANIA**	
RADIO TIRANA, Shijak	
6137.8 **SIERRA LEONE**	
RADIO UNAMSIL, Freetown	
6139.8 **COLOMBIA**	
†RADIO MELODIA, Santafé de Bogotá	
6140 **BURUNDI**	
R DIF DU BURUNDI, Gitega	
CANADA	
†R CANADA INTL, Sackville, NB	
CHINA (TAIWAN)	
†CBS	
CUBA	
†RADIO HABANA CUBA, Havana	
†RADIO REBELDE, Havana	
FINLAND	
YLE RADIO FINLAND, Pori	
GERMANY	
DEUTSCHE WELLE, Jülich	
IRAN	
VO THE ISLAMIC REP, Sirjan	
ROMANIA	
R ROMANIA INTL, Bucharest	
UNITED KINGDOM	
†BBC, Via Oman	
URUGUAY	
†RADIO MONTE CARLO, Montevideo	
USA	
(con'd) †R FARDA, Via Tajikistan	

World Time 0 1 2 3 4 5 6 7 8 9 10 11 12 13 14 15 16 17 18 19 20 21 22 23 24

Ⓦ • S Africa • 50/100 kW
Ⓦ M-Sa • S Africa • 50/100 kW
S Africa • 100 kW
Tu-Sa • C America • 250 kW
Ⓦ • E Europe & Mideast • 100 kW
Ⓢ • S Europe • 100 kW
⤶ • M-Sa • E Europe & Mideast • 100 kW
DS • 10 kW
Irr • DS • 10 kW
DS • 7.5 kW • ⤶
Irr • DS • 7.5 kW • ⤶
Ⓦ • Europe • 100 kW
Ⓦ • E North Am & C America • 500 kW
C Africa & E Africa • 250 kW
E Asia • EDUCATIONAL-2 • 100 kW
E Asia • 100 kW
DS-1 • 30 kW
Ⓦ • W Europe • 100 kW
Ⓦ • E Europe & W Asia • 500 kW
Ⓦ • W Africa & C Africa • 250 kW
Ⓦ • W North Am & C America • 250 kW
S Africa • 250 kW
Ⓦ • SE Asia • 250 kW
Ⓢ • E Asia • 250 kW
Ⓦ • W Asia & C Asia • 250 kW
Ⓦ • W Asia & C Asia • 250 kW
Ⓢ • S Africa • 50/100 kW
Ⓢ M-Sa • S Africa • 50/100 kW
Ⓦ • SE Asia • 250 kW
⤶ • M-Sa • Europe • 100 kW
ENGLISH, ETC • DS • 1 kW
Irr • DS • 5 kW
FRENCH, ETC • DS • 60 kW
DS • 60 kW
Ⓢ • E North Am & C America • 250 kW
Irr • Sa/Su • E Asia • CHINESE NETWORK
Irr • E Asia • CHINESE NETWORK
Ⓦ Su • C America • "ALO PRESIDENTE" • 50 kW
C America • 50 kW • ALT. FREQ. TO 11655 kHz
Ⓢ • E Europe • 250 kW
Europe • 100 kW
Ⓦ • W Asia & S Asia • 500 kW
Ⓦ • W Europe • 250 kW
S Asia • 250 kW
Ⓦ M-Sa • S Asia • 250 kW
Ⓦ Su • S Asia • 250 kW
DS • 1.5 kW
Irr • DS • 1.5 kW
Ⓦ • Mideast & W Asia • 100 kW

0 1 2 3 4 5 6 7 8 9 10 11 12 13 14 15 16 17 18 19 20 21 22 23 24

ENGLISH ▬ ARABIC ☒☒ CHINESE ☐☐☐ FRENCH ═══ GERMAN ▬▬ RUSSIAN ═══ SPANISH ═══ OTHER ▬

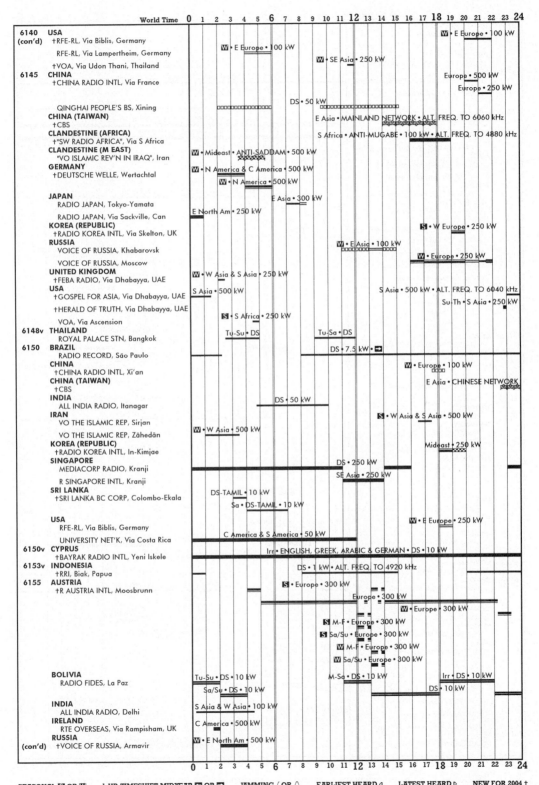

| World Time | 0 | 1 | 2 | 3 | 4 | 5 | 6 | 7 | 8 | 9 | 10 | 11 | 12 | 13 | 14 | 15 | 16 | 17 | 18 | 19 | 20 | 21 | 22 | 23 | 24 |

6140 USA
(con'd) †RFE-RL, Via Biblis, Germany
      RFE-RL, Via Lampertheim, Germany
      †VOA, Via Udon Thani, Thailand
6145 CHINA
      †CHINA RADIO INTL, Via France

      QINGHAI PEOPLE'S BS, Xining
CHINA (TAIWAN)
      †CBS
CLANDESTINE (AFRICA)
      †"SW RADIO AFRICA", Via S Africa
CLANDESTINE (M EAST)
      "VO ISLAMIC REV'N IN IRAQ", Iran
GERMANY
      †DEUTSCHE WELLE, Wertachtal

JAPAN
      RADIO JAPAN, Tokyo-Yamata
      RADIO JAPAN, Via Sackville, Can
KOREA (REPUBLIC)
      †RADIO KOREA INTL, Via Skelton, UK
RUSSIA
      VOICE OF RUSSIA, Khabarovsk

      VOICE OF RUSSIA, Moscow
UNITED KINGDOM
      †FEBA RADIO, Via Dhabayya, UAE
USA
      †GOSPEL FOR ASIA, Via Dhabayya, UAE

      †HERALD OF TRUTH, Via Dhabayya, UAE

      VOA, Via Ascension
6148v THAILAND
      ROYAL PALACE STN, Bangkok
6150 BRAZIL
      RADIO RECORD, São Paulo
CHINA
      †CHINA RADIO INTL, Xi'an
CHINA (TAIWAN)
      †CBS
INDIA
      ALL INDIA RADIO, Itanagar
IRAN
      VO THE ISLAMIC REP, Sirjan

      VO THE ISLAMIC REP, Zāhedān
KOREA (REPUBLIC)
      †RADIO KOREA INTL, In-Kimjae
SINGAPORE
      MEDIACORP RADIO, Kranji

      R SINGAPORE INTL, Kranji
SRI LANKA
      †SRI LANKA BC CORP, Colombo-Ekala

USA
      RFE-RL, Via Biblis, Germany
      UNIVERSITY NET'K, Via Costa Rica
6150v CYPRUS
      †BAYRAK RADIO INTL, Yeni Iskele
6153v INDONESIA
      †RRI, Biak, Papua
6155 AUSTRIA
      †R AUSTRIA INTL, Moosbrunn

BOLIVIA
      RADIO FIDES, La Paz

INDIA
      ALL INDIA RADIO, Delhi
IRELAND
      RTE OVERSEAS, Via Rampisham, UK
RUSSIA
(con'd) †VOICE OF RUSSIA, Armavir

| | 0 | 1 | 2 | 3 | 4 | 5 | 6 | 7 | 8 | 9 | 10 | 11 | 12 | 13 | 14 | 15 | 16 | 17 | 18 | 19 | 20 | 21 | 22 | 23 | 24 |

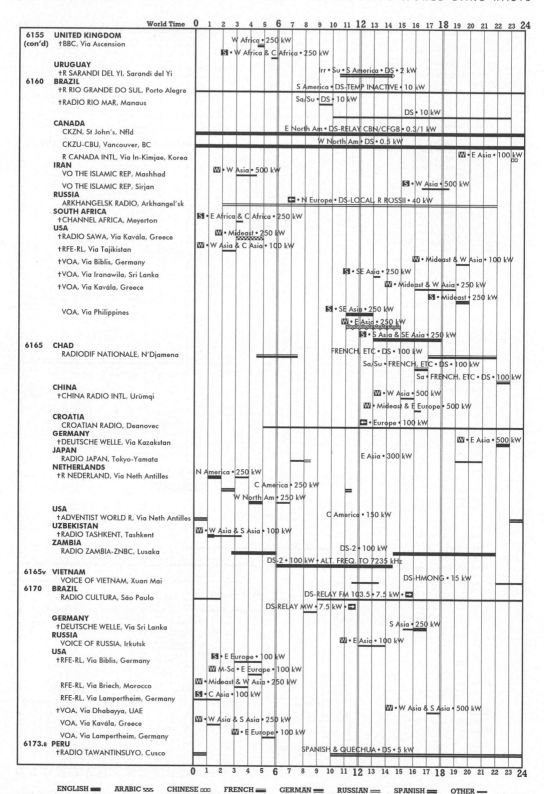

| | | World Time | 0 | 1 | 2 | 3 | 4 | 5 | 6 | 7 | 8 | 9 | 10 | 11 | 12 | 13 | 14 | 15 | 16 | 17 | 18 | 19 | 20 | 21 | 22 | 23 | 24 |

6155 UNITED KINGDOM
(con'd) †BBC, Via Ascension — W Africa • 250 kW; S • W Africa & C Africa • 250 kW

URUGUAY
†R SARANDI DEL YI, Sarandi del Yi — Irr • Su • S America • DS • 2 kW
6160 BRAZIL
†R RIO GRANDE DO SUL, Porto Alegre — S America • DS-TEMP INACTIVE • 10 kW
†RADIO RIO MAR, Manaus — Sa/Su • DS • 10 kW; DS • 10 kW

CANADA
CKZN, St John's, Nfld — E North Am • DS-RELAY CBN/CFGB • 0.3/1 kW
CKZU-CBU, Vancouver, BC — W North Am • DS • 0.5 kW
R CANADA INTL, Via In-Kimjae, Korea — W • E Asia • 100 kW
IRAN
VO THE ISLAMIC REP, Mashhad — W • W Asia • 500 kW
VO THE ISLAMIC REP, Sirjan — S • W Asia • 500 kW
RUSSIA
ARKHANGELSK RADIO, Arkhangel'sk — N Europe • DS-LOCAL, R ROSSII • 40 kW
SOUTH AFRICA
†CHANNEL AFRICA, Meyerton — S • E Africa & C Africa • 250 kW
USA
†RADIO SAWA, Via Kavála, Greece — W • Mideast • 250 kW
†RFE-RL, Via Tajikistan — W • W Asia & C Asia • 100 kW
†VOA, Via Biblis, Germany — W • Mideast & W Asia • 100 kW
†VOA, Via Iranawila, Sri Lanka — S • SE Asia • 250 kW; W • Mideast & W Asia • 250 kW
†VOA, Via Kavála, Greece — S • Mideast • 250 kW
VOA, Via Philippines — S • SE Asia • 250 kW; W • E Asia • 250 kW; S • S Asia & SE Asia • 250 kW

6165 CHAD
RADIODIF NATIONALE, N'Djamena — FRENCH, ETC • DS • 100 kW; Sa/Su • FRENCH, ETC • DS • 100 kW; Sa • FRENCH, ETC • DS • 100 kW

CHINA
†CHINA RADIO INTL, Urümqi — W • W Asia • 500 kW; W • Mideast & E Europe • 500 kW
CROATIA
CROATIAN RADIO, Deanovec — Europe • 100 kW
GERMANY
†DEUTSCHE WELLE, Via Kazakstan — W • E Asia • 500 kW
JAPAN
RADIO JAPAN, Tokyo-Yamata — E Asia • 300 kW
NETHERLANDS
†R NEDERLAND, Via Neth Antilles — N America • 250 kW; C America • 250 kW; W North Am • 250 kW; C America • 150 kW
USA
†ADVENTIST WORLD R, Via Neth Antilles —
UZBEKISTAN
†RADIO TASHKENT, Tashkent — W • W Asia & S Asia • 100 kW
ZAMBIA
RADIO ZAMBIA-ZNBC, Lusaka — DS-2 • 100 kW; DS-2 • 100 kW • ALT. FREQ. TO 7235 kHz

6165v VIETNAM
VOICE OF VIETNAM, Xuan Mai — DS-HMONG • 15 kW
6170 BRAZIL
RADIO CULTURA, São Paulo — DS-RELAY FM 103.5 • 7.5 kW; DS-RELAY MW • 7.5 kW

GERMANY
†DEUTSCHE WELLE, Via Sri Lanka — S Asia • 250 kW
RUSSIA
VOICE OF RUSSIA, Irkutsk — W • E Asia • 100 kW
USA
†RFE-RL, Via Biblis, Germany — S • E Europe • 100 kW; W M-Sa • E Europe • 100 kW
RFE-RL, Via Briech, Morocco — W • Mideast & W Asia • 250 kW
RFE-RL, Via Lampertheim, Germany — S • C Asia • 100 kW
†VOA, Via Dhabayya, UAE — W • W Asia & S Asia • 500 kW
VOA, Via Kavála, Greece — W • W Asia & S Asia • 250 kW
VOA, Via Lampertheim, Germany — W • E Europe • 100 kW
6173.8 PERU
†RADIO TAWANTINSUYO, Cusco — SPANISH & QUECHUA • DS • 5 kW

| | | 0 | 1 | 2 | 3 | 4 | 5 | 6 | 7 | 8 | 9 | 10 | 11 | 12 | 13 | 14 | 15 | 16 | 17 | 18 | 19 | 20 | 21 | 22 | 23 | 24 |

ENGLISH ▬ ARABIC ▨ CHINESE ▢▢▢ FRENCH ▬▬ GERMAN ▬ RUSSIAN ═ SPANISH ▬ OTHER ▬

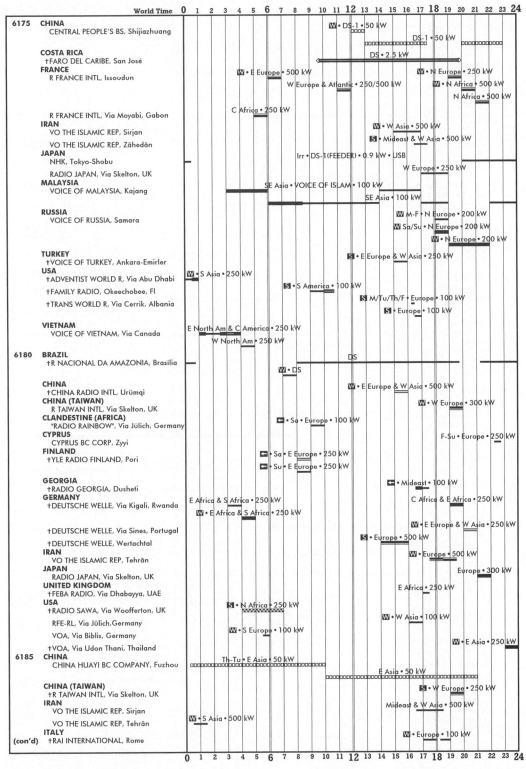

	World Time	0 1 2 3 4 5 6 7 8 9 10 11 12 13 14 15 16 17 18 19 20 21 22 23 24

6175　CHINA
　CENTRAL PEOPLE'S BS, Shijiazhuang

COSTA RICA
　†FARO DEL CARIBE, San José
FRANCE
　R FRANCE INTL, Issoudun

　R FRANCE INTL, Via Moyabi, Gabon
IRAN
　VO THE ISLAMIC REP, Sirjan
　VO THE ISLAMIC REP, Zāhedān
JAPAN
　NHK, Tokyo-Shobu
　RADIO JAPAN, Via Skelton, UK
MALAYSIA
　VOICE OF MALAYSIA, Kajang

RUSSIA
　VOICE OF RUSSIA, Samara

TURKEY
　†VOICE OF TURKEY, Ankara-Emirler
USA
　†ADVENTIST WORLD R, Via Abu Dhabi
　†FAMILY RADIO, Okeechobee, Fl
　†TRANS WORLD R, Via Cerrik, Albania

VIETNAM
　VOICE OF VIETNAM, Via Canada

6180　BRAZIL
　†R NACIONAL DA AMAZONIA, Brasília

CHINA
　†CHINA RADIO INTL, Urümqi
CHINA (TAIWAN)
　R TAIWAN INTL, Via Skelton, UK
CLANDESTINE (AFRICA)
　"RADIO RAINBOW", Via Jülich, Germany
CYPRUS
　CYPRUS BC CORP, Zyyi
FINLAND
　†YLE RADIO FINLAND, Pori

GEORGIA
　†RADIO GEORGIA, Dusheti
GERMANY
　†DEUTSCHE WELLE, Via Kigali, Rwanda

　†DEUTSCHE WELLE, Via Sines, Portugal
　†DEUTSCHE WELLE, Wertachtal
IRAN
　VO THE ISLAMIC REP, Tehrān
JAPAN
　RADIO JAPAN, Via Skelton, UK
UNITED KINGDOM
　†FEBA RADIO, Via Dhabayya, UAE
USA
　†RADIO SAWA, Via Woofferton, UK
　RFE-RL, Via Jülich, Germany
　VOA, Via Biblis, Germany
　†VOA, Via Udon Thani, Thailand
6185　CHINA
　CHINA HUAYI BC COMPANY, Fuzhou

CHINA (TAIWAN)
　†R TAIWAN INTL, Via Skelton, UK
IRAN
　VO THE ISLAMIC REP, Sirjan
　VO THE ISLAMIC REP, Tehrān
ITALY
(con'd)　†RAI INTERNATIONAL, Rome

Labels within chart:
- 6175 CHINA: W•DS-1•50 kW; DS-1•50 kW
- COSTA RICA: DS•2.5 kW
- FRANCE: W•E Europe•500 kW; W Europe & Atlantic•250/500 kW; W•N Europe•250 kW; W•N Africa•500 kW; N Africa•500 kW; C Africa•250 kW
- IRAN: W•W Asia•500 kW; S•Mideast & W Asia•500 kW
- JAPAN: Irr•DS-1(FEEDER)•0.9 kW•USB; W Europe•250 kW
- MALAYSIA: SE Asia•VOICE OF ISLAM•100 kW; SE Asia•100 kW
- RUSSIA: W M-F•N Europe•200 kW; W Sa/Su•N Europe•200 kW; W•N Europe•200 kW
- TURKEY: S•E Europe & W Asia•250 kW
- USA ADVENTIST: W•S Asia•250 kW
- FAMILY RADIO: S•S America•100 kW
- TRANS WORLD R: S M/Tu/Th/F•Europe•100 kW; S•Europe•100 kW
- VIETNAM: E North Am & C America•250 kW; W North Am•250 kW
- 6180 BRAZIL: DS; W•DS
- CHINA RADIO INTL: W•E Europe & W Asia•500 kW
- CHINA TAIWAN: W•W Europe•300 kW
- CLANDESTINE: ⇦•Sa•Europe•100 kW
- CYPRUS: F-Su•Europe•250 kW
- FINLAND: ⇦•Sa•E Europe•250 kW; ⇦•Su•E Europe•250 kW
- GEORGIA: ⇦•Mideast•100 kW
- GERMANY Kigali: E Africa & S Africa•250 kW; W•E Africa & S Africa•250 kW; C Africa & E Africa•250 kW
- DEUTSCHE WELLE Sines: W•E Europe & W Asia•250 kW; S•Europe•500 kW
- DEUTSCHE WELLE Wertachtal: W•Europe•500 kW
- RADIO JAPAN Skelton: Europe•300 kW
- FEBA RADIO: E Africa•250 kW
- RADIO SAWA: S•N Africa•250 kW
- RFE-RL: W•W Asia•100 kW
- VOA Biblis: W•S Europe•100 kW
- VOA Udon Thani: W•E Asia•250 kW
- 6185 CHINA HUAYI: Th-Tu•E Asia•50 kW; E Asia•50 kW
- CHINA TAIWAN: S•W Europe•250 kW
- IRAN Sirjan: Mideast & W Asia•500 kW
- IRAN Tehrān: W•S Asia•500 kW
- ITALY: W•Europe•100 kW

	0 1 2 3 4 5 6 7 8 9 10 11 12 13 14 15 16 17 18 19 20 21 22 23 24

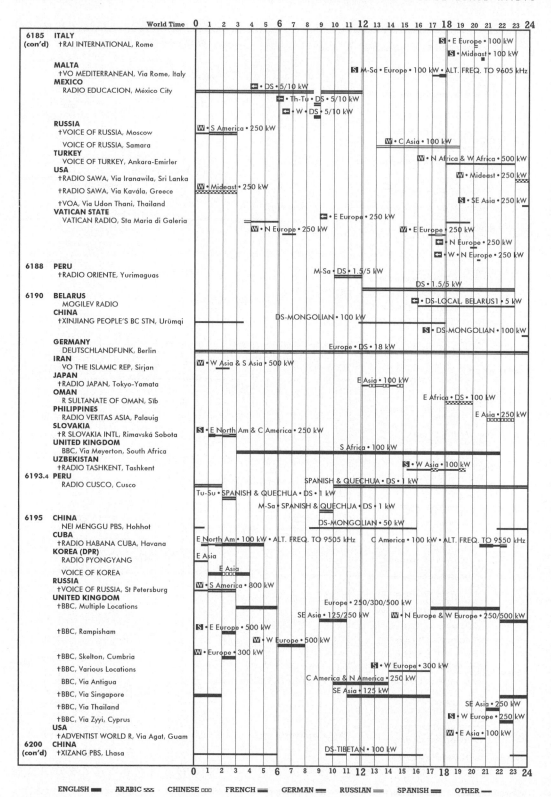

World Time

6185 ITALY
(con'd) †RAI INTERNATIONAL, Rome
S • E Europe • 100 kW
S • Mideast • 100 kW

MALTA
†VO MEDITERRANEAN, Via Rome, Italy
M-Sa • Europe • 100 kW • ALT. FREQ. TO 9605 kHz
MEXICO
RADIO EDUCACION, México City
DS • 5/10 kW
Th-Tu • DS • 5/10 kW
W • DS • 5/10 kW

RUSSIA
†VOICE OF RUSSIA, Moscow
W • S America • 250 kW
VOICE OF RUSSIA, Samara
W • C Asia • 100 kW
TURKEY
VOICE OF TURKEY, Ankara-Emirler
W • N Africa & W Africa • 500 kW
USA
†RADIO SAWA, Via Iranawila, Sri Lanka
W • Mideast • 250 kW
†RADIO SAWA, Via Kavála, Greece
W • Mideast • 250 kW
†VOA, Via Udon Thani, Thailand
S • SE Asia • 250 kW
VATICAN STATE
VATICAN RADIO, Sta Maria di Galeria
• E Europe • 250 kW
W • N Europe • 250 kW
W • E Europe • 250 kW
• N Europe • 250 kW
• W • N Europe • 250 kW

6188 PERU
†RADIO ORIENTE, Yurimaguas
M-Sa • DS • 1.5/5 kW
DS • 1.5/5 kW

6190 BELARUS
MOGILEV RADIO
DS-LOCAL, BELARUS1 • 5 kW
CHINA
†XINJIANG PEOPLE'S BC STN, Urümqi
DS-MONGOLIAN • 100 kW
S • DS-MONGOLIAN • 100 kW
GERMANY
DEUTSCHLANDFUNK, Berlin
Europe • DS • 18 kW
IRAN
VO THE ISLAMIC REP, Sirjan
W • W Asia & S Asia • 500 kW
JAPAN
†RADIO JAPAN, Tokyo-Yamata
E Asia • 100 kW
OMAN
R SULTANATE OF OMAN, Sīb
E Africa • DS • 100 kW
PHILIPPINES
RADIO VERITAS ASIA, Palauig
E Asia • 250 kW
SLOVAKIA
†R SLOVAKIA INTL, Rimavská Sobota
S • E North Am & C America • 250 kW
UNITED KINGDOM
BBC, Via Meyerton, South Africa
S Africa • 100 kW
UZBEKISTAN
†RADIO TASHKENT, Tashkent
S • W Asia • 100 kW
6193.4 PERU
RADIO CUSCO, Cusco
SPANISH & QUECHUA • DS • 1 kW
Tu-Su • SPANISH & QUECHUA • DS • 1 kW
M-Sa • SPANISH & QUECHUA • DS • 1 kW

6195 CHINA
NEI MENGGU PBS, Hohhot
DS-MONGOLIAN • 50 kW
CUBA
†RADIO HABANA CUBA, Havana
E North Am • 100 kW • ALT. FREQ. TO 9505 kHz   C America • 100 kW • ALT. FREQ. TO 9550 kHz
KOREA (DPR)
RADIO PYONGYANG
E Asia
VOICE OF KOREA
E Asia
RUSSIA
†VOICE OF RUSSIA, St Petersburg
W • S America • 300 kW
UNITED KINGDOM
†BBC, Multiple Locations
Europe • 250/300/500 kW
SE Asia • 125/250 kW   W • N Europe & W Europe • 250/500 kW
†BBC, Rampisham
S • E Europe • 500 kW
W • W Europe • 500 kW
†BBC, Skelton, Cumbria
W • Europe • 300 kW
†BBC, Various Locations
S • W Europe • 300 kW
BBC, Via Antigua
C America & N America • 250 kW
†BBC, Via Singapore
SE Asia • 125 kW
†BBC, Via Thailand
SE Asia • 250 kW
†BBC, Via Zyyi, Cyprus
S • W Europe • 250 kW
USA
†ADVENTIST WORLD R, Via Agat, Guam
W • E Asia • 100 kW
6200 CHINA
(con'd) †XIZANG PBS, Lhasa
DS-TIBETAN • 100 kW

ENGLISH ▬   ARABIC ▧▧▧   CHINESE □□□   FRENCH ▬   GERMAN ▬   RUSSIAN ═   SPANISH ▬   OTHER ▬

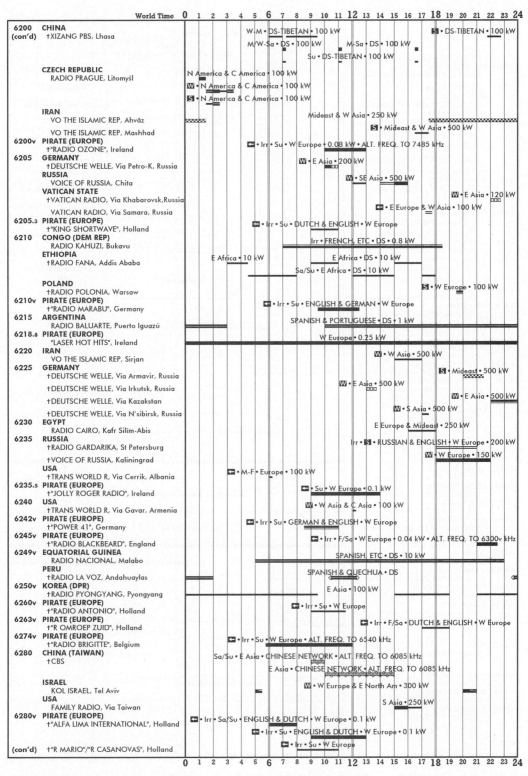

World Time	0 1 2 3 4 5 6 7 8 9 10 11 12 13 14 15 16 17 18 19 20 21 22 23 24
6200 (con'd) **CHINA** †XIZANG PBS, Lhasa	W·M · DS-TIBETAN · 100 kW · DS-TIBETAN · 100 kW
	M/W-Sa · DS · 100 kW M-Sa · DS · 100 kW
	Su · DS-TIBETAN · 100 kW
CZECH REPUBLIC RADIO PRAGUE, Litomyšl	N America & C America · 100 kW
	W · N America & C America · 100 kW
	S · N America & C America · 100 kW
IRAN VO THE ISLAMIC REP, Ahvāz	Mideast & W Asia · 250 kW
VO THE ISLAMIC REP, Mashhad	S · Mideast & W Asia · 500 kW
6200v PIRATE (EUROPE) †"RADIO OZONE", Ireland	⇦ · Irr · Su · W Europe · 0.08 kW · ALT. FREQ. TO 7485 kHz
6205 GERMANY †DEUTSCHE WELLE, Via Petro-K, Russia	W · E Asia · 200 kW
RUSSIA VOICE OF RUSSIA, Chita	W · SE Asia · 500 kW
VATICAN STATE †VATICAN RADIO, Via Khabarovsk,Russia	W · E Asia · 120 kW
VATICAN RADIO, Via Samara, Russia	⇦ · E Europe & W Asia · 100 kW
6205.3 PIRATE (EUROPE) †"KING SHORTWAVE", Holland	⇦ · Irr · Su · DUTCH & ENGLISH · W Europe
6210 CONGO (DEM REP) RADIO KAHUZI, Bukavu	Irr · FRENCH, ETC · DS · 0.8 kW
ETHIOPIA †RADIO FANA, Addis Ababa	E Africa · 10 kW E Africa · DS · 10 kW
	Sa/Su · E Africa · DS · 10 kW
POLAND †RADIO POLONIA, Warsaw	S · W Europe · 100 kW
6210v PIRATE (EUROPE) †"RADIO MARABU", Germany	⇦ · Irr · Su · ENGLISH & GERMAN · W Europe
6215 ARGENTINA RADIO BALUARTE, Puerto Iguazú	SPANISH & PORTUGUESE · DS · 1 kW
6218.8 PIRATE (EUROPE) "LASER HOT HITS", Ireland	W Europe · 0.25 kW
6220 IRAN VO THE ISLAMIC REP, Sirjan	W · W Asia · 500 kW
6225 GERMANY †DEUTSCHE WELLE, Via Armavir, Russia	S · Mideast · 500 kW
†DEUTSCHE WELLE, Via Irkutsk, Russia	W · E Asia · 500 kW
†DEUTSCHE WELLE, Via Kazakstan	W · E Asia · 500 kW
†DEUTSCHE WELLE, Via N'sibirsk, Russia	W · S Asia · 500 kW
6230 EGYPT RADIO CAIRO, Kafr Silīm-Abis	E Europe & Mideast · 250 kW
6235 RUSSIA †RADIO GARDARIKA, St Petersburg	Irr · S · RUSSIAN & ENGLISH · W Europe · 200 kW
†VOICE OF RUSSIA, Kaliningrad	W · W Europe · 150 kW
USA †TRANS WORLD R, Via Cerrik, Albania	⇦ · M-F · Europe · 100 kW
6235.5 PIRATE (EUROPE) †"JOLLY ROGER RADIO", Ireland	⇦ · Su · W Europe · 0.1 kW
6240 USA †TRANS WORLD R, Via Gavar, Armenia	W · W Asia & C Asia · 100 kW
6242v PIRATE (EUROPE) †"POWER 41", Germany	⇦ · Irr · Su · GERMAN & ENGLISH · W Europe
6245v PIRATE (EUROPE) †"RADIO BLACKBEARD", England	⇦ · Irr · F/Sa · W Europe · 0.04 kW · ALT. FREQ. TO 6300v kHz
6249v EQUATORIAL GUINEA RADIO NACIONAL, Malabo	SPANISH, ETC · DS · 10 kW
PERU †RADIO LA VOZ, Andahuaylas	SPANISH & QUECHUA · DS ◁
6250v KOREA (DPR) †RADIO PYONGYANG, Pyongyang	E Asia · 100 kW
6260v PIRATE (EUROPE) †"RADIO ANTONIO", Holland	⇦ · Irr · Su · W Europe
6263v PIRATE (EUROPE) †"R OMROEP ZUID", Holland	⇦ · Irr · F/Sa · DUTCH & ENGLISH · W Europe
6274v PIRATE (EUROPE) †"RADIO BRIGITTE", Belgium	⇦ · Irr · Su · W Europe · ALT. FREQ. TO 6540 kHz
6280 CHINA (TAIWAN) †CBS	Sa/Su · E Asia · CHINESE NETWORK · ALT. FREQ. TO 6085 kHz
	E Asia · CHINESE NETWORK · ALT. FREQ. TO 6085 kHz
ISRAEL KOL ISRAEL, Tel Aviv	W · W Europe & E North Am · 300 kW
USA FAMILY RADIO, Via Taiwan	S Asia · 250 kW
6280v PIRATE (EUROPE) †"ALFA LIMA INTERNATIONAL", Holland	⇦ · Irr · Sa/Su · ENGLISH & DUTCH · W Europe · 0.1 kW
	⇦ · Irr · Su · ENGLISH & DUTCH · W Europe · 0.1 kW
(con'd) †"R MARIO"/"R CASANOVAS", Holland	⇦ · Irr · Su · W Europe

	0 1 2 3 4 5 6 7 8 9 10 11 12 13 14 15 16 17 18 19 20 21 22 23 24

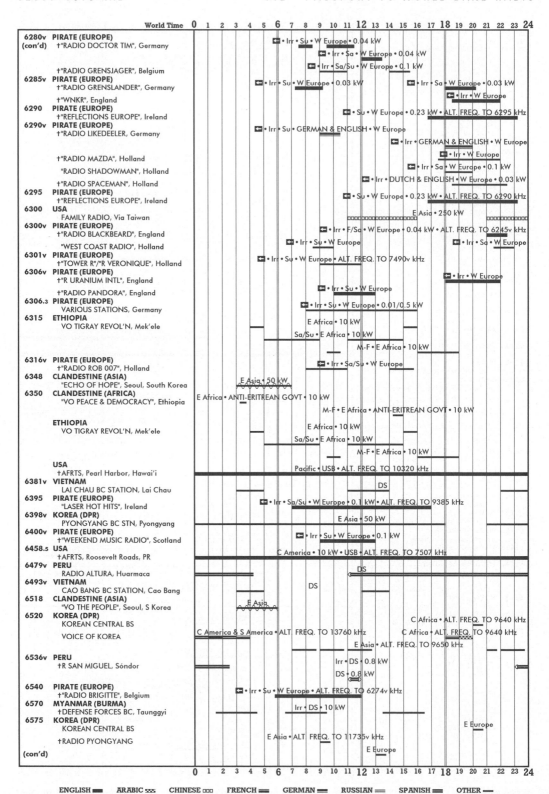

| World Time | 0 | 1 | 2 | 3 | 4 | 5 | 6 | 7 | 8 | 9 | 10 | 11 | 12 | 13 | 14 | 15 | 16 | 17 | 18 | 19 | 20 | 21 | 22 | 23 | 24 |

6280v PIRATE (EUROPE)
(con'd) †"RADIO DOCTOR TIM", Germany — Irr•Su•W Europe•0.04 kW; Irr•Sa•W Europe•0.04 kW

†"RADIO GRENSJAGER", Belgium — Irr•Sa/Su•W Europe•0.1 kW

6285v PIRATE (EUROPE)
†"RADIO GRENSLANDER", Germany — Irr•Su•W Europe•0.03 kW; Irr•Sa•W Europe•0.03 kW

†"WNKR", England — Irr•W Europe

6290 PIRATE (EUROPE)
†"REFLECTIONS EUROPE", Ireland — Su•W Europe•0.23 kW•ALT. FREQ. TO 6295 kHz

6290v PIRATE (EUROPE)
†"RADIO LIKEDEELER", Germany — Irr•Su•GERMAN & ENGLISH•W Europe; Irr•GERMAN & ENGLISH•W Europe

†"RADIO MAZDA", Holland — Irr•W Europe

"RADIO SHADOWMAN", Holland — Irr•Sa•W Europe•0.1 kW

†"RADIO SPACEMAN", Holland — Irr•DUTCH & ENGLISH•W Europe•0.03 kW

6295 PIRATE (EUROPE)
†"REFLECTIONS EUROPE", Ireland — Su•W Europe•0.23 kW•ALT. FREQ. TO 6290 kHz

6300 USA
FAMILY RADIO, Via Taiwan — E Asia•250 kW

6300v PIRATE (EUROPE)
†"RADIO BLACKBEARD", England — Irr•F/Sa•W Europe•0.04 kW•ALT. FREQ. TO 6245v kHz; Irr•Sa•W Europe

"WEST COAST RADIO", Holland — Irr•Su•W Europe

6301v PIRATE (EUROPE)
†"TOWER R"/"R VERONIQUE", Holland — Irr•Su•W Europe•ALT. FREQ. TO 7490v kHz

6306v PIRATE (EUROPE)
†"R URANIUM INTL", England — Irr•W Europe

†"RADIO PANDORA", England — Irr•Su•W Europe

6306.3 PIRATE (EUROPE)
VARIOUS STATIONS, Germany — Irr•Su•W Europe•0.01/0.5 kW

6315 ETHIOPIA
VO TIGRAY REVOL'N, Mek'ele — E Africa•10 kW; Sa/Su•E Africa•10 kW; M-F•E Africa•10 kW

6316v PIRATE (EUROPE)
†"RADIO ROB 007", Holland — Irr•Sa/Su•W Europe

6348 CLANDESTINE (ASIA)
"ECHO OF HOPE", Seoul, South Korea — E Asia•50 kW

6350 CLANDESTINE (AFRICA)
"VO PEACE & DEMOCRACY", Ethiopia — E Africa•ANTI-ERITREAN GOVT•10 kW; M-F•E Africa•ANTI-ERITREAN GOVT•10 kW

ETHIOPIA
VO TIGRAY REVOL'N, Mek'ele — E Africa•10 kW; Sa/Su•E Africa•10 kW; M-F•E Africa•10 kW

USA
†AFRTS, Pearl Harbor, Hawai'i — Pacific•USB•ALT. FREQ. TO 10320 kHz

6381v VIETNAM
LAI CHAU BC STATION, Lai Chau — DS

6395 PIRATE (EUROPE)
"LASER HOT HITS", Ireland — Irr•Sa/Su•W Europe•0.1 kW•ALT. FREQ. TO 9385 kHz

6398v KOREA (DPR)
PYONGYANG BC STN, Pyongyang — E Asia•50 kW

6400v PIRATE (EUROPE)
†"WEEKEND MUSIC RADIO", Scotland — Irr•Su•W Europe•0.1 kW

6458.5 USA
†AFRTS, Roosevelt Roads, PR — C America•10 kW•USB•ALT. FREQ. TO 7507 kHz

6479v PERU
RADIO ALTURA, Huarmaca — DS

6493v VIETNAM
CAO BANG BC STATION, Cao Bang — DS

6518 CLANDESTINE (ASIA)
"VO THE PEOPLE", Seoul, S Korea — E Asia

6520 KOREA (DPR)
KOREAN CENTRAL BS — C Africa•ALT. FREQ. TO 9640 kHz

VOICE OF KOREA — C America & S America•ALT. FREQ. TO 13760 kHz; C Africa•ALT. FREQ. TO 9640 kHz; E Asia•ALT. FREQ. TO 9650 kHz

6536v PERU
†R SAN MIGUEL, Sóndor — Irr•DS•0.8 kW; DS•0.8 kW

6540 PIRATE (EUROPE)
†"RADIO BRIGITTE", Belgium — Irr•Su•W Europe•ALT. FREQ. TO 6274v kHz

6570 MYANMAR (BURMA)
†DEFENSE FORCES BC, Taunggyi — Irr•DS•10 kW

6575 KOREA (DPR)
KOREAN CENTRAL BS — E Europe

†RADIO PYONGYANG — E Asia•ALT. FREQ. TO 11735v kHz; E Europe

(con'd)

ENGLISH ▬ ARABIC ▨ CHINESE ▭▭▭ FRENCH ▬▬ GERMAN ▬ RUSSIAN ═ SPANISH ▬ OTHER ▬

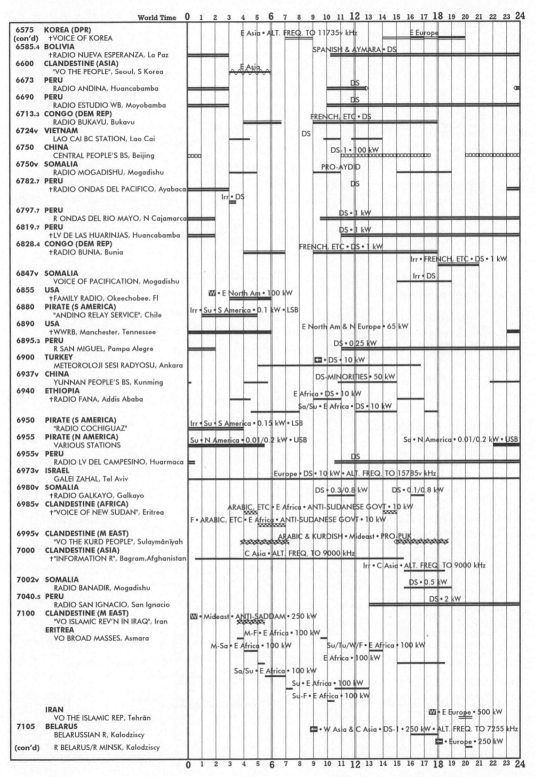

World Time 0 1 2 3 4 5 6 7 8 9 10 11 12 13 14 15 16 17 18 19 20 21 22 23 24

Freq	Station	Details
6575 (con'd)	**KOREA (DPR)** †VOICE OF KOREA	E Asia • ALT. FREQ. TO 11735v kHz E Europe
6585.4	**BOLIVIA** †RADIO NUEVA ESPERANZA, La Paz	SPANISH & AYMARA • DS
6600	**CLANDESTINE (ASIA)** "VO THE PEOPLE", Seoul, S Korea	E Asia
6673	**PERU** RADIO ANDINA, Huancabamba	DS
6690	**PERU** RADIO ESTUDIO WB, Moyobamba	DS
6713.3	**CONGO (DEM REP)** RADIO BUKAVU, Bukavu	FRENCH, ETC • DS
6724v	**VIETNAM** LAO CAI BC STATION, Lao Cai	DS
6750	**CHINA** CENTRAL PEOPLE'S BS, Beijing	DS-1 • 100 kW
6750v	**SOMALIA** RADIO MOGADISHU, Mogadishu	PRO-AYDID
6782.7	**PERU** †RADIO ONDAS DEL PACIFICO, Ayabaca	DS
		Irr • DS
6797.7	**PERU** R ONDAS DEL RIO MAYO, N Cajamarca	DS • 1 kW
6819.7	**PERU** †LV DE LAS HUARINJAS, Huancabamba	DS • 1 kW
6828.4	**CONGO (DEM REP)** †RADIO BUNIA, Bunia	FRENCH, ETC • DS • 1 kW Irr • FRENCH, ETC • DS • 1 kW
6847v	**SOMALIA** VOICE OF PACIFICATION, Mogadishu	Irr • DS
6855	**USA** †FAMILY RADIO, Okeechobee, Fl	W • E North Am • 100 kW
6880	**PIRATE (S AMERICA)** "ANDINO RELAY SERVICE", Chile	Irr • Su • S America • 0.1 kW • LSB
6890	**USA** †WWRB, Manchester, Tennessee	E North Am & N Europe • 65 kW
6895.3	**PERU** R SAN MIGUEL, Pampa Alegre	DS • 0.25 kW
6900	**TURKEY** METEOROLOJI SESI RADYOSU, Ankara	• DS • 10 kW
6937v	**CHINA** YUNNAN PEOPLE'S BS, Kunming	DS-MINORITIES • 50 kW
6940	**ETHIOPIA** †RADIO FANA, Addis Ababa	E Africa • DS • 10 kW Sa/Su • E Africa • DS • 10 kW
6950	**PIRATE (S AMERICA)** "RADIO COCHIGUAZ"	Irr • Su • S America • 0.15 kW • LSB
6955	**PIRATE (N AMERICA)** VARIOUS STATIONS	Su • N America • 0.01/0.2 kW • USB Sa • N America • 0.01/0.2 kW • USB
6955v	**PERU** RADIO LV DEL CAMPESINO, Huarmaca	DS
6973v	**ISRAEL** GALEI ZAHAL, Tel Aviv	Europe • DS • 10 kW • ALT. FREQ. TO 15785v kHz
6980v	**SOMALIA** †RADIO GALKAYO, Galkayo	DS • 0.3/0.8 kW DS • 0.1/0.8 kW
6985v	**CLANDESTINE (AFRICA)** †"VOICE OF NEW SUDAN", Eritrea	ARABIC, ETC • E Africa • ANTI-SUDANESE GOVT • 10 kW F • ARABIC, ETC • E Africa • ANTI-SUDANESE GOVT • 10 kW
6995v	**CLANDESTINE (M EAST)** "VO THE KURD PEOPLE", Sulaymānīyah	ARABIC & KURDISH • Mideast • PRO-PUK
7000	**CLANDESTINE (ASIA)** †"INFORMATION R", Bagram, Afghanistan	C Asia • ALT. FREQ. TO 9000 kHz Irr • C Asia • ALT. FREQ. TO 9000 kHz
7002v	**SOMALIA** RADIO BANADIR, Mogadishu	DS • 0.5 kW
7040.5	**PERU** RADIO SAN IGNACIO, San Ignacio	DS • 2 kW
7100	**CLANDESTINE (M EAST)** "VO ISLAMIC REV'N IN IRAQ", Iran	W • Mideast • ANTI-SADDAM • 250 kW
	ERITREA VO BROAD MASSES, Asmara	M-F • E Africa • 100 kW Su/Tu/W/F • E Africa • 100 kW M-Sa • E Africa • 100 kW E Africa • 100 kW Sa/Su • E Africa • 100 kW Su • E Africa • 100 kW Su-F • E Africa • 100 kW
	IRAN VO THE ISLAMIC REP, Tehrān	W • E Europe • 500 kW
7105	**BELARUS** BELARUSSIAN R, Kalodziscy	• W Asia & C Asia • DS-1 • 250 kW • ALT. FREQ. TO 7255 kHz
(con'd)	R BELARUS/R MINSK, Kalodziscy	• Europe • 250 kW

0 1 2 3 4 5 6 7 8 9 10 11 12 13 14 15 16 17 18 19 20 21 22 23 24

SEASONAL ⑤ OR Ⓦ   1-HR TIMESHIFT MIDYEAR ⬅ OR ➡   JAMMING / OR ∧   EARLIEST HEARD ◁   LATEST HEARD ▷   NEW FOR 2004 †

World Time 0 1 2 3 4 5 6 7 8 9 10 11 12 13 14 15 16 17 18 19 20 21 22 23 24

kHz	Country / Station	Schedule
7105 (con'd)	**BELARUS** R BELARUS/R MINSK, Kalodziscy	⇐ • F • Europe • 250 kW
		⇐ • M • Europe • 250 kW
		⇐ • Tu/Th • Europe • 250 kW
		⇐ • W/Sa/Su • Europe • 250 kW
		⇐ • F/Su • Europe • 250 kW
		⇐ • M-Th/Sa • Europe • 250 kW
		⇐ • Su/W/Sa • Europe • 250 kW
	CHINA NEI MENGGU PBS, Hohhot	DS • 50 kW
	CHINA (TAIWAN) †CBS	E Asia • NEWS NETWORK • ALT. FREQ. TO 7385 kHz
	GERMANY †DEUTSCHE WELLE, Wertachtal	S • W Asia & C Asia • 500 kW
		S • E Europe & W Asia • 500 kW
	†RADIO SANTEC, Jülich	W Su • Mideast • 100 kW
	HUNGARY †RADIO BUDAPEST, Jászberény	W • Europe • 250 kW • ALT. FREQ. TO 9655 kHz
	INDIA ALL INDIA RADIO, Lucknow	Su • DS • 50 kW
		DS • 50 kW
		ENGLISH, ETC • DS • 50 kW
	IRAN VO THE ISLAMIC REP, Tehrān	W Europe • 500 kW
	MADAGASCAR †RTV MALAGASY, Antananarivo	Irr • DS-1 • 30 kW • USB • ALT. FREQ. TO 7155 kHz
	ROMANIA †R ROMANIA INTL, Bucharest	W • E Europe • 50 kW
		S • S Europe • 50 kW
		W • W Europe • 250 kW
	†R ROMANIA INTL, Galbeni	S • Europe • 120 kW
	RUSSIA VOICE OF RUSSIA, Samara	W • C Asia • 250 kW
	UNITED KINGDOM †BBC, Rampisham	W • S Europe • 500 kW
		W M/W • S Europe • 500 kW
	†BBC, Via Ascension	S • C Africa & E Africa • 250 kW
		W • W Africa • 250 kW
		W Africa & C Africa • 250 kW
		W Africa • 250 kW
	†BBC, Via Lampertheim, Germany	W • E Europe • 100 kW
	†BBC, Via Oman	SE Asia • 250 kW
	†BBC, Via Singapore	E Asia • 100 kW
	†BBC, Via Thailand	SE Asia • 250 kW
	†BIBLE VOICE, Via Dhabayya, UAE	W • S Asia • 250 kW
	†FEBA RADIO, Via Dhabayya, UAE	W • S Asia • 250 kW
	USA †ADVENTIST WORLD R, Via Agat, Guam	W • E Asia • 100 kW
	†RADIO SAWA, Via Kavála, Greece	S • Mideast • 250 kW
	RFE-RL, Via Jülich, Germany	W • W Asia & C Asia • 100 kW
	†RFE-RL, Via Kavála, Greece	W • Mideast • 250 kW
	†VOA, Via Ascension	S • C Africa & S Africa • 250 kW
	†VOA, Via Briech, Morocco	W • Europe • 250 kW
	†VOA, Via São Tomé	W • W Africa & C Africa • 100 kW
	UZBEKISTAN †RADIO TASHKENT, Tashkent	W • Europe • 50 kW
7110	**BELARUS** GRODNO RADIO	⇐ • DS-LOCAL, BELARUS1 • 5 kW
	CHINA †CHINA RADIO INTL, Hohhot	E Asia • 50 kW
	†CHINA RADIO INTL, Jinhua	W • Europe • 600 kW
	ETHIOPIA RADIO ETHIOPIA, Gedja	DS • 100 kW
		Su • DS • 100 kW
		Sa/Su • DS • 100 kW
		M-F • DS • 100 kW
	UGANDA RADIO UGANDA, Kampala	ENGLISH, ETC • DS-BLUE CHANNEL • 10 kW
	UNITED KINGDOM †BBC, Via Biblis, Germany	S M-F • S Europe • 100 kW
		W M-F • S Europe • 100 kW
	†WALES RADIO INTL, Skelton, Cumbria	W F • Europe • 300 kW

0 1 2 3 4 5 6 7 8 9 10 11 12 13 14 15 16 17 18 19 20 21 22 23 24

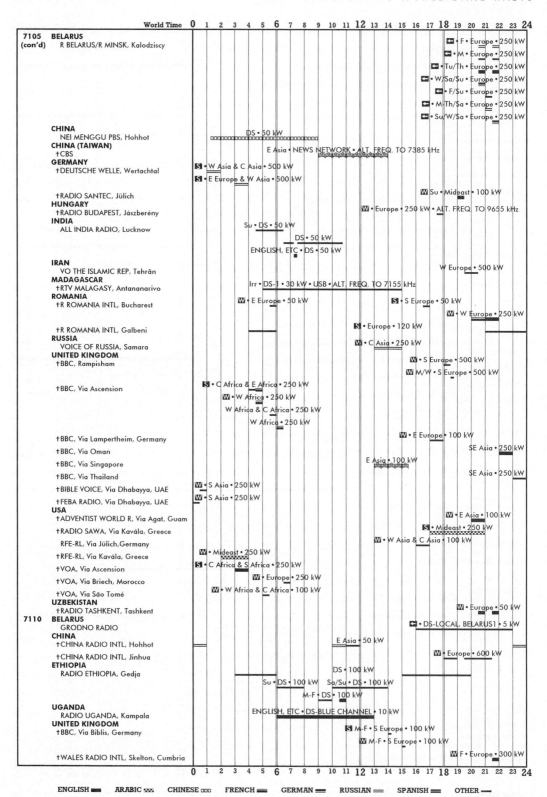

ENGLISH ARABIC CHINESE FRENCH GERMAN RUSSIAN SPANISH OTHER

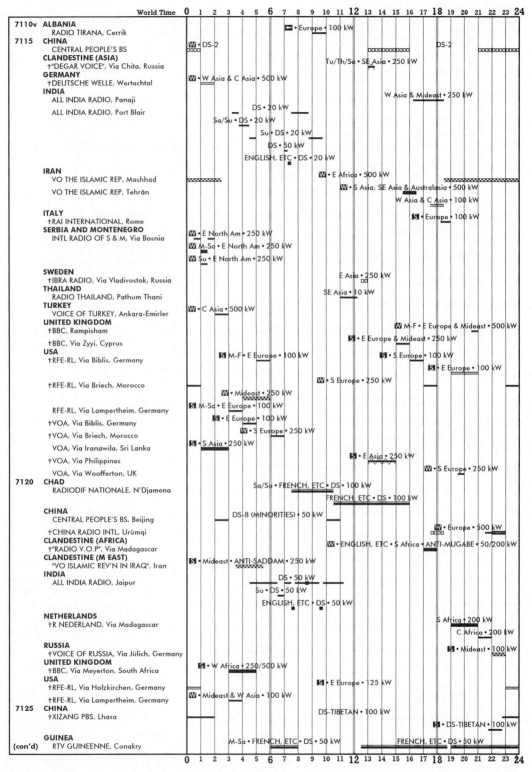

	World Time	0 1 2 3 4 5 6 7 8 9 10 11 12 13 14 15 16 17 18 19 20 21 22 23 24
7110v	**ALBANIA**	
	RADIO TIRANA, Cerrik	⊏ • Europe • 100 kW
7115	**CHINA**	
	CENTRAL PEOPLE'S BS	W • DS-2 / DS-2
	CLANDESTINE (ASIA)	
	†"DEGAR VOICE", Via Chita, Russia	Tu/Th/Sa • SE Asia • 250 kW
	GERMANY	
	†DEUTSCHE WELLE, Wertachtal	W • W Asia & C Asia • 500 kW / W Asia & Mideast • 250 kW
	INDIA	
	ALL INDIA RADIO, Panaji	DS • 20 kW
	ALL INDIA RADIO, Port Blair	Sa/Su • DS • 20 kW
		Su • DS • 20 kW
		DS • 50 kW
		ENGLISH, ETC • DS • 20 kW
	IRAN	
	VO THE ISLAMIC REP, Mashhad	W • E Africa • 500 kW
	VO THE ISLAMIC REP, Tehrān	W • S Asia, SE Asia & Australasia • 500 kW
		W Asia & C Asia • 100 kW
	ITALY	
	†RAI INTERNATIONAL, Rome	S • Europe • 100 kW
	SERBIA AND MONTENEGRO	
	INTL RADIO OF S & M, Via Bosnia	W • E North Am • 250 kW
		W M-Sa • E North Am • 250 kW
		W Su • E North Am • 250 kW
	SWEDEN	
	†IBRA RADIO, Via Vladivostok, Russia	E Asia • 250 kW
	THAILAND	
	RADIO THAILAND, Pathum Thani	SE Asia • 10 kW
	TURKEY	
	VOICE OF TURKEY, Ankara-Emirler	W • C Asia • 500 kW
	UNITED KINGDOM	
	†BBC, Rampisham	W M-F • E Europe & Mideast • 500 kW
	†BBC, Via Zyyi, Cyprus	S • E Europe & Mideast • 250 kW
	USA	
	†RFE-RL, Via Biblis, Germany	S M-F • E Europe • 100 kW / S • S Europe • 100 kW / S • E Europe • 100 kW
	†RFE-RL, Via Briech, Morocco	W • S Europe • 250 kW
		W • Mideast • 250 kW
	RFE-RL, Via Lampertheim, Germany	S M-Sa • E Europe • 100 kW
	†VOA, Via Biblis, Germany	S • E Europe • 100 kW
	†VOA, Via Briech, Morocco	W • S Europe • 250 kW
	VOA, Via Iranawila, Sri Lanka	S • S Asia • 250 kW
	†VOA, Via Philippines	S • E Asia • 250 kW
	VOA, Via Woofferton, UK	W • S Europe • 250 kW
7120	**CHAD**	
	RADIODIF NATIONALE, N'Djamena	Sa/Su • FRENCH, ETC • DS • 100 kW / FRENCH, ETC • DS • 100 kW
	CHINA	
	CENTRAL PEOPLE'S BS, Beijing	DS-8 (MINORITIES) • 50 kW
	†CHINA RADIO INTL, Urümqi	W • Europe • 500 kW
	CLANDESTINE (AFRICA)	
	†"RADIO V.O.P", Via Madagascar	W • ENGLISH, ETC • S Africa • ANTI-MUGABE • 50/200 kW
	CLANDESTINE (M EAST)	
	"VO ISLAMIC REV'N IN IRAQ", Iran	S • Mideast • ANTI-SADDAM • 250 kW
	INDIA	
	ALL INDIA RADIO, Jaipur	DS • 50 kW
		Su • DS • 50 kW
		ENGLISH, ETC • DS • 50 kW
	NETHERLANDS	
	†R NEDERLAND, Via Madagascar	S Africa • 200 kW
		C Africa • 200 kW
	RUSSIA	
	†VOICE OF RUSSIA, Via Jülich, Germany	S • Mideast • 100 kW
	UNITED KINGDOM	
	†BBC, Via Meyerton, South Africa	S • W Africa • 250/500 kW
	USA	
	†RFE-RL, Via Holzkirchen, Germany	S • E Europe • 125 kW
	†RFE-RL, Via Lampertheim, Germany	W • Mideast & W Asia • 100 kW
7125	**CHINA**	
	†XIZANG PBS, Lhasa	DS-TIBETAN • 100 kW / S • DS-TIBETAN • 100 kW
	GUINEA	
(con'd)	RTV GUINEENNE, Conakry	M-Sa • FRENCH, ETC • DS • 50 kW / FRENCH, ETC • DS • 50 kW

| | World Time | 0 1 2 3 4 5 6 7 8 9 10 11 12 13 14 15 16 17 18 19 20 21 22 23 24 |

SEASONAL S OR W   1-HR TIMESHIFT MIDYEAR ⊏ OR ⊐   JAMMING / OR /\   EARLIEST HEARD ◁   LATEST HEARD ▷   NEW FOR 2004 †

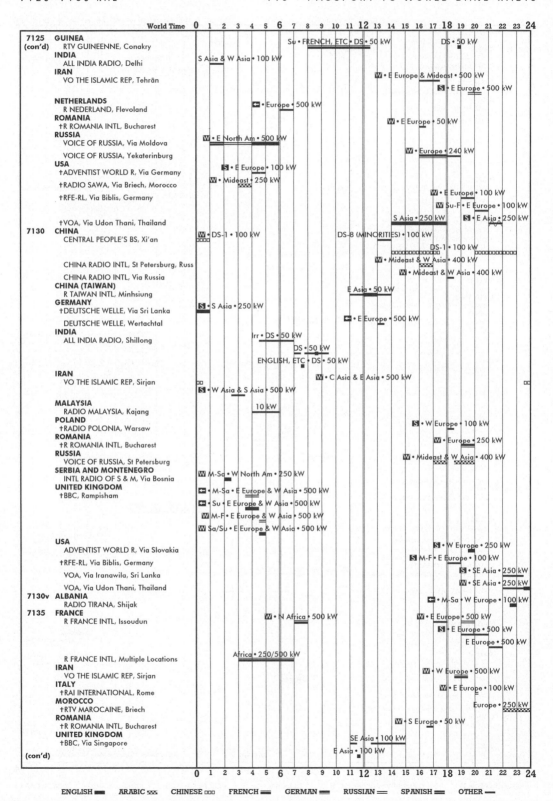

| World Time | 0 | 1 | 2 | 3 | 4 | 5 | 6 | 7 | 8 | 9 | 10 | 11 | 12 | 13 | 14 | 15 | 16 | 17 | 18 | 19 | 20 | 21 | 22 | 23 | 24 |

7125 **GUINEA**
(con'd) RTV GUINEENNE, Conakry — Su • FRENCH, ETC • DS • 50 kW — DS • 50 kW
INDIA
ALL INDIA RADIO, Delhi — S Asia & W Asia • 100 kW
IRAN
VO THE ISLAMIC REP, Tehrän — W • E Europe & Mideast • 500 kW — S • E Europe • 500 kW
NETHERLANDS
R NEDERLAND, Flevoland — ◻ • Europe • 500 kW
ROMANIA
†R ROMANIA INTL, Bucharest — W • E Europe • 50 kW
RUSSIA
VOICE OF RUSSIA, Via Moldova — W • E North Am • 500 kW
VOICE OF RUSSIA, Yekaterinburg — W • Europe • 240 kW
USA
†ADVENTIST WORLD R, Via Germany — S • E Europe • 100 kW
†RADIO SAWA, Via Briech, Morocco — W • Mideast • 250 kW
†RFE-RL, Via Biblis, Germany — W • E Europe • 100 kW — W Su-F • E Europe • 100 kW
†VOA, Via Udon Thani, Thailand — S Asia • 250 kW — S • E Asia • 250 kW

7130 **CHINA**
CENTRAL PEOPLE'S BS, Xi'an — W • DS-1 • 100 kW — DS-8 (MINORITIES) • 100 kW — DS-1 • 100 kW
CHINA RADIO INTL, St Petersburg, Russ — W • Mideast & W Asia • 400 kW
CHINA RADIO INTL, Via Russia — W • Mideast & W Asia • 400 kW
CHINA (TAIWAN)
R TAIWAN INTL, Minhsiung — E Asia • 50 kW
GERMANY
†DEUTSCHE WELLE, Via Sri Lanka — S • S Asia • 250 kW
DEUTSCHE WELLE, Wertachtal — ◻ • E Europe • 500 kW
INDIA
ALL INDIA RADIO, Shillong — Irr • DS • 50 kW — DS • 50 kW — ENGLISH, ETC • DS • 50 kW
IRAN
VO THE ISLAMIC REP, Sirjan — W • C Asia & E Asia • 500 kW — S • W Asia & S Asia • 500 kW
MALAYSIA
RADIO MALAYSIA, Kajang — 10 kW
POLAND
†RADIO POLONIA, Warsaw — S • W Europe • 100 kW
ROMANIA
†R ROMANIA INTL, Bucharest — W • Europe • 250 kW
RUSSIA
VOICE OF RUSSIA, St Petersburg — W • Mideast & W Asia • 400 kW
SERBIA AND MONTENEGRO
INTL RADIO OF S & M, Via Bosnia — W M-Sa • W North Am • 250 kW
UNITED KINGDOM
†BBC, Rampisham — ◻ • M-Sa • E Europe & W Asia • 500 kW — ◻ • Su • E Europe & W Asia • 500 kW — W M-F • E Europe & W Asia • 500 kW — W Sa/Su • E Europe & W Asia • 500 kW
USA
ADVENTIST WORLD R, Via Slovakia — S • W Europe • 250 kW
†RFE-RL, Via Biblis, Germany — S M-F • E Europe • 100 kW
VOA, Via Iranawila, Sri Lanka — S • SE Asia • 250 kW
VOA, Via Udon Thani, Thailand — W • SE Asia • 250 kW

7130v **ALBANIA**
RADIO TIRANA, Shijak — ◻ • M-Sa • W Europe • 100 kW
7135 **FRANCE**
R FRANCE INTL, Issoudun — W • N Africa • 500 kW — W • E Europe • 500 kW — S • E Europe • 500 kW — E Europe • 500 kW
R FRANCE INTL, Multiple Locations — Africa • 250/500 kW
IRAN
VO THE ISLAMIC REP, Sirjan — W • W Europe • 500 kW
ITALY
†RAI INTERNATIONAL, Rome — W • E Europe • 100 kW
MOROCCO
†RTV MAROCAINE, Briech — Europe • 250 kW
ROMANIA
†R ROMANIA INTL, Bucharest — W • S Europe • 50 kW
UNITED KINGDOM
†BBC, Via Singapore — SE Asia • 100 kW — E Asia • 100 kW

(con'd)

| | 0 | 1 | 2 | 3 | 4 | 5 | 6 | 7 | 8 | 9 | 10 | 11 | 12 | 13 | 14 | 15 | 16 | 17 | 18 | 19 | 20 | 21 | 22 | 23 | 24 |

ENGLISH ▬ ARABIC ░░ CHINESE ▢▢▢ FRENCH ▬ GERMAN ▬ RUSSIAN ═ SPANISH ▬ OTHER ▬

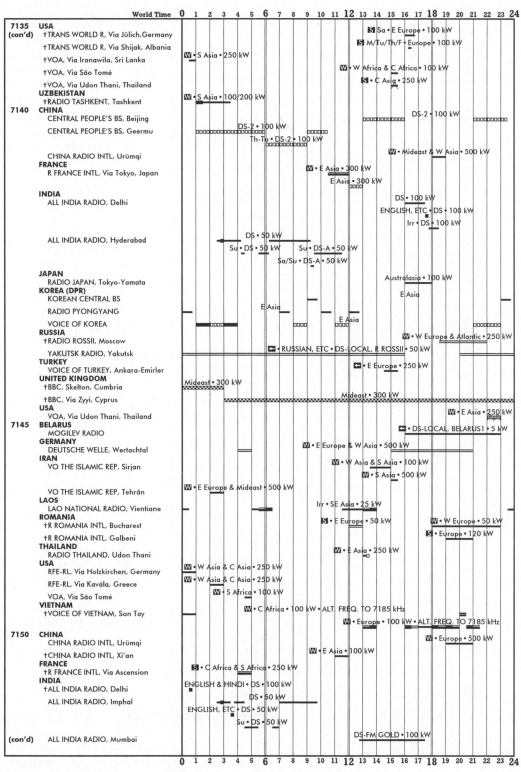

	World Time	0	1	2	3	4	5	6	7	8	9	10	11	12	13	14	15	16	17	18	19	20	21	22	23	24

7135 (con'd) **USA**
- †TRANS WORLD R, Via Jülich, Germany — S • Sa • E Europe • 100 kW
- †TRANS WORLD R, Via Shijak, Albania — S • M/Tu/Th/F • Europe • 100 kW
- †VOA, Via Iranawila, Sri Lanka — W • S Asia • 250 kW
- †VOA, Via São Tomé — W • W Africa & C Africa • 100 kW
- †VOA, Via Udon Thani, Thailand — S • C Asia • 250 kW

UZBEKISTAN
- †RADIO TASHKENT, Tashkent — W • S Asia • 100/200 kW

7140 CHINA
- CENTRAL PEOPLE'S BS, Beijing — DS-2 • 100 kW ... DS-2 • 100 kW
- CENTRAL PEOPLE'S BS, Geermu — Th-Tu • DS-2 • 100 kW
- CHINA RADIO INTL, Urümqi — W • Mideast & W Asia • 500 kW

FRANCE
- R FRANCE INTL, Via Tokyo, Japan — W • E Asia • 300 kW / E Asia • 300 kW

INDIA
- ALL INDIA RADIO, Delhi — DS • 100 kW / ENGLISH, ETC • DS • 100 kW / Irr • DS • 100 kW
- ALL INDIA RADIO, Hyderabad — DS • 50 kW / Su • DS • 50 kW / Su • DS-A • 50 kW / Sa/Su • DS-A • 50 kW

JAPAN
- RADIO JAPAN, Tokyo-Yamata — Australasia • 100 kW

KOREA (DPR)
- KOREAN CENTRAL BS — E Asia
- RADIO PYONGYANG — E Asia
- VOICE OF KOREA — E Asia

RUSSIA
- †RADIO ROSSII, Moscow — W • W Europe & Atlantic • 250 kW
- YAKUTSK RADIO, Yakutsk — RUSSIAN, ETC • DS-LOCAL, R ROSSII • 50 kW

TURKEY
- VOICE OF TURKEY, Ankara-Emirler — E Europe • 250 kW

UNITED KINGDOM
- †BBC, Skelton, Cumbria — Mideast • 300 kW
- †BBC, Via Zyyi, Cyprus — Mideast • 300 kW

USA
- VOA, Via Udon Thani, Thailand — W • E Asia • 250 kW

7145 BELARUS
- MOGILEV RADIO — DS-LOCAL, BELARUS1 • 5 kW

GERMANY
- DEUTSCHE WELLE, Wertachtal — W • E Europe & W Asia • 500 kW

IRAN
- VO THE ISLAMIC REP, Sirjan — W • W Asia & S Asia • 100 kW / W • S Asia • 500 kW
- VO THE ISLAMIC REP, Tehrān — W • E Europe & Mideast • 500 kW

LAOS
- LAO NATIONAL RADIO, Vientiane — Irr • SE Asia • 25 kW

ROMANIA
- †R ROMANIA INTL, Bucharest — S • E Europe • 50 kW / W • W Europe • 50 kW
- †R ROMANIA INTL, Galbeni — S • Europe • 120 kW

THAILAND
- RADIO THAILAND, Udon Thani — W • E Asia • 250 kW

USA
- RFE-RL, Via Holzkirchen, Germany — W • W Asia & C Asia • 250 kW
- RFE-RL, Via Kavála, Greece — W • W Asia & C Asia • 250 kW
- VOA, Via São Tomé — W • S Africa • 100 kW

VIETNAM
- †VOICE OF VIETNAM, Son Tay — W • C Africa • 100 kW • ALT FREQ. TO 7185 kHz / W • Europe • 100 kW • ALT. FREQ. TO 7185 kHz / W • Europe • 500 kW

7150 CHINA
- CHINA RADIO INTL, Urümqi — W • E Asia • 100 kW
- †CHINA RADIO INTL, Xi'an

FRANCE
- †R FRANCE INTL, Via Ascension — S • C Africa & S Africa • 250 kW

INDIA
- †ALL INDIA RADIO, Delhi — ENGLISH & HINDI • DS • 100 kW / DS • 50 kW
- ALL INDIA RADIO, Imphal — ENGLISH, ETC • DS • 50 kW / Su • DS • 50 kW
- (con'd) ALL INDIA RADIO, Mumbai — DS-FM GOLD • 100 kW

	0	1	2	3	4	5	6	7	8	9	10	11	12	13	14	15	16	17	18	19	20	21	22	23	24

SEASONAL **S** OR **W**   1-HR TIMESHIFT MIDYEAR ⊟ OR ⊡   JAMMING / OR ∧   EARLIEST HEARD ◁   LATEST HEARD ▷   NEW FOR 2004 †

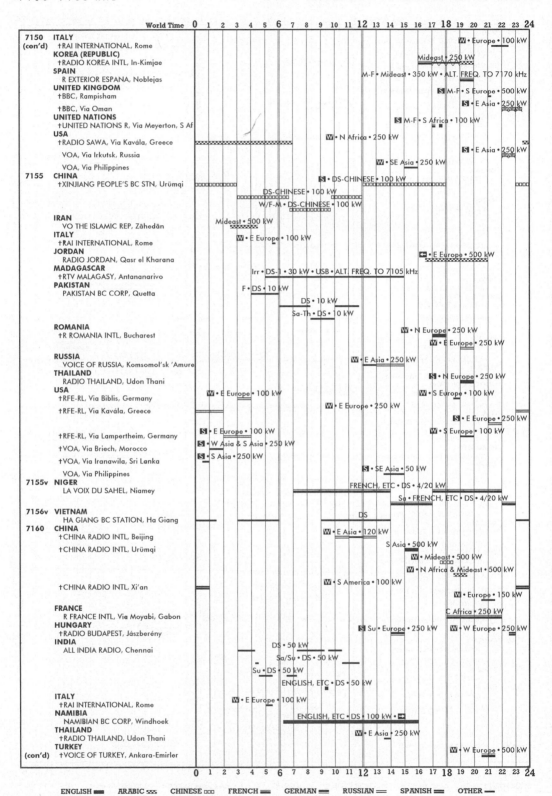

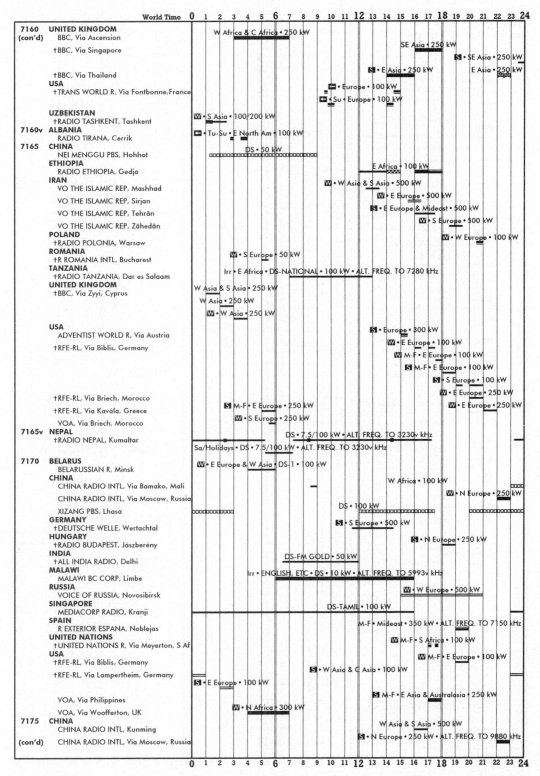

7160	**UNITED KINGDOM**		
(con'd)	BBC, Via Ascension	W Africa & C Africa • 250 kW	
	†BBC, Via Singapore	SE Asia • 250 kW	S SE Asia • 250 kW
	†BBC, Via Thailand	S • E Asia • 250 kW	E Asia • 250 kW
	USA		
	†TRANS WORLD R, Via Fontbonne, France	⬅ • Europe • 100 kW	
		⬅ • Su • Europe • 100 kW	
	UZBEKISTAN		
	†RADIO TASHKENT, Tashkent	W • S Asia • 100/200 kW	
7160v	**ALBANIA**		
	RADIO TIRANA, Cerrik	⬅ • Tu-Su • E North Am • 100 kW	
7165	**CHINA**		
	NEI MENGGU PBS, Hohhot	DS • 50 kW	
	ETHIOPIA		
	RADIO ETHIOPIA, Gedja	E Africa • 100 kW	
	IRAN		
	VO THE ISLAMIC REP, Mashhad	W • W Asia & S Asia • 500 kW	
	VO THE ISLAMIC REP, Sirjan	W • E Europe • 500 kW	
	VO THE ISLAMIC REP, Tehrān	S • E Europe & Mideast • 500 kW	
	VO THE ISLAMIC REP, Zāhedān	W • S Europe • 500 kW	
	POLAND		
	†RADIO POLONIA, Warsaw	W • W Europe • 100 kW	
	ROMANIA		
	†R ROMANIA INTL, Bucharest	W • S Europe • 50 kW	
	TANZANIA		
	†RADIO TANZANIA, Dar es Salaam	Irr • E Africa • DS-NATIONAL • 100 kW • ALT. FREQ. TO 7280 kHz	
	UNITED KINGDOM		
	†BBC, Via Zyyi, Cyprus	W Asia & S Asia • 250 kW	
		W Asia • 250 kW	
		W • W Asia • 250 kW	
	USA		
	ADVENTIST WORLD R, Via Austria	S • Europe • 300 kW	
	†RFE-RL, Via Biblis, Germany	W • E Europe • 100 kW	
		W • M-F • E Europe • 100 kW	
		S • M-F • E Europe • 100 kW	
		S • S Europe • 100 kW	
		W • E Europe • 250 kW	
	†RFE-RL, Via Briech, Morocco	S M-F • E Europe • 250 kW	
	†RFE-RL, Via Kavála, Greece	W • S Europe • 250 kW	W • E Europe • 250 kW
	VOA, Via Briech, Morocco		
7165v	**NEPAL**		
	†RADIO NEPAL, Kumaltar	DS • 7.5/100 kW • ALT. FREQ. TO 3230v kHz	
		Sa/Holidays • DS • 7.5/100 kW • ALT. FREQ. TO 3230v kHz	
7170	**BELARUS**		
	BELARUSSIAN R, Minsk	W • E Europe & W Asia • DS-1 • 100 kW	
	CHINA		
	CHINA RADIO INTL, Via Bamako, Mali	W Africa • 100 kW	
	CHINA RADIO INTL, Via Moscow, Russia	W • N Europe • 250 kW	
	XIZANG PBS, Lhasa	DS • 100 kW	
	GERMANY		
	†DEUTSCHE WELLE, Wertachtal	S • S Europe • 500 kW	
	HUNGARY		
	†RADIO BUDAPEST, Jászberény	S • N Europe • 250 kW	
	INDIA		
	†ALL INDIA RADIO, Delhi	DS-FM GOLD • 50 kW	
	MALAWI		
	MALAWI BC CORP, Limbe	Irr • ENGLISH, ETC • DS • 10 kW • ALT. FREQ. TO 5993v kHz	
	RUSSIA		
	VOICE OF RUSSIA, Novosibirsk	W • W Europe • 500 kW	
	SINGAPORE		
	MEDIACORP RADIO, Kranji	DS-TAMIL • 100 kW	
	SPAIN		
	R EXTERIOR ESPANA, Noblejas	M-F • Mideast • 350 kW • ALT. FREQ. TO 7150 kHz	
	UNITED NATIONS		
	†UNITED NATIONS R, Via Meyerton, S Af	W • M-F • S Africa • 100 kW	
	USA		
	†RFE-RL, Via Biblis, Germany	W • M-F • E Europe • 100 kW	
	†RFE-RL, Via Lampertheim, Germany	S • W Asia & C Asia • 100 kW	
		S • E Europe • 100 kW	
	VOA, Via Philippines	S M-F • E Asia & Australasia • 250 kW	
	VOA, Via Woofferton, UK	W • N Africa • 300 kW	
7175	**CHINA**		
	CHINA RADIO INTL, Kunming	W Asia & S Asia • 500 kW	
(con'd)	CHINA RADIO INTL, Via Moscow, Russia	S • N Europe • 250 kW • ALT. FREQ. TO 9880 kHz	

SEASONAL S OR W   1-HR TIMESHIFT MIDYEAR ⬅ OR ➡   JAMMING / OR ∧   EARLIEST HEARD ◁   LATEST HEARD ▷   NEW FOR 2004 †

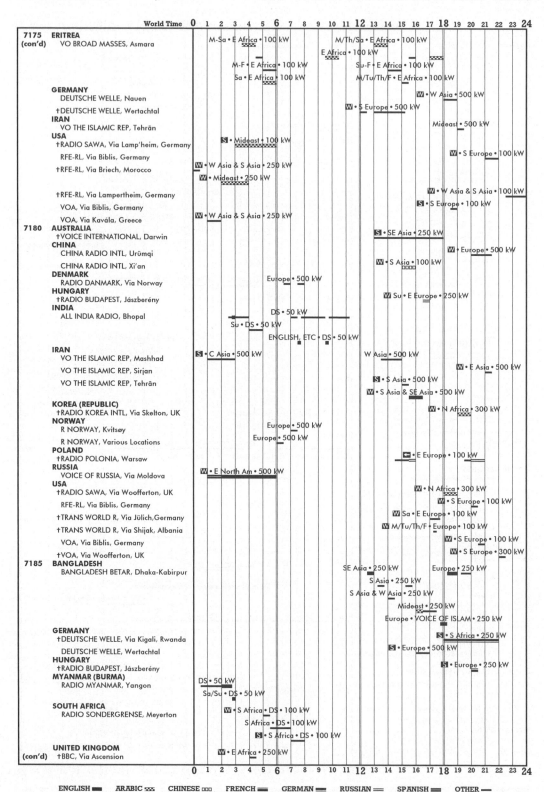

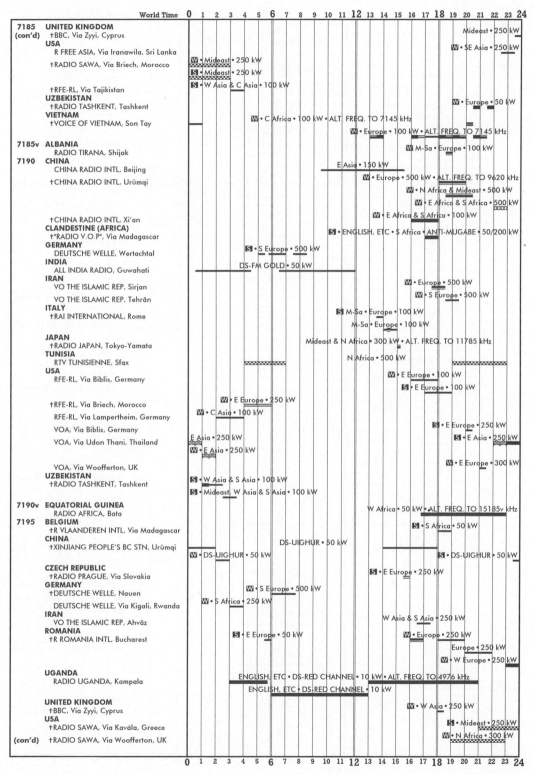

World Time	7185
7185 (con'd)	**UNITED KINGDOM** †BBC, Via Zyyi, Cyprus — Mideast • 250 kW
	USA R FREE ASIA, Via Iranawila, Sri Lanka — W • SE Asia • 250 kW
	†RADIO SAWA, Via Briech, Morocco — W • Mideast • 250 kW / S • Mideast • 250 kW
	†RFE-RL, Via Tajikistan — S • W Asia & C Asia • 100 kW
	UZBEKISTAN †RADIO TASHKENT, Tashkent — W • Europe • 50 kW
	VIETNAM †VOICE OF VIETNAM, Son Tay — W • C Africa • 100 kW • ALT. FREQ. TO 7145 kHz / W • Europe • 100 kW • ALT. FREQ. TO 7145 kHz
7185v	**ALBANIA** RADIO TIRANA, Shijak — W M-Sa • Europe • 100 kW
7190	**CHINA** CHINA RADIO INTL, Beijing — E Asia • 150 kW
	†CHINA RADIO INTL, Urümqi — W • Europe • 500 kW • ALT. FREQ. TO 9620 kHz / W • N Africa & Mideast • 500 kW / W • E Africa & S Africa • 500 kW
	†CHINA RADIO INTL, Xi'an — W • E Africa & S Africa • 100 kW
	CLANDESTINE (AFRICA) †"RADIO V.O.P.", Via Madagascar — S • ENGLISH, ETC • S Africa • ANTI-MUGABE • 50/200 kW
	GERMANY DEUTSCHE WELLE, Wertachtal — S • S Europe • 500 kW
	INDIA ALL INDIA RADIO, Guwahati — DS-FM GOLD • 50 kW
	IRAN VO THE ISLAMIC REP, Sirjan — W • Europe • 500 kW
	VO THE ISLAMIC REP, Tehrān — W • S Europe • 500 kW
	ITALY †RAI INTERNATIONAL, Rome — S M-Sa • Europe • 100 kW / M-Sa • Europe • 100 kW
	JAPAN †RADIO JAPAN, Tokyo-Yamata — Mideast & N Africa • 300 kW • ALT. FREQ. TO 11785 kHz
	TUNISIA RTV TUNISIENNE, Sfax — N Africa • 500 kW
	USA RFE-RL, Via Biblis, Germany — W • E Europe • 100 kW / S • E Europe • 100 kW
	†RFE-RL, Via Briech, Morocco — W • E Europe • 250 kW
	RFE-RL, Via Lampertheim, Germany — W • C Asia • 100 kW
	VOA, Via Biblis, Germany — S • E Europe • 250 kW
	VOA, Via Udon Thani, Thailand — E Asia • 250 kW / S • E Asia • 250 kW / W • E Asia • 250 kW
	VOA, Via Woofferton, UK — W • E Europe • 300 kW
	UZBEKISTAN †RADIO TASHKENT, Tashkent — S • W Asia & S Asia • 100 kW / S • Mideast, W Asia & S Asia • 100 kW
7190v	**EQUATORIAL GUINEA** RADIO AFRICA, Bata — W Africa • 50 kW • ALT. FREQ. TO 15185v kHz
7195	**BELGIUM** †R VLAANDEREN INTL, Via Madagascar — S • S Africa • 50 kW
	CHINA †XINJIANG PEOPLE'S BC STN, Urümqi — DS-UIGHUR • 50 kW / W • DS-UIGHUR • 50 kW / S • DS-UIGHUR • 50 kW
	CZECH REPUBLIC †RADIO PRAGUE, Via Slovakia — S • E Europe • 250 kW
	GERMANY †DEUTSCHE WELLE, Nauen — W • S Europe • 500 kW
	DEUTSCHE WELLE, Via Kigali, Rwanda — W • S Africa • 250 kW
	IRAN VO THE ISLAMIC REP, Ahvāz — W Asia & S Asia • 250 kW
	ROMANIA †R ROMANIA INTL, Bucharest — S • E Europe • 50 kW / W • Europe • 250 kW / Europe • 250 kW / W • W Europe • 250 kW
	UGANDA RADIO UGANDA, Kampala — ENGLISH, ETC • DS-RED CHANNEL • 10 kW • ALT. FREQ. TO 4976 kHz / ENGLISH, ETC • DS-RED CHANNEL • 10 kW
	UNITED KINGDOM †BBC, Via Zyyi, Cyprus — W • W Asia • 250 kW
	USA †RADIO SAWA, Via Kavála, Greece — S • Mideast • 250 kW
(con'd)	†RADIO SAWA, Via Woofferton, UK — W • N Africa • 300 kW

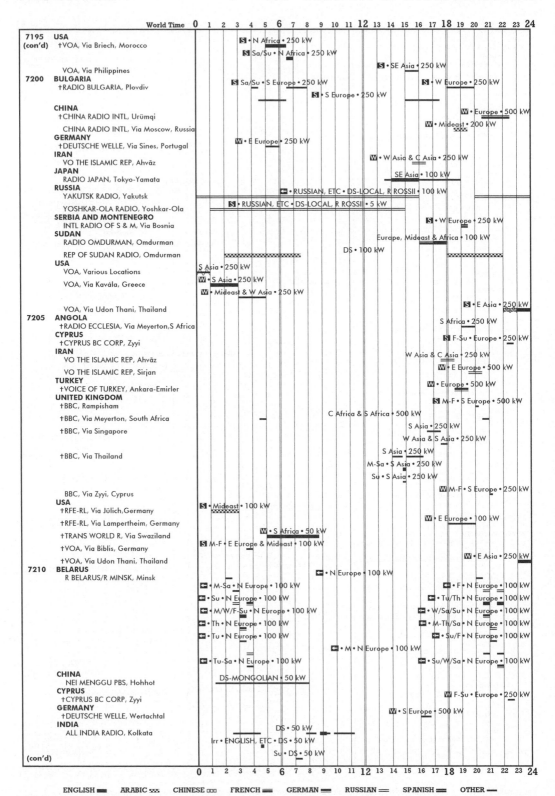

	World Time	0 1 2 3 4 5 6 7 8 9 10 11 12 13 14 15 16 17 18 19 20 21 22 23 24
7195 (con'd)	**USA** †VOA, Via Briech, Morocco	S • N Africa • 250 kW / S Sa/Su • N Africa • 250 kW
	VOA, Via Philippines	S • SE Asia • 250 kW
7200	**BULGARIA** †RADIO BULGARIA, Plovdiv	S Sa/Su • S Europe • 250 kW / S • W Europe • 250 kW / S • S Europe • 250 kW
	CHINA †CHINA RADIO INTL, Urümqi	W • Europe • 500 kW
	CHINA RADIO INTL, Via Moscow, Russia	W • Mideast • 200 kW
	GERMANY †DEUTSCHE WELLE, Via Sines, Portugal	W • E Europe • 250 kW
	IRAN VO THE ISLAMIC REP, Ahvāz	W • W Asia & C Asia • 250 kW
	JAPAN RADIO JAPAN, Tokyo-Yamata	SE Asia • 100 kW
	RUSSIA YAKUTSK RADIO, Yakutsk	RUSSIAN, ETC • DS-LOCAL, R ROSSII • 100 kW
	YOSHKAR-OLA RADIO, Yoshkar-Ola	S • RUSSIAN, ETC • DS-LOCAL, R ROSSII • 5 kW
	SERBIA AND MONTENEGRO INTL RADIO OF S & M, Via Bosnia	S • W Europe • 250 kW
	SUDAN RADIO OMDURMAN, Omdurman	Europe, Mideast & Africa • 100 kW
	REP OF SUDAN RADIO, Omdurman	DS • 100 kW
	USA VOA, Various Locations	S Asia • 250 kW
	VOA, Via Kavála, Greece	W • S Asia • 250 kW
		W • Mideast & W Asia • 250 kW
	VOA, Via Udon Thani, Thailand	S • E Asia • 250 kW
7205	**ANGOLA** †RADIO ECCLESIA, Via Meyerton, S Africa	S Africa • 250 kW
	CYPRUS †CYPRUS BC CORP, Zyyi	S F-Su • Europe • 250 kW
	IRAN VO THE ISLAMIC REP, Ahvāz	W Asia & C Asia • 250 kW
	VO THE ISLAMIC REP, Sirjan	W • E Europe • 500 kW
	TURKEY †VOICE OF TURKEY, Ankara-Emirler	W • Europe • 500 kW
	UNITED KINGDOM †BBC, Rampisham	S M-F • S Europe • 500 kW
	†BBC, Via Meyerton, South Africa	C Africa & S Africa • 500 kW
	†BBC, Via Singapore	S Asia • 250 kW / W Asia & S Asia • 250 kW
	†BBC, Via Thailand	S Asia • 250 kW / M-Sa • S Asia • 250 kW / Su • S Asia • 250 kW
	BBC, Via Zyyi, Cyprus	W M-F • S Europe • 250 kW
	USA †RFE-RL, Via Jülich, Germany	S • Mideast • 100 kW
	†RFE-RL, Via Lampertheim, Germany	W • E Europe • 100 kW
	†TRANS WORLD R, Via Swaziland	W • S Africa • 50 kW
	†VOA, Via Biblis, Germany	S M-F • E Europe & Mideast • 100 kW
	†VOA, Via Udon Thani, Thailand	W • E Asia • 250 kW
7210	**BELARUS** R BELARUS/R MINSK, Minsk	• N Europe • 100 kW
		• M-Sa • N Europe • 100 kW / • F • N Europe • 100 kW
		• Su • N Europe • 100 kW / • Tu/Th • N Europe • 100 kW
		• M/W/F-Su • N Europe • 100 kW / • W/Sa/Su • N Europe • 100 kW
		• Th • N Europe • 100 kW / • M-Th/Sa • N Europe • 100 kW
		• Tu • N Europe • 100 kW / • Su/F • N Europe • 100 kW
		• M • N Europe • 100 kW
		• Tu-Sa • N Europe • 100 kW / • Su/W/Sa • N Europe • 100 kW
	CHINA NEI MENGGU PBS, Hohhot	DS-MONGOLIAN • 50 kW
	CYPRUS †CYPRUS BC CORP, Zyyi	W F-Su • Europe • 250 kW
	GERMANY †DEUTSCHE WELLE, Wertachtal	W • S Europe • 500 kW
	INDIA ALL INDIA RADIO, Kolkata	DS • 50 kW
		Irr • ENGLISH, ETC • DS • 50 kW
		Su • DS • 50 kW
(con'd)		0 1 2 3 4 5 6 7 8 9 10 11 12 13 14 15 16 17 18 19 20 21 22 23 24

ENGLISH ▬   ARABIC ⋙   CHINESE ▫▫▫   FRENCH ▬   GERMAN ▬   RUSSIAN ═   SPANISH ▬   OTHER ▬

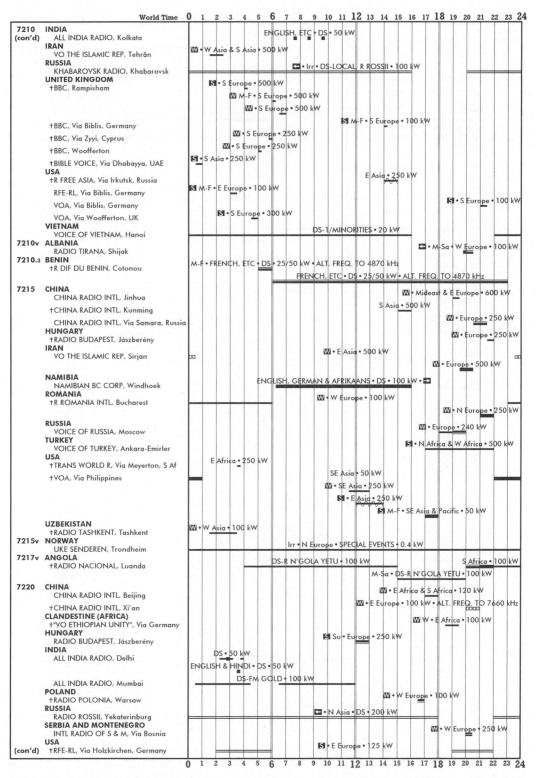

World Time	0 1 2 3 4 5 6 7 8 9 10 11 12 13 14 15 16 17 18 19 20 21 22 23 24

7210 INDIA
(con'd)   ALL INDIA RADIO, Kolkata — ENGLISH, ETC • DS • 50 kW
IRAN
    VO THE ISLAMIC REP, Tehrān — W • W Asia & S Asia • 500 kW
RUSSIA
    KHABAROVSK RADIO, Khabarovsk — Irr • DS-LOCAL, R ROSSII • 100 kW
UNITED KINGDOM
    †BBC, Rampisham — S • S Europe • 500 kW
        W • M-F • S Europe • 500 kW
        W • S Europe • 500 kW
        S • M-F • S Europe • 100 kW
    †BBC, Via Biblis, Germany — W • S Europe • 250 kW
    †BBC, Via Zyyi, Cyprus — W • S Europe • 250 kW
    †BBC, Woofferton
    †BIBLE VOICE, Via Dhabayya, UAE — S • S Asia • 250 kW
USA
    †R FREE ASIA, Via Irkutsk, Russia — E Asia • 250 kW
    RFE-RL, Via Biblis, Germany — S • M-F • E Europe • 100 kW
    VOA, Via Biblis, Germany — S • S Europe • 100 kW
    VOA, Via Woofferton, UK — S • S Europe • 300 kW
VIETNAM
    VOICE OF VIETNAM, Hanoi — DS-1/MINORITIES • 20 kW
7210v ALBANIA
    RADIO TIRANA, Shijak — M-Sa • W Europe • 100 kW
7210.3 BENIN
    †R DIF DU BENIN, Cotonou — M-F • FRENCH, ETC • DS • 25/50 kW • ALT. FREQ. TO 4870 kHz
        FRENCH, ETC • DS • 25/50 kW • ALT. FREQ. TO 4870 kHz

7215 CHINA
    CHINA RADIO INTL, Jinhua — W • Mideast & E Europe • 600 kW
    †CHINA RADIO INTL, Kunming — S Asia • 500 kW
    CHINA RADIO INTL, Via Samara, Russia — W • Europe • 250 kW
HUNGARY
    †RADIO BUDAPEST, Jászberény — W • Europe • 250 kW
IRAN
    VO THE ISLAMIC REP, Sirjan — W • E Asia • 500 kW
        W • Europe • 500 kW
NAMIBIA
    NAMIBIAN BC CORP, Windhoek — ENGLISH, GERMAN & AFRIKAANS • DS • 100 kW
ROMANIA
    †R ROMANIA INTL, Bucharest — W • W Europe • 100 kW
        W • N Europe • 250 kW
RUSSIA
    VOICE OF RUSSIA, Moscow — W • Europe • 240 kW
TURKEY
    VOICE OF TURKEY, Ankara-Emirler — S • N Africa & W Africa • 500 kW
USA
    †TRANS WORLD R, Via Meyerton, S Af — E Africa • 250 kW
    †VOA, Via Philippines — SE Asia • 50 kW
        W • SE Asia • 250 kW
        S • E Asia • 250 kW
        S • M-F • SE Asia & Pacific • 50 kW
UZBEKISTAN
    †RADIO TASHKENT, Tashkent — W • W Asia • 100 kW
7215v NORWAY
    UKE SENDEREN, Trondheim — Irr • N Europe • SPECIAL EVENTS • 0.4 kW
7217v ANGOLA
    †RADIO NACIONAL, Luanda — DS-R N'GOLA YETU • 100 kW
        S Africa • 100 kW
        M-Sa • DS-R N'GOLA YETU • 100 kW

7220 CHINA
    CHINA RADIO INTL, Beijing — W • E Africa & S Africa • 120 kW
    †CHINA RADIO INTL, Xi'an — W • E Europe • 100 kW • ALT. FREQ. TO 7660 kHz
CLANDESTINE (AFRICA)
    †"VO ETHIOPIAN UNITY", Via Germany — W • E Africa • 100 kW
HUNGARY
    RADIO BUDAPEST, Jászberény — S • Su • Europe • 250 kW
INDIA
    ALL INDIA RADIO, Delhi — DS • 50 kW
        ENGLISH & HINDI • DS • 50 kW
    ALL INDIA RADIO, Mumbai — DS-FM GOLD • 100 kW
POLAND
    †RADIO POLONIA, Warsaw — W • W Europe • 100 kW
RUSSIA
    RADIO ROSSII, Yekaterinburg — N Asia • DS • 200 kW
SERBIA AND MONTENEGRO
    INTL RADIO OF S & M, Via Bosnia — W • W Europe • 250 kW
USA
(con'd)   †RFE-RL, Via Holzkirchen, Germany — S • E Europe • 125 kW

	0 1 2 3 4 5 6 7 8 9 10 11 12 13 14 15 16 17 18 19 20 21 22 23 24

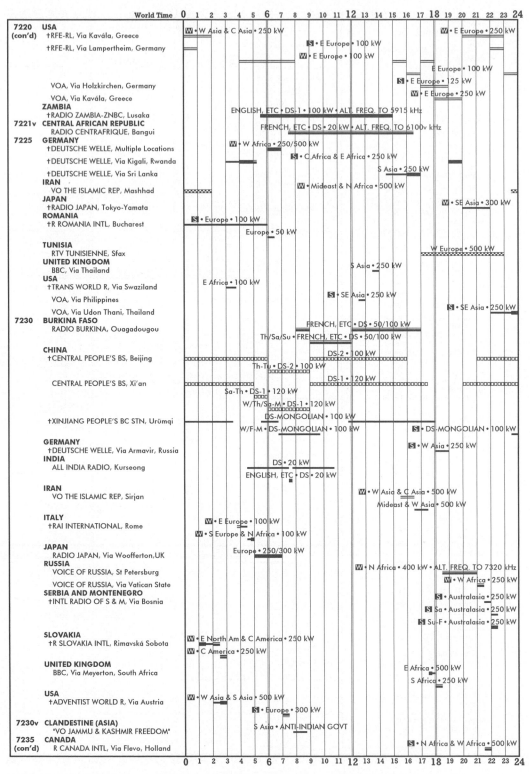

	World Time	0 1 2 3 4 5 6 7 8 9 10 11 12 13 14 15 16 17 18 19 20 21 22 23 24
7220 (con'd)	USA †RFE-RL, Via Kavála, Greece	W•W Asia & C Asia•250 kW ... W•E Europe•250 kW
	†RFE-RL, Via Lampertheim, Germany	S•E Europe•100 kW / W•E Europe•100 kW
	VOA, Via Holzkirchen, Germany	E Europe•100 kW
		S•E Europe•125 kW
	VOA, Via Kavála, Greece	W•E Europe•250 kW
	ZAMBIA †RADIO ZAMBIA-ZNBC, Lusaka	ENGLISH, ETC•DS-1•100 kW•ALT. FREQ. TO 5915 kHz
7221v	CENTRAL AFRICAN REPUBLIC RADIO CENTRAFRIQUE, Bangui	FRENCH, ETC•DS•20 kW•ALT. FREQ. TO 6100v kHz
7225	GERMANY †DEUTSCHE WELLE, Multiple Locations	W•W Africa•250/500 kW
	†DEUTSCHE WELLE, Via Kigali, Rwanda	S•C Africa & E Africa•250 kW
	†DEUTSCHE WELLE, Via Sri Lanka	S Asia•250 kW
	IRAN VO THE ISLAMIC REP, Mashhad	W•Mideast & N Africa•500 kW
	JAPAN †RADIO JAPAN, Tokyo-Yamata	W•SE Asia•300 kW
	ROMANIA †R ROMANIA INTL, Bucharest	S•Europe•100 kW
		Europe•50 kW
	TUNISIA RTV TUNISIENNE, Sfax	W Europe•500 kW
	UNITED KINGDOM BBC, Via Thailand	S Asia•250 kW
	USA †TRANS WORLD R, Via Swaziland	E Africa•100 kW
	VOA, Via Philippines	S•SE Asia•250 kW
	VOA, Via Udon Thani, Thailand	S•SE Asia•250 kW
7230	BURKINA FASO RADIO BURKINA, Ouagadougou	FRENCH, ETC•DS•50/100 kW / Th/Sa/Su•FRENCH, ETC•DS•50/100 kW
	CHINA †CENTRAL PEOPLE'S BS, Beijing	DS-2•100 kW / Th-Tu•DS-2•100 kW
	CENTRAL PEOPLE'S BS, Xi'an	DS-1•120 kW / Sa-Th•DS-1•120 kW / W/Th/Sa-M•DS-1•120 kW
	†XINJIANG PEOPLE'S BC STN, Urümqi	DS-MONGOLIAN•100 kW / W/F-M•DS-MONGOLIAN•100 kW / S•DS-MONGOLIAN•100 kW
	GERMANY †DEUTSCHE WELLE, Via Armavir, Russia	S•W Asia•250 kW
	INDIA ALL INDIA RADIO, Kurseong	DS•20 kW / ENGLISH, ETC•DS•20 kW
	IRAN VO THE ISLAMIC REP, Sirjan	W•W Asia & C Asia•500 kW / Mideast & W Asia•500 kW
	ITALY †RAI INTERNATIONAL, Rome	W•E Europe•100 kW / W•S Europe & N Africa•100 kW
	JAPAN RADIO JAPAN, Via Woofferton, UK	Europe•250/300 kW
	RUSSIA VOICE OF RUSSIA, St Petersburg	W•N Africa•400 kW•ALT. FREQ. TO 7320 kHz
	VOICE OF RUSSIA, Via Vatican State	W•W Africa•250 kW
	SERBIA AND MONTENEGRO †INTL RADIO OF S & M, Via Bosnia	S•Australasia•250 kW / S•Sa•Australasia•250 kW / S•Su-F•Australasia•250 kW
	SLOVAKIA †R SLOVAKIA INTL, Rimavská Sobota	W•E North Am & C America•250 kW / W•C America•250 kW
	UNITED KINGDOM BBC, Via Meyerton, South Africa	E Africa•500 kW / S Africa•250 kW
	USA †ADVENTIST WORLD R, Via Austria	W•W Asia & S Asia•500 kW / S•Europe•300 kW
7230v	CLANDESTINE (ASIA) "VO JAMMU & KASHMIR FREEDOM"	S Asia•ANTI-INDIAN GOVT
7235 (con'd)	CANADA R CANADA INTL, Via Flevo, Holland	S•N Africa & W Africa•500 kW

0 1 2 3 4 5 6 7 8 9 10 11 12 13 14 15 16 17 18 19 20 21 22 23 24

ENGLISH ▬ ARABIC ▨ CHINESE ▫▫▫ FRENCH ▬ GERMAN ▬ RUSSIAN ═ SPANISH ▬ OTHER ▬

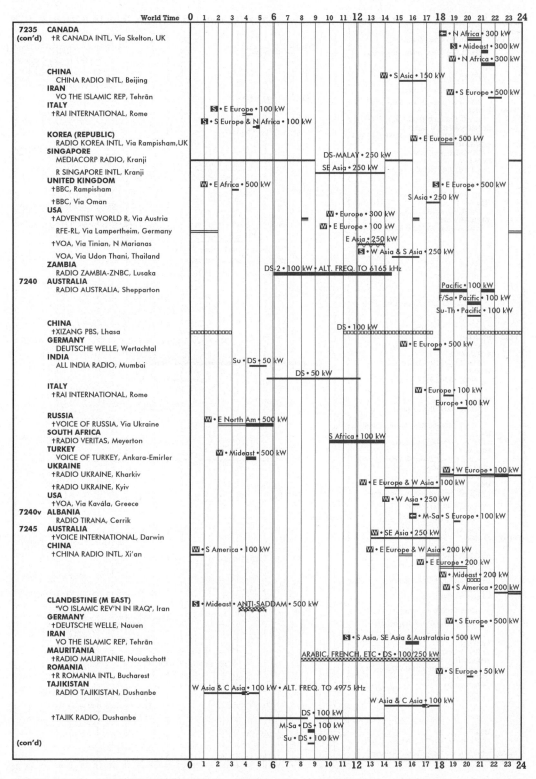

World Time	0 1 2 3 4 5 6 7 8 9 10 11 12 13 14 15 16 17 18 19 20 21 22 23 24

7235 **CANADA**
(con'd)   †R CANADA INTL, Via Skelton, UK — N Africa • 300 kW / Mideast • 300 kW / N Africa • 300 kW

CHINA
   CHINA RADIO INTL, Beijing — W • S Asia • 150 kW
IRAN
   VO THE ISLAMIC REP, Tehrān — W • S Europe • 500 kW
ITALY
   †RAI INTERNATIONAL, Rome — S • E Europe • 100 kW / S • S Europe & N Africa • 100 kW

KOREA (REPUBLIC)
   RADIO KOREA INTL, Via Rampisham, UK — W • E Europe • 500 kW
SINGAPORE
   MEDIACORP RADIO, Kranji — DS-MALAY • 250 kW
   R SINGAPORE INTL, Kranji — SE Asia • 250 kW
UNITED KINGDOM
   †BBC, Rampisham — W • E Africa • 500 kW / S • E Europe • 500 kW
   †BBC, Via Oman — S Asia • 250 kW
USA
   †ADVENTIST WORLD R, Via Austria — W • Europe • 300 kW
   RFE-RL, Via Lampertheim, Germany — W • E Europe • 100 kW
   †VOA, Via Tinian, N Marianas — E Asia • 250 kW
   VOA, Via Udon Thani, Thailand — S • W Asia & S Asia • 250 kW
ZAMBIA
   RADIO ZAMBIA-ZNBC, Lusaka — DS-2 • 100 kW • ALT. FREQ. TO 6165 kHz
7240 **AUSTRALIA**
   RADIO AUSTRALIA, Shepparton — Pacific • 100 kW / F/Sa • Pacific • 100 kW / Su-Th • Pacific • 100 kW

CHINA
   †XIZANG PBS, Lhasa — DS • 100 kW
GERMANY
   DEUTSCHE WELLE, Wertachtal — W • E Europe • 500 kW
INDIA
   ALL INDIA RADIO, Mumbai — Su • DS • 50 kW / DS • 50 kW

ITALY
   †RAI INTERNATIONAL, Rome — W • Europe • 100 kW / Europe • 100 kW
RUSSIA
   †VOICE OF RUSSIA, Via Ukraine — W • E North Am • 500 kW
SOUTH AFRICA
   †RADIO VERITAS, Meyerton — S Africa • 100 kW
TURKEY
   VOICE OF TURKEY, Ankara-Emirler — W • Mideast • 500 kW
UKRAINE
   †RADIO UKRAINE, Kharkiv — W • W Europe • 100 kW
   †RADIO UKRAINE, Kyiv — W • E Europe & W Asia • 100 kW
USA
   †VOA, Via Kavála, Greece — W • W Asia • 250 kW
7240v **ALBANIA**
   RADIO TIRANA, Cerrik — M-Sa • S Europe • 100 kW
7245 **AUSTRALIA**
   †VOICE INTERNATIONAL, Darwin — W • SE Asia • 250 kW
CHINA
   †CHINA RADIO INTL, Xi'an — W • S America • 100 kW / W • E Europe & W Asia • 200 kW / W • E Europe • 200 kW / W • Mideast • 200 kW / W • S America • 200 kW

CLANDESTINE (M EAST)
   "VO ISLAMIC REV'N IN IRAQ", Iran — S • Mideast • ANTI-SADDAM • 500 kW
GERMANY
   †DEUTSCHE WELLE, Nauen — W • S Europe • 500 kW
IRAN
   VO THE ISLAMIC REP, Tehrān — S • S Asia, SE Asia & Australasia • 500 kW
MAURITANIA
   †RADIO MAURITANIE, Nouakchott — ARABIC, FRENCH, ETC • DS • 100/250 kW
ROMANIA
   †R ROMANIA INTL, Bucharest — W • S Europe • 50 kW
TAJIKISTAN
   RADIO TAJIKISTAN, Dushanbe — W Asia & C Asia • 100 kW • ALT. FREQ. TO 4975 kHz / W Asia & C Asia • 100 kW
   †TAJIK RADIO, Dushanbe — DS • 100 kW / M-Sa • DS • 100 kW / Su • DS • 100 kW

(con'd)

0 1 2 3 4 5 6 7 8 9 10 11 12 13 14 15 16 17 18 19 20 21 22 23 24

SEASONAL ⑤ OR Ⓦ   1-HR TIMESHIFT MIDYEAR ⇦ OR ⇨   JAMMING / OR ∧   EARLIEST HEARD ◁   LATEST HEARD ▷   NEW FOR 2004 †

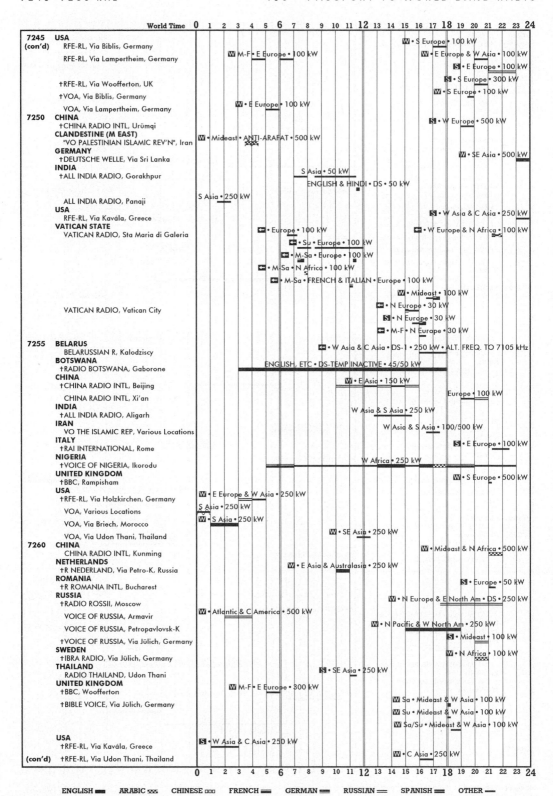

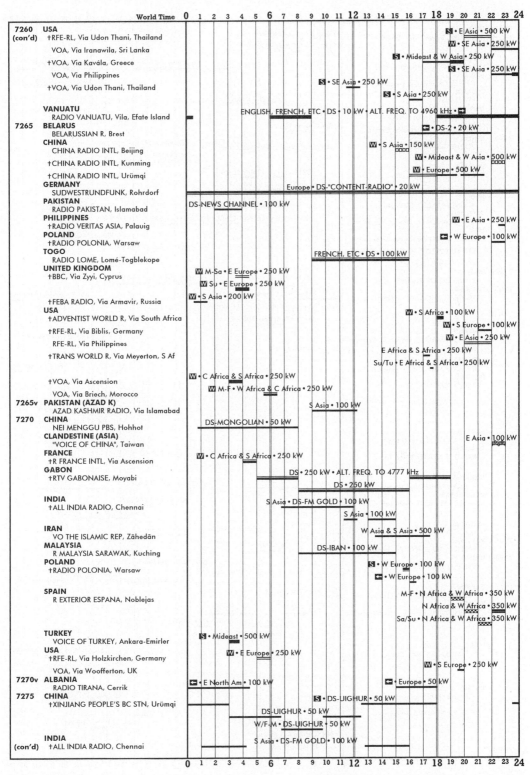

7260	USA		
(con'd)	†RFE-RL, Via Udon Thani, Thailand		S • E Asia • 500 kW
	VOA, Via Iranawila, Sri Lanka		W • SE Asia • 250 kW
	†VOA, Via Kavála, Greece		S • Mideast & W Asia • 250 kW
	VOA, Via Philippines		S • SE Asia • 250 kW
	†VOA, Via Udon Thani, Thailand	S • SE Asia • 250 kW	
			S • S Asia • 250 kW
	VANUATU		
	RADIO VANUATU, Vila, Efate Island	ENGLISH, FRENCH, ETC • DS • 10 kW • ALT. FREQ. TO 4960 kHz •	
7265	BELARUS		
	BELARUSSIAN R, Brest		• DS-2 • 20 kW
	CHINA		
	CHINA RADIO INTL, Beijing	W • S Asia • 150 kW	
	†CHINA RADIO INTL, Kunming		W • Mideast & W Asia • 500 kW
	†CHINA RADIO INTL, Urümqi		W • Europe • 500 kW
	GERMANY		
	SUDWESTRUNDFUNK, Rohrdorf	Europe • DS-"CONTENT-RADIO" • 20 kW	
	PAKISTAN		
	RADIO PAKISTAN, Islamabad	DS-NEWS CHANNEL • 100 kW	
	PHILIPPINES		
	†RADIO VERITAS ASIA, Palauig		W • E Asia • 250 kW
	POLAND		
	†RADIO POLONIA, Warsaw		• W Europe • 100 kW
	TOGO		
	RADIO LOME, Lomé-Togblekope	FRENCH, ETC • DS • 100 kW	
	UNITED KINGDOM		
	†BBC, Via Zyyi, Cyprus	W M-Sa • E Europe • 250 kW	
		W Su • E Europe • 250 kW	
	†FEBA RADIO, Via Armavir, Russia	W • S Asia • 200 kW	
	USA		
	†ADVENTIST WORLD R, Via South Africa		W • S Africa • 100 kW
	†RFE-RL, Via Biblis, Germany		W • S Europe • 100 kW
	RFE-RL, Via Philippines		W • E Asia • 250 kW
	†TRANS WORLD R, Via Meyerton, S Af	E Africa & S Africa • 250 kW	
		Su/Tu • E Africa & S Africa • 250 kW	
	†VOA, Via Ascension	W • C Africa & S Africa • 250 kW	
	VOA, Via Briech, Morocco	W M-F • W Africa & C Africa • 250 kW	
7265v	PAKISTAN (AZAD K)		
	AZAD KASHMIR RADIO, Via Islamabad	S Asia • 100 kW	
7270	CHINA		
	NEI MENGGU PBS, Hohhot	DS-MONGOLIAN • 50 kW	
	CLANDESTINE (ASIA)		
	"VOICE OF CHINA", Taiwan		E Asia • 100 kW
	FRANCE		
	†R FRANCE INTL, Via Ascension	W • C Africa & S Africa • 250 kW	
	GABON		
	†RTV GABONAISE, Moyabi	DS • 250 kW • ALT. FREQ. TO 4777 kHz	
		DS • 250 kW	
	INDIA		
	†ALL INDIA RADIO, Chennai	S Asia • DS-FM GOLD • 100 kW	
		S Asia • 100 kW	
	IRAN		
	VO THE ISLAMIC REP, Zāhedān	W Asia & S Asia • 500 kW	
	MALAYSIA		
	R MALAYSIA SARAWAK, Kuching	DS-IBAN • 100 kW	
	POLAND		
	†RADIO POLONIA, Warsaw	S • W Europe • 100 kW	
		• W Europe • 100 kW	
	SPAIN		
	R EXTERIOR ESPANA, Noblejas		M-F • N Africa & W Africa • 350 kW
			N Africa & W Africa • 350 kW
			Sa/Su • N Africa & W Africa • 350 kW
	TURKEY		
	VOICE OF TURKEY, Ankara-Emirler	S • Mideast • 500 kW	
	USA		
	†RFE-RL, Via Holzkirchen, Germany	W • E Europe • 250 kW	
	VOA, Via Woofferton, UK		W • S Europe • 250 kW
7270v	ALBANIA		
	RADIO TIRANA, Cerrik	• E North Am • 100 kW	• Europe • 50 kW
7275	CHINA		
	†XINJIANG PEOPLE'S BC STN, Urümqi	S • DS-UIGHUR • 50 kW	
		DS-UIGHUR • 50 kW	
		W/F-M • DS-UIGHUR • 50 kW	
	INDIA		
(con'd)	†ALL INDIA RADIO, Chennai	S Asia • DS-FM GOLD • 100 kW	

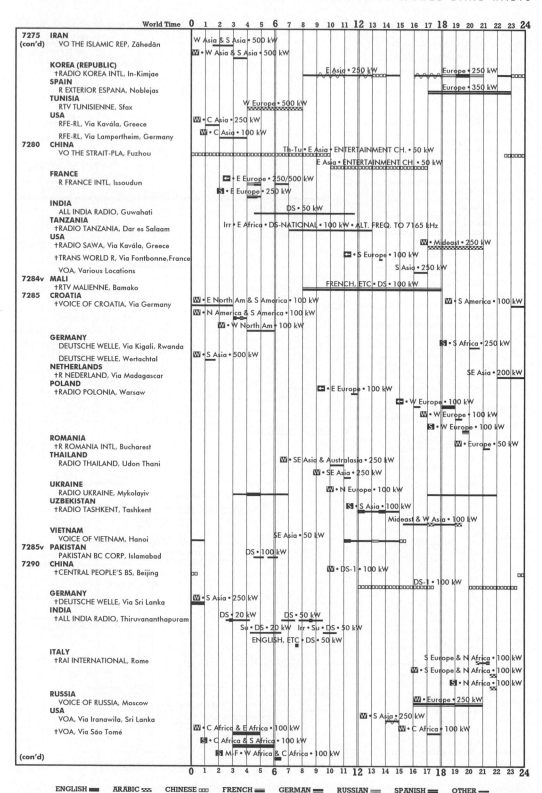

		World Time	0 1 2 3 4 5 6 7 8 9 10 11 12 13 14 15 16 17 18 19 20 21 22 23 24

7275 **IRAN**
(con'd) VO THE ISLAMIC REP, Zāhedān — W Asia & S Asia • 500 kW / Ⓦ • W Asia & S Asia • 500 kW

KOREA (REPUBLIC)
†RADIO KOREA INTL, In-Kimjae — E Asia • 250 kW / Europe • 250 kW

SPAIN
R EXTERIOR ESPANA, Noblejas — Europe • 350 kW

TUNISIA
RTV TUNISIENNE, Sfax — W Europe • 500 kW

USA
RFE-RL, Via Kavála, Greece — Ⓦ • C Asia • 250 kW
RFE-RL, Via Lampertheim, Germany — Ⓦ • C Asia • 100 kW

7280 **CHINA**
VO THE STRAIT-PLA, Fuzhou — Th-Tu • E Asia • ENTERTAINMENT CH. • 50 kW / E Asia • ENTERTAINMENT CH • 50 kW

FRANCE
R FRANCE INTL, Issoudun — ▣ • E Europe • 250/500 kW / Ⓢ • E Europe • 250 kW

INDIA
ALL INDIA RADIO, Guwahati — DS • 50 kW

TANZANIA
†RADIO TANZANIA, Dar es Salaam — Irr • E Africa • DS-NATIONAL • 100 kW • ALT. FREQ. TO 7165 kHz

USA
†RADIO SAWA, Via Kavála, Greece — Ⓦ • Mideast • 250 kW
†TRANS WORLD R, Via Fontbonne, France — ▣ • S Europe • 100 kW
VOA, Various Locations — S Asia • 250 kW

7284v **MALI**
†RTV MALIENNE, Bamako — FRENCH, ETC • DS • 100 kW

7285 **CROATIA**
†VOICE OF CROATIA, Via Germany — Ⓦ • E North Am & S America • 100 kW / Ⓦ • S America • 100 kW
Ⓦ • N America & S America • 100 kW
Ⓦ • W North Am • 100 kW

GERMANY
DEUTSCHE WELLE, Via Kigali, Rwanda — Ⓢ • S Africa • 250 kW
DEUTSCHE WELLE, Wertachtal — Ⓦ • S Asia • 500 kW

NETHERLANDS
†R NEDERLAND, Via Madagascar — SE Asia • 200 kW

POLAND
†RADIO POLONIA, Warsaw — ▣ • E Europe • 100 kW / ▣ • W Europe • 100 kW / Ⓦ • W Europe • 100 kW / Ⓢ • W Europe • 100 kW

ROMANIA
†R ROMANIA INTL, Bucharest — Ⓦ • Europe • 50 kW

THAILAND
RADIO THAILAND, Udon Thani — Ⓦ • SE Asia & Australasia • 250 kW / Ⓦ • SE Asia • 250 kW

UKRAINE
RADIO UKRAINE, Mykolayiv — Ⓦ • N Europe • 100 kW

UZBEKISTAN
†RADIO TASHKENT, Tashkent — Ⓢ • S Asia • 100 kW / Mideast & W Asia • 100 kW

VIETNAM
VOICE OF VIETNAM, Hanoi — SE Asia • 50 kW

7285v **PAKISTAN**
PAKISTAN BC CORP, Islamabad — DS • 100 kW

7290 **CHINA**
†CENTRAL PEOPLE'S BS, Beijing — Ⓦ • DS-1 • 100 kW / DS-1 • 100 kW

GERMANY
†DEUTSCHE WELLE, Via Sri Lanka — Ⓦ • S Asia • 250 kW

INDIA
†ALL INDIA RADIO, Thiruvananthapuram — DS • 20 kW / DS • 50 kW / Su • DS • 20 kW / Irr • Su • DS • 50 kW / ENGLISH, ETC • DS • 50 kW

ITALY
†RAI INTERNATIONAL, Rome — S Europe & N Africa • 100 kW / Ⓦ • S Europe & N Africa • 100 kW / Ⓢ • N Africa • 100 kW

RUSSIA
VOICE OF RUSSIA, Moscow — Ⓦ • Europe • 250 kW

USA
VOA, Via Iranawila, Sri Lanka — Ⓦ • S Asia • 250 kW
†VOA, Via São Tomé — Ⓦ • C Africa & E Africa • 100 kW / Ⓦ • C Africa • 100 kW / Ⓢ • C Africa & S Africa • 100 kW / Ⓢ • M-F • W Africa & C Africa • 100 kW

(con'd)

World Time	0 1 2 3 4 5 6 7 8 9 10 11 12 13 14 15 16 17 18 19 20 21 22 23 24

ENGLISH ▬   ARABIC ⨯⨯⨯   CHINESE □□□   FRENCH ▬▬   GERMAN ▬▬   RUSSIAN ═══   SPANISH ▬▬   OTHER ▬

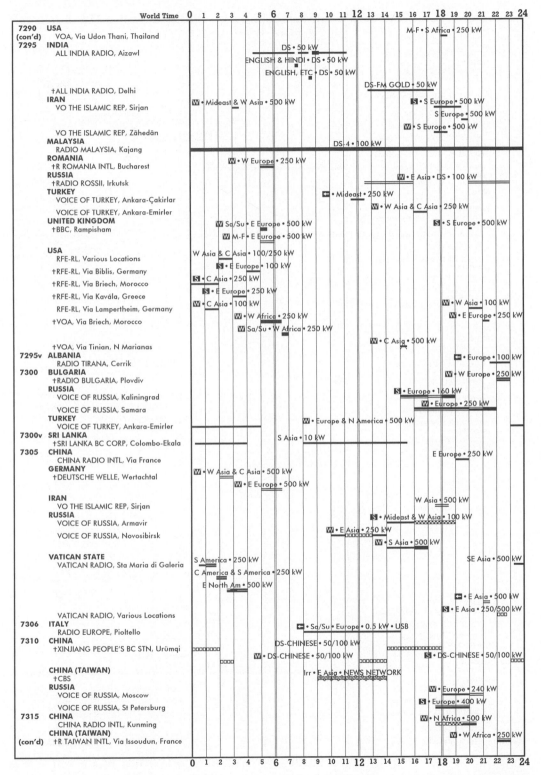

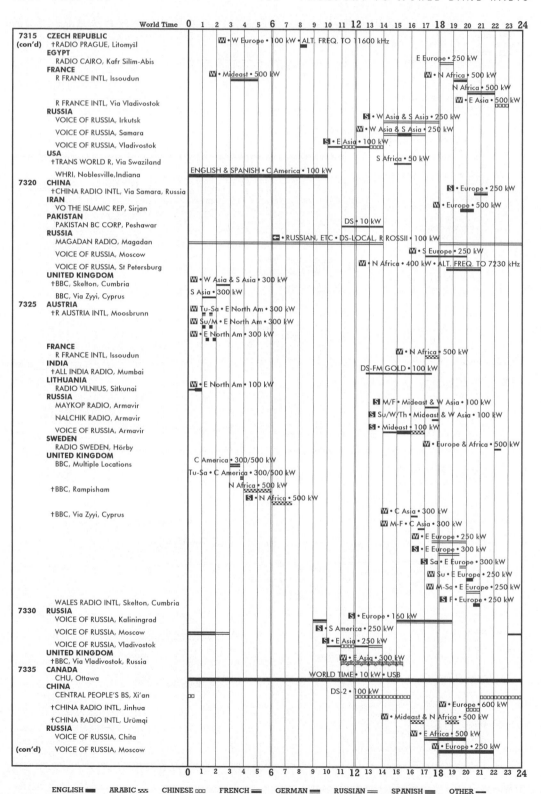

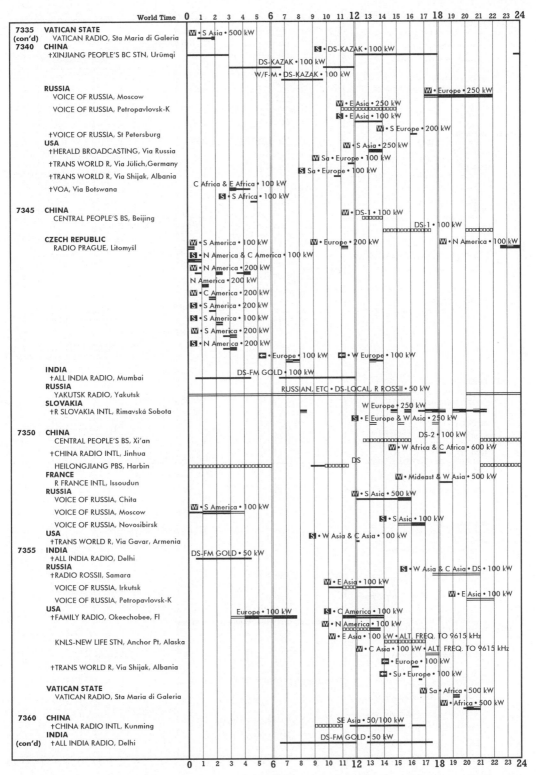

| World Time | 0 | 1 | 2 | 3 | 4 | 5 | 6 | 7 | 8 | 9 | 10 | 11 | 12 | 13 | 14 | 15 | 16 | 17 | 18 | 19 | 20 | 21 | 22 | 23 | 24 |

7335 VATICAN STATE
(con'd) VATICAN RADIO, Sta Maria di Galeria — W • S Asia • 500 kW

7340 CHINA
†XINJIANG PEOPLE'S BC STN, Urümqi — S • DS-KAZAK • 100 kW / DS-KAZAK • 100 kW / W/F-M • DS-KAZAK • 100 kW

RUSSIA
VOICE OF RUSSIA, Moscow — W • Europe • 250 kW
VOICE OF RUSSIA, Petropavlovsk-K — W • E Asia • 250 kW / S • E Asia • 100 kW / W • S Europe • 200 kW

†VOICE OF RUSSIA, St Petersburg
USA
†HERALD BROADCASTING, Via Russia — W • S Asia • 250 kW
†TRANS WORLD R, Via Jülich, Germany — W Sa • Europe • 100 kW / S Sa • Europe • 100 kW
†TRANS WORLD R, Via Shijak, Albania
†VOA, Via Botswana — C Africa & E Africa • 100 kW / S • S Africa • 100 kW

7345 CHINA
CENTRAL PEOPLE'S BS, Beijing — W • DS-1 • 100 kW / DS-1 • 100 kW

CZECH REPUBLIC
RADIO PRAGUE, Litomyšl — W • S America • 100 kW / W • Europe • 200 kW / W • N America • 100 kW
S • N America & C America • 100 kW
W • N America • 200 kW
N America • 200 kW
W • C America • 200 kW
S • S America • 200 kW
S • S America • 100 kW
W • S America • 200 kW
S • N America • 200 kW
⇆ • Europe • 100 kW   ⇆ • W Europe • 100 kW

INDIA
†ALL INDIA RADIO, Mumbai — DS-FM GOLD • 100 kW
RUSSIA
YAKUTSK RADIO, Yakutsk — RUSSIAN, ETC • DS-LOCAL, R ROSSII • 50 kW
SLOVAKIA
†R SLOVAKIA INTL, Rimavská Sobota — W Europe • 250 kW / S • E Europe & W Asia • 250 kW

7350 CHINA
CENTRAL PEOPLE'S BS, Xi'an — DS-2 • 100 kW
†CHINA RADIO INTL, Jinhua — W • W Africa & C Africa • 600 kW
HEILONGJIANG PBS, Harbin — DS
FRANCE
R FRANCE INTL, Issoudun — W • Mideast & W Asia • 500 kW
RUSSIA
VOICE OF RUSSIA, Chita — W • S Asia • 500 kW
VOICE OF RUSSIA, Moscow — W • S America • 100 kW
VOICE OF RUSSIA, Novosibirsk — S • S Asia • 100 kW
USA
†TRANS WORLD R, Via Gavar, Armenia — S • W Asia & C Asia • 100 kW

7355 INDIA
†ALL INDIA RADIO, Delhi — DS-FM GOLD • 50 kW
RUSSIA
†RADIO ROSSII, Samara — S • W Asia & C Asia • DS • 100 kW
VOICE OF RUSSIA, Irkutsk — W • E Asia • 100 kW
VOICE OF RUSSIA, Petropavlovsk-K — W • E Asia • 100 kW
USA
†FAMILY RADIO, Okeechobee, Fl — Europe • 100 kW / S • C America • 100 kW / W • N America • 100 kW / W • E Asia • 100 kW • ALT. FREQ. TO 9615 kHz
KNLS-NEW LIFE STN, Anchor Pt, Alaska — W • C Asia • 100 kW • ALT. FREQ. TO 9615 kHz
†TRANS WORLD R, Via Shijak, Albania — ⇆ • Europe • 100 kW / ⇆ • Su • Europe • 100 kW

VATICAN STATE
VATICAN RADIO, Sta Maria di Galeria — W Sa • Africa • 500 kW / W • Africa • 500 kW

7360 CHINA
†CHINA RADIO INTL, Kunming — SE Asia • 50/100 kW
INDIA
(con'd) †ALL INDIA RADIO, Delhi — DS-FM GOLD • 50 kW

| | 0 | 1 | 2 | 3 | 4 | 5 | 6 | 7 | 8 | 9 | 10 | 11 | 12 | 13 | 14 | 15 | 16 | 17 | 18 | 19 | 20 | 21 | 22 | 23 | 24 |

SEASONAL S OR W   1-HR TIMESHIFT MIDYEAR ⇆ OR ⇥   JAMMING / OR ∧   EARLIEST HEARD ◁   LATEST HEARD ▷   NEW FOR 2004 †

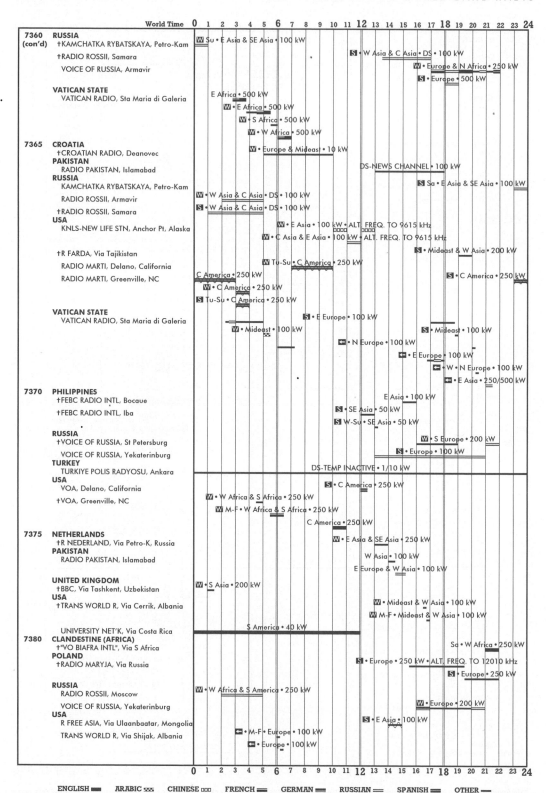

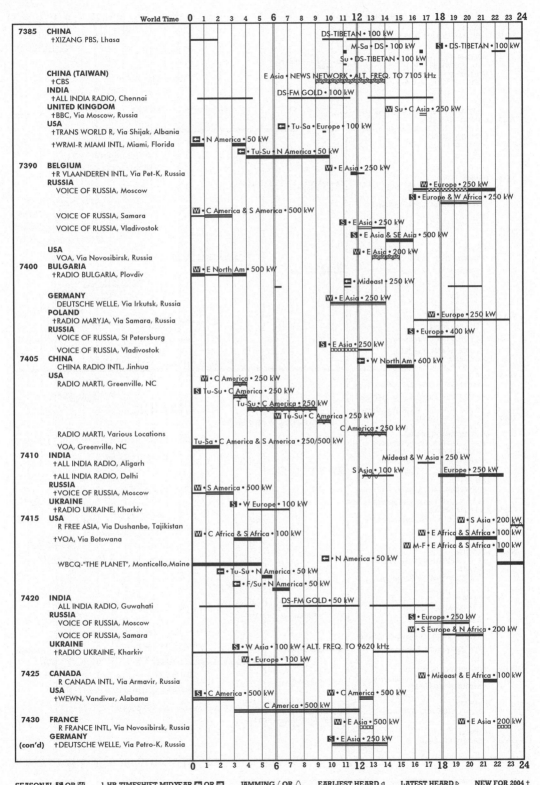

World Time 0 1 2 3 4 5 6 7 8 9 10 11 12 13 14 15 16 17 18 19 20 21 22 23 24

7385 CHINA
†XIZANG PBS, Lhasa
  DS-TIBETAN • 100 kW
  M-Sa • DS • 100 kW
  S • DS-TIBETAN • 100 kW
  Su • DS-TIBETAN • 100 kW

CHINA (TAIWAN)
†CBS
  E Asia • NEWS NETWORK • ALT. FREQ. TO 7105 kHz
INDIA
†ALL INDIA RADIO, Chennai
  DS-FM GOLD • 100 kW
UNITED KINGDOM
†BBC, Via Moscow, Russia
  W Su • C Asia • 250 kW
USA
†TRANS WORLD R, Via Shijak, Albania
  ⟷ • Tu-Sa • Europe • 100 kW
†WRMI-R MIAMI INTL, Miami, Florida
  ⟷ • N America • 50 kW
  ⟷ • Tu-Su • N America • 50 kW

7390 BELGIUM
†R VLAANDEREN INTL, Via Pet-K, Russia
  W • E Asia • 250 kW
RUSSIA
VOICE OF RUSSIA, Moscow
  W • Europe • 250 kW
  S • Europe & W Africa • 250 kW
VOICE OF RUSSIA, Samara
  W • C America & S America • 500 kW
VOICE OF RUSSIA, Vladivostok
  S • E Asia • 250 kW
  S • E Asia & SE Asia • 500 kW
USA
VOA, Via Novosibirsk, Russia
  W • E Asia • 200 kW
7400 BULGARIA
†RADIO BULGARIA, Plovdiv
  W • E North Am • 500 kW
  ⟷ • Mideast • 250 kW
GERMANY
DEUTSCHE WELLE, Via Irkutsk, Russia
  W • E Asia • 250 kW
POLAND
†RADIO MARYJA, Via Samara, Russia
  W • Europe • 250 kW
RUSSIA
VOICE OF RUSSIA, St Petersburg
  S • Europe • 400 kW
VOICE OF RUSSIA, Vladivostok
  S • E Asia • 250 kW
7405 CHINA
CHINA RADIO INTL, Jinhua
  ⟷ • W North Am • 600 kW
USA
RADIO MARTI, Greenville, NC
  W • C America • 250 kW
  S Tu-Su • C America • 250 kW
  Tu-Su • C America • 250 kW
  W Tu-Su • C America • 250 kW
  C America • 250 kW
RADIO MARTI, Various Locations
  Tu-Sa • C America & S America • 250/500 kW
VOA, Greenville, NC
7410 INDIA
†ALL INDIA RADIO, Aligarh
  Mideast & W Asia • 250 kW
†ALL INDIA RADIO, Delhi
  S Asia • 100 kW
  Europe • 250 kW
RUSSIA
†VOICE OF RUSSIA, Moscow
  W • S America • 500 kW
UKRAINE
†RADIO UKRAINE, Kharkiv
  S • W Europe • 100 kW
7415 USA
R FREE ASIA, Via Dushanbe, Tajikistan
  W • S Asia • 200 kW
†VOA, Via Botswana
  W • C Africa & S Africa • 100 kW
  W • E Africa & S Africa • 100 kW
  W M-F • E Africa & S Africa • 100 kW
WBCQ-"THE PLANET", Monticello, Maine
  ⟷ • N America • 50 kW
  ⟷ • Tu-Su • N America • 50 kW
  ⟷ • F/Su • N America • 50 kW

7420 INDIA
ALL INDIA RADIO, Guwahati
  DS-FM GOLD • 50 kW
RUSSIA
VOICE OF RUSSIA, Moscow
  S • Europe • 250 kW
VOICE OF RUSSIA, Samara
  W • S Europe & N Africa • 200 kW
UKRAINE
†RADIO UKRAINE, Kharkiv
  S • W Asia • 100 kW • ALT. FREQ. TO 9620 kHz
  W • Europe • 100 kW

7425 CANADA
R CANADA INTL, Via Armavir, Russia
  W • Mideast & E Africa • 100 kW
USA
†WEWN, Vandiver, Alabama
  S • C America • 500 kW
  W • C America • 500 kW
  C America • 500 kW

7430 FRANCE
R FRANCE INTL, Via Novosibirsk, Russia
  W • E Asia • 500 kW
  W • E Asia • 200 kW
GERMANY
(con'd) †DEUTSCHE WELLE, Via Petro-K, Russia
  S • E Asia • 250 kW

0 1 2 3 4 5 6 7 8 9 10 11 12 13 14 15 16 17 18 19 20 21 22 23 24

SEASONAL Ⓢ OR Ⓦ   1-HR TIMESHIFT MIDYEAR ⟷ OR ⟹   JAMMING / OR ∧   EARLIEST HEARD ◁   LATEST HEARD ▷   NEW FOR 2004 †

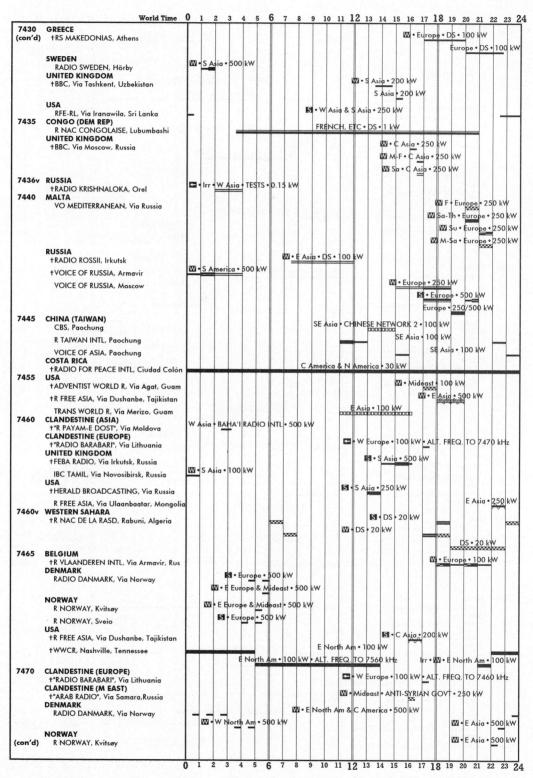

World Time		
7430 **GREECE**		
(con'd) †RS MAKEDONIAS, Athens	W • Europe • DS • 100 kW	
	Europe • DS • 100 kW	
SWEDEN		
RADIO SWEDEN, Hörby	W • S Asia • 500 kW	
UNITED KINGDOM		
†BBC, Via Tashkent, Uzbekistan	W • S Asia • 200 kW	
	S Asia • 200 kW	
USA		
RFE-RL, Via Iranawila, Sri Lanka	S • W Asia & S Asia • 250 kW	
7435 CONGO (DEM REP)		
R NAC CONGOLAISE, Lubumbashi	FRENCH, ETC • DS • 1 kW	
UNITED KINGDOM		
†BBC, Via Moscow, Russia	W • C Asia • 250 kW	
	W • M-F • C Asia • 250 kW	
	W • Sa • C Asia • 250 kW	
7436v RUSSIA		
†RADIO KRISHNALOKA, Orel	Irr • W Asia • TESTS • 0.15 kW	
7440 MALTA		
VO MEDITERRANEAN, Via Russia	W • F • Europe • 250 kW	
	W • Sa-Th • Europe • 250 kW	
	W • Su • Europe • 250 kW	
	W • M-Sa • Europe • 250 kW	
RUSSIA		
†RADIO ROSSII, Irkutsk	W • E Asia • DS • 100 kW	
†VOICE OF RUSSIA, Armavir	W • S America • 500 kW	
VOICE OF RUSSIA, Moscow	W • Europe • 250 kW	
	S • Europe • 500 kW	
	Europe • 250/500 kW	
7445 CHINA (TAIWAN)		
CBS, Paochung	SE Asia • CHINESE NETWORK 2 • 100 kW	
R TAIWAN INTL, Paochung	SE Asia • 100 kW	
VOICE OF ASIA, Paochung	SE Asia • 100 kW	
COSTA RICA		
†RADIO FOR PEACE INTL, Ciudad Colón	C America & N America • 30 kW	
7455 USA		
†ADVENTIST WORLD R, Via Agat, Guam	W • Mideast • 100 kW	
†R FREE ASIA, Via Dushanbe, Tajikistan	W • E Asia • 500 kW	
TRANS WORLD R, Via Merizo, Guam	E Asia • 100 kW	
7460 CLANDESTINE (ASIA)		
†"R PAYAM-E DOST", Via Moldova	W Asia • BAHA'I RADIO INTL • 500 kW	
CLANDESTINE (EUROPE)		
†"RADIO BARABARI", Via Lithuania	W Europe • 100 kW • ALT. FREQ. TO 7470 kHz	
UNITED KINGDOM		
†FEBA RADIO, Via Irkutsk, Russia	S • S Asia • 500 kW	
IBC TAMIL, Via Novosibirsk, Russia	W • S Asia • 100 kW	
USA		
†HERALD BROADCASTING, Via Russia	S • S Asia • 250 kW	
R FREE ASIA, Via Ulaanbaatar, Mongolia	E Asia • 250 kW	
7460v WESTERN SAHARA		
†R NAC DE LA RASD, Rabuni, Algeria	S • DS • 20 kW	
	W • DS • 20 kW	
	DS • 20 kW	
7465 BELGIUM		
†R VLAANDEREN INTL, Via Armavir, Rus	W • Europe • 100 kW	
DENMARK		
RADIO DANMARK, Via Norway	S • Europe • 500 kW	
	W • E Europe & Mideast • 500 kW	
NORWAY		
R NORWAY, Kvitsøy	W • E Europe & Mideast • 500 kW	
R NORWAY, Sveio	S • Europe • 500 kW	
USA		
†R FREE ASIA, Via Dushanbe, Tajikistan	S • C Asia • 200 kW	
†WWCR, Nashville, Tennessee	E North Am • 100 kW	
	E North Am • 100 kW • ALT. FREQ. TO 7560 kHz Irr • W • E North Am • 100 kW	
7470 CLANDESTINE (EUROPE)		
†"RADIO BARABARI", Via Lithuania	W Europe • 100 kW • ALT. FREQ. TO 7460 kHz	
CLANDESTINE (M EAST)		
†"ARAB RADIO", Via Samara, Russia	W • Mideast • ANTI-SYRIAN GOVT • 250 kW	
DENMARK		
RADIO DANMARK, Via Norway	W • E North Am & C America • 500 kW	
	W • W North Am • 500 kW	
	W • E Asia • 500 kW	
NORWAY		
(con'd) R NORWAY, Kvitsøy	W • E Asia • 500 kW	

ENGLISH ▬ ARABIC ⁓ CHINESE ░ FRENCH ═ GERMAN ▬ RUSSIAN ═ SPANISH ▬ OTHER ▬

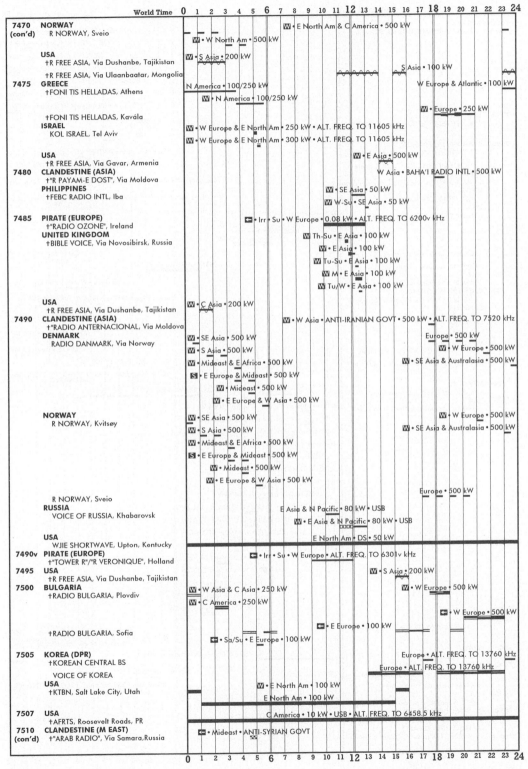

World Time 0 1 2 3 4 5 6 7 8 9 10 11 12 13 14 15 16 17 18 19 20 21 22 23 24

Freq	Station	
7470 (con'd)	**NORWAY** R NORWAY, Sveio	W • E North Am & C America • 500 kW / W • W North Am • 500 kW
	USA †R FREE ASIA, Via Dushanbe, Tajikistan	W • S Asia • 200 kW
	†R FREE ASIA, Via Ulaanbaatar, Mongolia	S Asia • 100 kW
7475	**GREECE** †FONI TIS HELLADAS, Athens	N America • 100/250 kW / W • N America • 100/250 kW / W Europe & Atlantic • 100 kW
	†FONI TIS HELLADAS, Kavála	W • Europe • 250 kW
	ISRAEL KOL ISRAEL, Tel Aviv	W • W Europe & E North Am • 250 kW • ALT. FREQ. TO 11605 kHz / W • W Europe & E North Am • 300 kW • ALT. FREQ. TO 11605 kHz
	USA †R FREE ASIA, Via Gavar, Armenia	W • E Asia • 500 kW
7480	**CLANDESTINE (ASIA)** †"R PAYAM-E DOST", Via Moldova	W Asia • BAHA'I RADIO INTL • 500 kW
	PHILIPPINES †FEBC RADIO INTL, Iba	W • SE Asia • 50 kW / W • W-Su • SE Asia • 50 kW
7485	**PIRATE (EUROPE)** †"RADIO OZONE", Ireland	⇇ • Irr • Su • W Europe • 0.08 kW • ALT. FREQ. TO 6200v kHz
	UNITED KINGDOM †BIBLE VOICE, Via Novosibirsk, Russia	W • Th-Su • E Asia • 100 kW / W • E Asia • 100 kW / W • Tu-Su • E Asia • 100 kW / W • M • E Asia • 100 kW / W • Tu/W • E Asia • 100 kW
	USA †R FREE ASIA, Via Dushanbe, Tajikistan	W • C Asia • 200 kW
7490	**CLANDESTINE (ASIA)** †"RADIO ANTERNACIONAL", Via Moldova	W • W Asia • ANTI-IRANIAN GOVT • 500 kW • ALT. FREQ. TO 7520 kHz
	DENMARK RADIO DANMARK, Via Norway	W • SE Asia • 500 kW / Europe • 500 kW / W • S Asia • 500 kW / W • W Europe • 500 kW / W • Mideast & E Africa • 500 kW / W • SE Asia & Australasia • 500 kW / S • E Europe & Mideast • 500 kW / W • Mideast • 500 kW / W • E Europe & W Asia • 500 kW
	NORWAY R NORWAY, Kvitsøy	W • SE Asia • 500 kW / W • W Europe • 500 kW / W • S Asia • 500 kW / W • SE Asia & Australasia • 500 kW / W • Mideast & E Africa • 500 kW / S • E Europe & Mideast • 500 kW / W • Mideast • 500 kW / W • E Europe & W Asia • 500 kW
	R NORWAY, Sveio	Europe • 500 kW
	RUSSIA VOICE OF RUSSIA, Khabarovsk	E Asia & N Pacific • 80 kW • USB / W • E Asia & N Pacific • 80 kW • USB
	USA WJIE SHORTWAVE, Upton, Kentucky	E North Am • DS • 50 kW
7490v	**PIRATE (EUROPE)** †"TOWER R"/"R VERONIQUE", Holland	⇇ • Irr • Su • W Europe • ALT. FREQ. TO 6301v kHz
7495	**USA** †R FREE ASIA, Via Dushanbe, Tajikistan	W • S Asia • 200 kW
7500	**BULGARIA** †RADIO BULGARIA, Plovdiv	W • W Asia & C Asia • 250 kW / W • W Europe • 500 kW / W • C America • 250 kW / ⇇ • W Europe • 500 kW
	†RADIO BULGARIA, Sofia	⇇ • E Europe • 100 kW / ⇇ • Sa/Su • E Europe • 100 kW
7505	**KOREA (DPR)** †KOREAN CENTRAL BS	Europe • ALT. FREQ. TO 13760 kHz
	VOICE OF KOREA	Europe • ALT. FREQ. TO 13760 kHz
	USA †KTBN, Salt Lake City, Utah	W • E North Am • 100 kW / E North Am • 100 kW
7507	**USA** †AFRTS, Roosevelt Roads, PR	C America • 10 kW • USB • ALT. FREQ. TO 6458.5 kHz
7510 (con'd)	**CLANDESTINE (M EAST)** †"ARAB RADIO", Via Samara, Russia	⇇ • Mideast • ANTI-SYRIAN GOVT

0 1 2 3 4 5 6 7 8 9 10 11 12 13 14 15 16 17 18 19 20 21 22 23 24

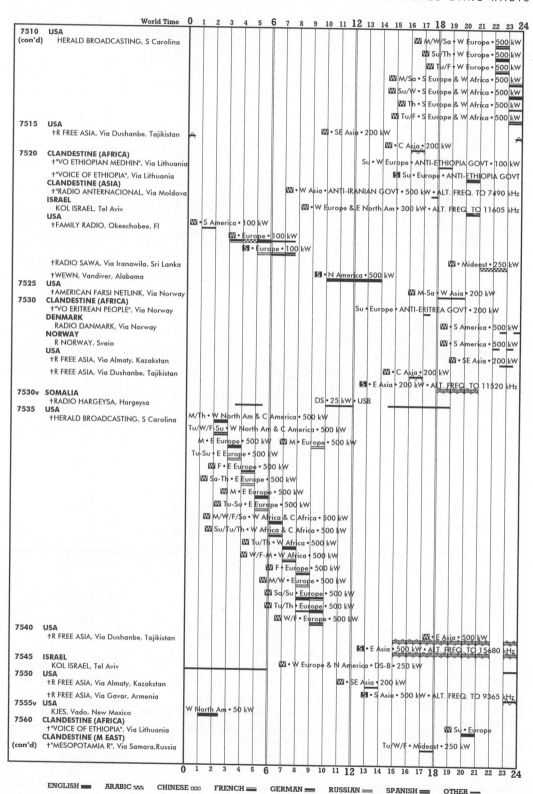

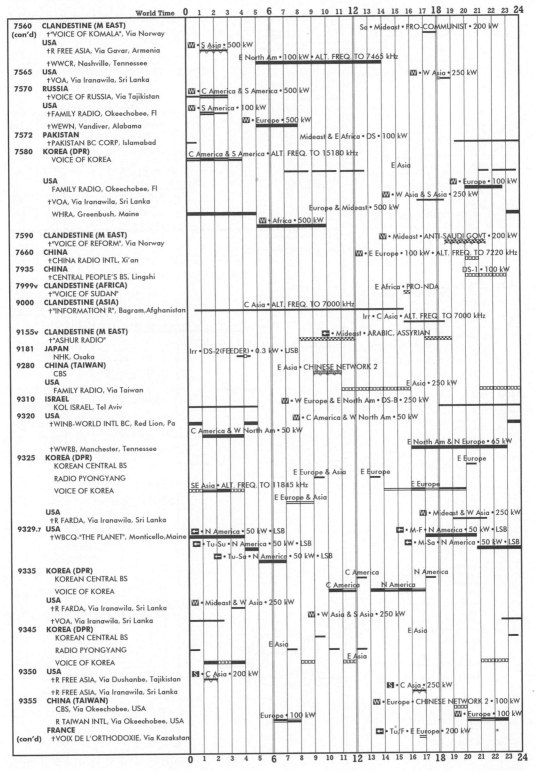

World Time	0 1 2 3 4 5 6 7 8 9 10 11 12 13 14 15 16 17 18 19 20 21 22 23 24

7560 (con'd) CLANDESTINE (M EAST)
†"VOICE OF KOMALA", Via Norway — Sa • Mideast • PRO-COMMUNIST • 200 kW
USA
†R FREE ASIA, Via Gavar, Armenia — W • S Asia • 500 kW
†WWCR, Nashville, Tennessee — E North Am • 100 kW • ALT. FREQ. TO 7465 kHz

7565 USA
†VOA, Via Iranawila, Sri Lanka — W • W Asia • 250 kW

7570 RUSSIA
†VOICE OF RUSSIA, Via Tajikistan — W • C America & S America • 500 kW
USA
†FAMILY RADIO, Okeechobee, Fl — W • S America • 100 kW
†WEWN, Vandiver, Alabama — W • Europe • 500 kW

7572 PAKISTAN
†PAKISTAN BC CORP, Islamabad — Mideast & E Africa • DS • 100 kW

7580 KOREA (DPR)
VOICE OF KOREA — C America & S America • ALT. FREQ. TO 15180 kHz — E Asia
USA
FAMILY RADIO, Okeechobee, Fl — W • Europe • 100 kW
†VOA, Via Iranawila, Sri Lanka — W • W Asia & S Asia • 250 kW
WHRA, Greenbush, Maine — Europe & Mideast • 500 kW — W • Africa • 500 kW

7590 CLANDESTINE (M EAST)
†"VOICE OF REFORM", Via Norway — W • Mideast • ANTI-SAUDI GOVT • 200 kW

7660 CHINA
†CHINA RADIO INTL, Xi'an — W • E Europe • 100 kW • ALT. FREQ. TO 7220 kHz

7935 CHINA
†CENTRAL PEOPLE'S BS, Lingshi — DS-1 • 100 kW

7999v CLANDESTINE (AFRICA)
†"VOICE OF SUDAN" — E Africa • PRO-NDA

9000 CLANDESTINE (ASIA)
†"INFORMATION R", Bagram, Afghanistan — C Asia • ALT. FREQ. TO 7000 kHz — Irr • C Asia • ALT. FREQ. TO 7000 kHz

9155v CLANDESTINE (M EAST)
†"ASHUR RADIO" — • Mideast • ARABIC, ASSYRIAN

9181 JAPAN
NHK, Osaka — Irr • DS-2 (FEEDER) • 0.3 kW • USB

9280 CHINA (TAIWAN)
CBS — E Asia • CHINESE NETWORK 2
USA
FAMILY RADIO, Via Taiwan — E Asia • 250 kW

9310 ISRAEL
KOL ISRAEL, Tel Aviv — W • W Europe & E North Am • DS-B • 250 kW

9320 USA
†WINB-WORLD INTL BC, Red Lion, Pa — W • C America & W North Am • 50 kW — C America & W North Am • 50 kW
†WWRB, Manchester, Tennessee — E North Am & N Europe • 65 kW

9325 KOREA (DPR)
KOREAN CENTRAL BS — E Europe
RADIO PYONGYANG — E Europe & Asia — E Europe — E Europe
VOICE OF KOREA — SE Asia • ALT. FREQ. TO 11845 kHz — E Europe & Asia
USA
†R FARDA, Via Iranawila, Sri Lanka — W • Mideast & W Asia • 250 kW

9329.7 USA
†WBCQ-"THE PLANET", Monticello, Maine — • N America • 50 kW • LSB — M-F • N America • 50 kW • LSB
— • Tu-Su • N America • 50 kW • LSB — M-Sa • N America • 50 kW • LSB
— • Tu-Sa • N America • 50 kW • LSB

9335 KOREA (DPR)
KOREAN CENTRAL BS — C America — N America
VOICE OF KOREA — C America — N America
USA
†R FARDA, Via Iranawila, Sri Lanka — W • Mideast & W Asia • 250 kW
†VOA, Via Iranawila, Sri Lanka — W • W Asia & S Asia • 250 kW

9345 KOREA (DPR)
KOREAN CENTRAL BS — E Asia
RADIO PYONGYANG — E Asia
VOICE OF KOREA — E Asia

9350 USA
†R FREE ASIA, Via Dushanbe, Tajikistan — S • C Asia • 200 kW
†R FREE ASIA, Via Iranawila, Sri Lanka — S • C Asia • 250 kW

9355 CHINA (TAIWAN)
CBS, Via Okeechobee, USA — W • Europe • CHINESE NETWORK 2 • 100 kW
R TAIWAN INTL, Via Okeechobee, USA — Europe • 100 kW — W • Europe • 100 kW
FRANCE
(con'd) †VOIX DE L'ORTHODOXIE, Via Kazakstan — • Tu/F • E Europe • 200 kW

	0 1 2 3 4 5 6 7 8 9 10 11 12 13 14 15 16 17 18 19 20 21 22 23 24

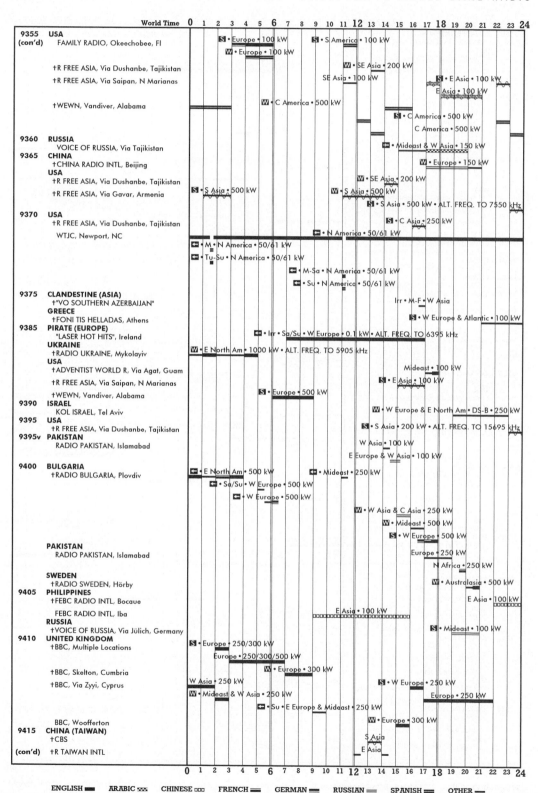

World Time 0 1 2 3 4 5 6 7 8 9 10 11 12 13 14 15 16 17 18 19 20 21 22 23 24

Freq	Station	
9355 (con'd)	**USA** FAMILY RADIO, Okeechobee, Fl	S • Europe • 100 kW / S • S America • 100 kW / W • Europe • 100 kW
	†R FREE ASIA, Via Dushanbe, Tajikistan	W • SE Asia • 200 kW
	†R FREE ASIA, Via Saipan, N Marianas	SE Asia • 100 kW / S • E Asia • 100 kW / E Asia • 100 kW
	†WEWN, Vandiver, Alabama	W • C America • 500 kW / S • C America • 500 kW / C America • 500 kW
9360	**RUSSIA** VOICE OF RUSSIA, Via Tajikistan	• Mideast & W Asia • 150 kW
9365	**CHINA** †CHINA RADIO INTL, Beijing	W • Europe • 150 kW
	USA †R FREE ASIA, Via Dushanbe, Tajikistan	W • SE Asia • 200 kW
	†R FREE ASIA, Via Gavar, Armenia	S • S Asia • 500 kW / W • S Asia • 500 kW / S • S Asia • 500 kW • ALT. FREQ. TO 7550 kHz
9370	**USA** †R FREE ASIA, Via Dushanbe, Tajikistan	S • C Asia • 250 kW
	WTJC, Newport, NC	• N America • 50/61 kW / • M • N America • 50/61 kW / • Tu-Su • N America • 50/61 kW / • M-Sa • N America • 50/61 kW / • Su • N America • 50/61 kW
9375	**CLANDESTINE (ASIA)** †"VO SOUTHERN AZERBAIJAN"	Irr • M-F • W Asia
	GREECE †FONI TIS HELLADAS, Athens	S • W Europe & Atlantic • 100 kW
9385	**PIRATE (EUROPE)** "LASER HOT HITS", Ireland	• Irr • Sa/Su • W Europe • 0.1 kW • ALT. FREQ. TO 6395 kHz
	UKRAINE †RADIO UKRAINE, Mykolayiv	W • E North Am • 1000 kW • ALT. FREQ. TO 5905 kHz
	USA †ADVENTIST WORLD R, Via Agat, Guam	Mideast • 100 kW
	†R FREE ASIA, Via Saipan, N Marianas	S • E Asia • 100 kW
	†WEWN, Vandiver, Alabama	S • Europe • 500 kW
9390	**ISRAEL** KOL ISRAEL, Tel Aviv	W • W Europe & E North Am • DS-B • 250 kW
9395	**USA** †R FREE ASIA, Via Dushanbe, Tajikistan	S • S Asia • 200 kW • ALT. FREQ. TO 15695 kHz
9395v	**PAKISTAN** RADIO PAKISTAN, Islamabad	W Asia • 100 kW / E Europe & W Asia • 100 kW
9400	**BULGARIA** †RADIO BULGARIA, Plovdiv	• E North Am • 500 kW / • Mideast • 250 kW / • Sa/Su • W Europe • 500 kW / • W Europe • 500 kW
	PAKISTAN RADIO PAKISTAN, Islamabad	W • W Asia & C Asia • 250 kW / W • Mideast • 500 kW / S • W Europe • 500 kW / Europe • 250 kW / N Africa • 250 kW
	SWEDEN †RADIO SWEDEN, Hörby	W • Australasia • 500 kW
9405	**PHILIPPINES** †FEBC RADIO INTL, Bocaue	E Asia • 100 kW
	FEBC RADIO INTL, Iba	E Asia • 100 kW
	RUSSIA †VOICE OF RUSSIA, Via Jülich, Germany	S • Mideast • 100 kW
9410	**UNITED KINGDOM** †BBC, Multiple Locations	S • Europe • 250/300 kW / Europe • 250/300/500 kW
	†BBC, Skelton, Cumbria	W • Europe • 300 kW
	†BBC, Via Zyyi, Cyprus	W Asia • 250 kW / S • W Europe • 250 kW / W • Mideast & W Asia • 250 kW / Europe • 250 kW / • Su • E Europe & Mideast • 250 kW
	BBC, Woofferton	W • Europe • 300 kW
9415	**CHINA (TAIWAN)** †CBS	S Asia
(con'd)	†R TAIWAN INTL	E Asia

0 1 2 3 4 5 6 7 8 9 10 11 12 13 14 15 16 17 18 19 20 21 22 23 24

ENGLISH ▬ ARABIC ⌇⌇⌇ CHINESE □□□ FRENCH ══ GERMAN ▬▬ RUSSIAN ══ SPANISH ══ OTHER ▬

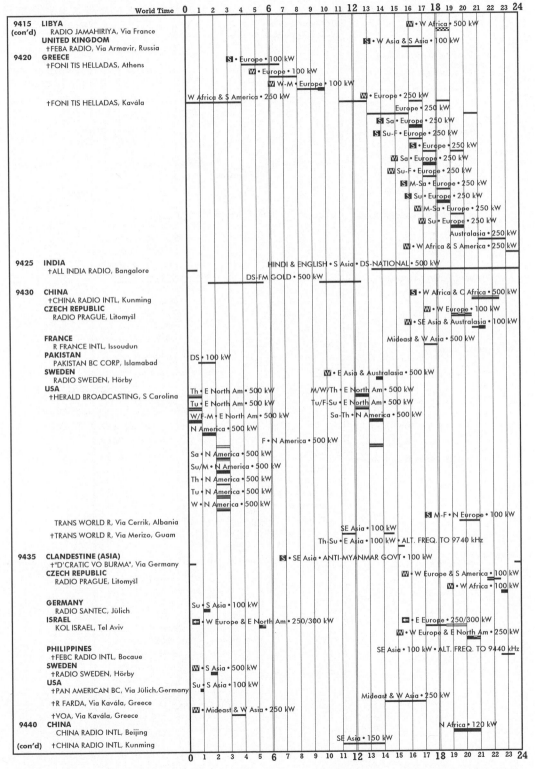

World Time

9415 (con'd)	**LIBYA**
	RADIO JAMAHIRIYA, Via France
	UNITED KINGDOM
	†FEBA RADIO, Via Armavir, Russia
9420	**GREECE**
	†FONI TIS HELLADAS, Athens
	†FONI TIS HELLADAS, Kavála
9425	**INDIA**
	†ALL INDIA RADIO, Bangalore
9430	**CHINA**
	†CHINA RADIO INTL, Kunming
	CZECH REPUBLIC
	RADIO PRAGUE, Litomyšl
	FRANCE
	R FRANCE INTL, Issoudun
	PAKISTAN
	PAKISTAN BC CORP, Islamabad
	SWEDEN
	RADIO SWEDEN, Hörby
	USA
	†HERALD BROADCASTING, S Carolina
	TRANS WORLD R, Via Cerrik, Albania
	†TRANS WORLD R, Via Merizo, Guam
9435	**CLANDESTINE (ASIA)**
	†"D'CRATIC VO BURMA", Via Germany
	CZECH REPUBLIC
	RADIO PRAGUE, Litomyšl
	GERMANY
	RADIO SANTEC, Jülich
	ISRAEL
	KOL ISRAEL, Tel Aviv
	PHILIPPINES
	†FEBC RADIO INTL, Bocaue
	SWEDEN
	†RADIO SWEDEN, Hörby
	USA
	†PAN AMERICAN BC, Via Jülich, Germany
	†R FARDA, Via Kavála, Greece
	†VOA, Via Kavála, Greece
9440	**CHINA**
	CHINA RADIO INTL, Beijing
(con'd)	†CHINA RADIO INTL, Kunming

Chart entries:

9415 LIBYA — RADIO JAMAHIRIYA, Via France: W • W Africa • 500 kW

UNITED KINGDOM — †FEBA RADIO, Via Armavir, Russia: S • W Asia & S Asia • 100 kW

9420 GREECE — †FONI TIS HELLADAS, Athens:
S • Europe • 100 kW
W • Europe • 100 kW
W-M • Europe • 100 kW

†FONI TIS HELLADAS, Kavála:
W Africa & S America • 250 kW
W • Europe • 250 kW
Europe • 250 kW
S Sa • Europe • 250 kW
S Su-F • Europe • 250 kW
S • Europe • 250 kW
W Sa • Europe • 250 kW
W Su-F • Europe • 250 kW
S M-Sa • Europe • 250 kW
S Su • Europe • 250 kW
W M-Sa • Europe • 250 kW
W Su • Europe • 250 kW
Australasia • 250 kW
W • W Africa & S America • 250 kW

9425 INDIA — †ALL INDIA RADIO, Bangalore:
HINDI & ENGLISH • S Asia • DS-NATIONAL • 500 kW
DS-FM GOLD • 500 kW

9430 CHINA — †CHINA RADIO INTL, Kunming: S • W Africa & C Africa • 500 kW

CZECH REPUBLIC — RADIO PRAGUE, Litomyšl:
W • W Europe • 100 kW
W • SE Asia & Australasia • 100 kW

FRANCE — R FRANCE INTL, Issoudun: Mideast & W Asia • 500 kW

PAKISTAN — PAKISTAN BC CORP, Islamabad: DS • 100 kW

SWEDEN — RADIO SWEDEN, Hörby: W • E Asia & Australasia • 500 kW

USA — †HERALD BROADCASTING, S Carolina:
Th • E North Am • 500 kW   M/W/Th • E North Am • 500 kW
Tu • E North Am • 500 kW   Tu/F-Su • E North Am • 500 kW
W/F-M • E North Am • 500 kW   Sa-Th • N America • 500 kW
N America • 500 kW
F • N America • 500 kW
Sa • N America • 500 kW
Su/M • N America • 500 kW
Th • N America • 500 kW
Tu • N America • 500 kW
W • N America • 500 kW
S M-F • N Europe • 100 kW

TRANS WORLD R, Via Cerrik, Albania: SE Asia • 100 kW

†TRANS WORLD R, Via Merizo, Guam: Th-Su • E Asia • 100 kW • ALT. FREQ. TO 9740 kHz

9435 CLANDESTINE (ASIA) — †"D'CRATIC VO BURMA", Via Germany: S • SE Asia • ANTI-MYANMAR GOVT • 100 kW

CZECH REPUBLIC — RADIO PRAGUE, Litomyšl:
W • W Europe & S America • 100 kW
W • W Africa • 100 kW

GERMANY — RADIO SANTEC, Jülich: Su • S Asia • 100 kW

ISRAEL — KOL ISRAEL, Tel Aviv:
⇦ • W Europe & E North Am • 250/300 kW
⇦ • E Europe • 250/300 kW
W • W Europe & E North Am • 250 kW

PHILIPPINES — †FEBC RADIO INTL, Bocaue: SE Asia • 100 kW • ALT. FREQ. TO 9440 kHz

SWEDEN — †RADIO SWEDEN, Hörby: W • S Asia • 500 kW

USA — †PAN AMERICAN BC, Via Jülich, Germany: Su • S Asia • 100 kW

†R FARDA, Via Kavála, Greece: Mideast & W Asia • 250 kW

†VOA, Via Kavála, Greece: W • Mideast & W Asia • 250 kW

9440 CHINA — CHINA RADIO INTL, Beijing: N Africa • 120 kW

(con'd) †CHINA RADIO INTL, Kunming: SE Asia • 150 kW

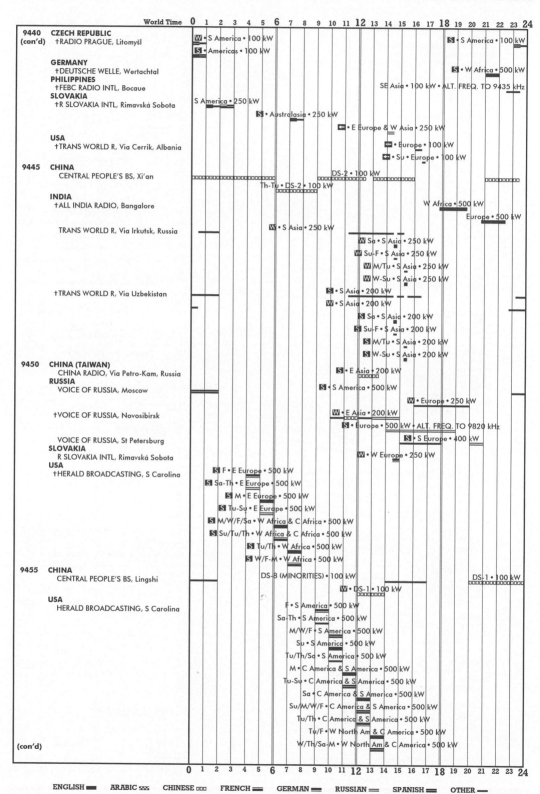

| World Time | 0 | 1 | 2 | 3 | 4 | 5 | 6 | 7 | 8 | 9 | 10 | 11 | 12 | 13 | 14 | 15 | 16 | 17 | 18 | 19 | 20 | 21 | 22 | 23 | 24 |

9440 (con'd) **CZECH REPUBLIC**
†RADIO PRAGUE, Litomyšl — W • S America • 100 kW / S • Americas • 100 kW / S • S America • 100 kW

GERMANY
†DEUTSCHE WELLE, Wertachtal — S • W Africa • 500 kW

PHILIPPINES
†FEBC RADIO INTL, Bocaue — SE Asia • 100 kW • ALT. FREQ. TO 9435 kHz

SLOVAKIA
†R SLOVAKIA INTL, Rimavská Sobota — S America • 250 kW / S • Australasia • 250 kW

USA
†TRANS WORLD R, Via Cerrik, Albania — E Europe & W Asia • 250 kW / Europe • 100 kW / Su • Europe • 100 kW

9445 **CHINA**
CENTRAL PEOPLE'S BS, Xi'an — DS-2 • 100 kW / Th-Tu • DS-2 • 100 kW

INDIA
†ALL INDIA RADIO, Bangalore — W Africa • 500 kW / Europe • 500 kW

TRANS WORLD R, Via Irkutsk, Russia — W • S Asia • 250 kW / W Sa • S Asia • 250 kW / W Su-F • S Asia • 250 kW / W M/Tu • S Asia • 250 kW / W W-Su • S Asia • 250 kW

†TRANS WORLD R, Via Uzbekistan — S • S Asia • 200 kW / W • S Asia • 200 kW / S Sa • S Asia • 200 kW / S Su-F • S Asia • 200 kW / S M/Tu • S Asia • 200 kW / S W-Su • S Asia • 200 kW

9450 **CHINA (TAIWAN)**
CHINA RADIO, Via Petro-Kam, Russia — S • E Asia • 200 kW

RUSSIA
VOICE OF RUSSIA, Moscow — S • S America • 500 kW / W • Europe • 250 kW

†VOICE OF RUSSIA, Novosibirsk — W • E Asia • 200 kW / S • Europe • 500 kW • ALT. FREQ. TO 9820 kHz

VOICE OF RUSSIA, St Petersburg — S • S Europe • 400 kW

SLOVAKIA
R SLOVAKIA INTL, Rimavská Sobota — W • W Europe • 250 kW

USA
†HERALD BROADCASTING, S Carolina — S F • E Europe • 500 kW / S Sa-Th • E Europe • 500 kW / S M • E Europe • 500 kW / S Tu-Su • E Europe • 500 kW / S M/W/F/Sa • W Africa & C Africa • 500 kW / S Su/Tu/Th • W Africa & C Africa • 500 kW / S Tu/Th • W Africa • 500 kW / S W/F-M • W Africa • 500 kW

9455 **CHINA**
CENTRAL PEOPLE'S BS, Lingshi — DS-8 (MINORITIES) • 100 kW / W • DS-1 • 100 kW / DS-1 • 100 kW

USA
HERALD BROADCASTING, S Carolina — F • S America • 500 kW / Sa-Th • S America • 500 kW / M/W/F • S America • 500 kW / Su • S America • 500 kW / Tu/Th/Sa • S America • 500 kW / M • C America & S America • 500 kW / Tu-Su • C America & S America • 500 kW / Sa • C America & S America • 500 kW / Su/M/W/F • C America & S America • 500 kW / Tu/Th • C America & S America • 500 kW / Tu/F • W North Am & C America • 500 kW / W/Th/Sa-M • W North Am & C America • 500 kW

(con'd)

| 0 | 1 | 2 | 3 | 4 | 5 | 6 | 7 | 8 | 9 | 10 | 11 | 12 | 13 | 14 | 15 | 16 | 17 | 18 | 19 | 20 | 21 | 22 | 23 | 24 |

ENGLISH ■■ ARABIC ⁓⁓⁓ CHINESE ▫▫▫ FRENCH ▬▬ GERMAN ▬▬ RUSSIAN ══ SPANISH ▬▬ OTHER ▬▬

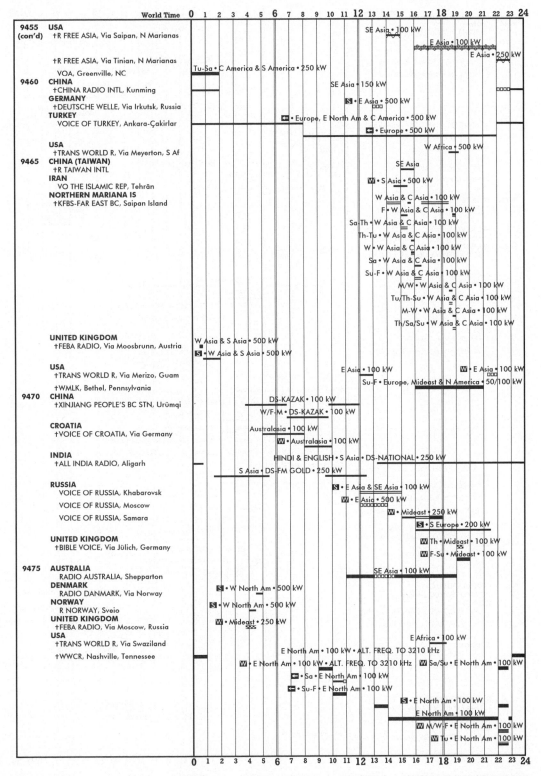

World Time

		9455	USA
9455 (con'd)		USA	†R FREE ASIA, Via Saipan, N Marianas
			†R FREE ASIA, Via Tinian, N Marianas
			VOA, Greenville, NC
9460		CHINA	†CHINA RADIO INTL, Kunming
		GERMANY	†DEUTSCHE WELLE, Via Irkutsk, Russia
		TURKEY	VOICE OF TURKEY, Ankara-Çakirlar
		USA	†TRANS WORLD R, Via Meyerton, S Af
9465		CHINA (TAIWAN)	†R TAIWAN INTL
		IRAN	VO THE ISLAMIC REP, Tehrān
		NORTHERN MARIANA IS	†KFBS-FAR EAST BC, Saipan Island
		UNITED KINGDOM	†FEBA RADIO, Via Moosbrunn, Austria
		USA	†TRANS WORLD R, Via Merizo, Guam
			†WMLK, Bethel, Pennsylvania
9470		CHINA	†XINJIANG PEOPLE'S BC STN, Urümqi
		CROATIA	†VOICE OF CROATIA, Via Germany
		INDIA	†ALL INDIA RADIO, Aligarh
		RUSSIA	VOICE OF RUSSIA, Khabarovsk
			VOICE OF RUSSIA, Moscow
			VOICE OF RUSSIA, Samara
		UNITED KINGDOM	†BIBLE VOICE, Via Jülich, Germany
9475		AUSTRALIA	RADIO AUSTRALIA, Shepparton
		DENMARK	RADIO DANMARK, Via Norway
		NORWAY	R NORWAY, Sveio
		UNITED KINGDOM	†FEBA RADIO, Via Moscow, Russia
		USA	†TRANS WORLD R, Via Swaziland
			†WWCR, Nashville, Tennessee

SE Asia • 100 kW
E Asia • 100 kW
E Asia • 250 kW
Tu-Sa • C America & S America • 250 kW
SE Asia • 150 kW
S • E Asia • 500 kW
⟷ • Europe, E North Am & C America • 500 kW
⟷ • Europe • 500 kW
W Africa • 500 kW
SE Asia
W • S Asia • 500 kW
W Asia & C Asia • 100 kW
F • W Asia & C Asia • 100 kW
Sa-Th • W Asia & C Asia • 100 kW
Th-Tu • W Asia & C Asia • 100 kW
W • W Asia & C Asia • 100 kW
Sa • W Asia & C Asia • 100 kW
Su-F • W Asia & C Asia • 100 kW
M/W • W Asia & C Asia • 100 kW
Tu/Th-Su • W Asia & C Asia • 100 kW
M-W • W Asia & C Asia • 100 kW
Th/Sa/Su • W Asia & C Asia • 100 kW
W Asia & S Asia • 500 kW
S • W Asia & S Asia • 500 kW
E Asia • 100 kW
W • E Asia • 100 kW
Su-F • Europe, Mideast & N America • 50/100 kW
DS-KAZAK • 100 kW
W/F-M • DS-KAZAK • 100 kW
Australasia • 100 kW
W • Australasia • 100 kW
HINDI & ENGLISH • S Asia • DS-NATIONAL • 250 kW
S Asia • DS-FM GOLD • 250 kW
S • E Asia & SE Asia • 100 kW
W • E Asia • 500 kW
W • Mideast • 250 kW
S • S Europe • 200 kW
W Th • Mideast • 100 kW
W F-Su • Mideast • 100 kW
SE Asia • 100 kW
S • W North Am • 500 kW
S • W North Am • 500 kW
W • Mideast • 250 kW
E Africa • 100 kW
E North Am • 100 kW • ALT. FREQ. TO 3210 kHz
W • E North Am • 100 kW • ALT. FREQ. TO 3210 kHz
W Sa/Su • E North Am • 100 kW
⟷ • Sa • E North Am • 100 kW
⟷ • Su-F • E North Am • 100 kW
S • E North Am • 100 kW
E North Am • 100 kW
W M/W-F • E North Am • 100 kW
W Tu • E North Am • 100 kW

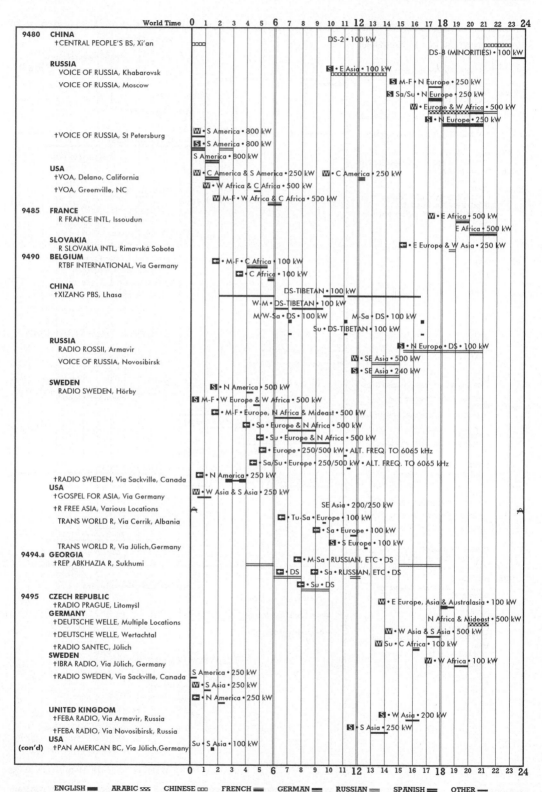

| | World Time | 0 | 1 | 2 | 3 | 4 | 5 | 6 | 7 | 8 | 9 | 10 | 11 | 12 | 13 | 14 | 15 | 16 | 17 | 18 | 19 | 20 | 21 | 22 | 23 | 24 |

9480 CHINA
　†CENTRAL PEOPLE'S BS, Xi'an — DS-2 • 100 kW; DS-8 (MINORITIES) • 100 kW

RUSSIA
　VOICE OF RUSSIA, Khabarovsk — S • E Asia • 100 kW
　VOICE OF RUSSIA, Moscow — M-F • N Europe • 250 kW; Sa/Su • N Europe • 250 kW; W • Europe & W Africa • 500 kW; S • N Europe • 250 kW
　†VOICE OF RUSSIA, St Petersburg — W • S America • 800 kW; S • S America • 800 kW; S America • 800 kW

USA
　†VOA, Delano, California — W • C America & S America • 250 kW; W • C America • 250 kW
　†VOA, Greenville, NC — W • W Africa & C Africa • 500 kW; W M-F • W Africa & C Africa • 500 kW

9485 FRANCE
　R FRANCE INTL, Issoudun — W • E Africa • 500 kW; E Africa • 500 kW

SLOVAKIA
　R SLOVAKIA INTL, Rimavská Sobota — E Europe & W Asia • 250 kW
9490 BELGIUM
　RTBF INTERNATIONAL, Via Germany — M-F • C Africa • 100 kW; C Africa • 100 kW

CHINA
　†XIZANG PBS, Lhasa — DS-TIBETAN • 100 kW; W-M • DS-TIBETAN • 100 kW; M/W-Sa • DS • 100 kW; M-Sa • DS • 100 kW; Su • DS-TIBETAN • 100 kW

RUSSIA
　RADIO ROSSII, Armavir — S • N Europe • DS • 100 kW
　VOICE OF RUSSIA, Novosibirsk — W • SE Asia • 500 kW; S • SE Asia • 240 kW

SWEDEN
　RADIO SWEDEN, Hörby — S • N America • 500 kW; S M-F • W Europe & W Africa • 500 kW; M-F • Europe, N Africa & Mideast • 500 kW; Sa • Europe & N Africa • 500 kW; Su • Europe & N Africa • 500 kW; Europe • 250/500 kW • ALT. FREQ TO 6065 kHz; Sa/Su • Europe • 250/500 kW • ALT. FREQ. TO 6065 kHz

　†RADIO SWEDEN, Via Sackville, Canada — N America • 250 kW
USA
　†GOSPEL FOR ASIA, Via Germany — W • W Asia & S Asia • 250 kW
　†R FREE ASIA, Various Locations — SE Asia • 200/250 kW
　TRANS WORLD R, Via Cerrik, Albania — Tu-Sa • Europe • 100 kW; Sa • Europe • 100 kW; S • S Europe • 100 kW

　TRANS WORLD R, Via Jülich, Germany
9494.8 GEORGIA
　†REP ABKHAZIA R, Sukhumi — M-Sa • RUSSIAN, ETC • DS; DS; Sa • RUSSIAN, ETC • DS; Su • DS

9495 CZECH REPUBLIC
　†RADIO PRAGUE, Litomyšl — W • E Europe, Asia & Australasia • 100 kW
GERMANY
　†DEUTSCHE WELLE, Multiple Locations — N Africa & Mideast • 500 kW
　†DEUTSCHE WELLE, Wertachtal — W • W Asia & S Asia • 500 kW
　†RADIO SANTEC, Jülich — W Su • C Africa • 100 kW
SWEDEN
　†IBRA RADIO, Via Jülich, Germany — W • W Africa • 100 kW
　†RADIO SWEDEN, Via Sackville, Canada — S America • 250 kW; W • S Asia • 250 kW; N America • 250 kW

UNITED KINGDOM
　†FEBA RADIO, Via Armavir, Russia — S • W Asia • 200 kW
　†FEBA RADIO, Via Novosibirsk, Russia — S • S Asia • 250 kW
USA
(con'd) †PAN AMERICAN BC, Via Jülich, Germany — Su • S Asia • 100 kW

| | 0 | 1 | 2 | 3 | 4 | 5 | 6 | 7 | 8 | 9 | 10 | 11 | 12 | 13 | 14 | 15 | 16 | 17 | 18 | 19 | 20 | 21 | 22 | 23 | 24 |

ENGLISH ▬   ARABIC ⧈⧈⧈   CHINESE □□□   FRENCH ▬   GERMAN ▬   RUSSIAN ══   SPANISH ▬   OTHER ▬

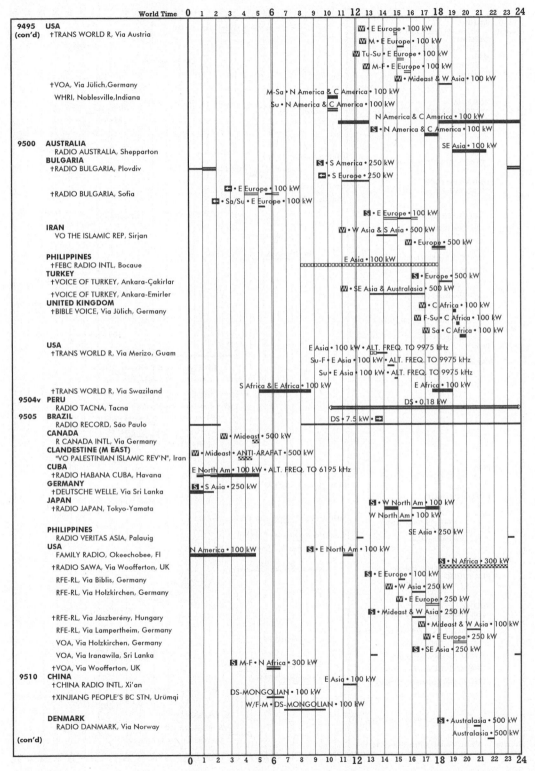

	World Time	0 1 2 3 4 5 6 7 8 9 10 11 12 13 14 15 16 17 18 19 20 21 22 23 24
9495 (con'd)	**USA** †TRANS WORLD R, Via Austria	W • E Europe • 100 kW
		W • M • E Europe • 100 kW
		W • Tu-Su • E Europe • 100 kW
		W • M-F • E Europe • 100 kW
	†VOA, Via Jülich, Germany	W • Mideast & W Asia • 100 kW
	WHRI, Noblesville, Indiana	M-Sa • N America & C America • 100 kW
		Su • N America & C America • 100 kW
		N America & C America • 100 kW
		S • N America & C America • 100 kW
9500	**AUSTRALIA** RADIO AUSTRALIA, Shepparton	SE Asia • 100 kW
	BULGARIA †RADIO BULGARIA, Plovdiv	S • S America • 250 kW
		• S Europe • 250 kW
	†RADIO BULGARIA, Sofia	• E Europe • 100 kW
		• Sa/Su • E Europe • 100 kW
	IRAN VO THE ISLAMIC REP, Sirjan	S • E Europe • 100 kW
		W • W Asia & S Asia • 500 kW
		W • Europe • 500 kW
	PHILIPPINES †FEBC RADIO INTL, Bocaue	E Asia • 100 kW
	TURKEY †VOICE OF TURKEY, Ankara-Çakirlar	S • Europe • 500 kW
	†VOICE OF TURKEY, Ankara-Emirler	W • SE Asia & Australasia • 500 kW
	UNITED KINGDOM †BIBLE VOICE, Via Jülich, Germany	W • C Africa • 100 kW
		W • F-Su • C Africa • 100 kW
		W • Sa • C Africa • 100 kW
	USA †TRANS WORLD R, Via Merizo, Guam	E Asia • 100 kW • ALT. FREQ. TO 9975 kHz
		Su-F • E Asia • 100 kW • ALT. FREQ. TO 9975 kHz
		Su • E Asia • 100 kW • ALT. FREQ. TO 9975 kHz
	†TRANS WORLD R, Via Swaziland	S Africa & E Africa • 100 kW
		E Africa • 100 kW
9504v	**PERU** RADIO TACNA, Tacna	DS • 0.18 kW
9505	**BRAZIL** RADIO RECORD, São Paulo	DS • 7.5 kW •
	CANADA R CANADA INTL, Via Germany	W • Mideast • 500 kW
	CLANDESTINE (M EAST) "VO PALESTINIAN ISLAMIC REV'N", Iran	W • Mideast • ANTI-ARAFAT • 500 kW
	CUBA †RADIO HABANA CUBA, Havana	E North Am • 100 kW • ALT. FREQ. TO 6195 kHz
	GERMANY †DEUTSCHE WELLE, Via Sri Lanka	S • S Asia • 250 kW
	JAPAN †RADIO JAPAN, Tokyo-Yamata	S • W North Am • 100 kW
		W North Am • 100 kW
	PHILIPPINES RADIO VERITAS ASIA, Palauig	SE Asia • 250 kW
	USA FAMILY RADIO, Okeechobee, Fl	N America • 100 kW
		S • E North Am • 100 kW
	†RADIO SAWA, Via Woofferton, UK	S • N Africa • 300 kW
	RFE-RL, Via Biblis, Germany	S • E Europe • 100 kW
	RFE-RL, Via Holzkirchen, Germany	W • W Asia • 250 kW
		W • E Europe • 250 kW
	†RFE-RL, Via Jászberény, Hungary	S • Mideast & W Asia • 250 kW
	RFE-RL, Via Lampertheim, Germany	W • Mideast & W Asia • 100 kW
	VOA, Via Holzkirchen, Germany	W • E Europe • 250 kW
	VOA, Via Iranawila, Sri Lanka	S • SE Asia • 250 kW
	VOA, Via Woofferton, UK	S • M-F • N Africa • 300 kW
9510	**CHINA** †CHINA RADIO INTL, Xi'an	E Asia • 100 kW
	†XINJIANG PEOPLE'S BC STN, Urümqi	DS-MONGOLIAN • 100 kW
		W/F-M • DS-MONGOLIAN • 100 kW
	DENMARK RADIO DANMARK, Via Norway	S • Australasia • 500 kW
		Australasia • 500 kW
(con'd)		

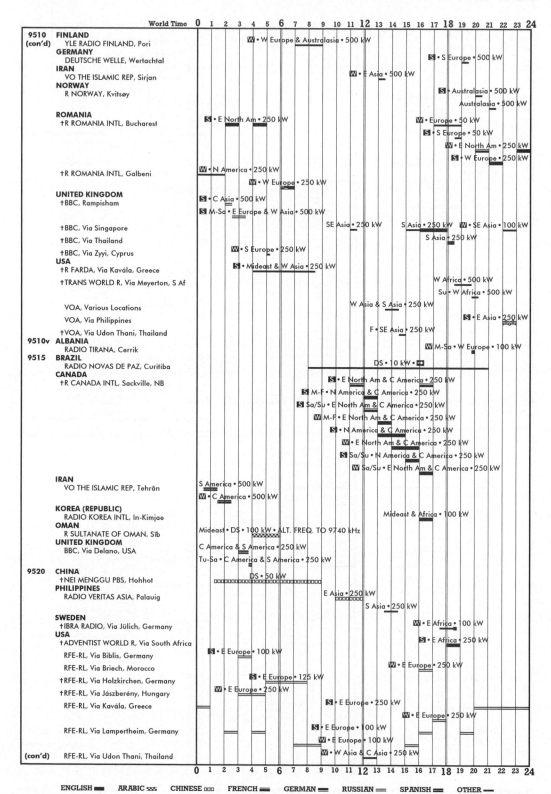

World Time 0 1 2 3 4 5 6 7 8 9 10 11 12 13 14 15 16 17 18 19 20 21 22 23 24

9510 **(con'd)**	**FINLAND** YLE RADIO FINLAND, Pori
	GERMANY DEUTSCHE WELLE, Wertachtal
	IRAN VO THE ISLAMIC REP, Sirjan
	NORWAY R NORWAY, Kvitsøy
	ROMANIA †R ROMANIA INTL, Bucharest
	†R ROMANIA INTL, Galbeni
	UNITED KINGDOM †BBC, Rampisham
	†BBC, Via Singapore
	†BBC, Via Thailand
	†BBC, Via Zyyi, Cyprus
	USA †R FARDA, Via Kavála, Greece
	†TRANS WORLD R, Via Meyerton, S Af
	VOA, Various Locations
	VOA, Via Philippines
	†VOA, Via Udon Thani, Thailand
9510v	**ALBANIA** RADIO TIRANA, Cerrik
9515	**BRAZIL** RADIO NOVAS DE PAZ, Curitiba
	CANADA †R CANADA INTL, Sackville, NB
	IRAN VO THE ISLAMIC REP, Tehrān
	KOREA (REPUBLIC) RADIO KOREA INTL, In-Kimjae
	OMAN R SULTANATE OF OMAN, Sīb
	UNITED KINGDOM BBC, Via Delano, USA
9520	**CHINA** †NEI MENGGU PBS, Hohhot
	PHILIPPINES RADIO VERITAS ASIA, Palauig
	SWEDEN †IBRA RADIO, Via Jülich, Germany
	USA †ADVENTIST WORLD R, Via South Africa
	RFE-RL, Via Biblis, Germany
	RFE-RL, Via Briech, Morocco
	†RFE-RL, Via Holzkirchen, Germany
	†RFE-RL, Via Jászberény, Hungary
	RFE-RL, Via Kavála, Greece
	RFE-RL, Via Lampertheim, Germany
(con'd)	RFE-RL, Via Udon Thani, Thailand

Program contents:
- W • W Europe & Australasia • 500 kW
- S • S Europe • 500 kW
- W • E Asia • 500 kW
- S • Australasia • 500 kW
- Australasia • 500 kW
- S • E North Am • 250 kW
- W • Europe • 50 kW
- S • S Europe • 50 kW
- W • E North Am • 250 kW
- S • W Europe • 250 kW
- W • N America • 250 kW
- W • W Europe • 250 kW
- S • C Asia • 500 kW
- S • M-Sa • E Europe & W Asia • 500 kW
- SE Asia • 250 kW
- S Asia • 250 kW
- W • SE Asia • 100 kW
- S Asia • 250 kW
- W • S Europe • 250 kW
- S • Mideast & W Asia • 250 kW
- W Africa • 500 kW
- Su • W Africa • 500 kW
- W Asia & S Asia • 250 kW
- S • E Asia • 250 kW
- F • SE Asia • 250 kW
- W M-Sa • W Europe • 100 kW
- DS • 10 kW •
- S • E North Am & C America • 250 kW
- S M-F • N America & C America • 250 kW
- S Sa/Su • E North Am & C America • 250 kW
- W M-F • E North Am & C America • 250 kW
- S • N America & C America • 250 kW
- W • E North Am & C America • 250 kW
- S Sa/Su • N America & C America • 250 kW
- W Sa/Su • E North Am & C America • 250 kW
- S America • 500 kW
- W • C America • 500 kW
- Mideast & Africa • 100 kW
- Mideast • DS • 100 kW • ALT. FREQ. TO 9740 kHz
- C America & S America • 250 kW
- Tu-Sa • C America & S America • 250 kW
- DS • 50 kW
- E Asia • 250 kW
- S Asia • 250 kW
- W • E Africa • 100 kW
- S • E Africa • 250 kW
- S • E Europe • 100 kW
- W • E Europe • 250 kW
- S • E Europe • 125 kW
- W • E Europe • 250 kW
- S • E Europe • 250 kW
- W • E Europe • 250 kW
- S • E Europe • 100 kW
- W • E Europe • 100 kW
- W • W Asia & C Asia • 250 kW

0 1 2 3 4 5 6 7 8 9 10 11 12 13 14 15 16 17 18 19 20 21 22 23 24

ENGLISH ▬ ARABIC ░░ CHINESE ▭▭▭ FRENCH ═══ GERMAN ▬▬ RUSSIAN ══ SPANISH ▬▬ OTHER ▬▬

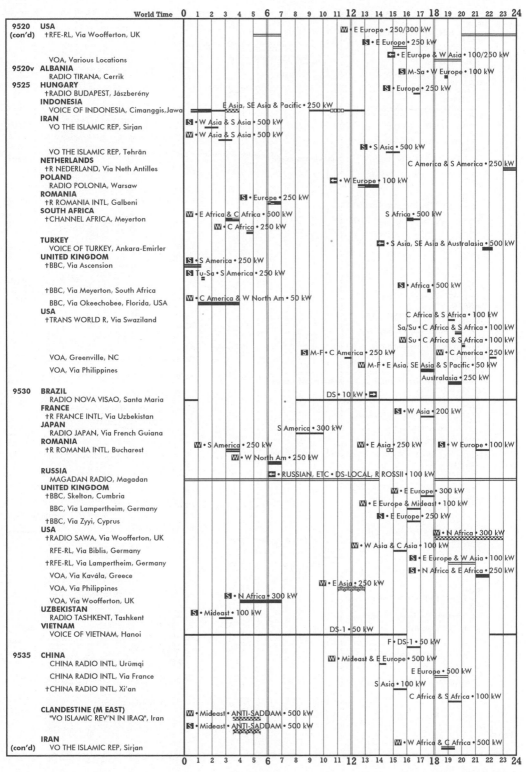

World Time		
9520 **USA** (con'd) †RFE-RL, Via Woofferton, UK		W • E Europe • 250/300 kW
		S • E Europe • 250 kW
VOA, Various Locations		⇦ • E Europe & W Asia • 100/250 kW
9520v **ALBANIA** RADIO TIRANA, Cerrik		S M-Sa • W Europe • 100 kW
9525 **HUNGARY** †RADIO BUDAPEST, Jászberény		S • Europe • 250 kW
INDONESIA VOICE OF INDONESIA, Cimanggis, Jawa	E Asia, SE Asia & Pacific • 250 kW	
IRAN VO THE ISLAMIC REP, Sirjan	S • W Asia & S Asia • 500 kW	
	W • W Asia & S Asia • 500 kW	
VO THE ISLAMIC REP, Tehrān		S • S Asia • 500 kW
NETHERLANDS †R NEDERLAND, Via Neth Antilles		C America & S America • 250 kW
POLAND RADIO POLONIA, Warsaw		⇦ • W Europe • 100 kW
ROMANIA †R ROMANIA INTL, Galbeni	S • Europe • 250 kW	
SOUTH AFRICA †CHANNEL AFRICA, Meyerton	W • E Africa & C Africa • 500 kW	S Africa • 500 kW
	W • C Africa • 250 kW	
TURKEY VOICE OF TURKEY, Ankara-Emirler		⇨ • S Asia, SE Asia & Australasia • 500 kW
UNITED KINGDOM †BBC, Via Ascension	S • S America • 250 kW	
	S Tu-Sa • S America • 250 kW	
†BBC, Via Meyerton, South Africa		S • Africa • 500 kW
BBC, Via Okeechobee, Florida, USA	W • C America & W North Am • 50 kW	
USA †TRANS WORLD R, Via Swaziland		C Africa & S Africa • 100 kW
		Sa/Su • C Africa & S Africa • 100 kW
		W Su • C Africa & S Africa • 100 kW
VOA, Greenville, NC	S M-F • C America • 250 kW	W • C America • 250 kW
VOA, Via Philippines		W M-F • E Asia, SE Asia & S Pacific • 50 kW
		Australasia • 250 kW
9530 **BRAZIL** RADIO NOVA VISAO, Santa Maria	DS • 10 kW • ⇨	
FRANCE †R FRANCE INTL, Via Uzbekistan		S • W Asia • 200 kW
JAPAN RADIO JAPAN, Via French Guiana	S America • 300 kW	
ROMANIA †R ROMANIA INTL, Bucharest	W • S America • 250 kW	W • E Asia • 250 kW S • W Europe • 100 kW
	W • W North Am • 250 kW	
RUSSIA MAGADAN RADIO, Magadan	⇦ • RUSSIAN, ETC • DS-LOCAL, R ROSSII • 100 kW	
UNITED KINGDOM †BBC, Skelton, Cumbria		W • E Europe • 300 kW
BBC, Via Lampertheim, Germany		W • E Europe & Mideast • 100 kW
†BBC, Via Zyyi, Cyprus		S • E Europe • 250 kW
USA †RADIO SAWA, Via Woofferton, UK		W • N Africa • 300 kW
RFE-RL, Via Biblis, Germany		W • W Asia & C Asia • 100 kW
†RFE-RL, Via Lampertheim, Germany		S • E Europe & W Asia • 100 kW
		S • N Africa & E Africa • 250 kW
VOA, Via Kavála, Greece		W • E Asia • 250 kW
VOA, Via Philippines		
VOA, Via Woofferton, UK	S • N Africa • 300 kW	
UZBEKISTAN RADIO TASHKENT, Tashkent	S • Mideast • 100 kW	
VIETNAM VOICE OF VIETNAM, Hanoi	DS-1 • 50 kW	
		F • DS-1 • 50 kW
9535 **CHINA** CHINA RADIO INTL, Urümqi		W • Mideast & E Europe • 500 kW
CHINA RADIO INTL, Via France		E Europe • 500 kW
†CHINA RADIO INTL, Xi'an		S Asia • 100 kW
		C Africa & S Africa • 100 kW
CLANDESTINE (M EAST) "VO ISLAMIC REV'N IN IRAQ", Iran	W • Mideast • ANTI-SADDAM • 500 kW	
	S • Mideast • ANTI-SADDAM • 500 kW	
IRAN (con'd) VO THE ISLAMIC REP, Sirjan		W • W Africa & C Africa • 500 kW

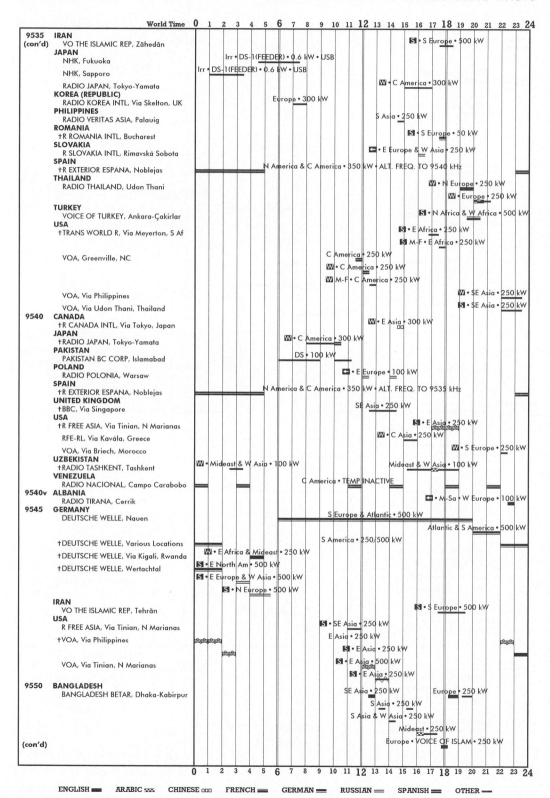

| World Time | 0 | 1 | 2 | 3 | 4 | 5 | 6 | 7 | 8 | 9 | 10 | 11 | 12 | 13 | 14 | 15 | 16 | 17 | 18 | 19 | 20 | 21 | 22 | 23 | 24 |

9535
(con'd)   **IRAN**
VO THE ISLAMIC REP, Zāhedān — S · S Europe · 500 kW
JAPAN
NHK, Fukuoka — Irr · DS-1(FEEDER) · 0.6 kW · USB
NHK, Sapporo — Irr · DS-1(FEEDER) · 0.6 kW · USB
RADIO JAPAN, Tokyo-Yamata — W · C America · 300 kW
KOREA (REPUBLIC)
RADIO KOREA INTL, Via Skelton, UK — Europe · 300 kW
PHILIPPINES
RADIO VERITAS ASIA, Palauig — S Asia · 250 kW
ROMANIA
†R ROMANIA INTL, Bucharest — S · S Europe · 50 kW
SLOVAKIA
R SLOVAKIA INTL, Rimavská Sobota — · E Europe & W Asia · 250 kW
SPAIN
†R EXTERIOR ESPANA, Noblejas — N America & C America · 350 kW · ALT. FREQ. TO 9540 kHz
THAILAND
RADIO THAILAND, Udon Thani — W · N Europe · 250 kW
W · Europe · 250 kW
TURKEY
VOICE OF TURKEY, Ankara-Çakirlar — S · N Africa & W Africa · 500 kW
USA
†TRANS WORLD R, Via Meyerton, S Af — S · E Africa · 250 kW
S · M-F · E Africa · 250 kW
VOA, Greenville, NC — C America · 250 kW
W · C America · 250 kW
W M-F · C America · 250 kW
VOA, Via Philippines — W · SE Asia · 250 kW
VOA, Via Udon Thani, Thailand — S · SE Asia · 250 kW
9540   **CANADA**
†R CANADA INTL, Via Tokyo, Japan — W · E Asia · 300 kW
JAPAN
†RADIO JAPAN, Tokyo-Yamata — W · C America · 300 kW
PAKISTAN
PAKISTAN BC CORP, Islamabad — DS · 100 kW
POLAND
RADIO POLONIA, Warsaw — · E Europe · 100 kW
SPAIN
†R EXTERIOR ESPANA, Noblejas — N America & C America · 350 kW · ALT. FREQ. TO 9535 kHz
UNITED KINGDOM
†BBC, Via Singapore — SE Asia · 250 kW
USA
†R FREE ASIA, Via Tinian, N Marianas — S · E Asia · 250 kW
RFE-RL, Via Kavála, Greece — W · C Asia · 250 kW
VOA, Via Briech, Morocco — W · S Europe · 250 kW
UZBEKISTAN
†RADIO TASHKENT, Tashkent — W · Mideast & W Asia · 100 kW   Mideast & W Asia · 100 kW
VENEZUELA
RADIO NACIONAL, Campo Carabobo — C America · TEMP INACTIVE
9540v   ALBANIA
RADIO TIRANA, Cerrik — · M-Sa · W Europe · 100 kW
9545   GERMANY
DEUTSCHE WELLE, Nauen — S Europe & Atlantic · 500 kW
Atlantic & S America · 500 kW
†DEUTSCHE WELLE, Various Locations — S America · 250/500 kW
†DEUTSCHE WELLE, Via Kigali, Rwanda — W · E Africa & Mideast · 250 kW
†DEUTSCHE WELLE, Wertachtal — S · E North Am · 500 kW
S · E Europe & W Asia · 500 kW
S · N Europe · 500 kW
IRAN
VO THE ISLAMIC REP, Tehrān — S · S Europe · 500 kW
USA
R FREE ASIA, Via Tinian, N Marianas — S · SE Asia · 250 kW
†VOA, Via Philippines — E Asia · 250 kW
S · E Asia · 250 kW
VOA, Via Tinian, N Marianas — S · E Asia · 500 kW
S · E Asia · 250 kW
9550   BANGLADESH
BANGLADESH BETAR, Dhaka-Kabirpur — SE Asia · 250 kW   Europe · 250 kW
S Asia · 250 kW
S Asia & W Asia · 250 kW
Mideast · 250 kW
(con'd) — Europe · VOICE OF ISLAM · 250 kW

| | 0 | 1 | 2 | 3 | 4 | 5 | 6 | 7 | 8 | 9 | 10 | 11 | 12 | 13 | 14 | 15 | 16 | 17 | 18 | 19 | 20 | 21 | 22 | 23 | 24 |

ENGLISH ▬   ARABIC ⋙   CHINESE ☐☐☐   FRENCH ▬   GERMAN ▬   RUSSIAN ═   SPANISH ▬   OTHER ▬

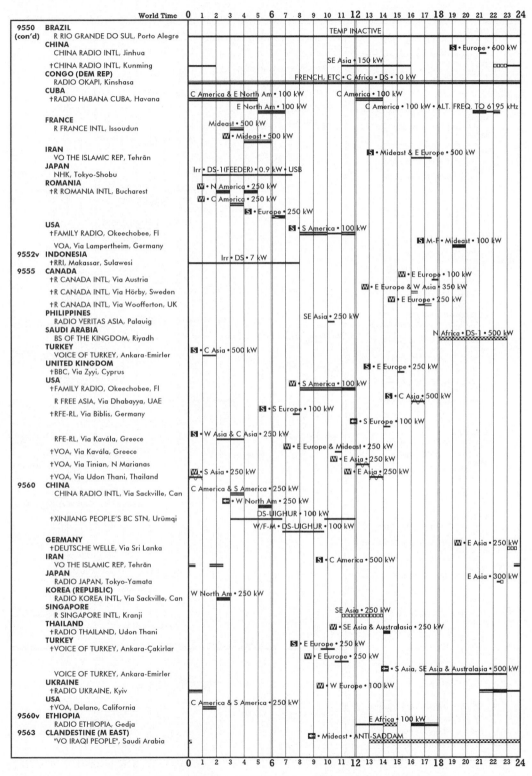

	World Time	0 1 2 3 4 5 6 7 8 9 10 11 12 13 14 15 16 17 18 19 20 21 22 23 24
9550 (con'd)	BRAZIL R RIO GRANDE DO SUL, Porto Alegre	TEMP INACTIVE
	CHINA CHINA RADIO INTL, Jinhua	Ⓢ • Europe • 600 kW
	†CHINA RADIO INTL, Kunming	SE Asia • 150 kW
	CONGO (DEM REP) RADIO OKAPI, Kinshasa	FRENCH, ETC • C Africa • DS • 10 kW
	CUBA †RADIO HABANA CUBA, Havana	C America & E North Am • 100 kW C America • 100 kW
		E North Am • 100 kW C America • 100 kW • ALT. FREQ. TO 6195 kHz
	FRANCE R FRANCE INTL, Issoudun	Mideast • 500 kW
		Ⓦ • Mideast • 500 kW
	IRAN VO THE ISLAMIC REP, Tehrān	Ⓢ • Mideast & E Europe • 500 kW
	JAPAN NHK, Tokyo-Shobu	Irr • DS-1(FEEDER) • 0.9 kW • USB
	ROMANIA †R ROMANIA INTL, Bucharest	Ⓦ • N America • 250 kW
		Ⓦ • C America • 250 kW
		Ⓢ • Europe • 250 kW
	USA †FAMILY RADIO, Okeechobee, Fl	Ⓢ • S America • 100 kW
	VOA, Via Lampertheim, Germany	Ⓢ M-F • Mideast • 100 kW
9552v	INDONESIA †RRI, Makassar, Sulawesi	Irr • DS • 7 kW
9555	CANADA †R CANADA INTL, Via Austria	Ⓦ • E Europe • 100 kW
	†R CANADA INTL, Via Hörby, Sweden	Ⓦ • E Europe & W Asia • 350 kW
	†R CANADA INTL, Via Woofferton, UK	Ⓦ • E Europe • 250 kW
	PHILIPPINES RADIO VERITAS ASIA, Palauig	SE Asia • 250 kW
	SAUDI ARABIA BS OF THE KINGDOM, Riyadh	N Africa • DS-1 • 500 kW
	TURKEY VOICE OF TURKEY, Ankara-Emirler	Ⓢ • C Asia • 500 kW
	UNITED KINGDOM †BBC, Via Zyyi, Cyprus	Ⓢ • E Europe • 250 kW
	USA †FAMILY RADIO, Okeechobee, Fl	Ⓦ • S America • 100 kW
	R FREE ASIA, Via Dhabayya, UAE	Ⓢ • C Asia • 500 kW
	†RFE-RL, Via Biblis, Germany	Ⓢ • S Europe • 100 kW
		⇆ • S Europe • 100 kW
	RFE-RL, Via Kavála, Greece	Ⓢ • W Asia & C Asia • 250 kW
	†VOA, Via Kavála, Greece	Ⓦ • E Europe & Mideast • 250 kW
	†VOA, Via Tinian, N Marianas	Ⓦ • E Asia • 250 kW
	†VOA, Via Udon Thani, Thailand	Ⓦ • S Asia • 250 kW Ⓦ • E Asia • 250 kW
9560	CHINA CHINA RADIO INTL, Via Sackville, Can	C America & S America • 250 kW
		⇆ • W North Am • 250 kW
	†XINJIANG PEOPLE'S BC STN, Urümqi	DS-UIGHUR • 100 kW
		W/F-M • DS-UIGHUR • 100 kW
	GERMANY †DEUTSCHE WELLE, Via Sri Lanka	Ⓦ • E Asia • 250 kW
	IRAN VO THE ISLAMIC REP, Tehrān	Ⓢ • C America • 500 kW
	JAPAN RADIO JAPAN, Tokyo-Yamata	E Asia • 300 kW
	KOREA (REPUBLIC) RADIO KOREA INTL, Via Sackville, Can	W North Am • 250 kW
	SINGAPORE R SINGAPORE INTL, Kranji	SE Asia • 250 kW
	THAILAND †RADIO THAILAND, Udon Thani	Ⓦ • SE Asia & Australasia • 250 kW
	TURKEY †VOICE OF TURKEY, Ankara-Çakirlar	Ⓢ • E Europe • 250 kW
		Ⓦ • E Europe • 250 kW
	VOICE OF TURKEY, Ankara-Emirler	⇆ • S Asia, SE Asia & Australasia • 500 kW
	UKRAINE †RADIO UKRAINE, Kyiv	Ⓦ • W Europe • 100 kW
	USA †VOA, Delano, California	C America & S America • 250 kW
9560v	ETHIOPIA RADIO ETHIOPIA, Gedja	E Africa • 100 kW
9563	CLANDESTINE (M EAST) "VO IRAQI PEOPLE", Saudi Arabia	⇆ • Mideast • ANTI-SADDAM

0 1 2 3 4 5 6 7 8 9 10 11 12 13 14 15 16 17 18 19 20 21 22 23 24

SEASONAL Ⓢ OR Ⓦ   1-HR TIMESHIFT MIDYEAR ⇆ OR ⇉   JAMMING / OR ∧   EARLIEST HEARD ◁   LATEST HEARD ▷   NEW FOR 2004 †

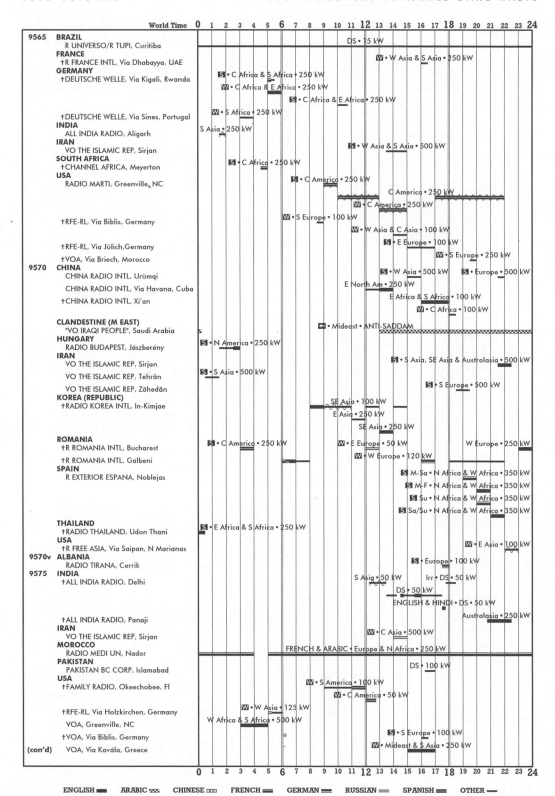

	World Time	0 1 2 3 4 5 6 7 8 9 10 11 12 13 14 15 16 17 18 19 20 21 22 23 24
9565	**BRAZIL**	
	R UNIVERSO/R TUPI, Curitiba	DS • 15 kW
	FRANCE	
	†R FRANCE INTL, Via Dhabayya, UAE	W • W Asia & S Asia • 250 kW
	GERMANY	
	†DEUTSCHE WELLE, Via Kigali, Rwanda	S • C Africa & S Africa • 250 kW
		W • C Africa & E Africa • 250 kW
		S • C Africa & E Africa • 250 kW
	†DEUTSCHE WELLE, Via Sines, Portugal	W • S Africa • 250 kW
	INDIA	
	ALL INDIA RADIO, Aligarh	S Asia • 250 kW
	IRAN	
	VO THE ISLAMIC REP, Sirjan	S • W Asia & S Asia • 500 kW
	SOUTH AFRICA	
	†CHANNEL AFRICA, Meyerton	S • C Africa • 250 kW
	USA	
	RADIO MARTI, Greenville, NC	S • C America • 250 kW
		C America • 250 kW
		W • C America • 250 kW
	†RFE-RL, Via Biblis, Germany	W • S Europe • 100 kW
		W • W Asia & C Asia • 100 kW
	†RFE-RL, Via Jülich, Germany	S • E Europe • 100 kW
	†VOA, Via Briech, Morocco	W • S Europe • 250 kW
9570	**CHINA**	
	CHINA RADIO INTL, Urümqi	S • W Asia • 500 kW　S • Europe • 500 kW
	CHINA RADIO INTL, Via Havana, Cuba	E North Am • 250 kW
	†CHINA RADIO INTL, Xi'an	E Africa & S Africa • 100 kW
		W • C Africa • 100 kW
	CLANDESTINE (M EAST)	
	"VO IRAQI PEOPLE", Saudi Arabia	□ • Mideast • ANTI-SADDAM
	HUNGARY	
	RADIO BUDAPEST, Jászberény	S • N America • 250 kW
	IRAN	
	VO THE ISLAMIC REP, Sirjan	S • S Asia, SE Asia & Australasia • 500 kW
	VO THE ISLAMIC REP, Tehrān	S • S Asia • 500 kW
	VO THE ISLAMIC REP, Zāhedān	S • S Europe • 500 kW
	KOREA (REPUBLIC)	
	†RADIO KOREA INTL, In-Kimjae	SE Asia • 100 kW
		E Asia • 250 kW
		SE Asia • 250 kW
	ROMANIA	
	†R ROMANIA INTL, Bucharest	S • C America • 250 kW　W • E Europe • 50 kW　W Europe • 250 kW
	†R ROMANIA INTL, Galbeni	W • W Europe • 120 kW
	SPAIN	
	R EXTERIOR ESPANA, Noblejas	S M-Sa • N Africa & W Africa • 350 kW
		S M-F • N Africa & W Africa • 350 kW
		S Su • N Africa & W Africa • 350 kW
		S Sa/Su • N Africa & W Africa • 350 kW
	THAILAND	
	†RADIO THAILAND, Udon Thani	S • E Africa & S Africa • 250 kW
	USA	
	†R FREE ASIA, Via Saipan, N Marianas	W • E Asia • 100 kW
9570v	**ALBANIA**	
	RADIO TIRANA, Cerrik	S • Europe • 100 kW
9575	**INDIA**	
	†ALL INDIA RADIO, Delhi	S Asia • 50 kW　Irr • DS • 50 kW
		DS • 50 kW
		ENGLISH & HINDI • DS • 50 kW
	†ALL INDIA RADIO, Panaji	Australasia • 250 kW
	IRAN	
	VO THE ISLAMIC REP, Sirjan	W • C Asia • 500 kW
	MOROCCO	
	RADIO MEDI UN, Nador	FRENCH & ARABIC • Europe & N Africa • 250 kW
	PAKISTAN	
	PAKISTAN BC CORP, Islamabad	DS • 100 kW
	USA	
	†FAMILY RADIO, Okeechobee, Fl	W • S America • 100 kW
		W • C America • 50 kW
	†RFE-RL, Via Holzkirchen, Germany	W • W Asia • 125 kW
	VOA, Greenville, NC	W Africa & S Africa • 500 kW
	†VOA, Via Biblis, Germany	S • S Europe • 100 kW
(con'd)	VOA, Via Kavála, Greece	W • Mideast & S Asia • 250 kW

	0 1 2 3 4 5 6 7 8 9 10 11 12 13 14 15 16 17 18 19 20 21 22 23 24

ENGLISH ▬　ARABIC ▨　CHINESE ▦　FRENCH ▬　GERMAN ▬　RUSSIAN ═　SPANISH ▬　OTHER ▬

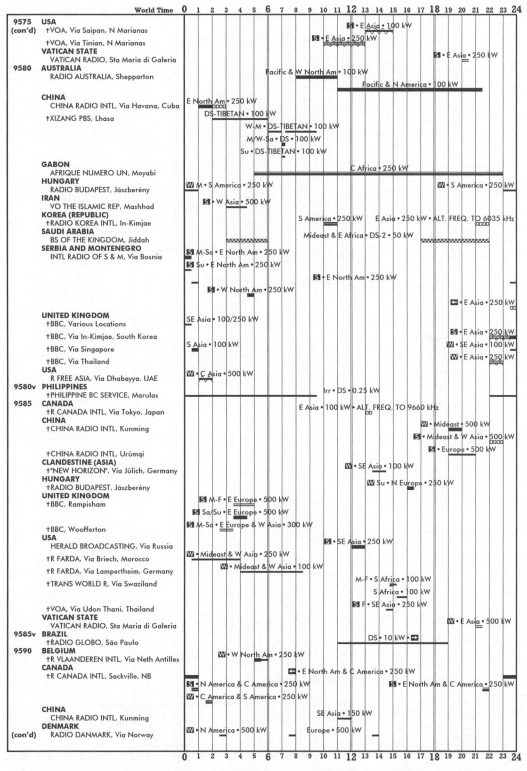

World Time

9575 **USA**
(con'd) †VOA, Via Saipan, N Marianas — S • E Asia • 100 kW

†VOA, Via Tinian, N Marianas — S • E Asia • 250 kW
VATICAN STATE
VATICAN RADIO, Sta Maria di Galeria — S • E Asia • 250 kW
9580 **AUSTRALIA**
RADIO AUSTRALIA, Shepparton — Pacific & W North Am • 100 kW
— Pacific & N America • 100 kW

CHINA
CHINA RADIO INTL, Via Havana, Cuba — E North Am • 250 kW
†XIZANG PBS, Lhasa — DS-TIBETAN • 100 kW
— W-M • DS-TIBETAN • 100 kW
— M/W-Sa • DS • 100 kW
— Su • DS-TIBETAN • 100 kW

GABON
AFRIQUE NUMERO UN, Moyabi — C Africa • 250 kW
HUNGARY
RADIO BUDAPEST, Jászberény — W M • S America • 250 kW   W • S America • 250 kW
IRAN
VO THE ISLAMIC REP, Mashhad — S • W Asia • 500 kW
KOREA (REPUBLIC)
†RADIO KOREA INTL, In-Kimjae — S America • 250 kW   E Asia • 250 kW • ALT. FREQ. TO 6035 kHz
SAUDI ARABIA
BS OF THE KINGDOM, Jiddah — Mideast & E Africa • DS-2 • 50 kW
SERBIA AND MONTENEGRO
INTL RADIO OF S & M, Via Bosnia — S M-Sa • E North Am • 250 kW
— S Su • E North Am • 250 kW
— S • E North Am • 250 kW
— S • W North Am • 250 kW
— ⬅ • E Asia • 250 kW

UNITED KINGDOM
†BBC, Various Locations — SE Asia • 100/250 kW
†BBC, Via In-Kimjae, South Korea — S Asia • 100 kW   S • E Asia • 250 kW
†BBC, Via Singapore — W • SE Asia • 100 kW
†BBC, Via Thailand — W • E Asia • 250 kW
USA
R FREE ASIA, Via Dhabayya, UAE — W • C Asia • 500 kW
9580v **PHILIPPINES**
†PHILIPPINE BC SERVICE, Marulas — Irr • DS • 0.25 kW
9585 **CANADA**
†R CANADA INTL, Via Tokyo, Japan — E Asia • 100 kW • ALT. FREQ. TO 9660 kHz
CHINA
†CHINA RADIO INTL, Kunming — W • Mideast • 500 kW
— S • Mideast & W Asia • 500 kW
— S • Europe • 500 kW
†CHINA RADIO INTL, Urümqi
CLANDESTINE (ASIA)
†"NEW HORIZON", Via Jülich, Germany — W • SE Asia • 100 kW
HUNGARY
†RADIO BUDAPEST, Jászberény — W Su • N Europe • 250 kW
UNITED KINGDOM
†BBC, Rampisham — S M-F • E Europe • 500 kW
— S Sa/Su • E Europe • 500 kW
— S M-Sa • E Europe & W Asia • 300 kW
†BBC, Woofferton
USA
HERALD BROADCASTING, Via Russia — S • SE Asia • 250 kW
†R FARDA, Via Briech, Morocco — W • Mideast & W Asia • 250 kW
†R FARDA, Via Lampertheim, Germany — W • Mideast & W Asia • 100 kW
†TRANS WORLD R, Via Swaziland — M-F • S Africa • 100 kW
— S Africa • 100 kW
†VOA, Via Udon Thani, Thailand — S F • SE Asia • 250 kW
VATICAN STATE
VATICAN RADIO, Sta Maria di Galeria — W • E Asia • 500 kW
9585v **BRAZIL**
†RADIO GLOBO, São Paulo — DS • 10 kW • ➡
9590 **BELGIUM**
†R VLAANDEREN INTL, Via Neth Antilles — W • W North Am • 250 kW
CANADA
†R CANADA INTL, Sackville, NB — ⬅ • E North Am & C America • 250 kW
— S • N America & C America • 250 kW   S • E North Am & C America • 250 kW
— W • C America & S America • 250 kW

CHINA
CHINA RADIO INTL, Kunming — SE Asia • 150 kW
DENMARK
(con'd) RADIO DANMARK, Via Norway — W • N America • 500 kW   Europe • 500 kW

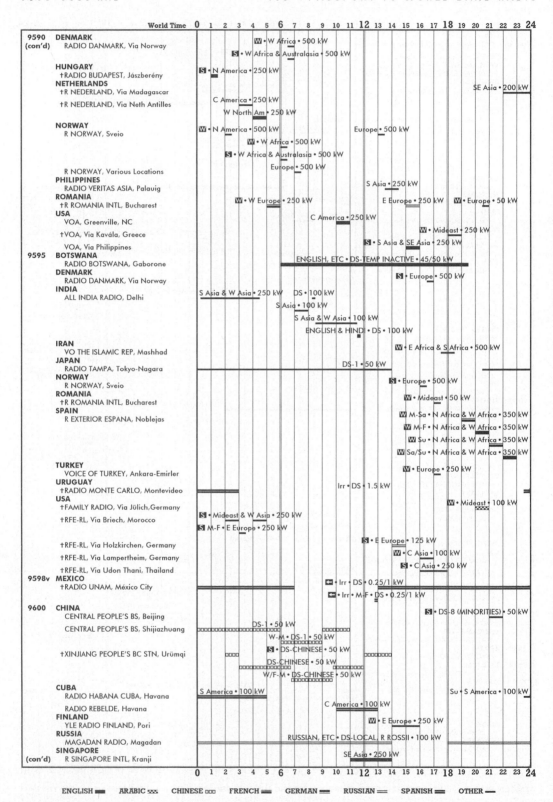

World Time 0 1 2 3 4 5 6 7 8 9 10 11 12 13 14 15 16 17 18 19 20 21 22 23 24

9590
(con'd) **DENMARK**
　　　RADIO DANMARK, Via Norway

HUNGARY
　†RADIO BUDAPEST, Jászberény
NETHERLANDS
　†R NEDERLAND, Via Madagascar
　†R NEDERLAND, Via Neth Antilles

NORWAY
　R NORWAY, Sveio

　R NORWAY, Various Locations
PHILIPPINES
　RADIO VERITAS ASIA, Palauig
ROMANIA
　†R ROMANIA INTL, Bucharest
USA
　VOA, Greenville, NC
　†VOA, Via Kavála, Greece
　VOA, Via Philippines
9595 **BOTSWANA**
　RADIO BOTSWANA, Gaborone
DENMARK
　RADIO DANMARK, Via Norway
INDIA
　ALL INDIA RADIO, Delhi

IRAN
　VO THE ISLAMIC REP, Mashhad
JAPAN
　RADIO TAMPA, Tokyo-Nagara
NORWAY
　R NORWAY, Sveio
ROMANIA
　†R ROMANIA INTL, Bucharest
SPAIN
　R EXTERIOR ESPANA, Noblejas

TURKEY
　VOICE OF TURKEY, Ankara-Emirler
URUGUAY
　†RADIO MONTE CARLO, Montevideo
USA
　†FAMILY RADIO, Via Jülich, Germany
　†RFE-RL, Via Briech, Morocco

　†RFE-RL, Via Holzkirchen, Germany
　†RFE-RL, Via Lampertheim, Germany
　†RFE-RL, Via Udon Thani, Thailand
9598v **MEXICO**
　†RADIO UNAM, México City

9600 **CHINA**
　CENTRAL PEOPLE'S BS, Beijing
　CENTRAL PEOPLE'S BS, Shijiazhuang

　†XINJIANG PEOPLE'S BC STN, Urümqi

CUBA
　RADIO HABANA CUBA, Havana
　RADIO REBELDE, Havana
FINLAND
　YLE RADIO FINLAND, Pori
RUSSIA
　MAGADAN RADIO, Magadan
SINGAPORE
(con'd) R SINGAPORE INTL, Kranji

ENGLISH ▬　ARABIC ⧉　CHINESE ☐☐☐　FRENCH ▬　GERMAN ▬　RUSSIAN ══　SPANISH ▬　OTHER ▬

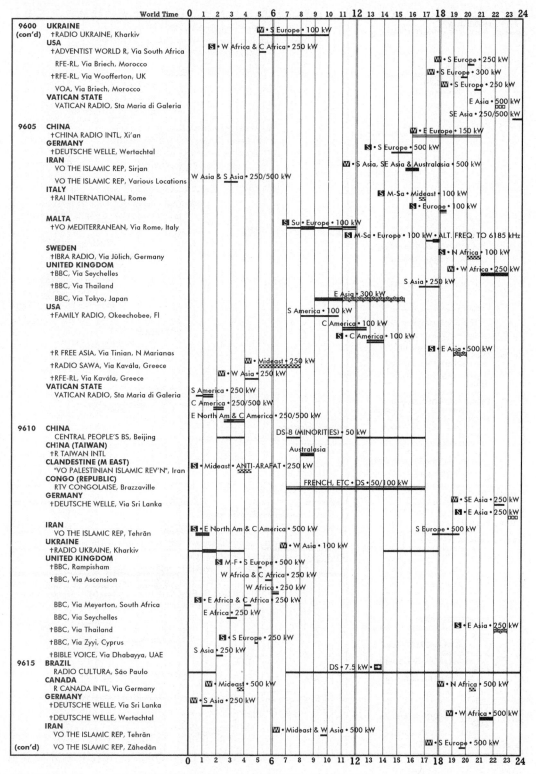

World Time: 0 1 2 3 4 5 6 7 8 9 10 11 12 13 14 15 16 17 18 19 20 21 22 23 24

9600 **UKRAINE**
(con'd) †RADIO UKRAINE, Kharkiv — W • S Europe • 100 kW
USA
†ADVENTIST WORLD R, Via South Africa — S • W Africa & C Africa • 250 kW
RFE-RL, Via Briech, Morocco — W • S Europe • 250 kW
†RFE-RL, Via Woofferton, UK — W • S Europe • 300 kW
VOA, Via Briech, Morocco — W • S Europe • 250 kW
VATICAN STATE
VATICAN RADIO, Sta Maria di Galeria — E Asia • 500 kW / SE Asia • 250/500 kW

9605 **CHINA**
†CHINA RADIO INTL, Xi'an — W • E Europe • 150 kW
GERMANY
†DEUTSCHE WELLE, Wertachtal — S • S Europe • 500 kW
IRAN
VO THE ISLAMIC REP, Sirjan — W • S Asia, SE Asia & Australasia • 500 kW
VO THE ISLAMIC REP, Various Locations — W Asia & S Asia • 250/500 kW
ITALY
†RAI INTERNATIONAL, Rome — S M-Sa • Mideast • 100 kW / S • Europe • 100 kW
MALTA
†VO MEDITERRANEAN, Via Rome, Italy — S Su • Europe • 100 kW / S M-Sa • Europe • 100 kW • ALT. FREQ. TO 6185 kHz
SWEDEN
†IBRA RADIO, Via Jülich, Germany — S • N Africa • 100 kW
UNITED KINGDOM
†BBC, Via Seychelles — W • W Africa • 250 kW
†BBC, Via Thailand — S Asia • 250 kW
BBC, Via Tokyo, Japan — E Asia • 300 kW
USA
†FAMILY RADIO, Okeechobee, Fl — S America • 100 kW / C America • 100 kW / S • C America • 100 kW
†R FREE ASIA, Via Tinian, N Marianas — S • E Asia • 500 kW
†RADIO SAWA, Via Kavála, Greece — W • Mideast • 250 kW
†RFE-RL, Via Kavála, Greece — W • W Asia • 250 kW
VATICAN STATE
VATICAN RADIO, Sta Maria di Galeria — S America • 250 kW / C America • 250/500 kW / E North Am & C America • 250/500 kW

9610 **CHINA**
CENTRAL PEOPLE'S BS, Beijing — DS-8 (MINORITIES) • 50 kW
CHINA (TAIWAN)
†R TAIWAN INTL — Australasia
CLANDESTINE (M EAST)
"VO PALESTINIAN ISLAMIC REV'N", Iran — S • Mideast • ANTI-ARAFAT • 250 kW
CONGO (REPUBLIC)
RTV CONGOLAISE, Brazzaville — FRENCH, ETC • DS • 50/100 kW
GERMANY
†DEUTSCHE WELLE, Via Sri Lanka — W • SE Asia • 250 kW / S • E Asia • 250 kW
IRAN
VO THE ISLAMIC REP, Tehrän — S • E North Am & C America • 500 kW / S Europe • 500 kW
UKRAINE
†RADIO UKRAINE, Kharkiv — W • W Asia • 100 kW
UNITED KINGDOM
†BBC, Rampisham — S M-F • S Europe • 500 kW / W Africa & C Africa • 250 kW
†BBC, Via Ascension — W Africa • 250 kW
BBC, Via Meyerton, South Africa — S • E Africa & C Africa • 250 kW
BBC, Via Seychelles — E Africa • 250 kW / S • E Asia • 250 kW
†BBC, Via Thailand — S • S Europe • 250 kW
†BBC, Via Zyyi, Cyprus — S Asia • 250 kW
†BIBLE VOICE, Via Dhabayya, UAE

9615 **BRAZIL**
RADIO CULTURA, São Paulo — DS • 7.5 kW •
CANADA
R CANADA INTL, Via Germany — W • Mideast • 500 kW / W • N Africa • 500 kW
GERMANY
†DEUTSCHE WELLE, Via Sri Lanka — W • S Asia • 250 kW
†DEUTSCHE WELLE, Wertachtal — W • W Africa • 500 kW
IRAN
VO THE ISLAMIC REP, Tehrän — W • Mideast & W Asia • 500 kW
(con'd) VO THE ISLAMIC REP, Zähedän — W • S Europe • 500 kW

0 1 2 3 4 5 6 7 8 9 10 11 12 13 14 15 16 17 18 19 20 21 22 23 24

SEASONAL S OR W   1-HR TIMESHIFT MIDYEAR ⇦ OR ⇨   JAMMING / OR /\   EARLIEST HEARD ◁   LATEST HEARD ▷   NEW FOR 2004 †

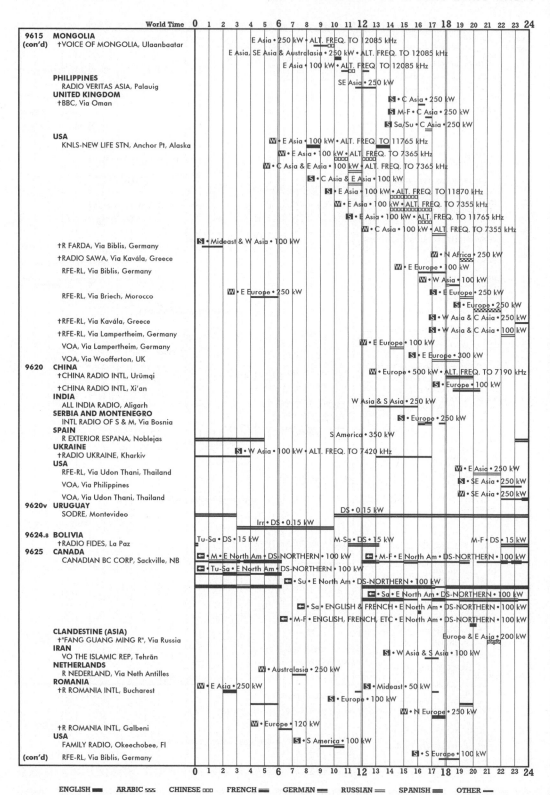

World Time 0 1 2 3 4 5 6 7 8 9 10 11 12 13 14 15 16 17 18 19 20 21 22 23 24

9615 **MONGOLIA**
(con'd) †VOICE OF MONGOLIA, Ulaanbaatar
E Asia • 250 kW • ALT. FREQ. TO 12085 kHz
E Asia, SE Asia & Australasia • 250 kW • ALT. FREQ. TO 12085 kHz
E Asia • 100 kW • ALT. FREQ. TO 12085 kHz

PHILIPPINES
RADIO VERITAS ASIA, Palauig
SE Asia • 250 kW
UNITED KINGDOM
†BBC, Via Oman
S • C Asia • 250 kW
S M-F • C Asia • 250 kW
S Sa/Su • C Asia • 250 kW

USA
KNLS-NEW LIFE STN, Anchor Pt, Alaska
W • E Asia • 100 kW • ALT. FREQ. TO 11765 kHz
W • E Asia • 100 kW • ALT. FREQ. TO 7365 kHz
W • C Asia & E Asia • 100 kW • ALT. FREQ. TO 7365 kHz
S • C Asia & E Asia • 100 kW
S • E Asia • 100 kW • ALT. FREQ. TO 11870 kHz
W • E Asia • 100 kW • ALT. FREQ. TO 7355 kHz
S • E Asia • 100 kW • ALT. FREQ. TO 11765 kHz
W • C Asia • 100 kW • ALT. FREQ. TO 7355 kHz

†R FARDA, Via Biblis, Germany
S • Mideast & W Asia • 100 kW
†RADIO SAWA, Via Kavála, Greece
W • N Africa • 250 kW
RFE-RL, Via Biblis, Germany
W • E Europe • 100 kW
W • W Asia • 100 kW
RFE-RL, Via Briech, Morocco
W • E Europe • 250 kW
S • E Europe • 250 kW
S • Europe • 250 kW
†RFE-RL, Via Kavála, Greece
S • W Asia & C Asia • 250 kW
†RFE-RL, Via Lampertheim, Germany
S • W Asia & C Asia • 100 kW
VOA, Via Lampertheim, Germany
W • E Europe • 100 kW
VOA, Via Woofferton, UK
S • E Europe • 300 kW
9620 **CHINA**
†CHINA RADIO INTL, Urümqi
W • Europe • 500 kW • ALT. FREQ. TO 7190 kHz
†CHINA RADIO INTL, Xi'an
S • Europe • 100 kW
INDIA
ALL INDIA RADIO, Aligarh
W Asia & S Asia • 250 kW
SERBIA AND MONTENEGRO
INTL RADIO OF S & M, Via Bosnia
S • Europe • 250 kW
SPAIN
R EXTERIOR ESPANA, Noblejas
S America • 350 kW
UKRAINE
†RADIO UKRAINE, Kharkiv
S • W Asia • 100 kW • ALT. FREQ. TO 7420 kHz
USA
RFE-RL, Via Udon Thani, Thailand
W • E Asia • 250 kW
VOA, Via Philippines
S • SE Asia • 250 kW
VOA, Via Udon Thani, Thailand
W • SE Asia • 250 kW
9620v **URUGUAY**
SODRE, Montevideo
DS • 0.15 kW
Irr • DS • 0.15 kW

9624.8 **BOLIVIA**
†RADIO FIDES, La Paz
Tu-Sa • DS • 15 kW   M-Sa • DS • 15 kW   M-F • DS • 15 kW
9625 **CANADA**
CANADIAN BC CORP, Sackville, NB
M • E North Am • DS-NORTHERN • 100 kW   M-F • E North Am • DS-NORTHERN • 100 kW
Tu-Sa • E North Am • DS-NORTHERN • 100 kW
Su • E North Am • DS-NORTHERN • 100 kW
Sa • E North Am • DS-NORTHERN • 100 kW
Sa • ENGLISH & FRENCH • E North Am • DS-NORTHERN • 100 kW
M-F • ENGLISH, FRENCH, ETC • E North Am • DS-NORTHERN • 100 kW

CLANDESTINE (ASIA)
†"FANG GUANG MING R", Via Russia
Europe & E Asia • 200 kW
IRAN
VO THE ISLAMIC REP, Tehrān
S • W Asia & S Asia • 100 kW
NETHERLANDS
R NEDERLAND, Via Neth Antilles
W • Australasia • 250 kW
ROMANIA
†R ROMANIA INTL, Bucharest
W • E Asia • 250 kW
S • Mideast • 50 kW
S • Europe • 100 kW
W • N Europe • 250 kW
†R ROMANIA INTL, Galbeni
W • Europe • 120 kW
USA
FAMILY RADIO, Okeechobee, Fl
S • S America • 100 kW
(con'd) RFE-RL, Via Biblis, Germany
S • S Europe • 100 kW

0 1 2 3 4 5 6 7 8 9 10 11 12 13 14 15 16 17 18 19 20 21 22 23 24

ENGLISH ■■   ARABIC ▨▨   CHINESE ▫▫▫   FRENCH ▬▬   GERMAN ▬▬   RUSSIAN ══   SPANISH ▬▬   OTHER ▬

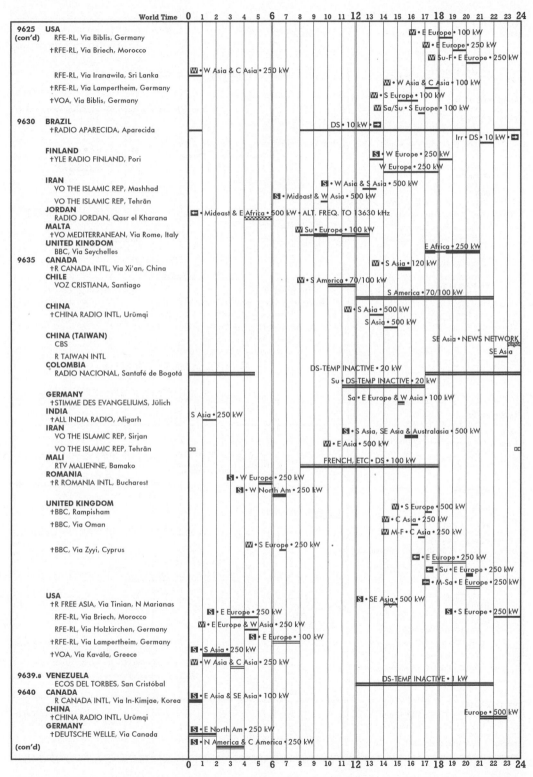

World Time

Freq	Country / Station	Details
9625 (con'd)	USA	
	RFE-RL, Via Biblis, Germany	W • E Europe • 100 kW
	†RFE-RL, Via Briech, Morocco	W • E Europe • 250 kW / W Su-F • E Europe • 250 kW
	RFE-RL, Via Iranawila, Sri Lanka	W • W Asia & C Asia • 250 kW
	†RFE-RL, Via Lampertheim, Germany	W • W Asia & C Asia • 100 kW
	†VOA, Via Biblis, Germany	W • S Europe • 100 kW / W Sa/Su • S Europe • 100 kW
9630	BRAZIL	
	†RADIO APARECIDA, Aparecida	DS • 10 kW • → / Irr • DS • 10 kW • →
	FINLAND	
	†YLE RADIO FINLAND, Pori	S • W Europe • 250 kW / W Europe • 250 kW
	IRAN	
	VO THE ISLAMIC REP, Mashhad	S • W Asia & S Asia • 500 kW
	VO THE ISLAMIC REP, Tehrān	S • Mideast & W Asia • 500 kW
	JORDAN	
	RADIO JORDAN, Qasr el Kharana	← • Mideast & E Africa • 500 kW • ALT. FREQ. TO 13630 kHz
	MALTA	
	†VO MEDITERRANEAN, Via Rome, Italy	W Su • Europe • 100 kW
	UNITED KINGDOM	
	BBC, Via Seychelles	E Africa • 250 kW
9635	CANADA	
	†R CANADA INTL, Via Xi'an, China	W • S Asia • 120 kW
	CHILE	
	VOZ CRISTIANA, Santiago	W • S America • 70/100 kW / S America • 70/100 kW
	CHINA	
	†CHINA RADIO INTL, Urümqi	W • S Asia • 500 kW / S Asia • 500 kW
	CHINA (TAIWAN)	
	CBS	SE Asia • NEWS NETWORK
	R TAIWAN INTL	SE Asia
	COLOMBIA	
	RADIO NACIONAL, Santafé de Bogotá	DS-TEMP INACTIVE • 20 kW / Su • DS-TEMP INACTIVE • 20 kW
	GERMANY	
	†STIMME DES EVANGELIUMS, Jülich	Sa • E Europe & W Asia • 100 kW
	INDIA	
	†ALL INDIA RADIO, Aligarh	S Asia • 250 kW
	IRAN	
	VO THE ISLAMIC REP, Sirjan	S • S Asia, SE Asia & Australasia • 500 kW
	VO THE ISLAMIC REP, Tehrān	W • E Asia • 500 kW
	MALI	
	RTV MALIENNE, Bamako	FRENCH, ETC • DS • 100 kW
	ROMANIA	
	†R ROMANIA INTL, Bucharest	S • W Europe • 250 kW / S • W North Am • 250 kW
	UNITED KINGDOM	
	†BBC, Rampisham	W • S Europe • 500 kW
	†BBC, Via Oman	W • C Asia • 250 kW / W M-F • C Asia • 250 kW
	†BBC, Via Zyyi, Cyprus	W • S Europe • 250 kW / ← • E Europe • 250 kW / ← • Su • E Europe • 250 kW / ← • M-Sa • E Europe • 250 kW
	USA	
	†R FREE ASIA, Via Tinian, N Marianas	S • SE Asia • 500 kW
	RFE-RL, Via Briech, Morocco	S • E Europe • 250 kW / S • S Europe • 250 kW
	RFE-RL, Via Holzkirchen, Germany	W • E Europe & W Asia • 250 kW
	†RFE-RL, Via Lampertheim, Germany	S • E Europe • 100 kW
	†VOA, Via Kavála, Greece	S • S Asia • 250 kW / W • W Asia & C Asia • 250 kW
9639.8	VENEZUELA	
	ECOS DEL TORBES, San Cristóbal	DS-TEMP INACTIVE • 1 kW
9640	CANADA	
	R CANADA INTL, Via In-Kimjae, Korea	S • E Asia & SE Asia • 100 kW
	CHINA	
	†CHINA RADIO INTL, Urümqi	Europe • 500 kW
	GERMANY	
	†DEUTSCHE WELLE, Via Canada	S • E North Am • 250 kW / S • N America & C America • 250 kW
(con'd)		

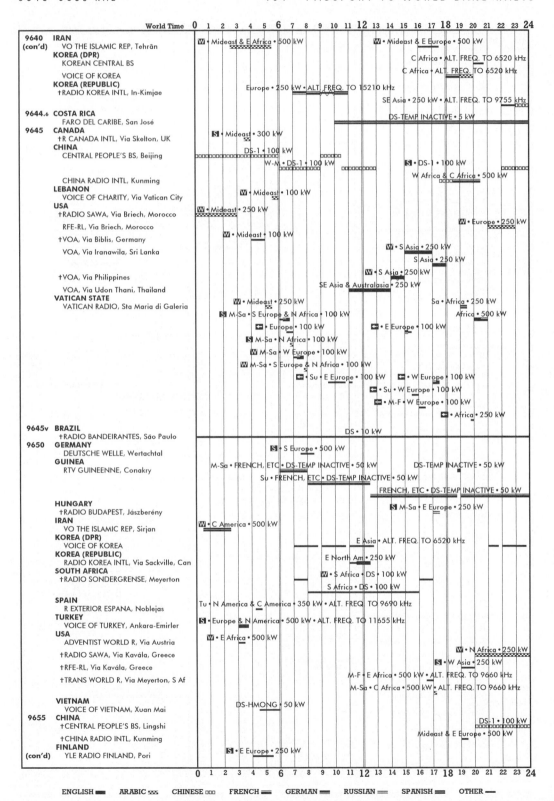

World Time	0 1 2 3 4 5 6 7 8 9 10 11 12 13 14 15 16 17 18 19 20 21 22 23 24
9640 **IRAN**	
(con'd) VO THE ISLAMIC REP, Tehrān	W • Mideast & E Africa • 500 kW W • Mideast & E Europe • 500 kW
KOREA (DPR)	
KOREAN CENTRAL BS	C Africa • ALT. FREQ. TO 6520 kHz
VOICE OF KOREA	C Africa • ALT. FREQ. TO 6520 kHz
KOREA (REPUBLIC)	
†RADIO KOREA INTL, In-Kimjae	Europe • 250 kW • ALT. FREQ. TO 15210 kHz
	SE Asia • 250 kW • ALT. FREQ. TO 9755 kHz
9644.6 COSTA RICA	
FARO DEL CARIBE, San José	DS-TEMP INACTIVE • 5 kW
9645 CANADA	
†R CANADA INTL, Via Skelton, UK	S • Mideast • 300 kW
CHINA	
CENTRAL PEOPLE'S BS, Beijing	DS-1 • 100 kW
	W-M • DS-1 • 100 kW
	S • DS-1 • 100 kW
CHINA RADIO INTL, Kunming	W Africa & C Africa • 500 kW
LEBANON	
VOICE OF CHARITY, Via Vatican City	W • Mideast • 100 kW
USA	
†RADIO SAWA, Via Briech, Morocco	W • Mideast • 250 kW
RFE-RL, Via Briech, Morocco	W • Europe • 250 kW
†VOA, Via Biblis, Germany	W • Mideast • 100 kW
VOA, Via Iranawila, Sri Lanka	W • S Asia • 250 kW
	S Asia • 250 kW
†VOA, Via Philippines	W • S Asia • 250 kW
VOA, Via Udon Thani, Thailand	SE Asia & Australasia • 250 kW
VATICAN STATE	
VATICAN RADIO, Sta Maria di Galeria	W • Mideast • 250 kW Sa • Africa • 250 kW
	S • M-Sa • S Europe & N Africa • 100 kW Africa • 500 kW
	• Europe • 100 kW • E Europe • 100 kW
	S • M-Sa • N Africa • 100 kW
	W • M-Sa • W Europe • 100 kW
	W • M-Sa • S Europe & N Africa • 100 kW
	• Su • E Europe • 100 kW • W Europe • 100 kW
	• Su • W Europe • 100 kW
	• M-F • W Europe • 100 kW
	• Africa • 250 kW
9645v BRAZIL	
†RADIO BANDEIRANTES, São Paulo	DS • 10 kW
9650 GERMANY	
DEUTSCHE WELLE, Wertachtal	S • S Europe • 500 kW
GUINEA	
RTV GUINEENNE, Conakry	M-Sa • FRENCH, ETC • DS-TEMP INACTIVE • 50 kW DS-TEMP INACTIVE • 50 kW
	Su • FRENCH, ETC • DS-TEMP INACTIVE • 50 kW
	FRENCH, ETC • DS-TEMP INACTIVE • 50 kW
HUNGARY	
†RADIO BUDAPEST, Jászberény	S • M-Sa • E Europe • 250 kW
IRAN	
VO THE ISLAMIC REP, Sirjan	W • C America • 500 kW
KOREA (DPR)	
VOICE OF KOREA	E Asia • ALT. FREQ. TO 6520 kHz
KOREA (REPUBLIC)	
RADIO KOREA INTL, Via Sackville, Can	E North Am • 250 kW
SOUTH AFRICA	
†RADIO SONDERGRENSE, Meyerton	W • S Africa • DS • 100 kW
	S Africa • DS • 100 kW
SPAIN	
R EXTERIOR ESPANA, Noblejas	Tu • N America & C America • 350 kW • ALT. FREQ. TO 9690 kHz
TURKEY	
VOICE OF TURKEY, Ankara-Emirler	S • Europe & N America • 500 kW • ALT. FREQ. TO 11655 kHz
USA	
ADVENTIST WORLD R, Via Austria	W • E Africa • 500 kW
†RADIO SAWA, Via Kavála, Greece	W • N Africa • 250 kW
†RFE-RL, Via Kavála, Greece	S • W Asia • 250 kW
†TRANS WORLD R, Via Meyerton, S Af	M-F • E Africa • 500 kW • ALT. FREQ. TO 9660 kHz
	M-Sa • C Africa • 500 kW • ALT. FREQ. TO 9660 kHz
VIETNAM	
VOICE OF VIETNAM, Xuan Mai	DS-HMONG • 50 kW
9655 CHINA	
†CENTRAL PEOPLE'S BS, Lingshi	DS-1 • 100 kW
†CHINA RADIO INTL, Kunming	Mideast & E Europe • 500 kW
FINLAND	
(con'd) YLE RADIO FINLAND, Pori	S • E Europe • 250 kW

0 1 2 3 4 5 6 7 8 9 10 11 12 13 14 15 16 17 18 19 20 21 22 23 24

ENGLISH ▬   ARABIC ░░░   CHINESE □□□   FRENCH ═══   GERMAN ▬▬   RUSSIAN ══   SPANISH ▬▬   OTHER ──

World Time

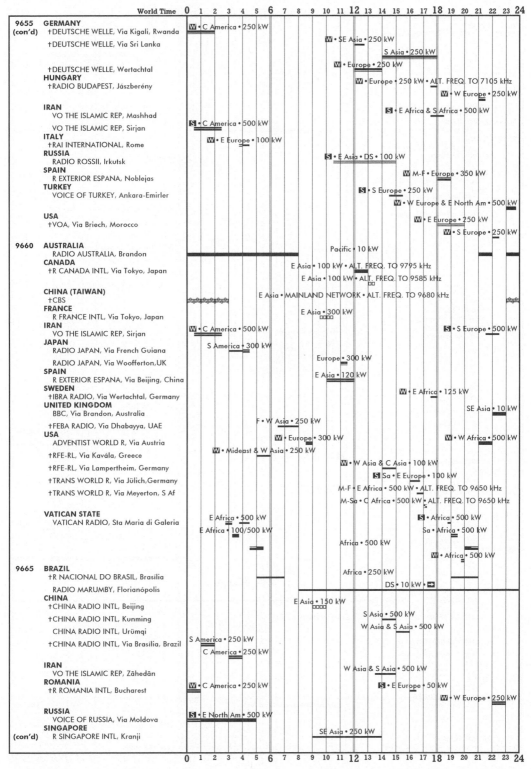

9655 (con'd)	**GERMANY**
	†DEUTSCHE WELLE, Via Kigali, Rwanda
	†DEUTSCHE WELLE, Via Sri Lanka
	†DEUTSCHE WELLE, Wertachtal
	HUNGARY
	†RADIO BUDAPEST, Jászberény
	IRAN
	VO THE ISLAMIC REP, Mashhad
	VO THE ISLAMIC REP, Sirjan
	ITALY
	†RAI INTERNATIONAL, Rome
	RUSSIA
	RADIO ROSSII, Irkutsk
	SPAIN
	R EXTERIOR ESPANA, Noblejas
	TURKEY
	VOICE OF TURKEY, Ankara-Emirler
	USA
	†VOA, Via Briech, Morocco
9660	**AUSTRALIA**
	RADIO AUSTRALIA, Brandon
	CANADA
	†R CANADA INTL, Via Tokyo, Japan
	CHINA (TAIWAN)
	†CBS
	FRANCE
	R FRANCE INTL, Via Tokyo, Japan
	IRAN
	VO THE ISLAMIC REP, Sirjan
	JAPAN
	RADIO JAPAN, Via French Guiana
	RADIO JAPAN, Via Woofferton, UK
	SPAIN
	R EXTERIOR ESPANA, Via Beijing, China
	SWEDEN
	†IBRA RADIO, Via Wertachtal, Germany
	UNITED KINGDOM
	BBC, Via Brandon, Australia
	†FEBA RADIO, Via Dhabayya, UAE
	USA
	ADVENTIST WORLD R, Via Austria
	†RFE-RL, Via Kavála, Greece
	†RFE-RL, Via Lampertheim, Germany
	†TRANS WORLD R, Via Jülich, Germany
	†TRANS WORLD R, Via Meyerton, S Af
	VATICAN STATE
	VATICAN RADIO, Sta Maria di Galeria
9665	**BRAZIL**
	†R NACIONAL DO BRASIL, Brasilia
	RADIO MARUMBY, Florianópolis
	CHINA
	†CHINA RADIO INTL, Beijing
	†CHINA RADIO INTL, Kunming
	CHINA RADIO INTL, Urümqi
	†CHINA RADIO INTL, Via Brasilia, Brazil
	IRAN
	VO THE ISLAMIC REP, Zähedän
	ROMANIA
	†R ROMANIA INTL, Bucharest
	RUSSIA
	VOICE OF RUSSIA, Via Moldova
	SINGAPORE
(con'd)	R SINGAPORE INTL, Kranji

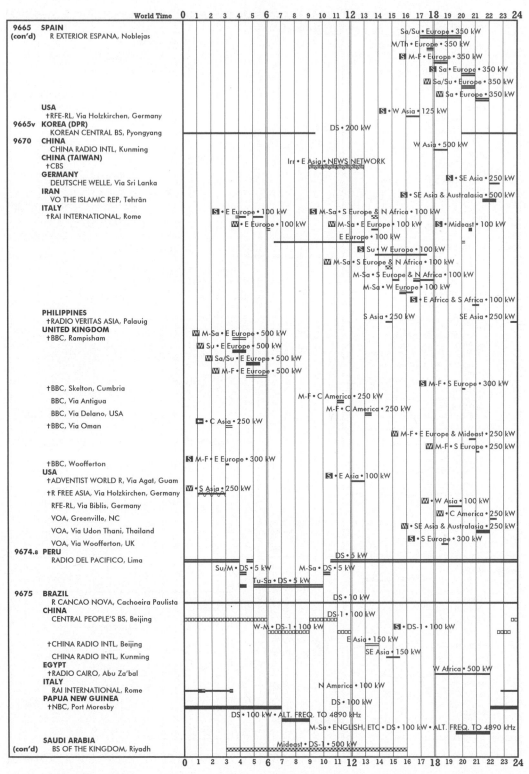

		World Time	0 1 2 3 4 5 6 7 8 9 10 11 12 13 14 15 16 17 18 19 20 21 22 23 24

9665 SPAIN
(con'd)   R EXTERIOR ESPANA, Noblejas
Sa/Su • Europe • 350 kW
M/Th • Europe • 350 kW
⑤ M-F • Europe • 350 kW
⑤ Sa • Europe • 350 kW
Ⓦ Sa/Su • Europe • 350 kW
Ⓦ Sa • Europe • 350 kW

USA
†RFE-RL, Via Holzkirchen, Germany
⑤ • W Asia • 125 kW
9665v KOREA (DPR)
KOREAN CENTRAL BS, Pyongyang
DS • 200 kW
9670 CHINA
CHINA RADIO INTL, Kunming
W Asia • 500 kW
CHINA (TAIWAN)
†CBS
Irr • E Asia • NEWS NETWORK
GERMANY
DEUTSCHE WELLE, Via Sri Lanka
⑤ • SE Asia • 250 kW
IRAN
VO THE ISLAMIC REP, Tehrān
⑤ • SE Asia & Australasia • 500 kW
ITALY
†RAI INTERNATIONAL, Rome
⑤ • E Europe • 100 kW   ⑤ M-Sa • S Europe & N Africa • 100 kW
Ⓦ • E Europe • 100 kW   Ⓦ M-Sa • E Europe • 100 kW   ⑤ • Mideast • 100 kW
E Europe • 100 kW
⑤ Su • W Europe • 100 kW
Ⓦ M-Sa • S Europe & N Africa • 100 kW
M-Sa • S Europe & N Africa • 100 kW
M-Sa • W Europe • 100 kW
⑤ • E Africa & S Africa • 100 kW

PHILIPPINES
†RADIO VERITAS ASIA, Palauig
S Asia • 250 kW   SE Asia • 250 kW
UNITED KINGDOM
†BBC, Rampisham
Ⓦ M-Sa • E Europe • 500 kW
Ⓦ Su • E Europe • 500 kW
Ⓦ Sa/Su • E Europe • 500 kW
Ⓦ M-F • E Europe • 500 kW
⑤ M-F • S Europe • 300 kW

†BBC, Skelton, Cumbria
M-F • C America • 250 kW
BBC, Via Antigua
M-F • C America • 250 kW
BBC, Via Delano, USA
• C Asia • 250 kW
†BBC, Via Oman
Ⓦ M-F • E Europe & Mideast • 250 kW
Ⓦ M-F • S Europe • 250 kW
†BBC, Woofferton
⑤ M-F • E Europe • 300 kW
USA
†ADVENTIST WORLD R, Via Agat, Guam
⑤ • E Asia • 100 kW
†R FREE ASIA, Via Holzkirchen, Germany
Ⓦ • S Asia • 250 kW
RFE-RL, Via Biblis, Germany
Ⓦ • W Asia • 100 kW
VOA, Greenville, NC
Ⓦ • C America • 250 kW
VOA, Via Udon Thani, Thailand
Ⓦ • SE Asia & Australasia • 250 kW
VOA, Via Woofferton, UK
⑤ • S Europe • 300 kW
9674.8 PERU
RADIO DEL PACIFICO, Lima
DS • 5 kW
Su/M • DS • 5 kW   M-Sa • DS • 5 kW
Tu-Sa • DS • 5 kW

9675 BRAZIL
R CANCAO NOVA, Cachoeira Paulista
DS • 10 kW
CHINA
CENTRAL PEOPLE'S BS, Beijing
DS-1 • 100 kW
W-M • DS-1 • 100 kW   ⑤ • DS-1 • 100 kW
†CHINA RADIO INTL, Beijing
E Asia • 150 kW
CHINA RADIO INTL, Kunming
SE Asia • 150 kW
EGYPT
†RADIO CAIRO, Abu Za'bal
W Africa • 500 kW
ITALY
RAI INTERNATIONAL, Rome
N America • 100 kW
PAPUA NEW GUINEA
†NBC, Port Moresby
DS • 100 kW
DS • 100 kW • ALT. FREQ. TO 4890 kHz
M-Sa • ENGLISH, ETC • DS • 100 kW • ALT. FREQ. TO 4890 kHz
SAUDI ARABIA
(con'd)   BS OF THE KINGDOM, Riyadh
Mideast • DS-1 • 500 kW

	0 1 2 3 4 5 6 7 8 9 10 11 12 13 14 15 16 17 18 19 20 21 22 23 24

ENGLISH ▬ ARABIC ▨ CHINESE □□□ FRENCH ═ GERMAN ▬ RUSSIAN ═ SPANISH ▬ OTHER ─

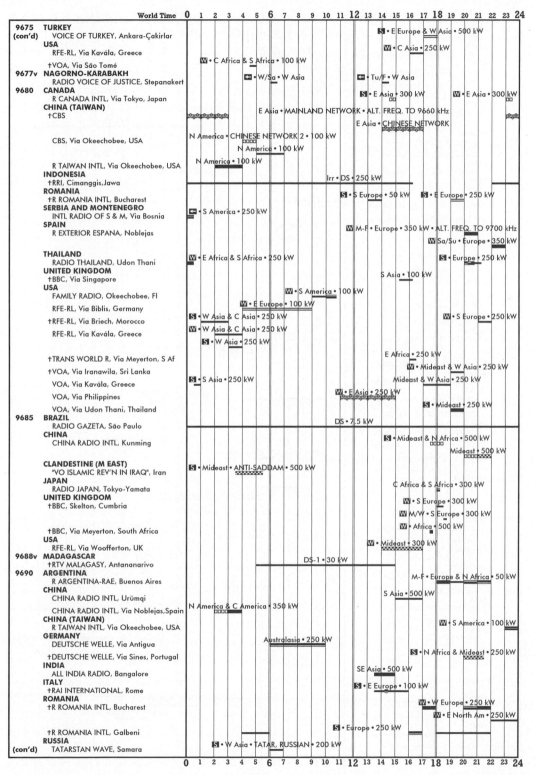

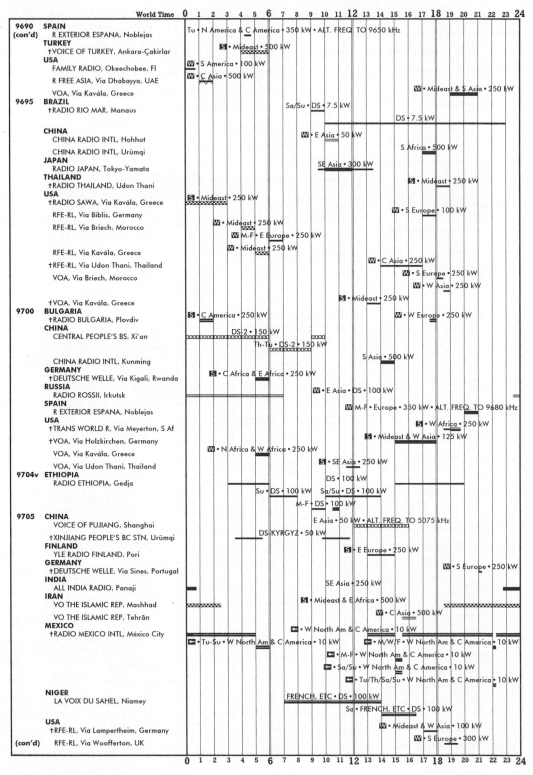

	World Time	0 1 2 3 4 5 6 7 8 9 10 11 12 13 14 15 16 17 18 19 20 21 22 23 24
9690 (con'd)	**SPAIN** R EXTERIOR ESPANA, Noblejas	Tu • N America & C America • 350 kW • ALT. FREQ. TO 9650 kHz
	TURKEY †VOICE OF TURKEY, Ankara-Çakirlar	S • Mideast • 500 kW
	USA FAMILY RADIO, Okeechobee, Fl	W • S America • 100 kW
	R FREE ASIA, Via Dhabayya, UAE	W • C Asia • 500 kW
	VOA, Via Kavála, Greece	W • Mideast & S Asia • 250 kW
9695	**BRAZIL** †RADIO RIO MAR, Manaus	Sa/Su • DS • 7.5 kW DS • 7.5 kW
	CHINA CHINA RADIO INTL, Hohhot	W • E Asia • 50 kW
	CHINA RADIO INTL, Urümqi	S Africa • 500 kW
	JAPAN RADIO JAPAN, Tokyo-Yamata	SE Asia • 300 kW
	THAILAND †RADIO THAILAND, Udon Thani	S • Mideast • 250 kW
	USA †RADIO SAWA, Via Kavála, Greece	S • Mideast • 250 kW
	RFE-RL, Via Biblis, Germany	W • S Europe • 100 kW
	RFE-RL, Via Briech, Morocco	W • Mideast • 250 kW M-F • E Europe • 250 kW
	RFE-RL, Via Kavála, Greece	W • Mideast • 250 kW
	†RFE-RL, Via Udon Thani, Thailand	W • C Asia • 250 kW
	VOA, Via Briech, Morocco	W • S Europe • 250 kW
		W • W Asia • 250 kW
	†VOA, Via Kavála, Greece	S • Mideast • 250 kW
9700	**BULGARIA** †RADIO BULGARIA, Plovdiv	S • C America • 250 kW W • W Europe • 250 kW
	CHINA CENTRAL PEOPLE'S BS, Xi'an	DS-2 • 150 kW Th-Tu • DS-2 • 150 kW
	CHINA RADIO INTL, Kunming	S Asia • 500 kW
	GERMANY †DEUTSCHE WELLE, Via Kigali, Rwanda	S • C Africa & E Africa • 250 kW
	RUSSIA RADIO ROSSII, Irkutsk	W • E Asia • DS • 100 kW
	SPAIN R EXTERIOR ESPANA, Noblejas	W M-F • Europe • 350 kW • ALT. FREQ. TO 9680 kHz
	USA †TRANS WORLD R, Via Meyerton, S Af	S • W Africa • 250 kW
	†VOA, Via Holzkirchen, Germany	S • Mideast & W Asia • 125 kW
	VOA, Via Kavála, Greece	W • N Africa & W Africa • 250 kW
	VOA, Via Udon Thani, Thailand	S • SE Asia • 250 kW
9704v	**ETHIOPIA** RADIO ETHIOPIA, Gedja	DS • 100 kW Su • DS • 100 kW Sa/Su • DS • 100 kW M-F • DS • 100 kW
9705	**CHINA** VOICE OF PUJIANG, Shanghai	E Asia • 50 kW • ALT. FREQ. TO 5075 kHz
	†XINJIANG PEOPLE'S BC STN, Urümqi	DS KYRGYZ • 50 kW
	FINLAND YLE RADIO FINLAND, Pori	S • E Europe • 250 kW
	GERMANY †DEUTSCHE WELLE, Via Sines, Portugal	W • S Europe • 250 kW
	INDIA ALL INDIA RADIO, Panaji	SE Asia • 250 kW
	IRAN VO THE ISLAMIC REP, Mashhad	S • Mideast & E Africa • 500 kW
	VO THE ISLAMIC REP, Tehrān	W • C Asia • 500 kW
	MEXICO †RADIO MEXICO INTL, México City	⇨ • W North Am & C America • 10 kW
		⇨ • Tu-Su • W North Am & C America • 10 kW ⇨ • M/W/F • W North Am & C America • 10 kW
		⇨ • M-F • W North Am & C America • 10 kW
		⇨ • Sa/Su • W North Am & C America • 10 kW
		⇨ • Tu/Th/Sa/Su • W North Am & C America • 10 kW
	NIGER LA VOIX DU SAHEL, Niamey	FRENCH, ETC • DS • 100 kW Sa • FRENCH, ETC • DS • 100 kW
	USA †RFE-RL, Via Lampertheim, Germany	W • Mideast & W Asia • 100 kW
(con'd)	RFE-RL, Via Woofferton, UK	W • S Europe • 300 kW

World Time   0 1 2 3 4 5 6 7 8 9 10 11 12 13 14 15 16 17 18 19 20 21 22 23 24

ENGLISH ■■■   ARABIC ⋙   CHINESE ⊡⊡⊡   FRENCH ══   GERMAN ▬▬   RUSSIAN ══   SPANISH ▬▬   OTHER ──

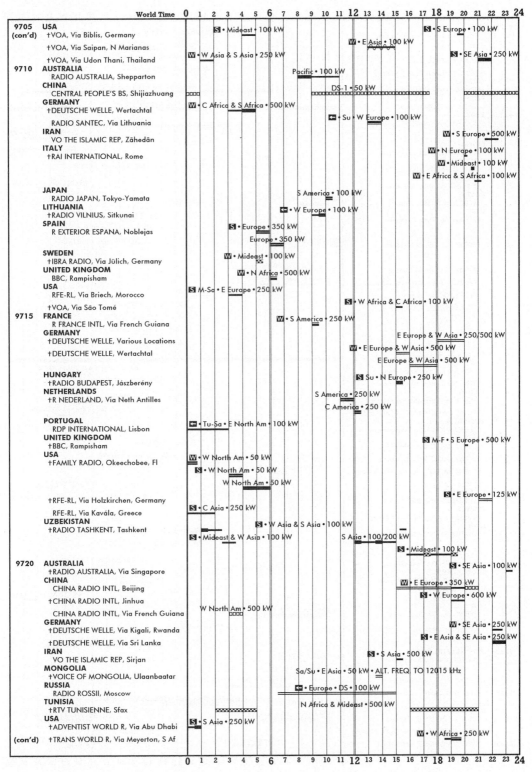

World Time 0 1 2 3 4 5 6 7 8 9 10 11 12 13 14 15 16 17 18 19 20 21 22 23 24

9705
(con'd)   USA
   †VOA, Via Biblis, Germany — S • Mideast • 100 kW — S • S Europe • 100 kW
   †VOA, Via Saipan, N Marianas — W • E Asia • 100 kW
   †VOA, Via Udon Thani, Thailand — W • W Asia & S Asia • 250 kW — S • SE Asia • 250 kW

9710   AUSTRALIA
   RADIO AUSTRALIA, Shepparton — Pacific • 100 kW
   CHINA
     CENTRAL PEOPLE'S BS, Shijiazhuang — DS-1 • 50 kW
   GERMANY
   †DEUTSCHE WELLE, Wertachtal — W • C Africa & S Africa • 500 kW
   RADIO SANTEC, Via Lithuania — ⟷ • Su • W Europe • 100 kW
   IRAN
     VO THE ISLAMIC REP, Zāhedān — W • S Europe • 500 kW
   ITALY
   †RAI INTERNATIONAL, Rome — W • N Europe • 100 kW
     — W • Mideast • 100 kW
     — W • E Africa & S Africa • 100 kW
   JAPAN
     RADIO JAPAN, Tokyo-Yamata — S America • 100 kW
   LITHUANIA
   †RADIO VILNIUS, Sitkunai — ⟷ • W Europe • 100 kW
   SPAIN
     R EXTERIOR ESPANA, Noblejas — S • Europe • 350 kW
     — Europe • 350 kW
   SWEDEN
   †IBRA RADIO, Via Jülich, Germany — W • Mideast • 100 kW
   UNITED KINGDOM
     BBC, Rampisham — W • N Africa • 500 kW
   USA
     RFE-RL, Via Briech, Morocco — S • M-Sa • E Europe • 250 kW
   †VOA, Via São Tomé — S • W Africa & C Africa • 100 kW

9715   FRANCE
     R FRANCE INTL, Via French Guiana — W • S America • 250 kW
   GERMANY
   †DEUTSCHE WELLE, Various Locations — E Europe & W Asia • 250/500 kW
   †DEUTSCHE WELLE, Wertachtal — W • E Europe & W Asia • 500 kW
     — E Europe & W Asia • 500 kW
   HUNGARY
   †RADIO BUDAPEST, Jászberény — S • Su • N Europe • 250 kW
   NETHERLANDS
   †R NEDERLAND, Via Neth Antilles — S America • 250 kW
     — C America • 250 kW
   PORTUGAL
     RDP INTERNATIONAL, Lisbon — ⟷ • Tu-Sa • E North Am • 100 kW
   UNITED KINGDOM
   †BBC, Rampisham — S • M-F • S Europe • 500 kW
   USA
   †FAMILY RADIO, Okeechobee, Fl — W • W North Am • 50 kW
     — S • W North Am • 50 kW
     — W North Am • 50 kW
   †RFE-RL, Via Holzkirchen, Germany — S • E Europe • 125 kW
   RFE-RL, Via Kavála, Greece — S • C Asia • 250 kW
   UZBEKISTAN
   †RADIO TASHKENT, Tashkent — S • W Asia & S Asia • 100 kW
     — S • Mideast & W Asia • 100 kW
     — S Asia • 100/200 kW
     — S • Mideast • 100 kW

9720   AUSTRALIA
   †RADIO AUSTRALIA, Via Singapore — S • SE Asia • 100 kW
   CHINA
     CHINA RADIO INTL, Beijing — W • E Europe • 350 kW
   †CHINA RADIO INTL, Jinhua — S • W Europe • 600 kW
     CHINA RADIO INTL, Via French Guiana — W North Am • 500 kW
   GERMANY
   †DEUTSCHE WELLE, Via Kigali, Rwanda — W • SE Asia • 250 kW
   †DEUTSCHE WELLE, Via Sri Lanka — S • E Asia & SE Asia • 250 kW
   IRAN
     VO THE ISLAMIC REP, Sirjan — S • S Asia • 500 kW
   MONGOLIA
   †VOICE OF MONGOLIA, Ulaanbaatar — Sa/Su • E Asia • 50 kW • ALT. FREQ. TO 12015 kHz
   RUSSIA
     RADIO ROSSII, Moscow — ⟷ • Europe • DS • 100 kW
   TUNISIA
   †RTV TUNISIENNE, Sfax — N Africa & Mideast • 500 kW
   USA
   †ADVENTIST WORLD R, Via Abu Dhabi — S • S Asia • 250 kW
(con'd)   †TRANS WORLD R, Via Meyerton, S Af — W • W Africa • 250 kW

SEASONAL S OR W   1-HR TIMESHIFT MIDYEAR ⟸ OR ⟹   JAMMING / OR ∧   EARLIEST HEARD ◁   LATEST HEARD ▷   NEW FOR 2004 †

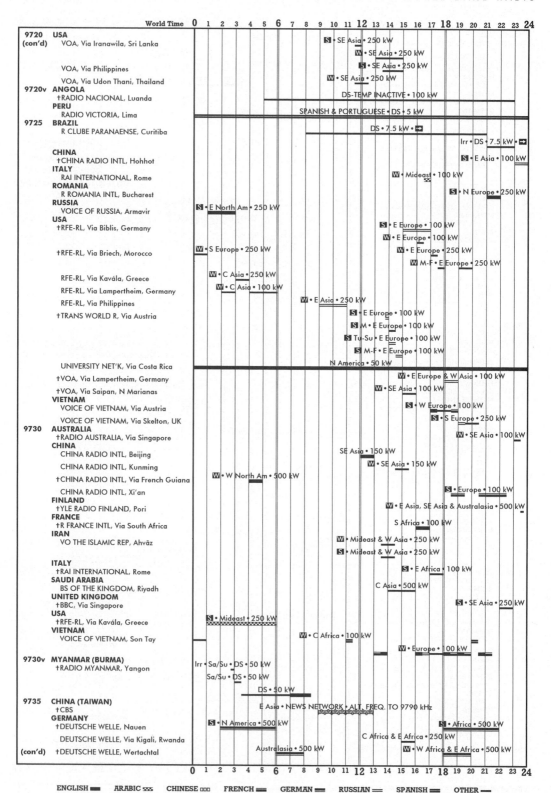

		World Time	

9720 USA
(con'd)   VOA, Via Iranawila, Sri Lanka — S • SE Asia • 250 kW
     W • SE Asia • 250 kW
     VOA, Via Philippines — S • SE Asia • 250 kW
     VOA, Via Udon Thani, Thailand — W • SE Asia • 250 kW
9720v ANGOLA
     †RADIO NACIONAL, Luanda — DS-TEMP INACTIVE • 100 kW
PERU
     RADIO VICTORIA, Lima — SPANISH & PORTUGUESE • DS • 5 kW
9725 BRAZIL
     R CLUBE PARANAENSE, Curitiba — DS • 7.5 kW •
     Irr • DS • 7.5 kW •
CHINA
     †CHINA RADIO INTL, Hohhot — S • E Asia • 100 kW
ITALY
     RAI INTERNATIONAL, Rome — W • Mideast • 100 kW
ROMANIA
     R ROMANIA INTL, Bucharest — S • N Europe • 250 kW
RUSSIA
     VOICE OF RUSSIA, Armavir — S • E North Am • 250 kW
USA
     †RFE-RL, Via Biblis, Germany — S • E Europe • 100 kW
     W • E Europe • 100 kW
     †RFE-RL, Via Briech, Morocco — W • S Europe • 250 kW
     W • E Europe • 250 kW
     W M-F • E Europe • 250 kW
     RFE-RL, Via Kavála, Greece — W • C Asia • 250 kW
     RFE-RL, Via Lampertheim, Germany — W • C Asia • 100 kW
     RFE-RL, Via Philippines — W • E Asia • 250 kW
     †TRANS WORLD R, Via Austria — S • E Europe • 100 kW
     S M • E Europe • 100 kW
     S Tu-Su • E Europe • 100 kW
     S M-F • E Europe • 100 kW
     UNIVERSITY NET'K, Via Costa Rica — N America • 50 kW
     †VOA, Via Lampertheim, Germany — W • E Europe & W Asia • 100 kW
     †VOA, Via Saipan, N Marianas — W • SE Asia • 100 kW
VIETNAM
     VOICE OF VIETNAM, Via Austria — S • W Europe • 100 kW
     VOICE OF VIETNAM, Via Skelton, UK — S • S Europe • 250 kW
9730 AUSTRALIA
     †RADIO AUSTRALIA, Via Singapore — W • SE Asia • 100 kW
CHINA
     CHINA RADIO INTL, Beijing — SE Asia • 150 kW
     CHINA RADIO INTL, Kunming — W • SE Asia • 150 kW
     †CHINA RADIO INTL, Via French Guiana — W • W North Am • 500 kW
     CHINA RADIO INTL, Xi'an — S • Europe • 100 kW
FINLAND
     †YLE RADIO FINLAND, Pori — W • E Asia, SE Asia & Australasia • 500 kW
FRANCE
     †R FRANCE INTL, Via South Africa — S Africa • 100 kW
IRAN
     VO THE ISLAMIC REP, Ahvāz — W • Mideast & W Asia • 250 kW
     S • Mideast & W Asia • 250 kW
ITALY
     †RAI INTERNATIONAL, Rome — S • E Africa • 100 kW
SAUDI ARABIA
     BS OF THE KINGDOM, Riyadh — C Asia • 500 kW
UNITED KINGDOM
     †BBC, Via Singapore — S • SE Asia • 250 kW
USA
     †RFE-RL, Via Kavála, Greece — S • Mideast • 250 kW
VIETNAM
     VOICE OF VIETNAM, Son Tay — W • C Africa • 100 kW
     W • Europe • 100 kW
9730v MYANMAR (BURMA)
     †RADIO MYANMAR, Yangon — Irr • Sa/Su • DS • 50 kW
     Sa/Su • DS • 50 kW
     DS • 50 kW
9735 CHINA (TAIWAN)
     †CBS — E Asia • NEWS NETWORK • ALT. FREQ. TO 9790 kHz
GERMANY
     †DEUTSCHE WELLE, Nauen — S • N America • 500 kW
     S • Africa • 500 kW
     DEUTSCHE WELLE, Via Kigali, Rwanda — C Africa & E Africa • 250 kW
(con'd)   †DEUTSCHE WELLE, Wertachtal — Australasia • 500 kW
     W • W Africa & E Africa • 500 kW

ENGLISH ▬   ARABIC ⊠   CHINESE ▫▫▫   FRENCH ═   GERMAN ▬   RUSSIAN ═   SPANISH ▬   OTHER ▬

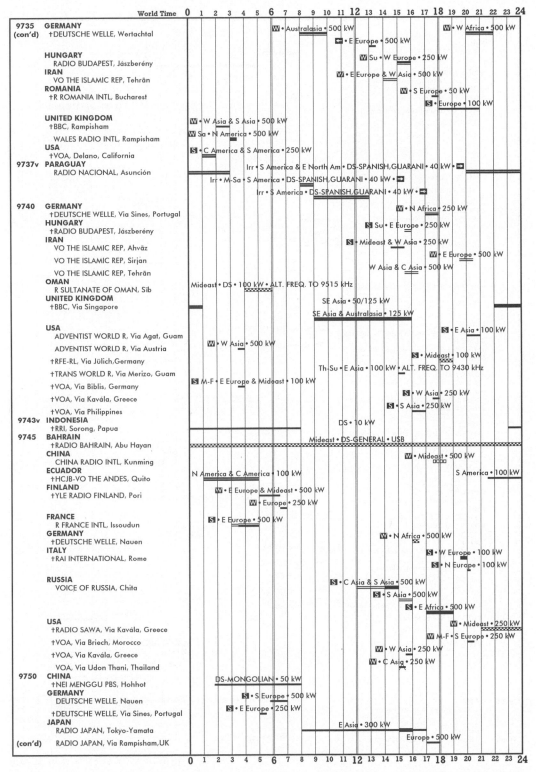

World Time 0 1 2 3 4 5 6 7 8 9 10 11 12 13 14 15 16 17 18 19 20 21 22 23 24

9735 GERMANY
(con'd) †DEUTSCHE WELLE, Wertachtal
W • Australasia • 500 kW
W • W Africa • 500 kW
⮂ • E Europe • 500 kW

HUNGARY
RADIO BUDAPEST, Jászberény
W Su • W Europe • 250 kW

IRAN
VO THE ISLAMIC REP, Tehrān
W • E Europe & W Asia • 500 kW

ROMANIA
†R ROMANIA INTL, Bucharest
W • S Europe • 50 kW
S • Europe • 100 kW

UNITED KINGDOM
†BBC, Rampisham
W • W Asia & S Asia • 500 kW

WALES RADIO INTL, Rampisham
W Sa • N America • 500 kW

USA
†VOA, Delano, California
S • C America & S America • 250 kW

9737v PARAGUAY
RADIO NACIONAL, Asunción
Irr • S America & E North Am • DS-SPANISH,GUARANI • 40 kW • ⮂
Irr • M-Sa • S America • DS-SPANISH,GUARANI • 40 kW • ⮂
Irr • S America • DS-SPANISH,GUARANI • 40 kW • ⮂

9740 GERMANY
†DEUTSCHE WELLE, Via Sines, Portugal
W • N Africa • 250 kW

HUNGARY
†RADIO BUDAPEST, Jászberény
S Su • E Europe • 250 kW

IRAN
VO THE ISLAMIC REP, Ahvāz
S • Mideast & W Asia • 250 kW

VO THE ISLAMIC REP, Sirjan
W • E Europe • 500 kW

VO THE ISLAMIC REP, Tehrān
W Asia & C Asia • 500 kW

OMAN
R SULTANATE OF OMAN, Sīb
Mideast • DS • 100 kW • ALT. FREQ. TO 9515 kHz

UNITED KINGDOM
†BBC, Via Singapore
SE Asia • 50/125 kW
SE Asia & Australasia • 125 kW

USA
ADVENTIST WORLD R, Via Agat, Guam
S • E Asia • 100 kW

ADVENTIST WORLD R, Via Austria
W • W Asia • 500 kW

†RFE-RL, Via Jülich, Germany
S • Mideast • 100 kW

†TRANS WORLD R, Via Merizo, Guam
Th-Su • E Asia • 100 kW • ALT. FREQ. TO 9430 kHz

†VOA, Via Biblis, Germany
S M-F • E Europe & Mideast • 100 kW

†VOA, Via Kavála, Greece
S • W Asia • 250 kW

†VOA, Via Philippines
S • S Asia • 250 kW

9743v INDONESIA
†RRI, Sorong, Papua
DS • 10 kW

9745 BAHRAIN
†RADIO BAHRAIN, Abu Hayan
Mideast • DS-GENERAL • USB

CHINA
CHINA RADIO INTL, Kunming
W • Mideast • 500 kW

ECUADOR
†HCJB-VO THE ANDES, Quito
N America & C America • 100 kW
S America • 100 kW

FINLAND
†YLE RADIO FINLAND, Pori
W • E Europe & Mideast • 500 kW
W • Europe • 250 kW

FRANCE
R FRANCE INTL, Issoudun
S • E Europe • 500 kW

GERMANY
†DEUTSCHE WELLE, Nauen
W • N Africa • 500 kW

ITALY
†RAI INTERNATIONAL, Rome
S • W Europe • 100 kW
S • N Europe • 100 kW

RUSSIA
VOICE OF RUSSIA, Chita
S • C Asia & S Asia • 500 kW
S • S Asia • 500 kW
S • E Africa • 500 kW

USA
†RADIO SAWA, Via Kavála, Greece
W • Mideast • 250 kW
W M-F • S Europe • 250 kW

†VOA, Via Briech, Morocco
W • W Asia • 250 kW

†VOA, Via Kavála, Greece
W • C Asia • 250 kW

VOA, Via Udon Thani, Thailand

9750 CHINA
†NEI MENGGU PBS, Hohhot
DS-MONGOLIAN • 50 kW

GERMANY
DEUTSCHE WELLE, Nauen
S • S Europe • 500 kW

†DEUTSCHE WELLE, Via Sines, Portugal
S • E Europe • 250 kW

JAPAN
RADIO JAPAN, Tokyo-Yamata
E Asia • 300 kW

(con'd) RADIO JAPAN, Via Rampisham, UK
Europe • 500 kW

0 1 2 3 4 5 6 7 8 9 10 11 12 13 14 15 16 17 18 19 20 21 22 23 24

SEASONAL S OR W   1-HR TIMESHIFT MIDYEAR ⮂ OR ⮂   JAMMING / OR ⋀   EARLIEST HEARD ◁   LATEST HEARD ▷   NEW FOR 2004 †

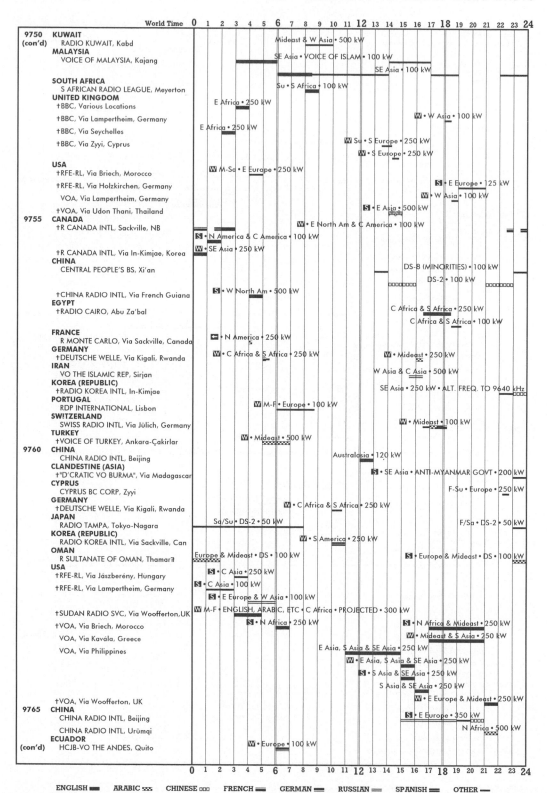

World Time

9750 (con'd)	KUWAIT
	RADIO KUWAIT, Kabd — Mideast & W Asia • 500 kW
	MALAYSIA
	VOICE OF MALAYSIA, Kajang — SE Asia • VOICE OF ISLAM • 100 kW
	— SE Asia • 100 kW
	SOUTH AFRICA
	S AFRICAN RADIO LEAGUE, Meyerton — Su • S Africa • 100 kW
	UNITED KINGDOM
	†BBC, Various Locations — E Africa • 250 kW
	†BBC, Via Lampertheim, Germany — W • W Asia • 100 kW
	†BBC, Via Seychelles — E Africa • 250 kW
	†BBC, Via Zyyi, Cyprus — W Su • S Europe • 250 kW / W • S Europe • 250 kW
	USA
	†RFE-RL, Via Briech, Morocco — W M-Sa • E Europe • 250 kW
	†RFE-RL, Via Holzkirchen, Germany — S • E Europe • 125 kW
	VOA, Via Lampertheim, Germany — W • W Asia • 100 kW
	†VOA, Via Udon Thani, Thailand — S • E Asia • 500 kW
9755	CANADA
	†R CANADA INTL, Sackville, NB — W • E North Am & C America • 100 kW / S • N America & C America • 100 kW
	†R CANADA INTL, Via In-Kimjae, Korea — W • SE Asia • 250 kW
	CHINA
	CENTRAL PEOPLE'S BS, Xi'an — DS-8 (MINORITIES) • 100 kW / DS-2 • 100 kW
	†CHINA RADIO INTL, Via French Guiana — S • W North Am • 500 kW
	EGYPT
	†RADIO CAIRO, Abu Za'bal — C Africa & S Africa • 250 kW / C Africa & S Africa • 100 kW
	FRANCE
	R MONTE CARLO, Via Sackville, Canada — • N America • 250 kW
	GERMANY
	†DEUTSCHE WELLE, Via Kigali, Rwanda — W • C Africa & S Africa • 250 kW / W • Mideast • 250 kW
	IRAN
	VO THE ISLAMIC REP, Sirjan — W Asia & C Asia • 500 kW
	KOREA (REPUBLIC)
	†RADIO KOREA INTL, In-Kimjae — SE Asia • 250 kW • ALT. FREQ. TO 9640 kHz
	PORTUGAL
	RDP INTERNATIONAL, Lisbon — W M-F • Europe • 100 kW
	SWITZERLAND
	SWISS RADIO INTL, Via Jülich, Germany — W • Mideast • 100 kW
	TURKEY
	†VOICE OF TURKEY, Ankara-Çakirlar — W • Mideast • 500 kW
9760	CHINA
	CHINA RADIO INTL, Beijing — Australasia • 120 kW
	CLANDESTINE (ASIA)
	†"D'CRATIC VO BURMA", Via Madagascar — S • SE Asia • ANTI-MYANMAR GOVT • 200 kW
	CYPRUS
	CYPRUS BC CORP, Zyyi — F-Su • Europe • 250 kW
	GERMANY
	†DEUTSCHE WELLE, Via Kigali, Rwanda — W • C Africa & S Africa • 250 kW
	JAPAN
	RADIO TAMPA, Tokyo-Nagara — Sa/Su • DS-2 • 50 kW / F/Sa • DS-2 • 50 kW
	KOREA (REPUBLIC)
	RADIO KOREA INTL, Via Sackville, Can — W • S America • 250 kW
	OMAN
	R SULTANATE OF OMAN, Thamarit — Europe & Mideast • DS • 100 kW / S • Europe & Mideast • DS • 100 kW
	USA
	†RFE-RL, Via Jászberény, Hungary — S • C Asia • 250 kW
	†RFE-RL, Via Lampertheim, Germany — S • C Asia • 100 kW
	— S • E Europe & W Asia • 100 kW
	†SUDAN RADIO SVC, Via Woofferton, UK — W M-F • ENGLISH, ARABIC, ETC • C Africa • PROJECTED • 300 kW
	†VOA, Via Briech, Morocco — S • N Africa • 250 kW / S • N Africa & Mideast • 250 kW
	VOA, Via Kavála, Greece — W • Mideast & S Asia • 250 kW
	VOA, Via Philippines — E Asia, S Asia & SE Asia • 250 kW / W • E Asia, S Asia & SE Asia • 250 kW / S • S Asia & SE Asia • 250 kW / S Asia & SE Asia • 250 kW
	†VOA, Via Woofferton, UK — W • E Europe & Mideast • 250 kW
9765	CHINA
	CHINA RADIO INTL, Beijing — S • E Europe • 350 kW
	CHINA RADIO INTL, Urümqi — N Africa • 500 kW
	ECUADOR
(con'd)	HCJB-VO THE ANDES, Quito — W • Europe • 100 kW

0 1 2 3 4 5 6 7 8 9 10 11 12 13 14 15 16 17 18 19 20 21 22 23 24

ENGLISH ▬ ARABIC ░ CHINESE ▫▫▫ FRENCH ═ GERMAN ▬ RUSSIAN ═ SPANISH ▭ OTHER ▬

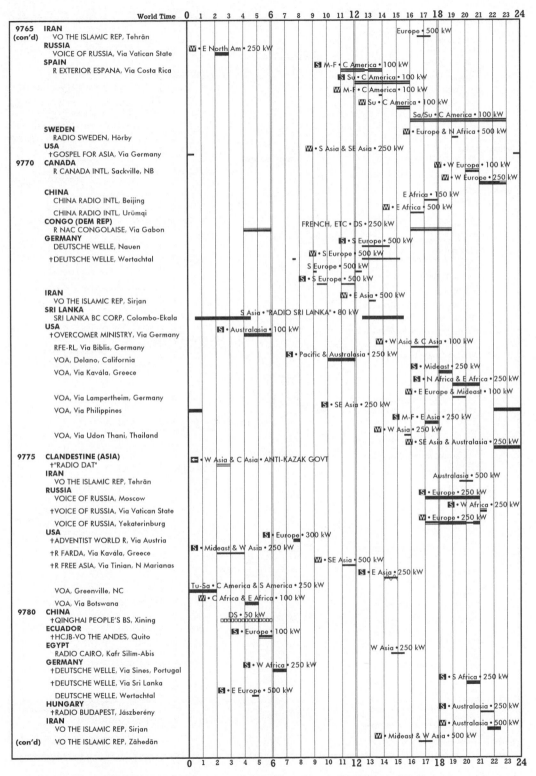

World Time 0 1 2 3 4 5 6 7 8 9 10 11 12 13 14 15 16 17 18 19 20 21 22 23 24

9765 **IRAN**
(con'd) VO THE ISLAMIC REP, Tehrān
Europe • 500 kW
RUSSIA
VOICE OF RUSSIA, Via Vatican State
W • E North Am • 250 kW
SPAIN
R EXTERIOR ESPANA, Via Costa Rica
S M-F • C America • 100 kW
S Su • C America • 100 kW
W M-F • C America • 100 kW
W Su • C America • 100 kW
Sa/Su • C America • 100 kW

SWEDEN
RADIO SWEDEN, Hörby
W • Europe & N Africa • 500 kW
USA
†GOSPEL FOR ASIA, Via Germany
W • S Asia & SE Asia • 250 kW
9770 **CANADA**
R CANADA INTL, Sackville, NB
W • W Europe • 100 kW
W • W Europe • 250 kW

CHINA
CHINA RADIO INTL, Beijing
E Africa • 150 kW
CHINA RADIO INTL, Urümqi
W • E Africa • 500 kW
CONGO (DEM REP)
R NAC CONGOLAISE, Via Gabon
FRENCH, ETC • DS • 250 kW
GERMANY
DEUTSCHE WELLE, Nauen
S • S Europe • 500 kW
†DEUTSCHE WELLE, Wertachtal
W • S Europe • 500 kW
S Europe • 500 kW
S • S Europe • 500 kW

IRAN
VO THE ISLAMIC REP, Sirjan
W • E Asia • 500 kW
SRI LANKA
SRI LANKA BC CORP, Colombo-Ekala
S Asia • "RADIO SRI LANKA" • 80 kW
USA
†OVERCOMER MINISTRY, Via Germany
S • Australasia • 100 kW
RFE-RL, Via Biblis, Germany
W • W Asia & C Asia • 100 kW
VOA, Delano, California
S • Pacific & Australasia • 250 kW
VOA, Via Kavála, Greece
S • Mideast • 250 kW
S • N Africa & E Africa • 250 kW
VOA, Via Lampertheim, Germany
W • E Europe & Mideast • 100 kW
VOA, Via Philippines
S • SE Asia • 250 kW
S M-F • E Asia • 250 kW
VOA, Via Udon Thani, Thailand
W • W Asia • 250 kW
W • SE Asia & Australasia • 250 kW

9775 **CLANDESTINE (ASIA)**
†"RADIO DAT"
⇦ • W Asia & C Asia • ANTI-KAZAK GOVT
IRAN
VO THE ISLAMIC REP, Tehrān
Australasia • 500 kW
RUSSIA
VOICE OF RUSSIA, Moscow
S • Europe • 250 kW
†VOICE OF RUSSIA, Via Vatican State
S • W Africa • 250 kW
VOICE OF RUSSIA, Yekaterinburg
W • Europe • 250 kW
USA
†ADVENTIST WORLD R, Via Austria
S • Europe • 300 kW
†R FARDA, Via Kavála, Greece
S • Mideast & W Asia • 250 kW
†R FREE ASIA, Via Tinian, N Marianas
W • SE Asia • 500 kW
S • E Asia • 250 kW
VOA, Greenville, NC
Tu-Sa • C America & S America • 250 kW
VOA, Via Botswana
W • C Africa & E Africa • 100 kW
9780 **CHINA**
†QINGHAI PEOPLE'S BS, Xining
DS • 50 kW
ECUADOR
†HCJB-VO THE ANDES, Quito
S • Europe • 100 kW
EGYPT
RADIO CAIRO, Kafr Silim-Abis
W Asia • 250 kW
GERMANY
†DEUTSCHE WELLE, Via Sines, Portugal
S • W Africa • 250 kW
†DEUTSCHE WELLE, Via Sri Lanka
S • S Africa • 250 kW
DEUTSCHE WELLE, Wertachtal
S • E Europe • 500 kW
HUNGARY
†RADIO BUDAPEST, Jászberény
S • Australasia • 250 kW
IRAN
VO THE ISLAMIC REP, Sirjan
W • Australasia • 500 kW
(con'd) VO THE ISLAMIC REP, Zāhedān
W • Mideast & W Asia • 500 kW

0 1 2 3 4 5 6 7 8 9 10 11 12 13 14 15 16 17 18 19 20 21 22 23 24

SEASONAL 🅂 OR 🅆   1-HR TIMESHIFT MIDYEAR ⇦ OR ⇨   JAMMING / OR ∧   EARLIEST HEARD ◁   LATEST HEARD ▷   NEW FOR 2004 †

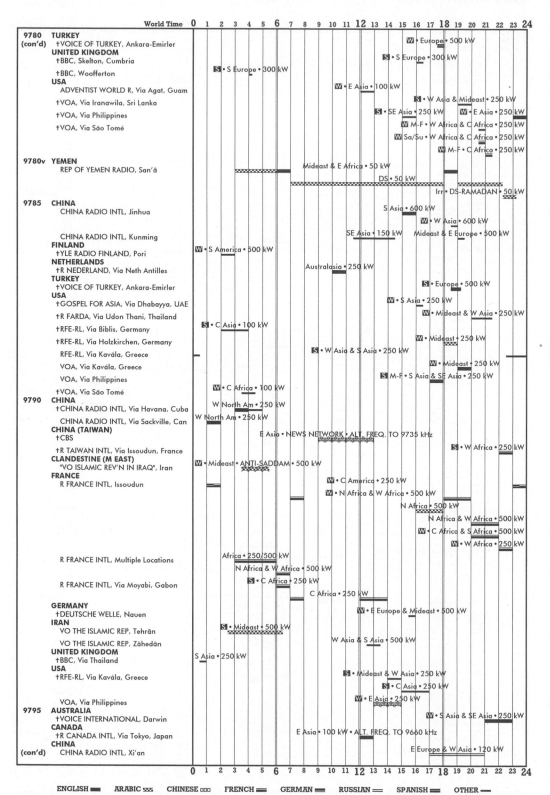

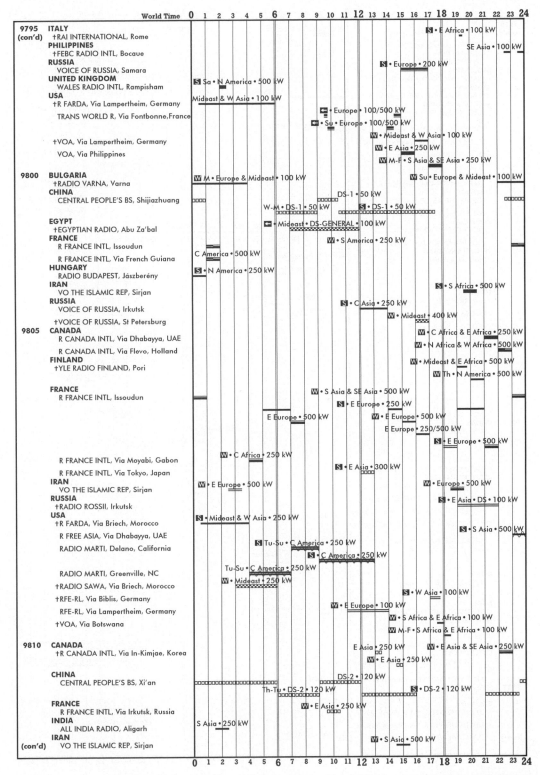

| World Time | 0 | 1 | 2 | 3 | 4 | 5 | 6 | 7 | 8 | 9 | 10 | 11 | 12 | 13 | 14 | 15 | 16 | 17 | 18 | 19 | 20 | 21 | 22 | 23 | 24 |

9795 ITALY
(con'd) †RAI INTERNATIONAL, Rome — S • E Africa • 100 kW

PHILIPPINES
†FEBC RADIO INTL, Bocaue — SE Asia • 100 kW

RUSSIA
VOICE OF RUSSIA, Samara — S • Europe • 200 kW

UNITED KINGDOM
WALES RADIO INTL, Rampisham — S Sa • N America • 500 kW

USA
†R FARDA, Via Lampertheim, Germany — Mideast & W Asia • 100 kW

TRANS WORLD R, Via Fontbonne, France — • Europe • 100/500 kW
• Su • Europe • 100/500 kW

†VOA, Via Lampertheim, Germany — W • Mideast & W Asia • 100 kW

VOA, Via Philippines — W • E Asia • 250 kW
W M-F • S Asia & SE Asia • 250 kW

9800 BULGARIA
†RADIO VARNA, Varna — W M • Europe & Mideast • 100 kW   W Su • Europe & Mideast • 100 kW

CHINA
CENTRAL PEOPLE'S BS, Shijiazhuang — DS-1 • 50 kW
W-M • DS-1 • 50 kW   S • DS-1 • 50 kW

EGYPT
†EGYPTIAN RADIO, Abu Za'bal — • Mideast • DS-GENERAL • 100 kW
W • S America • 250 kW

FRANCE
R FRANCE INTL, Issoudun

R FRANCE INTL, Via French Guiana — C America • 500 kW

HUNGARY
RADIO BUDAPEST, Jászberény — S • N America • 250 kW

IRAN
VO THE ISLAMIC REP, Sirjan — S • S Africa • 500 kW

RUSSIA
VOICE OF RUSSIA, Irkutsk — S • C Asia • 250 kW

†VOICE OF RUSSIA, St Petersburg — W • Mideast • 400 kW

9805 CANADA
R CANADA INTL, Via Dhabayya, UAE — W • C Africa & E Africa • 250 kW

R CANADA INTL, Via Flevo, Holland — W • N Africa & W Africa • 500 kW

FINLAND
†YLE RADIO FINLAND, Pori — W • Mideast & E Africa • 500 kW
W Th • N America • 500 kW

FRANCE
R FRANCE INTL, Issoudun — W • S Asia & SE Asia • 500 kW
S • E Europe • 250 kW
E Europe • 500 kW   W • E Europe • 500 kW
E Europe • 250/500 kW
S • E Europe • 500 kW

R FRANCE INTL, Via Moyabi, Gabon — W • C Africa • 250 kW

R FRANCE INTL, Via Tokyo, Japan — S • E Asia • 300 kW

IRAN
VO THE ISLAMIC REP, Sirjan — W • E Europe • 500 kW   W • Europe • 500 kW

RUSSIA
†RADIO ROSSII, Irkutsk — S • E Asia • DS • 100 kW

USA
†R FARDA, Via Briech, Morocco — S • Mideast & W Asia • 250 kW

R FREE ASIA, Via Dhabayya, UAE — S • S Asia • 500 kW

RADIO MARTI, Delano, California — S Tu-Su • C America • 250 kW
S • C America • 250 kW

RADIO MARTI, Greenville, NC — Tu-Su • C America • 250 kW

†RADIO SAWA, Via Briech, Morocco — W • Mideast • 250 kW

†RFE-RL, Via Biblis, Germany — S • W Asia • 100 kW

RFE-RL, Via Lampertheim, Germany — W • E Europe • 100 kW

†VOA, Via Botswana — W • S Africa & E Africa • 100 kW
W M-F • S Africa & E Africa • 100 kW

9810 CANADA
†R CANADA INTL, Via In-Kimjae, Korea — E Asia • 250 kW   W • E Asia & SE Asia • 250 kW
W • E Asia • 250 kW

CHINA
CENTRAL PEOPLE'S BS, Xi'an — DS-2 • 120 kW
Th-Tu • DS-2 • 120 kW   S • DS-2 • 120 kW

FRANCE
R FRANCE INTL, Via Irkutsk, Russia — W • E Asia • 250 kW

INDIA
ALL INDIA RADIO, Aligarh — S Asia • 250 kW

IRAN
(con'd) VO THE ISLAMIC REP, Sirjan — W • S Asia • 500 kW

| World Time | 0 | 1 | 2 | 3 | 4 | 5 | 6 | 7 | 8 | 9 | 10 | 11 | 12 | 13 | 14 | 15 | 16 | 17 | 18 | 19 | 20 | 21 | 22 | 23 | 24 |

SEASONAL S OR W   1-HR TIMESHIFT MIDYEAR ⬅ OR ➡   JAMMING / OR ∧   EARLIEST HEARD ◁   LATEST HEARD ▷   NEW FOR 2004 †

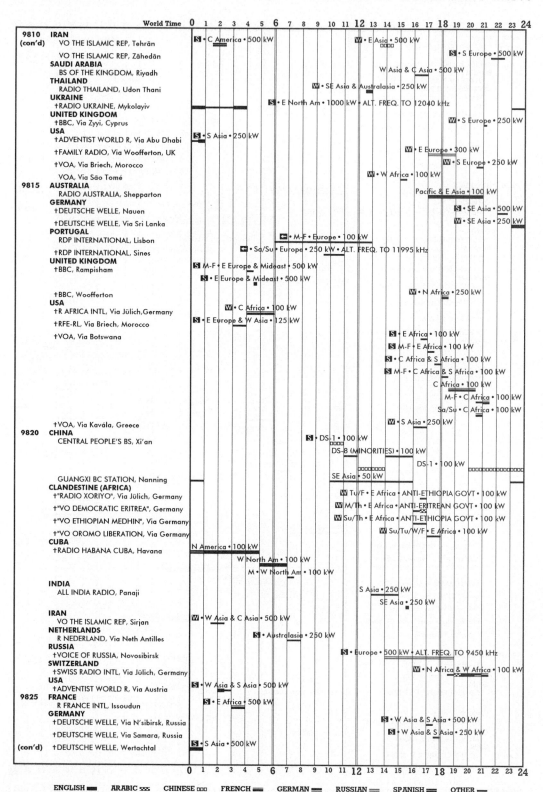

World Time 0 1 2 3 4 5 6 7 8 9 10 11 12 13 14 15 16 17 18 19 20 21 22 23 24

9810 (con'd) **IRAN**	
VO THE ISLAMIC REP, Tehrān	S • C America • 500 kW / W • E Asia • 500 kW
VO THE ISLAMIC REP, Zāhedān	S • S Europe • 500 kW
SAUDI ARABIA	
BS OF THE KINGDOM, Riyadh	W Asia & C Asia • 500 kW
THAILAND	
RADIO THAILAND, Udon Thani	W • SE Asia & Australasia • 250 kW
UKRAINE	
†RADIO UKRAINE, Mykolayiv	S • E North Am • 1000 kW • ALT. FREQ. TO 12040 kHz
UNITED KINGDOM	
†BBC, Via Zyyi, Cyprus	W • S Europe • 250 kW
USA	
†ADVENTIST WORLD R, Via Abu Dhabi	S • S Asia • 250 kW
†FAMILY RADIO, Via Woofferton, UK	W • E Europe • 300 kW
†VOA, Via Briech, Morocco	W • S Europe • 250 kW
VOA, Via São Tomé	W • W Africa • 100 kW
9815 **AUSTRALIA**	
RADIO AUSTRALIA, Shepparton	Pacific & E Asia • 100 kW
GERMANY	
†DEUTSCHE WELLE, Nauen	S • SE Asia • 500 kW
†DEUTSCHE WELLE, Via Sri Lanka	W • SE Asia • 250 kW
PORTUGAL	
RDP INTERNATIONAL, Lisbon	• M-F • Europe • 100 kW
†RDP INTERNATIONAL, Sines	• Sa/Su • Europe • 250 kW • ALT. FREQ. TO 11995 kHz
UNITED KINGDOM	
†BBC, Rampisham	S • M-F • E Europe & Mideast • 500 kW / S • E Europe & Mideast • 500 kW
†BBC, Woofferton	W • N Africa • 250 kW
USA	
†R AFRICA INTL, Via Jülich, Germany	W • C Africa • 100 kW
†RFE-RL, Via Briech, Morocco	S • E Europe & W Asia • 125 kW
†VOA, Via Botswana	S • E Africa • 100 kW
	S • M-F • E Africa • 100 kW
	S • C Africa & S Africa • 100 kW
	S • M-F • C Africa & S Africa • 100 kW
	C Africa • 100 kW
	M-F • C Africa • 100 kW
	Sa/Su • C Africa • 100 kW
†VOA, Via Kavála, Greece	W • S Asia • 250 kW
9820 **CHINA**	
CENTRAL PEOPLE'S BS, Xi'an	S • DS-1 • 100 kW
	DS-8 (MINORITIES) • 100 kW
	DS-1 • 100 kW
GUANGXI BC STATION, Nanning	SE Asia • 50 kW
CLANDESTINE (AFRICA)	
†"RADIO XORIYO", Via Jülich, Germany	W • Tu/F • E Africa • ANTI-ETHIOPIA GOVT • 100 kW
†"VO DEMOCRATIC ERITREA", Germany	W • M/Th • E Africa • ANTI-ERITREAN GOVT • 100 kW
†"VO ETHIOPIAN MEDHIN", Via Germany	W • Su/Th • E Africa • ANTI-ETHIOPIA GOVT • 100 kW
†"VO OROMO LIBERATION", Via Germany	W • Su/Tu/W/F • E Africa • 100 kW
CUBA	
†RADIO HABANA CUBA, Havana	N America • 100 kW
	W North Am • 100 kW
	M • W North Am • 100 kW
INDIA	
ALL INDIA RADIO, Panaji	S Asia • 250 kW
	SE Asia • 250 kW
IRAN	
VO THE ISLAMIC REP, Sirjan	W • W Asia & C Asia • 500 kW
NETHERLANDS	
R NEDERLAND, Via Neth Antilles	S • Australasia • 250 kW
RUSSIA	
†VOICE OF RUSSIA, Novosibirsk	S • Europe • 500 kW • ALT. FREQ. TO 9450 kHz
SWITZERLAND	
†SWISS RADIO INTL, Via Jülich, Germany	W • N Africa & W Africa • 100 kW
USA	
†ADVENTIST WORLD R, Via Austria	S • W Asia & S Asia • 500 kW
9825 **FRANCE**	
R FRANCE INTL, Issoudun	S • E Africa • 500 kW
GERMANY	
†DEUTSCHE WELLE, Via N'sibirsk, Russia	S • W Asia & S Asia • 500 kW
†DEUTSCHE WELLE, Via Samara, Russia	S • W Asia & S Asia • 250 kW
(con'd) †DEUTSCHE WELLE, Wertachtal	S • S Asia • 500 kW

0 1 2 3 4 5 6 7 8 9 10 11 12 13 14 15 16 17 18 19 20 21 22 23 24

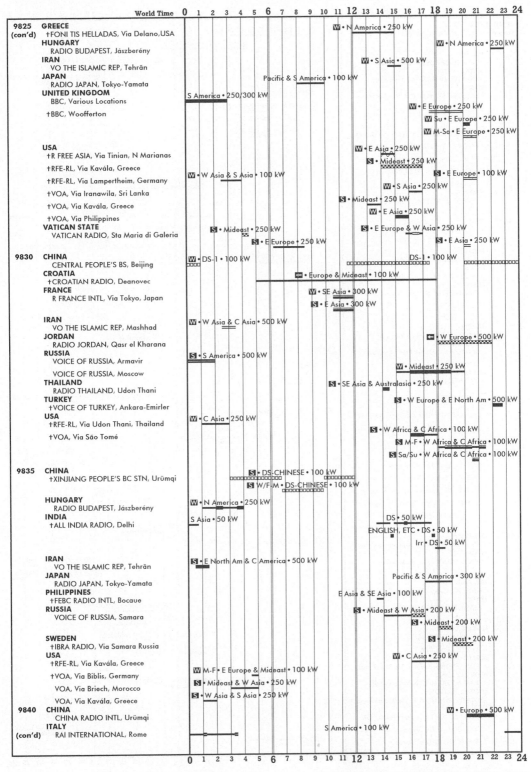

World Time	0 1 2 3 4 5 6 7 8 9 10 11 12 13 14 15 16 17 18 19 20 21 22 23 24
9825 **GREECE**	
(con'd) †FONI TIS HELLADAS, Via Delano, USA	W • N America • 250 kW
HUNGARY	
RADIO BUDAPEST, Jászberény	W • N America • 250 kW
IRAN	
VO THE ISLAMIC REP, Tehrän	W • S Asia • 500 kW
JAPAN	
RADIO JAPAN, Tokyo-Yamata	Pacific & S America • 100 kW
UNITED KINGDOM	
BBC, Various Locations	S America • 250/300 kW
†BBC, Woofferton	W • E Europe • 250 kW
	W • Su • E Europe • 250 kW
	W • M-Sa • E Europe • 250 kW
USA	
†R FREE ASIA, Via Tinian, N Marianas	W • E Asia • 250 kW
†RFE-RL, Via Kavála, Greece	S • Mideast • 250 kW
†RFE-RL, Via Lampertheim, Germany	W • W Asia & S Asia • 100 kW S • E Europe • 100 kW
†VOA, Via Iranawila, Sri Lanka	W • S Asia • 250 kW
†VOA, Via Kavála, Greece	S • Mideast • 250 kW
†VOA, Via Philippines	W • E Asia • 250 kW
VATICAN STATE	
VATICAN RADIO, Sta Maria di Galeria	S • Mideast • 250 kW S • E Europe & W Asia • 250 kW
	S • E Europe • 250 kW S • E Asia • 250 kW
9830 **CHINA**	
CENTRAL PEOPLE'S BS, Beijing	W • DS-1 • 100 kW DS-1 • 100 kW
CROATIA	
†CROATIAN RADIO, Deanovec	• Europe & Mideast • 100 kW
FRANCE	
R FRANCE INTL, Via Tokyo, Japan	W • SE Asia • 300 kW
	S • E Asia • 300 kW
IRAN	
VO THE ISLAMIC REP, Mashhad	W • W Asia & C Asia • 500 kW
JORDAN	
RADIO JORDAN, Qasr el Kharana	• W Europe • 500 kW
RUSSIA	
VOICE OF RUSSIA, Armavir	S • S America • 500 kW
VOICE OF RUSSIA, Moscow	W • Mideast • 250 kW
THAILAND	
RADIO THAILAND, Udon Thani	S • SE Asia & Australasia • 250 kW
TURKEY	
†VOICE OF TURKEY, Ankara-Emirler	S • W Europe & E North Am • 500 kW
USA	
†RFE-RL, Via Udon Thani, Thailand	W • C Asia • 250 kW
†VOA, Via São Tomé	S • W Africa & C Africa • 100 kW
	S • M-F • W Africa & C Africa • 100 kW
	S • Sa/Su • W Africa & C Africa • 100 kW
9835 **CHINA**	
†XINJIANG PEOPLE'S BC STN, Urümqi	S • DS-CHINESE • 100 kW
	S • W/F-M • DS-CHINESE • 100 kW
HUNGARY	
RADIO BUDAPEST, Jászberény	W • N America • 250 kW
INDIA	
†ALL INDIA RADIO, Delhi	S Asia • 50 kW
	DS • 50 kW
	ENGLISH, ETC • DS • 50 kW
	Irr • DS • 50 kW
IRAN	
VO THE ISLAMIC REP, Tehrän	S • E North Am & C America • 500 kW
JAPAN	
RADIO JAPAN, Tokyo-Yamata	Pacific & S America • 300 kW
PHILIPPINES	
†FEBC RADIO INTL, Bocaue	E Asia & SE Asia • 100 kW
RUSSIA	
VOICE OF RUSSIA, Samara	S • Mideast & W Asia • 200 kW
	S • Mideast • 200 kW
SWEDEN	
†IBRA RADIO, Via Samara Russia	S • Mideast • 200 kW
USA	
†RFE-RL, Via Kavála, Greece	W • C Asia • 250 kW
†VOA, Via Biblis, Germany	W • M-F • E Europe & Mideast • 100 kW
VOA, Via Briech, Morocco	S • Mideast & W Asia • 250 kW
VOA, Via Kavála, Greece	S • W Asia & S Asia • 250 kW
9840 **CHINA**	
CHINA RADIO INTL, Urümqi	W • Europe • 500 kW
ITALY	
(con'd) RAI INTERNATIONAL, Rome	S America • 100 kW

	0 1 2 3 4 5 6 7 8 9 10 11 12 13 14 15 16 17 18 19 20 21 22 23 24

SEASONAL S OR W   1-HR TIMESHIFT MIDYEAR ⇨ OR ⇨   JAMMING / OR /\   EARLIEST HEARD ◁   LATEST HEARD ▷   NEW FOR 2004 †

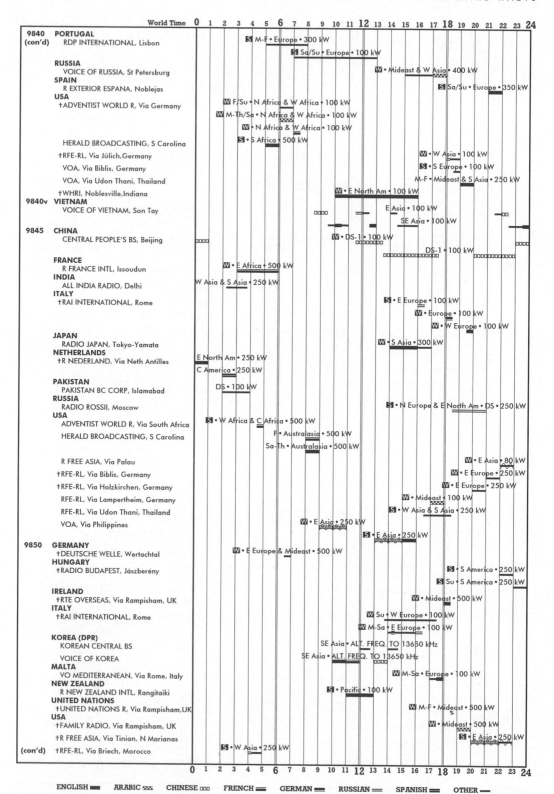

World Time 0 1 2 3 4 5 6 7 8 9 10 11 12 13 14 15 16 17 18 19 20 21 22 23 24

9840
(con'd) PORTUGAL
RDP INTERNATIONAL, Lisbon — S M-F • Europe • 300 kW / S Sa/Su • Europe • 100 kW

RUSSIA
VOICE OF RUSSIA, St Petersburg — W • Mideast & W Asia • 400 kW
SPAIN
R EXTERIOR ESPANA, Noblejas — S Sa/Su • Europe • 350 kW
USA
†ADVENTIST WORLD R, Via Germany — W F/Su • N Africa & W Africa • 100 kW / W M-Th/Sa • N Africa & W Africa • 100 kW / W • N Africa & W Africa • 100 kW / S • S Africa • 500 kW

HERALD BROADCASTING, S Carolina

†RFE-RL, Via Jülich, Germany — W • W Asia • 100 kW
VOA, Via Biblis, Germany — S • S Europe • 100 kW
VOA, Via Udon Thani, Thailand — M-F • Mideast & S Asia • 250 kW
†WHRI, Noblesville, Indiana — W • E North Am • 100 kW

9840v VIETNAM
VOICE OF VIETNAM, Son Tay — E Asia • 100 kW / SE Asia • 100 kW

9845 CHINA
CENTRAL PEOPLE'S BS, Beijing — W • DS-1 • 100 kW / DS-1 • 100 kW

FRANCE
R FRANCE INTL, Issoudun — W • E Africa • 500 kW
INDIA
ALL INDIA RADIO, Delhi — W Asia & S Asia • 250 kW
ITALY
†RAI INTERNATIONAL, Rome — S • E Europe • 100 kW / W • Europe • 100 kW / W • W Europe • 100 kW

JAPAN
RADIO JAPAN, Tokyo-Yamata — W • S Asia • 300 kW
NETHERLANDS
†R NEDERLAND, Via Neth Antilles — E North Am • 250 kW / C America • 250 kW

PAKISTAN
PAKISTAN BC CORP, Islamabad — DS • 100 kW
RUSSIA
RADIO ROSSII, Moscow — S • N Europe & E North Am • DS • 250 kW
USA
ADVENTIST WORLD R, Via South Africa — S • W Africa & C Africa • 500 kW
HERALD BROADCASTING, S Carolina — F • Australasia • 500 kW / Sa-Th • Australasia • 500 kW

R FREE ASIA, Via Palau — W • E Asia • 80 kW
†RFE-RL, Via Biblis, Germany — W • E Europe • 250 kW
†RFE-RL, Via Holzkirchen, Germany — W • E Europe • 250 kW
RFE-RL, Via Lampertheim, Germany — W • Mideast • 100 kW
RFE-RL, Via Udon Thani, Thailand — S • W Asia & S Asia • 250 kW
VOA, Via Philippines — W • E Asia • 250 kW / S • E Asia • 250 kW

9850 GERMANY
†DEUTSCHE WELLE, Wertachtal — W • E Europe & Mideast • 500 kW
HUNGARY
†RADIO BUDAPEST, Jászberény — S • S America • 250 kW / S Su • S America • 250 kW

IRELAND
†RTE OVERSEAS, Via Rampisham, UK — W • Mideast • 500 kW
ITALY
†RAI INTERNATIONAL, Rome — W Su • W Europe • 100 kW / W M-Sa • E Europe • 100 kW

KOREA (DPR)
KOREAN CENTRAL BS — SE Asia • ALT. FREQ. TO 13650 kHz
VOICE OF KOREA — SE Asia • ALT. FREQ. TO 13650 kHz
MALTA
VO MEDITERRANEAN, Via Rome, Italy — W M-Sa • Europe • 100 kW
NEW ZEALAND
R NEW ZEALAND INTL, Rangitaiki — S • Pacific • 100 kW
UNITED NATIONS
†UNITED NATIONS R, Via Rampisham, UK — W M-F • Mideast • 500 kW
USA
†FAMILY RADIO, Via Rampisham, UK — W • Mideast • 500 kW
†R FREE ASIA, Via Tinian, N Marianas — S • E Asia • 250 kW
(con'd) †RFE-RL, Via Briech, Morocco — S • W Asia • 250 kW

0 1 2 3 4 5 6 7 8 9 10 11 12 13 14 15 16 17 18 19 20 21 22 23 24

ENGLISH ▬ ARABIC ≋ CHINESE ▯▯▯ FRENCH ═ GERMAN ▬ RUSSIAN ══ SPANISH ▬ OTHER ▬

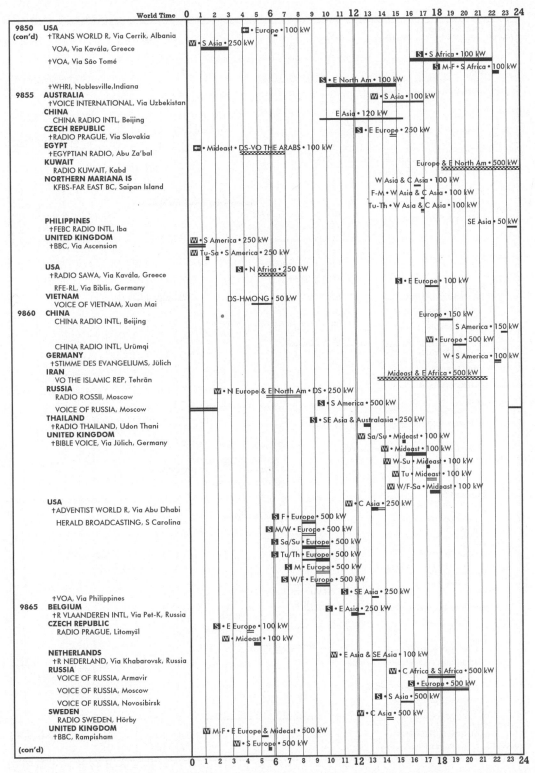

World Time 0 1 2 3 4 5 6 7 8 9 10 11 12 13 14 15 16 17 18 19 20 21 22 23 24

9850
(con'd)

USA
†TRANS WORLD R, Via Cerrik, Albania — ⬅ • Europe • 100 kW
VOA, Via Kavála, Greece — W • S Asia • 250 kW
†VOA, Via São Tomé — S • S Africa • 100 kW / S • M-F • S Africa • 100 kW

†WHRI, Noblesville, Indiana — S • E North Am • 100 kW
9855 **AUSTRALIA**
†VOICE INTERNATIONAL, Via Uzbekistan — W • S Asia • 100 kW
CHINA
CHINA RADIO INTL, Beijing — E Asia • 120 kW
CZECH REPUBLIC
†RADIO PRAGUE, Via Slovakia — S • E Europe • 250 kW
EGYPT
†EGYPTIAN RADIO, Abu Za'bal — ⬅ • Mideast • DS-VO THE ARABS • 100 kW
KUWAIT
RADIO KUWAIT, Kabd — Europe & E North Am • 500 kW
NORTHERN MARIANA IS
KFBS-FAR EAST BC, Saipan Island — W Asia & C Asia • 100 kW / F-M • W Asia & C Asia • 100 kW / Tu-Th • W Asia & C Asia • 100 kW

PHILIPPINES
†FEBC RADIO INTL, Iba — SE Asia • 50 kW
UNITED KINGDOM
†BBC, Via Ascension — W • S America • 250 kW / W Tu-Sa • S America • 250 kW

USA
†RADIO SAWA, Via Kavála, Greece — S • N Africa • 250 kW
RFE-RL, Via Biblis, Germany — S • E Europe • 100 kW
VIETNAM
VOICE OF VIETNAM, Xuan Mai — DS-HMONG • 50 kW
9860 **CHINA**
CHINA RADIO INTL, Beijing — Europe • 150 kW / S America • 150 kW

CHINA RADIO INTL, Urümqi — W • Europe • 500 kW / W • S America • 100 kW
GERMANY
†STIMME DES EVANGELIUMS, Jülich
IRAN
VO THE ISLAMIC REP, Tehrän — Mideast & E Africa • 500 kW
RUSSIA
RADIO ROSSII, Moscow — W • N Europe & E North Am • DS • 250 kW

VOICE OF RUSSIA, Moscow — S • S America • 500 kW
THAILAND
†RADIO THAILAND, Udon Thani — S • SE Asia & Australasia • 250 kW
UNITED KINGDOM
†BIBLE VOICE, Via Jülich, Germany — W Sa/Su • Mideast • 100 kW / W • Mideast • 100 kW / W W-Su • Mideast • 100 kW / W Tu • Mideast • 100 kW / W W/F-Sa • Mideast • 100 kW

USA
†ADVENTIST WORLD R, Via Abu Dhabi — W • C Asia • 250 kW
HERALD BROADCASTING, S Carolina — S F • Europe • 500 kW / S M/W • Europe • 500 kW / S Sa/Su • Europe • 500 kW / S Tu/Th • Europe • 500 kW / S M • Europe • 500 kW / S W/F • Europe • 500 kW

†VOA, Via Philippines — S • SE Asia • 250 kW
9865 **BELGIUM**
†R VLAANDEREN INTL, Via Pet-K, Russia — S • E Asia • 250 kW
CZECH REPUBLIC
RADIO PRAGUE, Litomyšl — S • E Europe • 100 kW / W • Mideast • 100 kW

NETHERLANDS
†R NEDERLAND, Via Khabarovsk, Russia — W • E Asia & SE Asia • 100 kW
RUSSIA
VOICE OF RUSSIA, Armavir — W • C Africa & S Africa • 500 kW / S • Europe • 500 kW
VOICE OF RUSSIA, Moscow — S • S Asia • 500 kW
VOICE OF RUSSIA, Novosibirsk — W • C Asia • 500 kW
SWEDEN
RADIO SWEDEN, Hörby
UNITED KINGDOM
†BBC, Rampisham — W M-F • E Europe & Mideast • 500 kW / W • S Europe • 500 kW

(con'd)

0 1 2 3 4 5 6 7 8 9 10 11 12 13 14 15 16 17 18 19 20 21 22 23 24

SEASONAL S OR W   1-HR TIMESHIFT MIDYEAR ⬅ OR ➡   JAMMING / OR ∧   EARLIEST HEARD ◁   LATEST HEARD ▷   NEW FOR 2004 †

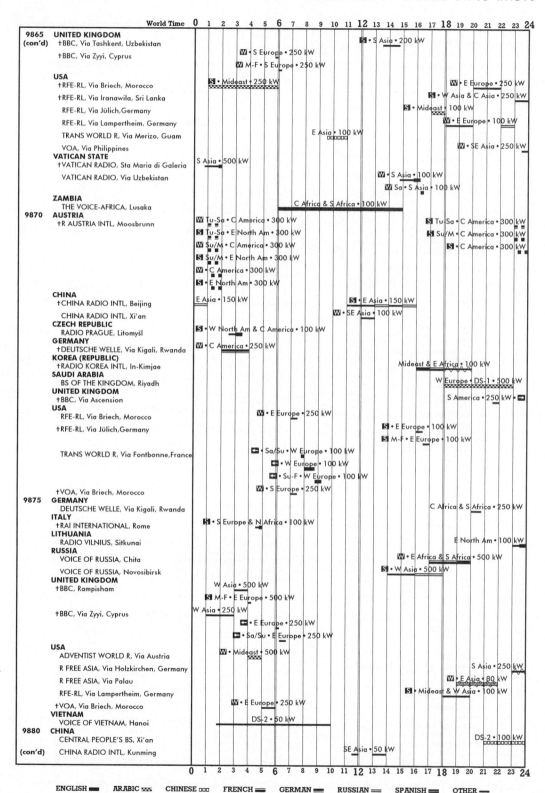

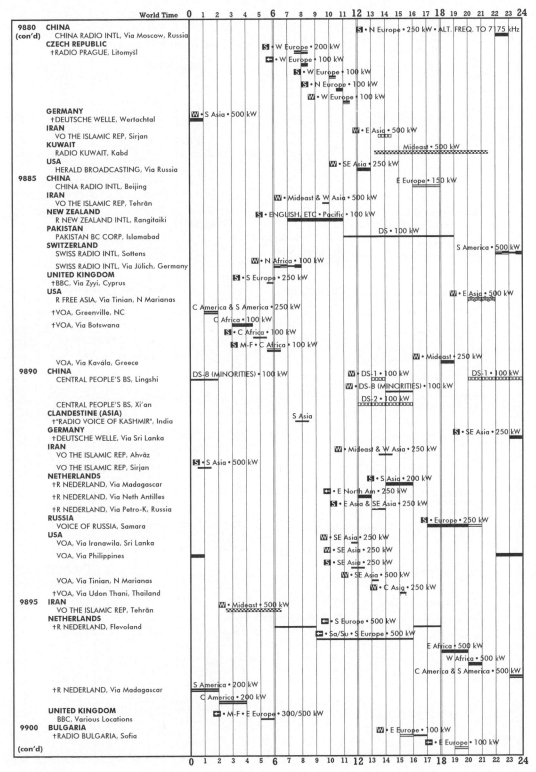

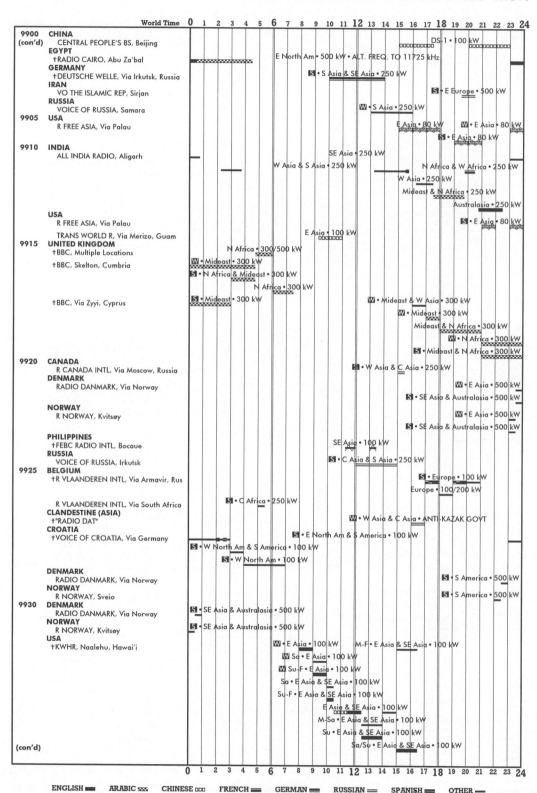

	World Time	0 1 2 3 4 5 6 7 8 9 10 11 12 13 14 15 16 17 18 19 20 21 22 23 24

9900 (con'd)
CHINA
 CENTRAL PEOPLE'S BS, Beijing — DS-1 • 100 kW
EGYPT
 †RADIO CAIRO, Abu Za'bal — E North Am • 500 kW • ALT. FREQ. TO 11725 kHz
GERMANY
 †DEUTSCHE WELLE, Via Irkutsk, Russia — S • S Asia & SE Asia • 250 kW
IRAN
 VO THE ISLAMIC REP, Sirjan — S • E Europe • 500 kW
RUSSIA
 VOICE OF RUSSIA, Samara — W • S Asia • 250 kW

9905 **USA**
 R FREE ASIA, Via Palau — E Asia • 80 kW / W • E Asia • 80 kW / S • E Asia • 80 kW

9910 **INDIA**
 ALL INDIA RADIO, Aligarh — SE Asia • 250 kW / W Asia & S Asia • 250 kW / N Africa & W Africa • 250 kW / W Asia • 250 kW / Mideast & N Africa • 250 kW / Australasia • 250 kW

USA
 R FREE ASIA, Via Palau — S • E Asia • 80 kW

 TRANS WORLD R, Via Merizo, Guam — E Asia • 100 kW

9915 **UNITED KINGDOM**
 †BBC, Multiple Locations — N Africa • 300/500 kW
 †BBC, Skelton, Cumbria — W • Mideast • 300 kW / S • N Africa & Mideast • 300 kW / N Africa • 300 kW

 †BBC, Via Zyyi, Cyprus — S • Mideast • 300 kW / W • Mideast & W Asia • 300 kW / W • Mideast • 300 kW / Mideast & N Africa • 300 kW / W • N Africa • 300 kW / S • Mideast & N Africa • 300 kW

9920 **CANADA**
 R CANADA INTL, Via Moscow, Russia — S • W Asia & C Asia • 250 kW
DENMARK
 RADIO DANMARK, Via Norway — W • E Asia • 500 kW / S • SE Asia & Australasia • 500 kW

NORWAY
 R NORWAY, Kvitsøy — W • E Asia • 500 kW / S • SE Asia & Australasia • 500 kW

PHILIPPINES
 †FEBC RADIO INTL, Bocaue — SE Asia • 100 kW
RUSSIA
 VOICE OF RUSSIA, Irkutsk — S • C Asia & S Asia • 250 kW

9925 **BELGIUM**
 †R VLAANDEREN INTL, Via Armavir, Rus — S • Europe • 100 kW / Europe • 100/200 kW

 R VLAANDEREN INTL, Via South Africa — S • C Africa • 250 kW
CLANDESTINE (ASIA)
 †"RADIO DAT" — W • W Asia & C Asia • ANTI-KAZAK GOVT
CROATIA
 †VOICE OF CROATIA, Via Germany — S • E North Am & S America • 100 kW / S • W North Am & S America • 100 kW / S • W North Am • 100 kW

DENMARK
 RADIO DANMARK, Via Norway — S • S America • 500 kW
NORWAY
 R NORWAY, Sveio — S • S America • 500 kW

9930 **DENMARK**
 RADIO DANMARK, Via Norway — S • SE Asia & Australasia • 500 kW
NORWAY
 R NORWAY, Kvitsøy — S • SE Asia & Australasia • 500 kW
USA
 †KWHR, Naalehu, Hawai'i — W • E Asia • 100 kW / M-F • E Asia & SE Asia • 100 kW / W Sa • E Asia • 100 kW / W Su-F • E Asia • 100 kW / Sa • E Asia & SE Asia • 100 kW / Su-F • E Asia & SE Asia • 100 kW / E Asia & SE Asia • 100 kW / M-Sa • E Asia & SE Asia • 100 kW / Su • E Asia & SE Asia • 100 kW / Sa/Su • E Asia & SE Asia • 100 kW

(con'd)

	0 1 2 3 4 5 6 7 8 9 10 11 12 13 14 15 16 17 18 19 20 21 22 23 24

ENGLISH ▬ ARABIC ⨯⨯⨯ CHINESE □□□ FRENCH ▬ GERMAN ▬ RUSSIAN ═ SPANISH ▬ OTHER ▬

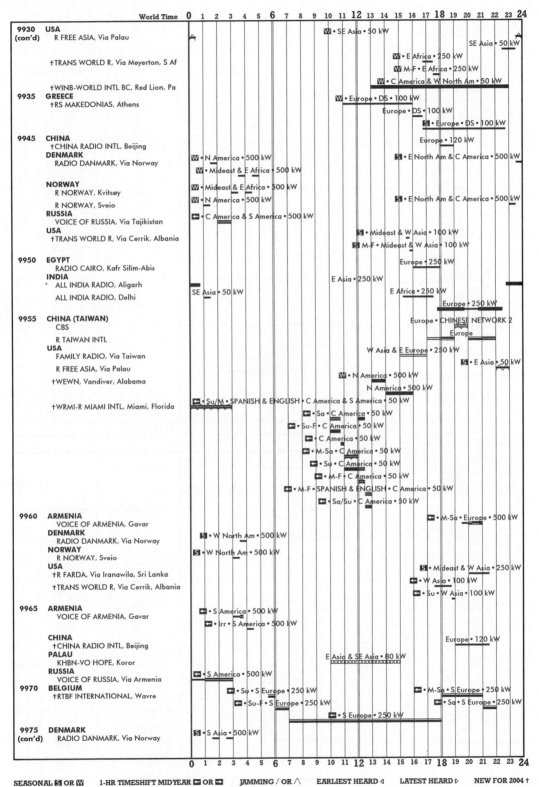

9930 (con'd)	USA	R FREE ASIA, Via Palau
		†TRANS WORLD R, Via Meyerton, S Af
		†WINB-WORLD INTL BC, Red Lion, Pa
9935	GREECE	†RS MAKEDONIAS, Athens
9945	CHINA	†CHINA RADIO INTL, Beijing
	DENMARK	RADIO DANMARK, Via Norway
	NORWAY	R NORWAY, Kvitsøy
		R NORWAY, Sveio
	RUSSIA	VOICE OF RUSSIA, Via Tajikistan
	USA	†TRANS WORLD R, Via Cerrik, Albania
9950	EGYPT	RADIO CAIRO, Kafr Silim-Abis
	INDIA	ALL INDIA RADIO, Aligarh
		ALL INDIA RADIO, Delhi
9955	CHINA (TAIWAN)	CBS
		R TAIWAN INTL
	USA	FAMILY RADIO, Via Taiwan
		R FREE ASIA, Via Palau
		†WEWN, Vandiver, Alabama
		†WRMI-R MIAMI INTL, Miami, Florida
9960	ARMENIA	VOICE OF ARMENIA, Gavar
	DENMARK	RADIO DANMARK, Via Norway
	NORWAY	R NORWAY, Sveio
	USA	†R FARDA, Via Iranawila, Sri Lanka
		†TRANS WORLD R, Via Cerrik, Albania
9965	ARMENIA	VOICE OF ARMENIA, Gavar
	CHINA	†CHINA RADIO INTL, Beijing
	PALAU	KHBN-VO HOPE, Koror
	RUSSIA	VOICE OF RUSSIA, Via Armenia
9970	BELGIUM	†RTBF INTERNATIONAL, Wavre
9975 (con'd)	DENMARK	RADIO DANMARK, Via Norway

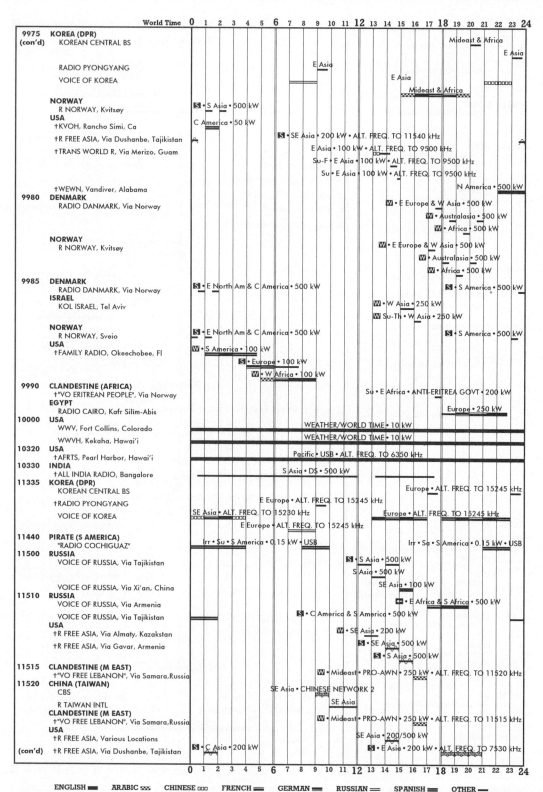

| | | World Time | 0 | 1 | 2 | 3 | 4 | 5 | 6 | 7 | 8 | 9 | 10 | 11 | 12 | 13 | 14 | 15 | 16 | 17 | 18 | 19 | 20 | 21 | 22 | 23 | 24 |

9975 (con'd) KOREA (DPR)
  KOREAN CENTRAL BS — Mideast & Africa / E Asia

  RADIO PYONGYANG — E Asia
  VOICE OF KOREA — E Asia / Mideast & Africa

  NORWAY
  R NORWAY, Kvitsøy — S • S Asia • 500 kW
  USA
  †KVOH, Rancho Simi, Ca — C America • 50 kW

  †R FREE ASIA, Via Dushanbe, Tajikistan — S • SE Asia • 200 kW • ALT. FREQ. TO 11540 kHz
  †TRANS WORLD R, Via Merizo, Guam — E Asia • 100 kW • ALT. FREQ. TO 9500 kHz
    Su-F • E Asia • 100 kW • ALT. FREQ. TO 9500 kHz
    Su • E Asia • 100 kW • ALT. FREQ. TO 9500 kHz

  †WEWN, Vandiver, Alabama — N America • 500 kW
9980 DENMARK
  RADIO DANMARK, Via Norway — W • E Europe & W Asia • 500 kW
    W • Australasia • 500 kW
    W • Africa • 500 kW

  NORWAY
  R NORWAY, Kvitsøy — W • E Europe & W Asia • 500 kW
    W • Australasia • 500 kW
    W • Africa • 500 kW

9985 DENMARK
  RADIO DANMARK, Via Norway — S • E North Am & C America • 500 kW / S • S America • 500 kW
  ISRAEL
  KOL ISRAEL, Tel Aviv — W • W Asia • 250 kW
    W Su-Th • W Asia • 250 kW

  NORWAY
  R NORWAY, Sveio — S • E North Am & C America • 500 kW / S • S America • 500 kW
  USA
  †FAMILY RADIO, Okeechobee, Fl — W • S America • 100 kW
    S • Europe • 100 kW
    W • W Africa • 100 kW

9990 CLANDESTINE (AFRICA)
  †"VO ERITREAN PEOPLE", Via Norway — Su • E Africa • ANTI-ERITREA GOVT • 200 kW
  EGYPT
  RADIO CAIRO, Kafr Silim-Abis — Europe • 250 kW
10000 USA
  WWV, Fort Collins, Colorado — WEATHER/WORLD TIME • 10 kW
  WWVH, Kekaha, Hawai'i — WEATHER/WORLD TIME • 10 kW
10320 USA
  †AFRTS, Pearl Harbor, Hawai'i — Pacific • USB • ALT. FREQ. TO 6350 kHz
10330 INDIA
  †ALL INDIA RADIO, Bangalore — S Asia • DS • 500 kW
11335 KOREA (DPR)
  KOREAN CENTRAL BS — Europe • ALT. FREQ. TO 15245 kHz
  †RADIO PYONGYANG — E Europe • ALT. FREQ. TO 15245 kHz
  VOICE OF KOREA — SE Asia • ALT. FREQ. TO 15230 kHz / Europe • ALT. FREQ. TO 15245 kHz
    E Europe • ALT. FREQ. TO 15245 kHz

11440 PIRATE (S AMERICA)
  "RADIO COCHIGUAZ" — Irr • Su • S America • 0.15 kW • USB / Irr • Sa • S America • 0.15 kW • USB
11500 RUSSIA
  VOICE OF RUSSIA, Via Tajikistan — S • S Asia • 500 kW
    S Asia • 500 kW

  VOICE OF RUSSIA, Via Xi'an, China — SE Asia • 100 kW
11510 RUSSIA
  VOICE OF RUSSIA, Via Armenia — • E Africa & S Africa • 500 kW
  VOICE OF RUSSIA, Via Tajikistan — S • C America & S America • 500 kW
  USA
  †R FREE ASIA, Via Almaty, Kazakstan — W • SE Asia • 200 kW
  †R FREE ASIA, Via Gavar, Armenia — S • SE Asia • 500 kW
    S • S Asia • 500 kW

11515 CLANDESTINE (M EAST)
  †"VO FREE LEBANON", Via Samara, Russia — W • Mideast • PRO-AWN • 250 kW • ALT. FREQ. TO 11520 kHz
11520 CHINA (TAIWAN)
  CBS — SE Asia • CHINESE NETWORK 2

  R TAIWAN INTL — SE Asia
  CLANDESTINE (M EAST)
  †"VO FREE LEBANON", Via Samara, Russia — W • Mideast • PRO-AWN • 250 kW • ALT. FREQ. TO 11515 kHz
  USA
  †R FREE ASIA, Various Locations — SE Asia • 200/500 kW
(con'd) †R FREE ASIA, Via Dushanbe, Tajikistan — S • C Asia • 200 kW / S • E Asia • 200 kW • ALT. FREQ. TO 7530 kHz

| | World Time | 0 | 1 | 2 | 3 | 4 | 5 | 6 | 7 | 8 | 9 | 10 | 11 | 12 | 13 | 14 | 15 | 16 | 17 | 18 | 19 | 20 | 21 | 22 | 23 | 24 |

ENGLISH ▬ ARABIC ▨ CHINESE ▭▭▭ FRENCH ▬▬ GERMAN ▬▬▬ RUSSIAN ═══ SPANISH ▬▬▬ OTHER ▬▬

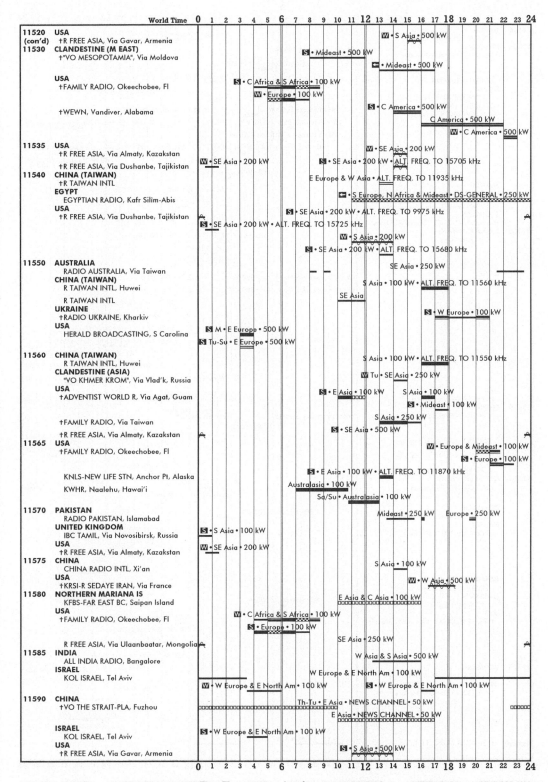

		World Time	0 1 2 3 4 5 6 7 8 9 10 11 12 13 14 15 16 17 18 19 20 21 22 23 24

11520 USA
(con'd)   †R FREE ASIA, Via Gavar, Armenia — Ⓦ • S Asia • 500 kW

11530 CLANDESTINE (M EAST)
   †"VO MESOPOTAMIA", Via Moldova — Ⓢ • Mideast • 500 kW
   — ⬅ • Mideast • 500 kW

USA
   †FAMILY RADIO, Okeechobee, Fl — Ⓢ • C Africa & S Africa • 100 kW
   — Ⓦ • Europe • 100 kW

   †WEWN, Vandiver, Alabama — Ⓢ • C America • 500 kW
   — C America • 500 kW
   — Ⓦ • C America • 500 kW

11535 USA
   †R FREE ASIA, Via Almaty, Kazakstan — Ⓦ • SE Asia • 200 kW
   †R FREE ASIA, Via Dushanbe, Tajikistan — Ⓦ • SE Asia • 200 kW — Ⓢ • SE Asia • 200 kW • ALT. FREQ. TO 15705 kHz

11540 CHINA (TAIWAN)
   †R TAIWAN INTL — E Europe & W Asia • ALT. FREQ. TO 11935 kHz

EGYPT
   EGYPTIAN RADIO, Kafr Silim-Abis — ⬅ • S Europe, N Africa & Mideast • DS-GENERAL • 250 kW

USA
   †R FREE ASIA, Via Dushanbe, Tajikistan — Ⓢ • SE Asia • 200 kW • ALT. FREQ. TO 9975 kHz
   — Ⓢ • SE Asia • 200 kW • ALT. FREQ. TO 15725 kHz
   — Ⓦ • S Asia • 200 kW
   — Ⓢ • SE Asia • 200 kW • ALT. FREQ. TO 15680 kHz

11550 AUSTRALIA
   RADIO AUSTRALIA, Via Taiwan — SE Asia • 250 kW

CHINA (TAIWAN)
   R TAIWAN INTL, Huwei — S Asia • 100 kW • ALT. FREQ. TO 11560 kHz

   R TAIWAN INTL — SE Asia

UKRAINE
   †RADIO UKRAINE, Kharkiv — Ⓦ • W Europe • 100 kW

USA
   HERALD BROADCASTING, S Carolina — Ⓢ M • E Europe • 500 kW
   — Ⓢ Tu-Su • E Europe • 500 kW

11560 CHINA (TAIWAN)
   R TAIWAN INTL, Huwei — S Asia • 100 kW • ALT. FREQ. TO 11550 kHz

CLANDESTINE (ASIA)
   "VO KHMER KROM", Via Vlad'k, Russia — Ⓦ Tu • SE Asia • 250 kW

USA
   †ADVENTIST WORLD R, Via Agat, Guam — Ⓢ • E Asia • 100 kW — S Asia • 100 kW
   — Ⓢ • Mideast • 100 kW

   †FAMILY RADIO, Via Taiwan — S Asia • 250 kW

   †R FREE ASIA, Via Almaty, Kazakstan — Ⓢ • SE Asia • 500 kW

11565 USA
   †FAMILY RADIO, Okeechobee, Fl — Ⓦ • Europe & Mideast • 100 kW
   — Ⓢ • Europe • 100 kW

   KNLS-NEW LIFE STN, Anchor Pt, Alaska — Ⓢ • E Asia • 100 kW • ALT. FREQ. TO 11870 kHz

   KWHR, Naalehu, Hawai'i — Australasia • 100 kW
   — Sa/Su • Australasia • 100 kW

11570 PAKISTAN
   RADIO PAKISTAN, Islamabad — Mideast • 250 kW — Europe • 250 kW

UNITED KINGDOM
   IBC TAMIL, Via Novosibirsk, Russia — Ⓢ • S Asia • 100 kW

USA
   †R FREE ASIA, Via Almaty, Kazakstan — Ⓦ • SE Asia • 200 kW

11575 CHINA
   CHINA RADIO INTL, Xi'an — S Asia • 100 kW

USA
   †KRSI-R SEDAYE IRAN, Via France — Ⓦ • W Asia • 500 kW

11580 NORTHERN MARIANA IS
   KFBS-FAR EAST BC, Saipan Island — E Asia & C Asia • 100 kW

USA
   †FAMILY RADIO, Okeechobee, Fl — Ⓦ • C Africa & S Africa • 100 kW
   — Ⓢ • Europe • 100 kW

   R FREE ASIA, Via Ulaanbaatar, Mongolia — SE Asia • 250 kW

11585 INDIA
   ALL INDIA RADIO, Bangalore — W Asia & S Asia • 500 kW

ISRAEL
   KOL ISRAEL, Tel Aviv — W Europe & E North Am • 100 kW
   — Ⓦ • W Europe & E North Am • 100 kW — Ⓢ • W Europe & E North Am • 100 kW

11590 CHINA
   †VO THE STRAIT-PLA, Fuzhou — Th-Tu • E Asia • NEWS CHANNEL • 50 kW
   — E Asia • NEWS CHANNEL • 50 kW

ISRAEL
   KOL ISRAEL, Tel Aviv — Ⓢ • W Europe & E North Am • 100 kW

USA
   †R FREE ASIA, Via Gavar, Armenia — Ⓢ • S Asia • 500 kW

	World Time	0 1 2 3 4 5 6 7 8 9 10 11 12 13 14 15 16 17 18 19 20 21 22 23 24

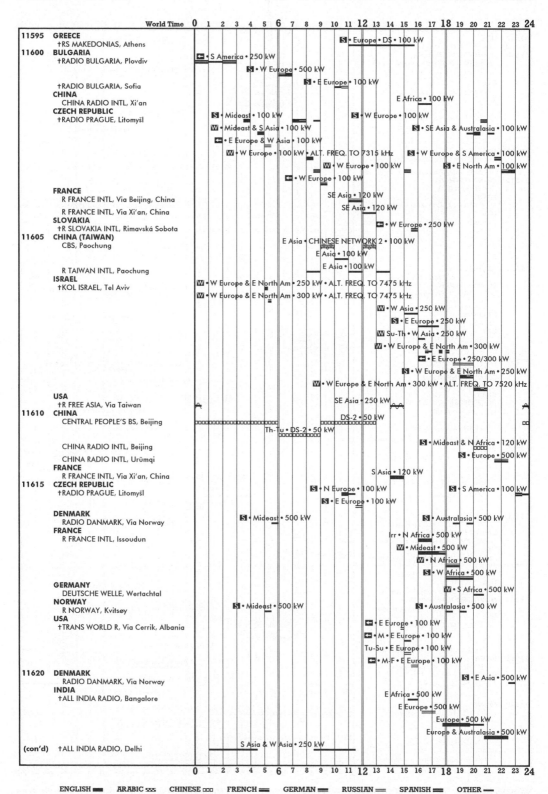

	World Time	0 1 2 3 4 5 6 7 8 9 10 11 12 13 14 15 16 17 18 19 20 21 22 23 24
11595	**GREECE**	
	†RS MAKEDONIAS, Athens	**S** • Europe • D**S** • 100 kW
11600	**BULGARIA**	
	†RADIO BULGARIA, Plovdiv	**□** • S America • 250 kW
		S • W Europe • 500 kW
	†RADIO BULGARIA, Sofia	**S** • E Europe • 100 kW
	CHINA	
	CHINA RADIO INTL, Xi'an	E Africa • 100 kW
	CZECH REPUBLIC	
	†RADIO PRAGUE, Litomyšl	**S** • Mideast • 100 kW　　　**S** • W Europe • 100 kW
		W • Mideast & S Asia • 100 kW
		S • SE Asia & Australasia • 100 kW
		□ • E Europe & W Asia • 100 kW
		W • W Europe • 100 kW • ALT. FREQ. TO 7315 kHz　　**S** • W Europe & S America • 100 kW
		W • W Europe • 100 kW　　　**S** • E North Am • 100 kW
		□ • W Europe • 100 kW
	FRANCE	
	R FRANCE INTL, Via Beijing, China	SE Asia • 120 kW
	R FRANCE INTL, Via Xi'an, China	SE Asia • 120 kW
	SLOVAKIA	
	†R SLOVAKIA INTL, Rimavská Sobota	**□** • W Europe • 250 kW
11605	**CHINA (TAIWAN)**	
	CBS, Paochung	E Asia • CHINESE NETWORK 2 • 100 kW
		E Asia • 100 kW
		E Asia • 100 kW
	R TAIWAN INTL, Paochung	
	ISRAEL	
	†KOL ISRAEL, Tel Aviv	**W** • W Europe & E North Am • 250 kW • ALT. FREQ. TO 7475 kHz
		W • W Europe & E North Am • 300 kW • ALT. FREQ. TO 7475 kHz
		W • W Asia • 250 kW
		S • E Europe • 250 kW
		W Su-Th • W Asia • 250 kW
		W • W Europe & E North Am • 300 kW
		□ • E Europe • 250/300 kW
		S • W Europe & E North Am • 250 kW
		W • W Europe & E North Am • 300 kW • ALT. FREQ. TO 7520 kHz
	USA	
	†R FREE ASIA, Via Taiwan	SE Asia • 250 kW
11610	**CHINA**	
	CENTRAL PEOPLE'S BS, Beijing	DS-2 • 50 kW
		Th-Tu • DS-2 • 50 kW
	CHINA RADIO INTL, Beijing	**S** • Mideast & N Africa • 120 kW
	CHINA RADIO INTL, Urümqi	**S** • Europe • 500 kW
	FRANCE	
	R FRANCE INTL, Via Xi'an, China	S Asia • 120 kW
11615	**CZECH REPUBLIC**	
	†RADIO PRAGUE, Litomyšl	**S** • N Europe • 100 kW　　　**S** • S America • 100 kW
		S • E Europe • 100 kW
	DENMARK	
	RADIO DANMARK, Via Norway	**S** • Mideast • 500 kW　　　**S** • Australasia • 500 kW
	FRANCE	
	R FRANCE INTL, Issoudun	Irr • N Africa • 500 kW
		W • Mideast • 500 kW
		W • N Africa • 500 kW
		S • W Africa • 500 kW
	GERMANY	
	DEUTSCHE WELLE, Wertachtal	**W** • S Africa • 500 kW
	NORWAY	
	R NORWAY, Kvitsøy	**S** • Mideast • 500 kW　　　**S** • Australasia • 500 kW
	USA	
	†TRANS WORLD R, Via Cerrik, Albania	**□** • E Europe • 100 kW
		□ • M • E Europe • 100 kW
		Tu-Su • E Europe • 100 kW
		□ • M-F • E Europe • 100 kW
11620	**DENMARK**	
	RADIO DANMARK, Via Norway	**S** • E Asia • 500 kW
	INDIA	
	†ALL INDIA RADIO, Bangalore	E Africa • 500 kW
		E Europe • 500 kW
		Europe • 500 kW
		Europe & Australasia • 500 kW
(con'd)	†ALL INDIA RADIO, Delhi	S Asia & W Asia • 250 kW
		0 1 2 3 4 5 6 7 8 9 10 11 12 13 14 15 16 17 18 19 20 21 22 23 24

ENGLISH ■　ARABIC ⁙　CHINESE ▭▭▭　FRENCH ▬　GERMAN ▬　RUSSIAN ═　SPANISH ▬　OTHER ▬

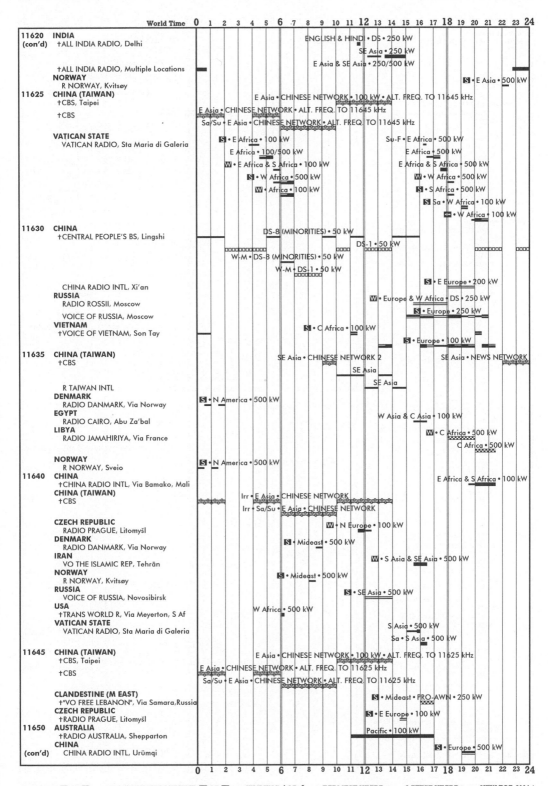

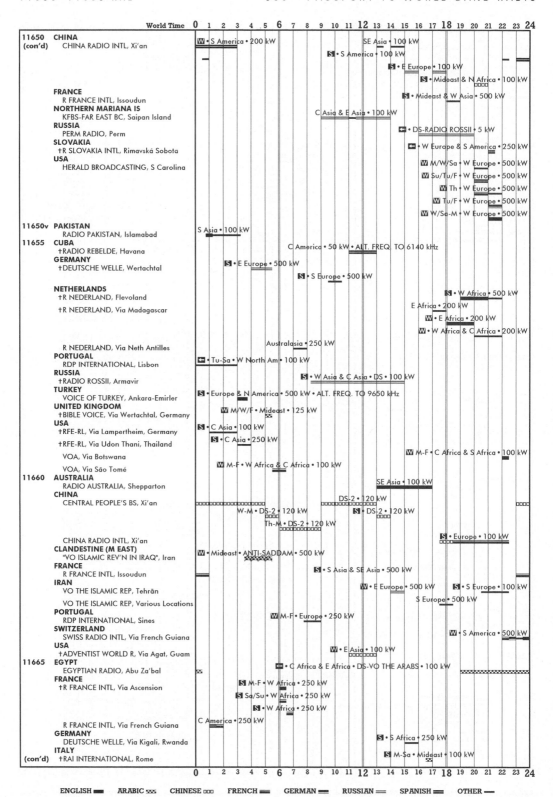

World Time 0 1 2 3 4 5 6 7 8 9 10 11 12 13 14 15 16 17 18 19 20 21 22 23 24

Frequency	Station	
11650 (con'd)	**CHINA** CHINA RADIO INTL, Xi'an	W • S America • 200 kW / SE Asia • 100 kW / S • S America • 100 kW / S • E Europe • 100 kW / S • Mideast & N Africa • 100 kW
	FRANCE R FRANCE INTL, Issoudun	S • Mideast & W Asia • 500 kW
	NORTHERN MARIANA IS KFBS-FAR EAST BC, Saipan Island	C Asia & E Asia • 100 kW
	RUSSIA PERM RADIO, Perm	• DS-RADIO ROSSII • 5 kW
	SLOVAKIA †R SLOVAKIA INTL, Rimavská Sobota	• W Europe & S America • 250 kW
	USA HERALD BROADCASTING, S Carolina	W M/W/Sa • W Europe • 500 kW / W Su/Tu/F • W Europe • 500 kW / W Th • W Europe • 500 kW / W Tu/F • W Europe • 500 kW / W W/Sa-M • W Europe • 500 kW
11650v	**PAKISTAN** RADIO PAKISTAN, Islamabad	S Asia • 100 kW
11655	**CUBA** †RADIO REBELDE, Havana	C America • 50 kW • ALT. FREQ. TO 6140 kHz
	GERMANY †DEUTSCHE WELLE, Wertachtal	S • E Europe • 500 kW / S • S Europe • 500 kW
	NETHERLANDS †R NEDERLAND, Flevoland	S • W Africa • 500 kW / E Africa • 200 kW
	†R NEDERLAND, Via Madagascar	W • E Africa • 200 kW / W • W Africa & C Africa • 200 kW
	R NEDERLAND, Via Neth Antilles	Australasia • 250 kW
	PORTUGAL RDP INTERNATIONAL, Lisbon	• Tu-Sa • W North Am • 100 kW
	RUSSIA †RADIO ROSSII, Armavir	S • W Asia & C Asia • DS • 100 kW
	TURKEY VOICE OF TURKEY, Ankara-Emirler	S • Europe & N America • 500 kW • ALT. FREQ. TO 9650 kHz
	UNITED KINGDOM †BIBLE VOICE, Via Wertachtal, Germany	W M/W/F • Mideast • 125 kW
	USA †RFE-RL, Via Lampertheim, Germany	S • C Asia • 100 kW
	†RFE-RL, Via Udon Thani, Thailand	S • C Asia • 250 kW
	VOA, Via Botswana	W M-F • C Africa & S Africa • 100 kW
	VOA, Via São Tomé	W M-F • W Africa & C Africa • 100 kW
11660	**AUSTRALIA** RADIO AUSTRALIA, Shepparton	SE Asia • 100 kW
	CHINA CENTRAL PEOPLE'S BS, Xi'an	DS-2 • 120 kW / W-M • DS-2 • 120 kW / S • DS-2 • 120 kW / Th-M • DS-2 • 120 kW
	CHINA RADIO INTL, Xi'an	S • Europe • 100 kW
	CLANDESTINE (M EAST) "VO ISLAMIC REV'N IN IRAQ", Iran	W • Mideast • ANTI-SADDAM • 500 kW
	FRANCE R FRANCE INTL, Issoudun	S • S Asia & SE Asia • 500 kW
	IRAN VO THE ISLAMIC REP, Tehrān	W • E Europe • 500 kW / S • S Europe • 100 kW
	VO THE ISLAMIC REP, Various Locations	S Europe • 500 kW
	PORTUGAL RDP INTERNATIONAL, Sines	W M-F • Europe • 250 kW
	SWITZERLAND SWISS RADIO INTL, Via French Guiana	W • S America • 500 kW
	USA †ADVENTIST WORLD R, Via Agat, Guam	W • E Asia • 100 kW
11665	**EGYPT** EGYPTIAN RADIO, Abu Za'bal	• C Africa & E Africa • DS-VO THE ARABS • 100 kW
	FRANCE †R FRANCE INTL, Via Ascension	S M-F • W Africa • 250 kW / S Sa/Su • W Africa • 250 kW / S • W Africa • 250 kW
	R FRANCE INTL, Via French Guiana	C America • 250 kW
	GERMANY DEUTSCHE WELLE, Via Kigali, Rwanda	S • S Africa • 250 kW
(con'd)	**ITALY** †RAI INTERNATIONAL, Rome	S M-Sa • Mideast • 100 kW

0 1 2 3 4 5 6 7 8 9 10 11 12 13 14 15 16 17 18 19 20 21 22 23 24

ENGLISH ▬ ARABIC ⠶⠶⠶ CHINESE ⠿⠿⠿ FRENCH ═══ GERMAN ▬▬ RUSSIAN ═══ SPANISH ▬▬ OTHER ──

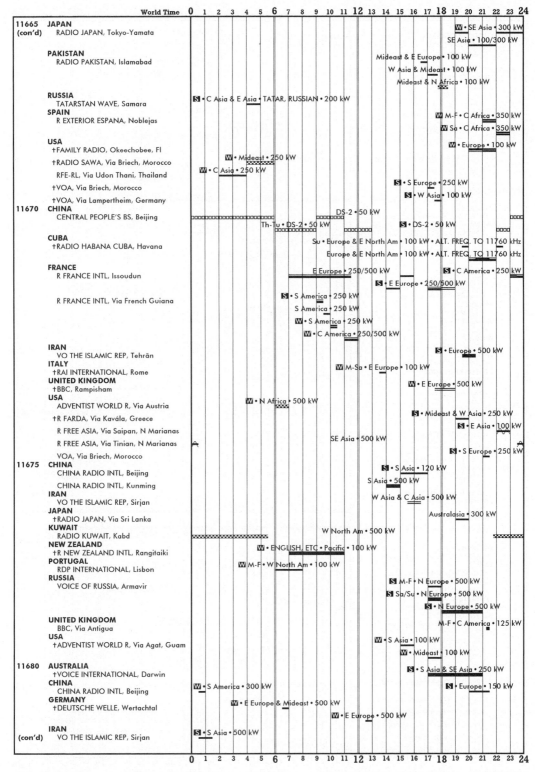

World Time 0 1 2 3 4 5 6 7 8 9 10 11 12 13 14 15 16 17 18 19 20 21 22 23 24

11665 JAPAN
(con'd) RADIO JAPAN, Tokyo-Yamata — W • SE Asia • 300 kW / SE Asia • 100/300 kW

PAKISTAN
RADIO PAKISTAN, Islamabad — Mideast & E Europe • 100 kW / W Asia & Mideast • 100 kW / Mideast & N Africa • 100 kW

RUSSIA
TATARSTAN WAVE, Samara — S • C Asia & E Asia • TATAR, RUSSIAN • 200 kW
SPAIN
R EXTERIOR ESPANA, Noblejas — W M-F • C Africa • 350 kW / W Sa • C Africa • 350 kW / W • Europe • 100 kW

USA
†FAMILY RADIO, Okeechobee, Fl — W • Mideast • 250 kW
†RADIO SAWA, Via Briech, Morocco — W • C Asia • 250 kW
RFE-RL, Via Udon Thani, Thailand
†VOA, Via Briech, Morocco — S • S Europe • 250 kW
†VOA, Via Lampertheim, Germany — S • W Asia • 100 kW

11670 CHINA
CENTRAL PEOPLE'S BS, Beijing — DS-2 • 50 kW / Th-Tu • DS-2 • 50 kW / S • DS-2 • 50 kW

CUBA
†RADIO HABANA CUBA, Havana — Su • Europe & E North Am • 100 kW • ALT. FREQ. TO 11760 kHz / Europe & E North Am • 100 kW • ALT. FREQ. TO 11760 kHz

FRANCE
R FRANCE INTL, Issoudun — E Europe • 250/500 kW / S • C America • 250 kW / S • E Europe • 250/500 kW

R FRANCE INTL, Via French Guiana — S • S America • 250 kW / S America • 250 kW / W • S America • 250 kW / W • C America • 250/500 kW

IRAN
VO THE ISLAMIC REP, Tehrān — S • Europe • 500 kW
ITALY
†RAI INTERNATIONAL, Rome — W M-Sa • E Europe • 100 kW
UNITED KINGDOM
†BBC, Rampisham — W • E Europe • 500 kW
USA
ADVENTIST WORLD R, Via Austria — W • N Africa • 500 kW
†R FARDA, Via Kavála, Greece — S • Mideast & W Asia • 250 kW
R FREE ASIA, Via Saipan, N Marianas — S • E Asia • 100 kW
R FREE ASIA, Via Tinian, N Marianas — SE Asia • 500 kW
VOA, Via Briech, Morocco — S • S Europe • 250 kW

11675 CHINA
CHINA RADIO INTL, Beijing — S • S Asia • 120 kW
CHINA RADIO INTL, Kunming — S Asia • 500 kW
IRAN
VO THE ISLAMIC REP, Sirjan — W Asia & C Asia • 500 kW
JAPAN
†RADIO JAPAN, Via Sri Lanka — Australasia • 300 kW
KUWAIT
RADIO KUWAIT, Kabd — W North Am • 500 kW
NEW ZEALAND
†R NEW ZEALAND INTL, Rangitaiki — W • ENGLISH, ETC • Pacific • 100 kW
PORTUGAL
RDP INTERNATIONAL, Lisbon — W M-F • W North Am • 100 kW
RUSSIA
VOICE OF RUSSIA, Armavir — S M-F • N Europe • 500 kW / S Sa/Su • N Europe • 500 kW / S • N Europe • 500 kW

UNITED KINGDOM
BBC, Via Antigua — M-F • C America • 125 kW
USA
†ADVENTIST WORLD R, Via Agat, Guam — W • S Asia • 100 kW / W • Mideast • 100 kW

11680 AUSTRALIA
†VOICE INTERNATIONAL, Darwin — S • S Asia & SE Asia • 250 kW
CHINA
CHINA RADIO INTL, Beijing — W • S America • 300 kW / S • Europe • 150 kW
GERMANY
†DEUTSCHE WELLE, Wertachtal — W • E Europe & Mideast • 500 kW / W • E Europe • 500 kW

IRAN
(con'd) VO THE ISLAMIC REP, Sirjan — S • S Asia • 500 kW

0 1 2 3 4 5 6 7 8 9 10 11 12 13 14 15 16 17 18 19 20 21 22 23 24

SEASONAL S OR W   1-HR TIMESHIFT MIDYEAR ⇦ OR ⇨   JAMMING / OR ∧   EARLIEST HEARD ◁   LATEST HEARD ▷   NEW FOR 2004 †

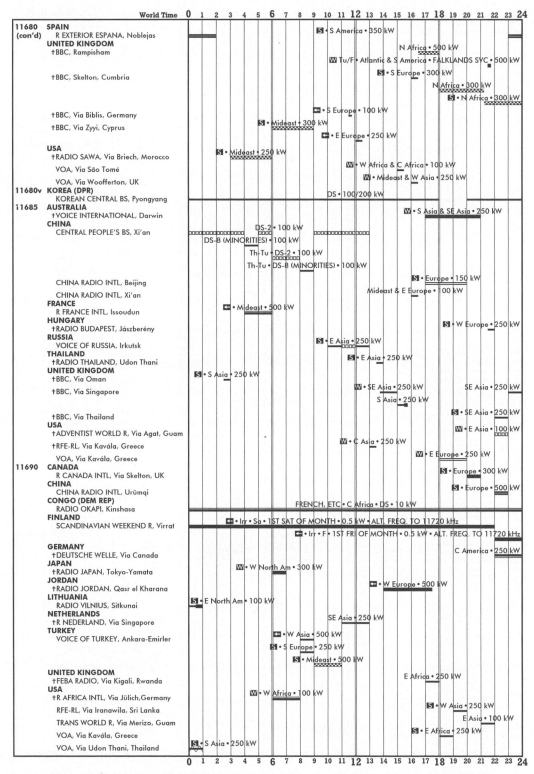

11680 (con'd)	**SPAIN** R EXTERIOR ESPANA, Noblejas — S · S America · 350 kW
	UNITED KINGDOM †BBC, Rampisham — N Africa · 500 kW / W Tu/F · Atlantic & S America · FALKLANDS SVC · 500 kW
	†BBC, Skelton, Cumbria — S · S Europe · 300 kW / N Africa · 300 kW / S · N Africa · 300 kW
	†BBC, Via Biblis, Germany — S Europe · 100 kW
	†BBC, Via Zyyi, Cyprus — S · Mideast · 300 kW / E Europe · 250 kW
	USA †RADIO SAWA, Via Briech, Morocco — S · Mideast · 250 kW
	VOA, Via São Tomé — W · W Africa & C Africa · 100 kW
	VOA, Via Woofferton, UK — W · Mideast & W Asia · 250 kW
11680v	**KOREA (DPR)** KOREAN CENTRAL BS, Pyongyang — DS · 100/200 kW
11685	**AUSTRALIA** †VOICE INTERNATIONAL, Darwin — W · S Asia & SE Asia · 250 kW
	CHINA CENTRAL PEOPLE'S BS, Xi'an — DS-2 · 100 kW / DS-8 (MINORITIES) · 100 kW / Th-Tu · DS-2 · 100 kW / Th-Tu · DS-8 (MINORITIES) · 100 kW
	CHINA RADIO INTL, Beijing — S · Europe · 150 kW
	CHINA RADIO INTL, Xi'an — Mideast & E Europe · 100 kW
	FRANCE R FRANCE INTL, Issoudun — Mideast · 500 kW
	HUNGARY †RADIO BUDAPEST, Jászberény — S · W Europe · 250 kW
	RUSSIA VOICE OF RUSSIA, Irkutsk — S · E Asia · 250 kW
	THAILAND †RADIO THAILAND, Udon Thani — S · E Asia · 250 kW
	UNITED KINGDOM †BBC, Via Oman — S · S Asia · 250 kW
	†BBC, Via Singapore — W · SE Asia · 250 kW / SE Asia · 250 kW / S Asia · 250 kW
	†BBC, Via Thailand — S · SE Asia · 250 kW
	USA †ADVENTIST WORLD R, Via Agat, Guam — W · E Asia · 100 kW
	†RFE-RL, Via Kavála, Greece — W · C Asia · 250 kW
	VOA, Via Kavála, Greece — W · E Europe · 250 kW
11690	**CANADA** R CANADA INTL, Via Skelton, UK — S · Europe · 300 kW
	CHINA CHINA RADIO INTL, Urümqi — S · Europe · 500 kW
	CONGO (DEM REP) RADIO OKAPI, Kinshasa — FRENCH, ETC · C Africa · DS · 10 kW
	FINLAND SCANDINAVIAN WEEKEND R, Virrat — Irr · Sa · 1ST SAT OF MONTH · 0.5 kW · ALT. FREQ. TO 11720 kHz / Irr · F · 1ST FRI OF MONTH · 0.5 kW · ALT. FREQ. TO 11720 kHz
	GERMANY †DEUTSCHE WELLE, Via Canada — C America · 250 kW
	JAPAN †RADIO JAPAN, Tokyo-Yamata — W · W North Am · 300 kW
	JORDAN †RADIO JORDAN, Qasr el Kharana — W Europe · 500 kW
	LITHUANIA RADIO VILNIUS, Sitkunai — S · E North Am · 100 kW
	NETHERLANDS †R NEDERLAND, Via Singapore — SE Asia · 250 kW
	TURKEY VOICE OF TURKEY, Ankara-Emirler — W Asia · 500 kW / S · S Europe · 250 kW / S · Mideast · 500 kW
	UNITED KINGDOM †FEBA RADIO, Via Kigali, Rwanda — E Africa · 250 kW
	USA †R AFRICA INTL, Via Jülich, Germany — W · W Africa · 100 kW
	RFE-RL, Via Iranawila, Sri Lanka — S · W Asia · 250 kW
	TRANS WORLD R, Via Merizo, Guam — E Asia · 100 kW
	VOA, Via Kavála, Greece — S · E Africa · 250 kW
	VOA, Via Udon Thani, Thailand — S · S Asia · 250 kW

ENGLISH ▬   ARABIC ▨▨▨   CHINESE ▫▫▫   FRENCH ▬   GERMAN ▬   RUSSIAN ▭   SPANISH ▭   OTHER ▬

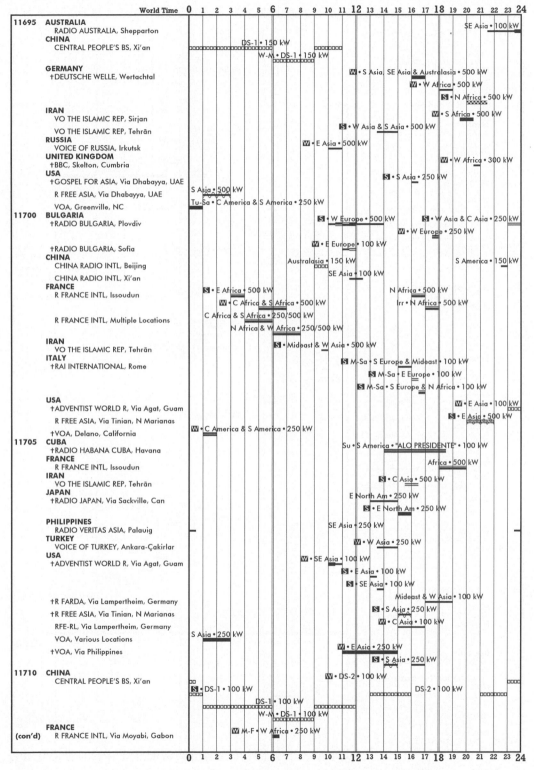

World Time 0 1 2 3 4 5 6 7 8 9 10 11 12 13 14 15 16 17 18 19 20 21 22 23 24

11695 AUSTRALIA
RADIO AUSTRALIA, Shepparton — SE Asia • 100 kW
CHINA
CENTRAL PEOPLE'S BS, Xi'an — DS-1 • 150 kW / W-M • DS-1 • 150 kW

GERMANY
†DEUTSCHE WELLE, Wertachtal — W • S Asia, SE Asia & Australasia • 500 kW / W • W Africa • 500 kW / S • N Africa • 500 kW

IRAN
VO THE ISLAMIC REP, Sirjan — W • S Africa • 500 kW
VO THE ISLAMIC REP, Tehrān — S • W Asia & S Asia • 500 kW
RUSSIA
VOICE OF RUSSIA, Irkutsk — W • E Asia • 500 kW
UNITED KINGDOM
†BBC, Skelton, Cumbria — W • W Africa • 300 kW
USA
†GOSPEL FOR ASIA, Via Dhabayya, UAE — S • S Asia • 250 kW
R FREE ASIA, Via Dhabayya, UAE — S Asia • 500 kW
VOA, Greenville, NC — Tu-Sa • C America & S America • 250 kW

11700 BULGARIA
†RADIO BULGARIA, Plovdiv — S • W Europe • 500 kW / S • W Asia & C Asia • 250 kW / W • W Europe • 250 kW

†RADIO BULGARIA, Sofia — W • E Europe • 100 kW
CHINA
CHINA RADIO INTL, Beijing — Australasia • 150 kW / S America • 150 kW
CHINA RADIO INTL, Xi'an — SE Asia • 100 kW
FRANCE
R FRANCE INTL, Issoudun — S • E Africa • 500 kW / N Africa • 500 kW / W • C Africa & S Africa • 500 kW / Irr • N Africa • 500 kW

R FRANCE INTL, Multiple Locations — C Africa & S Africa • 250/500 kW / N Africa & W Africa • 250/500 kW

IRAN
VO THE ISLAMIC REP, Tehrān — S • Mideast & W Asia • 500 kW
ITALY
†RAI INTERNATIONAL, Rome — S M-Sa • S Europe & Mideast • 100 kW / S M-Sa • E Europe • 100 kW / S M-Sa • S Europe & N Africa • 100 kW

USA
†ADVENTIST WORLD R, Via Agat, Guam — W • E Asia • 100 kW
R FREE ASIA, Via Tinian, N Marianas — S • E Asia • 500 kW
†VOA, Delano, California — W • C America & S America • 250 kW

11705 CUBA
†RADIO HABANA CUBA, Havana — Su • S America • "ALO PRESIDENTE" • 100 kW
FRANCE
R FRANCE INTL, Issoudun — Africa • 500 kW
IRAN
VO THE ISLAMIC REP, Tehrān — S • C Asia • 500 kW
JAPAN
†RADIO JAPAN, Via Sackville, Can — E North Am • 250 kW / S • E North Am • 250 kW

PHILIPPINES
RADIO VERITAS ASIA, Palauig — SE Asia • 250 kW
TURKEY
VOICE OF TURKEY, Ankara-Çakirlar — W • W Asia • 250 kW
USA
†ADVENTIST WORLD R, Via Agat, Guam — W • SE Asia • 100 kW / S • E Asia • 100 kW / S • SE Asia • 100 kW

†R FARDA, Via Lampertheim, Germany — Mideast & W Asia • 100 kW
†R FREE ASIA, Via Tinian, N Marianas — S • S Asia • 250 kW
RFE-RL, Via Lampertheim, Germany — W • C Asia • 100 kW
VOA, Various Locations — S Asia • 250 kW
†VOA, Via Philippines — W • E Asia • 250 kW / S • S Asia • 250 kW

11710 CHINA
CENTRAL PEOPLE'S BS, Xi'an — W • DS-2 • 100 kW / S • DS-1 • 100 kW / DS-2 • 100 kW / DS-1 • 100 kW / W-M • DS-1 • 100 kW

(con'd) FRANCE
R FRANCE INTL, Via Moyabi, Gabon — W M-F • W Africa • 250 kW

0 1 2 3 4 5 6 7 8 9 10 11 12 13 14 15 16 17 18 19 20 21 22 23 24

SEASONAL S OR W   1-HR TIMESHIFT MIDYEAR ⊏ OR ⊐   JAMMING / OR ∧   EARLIEST HEARD ◁   LATEST HEARD ▷   NEW FOR 2004 †

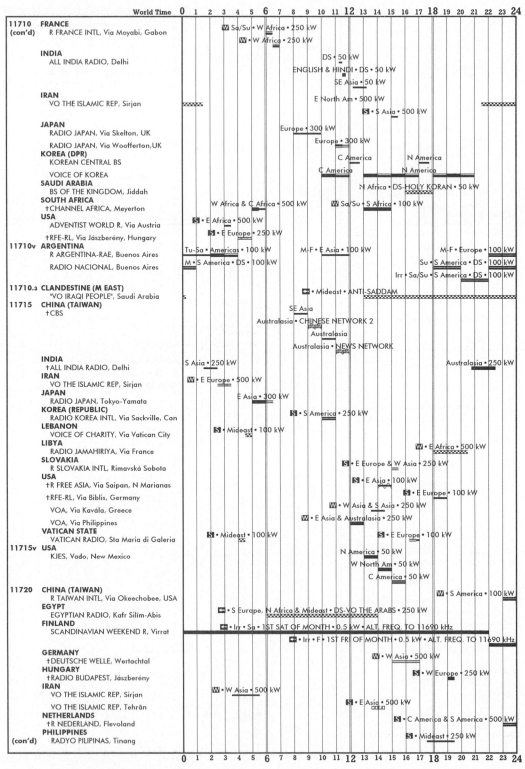

| World Time | 0 | 1 | 2 | 3 | 4 | 5 | 6 | 7 | 8 | 9 | 10 | 11 | 12 | 13 | 14 | 15 | 16 | 17 | 18 | 19 | 20 | 21 | 22 | 23 | 24 |

11710 FRANCE
(con'd)　R FRANCE INTL, Via Moyabi, Gabon — W•Sa/Su•W Africa•250 kW ; W•W Africa•250 kW

INDIA
ALL INDIA RADIO, Delhi — DS•50 kW ; ENGLISH & HINDI•DS•50 kW ; SE Asia•50 kW

IRAN
VO THE ISLAMIC REP, Sirjan — E North Am•500 kW ; S•S Asia•500 kW

JAPAN
RADIO JAPAN, Via Skelton, UK — Europe•300 kW
RADIO JAPAN, Via Woofferton, UK — Europe•300 kW
KOREA (DPR)
KOREAN CENTRAL BS — C America ; N America
VOICE OF KOREA — C America ; N America
SAUDI ARABIA
BS OF THE KINGDOM, Jiddah — N Africa•DS-HOLY KORAN•50 kW
SOUTH AFRICA
†CHANNEL AFRICA, Meyerton — W Africa & C Africa•500 kW ; W•Sa/Su•S Africa•100 kW
USA
ADVENTIST WORLD R, Via Austria — S•E Africa•500 kW
†RFE-RL, Via Jászberény, Hungary — S•E Europe•250 kW
11710v ARGENTINA
R ARGENTINA-RAE, Buenos Aires — Tu-Sa•Americas•100 kW ; M-F•E Asia•100 kW ; M-F•Europe•100 kW
RADIO NACIONAL, Buenos Aires — M•S America•DS•100 kW ; Su•S America•DS•100 kW ; Irr•Sa/Su•S America•DS•100 kW

11710.3 CLANDESTINE (M EAST)
"VO IRAQI PEOPLE", Saudi Arabia — •Mideast•ANTI-SADDAM
11715 CHINA (TAIWAN)
†CBS — SE Asia ; Australasia•CHINESE NETWORK 2 ; Australasia ; Australasia•NEWS NETWORK

INDIA
†ALL INDIA RADIO, Delhi — S Asia•250 kW ; Australasia•250 kW
IRAN
VO THE ISLAMIC REP, Sirjan — W•E Europe•500 kW
JAPAN
RADIO JAPAN, Tokyo-Yamata — E Asia•300 kW
KOREA (REPUBLIC)
RADIO KOREA INTL, Via Sackville, Can — S•S America•250 kW
LEBANON
VOICE OF CHARITY, Via Vatican City — S•Mideast•100 kW
LIBYA
RADIO JAMAHIRIYA, Via France — W•E Africa•500 kW
SLOVAKIA
R SLOVAKIA INTL, Rimavská Sobota — S•E Europe & W Asia•250 kW
USA
†R FREE ASIA, Via Saipan, N Marianas — S•E Asia•100 kW
†RFE-RL, Via Biblis, Germany — S•E Europe•100 kW
VOA, Via Kavála, Greece — W•W Asia & S Asia•250 kW
VOA, Via Philippines — W•E Asia & Australasia•250 kW
VATICAN STATE
VATICAN RADIO, Sta Maria di Galeria — S•Mideast•100 kW ; S•E Europe•100 kW
11715v USA
KJES, Vado, New Mexico — N America•50 kW ; W North Am•50 kW ; C America•50 kW

11720 CHINA (TAIWAN)
R TAIWAN INTL, Via Okeechobee, USA — W•S America•100 kW
EGYPT
EGYPTIAN RADIO, Kafr Silim-Abis — •S Europe, N Africa & Mideast•DS-VO THE ARABS•250 kW
FINLAND
SCANDINAVIAN WEEKEND R, Virrat — •Irr•Sa•1ST SAT OF MONTH•0.5 kW•ALT. FREQ. TO 11690 kHz ; •Irr•F•1ST FRI OF MONTH•0.5 kW•ALT. FREQ. TO 11690 kHz

GERMANY
†DEUTSCHE WELLE, Wertachtal — W•W Asia•500 kW
HUNGARY
†RADIO BUDAPEST, Jászberény — S•W Europe•250 kW
IRAN
VO THE ISLAMIC REP, Sirjan — W•W Asia•500 kW
VO THE ISLAMIC REP, Tehrān — S•E Asia•500 kW
NETHERLANDS
†R NEDERLAND, Flevoland — S•C America & S America•500 kW
PHILIPPINES
(con'd)　RADYO PILIPINAS, Tinang — S•Mideast•250 kW

| | 0 | 1 | 2 | 3 | 4 | 5 | 6 | 7 | 8 | 9 | 10 | 11 | 12 | 13 | 14 | 15 | 16 | 17 | 18 | 19 | 20 | 21 | 22 | 23 | 24 |

ENGLISH ▰▰　ARABIC ⬚⬚⬚　CHINESE ▫▫▫　FRENCH ▭▭　GERMAN ▬▬　RUSSIAN ═══　SPANISH ▬▬　OTHER ──

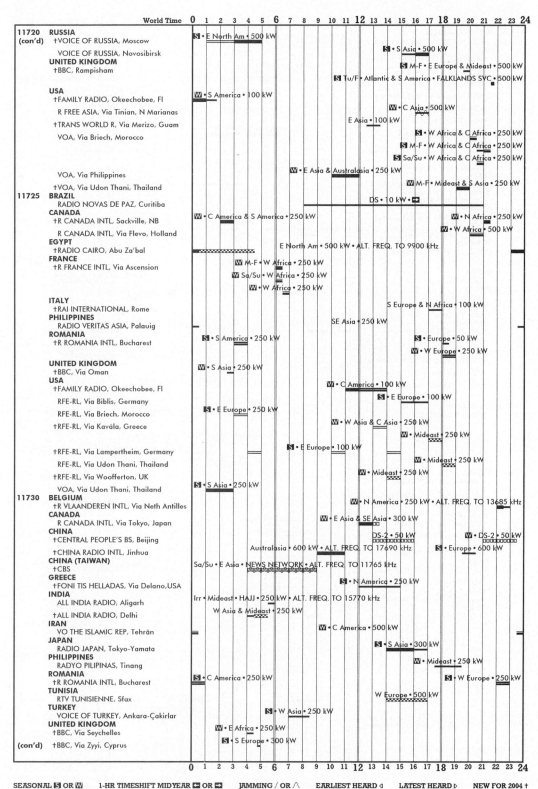

World Time

11720 **RUSSIA**	
(con'd) †VOICE OF RUSSIA, Moscow	S • E North Am • 500 kW
VOICE OF RUSSIA, Novosibirsk	S • S Asia • 500 kW
UNITED KINGDOM	
†BBC, Rampisham	M-F • E Europe & Mideast • 500 kW
	S Tu/F • Atlantic & S America • FALKLANDS SVC • 500 kW
USA	
†FAMILY RADIO, Okeechobee, Fl	W • S America • 100 kW
R FREE ASIA, Via Tinian, N Marianas	W • C Asia • 500 kW
†TRANS WORLD R, Via Merizo, Guam	E Asia • 100 kW
VOA, Via Briech, Morocco	S • W Africa & C Africa • 250 kW
	S M-F • W Africa & C Africa • 250 kW
	S Sa/Su • W Africa & C Africa • 250 kW
VOA, Via Philippines	W • E Asia & Australasia • 250 kW
†VOA, Via Udon Thani, Thailand	W M-F • Mideast & S Asia • 250 kW
11725 **BRAZIL**	
RADIO NOVAS DE PAZ, Curitiba	DS • 10 kW • ⊞
CANADA	
†R CANADA INTL, Sackville, NB	W • C America & S America • 250 kW
	W • N Africa • 250 kW
R CANADA INTL, Via Flevo, Holland	W • W Africa • 500 kW
EGYPT	
†RADIO CAIRO, Abu Za'bal	E North Am • 500 kW • ALT. FREQ. TO 9900 kHz
FRANCE	
†R FRANCE INTL, Via Ascension	W M-F • W Africa • 250 kW
	W Sa/Su • W Africa • 250 kW
	W • W Africa • 250 kW
ITALY	
†RAI INTERNATIONAL, Rome	S Europe & N Africa • 100 kW
PHILIPPINES	
RADIO VERITAS ASIA, Palauig	SE Asia • 250 kW
ROMANIA	
†R ROMANIA INTL, Bucharest	S • S America • 250 kW
	S • Europe • 50 kW
	W • W Europe • 250 kW
UNITED KINGDOM	
†BBC, Via Oman	W • S Asia • 250 kW
USA	
†FAMILY RADIO, Okeechobee, Fl	W • C America • 100 kW
RFE-RL, Via Biblis, Germany	S • E Europe • 100 kW
RFE-RL, Via Briech, Morocco	S • E Europe • 250 kW
†RFE-RL, Via Kavála, Greece	W • W Asia & C Asia • 250 kW
	W • Mideast • 250 kW
†RFE-RL, Via Lampertheim, Germany	S • E Europe • 100 kW
RFE-RL, Via Udon Thani, Thailand	W • Mideast • 250 kW
†RFE-RL, Via Woofferton, UK	W • Mideast • 250 kW
VOA, Via Udon Thani, Thailand	S • S Asia • 250 kW
11730 **BELGIUM**	
†R VLAANDEREN INTL, Via Neth Antilles	W • N America • 250 kW • ALT. FREQ. TO 13685 kHz
CANADA	
R CANADA INTL, Via Tokyo, Japan	W • E Asia & SE Asia • 300 kW
CHINA	
†CENTRAL PEOPLE'S BS, Beijing	DS-2 • 50 kW
	W • DS-2 • 50 kW
†CHINA RADIO INTL, Jinhua	Australasia • 600 kW • ALT. FREQ. TO 17690 kHz
	S • Europe • 600 kW
CHINA (TAIWAN)	
†CBS	Sa/Su • E Asia • NEWS NETWORK • ALT. FREQ. TO 11765 kHz
GREECE	
†FONI TIS HELLADAS, Via Delano,USA	S • N America • 250 kW
INDIA	
ALL INDIA RADIO, Aligarh	Irr • Mideast • HAJJ • 250 kW • ALT. FREQ. TO 15770 kHz
†ALL INDIA RADIO, Delhi	W Asia & Mideast • 250 kW
IRAN	
VO THE ISLAMIC REP, Tehrān	W • C America • 500 kW
JAPAN	
RADIO JAPAN, Tokyo-Yamata	S • S Asia • 300 kW
PHILIPPINES	
RADYO PILIPINAS, Tinang	W • Mideast • 250 kW
ROMANIA	
†R ROMANIA INTL, Bucharest	S • C America • 250 kW
	S • W Europe • 250 kW
TUNISIA	
RTV TUNISIENNE, Sfax	W Europe • 500 kW
TURKEY	
VOICE OF TURKEY, Ankara-Çakirlar	S • W Asia • 250 kW
UNITED KINGDOM	
†BBC, Via Seychelles	W • E Africa • 250 kW
(con'd) †BBC, Via Zyyi, Cyprus	S • S Europe • 300 kW

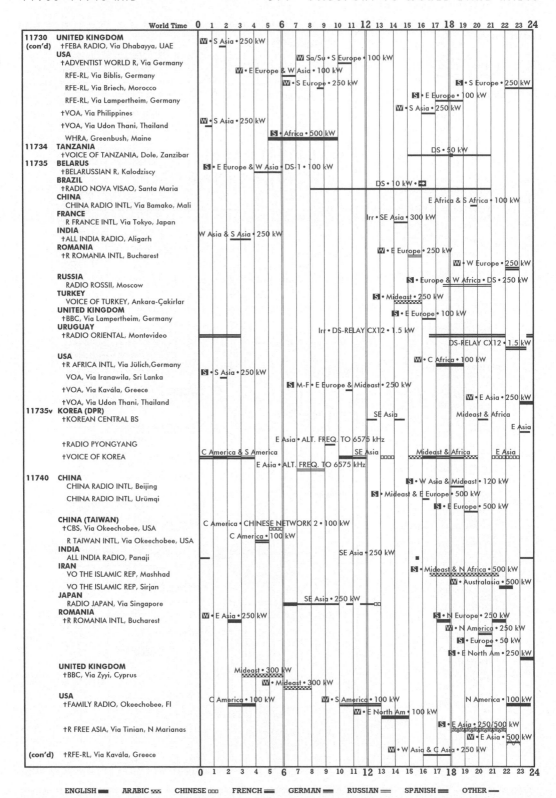

World Time	0 1 2 3 4 5 6 7 8 9 10 11 12 13 14 15 16 17 18 19 20 21 22 23 24
11730 (con'd) **UNITED KINGDOM** †FEBA RADIO, Via Dhabayya, UAE	W • S Asia • 250 kW
USA †ADVENTIST WORLD R, Via Germany	W Sa/Su • S Europe • 100 kW
RFE-RL, Via Biblis, Germany	W • E Europe & W Asia • 100 kW
RFE-RL, Via Briech, Morocco	W • S Europe • 250 kW / S • S Europe • 250 kW
RFE-RL, Via Lampertheim, Germany	S • E Europe • 100 kW
†VOA, Via Philippines	W • S Asia • 250 kW
†VOA, Via Udon Thani, Thailand	W • S Asia • 250 kW
WHRA, Greenbush, Maine	S • Africa • 500 kW
11734 TANZANIA †VOICE OF TANZANIA, Dole, Zanzibar	DS • 50 kW
11735 BELARUS †BELARUSSIAN R, Kalodziscy	S • E Europe & W Asia • DS-1 • 100 kW
BRAZIL †RADIO NOVA VISAO, Santa Maria	DS • 10 kW • ▣
CHINA CHINA RADIO INTL, Via Bamako, Mali	E Africa & S Africa • 100 kW
FRANCE R FRANCE INTL, Via Tokyo, Japan	Irr • SE Asia • 300 kW
INDIA †ALL INDIA RADIO, Aligarh	W Asia & S Asia • 250 kW
ROMANIA †R ROMANIA INTL, Bucharest	W • E Europe • 250 kW / W • W Europe • 250 kW
RUSSIA RADIO ROSSII, Moscow	S • Europe & W Africa • DS • 250 kW
TURKEY VOICE OF TURKEY, Ankara-Çakirlar	S • Mideast • 250 kW
UNITED KINGDOM †BBC, Via Lampertheim, Germany	S • E Europe • 100 kW
URUGUAY †RADIO ORIENTAL, Montevideo	Irr • DS-RELAY CX12 • 1.5 kW / DS-RELAY CX12 • 1.5 kW
USA †R AFRICA INTL, Via Jülich, Germany	W • C Africa • 100 kW
VOA, Via Iranawila, Sri Lanka	S • S Asia • 250 kW
†VOA, Via Kavála, Greece	S M-F • E Europe & Mideast • 250 kW
†VOA, Via Udon Thani, Thailand	W • E Asia • 250 kW
11735v KOREA (DPR) †KOREAN CENTRAL BS	SE Asia Mideast & Africa E Asia
†RADIO PYONGYANG	E Asia • ALT. FREQ. TO 6575 kHz
†VOICE OF KOREA	C America & S America SE Asia Mideast & Africa E Asia / E Asia • ALT. FREQ. TO 6575 kHz
11740 CHINA CHINA RADIO INTL, Beijing	S • W Asia & Mideast • 120 kW
CHINA RADIO INTL, Urümqi	S • Mideast & E Europe • 500 kW
	S • E Europe • 500 kW
CHINA (TAIWAN) †CBS, Via Okeechobee, USA	C America • CHINESE NETWORK 2 • 100 kW
R TAIWAN INTL, Via Okeechobee, USA	C America • 100 kW
INDIA ALL INDIA RADIO, Panaji	SE Asia • 250 kW
IRAN VO THE ISLAMIC REP, Mashhad	S • Mideast & N Africa • 500 kW
VO THE ISLAMIC REP, Sirjan	W • Australasia • 500 kW
JAPAN RADIO JAPAN, Via Singapore	SE Asia • 250 kW
ROMANIA †R ROMANIA INTL, Bucharest	W • E Asia • 250 kW / S • N Europe • 250 kW
	S • N America • 250 kW
	S • Europe • 50 kW
	S • E North Am • 250 kW
UNITED KINGDOM †BBC, Via Zyyi, Cyprus	Mideast • 300 kW / W • Mideast • 300 kW
USA †FAMILY RADIO, Okeechobee, Fl	C America • 100 kW / W • S America • 100 kW N America • 100 kW / W • E North Am • 100 kW
†R FREE ASIA, Via Tinian, N Marianas	S • E Asia • 250/500 kW / W • E Asia • 500 kW
(con'd) †RFE-RL, Via Kavála, Greece	W • W Asia & C Asia • 250 kW

World Time	0 1 2 3 4 5 6 7 8 9 10 11 12 13 14 15 16 17 18 19 20 21 22 23 24

ENGLISH ▬   ARABIC ☲   CHINESE ▦   FRENCH ▬   GERMAN ▬   RUSSIAN ═   SPANISH ▭   OTHER ▬

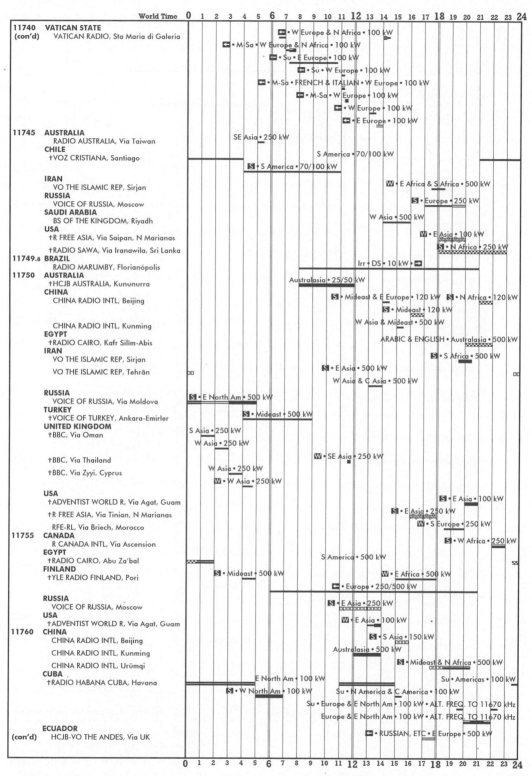

World Time

11740 **VATICAN STATE**
(con'd)   VATICAN RADIO, Sta Maria di Galeria
⬅ • W Europe & N Africa • 100 kW
⬅ • M-Sa • W Europe & N Africa • 100 kW
⬅ • Su • E Europe • 100 kW
⬅ • Su • W Europe • 100 kW
⬅ • M-Sa • FRENCH & ITALIAN • W Europe • 100 kW
⬅ • M-Sa • W Europe • 100 kW
⬅ • W Europe • 100 kW
⬅ • E Europe • 100 kW

11745 **AUSTRALIA**
RADIO AUSTRALIA, Via Taiwan   SE Asia • 250 kW
CHILE
†VOZ CRISTIANA, Santiago   S America • 70/100 kW
S • S America • 70/100 kW

IRAN
VO THE ISLAMIC REP, Sirjan   W • E Africa & S Africa • 500 kW
RUSSIA
VOICE OF RUSSIA, Moscow   S • Europe • 250 kW
SAUDI ARABIA
BS OF THE KINGDOM, Riyadh   W Asia • 500 kW
USA
†R FREE ASIA, Via Saipan, N Marianas   W • E Asia • 100 kW
†RADIO SAWA, Via Iranawila, Sri Lanka   S • N Africa • 250 kW

11749.8 **BRAZIL**
RADIO MARUMBY, Florianópolis   Irr • DS • 10 kW • ➡
11750 **AUSTRALIA**
†HCJB AUSTRALIA, Kununurra   Australasia • 25/50 kW
CHINA
CHINA RADIO INTL, Beijing   S • Mideast & E Europe • 120 kW   S • N Africa • 120 kW
S • Mideast • 120 kW

CHINA RADIO INTL, Kunming   W Asia & Mideast • 500 kW
EGYPT
†RADIO CAIRO, Kafr Silîm-Abis   ARABIC & ENGLISH • Australasia • 500 kW
IRAN
VO THE ISLAMIC REP, Sirjan   S • S Africa • 500 kW
VO THE ISLAMIC REP, Tehrān   S • E Asia • 500 kW
W Asia & C Asia • 500 kW

RUSSIA
VOICE OF RUSSIA, Via Moldova   S • E North Am • 500 kW
TURKEY
†VOICE OF TURKEY, Ankara-Emirler   S • Mideast • 500 kW
UNITED KINGDOM
†BBC, Via Oman   S Asia • 250 kW
W Asia • 250 kW

†BBC, Via Thailand   W • SE Asia • 250 kW

†BBC, Via Zyyi, Cyprus   W Asia • 250 kW
W • W Asia • 250 kW

USA
†ADVENTIST WORLD R, Via Agat, Guam   S • E Asia • 100 kW
†R FREE ASIA, Via Tinian, N Marianas   S • E Asia • 250 kW
RFE-RL, Via Briech, Morocco   W • S Europe • 250 kW
11755 **CANADA**
R CANADA INTL, Via Ascension   S • W Africa • 250 kW
EGYPT
†RADIO CAIRO, Abu Za'bal   S America • 500 kW
FINLAND
†YLE RADIO FINLAND, Pori   S • Mideast • 500 kW   W • E Africa • 500 kW
⬅ • Europe • 250/500 kW

RUSSIA
VOICE OF RUSSIA, Moscow   S • E Asia • 250 kW
USA
†ADVENTIST WORLD R, Via Agat, Guam   W • E Asia • 100 kW
11760 **CHINA**
CHINA RADIO INTL, Beijing   S • S Asia • 150 kW
CHINA RADIO INTL, Kunming   Australasia • 500 kW
CHINA RADIO INTL, Urümqi   S • Mideast & N Africa • 500 kW
CUBA
†RADIO HABANA CUBA, Havana   E North Am • 100 kW   Su • Americas • 100 kW
S • W North Am • 100 kW   Su • N America & C America • 100 kW
Su • Europe & E North Am • 100 kW • ALT. FREQ. TO 11670 kHz
Europe & E North Am • 100 kW • ALT. FREQ. TO 11670 kHz

ECUADOR
(con'd)   HCJB-VO THE ANDES, Via UK   ⬅ • RUSSIAN, ETC • E Europe • 500 kW

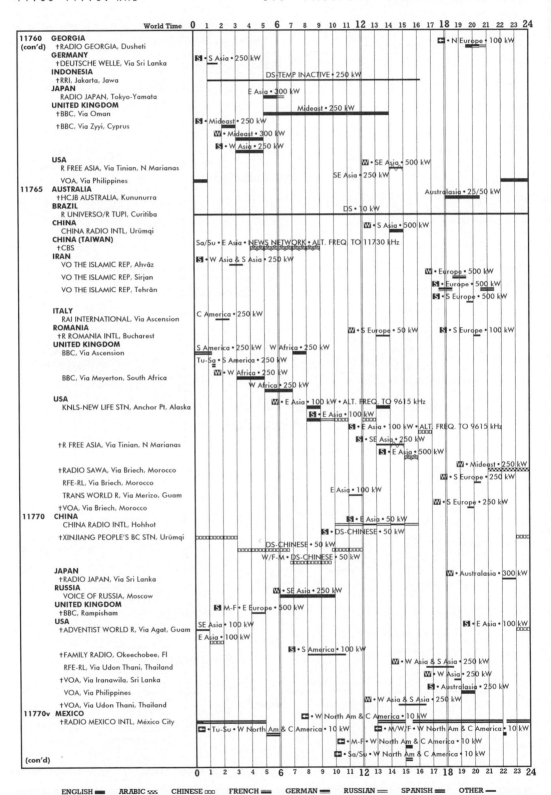

World Time 0 1 2 3 4 5 6 7 8 9 10 11 12 13 14 15 16 17 18 19 20 21 22 23 24

11760 **GEORGIA**
(con'd) †RADIO GEORGIA, Dusheti
　　　　　　　　　　　　　　　　　　　　　　　　 N Europe • 100 kW
　　　GERMANY
　　　　†DEUTSCHE WELLE, Via Sri Lanka　　　S • S Asia • 250 kW
　　　INDONESIA
　　　　†RRI, Jakarta, Jawa　　　　　　　　DS-TEMP INACTIVE • 250 kW
　　　JAPAN
　　　　RADIO JAPAN, Tokyo-Yamata　　　　E Asia • 300 kW
　　　UNITED KINGDOM
　　　　†BBC, Via Oman　　　　　　　　　　　　Mideast • 250 kW
　　　　†BBC, Via Zyyi, Cyprus　　　　　S • Mideast • 250 kW
　　　　　　　　　　　　　　　　　　　　W • Mideast • 300 kW
　　　　　　　　　　　　　　　　　　　　S • W Asia • 250 kW
　　　USA
　　　　R FREE ASIA, Via Tinian, N Marianas　　　　　　　　　W • SE Asia • 500 kW
　　　　VOA, Via Philippines　　　　　　　　　　　　SE Asia • 250 kW
11765 **AUSTRALIA**
　　　　†HCJB AUSTRALIA, Kununurra　　　　　　　　　　　　　　Australasia • 25/50 kW
　　　BRAZIL
　　　　R UNIVERSO/R TUPI, Curitiba　　　　　　DS • 10 kW
　　　CHINA
　　　　CHINA RADIO INTL, Urümqi　　　　　　　W • S Asia • 500 kW
　　　CHINA (TAIWAN)
　　　　†CBS　　　Sa/Su • E Asia • NEWS NETWORK • ALT. FREQ. TO 11730 kHz
　　　IRAN
　　　　VO THE ISLAMIC REP, Ahvāz　　　S • W Asia & S Asia • 250 kW
　　　　VO THE ISLAMIC REP, Sirjan　　　　　　　　　　　W • Europe • 500 kW
　　　　VO THE ISLAMIC REP, Tehrān　　　　　　　　　　S • Europe • 500 kW
　　　　　　　　　　　　　　　　　　　　　　　　S • S Europe • 500 kW
　　　ITALY
　　　　RAI INTERNATIONAL, Via Ascension　C America • 250 kW
　　　ROMANIA
　　　　†R ROMANIA INTL, Bucharest　　　　W • S Europe • 50 kW　　　S • S Europe • 100 kW
　　　UNITED KINGDOM
　　　　BBC, Via Ascension　　　S America • 250 kW　　W Africa • 250 kW
　　　　　　　　　　　　　Tu-Sa • S America • 250 kW
　　　　BBC, Via Meyerton, South Africa　　W • W Africa • 250 kW
　　　　　　　　　　　　　　　W Africa • 250 kW
　　　USA
　　　　KNLS-NEW LIFE STN, Anchor Pt, Alaska　　W • E Asia • 100 kW • ALT. FREQ. TO 9615 kHz
　　　　　　　　　　　　　　　　　　S • E Asia • 100 kW
　　　　　　　　　　　　　　　　　　　S • E Asia • 100 kW • ALT. FREQ. TO 9615 kHz
　　　　†R FREE ASIA, Via Tinian, N Marianas　　　　S • SE Asia • 250 kW
　　　　　　　　　　　　　　　　　　　　　S • E Asia • 500 kW
　　　　†RADIO SAWA, Via Briech, Morocco　　　　　　　　　W • Mideast • 250 kW
　　　　RFE-RL, Via Briech, Morocco　　　　　　　　　W • S Europe • 250 kW
　　　　TRANS WORLD R, Via Merizo, Guam　　E Asia • 100 kW
　　　　†VOA, Via Briech, Morocco　　　　　　　　　W • S Europe • 250 kW
11770 **CHINA**
　　　　CHINA RADIO INTL, Hohhot　　　　S • E Asia • 50 kW
　　　　　　　　　　　　　　　　　　S • DS-CHINESE • 50 kW
　　　　†XINJIANG PEOPLE'S BC STN, Urümqi
　　　　　　　　　　　　　　　DS-CHINESE • 50 kW
　　　　　　　　　　　　W/F-M • DS-CHINESE • 50 kW
　　　JAPAN
　　　　†RADIO JAPAN, Via Sri Lanka　　　　　　　　　　　　W • Australasia • 300 kW
　　　RUSSIA
　　　　VOICE OF RUSSIA, Moscow　　　W • SE Asia • 250 kW
　　　UNITED KINGDOM
　　　　†BBC, Rampisham　　　S • M-F • E Europe • 500 kW
　　　USA
　　　　†ADVENTIST WORLD R, Via Agat, Guam　SE Asia • 100 kW　　　　　　　S • E Asia • 100 kW
　　　　　　　　　　　　　　　　　　　E Asia • 100 kW
　　　　†FAMILY RADIO, Okeechobee, Fl　　　　S • S America • 100 kW
　　　　RFE-RL, Via Udon Thani, Thailand　　　　　　　W • W Asia & S Asia • 250 kW
　　　　†VOA, Via Iranawila, Sri Lanka　　　　　　　　W • W Asia • 250 kW
　　　　VOA, Via Philippines　　　　　　　　　　　S • Australasia • 250 kW
　　　　†VOA, Via Udon Thani, Thailand　　　　W • W Asia & S Asia • 250 kW
11770v **MEXICO**
　　　　†RADIO MEXICO INTL, México City　　　　W North Am & C America • 10 kW
　　　　　　　　　Tu-Su • W North Am & C America • 10 kW　　W North Am & C America • 10 kW
　　　　　　　　　　　　M-F • W North Am & C America • 10 kW
　　　　　　　　　　　Sa/Su • W North Am & C America • 10 kW

(con'd)

0 1 2 3 4 5 6 7 8 9 10 11 12 13 14 15 16 17 18 19 20 21 22 23 24

ENGLISH ▬　　ARABIC ⁓⁓⁓　　CHINESE □□□　　FRENCH ══　　GERMAN ▬▬　　RUSSIAN ══　　SPANISH ══　　OTHER ▬

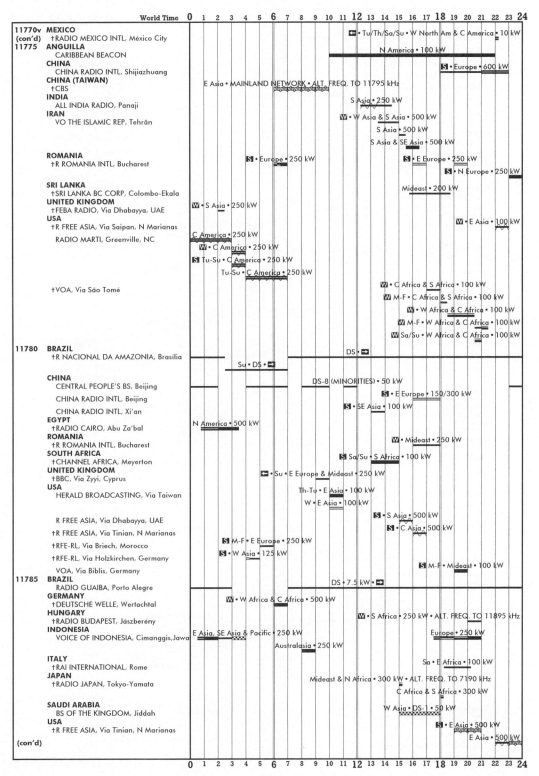

World Time | 0 1 2 3 4 5 6 7 8 9 10 11 12 13 14 15 16 17 18 19 20 21 22 23 24

11770v MEXICO
(con'd) †RADIO MEXICO INTL, México City — ◩ • Tu/Th/Sa/Su • W North Am & C America • 10 kW

11775 ANGUILLA
    CARIBBEAN BEACON — N America • 100 kW

CHINA
    CHINA RADIO INTL, Shijiazhuang — ⑤ • Europe • 600 kW

CHINA (TAIWAN)
    †CBS — E Asia • MAINLAND NETWORK • ALT. FREQ. TO 11795 kHz

INDIA
    ALL INDIA RADIO, Panaji — S Asia • 250 kW

IRAN
    VO THE ISLAMIC REP, Tehrān — ◪ • W Asia & S Asia • 500 kW
    S Asia • 500 kW
    S Asia & SE Asia • 500 kW

ROMANIA
    †R ROMANIA INTL, Bucharest — ⑤ • Europe • 250 kW
    ⑤ • E Europe • 250 kW
    ⑤ • N Europe • 250 kW

SRI LANKA
    †SRI LANKA BC CORP, Colombo-Ekala — Mideast • 200 kW

UNITED KINGDOM
    †FEBA RADIO, Via Dhabayya, UAE — ◪ • S Asia • 250 kW

USA
    †R FREE ASIA, Via Saipan, N Marianas — ◪ • E Asia • 100 kW

    RADIO MARTI, Greenville, NC — C America • 250 kW
    ◪ • C America • 250 kW
    ⑤ Tu-Su • C America • 250 kW
    Tu-Su • C America • 250 kW

    †VOA, Via São Tomé — ◪ • C Africa & S Africa • 100 kW
    ◪ M-F • C Africa & S Africa • 100 kW
    ◪ • W Africa & C Africa • 100 kW
    ◪ M-F • W Africa & C Africa • 100 kW
    ◪ Sa/Su • W Africa & C Africa • 100 kW

11780 BRAZIL
    †R NACIONAL DA AMAZONIA, Brasilia — DS • ◩
    Su • DS • ◩

CHINA
    CENTRAL PEOPLE'S BS, Beijing — DS-8 (MINORITIES) • 50 kW
    CHINA RADIO INTL, Beijing — ⑤ • E Europe • 150/300 kW
    CHINA RADIO INTL, Xi'an — ⑤ • SE Asia • 100 kW

EGYPT
    †RADIO CAIRO, Abu Za'bal — N America • 500 kW

ROMANIA
    †R ROMANIA INTL, Bucharest — ◪ • Mideast • 250 kW

SOUTH AFRICA
    †CHANNEL AFRICA, Meyerton — ⑤ Sa/Su • S Africa • 100 kW

UNITED KINGDOM
    †BBC, Via Zyyi, Cyprus — ◩ • Su • E Europe & Mideast • 250 kW

USA
    HERALD BROADCASTING, Via Taiwan — Th-Tu • E Asia • 100 kW
    W • E Asia • 100 kW

    R FREE ASIA, Via Dhabayya, UAE — ⑤ • S Asia • 500 kW
    †R FREE ASIA, Via Tinian, N Marianas — ⑤ • C Asia • 500 kW
    †RFE-RL, Via Briech, Morocco — ⑤ M-F • E Europe • 250 kW
    †RFE-RL, Via Holzkirchen, Germany — ⑤ • W Asia • 125 kW
    VOA, Via Biblis, Germany — ⑤ M-F • Mideast • 100 kW

11785 BRAZIL
    RADIO GUAIBA, Porto Alegre — DS • 7.5 kW • ◩

GERMANY
    †DEUTSCHE WELLE, Wertachtal — ◪ • W Africa & C Africa • 500 kW

HUNGARY
    †RADIO BUDAPEST, Jászberény — ◪ • S Africa • 250 kW • ALT. FREQ. TO 11895 kHz

INDONESIA
    VOICE OF INDONESIA, Cimanggis,Jawa — E Asia, SE Asia & Pacific • 250 kW
    Europe • 250 kW
    Australasia • 250 kW

ITALY
    †RAI INTERNATIONAL, Rome — Sa • E Africa • 100 kW

JAPAN
    †RADIO JAPAN, Tokyo-Yamata — Mideast & N Africa • 300 kW • ALT. FREQ. TO 7190 kHz
    C Africa & S Africa • 300 kW

SAUDI ARABIA
    BS OF THE KINGDOM, Jiddah — W Asia • DS-1 • 50 kW

USA
    †R FREE ASIA, Via Tinian, N Marianas — ⑤ • E Asia • 500 kW
    E Asia • 500 kW

(con'd)

0 1 2 3 4 5 6 7 8 9 10 11 12 13 14 15 16 17 18 19 20 21 22 23 24

SEASONAL ⑤ OR ◪   1-HR TIMESHIFT MIDYEAR ◩ OR ◪   JAMMING / OR ∧   EARLIEST HEARD ◁   LATEST HEARD ▷   NEW FOR 2004 †

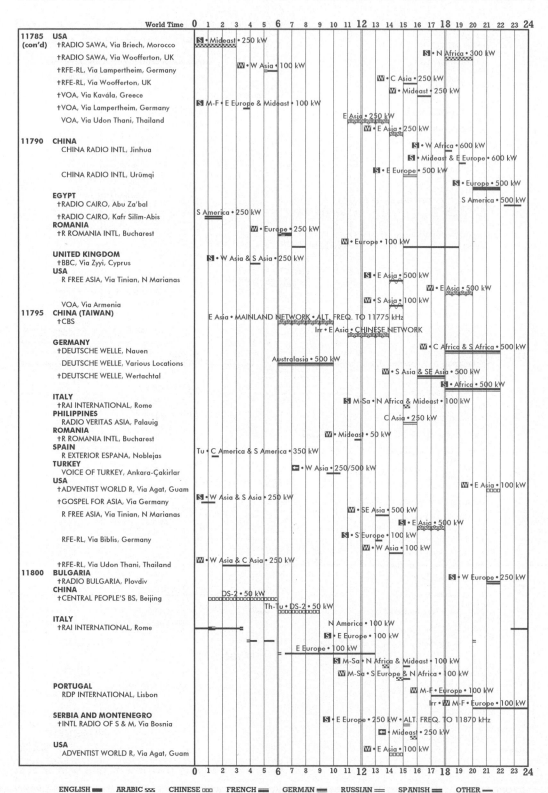

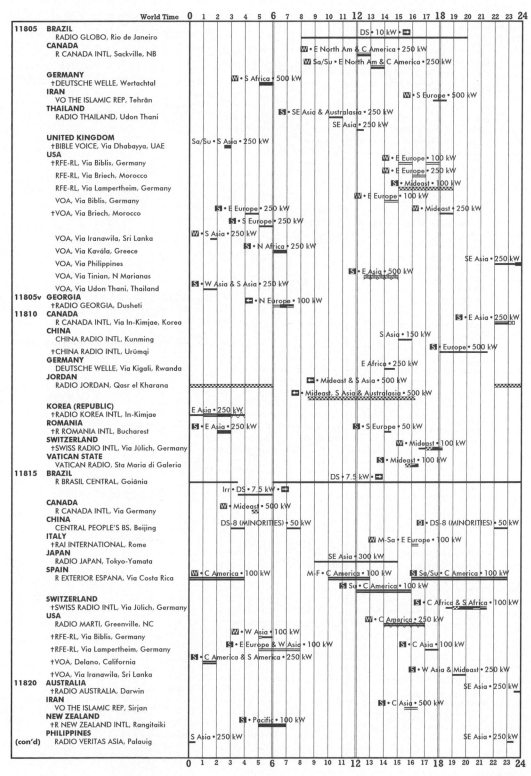

World Time 0 1 2 3 4 5 6 7 8 9 10 11 12 13 14 15 16 17 18 19 20 21 22 23 24

Freq	Station	
11805	**BRAZIL** RADIO GLOBO, Rio de Janeiro	DS • 10 kW • ➡
	CANADA R CANADA INTL, Sackville, NB	W • E North Am & C America • 250 kW / W Sa/Su • E North Am & C America • 250 kW
	GERMANY †DEUTSCHE WELLE, Wertachtal	W • S Africa • 500 kW
	IRAN VO THE ISLAMIC REP, Tehrān	W • S Europe • 500 kW
	THAILAND RADIO THAILAND, Udon Thani	S • SE Asia & Australasia • 250 kW / SE Asia • 250 kW
	UNITED KINGDOM †BIBLE VOICE, Via Dhabayya, UAE	Sa/Su • S Asia • 250 kW
	USA †RFE-RL, Via Biblis, Germany	W • E Europe • 100 kW
	RFE-RL, Via Briech, Morocco	W • E Europe • 250 kW
	RFE-RL, Via Lampertheim, Germany	S • Mideast • 100 kW
	VOA, Via Biblis, Germany	W • E Europe • 100 kW
	†VOA, Via Briech, Morocco	S • E Europe • 250 kW / W • Mideast • 250 kW
		S • S Europe • 250 kW
	VOA, Via Iranawila, Sri Lanka	W • S Asia • 250 kW
	VOA, Via Kavála, Greece	S • N Africa • 250 kW
	VOA, Via Philippines	SE Asia • 250 kW
	VOA, Via Tinian, N Marianas	S • E Asia • 500 kW
	VOA, Via Udon Thani, Thailand	S • W Asia & S Asia • 250 kW
11805v	**GEORGIA** †RADIO GEORGIA, Dusheti	➡ • N Europe • 100 kW
11810	**CANADA** R CANADA INTL, Via In-Kimjae, Korea	S • E Asia • 250 kW
	CHINA CHINA RADIO INTL, Kunming	S Asia • 150 kW
	†CHINA RADIO INTL, Urümqi	S • Europe • 500 kW
	GERMANY DEUTSCHE WELLE, Via Kigali, Rwanda	E Africa • 250 kW
	JORDAN RADIO JORDAN, Qasr el Kharana	➡ • Mideast & S Asia • 500 kW / ➡ • Mideast, S Asia & Australasia • 500 kW
	KOREA (REPUBLIC) †RADIO KOREA INTL, In-Kimjae	E Asia • 250 kW
	ROMANIA †R ROMANIA INTL, Bucharest	S • E Asia • 250 kW / S • S Europe • 50 kW
	SWITZERLAND †SWISS RADIO INTL, Via Jülich, Germany	W • Mideast • 100 kW
	VATICAN STATE VATICAN RADIO, Sta Maria di Galeria	S • Mideast • 100 kW
11815	**BRAZIL** R BRASIL CENTRAL, Goiânia	DS • 7.5 kW • ➡
		Irr • DS • 7.5 kW • ➡
	CANADA R CANADA INTL, Via Germany	W • Mideast • 500 kW
	CHINA CENTRAL PEOPLE'S BS, Beijing	DS-8 (MINORITIES) • 50 kW / 9 • DS-8 (MINORITIES) • 50 kW
	ITALY †RAI INTERNATIONAL, Rome	W M-Sa • E Europe • 100 kW
	JAPAN RADIO JAPAN, Tokyo-Yamata	SE Asia • 300 kW
	SPAIN R EXTERIOR ESPANA, Via Costa Rica	W • C America • 100 kW / M-F • C America • 100 kW / S Sa/Su • C America • 100 kW
		S Su • C America • 100 kW
	SWITZERLAND †SWISS RADIO INTL, Via Jülich, Germany	S • C Africa & S Africa • 100 kW
	USA RADIO MARTI, Greenville, NC	W • C America • 250 kW
	†RFE-RL, Via Biblis, Germany	W • W Asia • 100 kW
	†RFE-RL, Via Lampertheim, Germany	S • E Europe & W Asia • 100 kW / S • C Asia • 100 kW
	†VOA, Delano, California	S • C America & S America • 250 kW
	†VOA, Via Iranawila, Sri Lanka	S • W Asia & Mideast • 250 kW
11820	**AUSTRALIA** †RADIO AUSTRALIA, Darwin	SE Asia • 250 kW
	IRAN VO THE ISLAMIC REP, Sirjan	S • C Asia • 500 kW
	NEW ZEALAND †R NEW ZEALAND INTL, Rangitaiki	S • Pacific • 100 kW
(con'd)	**PHILIPPINES** RADIO VERITAS ASIA, Palauig	S Asia • 250 kW / SE Asia • 250 kW

0 1 2 3 4 5 6 7 8 9 10 11 12 13 14 15 16 17 18 19 20 21 22 23 24

SEASONAL **S** OR **W**   1-HR TIMESHIFT MIDYEAR ⬅ OR ➡   JAMMING / OR ∧   EARLIEST HEARD ◁   LATEST HEARD ▷   NEW FOR 2004 †

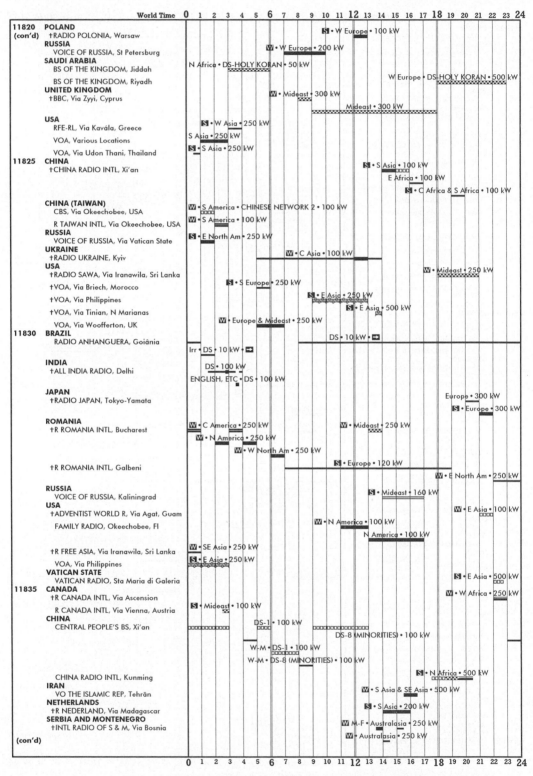

World Time 0 1 2 3 4 5 6 7 8 9 10 11 12 13 14 15 16 17 18 19 20 21 22 23 24

11820 POLAND
(con'd) †RADIO POLONIA, Warsaw — 𝕊 • W Europe • 100 kW
RUSSIA
  VOICE OF RUSSIA, St Petersburg — 𝕎 • W Europe • 200 kW
SAUDI ARABIA
  BS OF THE KINGDOM, Jiddah — N Africa • DS-HOLY KORAN • 50 kW
  BS OF THE KINGDOM, Riyadh — W Europe • DS-HOLY KORAN • 500 kW
UNITED KINGDOM
  †BBC, Via Zyyi, Cyprus — 𝕎 • Mideast • 300 kW
                          Mideast • 300 kW
USA
  RFE-RL, Via Kavála, Greece — 𝕊 • W Asia • 250 kW
  VOA, Various Locations — S Asia • 250 kW
  VOA, Via Udon Thani, Thailand — 𝕊 • S Asia • 250 kW
11825 CHINA
  †CHINA RADIO INTL, Xi'an — 𝕊 • S Asia • 100 kW
                            E Africa • 100 kW
                            𝕊 • C Africa & S Africa • 100 kW
CHINA (TAIWAN)
  CBS, Via Okeechobee, USA — 𝕎 • S America • CHINESE NETWORK 2 • 100 kW
  R TAIWAN INTL, Via Okeechobee, USA — 𝕎 • S America • 100 kW
RUSSIA
  VOICE OF RUSSIA, Via Vatican State — 𝕊 • E North Am • 250 kW
UKRAINE
  †RADIO UKRAINE, Kyiv — 𝕎 • C Asia • 100 kW
USA
  †RADIO SAWA, Via Iranawila, Sri Lanka — 𝕎 • Mideast • 250 kW
  †VOA, Via Briech, Morocco — 𝕊 • S Europe • 250 kW
  †VOA, Via Philippines — 𝕊 • E Asia • 250 kW
  †VOA, Via Tinian, N Marianas — 𝕊 • E Asia • 500 kW
  VOA, Via Woofferton, UK — 𝕎 • Europe & Mideast • 250 kW
11830 BRAZIL
  RADIO ANHANGUERA, Goiânia — DS • 10 kW • ➡
                              Irr • DS • 10 kW • ➡
INDIA
  †ALL INDIA RADIO, Delhi — DS • 100 kW
                           ENGLISH, ETC • DS • 100 kW
JAPAN
  †RADIO JAPAN, Tokyo-Yamata — Europe • 300 kW
                               𝕊 • Europe • 300 kW
ROMANIA
  †R ROMANIA INTL, Bucharest — 𝕎 • C America • 250 kW
                               𝕎 • N America • 250 kW   𝕎 • Mideast • 250 kW
                               𝕎 • W North Am • 250 kW
  †R ROMANIA INTL, Galbeni — 𝕊 • Europe • 120 kW
                             𝕎 • E North Am • 250 kW
RUSSIA
  VOICE OF RUSSIA, Kaliningrad — 𝕊 • Mideast • 160 kW
USA
  †ADVENTIST WORLD R, Via Agat, Guam — 𝕎 • E Asia • 100 kW
  FAMILY RADIO, Okeechobee, Fl — 𝕎 • N America • 100 kW
                                 N America • 100 kW
  †R FREE ASIA, Via Iranawila, Sri Lanka — 𝕎 • SE Asia • 250 kW
  VOA, Via Philippines — 𝕊 • E Asia • 250 kW
VATICAN STATE
  VATICAN RADIO, Sta Maria di Galeria — 𝕊 • E Asia • 500 kW
11835 CANADA
  †R CANADA INTL, Via Ascension — 𝕎 • W Africa • 250 kW
  R CANADA INTL, Via Vienna, Austria — 𝕊 • Mideast • 100 kW
CHINA
  CENTRAL PEOPLE'S BS, Xi'an — DS-1 • 100 kW
                              DS-8 (MINORITIES) • 100 kW
                              W-M • DS-1 • 100 kW
                              W-M • DS-8 (MINORITIES) • 100 kW
  CHINA RADIO INTL, Kunming — 𝕊 • N Africa • 500 kW
IRAN
  VO THE ISLAMIC REP, Tehrān — 𝕎 • S Asia & SE Asia • 500 kW
NETHERLANDS
  †R NEDERLAND, Via Madagascar — 𝕊 • S Asia • 200 kW
SERBIA AND MONTENEGRO
  †INTL RADIO OF S & M, Via Bosnia — 𝕎 M-F • Australasia • 250 kW
                                     𝕎 • Australasia • 250 kW
(con'd)

0 1 2 3 4 5 6 7 8 9 10 11 12 13 14 15 16 17 18 19 20 21 22 23 24

ENGLISH ▬   ARABIC ≈≈≈   CHINESE □□□   FRENCH ══   GERMAN ▬▬   RUSSIAN ══   SPANISH ══   OTHER ▬

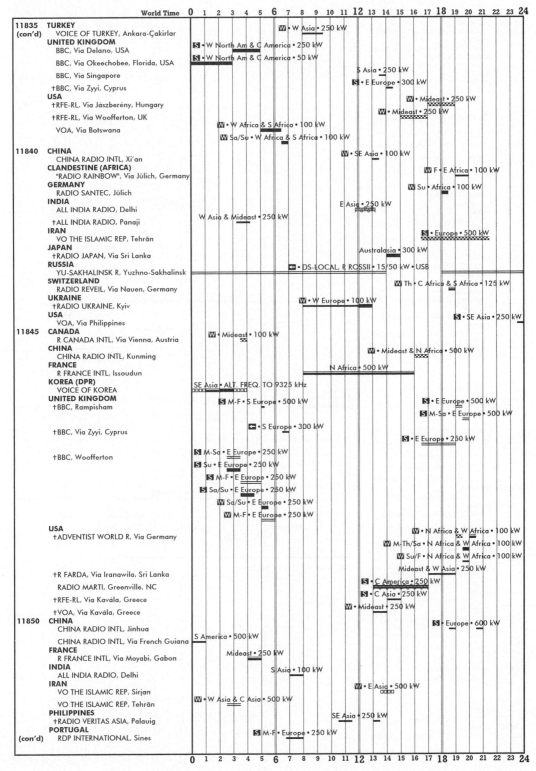

World Time 0 1 2 3 4 5 6 7 8 9 10 11 12 13 14 15 16 17 18 19 20 21 22 23 24

11835	
(con'd) **TURKEY**	
VOICE OF TURKEY, Ankara-Çakirlar	W • W Asia • 250 kW
UNITED KINGDOM	
BBC, Via Delano, USA	S • W North Am & C America • 250 kW
BBC, Via Okeechobee, Florida, USA	S • W North Am & C America • 50 kW
BBC, Via Singapore	S Asia • 250 kW
†BBC, Via Zyyi, Cyprus	S • E Europe • 300 kW
USA	
†RFE-RL, Via Jászberény, Hungary	W • Mideast • 250 kW
†RFE-RL, Via Woofferton, UK	W • Mideast • 250 kW
VOA, Via Botswana	W • W Africa & S Africa • 100 kW
	W Sa/Su • W Africa & S Africa • 100 kW
11840 **CHINA**	
CHINA RADIO INTL, Xi'an	W • SE Asia • 100 kW
CLANDESTINE (AFRICA)	
"RADIO RAINBOW", Via Jülich, Germany	W F • E Africa • 100 kW
GERMANY	
RADIO SANTEC, Jülich	W Su • Africa • 100 kW
INDIA	
ALL INDIA RADIO, Delhi	E Asia • 250 kW
†ALL INDIA RADIO, Panaji	W Asia & Mideast • 250 kW
IRAN	
VO THE ISLAMIC REP, Tehrān	S • Europe • 500 kW
JAPAN	
†RADIO JAPAN, Via Sri Lanka	Australasia • 300 kW
RUSSIA	
YU-SAKHALINSK R, Yuzhno-Sakhalinsk	• DS-LOCAL, R ROSSII • 15/50 kW • USB
SWITZERLAND	
RADIO REVEIL, Via Nauen, Germany	W Th • C Africa & S Africa • 125 kW
UKRAINE	
†RADIO UKRAINE, Kyiv	W • W Europe • 100 kW
USA	
VOA, Via Philippines	S • SE Asia • 250 kW
11845 **CANADA**	
R CANADA INTL, Via Vienna, Austria	W • Mideast • 100 kW
CHINA	
CHINA RADIO INTL, Kunming	W • Mideast & N Africa • 500 kW
FRANCE	
R FRANCE INTL, Issoudun	N Africa • 500 kW
KOREA (DPR)	
VOICE OF KOREA	SE Asia • ALT. FREQ. TO 9325 kHz
UNITED KINGDOM	
†BBC, Rampisham	S M-F • S Europe • 500 kW
	S • E Europe • 500 kW
	S M-Sa • E Europe • 500 kW
†BBC, Via Zyyi, Cyprus	• S Europe • 300 kW
	S • E Europe • 250 kW
†BBC, Woofferton	S M-Sa • E Europe • 250 kW
	S Su • E Europe • 250 kW
	S M-F • E Europe • 250 kW
	S Sa/Su • E Europe • 250 kW
	W Sa/Su • E Europe • 250 kW
	W M-F • E Europe • 250 kW
USA	
†ADVENTIST WORLD R, Via Germany	W • N Africa & W Africa • 100 kW
	W M-Th/Sa • N Africa & W Africa • 100 kW
	W Su/F • N Africa & W Africa • 100 kW
	Mideast & W Asia • 250 kW
†R FARDA, Via Iranawila, Sri Lanka	
RADIO MARTI, Greenville, NC	S • C America • 250 kW
†RFE-RL, Via Kavála, Greece	S • C Asia • 250 kW
†VOA, Via Kavála, Greece	W • Mideast • 250 kW
11850 **CHINA**	
CHINA RADIO INTL, Jinhua	S • Europe • 600 kW
CHINA RADIO INTL, Via French Guiana	S America • 500 kW
FRANCE	
R FRANCE INTL, Via Moyabi, Gabon	Mideast • 250 kW
INDIA	
ALL INDIA RADIO, Delhi	S Asia • 100 kW
IRAN	
VO THE ISLAMIC REP, Sirjan	W • E Asia • 500 kW
VO THE ISLAMIC REP, Tehrān	W • W Asia & C Asia • 500 kW
PHILIPPINES	
†RADIO VERITAS ASIA, Palauig	SE Asia • 250 kW
PORTUGAL	
(con'd) RDP INTERNATIONAL, Sines	S M-F • Europe • 250 kW

0 1 2 3 4 5 6 7 8 9 10 11 12 13 14 15 16 17 18 19 20 21 22 23 24

SEASONAL S OR W   1-HR TIMESHIFT MIDYEAR ⊏ OR ⊐   JAMMING / OR ∧   EARLIEST HEARD ◁   LATEST HEARD ▷   NEW FOR 2004 †

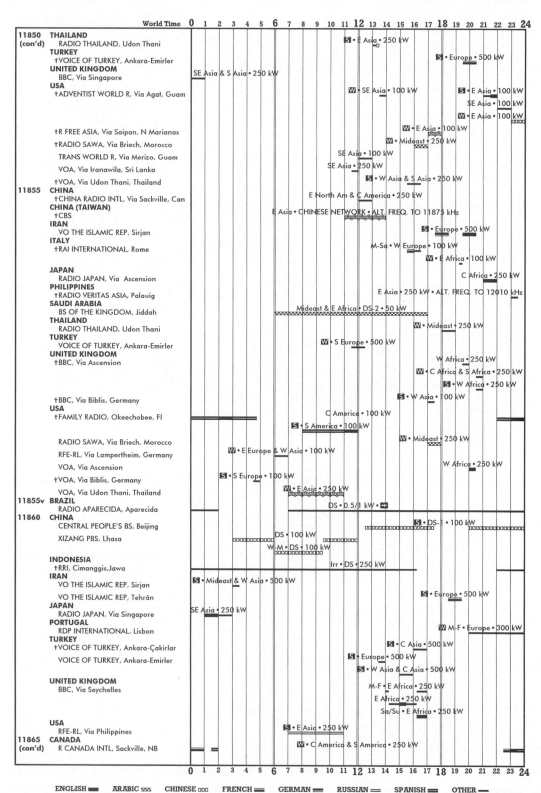

| | | World Time | 0 | 1 | 2 | 3 | 4 | 5 | 6 | 7 | 8 | 9 | 10 | 11 | 12 | 13 | 14 | 15 | 16 | 17 | 18 | 19 | 20 | 21 | 22 | 23 | 24 |

11850 THAILAND
(con'd)   RADIO THAILAND, Udon Thani — S • E Asia • 250 kW
TURKEY
†VOICE OF TURKEY, Ankara-Emirler — S • Europe • 500 kW
UNITED KINGDOM
BBC, Via Singapore — SE Asia & S Asia • 250 kW
USA
†ADVENTIST WORLD R, Via Agat, Guam — W • SE Asia • 100 kW / S • E Asia • 100 kW / SE Asia • 100 kW / W • E Asia • 100 kW
†R FREE ASIA, Via Saipan, N Marianas — W • E Asia • 100 kW
†RADIO SAWA, Via Briech, Morocco — W • Mideast • 250 kW
TRANS WORLD R, Via Merizo, Guam — SE Asia • 100 kW
VOA, Via Iranawila, Sri Lanka — SE Asia • 250 kW
†VOA, Via Udon Thani, Thailand — S • W Asia & S Asia • 250 kW

11855 CHINA
†CHINA RADIO INTL, Via Sackville, Can — E North Am & C America • 250 kW
CHINA (TAIWAN)
†CBS — E Asia • CHINESE NETWORK • ALT. FREQ. TO 11875 kHz
IRAN
VO THE ISLAMIC REP, Sirjan — S • Europe • 500 kW
ITALY
†RAI INTERNATIONAL, Rome — M-Sa • W Europe • 100 kW / W • E Africa • 100 kW
JAPAN
RADIO JAPAN, Via Ascension — C Africa • 250 kW
PHILIPPINES
†RADIO VERITAS ASIA, Palauig — E Asia • 250 kW • ALT. FREQ. TO 12010 kHz
SAUDI ARABIA
BS OF THE KINGDOM, Jiddah — Mideast & E Africa • DS-2 • 50 kW
THAILAND
RADIO THAILAND, Udon Thani — W • Mideast • 250 kW
TURKEY
VOICE OF TURKEY, Ankara-Emirler — W • S Europe • 500 kW
UNITED KINGDOM
†BBC, Via Ascension — W Africa • 250 kW / W • C Africa & S Africa • 250 kW / S • W Africa • 250 kW
†BBC, Via Biblis, Germany — S • W Asia • 100 kW
USA
†FAMILY RADIO, Okeechobee, Fl — C America • 100 kW / S • S America • 100 kW
RADIO SAWA, Via Briech, Morocco — W • Mideast • 250 kW
RFE-RL, Via Lampertheim, Germany — W • E Europe & W Asia • 100 kW
VOA, Via Ascension — W Africa • 250 kW
†VOA, Via Biblis, Germany — S • S Europe • 100 kW
VOA, Via Udon Thani, Thailand — W • E Asia • 250 kW

11855v BRAZIL
RADIO APARECIDA, Aparecida — DS • 0.5/1 kW • ■
11860 CHINA
CENTRAL PEOPLE'S BS, Beijing — S • DS-1 • 100 kW
XIZANG PBS, Lhasa — DS • 100 kW / W-M • DS • 100 kW
INDONESIA
†RRI, Cimanggis, Jawa — Irr • DS • 250 kW
IRAN
VO THE ISLAMIC REP, Sirjan — S • Mideast & W Asia • 500 kW
VO THE ISLAMIC REP, Tehrān — S • Europe • 500 kW
JAPAN
RADIO JAPAN, Via Singapore — SE Asia • 250 kW
PORTUGAL
RDP INTERNATIONAL, Lisbon — W • M-F • Europe • 300 kW
TURKEY
†VOICE OF TURKEY, Ankara-Çakirlar — S • C Asia • 500 kW
VOICE OF TURKEY, Ankara-Emirler — S • Europe • 500 kW / S • W Asia & C Asia • 500 kW
UNITED KINGDOM
BBC, Via Seychelles — M-F • E Africa • 250 kW / E Africa • 250 kW / Sa/Su • E Africa • 250 kW
USA
RFE-RL, Via Philippines — S • E Asia • 250 kW
11865 CANADA
(con'd)   R CANADA INTL, Sackville, NB — W • C America & S America • 250 kW

| | | 0 | 1 | 2 | 3 | 4 | 5 | 6 | 7 | 8 | 9 | 10 | 11 | 12 | 13 | 14 | 15 | 16 | 17 | 18 | 19 | 20 | 21 | 22 | 23 | 24 |

ENGLISH ▬   ARABIC ≋   CHINESE ▭▭▭   FRENCH ▭▭   GERMAN ▬   RUSSIAN ▭▭   SPANISH ▬   OTHER ▬

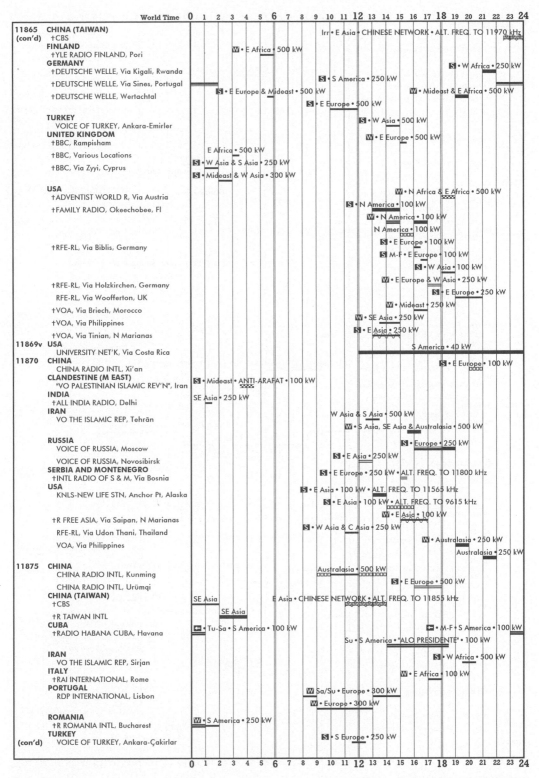

World Time   0 1 2 3 4 5 6 7 8 9 10 11 12 13 14 15 16 17 18 19 20 21 22 23 24

11865 **CHINA (TAIWAN)**
(con'd)   †CBS   Irr • E Asia • CHINESE NETWORK • ALT. FREQ. TO 11970 kHz
    FINLAND
     †YLE RADIO FINLAND, Pori   W • E Africa • 500 kW
    GERMANY
     †DEUTSCHE WELLE, Via Kigali, Rwanda   S • W Africa • 250 kW
     †DEUTSCHE WELLE, Via Sines, Portugal   S • S America • 250 kW
     †DEUTSCHE WELLE, Wertachtal   S • E Europe & Mideast • 500 kW   W • Mideast & E Africa • 500 kW
           S • E Europe • 500 kW
    TURKEY
     VOICE OF TURKEY, Ankara-Emirler   S • W Asia • 500 kW
    UNITED KINGDOM
     †BBC, Rampisham   W • E Europe • 500 kW
     †BBC, Various Locations   E Africa • 500 kW
     †BBC, Via Zyyi, Cyprus   S • W Asia & S Asia • 250 kW
           S • Mideast & W Asia • 300 kW
    USA
     †ADVENTIST WORLD R, Via Austria   W • N Africa & E Africa • 500 kW
     †FAMILY RADIO, Okeechobee, Fl   S • N America • 100 kW
           W • N America • 100 kW
           N America • 100 kW
     †RFE-RL, Via Biblis, Germany   S • E Europe • 100 kW
           S • M-F • E Europe • 100 kW
           S • W Asia • 100 kW
     †RFE-RL, Via Holzkirchen, Germany   W • E Europe & W Asia • 250 kW
     RFE-RL, Via Woofferton, UK   S • E Europe • 250 kW
     †VOA, Via Briech, Morocco   W • Mideast • 250 kW
     †VOA, Via Philippines   W • SE Asia • 250 kW
     †VOA, Via Tinian, N Marianas   S • E Asia • 250 kW

11869v **USA**
    UNIVERSITY NET'K, Via Costa Rica   S America • 40 kW
11870 **CHINA**
    CHINA RADIO INTL, Xi'an   S • E Europe • 100 kW
    CLANDESTINE (M EAST)
     "VO PALESTINIAN ISLAMIC REV'N", Iran   S • Mideast • ANTI-ARAFAT • 100 kW
    INDIA
     †ALL INDIA RADIO, Delhi   SE Asia • 250 kW
    IRAN
     VO THE ISLAMIC REP, Tehrān   W Asia & S Asia • 500 kW
           W • S Asia, SE Asia & Australasia • 500 kW
    RUSSIA
     VOICE OF RUSSIA, Moscow   S • Europe • 250 kW
     VOICE OF RUSSIA, Novosibirsk   S • E Asia • 250 kW
    SERBIA AND MONTENEGRO
     †INTL RADIO OF S & M, Via Bosnia   S • E Europe • 250 kW • ALT. FREQ. TO 11800 kHz
    USA
     KNLS-NEW LIFE STN, Anchor Pt, Alaska   S • E Asia • 100 kW • ALT. FREQ. TO 11565 kHz
           S • E Asia • 100 kW • ALT. FREQ. TO 9615 kHz
           W • E Asia • 100 kW
     †R FREE ASIA, Via Saipan, N Marianas
     RFE-RL, Via Udon Thani, Thailand   S • W Asia & C Asia • 250 kW
     VOA, Via Philippines   W • Australasia • 250 kW
           Australasia • 250 kW

11875 **CHINA**
    CHINA RADIO INTL, Kunming   Australasia • 500 kW
    CHINA RADIO INTL, Urümqi   S • E Europe • 500 kW
    CHINA (TAIWAN)
     †CBS   SE Asia   E Asia • CHINESE NETWORK • ALT. FREQ. TO 11855 kHz
     †R TAIWAN INTL   SE Asia
    CUBA
     †RADIO HABANA CUBA, Havana   ⇦ • Tu-Sa • S America • 100 kW   ⇦ • M-F • S America • 100 kW
           Su • S America • "ALO PRESIDENTE" • 100 kW
    IRAN
     VO THE ISLAMIC REP, Sirjan   S • W Africa • 500 kW
    ITALY
     †RAI INTERNATIONAL, Rome   W • E Africa • 100 kW
    PORTUGAL
     RDP INTERNATIONAL, Lisbon   W • Sa/Su • Europe • 300 kW
           W • Europe • 300 kW
    ROMANIA
     †R ROMANIA INTL, Bucharest   W • S America • 250 kW
    TURKEY
(con'd)   VOICE OF TURKEY, Ankara-Çakirlar   S • S Europe • 250 kW

World Time   0 1 2 3 4 5 6 7 8 9 10 11 12 13 14 15 16 17 18 19 20 21 22 23 24

SEASONAL S OR W   1-HR TIMESHIFT MIDYEAR ⇦ OR ⇨   JAMMING / OR ∧   EARLIEST HEARD ◁   LATEST HEARD ▷   NEW FOR 2004 †

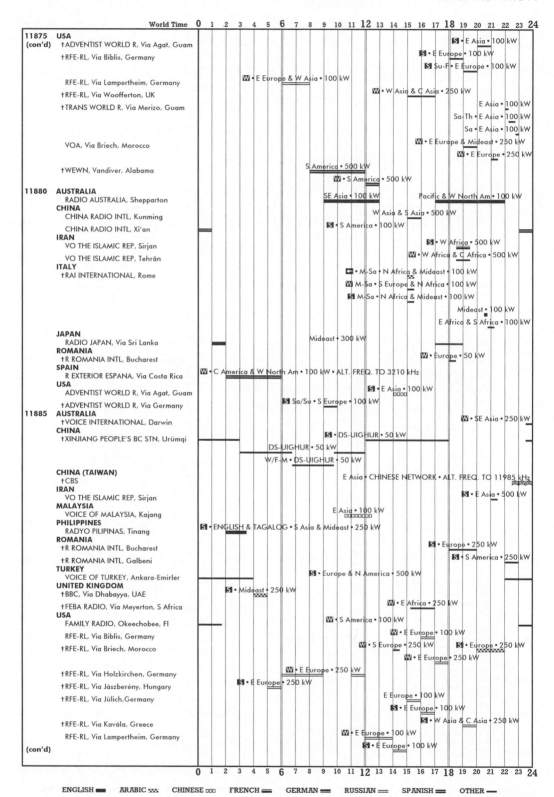

World Time | 0 1 2 3 4 5 6 7 8 9 10 11 12 13 14 15 16 17 18 19 20 21 22 23 24

11875 USA
(con'd) †ADVENTIST WORLD R, Via Agat, Guam — 🇸 • E Asia • 100 kW
†RFE-RL, Via Biblis, Germany — 🇸 • E Europe • 100 kW
🇸 • Su-F • E Europe • 100 kW
RFE-RL, Via Lampertheim, Germany — 🇼 • E Europe & W Asia • 100 kW
†RFE-RL, Via Woofferton, UK — 🇼 • W Asia & C Asia • 250 kW
†TRANS WORLD R, Via Merizo, Guam — E Asia • 100 kW
Sa-Th • E Asia • 100 kW
Sa • E Asia • 100 kW
VOA, Via Briech, Morocco — 🇼 • E Europe & Mideast • 250 kW
🇼 • E Europe • 250 kW
†WEWN, Vandiver, Alabama — S America • 500 kW
🇼 • S America • 500 kW
11880 AUSTRALIA
RADIO AUSTRALIA, Shepparton — SE Asia • 100 kW · Pacific & W North Am • 100 kW
CHINA
CHINA RADIO INTL, Kunming — W Asia & S Asia • 500 kW
CHINA RADIO INTL, Xi'an — 🇸 • S America • 100 kW
IRAN
VO THE ISLAMIC REP, Sirjan — 🇸 • W Africa • 500 kW
VO THE ISLAMIC REP, Tehrān — 🇼 • W Africa & C Africa • 500 kW
ITALY
†RAI INTERNATIONAL, Rome — ◄ • M-Sa • N Africa & Mideast • 100 kW
🇼 • M-Sa • S Europe & N Africa • 100 kW
🇸 • M-Sa • N Africa & Mideast • 100 kW
Mideast • 100 kW
E Africa & S Africa • 100 kW
JAPAN
RADIO JAPAN, Via Sri Lanka — Mideast • 300 kW
ROMANIA
†R ROMANIA INTL, Bucharest — 🇼 • Europe • 50 kW
SPAIN
R EXTERIOR ESPANA, Via Costa Rica — 🇼 • C America & W North Am • 100 kW • ALT. FREQ. TO 3210 kHz
USA
ADVENTIST WORLD R, Via Agat, Guam — 🇸 • E Asia • 100 kW
†ADVENTIST WORLD R, Via Germany — 🇸 • Sa/Su • S Europe • 100 kW
11885 AUSTRALIA
†VOICE INTERNATIONAL, Darwin — 🇼 • SE Asia • 250 kW
CHINA
†XINJIANG PEOPLE'S BC STN, Urümqi — 🇸 • DS-UIGHUR • 50 kW
DS-UIGHUR • 50 kW
W/F-M • DS-UIGHUR • 50 kW
CHINA (TAIWAN)
†CBS — E Asia • CHINESE NETWORK • ALT. FREQ. TO 11985 kHz
IRAN
VO THE ISLAMIC REP, Sirjan — 🇸 • E Asia • 500 kW
MALAYSIA
VOICE OF MALAYSIA, Kajang — E Asia • 100 kW
PHILIPPINES
RADYO PILIPINAS, Tinang — 🇸 • ENGLISH & TAGALOG • S Asia & Mideast • 250 kW
ROMANIA
†R ROMANIA INTL, Bucharest — 🇸 • Europe • 250 kW
†R ROMANIA INTL, Galbeni — 🇸 • S America • 250 kW
TURKEY
VOICE OF TURKEY, Ankara-Emirler — 🇸 • Europe & N America • 500 kW
UNITED KINGDOM
†BBC, Via Dhabayya, UAE — 🇸 • Mideast • 250 kW
†FEBA RADIO, Via Meyerton, S Africa — 🇼 • E Africa • 250 kW
USA
FAMILY RADIO, Okeechobee, Fl — 🇼 • S America • 100 kW
RFE-RL, Via Biblis, Germany — 🇼 • E Europe • 100 kW
†RFE-RL, Via Briech, Morocco — 🇼 • S Europe • 250 kW · 🇸 • Europe • 250 kW
🇼 • E Europe • 250 kW
†RFE-RL, Via Holzkirchen, Germany — 🇼 • E Europe • 250 kW
†RFE-RL, Via Jászberény, Hungary — 🇸 • E Europe • 250 kW
†RFE-RL, Via Jülich, Germany — E Europe • 100 kW
🇸 • E Europe • 100 kW
🇸 • W Asia & C Asia • 250 kW
†RFE-RL, Via Kavála, Greece — 🇼 • E Europe • 100 kW
RFE-RL, Via Lampertheim, Germany — 🇸 • E Europe • 100 kW
(con'd)

0 1 2 3 4 5 6 7 8 9 10 11 12 13 14 15 16 17 18 19 20 21 22 23 24

ENGLISH ▬   ARABIC ⚏⚏⚏   CHINESE ▫▫▫   FRENCH ▭▭   GERMAN ▬   RUSSIAN ═   SPANISH ▭▭   OTHER ▬

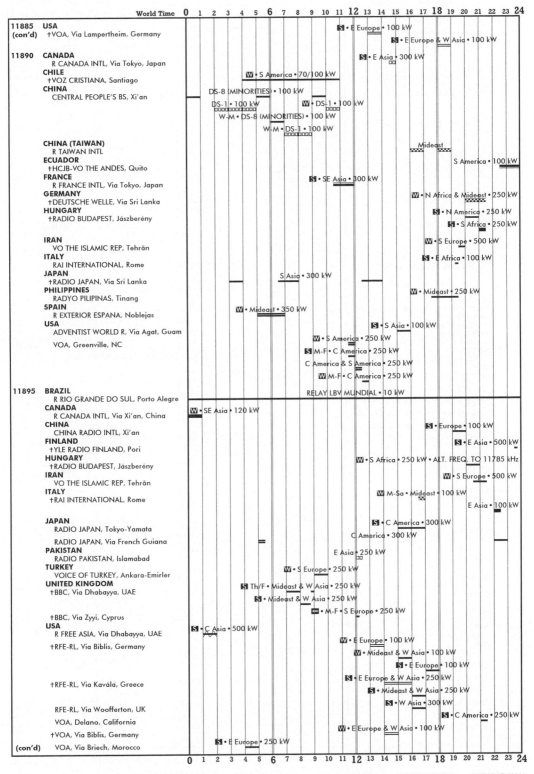

	World Time	0 1 2 3 4 5 6 7 8 9 10 11 12 13 14 15 16 17 18 19 20 21 22 23 24
11885 (con'd)	USA	
	†VOA, Via Lampertheim, Germany	S • E Europe • 100 kW
		S • E Europe & W Asia • 100 kW
11890	CANADA	
	R CANADA INTL, Via Tokyo, Japan	S • E Asia • 300 kW
	CHILE	
	†VOZ CRISTIANA, Santiago	W • S America • 70/100 kW
	CHINA	
	CENTRAL PEOPLE'S BS, Xi'an	DS-8 (MINORITIES) • 100 kW
		DS-1 • 100 kW W • DS-1 • 100 kW
		W-M • DS-8 (MINORITIES) • 100 kW
		W-M • DS-1 • 100 kW
	CHINA (TAIWAN)	
	R TAIWAN INTL	Mideast
	ECUADOR	S America • 100 kW
	†HCJB-VO THE ANDES, Quito	
	FRANCE	
	R FRANCE INTL, Via Tokyo, Japan	S • SE Asia • 300 kW
	GERMANY	
	†DEUTSCHE WELLE, Via Sri Lanka	W • N Africa & Mideast • 250 kW
	HUNGARY	
	†RADIO BUDAPEST, Jászberény	S • N America • 250 kW
		S • S Africa • 250 kW
	IRAN	
	VO THE ISLAMIC REP, Tehrān	W • S Europe • 500 kW
	ITALY	
	RAI INTERNATIONAL, Rome	S • E Africa • 100 kW
	JAPAN	
	†RADIO JAPAN, Via Sri Lanka	S Asia • 300 kW
	PHILIPPINES	
	RADYO PILIPINAS, Tinang	W • Mideast • 250 kW
	SPAIN	
	R EXTERIOR ESPANA, Noblejas	W • Mideast • 350 kW
	USA	
	ADVENTIST WORLD R, Via Agat, Guam	S • S Asia • 100 kW
		W • S America • 250 kW
	VOA, Greenville, NC	S M-F • C America • 250 kW
		C America & S America • 250 kW
		W M-F • C America • 250 kW
11895	BRAZIL	
	R RIO GRANDE DO SUL, Porto Alegre	RELAY LBV MUNDIAL • 10 kW
	CANADA	
	R CANADA INTL, Via Xi'an, China	W • SE Asia • 120 kW
	CHINA	
	CHINA RADIO INTL, Xi'an	S • Europe • 100 kW
	FINLAND	
	†YLE RADIO FINLAND, Pori	S • E Asia • 500 kW
	HUNGARY	
	†RADIO BUDAPEST, Jászberény	W • S Africa • 250 kW • ALT. FREQ. TO 11785 kHz
	IRAN	
	VO THE ISLAMIC REP, Tehrān	W • S Europe • 500 kW
	ITALY	
	†RAI INTERNATIONAL, Rome	W M-Sa • Mideast • 100 kW
		E Asia • 100 kW
	JAPAN	
	RADIO JAPAN, Tokyo-Yamata	S • C America • 300 kW
	RADIO JAPAN, Via French Guiana	C America • 300 kW
	PAKISTAN	
	RADIO PAKISTAN, Islamabad	E Asia • 250 kW
	TURKEY	
	VOICE OF TURKEY, Ankara-Emirler	W • S Europe • 250 kW
	UNITED KINGDOM	
	†BBC, Via Dhabayya, UAE	S Th/F • Mideast & W Asia • 250 kW
		S • Mideast & W Asia • 250 kW
	†BBC, Via Zyyi, Cyprus	• M-F • S Europe • 250 kW
	USA	
	R FREE ASIA, Via Dhabayya, UAE	S • C Asia • 500 kW
	†RFE-RL, Via Biblis, Germany	W • E Europe • 100 kW
		W • Mideast & W Asia • 100 kW
		S • E Europe • 100 kW
	†RFE-RL, Via Kavála, Greece	S • E Europe & W Asia • 250 kW
		S • Mideast & W Asia • 250 kW
	RFE-RL, Via Woofferton, UK	S • W Asia • 300 kW
	VOA, Delano, California	S • C America • 250 kW
	†VOA, Via Biblis, Germany	W • E Europe & W Asia • 100 kW
(con'd)	VOA, Via Briech, Morocco	S • E Europe • 250 kW

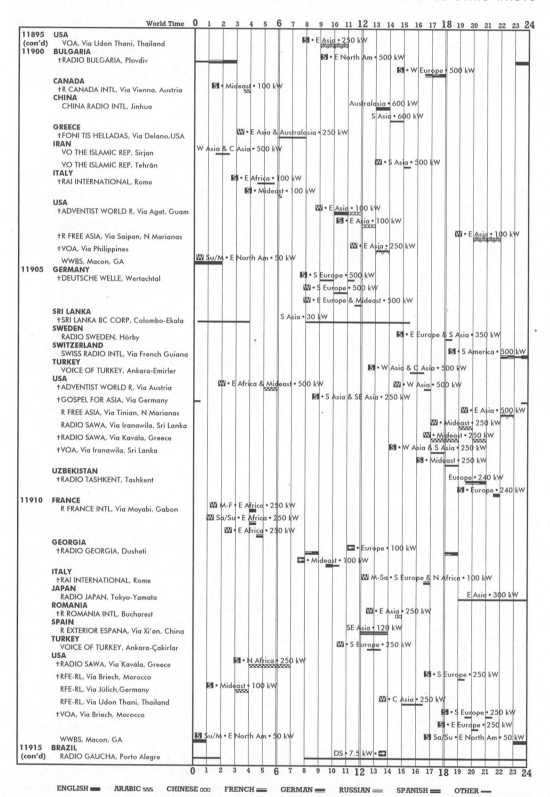

			World Time	0 1 2 3 4 5 6 7 8 9 10 11 12 13 14 15 16 17 18 19 20 21 22 23 24
11895 (con'd)	USA	VOA, Via Udon Thani, Thailand		S • E Asia • 250 kW
11900	BULGARIA	†RADIO BULGARIA, Plovdiv		S • E North Am • 500 kW
				S • W Europe • 500 kW
	CANADA	†R CANADA INTL, Via Vienna, Austria		S • Mideast • 100 kW
	CHINA	CHINA RADIO INTL, Jinhua		Australasia • 600 kW
				S Asia • 600 kW
	GREECE	†FONI TIS HELLADAS, Via Delano, USA		W • E Asia & Australasia • 250 kW
	IRAN	VO THE ISLAMIC REP, Sirjan		W Asia & C Asia • 500 kW
		VO THE ISLAMIC REP, Tehrān		W • S Asia • 500 kW
	ITALY	†RAI INTERNATIONAL, Rome		S • E Africa • 100 kW
				S • Mideast • 100 kW
	USA	†ADVENTIST WORLD R, Via Agat, Guam		W • E Asia • 100 kW
				S • E Asia • 100 kW
		†R FREE ASIA, Via Saipan, N Marianas		W • E Asia • 100 kW
		†VOA, Via Philippines		W • E Asia • 250 kW
		WWBS, Macon, GA		W Su/M • E North Am • 50 kW
11905	GERMANY	†DEUTSCHE WELLE, Wertachtal		S • S Europe • 500 kW
				W • S Europe • 500 kW
				W • E Europe & Mideast • 500 kW
	SRI LANKA	†SRI LANKA BC CORP, Colombo-Ekala		S Asia • 30 kW
	SWEDEN	RADIO SWEDEN, Hörby		S • E Europe & S Asia • 350 kW
	SWITZERLAND	SWISS RADIO INTL, Via French Guiana		S • S America • 500 kW
	TURKEY	VOICE OF TURKEY, Ankara-Emirler		S • W Asia & C Asia • 500 kW
	USA	†ADVENTIST WORLD R, Via Austria		W • E Africa & Mideast • 500 kW
				W • W Asia • 500 kW
		†GOSPEL FOR ASIA, Via Germany		S • S Asia & SE Asia • 250 kW
		R FREE ASIA, Via Tinian, N Marianas		W • E Asia • 500 kW
		RADIO SAWA, Via Iranawila, Sri Lanka		W • Mideast • 250 kW
		†RADIO SAWA, Via Kavála, Greece		W • Mideast • 250 kW
		†VOA, Via Iranawila, Sri Lanka		S • W Asia & S Asia • 250 kW
				S • Mideast • 250 kW
	UZBEKISTAN	†RADIO TASHKENT, Tashkent		Europe • 240 kW
				S • Europe • 240 kW
11910	FRANCE	R FRANCE INTL, Via Moyabi, Gabon		W M-F • E Africa • 250 kW
				W Sa/Su • E Africa • 250 kW
				W • E Africa • 250 kW
	GEORGIA	†RADIO GEORGIA, Dusheti		• Europe • 100 kW
				• Mideast • 100 kW
	ITALY	†RAI INTERNATIONAL, Rome		W M-Sa • S Europe & N Africa • 100 kW
	JAPAN	RADIO JAPAN, Tokyo-Yamata		E Asia • 300 kW
	ROMANIA	†R ROMANIA INTL, Bucharest		W • E Asia • 250 kW
	SPAIN	R EXTERIOR ESPANA, Via Xi'an, China		SE Asia • 120 kW
	TURKEY	VOICE OF TURKEY, Ankara-Çakirlar		W • S Europe • 250 kW
	USA	†RADIO SAWA, Via Kavála, Greece		S • N Africa • 250 kW
		†RFE-RL, Via Briech, Morocco		S • S Europe • 250 kW
		RFE-RL, Via Jülich, Germany		S • Mideast • 100 kW
		RFE-RL, Via Udon Thani, Thailand		W • C Asia • 250 kW
		†VOA, Via Briech, Morocco		S • S Europe • 250 kW
				S • E Europe • 250 kW
		WWBS, Macon, GA		S Su/M • E North Am • 50 kW
				S Sa/Su • E North Am • 50 kW
11915 (con'd)	BRAZIL	RADIO GAUCHA, Porto Alegre		DS • 7.5 kW • →

			World Time	0 1 2 3 4 5 6 7 8 9 10 11 12 13 14 15 16 17 18 19 20 21 22 23 24

ENGLISH ▬   ARABIC ﹏   CHINESE ☐☐☐   FRENCH ═   GERMAN ▬   RUSSIAN ⹀   SPANISH ▬   OTHER ▬

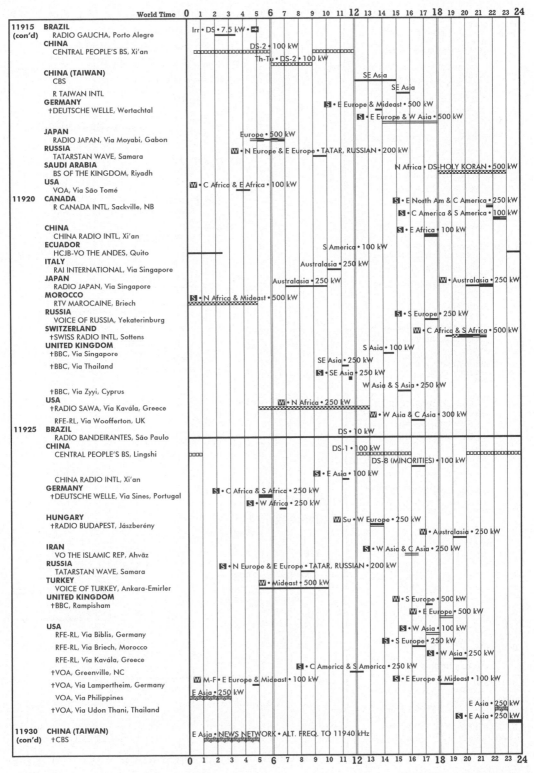

World Time 0 1 2 3 4 5 6 7 8 9 10 11 12 13 14 15 16 17 18 19 20 21 22 23 24

Frequency	Station	
11915 (con'd)	BRAZIL — RADIO GAUCHA, Porto Alegre	Irr • DS • 7.5 kW • ⇨
	CHINA — CENTRAL PEOPLE'S BS, Xi'an	DS-2 • 100 kW / Th-Tu • DS-2 • 100 kW
	CHINA (TAIWAN) — CBS	SE Asia
	R TAIWAN INTL	SE Asia
	GERMANY — †DEUTSCHE WELLE, Wertachtal	S • E Europe & Mideast • 500 kW / S • E Europe & W Asia • 500 kW
	JAPAN — RADIO JAPAN, Via Moyabi, Gabon	Europe • 500 kW
	RUSSIA — TATARSTAN WAVE, Samara	W • N Europe & E Europe • TATAR, RUSSIAN • 200 kW
	SAUDI ARABIA — BS OF THE KINGDOM, Riyadh	N Africa • DS HOLY KORAN • 500 kW
	USA — VOA, Via São Tomé	W • C Africa & E Africa • 100 kW
11920	CANADA — R CANADA INTL, Sackville, NB	S • E North Am & C America • 250 kW / S • C America & S America • 100 kW
	CHINA — CHINA RADIO INTL, Xi'an	S • E Africa • 100 kW
	ECUADOR — HCJB-VO THE ANDES, Quito	S America • 100 kW
	ITALY — RAI INTERNATIONAL, Via Singapore	Australasia • 250 kW
	JAPAN — RADIO JAPAN, Via Singapore	Australasia • 250 kW / W • Australasia • 250 kW
	MOROCCO — RTV MAROCAINE, Briech	S • N Africa & Mideast • 500 kW
	RUSSIA — VOICE OF RUSSIA, Yekaterinburg	S • S Europe • 250 kW
	SWITZERLAND — †SWISS RADIO INTL, Sottens	W • C Africa & S Africa • 500 kW
	UNITED KINGDOM — †BBC, Via Singapore	S Asia • 100 kW
	†BBC, Via Thailand	SE Asia • 250 kW / S • SE Asia • 250 kW
	†BBC, Via Zyyi, Cyprus	W Asia & S Asia • 250 kW
	USA — †RADIO SAWA, Via Kavála, Greece	W • N Africa • 250 kW
	RFE-RL, Via Woofferton, UK	W • W Asia & C Asia • 300 kW
11925	BRAZIL — RADIO BANDEIRANTES, São Paulo	DS • 10 kW
	CHINA — CENTRAL PEOPLE'S BS, Lingshi	DS-1 • 100 kW / DS-8 (MINORITIES) • 100 kW
	CHINA RADIO INTL, Xi'an	S • E Asia • 100 kW
	GERMANY — †DEUTSCHE WELLE, Via Sines, Portugal	S • C Africa & S Africa • 250 kW / S • W Africa • 250 kW
	HUNGARY — †RADIO BUDAPEST, Jászberény	W Su • W Europe • 250 kW / W • Australasia • 250 kW
	IRAN — VO THE ISLAMIC REP, Ahvāz	S • W Asia & C Asia • 250 kW
	RUSSIA — TATARSTAN WAVE, Samara	S • N Europe & E Europe • TATAR, RUSSIAN • 200 kW
	TURKEY — VOICE OF TURKEY, Ankara-Emirler	W • Mideast • 500 kW
	UNITED KINGDOM — †BBC, Rampisham	W • S Europe • 500 kW / W • E Europe • 500 kW
	USA — RFE-RL, Via Biblis, Germany	S • W Asia • 100 kW
	RFE-RL, Via Briech, Morocco	S • S Europe • 250 kW
	RFE-RL, Via Kavála, Greece	S • W Asia • 250 kW
	†VOA, Greenville, NC	S • C America & S America • 250 kW
	†VOA, Via Lampertheim, Germany	W M-F • E Europe & Mideast • 100 kW / S • E Europe & Mideast • 100 kW
	VOA, Via Philippines	E Asia • 250 kW
	†VOA, Via Udon Thani, Thailand	E Asia • 250 kW / S • E Asia • 250 kW
11930 (con'd)	CHINA (TAIWAN) — †CBS	E Asia • NEWS NETWORK • ALT. FREQ. TO 11940 kHz

0 1 2 3 4 5 6 7 8 9 10 11 12 13 14 15 16 17 18 19 20 21 22 23 24

SEASONAL S OR W   1-HR TIMESHIFT MIDYEAR ⇦ OR ⇨   JAMMING / OR ∧   EARLIEST HEARD ◁   LATEST HEARD ▷   NEW FOR 2004 †

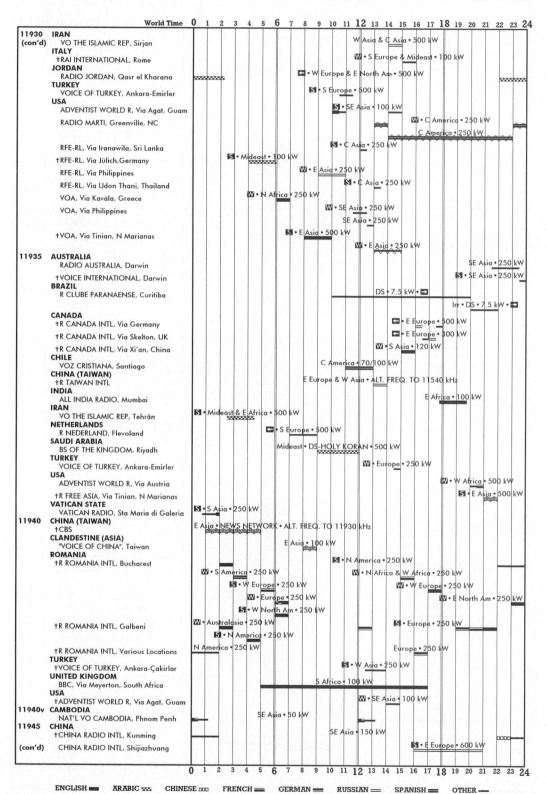

World Time	0 1 2 3 4 5 6 7 8 9 10 11 12 13 14 15 16 17 18 19 20 21 22 23 24
11930 IRAN	
(con'd) VO THE ISLAMIC REP, Sirjan	W Asia & C Asia • 500 kW
ITALY	
†RAI INTERNATIONAL, Rome	W • S Europe & Mideast • 100 kW
JORDAN	
RADIO JORDAN, Qasr el Kharana	⬛ • W Europe & E North Am • 500 kW
TURKEY	
VOICE OF TURKEY, Ankara-Emirler	S • S Europe • 500 kW
USA	
ADVENTIST WORLD R, Via Agat, Guam	S • SE Asia • 100 kW
RADIO MARTI, Greenville, NC	W • C America • 250 kW / C America • 250 kW
RFE-RL, Via Iranawila, Sri Lanka	S • C Asia • 250 kW
†RFE-RL, Via Jülich, Germany	S • Mideast • 100 kW
RFE-RL, Via Philippines	W • E Asia • 250 kW
RFE-RL, Via Udon Thani, Thailand	S • C Asia • 250 kW
VOA, Via Kavála, Greece	W • N Africa • 250 kW
VOA, Via Philippines	W • SE Asia • 250 kW / SE Asia • 250 kW
†VOA, Via Tinian, N Marianas	S • E Asia • 500 kW / W • E Asia • 250 kW
11935 AUSTRALIA	
RADIO AUSTRALIA, Darwin	SE Asia • 250 kW
†VOICE INTERNATIONAL, Darwin	S • SE Asia • 250 kW
BRAZIL	
R CLUBE PARANAENSE, Curitiba	DS • 7.5 kW • ⬛ / Irr • DS • 7.5 kW • ⬛
CANADA	
†R CANADA INTL, Via Germany	⬛ • E Europe • 500 kW
†R CANADA INTL, Via Skelton, UK	⬛ • E Europe • 300 kW
†R CANADA INTL, Via Xi'an, China	W • S Asia • 120 kW
CHILE	
VOZ CRISTIANA, Santiago	C America • 70/100 kW
CHINA (TAIWAN)	
†R TAIWAN INTL	E Europe & W Asia • ALT. FREQ. TO 11540 kHz
INDIA	
ALL INDIA RADIO, Mumbai	E Africa • 100 kW
IRAN	
VO THE ISLAMIC REP, Tehrān	S • Mideast & E Africa • 500 kW
NETHERLANDS	
R NEDERLAND, Flevoland	⬛ • S Europe • 500 kW
SAUDI ARABIA	
BS OF THE KINGDOM, Riyadh	Mideast • DS-HOLY KORAN • 500 kW
TURKEY	
VOICE OF TURKEY, Ankara-Emirler	W • Europe • 250 kW
USA	
ADVENTIST WORLD R, Via Austria	W • W Africa • 500 kW
†R FREE ASIA, Via Tinian, N Marianas	S • E Asia • 500 kW
VATICAN STATE	
VATICAN RADIO, Sta Maria di Galeria	S • S Asia • 250 kW
11940 CHINA (TAIWAN)	
†CBS	E Asia • NEWS NETWORK • ALT. FREQ. TO 11930 kHz
CLANDESTINE (ASIA)	
"VOICE OF CHINA", Taiwan	E Asia • 100 kW
ROMANIA	
†R ROMANIA INTL, Bucharest	S • N America • 250 kW / W • S America • 250 kW / W • N Africa & W Africa • 250 kW / S • W Europe • 250 kW / W • W Europe • 250 kW / W • Europe • 250 kW / W • E North Am • 250 kW / S • N North Am • 250 kW
†R ROMANIA INTL, Galbeni	W • Australasia • 250 kW / S • N America • 250 kW / S • Europe • 250 kW
†R ROMANIA INTL, Various Locations	N America • 250 kW / Europe • 250 kW
TURKEY	
†VOICE OF TURKEY, Ankara-Çakirlar	S • W Asia • 250 kW
UNITED KINGDOM	
BBC, Via Meyerton, South Africa	S Africa • 100 kW
USA	
†ADVENTIST WORLD R, Via Agat, Guam	W • SE Asia • 100 kW
11940v CAMBODIA	
NAT'L VO CAMBODIA, Phnom Penh	SE Asia • 50 kW
11945 CHINA	
†CHINA RADIO INTL, Kunming	SE Asia • 150 kW
(con'd) CHINA RADIO INTL, Shijiazhuang	S • E Europe • 600 kW
	0 1 2 3 4 5 6 7 8 9 10 11 12 13 14 15 16 17 18 19 20 21 22 23 24

ENGLISH ▬ ARABIC ≋ CHINESE ▭▭▭ FRENCH ═ GERMAN ▬ RUSSIAN ═ SPANISH ▬ OTHER ▬

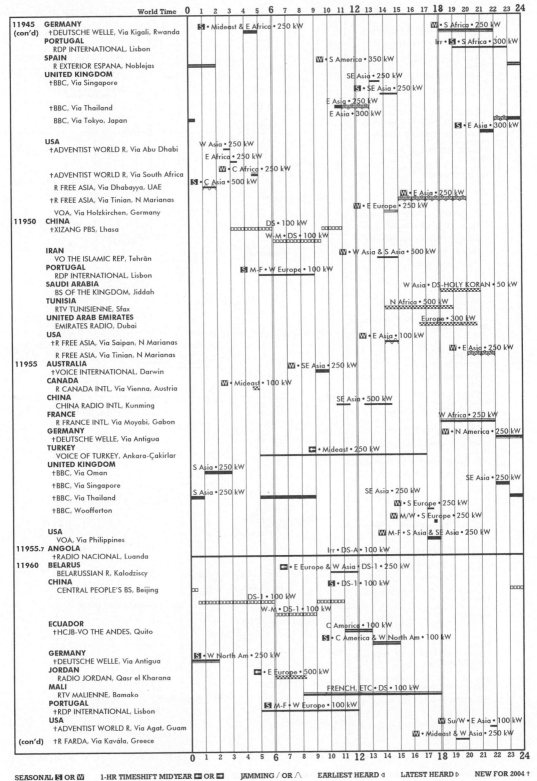

World Time

11945 **GERMANY**	
(con'd)	†DEUTSCHE WELLE, Via Kigali, Rwanda
	PORTUGAL
	RDP INTERNATIONAL, Lisbon
	SPAIN
	R EXTERIOR ESPANA, Noblejas
	UNITED KINGDOM
	†BBC, Via Singapore
	†BBC, Via Thailand
	BBC, Via Tokyo, Japan
	USA
	†ADVENTIST WORLD R, Via Abu Dhabi
	†ADVENTIST WORLD R, Via South Africa
	R FREE ASIA, Via Dhabayya, UAE
	†R FREE ASIA, Via Tinian, N Marianas
	VOA, Via Holzkirchen, Germany
11950 **CHINA**	†XIZANG PBS, Lhasa
	IRAN
	VO THE ISLAMIC REP, Tehrān
	PORTUGAL
	RDP INTERNATIONAL, Lisbon
	SAUDI ARABIA
	BS OF THE KINGDOM, Jiddah
	TUNISIA
	RTV TUNISIENNE, Sfax
	UNITED ARAB EMIRATES
	EMIRATES RADIO, Dubai
	USA
	†R FREE ASIA, Via Saipan, N Marianas
	R FREE ASIA, Via Tinian, N Marianas
11955 **AUSTRALIA**	†VOICE INTERNATIONAL, Darwin
	CANADA
	R CANADA INTL, Via Vienna, Austria
	CHINA
	CHINA RADIO INTL, Kunming
	FRANCE
	R FRANCE INTL, Via Moyabi, Gabon
	GERMANY
	†DEUTSCHE WELLE, Via Antigua
	TURKEY
	VOICE OF TURKEY, Ankara-Çakirlar
	UNITED KINGDOM
	†BBC, Via Oman
	†BBC, Via Singapore
	†BBC, Via Thailand
	†BBC, Woofferton
	USA
	VOA, Via Philippines
11955.7 ANGOLA	†RADIO NACIONAL, Luanda
11960 **BELARUS**	BELARUSSIAN R, Kalodziscy
	CHINA
	CENTRAL PEOPLE'S BS, Beijing
	ECUADOR
	†HCJB-VO THE ANDES, Quito
	GERMANY
	†DEUTSCHE WELLE, Via Antigua
	JORDAN
	RADIO JORDAN, Qasr el Kharana
	MALI
	RTV MALIENNE, Bamako
	PORTUGAL
	†RDP INTERNATIONAL, Lisbon
	USA
	†ADVENTIST WORLD R, Via Agat, Guam
(con'd)	†R FARDA, Via Kavála, Greece

Transmission target notes (left to right across the chart):

- †DEUTSCHE WELLE, Via Kigali, Rwanda — S • Mideast & E Africa • 250 kW; W • S Africa • 250 kW
- RDP INTERNATIONAL, Lisbon — Irr • S • S Africa • 300 kW
- R EXTERIOR ESPANA, Noblejas — W • S America • 350 kW
- †BBC, Via Singapore — SE Asia • 250 kW; S • SE Asia • 250 kW
- †BBC, Via Thailand — E Asia • 250 kW
- BBC, Via Tokyo, Japan — E Asia • 300 kW; S • E Asia • 300 kW
- †ADVENTIST WORLD R, Via Abu Dhabi — W Asia • 250 kW; E Africa • 250 kW
- †ADVENTIST WORLD R, Via South Africa — W • C Africa • 250 kW
- R FREE ASIA, Via Dhabayya, UAE — S • C Asia • 500 kW
- †R FREE ASIA, Via Tinian, N Marianas — W • E Asia • 250 kW
- VOA, Via Holzkirchen, Germany — W • E Europe • 250 kW
- †XIZANG PBS, Lhasa — DS • 100 kW; W-M • DS • 100 kW
- VO THE ISLAMIC REP, Tehrān — W • W Asia & S Asia • 500 kW
- RDP INTERNATIONAL, Lisbon — S • M-F • W Europe • 100 kW
- BS OF THE KINGDOM, Jiddah — W Asia • DS-HOLY KORAN • 50 kW
- RTV TUNISIENNE, Sfax — N Africa • 500 kW
- EMIRATES RADIO, Dubai — Europe • 300 kW
- †R FREE ASIA, Via Saipan, N Marianas — W • E Asia • 100 kW
- R FREE ASIA, Via Tinian, N Marianas — W • E Asia • 250 kW
- †VOICE INTERNATIONAL, Darwin — W • SE Asia • 250 kW
- R CANADA INTL, Via Vienna, Austria — W • Mideast • 100 kW
- CHINA RADIO INTL, Kunming — SE Asia • 500 kW
- R FRANCE INTL, Via Moyabi, Gabon — W Africa • 250 kW
- †DEUTSCHE WELLE, Via Antigua — W • N America • 250 kW
- VOICE OF TURKEY, Ankara-Çakirlar — • Mideast • 250 kW
- †BBC, Via Oman — S Asia • 250 kW; SE Asia • 250 kW
- †BBC, Via Singapore — S Asia • 250 kW; SE Asia • 250 kW
- †BBC, Woofferton — W • S Europe • 250 kW; W • M/W • S Europe • 250 kW
- VOA, Via Philippines — W • M-F • S Asia & SE Asia • 250 kW
- †RADIO NACIONAL, Luanda — Irr • DS-A • 100 kW
- BELARUSSIAN R, Kalodziscy — • E Europe & W Asia • DS-1 • 250 kW
- CENTRAL PEOPLE'S BS, Beijing — S • DS-1 • 100 kW; DS-1 • 100 kW; W-M • DS-1 • 100 kW
- †HCJB-VO THE ANDES, Quito — C America • 100 kW; S • C America & W North Am • 100 kW
- †DEUTSCHE WELLE, Via Antigua — S • W North Am • 250 kW
- RADIO JORDAN, Qasr el Kharana — • E Europe • 500 kW
- RTV MALIENNE, Bamako — FRENCH, ETC • DS • 100 kW
- †RDP INTERNATIONAL, Lisbon — S • M-F • W Europe • 100 kW
- †ADVENTIST WORLD R, Via Agat, Guam — W • Su/W • E Asia • 100 kW
- †R FARDA, Via Kavála, Greece — W • Mideast & W Asia • 250 kW

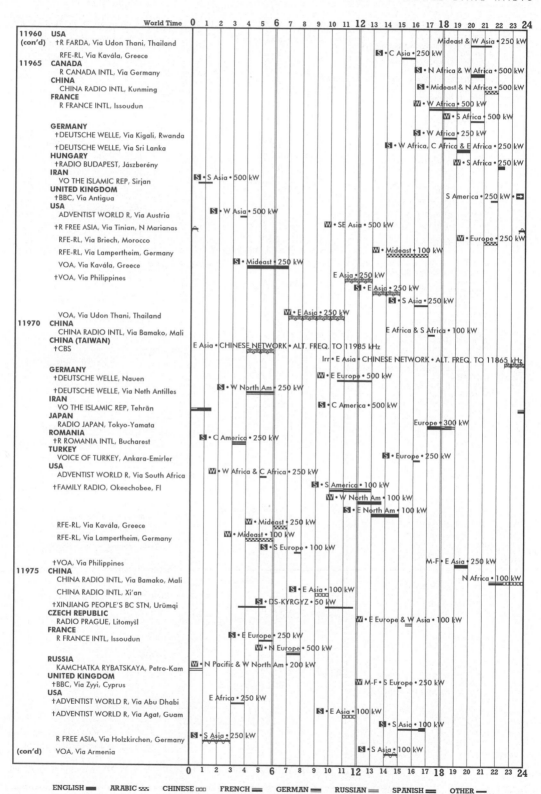

| World Time | 0 | 1 | 2 | 3 | 4 | 5 | 6 | 7 | 8 | 9 | 10 | 11 | 12 | 13 | 14 | 15 | 16 | 17 | 18 | 19 | 20 | 21 | 22 | 23 | 24 |

11960 **USA**
(con'd) †R FARDA, Via Udon Thani, Thailand — Mideast & W Asia • 250 kW
RFE-RL, Via Kavála, Greece — S • C Asia • 250 kW
11965 **CANADA**
R CANADA INTL, Via Germany — S • N Africa & W Africa • 500 kW
CHINA
CHINA RADIO INTL, Kunming — S • Mideast & N Africa • 500 kW
FRANCE
R FRANCE INTL, Issoudun — W • W Africa • 500 kW
W • S Africa • 500 kW
GERMANY
†DEUTSCHE WELLE, Via Kigali, Rwanda — S • W Africa • 250 kW
†DEUTSCHE WELLE, Via Sri Lanka — S • W Africa, C Africa & E Africa • 250 kW
HUNGARY
†RADIO BUDAPEST, Jászberény — W • S Africa • 250 kW
IRAN
VO THE ISLAMIC REP, Sirjan — S • S Asia • 500 kW
UNITED KINGDOM
†BBC, Via Antigua — S America • 250 kW •
USA
ADVENTIST WORLD R, Via Austria — S • W Asia • 500 kW
†R FREE ASIA, Via Tinian, N Marianas — W • SE Asia • 500 kW
RFE-RL, Via Briech, Morocco — W • Europe • 250 kW
RFE-RL, Via Lampertheim, Germany — W • Mideast • 100 kW
VOA, Via Kavála, Greece — S • Mideast • 250 kW
†VOA, Via Philippines — E Asia • 250 kW
S • E Asia • 250 kW
S • S Asia • 250 kW
11970 VOA, Via Udon Thani, Thailand — W • E Asia • 250 kW
CHINA
CHINA RADIO INTL, Via Bamako, Mali — E Africa & S Africa • 100 kW
CHINA (TAIWAN)
†CBS — E Asia • CHINESE NETWORK • ALT. FREQ. TO 11985 kHz
Irr • E Asia • CHINESE NETWORK • ALT. FREQ. TO 11865 kHz
GERMANY
†DEUTSCHE WELLE, Nauen — W • E Europe • 500 kW
†DEUTSCHE WELLE, Via Neth Antilles — S • W North Am • 250 kW
IRAN
VO THE ISLAMIC REP, Tehrān — S • C America • 500 kW
JAPAN
RADIO JAPAN, Tokyo-Yamata — Europe • 300 kW
ROMANIA
†R ROMANIA INTL, Bucharest — S • C America • 250 kW
TURKEY
VOICE OF TURKEY, Ankara-Emirler — S • Europe • 250 kW
USA
ADVENTIST WORLD R, Via South Africa — W • W Africa & C Africa • 250 kW
†FAMILY RADIO, Okeechobee, Fl — S • S America • 100 kW
W • W North Am • 100 kW
S • E North Am • 100 kW
RFE-RL, Via Kavála, Greece — W • Mideast • 250 kW
RFE-RL, Via Lampertheim, Germany — W • Mideast • 100 kW
S • S Europe • 100 kW
11975 †VOA, Via Philippines — M-F • E Asia • 250 kW
CHINA
CHINA RADIO INTL, Via Bamako, Mali — N Africa • 100 kW
CHINA RADIO INTL, Xi'an — S • E Asia • 100 kW
†XINJIANG PEOPLE'S BC STN, Urümqi — S • DS-KYRGYZ • 50 kW
CZECH REPUBLIC
RADIO PRAGUE, Litomyšl — W • E Europe & W Asia • 100 kW
FRANCE
R FRANCE INTL, Issoudun — S • E Europe • 250 kW
W • N Europe • 500 kW
RUSSIA
KAMCHATKA RYBATSKAYA, Petro-Kam — W • N Pacific & W North Am • 200 kW
UNITED KINGDOM
†BBC, Via Zyyi, Cyprus — W M-F • S Europe • 250 kW
USA
†ADVENTIST WORLD R, Via Abu Dhabi — E Africa • 250 kW
†ADVENTIST WORLD R, Via Agat, Guam — S • E Asia • 100 kW
S • S Asia • 100 kW
R FREE ASIA, Via Holzkirchen, Germany — S • S Asia • 250 kW
(con'd) VOA, Via Armenia — S • S Asia • 100 kW

| | 0 | 1 | 2 | 3 | 4 | 5 | 6 | 7 | 8 | 9 | 10 | 11 | 12 | 13 | 14 | 15 | 16 | 17 | 18 | 19 | 20 | 21 | 22 | 23 | 24 |

ENGLISH ▬ ARABIC ⌇⌇ CHINESE □□□ FRENCH ═ GERMAN ▬ RUSSIAN ═ SPANISH ═ OTHER ▬

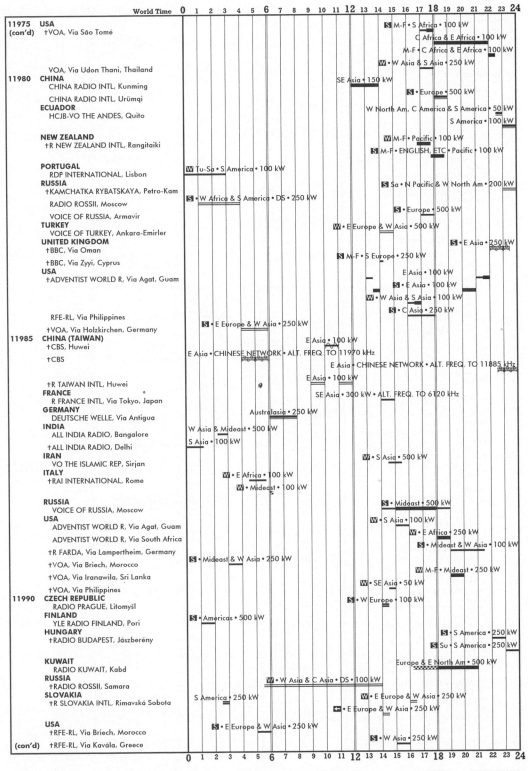

| World Time | 0 | 1 | 2 | 3 | 4 | 5 | 6 | 7 | 8 | 9 | 10 | 11 | 12 | 13 | 14 | 15 | 16 | 17 | 18 | 19 | 20 | 21 | 22 | 23 | 24 |

11975 USA
(con'd) †VOA, Via São Tomé
- M-F • S Africa • 100 kW
- C Africa & E Africa • 100 kW
- M-F • C Africa & E Africa • 100 kW
- W • W Asia & S Asia • 250 kW

VOA, Via Udon Thani, Thailand

11980 CHINA
CHINA RADIO INTL, Kunming — SE Asia • 150 kW
CHINA RADIO INTL, Urümqi — S • Europe • 500 kW
ECUADOR
HCJB-VO THE ANDES, Quito — W North Am, C America & S America • 50 kW
S America • 100 kW

NEW ZEALAND
†R NEW ZEALAND INTL, Rangitaiki
- W • M-F • Pacific • 100 kW
- S • M-F • ENGLISH, ETC • Pacific • 100 kW

PORTUGAL
RDP INTERNATIONAL, Lisbon — W • Tu-Sa • S America • 100 kW
RUSSIA
†KAMCHATKA RYBATSKAYA, Petro-Kam — S • Sa • N Pacific & W North Am • 200 kW
RADIO ROSSII, Moscow — S • W Africa & S America • DS • 250 kW
VOICE OF RUSSIA, Armavir — S • Europe • 500 kW
TURKEY
VOICE OF TURKEY, Ankara-Emirler — W • E Europe & W Asia • 500 kW
UNITED KINGDOM
†BBC, Via Oman — S • E Asia • 250 kW
†BBC, Via Zyyi, Cyprus — S • M-F • S Europe • 250 kW
USA
†ADVENTIST WORLD R, Via Agat, Guam
- E Asia • 100 kW
- S • E Asia • 100 kW
- W • W Asia & S Asia • 100 kW
- S • C Asia • 250 kW

RFE-RL, Via Philippines — S • E Europe & W Asia • 250 kW
†VOA, Via Holzkirchen, Germany

11985 CHINA (TAIWAN)
†CBS, Huwei — E Asia • 100 kW
†CBS — E Asia • CHINESE NETWORK • ALT. FREQ. TO 11970 kHz
E Asia • CHINESE NETWORK • ALT. FREQ. TO 11885 kHz

†R TAIWAN INTL, Huwei — E Asia • 100 kW
FRANCE
R FRANCE INTL, Via Tokyo, Japan — SE Asia • 300 kW • ALT. FREQ. TO 6120 kHz
GERMANY
DEUTSCHE WELLE, Via Antigua — Australasia • 250 kW
INDIA
ALL INDIA RADIO, Bangalore — W Asia & Mideast • 500 kW
†ALL INDIA RADIO, Delhi — S Asia • 100 kW
IRAN
VO THE ISLAMIC REP, Sirjan — W • S Asia • 500 kW
ITALY
†RAI INTERNATIONAL, Rome
- W • E Africa • 100 kW
- W • Mideast • 100 kW

RUSSIA
VOICE OF RUSSIA, Moscow — S • Mideast • 500 kW
USA
ADVENTIST WORLD R, Via Agat, Guam — W • S Asia • 100 kW
ADVENTIST WORLD R, Via South Africa — W • E Africa • 250 kW
†R FARDA, Via Lampertheim, Germany — S • Mideast & W Asia • 100 kW
†VOA, Via Briech, Morocco — S • Mideast & W Asia • 250 kW
†VOA, Via Iranawila, Sri Lanka — W • M-F • Mideast • 250 kW
†VOA, Via Philippines — W • SE Asia • 50 kW
11990 CZECH REPUBLIC
RADIO PRAGUE, Litomyšl — S • W Europe • 100 kW
FINLAND
YLE RADIO FINLAND, Pori — S • Americas • 500 kW
HUNGARY
†RADIO BUDAPEST, Jászberény
- S • S America • 250 kW
- S • Su • S America • 250 kW

KUWAIT
RADIO KUWAIT, Kabd — Europe & E North Am • 500 kW
RUSSIA
†RADIO ROSSII, Samara — W • W Asia & C Asia • DS • 100 kW
SLOVAKIA
†R SLOVAKIA INTL, Rimavská Sobota
- S America • 250 kW
- W • E Europe & W Asia • 250 kW
- E Europe & W Asia • 250 kW

USA
†RFE-RL, Via Briech, Morocco — S • E Europe & W Asia • 250 kW
(con'd) †RFE-RL, Via Kavála, Greece — S • W Asia • 250 kW

| | 0 | 1 | 2 | 3 | 4 | 5 | 6 | 7 | 8 | 9 | 10 | 11 | 12 | 13 | 14 | 15 | 16 | 17 | 18 | 19 | 20 | 21 | 22 | 23 | 24 |

SEASONAL **S** OR **W**   1-HR TIMESHIFT MIDYEAR ⇐ OR ⇒   JAMMING / OR /\   EARLIEST HEARD ◁   LATEST HEARD ▷   NEW FOR 2004 †

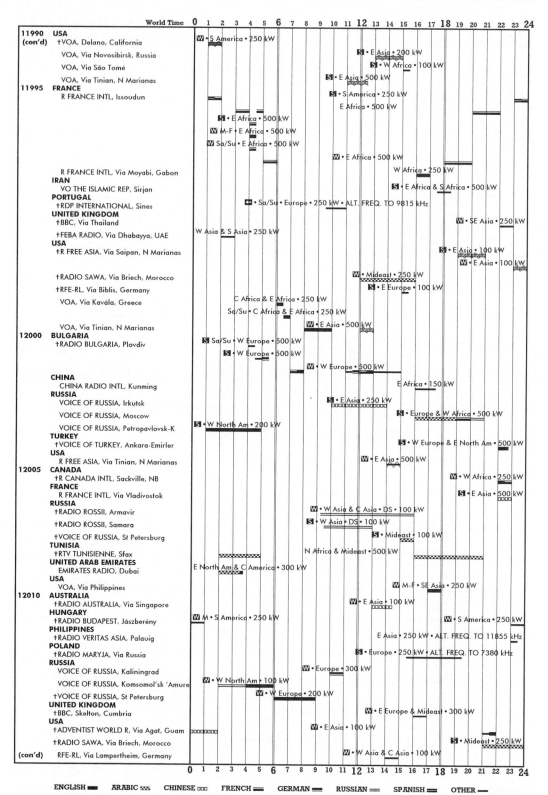

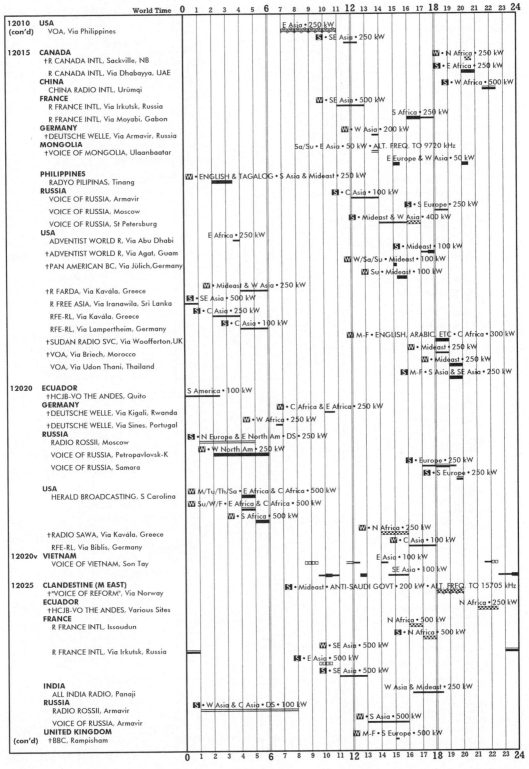

12010 (con'd)	**USA**	
	VOA, Via Philippines	E Asia • 250 kW
		S • SE Asia • 250 kW
12015	**CANADA**	
	†R CANADA INTL, Sackville, NB	W • N Africa • 250 kW
		S • E Africa • 250 kW
	R CANADA INTL, Via Dhabayya, UAE	
	CHINA	
	CHINA RADIO INTL, Urümqi	S • W Africa • 500 kW
	FRANCE	
	R FRANCE INTL, Via Irkutsk, Russia	W • SE Asia • 500 kW
	R FRANCE INTL, Via Moyabi, Gabon	S Africa • 250 kW
	GERMANY	
	†DEUTSCHE WELLE, Via Armavir, Russia	W • W Asia • 200 kW
	MONGOLIA	
	†VOICE OF MONGOLIA, Ulaanbaatar	Sa/Su • E Asia • 50 kW • ALT. FREQ. TO 9720 kHz
		E Europe & W Asia • 50 kW
	PHILIPPINES	
	RADYO PILIPINAS, Tinang	W • ENGLISH & TAGALOG • S Asia & Mideast • 250 kW
	RUSSIA	
	VOICE OF RUSSIA, Armavir	S • C Asia • 100 kW
	VOICE OF RUSSIA, Moscow	S • S Europe • 250 kW
	VOICE OF RUSSIA, St Petersburg	S • Mideast & W Asia • 400 kW
	USA	
	ADVENTIST WORLD R, Via Abu Dhabi	E Africa • 250 kW
	†ADVENTIST WORLD R, Via Agat, Guam	S • Mideast • 100 kW
	†PAN AMERICAN BC, Via Jülich, Germany	W/Sa/Su • Mideast • 100 kW
		W Su • Mideast • 100 kW
	†R FARDA, Via Kavála, Greece	W • Mideast & W Asia • 250 kW
	R FREE ASIA, Via Iranawila, Sri Lanka	S • SE Asia • 500 kW
	RFE-RL, Via Kavála, Greece	S • C Asia • 250 kW
	RFE-RL, Via Lampertheim, Germany	S • C Asia • 100 kW
	†SUDAN RADIO SVC, Via Woofferton, UK	W M-F • ENGLISH, ARABIC, ETC • C Africa • 300 kW
	†VOA, Via Briech, Morocco	W • Mideast • 250 kW
	VOA, Via Udon Thani, Thailand	W • Mideast • 250 kW
		S M-F • S Asia & SE Asia • 250 kW
12020	**ECUADOR**	
	†HCJB-VO THE ANDES, Quito	S America • 100 kW
	GERMANY	
	†DEUTSCHE WELLE, Via Kigali, Rwanda	W • C Africa & E Africa • 250 kW
	†DEUTSCHE WELLE, Via Sines, Portugal	W • W Africa • 250 kW
	RUSSIA	
	RADIO ROSSII, Moscow	S • N Europe & E North Am • DS • 250 kW
	VOICE OF RUSSIA, Petropavlovsk-K	W • W North Am • 250 kW
	VOICE OF RUSSIA, Samara	S • Europe • 250 kW
		S • S Europe • 250 kW
	USA	
	HERALD BROADCASTING, S Carolina	W M/Tu/Th/Sa • E Africa & C Africa • 500 kW
		W Su/W/F • E Africa & C Africa • 500 kW
		W • S Africa • 500 kW
	†RADIO SAWA, Via Kavála, Greece	W • N Africa • 250 kW
	RFE-RL, Via Biblis, Germany	W • C Africa • 100 kW
12020v	**VIETNAM**	
	VOICE OF VIETNAM, Son Tay	E Asia • 100 kW
		SE Asia • 100 kW
12025	**CLANDESTINE (M EAST)**	
	†"VOICE OF REFORM", Via Norway	S • Mideast • ANTI-SAUDI GOVT • 200 kW • ALT. FREQ. TO 15705 kHz
	ECUADOR	
	†HCJB-VO THE ANDES, Various Sites	N Africa • 250 kW
	FRANCE	
	R FRANCE INTL, Issoudun	N Africa • 500 kW
		S • N Africa • 500 kW
	R FRANCE INTL, Via Irkutsk, Russia	W • SE Asia • 500 kW
		S • E Asia • 500 kW
		S • SE Asia • 500 kW
	INDIA	
	ALL INDIA RADIO, Panaji	W Asia & Mideast • 250 kW
	RUSSIA	
	RADIO ROSSII, Armavir	S • W Asia & C Asia • DS • 100 kW
	VOICE OF RUSSIA, Armavir	W • S Asia • 500 kW
	UNITED KINGDOM	
(con'd)	†BBC, Rampisham	W M-F • S Europe • 500 kW

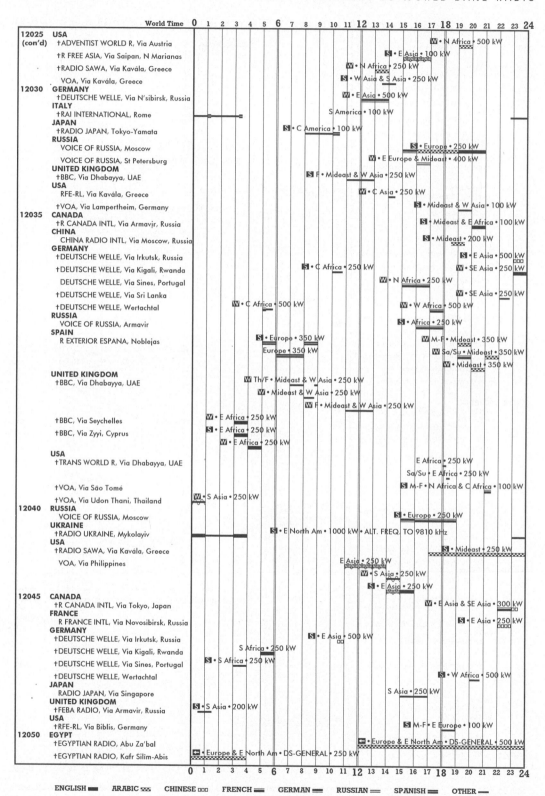

	World Time	0 1 2 3 4 5 6 7 8 9 10 11 12 13 14 15 16 17 18 19 20 21 22 23 24
12025 (con'd)	**USA** †ADVENTIST WORLD R, Via Austria	W • N Africa • 500 kW
	†R FREE ASIA, Via Saipan, N Marianas	S • E Asia • 100 kW
	†RADIO SAWA, Via Kavála, Greece	W • N Africa • 250 kW
	VOA, Via Kavála, Greece	S • W Asia & S Asia • 250 kW
12030	**GERMANY** †DEUTSCHE WELLE, Via N'sibirsk, Russia	W • E Asia • 500 kW
	ITALY †RAI INTERNATIONAL, Rome	S America • 100 kW
	JAPAN †RADIO JAPAN, Tokyo-Yamata	S • C America • 100 kW
	RUSSIA VOICE OF RUSSIA, Moscow	S • Europe • 250 kW
	VOICE OF RUSSIA, St Petersburg	W • E Europe & Mideast • 400 kW
	UNITED KINGDOM †BBC, Via Dhabayya, UAE	F • Mideast & W Asia • 250 kW
	USA RFE-RL, Via Kavála, Greece	W • C Asia • 250 kW
	†VOA, Via Lampertheim, Germany	S • Mideast & W Asia • 100 kW
12035	**CANADA** †R CANADA INTL, Via Armavir, Russia	S • Mideast & E Africa • 100 kW
	CHINA CHINA RADIO INTL, Via Moscow, Russia	S • Mideast • 200 kW
	GERMANY †DEUTSCHE WELLE, Via Irkutsk, Russia	S • E Asia • 500 kW
	†DEUTSCHE WELLE, Via Kigali, Rwanda	S • C Africa • 250 kW / W • SE Asia • 250 kW
	DEUTSCHE WELLE, Via Sines, Portugal	W • N Africa • 250 kW
	†DEUTSCHE WELLE, Via Sri Lanka	W • SE Asia • 250 kW
	†DEUTSCHE WELLE, Wertachtal	W • C Africa • 500 kW / W • W Africa • 500 kW
	RUSSIA VOICE OF RUSSIA, Armavir	S • Africa • 250 kW
	SPAIN R EXTERIOR ESPANA, Noblejas	S • Europe • 350 kW / W M-F • Mideast • 350 kW
		Europe • 350 kW / W Sa/Su • Mideast • 350 kW
		W • Mideast • 350 kW
	UNITED KINGDOM †BBC, Via Dhabayya, UAE	W Th/F • Mideast & W Asia • 250 kW
		W • Mideast & W Asia • 250 kW
		W F • Mideast & W Asia • 250 kW
	†BBC, Via Seychelles	W • E Africa • 250 kW
	†BBC, Via Zyyi, Cyprus	S • E Africa • 250 kW
		W • E Africa • 250 kW
	USA †TRANS WORLD R, Via Dhabayya, UAE	E Africa • 250 kW
		Sa/Su • E Africa • 250 kW
	†VOA, Via São Tomé	S M-F • N Africa & C Africa • 100 kW
	†VOA, Via Udon Thani, Thailand	W • S Asia • 250 kW
12040	**RUSSIA** VOICE OF RUSSIA, Moscow	S • Europe • 250 kW
	UKRAINE †RADIO UKRAINE, Mykolayiv	S • E North Am • 1000 kW • ALT. FREQ. TO 9810 kHz
	USA †RADIO SAWA, Via Kavála, Greece	S • Mideast • 250 kW
	VOA, Via Philippines	E Asia • 250 kW
		W • S Asia • 250 kW
		S • E Asia • 250 kW
12045	**CANADA** †R CANADA INTL, Via Tokyo, Japan	W • E Asia & SE Asia • 300 kW
	FRANCE R FRANCE INTL, Via Novosibirsk, Russia	S • E Asia • 250 kW
	GERMANY †DEUTSCHE WELLE, Via Irkutsk, Russia	S • E Asia • 500 kW
	†DEUTSCHE WELLE, Via Kigali, Rwanda	S Africa • 250 kW
	†DEUTSCHE WELLE, Via Sines, Portugal	S • S Africa • 250 kW
	†DEUTSCHE WELLE, Wertachtal	S • W Africa • 500 kW
	JAPAN RADIO JAPAN, Via Singapore	S Asia • 250 kW
	UNITED KINGDOM †FEBA RADIO, Via Armavir, Russia	S • S Asia • 200 kW
	USA †RFE-RL, Via Biblis, Germany	S M-F • E Europe • 100 kW
12050	**EGYPT** †EGYPTIAN RADIO, Abu Za'bal	• Europe & E North Am • DS-GENERAL • 500 kW
	†EGYPTIAN RADIO, Kafr Silim-Abis	• Europe & E North Am • DS-GENERAL • 250 kW

ENGLISH ▬ ARABIC ⌇⌇⌇ CHINESE ▢▢▢ FRENCH ═ GERMAN ▬▬ RUSSIAN ══ SPANISH ══ OTHER ▬

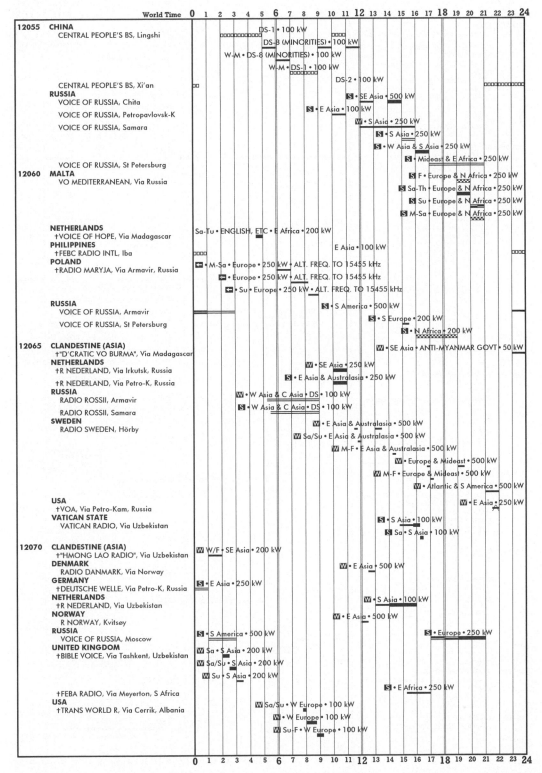

World Time | 0 1 2 3 4 5 6 7 8 9 10 11 12 13 14 15 16 17 18 19 20 21 22 23 24

12055 CHINA
CENTRAL PEOPLE'S BS, Lingshi
DS-1 • 100 kW
DS-8 (MINORITIES) • 100 kW
W-M • DS-8 (MINORITIES) • 100 kW
W-M • DS-1 • 100 kW
CENTRAL PEOPLE'S BS, Xi'an
DS-2 • 100 kW
RUSSIA
VOICE OF RUSSIA, Chita — S • SE Asia • 500 kW
VOICE OF RUSSIA, Petropavlovsk-K — S • E Asia • 100 kW
VOICE OF RUSSIA, Samara — W • S Asia • 250 kW
S • S Asia • 250 kW
S • W Asia & S Asia • 250 kW
VOICE OF RUSSIA, St Petersburg — S • Mideast & E Africa • 250 kW
12060 MALTA
VO MEDITERRANEAN, Via Russia
S • F • Europe & N Africa • 250 kW
Sa-Th • Europe & N Africa • 250 kW
S • Su • Europe & N Africa • 250 kW
S • M-Sa • Europe & N Africa • 250 kW

NETHERLANDS
†VOICE OF HOPE, Via Madagascar — Sa-Tu • ENGLISH, ETC • E Africa • 200 kW
PHILIPPINES
†FEBC RADIO INTL, Iba — E Asia • 100 kW
POLAND
†RADIO MARYJA, Via Armavir, Russia — M-Sa • Europe • 250 kW • ALT. FREQ. TO 15455 kHz
• Europe • 250 kW • ALT. FREQ. TO 15455 kHz
• Su • Europe • 250 kW • ALT. FREQ. TO 15455 kHz

RUSSIA
VOICE OF RUSSIA, Armavir — S • S America • 500 kW
VOICE OF RUSSIA, St Petersburg — S • S Europe • 200 kW
S • N Africa • 200 kW

12065 CLANDESTINE (ASIA)
†"D'CRATIC VO BURMA", Via Madagascar — W • SE Asia • ANTI-MYANMAR GOVT • 50 kW
NETHERLANDS
†R NEDERLAND, Via Irkutsk, Russia — W • SE Asia • 250 kW
†R NEDERLAND, Via Petro-K, Russia — S • E Asia & Australasia • 250 kW
RUSSIA
RADIO ROSSII, Armavir — W • W Asia & C Asia • DS • 100 kW
RADIO ROSSII, Samara — S • W Asia & C Asia • DS • 100 kW
SWEDEN
RADIO SWEDEN, Hörby — W • E Asia & Australasia • 500 kW
W Sa/Su • E Asia & Australasia • 500 kW
W M-F • E Asia & Australasia • 500 kW
W • Europe & Mideast • 500 kW
W M-F • Europe & Mideast • 500 kW
W • Atlantic & S America • 500 kW

USA
†VOA, Via Petro-Kam, Russia — W • E Asia • 250 kW
VATICAN STATE
VATICAN RADIO, Via Uzbekistan — S • S Asia • 100 kW
S Sa • S Asia • 100 kW

12070 CLANDESTINE (ASIA)
†"HMONG LAO RADIO", Via Uzbekistan — W W/F • SE Asia • 200 kW
DENMARK
RADIO DANMARK, Via Norway — W • E Asia • 500 kW
GERMANY
†DEUTSCHE WELLE, Via Petro-K, Russia — S • E Asia • 250 kW
NETHERLANDS
†R NEDERLAND, Via Uzbekistan — W • S Asia • 100 kW
NORWAY
R NORWAY, Kvitsøy — W • E Asia • 500 kW
RUSSIA
VOICE OF RUSSIA, Moscow — S • S America • 500 kW
S • Europe • 250 kW
UNITED KINGDOM
†BIBLE VOICE, Via Tashkent, Uzbekistan — W Sa • S Asia • 200 kW
W Sa/Su • S Asia • 200 kW
W Su • S Asia • 200 kW

†FEBA RADIO, Via Meyerton, S Africa — S • E Africa • 250 kW
USA
†TRANS WORLD R, Via Cerrik, Albania — W Sa/Su • W Europe • 100 kW
W • W Europe • 100 kW
W Su-F • W Europe • 100 kW

| 0 1 2 3 4 5 6 7 8 9 10 11 12 13 14 15 16 17 18 19 20 21 22 23 24

SEASONAL S OR W   1-HR TIMESHIFT MIDYEAR ⬅ OR ➡   JAMMING / OR ∧   EARLIEST HEARD ◁   LATEST HEARD ▷   NEW FOR 2004 †

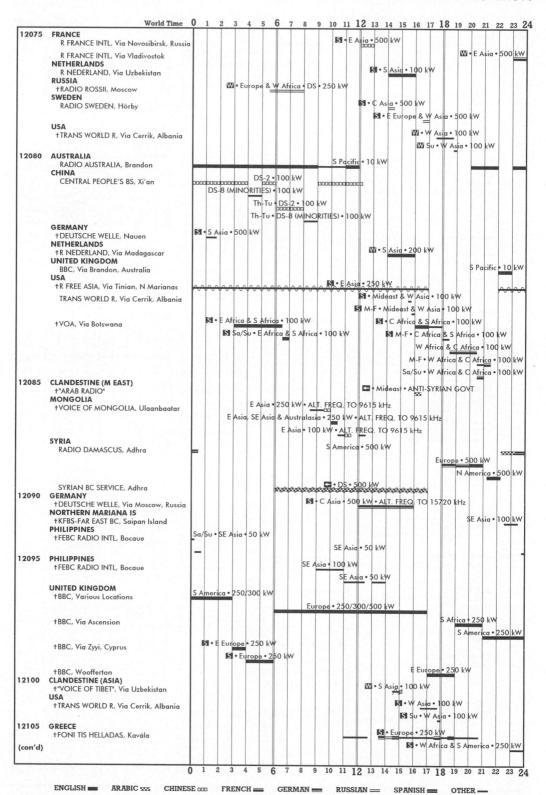

	World Time	0 1 2 3 4 5 6 7 8 9 10 11 12 13 14 15 16 17 18 19 20 21 22 23 24
12075	**FRANCE**	
	R FRANCE INTL, Via Novosibirsk, Russia	S • E Asia • 500 kW
	R FRANCE INTL, Via Vladivostok	W • E Asia • 500 kW
	NETHERLANDS	
	R NEDERLAND, Via Uzbekistan	S • S Asia • 100 kW
	RUSSIA	
	†RADIO ROSSII, Moscow	W • Europe & W Africa • DS • 250 kW
	SWEDEN	
	RADIO SWEDEN, Hörby	S • C Asia • 500 kW
		S • E Europe & W Asia • 500 kW
	USA	
	†TRANS WORLD R, Via Cerrik, Albania	W • W Asia • 100 kW
		W Su • W Asia • 100 kW
12080	**AUSTRALIA**	
	RADIO AUSTRALIA, Brandon	S Pacific • 10 kW
	CHINA	
	CENTRAL PEOPLE'S BS, Xi'an	DS-2 • 100 kW
		DS-8 (MINORITIES) • 100 kW
		Th-Tu • DS-2 • 100 kW
		Th-Tu • DS-8 (MINORITIES) • 100 kW
	GERMANY	
	†DEUTSCHE WELLE, Nauen	S • S Asia • 500 kW
	NETHERLANDS	
	†R NEDERLAND, Via Madagascar	W • S Asia • 200 kW
	UNITED KINGDOM	
	BBC, Via Brandon, Australia	S Pacific • 10 kW
	USA	
	†R FREE ASIA, Via Tinian, N Marianas	S • E Asia • 250 kW
		S • Mideast & W Asia • 100 kW
	TRANS WORLD R, Via Cerrik, Albania	S M-F • Mideast & W Asia • 100 kW
		S • E Africa & S Africa • 100 kW
		S • C Africa & S Africa • 100 kW
	†VOA, Via Botswana	S Sa/Su • E Africa & S Africa • 100 kW
		S M-F • C Africa & S Africa • 100 kW
		W Africa & C Africa • 100 kW
		M-F • W Africa & C Africa • 100 kW
		Sa/Su • W Africa & C Africa • 100 kW
12085	**CLANDESTINE (M EAST)**	
	†"ARAB RADIO"	• Mideast • ANTI-SYRIAN GOVT
	MONGOLIA	
	†VOICE OF MONGOLIA, Ulaanbaatar	E Asia • 250 kW • ALT. FREQ. TO 9615 kHz
		E Asia, SE Asia & Australasia • 250 kW • ALT. FREQ. TO 9615 kHz
		E Asia • 100 kW • ALT. FREQ. TO 9615 kHz
	SYRIA	
	RADIO DAMASCUS, Adhra	S America • 500 kW
		Europe • 500 kW
		N America • 500 kW
	SYRIAN BC SERVICE, Adhra	• DS • 500 kW
12090	**GERMANY**	
	†DEUTSCHE WELLE, Via Moscow, Russia	S • C Asia • 500 kW • ALT. FREQ. TO 15720 kHz
	NORTHERN MARIANA IS	
	†KFBS-FAR EAST BC, Saipan Island	SE Asia • 100 kW
	PHILIPPINES	
	†FEBC RADIO INTL, Bocaue	Sa/Su • SE Asia • 50 kW
		SE Asia • 50 kW
12095	**PHILIPPINES**	
	†FEBC RADIO INTL, Bocaue	SE Asia • 100 kW
		SE Asia • 50 kW
	UNITED KINGDOM	
	†BBC, Various Locations	S America • 250/300 kW
		Europe • 250/300/500 kW
	†BBC, Via Ascension	S Africa • 250 kW
		S America • 250 kW
	†BBC, Via Zyyi, Cyprus	S • E Europe • 250 kW
		S • Europe • 250 kW
	†BBC, Woofferton	E Europe • 250 kW
12100	**CLANDESTINE (ASIA)**	
	†"VOICE OF TIBET", Via Uzbekistan	W • S Asia • 100 kW
	USA	
	†TRANS WORLD R, Via Cerrik, Albania	S • W Asia • 100 kW
		S Su • W Asia • 100 kW
12105	**GREECE**	
	†FONI TIS HELLADAS, Kavála	S • Europe • 250 kW
(con'd)		S • W Africa & S America • 250 kW

ENGLISH ▬ ARABIC ⁓⁓⁓ CHINESE ▫▫▫ FRENCH ═ GERMAN ▬▬ RUSSIAN ═ SPANISH ▬ OTHER ▬

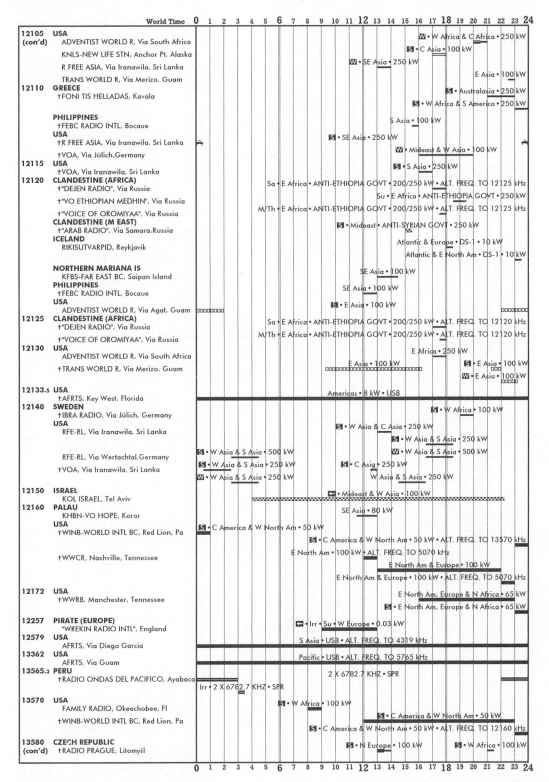

World Time

Freq	Country / Station	Schedule
12105 (con'd)	**USA** ADVENTIST WORLD R, Via South Africa	W • W Africa & C Africa • 250 kW
	KNLS-NEW LIFE STN, Anchor Pt, Alaska	S • C Asia • 100 kW
	R FREE ASIA, Via Iranawila, Sri Lanka	W • SE Asia • 250 kW
	TRANS WORLD R, Via Merizo, Guam	E Asia • 100 kW
12110	**GREECE** †FONI TIS HELLADAS, Kavála	S • Australasia • 250 kW / S • W Africa & S America • 250 kW
	PHILIPPINES †FEBC RADIO INTL, Bocaue	S Asia • 100 kW
	USA †R FREE ASIA, Via Iranawila, Sri Lanka	S • SE Asia • 250 kW
	†VOA, Via Jülich, Germany	W • Mideast & W Asia • 100 kW
12115	**USA** †VOA, Via Iranawila, Sri Lanka	S • S Asia • 250 kW
12120	**CLANDESTINE (AFRICA)** †"DEJEN RADIO", Via Russia	Sa • E Africa • ANTI-ETHIOPIA GOVT • 200/250 kW • ALT. FREQ. TO 12125 kHz
	†"VO ETHIOPIAN MEDHIN", Via Russia	Su • E Africa • ANTI-ETHIOPIA GOVT • 250 kW
	†"VOICE OF OROMIYAA", Via Russia	M/Th • E Africa • ANTI-ETHIOPIA GOVT • 200/250 kW • ALT. FREQ. TO 12125 kHz
	CLANDESTINE (M EAST) †"ARAB RADIO", Via Samara, Russia	S • Mideast • ANTI-SYRIAN GOVT • 250 kW
	ICELAND RIKISUTVARPID, Reykjavik	Atlantic & Europe • DS-1 • 10 kW / Atlantic & E North Am • DS-1 • 10 kW
	NORTHERN MARIANA IS KFBS-FAR EAST BC, Saipan Island	SE Asia • 100 kW
	PHILIPPINES †FEBC RADIO INTL, Bocaue	SE Asia • 100 kW
	USA ADVENTIST WORLD R, Via Agat, Guam	S • E Asia • 100 kW
12125	**CLANDESTINE (AFRICA)** †"DEJEN RADIO", Via Russia	Sa • E Africa • ANTI-ETHIOPIA GOVT • 200/250 kW • ALT. FREQ. TO 12120 kHz
	†"VOICE OF OROMIYAA", Via Russia	M/Th • E Africa • ANTI-ETHIOPIA GOVT • 200/250 kW • ALT. FREQ. TO 12120 kHz
12130	**USA** ADVENTIST WORLD R, Via South Africa	E Africa • 250 kW
	†TRANS WORLD R, Via Merizo, Guam	E Asia • 100 kW / S • E Asia • 100 kW / W • E Asia • 100 kW
12133.5	**USA** †AFRTS, Key West, Florida	Americas • B kW • USB
12140	**SWEDEN** †IBRA RADIO, Via Jülich, Germany	S • W Africa • 100 kW
	USA RFE-RL, Via Iranawila, Sri Lanka	S • W Asia & C Asia • 250 kW / S • W Asia & S Asia • 250 kW
	RFE-RL, Via Wertachtal, Germany	S • W Asia & S Asia • 500 kW / W • W Asia & S Asia • 500 kW
	†VOA, Via Iranawila, Sri Lanka	S • W Asia & S Asia • 250 kW / S • C Asia • 250 kW / W • W Asia & S Asia • 250 kW / W Asia & S Asia • 250 kW
12150	**ISRAEL** KOL ISRAEL, Tel Aviv	⬅ • Mideast & W Asia • 100 kW
12160	**PALAU** KHBN-VO HOPE, Koror	SE Asia • 80 kW
	USA †WINB-WORLD INTL BC, Red Lion, Pa	S • C America & W North Am • 50 kW / S • C America & W North Am • 50 kW • ALT. FREQ. TO 13570 kHz
	†WWCR, Nashville, Tennessee	E North Am • 100 kW • ALT. FREQ. TO 5070 kHz / E North Am & Europe • 100 kW / E North Am & Europe • 100 kW • ALT. FREQ. TO 5070 kHz
12172	**USA** †WWRB, Manchester, Tennessee	E North Am, Europe & N Africa • 65 kW / S • E North Am, Europe & N Africa • 65 kW
12257	**PIRATE (EUROPE)** "WREKIN RADIO INTL", England	⬅ • Irr • Su • W Europe • 0.03 kW
12579	**USA** AFRTS, Via Diego Garcia	S Asia • USB • ALT. FREQ. TO 4319 kHz
13362	**USA** AFRTS, Via Guam	Pacific • USB • ALT. FREQ. TO 5765 kHz
13565.3	**PERU** †RADIO ONDAS DEL PACIFICO, Ayabaca	2 X 6782.7 KHZ • SPR / Irr • 2 X 6782.7 KHZ • SPR
13570	**USA** FAMILY RADIO, Okeechobee, Fl	S • W Africa • 100 kW
	†WINB-WORLD INTL BC, Red Lion, Pa	S • C America & W North Am • 50 kW / S • C America & W North Am • 50 kW • ALT. FREQ. TO 12160 kHz
13580 (con'd)	**CZECH REPUBLIC** †RADIO PRAGUE, Litomyšl	S • N Europe • 100 kW / S • W Africa • 100 kW

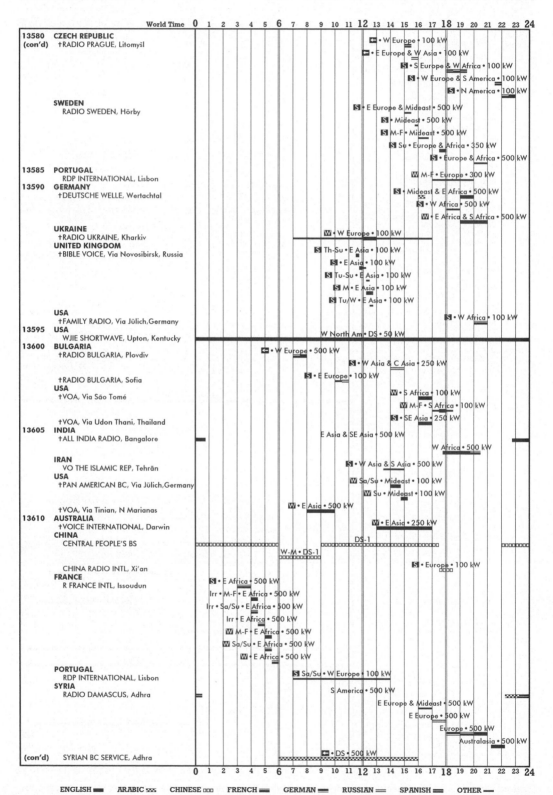

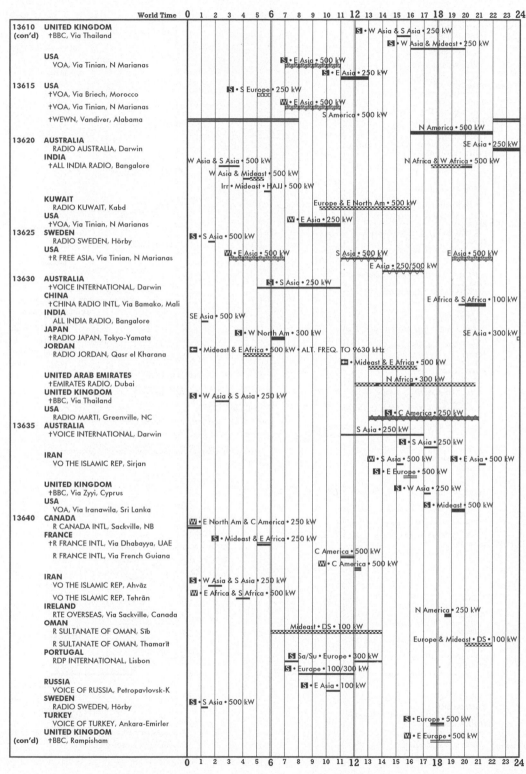

World Time

13610	**UNITED KINGDOM**	
(con'd)	†BBC, Via Thailand	**S** • W Asia & S Asia • 250 kW
		S • W Asia & Mideast • 250 kW
	USA	
	VOA, Via Tinian, N Marianas	**S** • E Asia • 500 kW
		S • E Asia • 250 kW
13615	**USA**	
	†VOA, Via Briech, Morocco	**S** • S Europe • 250 kW
	†VOA, Via Tinian, N Marianas	**W** • E Asia • 500 kW
	†WEWN, Vandiver, Alabama	S America • 500 kW
		N America • 500 kW
13620	**AUSTRALIA**	
	RADIO AUSTRALIA, Darwin	SE Asia • 250 kW
	INDIA	
	†ALL INDIA RADIO, Bangalore	W Asia & S Asia • 500 kW N Africa & W Africa • 500 kW
		W Asia & Mideast • 500 kW
		Irr • Mideast • HAJJ • 500 kW
	KUWAIT	
	RADIO KUWAIT, Kabd	Europe & E North Am • 500 kW
	USA	
	†VOA, Via Tinian, N Marianas	**W** • E Asia • 250 kW
13625	**SWEDEN**	
	RADIO SWEDEN, Hörby	**S** • S Asia • 500 kW
	USA	
	†R FREE ASIA, Via Tinian, N Marianas	**W** • E Asia • 500 kW S Asia • 500 kW E Asia • 500 kW
		E Asia • 250/500 kW
13630	**AUSTRALIA**	
	†VOICE INTERNATIONAL, Darwin	**S** • S Asia • 250 kW
	CHINA	
	†CHINA RADIO INTL, Via Bamako, Mali	E Africa & S Africa • 100 kW
	INDIA	
	ALL INDIA RADIO, Bangalore	SE Asia • 500 kW
	JAPAN	
	†RADIO JAPAN, Tokyo-Yamata	**S** • W North Am • 300 kW SE Asia • 300 kW
	JORDAN	
	RADIO JORDAN, Qasr el Kharana	**↔** • Mideast & E Africa • 500 kW • ALT. FREQ. TO 9630 kHz
		↔ • Mideast & E Africa • 500 kW
	UNITED ARAB EMIRATES	
	†EMIRATES RADIO, Dubai	N Africa • 300 kW
	UNITED KINGDOM	
	†BBC, Via Thailand	**S** • W Asia & S Asia • 250 kW
	USA	
	RADIO MARTI, Greenville, NC	**S** • C America • 250 kW
13635	**AUSTRALIA**	
	†VOICE INTERNATIONAL, Darwin	S Asia • 250 kW
		S • S Asia • 250 kW
	IRAN	
	VO THE ISLAMIC REP, Sirjan	**W** • S Asia • 500 kW **S** • E Asia • 500 kW
		S • E Europe • 500 kW
	UNITED KINGDOM	
	†BBC, Via Zyyi, Cyprus	**S** • W Asia • 250 kW
	USA	
	VOA, Via Iranawila, Sri Lanka	**S** • Mideast • 500 kW
13640	**CANADA**	
	R CANADA INTL, Sackville, NB	**W** • E North Am & C America • 250 kW
	FRANCE	
	†R FRANCE INTL, Via Dhabayya, UAE	**S** • Mideast & E Africa • 250 kW
	R FRANCE INTL, Via French Guiana	C America • 500 kW
		W • C America • 500 kW
	IRAN	
	VO THE ISLAMIC REP, Ahvāz	**S** • W Asia & S Asia • 250 kW
	VO THE ISLAMIC REP, Tehrān	**W** • E Africa & S Africa • 500 kW
	IRELAND	
	RTE OVERSEAS, Via Sackville, Canada	N America • 250 kW
	OMAN	
	R SULTANATE OF OMAN, Sīb	Mideast • DS • 100 kW
	R SULTANATE OF OMAN, Thamarīt	Europe & Mideast • DS • 100 kW
	PORTUGAL	
	RDP INTERNATIONAL, Lisbon	**S** • Sa/Su • Europe • 300 kW
		S • Europe • 100/300 kW
	RUSSIA	
	VOICE OF RUSSIA, Petropavlovsk-K	**S** • E Asia • 100 kW
	SWEDEN	
	RADIO SWEDEN, Hörby	**S** • S Asia • 500 kW
	TURKEY	
	VOICE OF TURKEY, Ankara-Emirler	**S** • Europe • 500 kW
	UNITED KINGDOM	
(con'd)	†BBC, Rampisham	**W** • E Europe • 500 kW

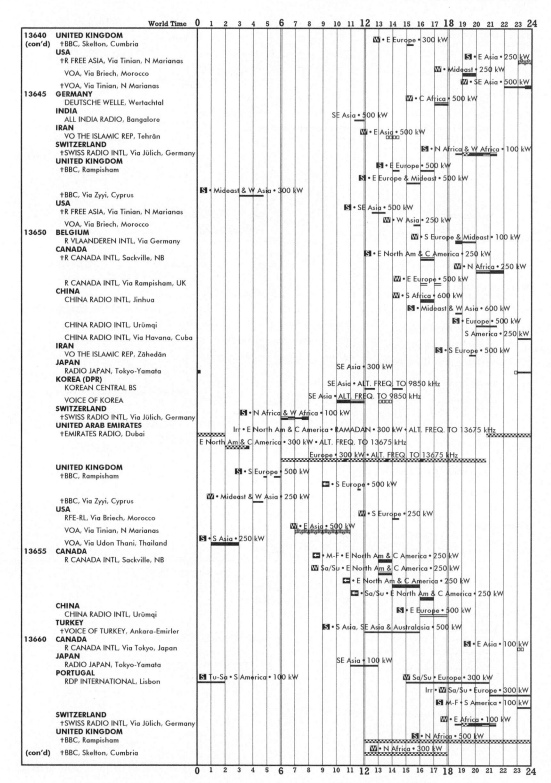

| | | World Time | 0 | 1 | 2 | 3 | 4 | 5 | 6 | 7 | 8 | 9 | 10 | 11 | 12 | 13 | 14 | 15 | 16 | 17 | 18 | 19 | 20 | 21 | 22 | 23 | 24 |

13640
(con'd)   UNITED KINGDOM
  †BBC, Skelton, Cumbria — **W** • E Europe • 300 kW
USA
  †R FREE ASIA, Via Tinian, N Marianas — **S** • E Asia • 250 kW
  VOA, Via Briech, Morocco — **W** • Mideast • 250 kW
  †VOA, Via Tinian, N Marianas — **W** • SE Asia • 500 kW
13645   GERMANY
  DEUTSCHE WELLE, Wertachtal — **W** • C Africa • 500 kW
INDIA
  ALL INDIA RADIO, Bangalore — SE Asia • 500 kW
IRAN
  VO THE ISLAMIC REP, Tehrān — **W** • E Asia • 500 kW
SWITZERLAND
  †SWISS RADIO INTL, Via Jülich, Germany — **S** • N Africa & W Africa • 100 kW
UNITED KINGDOM
  †BBC, Rampisham — **S** • E Europe • 500 kW
                    — **S** • E Europe & Mideast • 500 kW

  †BBC, Via Zyyi, Cyprus — **S** • Mideast & W Asia • 300 kW
USA
  †R FREE ASIA, Via Tinian, N Marianas — **S** • SE Asia • 500 kW
  VOA, Via Briech, Morocco — **W** • W Asia • 250 kW
13650   BELGIUM
  R VLAANDEREN INTL, Via Germany — **W** • S Europe & Mideast • 100 kW
CANADA
  †R CANADA INTL, Sackville, NB — **S** • E North Am & C America • 250 kW
                    — **W** • N Africa • 250 kW
  R CANADA INTL, Via Rampisham, UK — **W** • E Europe • 500 kW
CHINA
  CHINA RADIO INTL, Jinhua — **W** • S Africa • 600 kW
                    — **S** • Mideast & W Asia • 600 kW
  CHINA RADIO INTL, Urümqi — **S** • Europe • 500 kW
  CHINA RADIO INTL, Via Havana, Cuba — S America • 250 kW
IRAN
  VO THE ISLAMIC REP, Zāhedān — **S** • S Europe • 500 kW
JAPAN
  RADIO JAPAN, Tokyo-Yamata — SE Asia • 300 kW
KOREA (DPR)
  KOREAN CENTRAL BS — SE Asia • ALT. FREQ. TO 9850 kHz
  VOICE OF KOREA — SE Asia • ALT. FREQ. TO 9850 kHz
SWITZERLAND
  †SWISS RADIO INTL, Via Jülich, Germany — **S** • N Africa & W Africa • 100 kW
UNITED ARAB EMIRATES
  †EMIRATES RADIO, Dubai — Irr • E North Am & C America • RAMADAN • 300 kW • ALT. FREQ. TO 13675 kHz
                    — E North Am & C America • 300 kW • ALT. FREQ. TO 13675 kHz
                    — Europe • 300 kW • ALT. FREQ. TO 13675 kHz
UNITED KINGDOM
  †BBC, Rampisham — **S** • S Europe • 500 kW
                    — • S Europe • 500 kW
  †BBC, Via Zyyi, Cyprus — **W** • Mideast & W Asia • 250 kW
USA
  RFE-RL, Via Briech, Morocco — **W** • S Europe • 250 kW
  VOA, Via Tinian, N Marianas — **W** • E Asia • 500 kW
  VOA, Via Udon Thani, Thailand — **S** • S Asia • 250 kW
13655   CANADA
  R CANADA INTL, Sackville, NB — • M-F • E North Am & C America • 250 kW
                    — **W** • Sa/Su • E North Am & C America • 250 kW
                    — • E North Am & C America • 250 kW
                    — • Sa/Su • E North Am & C America • 250 kW
CHINA
  CHINA RADIO INTL, Urümqi — **S** • E Europe • 500 kW
TURKEY
  †VOICE OF TURKEY, Ankara-Emirler — **S** • S Asia, SE Asia & Australasia • 500 kW
13660   CANADA
  R CANADA INTL, Via Tokyo, Japan — **S** • E Asia • 100 kW
JAPAN
  RADIO JAPAN, Tokyo-Yamata — SE Asia • 100 kW
PORTUGAL
  RDP INTERNATIONAL, Lisbon — **S** Tu-Sa • S America • 100 kW
                    — **W** Sa/Su • Europe • 300 kW
                    — Irr • **W** Sa/Su • Europe • 300 kW
                    — **S** M-F • S America • 100 kW
SWITZERLAND
  †SWISS RADIO INTL, Via Jülich, Germany — **W** • E Africa • 100 kW
UNITED KINGDOM
  †BBC, Rampisham — **S** • N Africa • 500 kW
(con'd)   †BBC, Skelton, Cumbria — **W** • N Africa • 300 kW

| | World Time | 0 | 1 | 2 | 3 | 4 | 5 | 6 | 7 | 8 | 9 | 10 | 11 | 12 | 13 | 14 | 15 | 16 | 17 | 18 | 19 | 20 | 21 | 22 | 23 | 24 |

ENGLISH ▬ ARABIC ▨ CHINESE ▫▫▫ FRENCH ▦ GERMAN ▬ RUSSIAN ═ SPANISH ▬ OTHER ▬

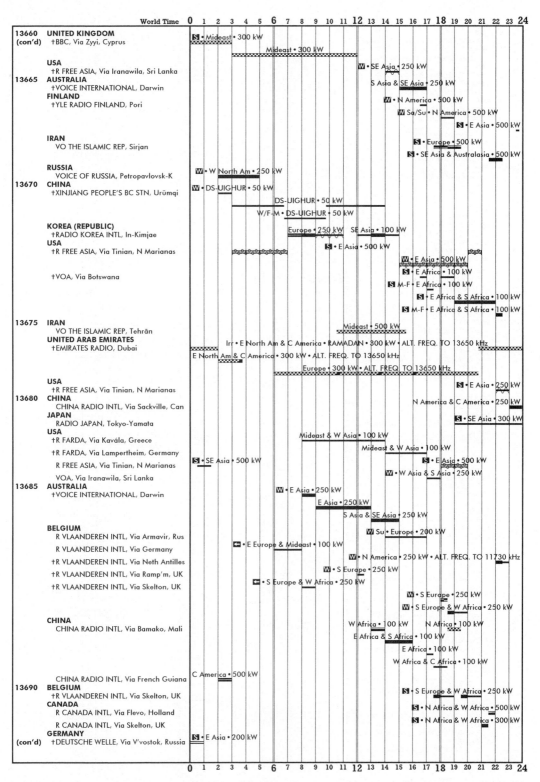

	World Time	0 1 2 3 4 5 6 7 8 9 10 11 12 13 14 15 16 17 18 19 20 21 22 23 24

13660 **UNITED KINGDOM**
(con'd)   †BBC, Via Zyyi, Cyprus — S • Mideast • 300 kW
Mideast • 300 kW

USA
     †R FREE ASIA, Via Iranawila, Sri Lanka — W • SE Asia • 250 kW
13665 **AUSTRALIA**
     †VOICE INTERNATIONAL, Darwin — S Asia & SE Asia • 250 kW
FINLAND
     †YLE RADIO FINLAND, Pori — W • N America • 500 kW
W Sa/Su • N America • 500 kW
S • E Asia • 500 kW

IRAN
     VO THE ISLAMIC REP, Sirjan — S • Europe • 500 kW
S • SE Asia & Australasia • 500 kW

RUSSIA
     VOICE OF RUSSIA, Petropavlovsk-K — W • W North Am • 250 kW
13670 **CHINA**
     †XINJIANG PEOPLE'S BC STN, Urümqi — W • DS-UIGHUR • 50 kW
DS-UIGHUR • 50 kW
W/F-M • DS-UIGHUR • 50 kW

KOREA (REPUBLIC)
     †RADIO KOREA INTL, In-Kimjae — Europe • 250 kW   SE Asia • 100 kW
USA
     †R FREE ASIA, Via Tinian, N Marianas — S • E Asia • 500 kW
W • E Asia • 500 kW

     †VOA, Via Botswana — S • E Africa • 100 kW
S M-F • E Africa • 100 kW
S • E Africa & S Africa • 100 kW
S M-F • E Africa & S Africa • 100 kW

13675 **IRAN**
     VO THE ISLAMIC REP, Tehrān — Mideast • 500 kW
UNITED ARAB EMIRATES
     †EMIRATES RADIO, Dubai — Irr • E North Am & C America • RAMADAN • 300 kW • ALT. FREQ. TO 13650 kHz
E North Am & C America • 300 kW • ALT. FREQ. TO 13650 kHz
Europe • 300 kW • ALT. FREQ. TO 13650 kHz

USA
     †R FREE ASIA, Via Tinian, N Marianas — S • E Asia • 250 kW
13680 **CHINA**
     CHINA RADIO INTL, Via Sackville, Can — N America & C America • 250 kW
JAPAN
     RADIO JAPAN, Tokyo-Yamata — S • SE Asia • 300 kW
USA
     †R FARDA, Via Kavála, Greece — Mideast & W Asia • 100 kW
     †R FARDA, Via Lampertheim, Germany — Mideast & W Asia • 100 kW
     R FREE ASIA, Via Tinian, N Marianas — S • SE Asia • 500 kW   S • E Asia • 500 kW
     VOA, Via Iranawila, Sri Lanka — W • W Asia & S Asia • 250 kW
13685 **AUSTRALIA**
     †VOICE INTERNATIONAL, Darwin — W • E Asia • 250 kW
E Asia • 250 kW
S Asia & SE Asia • 250 kW

BELGIUM
     R VLAANDEREN INTL, Via Armavir, Rus — W Su • Europe • 200 kW
     R VLAANDEREN INTL, Via Germany — ⇆ • E Europe & Mideast • 100 kW
     †R VLAANDEREN INTL, Via Neth Antilles — W • N America • 250 kW • ALT. FREQ. TO 11730 kHz
     †R VLAANDEREN INTL, Via Ramp'm, UK — W • S Europe • 250 kW
     †R VLAANDEREN INTL, Via Skelton, UK — ⇆ • S Europe & W Africa • 250 kW
W • S Europe • 250 kW
W • S Europe & W Africa • 250 kW

CHINA
     CHINA RADIO INTL, Via Bamako, Mali — W Africa • 100 kW   N Africa • 100 kW
E Africa & S Africa • 100 kW
E Africa • 100 kW
W Africa & C Africa • 100 kW

     CHINA RADIO INTL, Via French Guiana — C America • 500 kW
13690 **BELGIUM**
     †R VLAANDEREN INTL, Via Skelton, UK — S • S Europe & W Africa • 250 kW
CANADA
     R CANADA INTL, Via Flevo, Holland — S • N Africa & W Africa • 500 kW
     R CANADA INTL, Via Skelton, UK — S • N Africa & W Africa • 300 kW
GERMANY
(con'd)   †DEUTSCHE WELLE, Via V'vostok, Russia — S • E Asia • 200 kW

	0 1 2 3 4 5 6 7 8 9 10 11 12 13 14 15 16 17 18 19 20 21 22 23 24

SEASONAL S OR W   1-HR TIMESHIFT MIDYEAR ⇆ OR ⇉   JAMMING / OR ∧   EARLIEST HEARD ◁   LATEST HEARD ▷   NEW FOR 2004 †

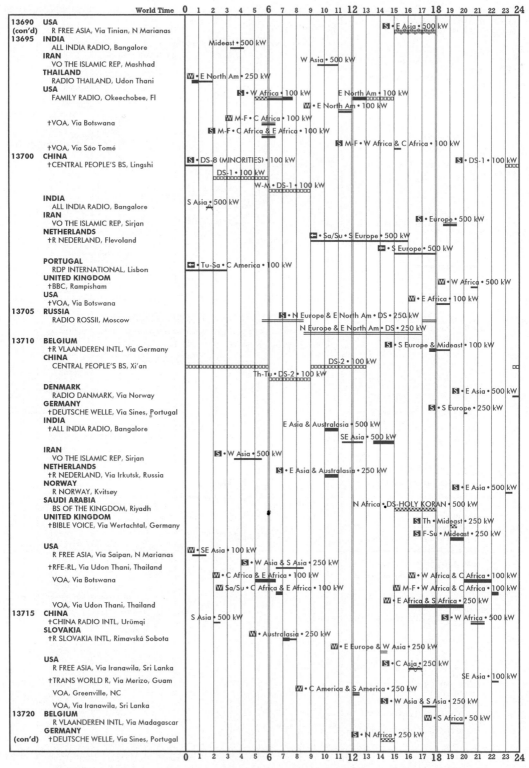

		World Time	0 1 2 3 4 5 6 7 8 9 10 11 12 13 14 15 16 17 18 19 20 21 22 23 24

13690 **USA**
(con'd)　R FREE ASIA, Via Tinian, N Marianas — S • E Asia • 500 kW

13695 **INDIA**
ALL INDIA RADIO, Bangalore — Mideast • 500 kW

IRAN
VO THE ISLAMIC REP, Mashhad — W Asia • 500 kW

THAILAND
RADIO THAILAND, Udon Thani — W • E North Am • 250 kW

USA
FAMILY RADIO, Okeechobee, Fl — S • W Africa • 100 kW　E North Am • 100 kW
W • E North Am • 100 kW

†VOA, Via Botswana — W M-F • C Africa • 100 kW
S M-F • C Africa & E Africa • 100 kW

†VOA, Via São Tomé — S M-F • W Africa & C Africa • 100 kW

13700 **CHINA**
†CENTRAL PEOPLE'S BS, Lingshi — S • DS-8 (MINORITIES) • 100 kW　S • DS-1 • 100 kW
DS-1 • 100 kW
W-M • DS-1 • 100 kW

INDIA
ALL INDIA RADIO, Bangalore — S Asia • 500 kW

IRAN
VO THE ISLAMIC REP, Sirjan — S • Europe • 500 kW

NETHERLANDS
†R NEDERLAND, Flevoland — • Sa/Su • S Europe • 500 kW
• S Europe • 500 kW

PORTUGAL
RDP INTERNATIONAL, Lisbon — • Tu-Sa • C America • 100 kW

UNITED KINGDOM
†BBC, Rampisham — W • W Africa • 500 kW

USA
†VOA, Via Botswana — W • E Africa • 100 kW

13705 **RUSSIA**
RADIO ROSSII, Moscow — S • N Europe & E North Am • DS • 250 kW
N Europe & E North Am • DS • 250 kW

13710 **BELGIUM**
†R VLAANDEREN INTL, Via Germany — S • S Europe & Mideast • 100 kW

CHINA
CENTRAL PEOPLE'S BS, Xi'an — DS-2 • 100 kW
Th-Tu • DS-2 • 100 kW

DENMARK
RADIO DANMARK, Via Norway — S • E Asia • 500 kW

GERMANY
†DEUTSCHE WELLE, Via Sines, Portugal — S • S Europe • 250 kW

INDIA
†ALL INDIA RADIO, Bangalore — E Asia & Australasia • 500 kW
SE Asia • 500 kW

IRAN
VO THE ISLAMIC REP, Sirjan — S • W Asia • 500 kW

NETHERLANDS
†R NEDERLAND, Via Irkutsk, Russia — S • E Asia & Australasia • 250 kW

NORWAY
R NORWAY, Kvitsøy — S • E Asia • 500 kW

SAUDI ARABIA
BS OF THE KINGDOM, Riyadh — N Africa • DS-HOLY KORAN • 500 kW

UNITED KINGDOM
†BIBLE VOICE, Via Wertachtal, Germany — S Th • Mideast • 250 kW
S F-Su • Mideast • 250 kW

USA
R FREE ASIA, Via Saipan, N Marianas — W • SE Asia • 100 kW

†RFE-RL, Via Udon Thani, Thailand — S • W Asia & S Asia • 250 kW

VOA, Via Botswana — W • C Africa & E Africa • 100 kW　W • W Africa & C Africa • 100 kW
W Sa/Su • C Africa & E Africa • 100 kW　W M-F • W Africa & C Africa • 100 kW

VOA, Via Udon Thani, Thailand — W • E Africa & S Africa • 250 kW

13715 **CHINA**
†CHINA RADIO INTL, Urümqi — S Asia • 500 kW　S • W Africa • 500 kW

SLOVAKIA
†R SLOVAKIA INTL, Rimavská Sobota — W • Australasia • 250 kW

USA
R FREE ASIA, Via Iranawila, Sri Lanka — W • E Europe & W Asia • 250 kW
S • C Asia • 250 kW

†TRANS WORLD R, Via Merizo, Guam — SE Asia • 100 kW

VOA, Greenville, NC — W • C America & S America • 250 kW

VOA, Via Iranawila, Sri Lanka — S • W Asia & S Asia • 250 kW

13720 **BELGIUM**
R VLAANDEREN INTL, Via Madagascar — W • S Africa • 50 kW

GERMANY
(con'd)　†DEUTSCHE WELLE, Via Sines, Portugal — S • N Africa • 250 kW

	0 1 2 3 4 5 6 7 8 9 10 11 12 13 14 15 16 17 18 19 20 21 22 23 24

ENGLISH ▬　ARABIC ▨▨▨　CHINESE ▢▢▢　FRENCH ▬▬　GERMAN ▬▬　RUSSIAN ══　SPANISH ▭▭　OTHER ▬

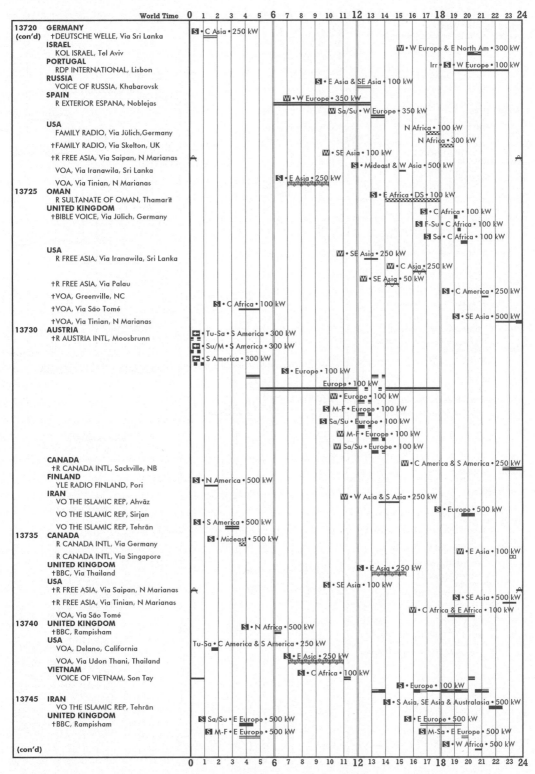

	World Time	0 1 2 3 4 5 6 7 8 9 10 11 12 13 14 15 16 17 18 19 20 21 22 23 24
13720 (con'd)	GERMANY †DEUTSCHE WELLE, Via Sri Lanka	S • C Asia • 250 kW
	ISRAEL KOL ISRAEL, Tel Aviv	W • W Europe & E North Am • 300 kW
	PORTUGAL RDP INTERNATIONAL, Lisbon	Irr • S • W Europe • 100 kW
	RUSSIA VOICE OF RUSSIA, Khabarovsk	S • E Asia & SE Asia • 100 kW
	SPAIN R EXTERIOR ESPANA, Noblejas	W • W Europe • 350 kW; W Sa/Su • W Europe • 350 kW
	USA FAMILY RADIO, Via Jülich, Germany	N Africa • 100 kW
	†FAMILY RADIO, Via Skelton, UK	N Africa • 300 kW
	†R FREE ASIA, Via Saipan, N Marianas	W • SE Asia • 100 kW
	VOA, Via Iranawila, Sri Lanka	S • Mideast & W Asia • 500 kW
	VOA, Via Tinian, N Marianas	S • E Asia • 250 kW
13725	OMAN R SULTANATE OF OMAN, Thamarīt	S • E Africa • DS • 100 kW
	UNITED KINGDOM †BIBLE VOICE, Via Jülich, Germany	S • C Africa • 100 kW; S F-Su • C Africa • 100 kW; S Sa • C Africa • 100 kW
	USA R FREE ASIA, Via Iranawila, Sri Lanka	W • SE Asia • 250 kW
		W • C Asia • 250 kW
	†R FREE ASIA, Via Palau	W • SE Asia • 50 kW
	†VOA, Greenville, NC	S • C America • 250 kW
	†VOA, Via São Tomé	S • C Africa • 100 kW
	†VOA, Via Tinian, N Marianas	S • SE Asia • 500 kW
13730	AUSTRIA †R AUSTRIA INTL, Moosbrunn	⇐ • Tu-Sa • S America • 300 kW; ⇐ • Su/M • S America • 300 kW; ⇐ • S America • 300 kW
		S • Europe • 100 kW
		Europe • 100 kW
		W • Europe • 100 kW; S M-F • Europe • 100 kW; S Sa/Su • Europe • 100 kW; W M-F • Europe • 100 kW; W Sa/Su • Europe • 100 kW
	CANADA †R CANADA INTL, Sackville, NB	W • C America & S America • 250 kW
	FINLAND YLE RADIO FINLAND, Pori	S • N America • 500 kW
	IRAN VO THE ISLAMIC REP, Ahvāz	W • W Asia & S Asia • 250 kW
	VO THE ISLAMIC REP, Sirjan	S • Europe • 500 kW
	VO THE ISLAMIC REP, Tehrān	S • S America • 500 kW
13735	CANADA R CANADA INTL, Via Germany	S • Mideast • 500 kW
	R CANADA INTL, Via Singapore	W • E Asia • 100 kW
	UNITED KINGDOM †BBC, Via Thailand	S • E Asia • 250 kW
	USA †R FREE ASIA, Via Saipan, N Marianas	S • SE Asia • 100 kW
	†R FREE ASIA, Via Tinian, N Marianas	S • SE Asia • 500 kW
	VOA, Via São Tomé	W • C Africa & E Africa • 100 kW
13740	UNITED KINGDOM †BBC, Rampisham	S • N Africa • 500 kW
	USA VOA, Delano, California	Tu-Sa • C America & S America • 250 kW
	VOA, Via Udon Thani, Thailand	S • E Asia • 250 kW
	VIETNAM VOICE OF VIETNAM, Son Tay	S • C Africa • 100 kW
		S • Europe • 100 kW
13745	IRAN VO THE ISLAMIC REP, Tehrān	S • S Asia, SE Asia & Australasia • 500 kW
	UNITED KINGDOM †BBC, Rampisham	S Sa/Su • E Europe • 500 kW; S M-F • E Europe • 500 kW; S • E Europe • 500 kW; S M-Sa • E Europe • 500 kW; S • W Africa • 500 kW
(con'd)		0 1 2 3 4 5 6 7 8 9 10 11 12 13 14 15 16 17 18 19 20 21 22 23 24

SEASONAL S OR W   1-HR TIMESHIFT MIDYEAR ⇐ OR ⇒   JAMMING / OR ∧   EARLIEST HEARD ◁   LATEST HEARD ▷   NEW FOR 2004 †

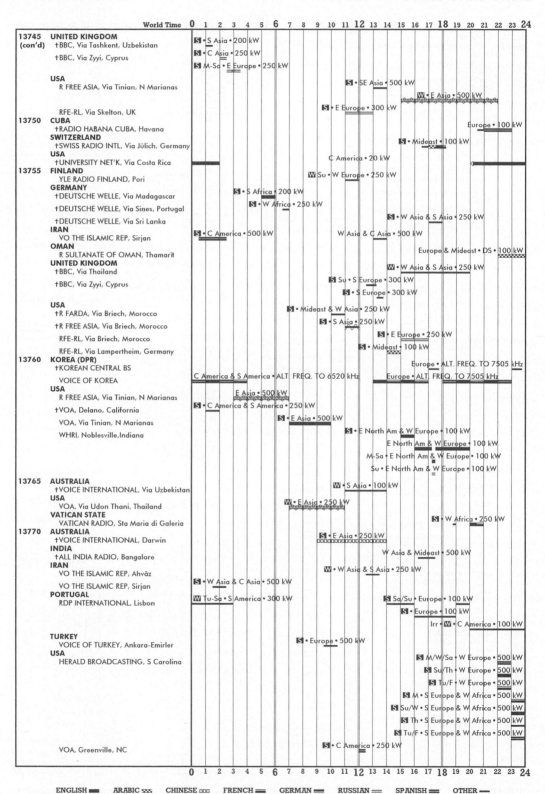

World Time 0 1 2 3 4 5 6 7 8 9 10 11 12 13 14 15 16 17 18 19 20 21 22 23 24

13745 **UNITED KINGDOM**
(con'd)   †BBC, Via Tashkent, Uzbekistan — **S** • S Asia • 200 kW
    †BBC, Via Zyyi, Cyprus — **S** • C Asia • 250 kW
    S M-Sa • E Europe • 250 kW

    USA
    R FREE ASIA, Via Tinian, N Marianas — **S** • SE Asia • 500 kW
    W • E Asia • 500 kW

    RFE-RL, Via Skelton, UK — **S** • E Europe • 300 kW
13750 **CUBA**
    †RADIO HABANA CUBA, Havana — Europe • 100 kW
    SWITZERLAND
    †SWISS RADIO INTL, Via Jülich, Germany — **S** • Mideast • 100 kW
    USA
    †UNIVERSITY NET'K, Via Costa Rica — C America • 20 kW
13755 **FINLAND**
    YLE RADIO FINLAND, Pori — **W** Su • W Europe • 250 kW
    GERMANY
    †DEUTSCHE WELLE, Via Madagascar — **S** • S Africa • 200 kW
    †DEUTSCHE WELLE, Via Sines, Portugal — **S** • W Africa • 250 kW

    †DEUTSCHE WELLE, Via Sri Lanka — **S** • W Asia & S Asia • 250 kW
    IRAN
    VO THE ISLAMIC REP, Sirjan — **S** • C America • 500 kW   W Asia & C Asia • 500 kW
    OMAN
    R SULTANATE OF OMAN, Thamarīt — Europe & Mideast • DS • 100 kW
    UNITED KINGDOM
    †BBC, Via Thailand — **W** • W Asia & S Asia • 250 kW
    †BBC, Via Zyyi, Cyprus — **S** Su • S Europe • 300 kW
    S • S Europe • 300 kW

    USA
    †R FARDA, Via Briech, Morocco — **S** • Mideast & W Asia • 250 kW
    †R FREE ASIA, Via Briech, Morocco — **S** • S Asia • 250 kW
    RFE-RL, Via Briech, Morocco — **S** • E Europe • 250 kW
    RFE-RL, Via Lampertheim, Germany — **S** • Mideast • 100 kW
13760 **KOREA (DPR)**
    †KOREAN CENTRAL BS — Europe • ALT. FREQ. TO 7505 kHz
    VOICE OF KOREA — C America & S America • ALT. FREQ. TO 6520 kHz   Europe • ALT. FREQ. TO 7505 kHz
    USA
    R FREE ASIA, Via Tinian, N Marianas — E Asia • 500 kW
    †VOA, Delano, California — **S** • C America & S America • 250 kW
    VOA, Via Tinian, N Marianas — **S** • E Asia • 500 kW
    WHRI, Noblesville, Indiana — **S** • E North Am & W Europe • 100 kW
    E North Am & W Europe • 100 kW
    M-Sa • E North Am & W Europe • 100 kW
    Su • E North Am & W Europe • 100 kW
13765 **AUSTRALIA**
    †VOICE INTERNATIONAL, Via Uzbekistan — **W** • S Asia • 100 kW
    USA
    VOA, Via Udon Thani, Thailand — **W** • E Asia • 250 kW
    VATICAN STATE
    VATICAN RADIO, Sta Maria di Galeria — **S** • W Africa • 250 kW
13770 **AUSTRALIA**
    †VOICE INTERNATIONAL, Darwin — **S** • E Asia • 250 kW
    INDIA
    †ALL INDIA RADIO, Bangalore — W Asia & Mideast • 500 kW
    IRAN
    VO THE ISLAMIC REP, Ahvāz — **W** • W Asia & S Asia • 250 kW
    VO THE ISLAMIC REP, Sirjan — **S** • W Asia & C Asia • 500 kW
    PORTUGAL
    RDP INTERNATIONAL, Lisbon — **W** Tu-Sa • S America • 300 kW
    S Sa/Su • Europe • 100 kW
    S • Europe • 100 kW
    Irr • **W** • C America • 100 kW

    TURKEY
    VOICE OF TURKEY, Ankara-Emirler — **S** • Europe • 500 kW
    USA
    HERALD BROADCASTING, S Carolina — **S** M/W/Sa • W Europe • 500 kW
    S Su/Th • W Europe • 500 kW
    S Tu/F • W Europe • 500 kW
    S M • S Europe & W Africa • 500 kW
    S Su/W • S Europe & W Africa • 500 kW
    S Th • S Europe & W Africa • 500 kW
    S Tu/F • S Europe & W Africa • 500 kW
    VOA, Greenville, NC — **S** • C America • 250 kW

0 1 2 3 4 5 6 7 8 9 10 11 12 13 14 15 16 17 18 19 20 21 22 23 24

ENGLISH ▬   ARABIC ⧖   CHINESE ☐☐☐   FRENCH ▬   GERMAN ▬   RUSSIAN ═   SPANISH ▬   OTHER ▬

World Time　0 1 2 3 4 5 6 7 8 9 10 11 12 13 14 15 16 17 18 19 20 21 22 23 24

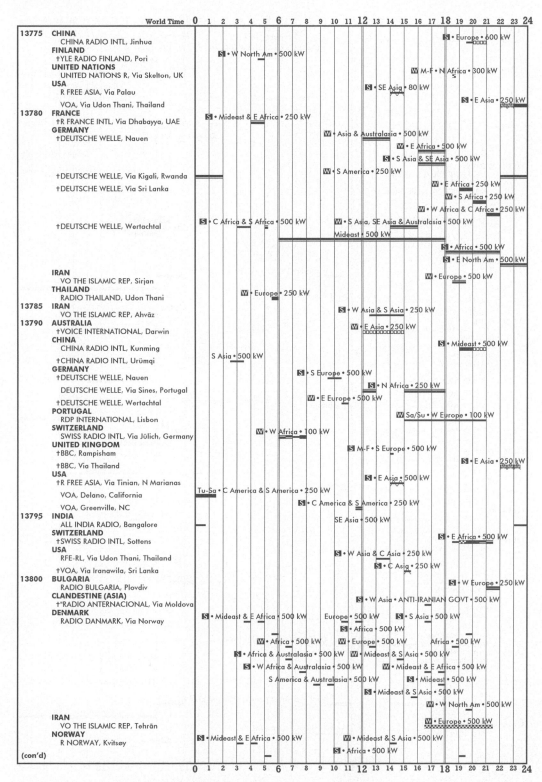

13775	**CHINA**
	CHINA RADIO INTL, Jinhua	S • Europe • 600 kW
	FINLAND
	†YLE RADIO FINLAND, Pori	S • W North Am • 500 kW
	UNITED NATIONS
	UNITED NATIONS R, Via Skelton, UK	W M-F • N Africa • 300 kW
	USA
	R FREE ASIA, Via Palau	S • SE Asia • 80 kW
	VOA, Via Udon Thani, Thailand	S • E Asia • 250 kW
13780	**FRANCE**
	†R FRANCE INTL, Via Dhabayya, UAE	S • Mideast & E Africa • 250 kW
	GERMANY
	†DEUTSCHE WELLE, Nauen	W • Asia & Australasia • 500 kW
		W • E Africa • 500 kW
		S • S Asia & SE Asia • 500 kW
	†DEUTSCHE WELLE, Via Kigali, Rwanda	W • S America • 250 kW
	†DEUTSCHE WELLE, Via Sri Lanka	W • E Africa • 250 kW
		W • S Africa • 250 kW
		W • W Africa & C Africa • 250 kW
	†DEUTSCHE WELLE, Wertachtal	S • C Africa & S Africa • 500 kW
		W • S Asia, SE Asia & Australasia • 500 kW
		Mideast • 500 kW
		S • Africa • 500 kW
		S • E North Am • 500 kW
	IRAN
	VO THE ISLAMIC REP, Sirjan	W • Europe • 500 kW
	THAILAND
	RADIO THAILAND, Udon Thani	W • Europe • 250 kW
13785	**IRAN**
	VO THE ISLAMIC REP, Ahvāz	S • W Asia & S Asia • 250 kW
13790	**AUSTRALIA**
	†VOICE INTERNATIONAL, Darwin	W • E Asia • 250 kW
	CHINA
	CHINA RADIO INTL, Kunming	S • Mideast • 500 kW
	†CHINA RADIO INTL, Urümqi	S Asia • 500 kW
	GERMANY
	†DEUTSCHE WELLE, Nauen	S • S Europe • 500 kW
	DEUTSCHE WELLE, Via Sines, Portugal	S • N Africa • 250 kW
	†DEUTSCHE WELLE, Wertachtal	W • E Europe • 500 kW
	PORTUGAL
	RDP INTERNATIONAL, Lisbon	W Sa/Su • W Europe • 100 kW
	SWITZERLAND
	SWISS RADIO INTL, Via Jülich, Germany	W • W Africa • 100 kW
	UNITED KINGDOM
	†BBC, Rampisham	S M-F • S Europe • 500 kW
	†BBC, Via Thailand	S • E Asia • 250 kW
	USA
	†R FREE ASIA, Via Tinian, N Marianas	S • E Asia • 500 kW
	VOA, Delano, California	Tu-Sa • C America & S America • 250 kW
	VOA, Greenville, NC	S • C America & S America • 250 kW
13795	**INDIA**
	ALL INDIA RADIO, Bangalore	SE Asia • 500 kW
	SWITZERLAND
	†SWISS RADIO INTL, Sottens	S • E Africa • 500 kW
	USA
	RFE-RL, Via Udon Thani, Thailand	S • W Asia & C Asia • 250 kW
		S • C Asia • 250 kW
	†VOA, Via Iranawila, Sri Lanka
13800	**BULGARIA**
	RADIO BULGARIA, Plovdiv	S • W Europe • 250 kW
	CLANDESTINE (ASIA)
	†"RADIO ANTERNACIONAL, Via Moldova	S • W Asia • ANTI-IRANIAN GOVT • 500 kW
	DENMARK
	RADIO DANMARK, Via Norway	S • Mideast & E Africa • 500 kW　Europe • 500 kW　S • S Asia • 500 kW
		S • Africa • 500 kW
		W • Africa • 500 kW　W • Europe • 500 kW　Africa • 500 kW
		S • Africa & Australasia • 500 kW　W • Mideast & S Asia • 500 kW
		S • W Africa & Australasia • 500 kW　W • Mideast & E Africa • 500 kW
		S America & Australasia • 500 kW　S • Mideast • 500 kW
		S • Mideast & S Asia • 500 kW
		W • W North Am • 500 kW
	IRAN
	VO THE ISLAMIC REP, Tehrān	W • Europe • 500 kW
	NORWAY
	R NORWAY, Kvitsøy	S • Mideast & E Africa • 500 kW　W • Mideast & S Asia • 500 kW
		S • Africa • 500 kW
(con'd)		

0 1 2 3 4 5 6 7 8 9 10 11 12 13 14 15 16 17 18 19 20 21 22 23 24

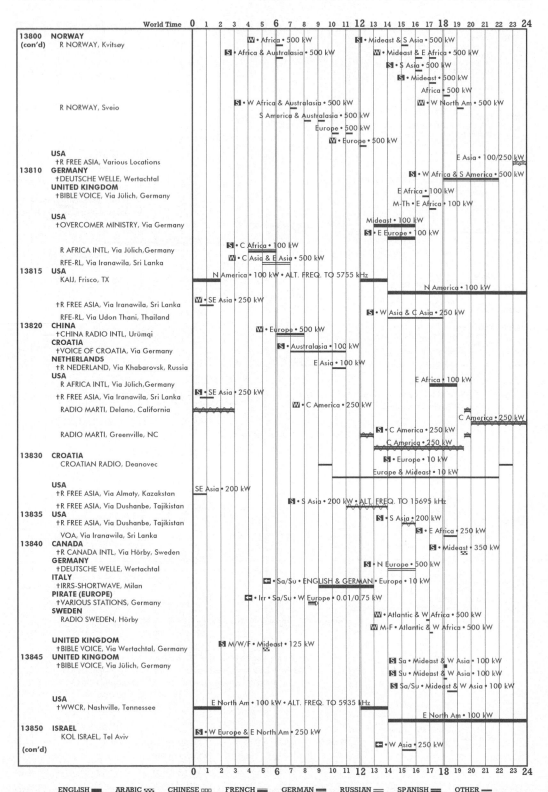

World Time 0 1 2 3 4 5 6 7 8 9 10 11 12 13 14 15 16 17 18 19 20 21 22 23 24

13800 **NORWAY**
(con'd) R NORWAY, Kvitsøy
  ☲ • Africa • 500 kW ☒ • Mideast & S Asia • 500 kW
  ☒ • Africa & Australasia • 500 kW ☲ • Mideast & E Africa • 500 kW
  ☒ • S Asia • 500 kW
  ☒ • Mideast • 500 kW
  Africa • 500 kW

  R NORWAY, Sveio
  ☒ • W Africa & Australasia • 500 kW ☲ • W North Am • 500 kW
  S America & Australasia • 500 kW
  Europe • 500 kW
  ☲ • Europe • 500 kW

  USA
  †R FREE ASIA, Various Locations E Asia • 100/250 kW
13810 **GERMANY**
  †DEUTSCHE WELLE, Wertachtal ☒ • W Africa & S America • 500 kW
  UNITED KINGDOM
  †BIBLE VOICE, Via Jülich, Germany E Africa • 100 kW
  M-Th • E Africa • 100 kW

  USA
  †OVERCOMER MINISTRY, Via Germany Mideast • 100 kW
  ☒ • E Europe • 100 kW

  R AFRICA INTL, Via Jülich, Germany ☒ • C Africa • 100 kW
  RFE-RL, Via Iranawila, Sri Lanka ☲ • C Asia & E Asia • 500 kW
13815 **USA**
  KAIJ, Frisco, TX N America • 100 kW • ALT. FREQ. TO 5755 kHz
  N America • 100 kW

  †R FREE ASIA, Via Iranawila, Sri Lanka ☲ • SE Asia • 250 kW
  RFE-RL, Via Udon Thani, Thailand ☒ • W Asia & C Asia • 250 kW
13820 **CHINA**
  †CHINA RADIO INTL, Urümqi ☲ • Europe • 500 kW
  CROATIA
  †VOICE OF CROATIA, Via Germany ☒ • Australasia • 100 kW
  NETHERLANDS
  †R NEDERLAND, Via Khabarovsk, Russia E Asia • 100 kW
  USA
  R AFRICA INTL, Via Jülich, Germany E Africa • 100 kW

  †R FREE ASIA, Via Iranawila, Sri Lanka ☒ • SE Asia • 250 kW
  RADIO MARTI, Delano, California ☲ • C America • 250 kW C America • 250 kW

  RADIO MARTI, Greenville, NC ☒ • C America • 250 kW
  C America • 250 kW
13830 **CROATIA**
  CROATIAN RADIO, Deanovec ☒ • Europe • 10 kW
  Europe & Mideast • 10 kW

  USA
  †R FREE ASIA, Via Almaty, Kazakstan SE Asia • 200 kW
  †R FREE ASIA, Via Dushanbe, Tajikistan ☒ • S Asia • 200 kW • ALT. FREQ. TO 15695 kHz
13835 **USA**
  †R FREE ASIA, Via Dushanbe, Tajikistan ☒ • S Asia • 200 kW
  VOA, Via Iranawila, Sri Lanka ☒ • E Africa • 250 kW
13840 **CANADA**
  †R CANADA INTL, Via Hörby, Sweden ☒ • Mideast • 350 kW
  GERMANY
  †DEUTSCHE WELLE, Wertachtal ☒ • N Europe • 500 kW
  ITALY
  †IRRS-SHORTWAVE, Milan ⬅ • Sa/Su • ENGLISH & GERMAN • Europe • 10 kW
  PIRATE (EUROPE)
  †VARIOUS STATIONS, Germany ⬅ • Irr • Sa/Su • W Europe • 0.01/0.75 kW ➡
  SWEDEN
  RADIO SWEDEN, Hörby ☲ • Atlantic & W Africa • 500 kW
  ☲ M-F • Atlantic & W Africa • 500 kW

  UNITED KINGDOM
  †BIBLE VOICE, Via Wertachtal, Germany ☒ M/W/F • Mideast • 125 kW
13845 **UNITED KINGDOM**
  †BIBLE VOICE, Via Jülich, Germany ☒ Sa • Mideast & W Asia • 100 kW
  ☒ Su • Mideast & W Asia • 100 kW
  ☒ Sa/Su • Mideast & W Asia • 100 kW

  USA
  †WWCR, Nashville, Tennessee E North Am • 100 kW • ALT. FREQ. TO 5935 kHz
  E North Am • 100 kW
13850 **ISRAEL**
  KOL ISRAEL, Tel Aviv ☒ • W Europe & E North Am • 250 kW
(con'd) ⬅ • W Asia • 250 kW

  0 1 2 3 4 5 6 7 8 9 10 11 12 13 14 15 16 17 18 19 20 21 22 23 24

ENGLISH ▬ ARABIC ﹏ CHINESE ▫▫▫ FRENCH ▬▬ GERMAN ▬▬ RUSSIAN ═ SPANISH ▬ OTHER ▬

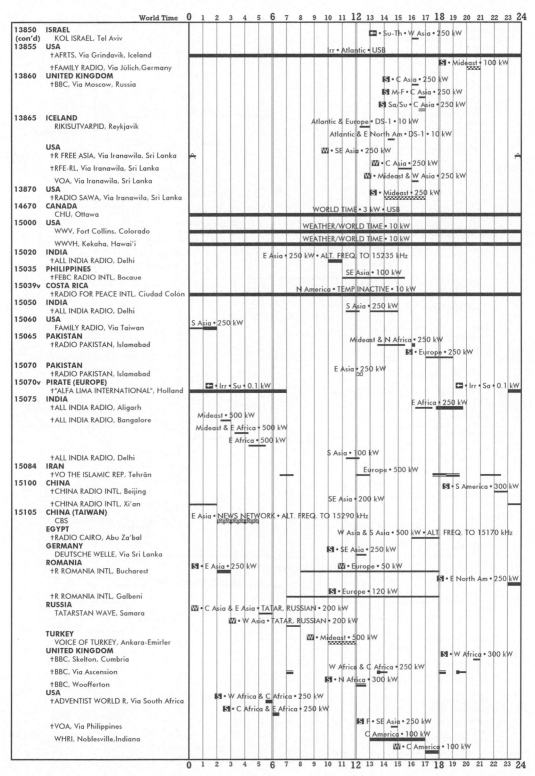

World Time: 0 1 2 3 4 5 6 7 8 9 10 11 12 13 14 15 16 17 18 19 20 21 22 23 24

- **13850** **ISRAEL** (con'd)
  - KOL ISRAEL, Tel Aviv — ⬌ • Su-Th • W Asia • 250 kW
- **13855** **USA**
  - †AFRTS, Via Grindavik, Iceland — Irr • Atlantic • USB
  - †FAMILY RADIO, Via Jülich, Germany — S • Mideast • 100 kW
- **13860** **UNITED KINGDOM**
  - †BBC, Via Moscow, Russia — S • C Asia • 250 kW; S M-F • C Asia • 250 kW; S Sa/Su • C Asia • 250 kW
- **13865** **ICELAND**
  - RIKISUTVARPID, Reykjavik — Atlantic & Europe • DS-1 • 10 kW; Atlantic & E North Am • DS-1 • 10 kW
  - **USA**
  - †R FREE ASIA, Via Iranawila, Sri Lanka — W • SE Asia • 250 kW
  - †RFE-RL, Via Iranawila, Sri Lanka — W • C Asia • 250 kW
  - VOA, Via Iranawila, Sri Lanka — W • Mideast & W Asia • 250 kW
- **13870** **USA**
  - †RADIO SAWA, Via Iranawila, Sri Lanka — S • Mideast • 250 kW
- **14670** **CANADA**
  - CHU, Ottawa — WORLD TIME • 3 kW • USB
- **15000** **USA**
  - WWV, Fort Collins, Colorado — WEATHER/WORLD TIME • 10 kW
  - WWVH, Kekaha, Hawai'i — WEATHER/WORLD TIME • 10 kW
- **15020** **INDIA**
  - †ALL INDIA RADIO, Delhi — E Asia • 250 kW • ALT. FREQ. TO 15235 kHz
- **15035** **PHILIPPINES**
  - †FEBC RADIO INTL, Bocaue — SE Asia • 100 kW
- **15039v** **COSTA RICA**
  - †RADIO FOR PEACE INTL, Ciudad Colón — N America • TEMP INACTIVE • 10 kW
- **15050** **INDIA**
  - †ALL INDIA RADIO, Delhi — S Asia • 250 kW
- **15060** **USA**
  - FAMILY RADIO, Via Taiwan — S Asia • 250 kW
- **15065** **PAKISTAN**
  - †RADIO PAKISTAN, Islamabad — Mideast & N Africa • 250 kW; S • Europe • 250 kW
- **15070** **PAKISTAN**
  - †RADIO PAKISTAN, Islamabad — E Asia • 250 kW
- **15070v** **PIRATE (EUROPE)**
  - †"ALFA LIMA INTERNATIONAL", Holland — ⬅ • Irr • Su • 0.1 kW; ⬅ • Irr • Sa • 0.1 kW
- **15075** **INDIA**
  - †ALL INDIA RADIO, Aligarh — E Africa • 250 kW
  - †ALL INDIA RADIO, Bangalore — Mideast • 500 kW; Mideast & E Africa • 500 kW; E Africa • 500 kW
  - †ALL INDIA RADIO, Delhi — S Asia • 100 kW
- **15084** **IRAN**
  - †VO THE ISLAMIC REP, Tehrān — Europe • 500 kW
- **15100** **CHINA**
  - †CHINA RADIO INTL, Beijing — S • S America • 300 kW
  - †CHINA RADIO INTL, Xi'an — SE Asia • 200 kW
- **15105** **CHINA (TAIWAN)**
  - CBS — E Asia • NEWS NETWORK • ALT. FREQ. TO 15290 kHz
  - **EGYPT**
  - †RADIO CAIRO, Abu Za'bal — W Asia & S Asia • 500 kW • ALT. FREQ. TO 15170 kHz
  - **GERMANY**
  - DEUTSCHE WELLE, Via Sri Lanka — S • SE Asia • 250 kW
  - **ROMANIA**
  - †R ROMANIA INTL, Bucharest — S • E Asia • 250 kW; W • Europe • 50 kW; S • E North Am • 250 kW
  - †R ROMANIA INTL, Galbeni — S • Europe • 120 kW
  - **RUSSIA**
  - TATARSTAN WAVE, Samara — W • C Asia & E Asia • TATAR, RUSSIAN • 200 kW; W • W Asia • TATAR, RUSSIAN • 200 kW
  - **TURKEY**
  - VOICE OF TURKEY, Ankara-Emirler — W • Mideast • 500 kW
  - **UNITED KINGDOM**
  - †BBC, Skelton, Cumbria — S • W Africa • 300 kW
  - †BBC, Via Ascension — W Africa & C Africa • 250 kW
  - †BBC, Woofferton — S • N Africa • 300 kW
  - **USA**
  - †ADVENTIST WORLD R, Via South Africa — S • W Africa & C Africa • 250 kW; S • C Africa & E Africa • 250 kW
  - †VOA, Via Philippines — S F • SE Asia • 250 kW
  - WHRI, Noblesville, Indiana — C America • 100 kW; W • C America • 100 kW

World Time: 0 1 2 3 4 5 6 7 8 9 10 11 12 13 14 15 16 17 18 19 20 21 22 23 24

SEASONAL S OR W   1-HR TIMESHIFT MIDYEAR ⬅ OR ➡   JAMMING / OR ∧   EARLIEST HEARD ◁   LATEST HEARD ▷   NEW FOR 2004 †

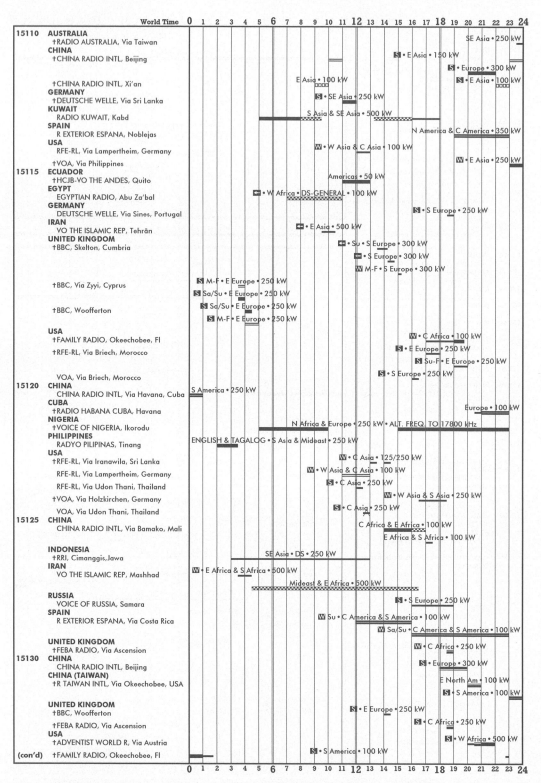

	World Time	0 1 2 3 4 5 6 7 8 9 10 11 12 13 14 15 16 17 18 19 20 21 22 23 24
15110	**AUSTRALIA**	
	†RADIO AUSTRALIA, Via Taiwan	SE Asia • 250 kW
	CHINA	
	†CHINA RADIO INTL, Beijing	⑤ • E Asia • 150 kW
		⑤ • Europe • 300 kW
	†CHINA RADIO INTL, Xi'an	E Asia • 100 kW ⑤ • E Asia • 100 kW
	GERMANY	
	†DEUTSCHE WELLE, Via Sri Lanka	⑤ • SE Asia • 250 kW
	KUWAIT	
	RADIO KUWAIT, Kabd	S Asia & SE Asia • 500 kW
	SPAIN	
	R EXTERIOR ESPANA, Noblejas	N America & C America • 350 kW
	USA	
	RFE-RL, Via Lampertheim, Germany	Ⓦ • W Asia & C Asia • 100 kW
	†VOA, Via Philippines	Ⓦ • E Asia • 250 kW
15115	**ECUADOR**	
	†HCJB-VO THE ANDES, Quito	Americas • 50 kW
	EGYPT	
	EGYPTIAN RADIO, Abu Za'bal	⬅ • W Africa • DS-GENERAL • 100 kW
	GERMANY	
	DEUTSCHE WELLE, Via Sines, Portugal	⑤ • S Europe • 250 kW
	IRAN	
	VO THE ISLAMIC REP, Tehrān	⬅ • E Asia • 500 kW
	UNITED KINGDOM	
	†BBC, Skelton, Cumbria	⬅ • Su • S Europe • 300 kW
		• S Europe • 300 kW
		Ⓦ M-F • S Europe • 300 kW
	†BBC, Via Zyyi, Cyprus	⑤ M-F • E Europe • 250 kW
		⑤ Sa/Su • E Europe • 250 kW
	†BBC, Woofferton	⑤ Sa/Su • E Europe • 250 kW
		⑤ M-F • E Europe • 250 kW
	USA	
	†FAMILY RADIO, Okeechobee, Fl	Ⓦ • C Africa • 100 kW
	†RFE-RL, Via Briech, Morocco	⑤ • E Europe • 250 kW
		⑤ Su-F • E Europe • 250 kW
	VOA, Via Briech, Morocco	⑤ • S Europe • 250 kW
15120	**CHINA**	
	CHINA RADIO INTL, Via Havana, Cuba	S America • 250 kW
	CUBA	
	†RADIO HABANA CUBA, Havana	Europe • 100 kW
	NIGERIA	
	†VOICE OF NIGERIA, Ikorodu	N Africa & Europe • 250 kW • ALT. FREQ. TO 17800 kHz
	PHILIPPINES	
	RADYO PILIPINAS, Tinang	ENGLISH & TAGALOG • S Asia & Mideast • 250 kW
	USA	
	†RFE-RL, Via Iranawila, Sri Lanka	Ⓦ • C Asia • 125/250 kW
	RFE-RL, Via Lampertheim, Germany	Ⓦ • W Asia & C Asia • 100 kW
	RFE-RL, Via Udon Thani, Thailand	⑤ • C Asia • 250 kW
	†VOA, Via Holzkirchen, Germany	Ⓦ • W Asia & S Asia • 250 kW
	VOA, Via Udon Thani, Thailand	⑤ • C Asia • 250 kW
15125	**CHINA**	
	CHINA RADIO INTL, Via Bamako, Mali	C Africa & E Africa • 100 kW
		E Africa & S Africa • 100 kW
	INDONESIA	
	†RRI, Cimanggis,Jawa	SE Asia • DS • 250 kW
	IRAN	
	VO THE ISLAMIC REP, Mashhad	Ⓦ • E Africa & S Africa • 500 kW
		Mideast & E Africa • 500 kW
	RUSSIA	
	VOICE OF RUSSIA, Samara	⑤ • S Europe • 250 kW
	SPAIN	
	R EXTERIOR ESPANA, Via Costa Rica	Ⓦ Su • C America & S America • 100 kW
		Ⓦ Sa/Su • C America & S America • 100 kW
	UNITED KINGDOM	
	†FEBA RADIO, Via Ascension	Ⓦ • C Africa • 250 kW
15130	**CHINA**	
	CHINA RADIO INTL, Beijing	⑤ • Europe • 300 kW
	CHINA (TAIWAN)	
	†R TAIWAN INTL, Via Okeechobee, USA	E North Am • 100 kW
		⑤ • S America • 100 kW
	UNITED KINGDOM	
	†BBC, Woofferton	⑤ • E Europe • 250 kW
	†FEBA RADIO, Via Ascension	⑤ • C Africa • 250 kW
	USA	
	†ADVENTIST WORLD R, Via Austria	⑤ • W Africa • 500 kW
(con'd)	†FAMILY RADIO, Okeechobee, Fl	⑤ • S America • 100 kW
		0 1 2 3 4 5 6 7 8 9 10 11 12 13 14 15 16 17 18 19 20 21 22 23 24

ENGLISH ▬ ARABIC ▧ CHINESE ⬚⬚⬚ FRENCH ▭ GERMAN ▤ RUSSIAN ═ SPANISH ▬ OTHER ▬

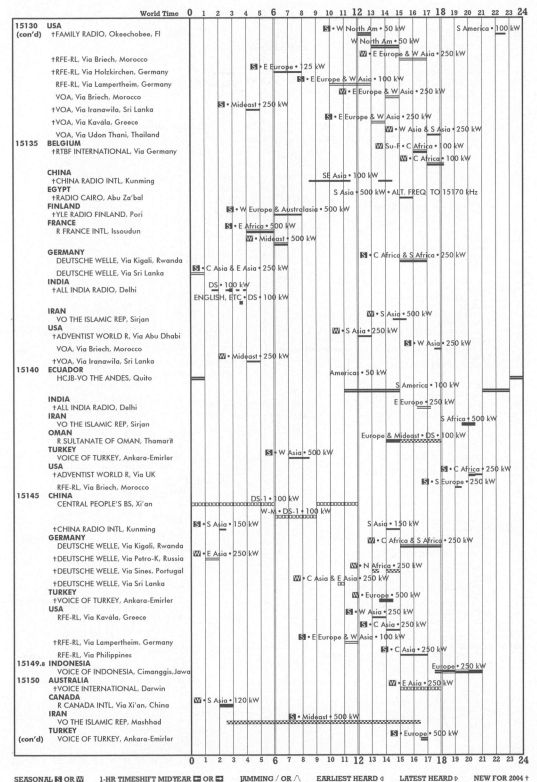

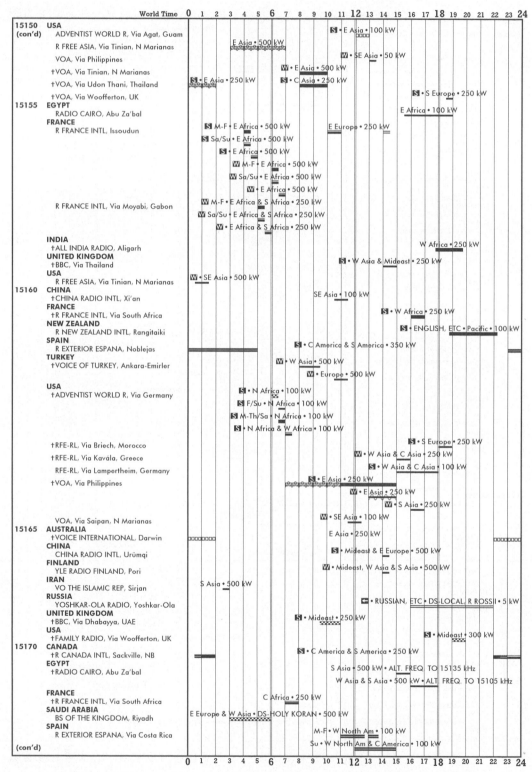

World Time	0 1 2 3 4 5 6 7 8 9 10 11 12 13 14 15 16 17 18 19 20 21 22 23 24
15150 USA	
(con'd) ADVENTIST WORLD R, Via Agat, Guam	🇸 • E Asia • 100 kW
R FREE ASIA, Via Tinian, N Marianas	E Asia • 500 kW
VOA, Via Philippines	🇼 • SE Asia • 50 kW
†VOA, Via Tinian, N Marianas	🇼 • E Asia • 500 kW
†VOA, Via Udon Thani, Thailand	🇸 • E Asia • 250 kW 🇸 • C Asia • 250 kW
†VOA, Via Woofferton, UK	🇸 • S Europe • 250 kW
15155 EGYPT	
RADIO CAIRO, Abu Za'bal	E Africa • 100 kW
FRANCE	
R FRANCE INTL, Issoudun	🇸 M-F • E Africa • 500 kW E Europe • 250 kW
	🇸 Sa/Su • E Africa • 500 kW
	🇸 • E Africa • 500 kW
	🇼 M-F • E Africa • 500 kW
	🇼 Sa/Su • E Africa • 500 kW
	🇼 • E Africa • 500 kW
R FRANCE INTL, Via Moyabi, Gabon	🇼 M-F • E Africa & S Africa • 250 kW
	🇼 Sa/Su • E Africa & S Africa • 250 kW
	🇼 • E Africa & S Africa • 250 kW
INDIA	
†ALL INDIA RADIO, Aligarh	W Africa • 250 kW
UNITED KINGDOM	
†BBC, Via Thailand	🇸 • W Asia & Mideast • 250 kW
USA	
R FREE ASIA, Via Tinian, N Marianas	🇼 • SE Asia • 500 kW
15160 CHINA	
†CHINA RADIO INTL, Xi'an	SE Asia • 100 kW
FRANCE	
†R FRANCE INTL, Via South Africa	🇸 • W Africa • 250 kW
NEW ZEALAND	
R NEW ZEALAND INTL, Rangitaiki	🇸 • ENGLISH, ETC • Pacific • 100 kW
SPAIN	
R EXTERIOR ESPANA, Noblejas	🇸 • C America & S America • 350 kW
TURKEY	
†VOICE OF TURKEY, Ankara-Emirler	🇼 • W Asia • 500 kW
	🇼 • Europe • 500 kW
USA	
†ADVENTIST WORLD R, Via Germany	🇸 • N Africa • 100 kW
	🇸 F/Su • N Africa • 100 kW
	🇸 M-Th/Sa • N Africa • 100 kW
	🇸 • N Africa & W Africa • 100 kW
†RFE-RL, Via Briech, Morocco	🇸 • S Europe • 250 kW
†RFE-RL, Via Kavála, Greece	🇼 • W Asia & C Asia • 250 kW
RFE-RL, Via Lampertheim, Germany	🇸 • W Asia & C Asia • 100 kW
†VOA, Via Philippines	🇸 • E Asia • 250 kW
	🇼 • E Asia • 250 kW
	🇼 • S Asia • 250 kW
VOA, Via Saipan, N Marianas	🇼 • SE Asia • 100 kW
15165 AUSTRALIA	
†VOICE INTERNATIONAL, Darwin	E Asia • 250 kW
CHINA	
CHINA RADIO INTL, Urümqi	🇸 • Mideast & E Europe • 500 kW
FINLAND	
YLE RADIO FINLAND, Pori	🇼 • Mideast, W Asia & S Asia • 500 kW
IRAN	
VO THE ISLAMIC REP, Sirjan	S Asia • 500 kW
RUSSIA	
YOSHKAR-OLA RADIO, Yoshkar-Ola	▣ • RUSSIAN, ETC • DS-LOCAL, R ROSSII • 5 kW
UNITED KINGDOM	
†BBC, Via Dhabayya, UAE	🇸 • Mideast • 250 kW
USA	
†FAMILY RADIO, Via Woofferton, UK	🇸 • Mideast • 300 kW
15170 CANADA	
†R CANADA INTL, Sackville, NB	🇸 • C America & S America • 250 kW
EGYPT	
†RADIO CAIRO, Abu Za'bal	S Asia • 500 kW • ALT. FREQ. TO 15135 kHz
	W Asia & S Asia • 500 kW • ALT. FREQ. TO 15105 kHz
FRANCE	
†R FRANCE INTL, Via South Africa	C Africa • 250 kW
SAUDI ARABIA	
BS OF THE KINGDOM, Riyadh	E Europe & W Asia • DS-HOLY KORAN • 500 kW
SPAIN	
R EXTERIOR ESPANA, Via Costa Rica	M-F • W North Am • 100 kW
	Su • W North Am & C America • 100 kW
(con'd)	

0 1 2 3 4 5 6 7 8 9 10 11 12 13 14 15 16 17 18 19 20 21 22 23 24

ENGLISH ▬   ARABIC ⋙   CHINESE ▦   FRENCH ▬   GERMAN ▬   RUSSIAN ═   SPANISH ▬   OTHER ▬

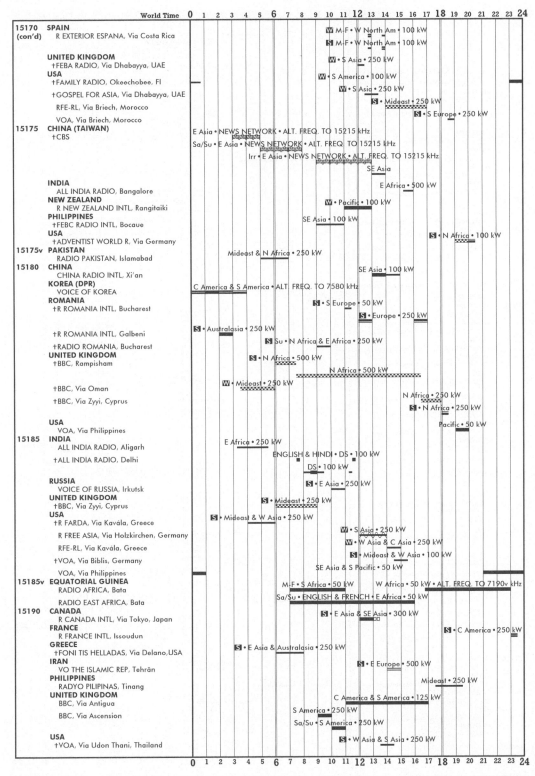

World Time	0 1 2 3 4 5 6 7 8 9 10 11 12 13 14 15 16 17 18 19 20 21 22 23 24

15170 **SPAIN**
(con'd)   R EXTERIOR ESPANA, Via Costa Rica
- W • M-F • W North Am • 100 kW
- S • M-F • W North Am • 100 kW

UNITED KINGDOM
†FEBA RADIO, Via Dhabayya, UAE
- W • S Asia • 250 kW

USA
†FAMILY RADIO, Okeechobee, Fl
- W • S America • 100 kW

†GOSPEL FOR ASIA, Via Dhabayya, UAE
- W • S Asia • 250 kW

RFE-RL, Via Briech, Morocco
- S • Mideast • 250 kW

VOA, Via Briech, Morocco
- S • S Europe • 250 kW

15175 **CHINA (TAIWAN)**
†CBS
- E Asia • NEWS NETWORK • ALT. FREQ. TO 15215 kHz
- Sa/Su • E Asia • NEWS NETWORK • ALT. FREQ. TO 15215 kHz
- Irr • E Asia • NEWS NETWORK • ALT. FREQ. TO 15215 kHz
- SE Asia

INDIA
ALL INDIA RADIO, Bangalore
- E Africa • 500 kW

NEW ZEALAND
R NEW ZEALAND INTL, Rangitaiki
- W • Pacific • 100 kW

PHILIPPINES
†FEBC RADIO INTL, Bocaue
- SE Asia • 100 kW

USA
†ADVENTIST WORLD R, Via Germany
- S • N Africa • 100 kW

15175v **PAKISTAN**
RADIO PAKISTAN, Islamabad
- Mideast & N Africa • 250 kW

15180 **CHINA**
CHINA RADIO INTL, Xi'an
- SE Asia • 100 kW

KOREA (DPR)
VOICE OF KOREA
- C America & S America • ALT. FREQ. TO 7580 kHz

ROMANIA
†R ROMANIA INTL, Bucharest
- S • S Europe • 50 kW
- S • Europe • 250 kW

†R ROMANIA INTL, Galbeni
- S • Australasia • 250 kW

†RADIO ROMANIA, Bucharest
- S • Su • N Africa & E Africa • 250 kW

UNITED KINGDOM
†BBC, Rampisham
- S • N Africa • 500 kW
- N Africa • 500 kW

†BBC, Via Oman
- W • Mideast • 250 kW

†BBC, Via Zyyi, Cyprus
- N Africa • 250 kW
- S • N Africa • 250 kW

USA
VOA, Via Philippines
- Pacific • 50 kW

15185 **INDIA**
ALL INDIA RADIO, Aligarh
- E Africa • 250 kW

†ALL INDIA RADIO, Delhi
- ENGLISH & HINDI • DS • 100 kW
- DS • 100 kW

RUSSIA
VOICE OF RUSSIA, Irkutsk
- S • E Asia • 250 kW

UNITED KINGDOM
†BBC, Via Zyyi, Cyprus
- S • Mideast • 250 kW

USA
†R FARDA, Via Kavála, Greece
- S • Mideast & W Asia • 250 kW

R FREE ASIA, Via Holzkirchen, Germany
- W • S Asia • 250 kW

RFE-RL, Via Kavála, Greece
- W • W Asia & C Asia • 250 kW

†VOA, Via Biblis, Germany
- S • Mideas & W Asia • 100 kW

VOA, Via Philippines
- SE Asia & S Pacific • 50 kW

15185v **EQUATORIAL GUINEA**
RADIO AFRICA, Bata
- M-F • S Africa • 50 kW   W Africa • 50 kW • ALT. FREQ. TO 7190v kHz

RADIO EAST AFRICA, Bata
- Sa/Su • ENGLISH & FRENCH • E Africa • 50 kW

15190 **CANADA**
R CANADA INTL, Via Tokyo, Japan
- S • E Asia & SE Asia • 300 kW

FRANCE
R FRANCE INTL, Issoudun
- S • C America • 250 kW

GREECE
†FONI TIS HELLADAS, Via Delano, USA
- S • E Asia & Australasia • 250 kW

IRAN
VO THE ISLAMIC REP, Tehrän
- S • E Europe • 500 kW

PHILIPPINES
RADYO PILIPINAS, Tinang
- Mideast • 250 kW

UNITED KINGDOM
BBC, Via Antigua
- C America & S America • 125 kW

BBC, Via Ascension
- S America • 250 kW
- Sa/Su • S America • 250 kW

USA
†VOA, Via Udon Thani, Thailand
- S • W Asia & S Asia • 250 kW

	0 1 2 3 4 5 6 7 8 9 10 11 12 13 14 15 16 17 18 19 20 21 22 23 24

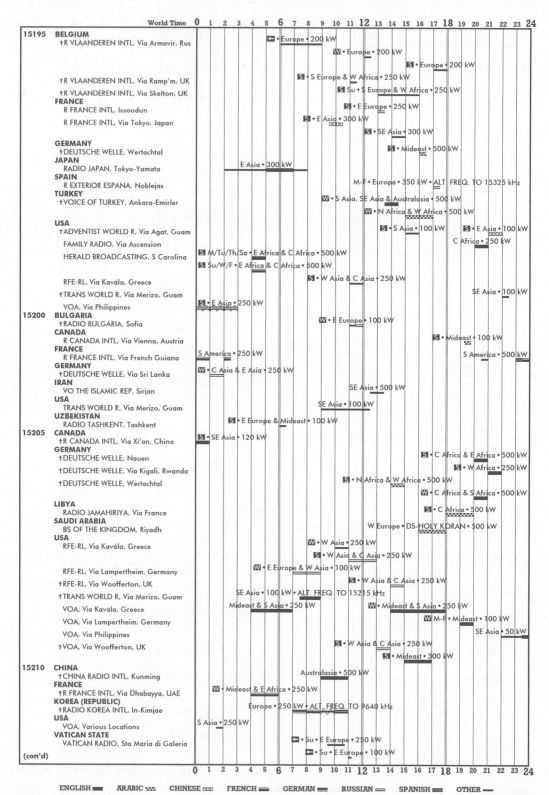

	World Time	0 1 2 3 4 5 6 7 8 9 10 11 12 13 14 15 16 17 18 19 20 21 22 23 24
15195	BELGIUM	
	†R VLAANDEREN INTL, Via Armavir, Rus	⇆ • Europe • 200 kW
		W • Europe • 200 kW
		S • Europe • 200 kW
	†R VLAANDEREN INTL, Via Ramp'm, UK	S • S Europe & W Africa • 250 kW
	†R VLAANDEREN INTL, Via Skelton, UK	Su • S Europe & W Africa • 250 kW
	FRANCE	
	R FRANCE INTL, Issoudun	S • E Europe • 250 kW
	R FRANCE INTL, Via Tokyo, Japan	S • E Asia • 300 kW
		S • SE Asia • 300 kW
	GERMANY	
	†DEUTSCHE WELLE, Wertachtal	S • Mideast • 500 kW
	JAPAN	
	RADIO JAPAN, Tokyo-Yamata	E Asia • 300 kW
	SPAIN	
	R EXTERIOR ESPANA, Noblejas	M-F • Europe • 350 kW • ALT. FREQ. TO 15325 kHz
	TURKEY	
	†VOICE OF TURKEY, Ankara-Emirler	W • S Asia, SE Asia & Australasia • 500 kW
		W • N Africa & W Africa • 500 kW
	USA	
	†ADVENTIST WORLD R, Via Agat, Guam	S • S Asia • 100 kW ⋯⋯ S • E Asia • 100 kW
	FAMILY RADIO, Via Ascension	C Africa • 250 kW
	HERALD BROADCASTING, S Carolina	S M/Tu/Th/Sa • E Africa & C Africa • 500 kW
		S Su/W/F • E Africa & C Africa • 500 kW
	RFE-RL, Via Kavála, Greece	S • W Asia & C Asia • 250 kW
	†TRANS WORLD R, Via Merizo, Guam	SE Asia • 100 kW
	VOA, Via Philippines	S • E Asia • 250 kW
15200	BULGARIA	
	†RADIO BULGARIA, Sofia	W • E Europe • 100 kW
	CANADA	
	R CANADA INTL, Via Vienna, Austria	S • Mideast • 100 kW
	FRANCE	
	R FRANCE INTL, Via French Guiana	S America • 250 kW ⋯⋯ S America • 500 kW
	GERMANY	
	†DEUTSCHE WELLE, Via Sri Lanka	W • C Asia & E Asia • 250 kW
	IRAN	
	VO THE ISLAMIC REP, Sirjan	SE Asia • 500 kW
	USA	
	TRANS WORLD R, Via Merizo, Guam	SE Asia • 100 kW
	UZBEKISTAN	
	RADIO TASHKENT, Tashkent	S • E Europe & Mideast • 100 kW
15205	CANADA	
	†R CANADA INTL, Via Xi'an, China	S • SE Asia • 120 kW
	GERMANY	
	†DEUTSCHE WELLE, Nauen	S • C Africa & E Africa • 500 kW
		S • W Africa • 250 kW
	†DEUTSCHE WELLE, Via Kigali, Rwanda	S • N Africa & W Africa • 500 kW
	†DEUTSCHE WELLE, Wertachtal	W • C Africa & S Africa • 500 kW
	LIBYA	
	RADIO JAMAHIRIYA, Via France	S • C Africa • 500 kW
	SAUDI ARABIA	
	BS OF THE KINGDOM, Riyadh	W Europe • DS-HOLY KORAN • 500 kW
	USA	
	RFE-RL, Via Kavála, Greece	W • W Asia • 250 kW
		S • W Asia & C Asia • 250 kW
	RFE-RL, Via Lampertheim, Germany	W • E Europe & W Asia • 100 kW
	†RFE-RL, Via Woofferton, UK	S • W Asia & C Asia • 250 kW
	†TRANS WORLD R, Via Merizo, Guam	SE Asia • 100 kW • ALT. FREQ. TO 15215 kHz
	VOA, Via Kavála, Greece	Mideast & S Asia • 250 kW ⋯⋯ W • Mideast & S Asia • 250 kW
	VOA, Via Lampertheim, Germany	W M-F • Mideast • 100 kW
	VOA, Via Philippines	SE Asia • 50 kW
	†VOA, Via Woofferton, UK	S • W Asia & C Asia • 250 kW
		S • Mideast • 300 kW
15210	CHINA	
	†CHINA RADIO INTL, Kunming	Australasia • 500 kW
	FRANCE	
	†R FRANCE INTL, Via Dhabayya, UAE	W • Mideast & E Africa • 250 kW
	KOREA (REPUBLIC)	
	†RADIO KOREA INTL, In-Kimjae	Europe • 250 kW • ALT. FREQ. TO 9640 kHz
	USA	
	VOA, Various Locations	S Asia • 250 kW
	VATICAN STATE	
	VATICAN RADIO, Sta Maria di Galeria	⇆ • Su • E Europe • 250 kW
		⇆ • Su • E Europe • 100 kW
(con'd)		

0 1 2 3 4 5 6 7 8 9 10 11 12 13 14 15 16 17 18 19 20 21 22 23 24

ENGLISH ▬ ARABIC ░░░ CHINESE □□□ FRENCH ▬ GERMAN ▬ RUSSIAN ═══ SPANISH ▬ OTHER ▬

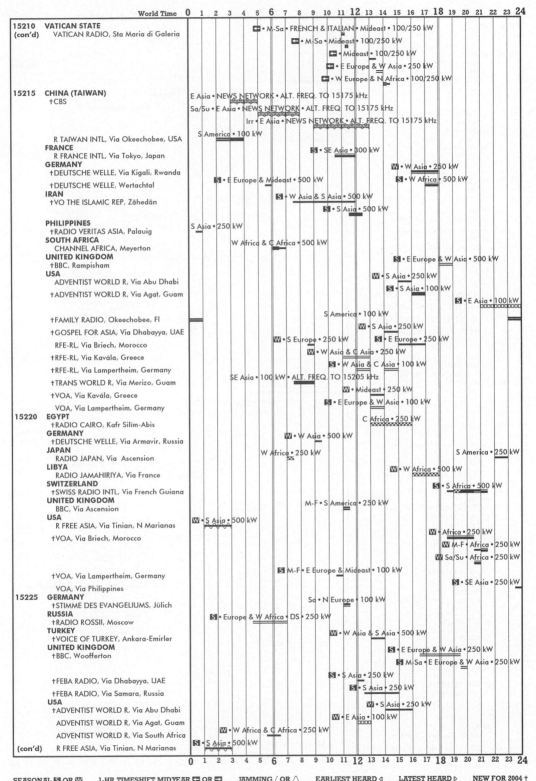

World Time 0 1 2 3 4 5 6 7 8 9 10 11 12 13 14 15 16 17 18 19 20 21 22 23 24

15210 **VATICAN STATE**
(con'd) VATICAN RADIO, Sta Maria di Galeria
- M-Sa • FRENCH & ITALIAN • Mideast • 100/250 kW
- M-Sa • Mideast • 100/250 kW
- Mideast • 100/250 kW
- E Europe & W Asia • 250 kW
- W Europe & N Africa • 100/250 kW

15215 **CHINA (TAIWAN)**
†CBS
E Asia • NEWS NETWORK • ALT. FREQ. TO 15175 kHz
Sa/Su • E Asia • NEWS NETWORK • ALT. FREQ. TO 15175 kHz
Irr • E Asia • NEWS NETWORK • ALT. FREQ. TO 15175 kHz

R TAIWAN INTL, Via Okeechobee, USA — S America • 100 kW
FRANCE
R FRANCE INTL, Via Tokyo, Japan — SE Asia • 300 kW
GERMANY
†DEUTSCHE WELLE, Via Kigali, Rwanda — W • W Asia • 250 kW
†DEUTSCHE WELLE, Wertachtal — S • E Europe & Mideast • 500 kW / W • W Africa • 500 kW
IRAN
†VO THE ISLAMIC REP, Zähedän — S • W Asia & S Asia • 500 kW / S • S Asia • 500 kW

PHILIPPINES
†RADIO VERITAS ASIA, Palauig — S Asia • 250 kW
SOUTH AFRICA
CHANNEL AFRICA, Meyerton — W Africa & C Africa • 500 kW
UNITED KINGDOM
†BBC, Rampisham — S • E Europe & W Asia • 500 kW
USA
ADVENTIST WORLD R, Via Abu Dhabi — W • S Asia • 250 kW
†ADVENTIST WORLD R, Via Agat, Guam — S • S Asia • 100 kW / S • E Asia • 100 kW

†FAMILY RADIO, Okeechobee, Fl — S America • 100 kW
†GOSPEL FOR ASIA, Via Dhabayya, UAE — W • S Asia • 250 kW
RFE-RL, Via Briech, Morocco — W • S Europe • 250 kW / S • E Europe • 250 kW
†RFE-RL, Via Kavála, Greece — W • W Asia & C Asia • 250 kW
†RFE-RL, Via Lampertheim, Germany — S • W Asia & C Asia • 100 kW
†TRANS WORLD R, Via Merizo, Guam — SE Asia • 100 kW • ALT. FREQ. TO 15205 kHz
†VOA, Via Kavála, Greece — W • Mideast • 250 kW
VOA, Via Lampertheim, Germany — S • E Europe & W Asia • 100 kW

15220 **EGYPT**
†RADIO CAIRO, Kafr Silim-Abis — C Africa • 250 kW
GERMANY
†DEUTSCHE WELLE, Via Armavir, Russia — W • W Asia • 500 kW
JAPAN
RADIO JAPAN, Via Ascension — W Africa • 250 kW / S America • 250 kW
LIBYA
RADIO JAMAHIRIYA, Via France — W • W Africa • 500 kW
SWITZERLAND
†SWISS RADIO INTL, Via French Guiana — S • S Africa • 500 kW
UNITED KINGDOM
BBC, Via Ascension — M-F • S America • 250 kW
USA
R FREE ASIA, Via Tinian, N Marianas — W • S Asia • 500 kW
†VOA, Via Briech, Morocco — W • Africa • 250 kW / W M-F • Africa • 250 kW / W Sa/Su • Africa • 250 kW

†VOA, Via Lampertheim, Germany — S M-F • E Europe & Mideast • 100 kW
VOA, Via Philippines — S • SE Asia • 250 kW

15225 **GERMANY**
†STIMME DES EVANGELIUMS, Jülich — Sa • N Europe • 100 kW
RUSSIA
†RADIO ROSSII, Moscow — S • Europe & W Africa • DS 250 kW
TURKEY
†VOICE OF TURKEY, Ankara-Emirler — W • W Asia & S Asia • 500 kW
UNITED KINGDOM
†BBC, Woofferton — S • E Europe & W Asia • 250 kW / S M-Sa • E Europe & W Asia • 250 kW

†FEBA RADIO, Via Dhabayya, UAE — S • S Asia • 250 kW
†FEBA RADIO, Via Samara, Russia — S • S Asia • 250 kW
USA
†ADVENTIST WORLD R, Via Abu Dhabi — W • S Asia • 250 kW
ADVENTIST WORLD R, Via Agat, Guam — W • E Asia • 100 kW
ADVENTIST WORLD R, Via South Africa — W • W Africa & C Africa • 250 kW
(con'd) R FREE ASIA, Via Tinian, N Marianas — S • S Asia • 500 kW

0 1 2 3 4 5 6 7 8 9 10 11 12 13 14 15 16 17 18 19 20 21 22 23 24

SEASONAL S OR W   1-HR TIMESHIFT MIDYEAR ⇐ OR ⇒   JAMMING / OR ∧   EARLIEST HEARD ◁   LATEST HEARD ▷   NEW FOR 2004 †

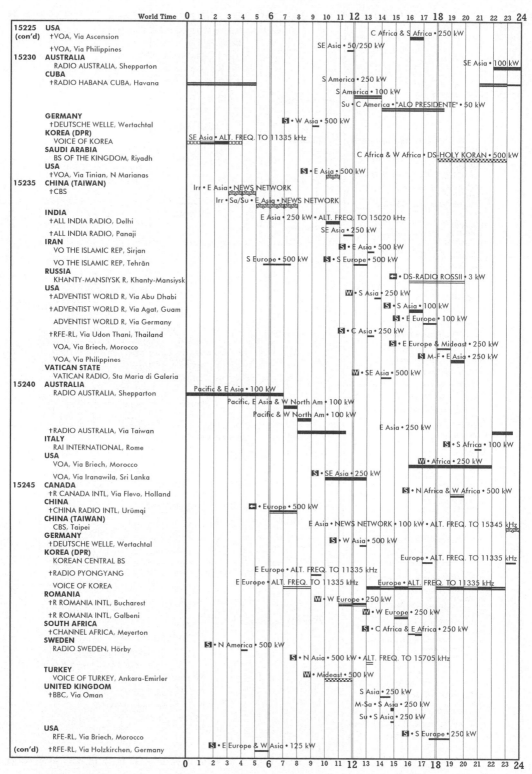

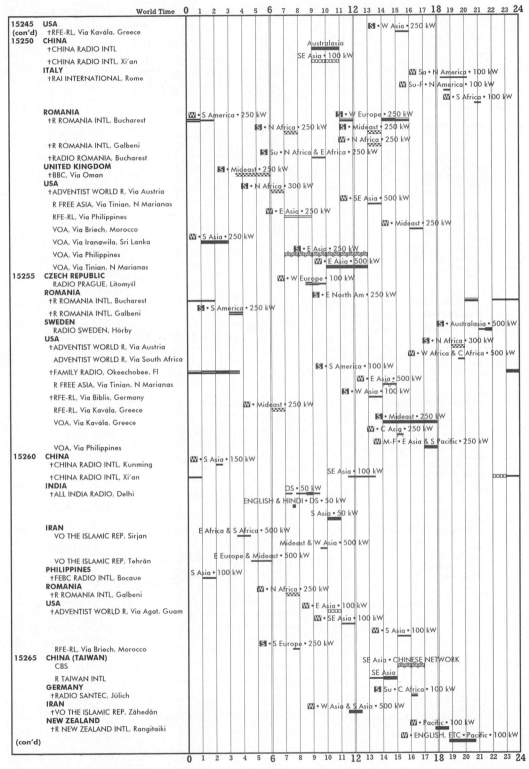

World Time

	0 1 2 3 4 5 6 7 8 9 10 11 12 13 14 15 16 17 18 19 20 21 22 23 24
15245 (con'd)	USA
	†RFE-RL, Via Kavála, Greece — S • W Asia • 250 kW
15250	CHINA
	†CHINA RADIO INTL — Australasia / SE Asia • 100 kW
	†CHINA RADIO INTL, Xi'an
	ITALY
	†RAI INTERNATIONAL, Rome — W Sa • N America • 100 kW / W Su-F • N America • 100 kW / W • S Africa • 100 kW
	ROMANIA
	†R ROMANIA INTL, Bucharest — W • S America • 250 kW / S • W Europe • 250 kW / S • N Africa • 250 kW / S • Mideast • 250 kW / W • N Africa • 250 kW
	†R ROMANIA INTL, Galbeni
	†RADIO ROMANIA, Bucharest — S Su • N Africa & E Africa • 250 kW
	UNITED KINGDOM
	†BBC, Via Oman — S • Mideast • 250 kW
	USA
	†ADVENTIST WORLD R, Via Austria — S • N Africa • 300 kW
	R FREE ASIA, Via Tinian, N Marianas — S • SE Asia • 500 kW
	RFE-RL, Via Philippines — W • E Asia • 250 kW
	VOA, Via Briech, Morocco — W • Mideast • 250 kW
	VOA, Via Iranawila, Sri Lanka — W • S Asia • 250 kW
	VOA, Via Philippines — S • E Asia • 250 kW
	VOA, Via Tinian, N Marianas — W • E Asia • 500 kW
15255	CZECH REPUBLIC
	RADIO PRAGUE, Litomyšl — W • W Europe • 100 kW
	ROMANIA
	†R ROMANIA INTL, Bucharest — S • E North Am • 250 kW
	†R ROMANIA INTL, Galbeni — S • S America • 250 kW
	SWEDEN
	RADIO SWEDEN, Hörby — S • Australasia • 500 kW
	USA
	†ADVENTIST WORLD R, Via Austria — S • N Africa • 300 kW
	ADVENTIST WORLD R, Via South Africa — W • W Africa & C Africa • 500 kW
	†FAMILY RADIO, Okeechobee, Fl — S • S America • 100 kW
	R FREE ASIA, Via Tinian, N Marianas — W • E Asia • 500 kW
	†RFE-RL, Via Biblis, Germany — S • W Asia • 100 kW
	RFE-RL, Via Kavála, Greece — W • Mideast • 250 kW
	VOA, Via Kavála, Greece — S • Mideast • 250 kW / W • C Asia • 250 kW / W M-F • E Asia & S Pacific • 250 kW
	VOA, Via Philippines
15260	CHINA
	†CHINA RADIO INTL, Kunming — W • S Asia • 150 kW
	†CHINA RADIO INTL, Xi'an — SE Asia • 100 kW
	INDIA
	†ALL INDIA RADIO, Delhi — DS • 50 kW / ENGLISH & HINDI • DS • 50 kW / S Asia • 50 kW
	IRAN
	VO THE ISLAMIC REP, Sirjan — E Africa & S Africa • 500 kW / Mideast & W Asia • 500 kW / E Europe & Mideast • 500 kW
	PHILIPPINES
	†FEBC RADIO INTL, Bocaue — S Asia • 100 kW
	ROMANIA
	†R ROMANIA INTL, Galbeni — W • N Africa • 250 kW
	USA
	†ADVENTIST WORLD R, Via Agat, Guam — W • E Asia • 100 kW / W • SE Asia • 100 kW / W • S Asia • 100 kW
	RFE-RL, Via Briech, Morocco — S • S Europe • 250 kW
15265	CHINA (TAIWAN)
	CBS — SE Asia • CHINESE NETWORK
	R TAIWAN INTL — SE Asia
	GERMANY
	†RADIO SANTEC, Jülich — S Su • C Africa • 100 kW
	IRAN
	†VO THE ISLAMIC REP, Zähedän — W • W Asia & S Asia • 500 kW
	NEW ZEALAND
	†R NEW ZEALAND INTL, Rangitaiki — W • Pacific • 100 kW / W • ENGLISH, ETC • Pacific • 100 kW
(con'd)	

| | 0 1 2 3 4 5 6 7 8 9 10 11 12 13 14 15 16 17 18 19 20 21 22 23 24 |

SEASONAL S OR W   1-HR TIMESHIFT MIDYEAR ⇐ OR ⇒   JAMMING / OR ∧   EARLIEST HEARD ◁   LATEST HEARD ▷   NEW FOR 2004 †

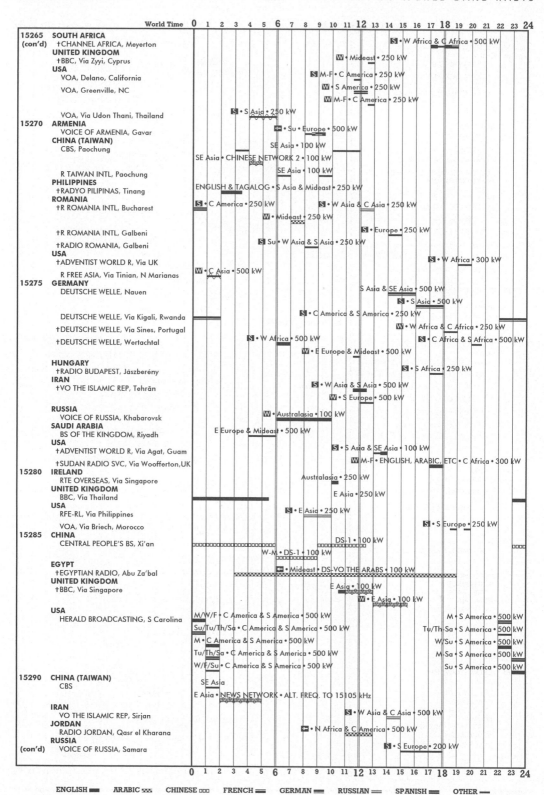

World Time 0 1 2 3 4 5 6 7 8 9 10 11 12 13 14 15 16 17 18 19 20 21 22 23 24

Freq	Country / Station	Details
15265 (con'd)	**SOUTH AFRICA** †CHANNEL AFRICA, Meyerton	S • W Africa & C Africa • 500 kW
	UNITED KINGDOM †BBC, Via Zyyi, Cyprus	W • Mideast • 250 kW
	USA VOA, Delano, California	S M-F • C America • 250 kW
	VOA, Greenville, NC	W • S America • 250 kW
		W M-F • C America • 250 kW
	VOA, Via Udon Thani, Thailand	S • S Asia • 250 kW
15270	**ARMENIA** VOICE OF ARMENIA, Gavar	• Su • Europe • 500 kW
	CHINA (TAIWAN) CBS, Paochung	SE Asia • 100 kW
		SE Asia • CHINESE NETWORK 2 • 100 kW
	R TAIWAN INTL, Paochung	SE Asia • 100 kW
	PHILIPPINES †RADYO PILIPINAS, Tinang	ENGLISH & TAGALOG • S Asia & Mideast • 250 kW
	ROMANIA †R ROMANIA INTL, Bucharest	S • C America • 250 kW S • W Asia & C Asia • 250 kW
		W • Mideast • 250 kW
	†R ROMANIA INTL, Galbeni	S • Europe • 250 kW
	†RADIO ROMANIA, Galbeni	S Su • W Asia & S Asia • 250 kW
	USA †ADVENTIST WORLD R, Via UK	S • W Africa • 300 kW
	R FREE ASIA, Via Tinian, N Marianas	W • C Asia • 500 kW
15275	**GERMANY** DEUTSCHE WELLE, Nauen	S Asia & SE Asia • 500 kW
		S • S Asia • 500 kW
	DEUTSCHE WELLE, Via Kigali, Rwanda	S • C America & S America • 250 kW
	†DEUTSCHE WELLE, Via Sines, Portugal	W • W Africa & C Africa • 250 kW
	†DEUTSCHE WELLE, Wertachtal	S • W Africa • 500 kW S • C Africa & S Africa • 500 kW
		W • E Europe & Mideast • 500 kW
	HUNGARY †RADIO BUDAPEST, Jászberény	S • S Africa • 250 kW
	IRAN †VO THE ISLAMIC REP, Tehrān	S • W Asia & S Asia • 500 kW
		W • S Europe • 500 kW
	RUSSIA VOICE OF RUSSIA, Khabarovsk	W • Australasia • 100 kW
	SAUDI ARABIA BS OF THE KINGDOM, Riyadh	E Europe & Mideast • 500 kW
	USA †ADVENTIST WORLD R, Via Agat, Guam	S • S Asia & SE Asia • 100 kW
	†SUDAN RADIO SVC, Via Woofferton, UK	W M-F • ENGLISH, ARABIC, ETC • C Africa • 300 kW
15280	**IRELAND** RTE OVERSEAS, Via Singapore	Australasia • 250 kW
	UNITED KINGDOM BBC, Via Thailand	E Asia • 250 kW
	USA RFE-RL, Via Philippines	S • E Asia • 250 kW
	VOA, Via Briech, Morocco	S • S Europe • 250 kW
15285	**CHINA** CENTRAL PEOPLE'S BS, Xi'an	DS-1 • 100 kW
		W-M • DS-1 • 100 kW
	EGYPT †EGYPTIAN RADIO, Abu Za'bal	• Mideast • DS-VO THE ARABS • 100 kW
	UNITED KINGDOM †BBC, Via Singapore	E Asia • 100 kW
		W • E Asia • 100 kW
	USA HERALD BROADCASTING, S Carolina	M/W/F • C America & S America • 500 kW M • S America • 500 kW
		Su/Tu/Th/Sa • C America & S America • 500 kW Tu/Th-Sa • S America • 500 kW
		M • C America & S America • 500 kW W/Su • S America • 500 kW
		Tu/Th/Sa • C America & S America • 500 kW M-Sa • S America • 500 kW
		W/F/Su • C America & S America • 500 kW Su • S America • 500 kW
15290	**CHINA (TAIWAN)** CBS	SE Asia
		E Asia • NEWS NETWORK • ALT. FREQ. TO 15105 kHz
	IRAN VO THE ISLAMIC REP, Sirjan	S • W Asia & C Asia • 500 kW
	JORDAN RADIO JORDAN, Qasr el Kharana	• N Africa & C America • 500 kW
	RUSSIA (con'd) VOICE OF RUSSIA, Samara	S • S Europe • 200 kW

0 1 2 3 4 5 6 7 8 9 10 11 12 13 14 15 16 17 18 19 20 21 22 23 24

ENGLISH ▪▪ ARABIC ⋙ CHINESE ▫▫▫ FRENCH ▬ GERMAN ▬ RUSSIAN ═ SPANISH ▬ OTHER ▬

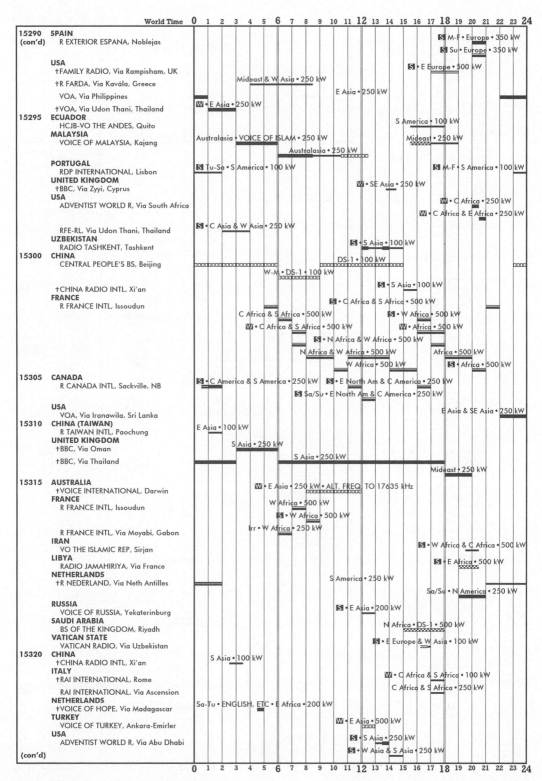

World Time	0 1 2 3 4 5 6 7 8 9 10 11 12 13 14 15 16 17 18 19 20 21 22 23 24
15290 **SPAIN**	
(con'd) R EXTERIOR ESPANA, Noblejas	S M-F • Europe • 350 kW
	S Su • Europe • 350 kW
USA	
†FAMILY RADIO, Via Rampisham, UK	S • E Europe • 500 kW
†R FARDA, Via Kavála, Greece	Mideast & W Asia • 250 kW
VOA, Via Philippines	E Asia • 250 kW
†VOA, Via Udon Thani, Thailand	W • E Asia • 250 kW
15295 **ECUADOR**	
HCJB-VO THE ANDES, Quito	S America • 100 kW
MALAYSIA	
VOICE OF MALAYSIA, Kajang	Australasia • VOICE OF ISLAM • 250 kW — Mideast • 250 kW
	Australasia • 250 kW
PORTUGAL	
RDP INTERNATIONAL, Lisbon	S Tu-Sa • S America • 100 kW — S M-F • S America • 100 kW
UNITED KINGDOM	
†BBC, Via Zyyi, Cyprus	W • SE Asia • 250 kW
USA	
ADVENTIST WORLD R, Via South Africa	W • C Africa • 250 kW
	W • C Africa & E Africa • 250 kW
RFE-RL, Via Udon Thani, Thailand	S • C Asia & W Asia • 250 kW
UZBEKISTAN	
RADIO TASHKENT, Tashkent	S • S Asia • 100 kW
15300 **CHINA**	
CENTRAL PEOPLE'S BS, Beijing	DS-1 • 100 kW
	W-M • DS-1 • 100 kW
†CHINA RADIO INTL, Xi'an	S • S Asia • 100 kW
FRANCE	
R FRANCE INTL, Issoudun	S • C Africa & S Africa • 500 kW
	C Africa & S Africa • 500 kW — S • W Africa • 500 kW
	W • C Africa & S Africa • 500 kW — W • Africa • 500 kW
	S • N Africa & W Africa • 500 kW
	N Africa & W Africa • 500 kW — Africa • 500 kW
	W Africa • 500 kW — S • Africa • 500 kW
15305 **CANADA**	
R CANADA INTL, Sackville, NB	S • C America & S America • 250 kW — S • E North Am & C America • 250 kW
	S Sa/Su • E North Am & C America • 250 kW
USA	
VOA, Via Iranawila, Sri Lanka	E Asia & SE Asia • 250 kW
15310 **CHINA (TAIWAN)**	
R TAIWAN INTL, Paochung	E Asia • 100 kW
UNITED KINGDOM	
†BBC, Via Oman	S Asia • 250 kW
†BBC, Via Thailand	S Asia • 250 kW
	Mideast • 250 kW
15315 **AUSTRALIA**	
†VOICE INTERNATIONAL, Darwin	W • E Asia • 250 kW • ALT. FREQ. TO 17635 kHz
FRANCE	
R FRANCE INTL, Issoudun	W Africa • 500 kW
	S • W Africa • 500 kW
R FRANCE INTL, Via Moyabi, Gabon	Irr • W Africa • 250 kW
IRAN	
VO THE ISLAMIC REP, Sirjan	S • W Africa & C Africa • 500 kW
LIBYA	
RADIO JAMAHIRIYA, Via France	S • E Africa • 500 kW
NETHERLANDS	
†R NEDERLAND, Via Neth Antilles	S America • 250 kW
	Sa/Su • N America • 250 kW
RUSSIA	
VOICE OF RUSSIA, Yekaterinburg	S • E Asia • 200 kW
SAUDI ARABIA	
BS OF THE KINGDOM, Riyadh	N Africa • DS-1 • 500 kW
VATICAN STATE	
VATICAN RADIO, Via Uzbekistan	S • E Europe & W Asia • 100 kW
15320 **CHINA**	
†CHINA RADIO INTL, Xi'an	S Asia • 100 kW
ITALY	
†RAI INTERNATIONAL, Rome	W • C Africa & S Africa • 100 kW
RAI INTERNATIONAL, Via Ascension	C Africa & S Africa • 250 kW
NETHERLANDS	
†VOICE OF HOPE, Via Madagascar	Sa-Tu • ENGLISH, ETC • E Africa • 200 kW
TURKEY	
VOICE OF TURKEY, Ankara-Emirler	W • E Asia • 500 kW
USA	
ADVENTIST WORLD R, Via Abu Dhabi	S • S Asia • 250 kW
	S • W Asia & S Asia • 250 kW
(con'd)	

SEASONAL S OR W　　1-HR TIMESHIFT MIDYEAR ⇦ OR ⇨　　JAMMING / OR ∧　　EARLIEST HEARD ◁　　LATEST HEARD ▷　　NEW FOR 2004 †

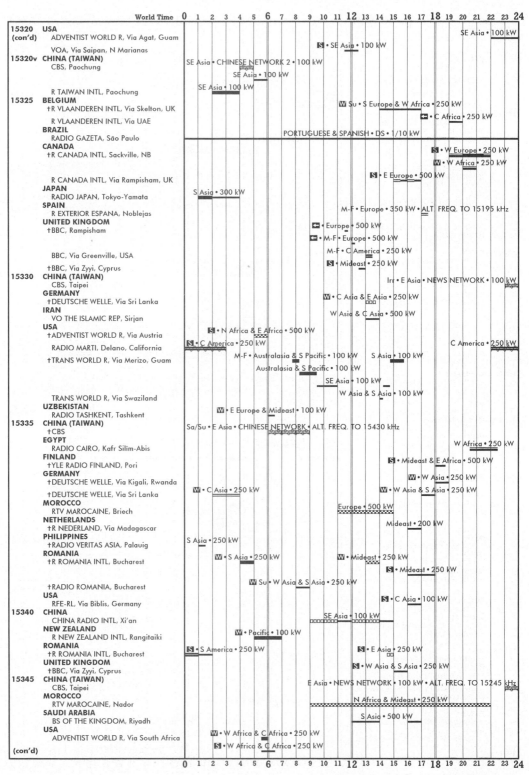

World Time	0 1 2 3 4 5 6 7 8 9 10 11 12 13 14 15 16 17 18 19 20 21 22 23 24
15320 USA (con'd)	
ADVENTIST WORLD R, Via Agat, Guam	SE Asia • 100 kW
VOA, Via Saipan, N Marianas	S • SE Asia • 100 kW
15320v CHINA (TAIWAN) CBS, Paochung	SE Asia • CHINESE NETWORK 2 • 100 kW / SE Asia • 100 kW
R TAIWAN INTL, Paochung	SE Asia • 100 kW
15325 BELGIUM †R VLAANDEREN INTL, Via Skelton, UK	W Su • S Europe & W Africa • 250 kW
R VLAANDEREN INTL, Via UAE	• C Africa • 250 kW
BRAZIL RADIO GAZETA, São Paulo	PORTUGUESE & SPANISH • DS • 1/10 kW
CANADA †R CANADA INTL, Sackville, NB	S • W Europe • 250 kW / W • W Africa • 250 kW
R CANADA INTL, Via Rampisham, UK	S • E Europe • 500 kW
JAPAN RADIO JAPAN, Tokyo-Yamata	S Asia • 300 kW
SPAIN R EXTERIOR ESPANA, Noblejas	M-F • Europe • 350 kW • ALT. FREQ. TO 15195 kHz
UNITED KINGDOM †BBC, Rampisham	• Europe • 500 kW
	• M-F • Europe • 500 kW
BBC, Via Greenville, USA	M-F • C America • 250 kW
†BBC, Via Zyyi, Cyprus	S • Mideast • 250 kW
15330 CHINA (TAIWAN) CBS, Taipei	Irr • E Asia • NEWS NETWORK • 100 kW
GERMANY †DEUTSCHE WELLE, Via Sri Lanka	W • C Asia & E Asia • 250 kW
IRAN VO THE ISLAMIC REP, Sirjan	W Asia & C Asia • 500 kW
USA †ADVENTIST WORLD R, Via Austria	S • N Africa & E Africa • 500 kW
RADIO MARTI, Delano, California	S • C America • 250 kW / C America • 250 kW
†TRANS WORLD R, Via Merizo, Guam	M-F • Australasia & S Pacific • 100 kW / S Asia • 100 kW
	Australasia & S Pacific • 100 kW
	SE Asia • 100 kW
	W Asia & S Asia • 100 kW
TRANS WORLD R, Via Swaziland	
UZBEKISTAN RADIO TASHKENT, Tashkent	W • E Europe & Mideast • 100 kW
15335 CHINA (TAIWAN) †CBS	Sa/Su • E Asia • CHINESE NETWORK • ALT. FREQ. TO 15430 kHz
EGYPT RADIO CAIRO, Kafr Silim-Abis	W Africa • 250 kW
FINLAND †YLE RADIO FINLAND, Pori	S • Mideast & E Africa • 500 kW
GERMANY †DEUTSCHE WELLE, Via Kigali, Rwanda	W • W Asia • 250 kW
†DEUTSCHE WELLE, Via Sri Lanka	W • C Asia • 250 kW / W • W Asia & S Asia • 250 kW
MOROCCO RTV MAROCAINE, Briech	Europe • 500 kW
NETHERLANDS †R NEDERLAND, Via Madagascar	Mideast • 200 kW
PHILIPPINES †RADIO VERITAS ASIA, Palauig	S Asia • 250 kW
ROMANIA †R ROMANIA INTL, Bucharest	W • S Asia • 250 kW / W • Mideast • 250 kW
	S • Mideast • 250 kW
†RADIO ROMANIA, Bucharest	W Su • W Asia & S Asia • 250 kW
USA RFE-RL, Via Biblis, Germany	S • C Asia • 100 kW
15340 CHINA CHINA RADIO INTL, Xi'an	SE Asia • 100 kW
NEW ZEALAND R NEW ZEALAND INTL, Rangitaiki	W • Pacific • 100 kW
ROMANIA †R ROMANIA INTL, Bucharest	S • S America • 250 kW / S • E Asia • 250 kW
UNITED KINGDOM †BBC, Via Zyyi, Cyprus	S • W Asia & S Asia • 250 kW
15345 CHINA (TAIWAN) CBS, Taipei	E Asia • NEWS NETWORK • 100 kW • ALT. FREQ. TO 15245 kHz
MOROCCO RTV MAROCAINE, Nador	N Africa & Mideast • 250 kW
SAUDI ARABIA BS OF THE KINGDOM, Riyadh	S Asia • 500 kW
USA ADVENTIST WORLD R, Via South Africa	W • W Africa & C Africa • 250 kW / S • W Africa & C Africa • 250 kW
(con'd)	

| World Time | 0 1 2 3 4 5 6 7 8 9 10 11 12 13 14 15 16 17 18 19 20 21 22 23 24 |

ENGLISH ▬ ARABIC ⋙ CHINESE ☐☐☐ FRENCH ▬ GERMAN ▬ RUSSIAN ═ SPANISH ▬ OTHER ▬

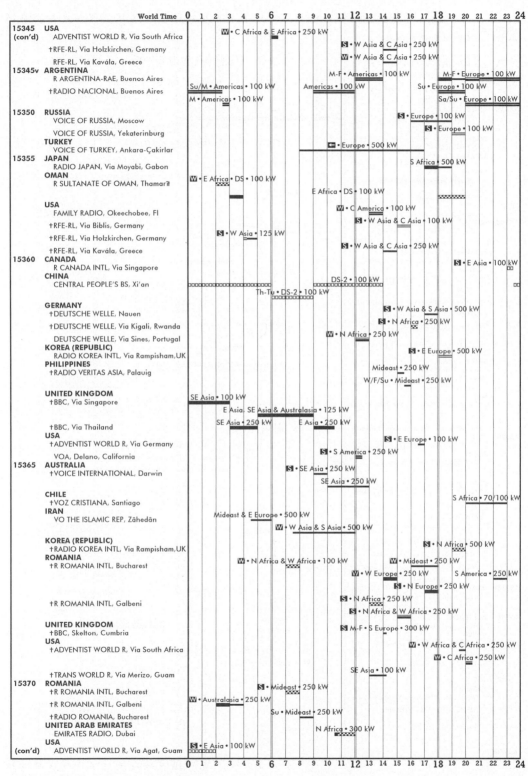

World Time

15345	**USA**
(con'd)	ADVENTIST WORLD R, Via South Africa — W • C Africa & E Africa • 250 kW
	†RFE-RL, Via Holzkirchen, Germany — S • W Asia & C Asia • 250 kW
	RFE-RL, Via Kavála, Greece — W • W Asia & C Asia • 250 kW
15345v	**ARGENTINA**
	R ARGENTINA-RAE, Buenos Aires — M-F • Americas • 100 kW / M-F • Europe • 100 kW
	†RADIO NACIONAL, Buenos Aires — Su/M • Americas • 100 kW / Americas • 100 kW / Su • Europe • 100 kW / M • Americas • 100 kW / Sa/Su • Europe • 100 kW
15350	**RUSSIA**
	VOICE OF RUSSIA, Moscow — S • Europe • 100 kW
	VOICE OF RUSSIA, Yekaterinburg — S • Europe • 100 kW
	TURKEY
	VOICE OF TURKEY, Ankara-Çakirlar — ⮂ • Europe • 500 kW
15355	**JAPAN**
	RADIO JAPAN, Via Moyabi, Gabon — S Africa • 500 kW
	OMAN
	R SULTANATE OF OMAN, Thamarīt — W • E Africa • DS • 100 kW / E Africa • DS • 100 kW
	USA
	FAMILY RADIO, Okeechobee, Fl — W • C America • 100 kW
	†RFE-RL, Via Biblis, Germany — S • W Asia & C Asia • 100 kW
	†RFE-RL, Via Holzkirchen, Germany — S • W Asia • 125 kW
	†RFE-RL, Via Kavála, Greece — S • W Asia & C Asia • 250 kW
15360	**CANADA**
	R CANADA INTL, Via Singapore — S • E Asia • 100 kW
	CHINA
	CENTRAL PEOPLE'S BS, Xi'an — DS-2 • 100 kW / Th-Tu • DS-2 • 100 kW
	GERMANY
	†DEUTSCHE WELLE, Nauen — S • W Asia & S Asia • 500 kW
	†DEUTSCHE WELLE, Via Kigali, Rwanda — S • N Africa • 250 kW
	DEUTSCHE WELLE, Via Sines, Portugal — W • N Africa • 250 kW
	KOREA (REPUBLIC)
	RADIO KOREA INTL, Via Rampisham, UK — S • E Europe • 500 kW
	PHILIPPINES
	†RADIO VERITAS ASIA, Palauig — Mideast • 250 kW / W/F/Su • Mideast • 250 kW
	UNITED KINGDOM
	†BBC, Via Singapore — SE Asia • 100 kW / E Asia, SE Asia & Australasia • 125 kW / SE Asia • 250 kW / E Asia • 250 kW
	†BBC, Via Thailand
	USA
	†ADVENTIST WORLD R, Via Germany — S • E Europe • 100 kW
	VOA, Delano, California — S • S America • 250 kW
15365	**AUSTRALIA**
	†VOICE INTERNATIONAL, Darwin — S • SE Asia • 250 kW / SE Asia • 250 kW
	CHILE
	†VOZ CRISTIANA, Santiago — S Africa • 70/100 kW
	IRAN
	VO THE ISLAMIC REP, Zāhedān — Mideast & E Europe • 500 kW / W • W Asia & S Asia • 500 kW
	KOREA (REPUBLIC)
	†RADIO KOREA INTL, Via Rampisham, UK — S • N Africa • 500 kW
	ROMANIA
	†R ROMANIA INTL, Bucharest — W • N Africa & W Africa • 100 kW / W • Mideast • 250 kW / W • W Europe • 250 kW / S America • 250 kW / S • N Europe • 250 kW
	†R ROMANIA INTL, Galbeni — S • N Africa • 250 kW / S • N Africa & W Africa • 250 kW
	UNITED KINGDOM
	†BBC, Skelton, Cumbria — S • M-F • S Europe • 300 kW
	USA
	†ADVENTIST WORLD R, Via South Africa — W • W Africa & C Africa • 250 kW / W • C Africa • 250 kW
	†TRANS WORLD R, Via Merizo, Guam — SE Asia • 100 kW
15370	**ROMANIA**
	†R ROMANIA INTL, Bucharest — S • Mideast • 250 kW
	†R ROMANIA INTL, Galbeni — W • Australasia • 250 kW
	†RADIO ROMANIA, Bucharest — Su • Mideast • 250 kW
	UNITED ARAB EMIRATES
	EMIRATES RADIO, Dubai — N Africa • 300 kW
	USA
(con'd)	ADVENTIST WORLD R, Via Agat, Guam — S • E Asia • 100 kW

0 1 2 3 4 5 6 7 8 9 10 11 12 13 14 15 16 17 18 19 20 21 22 23 24

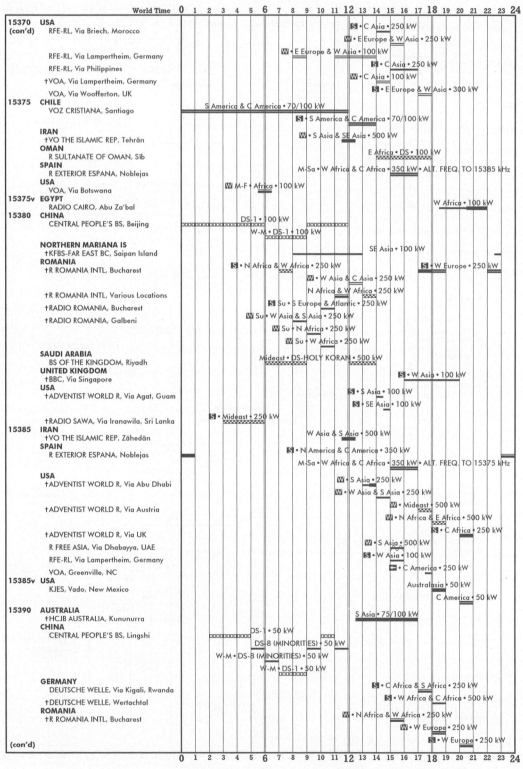

	World Time		
15370	**USA**		
(con'd)	RFE-RL, Via Briech, Morocco		S • C Asia • 250 kW
			W • E Europe & W Asia • 250 kW
	RFE-RL, Via Lampertheim, Germany		W • E Europe & W Asia • 100 kW
	RFE-RL, Via Philippines		S • C Asia • 250 kW
	†VOA, Via Lampertheim, Germany		W • C Asia • 100 kW
	VOA, Via Woofferton, UK		S • E Europe & W Asia • 300 kW
15375	**CHILE**		
	VOZ CRISTIANA, Santiago	S America & C America • 70/100 kW	
			S • S America & C America • 70/100 kW
	IRAN		
	†VO THE ISLAMIC REP, Tehrān		W • S Asia & SE Asia • 500 kW
	OMAN		
	R SULTANATE OF OMAN, Sīb		E Africa • DS • 100 kW
	SPAIN		
	R EXTERIOR ESPANA, Noblejas		M-Sa • W Africa & C Africa • 350 kW • ALT. FREQ. TO 15385 kHz
	USA		
	VOA, Via Botswana	W • M-F • Africa • 100 kW	
15375v	**EGYPT**		
	RADIO CAIRO, Abu Za'bal		W Africa • 100 kW
15380	**CHINA**		
	CENTRAL PEOPLE'S BS, Beijing	DS-1 • 100 kW	
		W-M • DS-1 • 100 kW	
	NORTHERN MARIANA IS		
	†KFBS-FAR EAST BC, Saipan Island		SE Asia • 100 kW
	ROMANIA		
	†R ROMANIA INTL, Bucharest	S • N Africa & W Africa • 250 kW	
			S • W Europe • 250 kW
		W • W Asia & C Asia • 250 kW	
	†R ROMANIA INTL, Various Locations	N Africa & W Africa • 250 kW	
		S • Su • S Europe & Atlantic • 250 kW	
	†RADIO ROMANIA, Bucharest	W • Su • W Asia & S Asia • 250 kW	
	†RADIO ROMANIA, Galbeni	W • Su • N Africa • 250 kW	
		W • Su • W Africa • 250 kW	
	SAUDI ARABIA		
	BS OF THE KINGDOM, Riyadh	Mideast • DS-HOLY KORAN • 500 kW	
	UNITED KINGDOM		
	†BBC, Via Singapore		S • W Asia • 100 kW
	USA		
	†ADVENTIST WORLD R, Via Agat, Guam		S • S Asia • 100 kW
			S • SE Asia • 100 kW
	†RADIO SAWA, Via Iranawila, Sri Lanka	S • Mideast • 250 kW	
15385	**IRAN**		
	†VO THE ISLAMIC REP, Zāhedān	W Asia & S Asia • 500 kW	
	SPAIN		
	R EXTERIOR ESPANA, Noblejas	S • N America & C America • 350 kW	
		M-Sa • W Africa & C Africa • 350 kW • ALT. FREQ. TO 15375 kHz	
	USA		
	†ADVENTIST WORLD R, Via Abu Dhabi	W • S Asia • 250 kW	
		W • W Asia & S Asia • 250 kW	
	†ADVENTIST WORLD R, Via Austria		W • Mideast • 500 kW
			W • N Africa & E Africa • 500 kW
			S • C Africa • 250 kW
	†ADVENTIST WORLD R, Via UK		S • S Asia • 500 kW
	R FREE ASIA, Via Dhabayya, UAE		S • W Asia • 100 kW
	RFE-RL, Via Lampertheim, Germany		
	VOA, Greenville, NC		← • C America • 250 kW
15385v	**USA**		
	KJES, Vado, New Mexico		Australasia • 50 kW
			C America • 50 kW
15390	**AUSTRALIA**		
	†HCJB AUSTRALIA, Kununurra		S Asia • 75/100 kW
	CHINA		
	CENTRAL PEOPLE'S BS, Lingshi	DS-1 • 50 kW	
		DS-8 (MINORITIES) • 50 kW	
		W-M • DS-8 (MINORITIES) • 50 kW	
		W-M • DS-1 • 50 kW	
	GERMANY		
	DEUTSCHE WELLE, Via Kigali, Rwanda		S • C Africa & S Africa • 250 kW
			S • W Africa & C Africa • 500 kW
	†DEUTSCHE WELLE, Wertachtal		
	ROMANIA		
	†R ROMANIA INTL, Bucharest		W • N Africa & W Africa • 250 kW
			W • W Europe • 250 kW
			S • W Europe • 250 kW
(con'd)			

ENGLISH ▬   ARABIC ▨   CHINESE ▫▫▫   FRENCH ▬   GERMAN ▬   RUSSIAN ══   SPANISH ▬   OTHER ▬

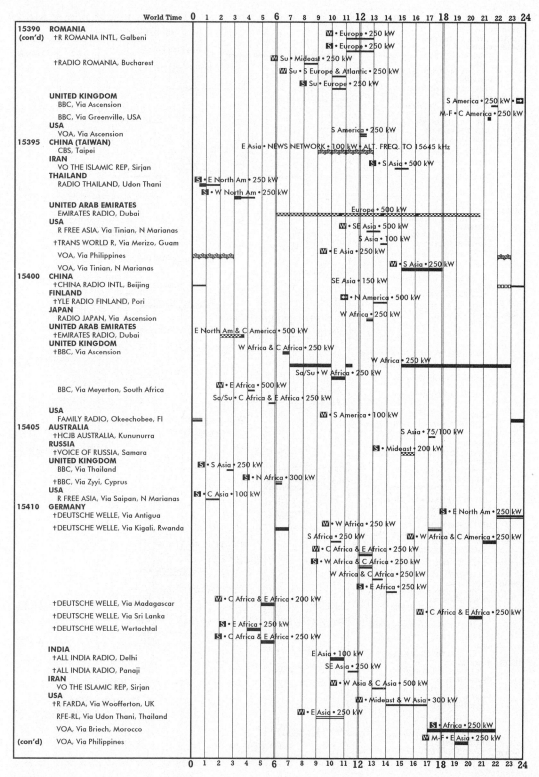

| | World Time | 0 | 1 | 2 | 3 | 4 | 5 | 6 | 7 | 8 | 9 | 10 | 11 | 12 | 13 | 14 | 15 | 16 | 17 | 18 | 19 | 20 | 21 | 22 | 23 | 24 |

15390 (con'd) ROMANIA
  †R ROMANIA INTL, Galbeni — ⓦ • Europe • 250 kW / ⓢ • Europe • 250 kW
  †RADIO ROMANIA, Bucharest — ⓦ Su • Mideast • 250 kW / ⓦ Su • S Europe & Atlantic • 250 kW / ⓢ Su • Europe • 250 kW

UNITED KINGDOM
  BBC, Via Ascension — S America • 250 kW •
  BBC, Via Greenville, USA — M-F • C America • 250 kW

USA
  VOA, Via Ascension — S America • 250 kW

15395 CHINA (TAIWAN)
  CBS, Taipei — E Asia • NEWS NETWORK • 100 kW • ALT. FREQ. TO 15645 kHz

IRAN
  VO THE ISLAMIC REP, Sirjan — ⓢ • S Asia • 500 kW

THAILAND
  RADIO THAILAND, Udon Thani — ⓢ • E North Am • 250 kW / ⓢ • W North Am • 250 kW

UNITED ARAB EMIRATES
  EMIRATES RADIO, Dubai — Europe • 500 kW

USA
  R FREE ASIA, Via Tinian, N Marianas — ⓦ • SE Asia • 500 kW
  †TRANS WORLD R, Via Merizo, Guam — S Asia • 100 kW
  VOA, Via Philippines — ⓦ • E Asia • 250 kW
  VOA, Via Tinian, N Marianas — ⓦ • S Asia • 250 kW

15400 CHINA
  †CHINA RADIO INTL, Beijing — SE Asia • 150 kW

FINLAND
  †YLE RADIO FINLAND, Pori — ⇨ • N America • 500 kW

JAPAN
  RADIO JAPAN, Via Ascension — W Africa • 250 kW

UNITED ARAB EMIRATES
  †EMIRATES RADIO, Dubai — E North Am & C America • 500 kW

UNITED KINGDOM
  †BBC, Via Ascension — W Africa & C Africa • 250 kW / W Africa • 250 kW / Sa/Su • W Africa • 250 kW
  BBC, Via Meyerton, South Africa — ⓦ • E Africa • 500 kW / Sa/Su • C Africa & E Africa • 250 kW

USA
  FAMILY RADIO, Okeechobee, Fl — ⓦ • S America • 100 kW

15405 AUSTRALIA
  †HCJB AUSTRALIA, Kununurra — S Asia • 75/100 kW

RUSSIA
  †VOICE OF RUSSIA, Samara — ⓢ • Mideast • 200 kW

UNITED KINGDOM
  BBC, Via Thailand — ⓢ • S Asia • 250 kW
  †BBC, Via Zyyi, Cyprus — ⓢ • N Africa • 300 kW

USA
  R FREE ASIA, Via Saipan, N Marianas — ⓢ • C Asia • 100 kW

15410 GERMANY
  †DEUTSCHE WELLE, Via Antigua — ⓢ • E North Am • 250 kW
  †DEUTSCHE WELLE, Via Kigali, Rwanda — ⓦ • W Africa • 250 kW / S Africa • 250 kW / ⓦ • W Africa & C America • 250 kW / ⓦ • C Africa & E Africa • 250 kW / ⓢ • W Africa & C Africa • 250 kW / W Africa & C Africa • 250 kW / ⓢ • E Africa • 250 kW
  †DEUTSCHE WELLE, Via Madagascar — ⓦ • C Africa & E Africa • 200 kW / ⓦ • C Africa & E Africa • 250 kW
  †DEUTSCHE WELLE, Via Sri Lanka — ⓢ • E Africa • 250 kW
  †DEUTSCHE WELLE, Wertachtal — ⓢ • C Africa & E Africa • 250 kW

INDIA
  †ALL INDIA RADIO, Delhi — E Asia • 100 kW
  †ALL INDIA RADIO, Panaji — SE Asia • 250 kW

IRAN
  VO THE ISLAMIC REP, Sirjan — ⓦ • W Asia & C Asia • 500 kW

USA
  †R FARDA, Via Woofferton, UK — ⓦ • Mideast & W Asia • 300 kW
  RFE-RL, Via Udon Thani, Thailand — ⓦ • E Asia • 250 kW
  VOA, Via Briech, Morocco — ⓢ • Africa • 250 kW

(con'd) VOA, Via Philippines — ⓦ M-F • E Asia • 250 kW

| | | 0 | 1 | 2 | 3 | 4 | 5 | 6 | 7 | 8 | 9 | 10 | 11 | 12 | 13 | 14 | 15 | 16 | 17 | 18 | 19 | 20 | 21 | 22 | 23 | 24 |

SEASONAL ⓢ OR ⓦ   1-HR TIMESHIFT MIDYEAR ⇦ OR ⇨   JAMMING / OR ⋀   EARLIEST HEARD ◁   LATEST HEARD ▷   NEW FOR 2004 †

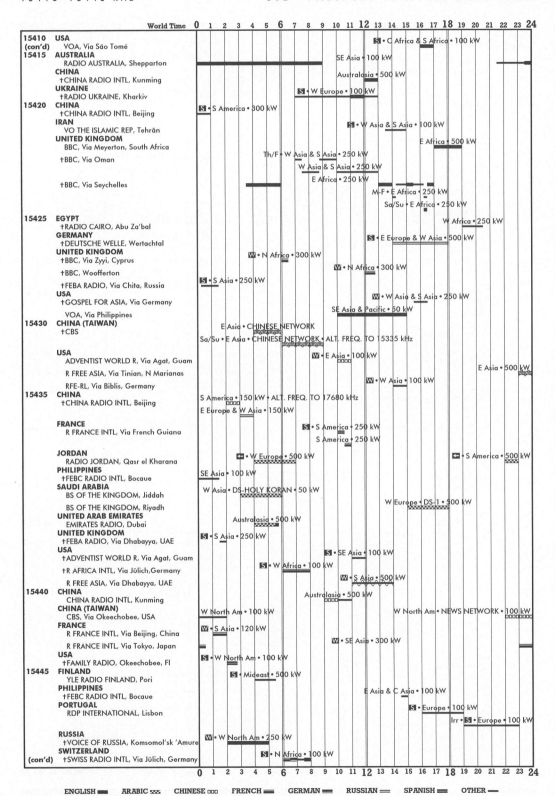

World Time 0 1 2 3 4 5 6 7 8 9 10 11 12 13 14 15 16 17 18 19 20 21 22 23 24

15410 (con'd)	USA	VOA, Via São Tomé — C Africa & S Africa • 100 kW
15415	AUSTRALIA	RADIO AUSTRALIA, Shepparton — SE Asia • 100 kW
	CHINA	†CHINA RADIO INTL, Kunming — Australasia • 500 kW
	UKRAINE	†RADIO UKRAINE, Kharkiv — S • W Europe • 100 kW
15420	CHINA	†CHINA RADIO INTL, Beijing — S • S America • 300 kW
	IRAN	VO THE ISLAMIC REP, Tehrān — S • W Asia & S Asia • 100 kW
	UNITED KINGDOM	BBC, Via Meyerton, South Africa — E Africa • 500 kW
		†BBC, Via Oman — Th/F • W Asia & S Asia • 250 kW / W Asia & S Asia • 250 kW
		†BBC, Via Seychelles — E Africa • 250 kW / M-F • E Africa • 250 kW / Sa/Su • E Africa • 250 kW
15425	EGYPT	†RADIO CAIRO, Abu Za'bal — W Africa • 250 kW
	GERMANY	†DEUTSCHE WELLE, Wertachtal — S • E Europe & W Asia • 500 kW
	UNITED KINGDOM	†BBC, Via Zyyi, Cyprus — W • N Africa • 300 kW
		†BBC, Woofferton — W • N Africa • 300 kW
		†FEBA RADIO, Via Chita, Russia — S • S Asia • 250 kW
	USA	†GOSPEL FOR ASIA, Via Germany — W • W Asia & S Asia • 250 kW
		VOA, Via Philippines — SE Asia & Pacific • 50 kW
15430	CHINA (TAIWAN)	†CBS — E Asia • CHINESE NETWORK / Sa/Su • E Asia • CHINESE NETWORK • ALT. FREQ. TO 15335 kHz
	USA	ADVENTIST WORLD R, Via Agat, Guam — W • E Asia • 100 kW
		R FREE ASIA, Via Tinian, N Marianas — E Asia • 500 kW
		RFE-RL, Via Biblis, Germany — W • W Asia • 100 kW
15435	CHINA	†CHINA RADIO INTL, Beijing — S America • 150 kW • ALT. FREQ. TO 17680 kHz / E Europe & W Asia • 150 kW
	FRANCE	R FRANCE INTL, Via French Guiana — S • S America • 250 kW / S America • 250 kW
	JORDAN	RADIO JORDAN, Qasr el Kharana — W Europe • 500 kW / S America • 500 kW
	PHILIPPINES	†FEBC RADIO INTL, Bocaue — SE Asia • 100 kW
	SAUDI ARABIA	BS OF THE KINGDOM, Jiddah — W Asia • DS-HOLY KORAN • 50 kW
		BS OF THE KINGDOM, Riyadh — W Europe • DS-1 • 500 kW
	UNITED ARAB EMIRATES	EMIRATES RADIO, Dubai — Australasia • 500 kW
	UNITED KINGDOM	†FEBA RADIO, Via Dhabayya, UAE — S • S Asia • 250 kW
	USA	†ADVENTIST WORLD R, Via Agat, Guam — S • SE Asia • 100 kW
		†R AFRICA INTL, Via Jülich, Germany — S • W Africa • 100 kW
		R FREE ASIA, Via Dhabayya, UAE — W • S Asia • 500 kW
15440	CHINA	CHINA RADIO INTL, Kunming — Australasia • 500 kW
	CHINA (TAIWAN)	CBS, Via Okeechobee, USA — W North Am • 100 kW / W North Am • NEWS NETWORK • 100 kW
	FRANCE	R FRANCE INTL, Via Beijing, China — W • S Asia • 120 kW
		R FRANCE INTL, Via Tokyo, Japan — W • SE Asia • 300 kW
	USA	†FAMILY RADIO, Okeechobee, Fl — S • W North Am • 100 kW
15445	FINLAND	YLE RADIO FINLAND, Pori — S • Mideast • 500 kW
	PHILIPPINES	†FEBC RADIO INTL, Bocaue — E Asia & C Asia • 100 kW
	PORTUGAL	RDP INTERNATIONAL, Lisbon — S • Europe • 100 kW / Irr • S • Europe • 100 kW
	RUSSIA	†VOICE OF RUSSIA, Komsomol'sk 'Amure — W • W North Am • 250 kW
	SWITZERLAND	†SWISS RADIO INTL, Via Jülich, Germany — S • N Africa • 100 kW
(con'd)		

0 1 2 3 4 5 6 7 8 9 10 11 12 13 14 15 16 17 18 19 20 21 22 23 24

ENGLISH ▬ ARABIC ⊠ CHINESE ▭▭▭ FRENCH ▬▬ GERMAN ▬▬ RUSSIAN ══ SPANISH ▬▬ OTHER ▬

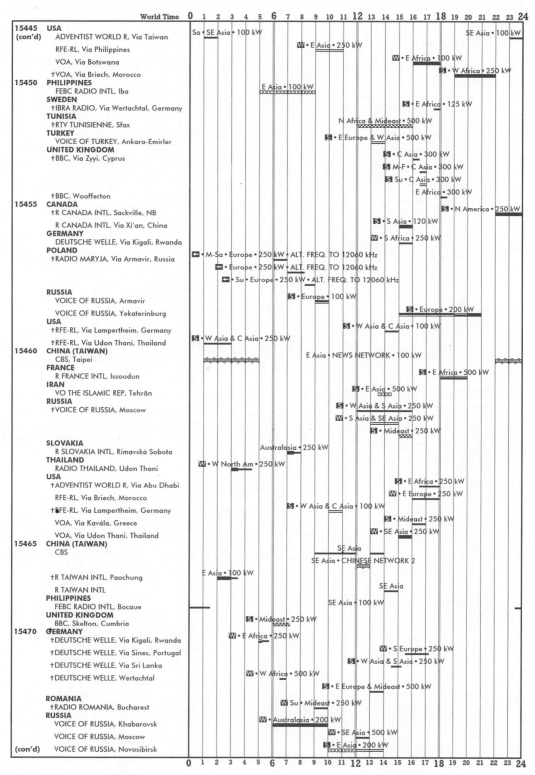

	World Time	0 1 2 3 4 5 6 7 8 9 10 11 12 13 14 15 16 17 18 19 20 21 22 23 24
15445 (con'd)	**USA**	
	ADVENTIST WORLD R, Via Taiwan	Sa • SE Asia • 100 kW SE Asia • 100 kW
	RFE-RL, Via Philippines	W • E Asia • 250 kW
	VOA, Via Botswana	W • E Africa • 100 kW
	†VOA, Via Briech, Morocco	S • W Africa • 250 kW
15450	**PHILIPPINES**	
	FEBC RADIO INTL, Iba	E Asia • 100 kW
	SWEDEN	
	†IBRA RADIO, Via Wertachtal, Germany	S • E Africa • 125 kW
	TUNISIA	
	†RTV TUNISIENNE, Sfax	N Africa & Mideast • 500 kW
	TURKEY	
	VOICE OF TURKEY, Ankara-Emirler	S • E Europe & W Asia • 500 kW
	UNITED KINGDOM	
	†BBC, Via Zyyi, Cyprus	S • C Asia • 300 kW
		S • M-F • C Asia • 300 kW
		S • Su • C Asia • 300 kW
		E Africa • 300 kW
	†BBC, Woofferton	
15455	**CANADA**	
	†R CANADA INTL, Sackville, NB	S • N America • 250 kW
	R CANADA INTL, Via Xi'an, China	S • S Asia • 120 kW
	GERMANY	
	DEUTSCHE WELLE, Via Kigali, Rwanda	W • S Africa • 250 kW
	POLAND	
	†RADIO MARYJA, Via Armavir, Russia	M-Sa • Europe • 250 kW • ALT. FREQ. TO 12060 kHz
		Europe • 250 kW • ALT. FREQ. TO 12060 kHz
		Su • Europe • 250 kW • ALT. FREQ. TO 12060 kHz
	RUSSIA	
	VOICE OF RUSSIA, Armavir	S • Europe • 100 kW
	VOICE OF RUSSIA, Yekaterinburg	S • Europe • 200 kW
	USA	
	†RFE-RL, Via Lampertheim, Germany	S • W Asia & C Asia • 100 kW
	†RFE-RL, Via Udon Thani, Thailand	S • W Asia & C Asia • 250 kW
15460	**CHINA (TAIWAN)**	
	CBS, Taipei	E Asia • NEWS NETWORK • 100 kW
	FRANCE	
	R FRANCE INTL, Issoudun	S • E Africa • 500 kW
	IRAN	
	VO THE ISLAMIC REP, Tehrān	S • E Asia • 500 kW
	RUSSIA	
	†VOICE OF RUSSIA, Moscow	S • W Asia & S Asia • 250 kW
		W • S Asia & SE Asia • 250 kW
		S • Mideast • 250 kW
	SLOVAKIA	
	R SLOVAKIA INTL, Rimavská Sobota	Australasia • 250 kW
	THAILAND	
	RADIO THAILAND, Udon Thani	W • W North Am • 250 kW
	USA	
	†ADVENTIST WORLD R, Via Abu Dhabi	S • E Africa • 250 kW
	RFE-RL, Via Briech, Morocco	W • E Europe • 250 kW
	†RFE-RL, Via Lampertheim, Germany	S • W Asia & C Asia • 100 kW
	VOA, Via Kavála, Greece	S • Mideast • 250 kW
	VOA, Via Udon Thani, Thailand	W • SE Asia • 250 kW
15465	**CHINA (TAIWAN)**	
	CBS	SE Asia
		SE Asia • CHINESE NETWORK 2
	†R TAIWAN INTL, Paochung	E Asia • 100 kW
	R TAIWAN INTL	SE Asia
	PHILIPPINES	
	FEBC RADIO INTL, Bocaue	SE Asia • 100 kW
	UNITED KINGDOM	
	BBC, Skelton, Cumbria	
15470	**GERMANY**	
	†DEUTSCHE WELLE, Via Kigali, Rwanda	S • Mideast • 250 kW
		W • E Africa • 250 kW
	†DEUTSCHE WELLE, Via Sines, Portugal	W • S Europe • 250 kW
	†DEUTSCHE WELLE, Via Sri Lanka	S • W Asia & S Asia • 250 kW
	†DEUTSCHE WELLE, Wertachtal	W • W Africa • 500 kW
		S • E Europe & Mideast • 500 kW
	ROMANIA	
	†RADIO ROMANIA, Bucharest	W Su • Mideast • 250 kW
	RUSSIA	
	VOICE OF RUSSIA, Khabarovsk	W • Australasia • 200 kW
	VOICE OF RUSSIA, Moscow	S • SE Asia • 500 kW
(con'd)	VOICE OF RUSSIA, Novosibirsk	S • E Asia • 200 kW

0 1 2 3 4 5 6 7 8 9 10 11 12 13 14 15 16 17 18 19 20 21 22 23 24

SEASONAL S OR W   1-HR TIMESHIFT MIDYEAR ◱ OR ◲   JAMMING / OR /\   EARLIEST HEARD ◁   LATEST HEARD ▷   NEW FOR 2004 †

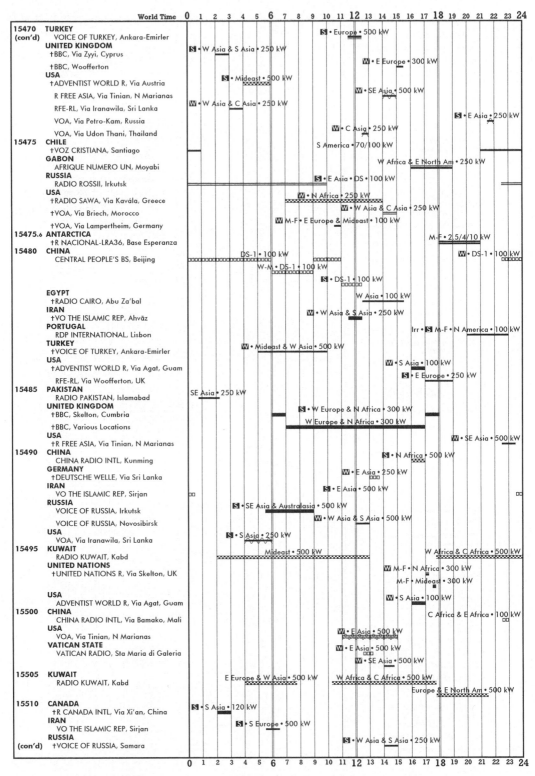

| World Time | 0 | 1 | 2 | 3 | 4 | 5 | 6 | 7 | 8 | 9 | 10 | 11 | 12 | 13 | 14 | 15 | 16 | 17 | 18 | 19 | 20 | 21 | 22 | 23 | 24 |

15470 TURKEY
(con'd) VOICE OF TURKEY, Ankara-Emirler — S • Europe • 500 kW
UNITED KINGDOM
†BBC, Via Zyyi, Cyprus — S • W Asia & S Asia • 250 kW
†BBC, Woofferton — W • E Europe • 300 kW
USA
†ADVENTIST WORLD R, Via Austria — S • Mideast • 500 kW
R FREE ASIA, Via Tinian, N Marianas — W • SE Asia • 500 kW
RFE-RL, Via Iranawila, Sri Lanka — W • W Asia & C Asia • 250 kW
VOA, Via Petro-Kam, Russia — S • E Asia • 250 kW
VOA, Via Udon Thani, Thailand — W • C Asia • 250 kW

15475 CHILE
†VOZ CRISTIANA, Santiago — S America • 70/100 kW
GABON
AFRIQUE NUMERO UN, Moyabi — W Africa & E North Am • 250 kW
RUSSIA
RADIO ROSSII, Irkutsk — S • E Asia • DS • 100 kW
USA
†RADIO SAWA, Via Kavála, Greece — W • N Africa • 250 kW
†VOA, Via Briech, Morocco — W • W Asia & C Asia • 250 kW
†VOA, Via Lampertheim, Germany — W M-F • E Europe & Mideast • 100 kW

15475.6 ANTARCTICA
†R NACIONAL-LRA36, Base Esperanza — M-F • 2,5/4/10 kW

15480 CHINA
CENTRAL PEOPLE'S BS, Beijing — DS-1 • 100 kW   W • DS-1 • 100 kW
W-M • DS-1 • 100 kW
S • DS-1 • 100 kW
EGYPT
†RADIO CAIRO, Abu Za'bal — W Asia • 100 kW
IRAN
†VO THE ISLAMIC REP, Ahvãz — W • W Asia & S Asia • 250 kW
PORTUGAL
RDP INTERNATIONAL, Lisbon — Irr • S M-F • N America • 100 kW
TURKEY
†VOICE OF TURKEY, Ankara-Emirler — W • Mideast & W Asia • 500 kW
USA
†ADVENTIST WORLD R, Via Agat, Guam — W • S Asia • 100 kW
RFE-RL, Via Woofferton, UK — S • E Europe • 250 kW

15485 PAKISTAN
RADIO PAKISTAN, Islamabad — SE Asia • 250 kW
UNITED KINGDOM
†BBC, Skelton, Cumbria — S • W Europe & N Africa • 300 kW
†BBC, Various Locations — W Europe & N Africa • 300 kW
USA
†R FREE ASIA, Via Tinian, N Marianas — W • SE Asia • 500 kW

15490 CHINA
CHINA RADIO INTL, Kunming — S • N Africa • 500 kW
GERMANY
†DEUTSCHE WELLE, Via Sri Lanka — W • E Asia • 250 kW
IRAN
VO THE ISLAMIC REP, Sirjan — S • E Asia • 500 kW
RUSSIA
VOICE OF RUSSIA, Irkutsk — S • SE Asia & Australasia • 500 kW
VOICE OF RUSSIA, Novosibirsk — W • W Asia & S Asia • 500 kW
USA
VOA, Via Iranawila, Sri Lanka — S • S Asia • 250 kW

15495 KUWAIT
RADIO KUWAIT, Kabd — Mideast • 500 kW   W Africa & C Africa • 500 kW
UNITED NATIONS
†UNITED NATIONS R, Via Skelton, UK — W M-F • N Africa • 300 kW
M-F • Mideast • 300 kW
USA
ADVENTIST WORLD R, Via Agat, Guam — W • S Asia • 100 kW

15500 CHINA
CHINA RADIO INTL, Via Bamako, Mali — C Africa & E Africa • 100 kW
USA
VOA, Via Tinian, N Marianas — W • E Asia • 500 kW
VATICAN STATE
VATICAN RADIO, Sta Maria di Galeria — W • E Asia • 500 kW
W • SE Asia • 500 kW

15505 KUWAIT
RADIO KUWAIT, Kabd — E Europe & W Asia • 500 kW   W Africa & C Africa • 500 kW
Europe & E North Am • 500 kW

15510 CANADA
†R CANADA INTL, Via Xi'an, China — S • S Asia • 120 kW
IRAN
VO THE ISLAMIC REP, Sirjan — S • S Europe • 500 kW
RUSSIA
(con'd) †VOICE OF RUSSIA, Samara — S • W Asia & S Asia • 250 kW

| 0 | 1 | 2 | 3 | 4 | 5 | 6 | 7 | 8 | 9 | 10 | 11 | 12 | 13 | 14 | 15 | 16 | 17 | 18 | 19 | 20 | 21 | 22 | 23 | 24 |

ENGLISH ▬   ARABIC ⋙   CHINESE ▫▫▫   FRENCH ▭   GERMAN ▬   RUSSIAN ═   SPANISH ▭   OTHER ▬

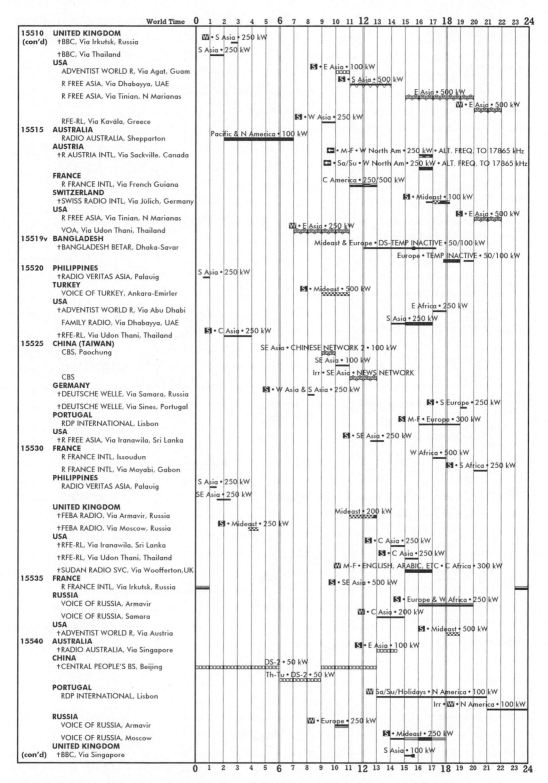

World Time

Freq	Country / Station	Target / Details
15510 (con'd)	**UNITED KINGDOM**	
	†BBC, Via Irkutsk, Russia	W • S Asia • 250 kW
	†BBC, Via Thailand	S Asia • 250 kW
	USA	
	ADVENTIST WORLD R, Via Agat, Guam	S • E Asia • 100 kW
	R FREE ASIA, Via Dhabayya, UAE	S • S Asia • 500 kW
	R FREE ASIA, Via Tinian, N Marianas	E Asia • 500 kW
		W • E Asia • 500 kW
	RFE-RL, Via Kavála, Greece	S • W Asia • 250 kW
15515	**AUSTRALIA**	
	RADIO AUSTRALIA, Shepparton	Pacific & N America • 100 kW
	AUSTRIA	
	†R AUSTRIA INTL, Via Sackville, Canada	⇇ • M-F • W North Am • 250 kW • ALT. FREQ. TO 17865 kHz
		⇇ • Sa/Su • W North Am • 250 kW • ALT. FREQ. TO 17865 kHz
	FRANCE	
	R FRANCE INTL, Via French Guiana	C America • 250/500 kW
	SWITZERLAND	
	†SWISS RADIO INTL, Via Jülich, Germany	S • Mideast • 100 kW
	USA	
	R FREE ASIA, Via Tinian, N Marianas	S • E Asia • 500 kW
	VOA, Via Udon Thani, Thailand	W • E Asia • 250 kW
15519v	**BANGLADESH**	
	†BANGLADESH BETAR, Dhaka-Savar	Mideast & Europe • DS-TEMP INACTIVE • 50/100 kW
		Europe • TEMP INACTIVE • 50/100 kW
15520	**PHILIPPINES**	
	†RADIO VERITAS ASIA, Palauig	S Asia • 250 kW
	TURKEY	
	VOICE OF TURKEY, Ankara-Emirler	S • Mideast • 500 kW
	USA	
	†ADVENTIST WORLD R, Via Abu Dhabi	E Africa • 250 kW
	FAMILY RADIO, Via Dhabayya, UAE	S Asia • 250 kW
	†RFE-RL, Via Udon Thani, Thailand	S • C Asia • 250 kW
15525	**CHINA (TAIWAN)**	
	CBS, Paochung	SE Asia • CHINESE NETWORK 2 • 100 kW
		SE Asia • 100 kW
	CBS	Irr • SE Asia • NEWS NETWORK
	GERMANY	
	†DEUTSCHE WELLE, Via Samara, Russia	S • W Asia & S Asia • 250 kW
	†DEUTSCHE WELLE, Via Sines, Portugal	S • S Europe • 250 kW
	PORTUGAL	
	RDP INTERNATIONAL, Lisbon	S • M-F • Europe • 300 kW
	USA	
	†R FREE ASIA, Via Iranawila, Sri Lanka	S • SE Asia • 250 kW
15530	**FRANCE**	
	R FRANCE INTL, Issoudun	W Africa • 500 kW
	R FRANCE INTL, Via Moyabi, Gabon	S • S Africa • 250 kW
	PHILIPPINES	
	RADIO VERITAS ASIA, Palauig	S Asia • 250 kW
		SE Asia • 250 kW
	UNITED KINGDOM	
	†FEBA RADIO, Via Armavir, Russia	Mideast • 200 kW
	†FEBA RADIO, Via Moscow, Russia	S • Mideast • 250 kW
	USA	
	†RFE-RL, Via Iranawila, Sri Lanka	S • C Asia • 250 kW
	†RFE-RL, Via Udon Thani, Thailand	S • C Asia • 250 kW
	†SUDAN RADIO SVC, Via Woofferton, UK	W M-F • ENGLISH, ARABIC, ETC • C Africa • 300 kW
15535	**FRANCE**	
	R FRANCE INTL, Via Irkutsk, Russia	S • SE Asia • 500 kW
	RUSSIA	
	VOICE OF RUSSIA, Armavir	S • Europe & W Africa • 250 kW
	VOICE OF RUSSIA, Samara	W • C Asia • 200 kW
	USA	
	†ADVENTIST WORLD R, Via Austria	S • Mideast • 500 kW
15540	**AUSTRALIA**	
	†RADIO AUSTRALIA, Via Singapore	S • E Asia • 100 kW
	CHINA	
	†CENTRAL PEOPLE'S BS, Beijing	DS-2 • 50 kW
		Th-Tu • DS-2 • 50 kW
	PORTUGAL	
	RDP INTERNATIONAL, Lisbon	W Sa/Su/Holidays • N America • 100 kW
		Irr • W • N America • 100 kW
	RUSSIA	
	VOICE OF RUSSIA, Armavir	W • Europe • 250 kW
	VOICE OF RUSSIA, Moscow	S • Mideast • 250 kW
	UNITED KINGDOM	
(con'd)	†BBC, Via Singapore	S Asia • 100 kW

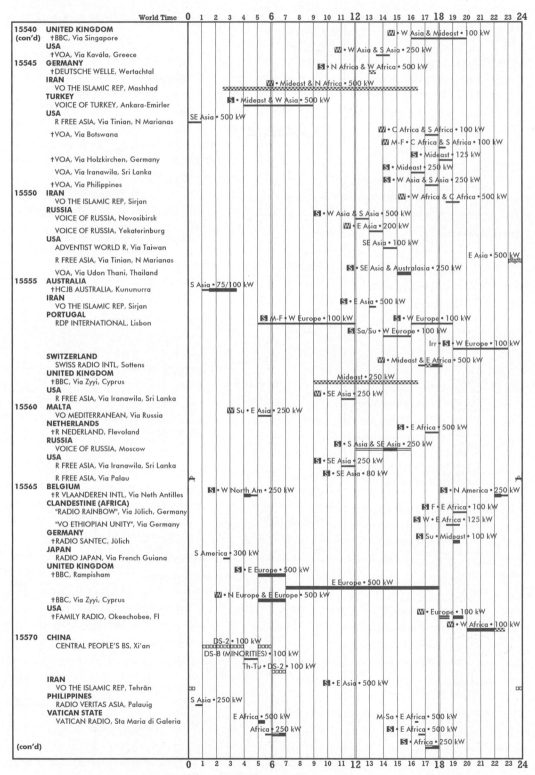

15540	**UNITED KINGDOM**	
(con'd)	†BBC, Via Singapore	W • W Asia & Mideast • 100 kW
	USA	
	†VOA, Via Kavála, Greece	W • W Asia & S Asia • 250 kW
15545	**GERMANY**	
	†DEUTSCHE WELLE, Wertachtal	S • N Africa & W Africa • 500 kW
	IRAN	
	VO THE ISLAMIC REP, Mashhad	W • Mideast & N Africa • 500 kW
	TURKEY	
	VOICE OF TURKEY, Ankara-Emirler	S • Mideast & W Asia • 500 kW
	USA	
	R FREE ASIA, Via Tinian, N Marianas	SE Asia • 500 kW
	†VOA, Via Botswana	W • C Africa & S Africa • 100 kW / W M-F • C Africa & S Africa • 100 kW
		S • Mideast • 125 kW
	†VOA, Via Holzkirchen, Germany	
	VOA, Via Iranawila, Sri Lanka	S • Mideast • 250 kW
	†VOA, Via Philippines	S • W Asia & S Asia • 250 kW
15550	**IRAN**	
	VO THE ISLAMIC REP, Sirjan	W • W Africa & C Africa • 500 kW
	RUSSIA	
	VOICE OF RUSSIA, Novosibirsk	S • W Asia & S Asia • 500 kW
	VOICE OF RUSSIA, Yekaterinburg	W • E Asia • 200 kW
	USA	
	ADVENTIST WORLD R, Via Taiwan	SE Asia • 100 kW / E Asia • 500 kW
	R FREE ASIA, Via Tinian, N Marianas	
	VOA, Via Udon Thani, Thailand	S • SE Asia & Australasia • 250 kW
15555	**AUSTRALIA**	
	†HCJB AUSTRALIA, Kununurra	S Asia • 75/100 kW
	IRAN	
	VO THE ISLAMIC REP, Sirjan	S • E Asia • 500 kW
	PORTUGAL	
	RDP INTERNATIONAL, Lisbon	S M-F • W Europe • 100 kW / S • W Europe • 100 kW
		S Sa/Su • W Europe • 100 kW
		Irr • S • W Europe • 100 kW
	SWITZERLAND	
	SWISS RADIO INTL, Sottens	W • Mideast & E Africa • 500 kW
	UNITED KINGDOM	
	†BBC, Via Zyyi, Cyprus	Mideast • 250 kW
	USA	
	R FREE ASIA, Via Iranawila, Sri Lanka	W • SE Asia • 250 kW
15560	**MALTA**	
	VO MEDITERRANEAN, Via Russia	W Su • E Asia • 250 kW
	NETHERLANDS	
	†R NEDERLAND, Flevoland	S • E Africa • 500 kW
	RUSSIA	
	VOICE OF RUSSIA, Moscow	S • S Asia & SE Asia • 250 kW
	USA	
	R FREE ASIA, Via Iranawila, Sri Lanka	S • SE Asia • 250 kW
	R FREE ASIA, Via Palau	S • SE Asia • 80 kW
15565	**BELGIUM**	
	†R VLAANDEREN INTL, Via Neth Antilles	S • W North Am • 250 kW / S • N America • 250 kW
	CLANDESTINE (AFRICA)	
	"RADIO RAINBOW", Via Jülich, Germany	S F • E Africa • 100 kW
	"VO ETHIOPIAN UNITY", Via Germany	S W • E Africa • 125 kW
	GERMANY	
	†RADIO SANTEC, Jülich	S Su • Mideast • 100 kW
	JAPAN	
	RADIO JAPAN, Via French Guiana	S America • 300 kW
	UNITED KINGDOM	
	†BBC, Rampisham	S • E Europe • 500 kW / E Europe • 500 kW
	†BBC, Via Zyyi, Cyprus	W • N Europe & E Europe • 500 kW
	USA	
	†FAMILY RADIO, Okeechobee, Fl	W • Europe • 100 kW
		W • W Africa • 100 kW
15570	**CHINA**	
	CENTRAL PEOPLE'S BS, Xi'an	DS-2 • 100 kW
		DS-8 (MINORITIES) • 100 kW
		Th-Tu • DS-2 • 100 kW
	IRAN	
	VO THE ISLAMIC REP, Tehrān	S • E Asia • 500 kW
	PHILIPPINES	
	RADIO VERITAS ASIA, Palauig	S Asia • 250 kW
	VATICAN STATE	
	VATICAN RADIO, Sta Maria di Galeria	E Africa • 500 kW / M-Sa • E Africa • 500 kW
		Africa • 250 kW / S • E Africa • 500 kW
		S • Africa • 250 kW
(con'd)		

ENGLISH ▬   ARABIC ▨   CHINESE ▫▫▫   FRENCH ▭   GERMAN ▬   RUSSIAN ▭   SPANISH ▬   OTHER ▬

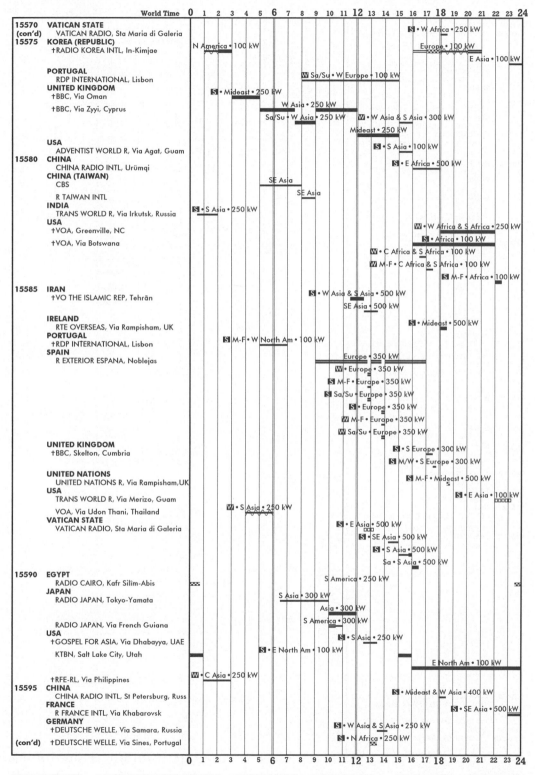

World Time																								
	0	1	2	3	4	5	6	7	8	9	10	11	12	13	14	15	16	17	18	19	20	21	22	23	24

15570 VATICAN STATE
(con'd) VATICAN RADIO, Sta Maria di Galeria — Ⓢ • W Africa • 250 kW
15575 KOREA (REPUBLIC)
 †RADIO KOREA INTL, In-Kimjae — N America • 100 kW / Europe • 100 kW / E Asia • 100 kW

PORTUGAL
 RDP INTERNATIONAL, Lisbon — Ⓦ Sa/Su • W Europe • 100 kW
UNITED KINGDOM
 †BBC, Via Oman — Ⓢ • Mideast • 250 kW

 †BBC, Via Zyyi, Cyprus — W Asia • 250 kW / Sa/Su • W Asia • 250 kW / Ⓦ • W Asia & S Asia • 300 kW / Mideast • 250 kW

USA
 ADVENTIST WORLD R, Via Agat, Guam — Ⓢ • S Asia • 100 kW
15580 CHINA
 CHINA RADIO INTL, Urümqi — Ⓢ • E Africa • 500 kW
 CHINA (TAIWAN)
 CBS — SE Asia
 R TAIWAN INTL — SE Asia
INDIA
 TRANS WORLD R, Via Irkutsk, Russia — Ⓢ • S Asia • 250 kW
USA
 †VOA, Greenville, NC — Ⓦ • W Africa & S Africa • 250 kW / Ⓢ • Africa • 100 kW
 †VOA, Via Botswana — Ⓦ • C Africa & S Africa • 100 kW / Ⓦ M-F • C Africa & S Africa • 100 kW / Ⓦ M-F • Africa • 100 kW

15585 IRAN
 †VO THE ISLAMIC REP, Tehrān — Ⓢ • W Asia & S Asia • 500 kW / SE Asia • 500 kW

IRELAND
 RTE OVERSEAS, Via Rampisham, UK — Ⓢ • Mideast • 500 kW
PORTUGAL
 †RDP INTERNATIONAL, Lisbon — Ⓢ M-F • W North Am • 100 kW
SPAIN
 R EXTERIOR ESPANA, Noblejas — Europe • 350 kW / Ⓦ • Europe • 350 kW / Ⓢ M-F • Europe • 350 kW / Ⓢ Sa/Su • Europe • 350 kW / Ⓢ • Europe • 350 kW / Ⓦ M-F • Europe • 350 kW / Ⓦ Sa/Su • Europe • 350 kW

UNITED KINGDOM
 †BBC, Skelton, Cumbria — Ⓢ • S Europe • 300 kW / Ⓢ M/W • S Europe • 300 kW

UNITED NATIONS
 UNITED NATIONS R, Via Rampisham,UK — Ⓢ M-F • Mideast • 500 kW
USA
 TRANS WORLD R, Via Merizo, Guam — Ⓢ • E Asia • 100 kW
 VOA, Via Udon Thani, Thailand — Ⓦ • S Asia • 250 kW
VATICAN STATE
 VATICAN RADIO, Sta Maria di Galeria — Ⓢ • E Asia • 500 kW / Ⓢ • SE Asia • 500 kW / Ⓢ • S Asia • 500 kW / Sa • S Asia • 500 kW

15590 EGYPT
 RADIO CAIRO, Kafr Silim-Abis — S America • 250 kW
JAPAN
 RADIO JAPAN, Tokyo-Yamata — S Asia • 300 kW / Asia • 300 kW
 RADIO JAPAN, Via French Guiana — S America • 300 kW
USA
 †GOSPEL FOR ASIA, Via Dhabayya, UAE — Ⓢ • S Asia • 250 kW
 KTBN, Salt Lake City, Utah — Ⓢ • E North Am • 100 kW / E North Am • 100 kW

 †RFE-RL, Via Philippines — Ⓦ • C Asia • 250 kW
15595 CHINA
 CHINA RADIO INTL, St Petersburg, Russ — Ⓢ • Mideast & W Asia • 400 kW
 FRANCE
 R FRANCE INTL, Via Khabarovsk — Ⓢ • SE Asia • 500 kW
 GERMANY
 †DEUTSCHE WELLE, Via Samara, Russia — Ⓢ • W Asia & S Asia • 250 kW
(con'd) †DEUTSCHE WELLE, Via Sines, Portugal — Ⓢ • N Africa • 250 kW

	0	1	2	3	4	5	6	7	8	9	10	11	12	13	14	15	16	17	18	19	20	21	22	23	24

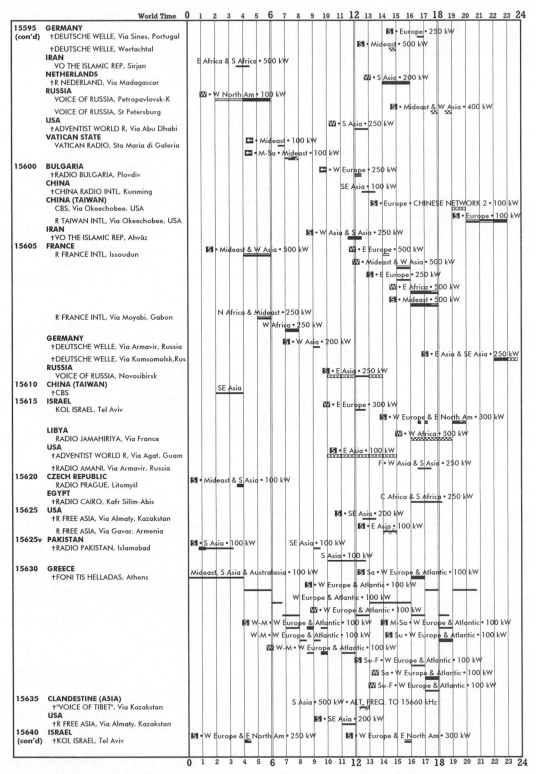

15595	**GERMANY**
(con'd)	†DEUTSCHE WELLE, Via Sines, Portugal
	†DEUTSCHE WELLE, Wertachtal
	IRAN
	VO THE ISLAMIC REP, Sirjan
	NETHERLANDS
	†R NEDERLAND, Via Madagascar
	RUSSIA
	VOICE OF RUSSIA, Petropavlovsk-K
	VOICE OF RUSSIA, St Petersburg
	USA
	†ADVENTIST WORLD R, Via Abu Dhabi
	VATICAN STATE
	VATICAN RADIO, Sta Maria di Galeria
15600	**BULGARIA**
	†RADIO BULGARIA, Plovdiv
	CHINA
	†CHINA RADIO INTL, Kunming
	CHINA (TAIWAN)
	CBS, Via Okeechobee, USA
	R TAIWAN INTL, Via Okeechobee, USA
	IRAN
	†VO THE ISLAMIC REP, Ahvāz
15605	**FRANCE**
	R FRANCE INTL, Issoudun
	R FRANCE INTL, Via Moyabi, Gabon
	GERMANY
	†DEUTSCHE WELLE, Via Armavir, Russia
	†DEUTSCHE WELLE, Via Komsomolsk,Rus
	RUSSIA
	VOICE OF RUSSIA, Novosibirsk
15610	**CHINA (TAIWAN)**
	†CBS
15615	**ISRAEL**
	KOL ISRAEL, Tel Aviv
	LIBYA
	RADIO JAMAHIRIYA, Via France
	USA
	†ADVENTIST WORLD R, Via Agat, Guam
	†RADIO AMANI, Via Armavir, Russia
15620	**CZECH REPUBLIC**
	RADIO PRAGUE, Litomyšl
	EGYPT
	†RADIO CAIRO, Kafr Silīm-Abis
15625	**USA**
	†R FREE ASIA, Via Almaty, Kazakstan
	R FREE ASIA, Via Gavar, Armenia
15625v	**PAKISTAN**
	†RADIO PAKISTAN, Islamabad
15630	**GREECE**
	†FONI TIS HELLADAS, Athens
15635	**CLANDESTINE (ASIA)**
	†"VOICE OF TIBET", Via Kazakstan
	USA
	†R FREE ASIA, Via Almaty, Kazakstan
15640	**ISRAEL**
(con'd)	†KOL ISRAEL, Tel Aviv

ENGLISH ▬   ARABIC ⟨⟨⟨   CHINESE ▭▭▭   FRENCH ═══   GERMAN ▬▬▬   RUSSIAN ══   SPANISH ▭▭▭   OTHER ▬▬

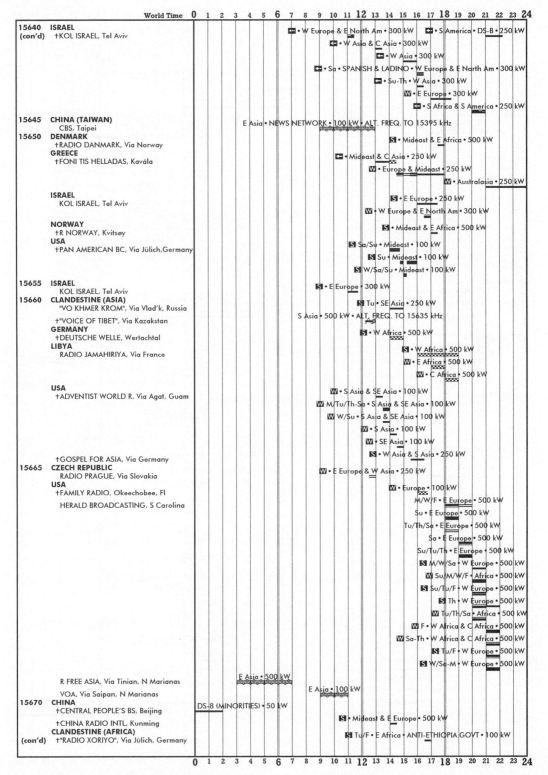

World Time

15640 **ISRAEL**		
(con'd) †KOL ISRAEL, Tel Aviv	• W Europe & E North Am • 300 kW	• S America • DS-B • 250 kW
	• W Asia & C Asia • 300 kW	
	• W Asia • 300 kW	
	• Sa • SPANISH & LADINO • W Europe & E North Am • 300 kW	
	• Su-Th • W Asia • 300 kW	
	W • E Europe • 300 kW	
	• S Africa & S America • 250 kW	
15645 **CHINA (TAIWAN)**	E Asia • NEWS NETWORK • 100 kW • ALT. FREQ. TO 15395 kHz	
CBS, Taipei		
15650 **DENMARK**	S • Mideast & E Africa • 500 kW	
†RADIO DANMARK, Via Norway		
GREECE	• Mideast & C Asia • 250 kW	
†FONI TIS HELLADAS, Kavála	W • Europe & Mideast • 250 kW	
	W • Australasia • 250 kW	
ISRAEL	S • E Europe • 250 kW	
KOL ISRAEL, Tel Aviv	W • W Europe & E North Am • 300 kW	
NORWAY	S • Mideast & E Africa • 500 kW	
†R NORWAY, Kvitsøy		
USA	S Sa/Su • Mideast • 100 kW	
†PAN AMERICAN BC, Via Jülich,Germany	S Su • Mideast • 100 kW	
	W/Sa/Su • Mideast • 100 kW	
15655 **ISRAEL**	S • E Europe • 300 kW	
KOL ISRAEL, Tel Aviv		
15660 **CLANDESTINE (ASIA)**	S Tu • SE Asia • 250 kW	
"VO KHMER KROM", Via Vlad'k, Russia		
†"VOICE OF TIBET", Via Kazakstan	S Asia • 500 kW • ALT. FREQ. TO 15635 kHz	
GERMANY	S • W Africa • 500 kW	
†DEUTSCHE WELLE, Wertachtal		
LIBYA	S • W Africa • 500 kW	
RADIO JAMAHIRIYA, Via France	W • E Africa • 500 kW	
	W • C Africa • 500 kW	
USA	W • S Asia & SE Asia • 100 kW	
†ADVENTIST WORLD R, Via Agat, Guam	W M/Tu/Th-Sa • S Asia & SE Asia • 100 kW	
	W/Su • S Asia & SE Asia • 100 kW	
	W • S Asia • 100 kW	
	W • SE Asia • 100 kW	
	S • W Asia & S Asia • 250 kW	
†GOSPEL FOR ASIA, Via Germany		
15665 **CZECH REPUBLIC**	W • E Europe & W Asia • 250 kW	
RADIO PRAGUE, Via Slovakia		
USA	W • Europe • 100 kW	
†FAMILY RADIO, Okeechobee, Fl		
HERALD BROADCASTING, S Carolina	M/W/F • E Europe • 500 kW	
	Su • E Europe • 500 kW	
	Tu/Th/Sa • E Europe • 500 kW	
	Sa • E Europe • 500 kW	
	Su/Tu/Th • E Europe • 500 kW	
	S M/W/Sa • W Europe • 500 kW	
	W Su/M/W/F • Africa • 500 kW	
	S Su/Tu/F • W Europe • 500 kW	
	S Th • W Europe • 500 kW	
	W Tu/Th/Sa • Africa • 500 kW	
	W F • W Africa & C Africa • 500 kW	
	W Sa-Th • W Africa & C Africa • 500 kW	
	S Tu/F • W Europe • 500 kW	
	S W/Sa-M • W Europe • 500 kW	
R FREE ASIA, Via Tinian, N Marianas	E Asia • 500 kW	
VOA, Via Saipan, N Marianas	E Asia • 100 kW	
15670 **CHINA**	DS-8 (MINORITIES) • 50 kW	
†CENTRAL PEOPLE'S BS, Beijing		
†CHINA RADIO INTL, Kunming	S • Mideast & E Europe • 500 kW	
CLANDESTINE (AFRICA)		
(con'd) †"RADIO XORIYO", Via Jülich, Germany	S Tu/F • E Africa • ANTI-ETHIOPIA GOVT • 100 kW	

SEASONAL S OR W 1-HR TIMESHIFT MIDYEAR ⮜ OR ⮞ JAMMING / OR /\ EARLIEST HEARD ◁ LATEST HEARD ▷ NEW FOR 2004 †

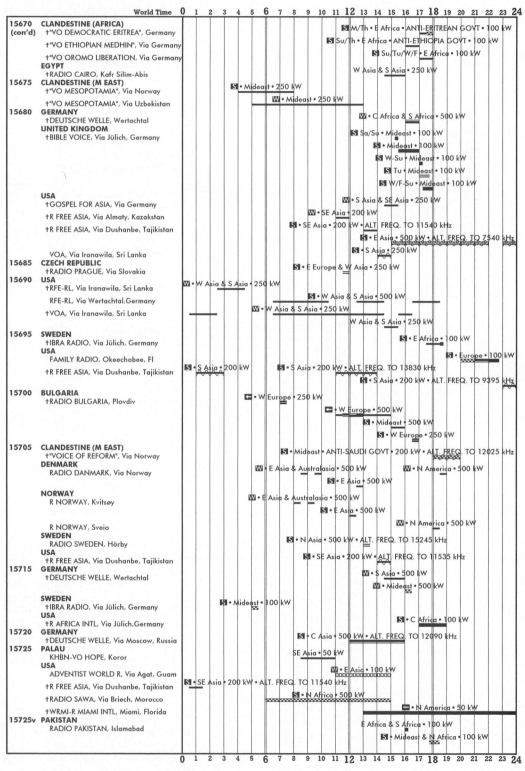

World Time		
15670 (con'd)	**CLANDESTINE (AFRICA)**	
	†"VO DEMOCRATIC ERITREA", Germany	S M/Th • E Africa • ANTI-ERITREAN GOVT • 100 kW
	†"VO ETHIOPIAN MEDHIN", Via Germany	S Su/Th • E Africa • ANTI-ETHIOPIA GOVT • 100 kW
	†"VO OROMO LIBERATION, Via Germany	S Su/Tu/W/F • E Africa • 100 kW
	EGYPT	
	†RADIO CAIRO, Kafr Silim-Abis	W Asia & S Asia • 250 kW
15675	**CLANDESTINE (M EAST)**	
	†"VO MESOPOTAMIA", Via Norway	S • Mideast • 250 kW
	†"VO MESOPOTAMIA", Via Uzbekistan	W • Mideast • 250 kW
15680	**GERMANY**	
	†DEUTSCHE WELLE, Wertachtal	W • C Africa & S Africa • 500 kW
	UNITED KINGDOM	
	†BIBLE VOICE, Via Jülich, Germany	S Sa/Su • Mideast • 100 kW
		S • Mideast • 100 kW
		S W–Su • Mideast • 100 kW
		S Tu • Mideast • 100 kW
		S W/F–Su • Mideast • 100 kW
	USA	
	†GOSPEL FOR ASIA, Via Germany	W • S Asia & SE Asia • 250 kW
	†R FREE ASIA, Via Almaty, Kazakstan	W • SE Asia • 200 kW
	†R FREE ASIA, Via Dushanbe, Tajikistan	S • SE Asia • 200 kW • ALT. FREQ. TO 11540 kHz
		S • E Asia • 500 kW • ALT. FREQ. TO 7540 kHz
	VOA, Via Iranawila, Sri Lanka	S • S Asia • 250 kW
15685	**CZECH REPUBLIC**	
	†RADIO PRAGUE, Via Slovakia	S • E Europe & W Asia • 250 kW
15690	**USA**	
	†RFE-RL, Via Iranawila, Sri Lanka	W • W Asia & S Asia • 250 kW
	RFE-RL, Via Wertachtal, Germany	S • W Asia & S Asia • 500 kW
	†VOA, Via Iranawila, Sri Lanka	W • W Asia & S Asia • 250 kW
		W Asia & S Asia • 250 kW
15695	**SWEDEN**	
	†IBRA RADIO, Via Jülich, Germany	S • E Africa • 100 kW
	USA	
	FAMILY RADIO, Okeechobee, Fl	S • Europe • 100 kW
		S • S Asia • 200 kW S • S Asia • 200 kW • ALT. FREQ. TO 13830 kHz
	†R FREE ASIA, Via Dushanbe, Tajikistan	S • S Asia • 200 kW • ALT. FREQ. TO 9395 kHz
15700	**BULGARIA**	
	†RADIO BULGARIA, Plovdiv	⬅ • W Europe • 250 kW
		⬅ • W Europe • 500 kW
		S • Mideast • 500 kW
		S • W Europe • 250 kW
15705	**CLANDESTINE (M EAST)**	
	†"VOICE OF REFORM", Via Norway	S • Mideast • ANTI-SAUDI GOVT • 200 kW • ALT. FREQ. TO 12025 kHz
	DENMARK	
	RADIO DANMARK, Via Norway	W • E Asia & Australasia • 500 kW W • N America • 500 kW
		S • E Asia • 500 kW
	NORWAY	
	R NORWAY, Kvitsøy	W • E Asia & Australasia • 500 kW
		S • E Asia • 500 kW
	R NORWAY, Sveio	W • N America • 500 kW
	SWEDEN	
	RADIO SWEDEN, Hörby	S • N Asia • 500 kW • ALT. FREQ. TO 15245 kHz
	USA	
	†R FREE ASIA, Via Dushanbe, Tajikistan	S • SE Asia • 200 kW • ALT. FREQ. TO 11535 kHz
15715	**GERMANY**	
	†DEUTSCHE WELLE, Wertachtal	W • S Asia • 500 kW
		W • Mideast • 500 kW
	SWEDEN	
	†IBRA RADIO, Via Jülich, Germany	S • Mideast • 100 kW
	USA	
	†R AFRICA INTL, Via Jülich, Germany	S • C Africa • 100 kW
15720	**GERMANY**	
	†DEUTSCHE WELLE, Via Moscow, Russia	S • C Asia • 500 kW • ALT. FREQ. TO 12090 kHz
15725	**PALAU**	
	KHBN-VO HOPE, Koror	SE Asia • 50 kW
	USA	
	ADVENTIST WORLD R, Via Agat, Guam	W • E Asia • 100 kW
	†R FREE ASIA, Via Dushanbe, Tajikistan	S • SE Asia • 200 kW • ALT. FREQ. TO 11540 kHz
	†RADIO SAWA, Via Briech, Morocco	S • N Africa • 500 kW
	†WRMI-R MIAMI INTL, Miami, Florida	⬅ • N America • 50 kW
15725v	**PAKISTAN**	
	RADIO PAKISTAN, Islamabad	E Africa & S Africa • 100 kW
		S • Mideast & N Africa • 100 kW

ENGLISH ▬   ARABIC ⁙   CHINESE ▫▫▫   FRENCH ▬▬   GERMAN ▬▬   RUSSIAN ══   SPANISH ▬▬   OTHER —

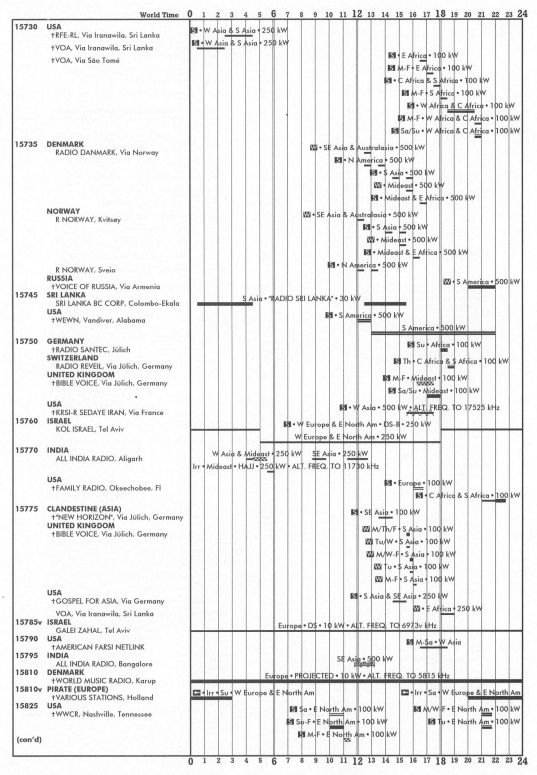

| World Time | 0 | 1 | 2 | 3 | 4 | 5 | 6 | 7 | 8 | 9 | 10 | 11 | 12 | 13 | 14 | 15 | 16 | 17 | 18 | 19 | 20 | 21 | 22 | 23 | 24 |

15730 USA
  †RFE-RL, Via Iranawila, Sri Lanka — S • W Asia & S Asia • 250 kW
  †VOA, Via Iranawila, Sri Lanka — S • W Asia & S Asia • 250 kW
  †VOA, Via São Tomé — S • E Africa • 100 kW
  S M-F • E Africa • 100 kW
  S • C Africa & S Africa • 100 kW
  S M-F • S Africa • 100 kW
  S • W Africa & C Africa • 100 kW
  S M-F • W Africa & C Africa • 100 kW
  S Sa/Su • W Africa & C Africa • 100 kW

15735 DENMARK
  RADIO DANMARK, Via Norway — W • SE Asia & Australasia • 500 kW
  S • N America • 500 kW
  S • S Asia • 500 kW
  W • Mideast • 500 kW
  S • Mideast & E Africa • 500 kW

  NORWAY
  R NORWAY, Kvitsøy — W • SE Asia & Australasia • 500 kW
  S • S Asia • 500 kW
  W • Mideast • 500 kW
  S • Mideast & E Africa • 500 kW
  S • N America • 500 kW

  R NORWAY, Sveio
  RUSSIA
  †VOICE OF RUSSIA, Via Armenia — W • S America • 500 kW
15745 SRI LANKA
  SRI LANKA BC CORP, Colombo-Ekala — S Asia • "RADIO SRI LANKA" • 30 kW
  USA
  †WEWN, Vandiver, Alabama — S • S America • 500 kW
  S America • 500 kW

15750 GERMANY
  †RADIO SANTEC, Jülich — S Su • Africa • 100 kW
  SWITZERLAND
  RADIO REVEIL, Via Jülich, Germany — S Th • C Africa & S Africa • 100 kW
  UNITED KINGDOM
  †BIBLE VOICE, Via Jülich, Germany — S M-F • Mideast • 100 kW
  S Sa/Su • Mideast • 100 kW

  USA
  †KRSI-R SEDAYE IRAN, Via France — S • W Asia • 500 kW • ALT. FREQ. TO 17525 kHz
15760 ISRAEL
  KOL ISRAEL, Tel Aviv — S • W Europe & E North Am • DS-B • 250 kW
  W Europe & E North Am • 250 kW

15770 INDIA
  ALL INDIA RADIO, Aligarh — W Asia & Mideast • 250 kW   SE Asia • 250 kW
  Irr • Mideast • HAJJ • 250 kW • ALT. FREQ. TO 11730 kHz

  USA
  †FAMILY RADIO, Okeechobee, Fl — S • Europe • 100 kW
  S • C Africa & S Africa • 100 kW

15775 CLANDESTINE (ASIA)
  †"NEW HORIZON", Via Jülich, Germany — S • SE Asia • 100 kW
  UNITED KINGDOM
  †BIBLE VOICE, Via Jülich, Germany — W M/Th/F • S Asia • 100 kW
  W Tu/W • S Asia • 100 kW
  W M/W-F • S Asia • 100 kW
  W Tu • S Asia • 100 kW
  W M-F • S Asia • 100 kW

  USA
  †GOSPEL FOR ASIA, Via Germany — S • S Asia & SE Asia • 250 kW
  VOA, Via Iranawila, Sri Lanka — W • E Africa • 250 kW
15785v ISRAEL
  GALEI ZAHAL, Tel Aviv — Europe • DS • 10 kW • ALT. FREQ. TO 6973v kHz
15790 USA
  †AMERICAN FARSI NETLINK — S M-Sa • W Asia
15795 INDIA
  ALL INDIA RADIO, Bangalore — SE Asia • 500 kW
15810 DENMARK
  †WORLD MUSIC RADIO, Karup — Europe • PROJECTED • 10 kW • ALT. FREQ. TO 5815 kHz
15810v PIRATE (EUROPE)
  †VARIOUS STATIONS, Holland — ← • Irr • Su • W Europe & E North Am   ← • Irr • Sa • W Europe & E North Am
15825 USA
  †WWCR, Nashville, Tennessee — S Sa • E North Am • 100 kW   S M/W-F • E North Am • 100 kW
  S Su-F • E North Am • 100 kW   S Tu • E North Am • 100 kW
  S M-F • E North Am • 100 kW

(con'd)

| 0 | 1 | 2 | 3 | 4 | 5 | 6 | 7 | 8 | 9 | 10 | 11 | 12 | 13 | 14 | 15 | 16 | 17 | 18 | 19 | 20 | 21 | 22 | 23 | 24 |

SEASONAL S OR W   1-HR TIMESHIFT MIDYEAR ← OR →   JAMMING / OR ∧   EARLIEST HEARD ◁   LATEST HEARD ▷   NEW FOR 2004 †

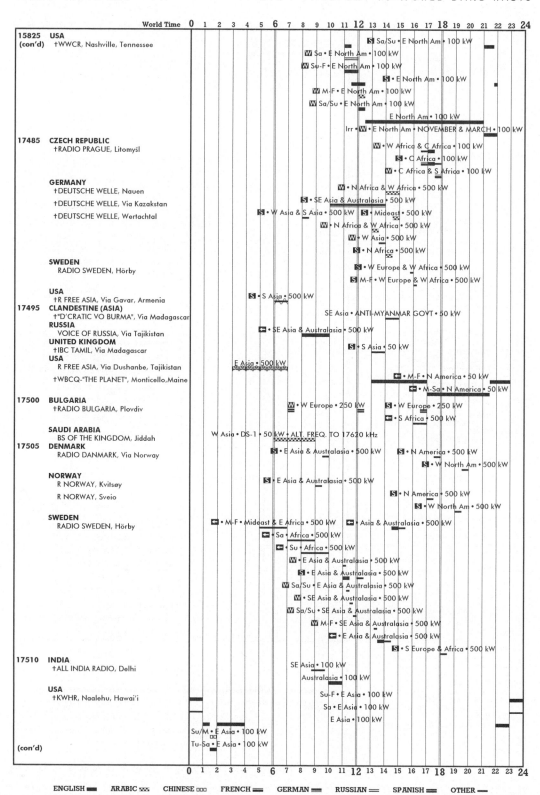

World Time	0 1 2 3 4 5 6 7 8 9 10 11 12 13 14 15 16 17 18 19 20 21 22 23 24

15825 USA
(con'd) †WWCR, Nashville, Tennessee
- S Sa/Su • E North Am • 100 kW
- W Sa • E North Am • 100 kW
- W Su-F • E North Am • 100 kW
- S • E North Am • 100 kW
- W M-F • E North Am • 100 kW
- W Sa/Su • E North Am • 100 kW
- E North Am • 100 kW
- Irr • W • E North Am • NOVEMBER & MARCH • 100 kW

17485 CZECH REPUBLIC
†RADIO PRAGUE, Litomyšl
- W • W Africa & C Africa • 100 kW
- S • C Africa • 100 kW
- W • C Africa & S Africa • 100 kW

GERMANY
†DEUTSCHE WELLE, Nauen
- W • N Africa & W Africa • 500 kW

†DEUTSCHE WELLE, Via Kazakstan
- S • SE Asia & Australasia • 500 kW

†DEUTSCHE WELLE, Wertachtal
- S • W Asia & S Asia • 500 kW   S • Mideast • 500 kW
- W • N Africa & W Africa • 500 kW
- W • W Asia • 500 kW
- S • N Africa • 500 kW

SWEDEN
RADIO SWEDEN, Hörby
- S • W Europe & W Africa • 500 kW
- S M-F • W Europe & W Africa • 500 kW

USA
†R FREE ASIA, Via Gavar, Armenia
- S • S Asia • 500 kW

17495 CLANDESTINE (ASIA)
†"D'CRATIC VO BURMA", Via Madagascar
- SE Asia • ANTI-MYANMAR GOVT • 50 kW

RUSSIA
VOICE OF RUSSIA, Via Tajikistan
- • SE Asia & Australasia • 500 kW

UNITED KINGDOM
†IBC TAMIL, Via Madagascar
- S • S Asia • 50 kW

USA
R FREE ASIA, Via Dushanbe, Tajikistan
- E Asia • 500 kW

†WBCQ-"THE PLANET", Monticello, Maine
- • M-F • N America • 50 kW
- • M-Sa • N America • 50 kW

17500 BULGARIA
†RADIO BULGARIA, Plovdiv
- W • W Europe • 250 kW   S • W Europe • 250 kW
- • S Africa • 500 kW

SAUDI ARABIA
BS OF THE KINGDOM, Jiddah
- W Asia • DS-1 • 50 kW • ALT. FREQ. TO 17620 kHz

17505 DENMARK
RADIO DANMARK, Via Norway
- S • E Asia & Australasia • 500 kW   S • N America • 500 kW
- S • W North Am • 500 kW

NORWAY
R NORWAY, Kvitsøy
- S • E Asia & Australasia • 500 kW

R NORWAY, Sveio
- S • N America • 500 kW
- S • W North Am • 500 kW

SWEDEN
RADIO SWEDEN, Hörby
- • M-F • Mideast & E Africa • 500 kW   • Asia & Australasia • 500 kW
- • Sa • Africa • 500 kW
- • Su • Africa • 500 kW
- W • E Asia & Australasia • 500 kW
- S • E Asia & Australasia • 500 kW
- W Sa/Su • E Asia & Australasia • 500 kW
- W • SE Asia & Australasia • 500 kW
- W Sa/Su • SE Asia & Australasia • 500 kW
- W M-F • SE Asia & Australasia • 500 kW
- • E Asia & Australasia • 500 kW
- S • S Europe & Africa • 500 kW

17510 INDIA
†ALL INDIA RADIO, Delhi
- SE Asia • 100 kW
- Australasia • 100 kW

USA
†KWHR, Naalehu, Hawai'i
- Su-F • E Asia • 100 kW
- Sa • E Asia • 100 kW
- E Asia • 100 kW
- Su/M • E Asia • 100 kW
- Tu-Sa • E Asia • 100 kW

(con'd)

	0 1 2 3 4 5 6 7 8 9 10 11 12 13 14 15 16 17 18 19 20 21 22 23 24

ENGLISH ▬   ARABIC ▩   CHINESE ▭▭▭   FRENCH ▬▬   GERMAN ▬▬   RUSSIAN ══   SPANISH ▬▬   OTHER ▬

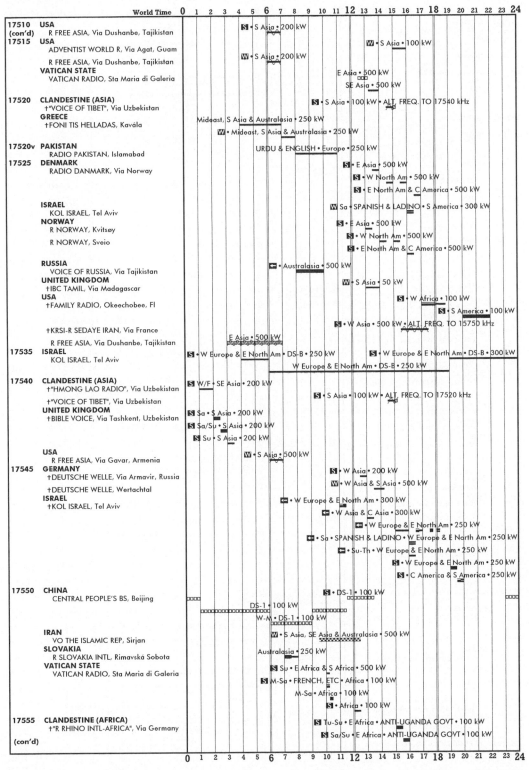

17510 (con'd)	**USA** R FREE ASIA, Via Dushanbe, Tajikistan	S • S Asia • 200 kW
17515	**USA** ADVENTIST WORLD R, Via Agat, Guam	W • S Asia • 100 kW
	R FREE ASIA, Via Dushanbe, Tajikistan	W • S Asia • 200 kW
	VATICAN STATE VATICAN RADIO, Sta Maria di Galeria	E Asia • 500 kW / SE Asia • 500 kW
17520	**CLANDESTINE (ASIA)** †"VOICE OF TIBET", Via Uzbekistan	S • S Asia • 100 kW • ALT. FREQ. TO 17540 kHz
	GREECE †FONI TIS HELLADAS, Kavála	Mideast, S Asia & Australasia • 250 kW / W • Mideast, S Asia & Australasia • 250 kW
17520v	**PAKISTAN** RADIO PAKISTAN, Islamabad	URDU & ENGLISH • Europe • 250 kW
17525	**DENMARK** RADIO DANMARK, Via Norway	S • E Asia • 500 kW / S • W North Am • 500 kW / S • E North Am & C America • 500 kW
	ISRAEL KOL ISRAEL, Tel Aviv	W Sa • SPANISH & LADINO • S America • 300 kW
	NORWAY R NORWAY, Kvitsøy	S • E Asia • 500 kW
	R NORWAY, Sveio	S • W North Am • 500 kW / S • E North Am & C America • 500 kW
	RUSSIA VOICE OF RUSSIA, Via Tajikistan	⮂ • Australasia • 500 kW
	UNITED KINGDOM †IBC TAMIL, Via Madagascar	W • S Asia • 50 kW
	USA †FAMILY RADIO, Okeechobee, Fl	S • W Africa • 100 kW / S • S America • 100 kW
	†KRSI-R SEDAYE IRAN, Via France	S • W Asia • 500 kW • ALT. FREQ. TO 15750 kHz
	R FREE ASIA, Via Dushanbe, Tajikistan	E Asia • 500 kW
17535	**ISRAEL** KOL ISRAEL, Tel Aviv	S • W Europe & E North Am • DS-B • 250 kW / S • W Europe & E North Am • DS-B • 300 kW / W Europe & E North Am • DS-B • 250 kW
17540	**CLANDESTINE (ASIA)** †"HMONG LAO RADIO", Via Uzbekistan	S W/F • SE Asia • 200 kW
	†"VOICE OF TIBET", Via Uzbekistan	S • S Asia • 100 kW • ALT. FREQ. TO 17520 kHz
	UNITED KINGDOM †BIBLE VOICE, Via Tashkent, Uzbekistan	S Sa • S Asia • 200 kW / S Sa/Su • S Asia • 200 kW / S Su • S Asia • 200 kW
	USA R FREE ASIA, Via Gavar, Armenia	W • S Asia • 500 kW
17545	**GERMANY** †DEUTSCHE WELLE, Via Armavir, Russia	S • W Asia • 200 kW / W • W Asia & S Asia • 500 kW
	†DEUTSCHE WELLE, Wertachtal	⮂ • W Europe & E North Am • 300 kW
	ISRAEL †KOL ISRAEL, Tel Aviv	⮂ • W Asia & C Asia • 300 kW / ⮂ • W Europe & E North Am • 250 kW / ⮂ • Sa • SPANISH & LADINO • W Europe & E North Am • 250 kW / ⮂ • Su-Th • W Europe & E North Am • 250 kW / S • W Europe & E North Am • 250 kW / S • C America & S America • 250 kW
17550	**CHINA** CENTRAL PEOPLE'S BS, Beijing	S • DS-1 • 100 kW / DS-1 • 100 kW / W-M • DS-1 • 100 kW
	IRAN VO THE ISLAMIC REP, Sirjan	W • S Asia, SE Asia & Australasia • 500 kW
	SLOVAKIA R SLOVAKIA INTL, Rimavská Sobota	Australasia • 250 kW
	VATICAN STATE VATICAN RADIO, Sta Maria di Galeria	S Su • E Africa & S Africa • 500 kW / S M-Sa • FRENCH, ETC • Africa • 100 kW / M-Sa • Africa • 100 kW / S • Africa • 100 kW
17555	**CLANDESTINE (AFRICA)** †"R RHINO INTL-AFRICA", Via Germany	S Tu-Su • E Africa • ANTI-UGANDA GOVT • 100 kW / S Sa/Su • E Africa • ANTI-UGANDA GOVT • 100 kW
(con'd)		

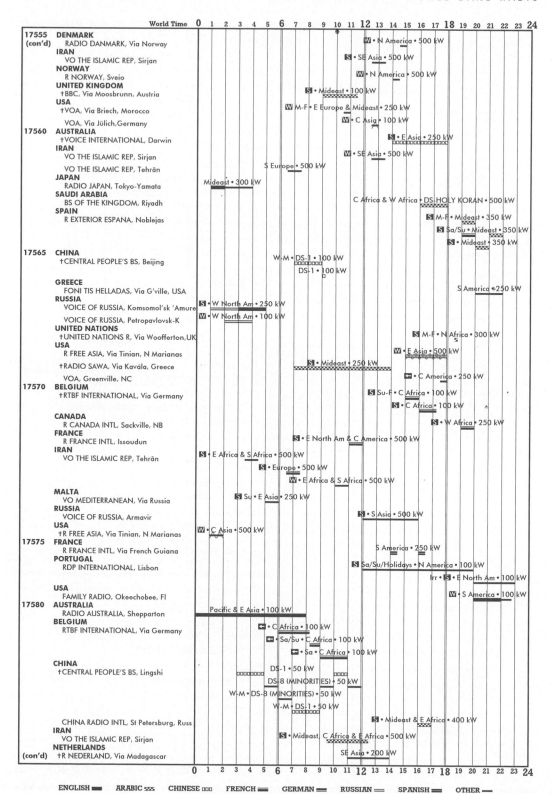

World Time   0 1 2 3 4 5 6 7 8 9 10 11 12 13 14 15 16 17 18 19 20 21 22 23 24

17555 **DENMARK**
(con'd)   RADIO DANMARK, Via Norway — **W** • N America • 500 kW
           IRAN
           VO THE ISLAMIC REP, Sirjan — **S** • SE Asia • 500 kW
           NORWAY
           R NORWAY, Sveio — **W** • N America • 500 kW
           UNITED KINGDOM
           †BBC, Via Moosbrunn, Austria — **S** • Mideast • 100 kW
           USA
           †VOA, Via Briech, Morocco — **W** M-F • E Europe & Mideast • 250 kW
           VOA, Via Jülich, Germany — **W** • C Asia • 100 kW
17560 **AUSTRALIA**
           †VOICE INTERNATIONAL, Darwin — **S** • E Asia • 250 kW
           IRAN
           VO THE ISLAMIC REP, Sirjan — **W** • SE Asia • 500 kW
           VO THE ISLAMIC REP, Tehrān — S Europe • 500 kW
           JAPAN
           RADIO JAPAN, Tokyo-Yamata — Mideast • 300 kW
           SAUDI ARABIA
           BS OF THE KINGDOM, Riyadh — C Africa & W Africa • DS-HOLY KORAN • 500 kW
           SPAIN
           R EXTERIOR ESPANA, Noblejas — **S** M-F • Mideast • 350 kW
                                        — **S** Sa/Su • Mideast • 350 kW
                                        — **S** • Mideast • 350 kW
17565 **CHINA**
           †CENTRAL PEOPLE'S BS, Beijing — W-M • DS-1 • 100 kW
                                          DS-1 • 100 kW
           GREECE
           FONI TIS HELLADAS, Via G'ville, USA — S America • 250 kW
           RUSSIA
           VOICE OF RUSSIA, Komsomol'sk 'Amure — **S** • W North Am • 250 kW
           VOICE OF RUSSIA, Petropavlovsk-K — **W** • W North Am • 100 kW
           UNITED NATIONS
           †UNITED NATIONS R, Via Woofferton,UK — **S** M-F • N Africa • 300 kW
           USA
           R FREE ASIA, Via Tinian, N Marianas — **W** • E Asia • 500 kW
           †RADIO SAWA, Via Kavála, Greece — **S** • Mideast • 250 kW
           VOA, Greenville, NC — **◻** • C America • 250 kW
17570 **BELGIUM**
           †RTBF INTERNATIONAL, Via Germany — **S** Su-F • C Africa • 100 kW
                                             — **S** • C Africa • 100 kW
           CANADA
           R CANADA INTL, Sackville, NB — **S** • W Africa • 250 kW
           FRANCE
           R FRANCE INTL, Issoudun — **S** • E North Am & C America • 500 kW
           IRAN
           VO THE ISLAMIC REP, Tehrān — **S** • E Africa & S Africa • 500 kW
                                       — **S** • Europe • 500 kW
                                       — **W** • E Africa & S Africa • 500 kW
           MALTA
           VO MEDITERRANEAN, Via Russia — **S** Su • E Asia • 250 kW
           RUSSIA
           VOICE OF RUSSIA, Armavir — **S** • S Asia • 500 kW
           USA
           †R FREE ASIA, Via Tinian, N Marianas — **W** • C Asia • 500 kW
17575 **FRANCE**
           R FRANCE INTL, Via French Guiana — S America • 250 kW
           PORTUGAL
           RDP INTERNATIONAL, Lisbon — **S** Sa/Su/Holidays • N America • 100 kW
                                      — Irr • **S** • E North Am • 100 kW
           USA
           FAMILY RADIO, Okeechobee, Fl — **W** • S America • 100 kW
17580 **AUSTRALIA**
           RADIO AUSTRALIA, Shepparton — Pacific & E Asia • 100 kW
           BELGIUM
           RTBF INTERNATIONAL, Via Germany — **◻** • C Africa • 100 kW
                                           — **◻** Sa/Su • C Africa • 100 kW
                                           — **◻** • Sa • C Africa • 100 kW
           CHINA
           †CENTRAL PEOPLE'S BS, Lingshi — DS-1 • 50 kW
                                          DS-8 (MINORITIES) • 50 kW
                                          W-M • DS-8 (MINORITIES) • 50 kW
                                          W-M • DS-1 • 50 kW
           CHINA RADIO INTL, St Petersburg, Russ — **S** • Mideast & E Africa • 400 kW
           IRAN
           VO THE ISLAMIC REP, Sirjan — **S** • Mideast, C Africa & E Africa • 500 kW
           NETHERLANDS
(con'd)   †R NEDERLAND, Via Madagascar — SE Asia • 200 kW

0 1 2 3 4 5 6 7 8 9 10 11 12 13 14 15 16 17 18 19 20 21 22 23 24

ENGLISH ▬   ARABIC ⋙   CHINESE ☐☐☐   FRENCH ══   GERMAN ▬   RUSSIAN ══   SPANISH ══   OTHER ▬

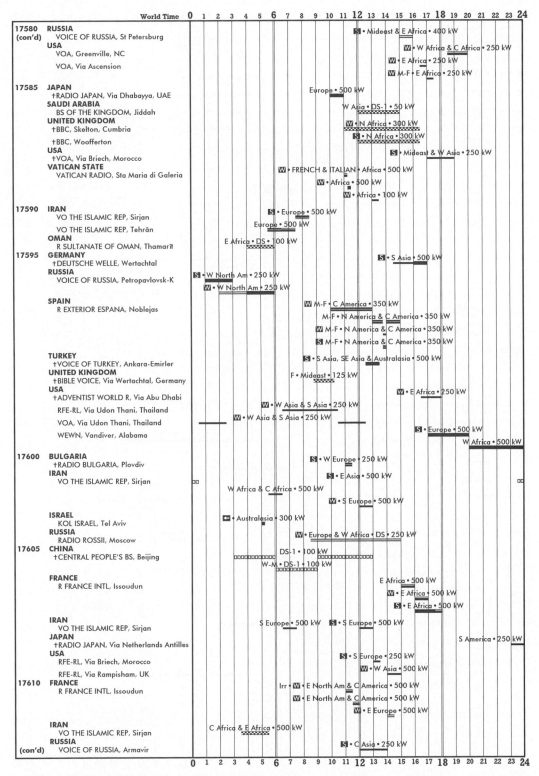

World Time

17580 (con'd) RUSSIA
VOICE OF RUSSIA, St Petersburg — [S] • Mideast & E Africa • 400 kW
USA
VOA, Greenville, NC — [W] • W Africa & C Africa • 250 kW
VOA, Via Ascension — [W] • E Africa • 250 kW / [W] M-F • E Africa • 250 kW

17585 JAPAN
†RADIO JAPAN, Via Dhabayya, UAE — Europe • 500 kW
SAUDI ARABIA
BS OF THE KINGDOM, Jiddah — W Asia • DS-1 • 50 kW
UNITED KINGDOM
†BBC, Skelton, Cumbria — [W] • N Africa • 300 kW
†BBC, Woofferton — [S] • N Africa • 300 kW
USA
†VOA, Via Briech, Morocco — [S] • Mideast & W Asia • 250 kW
VATICAN STATE
VATICAN RADIO, Sta Maria di Galeria — [W] • FRENCH & ITALIAN • Africa • 500 kW
[W] • Africa • 500 kW
[W] • Africa • 100 kW

17590 IRAN
VO THE ISLAMIC REP, Sirjan — [S] • Europe • 500 kW
VO THE ISLAMIC REP, Tehrān — Europe • 500 kW
OMAN
R SULTANATE OF OMAN, Thamarīt — E Africa • DS • 100 kW
17595 GERMANY
†DEUTSCHE WELLE, Wertachtal — [S] • S Asia • 500 kW
RUSSIA
VOICE OF RUSSIA, Petropavlovsk-K — [S] • W North Am • 250 kW
[W] • W North Am • 250 kW

SPAIN
R EXTERIOR ESPANA, Noblejas — [W] M-F • C America • 350 kW
M-F • N America & C America • 350 kW
[W] M-F • N America & C America • 350 kW
[S] M-F • N America & C America • 350 kW

TURKEY
†VOICE OF TURKEY, Ankara-Emirler — [S] • S Asia, SE Asia & Australasia • 500 kW
UNITED KINGDOM
†BIBLE VOICE, Via Wertachtal, Germany — F • Mideast • 125 kW
USA
†ADVENTIST WORLD R, Via Abu Dhabi — [W] • E Africa • 250 kW
RFE-RL, Via Udon Thani, Thailand — [W] • W Asia & S Asia • 250 kW
VOA, Via Udon Thani, Thailand — [W] • W Asia & S Asia • 250 kW
WEWN, Vandiver, Alabama — [S] • Europe • 500 kW
W Africa • 500 kW

17600 BULGARIA
†RADIO BULGARIA, Plovdiv — [S] • W Europe • 250 kW
IRAN
VO THE ISLAMIC REP, Sirjan — [S] • E Asia • 500 kW
W Africa & C Africa • 500 kW
[W] • S Europe • 500 kW

ISRAEL
KOL ISRAEL, Tel Aviv — Australasia • 300 kW
RUSSIA
RADIO ROSSII, Moscow — [W] • Europe & W Africa • DS • 250 kW
17605 CHINA
†CENTRAL PEOPLE'S BS, Beijing — DS-1 • 100 kW
W-M • DS-1 • 100 kW

FRANCE
R FRANCE INTL, Issoudun — E Africa • 500 kW
[W] • E Africa • 500 kW
[S] • E Africa • 500 kW

IRAN
VO THE ISLAMIC REP, Sirjan — S Europe • 500 kW / [S] • S Europe • 500 kW
JAPAN
†RADIO JAPAN, Via Netherlands Antilles — S America • 250 kW
USA
RFE-RL, Via Briech, Morocco — [S] • S Europe • 250 kW
RFE-RL, Via Rampisham, UK — [W] • W Asia • 500 kW
17610 FRANCE
R FRANCE INTL, Issoudun — Irr • [W] • E North Am & C America • 500 kW
[W] • E North Am & C America • 500 kW
[W] • E Europe • 500 kW

IRAN
VO THE ISLAMIC REP, Sirjan — C Africa & E Africa • 500 kW
RUSSIA
(con'd) VOICE OF RUSSIA, Armavir — [S] • C Asia • 250 kW

SEASONAL [S] OR [W]   1-HR TIMESHIFT MIDYEAR ⇆ OR ⇨   JAMMING / OR ∧   EARLIEST HEARD ◁   LATEST HEARD ▷   NEW FOR 2004 †

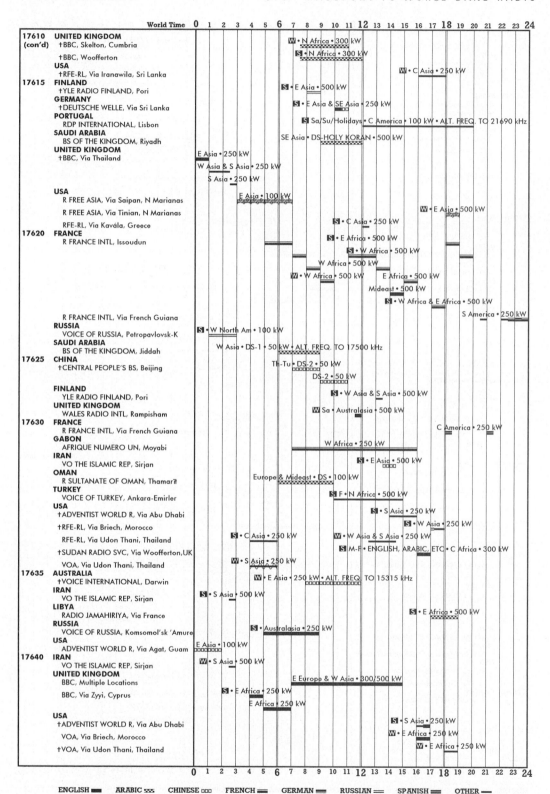

	World Time	0 1 2 3 4 5 6 7 8 9 10 11 12 13 14 15 16 17 18 19 20 21 22 23 24

17610 UNITED KINGDOM
(con'd) †BBC, Skelton, Cumbria — Ⓦ • N Africa • 300 kW

  †BBC, Woofferton — Ⓢ N Africa • 300 kW
USA
  †RFE-RL, Via Iranawila, Sri Lanka — Ⓦ • C Asia • 250 kW
17615 FINLAND
  †YLE RADIO FINLAND, Pori — Ⓢ • E Asia • 500 kW
GERMANY
  †DEUTSCHE WELLE, Via Sri Lanka — Ⓢ • E Asia & SE Asia • 250 kW
PORTUGAL
  RDP INTERNATIONAL, Lisbon — Ⓢ Sa/Su/Holidays • C America • 100 kW • ALT. FREQ. TO 21690 kHz
SAUDI ARABIA
  BS OF THE KINGDOM, Riyadh — SE Asia • DS-HOLY KORAN • 500 kW
UNITED KINGDOM
  †BBC, Via Thailand — E Asia • 250 kW

  — W Asia & S Asia • 250 kW

  — S Asia • 250 kW

USA
  R FREE ASIA, Via Saipan, N Marianas — E Asia • 100 kW

  R FREE ASIA, Via Tinian, N Marianas — Ⓦ • E Asia • 500 kW

  RFE-RL, Via Kavála, Greece — Ⓢ • C Asia • 250 kW
17620 FRANCE
  R FRANCE INTL, Issoudun — Ⓢ • E Africa • 500 kW

  — Ⓢ • W Africa • 500 kW

  — W Africa • 500 kW

  — Ⓦ • W Africa • 500 kW   E Africa • 500 kW

  — Mideast • 500 kW

  — Ⓢ • W Africa & E Africa • 500 kW

  R FRANCE INTL, Via French Guiana — S America • 250 kW
RUSSIA
  VOICE OF RUSSIA, Petropavlovsk-K — Ⓢ • W North Am • 100 kW
SAUDI ARABIA
  BS OF THE KINGDOM, Jiddah — W Asia • DS-1 • 50 kW • ALT. FREQ. TO 17500 kHz
17625 CHINA
  †CENTRAL PEOPLE'S BS, Beijing — Th-Tu • DS-2 • 50 kW

  — DS-2 • 50 kW

FINLAND
  YLE RADIO FINLAND, Pori — Ⓢ • W Asia & S Asia • 500 kW
UNITED KINGDOM
  WALES RADIO INTL, Rampisham — Ⓦ Sa • Australasia • 500 kW
17630 FRANCE
  R FRANCE INTL, Via French Guiana — C America • 250 kW
GABON
  AFRIQUE NUMERO UN, Moyabi — W Africa • 250 kW
IRAN
  VO THE ISLAMIC REP, Sirjan — Ⓢ • E Asia • 500 kW
OMAN
  R SULTANATE OF OMAN, Thamarīt — Europe & Mideast • DS • 100 kW
TURKEY
  VOICE OF TURKEY, Ankara-Emirler — Ⓢ F • N Africa • 500 kW
USA
  †ADVENTIST WORLD R, Via Abu Dhabi — Ⓢ • S Asia • 250 kW

  †RFE-RL, Via Briech, Morocco — Ⓢ • W Asia • 250 kW

  RFE-RL, Via Udon Thani, Thailand — Ⓢ • C Asia • 250 kW   Ⓦ • W Asia & S Asia • 250 kW

  †SUDAN RADIO SVC, Via Woofferton,UK — Ⓢ M-F • ENGLISH, ARABIC, ETC • C Africa • 300 kW

  VOA, Via Udon Thani, Thailand — Ⓦ • S Asia • 250 kW
17635 AUSTRALIA
  †VOICE INTERNATIONAL, Darwin — Ⓦ • E Asia • 250 kW • ALT. FREQ. TO 15315 kHz
IRAN
  VO THE ISLAMIC REP, Sirjan — Ⓢ • S Asia • 500 kW
LIBYA
  RADIO JAMAHIRIYA, Via France — Ⓢ • E Africa • 500 kW
RUSSIA
  VOICE OF RUSSIA, Komsomol'sk 'Amure — Ⓢ • Australasia • 250 kW
USA
  ADVENTIST WORLD R, Via Agat, Guam — E Asia • 100 kW
17640 IRAN
  VO THE ISLAMIC REP, Sirjan — Ⓦ • S Asia • 500 kW
UNITED KINGDOM
  BBC, Multiple Locations — E Europe & W Asia • 300/500 kW

  BBC, Via Zyyi, Cyprus — Ⓢ • E Africa • 250 kW

  — E Africa • 250 kW

USA
  †ADVENTIST WORLD R, Via Abu Dhabi — Ⓢ • S Asia • 250 kW

  VOA, Via Briech, Morocco — Ⓦ • E Africa • 250 kW

  †VOA, Via Udon Thani, Thailand — Ⓦ • E Africa • 250 kW

	0 1 2 3 4 5 6 7 8 9 10 11 12 13 14 15 16 17 18 19 20 21 22 23 24

ENGLISH ▬   ARABIC ⧓⧓⧓   CHINESE □□□   FRENCH ▬   GERMAN ▬   RUSSIAN ══   SPANISH ▬   OTHER ▬

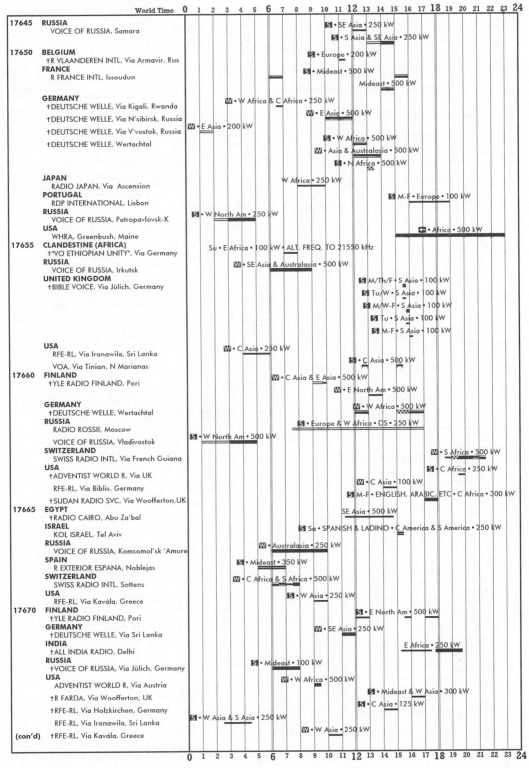

World Time scale: 0 1 2 3 4 5 6 7 8 9 10 11 12 13 14 15 16 17 18 19 20 21 22 23 24

17645 RUSSIA
VOICE OF RUSSIA, Samara
S • SE Asia • 250 kW
S • S Asia & SE Asia • 250 kW

17650 BELGIUM
†R VLAANDEREN INTL, Via Armavir, Rus
S • Europe • 200 kW
FRANCE
R FRANCE INTL, Issoudun
S • Mideast • 500 kW
Mideast • 500 kW

GERMANY
†DEUTSCHE WELLE, Via Kigali, Rwanda
W • W Africa & C Africa • 250 kW
†DEUTSCHE WELLE, Via N'sibirsk, Russia
W • E Asia • 500 kW
†DEUTSCHE WELLE, Via V'vostok, Russia
W • E Asia • 200 kW
†DEUTSCHE WELLE, Wertachtal
S • W Africa • 500 kW
W • Asia & Australasia • 500 kW
S • N Africa • 500 kW

JAPAN
RADIO JAPAN, Via Ascension
W Africa • 250 kW
PORTUGAL
RDP INTERNATIONAL, Lisbon
S M-F • Europe • 100 kW
RUSSIA
VOICE OF RUSSIA, Petropavlovsk-K
S • W North Am • 250 kW
USA
WHRA, Greenbush, Maine
• Africa • 500 kW

17655 CLANDESTINE (AFRICA)
†"VO ETHIOPIAN UNITY", Via Germany
Su • E Africa • 100 kW • ALT. FREQ. TO 21550 kHz
RUSSIA
VOICE OF RUSSIA, Irkutsk
W • SE Asia & Australasia • 500 kW
UNITED KINGDOM
†BIBLE VOICE, Via Jülich, Germany
S M/Th/F • S Asia • 100 kW
S Tu/W • S Asia • 100 kW
S M/W-F • S Asia • 100 kW
S Tu • S Asia • 100 kW
S M-F • S Asia • 100 kW

USA
RFE-RL, Via Iranawila, Sri Lanka
W • C Asia • 250 kW
VOA, Via Tinian, N Marianas
S • C Asia • 500 kW

17660 FINLAND
†YLE RADIO FINLAND, Pori
W • C Asia & E Asia • 500 kW
W • E North Am • 500 kW

GERMANY
†DEUTSCHE WELLE, Wertachtal
W • W Africa • 500 kW
RUSSIA
RADIO ROSSII, Moscow
S • Europe & W Africa • DS • 250 kW
VOICE OF RUSSIA, Vladivostok
S • W North Am • 500 kW
SWITZERLAND
SWISS RADIO INTL, Via French Guiana
W • S Africa • 500 kW
USA
†ADVENTIST WORLD R, Via UK
S • C Africa • 250 kW
RFE-RL, Via Biblis, Germany
W • C Asia • 100 kW
†SUDAN RADIO SVC, Via Woofferton,UK
S M-F • ENGLISH, ARABIC, ETC • C Africa • 300 kW

17665 EGYPT
†RADIO CAIRO, Abu Za'bal
SE Asia • 500 kW
ISRAEL
KOL ISRAEL, Tel Aviv
S Sa • SPANISH & LADINO • C America & S America • 250 kW
RUSSIA
VOICE OF RUSSIA, Komsomol'sk 'Amure
W • Australasia • 250 kW
SPAIN
R EXTERIOR ESPANA, Noblejas
S • Mideast • 350 kW
SWITZERLAND
SWISS RADIO INTL, Sottens
W • C Africa & S Africa • 500 kW
USA
RFE-RL, Via Kavála, Greece
S • W Asia • 250 kW

17670 FINLAND
†YLE RADIO FINLAND, Pori
S • E North Am • 500 kW
GERMANY
†DEUTSCHE WELLE, Via Sri Lanka
W • SE Asia • 250 kW
INDIA
†ALL INDIA RADIO, Delhi
E Africa • 250 kW
RUSSIA
†VOICE OF RUSSIA, Via Jülich, Germany
S • Mideast • 100 kW
USA
ADVENTIST WORLD R, Via Austria
W • W Africa • 500 kW
†R FARDA, Via Woofferton, UK
S • Mideast & W Asia • 300 kW
†RFE-RL, Via Holzkirchen, Germany
S • C Asia • 125 kW
RFE-RL, Via Iranawila, Sri Lanka
S • W Asia & S Asia • 250 kW
(con'd) †RFE-RL, Via Kavála, Greece
W • W Asia • 250 kW

World Time scale: 0 1 2 3 4 5 6 7 8 9 10 11 12 13 14 15 16 17 18 19 20 21 22 23 24

SEASONAL S OR W   1-HR TIMESHIFT MIDYEAR ⬅ OR ➡   JAMMING / OR ∧   EARLIEST HEARD ◁   LATEST HEARD ▷   NEW FOR 2004 †

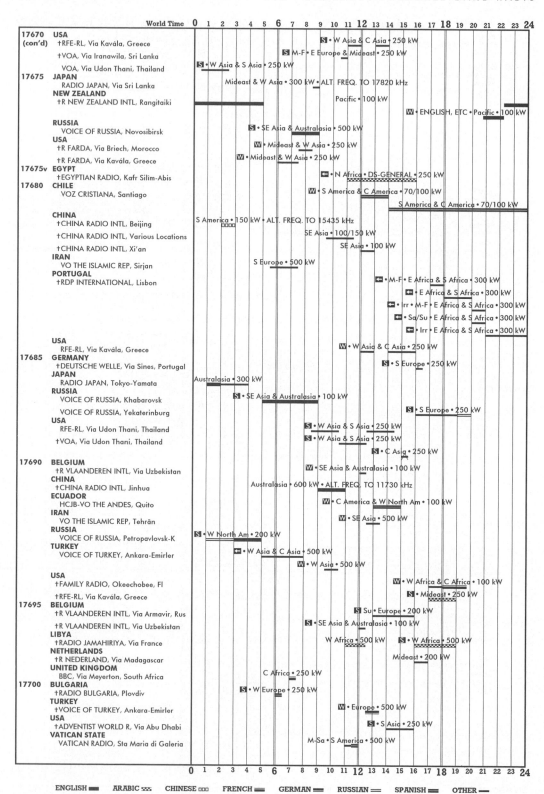

	World Time	0 1 2 3 4 5 6 7 8 9 10 11 12 13 14 15 16 17 18 19 20 21 22 23 24
17670	**USA**	
(con'd)	†RFE-RL, Via Kavála, Greece	S • W Asia & C Asia • 250 kW
	†VOA, Via Iranawila, Sri Lanka	S • M-F • E Europe & Mideast • 250 kW
	VOA, Via Udon Thani, Thailand	S • W Asia & S Asia • 250 kW
17675	**JAPAN**	
	RADIO JAPAN, Via Sri Lanka	Mideast & W Asia • 300 kW • ALT FREQ. TO 17820 kHz
	NEW ZEALAND	
	†R NEW ZEALAND INTL, Rangitaiki	Pacific • 100 kW
		W • ENGLISH, ETC • Pacific • 100 kW
	RUSSIA	
	VOICE OF RUSSIA, Novosibirsk	S • SE Asia & Australasia • 500 kW
	USA	
	†R FARDA, Via Briech, Morocco	W • Mideast & W Asia • 250 kW
	†R FARDA, Via Kavála, Greece	W • Mideast & W Asia • 250 kW
17675v	**EGYPT**	
	†EGYPTIAN RADIO, Kafr Silim-Abis	N Africa • DS-GENERAL • 250 kW
17680	**CHILE**	
	VOZ CRISTIANA, Santiago	W • S America & C America • 70/100 kW
		S America & C America • 70/100 kW
	CHINA	
	†CHINA RADIO INTL, Beijing	S America • 150 kW • ALT. FREQ. TO 15435 kHz
	†CHINA RADIO INTL, Various Locations	SE Asia • 100/150 kW
	†CHINA RADIO INTL, Xi'an	SE Asia • 100 kW
	IRAN	
	VO THE ISLAMIC REP, Sirjan	S Europe • 500 kW
	PORTUGAL	
	†RDP INTERNATIONAL, Lisbon	M-F • E Africa & S Africa • 300 kW
		E Africa & S Africa • 300 kW
		Irr • M-F • E Africa & S Africa • 300 kW
		Sa/Su • E Africa & S Africa • 300 kW
		Irr • E Africa & S Africa • 300 kW
	USA	
	RFE-RL, Via Kavála, Greece	W • W Asia & C Asia • 250 kW
17685	**GERMANY**	
	†DEUTSCHE WELLE, Via Sines, Portugal	S • S Europe • 250 kW
	JAPAN	
	RADIO JAPAN, Tokyo-Yamata	Australasia • 300 kW
	RUSSIA	
	VOICE OF RUSSIA, Khabarovsk	S • SE Asia & Australasia • 100 kW
	VOICE OF RUSSIA, Yekaterinburg	S • S Europe • 250 kW
	USA	
	RFE-RL, Via Udon Thani, Thailand	S • W Asia & S Asia • 250 kW
	†VOA, Via Udon Thani, Thailand	S • W Asia & S Asia • 250 kW
		S • C Asia • 250 kW
17690	**BELGIUM**	
	†R VLAANDEREN INTL, Via Uzbekistan	W • SE Asia & Australasia • 100 kW
	CHINA	
	†CHINA RADIO INTL, Jinhua	Australasia • 600 kW • ALT. FREQ. TO 11730 kHz
	ECUADOR	
	HCJB-VO THE ANDES, Quito	W • C America & W North Am • 100 kW
	IRAN	
	VO THE ISLAMIC REP, Tehrān	W • SE Asia • 500 kW
	RUSSIA	
	VOICE OF RUSSIA, Petropavlovsk-K	S • W North Am • 200 kW
	TURKEY	
	VOICE OF TURKEY, Ankara-Emirler	W • W Asia & C Asia • 500 kW
		W • W Asia • 500 kW
	USA	
	†FAMILY RADIO, Okeechobee, Fl	W • W Africa & C Africa • 100 kW
		S • Mideast • 250 kW
	†RFE-RL, Via Kavála, Greece	
17695	**BELGIUM**	
	†R VLAANDEREN INTL, Via Armavir, Rus	S • Su • Europe • 200 kW
	†R VLAANDEREN INTL, Via Uzbekistan	S • SE Asia & Australasia • 100 kW
	LIBYA	
	†RADIO JAMAHIRIYA, Via France	W Africa • 500 kW	S • W Africa • 500 kW
	NETHERLANDS	
	†R NEDERLAND, Via Madagascar	Mideast • 200 kW
	UNITED KINGDOM	
	BBC, Via Meyerton, South Africa	C Africa • 250 kW
17700	**BULGARIA**	
	†RADIO BULGARIA, Plovdiv	S • W Europe • 250 kW
	TURKEY	
	†VOICE OF TURKEY, Ankara-Emirler	W • Europe • 500 kW
	USA	
	†ADVENTIST WORLD R, Via Abu Dhabi	S • S Asia • 250 kW
	VATICAN STATE	
	VATICAN RADIO, Sta Maria di Galeria	M-Sa • S America • 500 kW

World Time	0 1 2 3 4 5 6 7 8 9 10 11 12 13 14 15 16 17 18 19 20 21 22 23 24

ENGLISH ▬ ARABIC ⧓⧓⧓ CHINESE □□□ FRENCH ▬ GERMAN ▬ RUSSIAN ═══ SPANISH ▬ OTHER ▬

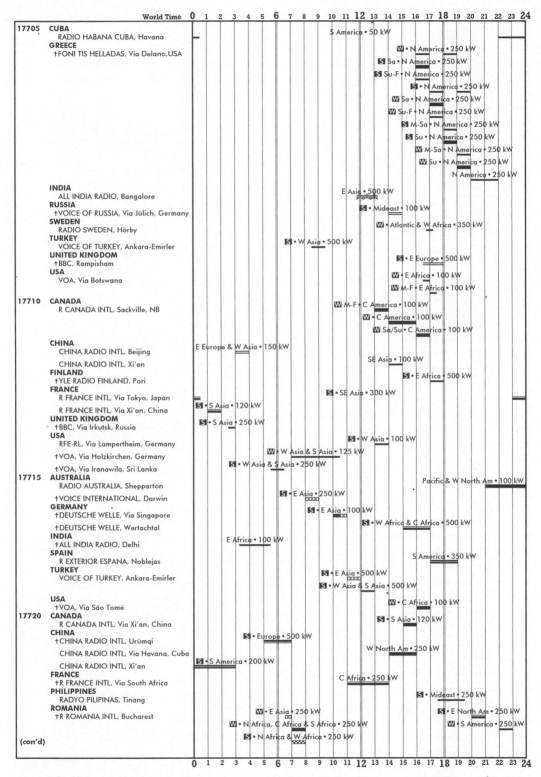

	World Time	0 1 2 3 4 5 6 7 8 9 10 11 12 13 14 15 16 17 18 19 20 21 22 23 24
17705	**CUBA** RADIO HABANA CUBA, Havana	S America • 50 kW
	GREECE †FONI TIS HELLADAS, Via Delano,USA	W • N America • 250 kW
		S Sa • N America • 250 kW
		S Su-F • N America • 250 kW
		S • N America • 250 kW
		W Sa • N America • 250 kW
		W Su-F • N America • 250 kW
		S M-Sa • N America • 250 kW
		S Su • N America • 250 kW
		W M-Sa • N America • 250 kW
		W Su • N America • 250 kW
		N America • 250 kW
	INDIA ALL INDIA RADIO, Bangalore	E Asia • 500 kW
	RUSSIA †VOICE OF RUSSIA, Via Jülich, Germany	S • Mideast • 100 kW
	SWEDEN RADIO SWEDEN, Hörby	W • Atlantic & W Africa • 350 kW
	TURKEY VOICE OF TURKEY, Ankara-Emirler	S • W Asia • 500 kW
	UNITED KINGDOM †BBC, Rampisham	S • E Europe • 500 kW
	USA VOA, Via Botswana	W • E Africa • 100 kW
		W M-F • E Africa • 100 kW
17710	**CANADA** R CANADA INTL, Sackville, NB	W M-F • C America • 100 kW
		W • C America • 100 kW
		W Sa/Su • C America • 100 kW
	CHINA CHINA RADIO INTL, Beijing	E Europe & W Asia • 150 kW
	CHINA RADIO INTL, Xi'an	SE Asia • 100 kW
	FINLAND †YLE RADIO FINLAND, Pori	S • E Africa • 500 kW
	FRANCE R FRANCE INTL, Via Tokyo, Japan	S • SE Asia • 300 kW
	R FRANCE INTL, Via Xi'an, China	S • S Asia • 120 kW
	UNITED KINGDOM †BBC, Via Irkutsk, Russia	S • S Asia • 250 kW
	USA RFE-RL, Via Lampertheim, Germany	S • W Asia • 100 kW
	†VOA, Via Holzkirchen, Germany	W • W Asia & S Asia • 125 kW
	†VOA, Via Iranawila, Sri Lanka	S • W Asia & S Asia • 250 kW
17715	**AUSTRALIA** RADIO AUSTRALIA, Shepparton	Pacific & W North Am • 100 kW
	†VOICE INTERNATIONAL, Darwin	S • E Asia • 250 kW
	GERMANY †DEUTSCHE WELLE, Via Singapore	S • E Asia • 100 kW
	†DEUTSCHE WELLE, Wertachtal	S • W Africa & C Africa • 500 kW
	INDIA †ALL INDIA RADIO, Delhi	E Africa • 100 kW
	SPAIN R EXTERIOR ESPANA, Noblejas	S America • 350 kW
	TURKEY VOICE OF TURKEY, Ankara-Emirler	S • E Asia • 500 kW
		S • W Asia & S Asia • 500 kW
	USA †VOA, Via São Tomé	W • C Africa • 100 kW
17720	**CANADA** R CANADA INTL, Via Xi'an, China	S • S Asia • 120 kW
	CHINA †CHINA RADIO INTL, Urümqi	S • Europe • 500 kW
	CHINA RADIO INTL, Via Havana, Cuba	W North Am • 250 kW
	CHINA RADIO INTL, Xi'an	S • S America • 200 kW
	FRANCE †R FRANCE INTL, Via South Africa	C Africa • 250 kW
	PHILIPPINES RADYO PILIPINAS, Tinang	S • Mideast • 250 kW
	ROMANIA †R ROMANIA INTL, Bucharest	S • E North Am • 250 kW
		W • E Asia • 250 kW
		W • N Africa, C Africa & S Africa • 250 kW
		W • S America • 250 kW
		S • N Africa & W Africa • 250 kW
(con'd)		0 1 2 3 4 5 6 7 8 9 10 11 12 13 14 15 16 17 18 19 20 21 22 23 24

SEASONAL S OR W   1-HR TIMESHIFT MIDYEAR ⬅ OR ➡   JAMMING / OR /\   EARLIEST HEARD ◁   LATEST HEARD ▷   NEW FOR 2004 †

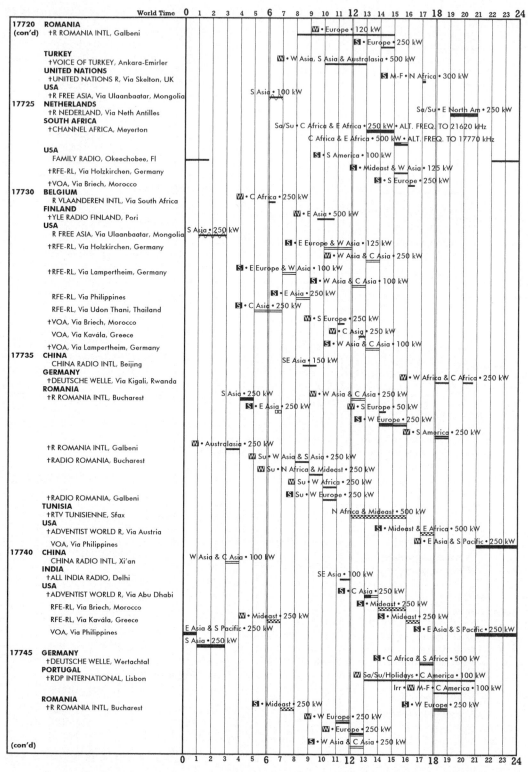

World Time	0 1 2 3 4 5 6 7 8 9 10 11 12 13 14 15 16 17 18 19 20 21 22 23 24
17720 ROMANIA	
(con'd) †R ROMANIA INTL, Galbeni	W • Europe • 120 kW
	S • Europe • 250 kW
TURKEY	
†VOICE OF TURKEY, Ankara-Emirler	W • W Asia, S Asia & Australasia • 500 kW
UNITED NATIONS	
†UNITED NATIONS R, Via Skelton, UK	S • M-F • N Africa • 300 kW
USA	
†R FREE ASIA, Via Ulaanbaatar, Mongolia	S Asia • 100 kW
17725 NETHERLANDS	
†R NEDERLAND, Via Neth Antilles	Sa/Su • E North Am • 250 kW
SOUTH AFRICA	
†CHANNEL AFRICA, Meyerton	Sa/Su • C Africa & E Africa • 250 kW • ALT. FREQ. TO 21620 kHz
	C Africa & E Africa • 500 kW • ALT. FREQ. TO 17770 kHz
USA	
FAMILY RADIO, Okeechobee, Fl	S • S America • 100 kW
†RFE-RL, Via Holzkirchen, Germany	S • Mideast & W Asia • 125 kW
†VOA, Via Briech, Morocco	S • S Europe • 250 kW
17730 BELGIUM	
R VLAANDEREN INTL, Via South Africa	W • C Africa • 250 kW
FINLAND	
†YLE RADIO FINLAND, Pori	W • E Asia • 500 kW
USA	
R FREE ASIA, Via Ulaanbaatar, Mongolia	S Asia • 250 kW
†RFE-RL, Via Holzkirchen, Germany	S • E Europe & W Asia • 125 kW
	W • W Asia & C Asia • 250 kW
†RFE-RL, Via Lampertheim, Germany	S • E Europe & W Asia • 100 kW
	S • W Asia & C Asia • 100 kW
RFE-RL, Via Philippines	S • E Asia • 250 kW
RFE-RL, Via Udon Thani, Thailand	S • C Asia • 250 kW
†VOA, Via Briech, Morocco	W • S Europe • 250 kW
VOA, Via Kavála, Greece	W • C Asia • 250 kW
†VOA, Via Lampertheim, Germany	S • W Asia & C Asia • 100 kW
17735 CHINA	
CHINA RADIO INTL, Beijing	SE Asia • 150 kW
GERMANY	
†DEUTSCHE WELLE, Via Kigali, Rwanda	W • W Africa & C Africa • 250 kW
ROMANIA	
†R ROMANIA INTL, Bucharest	S Asia • 250 kW
	W • W Asia & C Asia • 250 kW
	S • E Asia • 250 kW
	W • S Europe • 50 kW
	S • W Europe • 250 kW
	W • S America • 250 kW
†R ROMANIA INTL, Galbeni	W • Australasia • 250 kW
†RADIO ROMANIA, Bucharest	W Su • W Asia & S Asia • 250 kW
	W Su • N Africa & Mideast • 250 kW
	W Su • W Africa • 250 kW
†RADIO ROMANIA, Galbeni	S Su • W Europe • 250 kW
TUNISIA	
†RTV TUNISIENNE, Sfax	N Africa & Mideast • 500 kW
USA	
†ADVENTIST WORLD R, Via Austria	S • Mideast & E Africa • 500 kW
VOA, Via Philippines	W • E Asia & S Pacific • 250 kW
17740 CHINA	
CHINA RADIO INTL, Xi'an	W Asia & C Asia • 100 kW
INDIA	
†ALL INDIA RADIO, Delhi	SE Asia • 100 kW
USA	
†ADVENTIST WORLD R, Via Abu Dhabi	S • C Asia • 250 kW
RFE-RL, Via Briech, Morocco	S • Mideast • 250 kW
RFE-RL, Via Kavála, Greece	W • Mideast • 250 kW
	S • Mideast • 250 kW
VOA, Via Philippines	E Asia & S Pacific • 250 kW
	S • E Asia & S Pacific • 250 kW
	S Asia • 250 kW
17745 GERMANY	
†DEUTSCHE WELLE, Wertachtal	S • C Africa & S Africa • 500 kW
PORTUGAL	
†RDP INTERNATIONAL, Lisbon	W Sa/Su/Holidays • C America • 100 kW
	Irr • W M-F • C America • 100 kW
ROMANIA	
†R ROMANIA INTL, Bucharest	S • Mideast • 250 kW
	S • W Europe • 250 kW
	W • W Europe • 250 kW
	W • Europe • 250 kW
(con'd)	S • W Asia & C Asia • 250 kW

0 1 2 3 4 5 6 7 8 9 10 11 12 13 14 15 16 17 18 19 20 21 22 23 24

ENGLISH ▬   ARABIC ▨   CHINESE ▫▫▫   FRENCH ═══   GERMAN ══   RUSSIAN ══   SPANISH ══   OTHER ▬

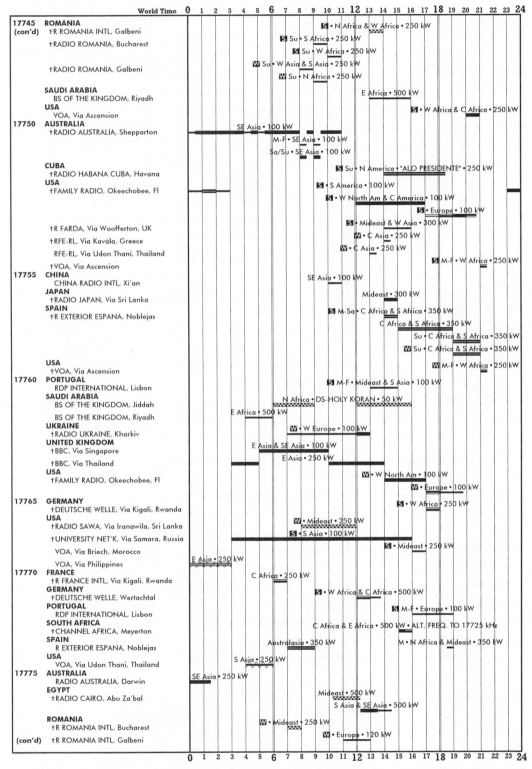

| | | World Time | 0 | 1 | 2 | 3 | 4 | 5 | 6 | 7 | 8 | 9 | 10 | 11 | 12 | 13 | 14 | 15 | 16 | 17 | 18 | 19 | 20 | 21 | 22 | 23 | 24 |

17745 ROMANIA
(con'd) †R ROMANIA INTL, Galbeni — S • N Africa & W Africa • 250 kW
†RADIO ROMANIA, Bucharest — S Su • S Africa • 250 kW
— S Su • W Africa • 250 kW
†RADIO ROMANIA, Galbeni — W Su • W Asia & S Asia • 250 kW
— W Su • N Africa • 250 kW

SAUDI ARABIA
BS OF THE KINGDOM, Riyadh — E Africa • 500 kW
USA
VOA, Via Ascension — S • W Africa & C Africa • 250 kW

17750 AUSTRALIA
†RADIO AUSTRALIA, Shepparton — SE Asia • 100 kW
— M-F • SE Asia • 100 kW
— Sa/Su • SE Asia • 100 kW

CUBA
†RADIO HABANA CUBA, Havana — S Su • N America • "ALO PRESIDENTE" • 250 kW
USA
†FAMILY RADIO, Okeechobee, Fl — S • S America • 100 kW
— S • W North Am & C America • 100 kW
— S • Europe • 100 kW
†R FARDA, Via Woofferton, UK — S • Mideast & W Asia • 300 kW
†RFE-RL, Via Kavála, Greece — W • C Asia • 250 kW
RFE-RL, Via Udon Thani, Thailand — W • C Asia • 250 kW
†VOA, Via Ascension — S • M-F • W Africa • 250 kW

17755 CHINA
CHINA RADIO INTL, Xi'an — SE Asia • 100 kW
JAPAN
†RADIO JAPAN, Via Sri Lanka — Mideast • 300 kW
SPAIN
†R EXTERIOR ESPANA, Noblejas — S M-Sa • C Africa & S Africa • 350 kW
— C Africa & S Africa • 350 kW
— Su • C Africa & S Africa • 350 kW
— W Su • C Africa & S Africa • 350 kW

USA
†VOA, Via Ascension — W • M-F • W Africa • 250 kW
17760 PORTUGAL
RDP INTERNATIONAL, Lisbon — S M-F • Mideast & S Asia • 100 kW
SAUDI ARABIA
BS OF THE KINGDOM, Jiddah — N Africa • DS-HOLY KORAN • 50 kW
BS OF THE KINGDOM, Riyadh — E Africa • 500 kW
UKRAINE
†RADIO UKRAINE, Kharkiv — W • W Europe • 100 kW
UNITED KINGDOM
†BBC, Via Singapore — E Asia & SE Asia • 100 kW
†BBC, Via Thailand — E Asia • 250 kW
USA
†FAMILY RADIO, Okeechobee, Fl — W • W North Am • 100 kW
— W • Europe • 100 kW

17765 GERMANY
†DEUTSCHE WELLE, Via Kigali, Rwanda — S • W Africa • 250 kW
USA
†RADIO SAWA, Via Iranawila, Sri Lanka — W • Mideast • 250 kW
†UNIVERSITY NET'K, Via Samara, Russia — S • S Asia • 100 kW
VOA, Via Briech, Morocco — S • Mideast • 250 kW
VOA, Via Philippines — E Asia • 250 kW

17770 FRANCE
†R FRANCE INTL, Via Kigali, Rwanda — C Africa • 250 kW
GERMANY
†DEUTSCHE WELLE, Wertachtal — S • W Africa & C Africa • 500 kW
PORTUGAL
RDP INTERNATIONAL, Lisbon — S M-F • Europe • 100 kW
SOUTH AFRICA
†CHANNEL AFRICA, Meyerton — C Africa & E Africa • 500 kW • ALT. FREQ. TO 17725 kHz
SPAIN
R EXTERIOR ESPANA, Noblejas — Australasia • 350 kW — M • N Africa & Mideast • 350 kW
USA
VOA, Via Udon Thani, Thailand — S Asia • 250 kW

17775 AUSTRALIA
RADIO AUSTRALIA, Darwin — SE Asia • 250 kW
EGYPT
†RADIO CAIRO, Abu Za'bal — Mideast • 500 kW
— S Asia & SE Asia • 500 kW

ROMANIA
†R ROMANIA INTL, Bucharest — W • Mideast • 250 kW
(con'd) †R ROMANIA INTL, Galbeni — W • Europe • 120 kW

| | | 0 | 1 | 2 | 3 | 4 | 5 | 6 | 7 | 8 | 9 | 10 | 11 | 12 | 13 | 14 | 15 | 16 | 17 | 18 | 19 | 20 | 21 | 22 | 23 | 24 |

SEASONAL S OR W   1-HR TIMESHIFT MIDYEAR ⊟ OR ⊞   JAMMING / OR ∧   EARLIEST HEARD ◁   LATEST HEARD ▷   NEW FOR 2004 †

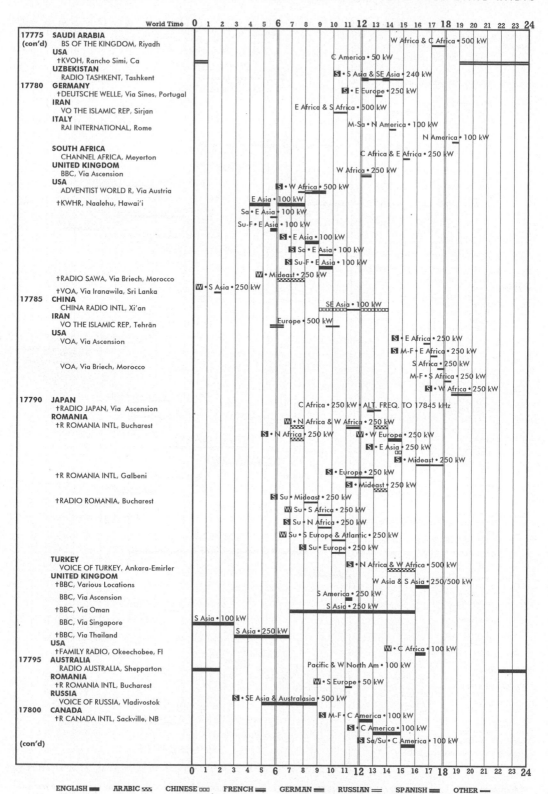

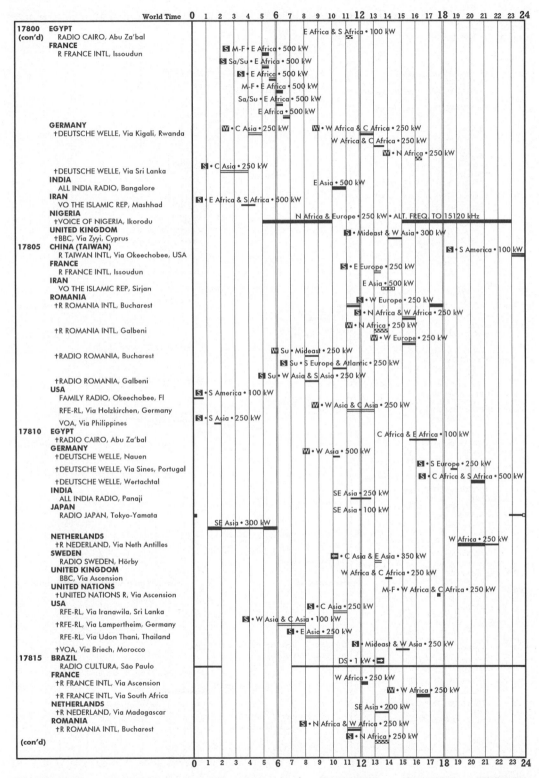

World Time	0 1 2 3 4 5 6 7 8 9 10 11 12 13 14 15 16 17 18 19 20 21 22 23 24

17800
(con'd)

EGYPT
RADIO CAIRO, Abu Za'bal — E Africa & S Africa • 100 kW

FRANCE
R FRANCE INTL, Issoudun
- S M-F • E Africa • 500 kW
- S Sa/Su • E Africa • 500 kW
- S • E Africa • 500 kW
- M-F • E Africa • 500 kW
- Sa/Su • E Africa • 500 kW
- E Africa • 500 kW

GERMANY
†DEUTSCHE WELLE, Via Kigali, Rwanda
- W • C Asia • 250 kW
- W • W Africa & C Africa • 250 kW
- W Africa & C Africa • 250 kW
- W • N Africa • 250 kW

†DEUTSCHE WELLE, Via Sri Lanka
- S • C Asia • 250 kW

INDIA
ALL INDIA RADIO, Bangalore — E Asia • 500 kW

IRAN
VO THE ISLAMIC REP, Mashhad — S • E Africa & S Africa • 500 kW

NIGERIA
†VOICE OF NIGERIA, Ikorodu — N Africa & Europe • 250 kW • ALT. FREQ. TO 15120 kHz

UNITED KINGDOM
†BBC, Via Zyyi, Cyprus — S • Mideast & W Asia • 300 kW

17805

CHINA (TAIWAN)
R TAIWAN INTL, Via Okeechobee, USA — S • S America • 100 kW

FRANCE
R FRANCE INTL, Issoudun — S • E Europe • 250 kW

IRAN
VO THE ISLAMIC REP, Sirjan — E Asia • 500 kW

ROMANIA
†R ROMANIA INTL, Bucharest
- S • W Europe • 250 kW
- S • N Africa & W Africa • 250 kW

†R ROMANIA INTL, Galbeni
- W • N Africa • 250 kW
- W • W Europe • 250 kW

†RADIO ROMANIA, Bucharest
- W Su • Mideast • 250 kW
- S Su • S Europe & Atlantic • 250 kW

†RADIO ROMANIA, Galbeni
- S Su • W Asia & S Asia • 250 kW

USA
FAMILY RADIO, Okeechobee, Fl — S • S America • 100 kW

RFE-RL, Via Holzkirchen, Germany — W • W Asia & C Asia • 250 kW

VOA, Via Philippines — S • S Asia • 250 kW

17810

EGYPT
†RADIO CAIRO, Abu Za'bal — C Africa & E Africa • 100 kW

GERMANY
†DEUTSCHE WELLE, Nauen — W • W Asia • 500 kW

†DEUTSCHE WELLE, Via Sines, Portugal — S • S Europe • 250 kW

†DEUTSCHE WELLE, Wertachtal — S • C Africa & S Africa • 500 kW

INDIA
ALL INDIA RADIO, Panaji — SE Asia • 250 kW

JAPAN
RADIO JAPAN, Tokyo-Yamata — SE Asia • 100 kW
SE Asia • 300 kW

NETHERLANDS
†R NEDERLAND, Via Neth Antilles — W Africa • 250 kW

SWEDEN
RADIO SWEDEN, Hörby — • C Asia & E Asia • 350 kW

UNITED KINGDOM
BBC, Via Ascension — W Africa & C Africa • 250 kW

UNITED NATIONS
†UNITED NATIONS R, Via Ascension — M-F • W Africa & C Africa • 250 kW

USA
RFE-RL, Via Iranawila, Sri Lanka — S • C Asia • 250 kW

†RFE-RL, Via Lampertheim, Germany — S • W Asia & C Asia • 100 kW

RFE-RL, Via Udon Thani, Thailand — S • E Asia • 250 kW

†VOA, Via Briech, Morocco — S • Mideast & W Asia • 250 kW

17815

BRAZIL
RADIO CULTURA, São Paulo — DS • 1 kW •

FRANCE
†R FRANCE INTL, Via Ascension — W Africa • 250 kW

†R FRANCE INTL, Via South Africa — W • W Africa • 250 kW

NETHERLANDS
†R NEDERLAND, Via Madagascar — SE Asia • 200 kW

ROMANIA
†R ROMANIA INTL, Bucharest
- S • N Africa & W Africa • 250 kW
- S • N Africa • 250 kW

(con'd)

	0 1 2 3 4 5 6 7 8 9 10 11 12 13 14 15 16 17 18 19 20 21 22 23 24

SEASONAL S OR W   1-HR TIMESHIFT MIDYEAR ⬅ OR ➡   JAMMING / OR /\   EARLIEST HEARD ◁   LATEST HEARD ▷   NEW FOR 2004 †

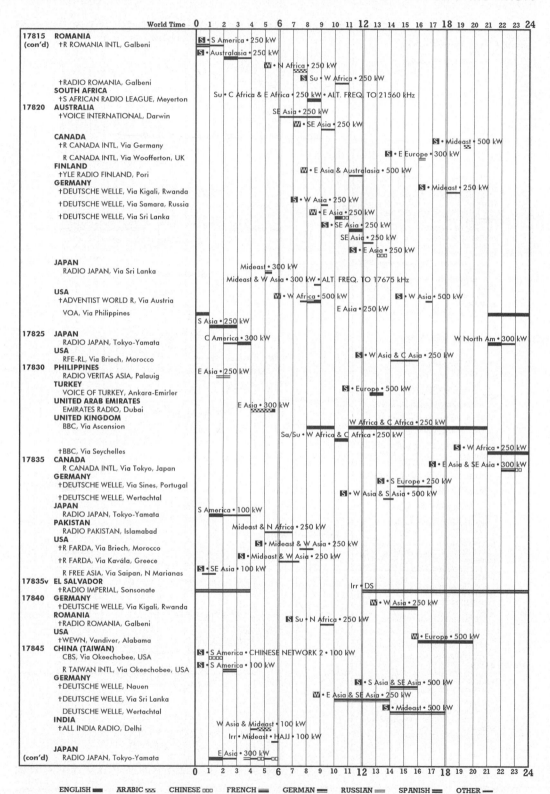

17815 **ROMANIA**	
(con'd) †R ROMANIA INTL, Galbeni	S America • 250 kW
	Australasia • 250 kW
	W • N Africa • 250 kW
	S Su • W Africa • 250 kW
†RADIO ROMANIA, Galbeni	
SOUTH AFRICA	
†S AFRICAN RADIO LEAGUE, Meyerton	Su • C Africa & E Africa • 250 kW • ALT. FREQ. TO 21560 kHz
17820 **AUSTRALIA**	
†VOICE INTERNATIONAL, Darwin	SE Asia • 250 kW
	W • SE Asia • 250 kW
CANADA	
†R CANADA INTL, Via Germany	S • Mideast • 500 kW
R CANADA INTL, Via Woofferton, UK	S • E Europe • 300 kW
FINLAND	
†YLE RADIO FINLAND, Pori	W • E Asia & Australasia • 500 kW
GERMANY	
†DEUTSCHE WELLE, Via Kigali, Rwanda	S • Mideast • 250 kW
†DEUTSCHE WELLE, Via Samara, Russia	S • W Asia • 250 kW
†DEUTSCHE WELLE, Via Sri Lanka	W • E Asia • 250 kW
	S • SE Asia • 250 kW
	SE Asia • 250 kW
	S • E Asia • 250 kW
JAPAN	
RADIO JAPAN, Via Sri Lanka	Mideast • 300 kW
	Mideast & W Asia • 300 kW • ALT. FREQ. TO 17675 kHz
USA	
†ADVENTIST WORLD R, Via Austria	W • W Africa • 500 kW S • W Asia • 500 kW
VOA, Via Philippines	E Asia • 250 kW
	S Asia • 250 kW
17825 **JAPAN**	C America • 300 kW W North Am • 300 kW
RADIO JAPAN, Tokyo-Yamata	
USA	
RFE-RL, Via Briech, Morocco	S • W Asia & C Asia • 250 kW
17830 **PHILIPPINES**	E Asia • 250 kW
RADIO VERITAS ASIA, Palauig	
TURKEY	
VOICE OF TURKEY, Ankara-Emirler	S • Europe • 500 kW
UNITED ARAB EMIRATES	
EMIRATES RADIO, Dubai	E Asia • 300 kW
UNITED KINGDOM	
BBC, Via Ascension	W Africa & C Africa • 250 kW
	Sa/Su • W Africa & C Africa • 250 kW
†BBC, Via Seychelles	S • W Africa • 250 kW
17835 **CANADA**	
R CANADA INTL, Via Tokyo, Japan	S • E Asia & SE Asia • 300 kW
GERMANY	
†DEUTSCHE WELLE, Via Sines, Portugal	S • S Europe • 250 kW
†DEUTSCHE WELLE, Wertachtal	S • W Asia & S Asia • 500 kW
JAPAN	
RADIO JAPAN, Tokyo-Yamata	S America • 100 kW
PAKISTAN	
RADIO PAKISTAN, Islamabad	Mideast & N Africa • 250 kW
USA	
†R FARDA, Via Briech, Morocco	S • Mideast & W Asia • 250 kW
†R FARDA, Via Kavála, Greece	S • Mideast & W Asia • 250 kW
R FREE ASIA, Via Saipan, N Marianas	S • SE Asia • 100 kW
17835v **EL SALVADOR**	
†RADIO IMPERIAL, Sonsonate	Irr • DS
17840 **GERMANY**	
†DEUTSCHE WELLE, Via Kigali, Rwanda	W • W Asia • 250 kW
ROMANIA	
†RADIO ROMANIA, Galbeni	S Su • N Africa • 250 kW
USA	
†WEWN, Vandiver, Alabama	W • Europe • 500 kW
17845 **CHINA (TAIWAN)**	
CBS, Via Okeechobee, USA	S • S America • CHINESE NETWORK 2 • 100 kW
R TAIWAN INTL, Via Okeechobee, USA	S • S America • 100 kW
GERMANY	
†DEUTSCHE WELLE, Nauen	S • S Asia & SE Asia • 500 kW
†DEUTSCHE WELLE, Via Sri Lanka	W • E Asia & SE Asia • 250 kW
DEUTSCHE WELLE, Wertachtal	S • Mideast • 500 kW
INDIA	
†ALL INDIA RADIO, Delhi	W Asia & Mideast • 100 kW
	Irr • Mideast • HAJJ • 100 kW
JAPAN	
(con'd) RADIO JAPAN, Tokyo-Yamata	E Asia • 300 kW

ENGLISH ▬ ARABIC ※ CHINESE □□□ FRENCH ══ GERMAN ▬▬ RUSSIAN ═══ SPANISH ▬ OTHER ▬▬

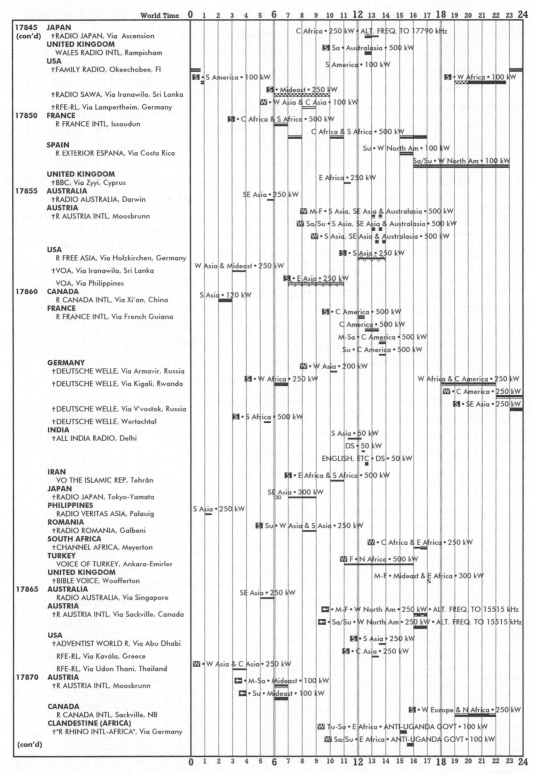

World Time   0 1 2 3 4 5 6 7 8 9 10 11 12 13 14 15 16 17 18 19 20 21 22 23 24

17845 **JAPAN**
(con'd) †RADIO JAPAN, Via Ascension — C Africa • 250 kW • ALT. FREQ. TO 17790 kHz
UNITED KINGDOM
  WALES RADIO INTL, Rampisham — S Sa • Australasia • 500 kW
USA
†FAMILY RADIO, Okeechobee, Fl — S America • 100 kW ; S • S America • 100 kW ; S • W Africa • 100 kW

†RADIO SAWA, Via Iranawila, Sri Lanka — S • Mideast • 250 kW

†RFE-RL, Via Lampertheim, Germany — W • W Asia & C Asia • 100 kW
17850 **FRANCE**
  R FRANCE INTL, Issoudun — S • C Africa & S Africa • 500 kW ; C Africa & S Africa • 500 kW

SPAIN
  R EXTERIOR ESPANA, Via Costa Rica — Su • W North Am • 100 kW ; Sa/Su • W North Am • 100 kW

UNITED KINGDOM
†BBC, Via Zyyi, Cyprus — E Africa • 250 kW
17855 **AUSTRALIA**
†RADIO AUSTRALIA, Darwin — SE Asia • 250 kW
AUSTRIA
†R AUSTRIA INTL, Moosbrunn — W M-F • S Asia, SE Asia & Australasia • 500 kW ; W Sa/Su • S Asia, SE Asia & Australasia • 500 kW ; W • S Asia, SE Asia & Australasia • 500 kW

USA
  R FREE ASIA, Via Holzkirchen, Germany — S • S Asia • 250 kW

†VOA, Via Iranawila, Sri Lanka — W Asia & Mideast • 250 kW

VOA, Via Philippines — S • E Asia • 250 kW
17860 **CANADA**
  R CANADA INTL, Via Xi'an, China — S Asia • 120 kW
FRANCE
  R FRANCE INTL, Via French Guiana — S • C America • 500 kW ; C America • 500 kW ; M-Sa • C America • 500 kW ; Su • C America • 500 kW

GERMANY
†DEUTSCHE WELLE, Via Armavir, Russia — W • W Asia • 200 kW
†DEUTSCHE WELLE, Via Kigali, Rwanda — S • W Africa • 250 kW ; W Africa & C America • 250 kW ; W • C America • 250 kW ; S • SE Asia • 250 kW

†DEUTSCHE WELLE, Via V'vostok, Russia

†DEUTSCHE WELLE, Wertachtal — S • S Africa • 500 kW
INDIA
†ALL INDIA RADIO, Delhi — S Asia • 50 kW ; DS • 50 kW ; ENGLISH, ETC • DS • 50 kW

IRAN
  VO THE ISLAMIC REP, Tehrän — S • E Africa & S Africa • 500 kW
JAPAN
†RADIO JAPAN, Tokyo-Yamata — SE Asia • 300 kW
PHILIPPINES
  RADIO VERITAS ASIA, Palauig — S Asia • 250 kW
ROMANIA
†RADIO ROMANIA, Galbeni — S • Su • W Asia & S Asia • 250 kW
SOUTH AFRICA
†CHANNEL AFRICA, Meyerton — W • C Africa & E Africa • 250 kW
TURKEY
  VOICE OF TURKEY, Ankara-Emirler — W F • N Africa • 500 kW
UNITED KINGDOM
†BIBLE VOICE, Woofferton — M-F • Mideast & E Africa • 300 kW
17865 **AUSTRALIA**
  RADIO AUSTRALIA, Via Singapore — SE Asia • 250 kW
AUSTRIA
†R AUSTRIA INTL, Via Sackville, Canada — ⯈ • M-F • W North Am • 250 kW • ALT. FREQ. TO 15515 kHz ; ⯈ • Sa/Su • W North Am • 250 kW • ALT. FREQ. TO 15515 kHz

USA
†ADVENTIST WORLD R, Via Abu Dhabi — S • S Asia • 250 kW

RFE-RL, Via Kavála, Greece — S • C Asia • 250 kW

RFE-RL, Via Udon Thani, Thailand — W • W Asia & C Asia • 250 kW
17870 **AUSTRIA**
†R AUSTRIA INTL, Moosbrunn — ⯇ • M-Sa • Mideast • 100 kW ; ⯇ • Su • Mideast • 100 kW

CANADA
  R CANADA INTL, Sackville, NB — S • W Europe & N Africa • 250 kW
CLANDESTINE (AFRICA)
†"R RHINO INTL-AFRICA", Via Germany — W Tu-Su • E Africa • ANTI-UGANDA GOVT • 100 kW ; W Sa/Su • E Africa • ANTI-UGANDA GOVT • 100 kW

(con'd)

0 1 2 3 4 5 6 7 8 9 10 11 12 13 14 15 16 17 18 19 20 21 22 23 24

SEASONAL S OR W   1-HR TIMESHIFT MIDYEAR ⯇ OR ⯈   JAMMING / OR ∧   EARLIEST HEARD ◁   LATEST HEARD ▷   NEW FOR 2004 †

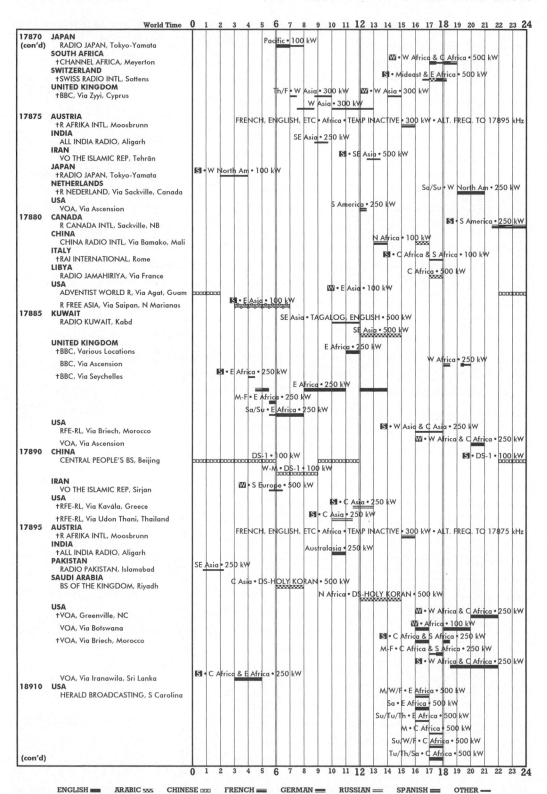

World Time		
17870 **JAPAN**		
(con'd) RADIO JAPAN, Tokyo-Yamata	Pacific • 100 kW	
SOUTH AFRICA		
†CHANNEL AFRICA, Meyerton	W • W Africa & C Africa • 500 kW	
SWITZERLAND		
†SWISS RADIO INTL, Sottens	S • Mideast & E Africa • 500 kW	
UNITED KINGDOM		
†BBC, Via Zyyi, Cyprus	Th/F • W Asia • 300 kW W • W Asia • 300 kW	
	W Asia • 300 kW	
17875 **AUSTRIA**		
†R AFRIKA INTL, Moosbrunn	FRENCH, ENGLISH, ETC • Africa • TEMP INACTIVE • 300 kW • ALT. FREQ. TO 17895 kHz	
INDIA		
ALL INDIA RADIO, Aligarh	SE Asia • 250 kW	
IRAN		
VO THE ISLAMIC REP, Tehrān	S • SE Asia • 500 kW	
JAPAN		
†RADIO JAPAN, Tokyo-Yamata	S • W North Am • 100 kW	
NETHERLANDS		
†R NEDERLAND, Via Sackville, Canada	Sa/Su • W North Am • 250 kW	
USA		
VOA, Via Ascension	S America • 250 kW	
17880 **CANADA**		
R CANADA INTL, Sackville, NB	S • S America • 250 kW	
CHINA		
CHINA RADIO INTL, Via Bamako, Mali	N Africa • 100 kW	
ITALY		
†RAI INTERNATIONAL, Rome	S • C Africa & S Africa • 100 kW	
LIBYA		
RADIO JAMAHIRIYA, Via France	C Africa • 500 kW	
USA		
ADVENTIST WORLD R, Via Agat, Guam	W • E Asia • 100 kW	
R FREE ASIA, Via Saipan, N Marianas	S • E Asia • 100 kW	
17885 **KUWAIT**		
RADIO KUWAIT, Kabd	SE Asia • TAGALOG, ENGLISH • 500 kW	
	SE Asia • 500 kW	
UNITED KINGDOM		
†BBC, Various Locations	E Africa • 250 kW	
BBC, Via Ascension	W Africa • 250 kW	
†BBC, Via Seychelles	S • E Africa • 250 kW	
	E Africa • 250 kW	
	M-F • E Africa • 250 kW	
	Sa/Su • E Africa • 250 kW	
USA		
RFE-RL, Via Briech, Morocco	S • W Asia & C Asia • 250 kW	
VOA, Via Ascension	W • W Africa & C Africa • 250 kW	
17890 **CHINA**		
CENTRAL PEOPLE'S BS, Beijing	DS-1 • 100 kW S • DS-1 • 100 kW	
	W-M • DS-1 • 100 kW	
IRAN		
VO THE ISLAMIC REP, Sirjan	W • S Europe • 500 kW	
USA		
†RFE-RL, Via Kavála, Greece	S • C Asia • 250 kW	
†RFE-RL, Via Udon Thani, Thailand	S • C Asia • 250 kW	
17895 **AUSTRIA**		
†R AFRIKA INTL, Moosbrunn	FRENCH, ENGLISH, ETC • Africa • TEMP INACTIVE • 300 kW • ALT. FREQ. TO 17875 kHz	
INDIA		
†ALL INDIA RADIO, Aligarh	Australasia • 250 kW	
PAKISTAN		
RADIO PAKISTAN, Islamabad	SE Asia • 250 kW	
SAUDI ARABIA		
BS OF THE KINGDOM, Riyadh	C Asia • DS-HOLY KORAN • 500 kW	
	N Africa • DS-HOLY KORAN • 500 kW	
USA		
†VOA, Greenville, NC	W • W Africa & C Africa • 250 kW	
VOA, Via Botswana	W • Africa • 100 kW	
†VOA, Via Briech, Morocco	S • C Africa & S Africa • 250 kW	
	M-F • C Africa & S Africa • 250 kW	
	S • W Africa & C Africa • 250 kW	
VOA, Via Iranawila, Sri Lanka	S • C Africa & E Africa • 250 kW	
18910 **USA**		
HERALD BROADCASTING, S Carolina	M/W/F • E Africa • 500 kW	
	Sa • E Africa • 500 kW	
	Su/Tu/Th • E Africa • 500 kW	
	M • C Africa • 500 kW	
	Su/W/F • C Africa • 500 kW	
	Tu/Th/Sa • C Africa • 500 kW	
(con'd)		

ENGLISH ▬   ARABIC ▨   CHINESE ▫▫▫   FRENCH ▬   GERMAN ▬   RUSSIAN ═   SPANISH ▬   OTHER ▬

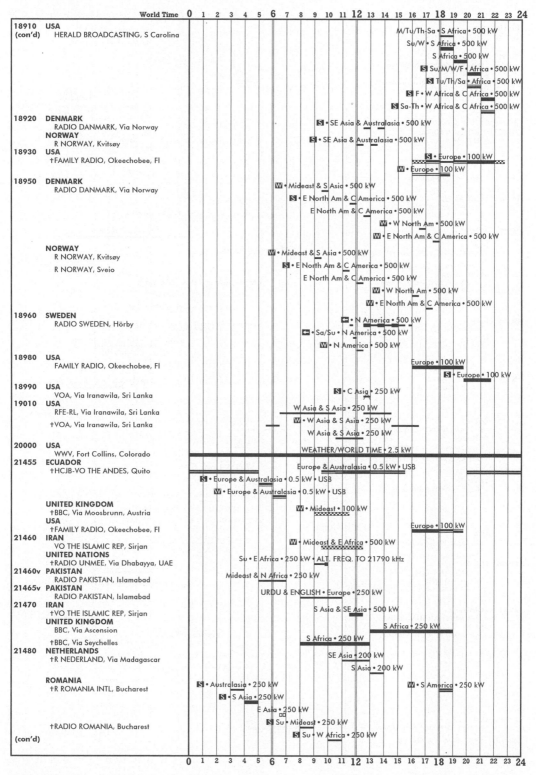

World Time	0 1 2 3 4 5 6 7 8 9 10 11 12 13 14 15 16 17 18 19 20 21 22 23 24

18910 **USA**
(con'd) HERALD BROADCASTING, S Carolina
- M/Tu/Th·Sa • S Africa • 500 kW
- Su/W • S Africa • 500 kW
- S Africa • 500 kW
- ⑤ Su/M/W/F • Africa • 500 kW
- ⑤ Tu/Th/Sa • Africa • 500 kW
- ⑤ F • W Africa & C Africa • 500 kW
- ⑤ Sa-Th • W Africa & C Africa • 500 kW

18920 **DENMARK**
RADIO DANMARK, Via Norway
- ⑤ • SE Asia & Australasia • 500 kW
NORWAY
R NORWAY, Kvitsøy
- ⑤ • SE Asia & Australasia • 500 kW
18930 **USA**
†FAMILY RADIO, Okeechobee, Fl
- ⑤ • Europe • 100 kW
- Ⓦ • Europe • 100 kW

18950 **DENMARK**
RADIO DANMARK, Via Norway
- Ⓦ • Mideast & S Asia • 500 kW
- ⑤ • E North Am & C America • 500 kW
- E North Am & C America • 500 kW
- Ⓦ • W North Am • 500 kW
- Ⓦ • E North Am & C America • 500 kW

NORWAY
R NORWAY, Kvitsøy
- Ⓦ • Mideast & S Asia • 500 kW
R NORWAY, Sveio
- ⑤ • E North Am & C America • 500 kW
- E North Am & C America • 500 kW
- Ⓦ • W North Am • 500 kW
- Ⓦ • E North Am & C America • 500 kW

18960 **SWEDEN**
RADIO SWEDEN, Hörby
- ⬌ • N America • 500 kW
- ⬌ • Sa/Su • N America • 500 kW
- Ⓦ • N America • 500 kW

18980 **USA**
FAMILY RADIO, Okeechobee, Fl
- Europe • 100 kW
- ⑤ • Europe • 100 kW

18990 **USA**
VOA, Via Iranawila, Sri Lanka
- ⑤ • C Asia • 250 kW
19010 **USA**
RFE-RL, Via Iranawila, Sri Lanka
- W Asia & S Asia • 250 kW
†VOA, Via Iranawila, Sri Lanka
- Ⓦ • W Asia & S Asia • 250 kW
- W Asia & S Asia • 250 kW

20000 **USA**
WWV, Fort Collins, Colorado
- WEATHER/WORLD TIME • 2.5 kW
21455 **ECUADOR**
†HCJB-VO THE ANDES, Quito
- Europe & Australasia • 0.5 kW • USB
- ⑤ • Europe & Australasia • 0.5 kW • USB
- Ⓦ • Europe & Australasia • 0.5 kW • USB

UNITED KINGDOM
†BBC, Via Moosbrunn, Austria
- Ⓦ • Mideast • 100 kW
USA
†FAMILY RADIO, Okeechobee, Fl
- Europe • 100 kW
21460 **IRAN**
VO THE ISLAMIC REP, Sirjan
- Ⓦ • Mideast & E Africa • 500 kW
UNITED NATIONS
†RADIO UNMEE, Via Dhabayya, UAE
- Su • E Africa • 250 kW • ALT. FREQ. TO 21790 kHz
21460v **PAKISTAN**
RADIO PAKISTAN, Islamabad
- Mideast & N Africa • 250 kW
21465v **PAKISTAN**
RADIO PAKISTAN, Islamabad
- URDU & ENGLISH • Europe • 250 kW
21470 **IRAN**
†VO THE ISLAMIC REP, Sirjan
- S Asia & SE Asia • 500 kW
UNITED KINGDOM
BBC, Via Ascension
- S Africa • 250 kW
†BBC, Via Seychelles
- S Africa • 250 kW
21480 **NETHERLANDS**
†R NEDERLAND, Via Madagascar
- SE Asia • 200 kW
- S Asia • 200 kW

ROMANIA
†R ROMANIA INTL, Bucharest
- ⑤ • Australasia • 250 kW
- Ⓦ • S America • 250 kW
- ⑤ • S Asia • 250 kW
- E Asia • 250 kW
†RADIO ROMANIA, Bucharest
- ⑤ Su • Mideast • 250 kW
- ⑤ Su • W Africa • 250 kW
(con'd)

	0 1 2 3 4 5 6 7 8 9 10 11 12 13 14 15 16 17 18 19 20 21 22 23 24

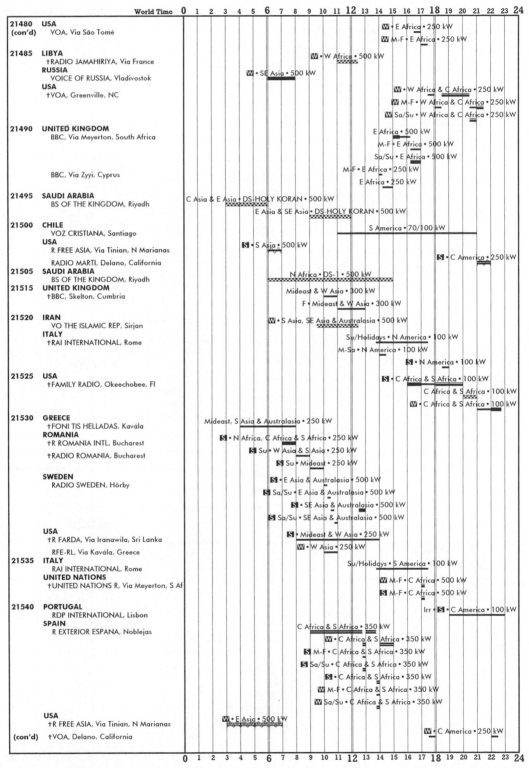

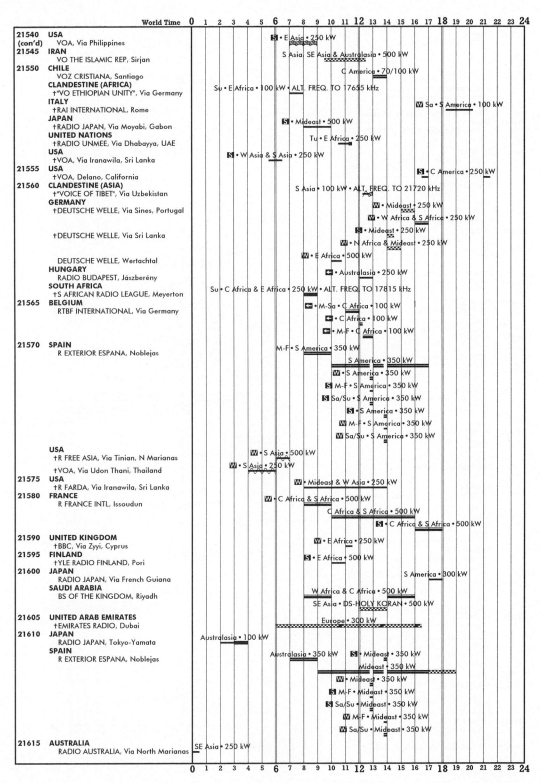

World Time	0 1 2 3 4 5 6 7 8 9 10 11 12 13 14 15 16 17 18 19 20 21 22 23 24
21540 **USA** (con'd) VOA, Via Philippines	**S** • E Asia • 250 kW
21545 IRAN VO THE ISLAMIC REP, Sirjan	S Asia, SE Asia & Australasia • 500 kW
21550 CHILE VOZ CRISTIANA, Santiago	C America • 70/100 kW
CLANDESTINE (AFRICA) †"VO ETHIOPIAN UNITY", Via Germany	Su • E Africa • 100 kW • ALT. FREQ. TO 17655 kHz
ITALY †RAI INTERNATIONAL, Rome	**W** Sa • S America • 100 kW
JAPAN †RADIO JAPAN, Via Moyabi, Gabon	**S** • Mideast • 500 kW
UNITED NATIONS †RADIO UNMEE, Via Dhabayya, UAE	Tu • E Africa • 250 kW
USA †VOA, Via Iranawila, Sri Lanka	**S** • W Asia & S Asia • 250 kW
21555 USA †VOA, Delano, California	**S** • C America • 250 kW
21560 CLANDESTINE (ASIA) †"VOICE OF TIBET", Via Uzbekistan	S Asia • 100 kW • ALT. FREQ. TO 21720 kHz
GERMANY †DEUTSCHE WELLE, Via Sines, Portugal	**W** • Mideast • 250 kW **W** • W Africa & S Africa • 250 kW
†DEUTSCHE WELLE, Via Sri Lanka	**S** • Mideast • 250 kW **W** • N Africa & Mideast • 250 kW
DEUTSCHE WELLE, Wertachtal	**W** • E Africa • 500 kW
HUNGARY RADIO BUDAPEST, Jászberény	⊟ • Australasia • 250 kW
SOUTH AFRICA †S AFRICAN RADIO LEAGUE, Meyerton	Su • C Africa & E Africa • 250 kW • ALT. FREQ. TO 17815 kHz
21565 BELGIUM RTBF INTERNATIONAL, Via Germany	⊟ • M-Sa • C Africa • 100 kW ⊟ • C Africa • 100 kW ⊟ • M-F • C Africa • 100 kW
21570 SPAIN R EXTERIOR ESPANA, Noblejas	M-F • S America • 350 kW S America • 350 kW **W** • S America • 350 kW **S** M-F • S America • 350 kW **S** Sa/Su • S America • 350 kW **S** • S America • 350 kW **W** M-F • S America • 350 kW **W** Sa/Su • S America • 350 kW
USA †R FREE ASIA, Via Tinian, N Marianas	**W** • S Asia • 500 kW
†VOA, Via Udon Thani, Thailand	**W** • S Asia • 250 kW
21575 USA †R FARDA, Via Iranawila, Sri Lanka	**W** • Mideast & W Asia • 250 kW
21580 FRANCE R FRANCE INTL, Issoudun	**W** • C Africa & S Africa • 500 kW C Africa & S Africa • 500 kW **S** • C Africa & S Africa • 500 kW
21590 UNITED KINGDOM †BBC, Via Zyyi, Cyprus	**W** • E Africa • 250 kW
21595 FINLAND †YLE RADIO FINLAND, Pori	**S** • E Africa • 500 kW
21600 JAPAN RADIO JAPAN, Via French Guiana	S America • 300 kW
SAUDI ARABIA BS OF THE KINGDOM, Riyadh	W Africa & C Africa • 500 kW SE Asia • DS-HOLY KORAN • 500 kW
21605 UNITED ARAB EMIRATES †EMIRATES RADIO, Dubai	Europe • 300 kW
21610 JAPAN RADIO JAPAN, Tokyo-Yamata	Australasia • 100 kW
SPAIN R EXTERIOR ESPANA, Noblejas	Australasia • 350 kW **S** • Mideast • 350 kW Mideast • 350 kW **W** • Mideast • 350 kW **S** M-F • Mideast • 350 kW **S** Sa/Su • Mideast • 350 kW **W** M-F • Mideast • 350 kW **W** Sa/Su • Mideast • 350 kW
21615 AUSTRALIA RADIO AUSTRALIA, Via North Marianas	SE Asia • 250 kW
	0 1 2 3 4 5 6 7 8 9 10 11 12 13 14 15 16 17 18 19 20 21 22 23 24

SEASONAL **S** OR **W**   1-HR TIMESHIFT MIDYEAR ⊟ OR ⊡   JAMMING / OR /\   EARLIEST HEARD ◁   LATEST HEARD ▷   NEW FOR 2004 †

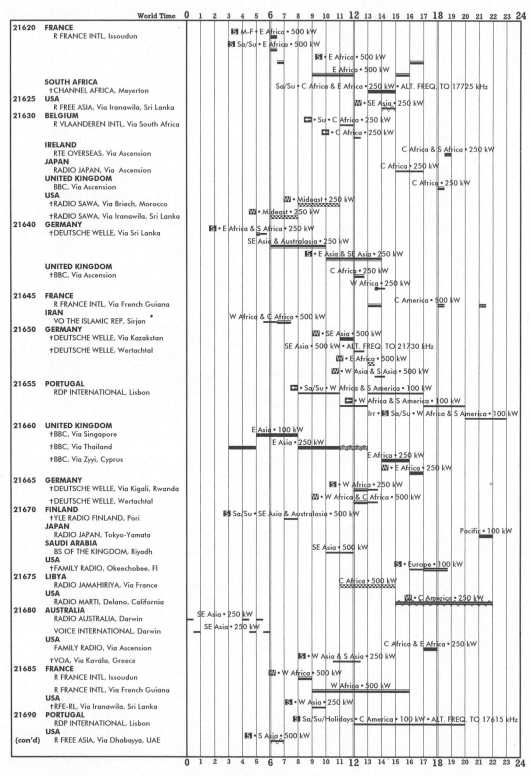

World Time					

21620 FRANCE
R FRANCE INTL, Issoudun

SOUTH AFRICA
†CHANNEL AFRICA, Meyerton

21625 USA
R FREE ASIA, Via Iranawila, Sri Lanka

21630 BELGIUM
R VLAANDEREN INTL, Via South Africa

IRELAND
RTE OVERSEAS, Via Ascension

JAPAN
RADIO JAPAN, Via Ascension

UNITED KINGDOM
BBC, Via Ascension

USA
†RADIO SAWA, Via Briech, Morocco

†RADIO SAWA, Via Iranawila, Sri Lanka

21640 GERMANY
†DEUTSCHE WELLE, Via Sri Lanka

UNITED KINGDOM
†BBC, Via Ascension

21645 FRANCE
R FRANCE INTL, Via French Guiana

IRAN
VO THE ISLAMIC REP, Sirjan

21650 GERMANY
†DEUTSCHE WELLE, Via Kazakstan

†DEUTSCHE WELLE, Wertachtal

21655 PORTUGAL
RDP INTERNATIONAL, Lisbon

21660 UNITED KINGDOM
†BBC, Via Singapore

†BBC, Via Thailand

†BBC, Via Zyyi, Cyprus

21665 GERMANY
†DEUTSCHE WELLE, Via Kigali, Rwanda

†DEUTSCHE WELLE, Wertachtal

21670 FINLAND
†YLE RADIO FINLAND, Pori

JAPAN
RADIO JAPAN, Tokyo-Yamata

SAUDI ARABIA
BS OF THE KINGDOM, Riyadh

USA
†FAMILY RADIO, Okeechobee, Fl

21675 LIBYA
RADIO JAMAHIRIYA, Via France

USA
RADIO MARTI, Delano, California

21680 AUSTRALIA
RADIO AUSTRALIA, Darwin

VOICE INTERNATIONAL, Darwin

USA
FAMILY RADIO, Via Ascension

†VOA, Via Kavála, Greece

21685 FRANCE
R FRANCE INTL, Issoudun

R FRANCE INTL, Via French Guiana

USA
†RFE-RL, Via Iranawila, Sri Lanka

21690 PORTUGAL
RDP INTERNATIONAL, Lisbon

USA
(con'd) R FREE ASIA, Via Dhabayya, UAE

ENGLISH ▬   ARABIC ▨   CHINESE □□□   FRENCH ▬▬   GERMAN ▬▬   RUSSIAN ══   SPANISH ══   OTHER ──

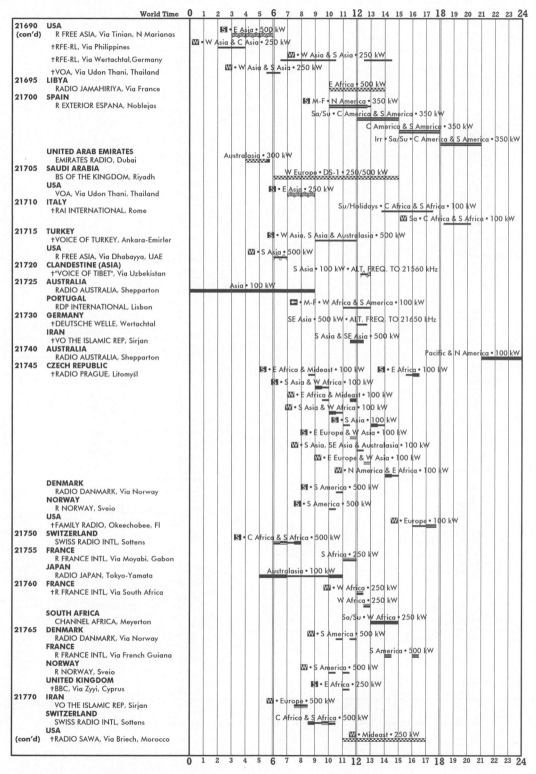

| | World Time | 0 | 1 | 2 | 3 | 4 | 5 | 6 | 7 | 8 | 9 | 10 | 11 | 12 | 13 | 14 | 15 | 16 | 17 | 18 | 19 | 20 | 21 | 22 | 23 | 24 |

21690 **USA**
(con'd)   R FREE ASIA, Via Tinian, N Marianas — 🅂 • E Asia • 500 kW
     †RFE-RL, Via Philippines — 🅆 • W Asia & C Asia • 250 kW
     †RFE-RL, Via Wertachtal, Germany — 🅆 • W Asia & S Asia • 250 kW
     †VOA, Via Udon Thani, Thailand — 🅆 • W Asia & S Asia • 250 kW

21695 **LIBYA**
     RADIO JAMAHIRIYA, Via France — E Africa • 500 kW

21700 **SPAIN**
     R EXTERIOR ESPANA, Noblejas — 🅂 M-F • N America • 350 kW
     Sa/Su • C America & S America • 350 kW
     C America & S America • 350 kW
     Irr • Sa/Su • C America & S America • 350 kW

   UNITED ARAB EMIRATES
     EMIRATES RADIO, Dubai — Australasia • 300 kW

21705 **SAUDI ARABIA**
     BS OF THE KINGDOM, Riyadh — W Europe • DS-1 • 250/500 kW
   USA
     VOA, Via Udon Thani, Thailand — 🅂 • E Asia • 250 kW

21710 **ITALY**
     †RAI INTERNATIONAL, Rome — Su/Holidays • C Africa & S Africa • 100 kW
     🅆 Sa • C Africa & S Africa • 100 kW

21715 **TURKEY**
     †VOICE OF TURKEY, Ankara-Emirler — 🅂 • W Asia, S Asia & Australasia • 500 kW
   USA
     R FREE ASIA, Via Dhabayya, UAE — 🅆 • S Asia • 500 kW

21720 **CLANDESTINE (ASIA)**
     †"VOICE OF TIBET", Via Uzbekistan — S Asia • 100 kW • ALT. FREQ. TO 21560 kHz

21725 **AUSTRALIA**
     RADIO AUSTRALIA, Shepparton — Asia • 100 kW
   PORTUGAL
     RDP INTERNATIONAL, Lisbon — ⬅ • M-F • W Africa & S America • 100 kW

21730 **GERMANY**
     †DEUTSCHE WELLE, Wertachtal — SE Asia • 500 kW • ALT. FREQ. TO 21650 kHz
   IRAN
     †VO THE ISLAMIC REP, Sirjan — S Asia & SE Asia • 500 kW

21740 **AUSTRALIA**
     RADIO AUSTRALIA, Shepparton — Pacific & N America • 100 kW

21745 **CZECH REPUBLIC**
     †RADIO PRAGUE, Litomyšl — 🅂 • E Africa & Mideast • 100 kW   🅂 • E Africa • 100 kW
     🅂 • S Asia & W Africa • 100 kW
     🅆 • E Africa & Mideast • 100 kW
     🅆 • S Asia & W Africa • 100 kW
     🅂 • S Asia • 100 kW
     🅂 • E Europe & W Asia • 100 kW
     🅆 • S Asia, SE Asia & Australasia • 100 kW
     🅆 • E Europe & W Asia • 100 kW
     🅆 • N America & E Africa • 100 kW

   DENMARK
     RADIO DANMARK, Via Norway — 🅂 • S America • 500 kW
   NORWAY
     R NORWAY, Sveio — 🅂 • S America • 500 kW
   USA
     †FAMILY RADIO, Okeechobee, Fl — 🅆 • Europe • 100 kW

21750 **SWITZERLAND**
     SWISS RADIO INTL, Sottens — 🅂 • C Africa & S Africa • 500 kW

21755 **FRANCE**
     R FRANCE INTL, Via Moyabi, Gabon — S Africa • 250 kW
   JAPAN
     RADIO JAPAN, Tokyo-Yamata — Australasia • 100 kW

21760 **FRANCE**
     †R FRANCE INTL, Via South Africa — 🅆 • W Africa • 250 kW
     W Africa • 250 kW

   SOUTH AFRICA
     CHANNEL AFRICA, Meyerton — Sa/Su • W Africa • 250 kW

21765 **DENMARK**
     RADIO DANMARK, Via Norway — 🅆 • S America • 500 kW
   FRANCE
     R FRANCE INTL, Via French Guiana — S America • 500 kW
   NORWAY
     R NORWAY, Sveio — 🅆 • S America • 500 kW
   UNITED KINGDOM
     †BBC, Via Zyyi, Cyprus — 🅂 • E Africa • 250 kW

21770 **IRAN**
     VO THE ISLAMIC REP, Sirjan — 🅆 • Europe • 500 kW
   SWITZERLAND
     SWISS RADIO INTL, Sottens — C Africa & S Africa • 500 kW
   USA
(con'd)   †RADIO SAWA, Via Briech, Morocco — 🅆 • Mideast • 250 kW

SEASONAL 🅂 OR 🅆   1-HR TIMESHIFT MIDYEAR ⬅ OR ➡   JAMMING / OR ∧   EARLIEST HEARD ◁   LATEST HEARD ▷   NEW FOR 2004 †

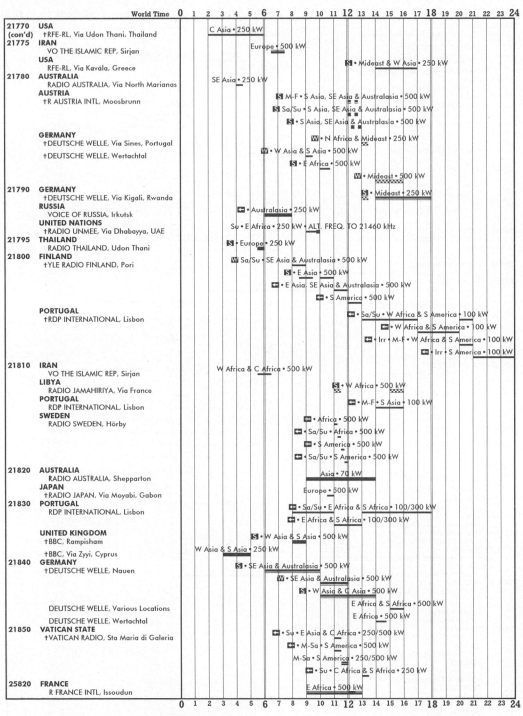

World Time 0 1 2 3 4 5 6 7 8 9 10 11 12 13 14 15 16 17 18 19 20 21 22 23 24

Freq	Country / Station	Details
21770 (con'd)	USA — †RFE-RL, Via Udon Thani, Thailand	C Asia • 250 kW
21775	IRAN — VO THE ISLAMIC REP, Sirjan	Europe • 500 kW
	USA — RFE-RL, Via Kavála, Greece	S • Mideast & W Asia • 250 kW
21780	AUSTRALIA — RADIO AUSTRALIA, Via North Marianas	SE Asia • 250 kW
	AUSTRIA — †R AUSTRIA INTL, Moosbrunn	S • M-F • S Asia, SE Asia & Australasia • 500 kW; S • Sa/Su • S Asia, SE Asia & Australasia • 500 kW; S • S Asia, SE Asia & Australasia • 500 kW
	GERMANY — †DEUTSCHE WELLE, Via Sines, Portugal	W • N Africa & Mideast • 250 kW
	†DEUTSCHE WELLE, Wertachtal	W • W Asia & S Asia • 500 kW; S • E Africa • 500 kW; W • Mideast • 500 kW
21790	GERMANY — †DEUTSCHE WELLE, Via Kigali, Rwanda	S • Mideast • 250 kW
	RUSSIA — VOICE OF RUSSIA, Irkutsk	• Australasia • 250 kW
	UNITED NATIONS — †RADIO UNMEE, Via Dhabayya, UAE	Su • E Africa • 250 kW • ALT. FREQ. TO 21460 kHz
21795	THAILAND — RADIO THAILAND, Udon Thani	S • Europe • 250 kW
21800	FINLAND — †YLE RADIO FINLAND, Pori	W • Sa/Su • SE Asia & Australasia • 500 kW; S • E Asia • 500 kW; • E Asia, SE Asia & Australasia • 500 kW; • S America • 500 kW
	PORTUGAL — †RDP INTERNATIONAL, Lisbon	• Sa/Su • W Africa & S America • 100 kW; • W Africa & S America • 100 kW; • Irr • M-F • W Africa & S America • 100 kW; • Irr • S America • 100 kW
21810	IRAN — VO THE ISLAMIC REP, Sirjan	W Africa & C Africa • 500 kW
	LIBYA — RADIO JAMAHIRIYA, Via France	S • W Africa • 500 kW
	PORTUGAL — RDP INTERNATIONAL, Lisbon	• M-F • S Asia • 100 kW
	SWEDEN — RADIO SWEDEN, Hörby	• Africa • 500 kW; • Sa/Su • Africa • 500 kW; • S America • 500 kW; • Sa/Su • S America • 500 kW
21820	AUSTRALIA — RADIO AUSTRALIA, Shepparton	Asia • 70 kW
	JAPAN — †RADIO JAPAN, Via Moyabi, Gabon	Europe • 500 kW
21830	PORTUGAL — RDP INTERNATIONAL, Lisbon	• Sa/Su • E Africa & S Africa • 100/300 kW; • E Africa & S Africa • 100/300 kW
	UNITED KINGDOM — †BBC, Rampisham	S • W Asia & S Asia • 500 kW
	†BBC, Via Zyyi, Cyprus	W Asia & S Asia • 250 kW
21840	GERMANY — †DEUTSCHE WELLE, Nauen	S • SE Asia & Australasia • 500 kW; W • SE Asia & Australasia • 500 kW; S • W Asia & C Asia • 500 kW
	DEUTSCHE WELLE, Various Locations	E Africa & S Africa • 500 kW
	DEUTSCHE WELLE, Wertachtal	E Africa • 500 kW
21850	VATICAN STATE — †VATICAN RADIO, Sta Maria di Galeria	• Su • E Asia & C Africa • 250/500 kW; • M-Sa • S America • 500 kW; M-Sa • S America • 250/500 kW; • Su • C Africa & S Africa • 250 kW
25820	FRANCE — R FRANCE INTL, Issoudun	E Africa • 500 kW

0 1 2 3 4 5 6 7 8 9 10 11 12 13 14 15 16 17 18 19 20 21 22 23 24

ENGLISH ▬   ARABIC ▨   CHINESE ▦   FRENCH ▬   GERMAN ▬   RUSSIAN ▬   SPANISH ▬   OTHER ▬